SPENCER A. RATHUS

HDEV 5

BRIEF CONTENTS

CONTENTS

Caiaimage/Sam Edwards/Getty Images

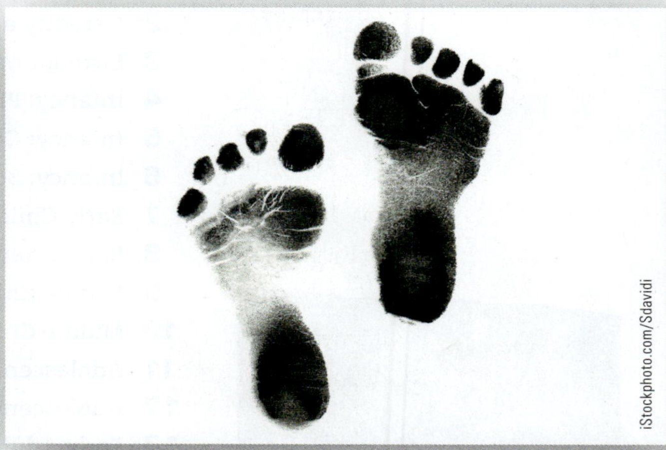

iStockphoto.com/Sdavidi

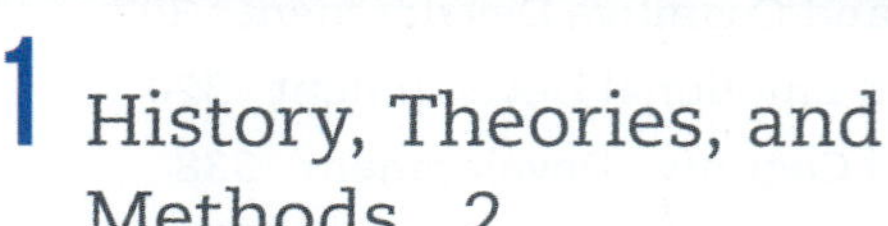

Joakim Leroy/E+/Getty Images

rubberball/Getty Images

11 Adolescence: Physical and Cognitive Development 218

12 Adolescence: Social and Emotional Development 240

13 Early Adulthood: Physical and Cognitive Development 256

14 Early Adulthood: Social and Emotional Development 276

15 Middle Adulthood: Physical and Cognitive Development 302

16 Middle Adulthood: Social and Emotional Development 320

17 Late Adulthood: Physical and Cognitive Development 338

18 Late Adulthood: Social and Emotional Development 360

19 Life's Final Chapter 380

1 History, Theories, and Methods

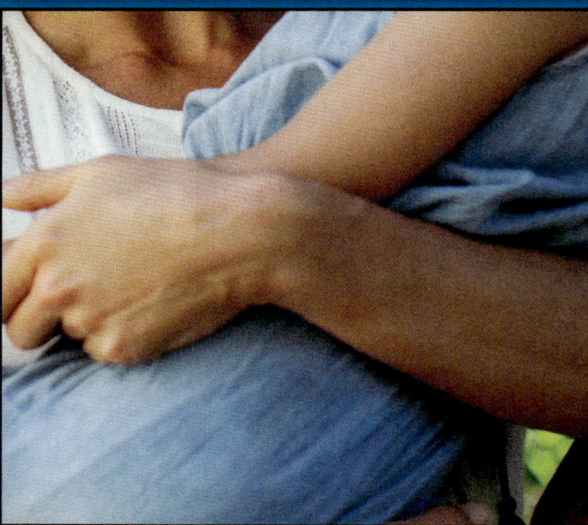

Caiaimage/Sam Edwards/Getty Images

LEARNING OUTCOMES

After studying this chapter, you will be able to...

- 1-1 Relate the history of the study of human development
- 1-2 Compare and contrast theories of human development
- 1-3 Enumerate key controversies in human development
- 1-4 Describe ways in which researchers study human development

After you finish this chapter, go to **PAGE 21** for **STUDY TOOLS**

This book has a story to tell. An important, remarkable story—your story. It is about the amazing journey you have already taken through childhood, and about the unfolding of your adult life. Billions of people have made this journey before. You have much in common with them. Yet you are unique, and things will happen to you, and because of you, that have never happened before.

You are unique, and things will happen to you, and because of you, that have never happened before.

1-1 THE DEVELOPMENT OF THE STUDY OF HUMAN DEVELOPMENT

Developmental psychology is the discipline that studies the physical, cognitive, social, and emotional development of humans. It focuses on the many influences on behavior, including the effects of the person's physical, social, and cultural environment, and how these factors interact to influence the developments that occur over time.

Scientific inquiry into human development has existed for little more than a century. In ancient times and in the Middle Ages, children often were viewed as innately evil and discipline was harsh. Legally, medieval children were treated as property and servants. They could be sent to the monastery, married without consultation, or convicted of crimes. Children were nurtured until they were seven years old, which was considered the "age of reason." Then they were expected to work alongside adults in the home and in the field.

The transition to modern thinking about children is marked by the writings of philosophers such as John Locke and Jean-Jacques Rousseau. Englishman John Locke (1632–1704) believed that the child came into the world as a *tabula rasa*—a "blank tablet" or clean slate—that was written on by experience. Locke did not believe that inborn predispositions toward good or evil played an important role in the conduct of the child. Instead, he focused on the role of the environment or of experience. Locke believed that social approval and disapproval are powerful shapers of behavior. But Jean-Jacques Rousseau (1712–1778), a Swiss-French philosopher, argued that children are inherently good and that, if allowed to express their natural impulses, they will develop into generous and moral individuals.

During the Industrial Revolution—a period from the late 18th century through the 19th century when machine-based production replaced much manual labor—family life came to be defined in terms of the nuclear unit of mother, father, and children rather than the extended family. Children became more visible, fostering awareness of childhood as a special time of life. Still, children often labored in factories from dawn to dusk through the early years of the 20th century.

In the 20th century, laws were passed to protect children from strenuous labor, to require that they attend school until a certain age, and to prevent them from getting married or being sexually exploited. Whereas children were once considered the property of parents, laws now protect children from abuse by parents and other adults. Juvenile courts see that children who break the law receive treatment in the criminal justice system.

developmental psychology the discipline that studies the physical, cognitive, social, and emotional development of humans.

TRUTH OR FICTION?

WHAT DO YOU THINK? FOLKLORE, COMMON SENSE, OR NONSENSE? SELECT T FOR "TRUTH" OR F FOR "FICTION," AND CHECK THE ACCURACY OF YOUR ANSWERS AS YOU READ THROUGH THE CHAPTER.

T	F	During the Middle Ages, children were often treated as miniature adults.
T	F	Nail biting and smoking cigarettes are signs of conflict experienced during early childhood.
T	F	Research with monkeys has helped psychologists understand the formation of attachment in humans.
T	F	To learn how a person develops over a lifetime, researchers have tracked some individuals for more than 50 years.

Various thoughts about child development coalesced into a field of scientific study in the 19th and early 20th centuries. G. Stanley Hall (1844–1924) is credited with founding child development as an academic discipline and bringing scientific attention to focus on the period of adolescence. French psychologist Alfred Binet (1857–1911), along with Theodore Simon (1872–1961), developed the first standardized intelligence test near the beginning of the 20th century. Binet's purpose was to identify public school children who were at risk of falling behind their peers in academic achievement. By the start of the 20th century, child development had emerged as a scientific field of study. Soon major theories of the developing child were proposed by theorists such as Arnold Gesell, Sigmund Freud, John B. Watson, and Jean Piaget.

The traditional focus of developmental psychologists has been on childhood and adolescence because of the dramatic physical and cognitive changes that occur during those years. But in the 20th century, psychologists began to take on a **life-span perspective**, in which they viewed human development as occurring throughout the individual's lifetime.

William Perry and Gisella Labouvie-Vief, for example, have studied the development of cognitive complexity from adolescence to late adulthood. K. W. Schaie and others have studied trends in various mental abilities throughout middle and late adulthood, showing that some abilities decline in middle and late adulthood, but others that represent the accumulation of decades of knowledge can advance into late adulthood. Though young adulthood is the time of peak physical development, people perform at their best on some of the most complex intellectual tasks during midlife, and many people are most well-adjusted during late adulthood.

Developmental psychologists and educators attempt to sort out the influences of heredity (maturation) and the environment (experience) in development. John Watson would have argued that this girl's preferences and skills are shaped by experience. Arnold Gesell might have preferred to focus on the expression of her inborn ability.

Tetra Images / Alamy Stock Photo

1-2 THEORIES OF DEVELOPMENT

life-span perspective perspective in which psychologists view human development as occurring throughout the individual's lifetime.

behaviorism Watson's view that science must study observable behavior only and investigate relationships between stimuli and responses.

Give me a dozen healthy infants, well-formed, and my own specified world to bring them up in, and I'll guarantee to train them to become any type of specialist I might suggest—doctor, lawyer, merchant, chief, and, yes, even beggar and thief, regardless of their talents, penchants, tendencies, abilities, vocations, and the race of their ancestors.

—*John B. Watson (1924, p. 82)*

TRUTH

(T) F During the Middle Ages, children were often treated as miniature adults.

It is true that during the Middle Ages, children were often treated as miniature adults. This does not mean that they were given more privileges, however. Instead, more was expected of them.

Theories are formulations of apparent relationships among observed events. They allow us to derive explanations and predictions. Many psychological theories combine statements about behavior (such as reflexes), mental processes (such as whether a reflex is intentional or not), and biological processes (such as maturation of the nervous system). A satisfactory theory allows us to predict behavior. For example, a theory about a reflex should allow us to predict the age at which it will drop out or be replaced by intentional behavior. John B. Watson (1878–1958), the founder of American **behaviorism**, viewed development in terms of learning theory. He generally agreed with Locke that children's ideas, preferences, and skills are shaped by experience. There has been a long-standing nature–nurture debate in the study of children. In his theoretical approach to understanding children, Watson came down on the side of nurture—the importance of the physical and social environments—as found, for example, in parental training and approval.

Arnold Gesell expressed the opposing idea that biological **maturation** was the main principle of development: "All things considered, the inevitability and surety of maturation are the most impressive characteristics of early development. It is the hereditary ballast which conserves and stabilizes growth of each individual infant" (Gesell, 1928, p. 378). Watson was talking about the behavior patterns that children develop, whereas Gesell was focusing mainly on physical aspects of growth and development.

Theories such as behavioral theory and maturational theory help developmentalists explain, predict, and influence the events they study. Let's consider theories that are popular among developmentalists today. They fall within broad perspectives on development.

Courtesy of the Ferdinand Hamburger Archives of The Johns Hopkins University

According to John B. Watson (1878–1958), the founder of American behaviorism, a theory about a reflex should allow us to predict the age at which it will drop out or be replaced by intentional behavior. Here Watson is demonstrating the grasp reflex of a newborn infant.

1-2a THE PSYCHOANALYTIC PERSPECTIVE

A number of theories fall within the psychoanalytic perspective. Each owes its origin to Sigmund Freud and views children—and adults—as caught in conflict. Early in development, the conflict is between the child and the world outside. The expression of basic drives, such as sex and aggression, conflict with parental expectations, social rules, moral codes, even laws. But the external limits—parental demands and social rules—are brought inside or *internalized*. Once internalization occurs, the conflict takes place between opposing *inner* forces. The child's observable behavior, thoughts, and feelings reflect the outcomes of these hidden battles.

Let's consider Freud's theory of **psychosexual development** and Erik Erikson's theory of psychosocial development. Each is a **stage theory** that sees children as developing through distinct periods of life. Each suggests that the child's experiences during early stages affect the child's emotional and social life at the time and later on.

SIGMUND FREUD'S THEORY OF PSYCHOSEXUAL DEVELOPMENT Sigmund Freud's (1856–1939) theory of psychosexual development focused on emotional and social development and on the origins of psychological traits such as dependence, obsessive neatness, and vanity. Freud theorized three parts of the personality: the *id*, *ego*, and *superego*. The id is present at birth and is *unconscious*. It represents biological drives and demands instant gratification, as suggested by a baby's wailing. The ego, or the conscious sense of self, begins to develop when children learn to obtain gratification consciously, without screaming or crying. The ego curbs the appetites of the id and makes plans that are in keeping with social conventions so that a person can find gratification but avoid social disapproval. The superego develops throughout infancy and early childhood. It brings inward the wishes and morals of the child's caregivers and other members of the community. Throughout the remainder of the child's life, the superego will monitor the intentions and behavior of the ego, hand down judgments of right and wrong,

FREUD'S THEORY OF PSYCHOSEXUAL DEVELOPMENT

Sigmund Freud's (1856–1939) theory of psychosexual development focused on emotional and social development and on the origins of psychological traits such as dependence, obsessive neatness, and vanity. According to Freud, there are five stages of psychosexual development:

- oral
- anal
- phallic
- latency
- genital

maturation the unfolding of genetically determined traits, structures, and functions.

psychosexual development the process by which libidinal energy is expressed through different erogenous zones during different stages of development.

stage theory a theory of development characterized by distinct periods of life.

and attempt to influence behavior through flooding the person with feelings of guilt and shame when the judgment is in the negative.

According to Freud, there are five stages of psychosexual development: *oral, anal, phallic, latency*, and *genital*. If a child receives too little or too much gratification during a stage, the child can become *fixated* in that stage. For example, during the first year of life, which Freud termed the *oral stage*, "oral" activities such as sucking and biting bring pleasure and gratification. If the child is weaned early or breast-fed too long, the child may become fixated on oral activities such as nail biting or smoking, or even show a "biting wit."

FICTION

T (F) Nail biting and smoking cigarettes are signs of conflict experienced during early childhood.

Actually, there is no evidence that nail biting and smoking cigarettes are signs of conflict experienced during early childhood. The statement must therefore be considered "fiction."

In the second, or *anal*, stage, gratification is obtained through control and elimination of waste products. Excessively strict or permissive toilet training can lead to the development of anal-retentive traits, such as perfectionism and neatness, or anal-expulsive traits, such as sloppiness and carelessness. In the third stage, the *phallic stage*, parent–child conflict may develop over masturbation, which many parents treat with punishment and threats. It is normal for children to develop strong sexual attachments to the parent of the other sex during the phallic stage and to begin to view the parent of the same sex as a rival.

By age five or six, Freud believed, children enter a *latency stage* during which sexual feelings remain unconscious, children turn to schoolwork, and they typically prefer playmates of their own sex. The final stage of psychosexual development, the *genital stage*, begins with the biological changes that usher in adolescence. Adolescents generally desire sexual gratification through intercourse with a member of the other sex. Freud believed that oral or anal stimulation, masturbation, and male–male or female–female sexual activity are immature forms of sexual conduct that reflect fixations at early stages of development.

psychosocial development
Erikson's theory, which emphasizes the importance of social relationships and conscious choice throughout eight stages of development.

Evaluation Freud's views about the anal stage have influenced child-care workers to recommend that toilet training not be started too early or handled punitively. His emphasis on the emotional needs of children has influenced educators to be more sensitive to the possible emotional reasons behind a child's misbehavior. Freud's work has also been criticized. For one thing, Freud developed his theory on the basis of contacts with adult patients (mostly women) (Hergenhahn & Henley, 2014), rather than observing children directly. Freud may also have inadvertently guided patients into expressing ideas that confirmed his views.

Some of Freud's own disciples, including Erik Erikson, believe that Freud placed too much emphasis on basic instincts and unconscious motives. He argues that people are motivated not only by drives such as sex and aggression but also by social relationships and conscious desires to achieve, to have aesthetic experiences, and to help others.

ERIK ERIKSON'S THEORY OF PSYCHOSOCIAL DEVELOPMENT Erik Erikson (1902–1994) modified Freud's theory and extended it through the adult years. Erikson's theory, like Freud's, focuses on the development of the emotional life and psychological traits, but Erikson focuses on social relationships rather than sexual or aggressive instincts. Therefore, Erikson speaks of **psychosocial development** rather than of *psychosexual development*. Furthermore, Erikson places greater emphasis on the ego, or the sense of self. Erikson (1963) extended Freud's five stages to eight to include the concerns of

ERIKSON'S THEORY OF PSYCHOSOCIAL DEVELOPMENT

Erik Erikson (1902–1994) modified Freud's psychosexual theory and extended it through the adult years. Erikson's theory, like Freud's, focuses on the development of the emotional life and psychological traits, but Erikson focuses on social relationships rather than sexual or aggressive instincts. He expanded Freud's five stages to eight, to include the stages of adult development.

Erik Erikson was concerned with the development of our sense of identity—who we are and what we stand for. He was especially concerned with the crisis in identity that affects adolescents in our culture. How would you describe this adolescent's apparent sense of identity?

adulthood. Rather than label his stages after parts of the body, Erikson labeled them after the **life crisis** that people might encounter during that stage.

Erikson proposed that social relationships and physical maturation give each stage its character. For example, the parent–child relationship and the infant's dependence and helplessness are responsible for the nature of the earliest stages of development.

Early experiences affect future developments. With parental support, most children resolve early life crises productively. Successful resolution of each crisis bolsters their sense of identity—of who they are and what they stand for—and their expectation of future success.

Erikson's views, like Freud's, have influenced child rearing, early childhood education, and child therapy. For example, Erikson's views about an adolescent **identity crisis** have entered the popular culture and have affected the way many parents and teachers deal with teenagers. Some schools help students master the crisis by means of life-adjustment courses and study units on self-understanding in social studies and literature classes.

WATSON: THE FOUNDER OF AMERICAN BEHAVIORISM

John B. Watson (1878–1958) is considered the founder of American behaviorism. He was a major force in early 20th century psychology, arguing that psychologists should study only observable behavior, not thoughts, fantasies, and other mental images. He viewed development in terms of learning theory. He generally agreed with Locke that children's ideas, preferences, and skills are shaped by experience. In the long-standing nature–nurture debate in the study of children, his theoretical approach to understanding children comes down on the side of nurture.

Evaluation Erikson's views are appealing in that they emphasize the importance of human consciousness and choice. They are also appealing in that they portray us as prosocial and helpful, whereas Freud portrayed us as selfish and needing to be compelled to comply with social rules. There is also some empirical support for the Eriksonian view that positive outcomes of early life crises help put us on the path to positive development (Gfellner & Armstrong, 2012; Marcia, 2010).

1-2b THE LEARNING PERSPECTIVE: BEHAVIORAL AND SOCIAL COGNITIVE THEORIES

During the 1930s, psychologists derived an ingenious method for helping five- and six-year-old children overcome bed-wetting from the behavioral perspective. Most children at this age wake up and go to the bathroom when their bladders are full. Bed wetters, though, sleep through bladder tension and reflexively urinate in bed. To address this problem, the psychologists placed a special pad beneath the sleeping child. Wetness in the pad closed an electrical circuit, causing a bell to ring and waking the sleeping child. After several repetitions, most children learned to wake up before they wet the pad. How? They learned through a technique called *classical conditioning*, which we explain in this section.

The so-called bell-and-pad method for bed-wetting is a more complicated example of learning theory being applied to human development. Most applications of learning theory to development are found in simpler, everyday events. In this section, we consider two theories of learning: behaviorism and social cognitive theory.

BEHAVIORISM John B. Watson argued that a scientific approach to development must focus on observable behavior only and not on things like thoughts, fantasies, and other mental images.

life crisis an internal conflict that attends each stage of psychosocial development.

identity crisis according to Erikson, a period of inner conflict during which one examines one's values and makes decisions about one's life roles.

FIG.1.1 SCHEMATIC REPRESENTATION OF CLASSICAL CONDITIONING

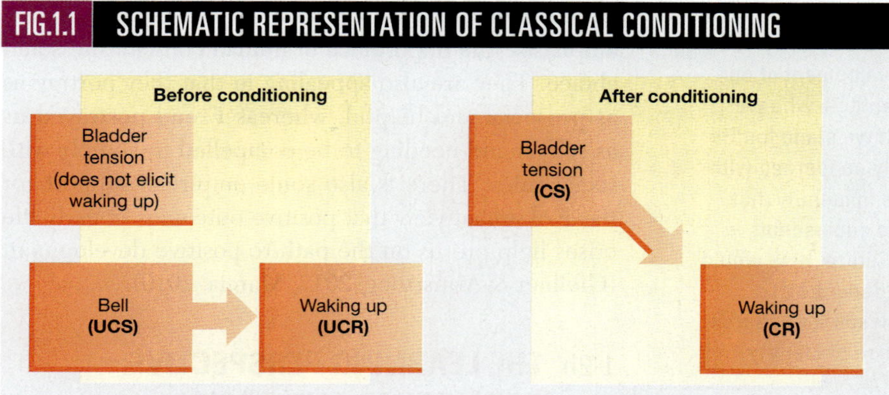

Before conditioning, the bell is an unlearned or unconditioned stimulus (UCS) that elicits waking up, which is an unlearned or unconditioned response (UCR). Bladder tension does not elicit waking up, which is the problem. During the conditioning procedure, bladder tension repeatedly precedes urination, which in turn causes the bell to ring. After several repetitions, bladder tension has become associated with the bell, making bladder tension into a learned or conditioned stimulus (CS) that causes the child to awaken. Awakening in response to bladder tension is a learned or conditioned response (CR).

Classical conditioning is a simple form of learning in which an originally neutral stimulus comes to bring forth, or elicit, the response usually brought forth by a second stimulus as a result of being paired repeatedly with the second stimulus. In the bell-and-pad method for bed-wetting, psychologists repeatedly pair tension in the children's bladders with a stimulus that awakens them (the bell). The children learn to respond to the bladder tension as if it were a bell; that is, they wake up (see Figure 1.1).

Behaviorists argue that much emotional learning is acquired through classical conditioning. In **operant conditioning** (a different kind of conditioning), children learn to do something because of its effects. B. F. Skinner introduced the key concept of **reinforcement**. Reinforcers are stimuli that increase the frequency of the behavior they follow. Most children learn to adjust their behavior to conform to social codes and rules to earn reinforcers such as the attention and approval of their parents and teachers. Other children, ironically, may learn to misbehave because misbehavior also draws attention. Any stimulus that increases the frequency of the responses preceding it serves as a reinforcer. Skinner distinguished between positive and negative reinforcers. **Positive reinforcers** increase the frequency of behaviors when they are *applied*. Food and approval usually serve as positive reinforcers. **Negative reinforcers** increase the frequency of behaviors when they are *removed*. Fear acts as a negative reinforcer in that its removal increases the frequency of the behaviors preceding it. Figure 1.2 compares positive and negative reinforcers.

Extinction results from repeated performance of operant behavior without reinforcement. After a number of trials, the operant behavior is no longer shown. Children's temper tantrums and crying at bedtime can often be extinguished by parents' remaining out of the bedroom after the children have been put to bed. Punishments are aversive events that suppress or *decrease* the frequency of the behavior they follow. (Figure 1.3 compares negative reinforcers with punishments.) Many learning theorists agree that punishment is undesirable in rearing children for reasons such as punishment does not in itself suggest an alternative acceptable form of behavior; punishment tends

classical conditioning a simple form of learning in which one stimulus comes to bring forth the response usually brought forth by a second stimulus by being paired repeatedly with the second stimulus.

operant conditioning a simple form of learning in which an organism learns to engage in behavior that is reinforced.

reinforcement the process of providing stimuli following responses that increase the frequency of the responses.

positive reinforcer a reinforcer that, when applied, increases the frequency of a response.

negative reinforcer a reinforcer that, when removed, increases the frequency of a response.

extinction the cessation of a response that is performed in the absence of reinforcement.

SKINNER AND BEHAVIORISM

B.F. Skinner, (1904–1990), picked up the behaviorist mandate from John Watson. Behaviorists argue that much emotional learning is acquired through conditioning. Skinner introduced the key concept of positive and negative reinforcement in operant conditioning. He was interested in popularizing his views on psychology and wrote a novel, *Walden Two*, which supported his views and achieved a sort of cult following.

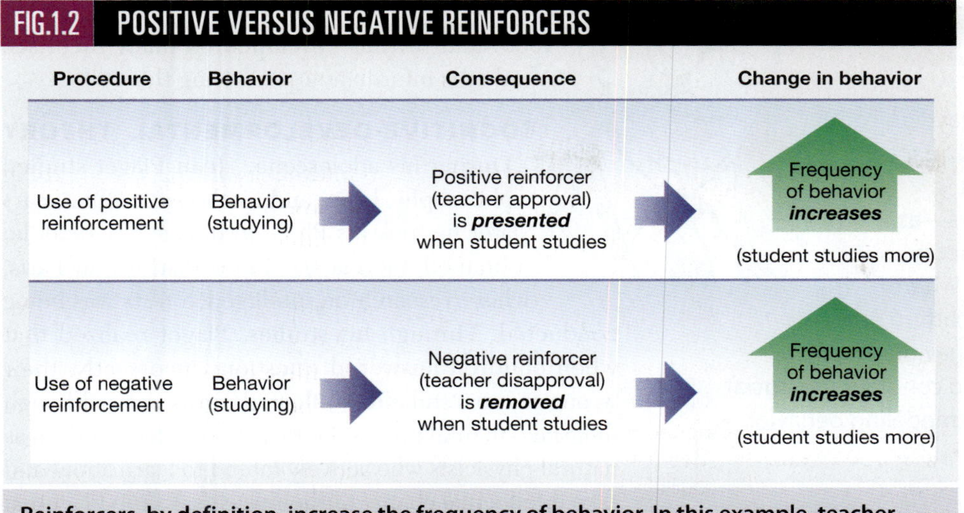

Reinforcers, by definition, increase the frequency of behavior. In this example, teacher approval is a positive reinforcer because it increases the frequency of behavior when it is *applied*. Teacher disapproval functions as a negative reinforcer because *removing* it increases behavior—in this case, studying. But teacher disapproval can backfire when other students show strong approval of a student's disobeying the teacher.

to suppress behavior only when its delivery is guaranteed; and punishment can create feelings of anger and hostility.

Research suggests that when teachers praise and attend to appropriate behavior and ignore misbehavior, studying and classroom behavior improve while disruptive and aggressive behaviors decrease (Coffee & Kratochwill, 2013; Jenkins et al., 2015). By ignoring misbehavior or by using *time out* from positive reinforcement, we can avoid reinforcing children for misbehavior. In using time out, children are placed in drab, restrictive environments for a specified time period such as 10 minutes when they behave disruptively.

Operant conditioning is used every day in the *socialization* of young children. Parents and peers influence children to acquire behavior patterns they consider to be appropriate to their gender through the elaborate use of rewards and punishments. Thus, boys may ignore other boys when they play with dolls and housekeeping toys but play with boys when they use transportation toys. Many children are thus taught to engage in behavior that may please others more than it pleases themselves.

SOCIAL COGNITIVE THEORY Behaviorists tend to limit their view of learning to conditioning. **Social cognitive theorists** such as Albert Bandura (1986, 2011, 2012) have shown that much learning also occurs by observing other people, reading, and viewing characters in the media. People may need practice to refine their skills, but they can acquire the basic know-how through observation.

Observational learning occurs when children observe how parents cook, clean, or repair a broken appliance. It takes place when adults watch supervisors sketch out sales strategies on a blackboard or hear them speak a foreign language. In social cognitive theory, the people after whom we pattern our own behavior are termed *models*.

FIG.1.3 NEGATIVE REINFORCERS VERSUS PUNISHMENTS

Procedure	Behavior	Consequence	Change in behavior
Use of negative reinforcement	Behavior (studying)	Negative reinforcer (teacher disapproval) is ***removed*** when student studies	Frequency of behavior ***increases*** (student studies more)
Use of punishment	Behavior (talking in class)	Punishment (detention) is ***presented*** when student talks in class	Frequency of behavior ***decreases*** (student talks less in class)

Both negative reinforcers and punishments tend to be aversive stimuli. Reinforcers, however, increase the frequency of behavior. Punishments decrease the frequency of behavior. Negative reinforcers increase the frequency of behavior when they are removed.

social cognitive theory a cognitively oriented learning theory that emphasizes observational learning.

BANDURA AND SOCIAL COGNITIVE THEORY

Albert Bandura (b. 1925), a leading social cognitive theorist, emphasized the role of social learning—that is, learning by observing others—as a key element in learning theory. He labeled the people after whom we, as children and adults, pattern our behavior "models." While behaviorists tend to limit their view of learning to conditioning, social cognitive theorists focus on modeling behavior.

EVALUATION OF LEARNING THEORIES Learning theories allow us to explain, predict, and influence many aspects of behavior. The use of the bell-and-pad method for bed-wetting would probably not have been derived from any other theoretical approach. Many of the teaching approaches used in educational TV shows are based on learning theory.

1-2c THE COGNITIVE PERSPECTIVE

Cognitive theorists focus on people's mental processes. They investigate the ways in which children perceive and mentally represent the world, how they develop thinking, logic, and problem-solving ability. One cognitive perspective is **cognitive-developmental theory**, advanced by Swiss biologist Jean Piaget (1896–1980) and further developed by many theorists. Another is information-processing theory.

COGNITIVE-DEVELOPMENTAL THEORY During his adolescence, Jean Piaget studied philosophy, logic, and mathematics, but years later he took his Ph.D. in biology. In 1920, he obtained a job at the Binet Institute in Paris, where research on intelligence tests was being conducted. Through his studies, Piaget realized that when children answered questions incorrectly, their wrong answers still often reflected consistent—although illogical—mental processes. Piaget regarded children as natural physicists who actively intend to learn about and take intellectual charge of their worlds. In the Piagetian view, children who squish their food and laugh enthusiastically are often acting as budding scientists. They are studying both the texture and consistency of their food, as well as their parents' response.

Piaget used concepts such as *schemes, adaptation, assimilation, accommodation*, and *equilibration* to describe and explain cognitive development. Piaget defines the **scheme** as a pattern of action or mental structure that is involved in acquiring or organizing knowledge. For example, newborn babies might be said to have a sucking scheme (others call this a *reflex*), responding to things put in their mouths as "things I can suck" versus "things I can't suck."

Adaptation refers to the interaction between the organism and the environment. According to Piaget, all organisms adapt to their environment. Adaptation consists of assimilation and accommodation, which occur throughout life. Cognitive **assimilation** refers to the process by which someone responds to new objects or events according to existing schemes or ways of organizing knowledge. Two-year-olds who refer to horses as

cognitive-developmental theory the stage theory that holds that the child's abilities to mentally represent the world and solve problems unfold as a result of the interaction of experience and the maturation of neurological structures.

scheme an action pattern or mental structure that is involved in the acquisition and organization of knowledge.

adaptation the interaction between the organism and the environment, consisting of assimilation and accommodation.

assimilation the incorporation of new events or knowledge into existing schemes.

PIAGET'S COGNITIVE-DEVELOPMENTAL THEORY

Cognitive theorists investigate the ways in which children perceive and mentally represent the world, how they develop thinking, logic, and problem-solving ability. One cognitive perspective is cognitive-developmental theory, advanced by Swiss biologist Jean Piaget (1896–1980). Piaget's early training as a biologist led him to view children as mentally assimilating and accommodating aspects of their environment.

Piaget used concepts such as schemes, adaptation, assimilation, accommodation, and equilibration to describe and explain cognitive development. In 1963, Piaget hypothesized that children's cognitive processes develop in an orderly sequence, or series, of stages. He identified four major stages of cognitive development: sensorimotor, preoperational, concrete operational, and formal operational.

"doggies" are assimilating horses into their dog scheme. Sometimes a novel object or event cannot be made to fit into an existing scheme. In that case, the scheme may be changed or a new scheme may be created to incorporate the new event. This process is called **accommodation**. Consider the sucking reflex. Infants accommodate by rejecting objects that are too large, that taste bad, or that are of the wrong texture or temperature.

Piaget theorized that when children can assimilate new events into existing schemes, they are in a state of cognitive harmony, or equilibrium. When something that does not fit happens, their state of equilibrium is disturbed and they may try to accommodate. The process of restoring equilibrium is termed **equilibration**. Piaget believed that the attempt to restore equilibrium lies at the heart of the natural curiosity of the child.

PIAGET'S STAGES OF COGNITIVE DEVELOPMENT

Piaget (1963) hypothesized that children's cognitive processes develop in an orderly sequence, or series, of stages. Piaget identified four major stages of cognitive development: *sensorimotor, preoperational, concrete operational*, and *formal operational*. These stages are discussed in subsequent chapters.

Because Piaget's theory focuses on cognitive development, its applications are primarily in educational settings. Teachers following Piaget's views actively engage the child in solving problems. They gear instruction to the child's developmental level and offer activities that challenge the child to advance to the next level.

Piaget's theory ends with formal operational thought. Life-span theorists such as William Perry note that college students' views on what they know and how they get to know what they know become more complex as they are exposed to the complexities of college thought. Gisella Labouvie-Vief notes that the "cognitively healthy" adult is more willing than the egocentric adolescent to compromise and cope with the world as it is, not as she or he would like it to be.

Evaluation Many researchers, using a variety of methods, find that Piaget may have underestimated the ages when children are capable of doing certain things. It also appears that many cognitive skills may develop gradually and not in distinct stages. Nevertheless, Piaget has provided a strong theoretical foundation for researchers concerned with sequences in cognitive development.

INFORMATION-PROCESSING THEORY Another face of the cognitive perspective is information processing (Brigham et al., 2011; Calvete & Orue, 2012). Many psychologists and educators speak of people as having working or short-term memory and a more permanent long-term memory (storage). If information has been placed in long-term memory, it must be retrieved before we can work on it. Retrieving information from our own long-term memories requires certain cues, without which the information may be lost.

Thus, many cognitive psychologists focus on information processing in people—the processes by which people encode (input) information, store it (in long-term memory), retrieve it (place it in short-term memory), and manipulate it to solve problems. Our strategies for solving problems are sometimes referred to as our *mental programs* or *software*. In this computer metaphor, our brains are the *hardware* that runs our mental programs. Our brains—containing billions of brain cells called *neurons*—become our most "personal" computers. When psychologists who study information processing contemplate cognitive development, they are likely to talk in terms of the *size* of the person's short-term memory and the *number of programs* she or he can run simultaneously.

The most obvious applications of information processing occur in teaching. For example, information-processing models alert teachers to the sequence of steps by which children acquire information, commit it to memory, and retrieve it to solve problems. By understanding this sequence, teachers can provide experiences that give students practice with each stage.

We now see that the brain is a sort of biological computer. Let us next see what other aspects of biology can be connected with development.

1-2d THE BIOLOGICAL PERSPECTIVE

The biological perspective directly relates to physical development: to gains in height and weight; development of the brain; and developments connected with hormones, reproduction, and heredity. Here we consider two biologically oriented theories of development, evolutionary psychology and ethology.

EVOLUTIONARY PSYCHOLOGY AND ETHOLOGY: "DOING WHAT COMES NATURALLY" Evolutionary psychology and ethology were heavily influenced by the 19th-century work of Charles Darwin and by the work of 20th-century ethologists Konrad Lorenz and Niko Tinbergen. **Ethology** is concerned with instinctive, or inborn, behavior patterns. According to the theory of evolution, there is a struggle for survival

accommodation the modification of existing schemes to permit the incorporation of new events or knowledge.

equilibration the creation of an equilibrium, or balance, between assimilation and accommodation.

ethology the study of behaviors that are specific to a species.

as various species and individuals compete for a limited quantity of resources. The combined genetic instructions from parents lead to variations among individuals. There are also sharper differences from parents, caused by sudden changes in genetic material called *mutations*. Those individuals whose traits are better adapted to their environments are more likely to survive (that is, to be naturally selected). Survival permits them to reach sexual maturity, select mates, and reproduce, thereby transmitting their features or traits to the next generation. What began as a minor variation or a mutation becomes embedded in more and more individuals over the generations—if it fosters survival.

The field of **evolutionary psychology** studies the ways in which adaptation and natural selection are connected with mental processes and behavior. One of the concepts of evolutionary psychology is that not only physical traits but also patterns of behavior, including social behavior, evolve and are transmitted genetically from generation to generation. In other words, behavior patterns that help an organism to survive and reproduce are likely to be transmitted to the next generation. Such behaviors are believed to include aggression, strategies of mate selection, even altruism—that is, self-sacrifice of the individual to help perpetuate the family group. The behavior patterns are termed *instinctive* or *species-specific* because they evolved within certain *species*.

The nervous systems of most, and perhaps all, animals are "prewired" to respond to some situations in specific ways. For example, birds raised in isolation from other birds build nests during the mating season even if they have never seen a nest or seen another bird building one. Nest-building could not have been learned. Birds raised in isolation also sing the songs typical of their species. These behaviors are *built in*, or instinctive. They are also referred to as inborn **fixed action patterns (FAPs)**.

evolutionary psychology the branch of psychology that deals with the ways in which humans' historical adaptations to the environment influence behavior and mental processes, with special focus on aggressive behavior and mating strategies.

fixed action pattern (FAP) a stereotyped pattern of behavior that is evoked by a "releasing stimulus"; an instinct.

ecology the branch of biology that deals with the relationships between living organisms and their environment.

ecological systems theory the view that explains child development in terms of the reciprocal influences between children and environmental settings.

microsystem the immediate settings with which the child interacts, such as the home, the school, and peers.

mesosystem the interlocking settings that influence the child, such as the interaction of the school and the larger community.

During prenatal development, genes and sex hormones are responsible for the physical development of female and male sex organs. Most theorists also believe that in many species, including humans, sex hormones can "masculinize" or "feminize" the embryonic brain by creating tendencies to behave in stereotypical masculine or feminine ways. Testosterone, the male sex hormone, seems to be connected with feelings of self-confidence, high activity levels, and—the negative side—aggressiveness (Hines, 2011; Nguyen et al., 2016; Rice & Sher, 2013).

Research into the ethological perspective suggests that instinct may play a role in human behavior. Two questions that ethological research seeks to answer are: What areas of human behavior and development, if any, involve instincts? How powerful are instincts in people?

1-2e THE ECOLOGICAL PERSPECTIVE

Ecology is the branch of biology that deals with the relationships between living organisms and their environment. The **ecological systems theory** of development addresses aspects of psychological, social, and emotional development as well as aspects of biological development. Ecological systems theorists explain development in terms of the interaction between people and the settings in which they live (Bronfenbrenner & Morris, 2006).

According to Urie Bronfenbrenner (1917–2005), for example, we need to focus on the two-way interactions between the child and the parents, not just maturational forces (nature) or child-rearing practices (nurture). Bronfenbrenner suggested that we can view the setting or contexts of human development as consisting of multiple systems, each embedded within the next larger context (Bronfenbrenner & Morris, 2006). From narrowest to widest, these systems are the microsystem, the mesosystem, the exosystem, the macrosystem, and the chronosystem (Figure 1.4).

The **microsystem** involves the interactions of the child and other people in the immediate setting, such as the home, the school, or the peer group. Initially, the microsystem is small, involving care-giving interactions with the parents or others, usually at home. As children get older, they do more, with more people, in more places.

The **mesosystem** involves the interactions of the various settings within the microsystem. For instance, the home and the school interact during parent–teacher conferences. The school and the larger community interact when children are taken on field trips. The ecological systems approach addresses the joint effect of two or more settings on the child.

FIG.1.4 THE CONTEXTS OF HUMAN DEVELOPMENT

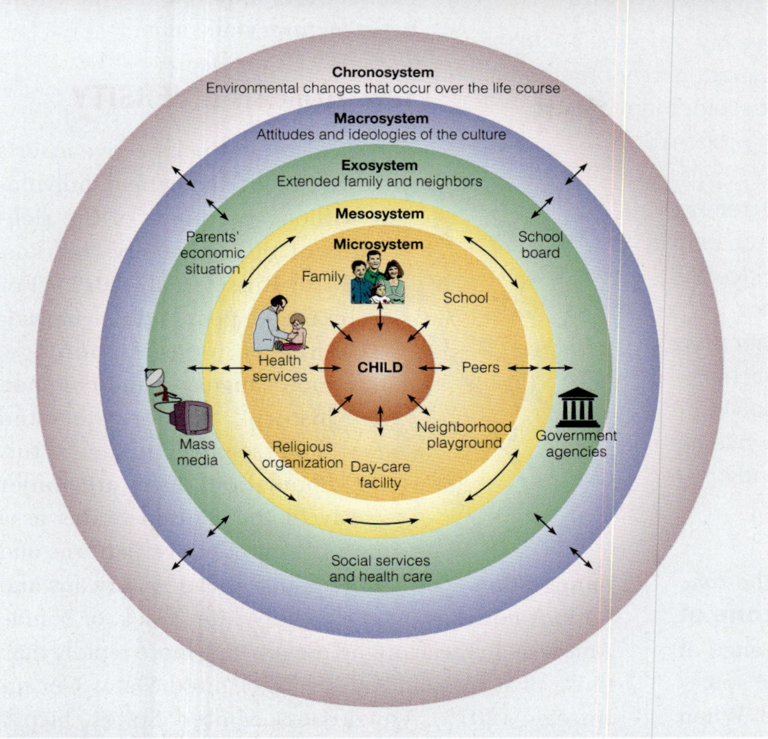

Psychologists and educators explain social and environmental influences on development in various ways. Urie Bronfenbrenner spoke of the importance of *ecological systems*, which affect development in various ways. The child's family, peers, and day-care facility, for example, are part of the child's microsystem and exert enormous influence. But the elements in the microsystem interact with other systems to influence the child. The parents' economic situation, for example, which is considered part of the child's exosystem, makes certain things possible for the child and rules out others.

The **exosystem** involves the institutions in which the child does not directly participate but which exert an indirect influence on the child. For example, the school board is part of the child's exosystem because board members put together programs for the child's education, determine what textbooks will be acceptable, and so forth. In similar fashion, the parents' workplaces and economic situations determine the hours during which they will be available to the child, and so on (Hong & Eamon, 2012; Tisdale & Pitt-Catsuphes, 2012). When some parents are unavailable, children may be more likely to misbehave at home or in school.

The **macrosystem** involves the interaction of children with the beliefs, values, expectations, and lifestyles of their cultural settings. Cross-cultural studies examine children's interactions with their macrosystem. Macrosystems exist within a particular culture. In the United States, the dual-earner family, the low-income single-parent household, and the family with father as sole breadwinner describe three different macrosystems. Each has its lifestyle, set of values, and expectations (Bronfenbrenner & Morris, 2006; Lustig, 2011).

The **chronosystem** considers the changes that occur over time. For example, the effects of divorce peak about a year after the event, and then children begin to recover. The breakup has more of an effect on boys than on girls. The ecological approach broadens the strategies for intervention in problems such as prevention of teenage pregnancy, child abuse, and juvenile offending, including substance use disorders (Kaminski & Stormshak, 2007; Latkin et al., 2013).

1-2f THE SOCIOCULTURAL PERSPECTIVE

The sociocultural perspective teaches that people are social beings who are affected by the cultures in which they live. Developmentalists use the term *sociocultural* in a couple of different ways. One refers quite specifically to the *sociocultural theory* of Russian psychologist Lev Semenovich Vygotsky (1896–1934). The other addresses the effect of human diversity on people, including such factors as ethnicity and gender.

VYGOTSKY'S SOCIOCULTURAL THEORY

Whereas genetics is concerned with the biological transmission of traits from generation to generation, Vygotsky's (1978) theory is concerned with the transmission of information and cognitive skills from generation to generation. The transmission of skills involves teaching and learning, but Vygotsky does not view learning in terms of conditioning. Rather, he focuses on how the child's social interaction with adults, largely in the home, organizes a child's learning experiences in such a way that the child can obtain cognitive skills—such as computation or reading skills—and use them to acquire information. Like Piaget, Vygotsky sees the child's functioning as adaptive, and the child adapts to his or her social and cultural interactions.

exosystem community institutions and settings that indirectly influence the child, such as the school board and the parents' workplaces.

macrosystem the basic institutions and ideologies that influence the child.

chronosystem the environmental changes that occur over time and have an effect on the child.

VYGOTSKY'S SOCIOCULTURAL THEORY

Lev Semenovich Vygotsky (1896–1934) was mainly concerned with the transmission of information from one generation to another. He explained the social influences on children's development of knowledge and skills in terms of their zone of proximal development and scaffolding.

The zone of proximal development (ZPD) refers to a range of tasks that a child can carry out with the help of someone who is more skilled, as in an apprenticeship. A scaffold is a temporary skeletal structure that enables workers to fabricate a building or other more permanent structure. In Vygotsky's theory, teachers and parents provide children with problem-solving methods that serve as cognitive scaffolding while the child gains the ability to function independently.

Key concepts in Vygotsky's theory include the *zone of proximal development* and *scaffolding*. The **zone of proximal development (ZPD)** refers to a range of tasks that a child can carry out with the help of someone who is more skilled, as in an apprenticeship. When learning with other people, children internalize—or bring inward—the conversations and explanations that help them gain the necessary skills (Vygotsky, 1962; Poehner, 2012; Thompson et al., 2016).

A *scaffold* is a temporary skeletal structure that enables workers to fabricate a building or other more permanent structure. In Vygotsky's theory, teachers and parents provide children with problem-solving methods that serve as cognitive **scaffolding** while the child gains the ability to function independently. For example, children may be offered scaffolding that enables them to use their fingers or their toes to do simple calculations. Eventually, the scaffolding is removed and the cognitive structures stand alone.

zone of proximal development (ZPD) Vygotsky's term for the situation in which a child carries out tasks with the help of someone who is more skilled.

scaffolding Vygotsky's term for temporary cognitive structures or methods of solving problems that help the child as he or she learns to function independently.

Len Rubenstein/Photolibrary/Getty Images; Brand X Pictures/Jupiter Images

According to Vygotsky's theory, teachers and parents provide children with problem-solving methods that serve as cognitive scaffolding.

1-2g HUMAN DIVERSITY

The sociocultural perspective asserts that we cannot understand individuals without awareness of the richness of their diversity (Markus, 2016; Russo et al., 2012). For example, people differ in their ethnicity (cultural heritage, race, language, and common history), their gender, and their socioeconomic status.

Population shifts are under way in the United States as a result of reproductive patterns and immigration. The numbers of African Americans and Latin Americans (who may be White, Black, or Native American in racial origin) are growing more rapidly than those of European Americans (United States Census Bureau. (2015). QuickFacts, United States. http://www.census.gov/quickfacts/table/PST045215/00). The cultural heritages, languages, and histories of ethnic minority groups are thus likely to have an increasing effect on the cultural life of the United States, yet it turns out that the dominant culture in the United States has often disparaged the traditions and languages of people from ethnic minority groups. For example, it has been considered harmful to rear children bilingually, although research suggests that bilingualism broadens children's knowledge of the various peoples of the world.

Studying diversity is also important so that students have appropriate educational experiences. To teach students and guide their learning, educators need to understand children's family values and cultural expectations. Issues that affect people from various ethnic groups include bilingualism, ethnic differences in intelligence test scores, the prevalence of suicide among members of different backgrounds, and patterns of child rearing among parents of various groups.

Gender is another aspect of human diversity. Gender is the psychological state of being male or being female, as influenced by cultural concepts of gender-appropriate behavior. Expectations of females and males are often polarized by cultural expectations. Males may differ from females in some respects, but history has created more burdens for women than men as a result. Historically, females have been discouraged from careers in the sciences, politics, and business. Recent research, however, shows that females are as capable as males of performing in so-called STEM fields (science, technology, engineering, and math) (e.g., Brown & Lent, 2016). Women today are making inroads into academic and vocational spheres—such as medicine, law, engineering, and the military—that were traditionally male preserves. Today, most college students in the United States are female, but there remain many parts of the world in which women are prevented from obtaining an education (Yousafazi & Lamb, 2013).

Contemporary psychologists and educators recognize that we cannot understand the development of individuals without reference to their diversity—for example, their cultural heritage, race, language, common history, gender, and socioeconomic status.

Derek Latta/Getty Images

Table 1.1 summarizes the theoretical perspectives on development.

1-3 CONTROVERSIES IN DEVELOPMENT

The discussion of theories of development reveals that developmentalists can see things in very different ways. Let us consider how they react to three of the most important debates in the field.

1-3a THE NATURE–NURTURE CONTROVERSY

Researchers are continually trying to sort out the extent to which human behavior is the result of **nature** (heredity) and of **nurture** (environmental influences). What aspects of behavior originate in our genes and are biologically programmed to unfold as time goes on, as long as minimal nutrition and social experience are provided? What aspects of behavior can be traced largely to such environmental influences as nutrition and learning?

Scientists seek the natural causes of development in children's genetic heritage, the functioning of the nervous system, and in maturation. Scientists seek the environmental causes of development in children's nutrition, cultural and family backgrounds, and opportunities to learn about the world, including cognitive stimulation during early childhood and formal education.

Some theorists (e.g., cognitive-developmental and biological theorists) lean heavily toward natural explanations of development, whereas others (e.g., learning theorists) lean more heavily toward environmental explanations. Today, though, nearly all researchers agree that nature and nurture play important roles in nearly every area of development. Consider the development of language. Language is based in structures found in certain areas of the brain. Thus, biology (nature) plays a vital role. Children also come to speak the languages spoken by their caretakers. Parent–child similarities in accent and vocabulary provide additional evidence for the role of learning (nurture) in language development.

1-3b THE CONTINUITY–DISCONTINUITY CONTROVERSY

Some developmentalists view human development as a continuous process in which the effects of learning mount gradually, with no major sudden qualitative changes. In contrast, other theorists believe that a number of rapid qualitative changes usher in new stages of development. Maturational theorists point out that the environment, even when enriched, profits us little until we are ready, or mature enough, to develop in a certain way. For example, newborn babies will not imitate their parents' speech, even when parents speak clearly and deliberately. Nor does aided practice in walking during the first few months after birth significantly accelerate the emergence of independent walking. The babies are not ready to do these things.

nature the processes within an organism that guide it to develop according to its genetic code.

nurture environmental factors that influence development.

TABLE 1.1 CHILD DEVELOPMENT PERSPECTIVES AND THEORIES

Perspective	Theory	Core Concepts	Is Nature or Nurture More Important?
The Psychoanalytic Perspective	**Theory of psychosexual development** (Sigmund Freud)	Social codes channel primitive impulses, resulting in unconscious conflict.	Interaction of nature and nurture: Maturation sets the stage for reacting to social influences.
	Theory of psychosocial development (Erik Erikson)	People undergo life crises that are largely based on social relationships, opportunities, and expectations.	Interaction of nature and nurture: Maturation sets the stage for reacting to social influences and opportunities.
The Learning Perspective: Behavioral and Social Cognitive Theories	**Behaviorism** (John B. Watson, Ivan Pavlov, B. F. Skinner)	Behavior is learned by association, as in classical and operant conditioning.	Nurture: Children are seen almost as blank tablets.
	Social cognitive theory (Albert Bandura and others)	Conditioning occurs, but people also learn by observing others and choose whether to display learned responses.	Emphasizes nurture but allows for the expression of natural tendencies.
The Cognitive Perspective	**Cognitive-developmental theory** (Jean Piaget)	Children adapt to the environment via assimilation to existing mental structures by accommodating to these structures.	Emphasizes nature but allows for influences of experience.
	Information-processing theory	Human cognitive functioning is compared to that of computers—how they input, manipulate, store, and output information.	Interaction of nature and nurture.
The Biological Perspective	**Ethology and evolution** (Charles Darwin, Konrad Lorenz, Niko Tinbergen)	Organisms are biologically "prewired" to develop certain adaptive responses during sensitive periods.	Emphasizes nature but experience is also critical; e.g., imprinting occurs during a sensitive period but experience determines the object of imprinting.
The Ecological Perspective	**Ecological systems theory** (Urie Bronfenbrenner)	Children's development occurs within interlocking systems, and development is enhanced by intervening in these systems.	Interaction of nature and nurture: Children's personalities and skills contribute to their development.
The Sociocultural Perspective	**Sociocultural theory** (Lev Vygotsky)	Children internalize sociocultural dialogues in developing problem-solving skills.	Interaction of nature and nurture: Nurture is discussed in social and cultural terms.
	Sociocultural perspective and human diversity	Development is influenced by factors such as cultural heritage, race, language, common history, gender, and socioeconomic status.	Nurture.

Stage theorists such as Sigmund Freud and Jean Piaget saw development as discontinuous. They saw biological changes as providing the potential for psychological changes. Freud focused on the ways in which biological developments might provide the basis for personality development. Piaget believed maturation of the nervous system allowed cognitive development.

Certain aspects of physical development do occur in stages. For example, from the age of two years to the onset of puberty, children gradually grow larger. Then the adolescent growth spurt occurs as rushes of hormones cause rapid biological changes in structure and function (as in the development of the sex organs) and in size. Psychologists disagree on whether developments in cognition occur in stages.

1-3c THE ACTIVE–PASSIVE CONTROVERSY

Historical views of children as willful and unruly suggest that people have generally seen children as active, even if mischievous (at best) or evil (at worst). John Locke introduced a view of children as passive beings (blank tablets); experience "wrote" features of personality and moral virtue on them.

At one extreme, educators who view children as passive may assume that they must be motivated to learn by their instructors. Such educators are likely to provide a rigorous traditional curriculum with a powerful system of rewards and punishments to promote absorption of the subject matter. At the other extreme, educators who view children as active may assume that they have a natural

Here we have a clear example of the importance of maturation in development. Adolescents undergo a growth spurt that disrupts a pattern of gradual gains in height and weight that persisted throughout most of childhood. Girls, interestingly, spurt earlier than boys. The girl and boy shown here are actually the same age, even though the girl towers over the boy. But her height advantage is temporary; when he spurts, he will quickly catch up to her and surpass her in height.

Mark Richard/PhotoEdit

love of learning. Such educators are likely to argue for open education and encourage children to explore and pursue their unique likes and talents.

These debates are theoretical. Scientists value theory for its ability to tie together observations and suggest new areas of investigation, but scientists also follow an **empirical** approach. That is, they engage in research methods, such as those described in the next section, to find evidence for or against various theoretical positions.

1-4 HOW DO WE STUDY DEVELOPMENT?

What is the relationship between intelligence and achievement? What are the effects of maternal use of aspirin and alcohol on the fetus? What are the effects of parental divorce on children? What are the effects of early retirement? We may have expressed opinions on such questions at one time or another, but scientists insist that such questions be answered by research. Strong arguments or reference to authority figures are not evidence. Scientific evidence is obtained only by gathering sound information and conducting research.

1-4a GATHERING INFORMATION

Researchers use various methods to gather information. For example, they may ask teachers or parents to report on the behavior of children, use interviews or questionnaires with adults, or study statistics compiled by the government or the United Nations. They also directly observe children in the laboratory, the playground, or the classroom. Let us discuss two ways of gathering information: the naturalistic-observation method and the case-study method.

NATURALISTIC OBSERVATION **Naturalistic-observation** studies are conducted in the field, that is, in the natural, or real-life, settings in which they happen. In field studies, investigators observe the natural behavior of children in settings such as homes, playgrounds, and classrooms and try not to interfere with it. Researchers may try to "blend into the woodwork" by sitting quietly in the back of a classroom or by observing the class through a one-way mirror.

Naturalistic-observation studies have been done with children of different cultures. For example, researchers have observed the motor behavior of Native American Hopi children who are strapped to cradle boards during their first year. You can read more about this in Chapter 5.

THE CASE STUDY The **case study** is a carefully drawn account of the behavior of an individual. Parents who keep diaries of their children's activities are involved in informal case studies. Case studies themselves often use a number of different kinds of information. In addition to direct observation, case studies may include questionnaires, **standardized tests**, and interviews. Information gleaned from public records may be included. Scientists who use the case-study method try to record all relevant factors in a person's behavior, and they are cautious in drawing conclusions about what leads to what.

empirical based on observation and experimentation.

naturalistic-observation a scientific method in which organisms are observed in their natural environments.

case study a carefully drawn biography of the life of an individual.

standardized test a test in which an individual's score is compared to the scores of a group of similar individuals.

1-4b CORRELATION: PUTTING THINGS TOGETHER

Researchers use the correlational method to determine whether one behavior or trait being studied is related to, or correlated with, another. Consider intelligence and achievement. These variables are assigned numbers such as intelligence test scores and grade point averages. Then the numbers or scores are mathematically related and expressed as a **correlation coefficient**—a number that varies between +1.00 and −1.00.

In general, the higher people score on intelligence tests, the better their academic performance (or income) is likely to be. The scores attained on intelligence tests are **positively correlated** (about +0.60 to +0.70) with overall academic achievement (and income). There is a **negative correlation** between adolescents' grades and delinquent acts. The higher an adolescent's grades, the less likely he or she is to engage in criminal behavior. Figure 1.5 illustrates the concepts of positive and negative correlations.

LIMITATIONS OF CORRELATIONAL INFORMATION Correlational information can reveal relationships between variables, but it does not show cause and effect. It may seem logical to assume that exposure to violent media makes people more aggressive, but it may also be that more aggressive people *choose* violent media. This research bias is termed a *selection factor*.

Similarly, studies report that children (especially boys) in divorced families tend to show more behavioral problems than children in intact families (Daryanani et al., 2016; Vélez et al., 2011). These studies, however, do not show that divorce causes these adjustment problems. It could be that the factors that led to divorce—such as parental conflict—also led to adjustment problems among the children (Hetherington, 2006). To investigate cause and effect, researchers turn to the experimental method.

1-4c THE EXPERIMENT: TRYING THINGS OUT

The experiment is the preferred method for investigating questions of cause and effect. In the **experiment**, a group of research participants receives a treatment and another group does not. The subjects are then observed to determine whether the treatment changes their behavior. Experiments are usually undertaken to test a **hypothesis**. For example, a researcher might hypothesize that TV violence will cause aggressive behavior in children.

INDEPENDENT AND DEPENDENT VARIABLES In an experiment to determine whether TV violence causes aggressive behavior, subjects in the experimental group would be shown a TV program containing violence, and its effects on behavior would be measured.

FIG.1.5 EXAMPLES OF POSITIVE AND NEGATIVE CORRELATIONS

When two variables are correlated positively, one increases as the other increases. Part A shows that there is a positive correlation between the amount of time studying and one's grades in school. In contrast, when two variables are correlated negatively, one decreases as the other one increases. As in Part B, a teenager's school grades are likely to decrease as he engages in more delinquent acts. But correlation does not show cause and effect. Do the teenager's grades fall off because of his engaging in more delinquent behavior? Do falling grades lead to more delinquency? Or could another factor explain *both* falling grades and increased delinquency?

correlation coefficient a number ranging from +1.00 to −1.00 that expresses the direction (positive or negative) and strength of the relationship between two variables.

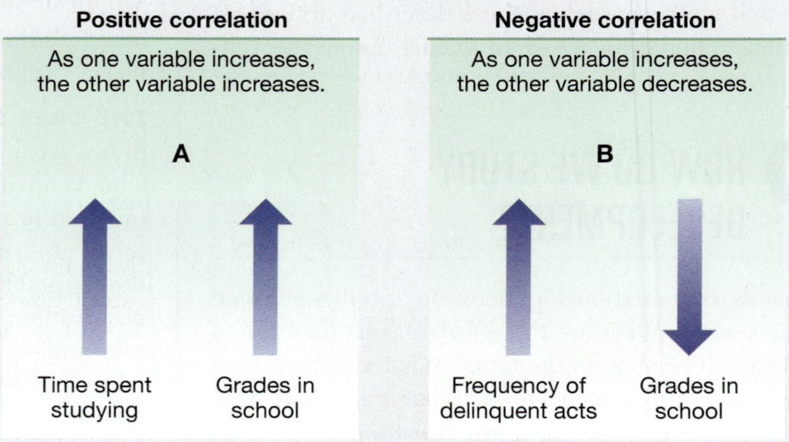

positive correlation a relationship between two variables in which one variable increases as the other increases.

negative correlation a relationship between two variables in which one variable increases as the other decreases.

experiment a method of scientific investigation that seeks to discover cause-and-effect relationships by introducing independent variables and observing their effects on dependent variables.

hypothesis a proposition to be tested.

TV violence would be considered an **independent variable**, a variable whose presence is manipulated by the experimenters so that its effects can be determined. The measured result—in this case, the child's behavior—is called a **dependent variable**. Its presence or level presumably depends on the independent variable.

EXPERIMENTAL AND CONTROL GROUPS Experiments use experimental and control groups. Subjects in the **experimental group** receive the treatment, whereas subjects in the **control group** do not. All other conditions are held constant for both groups. Thus, we can have confidence that experimental outcomes reflect the treatments and not chance factors.

RANDOM ASSIGNMENT Subjects should be assigned to experimental or control groups on a chance or random basis. We could not conclude much from an experiment on the effects of TV violence if the children were allowed to choose whether they would be in a group that watched TV violence or in a group that did not. A *selection factor* rather than the treatment might then be responsible for the results of the experiment.

Ethical and practical considerations also prevent researchers from doing experiments on the effects of many life circumstances, such as divorce or different patterns of child rearing. We cannot randomly assign some families to divorce or conflict and assign other families to "bliss." Nor can we randomly assign parents to rearing their children in an authoritarian or permissive manner. In some areas of investigation, we must settle for correlational evidence.

When experiments cannot ethically be performed on humans, researchers sometimes carry them out with animals and try to generalize the findings to humans. No researcher would separate human infants from their parents to study the effects of isolation on development, yet experimenters have deprived monkeys of early social experience. Such research has helped psychologists investigate the formation of parent–child bonds of attachment.

TRUTH

F Research with monkeys has helped psychologists understand the formation of attachment in humans.

It is true that research with monkeys has helped psychologists understand the formation of attachment in humans. Researchers have exposed monkeys and other nonhuman animals to conditions that it would be unethical to use with humans.

1-4d LONGITUDINAL RESEARCH: STUDYING DEVELOPMENT OVER TIME

The processes of development occur over time, and researchers have devised different strategies for comparing children of one age with children or adults of other ages. In **longitudinal research**, the same people are observed repeatedly over time, and changes in development, such as gains in height or changes in mental abilities, are recorded. In **cross-sectional research**, children of different ages are observed and compared. It is assumed that when a large number of children are chosen at random, the differences found in the older age groups are a reflection of how the younger children will develop, given time.

LONGITUDINAL STUDIES The Terman Studies of Genius, begun in the 1920s, tracked children with high IQ scores for more than 50 years. Male subjects, but not female subjects, went on to high achievements in the professional world. Why? Contemporary studies of women show that women with high intelligence generally match the achievements of men and suggest that women of the earlier era were held back by traditional gender-role expectations.

Most longitudinal studies span months or a few years, not decades. For example, briefer longitudinal studies have found that the children of divorced parents undergo the most severe adjustment problems within a few months of the divorce, peaking at about a year. By two or three years afterward, many children regain their equilibrium,

independent variable a condition in a scientific study that is manipulated so that its effects can be observed.

dependent variable a measure of an assumed effect of an independent variable.

experimental group a group made up of subjects who receive a treatment in an experiment.

control group a group made up of subjects in an experiment who do not receive the treatment but for whom all other conditions are comparable to those of subjects in the experimental group.

longitudinal research the study of developmental processes by taking repeated measures of the same group of participants at various stages of development.

cross-sectional research the study of developmental processes by taking measures of participants of different age groups at the same time.

as indicated by improved academic performance and social behavior (Hetherington, 2006; Moon, 2011).

Longitudinal studies have drawbacks. For example, it can be difficult to enlist volunteers to participate in a study that will last a lifetime. Many subjects fall out of touch as the years pass; others die. The researchers must be patient or arrange to enlist future generations of researchers.

TRUTH

T F To learn how a person develops over a lifetime, researchers have tracked some individuals for more than 50 years.

It is true that researchers have tracked some individuals for more than 50 years to learn how a person develops over a lifetime. The Terman study did just that. What are the advantages and disadvantages of longitudinal research as compared with cross-sectional research?

CROSS-SECTIONAL STUDIES Because of the drawbacks of longitudinal studies, most research that compares children of different ages is cross-sectional. In other words, most investigators gather data on what the "typical" six-month-old is doing by finding children who are six months old today. When they expand their research to the behavior of typical 12-month-olds, they seek another group of children, and so on.

A major challenge to cross-sectional research is the **cohort effect**. A cohort is a group of people born at about the same time. As a result, they experience cultural and other events unique to their age group. In other words, children and adults of different ages are not likely to have shared similar cultural backgrounds. People who are 80 years old today, for example, grew up without TV. Today's children are growing up taking iPods and the Internet for granted.

Children of past generations also grew up with different expectations about gender roles and appropriate social behavior. Women in the Terman study generally chose motherhood over careers because of the times. Today's girls are growing up with female role models who are astronauts and government officials.

In longitudinal studies, we know that we have the same individuals as they have developed over 5, 25, even 50 years or more. In cross-sectional research, we can only hope that they will be comparable.

CROSS-SEQUENTIAL RESEARCH **Cross-sequential research** combines the longitudinal and cross-sectional methods so that many of their individual drawbacks are overcome. In the cross-sequential study, the full span of the ideal longitudinal study is broken up into convenient segments (see Figure 1.6). Assume that we wish to follow the attitudes of children toward gender roles from the age of 4 through the age of 12. The typical longitudinal study would take eight years. We can, however, divide this eight-year span in half by attaining two samples of children (a cross-section) instead of one: four-year-olds and eight-year-olds. We would then interview, test, and observe each group at the beginning of the study (2018) and four years later (2022).

FIG.1.6 EXAMPLES OF CROSS-SEQUENTIAL RESEARCH

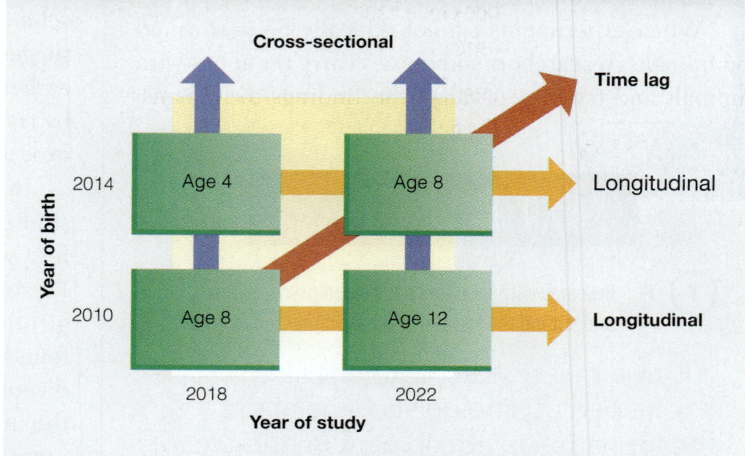

Cross-sequential research combines three methods: cross-sectional, longitudinal, and time lag. The child's age at the time of testing appears in the boxes. Vertical columns represent cross-sectional comparisons. Horizontal rows represent longitudinal comparisons. Diagonals represent time-lag comparisons.

cohort effect similarities in behavior among a group of peers that stem from the fact that group members were born at the same time in history.

cross-sequential research an approach that combines the longitudinal and cross-sectional methods by following individuals of different ages for abbreviated periods of time.

An obvious advantage to this collapsed method is that the study is completed in four years rather than eight years. Still, the testing and retesting of samples provides some of the continuity of the longitudinal study. By observing both samples at the age of eight (a **time-lag** comparison), we can also determine whether they are, in fact, comparable or whether the four-year difference in their birth date is associated with a cohort effect.

1-4e ETHICAL CONSIDERATIONS

Researchers adhere to ethical standards that are intended to promote the dignity of the individual, foster human welfare, and maintain scientific integrity. These standards also ensure that they do not use methods or treatments that harm subjects:

- Researchers are not to use methods that may do physical or psychological harm.
- Participants (and parents, if participants are minors) must be informed of the purposes of the research and about the research methods.
- Participants must provide voluntary consent to participate in the study.
- Participants may withdraw from the study at any time, for any reason.
- Participants should be offered information about the results of the study.
- The identities of the participants are to remain confidential.
- Researchers should present their research plans to a committee of their colleagues and gain the committee's approval before proceeding.

These guidelines present researchers with a number of hurdles to overcome before proceeding with and while conducting research, but because they protect the welfare of participants, the guidelines are valuable.

In this chapter we have defined developmental psychology, discussed its history as a discipline, explored theories of developmental psychology, and seen how developmental psychologists and educators conduct research into human development. In the next chapter, we return to the true beginnings of human development: heredity and prenatal development.

time-lag the study of developmental processes by taking measures of participants of the same age group at different times.

STUDY TOOLS 1

READY TO STUDY?

In the book, you can:

- ☐ Rip out the chapter review card at the back of the book for a handy summary of the chapter and key terms.
- ☐ Check your understanding of what you've read with the quizzes that follow.

ONLINE AT CENGAGEBRAIN.COM YOU CAN:

- ☐ Collect StudyBits while you read and study the chapter.
- ☐ Quiz yourself on key concepts.
- ☐ Find videos for further exploration.
- ☐ Prepare for tests with HDEV5 Flash Cards as well as those you create.

SELF-ASSESSMENTS

Fill-Ins

Answers can be found in the back of the book.

1. ___________ believed that a child came into the world as a tabula rasa.
2. Freud theorized that the personality has three parts: the id, the ego, and the ___________.
3. Erikson emphasized ___________ rather than psychosexual development.
4. In the bell-and-pad method for treating bed-wetting in children, psychologists repeatedly pair tension in the ___________ with a stimulus that awakens them.
5. According to Piaget, ___________ is the process by which a person responds to new objects or events with existing schemes.
6. According to evolutionary psychologists, organisms can inherit ___________-specific behaviors.
7. According to the ecological perspective, the ___________ involves the institutions in which the person does not directly participate but which exert an indirect influence on the person.
8. The ___________ Studies of Genius followed children with high IQ scores for more than 50 years.
9. There is usually a(n) ___________ correlation between time spent studying and grades in school.
10. Cross-___________ research combines cross-sectional research, longitudinal research, and time-lag research.

Multiple Choice

1. **Which of the following is the correct order for the stages of psychosexual development?**
   a. anal, oral, genital, phallic, latency
   b. oral, anal, phallic, latency, genital
   c. genital, phallic, anal, oral, latency
   d. phallic, latency, oral, genital, anal

2. **In operant conditioning, extinction results from repeated performance of operant behavior in the absence of**
   a. the conditioned stimulus.
   b. punishment.
   c. time out.
   d. reinforcement.

3. **Negative reinforcers differ from punishments in that**
   a. negative reinforcers increase the frequency of behavior when they are removed.
   b. punishments increase the frequency of behavior when they are removed.
   c. negative reinforcers decrease the frequency of behavior when they are removed.
   d. punishments decrease the frequency of behavior when they are removed.

4. **According to Bronfenbrenner, the ____________ involves the interactions of the child and other people in the immediate setting, such as the home, school, or peer group.**
   a. mesosystem
   b. macrosystem
   c. exosystem
   d. microsystem

5. **Which of the following kinds of theorists is likely to view development as continuous?**
   a. a psychoanalytic theorist
   b. a behaviorist
   c. a cognitive-developmental theorist
   d. a psychosocial theorist

6. **Which of the following is an example of development occurring discontinuously?**
   a. the adolescent growth spurt
   b. scaffolding
   c. acquiring social skills
   d. learning new vocabulary words

7. **In a ____________ sample, each member of a population has an equal chance of being selected to participate.**
   a. random
   b. selection
   c. stratified
   d. free

8. **More aggressive people are more likely to watch violent TV shows. Which of the following is true about this statement?**
   a. It shows that violent TV shows cause aggressive behavior.
   b. It shows that aggressive behavior leads to a preference for violent TV shows.
   c. It shows a relationship between aggressive behavior and violent TV shows.
   d. It shows cause and effect involving several unknown factors.

9. **Which of the following is true of all experiments?**
   a. Participants are blind as to the treatment they have received.
   b. Experimenters deceive the participants.
   c. Equal numbers of participants are assigned to the experimental and control groups.
   d. There are independent and dependent variables.

10. **Dr. Liu was interested in testing the effects of violent television on six-year-old children. She showed a particularly violent episode of *Power Rangers* to one group and a short nonviolent episode of an old Bill Cosby show to another group. She then observed the groups in the playground and measured their behaviors. What is the dependent variable in this study?**
    a. Bill Cosby and his family
    b. violent or nonviolent TV show
    c. the behavior on the playground
    d. the amount of time watching TV

2 Heredity and Prenatal Development

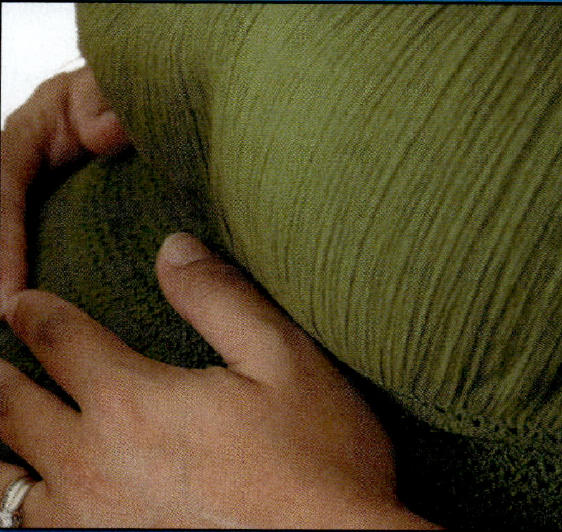

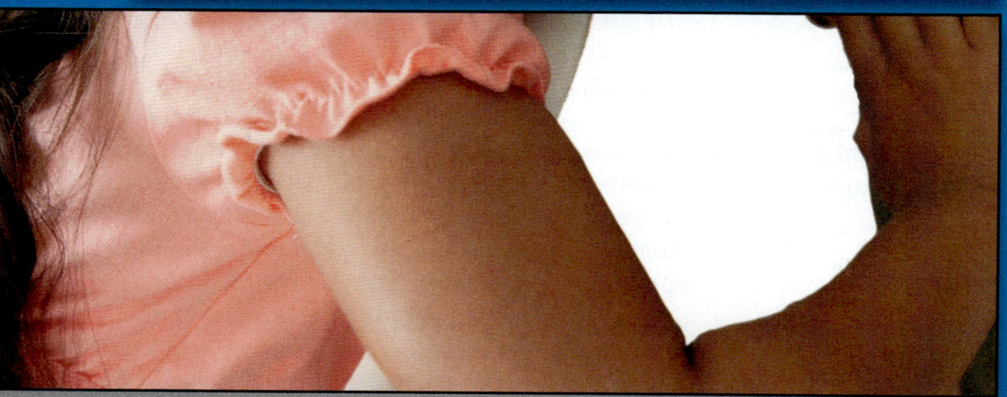

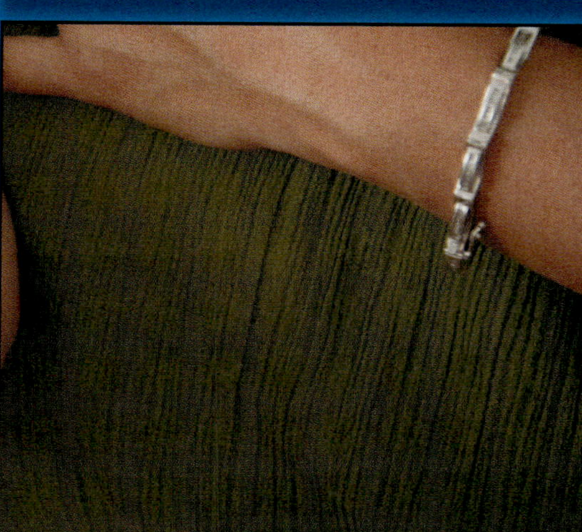

Hill Street Studios/Getty Images

LEARNING OUTCOMES

After studying this chapter, you will be able to...

- 2-1 Describe the influences of heredity on development
- 2-2 Describe the influences of the environment on development
- 2-3 Explain what happens in the process of conception
- 2-4 Recount the major events of prenatal development

After you finish this chapter, go to **PAGE 47** for **STUDY TOOLS**

Consider some of the facts of life. People cannot breathe underwater (without special equipment). Nor can people fly (without special equipment). Fish cannot learn to speak French or dance an Irish jig, even if you raise them in enriched environments and send them to finishing school. We cannot breathe underwater or fly because we have not inherited gills or wings.

> The structures we inherit make our behavior possible and place limits on it.

Fish are similarly limited by their heredity.

Heredity makes possible all things human. The structures we inherit make our behavior possible and place limits on it. The field of biology that studies heredity is called **genetics**. It is our heredity that determines that human embryos will grow arms rather than wings, lungs rather than gills, and hair rather than scales.

2-1 THE INFLUENCE OF HEREDITY ON DEVELOPMENT

Genetic influences are fundamental in the transmission of physical traits, such as height, hair texture, and eye color. Heredity appears to be a factor in almost all aspects of human behavior, personality, and mental processes (Plomin & Asbury, 2005; Plomin & Haworth, 2009; Stone et al., 2012). Examples include sociability, anxiety, social dominance, leadership, effectiveness as a parent, happiness, and even interest in arts and crafts (Blum et al., 2009; Ebstein et al., 2010; Sirgy, 2012). Genetic factors are also involved in psychological problems such as schizophrenia, depression, and dependence on nicotine, alcohol, and other substances (Leonardo & Hen, 2006; Lewis et al., 2013; Viding et al., 2013).

2-1a CHROMOSOMES AND GENES

Traits are transmitted by chromosomes and genes. **Chromosomes** are rod-shaped structures found in cells. Typical human cells contain 46 chromosomes organized into 23 pairs. Each chromosome contains thousands of segments called genes. **Genes** are the biochemical materials that regulate the development of traits. Some traits, such as blood type, appear to be transmitted by a single pair of genes, one of which is derived from each parent. Other traits are **polygenic**, that is, determined by several pairs of genes.

Our heredity is governed by 20,000 to 25,000 genes (Gonzaga-Jaurequi et al., 2012). Genes are segments of strands of **deoxyribonucleic acid (DNA)**. DNA takes the form of a double spiral, or helix, similar to a twisting ladder (see Figure 2.1). The "rungs" of the ladder consist of one of two pairs of bases, either adenine with thymine (A with T) or cytosine with guanine (C with G). The sequence of the rungs is the genetic code that will cause the developing organism to grow arms or wings, skin or scales.

genetics the branch of biology that studies heredity.

chromosomes rod-shaped structures composed of genes that are found within the nuclei of cells.

gene the basic unit of heredity. Genes are composed of deoxyribonucleic acid (DNA).

polygenic resulting from many genes.

deoxyribonucleic acid (DNA) genetic material that takes the form of a double helix composed of phosphates, sugars, and bases.

TRUTH OR FICTION?

T	F	Your father determined whether you are female or male.
T	F	Approximately 120 to 150 boys are conceived for every 100 girls.
T	F	Sperm travel randomly inside the woman's reproductive tract, so reaching the ovum is a matter of luck.
T	F	"Test-tube babies" are grown in a laboratory dish throughout their nine-month gestation period.
T	F	Newly fertilized egg cells survive without any nourishment from the mother for more than a week.
T	F	Fetuses suck their thumbs, sometimes for hours on end.
T	F	A father's age at the time of conception can influence the development of the fetus.

2-1b MITOSIS AND MEIOSIS

We begin life as a single cell, or zygote, that divides repeatedly. There are two types of cell division: *mitosis* and *meiosis*. In **mitosis**, strands of DNA break apart, or "unzip" (see Figure 2.2). The double helix then duplicates. The DNA forms two camps on either side of the cell, and then the cell divides. Each incomplete rung combines with the appropriate "partner" (i.e., G and C, A and T) to form a new complete ladder. The two resulting identical copies of the DNA strand separate when the cell divides; each becomes a member of a newly formed cell. As a result, the genetic code is identical in new cells unless **mutations** occur through radiation or other environmental influences. Mutations also occur by chance, but not often.

Sperm and ova ("egg cells") are produced through **meiosis**, or *reduction division*. In meiosis, the 46 chromosomes within the cell nucleus first line up into 23 pairs. The DNA ladders then unzip, leaving unpaired halves of chromosome. When the cell divides, one member of each pair goes to each newly formed cell. Each new cell nucleus contains only 23 chromosomes, not 46.

When a sperm cell fertilizes an ovum, we receive 23 chromosomes from our father's sperm cell and 23 from our mother's ovum, and the combined chromosomes form 23 pairs (see Figure 2.3). Twenty-two of the pairs are **autosomes**—pairs that look alike and possess genetic information concerning the same set of traits. The 23rd pair are **sex chromosomes**, which look different from other chromosomes and determine our sex. We all receive an X sex chromosome (so called because of its X shape) from our mothers. The father supplies either a Y or an X sex chromosome. If we receive another X sex chromosome from our fathers, we develop into females, and if a Y (named after its Y shape), males.

mitosis the form of cell division in which each chromosome splits lengthwise to double in number. Half of each chromosome combines with chemicals to retake its original form and then moves to the new cell.

mutation a sudden variation in a heritable characteristic, as by an accident that affects the composition of genes.

meiosis the form of cell division in which each pair of chromosomes splits so that one member of each pair moves to the new cell. As a result, each new cell has 23 chromosomes.

autosome a member of a pair of chromosomes (with the exception of sex chromosomes).

sex chromosome a chromosome in the shape of a Y (male) or X (female) that determines the anatomic sex of the child.

FIG.2.1 THE DOUBLE HELIX OF DNA

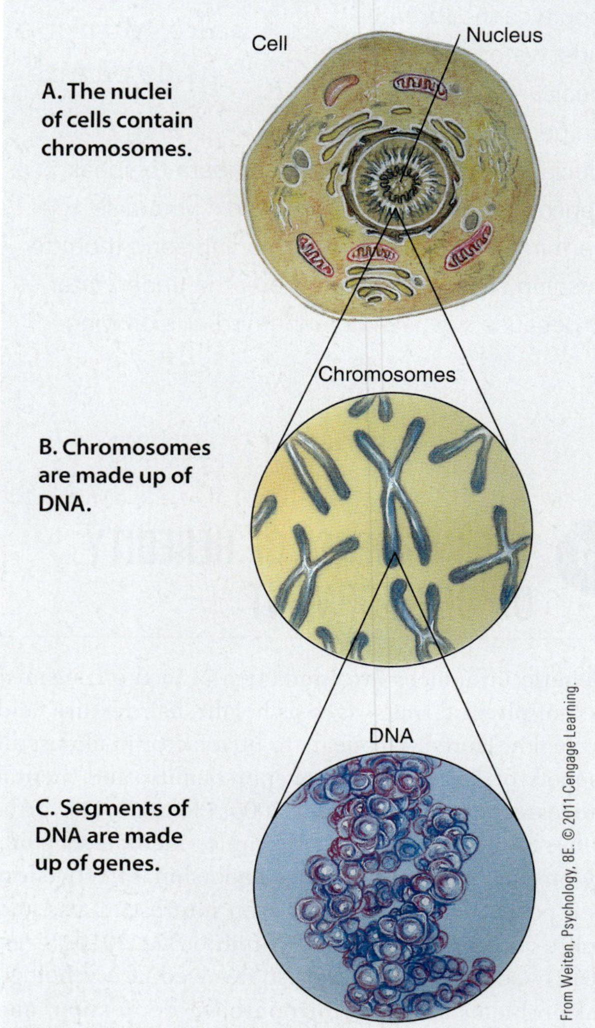
Cell
Nucleus
A. The nuclei of cells contain chromosomes.
Chromosomes
B. Chromosomes are made up of DNA.
DNA
C. Segments of DNA are made up of genes.
From Weiten, Psychology, 8E. © 2011 Cengage Learning.

Your genetic code determines your species and all those traits that can be inherited, from the color of your eyes to predispositions toward many psychological traits and abilities, including sociability and musical talent.

TRUTH

T F Your father determined whether you are female or male.

It is true that your father determined whether you are female or male. Fathers supply either an X or a Y sex chromosome, which determines whether the baby is female or male.

FIG.2.2 MITOSIS

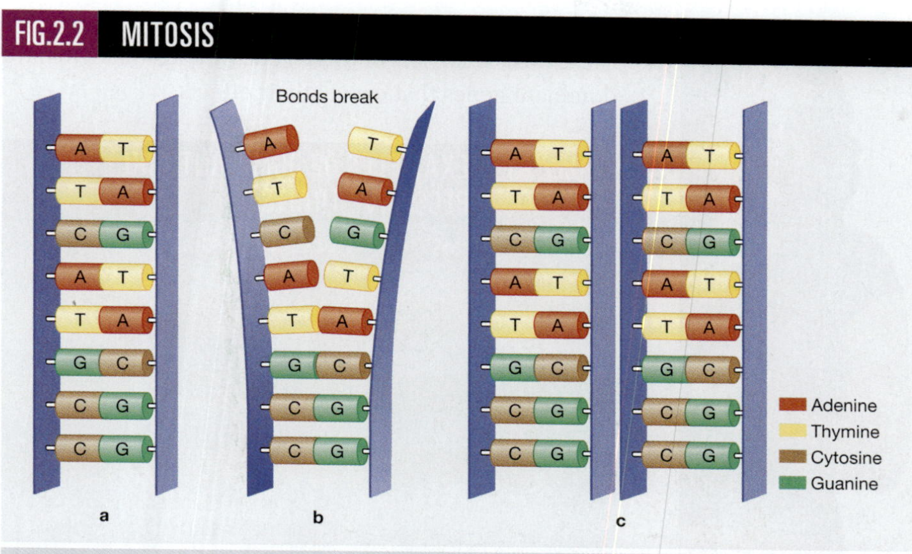

(a) A segment of a strand of DNA before mitosis. (b) During mitosis, chromosomal strands of DNA "unzip." (c) The double helix is rebuilt in the cell as each incomplete "rung" combines with appropriate molecules.

2-1c IDENTICAL AND FRATERNAL TWINS

Now and then, a zygote divides into two cells that separate so that each develops into an individual with the same genetic makeup. These individuals are identical twins, or **monozygotic (MZ) twins**. If the woman produces two ova in the same month and they are each fertilized by different sperm cells, they develop into fraternal twins, or **dizygotic (DZ) twins**. DZ twins run in families. If a woman is a twin, if her mother was a twin, or if she has previously borne twins, the chances rise that she will bear twins (Fellman, 2013).

As women reach the end of their childbearing years, **ovulation** becomes less regular, resulting in a number of months when more than one ovum is released. Thus, the chances of twins increase with parental age (Fellman, 2013). Fertility drugs also enhance the chances of multiple births by causing more than one ovum to ripen and be released during a woman's cycle (Fellman, 2013).

2-1d DOMINANT AND RECESSIVE TRAITS

Traits are determined by pairs of genes. Each member of a pair of genes is termed an **allele**. When both of the alleles for a trait, such as hair color, are the same, the person is said to be **homozygous** for that trait. When the alleles for a trait differ, the person is **heterozygous** for that trait. Some traits result from an "averaging" of the genetic instructions carried by the parents. When the effects of both alleles are shown, there is said to be incomplete dominance or codominance. When a *dominant* allele is paired with a *recessive* allele, the trait determined by the dominant allele appears in the offspring. For example, the offspring from the crossing of brown eyes with blue eyes have brown eyes, suggesting that brown eyes are a **dominant trait** and blue eyes are a **recessive trait**.

FIG.2.3 THE 23 PAIRS OF HUMAN CHROMOSOMES

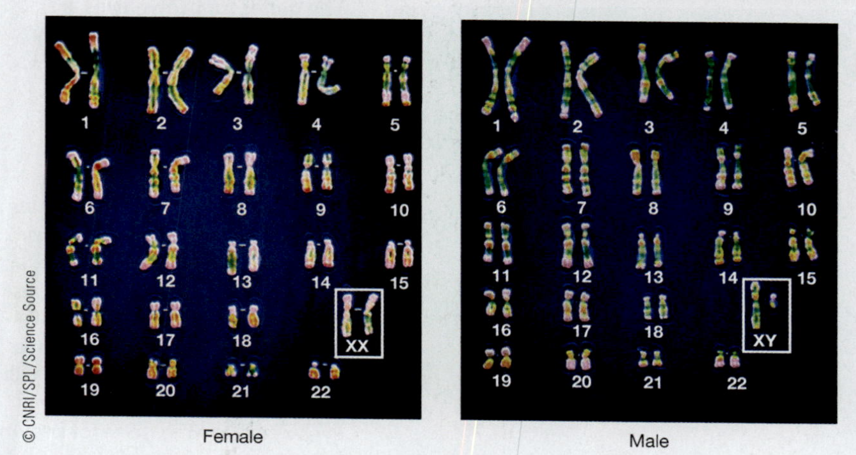

People normally have 23 pairs of chromosomes. Females have two X chromosomes, whereas males have an X and a Y sex chromosome.

monozygotic (MZ) twins twins that derive from a single zygote that has split into two; identical twins. Each MZ twin carries the same genetic code.

dizygotic (DZ) twins twins that derive from two zygotes; fraternal twins.

ovulation the releasing of an ovum from an ovary.

allele a member of a pair of genes.

homozygous having two identical alleles.

heterozygous having two different alleles.

dominant trait a trait that is expressed.

recessive trait a trait that is not expressed when the gene or genes involved have been paired with dominant genes.

rubberball/Getty Images

Identical twins. Monozygotic twins share 100% of their genes, whereas dizygotic twins share 50% of their genes. Identical twins are extremely close in appearance and also tend to share many psychological traits.

If one parent carried genes for only brown eyes and if the other parent carried genes for only blue eyes, the children would invariably have brown eyes. But brown-eyed parents can also carry recessive genes for blue eyes, as shown in Figure 2.4. If the recessive gene from one parent combines with the recessive gene from the other parent, the recessive trait will be shown. As suggested by Figure 2.4, approximately 25% of the children of brown-eyed parents who carry recessive blue eye color will have blue eyes. Table 2.1 shows a number of dominant and recessive traits in humans.

People who bear one dominant gene and one recessive gene for a trait are said to be **carriers** of the recessive gene. In the cases of recessive genes that cause illness, carriers of those genes are fortunate to have dominant genes that cancel their effects.

carrier a person who carries and transmits characteristics but does not exhibit them.

TABLE 2.1 EXAMPLES OF DOMINANT AND RECESSIVE TRAITS

Dominant Trait	Recessive Trait
Dark hair	Blond hair
Dark hair	Red hair
Curly hair	Straight hair
Normal color vision	Red-green color blindness
Normal vision	Myopia (nearsightedness)
Farsightedness	Normal vision
Normal pigmentation	Deficiency of pigmentation in skin, hair, and retina (albinism)
Normal sensitivity to touch	Extremely fragile skin
Normal hearing	Some forms of deafness
Dimples	Lack of dimpling
Type A blood	Type O blood
Type B blood	Type O blood
Tolerance of lactose	Lactose intolerance

2-1e CHROMOSOMAL AND GENETIC ABNORMALITIES

Chromosomal or genetic abnormalities can cause health problems. Some chromosomal disorders reflect abnormalities in the 22 pairs of autosomes (such as Down's syndrome); others reflect abnormalities in the sex

FIG.2.4 TRANSMISSION OF DOMINANT AND RECESSIVE TRAITS

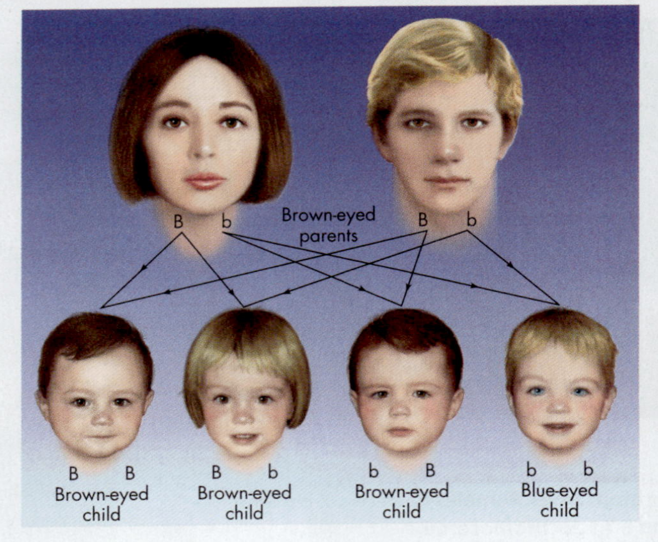

Did you know that you can have brown eyes but be carrying a gene for blue or green eyes? The genes for brown eyes are dominant—meaning that they are the ones that will be shown, and the genes for blue eyes are recessive. Here each of the two parents carries a gene for brown eyes (so they both have brown eyes) and a gene for blue eyes (which remain recessive, or hidden). Their children inherit the genes for brown or blue eyes by chance. Therefore, three out of four of their children will have brown eyes. Of the three, two will have a recessive gene for blue eyes as well as the gene for brown eyes. Only the fourth child, who inherits two genes for blue eyes, will actually have blue eyes.

chromosomes (e.g., XYY syndrome). Some genetic abnormalities, such as cystic fibrosis, are caused by a single pair of genes; others are caused by combinations of genes. Diabetes mellitus, epilepsy, and peptic ulcers are **multifactorial problems**; they reflect both a genetic predisposition and environmental contributors.

2-1f CHROMOSOMAL ABNORMALITIES

People normally have 46 chromosomes. Children with more or fewer chromosomes usually experience health problems or behavioral abnormalities. The risk of chromosomal abnormalities rises with the age of the parents (Desai et al., 2013; Sandin et al., 2012).

FIG.2.5 DOWN'S SYNDROME

© Michael Greenlar/The Image Works

People with Down's syndrome have characteristic features that include a rounded face, a protruding tongue, a broad, flat nose, and a sloping fold of skin over the inner corners of the eyes.

DOWN'S SYNDROME **Down's syndrome** is usually caused by an extra chromosome on the 21st pair, resulting in 47 chromosomes. The probability of having a child with Down's syndrome increases with the age of the parents. People with Down's syndrome have characteristic features that include a rounded face, a protruding tongue, a broad, flat nose, and a sloping fold of skin over the inner corners of the eyes (see Figure 2.5). They show deficits in cognitive development and motor development (van Gameren-Oosterom et al., 2013) and usually die from cardiovascular problems by middle age, although modern medicine has extended life appreciably.

SEX-LINKED CHROMOSOMAL ABNORMALITIES A number of disorders stem from an abnormal number of sex chromosomes and are therefore called **sex-linked chromosomal abnormalities**. Most individuals with an abnormal number of sex chromosomes are infertile. Beyond that common finding, there are many differences, some of them associated with "maleness" or "femaleness."

Approximately 1 male in 700–1,000 has an extra Y chromosome. The Y chromosome is associated with maleness, and the extra Y sex chromosome apparently heightens male secondary sex characteristics. For example, XYY males are somewhat taller than average and develop heavier beards. For these kinds of reasons, males with XYY sex chromosomal structure were once called "supermales." However, XYY "supermales" tend to have more problems than XY males. For example, they are often mildly delayed in language development.

Approximately 1 male in 500 has **Klinefelter syndrome**, which is caused by an extra X sex chromosome (an XXY sex chromosomal pattern). XXY males produce less of the male sex hormone **testosterone** than normal males. As a result, male primary and secondary sex characteristics—such as the testes, deepening of the voice, musculature, and the male pattern of body hair—do not develop properly. XXY males usually have enlarged breasts (gynecomastia) and are usually mildly mentally retarded, particularly in language skills (Skakkebaek et al., 2014). XXY males are typically treated with testosterone replacement therapy, which can foster growth of sex characteristics and elevate the mood, but they remain infertile.

Approximately 1 girl in 2,500 has a single X sex chromosome and as a result develops **Turner syndrome**. The external genitals of such girls are normal, but their ovaries are poorly developed and they produce little **estrogen**. Girls with this problem are shorter than average and infertile. Researchers have connected a specific pattern of cognitive deficits with low estrogen levels: problems in visual–spatial skills, mathematics, and nonverbal memory (Davenport et al., 2013). Yet a sample of women with Turner syndrome who are participating in a National Institutes

multifactorial problems problems that stem from the interaction of heredity and environmental factors.

Down's syndrome a chromosomal abnormality characterized by intellectual disabilities and caused by an extra chromosome in the 21st pair.

sex-linked chromosomal abnormalities abnormalities that are transmitted from generation to generation and carried by a sex chromosome.

Klinefelter syndrome a chromosomal disorder found among males that is caused by an extra X sex chromosome and that is characterized by infertility and mild intellectual disabilities.

testosterone a male sex hormone produced mainly by the testes.

Turner syndrome a chromosomal disorder found among females that is caused by having a single X sex chromosome and is characterized by infertility.

estrogen a female sex hormone produced mainly by the ovaries.

of Health (NIH) study found that women with Turner syndrome were more likely to have a bachelor's degree and be employed than their age-mates in the general population (Gould et al., 2013).

Approximately 1 girl in 1,000 has an XXX sex chromosomal structure, *Triple X syndrome*. Such girls are normal in appearance but tend to show lower-than-average language skills and poorer memory for recent events. Development of external sexual organs appears normal enough, although there is increased incidence of infertility (Lee et al., 2011).

GENETIC ABNORMALITIES

- Phenylketonuria
- Huntington's disease
- Sickle-cell anemia
- Tay-Sachs disease
- Cystic fibrosis
- Hemophilia
- Muscular dystrophy

© Image ideas/Jupiterimages

2-1g GENETIC ABNORMALITIES

A number of disorders have been attributed to genes.

PHENYLKETONURIA The enzyme disorder **phenylketonuria (PKU)** is transmitted by a recessive gene and affects about 1 child in 8,000. Children with PKU cannot metabolize an amino acid called phenylalanine, so it builds up in their bodies and impairs the functioning of the central nervous system, resulting in mental retardation, psychological disorders, and physical problems. There is no cure for PKU, but children with PKU can be placed on diets low in phenylalanine within three to six weeks of birth and develop normally (Casey, 2013; Dawson et al., 2011).

HUNTINGTON'S DISEASE **Huntington's disease (HD)** is a fatal, progressive degenerative disorder and a dominant trait, affecting approximately 1 American in 18,000. Physical symptoms include uncontrollable muscle movements. Psychological symptoms include loss of intellectual functioning and personality change (van Dujin et al., 2014). Because the onset of HD is delayed until middle adulthood, many individuals with the defect have borne children only to discover years later that they and possibly half their offspring will inevitably develop it. Medicines can help deal with some symptoms.

SICKLE-CELL ANEMIA **Sickle-cell anemia** is caused by a recessive gene. Sickle-cell anemia is most common among African Americans. Nearly 1 African American in 10 and 1 Latin American in 20 is a carrier. In sickle-cell anemia, red blood cells take on the shape of a sickle and clump together, obstructing small blood vessels and decreasing the oxygen supply. The lessened oxygen supply can impair cognitive skills and academic performance (Smith et al., 2013). Physical problems include painful and swollen joints, jaundice, and potentially fatal conditions such as pneumonia, stroke, and heart and kidney failure.

TAY-SACHS DISEASE **Tay-Sachs disease** is also caused by a recessive gene. It causes the central nervous system to degenerate, resulting in death. The disorder is most commonly found among children in Jewish families of Eastern European background. Approximately 1 in 30 Jewish Americans from this background carries the recessive gene for Tay-Sachs. Children with the disorder progressively lose control over their muscles, experience sensory losses, develop intellectual disabilities, become paralyzed, and usually die by about the age of five.

CYSTIC FIBROSIS **Cystic fibrosis**, also caused by a recessive gene, is the most common fatal hereditary disease among European Americans. Approximately 30,000 Americans have the disorder, but another 10 million (1 in every 31 people) are carriers (Cystic Fibrosis Foundation, 2014). Children with the disease suffer from excessive production of thick mucus that clogs the pancreas and lungs. Most victims die of respiratory infections in their 20s.

MARKA / Alamy Stock Photo

Richard Burton and Elizabeth Taylor, the co-stars of the movie *Cleopatra*. Burton was diagnosed with hemophilia.

phenylketonuria (PKU) a genetic abnormality in which phenylalanine builds up and causes intellectual disabilities.

Huntington's disease (HD) a fatal genetic neurological disorder whose onset is in middle age.

sickle-cell anemia a genetic disorder that decreases the blood's capacity to carry oxygen.

Tay-Sachs disease a fatal genetic neurological disorder.

cystic fibrosis a fatal genetic disorder in which mucus obstructs the lungs and pancreas.

SEX-LINKED GENETIC ABNORMALITIES Some genetic defects, such as **hemophilia**, are carried on only the X sex chromosome. For this reason, they are referred to as **sex-linked genetic abnormalities**. These defects also involve recessive genes. Females, who have two X sex chromosomes, are less likely than males to show sex-linked disorders because the genes that cause the disorder would have to be present on both of a female's sex chromosomes for the disorder to be expressed. Sex-linked diseases are more likely to afflict sons of female carriers because males have only one X sex chromosome, which they inherit from their mothers.

One form of **muscular dystrophy**, Duchenne muscular dystrophy, is sex-linked. Muscular dystrophy is characterized by a weakening of the muscles, which can lead to wasting away, inability to walk, and sometimes death. Other sex-linked abnormalities include diabetes, color blindness, and some types of night blindness.

2-1h GENETIC COUNSELING AND PRENATAL TESTING

It is possible to detect genetic abnormalities that are responsible for many diseases. **Genetic counselors** compile information about a couple's genetic heritage to explore whether their children might develop genetic abnormalities. Couples who face a high risk of passing along genetic defects to their children sometimes elect to adopt or not have children rather than conceive their own. In addition, **prenatal** testing can indicate whether the embryo or fetus is carrying genetic abnormalities.

Although we discuss amniocentesis and chorionic villus sampling, it should be noted that their use tends to be declining because blood tests and ultrasound are becoming more sophisticated and used more frequently. By the time an amniocentesis is normally scheduled, a woman today may have had several blood tests and ultrasounds, which provide evidence of chromosomal as well as genetic abnormalities, and also provide reasonably clear pictures of the embryo and fetus.

AMNIOCENTESIS **Amniocentesis** is usually performed on the mother at 14–16 weeks after conception, although many physicians now perform the procedure earlier ("early amniocentesis"). In this fetal-screening method, the health professional uses a syringe (needle) to withdraw fluid from the amniotic sac. The fluid contains cells that are sloughed off by the fetus. The cells are separated from the amniotic fluid, grown in a culture, and then examined microscopically for genetic and chromosomal abnormalities.

Amniocentesis was once routinely recommended for women who become pregnant past the age of 35 because the chances of Down's syndrome and other chromosomal abnormalities increase dramatically as women—or their mates!—approach or pass the age of 40. Amniocentesis also permits parents to learn the sex of their unborn child through examination of the sex chromosomes, but most parents learn the sex of their baby earlier by ultrasound. Amniocentesis carries some risk of **miscarriage**, although the extent of the risk is unclear.

CHORIONIC VILLUS SAMPLING **Chorionic villus sampling (CVS)** is similar to amniocentesis but is carried out between the 9th and 12th week of pregnancy. A small syringe is inserted through the vagina into the **uterus** and sucks out some threadlike projections (villi) from the outer membrane that envelops the amniotic sac and fetus. Results are available within days. CVS has not been used as frequently as amniocentesis because CVS carries a slightly greater risk of miscarriage. However, there is controversy as to how much amniocentesis and CVS increase the risk of miscarriage, and some health professionals assert that the risk of these procedures has been exaggerated (Akolekar et al., 2014; Ogilvie & Akolekar, 2013). Check with your physician for the latest information.

ULTRASOUND Health professionals also use sound waves that are too high in frequency to be heard by the human ear—**ultrasound**—to obtain information about the fetus. Ultrasound waves are reflected by

hemophilia a genetic disorder in which blood does not clot properly.

sex-linked genetic abnormalities abnormalities resulting from genes that are found on the X sex chromosome. They are more likely to be shown by male off spring (who do not have an opposing gene from a second X chromosome) than by female offspring.

muscular dystrophy a chronic disease characterized by a progressive wasting away of the muscles.

genetic counselors health workers who compile information about a couple's genetic heritage to advise them as to whether their children might develop genetic abnormalities.

prenatal before birth.

amniocentesis a procedure for drawing and examining fetal cells sloughed off into amniotic fluid to determine the presence of various disorders.

miscarriage the expulsion of an embryo or fetus before it can sustain life on its own, most often due to defective development.

chorionic villus sampling (CVS) a method for the prenatal detection of genetic abnormalities that samples the membrane enveloping the amniotic sac and fetus.

uterus the hollow organ within females in which the embryo and fetus develop.

ultrasound sound waves too high in pitch to be sensed by the human ear.

FIG.2.6 SONOGRAM

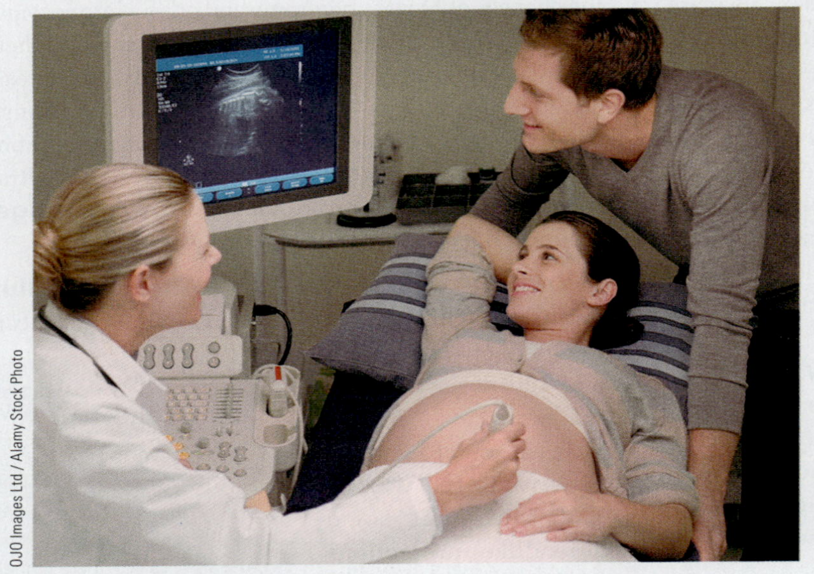

OJO Images Ltd / Alamy Stock Photo

The first baby pictures? In the ultrasound technique, sound waves that are too high in pitch for the human ear to hear are bounced off the fetus. A computer then assembles the information into a picture that enables health professionals to detect various abnormalities. Once the fetus reaches a certain age, the method also reveals its anatomic sex.

the fetus, and a computer uses the information to generate a picture of the fetus. The picture is termed a **sonogram** (see Figure 2.6).

Ultrasound is used to guide the syringe in amniocentesis and CVS by determining the position of the fetus. Ultrasound also is used to track the growth of the fetus, to determine fetal age and sex, and to detect multiple pregnancies and structural abnormalities. In the fourth and fifth months, ultrasound is usually used to perform complete anatomical scans of the fetus.

sonogram a procedure for using ultrasonic sound waves to create a picture of an embryo or fetus.

alpha-fetoprotein (AFP) assay a blood test that assesses the mother's blood level of alpha-fetoprotein, a substance that is linked with fetal neural tube defects.

genotype the genetic form or constitution of a person as determined by heredity.

phenotype the actual form or constitution of a person as determined by heredity and environmental factors.

BLOOD TESTS Parental blood tests can reveal the presence of genetic disorders such as sickle-cell anemia, Tay-Sachs disease, and cystic fibrosis. The **alpha-fetoprotein (AFP) assay** is used to detect neural tube defects such as spina bifida and certain chromosomal abnormalities. Neural tube defects cause an elevation in the AFP level in the mother's blood. Elevated AFP levels also are associated with increased risk of fetal death. Blood tests are also now testing for chromosomal abnormalities, and at three to four months of pregnancy they reveal the sex of the baby.

2-2 HEREDITY AND THE ENVIRONMENT

In addition to inheritance, the development of our traits is also influenced by nutrition, learning, exercise, and—unfortunately—accident and illness. A potential Shakespeare who is reared in poverty and never taught to read or write will not create a *Hamlet*. Our traits and behaviors therefore represent the interaction of heredity and environment. The sets of traits that we inherit from our parents are referred to as our **genotypes**. The actual sets of traits that we exhibit are called our **phenotypes**. Our phenotypes reflect both genetic and environmental influences.

Researchers have developed a number of strategies to help sort out the effects of heredity and the environment on development.

2-2a KINSHIP STUDIES

Researchers study the distribution of a trait or behavior among relatives who differ in degree of genetic closeness. The more closely people are related, the more genes they have in common. Parents and children have a 50% overlap in their genetic endowments, and so do siblings (brothers and sisters). Aunts and uncles have a 25% overlap with nieces and nephews, as do grandparents with grandchildren.

A potential Shakespeare who is reared in poverty and never taught to read or write will not create a *Hamlet*.

First cousins share 12.5% of their genetic endowment. If genes are implicated in a trait, people who are more closely related should be more likely to share it.

2-2b TWIN STUDIES: LOOKING IN THE GENETIC MIRROR

MZ twins share 100% of their genes, whereas DZ twins have a 50% overlap, just as other siblings do. If MZ twins show greater similarity on some trait or behavior than DZ twins do, a genetic basis for the trait or behavior is indicated.

MZ twins resemble each other more closely than DZ twins on a number of physical and psychological traits, even when the MZ twins are reared apart and the DZ twins are reared together (Bouchard & Loehlin, 2001). MZ twins are more likely to look alike and to be similar in height and weight (Dubois et al., 2012; Plomin et al., 2013). Heredity even affects their preference for coffee or tea (Luciano et al., 2005). MZ twins resemble one another more strongly than DZ twins in intelligence and personality traits (Hur, 2005; McCrae et al., 2000; Trzaskowski et al., 2013). MZ twins are also more likely to share psychological disorders such as **autism**, depression, schizophrenia, and vulnerability to alcoholism (Belmonte & Carper, 2006; Plomin et al., 2013; Ronald et al., 2006).

But one might ask whether MZ twins resemble each other so closely partly because they are often treated so similarly? One way to answer this question is to find and compare MZ twins who were reared apart. Except for the uterine environment, similarities between MZ twins reared apart would appear to be a result of heredity. In the Minnesota Study of Twins Reared Apart (McGue & Christensen, 2013), researchers have been measuring the physiological and psychological characteristics of 56 sets of MZ adult twins who were separated in infancy and reared in different homes. The MZ twins reared apart are about as similar as MZ twins reared together on measures of intelligence, personality, temperament, occupational and leisure-time interests, and social attitudes. Moreover, the similarities persist throughout life (McGue & Christensen, 2013). These traits would thus appear to have a genetic underpinning.

2-2c ADOPTION STUDIES

Adoption studies in which children are separated from their natural parents at an early age and reared by adoptive parents provide special opportunities for sorting out nature and nurture. When children who are reared by adoptive parents are nonetheless more similar to their natural parents in a trait, a powerful argument is made for a genetic role in the appearance of that trait.

Traits are determined by pairs of genes. One member of each pair comes from each parent in the process called conception, which we discuss next.

2-3 CONCEPTION: AGAINST ALL ODDS

Conception is the union of an ovum and a sperm cell. Conception, from one perspective, is the beginning of a new human life. From another perspective, though, conception is also the end of a fantastic voyage in which one of several hundred thousand ova produced by the woman unites with one of hundreds of millions of sperm produced by the man in the average ejaculate.

2-3a OVA

At birth, women have 300,000 to 400,000 ova in each ovary, although she will only ovulate some 500 of these during her lifetime (Adhikari & Liu, 2013). The ova, however, are immature in form. In addition to ova, the ovaries also produce the female hormones estrogen and progesterone. At puberty, in response to hormonal command, some ova begin to mature. Each month, an egg (occasionally more than one) is released from its ovarian follicle about midway through the menstrual cycle and enters a nearby fallopian tube (see Figure 2.7). It might take three to four days for an egg to be propelled by small, hairlike structures called cilia and, perhaps, by contractions in the wall of the tube, along the few inches of the fallopian tube to the uterus. Unlike sperm, eggs do not propel themselves. If the egg is not fertilized, it is discharged through the uterus and the vagina along with the **endometrium** that had formed to support an embryo, in the menstrual flow.

autism a developmental disorder characterized by failure to relate to others, communication problems, intolerance of change, and ritualistic behavior.

conception the union of a sperm cell and an ovum that occurs when the chromosomes of each of these cells combine to form 23 new pairs.

endometrium the inner lining of the uterus.

FIG.2.7 FEMALE REPRODUCTIVE ORGANS

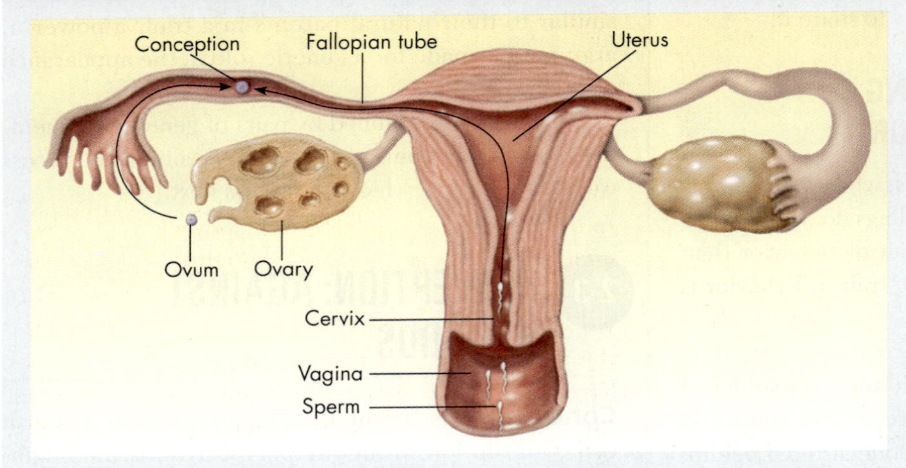

The ovaries release egg cells (ova), which find their ways into fallopian tubes—exactly how is not fully known. Fertilization normally takes place in a fallopian tube. The fertilized ovum begins to divide while it travels through the tube into the uterus, where it becomes implanted in the wall and grows to term.

Ova are much larger than sperm. The chicken egg and the six-inch ostrich egg are each just one cell, although the sperm of these birds are microscopic. Human ova are barely visible to the eye, but their bulk is still thousands of times larger than that of sperm cells.

TRUTH

(T) F Approximately 120 to 150 boys are conceived for every 100 girls.

It is true that approximately 120 to 150 boys are conceived for every 100 girls. Sperm with Y sex chromosomes swim more rapidly, resulting in the conception of more boys than girls.

2-3b SPERM CELLS

Sperm cells develop through several stages. They each begin with 46 chromosomes, but after meiosis, each sperm has 23 chromosomes, half with X sex chromosomes and half with Y. Each sperm cell is about 1/500th of an inch long, one of the smallest types of cells in the body. Sperm with Y sex chromosomes appear to swim faster than sperm with X sex chromosomes. This difference contributes to the conception of 120 to 150 boys for every 100 girls. Male fetuses suffer a higher rate of miscarriage than females, however, often during the first month of pregnancy. At birth, boys outnumber girls by a ratio of only 106 to 100. Boys also have a higher incidence of infant mortality, which further equalizes the numbers of girls and boys.

The 150 million or so sperm in the ejaculate may seem to be a wasteful investment because only one sperm can fertilize an ovum, but only 1 in 1,000 sperm will ever approach an ovum. Millions deposited in the vagina flow out of the woman's body because of gravity. Normal vaginal acidity kills many more sperm. Many surviving sperm then have to swim against the current of fluid coming from the cervix (see Figure 2.7).

Sperm that survive these initial obstacles may reach the fallopian tubes 60 to 90 minutes after ejaculation. About half the sperm enter the fallopian tube that does

not contain the egg. Perhaps 2,000 enter the correct tube. Fewer still manage to swim the final two inches against the currents generated by the cilia that line the tube. It is *not* true that sperm travel about at random inside the woman's reproductive tract. Sperm cells are apparently "egged on" (pardon the pun) by a change in calcium ions that occurs when an ovum is released (Olson et al., 2011).

FICTION

T (F) Sperm travel randomly inside the woman's reproductive tract, so reaching the ovum is a matter of luck.

It is not true that sperm travel about at random inside the woman's reproductive tract. The direction in which sperm travel is influenced by a change in calcium ions that occurs when an ovum is released.

Of all the sperm swarming around the egg, only one enters (see Figure 2.8). Ova are surrounded by a gelatinous layer that must be penetrated if fertilization is to occur. Many of the sperm that have completed their journey to the ovum secrete an enzyme that briefly thins the layer, but it enables only one sperm to penetrate. Once a sperm cell has entered, the layer thickens, locking other sperm out.

FIG.2.8 HUMAN SPERM SWARMING AROUND AN OVUM IN A FALLOPIAN TUBE

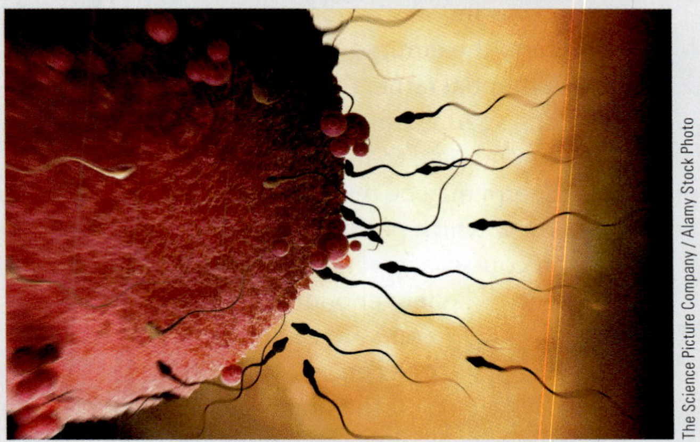

The Science Picture Company / Alamy Stock Photo

Hundreds of millions of sperm enter a woman during sexual intercourse. Thousands arrive in the fallopian tube with the ovum. Many attempt to enter the ovum, but only one succeeds because the surface of the ovum becomes impermeable to other sperm. It is believed that sperm locate the ovum through a rudimentary sense of smell.

The chromosomes from the sperm cell line up across from the corresponding chromosomes in the egg cell. They form 23 new pairs with a unique set of genetic instructions.

2-3c INFERTILITY AND ALTERNATIVE WAYS OF BECOMING PARENTS

Approximately one American couple in six or seven has fertility problems (path2parenthood, 2016). The term *infertility* usually is not applied until the couple has failed to conceive on their own for one year. Infertility was once viewed as a problem of the woman, but it turns out that the problem lies with the woman in only 40% of cases. The problem lies with the man in about 40% of cases, and the other 20% have unknown origins (path2parenthood, 2016).

CAUSES OF INFERTILITY A low sperm count—or lack of sperm—is the most common infertility problem in men. Men's fertility problems have a variety of causes: genetic factors, environmental poisons, diabetes, sexually transmitted infections (STIs), overheating of the testes (which happens now and then among athletes, such as long-distance runners), pressure (as from using narrow bicycle seats), aging, certain prescription and illicit drugs, and obesity (path2parenthood, 2016). Sometimes the sperm count is adequate, but other factors such as prostate or hormonal problems deform sperm or deprive them of their **motility**. Motility can also be impaired by the scar tissue from infections, such as STIs.

The most common problem in women is irregular ovulation or lack of ovulation. This problem can have many causes, including irregularities among the hormones that govern ovulation, stress, and malnutrition. So-called fertility drugs (e.g., clomiphene and pergonal) are made up of hormones that cause women to ovulate. These drugs may cause multiple births by stimulating more than one ovum to ripen during a month (path2parenthood, 2016).

Infections may scar the fallopian tubes and other organs, impeding the passage of sperm or ova. Such infections include **pelvic inflammatory disease (PID)**. PID can result from bacterial or viral infections, including the STIs gonorrhea and chlamydia. Antibiotics are usually helpful in treating bacterial infections, but infertility may be irreversible.

motility self-propulsion.

pelvic inflammatory disease (PID) an infection of the abdominal region that may have various causes and that may impair fertility.

Endometriosis can obstruct the fallopian tubes, where conception normally takes place. Endometriosis has become fairly common among women who delay childbearing. Each month, tissue develops to line the uterus in case the woman conceives. This tissue—the endometrium—is then sloughed off during menstruation. But some of it backs up into the abdomen through the fallopian tubes. It then collects in the abdomen, where it can cause abdominal pain and lessen the chances of conception. Physicians may treat endometriosis with hormones that temporarily prevent menstruation or through surgery.

endometriosis inflammation of endometrial tissue sloughed off into the abdominal cavity rather than out of the body during menstruation; the condition is characterized by abdominal pain and sometimes infertility.

artificial insemination injection of sperm into the uterus to fertilize an ovum.

in vitro fertilization (IVF) fertilization of an ovum in a laboratory dish.

Let's consider methods used to help infertile couples bear children.

ARTIFICIAL INSEMINATION Multiple ejaculations of men with low sperm counts can be collected and quickfrozen. The sperm can then be injected into the woman's uterus at the time of ovulation. This method is one **artificial insemination** procedure. Sperm from men with low sperm motility can also be injected into their partners' uteruses so that the sperm can begin their journey closer to the fallopian tubes. When a man has no sperm or an extremely low sperm count, his partner can be artificially inseminated with the sperm of a donor who resembles the man in physical traits. Some women who want a baby but do not have a partner also use artificial insemination.

IN VITRO FERTILIZATION So called "test-tube babies" are not actually grown in a test tube but are conceived through **in vitro fertilization (IVF)**, a method of

LGBT Family Building

Not only heterosexual couples want children. So do singles. And so do members of the lesbian, gay, bisexual, and transgendered community.

Some LGBT people have children from previous marriages or other relationships. But if they don't, and if they want children, they have to decide how to make it happen. Transgendered individuals who have had genital surgery are also sterile, so they cannot father or bear offspring.

Lesbians, of course, can conceive through sexual intercourse with a friend or confidant, but many prefer not to do so. They can also conceive through assisted productive technologies such as artificial insemination, intrauterine insemination (IUI), and in vitro fertilization (IVF). These methods require donor sperm, from either a known or an anonymous source. Artificial insemination is a low-technology method in which sperm are inserted directly into the uterus. If artificial insemination does not work, a woman may consider IVF.

Gay males will need a surrogate mother to become impregnated by their sperm and carry the embryo and fetus to term. The two potential fathers' sperm is analyzed, and either the sperm with the strongest likelihood to impregnate the surrogate are selected, or the sperm may be mixed so that the fathers do not know which partner actually fathered the child. Of course, actual fatherhood usually becomes clear enough in terms of the child's appearance and behavior as time goes on.

The American Fertility Association (www.theafa.org) invites all individuals who have fertility questions or issues to be in touch with them—heterosexual couples, would-be single parents, and lesbian, gay, bisexual, and transgendered couples.

Gary John Norman/Getty Images

They've got each other. How do they go about building a family?

conception in which ripened ova are removed surgically from the mother and placed in a laboratory dish. The father's sperm are also placed in the dish. One or more ova are fertilized and then injected into the mother's uterus to become implanted.

FICTION

T F "Test-tube babies" are grown in a laboratory dish throughout their nine-month gestation period.

It is not true that "Test-tube babies" are grown in a laboratory dish throughout their nine-month gestation period. So-called "Test-tube babies" are conceived in a laboratory dish, and then the embryos are implanted into the mother's uterus for gestation.

IVF may be used when the fallopian tubes are blocked because the ova need not travel through them. If the father's sperm are low in motility, they are sometimes injected directly into the ovum. A variation known as **donor IVF** can be used when the intended mother does not produce ova. An ovum from another woman is fertilized and injected into the uterus of the mother-to-be.

Because only a minority of attempts lead to births, it can take several attempts to achieve a pregnancy. Several embryos may be injected into the uterus at once, heightening the odds that one of the embryos will become implanted. IVF remains costly but is otherwise routine, if not guaranteed.

SURROGATE MOTHERS Surrogate mothers bring babies to term for other women who are infertile. Surrogate mothers may be artificially inseminated by the partners of infertile women, in which case the baby carries the genes of the father. But sometimes—as with 60-year-old singer-songwriter James Taylor and his 54-year-old wife—ova are surgically extracted from the biological mother, fertilized in vitro by the biological father, and then implanted in another woman's uterus, where the baby is brought to term. Surrogate mothers are usually paid and sign agreements to surrender the baby.

ADOPTION Adoption is another way for people to obtain children. Despite occasional conflicts that pit adoptive parents against biological parents who change their minds about giving up their children, most adoptions result in the formation of loving new families. Many Americans find it easier to adopt infants from other countries or with special needs.

SELECTING THE SEX OF YOUR CHILD Today, there is a reliable method for selecting the sex of a child prior to implantation: preimplantation genetic diagnosis (PGD). PGD was developed to detect genetic disorders, but it also reveals the sex of the embryo. In PGD, ova are fertilized in vitro. After a few days of cell division, a cell is extracted from each, and its sex chromosomal structure is examined microscopically to learn of its sex. Embryos of the desired sex are implanted in the woman's uterus, where one or more can grow to term. However, successful implantation cannot be guaranteed.

2-4 PRENATAL DEVELOPMENT

The most rapid and dramatic human developments are literally "out of sight" and take place in the uterus. Within nine months, a fetus develops from a nearly microscopic cell to a neonate about 20 inches long. Its weight increases a billionfold.

We can date pregnancy from the onset of the last menstrual period before conception, which makes the normal gestation period 280 days. We can also date pregnancy from the assumed date of fertilization, which normally occurs two weeks after the beginning of the woman's last menstrual cycle. With this accounting method, the gestation period is 266 days.

Prenatal development is divided into three periods: the germinal stage (approximately the first two weeks), the embryonic stage (the third through the eighth weeks), and the fetal stage (the third month through birth). Health professionals also commonly speak of prenatal development in terms of three trimesters of three months each.

donor IVF the transfer of a donor's ovum, fertilized in a laboratory dish, to the uterus of another woman.

TRUTH

 F Newly fertilized egg cells survive without any nourishment from the mother for more than a week.

It is true that newly fertilized egg cells survive without any nourishment from the mother for more than a week. And because of that, they make no gains in mass.

2-4a THE GERMINAL STAGE: WANDERINGS

Within 36 hours after conception, the zygote divides into two cells. It then divides repeatedly as it undergoes its three- to four-day journey to the uterus. Within another 36 hours, it has become 32 cells. The mass of dividing cells wanders about the uterus for another three to four days before it begins to implant in the uterine wall. Implantation takes another week or so. The period from conception to implantation is called the **germinal stage**.

A few days into the germinal stage, the dividing cell mass takes the form of a fluid-filled ball of cells called a **blastocyst**. In the blastocyst, cells begin to separate into groups that will eventually become different structures. The inner part of the blastocyst has two distinct layers that form a thickened mass of cells called the **embryonic disk**. These cells will become the embryo and eventually the fetus.

The outer part of the blastocyst, or **trophoblast**, at first consists of a single layer of cells, but it rapidly differentiates into four membranes that will protect and nourish the embryo. One membrane produces blood cells until the embryo's liver develops and takes over this function. Then it disappears. Another membrane develops into the **umbilical cord** and the blood vessels of the **placenta**. A third develops into the amniotic sac, and the fourth becomes the chorion, which will line the placenta.

The cluster of cells that will become the embryo and then the fetus is at first nourished only by the yolk of the egg cell. A blastocyst gains mass only when it receives nourishment from outside. For that to happen, it must be implanted in the uterine wall. Implantation may be accompanied by bleeding, which is usually normal, but bleeding can also be a sign of miscarriage. Most women who experience implantation bleeding, however, do not miscarry, but have normal pregnancies. Miscarriage usually stems from abnormalities in the developmental process. Approximately 10% to 20% of known pregnancies terminate in miscarriage. The actual figure is higher because many women miscarry before they knew they were pregnant (Miscarriage, 2016).

germinal stage the period of development between conception and the implantation of the embryo.

blastocyst a stage within the germinal period of prenatal development in which the zygote has the form of a sphere of cells surrounding a cavity of fluid.

embryonic disk the platelike inner part of the blastocyst that differentiates into the ectoderm, mesoderm, and endoderm of the embryo.

trophoblast the outer part of the blastocyst from which the amniotic sac, placenta, and umbilical cord develop.

umbilical cord a tube that connects the fetus to the placenta.

placenta an organ connected to the uterine wall and to the fetus by the umbilical cord. The placenta serves as a relay station between mother and fetus for the exchange of nutrients and wastes.

embryonic stage the stage of prenatal development that lasts from implantation through the eighth week of pregnancy; it is characterized by the development of the major organ systems.

cephalocaudal from head to tail.

proximodistal from the inner part (or axis) of the body outward.

ectoderm the outermost cell layer of the newly formed embryo from which the skin and nervous system develop.

neural tube a hollowed-out area in the blastocyst from which the nervous system develops.

2-4b THE EMBRYONIC STAGE

The **embryonic stage** begins with implantation and covers the first two months, during which the major organ systems differentiate. Development follows **cephalocaudal** (Latin for "head to tail") and **proximodistal** (Latin for "near to far") trends. Growth of the head takes precedence over growth of the lower parts of the body (see Figure 2.9). You can also think of the body as containing a central axis that coincides with the spinal cord. The growth of the organ systems near the spine occurs earlier than growth of the extremities. Relatively early maturation of the brain and organs that lie near the spine allows them to play key roles in further development.

During the embryonic stage, the outer layer of cells of the embryonic disk, or **ectoderm**, develops into the nervous system, sensory organs, nails, hair, teeth, and outer layer of skin. At approximately 21 days, two ridges appear in the embryo and fold to compose the **neural tube**, from which the nervous system will develop.

FIG.2.9 A HUMAN EMBRYO AT 7 WEEKS

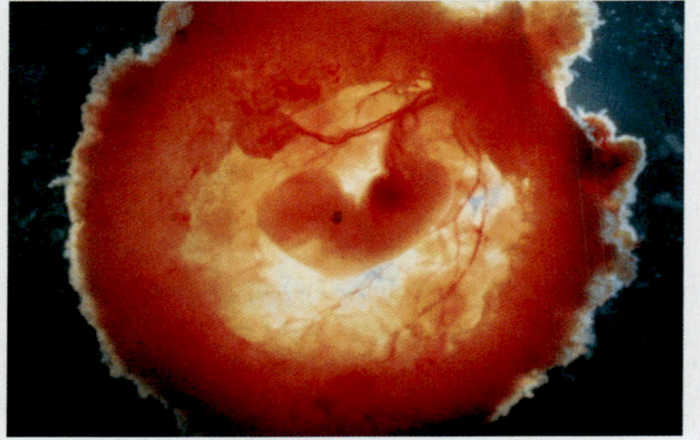

Petit Format/Nestle/Science source

By the time this photo was taken, the embryo's heart had already been beating for about a month. By another week, all the major organs systems will have formed, and the embryo will enter the fetal stage.

The inner layer, or **endoderm**, forms the digestive and respiratory systems, the liver, and the pancreas. A bit later, the mesoderm, a middle layer of cells, becomes differentiated. The **mesoderm** develops into the excretory, reproductive, and circulatory systems, the muscles, the skeleton, and the inner layer of the skin.

During the third week after conception, the head and blood vessels begin to form. Your heart started beating when you were only ¼ of an inch long and weighed a fraction of an ounce. The major organ systems develop during the first two months. Arm buds and leg buds begin to appear toward the end of the first month. Eyes, ears, nose, and mouth begin to take shape. By this time, the nervous system, including the brain, has also begun to develop. During the second month, the cells in the nervous system begin to "fire"; that is, they send messages among themselves. Most likely, it is random cell firing, and the "content" of such "messages" is anybody's guess. By the end of the second month, the embryo is looking quite human. The head has the lovely, round shape of your own, and the facial features have become quite distinct. All this detail is inscribed on an embryo that is only about one inch long and weighs 1/30th of an ounce. By the end of the embryonic period, teeth buds have formed. The embryo's kidneys are filtering acid from the blood, and its liver is producing red blood cells.

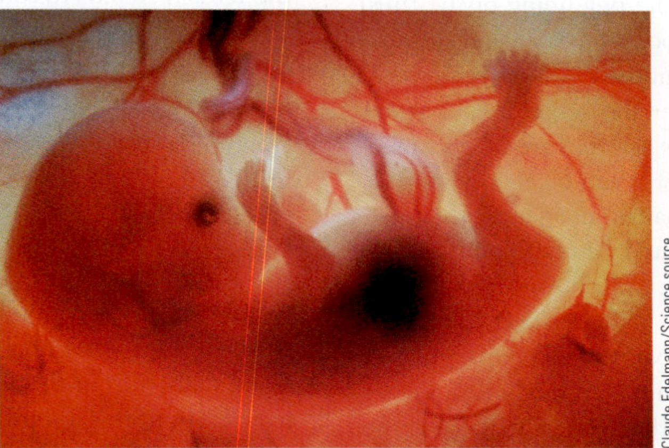

A human fetus at 12 weeks. Note how oversized the head is in relation to the rest of the body.

Claude Edelmann/Science source

SEXUAL DIFFERENTIATION By five to six weeks, the embryo is only one-quarter to one-half inch long. At this stage of development, both the internal and the external genitals resemble primitive female structures. By about the seventh week, the genetic code (XY or XX) begins to assert itself, causing sex organs to differentiate. Genetic activity on the Y sex chromosome causes the testes to begin to differentiate. The ovaries begin to differentiate if the Y chromosome is *absent*. By about three months after conception, males and females show distinct external genital structures. Once the testes have developed in the embryo, they begin to produce male sex hormones, or **androgens**, the most important of which is testosterone. Female embryos and fetuses produce small amounts of androgens, but they are usually not enough to cause sexual differentiation along male lines.

THE AMNIOTIC SAC The embryo and fetus develop within a protective **amniotic sac** in the uterus. This sac is surrounded by a clear membrane and contains **amniotic fluid**. The fluid serves as a kind of natural air bag or shock absorber, allowing the embryo and fetus to move around without injury. It also helps maintain an even temperature.

THE PLACENTA The **placenta** is a pancake-shaped mass of tissue that permits the embryo (and, later on, the fetus) to exchange nutrients and wastes with the mother. The placenta is unique in origin. It grows from material supplied by both the mother and the embryo. The fetus is connected to the placenta by the umbilical cord. The mother is connected to the placenta by blood vessels in the uterine wall.

Mother and embryo have separate circulatory systems. The placenta contains a membrane that permits oxygen and nutrients to reach the embryo from the mother, and permits

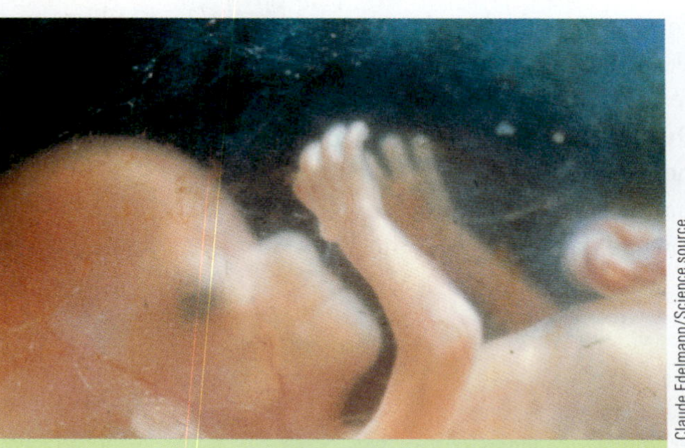

A human fetus at 4½ months. The organ systems are maturing and the fetus is making dramatic gains in size. It also looks unmistakably human.

Claude Edelmann/Science source

endoderm the inner layer of the embryo from which the lungs and digestive system develop.

mesoderm the central layer of the embryo from which the bones and muscles develop.

androgens male sex hormones.

amniotic sac the sac containing the fetus.

amniotic fluid fluid within the amniotic sac that suspends and protects the fetus.

placenta the organ formed in the lining of the uterus that provides nourishment for the fetus and elimination of its waste products.

carbon dioxide and waste products to pass to the mother from the embryo. The mother then eliminates them through her lungs and kidneys. Some harmful substances can also sneak through the placenta, including various "germs," such as the ones that cause syphilis and German measles, but HIV (the virus that causes AIDS) is more likely to be transmitted via bleeding that occurs at childbirth. (Check with your physician as to how to minimize this risk.) Some drugs—aspirin, narcotics, alcohol, tranquilizers, and others—do cross the placenta and affect the fetus.

The placenta also secretes hormones that preserve the pregnancy, prepare the breasts for nursing, and stimulate the uterine contractions that prompt childbirth. Ultimately, the placenta passes from the birth canal after the baby; for this reason, it is also called the afterbirth.

2-4c THE FETAL STAGE

The **fetal stage** lasts from the beginning of the third month until birth. The fetus begins to turn and respond to external stimulation at about the ninth or tenth week. By the end of the first trimester, the major organ systems have been formed. The fingers and toes are fully formed. The eyes and the sex of the fetus can be clearly seen.

The second trimester is characterized by further maturation of fetal organ systems and dramatic gains in size. The brain continues to mature, contributing to the fetus's ability to regulate its own basic body functions. The fetus advances from one ounce to two pounds in weight and grows four to five times in length, from about 3 inches to 14 inches. By the end of the second trimester, the fetus opens and shuts its eyes, sucks its thumb, alternates between wakefulness and sleep, and perceives light and sounds.

During the third trimester, the organ systems mature further. The fetus gains about 5½ pounds and doubles in length. During the seventh month, the fetus normally turns upside down in the uterus so that delivery will be head first. By the end of the seventh month, the fetus will have almost doubled in weight, gaining another 1 pound, 12 ounces, and will have increased another two inches in length. If born now, chances of survival are nearly 90%. If born at the end of the eighth month, the odds are overwhelmingly in favor of survival. Newborn boys average about 7½ pounds and newborn girls about 7 pounds.

fetal stage the stage that begins with the third month of pregnancy and ends with childbirth, during which organ systems mature and there are gains in size.

TRUTH

(T) F Fetuses suck their thumbs, sometimes for hours on end.

It is true that fetuses suck their thumbs. Sometimes they do so for hours on end.

FETAL PERCEPTION By the 13th week of pregnancy, the fetus responds to sound waves. Sontag and Richards (1938) rang a bell near the mother's abdomen, and the fetus responded with movements similar to those of the startle reflex shown after birth. During the third trimester, fetuses respond to sounds of different frequencies through a variety of movements and changes in heart rate, suggesting that they can discriminate pitch (Lecanuet et al., 2000).

An experiment by Anthony DeCasper and William Fifer (1980) is even more intriguing. In this study, women read the Dr. Seuss book *The Cat in the Hat* out loud twice daily during the final month and a half of pregnancy. After birth, their babies were given special pacifiers. Sucking on these pacifiers in one way would activate recordings of their mothers reading *The Cat in the Hat*, and sucking on them in another way would activate their mothers' readings of a book that was written in very different rhythms. The newborns "chose" to hear *The Cat in the Hat*. Fetal learning may be one basis for the development of attachment to the mother (DiPietro, 2010; James, 2010; Lee & Kisilevsky, 2013).

FETAL MOVEMENTS The mother usually feels the first fetal movements in the middle of the fourth month (Raynes-Greenough et al., 2013). By 29–30 weeks, the fetus moves its limbs so vigorously that the mother may complain of being kicked. The fetus also turns somersaults, which are clearly felt by the mother. The umbilical cord will not break or become dangerously wrapped around the fetus, no matter

Did you develop your appreciation of Dr. Seuss before you were born? In a fascinating experiment, mothers read *The Cat in the Hat* aloud twice a day during the final month and a half of pregnancy. Their newborns showed a preference for hearing *The Cat in the Hat* rather than another book.

Vince Bucci/Getty Images

how many acrobatic feats the fetus performs. As the fetus grows, it becomes cramped in the uterus, and movement is constricted, so that the fetus becomes markedly less active during the ninth month of pregnancy.

2-4d ENVIRONMENTAL INFLUENCES ON PRENATAL DEVELOPMENT

The developing fetus is subject to many environmental hazards. Scientific advances have made us keenly aware of the types of things that can go wrong and what we can do to prevent these problems.

NUTRITION It is a common misconception that fetuses "take what they need" from their mothers. However, maternal malnutrition has been linked to low birth weight, prematurity, retardation of brain development, cognitive deficiencies, behavioral problems, and even cardiovascular disease (Monk et al., 2013; de Souza et al., 2011). The effects of fetal malnutrition are sometimes overcome by a supportive, care-giving environment. Experiments with children who suffered from fetal malnutrition show that enriched day-care programs enhance intellectual and social skills by five years of age (Ramey et al., 1999). Supplementing the diets of pregnant women who might otherwise be deficient in their intake of calories and protein also shows modest positive effects on the motor development of infants (de Souza et al., 2011). On the other hand, maternal obesity is linked with a higher risk of **stillbirth** (Crane et al., 2013) and neural tube defects. Over the course of pregnancy, women who do not restrict their diet normally will gain 25–35 pounds. Overweight women may gain less, and slender women may gain more. Regular weight gains of about one-half pound per week during the first half of pregnancy and one pound per week thereafter are desirable.

> Maternal malnutrition has been linked to low birth weight, prematurity, retardation of brain development, cognitive deficiencies, behavioral problems, and even cardiovascular disease.

TERATOGENS AND HEALTH PROBLEMS OF THE MOTHER **Teratogens** are environmental agents that can harm the embryo or fetus. They include drugs taken by the mother, such as marijuana and alcohol, and substances that the mother's body produces, such as Rh-positive antibodies. Another class of teratogens is the heavy metals, such as lead and mercury, which are toxic to the embryo. Hormones are healthful in countless ways—for example, they help maintain pregnancy—but excessive quantities are harmful to the embryo. Exposure to radiation can also harm the embryo. Finally, disease-causing organisms—also called pathogens—such as bacteria and viruses are also teratogens.

CRITICAL PERIODS OF VULNERABILITY Exposure to particular teratogens is most harmful during **critical periods** that correspond to the times when organs are developing. For example, the heart develops rapidly in the third to fifth weeks after conception. As you can see in Figure 2.10 on page 42, the heart is most vulnerable to certain teratogens at this time. The arms and legs, which develop later, are most vulnerable in the fourth through eighth weeks. Because the major organ systems differentiate during the embryonic stage, the embryo is generally more vulnerable to teratogens than the fetus. Even so, many teratogens are harmful throughout the entire course of prenatal development.

Let's consider the effects of various health problems of the mother. We begin with sexually transmitted infections (STIs).

SEXUALLY TRANSMITTED INFECTIONS The **syphilis** bacterium can cause miscarriage, stillbirth, or **congenital** syphilis. Routine blood tests early in pregnancy can diagnose syphilis. The syphilis bacterium is vulnerable to antibiotics. The fetus will probably not contract syphilis if an infected mother is treated with antibiotics before the fourth month of pregnancy (Centers for Disease Control and Prevention, 2013). If the mother is not treated, the baby may be infected in utero and develop congenital syphilis. About 12% of those infected die.

stillbirth the birth of a dead fetus.

teratogens environmental influences or agents that can damage the embryo or fetus.

critical period in this usage, a period during which an embryo is particularly vulnerable to a certain teratogen.

syphilis a sexually transmitted infection that, in advanced stages, can attack major organ systems.

congenital present at birth and resulting from genetic or chromosomal abnormalities or from exposure to the prenatal environment.

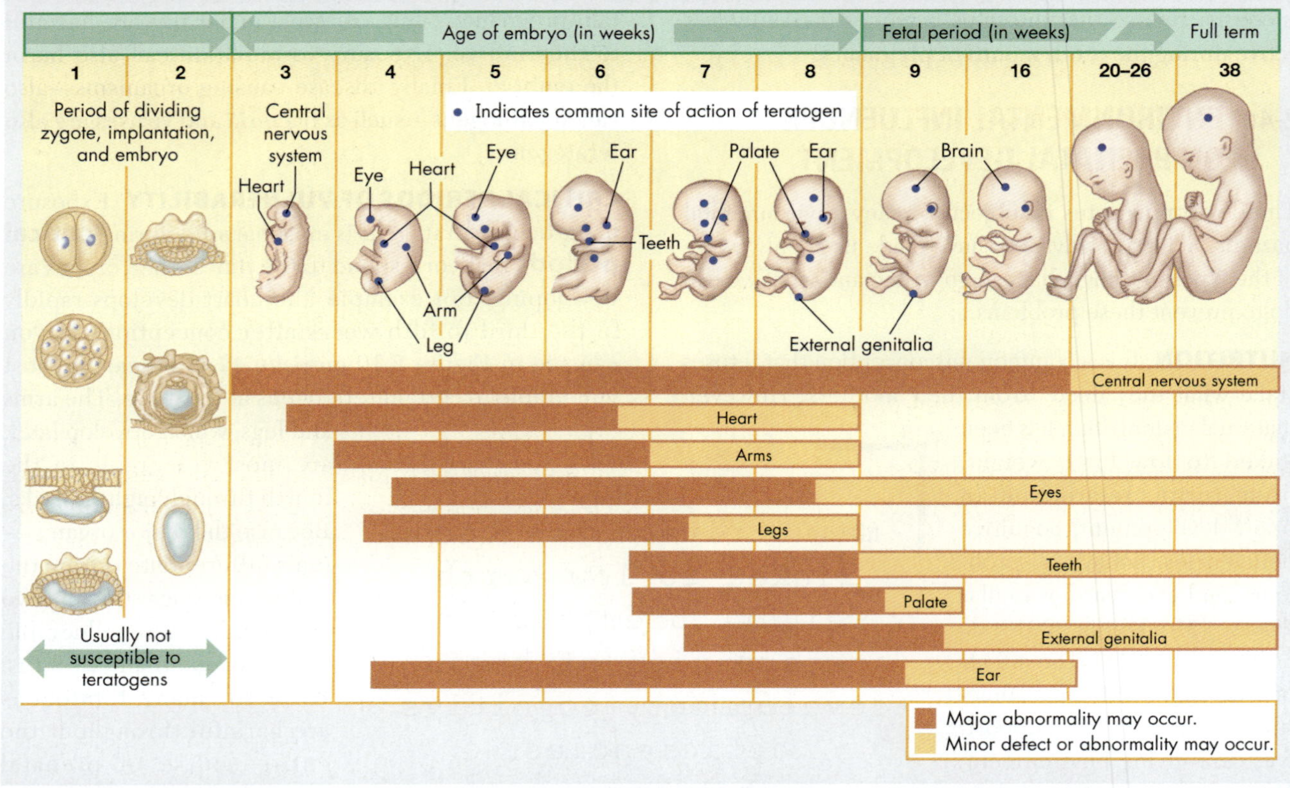

Specific teratogens are most harmful during certain periods of prenatal development.

HIV/AIDS (human immunodeficiency virus/acquired immunodeficiency syndrome) disables the body's immune system and leaves victims prey to a variety of fatal illnesses, including respiratory disorders and cancer. HIV/AIDS is lethal unless treated with a "cocktail" of antiviral drugs. Even then, the drugs do not work for everyone, and the eventual outcome remains in doubt.

HIV can be transmitted by sexual relations, blood transfusions, sharing hypodermic needles while shooting up drugs, childbirth, and breast feeding. During childbirth, blood vessels in the mother and baby rupture, enabling an exchange of blood and transmission of HIV. HIV is also found in breast milk. However, a majority of babies born to mothers with HIV/AIDS do not become infected themselves. It also appears that women can decrease the risk of their babies becoming infected with HIV by regular use of antiviral drugs such as Truvada (Callahan et al., 2015; Conniff & Evensen, 2016).

HIV/AIDS HIV stands for human immunodeficiency virus, which cripples the body's immune system. AIDS stands for acquired immunodeficiency syndrome, a condition in which the immune system is weakened such that it is vulnerable to diseases it would otherwise fight off.

rubella a viral infection that can cause retardation and heart disease in the embryo. Also called German measles.

About one-fourth of babies born to mothers infected with HIV become infected themselves. Maternal use of antiviral drugs decreases the likelihood of transmitting the virus. Check with your doctor about various ways of keeping the fetus and the birth process safe.

Ablestock/Jupiter Images

RUBELLA Rubella (German measles) is a viral infection. Women who are infected during the first 20 weeks of pregnancy stand at least a 20% chance of bearing children with birth defects such as deafness, intellectual disabilities, heart disease, or eye problems, including blindness.

Many adult women had rubella as children and became immune in this way. Women who are not immune are best vaccinated before they become pregnant, although they can be inoculated during pregnancy, if necessary.

PREECLAMPSIA **Preeclampsia** (also called **toxemia**) is a life-threatening disease characterized by high blood pressure that may afflict women late in the second or early in the third trimester. Women with toxemia often have **premature** or undersized babies. Toxemia also causes some 15% to 20% of pregnancy-related maternal deaths (Bangal et al., 2012; Verlohren et al., 2012). Preeclampsia appears to be linked to malnutrition, but the causes are unclear. Women who do not receive prenatal care are much more likely to die from preeclampsia than those who do receive prenatal care.

RH INCOMPATIBILITY In **Rh incompatibility**, antibodies produced by the mother are transmitted to a fetus or newborn infant and cause brain damage or death. Rh is a blood protein found in the red blood cells of some individuals. Rh incompatibility occurs when a woman who does not have this factor—and is thus Rh negative—is carrying an Rh-positive fetus, which can happen if the father is Rh positive. The negative–positive combination occurs in approximately 10% of American couples and becomes a problem in some resulting pregnancies. Rh incompatibility does not affect a first child because women will not have formed Rh antibodies. The chances of an exchange of blood are greatest during childbirth. If an exchange occurs, the mother produces Rh-positive antibodies to the baby's Rh-positive blood. These antibodies can enter the fetal bloodstream during subsequent deliveries, causing anemia, mental deficiency, or death.

If an Rh-negative mother is injected with Rh immunoglobulin within 72 hours after delivery of an Rh-positive baby, she will not develop the antibodies. A fetus or newborn child at risk of Rh disease may receive a blood transfusion to remove the mother's antibodies.

2-4e DRUGS TAKEN BY THE PARENTS

Rh antibodies can be lethal to children, but many other substances can have harmful effects. Even commonly used medications, such as aspirin, can be harmful to the fetus. If a woman is pregnant or thinks she may be, it is advisable for her to consult her obstetrician before taking any drugs, not just prescription medications. A physician usually can recommend a safe and effective substitute for a drug that could potentially harm a developing fetus.

preeclampsia (or **toxemia**) a life-threatening disease that can afflict pregnant women; it is characterized by high blood pressure.

premature born before the full term of gestation. Also referred to as preterm.

Rh incompatibility a condition in which antibodies produced by the mother are transmitted to the child, possibly causing brain damage or death.

Noble Stock/Jupiterimages

Drugs taken by the parents may be harmful to the embryo and fetus. Heavy drinking is connected with fetal alcohol syndrome (FAS), and there is no guaranteed safe small amount of alcohol. Cigarettes deprive the fetus of oxygen. Other drugs have other effects.

THALIDOMIDE **Thalidomide** was marketed in the 1960s as a treatment for insomnia and nausea and provides a dramatic example of critical periods of vulnerability to teratogens. A fetus's extremities undergo rapid development during the second month of pregnancy (see Figure 2.11). Thalidomide taken during this period almost invariably causes birth defects, such as missing or stunted limbs. The drug is no longer prescribed for pregnant women.

HORMONES Women at risk for miscarriages have been prescribed hormones to help maintain their pregnancies. **Progestin**—a synthetic version of naturally occurring progesterone—is chemically similar to male sex hormones and can masculinize the external sex organs of female embryos. **DES** (short for diethylstilbestrol), a powerful estrogen, often prescribed during the 1940s and 1950s to help prevent miscarriage, has been shown to have caused cervical, vaginal, and testicular cancers in some offspring. Among daughters of DES users, some 2% to 3% will develop cancer in the reproductive tract (Verloop et al., 2010, Gee et al., 2014).

VITAMINS Although pregnant women are often prescribed multivitamins to maintain their own health and to promote the development of their fetuses, high doses of vitamins A and D have been associated with central nervous system damage, small head size, and heart defects (Simpson et al., 2011; Wagner et al., 2014).

HEROIN AND METHADONE Maternal addiction to heroin or methadone is linked to low birth weight, prematurity, and toxemia. Narcotics such as heroin and methadone readily cross the placental membrane, and the fetuses of women who regularly use them can become addicted. Addicted newborns may be given the narcotic or a substitute shortly after birth so that they will not suffer serious withdrawal symptoms. The drug is then withdrawn gradually. Addicted newborns may also have behavioral effects, such as delays in motor and language development at the age of 12 months (Minnes et al., 2011).

thalidomide a sedative used in the 1960s that has been linked to birth defects, especially deformed or absent limbs.

Progestin a synthetic hormone used to maintain pregnancy that can cause masculinization of the fetus.

DES diethylstilbestrol, an estrogen that has been linked to cancer in the reproductive organs of children of women who used the hormone when pregnant.

fetal alcohol syndrome (FAS) a cluster of symptoms shown by children of women who drank heavily during pregnancy, including characteristic facial features and intellectual disabilities.

MARIJUANA (CANNABIS) Smoking marijuana during pregnancy apparently poses a number of risks for the fetus, including slower growth and low birth weight. The babies of women who regularly used marijuana show increased tremors and startling, suggesting immature development of the nervous system (Minnes et al., 2011).

Research into the cognitive effects of maternal prenatal use of marijuana suggests that cognitive skills, including learning and memory, may be impaired (Huizink, 2013). One study assessed the behavior of ten-year-olds who had been exposed prenatally to maternal use of marijuana (Goldschmidt et al., 2000), and suggested that prenatal use of marijuana was significantly related to increased hyperactivity, impulsivity, problems in paying attention, and increased delinquency and aggressive behavior.

COCAINE Pregnant women who abuse cocaine increase the risk of stillbirth, low birth weight, and birth defects. Infants exposed to cocaine prenatally are often excitable and irritable, or lethargic; sleep is disturbed (Richardson et al., 2013). There are suggestions of delays in cognitive development, even among preadolescents (Richardson et al., 2013).

Children who are exposed to cocaine prenatally also show problems at later ages. One study compared 189 children at four years of age who had been exposed to cocaine in utero with 185 four-year-olds who had not (Lewis et al., 2004). The children exposed to cocaine had much lower receptive and expressive language abilities.

ALCOHOL Because alcohol passes through the placenta, drinking by a pregnant woman poses risks for the embryo and fetus. Heavy drinking can be lethal and is also connected with deficiencies and deformities in growth. Some children of heavy drinkers develop **fetal alcohol syndrome (FAS)** (O'Leary et al., 2010; see Figure 2.11). Babies with FAS are often smaller than normal, and so are their brains. They have distinct facial features: widely spaced eyes, an underdeveloped upper jaw, a flattened nose. Psychological characteristics appear to reflect dysfunction of the brain.

The facial deformities of FAS diminish as the child moves into adolescence, and most children catch up in height and weight, but the intellectual, academic, and behavioral deficits of FAS persist. Maladaptive behaviors such as poor judgment, distractibility, and difficulty perceiving social cues are common (Kooistra et al., 2010). Although some health professionals allow pregnant women a glass of wine with dinner, there is no guaranteed safe minimal amount of alcohol (Kelly et al., 2013).

FIG.2.11 FETAL ALCOHOL SYNDROME (FAS)

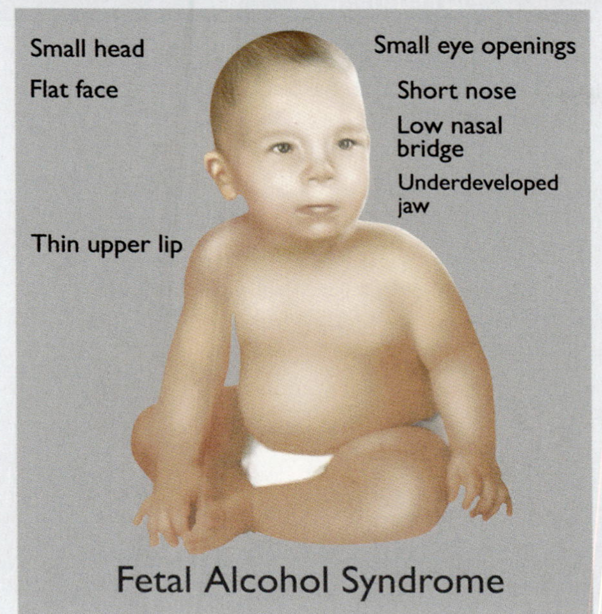

The children of many mothers who drank alcohol during pregnancy exhibit FAS. This syndrome is characterized by developmental lags and such facial features as an underdeveloped upper jaw, a flattened nose, and widely spaced eyes.

CAFFEINE Many pregnant women consume caffeine in the form of coffee, tea, soft drinks, chocolate, and nonprescription drugs. Some authors argue that research findings on caffeine's effects on the developing fetus have been inconsistent (Signorello & McLaughlin, 2004). However, some studies have found that pregnant women who take in a good deal of caffeine are more likely than nonusers to have a miscarriage or a low-birth-weight baby (Bakker et al., 2010; Sengpiel et al., 2013). Ask your doctor.

CIGARETTES Cigarette smoke contains many ingredients, including the stimulant nicotine, the gas carbon monoxide, and hydrocarbons ("tars"), which are carcinogens. Nicotine and carbon monoxide pass through the placenta and reach the fetus. Nicotine stimulates the fetus, but its long-term effects are uncertain. Carbon monoxide decreases the amount of oxygen available to the fetus. Oxygen deprivation is connected with impaired motor development, academic delays, learning and intellectual disabilities, and hyperactivity (Minnes et al., 2011).

ian nolan / Alamy Stock Photo

Pregnant women who smoke are likely to deliver smaller babies than nonsmokers (Anblagan et al., 2013). Their babies are more likely to be stillborn or to die soon after birth (Still-birth Collaborative Research Network Writing Group, 2011). Babies of fathers who smoke have higher rates of birth defects, infant mortality, lower birth weights, and cardiovascular problems (Misra et al., 2010).

2-4f ENVIRONMENTAL HAZARDS

Mothers know when they are ingesting drugs, but there are many other substances in the environment they may take in unknowingly. These substances are environmental hazards to which we are all exposed, and we refer to them collectively as pollution.

Prenatal exposure to heavy metals such as lead, mercury, and zinc may delay mental development at one and two years of age (Chen et al., 2014; Gorini et al., 2014). Polychlorinated biphenyls (PCBs), used in many industrial products, accumulate in fish that feed in polluted waters. Newborns whose mothers consumed PCB-contaminated fish from Lake Michigan were smaller and showed poorer motor functioning and memory defects (Jacobson et al., 1992). On the other hand, prenatal exposure to the low levels of metals that we now find in most developed countries may not be harmful (Foms et al., 2014).

Experiments with mice show that fetal exposure to radiation in high doses can damage the eyes, central nervous system, and skeleton (Buratovic et al., 2016; Hossain et al., 2005). Pregnant women exposed to atomic radiation during the bombings of Hiroshima and Nagasaki in World War II gave birth to babies who were likely to be intellectually disabled as well as physically deformed (Sadler, 2005). Pregnant women are advised to avoid unnecessary exposure to x-rays. (Ultrasound, which is not an x-ray, has not been shown to harm the fetus.)

2-4g PARENTS' AGE

What about the parents' age? Older fathers are more likely to produce abnormal sperm. The mother's age also matters. From a biological vantage point, the 20s may be the ideal age for women to bear children. Teenage mothers have a higher incidence of infant mortality and children with low birth weight (Save the Children, 2011). Girls who become pregnant in their early teens may place a burden on bodies that may not have adequately matured to facilitate pregnancy and childbirth (Save the Children, 2011).

Women's fertility declines gradually until the mid-30s, after which it declines more rapidly. Women possess all their ova in immature form at birth. Over 30 years, these cells are exposed to the environmental slings and arrows of toxic wastes, chemical pollutants, and radiation, thus increasing the risk of chromosomal abnormalities such as Down's syndrome. Women who wait until their 30s or 40s to have children also increase the likelihood of having miscarriages (Khalil et al., 2013). With adequate prenatal care, however, the risk of problems in pregnancy is relatively small, even for older first-time mothers (Williams et al., 2011).

DO MEN REALLY HAVE ALL THE TIME IN THE WORLD? The artist Pablo Picasso fathered children in his 70s. Strom Thurmond, a longtime U.S. senator, fathered a child in his 90s. It has been widely known that women's chances of conceiving children decline as they age. The traditional message has been "Women, you'd better hurry up. Men, you have all the time in the world."

TRUTH

(T) F A father's age at the time of conception can influence the development of the fetus.

It is true that a father's age at the time of conception can influence the development of the fetus. The older the father, the greater the risk of chromosomal abnormalities.

Not so, apparently. Older fathers are more likely to produce abnormal sperm, leading to fertility problems. But that's only the tip of the iceberg. University of Queensland researchers analyzed data from some 33,000 U.S. children and found that the older the father is at

FIG.2.12 AUTISM RISK INCREASES WITH PATERNAL AGE

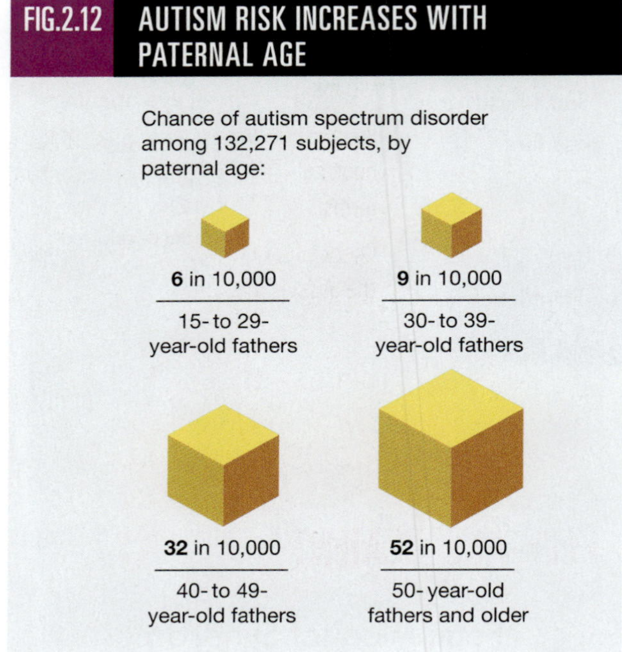

conception, the lower a child's score may be on tests of reading skills, reasoning, memory, and concentration. The ages of 29 and 30 are something of a turning point for men, because children conceived past these ages are at greater risk for the psychological disorders of schizophrenia and bipolar disorder. Children born to men past 40 also have a greater risk of autism, as shown in Figure 2.12 (Reichenberg et al., 2006).

These findings do not mean that the majority of children born to men past their reproductive "prime" will develop these problems, but it does mean that men's age, as women's, is related to risks for their children.

Whatever the age of the mother and father, the events of childbirth provide some of the most memorable moments in the lives of parents. In Chapter 3, we continue our voyage with the process of birth and the characteristics of the newborn child.

STUDY TOOLS 2

READY TO STUDY?

In the book, you can:

- ☐ Rip out the chapter review card at the back of the book for a handy summary of the chapter and key terms.
- ☐ Check your understanding of what you've read with the quizzes that follow.

ONLINE AT CENGAGEBRAIN.COM YOU CAN:

- ☐ Collect StudyBits while you read and study the chapter.
- ☐ Quiz yourself on key concepts.
- ☐ Find videos for further exploration.
- ☐ Prepare for tests with HDEV5 Flash Cards as well as those you create.

SELF-ASSESSMENT

Fill-Ins

Answers can be found in the back of the book.

1. ____________ are the biological materials that regulate the development of traits.
2. Dizygotic twins share ____________ % of their genes.
3. "Supermales" have ____________ sex-chromosomal structure.
4. ____________ -cell anemia is most common among African Americans.
5. Sperm are apparently guided toward an egg cell (ovum) by changes in ____________ ions.
6. Some women are infertile due to ____________, which can obstruct the fallopian tubes.
7. The outer layer of the blastocyst is the ____________.
8. The ____________ is a pancake-shaped mass of tissue that permits the embryo and fetus to exchange nutrients and wastes with the mother.
9. ____________ is a life-threatening disease characterized by high blood pressure that may afflict women late in the second or early in the third trimester.
10. Cigarette smoking by a pregnant woman is harmful to the fetus because it decreases the amount of ____________ available to the fetus.

Multiple Choice

1. **Which of the following is accurate about the age of the parents and possible health risks for a child?**
   a. Only the mother's age matters.
   b. The younger a female is, the greater the chances of a positive pregnancy outcome.
   c. Only the father's age matters.
   d. The age of both the mother and the father can matter.

2. **The arms and the legs are most vulnerable to teratogens**
   a. one to four weeks after conception.
   b. four to eight weeks after conception.
   c. eight to twelve weeks after conception.
   d. twelve to sixteen weeks after conception.

3. **Which of the following is not likely to be transmitted to the fetus through the placenta?**
   a. HIV
   b. aspirin
   c. narcotics
   d. alcohol

4. **About ____________ % of cases of infertility have unknown causes.**
   a. 20
   b. 40
   c. 60
   d. 80

5. **Which of the following is a sex-linked disease?**
   a. Tay-Sachs disease
   b. Huntington's disease
   c. hemophilia
   d. cystic fibrosis

6. **Girls with which one of the following disorders are infertile, have poorly developed ovaries, and attain shorter than average height?**
   a. Klinefelter syndrome
   b. supermale syndrome
   c. triple X syndrome
   d. Turner syndrome

7. **Which of the following is a dominant trait?**
   a. straight hair
   b. type O blood
   c. farsightedness
   d. lactose intolerance

8. **The period from conception to implantation is called the ____________ stage of prenatal development.**
   a. latency
   b. germinal
   c. fetal
   d. embryonic

9. **____________ is a powerful estrogen that was often prescribed during the 1940s and 1950s to help prevent miscarriage. Since then, it has been shown to cause cervical, vaginal, and testicular cancers in some off spring.**
   a. DES
   b. Progestin
   c. Vitamin A
   d. Thalidomide

10. **In ____________, antibodies produced by the mother are transmitted to a fetus or newborn infant and cause brain damage or death.**
    a. preeclampsia
    b. Rh incompatibility
    c. spina bifida
    d. FAS

3 Birth and the Newborn Baby: In the New World

iStockphoto.com/Sdavidi

LEARNING OUTCOMES

After studying this chapter, you will be able to...

- 3-1 Identify the stages of childbirth
- 3-2 Examine different methods of childbirth
- 3-3 Discuss potential problems with childbirth
- 3-4 Describe the postpartum period
- 3-5 Examine the characteristics of a neonate

After you finish this chapter, go to **PAGE 68** for **STUDY TOOLS**

During the last few weeks before she gave birth, Michele explained: "I couldn't get my mind off the pregnancy—what it was going to be like when I finally delivered Lisa. I'd had the amniocentesis, so I knew it was a girl. I'd had the ultrasounds, so all her fingers and toes had been counted, but I was still hoping and praying that everything would turn out all right. To be honest, I was also worried about the delivery. I had always been an A student, and I guess I wanted to earn an A in childbirth as well. Matt was understanding, and he was even helpful, but, you know, it wasn't him."

> Nearly all first-time mothers struggle through the last weeks of pregnancy and worry about the mechanics of delivery.

Nearly all first-time mothers struggle through the last weeks of pregnancy and worry about the mechanics of delivery. Childbirth is a natural function, of course, but so many of them have gone to classes to learn how to do what comes naturally! They worry about whether they'll get to the hospital or birthing center on time ("Is there gas in the car?" "Is it snowing?"). They worry about whether the baby will start breathing on its own properly. They may wonder if they'll do it on their own or need a C-section. They may also worry about whether it will hurt, and how much, and when they should ask for anesthetics, and, well, how to earn that A.

Close to full **term**, Michele and other women are sort of front-loaded and feel bent out of shape, and guess what? They are. The weight of the fetus may also be causing backaches. Will they deliver the baby, or will the baby—by being born—deliver them from discomfort? "Hanging in and having Lisa was a wonderful experience," Michele said in the end. "I think Matt should have had it."

COUNTDOWN ...

Early in the last month of pregnancy, the head of the fetus settles in the pelvis. This process is called *dropping* or *lightening*. Because lightening decreases pressure on the diaphragm, the mother may, in fact, feel lighter.

The first uterine contractions are called **Braxton-Hicks contractions**, or false labor contractions. They are relatively painless and may be experienced as early as the sixth month of pregnancy. They increase in frequency as the pregnancy progresses and may serve to tone the muscles that will be used in delivery. True labor contractions are more painful and regular, and are usually intensified by walking.

A day or so before labor begins, increased pelvic pressure from the fetus may rupture blood vessels in the birth canal so that blood appears in vaginal secretions. Mucus that had plugged the **cervix** and protected the uterus from infection becomes dislodged. About one woman in ten has a rush of warm liquid from the vagina at this time. This liquid is amniotic fluid, and its discharge means that the amniotic sac has burst. The sac usually does not burst until the end

term the typical nine-month period from conception to childbirth.

Braxton-Hicks contractions the first, usually painless, contractions of childbirth.

cervix the narrow lower end of the uterus, through which a baby passes to reach the vagina.

TRUTH OR FICTION?

T	F	The fetus signals the mother when it is ready to be born.
T	F	After birth, babies are held upside down and slapped on the buttocks to stimulate independent breathing.
T	F	Women who give birth according to the Lamaze method do not experience pain.
T	F	In the United States, nearly three of every ten births are by cesarean section.
T	F	It is abnormal to feel depressed following childbirth.
T	F	Parents must have extended early contact with their newborn children if adequate bonding is to take place.
T	F	More children in the United States die from sudden infant death syndrome (SIDS) than from cancer, heart disease, pneumonia, child abuse, AIDS, cystic fibrosis, and muscular dystrophy combined.

of the first stage of childbirth, as described later. Other signs that labor is beginning include indigestion, diarrhea, an ache in the small of the back, and cramps.

The fetus may actually signal the mother when it is "ready" to be born by secreting hormones that stimulate the placenta and uterus to secrete **prostaglandins** (Plunkett et al., 2011; Swaggart et al., 2015). Prostaglandins not only cause the cramping that women may feel before or during menstruation, they also excite the muscles of the uterus to engage in labor contractions. As labor progresses, the pituitary gland releases the hormone **oxytocin**, which stimulates contractions powerful enough to expel the baby.

TRUTH

T F The fetus signals the mother when it is ready to be born.

The fetus may actually signal the mother when it is "ready" to be born by secreting hormones that stimulate the placenta and uterus to secrete prostaglandins (Swaggart et al., 2015). Prostaglandins not only cause the cramping that women may feel before or during menstruation, they also excite the muscles of the uterus to engage in labor contractions.

3-1 THE STAGES OF CHILDBIRTH

Regular uterine contractions signal the beginning of childbirth. Childbirth occurs in three stages. In the first stage, uterine contractions **efface** and **dilate** the cervix, which needs to widen to about four inches (ten centimeters) to allow the baby to pass. Dilation of the cervix causes most of the pain of childbirth (see Figure 3.1).

The first stage is the longest stage. Among women undergoing their first deliveries, this stage may last from a few hours to more than a day. Subsequent pregnancies take less time. The first contractions are not usually all that painful and are spaced 10 to 20 minutes apart. They may last from 20 to 40 seconds each. As the process continues, the contractions become more powerful, frequent, and regular. Women are usually advised to go to the hospital or birthing center when the contractions are four to five minutes apart. Until the end of the first stage of labor, the mother is usually in a labor room.

If the woman is to be "prepped"—that is, if her pubic hair is to be shaved—it takes place now. The prep is intended to lower the chances of infection during delivery and to facilitate the performance of an **episiotomy**. A woman may be given an enema to prevent an involuntary bowel movement during labor. But many women find prepping and enemas degrading and seek obstetricians (physicians who treat women during pregnancy, labor, and recovery from childbirth) who do not perform them routinely.

During the first stage of childbirth, fetal monitoring may be used. One kind of monitor is an electronic device strapped around the woman's abdomen that measures the fetal heart rate as well as the mother's contractions. An abnormal heart rate alerts the medical staff to possible fetal distress so that appropriate steps can be taken, such as speeding up the delivery. When the cervix is nearly fully dilated, the head of the fetus begins to move into the vagina. This process is called **transition**. During transition, which lasts about 30 minutes or less, contractions are usually frequent and strong.

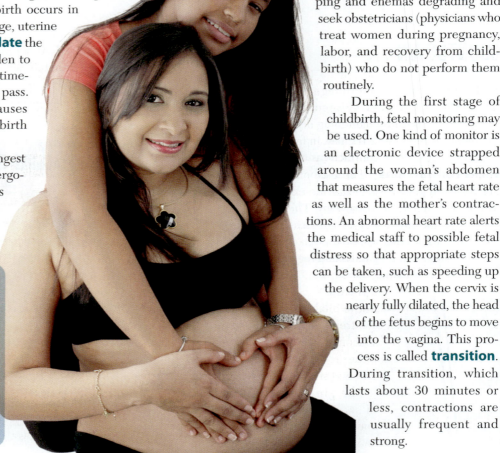

David Castillo Dominici / Alamy Stock Photo

prostaglandins hormones that stimulate uterine contractions.

oxytocin a hormone that stimulates labor contractions.

efface to become thin.

dilate to widen.

episiotomy a surgical incision between the birth canal and anus that widens the vaginal opening.

transition movement of the head of the fetus into the vagina.

FIG.3.1 STAGES OF CHILDBIRTH

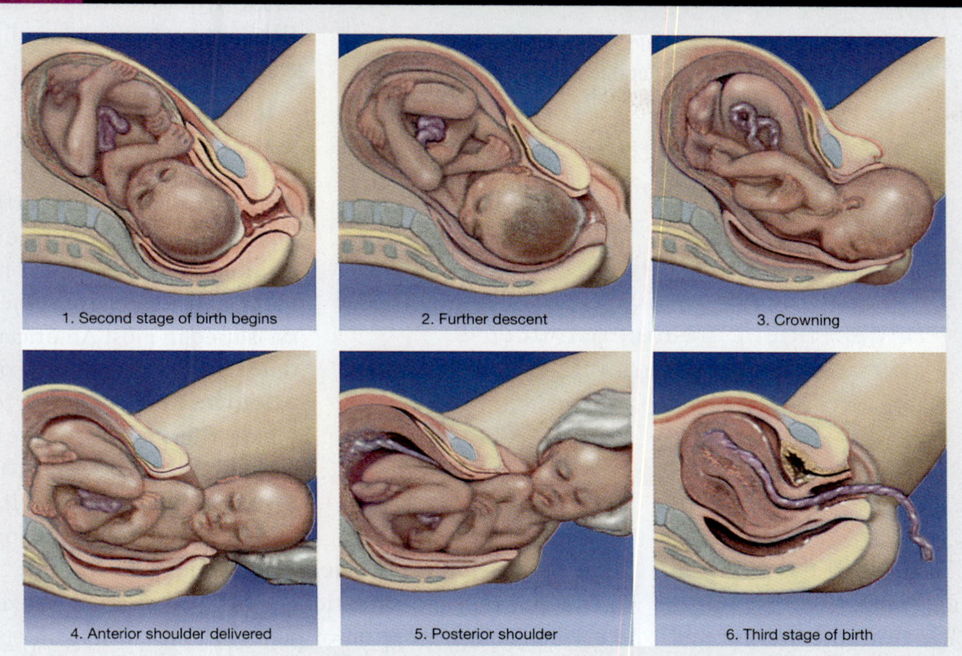

In the first stage, uterine contractions efface and dilate the cervix. The second stage begins with movement of the baby into the birth canal and ends with birth of the baby. During the third stage, the placenta separates from the uterine wall and is expelled through the birth canal.

The second stage of childbirth begins when the baby appears at the opening of the vagina (now called the *birth canal*). The second stage is briefer than the first, possibly lasting minutes or a few hours and ending with the birth of the baby. The woman may be taken to a delivery room for the second stage.

The contractions of the second stage stretch the skin surrounding the birth canal farther and propel the baby along. The baby's head is said to have crowned when it begins to emerge from the birth canal. Once crowning has occurred, the baby normally emerges completely within minutes.

The physician or nurse may perform an episiotomy once crowning takes place. The purpose of an episiotomy is to prevent random tearing when the area between the birth canal and the anus becomes severely stretched. Women are unlikely to feel the incision of the episiotomy because the pressure of the crowning head tends to numb the region between the vagina and the anus. The episiotomy, like prepping and the enema, is controversial and is not practiced in Europe. The incision may cause itching and discomfort as it heals. The incidence of the use of episiotomy in the United States has been declining, with some studies suggesting that the procedure causes as many problems as it prevents. Some health professionals argue that an episiotomy is warranted when the baby's shoulders are wide or if the baby's heart rate declines for a long period of time. The strongest predictor of whether a practitioner will choose to use episiotomy is not the condition of the mother or the baby, but rather whether the physician normally performs an episiotomy.

To clear the passageway for breathing from any obstructions, mucus is suctioned from the baby's mouth when the head emerges from the birth canal. When the baby is breathing adequately on its own, the umbilical cord is clamped and severed (see Figure 3.2). Mother and infant are now separate beings. The stump of the umbilical cord will dry and fall off on its own in about seven to ten days.

FIG.3.2 CUTTING THE UMBILICAL CORD

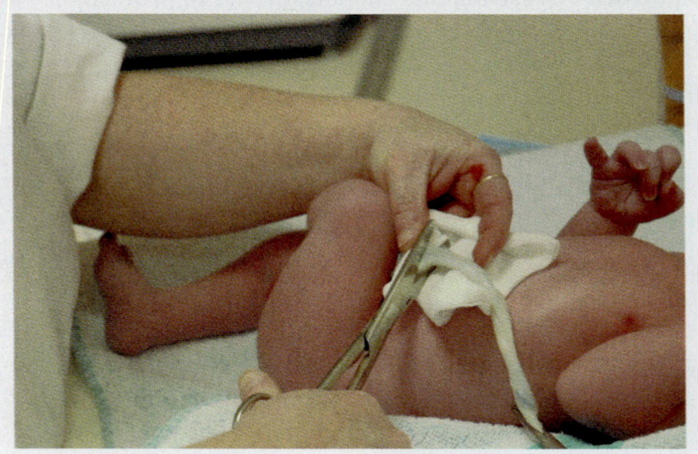

BSIP/Science Source

The stump of the cord dries and falls off in about seven to ten days.

Now the baby is frequently whisked away by a nurse, who will perform various procedures, including footprinting the baby, supplying an ID bracelet, putting antibiotic ointment or drops of silver nitrate into the baby's eyes to prevent bacterial infections, and giving the baby a vitamin K injection to help its blood clot properly if it bleeds (newborn babies do not manufacture vitamin K). While these procedures go on, the mother is in the third stage of labor.

FICTION

T (F) After birth, babies are held upside down and slapped on the buttocks to stimulate independent breathing.

It is no longer true that babies are held upside down and slapped on the buttocks to stimulate independent breathing, even though we often see this in old movies. To assist independent breathing, mucus is suctioned from the baby's nose and mouth when the head emerges from the birth canal.

The third stage of labor, also called the placental stage, lasts from minutes to an hour or more. During this stage, the placenta separates from the uterine wall and is expelled through the birth canal. Some bleeding is normal. The obstetrician sews the episiotomy, if one has been performed.

3-2 METHODS OF CHILDBIRTH

Childbirth was once a more intimate procedure that usually took place in the woman's home and involved her, perhaps a **midwife**, and family. This pattern is followed in many less developed nations today, but only rarely in the United States and other developed nations. Contemporary American childbirths usually take place in hospitals, where physicians use sophisticated instruments and anesthetics to protect mother and child from complications and discomfort. Modern medicine has saved lives, but childbearing has also become more impersonal. Some argue that modern methods wrest control from women over their own bodies. They even argue that anesthetics have denied many women the experience of giving birth, although many or most women admit that they appreciate having the experience "muted."

midwife an individual who helps women in childbirth.

anesthetics agents that lessen pain.

general anesthesia elimination of pain by putting a person to sleep.

local anesthetic reduction of pain in an area of the body.

neonate an infant from birth through the first four weeks of life.

natural childbirth childbirth without anesthesia.

3-2a ANESTHESIA

Although painful childbirth has historically been seen as the standard for women, today, at least some anesthesia is used in most American deliveries. Two types of **anesthetics** are used to lessen the pain associated with childbirth. **General anesthesia** achieves its anesthetic effect by putting the woman to sleep by means of an injected barbiturate. Tranquilizers and narcotics can be used to reduce anxiety and the perception of pain without causing sleep. General anesthesia reduces the responsiveness of the baby shortly after birth, but there is mixed evidence as to whether there are long-term negative effects (Eger et al., 2014).

Regional or **local anesthetics** deaden pain without putting the mother to sleep. With a *pudendal block*, the mother's external genitals are numbed by local injection. With an *epidural block* and a *spinal block*, anesthesia is injected into the spinal canal or spinal cord, temporarily numbing the body below the waist. Local anesthesia may have minor depressive effects on **neonates** shortly after birth, but the effects have not been shown to linger (Torpy et al., 2011).

In so-called **natural childbirth**, a woman uses no anesthesia. Instead, she is educated about the biological aspects of reproduction and delivery, encouraged to maintain physical fitness, and taught relaxation and breathing exercises.

3-2b HYPNOSIS AND BIOFEEDBACK

Hypnosis has been used to help clients stick to diets, quit smoking, and undergo dental treatments with less discomfort. It has also been used with some success as an alternative to anesthesia during childbirth (Camann, 2014; Landolt & Milling, 2011).

Biofeedback is a method that provides the woman in labor with continuous information as to what is

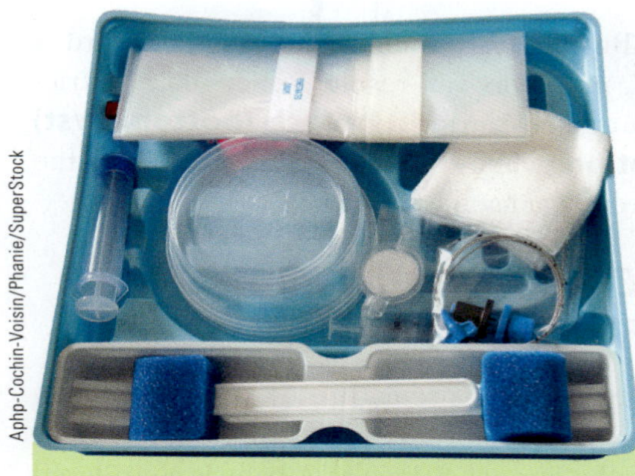

An epidural anesthesia kit. An *epidural block* permits the woman to stay awake but feel no sensation in the pelvis or below.

FIG.3.3 C-SECTIONS, UNITED STATES, 1996–2014

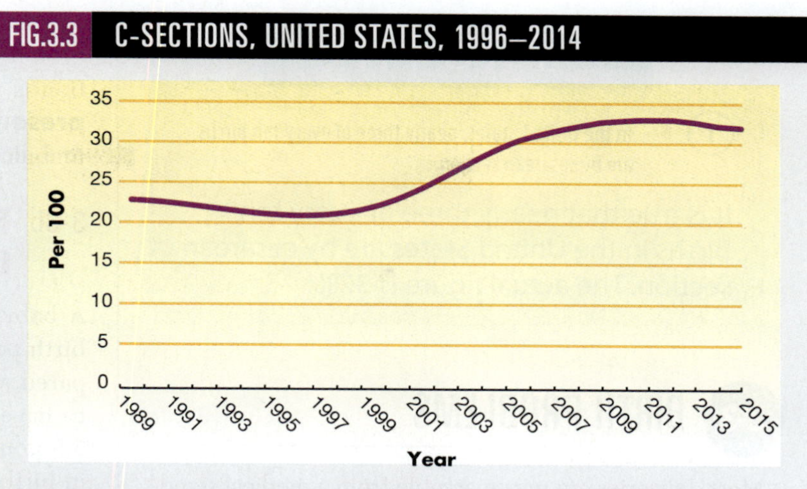

Since 1996, the percentage of American women undergoing C-sections mushroomed from 21% to 33% and appears to have leveled off at 32%–33%.

Source: U.S. National Center for Health Statistics (page last updated February 25, 2014). http://www.cdc.gov/nchs/fastats/delivery.htm. (Accessed September 16, 2014).

happening with various bodily functions. Muscle tension and blood pressure are among the functions that can be targeted. Studies suggest that helping women relax muscle tension may have some positive effects early during labor, but greater benefits have not so far been established (Loayza et al., 2011).

3-2c PREPARED CHILDBIRTH

In the **Lamaze method**, or prepared childbirth, women engage in breathing and relaxation exercises that lessen fear and pain and distract them from discomfort. The mother-to-be attends Lamaze classes with a "coach"—most often, her partner—who will aid her in the delivery room by doing things such as massaging her, timing the contractions, offering social support, and coaching her in patterns of breathing and relaxation. Women using the Lamaze method often report less pain and ask for less medication (Camann, 2014; Lothian, 2011).

FICTION

T (F) Women who give birth according to the Lamaze method do not experience pain.

It is not true that women who give birth according to the Lamaze method do not experience pain. However, women using the method often report less pain and ask for less medication.

3-2d CESAREAN SECTION

In a **cesarean section (C-section)**, the physician delivers the baby by surgery. The physician cuts through the mother's abdomen and uterus and physically removes the baby.

Physicians prefer C-sections to vaginal delivery when they believe that normal delivery may threaten the mother or child or may be more difficult than desired. One-third of all births (32.2%) in the United States are currently by C-section (Martin, 2013). To gain some perspective, note that C-sections accounted for only 23% of births in 1989 (see Figure 3.3). Some of the increase is due to medical advances, but some women request C-sections so they can control the time of the delivery, and some physicians perform them to prevent malpractice suits in case something goes wrong during a vaginal delivery.

C-sections are also performed when the physician wants to prevent the circulatory systems of the mother and baby from mixing, as might occur when there is (normal) bleeding during vaginal delivery. C-sections in such cases help prevent transmission of the viruses that cause genital herpes and AIDS. C-sections have been shown to reduce the risk of hypoxia (Roberts et al., 2015).

Lamaze method a childbirth method in which women are educated about childbirth, breathe in patterns that lessen pain during birth, and have a coach present.

cesarean section (C-section) delivery of a baby by abdominal surgery.

TRUTH

(T) F In the United States, nearly three of every ten births are by cesarean section.

It is true that nearly three of every ten births in the United States are by cesarean section. The actual figure is 32%.

3-3 BIRTH PROBLEMS

Most deliveries are unremarkable from a medical standpoint (although perhaps every delivery is most remarkable from the parents' point of view). Still, a number of problems can and do occur.

3-3a OXYGEN DEPRIVATION

Researchers use two terms to discuss oxygen deprivation: anoxia and hypoxia. **Anoxia** derives from roots meaning "without oxygen." **Hypoxia** derives from roots meaning "under" and "oxygen," the point again being that the baby does not receive enough oxygen in utero to develop properly. Prenatal oxygen deprivation can impair the development of the fetus's central nervous system, leading to cognitive problems, especially in memory and spatial relations; motor problems; and psychological disorders (Liu et al., 2011; Rennie & Rosenbloom, 2011). Prolonged cutoff of the baby's oxygen supply during delivery can also cause psychological and physical health problems, such as early-onset schizophrenia and cerebral palsy (Kotlicka-Antczak et al., 2014).

Oxygen deprivation can be caused by maternal disorders such as diabetes, by immaturity of the baby's respiratory system, and by accidents, some of which involve pressure against the umbilical cord during birth. Passage through the birth canal is tight, and the umbilical cord is usually squeezed during the process. If the squeezing is temporary, the effect is like holding one's breath for a moment and no problems are likely to ensue. But if constriction of the umbilical cord is prolonged, problems can result. Prolonged constriction is more likely during a **breech (bottom-first) presentation**, when the baby's body may press the umbilical cord against the birth canal.

anoxia absence of oxygen.

hypoxia less oxygen than required.

breech (bottom-first) presentation buttocks-first childbirth.

preterm born prior to 37 weeks of gestation.

small for gestational age descriptive of neonates who are small for their age.

3-3b PRETERM AND LOW-BIRTH-WEIGHT INFANTS

A baby is considered premature or **preterm** when birth occurs at or before 37 weeks of gestation compared with the normal 40 weeks. A baby is considered to have a low birth weight when it weighs less than 5.5 pounds (about 2,500 grams). When a baby is low in birth weight, even though it is born at full term, it is referred to as being **small for gestational age**. Mothers who smoke, abuse drugs, or are malnourished place their babies at risk of being small for gestational age. Small-for-gestational-age babies tend to remain shorter and lighter than their age-mates and show slight delays in learning and problems in attention when compared with their age-mates (Heinonen et al., 2011). Preterm babies are more likely than small-for-gestational-age babies to achieve normal heights and weights. Prematurity is more common in the case of multiple births—even twins (Kurosawa et al., 2012; Shiozaki et al., 2014).

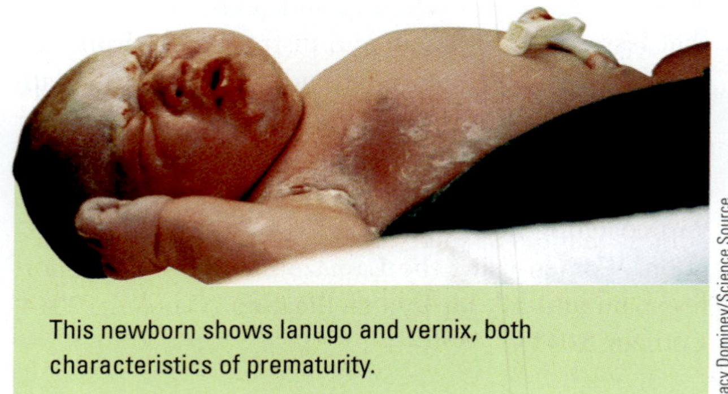

This newborn shows lanugo and vernix, both characteristics of prematurity.

Tracy Dominey/Science Source

RISKS ASSOCIATED WITH PREMATURITY AND LOW BIRTH WEIGHT Neonates weighing between 3.25 and 5.5 pounds are seven times more likely to die than infants of normal birth weight, whereas those weighing less than 3.3 pounds are nearly 100 times as likely to die (Save the Children, 2013; Strunk et al., 2012). By and large, the lower a child's birth weight, the more poorly he or she fares on measures of neurological development and cognitive functioning throughout the school years (Clark et al., 2013; Edwards et al., 2011).

There are also risks for motor development. One study compared 96 very low birth weight (VLBW) children with normal-term children at 6, 9, 12, and 18 months, correcting for age according to the expected date of delivery (Jeng et al., 2000). The median age at which the full-term infants began to walk was 12 months, compared with 14 months for the VLBW infants. By 18 months of age, all full-term infants were walking, compared to 89% of the VLBW infants.

SIGNS OF PREMATURITY Preterm babies are relatively thin because they have not yet formed the layer of fat that gives full-term children their round, robust appearance. They often have fine, downy hair, referred to as **lanugo**, and an oily white substance on the skin known as **vernix**. If the babies are born six weeks or more before term, their nipples will not have emerged. The testicles of boys born this early will not yet have descended into the scrotum. Boys with undescended testes at birth are at higher risk for testicular cancer later in life.

Preterm babies have immature muscles, so their sucking and breathing reflexes are weak. In addition, the walls of the tiny air sacs in their lungs may tend to stick together because the babies do not yet secrete substances that lubricate the walls of the sacs. As a result, babies born more than a month before full term may breathe irregularly or may suddenly stop breathing, evidence of **respiratory distress syndrome**. Preterm infants with respiratory distress syndrome show poorer development in cognitive, language, and motor skills over the first two years of development than full-term infants. Injecting pregnant women at risk for delivering preterm babies with corticosteroids increases the babies' chances of survival (Murphy et al., 2011).

TREATMENT OF PRETERM BABIES Because of their physical frailty, preterm infants usually remain in the hospital and are placed in **incubators**, which maintain a temperature-controlled environment and afford some protection from disease. The babies may be given oxygen, although excessive oxygen can cause permanent eye injury.

PARENTS AND PRETERM NEONATES Parents often do not treat preterm neonates as well as they treat full-term neonates. For one thing, preterm infants usually do not have the robust, appealing appearance of many full-term babies. Their cries are more high pitched and grating, and they are more irritable (Kaye & Shah, 2015; Gima et al., 2010). The demands of caring for preterm babies can be depressing to parents (Cheng et al., 2016; Welch et al., 2016). Mothers of preterm babies frequently report that they feel alienated from their babies and harbor feelings of failure, guilt, and low self-esteem (Baum et al., 2011; Vigod et al., 2011). Fear of hurting preterm babies can further discourage parents from handling them, but encouraging mothers to massage their preterm infants can help them cope with this fear (Feldman et al., 2014). Once they come home from the hospital, preterm infants remain more passive and less sociable than full-term infants (Korja et al., 2012). Preterm infants fare better when they have responsive and caring parents.

INTERVENTION PROGRAMS Preterm infants profit from early stimulation just as full-term babies do—being cuddled, rocked, talked to, and sung to; being exposed to recordings of their mothers' voices; having mobiles in view; and having live and recorded music in their environment (Nordhov et al., 2012). Other forms of stimulation include massage and "kangaroo care" (Johnston et al., 2011), in which the baby spends time each day lying skin to skin and chest to chest with a parent. By and large, stimulated preterm infants tend to gain weight more rapidly, show fewer respiratory problems, and make greater advances in motor, intellectual, and neurological development than control infants (Fucile & Gisel, 2010; Nordhov et al., 2010).

3-4 THE POSTPARTUM PERIOD

The **postpartum period** refers to the weeks following delivery, but there is no specific limit. The "parting" from the baby is frequently a happy experience. The family's long wait is over. Concerns about pregnancy and labor are over, fingers and toes have been counted, and despite some local discomfort, the mother finds her "load" to be lightened, most literally. According to the American Psychiatric Association (2014), however, about 70% of new mothers have periods of tearfulness, sadness, and irritability, which the Association refers to as the "baby blues."

lanugo fine, downy hair on premature babies.

vernix oily white substance on the skin of premature babies.

respiratory distress syndrome weak and irregular breathing, typical of preterm babies.

incubators a heated, protective container for premature infants.

postpartum period the period immediately following childbirth.

Maternal and Child Mortality Around the World

Modern medicine has made vast strides in decreasing the rates of maternal and infant mortality, but the advances are not equally spread throughout the world. Save the Children, a nonprofit relief and development organization, tracks the likelihood that a woman will die in childbirth and that an infant will die during its first year. The likelihood of maternal and infant mortality is connected with what Save the Children terms the *Mothers' Index*, which includes factors such as the lifetime risk of maternal death during pregnancy and delivery, the under-five mortality rate for children, the years of formal schooling of mothers, economic status (as measured by national income per person), and participation of women in national government—a measure of the extent to which a society empowers women. Figure 3.4 shows the various reasons why children die, according to a recent edition of *State of the World's Mothers* (Save the Children, 2015).

Why are maternal and infant mortality so low in Europe?

Number 1 on the *Mothers' Index* is Norway where the chances of the woman dying are about 1 in 14,900 and where only 3 infants in 1,000 die during the first five years (see Table 3.1). Women receive an average of 17 years of formal schooling (the same as in the United States), per capita income is $102,610, and 40% of national government seats are held by women (as compared to only 19% in the United States). In the United States, which ranks number 33 on the list, 1 in 1,800 women stands a lifetime risk of dying during pregnancy or childbirth, and a child has a 6.9 in 1,000 chance of dying under the age of 5. Half the countries in the world have a higher percentage

FIG.3.4 WHY DO YOUNG CHILDREN DIE?

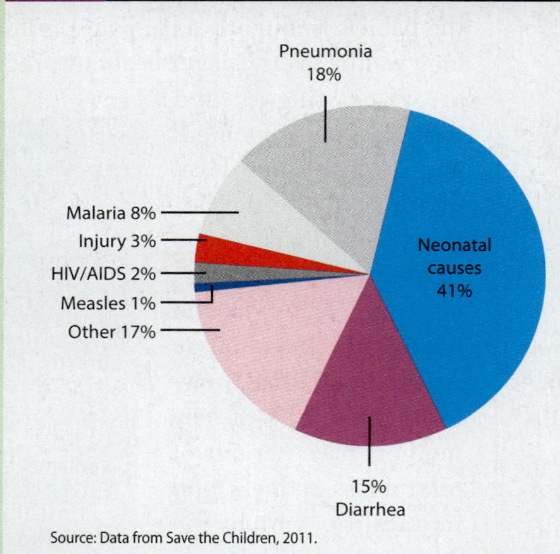

Source: Data from Save the Children, 2011.

Why do young children die? Estimates show that pneumonia, diarrhea, and malaria remain the leading killers of children under five worldwide. Together they account for 41% of child deaths. More than 40% of all under-five deaths occur in the first month of life. Most of these children could be saved by increasing coverage for known, affordable, and effective interventions. Ensuring proper nutrition is a critical aspect of prevention, since malnutrition contributes to more than a third of all child deaths.

of females in national government than the United States. The performance of the United States in the rankings is related to the large number of "nations within the nation." For example, there is great disparity in wealth, and richer Americans fare better in the rankings than poorer Americans. High-quality medical intervention is more available in some parts of the country than others. Many mobile Americans base their residence, in part, on the availability of good medicine.

TABLE 3.1 MATERNAL AND CHILD MORTALITY IN SELECTED COUNTRIES AS RELATED TO INCOME LEVEL AND EMPOWERMENT OF WOMEN

Readers may wonder why the United States ranks so low on this list. One answer is that states with above-average poverty rates, large rural populations, and less-than-average levels of education have the highest maternal and infant mortality rates. According to a recent report by the Centers for Disease Control's National Center for Health Statistics (http://www.cdc.gov/nchs/linked.htm), African American women have the highest infant mortality rate—13.60 per 1,000 live births as compared to 4.55 per 1,000 births for Cuban American women. European American women had 5.66 infant deaths per 1,000 births, as compared with 8.45 for Native Americans, 7.82 for Puerto Ricans, 5.47 for Mexican Americans, 4.67 for Asian Americans, and 4.65 for Central and South Americans. How do you explain these ethnic differences?

Country	Lifetime risk of maternal mortality (1 in number shown)	Under-five mortality rate (per 1,000 live births)	Average years of formal schooling for women	National income per person (in U.S. dollars)	Participation of women in national government (percentage of seats held by women)	Mothers' Index Rank
Norway	14,900	2.8	17.5	102,610	39.6	1
Ireland	5,500	3.8	18.6	43,110	19.9	22
Italy	17,100	3.6	16.0	35,860	30.1	12
France	4,300	4.2	16.0	43,460	25.7	23
Germany	11,000	3.9	16.5	47,270	36.9	8
Poland	19,800	5.2	15.5	13,240	22.1	28
Japan	12,100	2.9	15.3	46,330	11.6	32
Mexico	900	14.5	13.1	9,940	37.1	53
Sweden	13,600	3.0	15.8	61,760	43.6	5
Canada	5,200	5.2	15.8	52,200	28.2	20
United Kingdom	6,900	4.6	16.2	41,680	23.5	24
United States	1,800	6.9	16.4	53,470	19.5	33
Russia	2,600	10.1	14.7	13,850	14.5	56
China	1,800	12.7	13.1	6,560	23.6	61
Cuba	970	6.2	13.8	5,890	48.9	40
Israel	17,400	4.0	16.0	33,930	22.5	18
Nigeria	31	117.4	9.0	2,710	6.6	166
India	190	52.7	11.7	1,570	12.2	140
Afghanistan	49	97.3	9.7	690	24.8	152

Source: Save the Children (2013, 2014).

3-4a POSSIBLE PSYCHOLOGICAL PROBLEMS THAT MAY AFFECT THE MOTHER

So-called "baby blues" may be considered normal in that they are by experienced by the majority of new mothers (American Psychiatric Association, 2014). Researchers believe that they are often due to hormonal changes that accompany pregnancy and follow delivery (Brummelte & Galea, 2010). They last about ten days and are generally not severe enough to impair the mother's functioning.

About one woman in seven or eight experiences depression or anxiety postpartum. **Major depression with perinatal onset** is a serious mood disorder that begins about a month after delivery and may linger for weeks or months. Major depression with perinatal onset is characterized by serious sadness, feelings of hopelessness, helplessness, and worthlessness, difficulty concentrating, mood swings, and major changes in appetite (usually loss of appetite) and sleep patterns (frequently insomnia). Some women show obsessive concern with the well-being of their babies, which is also a sign of anxiety postpartum.

major depression with perinatal onset serious maternal depression following delivery; characterized by sadness, apathy, and feelings of worthlessness.

Many researchers suggest that major depression with perinatal onset is caused by a sudden drop in estrogen (O'Hara & McCabe, 2013). The focus is on physiological factors because of the major changes in body chemistry during and after pregnancy and because women around the world seem to experience similar disturbances in mood, even when their life experiences and support systems are radically different from those found in the United States (O'Hara & McCabe, 2013). But it should also be noted that stress can heighten symptoms of major depression with perinatal onset (Hillerer et al., 2012).

According to the American Psychiatric Association (2014), the yet more serious postpartum psychosis affects about 1 woman in 1,000. "Psychosis" may mean a break with reality. Mothers with this disorder may have delusional thoughts about the infant that place the infant at

Have We Found the Daddy Hormones?

Are oxytocin and vasopressin the "Daddy hormones"? Perhaps so, at least in prairie voles, which are a kind of tailless mouse, and sheep. These hormones are connected with the creation of mother–infant bonds in sheep, pair bonds in monogamous voles, and bonds of attachment between vole fathers and their young. Experimental research clearly shows that increasing vasopressin levels transform an indifferent male into a caring, monogamous, and protective mate and father (Keebaugh et al., 2015; Young, 2015).

Oxytocin and vasopressin are secreted by the pituitary gland, which secretes many hormones that are involved in reproduction and the nurturing of young. For example, prolactin regulates maternal behavior in lower mammals and stimulates the production of milk in women. Oxytocin stimulates labor but is also involved in social recognition and bonding. Vasopressin enables the body to conserve water by inhibiting urine production when fluid levels are low; however, it is also connected with paternal behavior patterns in some mammals. For example, male prairie voles form pair-bonds with female prairie voles after mating with them (Keebaugh et al., 2015). Mating stimulates the secretion of vasopressin, and vasopressin causes the previously promiscuous male to sing "I only have eyes for you."

Nature Photographers Ltd/Alamy Stock Photo

The hormones oxytocin and vasopressin stimulation formation of the bonds of attachment in voles. Do they play a similar role in humans?

After learning about their effects on voles, we may wonder how oxytocin and vasopressin may be connected with the formation of bonds between men and women and between men and children. And will perfume makers soon be lacing new scents with the the hormones?

risk of injury or death. Some women experience delusions that the infant is possessed by the devil. Some women have "command hallucinations" and experience a command to kill the infant as though it is coming from the outside.

Women who experience major depression with perinatal onset usually profit from social support and counseling. Drugs that increase estrogen levels or act as antidepressants may also help.

FICTION

T (F) It is abnormal to feel depressed following childbirth.

It is not abnormal to feel depressed following childbirth. Postpartum mood changes are so common that they are expected and may be considered normal, if not desired.

3-4b BONDING

Bonding—that is, the formation of bonds of attachment between parents and their children—is essential to the survival and well-being of children. Since the publication of controversial research by Marshall Klaus and John Kennell in the 1970s, many have wondered whether extended parent–infant contact is required during the first hours postpartum in order to foster parent–infant bonding (Klaus & Kennell, 1978). In their study, one group of mothers was randomly assigned to standard hospital procedure in which their babies were whisked away to the nursery shortly after birth. Throughout the remainder of the hospital stay, the babies visited their mothers only long enough to be fed. The other babies stayed after feeding and spent a total of five hours a day with their mothers. The hospital staff encouraged and reassured the group of mothers who had extended contact. Follow-ups over two years found that mothers with extended contact were more likely than control mothers to cuddle their babies, soothe them when they cried, and interact with them. Critics note that the Klaus and Kennell studies did not separate the benefits of extended contact from benefits attributable to parents' knowledge that they were in a special group and from the extra attention of the hospital staff.

Blend Images - Mike Kemp/Brand X Pictures/Getty Images

It has been debated whether extended early contact with an infant is needed for mother–infant bonding to take place. The consensus today seems to be that the bonding process is more flexible than Klaus and Kennell's 1970s research suggested.

FICTION

T (F) Parents must have extended early contact with their newborn children if adequate bonding is to take place.

It is not true that parents must have extended early contact with their newborn children if adequate bonding is to take place. Many parents, for example, adopt children who are a few years old and still bond well with them.

Parent–child bonding has been shown to be a complex process involving desire to have the child; parent–child familiarity with one another's sounds, odors, and tastes; and caring. On the other hand, serious maternal depression can delay bonding with newborns (Klier, 2006), but a Dutch study found that mother–infant attachment appears to be normal by the age of 14 months (Tharner et al., 2012). A history of rejection by parents can interfere with women's bonding with their own children (Brockington, 2011).

Despite the Klaus and Kennell studies, which made a brief splash in the 1970s, it is not necessary that parents have extended early contact with their newborn children for adequate bonding to occur. Many parents, for instance, adopt children at advanced ages and bond closely with them.

bonding formation of parent–infant attachment.

3-5 CHARACTERISTICS OF NEONATES

Many neonates come into the world looking a bit fuzzy, but even though they are utterly dependent on others, they are probably more aware of their surroundings than you had imagined. Neonates also make rapid adaptations to the world around them.

3-5a ASSESSING THE HEALTH OF NEONATES

The neonate's overall level of health is usually evaluated at birth according to the **Apgar scale** (see Table 3.2). Apgar scores are based on five signs of health: appearance, pulse, grimace, activity level, and respiratory effort. The neonate can receive a score of 0, 1, or 2 on each sign. The total Apgar score can therefore vary from 0 to 10. A score of 7 or above usually indicates that the baby is not in danger. A score below 4 suggests that the baby is in critical condition and requires medical attention. By one minute after birth, most normal babies attain scores of 8 to 10.

The **Brazelton Neonatal Behavioral Assessment Scale** measures neonates' reflexes and other behavior patterns. This test screens neonates for behavioral and neurological problems by assessing four areas of behavior: motor behavior, response to stress, adaptive behavior, and control over physiological state.

Apgar scale a measure of a newborn's health that assesses appearance, pulse, grimace, activity level, and respiratory effort.

Brazelton Neonatal Behavioral Assessment Scale a measure of a newborn's motor behavior, response to stress, adaptive behavior, and control over physiological state.

reflexe an unlearned, stereotypical response to a stimulus.

rooting reflex turning the mouth and head toward stroking of the cheek or the corner of the mouth.

Moro reflex arching the back, flinging out the arms and legs, and drawing them back to the chest in response to a sudden noise or change in position.

3-5b REFLEXES

Reflexes are simple, automatic, stereotypical responses that are elicited by certain types of stimulation. They occur without thinking. Reflexes are the most complicated motor activities displayed by neonates. Of these reflexes, most are exhibited by neonates very shortly after birth, disappear within a few months, and—if the behaviors still serve a purpose—are replaced by corresponding voluntary actions.

The Rooting Reflex

Cathy Melloan Resources / PhotoEdit

Pediatricians learn about a neonate's neural functioning by testing its reflexes. The absence or weakness of a reflex may indicate immaturity (as in prematurity), slowed responsiveness (which can result from anesthetics used during childbirth), brain injury, or retardation.

The rooting and sucking reflexes are basic to survival. In the **rooting reflex**, the baby turns the head and mouth toward a stimulus that strokes the cheek, chin, or corner of the mouth. The rooting reflex facilitates finding the mother's nipple in preparation for sucking. Babies will suck almost any object that touches their lips. The sucking reflex grows stronger during the first days after birth and can be lost if not stimulated. As the months go on, reflexive sucking becomes replaced by voluntary sucking.

In the startle or **Moro reflex**, the back arches and the legs and arms are flung out and then brought back toward the chest, with the arms in a hugging motion. The Moro reflex occurs when a baby's position is suddenly changed or when support for the head and neck is suddenly lost. It can also be elicited by loud noises, bumping the baby's crib, or jerking the baby's blanket. The Moro reflex is usually lost within six to seven months after birth. Absence of the Moro reflex can indicate immaturity or brain damage.

TABLE 3.2 THE APGAR SCALE

Points	0	1	2
Appearance: Color	Blue, pale	Body pink, extremities blue	Entirely pink
Pulse: Heart rate	Absent (not detectable)	Slow—below 100 beats/minute	Rapid—100–140 beats/minute
Grimace: Reflex irritability	No response	Grimace	Crying, coughing, sneezing
Activity level: Muscle tone	Completely flaccid, limp	Weak, inactive	Flexed arms and legs; resists extension
Respiratory effort: Breathing	Absent (infant is apneic)	Shallow, irregular, slow	Regular breathing; lusty crying

The Moro Reflex

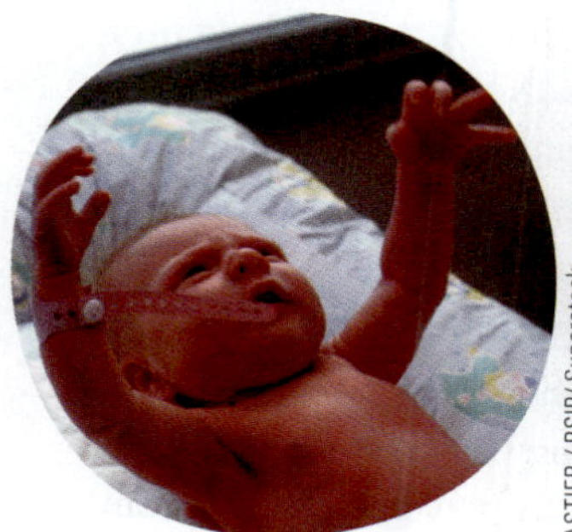

ASTIER / BSIP/ Superstock

The Grasping Reflex

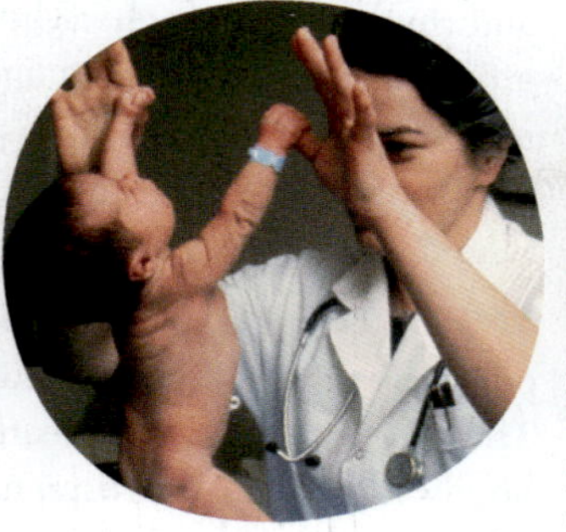

Petit Format/Science Source

The Stepping Reflex

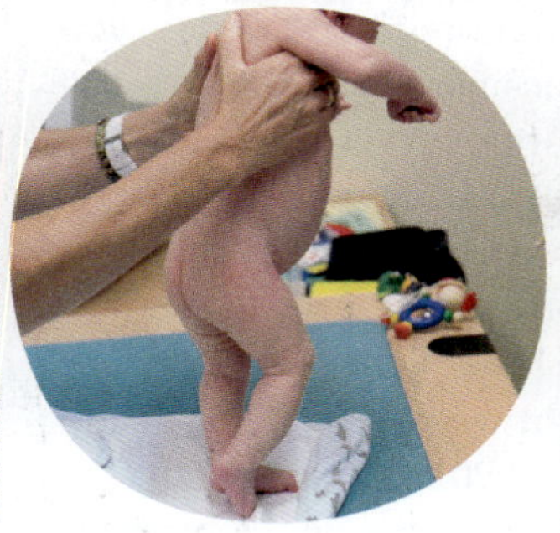

Picture Partners / Science Source

The Tonic-Neck Reflex

Edward Hattersley / Alamy Stock Photo

During the first few weeks following birth, babies show an increasing tendency to reflexively grasp fingers or other objects pressed against the palms of their hands. In this **grasping reflex**, or palmar reflex, they use four fingers only (the thumbs are not included). Absence of the grasping reflex may indicate depressed activity of the nervous system, which can stem from use of anesthetics during childbirth. The grasping reflex is usually lost within three to four months of age, and babies generally show voluntary grasping within five to six months.

Within one or two days after birth, babies show a reflex that mimics walking. When held under the arms and tilted forward so that the feet press against a solid surface, a baby will show a **stepping reflex** in which the feet advance one after the other. A full-term baby "walks" heel to toe, whereas a preterm infant is more likely to remain on tiptoe. The stepping reflex usually disappears by about three or four months of age.

In the **Babinski reflex**, the neonate fans or spreads the toes in response to stroking of the underside of the foot from heel to toes. The Babinski reflex normally disappears toward the end of the first year, to be replaced by curling downward of the toes.

The **tonic-neck reflex** is observed when the baby is lying on its back and turns its head to one side. The arm and leg on that side extend, while the limbs on the opposite side flex.

Some reflexes, such as breathing regularly and blinking the eye in response to a puff of air, remain with us for life. Others, such as the sucking and grasping reflexes, are gradually replaced after a number of months by voluntary sucking and grasping. Still others, such as the Moro and Babinski reflexes, disappear, indicating that the nervous system is maturing on schedule.

3-5c SENSORY CAPABILITIES

In 1890, William James, a founder of modern psychology, wrote that the neonate must sense the world "as one great blooming, buzzing confusion." The neonate emerges from being literally suspended in a temperature-controlled environment to being—again, in James's words—"assailed by eyes, ears, nose, skin, and entrails at once." We now describe the sensory capabilities of neonates, and we see that James, for all his eloquence, exaggerated their disorganization.

VISION Neonates can see, but they are nearsighted. They can best see objects that are about seven to nine inches from their eyes (Braddick & Atkinson, 2011). They also do not have the peripheral vision of older children. Neonates can visually detect movement, and many neonates can visually follow, or track, movement the first day after birth. In fact, they appear to prefer (i.e., they spend more time looking at) moving objects to stationary objects (Arterberry & Kellman, 2016).

Visual accommodation refers to the self-adjustments made by the eye's lens to bring objects into focus. Neonates show little or no visual accommodation; rather; they see as through a

© Design Pics/Leah Warkentin

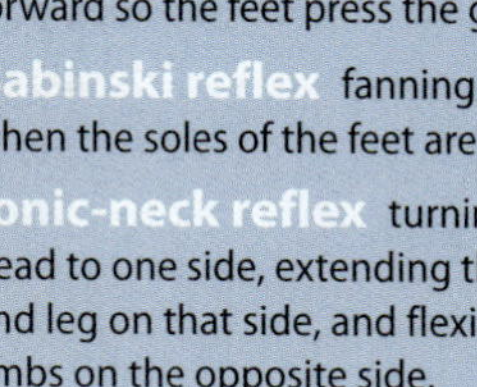

grasping reflex grasping objects that touch the palms.

stepping reflex taking steps when held under the arms and leaned forward so the feet press the ground.

Babinski reflex fanning the toes when the soles of the feet are stroked.

tonic-neck reflex turning the head to one side, extending the arm and leg on that side, and flexing the limbs on the opposite side.

visual accommodation automatic adjustments of the lenses to focus on objects.

fixed-focus camera. As noted above, objects placed about seven to nine inches away are in clearest focus for most neonates, but visual accommodation improves dramatically during a baby's first two months (Arterberry & Kellman, 2016).

Neonates do not have the muscle control to converge their eyes on an object that is close to them. For this reason, one eye may be staring off to the side while the other fixates on an object straight ahead. **Convergence** does not occur until seven or eight weeks of age for nearby objects (Arterberry & Kellman, 2016).

The degree to which neonates perceive color remains an open question. By four months, however, infants can see most of, if not all, the colors of the visible spectrum (Kimura et al., 2010).

Even at birth, babies do not just passively respond to visual stimuli. Babies placed in absolute darkness open their eyes wide and search around (Braddick & Atkinson, 2011).

> Neonates prefer their mothers' voices to those of other women, but they do not show similar preferences for the voices of their fathers.

HEARING Fetuses respond to sound months before they are born. Although the auditory pathways in the brain are not fully developed prior to birth, fetuses' middle and inner ears normally reach their mature shapes and sizes before birth. Normal neonates hear well unless their middle ears are clogged with amniotic fluid (Zhiqi et al., 2010). Most neonates turn their heads toward unusual sounds, such as the shaking of a rattle.

Neonates have the capacity to respond to sounds of different **amplitude** and **pitch**. They are more likely to respond to high-pitched sounds than to low-pitched sounds (Homae et al., 2011). By contrast, speaking or singing to infants softly, in a relatively low-pitched voice, can have a soothing effect (Conrad et al., 2011; Arterberry & Kellman, 2016).

The sense of hearing may play a role in the formation of affectional bonds between neonates and mothers that goes well beyond the soothing potential of the mothers' voices. Neonates prefer their mothers' voices to those of other women, but they do not show similar preferences for the voices of their fathers (DeCasper & Prescott, 1984; Freeman et al., 1993). This preference may reflect prenatal exposure to sounds produced by their mothers.

convergence inward movement of the eyes to focus on an object that is drawing nearer.

amplitude loudness (of sound waves).

pitch highness or lowness (of a sound), as determined by the frequency of sound waves.

Neonates are particularly responsive to the sounds and rhythms of speech, although they do not show preferences for specific languages. Neonates can discriminate different speech sounds, and they can discriminate new sounds of speech from those they have heard before (Gervain et al., 2011).

SMELL: THE NOSE KNOWS–EARLY Neonates can discriminate distinct odors, such as those of onions and licorice. They show more rapid breathing patterns and increased bodily movement in response to powerful odors. They also turn away from unpleasant odors, such as ammonia and vinegar, as early as the first day after birth (Werner & Bernstein, 2001). The nasal preferences of neonates are similar to those of older children and adults (Werner & Bernstein, 2001).

The sense of smell, like hearing, may provide a vehicle for mother–infant recognition and attachment (Lee et al., 2011). Neonates may be sensitive to the smell of milk because, when held by the mother, they tend to turn toward her nipple before they have had a chance to see or touch it. In one experiment, Macfarlane (1975, 1977) placed nursing pads above and to the sides of neonates' heads. One pad had absorbed milk from the mother, the other was clean. Neonates less than one week old spent more time turning to look at their mothers' pads than at the new pads.

Breast-fed 15-day-old infants also prefer their mother's underarm odor to odors produced by other milk- producing women and by other women. Bottle-fed infants do not show this preference (Cernoch & Porter, 1985; Porter et al., 1992). Underarm odor, along with odors from breast secretions, might contribute to the early development of recognition and attachment.

TASTE Neonates are sensitive to different tastes, and their preferences, as suggested by their facial expressions in response to various fluids, are like those of adults (Beauchamp & Mennella, 2011). Neonates swallow without showing any facial expression suggestive of a positive or negative response when distilled water is placed on their tongues. Sweet solutions are met with smiles, licking, and eager sucking, as in Figure 3.5a (Rosenstein & Oster, 1988). Neonates discriminate among solutions with salty, sour, and bitter tastes, as suggested by reactions in the lower part of the face (Rosenstein & Oster, 1988). Sour fluids elicit pursing of the lips, nose wrinkling, and eye blinking (see Figure 3.5b). Bitter solutions stimulate spitting, gagging, and sticking out the tongue (see Figure 3.5c).

FIG.3.5 FACIAL EXPRESSIONS ELICITED BY SWEET, SOUR, AND BITTER SOLUTIONS

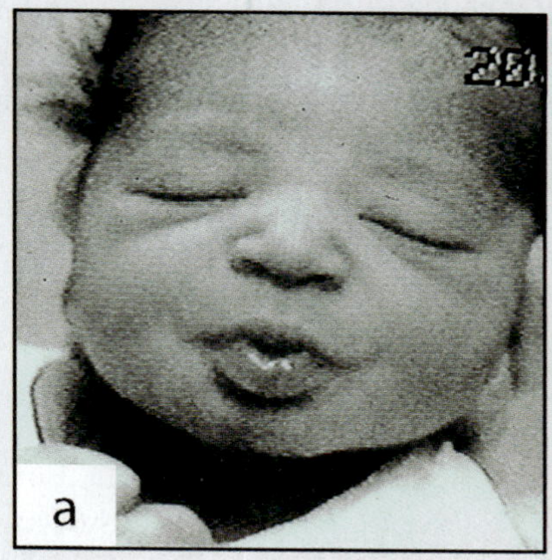

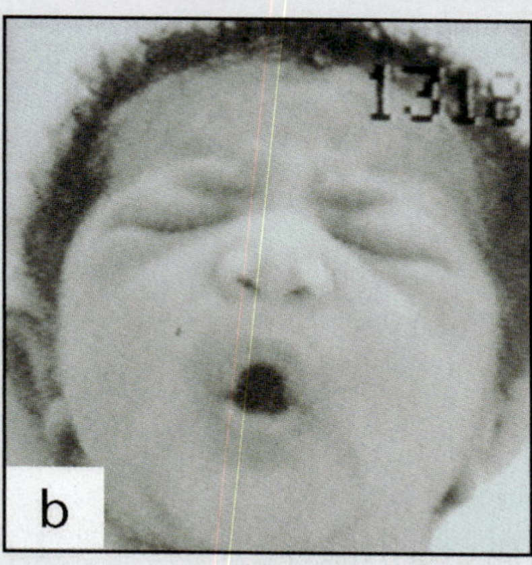

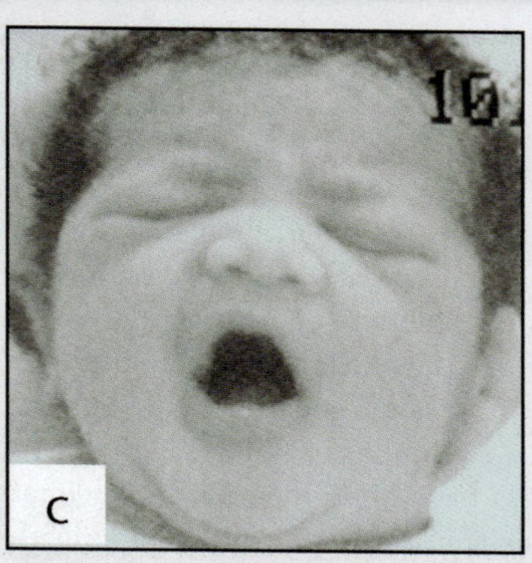

Courtesy of Rosenstein, D. S. and Oster, H. (1988)

Neonates are sensitive to different tastes, as shown by their facial expressions when tasting (a) sweet, (b) sour, and (c) bitter solutions.

Sweet solutions have a calming effect on neonates (Fernandes et al., 2011). One study found that sweeter solutions increase the heart rate, suggesting heightened arousal, but also slow down the rate of sucking (Crook & Lipsitt, 1976). Researchers interpret this finding to suggest an effort to savor the sweeter solution, to make the flavor last.

TOUCH The sense of touch is an extremely important avenue of learning and communication for babies. Not only do the skin senses provide information about the external world, but the sensations of skin against skin also appear to provide feelings of comfort and security that may be major factors in the formation of bonds of attachment between infants and their caregivers. Many reflexes—including the rooting, sucking, Babinski, and grasping reflexes, to name a few—are activated by pressure against the skin.

Ariel Skelley/Blend Images/Jupiter Images

The sensations of skin against skin appear to provide feelings of comfort and security that contribute to the formation of bonds of attachment between infants and their caregivers.

3-5d LEARNING: REALLY EARLY CHILDHOOD "EDUCATION"

The somewhat limited sensory capabilities of neonates suggest that they may not learn as rapidly as older children do. After all, we must sense clearly those things we are to learn about. Neonates do, however, seem capable of conditioning.

CLASSICAL CONDITIONING OF NEONATES In classical conditioning of neonates, involuntary responses are conditioned to new stimuli. In a typical study (Lipsitt, 2002), neonates were taught to blink in response to a tone. Blinking (the unconditioned response) was elicited by a puff of air directed toward the infant's eye (the unconditioned stimulus). A tone was sounded (the conditioned stimulus) as the puff of air was delivered. After repeated pairings, sounding the tone caused the neonate to blink (the conditioned response).

OPERANT CONDITIONING OF NEONATES Operant conditioning, like classical conditioning, can take place in neonates. The experiment from Chapter 2 in which neonates learned to suck on a pacifier in such a way as to activate a recording of their mothers reading *The Cat in the Hat* (DeCasper & Fifer, 1980; DeCasper & Spence, 1991) is a prime example of operant conditioning.

3-5e SLEEPING AND WAKING

As adults, we spend about one-third of our time sleeping. Neonates greatly outdo us, spending two-thirds of their time, or about 16 hours per day, in sleep. And, in one of life's basic challenges to parents, neonates do not sleep their 16 hours consecutively.

A number of different states of sleep and wakefulness have been identified in neonates and infants, as shown in Table 3.3. Although individual babies differ in the amount of time they spend in each of these states, sleep clearly predominates over wakefulness in the early days and weeks of life.

Different infants require different amounts of sleep and follow different patterns of sleep, but virtually all infants distribute their sleeping throughout the day and night through a series of naps. The typical infant has about six cycles of waking and sleeping in a 24-hour period. The longest nap typically approaches four and a half hours, and the neonate is usually awake for a little more than one hour during each cycle.

After a month or so, the infant has fewer but longer sleep periods and will usually take longer naps during the night. By the ages of about six months to one year, many infants begin to sleep through the night. Some infants start sleeping through the night earlier. A number of infants begin to sleep through the night for a week or so and then revert to their wakeful ways again for a while.

REM AND NON-REM SLEEP Sleep can be divided into **rapid-eye-movement (REM) sleep** and **non-rapid-eye-movement (non-REM) sleep** (see Figure 3.6). REM sleep is characterized by rapid eye movements that can be observed beneath closed lids. Adults who are roused during REM sleep report that they have been dreaming about 80% of the time. Is the same true of neonates?

rapid-eye-movement (REM) sleep a sleep period when dreams are likely, as suggested by rapid eye movements.

non-rapid-eye-movement (non-REM) sleep a sleep period when dreams are unlikely.

TABLE 3.3 STATES OF SLEEP AND WAKEFULNESS IN INFANCY

State	Comments
Quiet sleep (non-REM)	Regular breathing, eyes closed, no movement
Active sleep (REM)	Irregular breathing, eyes closed, rapid eye movement, muscle twitches
Drowsiness	Regular or irregular breathing, eyes open or closed, little movement
Alert inactivity	Regular breathing, eyes open, looking around, little body movement
Alert activity	Irregular breathing, eyes open, active body movement
Crying	Irregular breathing, eyes open or closed, thrashing of arms and legs, crying

Note from Figure 3.6 that neonates spend about half their time sleeping in REM sleep. As they develop, the percentage of sleeping time spent in REM sleep declines. By six months or so, REM sleep accounts for only about 30% of the baby's sleep. By two to three years, REM sleep drops off to about 20%–25% (Salzarulo & Ficca, 2002). There is a dramatic falling-off in the total number of hours spent in sleep as we develop (Blumberg & Seelke, 2010).

What is the function of REM sleep in neonates? Research with humans and other animals, including kittens and rat pups, suggests that the brain requires a certain amount of stimulation for the creation of proteins

FIG.3.6 REM AND NON-REM SLEEP

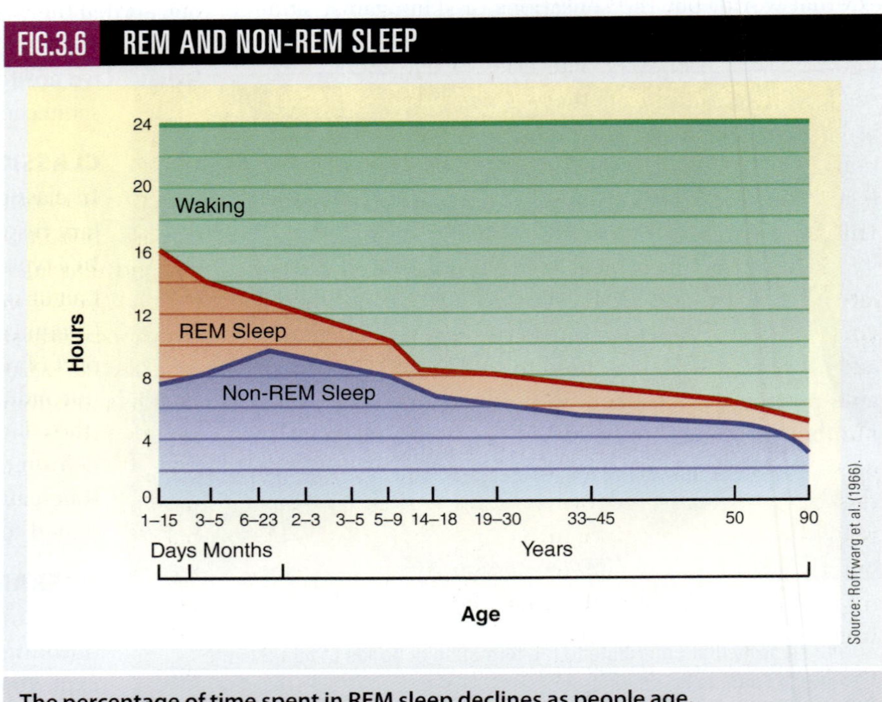

The percentage of time spent in REM sleep declines as people age.

that are involved in the development of neurons and synapses (Blumberg & Seelke, 2010). Perhaps neonates create this stimulation by means of REM sleep, which most closely parallels the waking state in terms of brain waves. Preterm babies spend an even greater proportion of their time in REM sleep, perhaps because they need relatively more stimulation of the brain.

CRYING No discussion of the sleeping and waking states of neonates would be complete without mentioning crying, a comment that parents will view as an understatement. The main reason babies cry seems to be simple enough. Studies suggest a one-word answer: pain (Out et al., 2010). Whether crying is healthful remains an open question, but some crying among babies seems to be universal.

Before parenthood, many people wonder whether they will be able to recognize the meaning of their babies' cries, but it usually does not take them long. Parents typically learn to distinguish cries that signify hunger, anger, and pain. The pitch of an infant's cries appears to provide information (Out et al., 2010). Adults perceive high-pitched crying to be more urgent, distressing, and sick sounding than low-pitched crying (Out et al., 2010; Zeifman, 2004). A sudden, loud, insistent cry associated with flexing and kicking of the legs may indicate colic, that is, pain resulting from gas or other sources of distress in the digestive tract. Crying from colic can be severe and persistent; it may last for hours (Barr et al., 2005; Gudmundsson, 2010). Much to the relief of parents, colic tends to disappear by the third to sixth month, as a baby's digestive system matures.

Certain high-pitched cries, when prolonged, may signify health problems. The cries of chronically distressed infants differ from those of nondistressed infants in both rhythm and pitch. Patterns of crying may be indicative of chromosomal abnormalities, infections, fetal malnutrition, and exposure to narcotics (Douglas & Hill, 2011).

Peaks of crying appear to be concentrated in the late afternoon and early evening (McGlaughlin & Grayson, 2001). Although some cries may seem extreme and random at first, they tend to settle into a recognizable pattern. Infants seem to produce about the same number of crying bouts during the first nine months or so, but the duration of the bouts lessens during this period (van Ijzendoorn & Hubbard, 2000). The response of the caregiver influences crying. It turns out that the more frequently mothers ignore their infants' crying bouts in the first nine weeks, the less frequently their infants cry in the following nine-week period (van Ijzendoorn & Hubbard, 2000). This finding should certainly not be interpreted to mean that infant crying is best ignored. At least at first, crying communicates pain and hunger, and these are conditions that it is advisable to correct. Persistent crying can strain the mother–infant relationship (Out et al., 2010).

SOOTHING Sucking seems to be a built-in tranquilizer. Sucking on a **pacifier** decreases crying and agitated movement in hungry neonates (Field, 1999; Shubert et al., 2016). Therefore, the soothing function of sucking need not be learned through experience. Sucking (drinking) a sweet solution also appears to have a soothing effect (Stevens et al., 2005).

Parents soothe infants by picking them up, patting them, caressing and rocking them, swaddling them (wrapping them in a blanket, reminiscent of the womb), and speaking to them in a low voice. Parents then usually try to find the specific cause of the distress by offering a bottle or pacifier or checking the diaper. Parents learn by trial and error what types of embraces and movements are likely to soothe their child, and infants learn quickly that crying is followed by being picked up or other interventions. Parents sometimes worry that if they pick up a crying baby quickly, they are reinforcing the baby for crying. In this way, they believe, the child may become spoiled and find it progressively more difficult to engage in self-soothing to get to sleep.

Fortunately, as infants mature and learn, crying tends to become replaced by less upsetting verbal requests for intervention. Among adults, of course, soothing techniques take very different forms—such as admission that one started the argument.

3-5f SUDDEN INFANT DEATH SYNDROME (SIDS)

It is true that more children die from **sudden infant death syndrome (SIDS)** than die from cancer, heart disease, pneumonia, child abuse, AIDS, cystic fibrosis, and muscular dystrophy combined (Lipsitt, 2003). SIDS—also known as crib death—is a disorder of infancy that apparently strikes while a baby is sleeping. In the typical case, a baby goes to sleep, apparently in perfect health, and is found dead the next morning. There is no sign that the baby struggled or was in pain.

SIDS is more common among the following: babies aged two to five months, babies who are put to sleep on their stomachs or their sides (sleeping prone decreases the oxygen supply to the brain),

pacifier a device such as an artificial nipple or teething ring that soothes babies when sucked.

sudden infant death syndrome (SIDS) the death, while sleeping, of apparently healthy babies who stop breathing.

premature and low-birth-weight infants, male babies, babies in families of lower socioeconomic status, bottle-fed babies, African American babies, babies of teenage mothers, babies whose mothers smoked during or after pregnancy or whose mothers used narcotics during pregnancy, babies of low birth weight, and babies who have respiratory infections.

The incidence of SIDS has been declining, in part because some cases of SIDS have been reattributed to accidental suffocation. Even so, some 2,000–3,000 infants in the United States still die each year of SIDS. It is the most common cause of death during the first year, and most of these deaths occur between two and five months of age (Käll & Lagercrantz, 2012). New parents frequently live in dread of SIDS and check regularly through the night to see if their babies are breathing. It is not abnormal, by the way, for babies occasionally to suspend breathing for a moment.

TRUTH

 **F** More children in the United States die from sudden infant death syndrome (SIDS) than from cancer, heart disease, pneumonia, child abuse, AIDS, cystic fibrosis, and muscular dystrophy combined.

It is true that in the United States, more children die from sudden infant death syndrome (SIDS) than than from all these other causes combined.

THE CHILDREN'S HOSPITAL BOSTON STUDY

Perhaps the most compelling study to date about the causes of SIDS was led by health professionals at the Children's Hospital Boston (Paterson et al., 2006). The study focused on an area in the brain stem called the **medulla**, which is involved in basic functions such as breathing and sleep-wake cycles. The medulla causes us to breathe if we are in need of oxygen. Researchers compared the medullas of babies who had died from SIDS with those of babies who had died at the same ages from other causes. They found that the medullas of the babies who died from SIDS were less sensitive to the brain chemical *serotonin*, a chemical that helps keep the medulla responsive. The problem was particularly striking in the brains of the boys, which could account for the sex difference in the incidence of SIDS.

medulla a part of the brain stem that regulates vital and automatic functions such as breathing and the sleep-wake cycle.

What should you do about SIDS? Following are some suggestions from the American Academy of Pediatrics (2012):

- Place your baby to sleep on her back for every sleep.
- Place your baby to sleep on a firm sleep surface. To learn more about crib safety, visit the Consumer Product Safety Commission Web site at www.cpsc.gov.
- Keep soft objects, loose bedding, or any objects that could increase the risk of entrapment, suffocation, or strangulation out of the crib.
- Place your baby to sleep in the same room where you sleep but not the same bed.
- Breast-feed as much and for as long as you can.
- Schedule and go to all well-child visits.
- Keep your baby away from smokers and places where people smoke.
- Do not let your baby get too hot.
- Offer a pacifier at nap time and bedtime.
- Do not use home cardiorespiratory monitors to help reduce the risk of SIDS.
- Do not use products that claim to reduce the risk of SIDS.

Perhaps within a few years we will have a screening test for SIDS and a method for preventing or controlling it. In the next chapter, we continue to follow physical development over the first two years.

STUDY TOOLS 3

READY TO STUDY?

In the book, you can:

- ☐ Check your understanding of what you've read with the quizzes below.
- ☐ Rip out the chapter review card at the back of the book to have a summary of the chapter and the key terms handy.

ONLINE AT CENGAGEBRAIN.COM YOU CAN:

- ☐ View a prenatal assessment and ultrasound in a short video.
- ☐ Prepare for tests with quizzes.
- ☐ Review the key terms with Flash Cards.
- ☐ Play games to master concepts.

SELF-ASSESSMENT

Fill-Ins

Answers can be found in the back of the book.

1. False labor contractions are technically called ____________-____________ contractions.
2. In a(n) ____________ block, anesthesia is injected into the spinal canal.
3. One sign of prematurity is ____________, an oily white substance on the skin.
4. The continent with the lowest risk of maternal mortality is ____________.
5. Major depression with perinatal onset is most likely related to changes in ____________.
6. Klaus and Kennell argued that extensive early contact is necessary to promote ____________.
7. The health of neonates is assessed using the five-point ____________ scale.
8. In the ____________ reflex, the baby turns the head and mouth toward a stimulus that strokes the cheek, chin, or corner of the mouth.
9. Fifteen-day-old breast-fed infants prefer their mothers' ____________ odor to those of other women.
10. The least common kind of maternal depression after delivery is ____________ ____________.

Multiple Choice

1. **What percentage of American deliveries is by C-section?**
   a. 11% c. 32%
   b. 22% d. 44%

2. **Injecting pregnant women at risk for delivering premature babies with ____________ increases the babies' chances of survival.**
   a. corticosteroids c. tetracycline
   b. gamma globulin d. saline solution

3. **The risk of maternal mortality during childbirth is highest in**
   a. China. c. Cuba.
   b. Egypt. d. Afghanistan.

4. **How many new mothers are likely to experience the "baby blues"?**
   a. 2 in 10 c. 7 in 10
   b. 4 in 10 d. 9 in 10

5. **In which of the following reflexes does the neonate fan its toes in response to stroking the underside of the foot?**
   a. stepping c. Babinski
   b. Moro d. tonic neck

6. **Neonates show**
   a. visual accommodation.
   b. nearsightedness.
   c. preference for the color blue.
   d. convergence of the eyes.

7. **Neonates show preference for**
   a. their mothers' voices. c. dogs' barks.
   b. their fathers' voices. d. music.

8. **According to the text, neonates have a taste preference for ____________ solutions.**
   a. sour c. sweet
   b. salty d. bitter

9. **Neonates spend about ____________ hours a day sleeping.**
   a. 6 c. 12
   b. 8 d. 16

10. **SIDS is more common among**
    a. female babies.
    b. babies who are put to sleep on their stomachs.
    c. babies of mothers in their 20s.
    d. European American babies.

4 Infancy: Physical Development

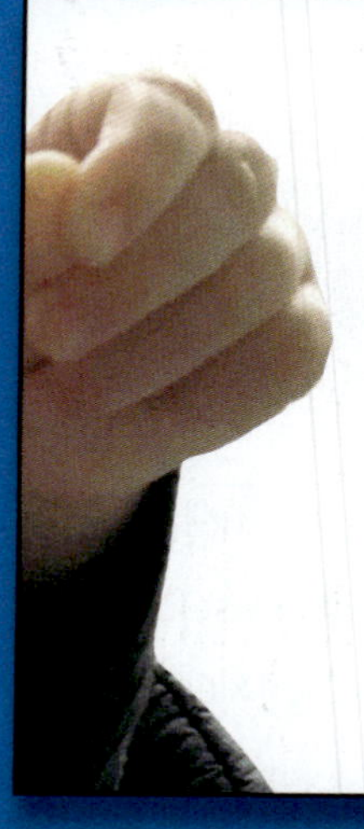
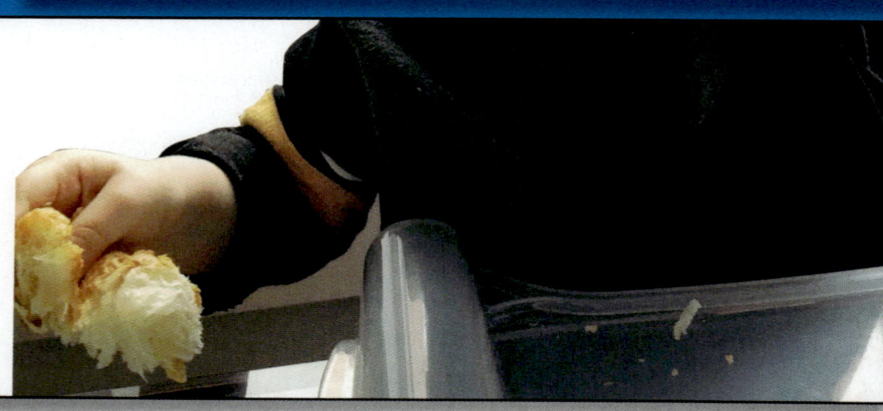

Spencer Rathus

LEARNING OUTCOMES

After studying this chapter, you will be able to...

- 4-1 Describe trends in the physical development of the infant
- 4-2 Describe the physical development of the brain and the nervous system
- 4-3 Describe the key events in the motor development of the infant
- 4-4 Describe patterns of sensory and perceptual development in infancy

After you finish this chapter, go to **PAGE 86** for **STUDY TOOLS**

What a fascinating creature the newborn is: tiny, delicate, apparently oblivious to its surroundings, yet perfectly formed and fully capable of letting its caregivers know when it is hungry, thirsty, or uncomfortable. And what a fascinating creature is this same child two years later: running, playing, talking, hugging, and kissing.

> It is hard to believe that only two short years—the years of infancy—bring about so many changes.

It is hard to believe that only two short years—the years of infancy—bring about so many changes. It seems that nearly every day brings a new accomplishment. But as we will see, not all infants share equally in the explosion of positive developments. Therefore, we will also enumerate some developmental problems and what can be done about them.

4-1 PHYSICAL GROWTH AND DEVELOPMENT

During the first two years, children make enormous strides in physical growth and development. In this section, we explore sequences of physical development, changes in height and weight, and nutrition. As we see next, development is "head first."

4-1a SEQUENCES OF PHYSICAL DEVELOPMENT

Three key sequences of physical development are cephalocaudal development, proximodistal development, and differentiation.

CEPHALOCAUDAL DEVELOPMENT Development proceeds from the upper part of the head to the lower parts of the body. When we consider the central role of the brain, which is contained within the skull, the cephalocaudal sequence appears quite logical. The brain regulates essential functions, such as heartbeat. Through the secretion of hormones, the brain also regulates the growth and development of the body and influences basic drives, such as hunger and thirst.

The head develops more rapidly than the rest of the body during the embryonic stage. By eight weeks after conception, the head constitutes half the entire length of the embryo. The brain develops more rapidly than the spinal cord. Arm buds form before leg buds. Most newborn babies have a strong, well-defined sucking reflex, although their legs are spindly and their limbs move back and forth only in diffuse excitement or agitation. Infants can hold up their heads before they gain control over their arms, their torsos, and, finally, their legs. They can sit up before they can crawl and walk.

iStockphoto.com/lostinbids

The lower parts of the body, because they get off to a later start, must do more growing to reach adult size. The head doubles in length between birth and maturity, but the torso, arms, and legs increase in length by three, four, and five times, respectively.

PROXIMODISTAL DEVELOPMENT Growth and development also proceed from the trunk outward, from the body's central axis toward the periphery.

TRUTH OR FICTION?

T	F	The head of the newborn child doubles in length by adulthood, but the legs increase in length by about five times.
T	F	Infants triple their birth weight within a year.
T	F	A newborn's brain weights about 25% of its adult weight, but grows to some 70% of its adult weight by the child's first birthday.
T	F	The cerebral cortex—the outer layer of the brain that is vital to human thought and reasoning—is only one-eighth of an inch thick.
T	F	Native American Hopi infants spend the first year of life strapped to a board, yet they begin to walk at about the same time as children who are reared in other cultures.

The proximodistal principle, too, makes sense. The brain and spinal cord follow a central axis down through the body, and it is essential that the nerves be in place before infants can gain control over their arms and legs. Consider also that the life functions of the newborn baby—heartbeat, respiration, digestion, and elimination of wastes—are all carried out by organ systems close to the central axis. These functions must be in operation or ready to operate when the child is born.

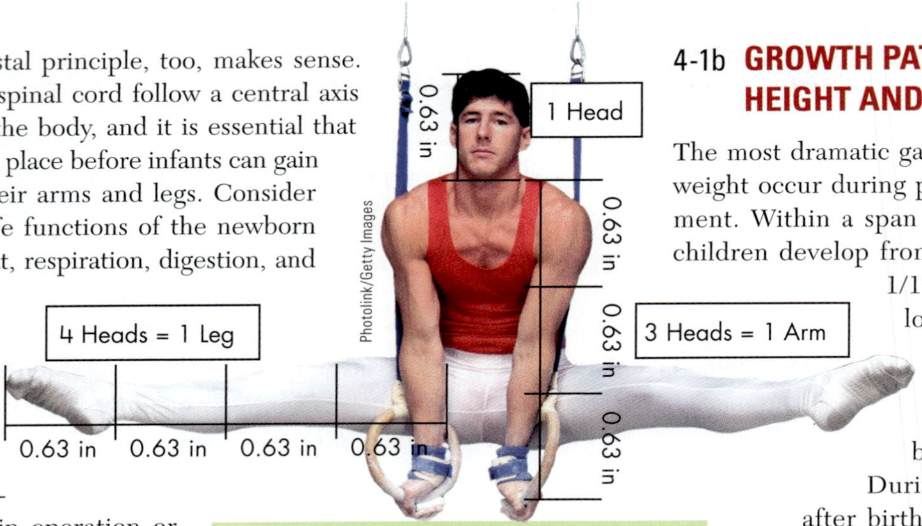

1 Head

0.63 in

0.63 in

0.63 in

0.63 in

3 Heads = 1 Arm

4 Heads = 1 Leg

0.63 in 0.63 in 0.63 in 0.63 in

Photolink/Getty Images

As we develop our body proportions change.

TRUTH

(T) F The head of the newborn child doubles in length by adulthood, but the legs increase in length by about five times.

It is true that the head of the newborn child doubles in length by adulthood, and the legs increase in length by about five times. The torso also increases by about three times and the arms by four times.

In terms of motor development, infants gain control over their trunks and their shoulders before they can control their arms, hands, and fingers. Similarly, infants gain control over their hips and upper legs before they can direct their lower legs, feet, and toes.

DIFFERENTIATION As children mature, their behaviors become less loose and global, and more specific and distinct, a tendency called **differentiation**. If a neonate's finger is pricked or burned, he or she may withdraw the finger but also thrash about, cry, and show general signs of distress. Toddlers may also cry, show distress, and withdraw the finger, but they are less likely to thrash about wildly. Thus, the response to pain has become more specific. An older child or adult is also likely to withdraw the finger, but less likely to wail (sometimes) and show general distress.

differentiation the processes by which behaviors and physical structures become specialized.

4-1b GROWTH PATTERNS IN HEIGHT AND WEIGHT

The most dramatic gains in height and weight occur during prenatal development. Within a span of nine months, children develop from a zygote about 1/175th of an inch long to a neonate about 20 inches in length. Weight increases by billions.

During the first year after birth, gains in height and weight are also dramatic, although not by the standards of prenatal gains. Infants usually double their birth weight in about five months and triple it by the first birthday (World Health Organization, 2010a, 2010b). Their height increases by about 50% in the first year, so that a child whose length at birth was 20 inches is likely to be about 30 inches tall at 12 months.

TRUTH

(T) F Infants triple their birth weight within a year.

It is true that infants triple their birth weight within a year. They usually double their birth weight in only five months.

Growth in infancy has long been viewed as a slow and steady process. Growth charts in pediatricians' offices resemble the smooth, continuous curves shown in Figure 4.1, but research suggests that infants actually grow in spurts. About 90%–95% of the time, they are not growing at all. One study measured the height of infants throughout their first 21 months (Lampl et al., 1992). The researchers found that the infants would remain the same size for 2 to 63 days and then would shoot up in length from one-fifth of an inch (0.5 centimeter) to a full inch (2.5 centimeters) in less than 24 hours.

Infants grow another four to six inches during the second year and gain another four to seven pounds. Boys generally reach half their adult height by their second birthday. Girls, however, mature more quickly than boys and are likely to reach half their adult height at the age of 18 months (World Health Organization, 2010a, 2010b). The growth rates of taller-than-average infants, as a group, tend to slow down. Those of shorter-than-average infants,

FIG.4.1 GROWTH CURVES FOR LENGTH (HEIGHT) AND WEIGHT FROM BIRTH TO AGE TWO YEARS

Birth to 24 months: Girls
Length-for-age and Weight-for-age percentiles

Published by the Centers for Disease Control and Prevention, November 1, 2009
SOURCE: WHO Child Growth Standards (http://www.who.int/childgrowth/en)

Birth to 24 months: Boys
Length-for-age and Weight-for-age percentiles

Published by the Centers for Disease Control and Prevention, November 1, 2009
SOURCE: WHO Child Growth Standards (http://www.who.int/childgrowth/en)

SAFER • HEALTHIER • PEOPLE™

Source: Kuczmarski et al. (2000, Figures 1–4).

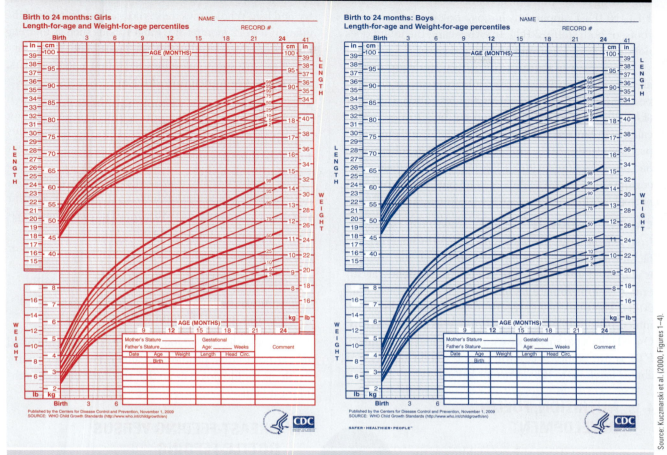

The curves indicate the percentiles for weight and length at different ages. Lines labeled 97th show the height and weight of children who are taller and heavier than 97% of children of a particular age. Lines marked 50th indicate the height and weight of the average child of a given age.

as a group, tend to speed up. I am not suggesting that there is no relationship between infant and adult heights or that we all wind up in an average range. Tall infants, as a group, wind up taller than short infants, but in most cases not by as much as seemed likely during infancy.

CHANGES IN BODY PROPORTIONS As mentioned earlier, development proceeds in a cephalocaudal manner. A few weeks after conception, an embryo is almost all head. At the beginning of the fetal stage, the head is about half the length of the unborn child. In the neonate, it is about one-fourth the length of the body. The head gradually diminishes in proportion to the rest of the body, even though it doubles in size by adulthood.

Typically, an adult's arms are nearly three times the length of the head. The legs are about four times as long. Among neonates, the arms and legs are about equal in length. Each is only about 1½ times the length of the head. By the first birthday, the neck has begun to lengthen, as have the arms and legs. The arms grow more rapidly than the legs at first; by the second birthday, the arms are actually longer than the legs, but soon the legs catch up with and surpass the arms in length.

FAILURE TO THRIVE Haley is four months old. Her mother, as she puts it, is breast-feeding Haley "all the time" because she is not gaining weight. Not gaining weight for a while is normal, but Haley is also irritable and feeds fitfully, sometimes refusing the breast entirely. Her pediatrician is evaluating her for a syndrome called **failure to thrive (FTT)**.

FTT is a serious disorder that impairs growth in infancy and early childhood. Yet FTT is sometimes a fuzzy diagnosis. Historically, researchers have spoken of biologically based (or "organic") FTT versus nonbiologically based

failure to thrive (FTT) a disorder of infancy and early childhood characterized by variable eating and inadequate gains in weight.

("nonorganic") FTT. The idea is that in organic FTT, an underlying health problem accounts for FTT. Nonorganic FTT (NOFTT) apparently has psychological roots, social roots, or both (Jaffe, 2011). In either case, the infant does not make normal gains in weight and size.

Regardless of the cause or causes, feeding problems are central. As in Haley's case, infants are more likely to be described as variable eaters and less often as hungry (Llewellyn, 2011). FTT is linked not only to slow physical growth but also to cognitive, behavioral, and emotional problems (Jaffe, 2011). One study found that children who had been diagnosed with FTT in infancy were smaller, less cognitively advanced, and more emotionally disturbed than normal children at the age of 8½ (Dykman et al., 2001).

CATCH-UP GROWTH A child's growth can be slowed from its genetically predetermined course by many organic factors, including illness and malnutrition. If the problem is alleviated, the child's rate of growth frequently accelerates to approximate its normal course (Parsons et al., 2011). The tendency to return to one's genetically determined pattern of growth is referred to as **canalization**. Once Haley's parents receive counseling and once Haley's FTT is overcome, Haley will put on weight rapidly and almost catch up to the norms for her age.

4-1c NUTRITION: FUELING DEVELOPMENT

The nutritional status of most children in the United States is good compared with that of children in developing countries (Save the Children, 2013). However, infants and young children from low-income families are more likely than other children to display signs of poor nutrition, such as anemia (a reduced number of red blood cells, causing paleness and weakness) and FTT (Save the Children, 2013).

From birth, infants should be fed either breast milk or an iron-fortified infant formula. The introduction of solid foods is not recommended until about four to six months of age, although the American Academy of Pediatrics recommends that infants be fed breast milk throughout the first year and longer if possible (Meek, 2011). The first solid food is usually iron-enriched cereal, followed by strained fruits, vegetables, meats, poultry, and fish. Whole cow's milk is normally delayed until the infant is 9 to 12 months old. Finger foods such as teething biscuits are introduced in the latter part of the first year.

Here are some guidelines for infant nutrition (U.S. Department of Agriculture, 2011):

- Build up to a variety of foods. Introduce new foods one at a time. The infant may be allergic to a new food, and introducing foods one at a time helps isolate their possible effects.
- Pay attention to the infant's appetite to help avoid overfeeding or underfeeding.
- Do not restrict fat and cholesterol too much. Infants need calories and some fat.
- Do not overdo high-fiber foods.
- Generally avoid items with added sugar and salt.
- Encourage eating of high-iron foods; infants need more iron, pound for pound, than adults do.

Parents who are on low-fat, high-fiber diets to ward off cardiovascular problems, cancer, and other health problems should not assume that the same diet is healthful for infants.

canalization the tendency of growth rates to return to normal after undergoing environmentally induced change.

RooM the Agency / Alamy Stock Photo

Breastfeeding is considered to be the gold standard for mothers in the United States and Canada today. What are the advantages of breastfeeding? Are their circumstances under which women might choose not to breastfeed their children?

4-1d BREAST-FEEDING VERSUS BOTTLE-FEEDING

In many developing nations, mothers have to breast-feed. Even in developed nations, where formula is readily available, breast milk is considered by most health professionals to be the "medical gold standard" (Karasahin, K. E., 2016). Over the past few decades, breastfeeding has become more popular, largely because of increased knowledge of its health benefits (U.S. Department of Health and Human Services, 2010). Today, most American mothers—more than 70%—breast-feed their children for at least a while, but only about two women in five continue to breast-feed after six months, and only one in five is still breast-feeding after one year (Centers for Disease Control and Prevention, 2010a).

Many women bottle-feed because they return to work after childbirth and are unavailable to breast-feed. Their partners, extended families, nannies,

THERE ARE NUMEROUS ADVANTAGES TO BREAST MILK (U.S. DEPARTMENT OF HEALTH AND HUMAN SERVICES, 2010)

- Breast milk conforms to human digestion processes (i.e., it is unlikely to upset the infant's stomach).
- Breast milk alone is adequate for the first six months after birth. Other foods can merely supplement breast milk through the first year.
- As the infant matures, the composition of breast milk changes to help meet the infant's changing needs.
- Breast milk contains the mother's antibodies and helps the infant ward off health problems ranging from ear infections, pneumonia, wheezing, bronchiolitis, and tetanus to chicken pox, bacterial meningitis, and typhoid fever.
- Breast milk helps protect against the form of cancer known as childhood lymphoma (a cancer of the lymph glands).
- Breast milk decreases the likelihood of developing serious cases of diarrhea.
- Infants who are nourished by breast milk are less likely to develop allergic responses and constipation.
- Breast-fed infants are less likely to develop obesity later in life.
- Breast-feeding promotes myelination and is associated with better neural and behavioral organization in the infant (Deoni et al., 2013).

or child-care workers give their children bottles during the day. Some mothers pump their milk and bottle it for use when they are away. Some parents bottle-feed because it permits both parents to share in feeding.

Breast-feeding also has health benefits for the mother: It reduces the risk of early breast cancer and ovarian cancer, and it builds the strength of bones, which can reduce the likelihood of hip fractures that result from osteoporosis following menopause. Breast-feeding also helps shrink the uterus after delivery.

There are downsides to breast-feeding. For example, breast milk is one of the bodily fluids that transmit HIV (Badiou S., et al., 2016). As many as one-third of infants born to mothers who are infected with HIV, the virus that causes AIDS, become infected during pregnancy, childbirth, or breastfeeding (Rose et al., 2014). Alcohol, many drugs, and environmental hazards such as polychlorinated biphenyls (PCBs) can also be transmitted through breast milk. Moreover, for breast milk to contain the necessary nutrients, mothers must be adequately nourished themselves. The mother also encounters the physical demands of producing and expelling milk, a tendency for soreness in the breasts, and the inconvenience of being continually available to meet the infant's feeding needs.

Alex Staroseltsev/Shutterstock.com

4-2 DEVELOPMENT OF THE BRAIN AND NERVOUS SYSTEM

The nervous system is a system of **nerves** involved in heartbeat, visual–motor coordination, thought and language, and so on.

4-2a DEVELOPMENT OF NEURONS

The basic units of the nervous system are cells called **neurons**. Neurons receive and transmit messages from one part of the body to another. The messages account for phenomena such as reflexes, the perception of an itch from a mosquito bite, the visual–motor coordination of a skier, the composition of a concerto, and the solution of a math problem.

People are born with about 100 billion neurons, most of which are in the brain. Neurons vary according to their functions and locations in the body. Some neurons in the brain are only a fraction of an inch in length, whereas neurons in the leg can grow several feet long. Each neuron possesses a cell body, dendrites, and an axon (see Figure 4.2 on page 76). **Dendrites** are short fibers that extend from the cell body and receive incoming messages from up to 1,000 adjoining transmitting neurons. The **axon** extends trunk-like from the cell body and accounts for much of the difference in length in neurons. An axon can be up to several feet in length if it is carrying messages

nerves bundles of axons from many neurons.

neurons cells in the nervous system that transmit messages.

dendrites rootlike parts of neurons that receive impulses from other neurons.

axon a long, thin part of a neuron that transmits impulses to other neurons through branching structures called axon terminals.

FIG.4.2 ANATOMY OF A NEURON

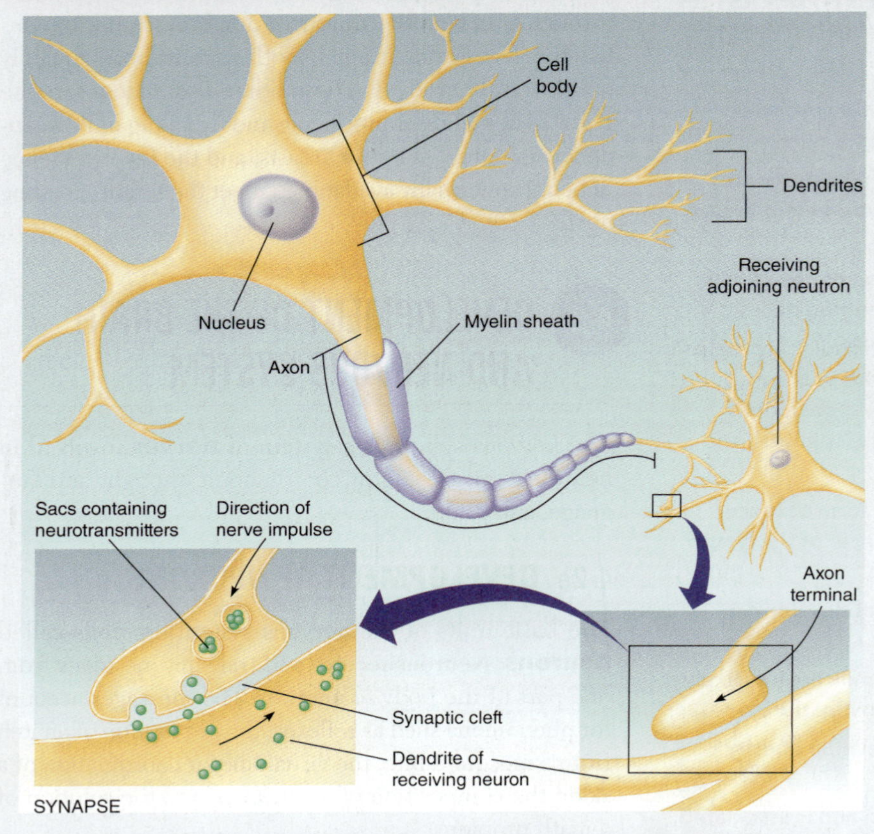

"Messages" enter neurons through dendrites, are transmitted along the axon, and are sent through axon terminals to muscles, glands, and other neurons. Neurons develop by proliferation of dendrites and axon terminals and through myelination.

current being carried along the axon is minimized, and messages are conducted more efficiently.

The term **myelination** refers to the process by which axons are coated with myelin. Myelination is not complete at birth, but rather is part of the maturation process that leads to the abilities to crawl and walk during the first year after birth. Myelination of the brain's prefrontal matter continues into the second decade of life and is connected with advances in working memory and language ability (Burgaleta, M., et al. 2016). Breakdown of myelin is believed to be associated with Alzheimer's disease, a source of cognitive decline that begins later in life.

In the disease **multiple sclerosis**, myelin is replaced by hard, fibrous tissue that disrupts the timing of neural transmission, interfering with muscle control (Zhang et al., 2016). Phenylketonuria (PKU) causes intellectual disability by inhibiting the formation of myelin in the brain (Velumian & Samoilova, 2014).

from the toes to the spine. Messages are released from axon terminals in the form of chemicals called **neurotransmitters**. These messages are received by the dendrites of adjoining neurons, muscles, or glands. As the child matures, axons lengthen, and dendrites and axon terminals proliferate.

MYELIN Many neurons are tightly wrapped with white, fatty **myelin sheaths** that give them the appearance of a string of white sausages. The high fat content of the myelin sheath insulates the neuron from electrically charged atoms in the fluids that encase the nervous system. In this way, leakage of the electric

neurotransmitters a chemical that transmits a neural impulse across a synapse from one neuron to another.

myelin sheaths a fatty, whitish substance that encases and insulates axons.

myelination the coating of axons with myelin.

multiple sclerosis a disorder in which hard fibrous tissue replaces myelin, impeding neural transmission.

4-2b DEVELOPMENT OF THE BRAIN

The brain of the neonate weighs a little less than a pound, or nearly one-fourth its adult weight. In keeping with the principles of cephalocaudal growth, an infant's brain triples in weight, reaching nearly 70% of its adult weight by the age of one year (see Figure 4.3). Let's look at the brain, as shown in Figure 4.4, and discuss the development of the structures within.

TRUTH

(T) F A newborn's brain weighs about 25% of its adult weight, but grows to some 70% of its adult weight by the child's first birthday.

It is true that a newborn's brain weighs about 25% of its adult weight, and that it mushrooms to some 70% of adult weight by the age of one year.

FIG.4.3 GROWTH OF BODY SYSTEMS AS A PERCENTAGE OF TOTAL POSTNATAL GROWTH

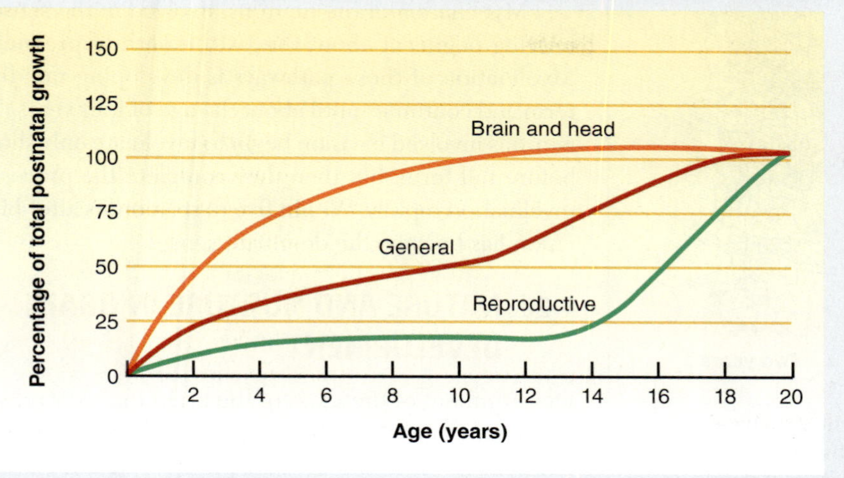

The brain will triple in weight by the infant's first birthday, reaching nearly 70% of its adult weight.

STRUCTURES OF THE BRAIN Many nerves that connect the spinal cord to higher levels of the brain pass through the **medulla**. The medulla, part of an area called the brain stem, is vital in the control of basic functions, such as heartbeat and respiration. Above the medulla lies the **cerebellum**. The cerebellum helps the child maintain balance, control motor behavior, and coordinate eye movements with bodily sensations.

The **cerebrum** is the crowning glory of the brain. It makes possible the breadth and depth of human learning, thought, memory, and language. The surface of the cerebrum consists of two hemispheres that become increasingly wrinkled as the child develops, coming to show ridges and valleys called fissures. This surface is the cerebral cortex. The cerebral cortex is only one-eighth of an inch thick, yet it is the seat of thought and reason. It is here that we receive sensory information from the world outside and command muscles to move.

FIG.4.4 STRUCTURES OF THE BRAIN

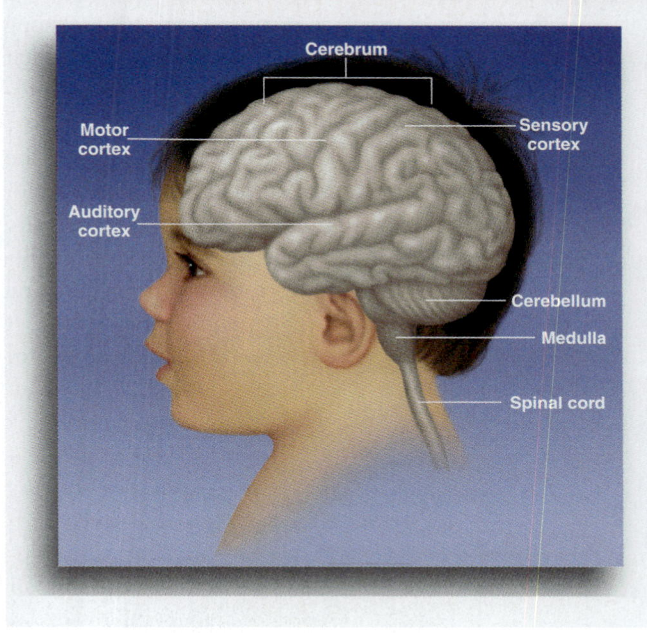

TRUTH

T F The cerebral cortex—the outer layer of the brain that is vital to human thought and reasoning—is only one-eighth of an inch thick.

It is true that the cerebral cortex—the outer layer of the brain that is vital to human thought and reasoning—is only one-eighth of an inch thick. (Look at a ruler and think about that for a while.)

GROWTH SPURTS OF THE BRAIN The first major growth spurt of the brain occurs during the fourth and fifth months of prenatal development, when neurons proliferate. A second growth spurt in the brain occurs between the 25th week of prenatal development and the end of the second year after birth. Whereas the first growth spurt of the brain is due to the formation of neurons, the second growth spurt is due primarily to the proliferation of dendrites and axon terminals (see Figure 4.5).

medulla an area of the lower, back part of the brain involved in heartbeat and respiration.

cerebellum the area of the lower, back part of the brain involved in coordination and balance.

cerebrum the largest, rounded part of the brain, responsible for learning, thought, memory, and language.

FIG.4.5 INCREASE IN NEURAL CONNECTIONS IN THE BRAIN

Neonate | Six months | Two years

Image Source/Jupiter Images; Stockbyte/Getty Images

A major growth spurt occurs between the 25th week of prenatal development and the end of the second year after birth, due primarily to the proliferation of dendrites and axon terminals.

BRAIN DEVELOPMENT IN INFANCY There is a link between what infants can do and myelination. At birth, the parts of the brain involved in heartbeat and respiration, sleeping and arousal, and reflex activity are fairly well myelinated and functional. Myelination of motor pathways allows neonates to show stereotyped reflexes, but otherwise neonates' physical activity tends to be random and ill-organized. Myelin develops rapidly along the major motor pathways from the cerebral cortex during the last month of pregnancy and continues to develop after birth. The development of intentional physical activity coincides with myelination as the unorganized movements of the neonate come under increasing control. Myelination of the nerves to muscles is largely developed by the age of two years, although myelination continues to some degree into adolescence.

Although neonates respond to touch and can see and hear quite well, the areas of the cortex that are involved in vision, hearing, and the skin senses are less well myelinated at birth. As myelination progresses and the interconnections between the various areas of the cortex thicken, children become increasingly capable of complex and integrated sensorimotor activities (Bartzokis et al., 2010).

Myelination of the neurons involved in the sense of hearing begins at about the sixth month of pregnancy. Myelination of these pathways is developing rapidly at term and continues until about the age of four years. The neurons involved in vision begin to myelinate only shortly before full term, but then they complete the process of myelination rapidly. Within five to six months after birth, vision has become the dominant sense.

4-2c NATURE AND NURTURE IN BRAIN DEVELOPMENT

Development of the areas of the brain that control sensation and movement begins as a result of maturation, but sensory stimulation and physical activity during early infancy also spur the development of these areas (Posner et al., 2013; Walker, 2016).

Research with animals shows how sensory stimulation sparks growth of the cortex. Researchers have given rats "amusement parks" with toys such as ladders, platforms, and boxes to demonstrate the effects of enriched environments. In these studies, rats exposed to the more complex environments develop heavier brains than control animals. The weight differences in part reflect more synapses per neuron (Anderson, 2011). On the other hand, animals reared in darkness show shrinkage of the visual cortex, impaired vision, and impaired visual–motor coordination (Anderson, 2011; Talaei & Salami, 2013). If they don't use it, they lose it.

The brain is also affected by experience. Infants actually have more connections among neurons than adults do. Connections that are activated by experience survive; others do not (Awasaki & Ito, 2016).

The great adaptability of the brain appears to be a double-edged sword. Adaptability allows us to develop different patterns of neural connections to meet the demands of different environments, but lack of stimulation—especially during critical early periods of development—can impair adaptability.

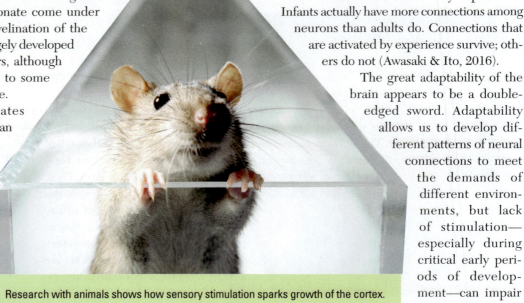

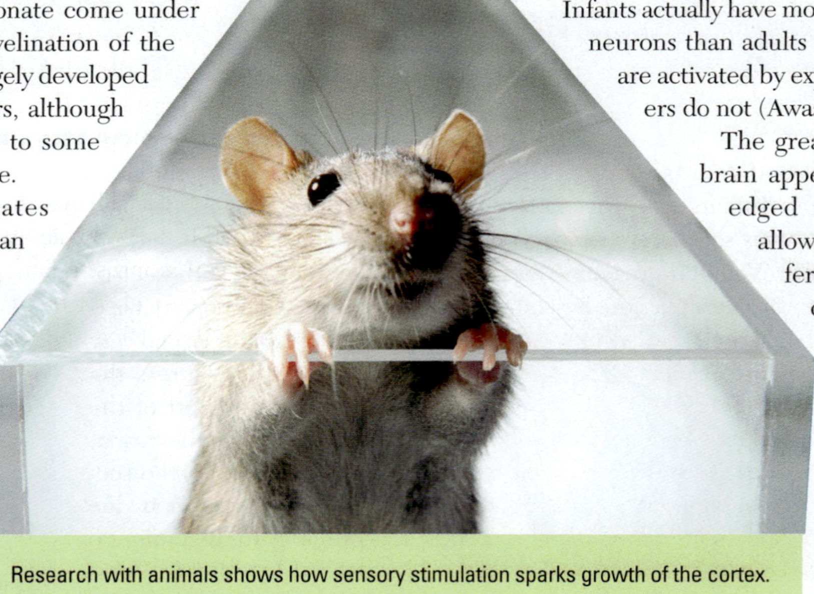

BonkersAboutScience/Alamy Stock Photo

Research with animals shows how sensory stimulation sparks growth of the cortex.

4-3 MOTOR DEVELOPMENT

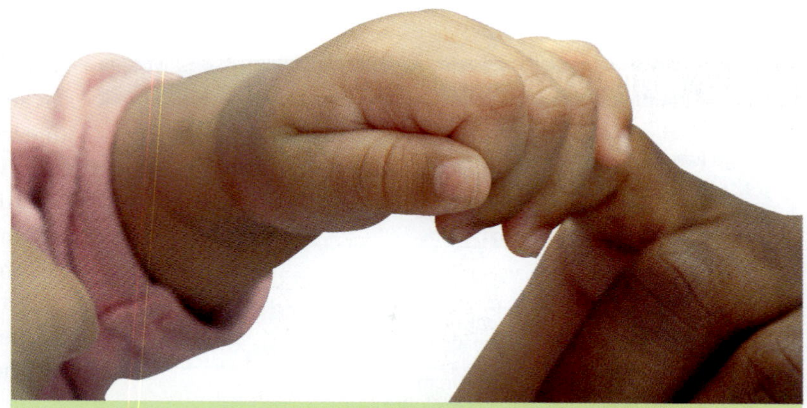
© Corbis

Grasping is reflexive in newborns. By a year, infants can pick up tiny objects.

Motor development involves the activity of muscles, leading to changes in posture, movement, and coordination of movement with the infant's developing sensory apparatus. Motor development provides some of the most fascinating changes in infants, because so much happens so fast.

Like physical development, motor development follows cephalocaudal and proximodistal patterns and differentiation. Infants gain control of their heads and upper torsos before they can effectively use their arms. This trend illustrates cephalocaudal development. Infants also can control their trunks and shoulders before they can use their hands and fingers, demonstrating the proximodistal trend.

4-3a LIFTING AND HOLDING THE TORSO AND HEAD

Neonates can move their heads slightly to the side. They can thus avoid suffocation if they are lying face down and their noses or mouths are obstructed by bedding. At about one month, infants can raise their heads. By about two months, they can also lift their chests while lying on their stomachs.

When neonates are held, their heads must be supported. But by three to six months of age, infants generally manage to hold their heads quite well so supporting the head is no longer necessary. Unfortunately, infants who can normally support their heads cannot do so when they are lifted or moved about in a jerky manner; infants who are handled carelessly can thus develop neck injuries.

4-3b CONTROL OF THE HANDS: GETTING A GRIP

The development of hand skills is an example of proximodistal development. Infants will track slowly moving objects with their eyes shortly after birth, but they will not reach for them. Voluntary reaching and grasping require visual–motor coordination. By about three months, infants will make clumsy swipes at objects. Between four and six months, infants become more successful at grasping objects (Daum et al., 2013). However, they may not know how to let go and may hold an object indefinitely, until their attention is diverted and the hand opens accidentally. Four to six months is a good age for giving children rattles, large plastic spoons, mobiles, and other brightly colored hanging toys that can be grasped but are harmless when they wind up in the mouth.

Grasping is reflexive at first. Voluntary holding replaces reflexive grasping by three to four months. Infants first use an **ulnar grasp**, holding objects clumsily between their fingers and their palm. By four to six months, they can transfer objects back and forth between hands. The oppositional thumb comes into play at about 9 to 12 months, enabling infants to pick up tiny objects in a **pincer grasp**. By about 11 months, infants can hold objects in each hand and inspect them in turn.

Another aspect of visual–motor coordination is stacking blocks. On average, children can stack two blocks at 15 months, three blocks at 18 months, and five blocks at 24 months (Wentworth et al., 2000).

4-3c LOCOMOTION

Locomotion is movement from one place to another. Children gain the capacity to move their bodies through a sequence of activities that includes rolling over, sitting up, crawling, creeping, walking, and running (see Figure 4.6). There is much variation in the ages at which infants first engage in these activities. Although the sequence mostly remains the same, some children will skip a step. For example, an infant may creep without ever having crawled.

Most infants can roll over, from back to stomach and from stomach to back, by about the age of six months. By about seven months, infants usually begin to sit up by themselves. At about eight to nine months, most infants begin to crawl, a motor activity in which they lie on their bellies and use their arms to pull themselves along. Creeping, in which infants move themselves along on their hands and knees, usually appears a month or so after crawling.

ulnar grasp grasping objects between the fingers and the palm.

pincer grasp grasping objects between the fingers and the thumb.

locomotion movement from one place to another.

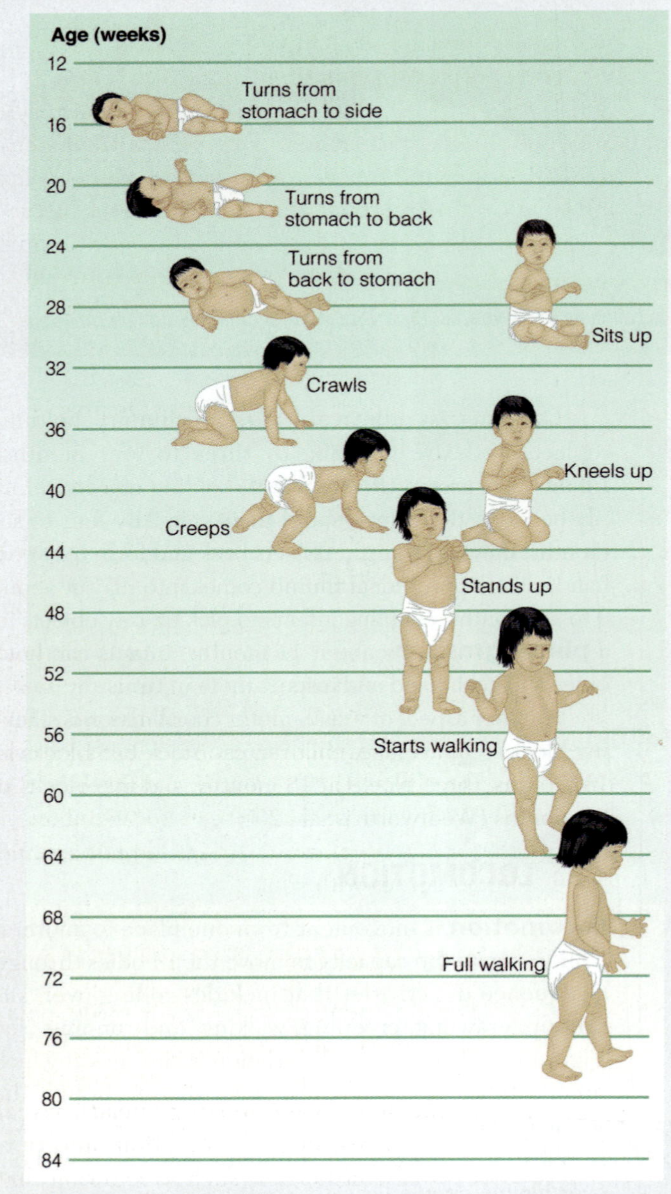

Motor development proceeds in an orderly sequence, but there is considerable variation in the timing of marker events.

Standing overlaps with crawling and creeping. Most infants can remain in a standing position by holding on to something at the age of eight or nine months. At this age, they may also be able to walk a bit with support. About two months later, they can pull themselves to a standing position by holding on to the sides of their cribs or other objects and can stand briefly without holding on. By 12 to 15 months or so, they walk by themselves, earning them the name **toddler**.

toddler a child who walks with short, uncertain steps.

Toddlers soon run about, supporting their relatively heavy heads and torsos by spreading their legs in a bowlegged fashion. Because they are top-heavy and inexperienced, they fall frequently. Many toddlers are skillful at navigating slopes (Adolph & Robinson, 2015). They walk down shallow slopes but prudently choose to slide or crawl down steep ones. Walking lends children new freedom. It allows them to get about rapidly and to grasp objects that were formerly out of reach. Give toddlers a large ball to toss and run after; it is an inexpensive and most enjoyable toy.

As children mature, their muscle strength, bone density, and balance and coordination improve. By the age of two years, they can climb steps one at a time, placing both feet on each step. They can run well, walk backward, kick a large ball, and jump several inches.

Both maturation (nature) and experience (nurture) are involved in motor development. Certain voluntary motor activities are not possible until the brain has matured in terms of myelination and the differentiation of the motor areas of the cortex. Although the neonate shows stepping and swimming reflexes, these behaviors are controlled by more primitive parts of the brain. They disappear when cortical development inhibits some functions of the lower parts of the brain; and, when they reappear, they differ in quality.

Infants also need some opportunity to experiment before they can engage in milestones such as sitting up and walking. Even so, many of these advances can apparently be attributed to maturation. In classic research, Wayne Dennis and Marsena Dennis (1940) reported on the motor development of Native American Hopi children who spent their first year strapped to a cradle board. Although denied a full year of experience in locomotion, the Hopi infants gained the capacity to walk early in their second year, about when other children do.

Can training accelerate the appearance of motor skills? In a classic study with identical twins, Arnold Gesell (1929) gave one twin extensive training in hand coordination, block building, and stair climbing from early infancy. The other twin was allowed to develop on his own. At first, the trained twin had better skills, but as time passed, the untrained twin became just as skilled.

The development of motor skills can be accelerated by training (Cole et al., 2013; Zelazo & Müller, 2010), but the effect seems slight.

TRUTH

T F Native American Hopi infants spend the first year of life strapped to a board, yet they begin to walk at about the same time as children who are reared in other cultures.

It is true that Native American Hopi infants spend the first year of life strapped to a board yet begin to walk at about the same time as children who are reared in other cultures. This finding is strong evidence of a powerful role for maturation.

Although being strapped to a cradle board did not permanently prevent the motor development of Hopi infants, Wayne Dennis (1960) reported that infants in an Iranian orphanage, who were exposed to extreme social and physical deprivation, were significantly set back in their motor development. They grew apathetic, and all aspects of development suffered. By contrast, however, the motor development of similar infants in a Lebanese orphanage accelerated dramatically in response to such minimal intervention as being propped up in their cribs and being given a few colorful toys (Sayegh & Dennis, 1965).

Nature provides the limits—the "reaction range"—for the expression of inherited traits. Nurture determines whether the child will develop skills that reach the upper limits of the range. Even such a fundamental skill as locomotion is determined by a complex interplay of maturational and environmental factors (Adolph & Robinson, 2015). There may be little purpose in trying to train children to enhance motor skills before they are ready. Once they are ready, however, teaching and practice do make a difference. One does not become an Olympic athlete without "good genes," but one also usually does not become an Olympic athlete without solid training.

4-4 SENSORY AND PERCEPTUAL DEVELOPMENT

Many things that are obvious to us are not so obvious to infants. You may know that a coffee cup is the same whether you see it from above or from the side, but make no such assumptions about the infant's knowledge. You may know that an infant's mother is the same size whether she is standing next to the infant or approaching from two blocks away, but do not assume that the infant agrees with you.

Native American Hopi children are traditionally strapped to a cradle board for the first year of life. Although they are denied the opportunity to experiment with various locomotive tasks, they begin to walk rapidly when they are unstrapped.

4-4a DEVELOPMENT OF VISION

Development of vision involves development of visual acuity or sharpness, development of peripheral vision (seeing things at the sides while looking ahead), visual preferences, depth perception, and perceptual constancies, such as knowing that an object remains the same object even though it may look different when seen from a different angle.

DEVELOPMENT OF VISUAL ACUITY AND PERIPHERAL VISION Newborns are extremely nearsighted, with vision beginning at about 20/600. The most dramatic gains in visual acuity are made between birth and six months of age, with acuity reaching about 20/50 (S. P. Johnson, 2011; Slater et al., 2010). By three to five years, visual acuity generally approximates adult levels (20/20 in the best cases).

Neonates also have poor peripheral vision (Disabato & Daniels, 2013). Adults can perceive objects that are nearly 90 degrees off to the side (i.e., directly to the left or right), although objects at these extremes are unclear. Neonates cannot perceive visual stimuli that are off to the side by an angle of more than 30 degrees, but their peripheral vision expands to an angle of about 45 degrees by the age of seven weeks. By six months, their peripheral vision is about equal to that of an adult.

Let us now consider the development of visual perception. We will see that infants frequently prefer the strange to the familiar and will avoid going off the deep end—sometimes.

VISUAL PREFERENCES Neonates look at stripes longer than at blobs. This finding has been used in much of the research on visual acuity. Classic research found that by the age of 8 to 12 weeks, most infants also show distinct preferences for curved lines over straight ones (Fantz et al., 1975).

Robert Fantz (1961) wondered whether there was something intrinsically interesting about the human face that drew the attention of infants. To investigate this question, he showed two-month-old infants the six disks in Figure 4.7. One disk contained human features, another newsprint, and still another a bull's eye. The remaining three disks were featureless but colored red, white, and yellow. In this study, the infants fixated significantly longer on the human face.

FIG.4.7 INFANT'S PREFERENCES FOR VISUAL STIMULI

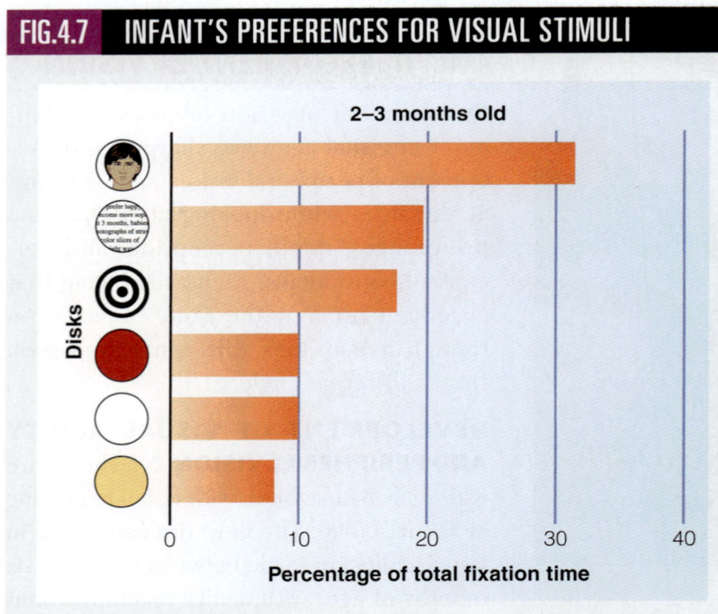

Infants appear to prefer complex to simple visual stimuli. By the time they are two months old, they also tend to show a preference for the human face.

Some studies suggest that the infants in Fantz's (1961) study may have preferred the human face because it had a complex, intriguing pattern of dots (eyes) within an outline, not because it was a face. But de Haan and Groen (2006) assert that "reading" faces (interpreting facial expressions) is important to infants because they do not understand verbal information as communicated through language.

Researchers therefore continue to ask whether humans come into the world "prewired" to prefer human stimuli to other stimuli that are just as complex, and—if so—what it is about human stimuli that draws attention. Some researchers—unlike de Haan and Groen—argue that neonates do not "prefer" faces because they are faces per se but because of the structure of their immature visual systems (Simion et al., 2001). A supportive study of 34 neonates found that the longer fixations on facelike stimuli resulted from a larger number of brief fixations (looks) rather than from a few prolonged fixations (Cassia et al., 2001). The infants' gaze, then, was sort of bouncing around from feature to feature rather than "staring" at the face in general. The researchers interpreted the finding to show that the stimulus properties of the visual object are more important than the fact that it represents a human face. Even so, of course, the "immature visual system" would be providing some "prewired" basis for attending to the face. Is there an evolutionary advantage to neonates' preferring faces? Perhaps. Let us note that among rhesus monkeys, neonatal face-to-face interactions appear to promote subsequent social behavior (Dettmer et al., 2016).

Learning also plays some role. For example, neonates can discriminate their mother's face from a stranger's after eight hours of mother–infant contact spread over four days (Bushnell, 2001).

Neonates appear to direct their attention to the edges of objects. This pattern persists for the first several weeks (S. P. Johnson, 2011). When they are given the opportunity to look at human faces, one-month-old infants tend to pay most attention to the "edges," that is, the chin, an ear, or the hairline. The eye movements of two-month-old infants move in from the edge (see Figure 4.8). The infants focus particularly on the eyes, although they also inspect other features such as the mouth and nose (Aslin, 2012).

Some researchers (e.g., Haith, 1979) explain infants' tendencies to scan from the edges of objects inward by noting that for the first several weeks, infants seem to be concerned with *where*

FIG.4.8 EYE MOVEMENTS OF 1- AND 2-MONTH-OLDS

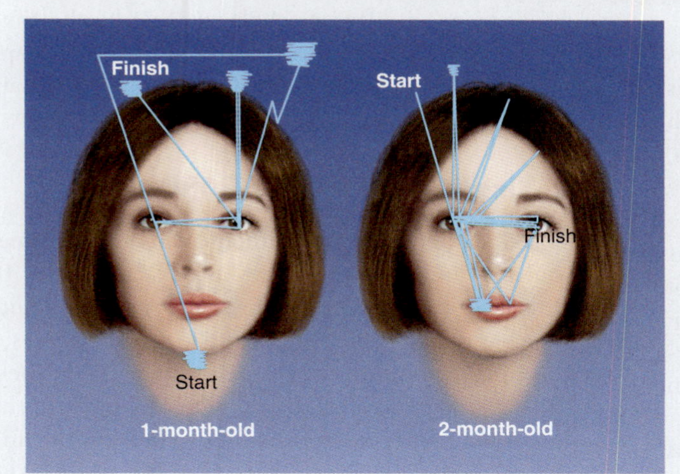

One-month-olds direct their attention to the edges of objects. Two-month-olds move in from the edge.

things are. Their attention is captured by movement and sharp contrasts in brightness and shape, such as those found where the edges of objects stand out against their backgrounds. But by about two months, infants tend to focus on the *what* of things, scanning systematically within the boundaries of objects (Aslin, 2012).

DEVELOPMENT OF DEPTH PERCEPTION Many infants respond to cues for depth by the time they are able to crawl (six to eight months of age or so), and most have the good sense to avoid "going off the deep end," that is, crawling off ledges and tabletops into open space (Campos et al., 1978).

In a classic study on depth perception, Gibson and Walk (1960) placed infants of various ages on a fabric-covered runway that ran across the center of a clever device called a visual cliff (see Figure 4.9). The visual cliff is a sheet of Plexiglas that covers a cloth with a checkerboard pattern. On one side, the cloth is placed immediately beneath the Plexiglas; on the other, it is dropped about four feet. In the Gibson and Walk study, eight out of ten infants who had begun to crawl refused to venture onto the seemingly unsupported surface, even when their mothers beckoned encouragingly from the other side.

Psychologists can assess infants' emotional responses to the visual cliff long before infants can crawl. For example, Campos and his colleagues (1970) found that one-month-old infants showed no change in heart rate when placed face down on the "cliff." They apparently did not perceive the depth of the cliff. At two months, infants showed decreases in heart rate when so placed, which psychologists interpret as a sign of interest. But the heart rates of nine-month-olds accelerated on the cliff, which is interpreted as a fear response. The study appears to suggest that infants profit from some experience crawling about (and, perhaps, accumulating some bumps) before they develop fear of heights. The nine-month-olds but not the two-month-olds had had such experience. Other studies support the view that infants usually do not develop fear of heights until they can move around (Dahl et al., 2013).

DEVELOPMENT OF PERCEPTUAL CONSTANCIES It may not surprise you that a 12-inch ruler is the same length whether it is two feet or six feet away or that a door across the room is a rectangle whether closed or ajar. Awareness of these facts depends not on sensation alone but on the development of perceptual constancies. **Perceptual constancy**

perceptual constancy
perceiving objects as maintaining their identity although sensations from them change as their positions change.

FIG.4.9 THE VISUAL CLIFF

This young explorer has the good sense not to crawl out onto an apparently unsupported surface, even when mother beckons from the other side.

is the tendency to perceive an object to be the same, even though the sensations produced by the object may differ under various conditions.

Consider again the example of the ruler. When it is two feet away, its image, as focused on the retina, has a certain "retinal size." From six feet away, the 12-inch ruler is only one-third as long in terms of retinal size, but we perceive it as being the same size because of size constancy. *Size constancy* is the tendency to perceive the same objects as being of the same size even though their retinal sizes vary as a function of their distance. From six feet away, a 36-inch yardstick casts an image equal in retinal size to the 12-inch ruler at two feet, but—if recognized as a yardstick—it is perceived as longer, again because of size constancy.

Bower (1974) conditioned 2½- to 3-month-old infants to turn their heads to the left when shown a 12-inch cube from a distance of three feet. He then presented them with three experimental stimuli: (1) a 12-inch cube nine feet away, whose retinal size was smaller than that of the original cube; (2) a 36-inch cube three feet away, whose retinal size was larger than that of the original cube; and (3) a 36-inch cube nine feet away, whose retinal size was the same as that of the original cube. The infants turned their heads most frequently in response to the first experimental cube, although its retinal image was only one-third the length of that to which they had been conditioned, suggesting that they had achieved size constancy. Later studies have confirmed Bower's finding that size constancy is present in early infancy. Some research suggests that even neonates possess rudimentary size constancy (Slater et al., 2010, Siegler et al., 2016).

Shape constancy is the tendency to perceive an object as having the same shape even though, when perceived from another angle, the shape projected onto the retina may change dramatically. When the top of a cup or a glass is seen from above, the visual sensations are in the shape of a circle. When seen from a slight angle, the sensations are elliptical. However, because of our familiarity with the object, we still perceive the rim of the cup or glass as being a circle. In the first few months after birth, infants see the features of their caregivers, bottles, cribs, and toys from all different angles so that by the time they are four or five months old, a broad grasp of shape constancy seems to be established, at least under certain conditions (Slater et al., 2010).

4-4b DEVELOPMENT OF HEARING

Neonates can crudely orient their heads in the direction of a sound (Burnham & Mattock, 2010). By 18 months of age, the accuracy of sound-localizing ability approaches that of adults. Sensitivity to sounds increases in the first few months of life (Burnham & Mattock, 2010). As infants mature, the range of the pitch of the sounds they can sense gradually expands to include the adult's range of 20 to 20,000 cycles per second. The ability to detect differences in the pitch and loudness of sounds improves considerably throughout the preschool years. Auditory acuity also improves gradually over the first several years (Burnham & Matlock, 2010), although infants' hearing can be so acute that many parents complain their napping infants will awaken at the slightest sound. This is especially true if parents have been overprotective in attempting to keep their rooms as silent as possible. Infants who are normally exposed to a backdrop of moderate noise levels become habituated to them and are not likely to awaken unless there is a sudden, sharp noise.

By the age of one month, infants perceive differences between speech sounds that are highly similar. In a classic study relying on the **habituation** method, infants of this age could activate a recording of "bah" by sucking on a nipple (Eimas et al., 1971). As time went on, habituation occurred, as shown by decreased sucking so as to hear the "bah" sound. Then the researchers switched from "bah" to "pah." If the sounds had seemed the same to the infants, their lethargic sucking patterns would have continued, but they immediately sucked harder, suggesting that they perceived the difference. Other researchers have found that within another month or two, infants reliably discriminate three-syllable words such as *marana* and *malana* (Kuhl et al., 2006).

Our auditory acuity develops gradually over the first few years of life, but we learn to locate sounds rather quickly.

© Alloy Photography/Veer

habituation becoming used to a stimulus and therefore paying less attention to it.

Infants can discriminate the sounds of their parent's voices by 3½ months of age. In classic research, infants of this age were oriented toward their parents as they reclined in infant seats. The experimenters (Spelke & Owsley, 1979) played recordings of the mother's or father's voice while the parents themselves remained inactive. The infants reliably looked at the parent whose voice was being played.

Young infants are capable of perceiving most of the speech sounds present in the world's languages. But after exposure to one's native language, infants gradually lose the capacity to discriminate those sounds that are not found in the native language (Werker & Hensch, 2015), as shown in Figure 4.10 (Werker, 1989).

Infants also learn at an early age to ignore small, meaningless variations in the sounds of their native language, for instance those caused by accents or head colds, as early as six months of age (Kuhl et al., 2006). Kuhl and her colleagues (1997) presented American and Swedish infants with pairs of sounds in either their own language or the other one. The infants were trained to look over their shoulder when they heard a difference in the sounds and to ignore sound pairs that seemed to be the same. The infants routinely ignored variations in sounds that were part of their language, because they apparently perceived them as the same sound. But the infants noticed slight variations in the sounds of the other language.

4-4c DEVELOPMENT OF COORDINATION OF THE SENSES

Young infants can recognize that objects experienced by one sense (e.g., vision) are the same as those experienced through another sense (e.g., touch). This ability has been demonstrated in infants as young as one month of age (Bushnell, 1993). One experiment demonstrating such understanding in five-month-olds showed that infants of this age tend to look longer at novel rather than familiar sources of stimulation. Féron and her colleagues (2006) first allowed five-month-old infants to handle groups of either two or three objects, presented one by one, to their right hand. The infants were then shown visual displays of either two or three objects. The infants looked longer at the group of objects that differed from the one they had handled, showing a transfer of information from the sense of touch to the sense of vision.

4-4d THE ACTIVE–PASSIVE CONTROVERSY IN PERCEPTUAL DEVELOPMENT

Newborn children may have more sophisticated sensory capabilities than you expected. Still, their ways of perceiving the world are largely mechanical, or passive. Neonates seem to be generally at the mercy of external stimuli. When a bright light strikes, they attend to it. If the light moves slowly across the plane of their vision, they track it.

As time passes, broad changes occur in the perceptual processes of children, and the child's role in perception appears to become decidedly more active. Developmental psychologist Eleanor Gibson (1969, 1991) noted a number of these changes:

1. Intentional action replaces "capture" (automatic responses to stimulation). Purposeful scanning and exploration of the environment take the place of mechanical movements and passive responses to stimulation.
2. Systematic search replaces unsystematic search.

FIG.4.10 DECLINING ABILITY TO DISCRIMINATE THE SOUNDS OF FOREIGN LANGUAGES

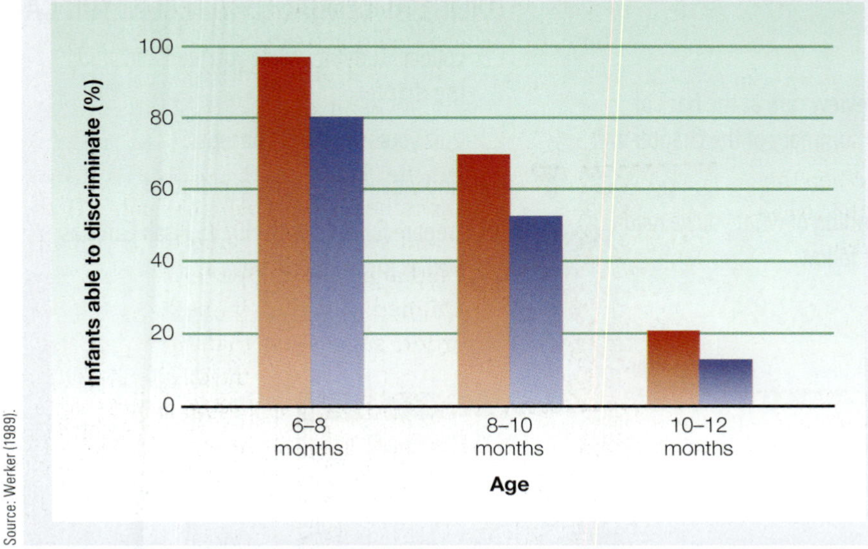

Infants show a decline in the ability to discriminate sounds not found in their native language. Before six months of age, infants from English-speaking families could discriminate sounds found in Hindi (red bars) and Salish, a Native American language (blue bars). By 10 to 12 months of age, they could no longer do so.

3. Attention becomes selective. Older children become capable of selecting the information they need from the welter of confusion in the environment.
4. Irrelevant information becomes ignored. That might mean shutting out the noise of cars in the street or radios in the neighborhood so as to focus on a book.

In short, children develop from passive, mechanical reactors to the world about them into active, purposeful seekers and organizers of sensory information.

4-4e NATURE AND NURTURE IN PERCEPTUAL DEVELOPMENT

The nature–nurture issue is found in perceptual development, as in other areas of development.

EVIDENCE FOR THE ROLE OF NATURE Compelling evidence supports the idea that inborn sensory capacities play a crucial role in perceptual development. Neonates arrive in the world with a good number of perceptual skills. They can see nearby objects quite well, and their hearing is usually fine. They are born with tendencies to track moving objects, to systematically scan the horizon, and to prefer certain kinds of stimuli. Preferences for different kinds of visual stimuli appear to unfold on schedule as the first months wear on. Sensory changes, as with motor changes, appear to be linked to maturation of the nervous system.

EVIDENCE FOR THE ROLE OF NURTURE Evidence that experience plays a crucial role in perceptual development is also compelling. Children and lower animals have critical periods in their perceptual development. Failure to receive adequate sensory stimulation during these periods can result in permanent sensory deficits (Cascio, 2010; Lomanowska & Melo, 2016. For example, newborn kittens raised with a patch over one eye wind up with few or no cells in the visual area of the cerebral cortex that would normally be stimulated by light that enters that eye. In effect, that eye becomes blind, even though sensory receptors in the eye itself may fire in response to light. On the other hand, if the eye of an adult cat is patched for the same amount of time, the animal will not lose vision. The critical period will have passed. Similarly, if health problems require that a child's eye must be patched for an extensive period of time during the first year, the child's visual acuity in that eye may be impaired.

Today most investigators would agree that nature and nurture interact to shape perceptual development. In the next chapter, we see how nature and nurture influence the development of thought and language in infants.

STUDY TOOLS 4

READY TO STUDY?

In the book, you can:

- ☐ Rip out the chapter review card at the back of the book for a handy summary of the chapter and key terms.
- ☐ Check your understanding of what you've read with the quizzes that follow.

ONLINE AT CENGAGEBRAIN.COM YOU CAN:

- ☐ Collect StudyBits while you read and study the chapter.
- ☐ Quiz yourself on key concepts.
- ☐ Find videos for further exploration.
- ☐ Prepare for tests with HDEV5 Flash Cards as well as those you create.

SELF-ASSESSMENTS

Fill-Ins

Answers can be found in the back of the book.

1. Failure to receive adequate sensory stimulation during a(n) ____________ period can result in permanent sensory deficits.
2. Boys generally reach half their adult height by their ____________ birthday.
3. Native American Hopi Indians typically spend the first year strapped to a(n) ____________ ____________.
4. The tendency to return to one's genetically determined pattern of growth following a period of deprivation is referred to as ____________.
5. Breast milk contains the mother's ____________ and helps the infant ward off health problems such as ear infections and pneumonia.
6. In the disease ____________ ____________, myelin is replaced by hard, fibrous tissue that disrupts the timing of neural transmission, interfering with muscle control.
7. The first major growth spurt of the brain occurs during the fourth and fifth months of prenatal development, due to the proliferation of ____________.
8. Animals reared in darkness show shrinkage of the ____________ ____________.
9. By 12 to 15 months or so, infants walk by themselves, earning them the name ____________.
10. Fantz shows two-month-old infants disks colored red, white, and yellow, and disks with newsprint, a bull's eye, and a human face. The infants fixated longest on the ____________.

Multiple Choice

1. The American Academy of Pediatrics recommends that infants be fed breast milk for at least

a. four to six months.
b. six to nine months.
c. one year.
d. two years.

2. Which of the following is untrue about breastfeeding?

a. Breast-feeding cannot transmit HIV.
b. Breast-feeding helps shrink the uterus after delivery.
c. Breast milk can transmit polychlorinated biphenyls.
d. Breast-feeding reduces the risk of ovarian cancer.

3. How long does it take for a child's brain to reach 70% of its adult weight?

a. one year
b. two years
c. three years
d. five years

4. Which part of the brain helps the child maintain balance?

a. the medulla
b. the amygdala
c. the auditory cortex
d. the cerebellum

5. Vision is the infant's dominant sense at

a. birth.
b. one–four months.
c. five–six months.
d. one year.

6. Myelination of motor pathways allows neonates to engage in

a. reflexes.
b. beating of the heart.
c. respiration.
d. the cycle of waking and sleeping.

7. Myelination of the neurons involved in the sense of hearing begins

a. in the germinal stage.
b. in the embryonic stage.
c. in the fetal stage.
d. after birth.

8. At three to four months of age, infants hold objects clumsily between their finger and their palm. This behavior is known as the

a. reflexive grasp.
b. proximodistal grasp.
c. pincer grasp.
d. ulnar grasp.

9. Which of the following is true of motor development?

a. Only nature is involved in motor development.
b. Only nurture is involved in motor development.
c. Nature and nurture are both involved in motor development.
d. Neither nature nor nurture is involved in motor development.

10. At what age does a child's visual acuity first approximate adult levels?

a. at birth
b. by one to two years of age
c. by three to five years of age
d. by six to ten years of age

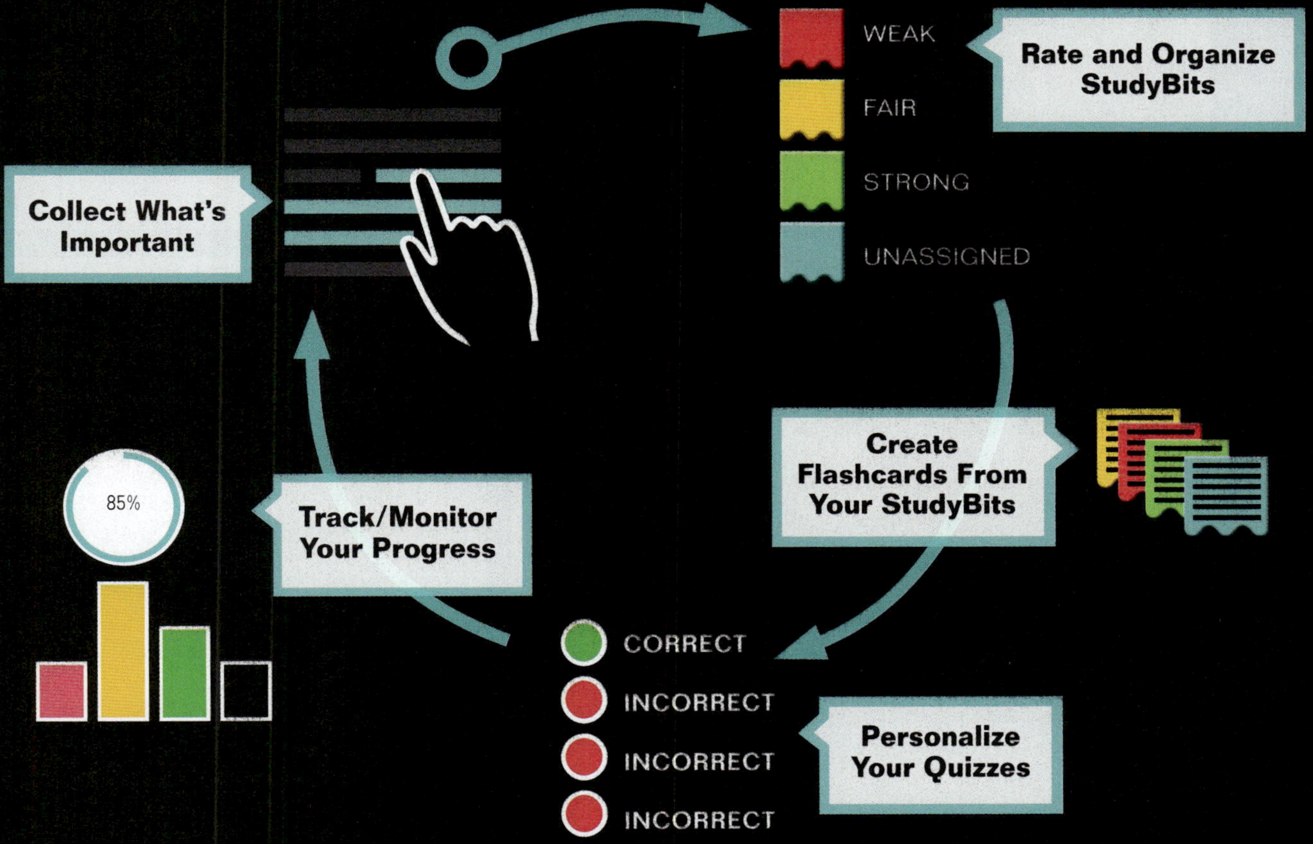

5 Infancy: Cognitive Development

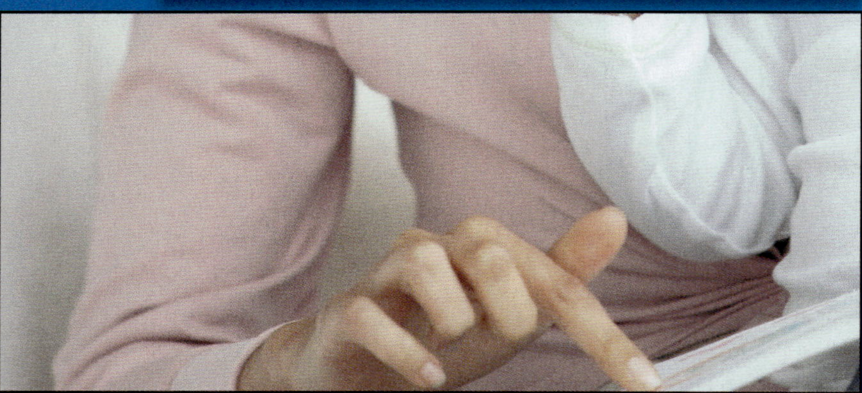

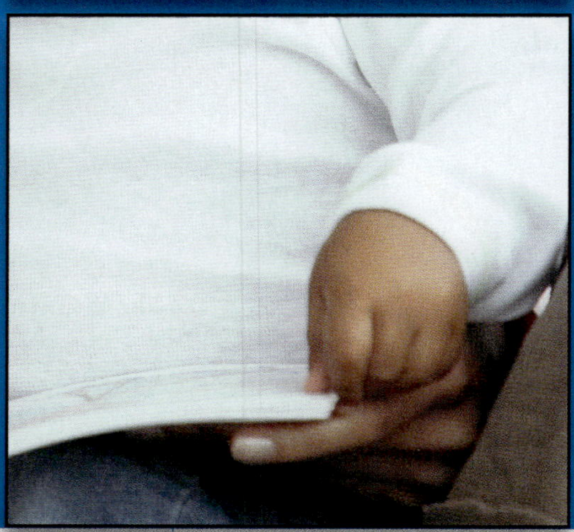

OJO Images Photography/Veer

LEARNING OUTCOMES

After studying this chapter, you will be able to...

5-1 Examine Jean Piaget's studies of cognitive development

5-2 Discuss the information-processing approach to cognitive development

5-3 Identify individual differences in intelligence among infants

5-4 Examine language development in infants

After you finish this chapter, go to **PAGE 108** for **STUDY TOOLS**

Laurent...resumes his experiments of the day before. He grabs in succession a celluloid swan, a box, etc., stretches out his arm and lets them fall. He distinctly varies the position of the fall. Sometimes he stretches out his arm vertically, sometimes he holds it obliquely, in front of or behind his eyes, etc. When the object falls in a new position, he lets it fall two or three times more on the same place, as though to study the spatial relation; then he modifies the situation.

Cognitive development focuses on the development of children's ways of perceiving and mentally representing the world.

Is this a description of a scientist at work? In a way, it is. Although Swiss psychologist Jean Piaget ([1936] 1963) was describing his 11-month-old son Laurent, children of this age frequently act like scientists, performing what Piaget called "experiments in order to see."

5-1 COGNITIVE DEVELOPMENT: JEAN PIAGET

Cognitive development focuses on the development of children's ways of perceiving and mentally representing the world. Piaget labeled children's concepts of the world *schemes*. He hypothesized that children try to use *assimilation* to absorb new events into existing schemes. When assimilation does not allow the child to make sense of novel events, children try to modify existing schemes through *accommodation*.

Piaget ([1936] 1963) hypothesized that cognitive processes develop in an orderly sequence of stages. Some children may advance more quickly than others, but the sequence remains constant (Taber, 2013; Tryphon & Voneche, 2013). Piaget identified four stages of cognitive development: sensorimotor, preoperational, concrete operational, and formal operational. In this chapter, we discuss the sensorimotor stage.

5-1a THE SENSORIMOTOR STAGE

Piaget's **sensorimotor stage** refers to the first two years of cognitive development, a time during which infants progress from responding to events with reflexes, or ready-made schemes, to goal-oriented behavior. Piaget divided the sensorimotor stage into six substages. In each substage, earlier forms of behavior are repeated, varied, and coordinated.

sensorimotor stage Piaget's first stage of cognitive development, which lasts through infancy and is generally characterized by increasingly complex coordination of sensory experiences with motor activity.

1. SIMPLE REFLEXES The first substage covers the first month after birth. It is dominated by the assimilation of sources of stimulation into inborn reflexes such as grasping or visual tracking. At birth, reflexes seem stereotypical and inflexible. But even within the first few hours, neonates begin to modify reflexes as a result of experience. For example, infants will adapt patterns of sucking to the shape of the nipple and the rate of flow of fluid. During the first month or so, however, infants

Steve Allen/Stockbyte/Jupiter Images

TRUTH OR FICTION?

T	F	For two-month-old infants, "out of sight" is truly "out of mind."
T	F	A one-hour-old infant may imitate an adult who sticks out his or her tongue.
T	F	Psychologists can begin to measure intelligence in infancy.
T	F	Infant crying is a primitive form of language.
T	F	You can advance children's development of pronunciation by correcting their errors.
T	F	Children are "prewired" to listen to language in such a way that they come to understand rules of grammar.

apparently make no connection between stimulation perceived through different sensory modalities. They make no effort to grasp objects that they visually track.

2. PRIMARY CIRCULAR REACTIONS The second substage, primary circular reactions, lasts from about one to four months of age and is characterized by the beginnings of the ability to coordinate various sensorimotor schemes. Infants tend to repeat stimulating actions that first occurred by chance. They may lift an arm repeatedly to bring it into view. **Primary circular reactions** focus on the infant's own body rather than on the external environment. Piaget noticed the following primary circular reaction in his son Laurent:

> *At 2 months 4 days, Laurent by chance discovers his right index finger and looks at it briefly. At 2 months 11 days, he inspects for a moment his open right hand, perceived by chance. At 2 months 17 days, he follows its spontaneous movement for a moment, then examines it several times while it searches for his nose or rubs his eye.*
>
> —Piaget ([1936] 1963, pp. 96–97)

Thus, Laurent, early in the third month, visually tracks the behavior of his hands, but his visual observations do not affect their movement. In terms of assimilation and accommodation, the child is attempting to assimilate the motor scheme (moving the hand) into the sensory scheme (looking at it). But the schemes do not automatically fit. Several days of apparent trial and error pass, during which the infant seems to be trying to make accommodations so that they will fit. By the third month, infants may examine objects repeatedly and intensely. It seems that the infant is no longer simply looking and seeing but is now "looking in order to see."

primary circular reactions the repetition of actions that first occurred by chance and that focus on the infant's own body.

secondary circular reactions the repetition of actions that produce an effect on the environment.

Because Laurent (and other infants) will repeat actions that allow them to see, cognitive-developmental psychologists consider sensorimotor coordination self-reinforcing. Laurent is acting on his hands to keep them in his field of vision. Piaget considers the desire to prolong stimulation to be as "basic" as the drives of hunger or thirst.

3. SECONDARY CIRCULAR REACTIONS The third substage lasts from about four to eight months and is characterized by **secondary circular reactions**, in which patterns of activity are repeated because of their effect on the environment. In the second substage (primary circular reactions), infants are focused on their own bodies, as in the example given with Laurent. In the third substage (secondary circular reactions), the focus shifts to objects and environmental events. Infants may now learn to pull strings in order to make a plastic face appear or to shake an object in order to hear it rattle.

4. COORDINATION OF SECONDARY SCHEMES In the fourth substage, which lasts from about 8 to 12 months of age, infants no longer act simply to prolong interesting occurrences. Now they can coordinate schemes to attain specific goals. Infants begin to show intentional, goal-directed behavior in which they differentiate between the means of achieving a goal and the goal or end itself. For example, they may lift a piece of cloth to reach a toy that they had seen a parent place under the cloth earlier. In this example, the scheme of picking up the cloth (the means) is coordinated with the scheme of reaching for the toy

Picture Partners/Alamy stock Photo

1. In the first substage, neonates assimilate sources of stimulation into reflexive responses.

Picture Partners/Alamy Stock Photo

2. In the second substage, infants repeat stimulating actions that first occurred by chance (primary circular reactions).

© Matt Brasier/Masterfile

3. In the third substage, patterns of activity are repeated because of their effect on the environment (secondary circular reactions).

(the goal or end). This example indicates that the infant has mentally represented the toy placed under the cloth.

During the fourth substage, infants also gain the capacity to imitate gestures and sounds that they had previously ignored. The imitation of a facial gesture implies that infants have mentally represented their own faces and can tell what parts of their faces they are moving through feedback from facial muscles.

5. TERTIARY CIRCULAR REACTIONS In the fifth substage, which lasts from about 12 to 18 months of age, Piaget looked on the behavior of infants as characteristic of budding scientists. Infants now engage in **tertiary circular reactions**, or purposeful adaptations of established schemes to specific situations. Behavior takes on a new experimental quality, and infants may vary their actions dozens of times in a deliberate trial-and-error fashion to learn how things work.

Piaget reported an example of tertiary circular reactions by his daughter Jacqueline. The episode was an experiment in which Piaget placed a stick outside Jacqueline's playpen, which had wooden bars (Piaget, 1963 [1936]). At first, Jacqueline grasped the stick and tried to pull it sideways into the playpen. The stick was too long and could not fit through the bars. After days of overt trial and error, however, Jacqueline discovered that she could bring the stick between the bars by turning it upright. In the sixth substage, described next, infants apparently engage in mental trial and error before displaying the correct overt response.

6. INVENTION OF NEW MEANS THROUGH MENTAL COMBINATIONS The sixth substage lasts from about 18 to 24 months of age. It serves as a transition between sensorimotor development and the development of symbolic thought. External exploration is replaced by mental exploration. At about 18 months, children may also use imitation to symbolize or stand for a plan of action.

Piaget presented his other children, Lucienne and Laurent, with the playpen and stick problem at the age of 18 months old. Rather than engage in overt trial and error, the 18-month-old children sat and studied the situation for a few moments. Then they grasped the stick, turned it upright, and brought it into the playpen with little overt effort. Lucienne and Laurent apparently mentally represented the stick and the bars of the playpen and perceived that the stick would not fit through as it was. They must then have rotated the mental image of the stick until they perceived a position that would allow the stick to pass between the bars.

5-1b DEVELOPMENT OF OBJECT PERMANENCE

The appearance of **object permanence** is an important aspect of sensorimotor development. Object permanence is the recognition that an object or person continues to exist when out of sight. For example, your textbook continues to exist when you leave it in the library after studying for the big test, and an infant's mother continues to exist even when she is in another room. The development of object permanence is tied into the development of infants' working memory and reasoning ability (Yermolayeva & Rakison, 2014; Reynolds & Romano, 2016).

tertiary circular reactions the purposeful adaptation of established schemes to new situations.

object permanence recognition that objects continue to exist when they are not in view.

Myrleen Pearson/PhotoEdit

David Mendelsohn/Masterfile

© Stephen Ausmus/Courtesy of the USDA

4. In the fourth substage, infants coordinate their behavior to attain specific goals (coordinating secondary schemes).

5. In the fifth substage, infants use overt trial and error to learn how things work (tertiary circular reactions).

6. In the sixth substage, infants use mental trial and error in solving problems.

Neonates show no tendency to respond to objects that are not within their immediate sensory grasp. By the age of two months, infants may show some surprise if an object (such as a toy duck) is placed behind a screen and then taken away so that when the screen is lifted, it is absent. However, they make no effort to search for the missing object. (See Figure 5.1.) Through the first six months or so, when the screen is placed between the object and the infant, the infant behaves as though the object is no longer there. It is true that "out of sight" is "out of mind" for two-month-old infants. Apparently, they do not yet reliably mentally represent objects they see.

There are some interesting advances in the development of the object concept by about the sixth month (Piaget's substage 3). For example, an infant at this age will tend to look for an object that has been dropped, behavior that suggests some form of object permanence. By this age, there is also reason to believe that the infant perceives a mental representation (image) of an object, such as a favorite toy, in response to sensory impressions of part of the object. This perception is shown by the infant's reaching for an object that is partly hidden.

A-not-B error the error made when an infant selects a familiar hiding place (A) for an object rather than a new hiding place, even after the infant has seen it hidden in the new place.

TRUTH

T F For two-month-old infants, "out of sight" is truly "out of mind."

It is true that "out of sight" is "out of mind" for two-month-old infants. They do not yet reliably mentally represent the objects they see.

By 8 to 12 months of age (Piaget's substage 4), infants will seek to retrieve objects that have been completely hidden. But in observing his own children, Piaget (1963 [1936]) noted an interesting error known as the **A-not-B error**. Piaget repeatedly hid a toy behind a screen (A), and each time, his infant removed the screen and retrieved the toy. Then, as the infant watched, Piaget

FIG.5.1 DEVELOPMENT OF OBJECT PERMANENCE

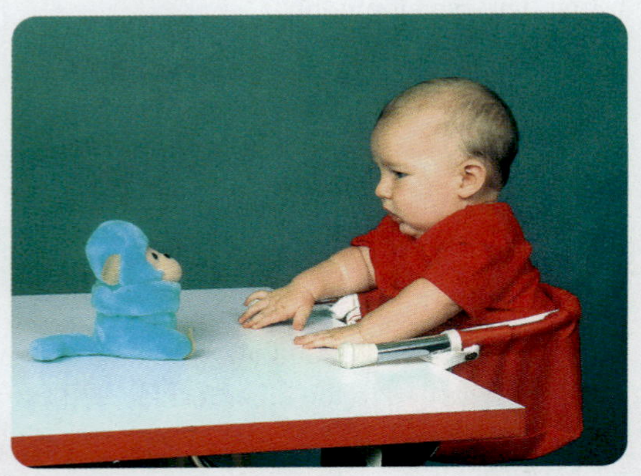

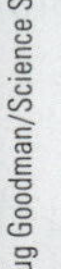
Doug Goodman/Science Source

Doug Goodman / Science Source

Doug Goodman / Science Source

Doug Goodman / Science Source

The infant in the top row is in the early part of the sensorimotor stage, in which "out of sight" is literally "out of mind." Once the toy is screened by the piece of paper, the infant loses interest in it. Piaget would have said that the toy is not yet "mentally represented." The older infant in the bottom row has mentally represented an object, and pushes through the towel to reach it after it has been screened from sight.

hid the toy behind another screen (B) in a different place. Still, the infant tried to recover the toy by pushing aside the first screen (A). It is as though the child had learned that a certain motor activity would reinstate the missing toy. The child's concept of the object did not, at this age, extend to recognition that objects usually remain in the place where they have been most recently mentally represented.

Under certain conditions, nine- to ten-month-old infants do not show the A-not-B error. They apparently need a certain degree of maturation of the front lobes of the cerebral cortex, which fosters the development of working memory and attention (Cuevas & Bell, 2010). Also, if infants are allowed to search for the object immediately after seeing it hidden, the error often does not occur. But if they are forced to wait five or more seconds before looking, they are likely to commit the A-not-B error (Wellman et al., 1986).

5-1c EVALUATION OF PIAGET'S THEORY

Piaget's theory remains a comprehensive model of infant cognition. Many of his observations of his own infants have been confirmed by others. The pattern and sequence of events he described have been observed among American, European, African, and Asian infants (Werner, 1988). Still, research has raised questions about the validity of many of Piaget's claims (Reed, 2013).

First, most researchers now agree that cognitive development is not as tied to discrete stages as Piaget suggested (Fuller, 2011; Reed, 2013). Although later developments seem to build on earlier ones, the process appears to be more gradual than discontinuous.

Second, Piaget emphasized the role of maturation, almost to the point of excluding adult and peer influences on cognitive development. However, these interpersonal influences have been shown to play roles in cognitive development (Nisbett, 2016; Reed, 2013).

Third, Piaget appears to have underestimated infants' competence (Reed, 2013). For example, infants display object permanence earlier than he believed (Moore & Meltzoff, 2008). Also consider studies on **deferred imitation** (imitation of an action that may have occurred hours, days, or even weeks earlier). The presence of deferred imitation suggests that children have mentally represented behavior patterns. Piaget believed that deferred imitation appears at about 18 months, but others have found that infants show deferred imitation as early as nine months. In one study, nine-month-old infants watched an adult perform behaviors such as pushing a button to produce a beep (Meltzoff et al., 2013). When given a chance to play with the same objects a day later, many infants imitated the actions they had witnessed.

5-2 INFORMATION PROCESSING

The **information-processing approach** to cognitive development focuses on how children manipulate or process information coming in from the environment or already stored in the mind. Infants' tools for processing information include their memory and imitation.

5-2a INFANTS' MEMORY

Many of the cognitive capabilities of infants—recognizing the faces of familiar people, developing object permanence, and, in fact, learning in any form—depend on one critical aspect of cognitive development: their memory (Bauer et al., 2010). Even neonates demonstrate memory for stimuli to which they have been exposed previously. For example, neonates adjust their rate of sucking to hear a recording of their mother reading a story she had read aloud during the last weeks of pregnancy, as discussed in Chapter 2 (DeCasper & Fifer, 1980; DeCasper et al., 2011).

Memory improves dramatically between two and six months of age and then again by 12 months (Pelphrey et al., 2004; Rose et al., 2011). The improvement may indicate that older infants are more capable than younger ones of encoding (i.e., storing) information, retrieving information already stored, or both (Patel et al., 2013).

A fascinating series of studies by Carolyn Rovee-Collier and her colleagues (Giles & Rovee-Collier, 2011; Rovee-Collier, 1993) illustrates some of these developmental changes in infant memory. As shown in Figure 5.2, one end of a ribbon was tied to a brightly colored mobile suspended above the infant's crib. The other end was tied to the infant's ankle, so that when the infant kicked, the mobile moved. Infants quickly learned to increase their rate of kicking. To measure memory, the infant's ankle was again fastened to the mobile after a period of one or more days had elapsed. In one study, two-month-olds remembered how to make the mobile move after delays of up to three days, and three-month-olds remembered for more than a week (Greco et al., 1986).

Infant memory can be improved if infants receive a reminder ("priming") before their memory is tested (Imuta et al., 2013).

deferred imitation the imitation of people and events that occurred in the past.

information-processing approach the view of cognitive development that focuses on how children manipulate sensory information and/or information stored in memory.

FIG.5.2 INVESTIGATING INFANT MEMORY

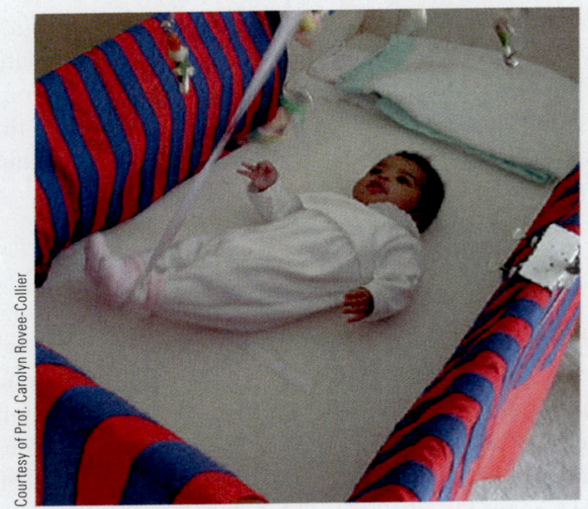

Courtesy of Prof. Carolyn Rovee-Collier

In this technique, developed by Carolyn Rovee-Collier, the infant's ankle is connected to a mobile by a ribbon. Infants quickly learn to kick to make the mobile move. Two- and three-month-olds remember how to perform this feat after a delay of a few days. If they are given a reminder, such as simply viewing the mobile, their memory lasts for two to four weeks.

In one study infants were shown the moving mobile on the day before the memory test, but they were not allowed to activate it. Under these conditions, three-month-olds remembered how to move the mobile after a 28-day delay (Rovee-Collier, 1993).

5-2b IMITATION: INFANT SEE, INFANT DO?

Imitation is the basis for much of human learning. Deferred imitation—that is, the imitation of actions after a time delay—occurs as early as six months of age (Campanella & Rovee-Collier, 2005; Schneider, 2015). To help them remember the imitated act, infants are usually permitted to practice it when they learn it. But in one study, 12-month-old infants were prevented from practicing the behavior they imitated. Yet they were able to demonstrate it four weeks later, suggesting that they had mentally represented the act (Klein & Meltzoff, 1999).

But infants can imitate certain actions at a much earlier age. Neonates only 0.7 to 71 hours old have been found to imitate adults who open their mouths or stick out their tongues (Meltzoff et al., 2013; Fogassi & Rizzolatti, 2013; see Figure 5.3).

TRUTH

(T) F A one-hour-old infant may imitate an adult who sticks out his or her tongue.

It is true that a one-hour-old infant may imitate an adult who sticks out his or her tongue. This feat is apparently made possible by mirror neurons.

Some studies have not found imitation in early infancy (Abravanel & DeYong, 1991), and one key factor may be the infants' age. The studies that find imitation generally have been done with very young infants—up to two weeks old—whereas the studies that do not find imitation have tended to use older infants. Therefore, the imitation of neonates is likely to be reflexive—and made possible, as we will see, by "mirror neurons." Thus, imitation might disappear when reflexes are "dropping out" and re-emerge when it has a firmer cognitive footing.

MIRROR NEURONS Many researchers believe that social organization and human culture are made possible by certain kinds of neurons that are present at birth. And

FIG.5.3 IMITATION IN INFANTS

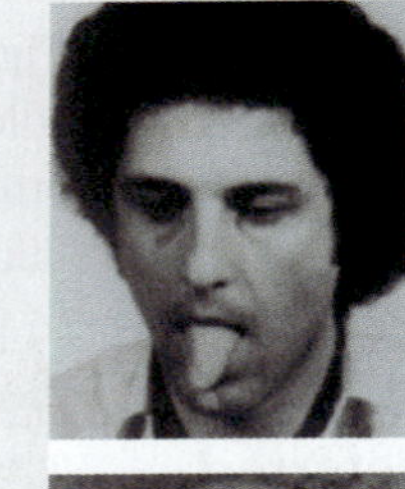

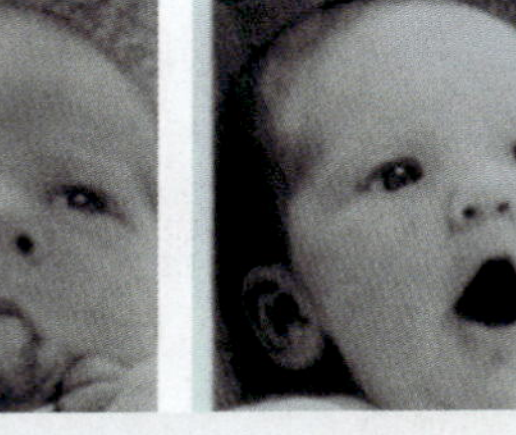
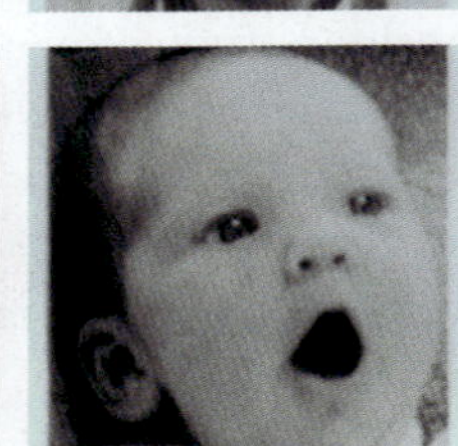
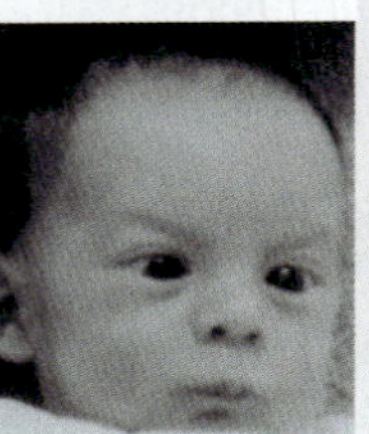

A.N. Meltzoff & M.K. Moore, "Imitation of facial and manual gestures by human neonates." Science, 1977, 198, 75–78.

These two- to three-week-old infants are imitating the facial gestures of an adult experimenter. How are we to interpret these findings? Can we say that the infants "knew" what the experimenter was doing and "chose" to imitate the behavior, or is there another explanation?

these neurons, like so many other important psychological discoveries, were found by accident (Cozolino, 2014; Fogassi & Rizzolatti, 2013).

A research team in Parma, Italy, headed by Vittorio Gallese and including Rizzolatti (Gallese et al., 1996), was recording the activity of individual neurons in monkeys' brains as the animals reached for objects. One of the researchers reached for an object that had been handled by a monkey, and quite to his surprise, a neuron in the monkey's brain fired in the same way it had fired when the animal had picked up the object. The research team followed up the phenomenon and discovered many such neurons in the frontal lobes of their monkeys, just before the motor cortex, which they dubbed *mirror neurons*. These *mirror neurons*, also found in humans, are activated when the individual performs a motor act or observes another individual engaging in the same act (Cattaneo et al., 2010; see Figure 5.4).

Mirror neurons in humans are also connected with emotions. Certain regions of the brain—particularly in the frontal lobe—are active when people experience emotions such as disgust, happiness, pain, and also when they observe another person experiencing an emotion (Rizzolati & Fabbri-Destro, 2011). It thus appears that there is a neural basis for empathy—that is, the identification or vicarious experiencing of feelings in others based on the observation of visual and other cues.

It has also been suggested that mirror neurons are connected with the built-in human capacity to acquire language (Corballis, 2010).

Photobac/Shutterstock.com

FIG.5.4 IMITATION IN INFANT MONKEYS

Gross L (2006) Evolution of Neonatal Imitation. PLoS Biol 4(9): e311. doi:10.1371/journal. pbio.0040311, © 2006 Public Library of Science

A newborn rhesus monkey imitates protrusion of the tongue, a feat made possible by mirror neurons, not by learning.

Mirror neurons are also apparently connected with gender differences in empathy (females show more of it) and the instinctive human ability to acquire language (Arbib, 2015; Brucker et al., 2015).

5-3 INDIVIDUAL DIFFERENCES IN COGNITIVE FUNCTIONING AMONG INFANTS

Cognitive development does not proceed in the same way or at the same pace for all infants. Efforts to understand the development of infant differences in cognitive development have relied on so-called scales of infant development or infant intelligence.

Measuring cognition or intelligence in infants is quite different from measuring it in adults. Infants cannot, of course, be assessed by asking them to explain the meanings of words, the similarity between concepts, or the rationales for social rules. One of the most important tests of intellectual development among infants—the Bayley Scales of Infant Development, constructed in 1933 by psychologist Nancy Bayley and revised since—contains very different kinds of items.

The Bayley test consists of mental-scale items and motor-scale items. The mental scale assesses verbal communication, perceptual skills, learning and memory, and problem-solving skills. The motor scale assesses gross motor skills, such as standing, walking, and climbing, and fine motor skills, as shown by the ability to manipulate the hands and fingers. A behavior rating scale based on examiner observation of the child during the test is also used. The behavior rating scale assesses attention span, goal directedness, persistence, and aspects of social and emotional development. Table 5.1 contains sample items from the mental and motor scales and shows the ages at which 50% of the infants taking the test passed the items.

TABLE 5.1	ITEMS FROM THE BAYLEY SCALES OF INFANT DEVELOPMENT (BSID–II)	
Age	**Mental-Scale Items**	**Motor-Scale Items**
1 month	The infant quiets when picked up.	The infant makes a postural adjustment when put to examiner's shoulder.
2 months	When examiner presents two objects (bell and rattle) above the infant in a crib, the infant glances back and forth from one to the other.	The infant holds his or her head steady when being carried about in a vertical position.
5 months	The infant is observed to transfer an object from one hand to the other during play.	When seated at a feeding-type table and presented with a sugar pill that is out of reach, the infant attempts to pick it up.
8 months	When an object (toy) in plain view of the infant (i.e., on a table) is covered by a cup, the infant removes the cup to retrieve the object.	The infant raises herself or himself into a sitting position.
12 months	The infant imitates words that are spoken by the examiner	When requested by the examiner, the infant stands up from a position in which she or he had been lying on her or his back on the floor.
14–16 months	The infant builds a tower with two cubes (blocks) after the examiner demonstrates the behavior.	The infant walks alone with good coordination.

Even though psychologists can begin to measure intelligence in infancy, they use items that differ from the kinds of items used with older children and adults. It remains unclear how well results obtained in infancy predict intellectual functioning at later ages.

F Psychologists can begin to measure intelligence in infancy.

It is true that psychologists begin to measure intelligence in infancy, but they use items that differ from the kinds of items used with older children and adults. (There is always controversy about what researchers are actually measuring when they set out to measure "intelligence.")

5-3a TESTING INFANTS: WHY AND WITH WHAT?

As you can imagine, it is no easy matter to test an infant. The items must be administered on a one-to-one basis by a patient tester, and it can be difficult to judge whether the infant is showing the targeted response. Why, then, do we test infants?

One reason is to screen infants for handicaps. A tester may be able to detect early signs of sensory or neurological problems, as suggested by development of visual–motor coordination. In addition to the Bayley scales, a number of tests have been developed to screen infants for such difficulties, including the Brazelton Neonatal Behavioral Assessment Scale (see Chapter 3) and the Denver Developmental Screening Test.

5-3b INSTABILITY OF INTELLIGENCE SCORES ATTAINED IN INFANCY

Researchers have also tried to use infant scales to predict development, but this effort has been less than successful. One study found that scores obtained during the first year of life correlated moderately at best with scores obtained a year later (Harris et al., 2005). Certain items on the Bayley scales appear to predict related intellectual skills later in childhood. For example, Bayley items measuring infant motor skills predict subsequent fine motor and visual–spatial skills at six to eight years of age (Siegel, 1992). Bayley language items also predict language skills at the same age (Siegel, 1992).

Another study found that the Bayley scales and socioeconomic status were able to predict cognitive development among low-birth-weight children from 18 months to four years of age (Dezoete et al., 2003). But overall scores on the Bayley and other infant scales apparently do not predict school grades or IQ scores among school children very well (Bornstein & Colombo, 2012). Predictability of teenage and adult intelligence test scores becomes stronger once children reach the ages of six or seven (Bornstein & Colombo, 2012). Perhaps the sensorimotor test items used during infancy are not that strongly related to the verbal and symbolic items used to assess intelligence at later ages.

The overall conclusion seems to be that the Bayley scales can identify gross lags in development and relative strengths and weaknesses. However, they are only moderate predictors of intelligence scores even one year later, and are still poorer predictors of scores taken beyond longer stretches of time.

5-3c USE OF VISUAL RECOGNITION MEMORY

In a continuing effort to find aspects of intelligence and cognition that might remain consistent from infancy through later childhood, a number of researchers have recently focused on visual recognition memory (Reynolds & Romano, 2016). **Visual recognition memory** is the ability to discriminate previously seen objects from novel objects. This procedure is based on *habituation*.

Let us consider longitudinal studies of this type. Susan Rose and her colleagues (Rose et al., 1992) showed seven-month-old infants pictures of two identical faces. After 20 seconds, the pictures were replaced with one picture of a new face and a second picture of the familiar face. The amount of time the infants spent looking at each face in the second set of pictures was recorded. Some infants spent more time looking at the new face than at the older face, suggesting that they had better memory for visual stimulation. The children were given standard IQ tests yearly from ages one through six. It was found that the children with greater visual recognition memory later attained higher IQ scores.

Rose and her colleagues (2001, 2015) also showed that, from age to age, individual differences in capacity for visual recognition memory are stable. This finding is important because intelligence—the quality that many researchers seek to predict from visual recognition memory—is also theorized to be a reasonably stable trait. Similarly, items on intelligence tests are age graded; that is, older children perform better than younger children, even as developing intelligence remains constant. So, too, with visual recognition memory. Capacity for visual recognition memory increases over the first year after birth (Rose et al., 2015).

A number of other studies have examined the relationship between either infant visual recognition memory or preference for novel stimulation (which is a related measure) and later IQ scores. In general, they show good predictive validity for broad cognitive abilities throughout childhood, including measures of intelligence and language ability (Heimann et al., 2006; Rose et al., 2015).

In sum, scales of infant development may provide useful data as screening devices, as research instruments, or simply as a way to describe the things that infants do and do not do, but their predictive power as intelligence tests has been disappointing. Tests of visual recognition hold better promise as predictors of intelligence at older ages.

Now let us turn our attention to a fascinating aspect of cognitive development, the development of language.

Infant intelligence scores are unstable; that is, a score in infancy cannot be considered to have accurate predictive power for scores obtained later in life.

John Lund/Annabelle Breakey/Blend Images/Corbis

5-4 LANGUAGE DEVELOPMENT

As children develop language skills, they often begin speaking about the things more closely connected with their environments and their needs. Children enjoy playing with language. In physical development, the most dramatic developments come early—fast and furious—long before the child is born. Language does not come quite as early, and its development may not seem quite so fast and furious. Nevertheless, during the years of infancy, most infants develop from creatures without language to little people who understand nearly all the things that are said to them and who relentlessly sputter words and simple sentences for all the world to hear.

5-4a EARLY VOCALIZATIONS

Children develop language according to an invariant sequence of steps, or stages, as outlined in Table 5.2. We begin with the **prelinguistic** vocalizations. True words are symbols of objects and events. Prelinguistic vocalizations, such as cooing and babbling, do not represent objects or actions, so infant crying is not a primitive form of language.

visual recognition memory the kind of memory shown in an infant's ability to discriminate previously seen objects from novel objects.

prelinguistic vocalizations made by the infant before the use of language.

FICTION

T (F) Infant crying is a primitive form of language.

It is not true that infant crying is a primitive form of language. In true language, words are symbols for objects or events. Cries may express discomfort, but they are not symbols.

Newborn children, as parents are well aware, have an unlearned but highly effective form of verbal expression: crying and more crying. Crying is about the only sound that infants make during the first month. During the second month, infants begin **cooing**. Infants use their tongues when they coo. For this reason, coos are more articulated than cries. Coos are often vowel-like and may resemble extended "oohs" and "ahs." Cooing appears linked to feelings of pleasure or positive excitement. Infants tend not to coo when they are hungry, tired, or in pain.

Cries and coos are innate but can be modified by experience (Volterra et al., 2004; Waxman & Goswami, 2012). When parents respond positively to cooing by talking to their infants, smiling at them, and imitating them, cooing increases. Early parent–child "conversations," in which parents respond to coos and then pause as the infant coos, may foster infant awareness of taking turns as a way of verbally relating to other people.

By about eight months of age, cooing decreases markedly. Somewhere between six and nine months, children begin to babble. **Babbling** is the first vocalizing that sounds like human speech. In babbling, infants frequently combine consonants and vowels, as in *ba*, *ga*, and, sometimes, the much valued *dada* (McCardle et al., 2009). At first, dada is purely coincidental (sorry, you dads), despite the family's jubilation over its appearance.

In verbal interactions between infants and adults, the adults frequently repeat the syllables produced by their infants. They are likely to say "dadada" or "bababa" instead of simply "da" or "ba." Such redundancy apparently helps infants discriminate these sounds from others and further encourages them to imitate their parents (Elkind, 2007; Waxman & Goswami, 2012).

After infants have been babbling for a few months, parents often believe that their children are having conversations with themselves. At 10 to 12 months, infants

cooing prelinguistic vowel-like sounds that reflect feelings of positive excitement.

babbling the child's first vocalizations that have the sounds of speech.

TABLE 5.2 MILESTONES IN LANGUAGE DEVELOPMENT IN INFANCY

Approximate Age	Vocalization and Language
Birth	• Cries.
12 weeks	• Cries less. • Smiles when talked to and nodded at. • Engages in squealing and gurgling sounds (cooing). • Sustains cooing for 15–20 seconds.
16 weeks	• Responds to human sounds more definitely. • Turns head, searching for the speaker. • Chuckles occasionally.
20 weeks	• Cooing becomes interspersed with consonant-like sounds. • Vocalizations differ from the sounds of mature language.
6 months	• Cooing changes to single-syllable babbling. • Neither vowels nor consonants have fixed pattern of recurrence. • Common utterances sound somewhat like *ma*, *mu*, *da*, or *di*.
8 months	• Continuous repetition (reduplication) enters into babbling. • Patterns of intonation become distinct. • Utterances can signal emphasis and emotion.
10 months	• Vocalizations mixed with sound play, such as gurgling, bubble blowing. • Makes effort to imitate sounds made by older people with mixed success.
12 months	• Identical sound sequences replicated more often. • Words (e.g., *mamma* or *dada*) emerge. • Many words and requests understood (e.g., "Show me your eyes").
18 months	• Repertoire of 3–50 words. • Explosive vocabulary growth. • Babbling consists of several syllables with intricate intonation. • Little effort to communicate information. • Little joining of words into spontaneous two-word utterances. • Understands nearly everything spoken.
24 months	• Vocabulary more than 50 words, naming everything in the environment. • Spontaneous creation of two-word sentences. • Clear efforts to communicate.

Source: Table items adapted from Lenneberg (1967, pp. 128–130).
Note: Ages are approximations. Slower development does not necessarily indicate language problems.

tend to repeat syllables, showing what linguists refer to as **echolalia**. Parents overhear them going on and on, repeating consonant–vowel combinations ("ah-bah-bah-bah-bah"), pausing, and then switching to other combinations.

Toward the end of the first year, infants are also using patterns of rising and falling **intonation** that resemble the sounds of adult speech. It may sound as though the infant is trying to speak the parents' language. Parents may think that their children are babbling in English or in whatever tongue is spoken in the home.

5-4b DEVELOPMENT OF VOCABULARY

Vocabulary development refers to the child's learning the meanings of words. In general, children's **receptive vocabulary** development outpaces their **expressive vocabulary** development (Klee & Stokes, 2011). At any given time, they can understand more words than they can use. One study, for example, found that 12-month-olds could speak an average of 13 words but could comprehend the meaning of 84 (Tamis-LeMonda et al., 2006). Infants usually understand much of what others are saying well before they themselves utter any words at all. Their ability to segment speech sounds into meaningful units—or words—before 12 months is a good predictor of their vocabulary at 24 months (Newman et al., 2006).

THE CHILD'S FIRST WORDS Ah, that long-awaited first word! What a milestone! Sad to say, many parents miss it. They are not quite sure when their infants utter their first word, often because the first word is not pronounced clearly or because pronunciation varies from usage to usage.

A child's first word typically is spoken between the ages of 11 and 13 months, but a range of 8 to 18 months is considered normal (Klee & Stokes, 2011). First words tend to be brief, consisting of one or two syllables. Each syllable is likely to consist of a consonant followed by a vowel. Vocabulary acquisition is slow at first. It may take children three or four months to achieve a vocabulary of 10 to 30 words after the first word is spoken.

By about 18 months of age, children may be producing up to 50 words. Many of them are quite familiar, such as *no*, *cookie*, *mama*, *hi*, and *eat*. Others, such as *all gone* and *bye-bye*, may not be found in the dictionary, but they function as words. That is, they are used consistently to symbolize the same meaning.

More than half (65%) of children's first words make up "general nominals" and "specific nominals" (Hoff, 2014; Tamis-LeMonda et al., 2014). General nominals are similar to nouns in that they include the names of classes of objects (*car*, *ball*), animals (*doggy*, *cat*), and people (*boy*, *girl*), but they also include both personal and relative pronouns (*she, that*). Specific nominals are proper nouns, such as *Daddy* and *Rover*. Words expressing movement are frequently found in early speech.

At about 18 to 22 months of age, there is a rapid burst in vocabulary (Tamis-LeMonda et al., 2006). The child's vocabulary may increase from 50 to more than 300 words in only a few months. This vocabulary spurt could also be called a naming explosion because almost 75% of the words added during this time are nouns. The rapid pace of vocabulary growth continues through the preschool years, with children acquiring an average of nine new words per day (Hoff, 2006).

OVEREXTENSION Young children try to talk about more objects than they have words for. To accomplish their linguistic feats, children often extend the meaning of one word to refer to things and actions for which they do not have words (E. K. Johnson, 2016). This process is called **overextension**. Eve Clark (1973, 1975) studied diaries of infants' language development and found that overextensions are generally based on perceived similarities in function or form between the original object or action and the new one. She provides the example of the word *mooi*, which one child originally used to designate the moon. The child then overextended *mooi* to designate all round objects, including the letter *o* and cookies and cakes. Overextensions gradually pull back to their proper references as the child's vocabulary and ability to classify objects develop (E. K. Johnson, 2016).

5-4c DEVELOPMENT OF SENTENCES

The infant's first sentences are typically one-word utterances, but they express complete ideas and therefore can be thought of as sentences. Roger Brown (1973) called brief expressions that have the meanings of sentences **telegraphic speech**. Adults who write telegrams (or, today, text messages) often use principles of syntax to cut out unnecessary words. "Home Tuesday" might stand for "I expect to be home on Tuesday." Similarly, only the essential words are used in children's telegraphic speech—in particular, nouns, verbs, and some modifiers.

echolalia the automatic repetition of sounds or words.

intonation the use of pitches of varying levels to help communicate meaning.

receptive vocabulary the number of words one understands.

expressive vocabulary the number of words one can use in the production of language.

overextension use of words in situations in which their meanings become extended.

telegraphic speech type of speech in which only the essential words are used.

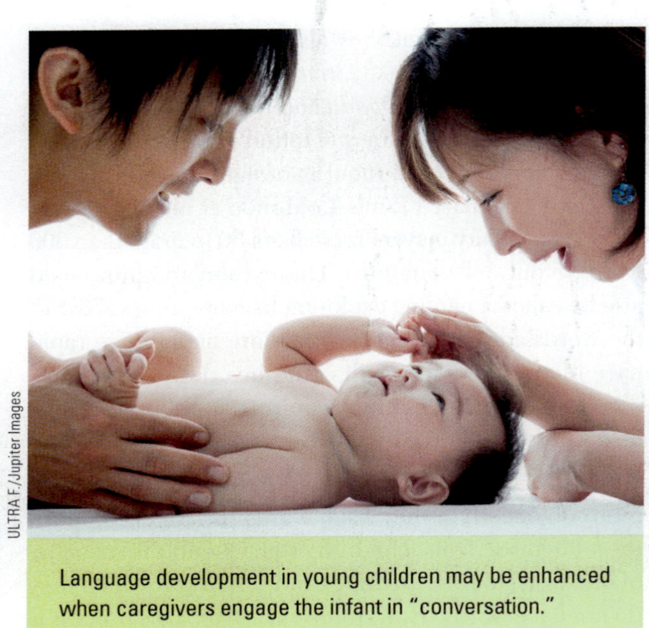
ULTRA F./Jupiter Images

Language development in young children may be enhanced when caregivers engage the infant in "conversation."

MEAN LENGTH OF UTTERANCE The **mean length of utterance (MLU)** is the average number of **morphemes** that communicators use in their sentences. Morphemes are the smallest units of meaning in a language. A morpheme may be a whole word or part of a word, such as a prefix or suffix. For example, the word *walked* consists of two morphemes: the verb *walk* and the suffix *ed*, which changes the verb to the past tense. In Figure 5.5, we see the relationship between chronological age and MLU for three children tracked by Roger Brown (1973, 1977): Lin, Victor, and Sarah.

The patterns of growth in MLU are similar for each child, showing swift upward movement, broken by intermittent and brief regressions. Figure 5.5 also shows something about individual differences. Lin was precocious compared with Victor and Sarah, extending her MLU at much earlier ages. But as suggested earlier, the receptive language of all three children would have exceeded their expressive language at any given time. Also, Lin's earlier extension of MLU does not guarantee that she will show more complex expressive language than Victor and Sarah at maturity.

Let us now consider the features of two types of telegraphic speech: the holophrase and two-word utterances.

HOLOPHRASES **Holophrases** are single words that are used to express complex meanings. For example, *Mama* may be used by the child to signify meanings as varied as "There goes Mama," "Come here, Mama," and "You are Mama." Most children readily teach their parents what they intend by augmenting their holophrases with gestures, intonations, and reinforcers. That is, they act delighted when parents do as requested and howl when they do not.

TWO-WORD SENTENCES When the child's vocabulary consists of 50 to 100 words (usually somewhere between 18 and 24 months of age), telegraphic two-word sentences begin to appear (Tamis-LeMonda

FIG.5.5 MEAN LENGTH OF UTTERANCE FOR THREE CHILDREN

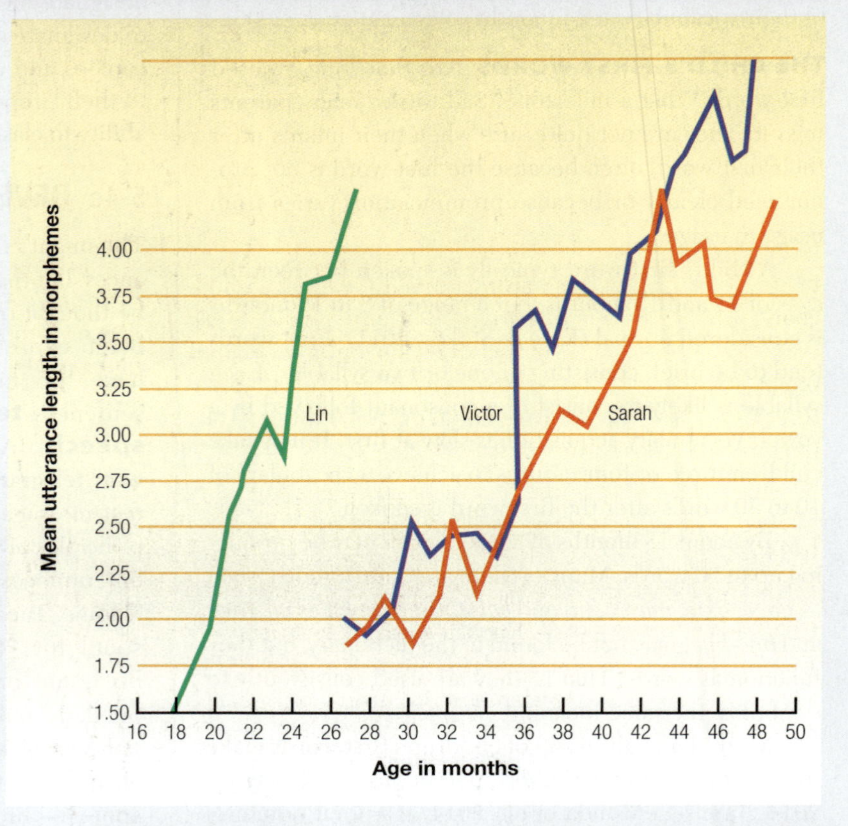

The mean length of utterance (MLU) increases rapidly once speech begins.

mean length of utterance (MLU) the average number of morphemes used in an utterance.

morpheme the smallest unit of meaning in a language.

holophrase a single word that is used to express complex meanings.

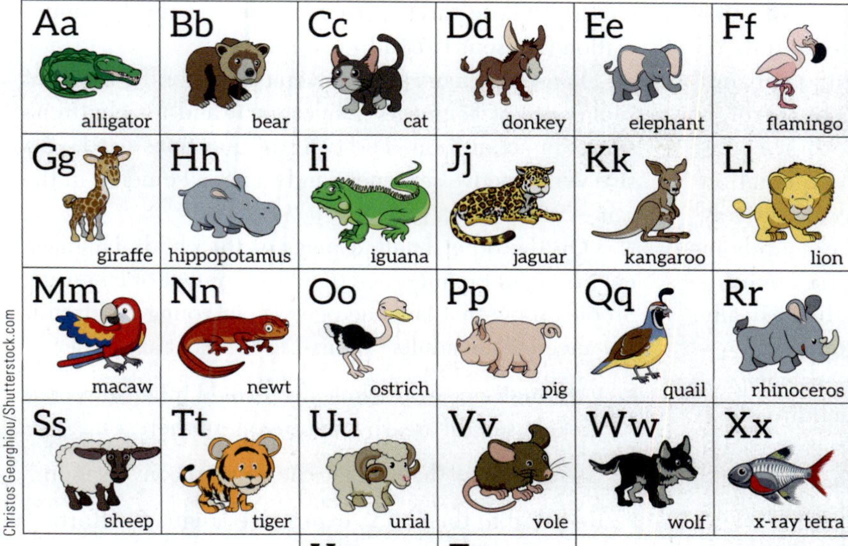

Christos Georghiou/Shutterstock.com

et al., 2006). In the sentence "That ball," the words *is* and *a* are implied.

Two-word sentences, although brief and telegraphic, show understanding of **syntax** (Slobin, 2001). The child will say "Sit chair," not "Chair sit," to tell a parent to sit in a chair. The child will say "My shoe," not "Shoe my," to show possession. "Mommy go" means Mommy is leaving, whereas "Go Mommy" expresses the wish for Mommy to go away.

5-4d THEORIES OF LANGUAGE DEVELOPMENT

Billions of children have learned the languages spoken by their parents and have passed them down, with minor changes, from generation to generation. But how do they do so? In discussing this question—and so many others—we refer to the possible roles of nature and nurture. Learning theorists have come down on the side of nurture, and those who point to a basic role for nature are said to hold a nativist view.

5-4e VIEWS THAT EMPHASIZE NURTURE

Learning plays an obvious role in language development. Children who are reared in English-speaking homes learn English, not Japanese or Russian. Learning theorists usually explain language development in terms of imitation and reinforcement.

THE ROLE OF IMITATION From a social cognitive perspective, parents serve as **models**. Children learn language, at least in part, by observation and imitation. Many vocabulary words, especially nouns and verbs, are learned by imitation. But imitative learning does not explain why children spontaneously utter phrases and sentences that they have not observed (Waxman & Goswami, 2012). Parents, for example, are unlikely to model utterances such as "Bye bye sock" and "All gone Daddy" but children say them. And children sometimes steadfastly avoid imitating certain language forms suggested by adults, even when the adults are insistent. Note the following exchange between two-year-old Ben and a (very frustrated) adult (Kuczaj, 1982, p. 48):

Ben: I like these candy. I like they.
Adult: You like them?
Ben: Yes, I like they.
Adult: Say them.
Ben: Them.
Adult: Say "I like them."
Ben: I like them.
Adult: Good.
Ben: I'm good. These candy good too.
Adult: Are they good?
Ben: Yes. I like they. You like they?

Ben is not resisting the adult because of obstinacy. He does repeat "I like them" when asked to do so. But when given the opportunity afterward to construct the object *them*, he reverts to using the subjective form *they*. Ben is likely at this period in his development to use his (erroneous) understanding of syntax spontaneously to actively produce his own language, rather than just imitate a model.

THE ROLE OF REINFORCEMENT B. F. Skinner (1957) allowed that prelinguistic vocalizations such as cooing and babbling may be inborn. But parents reinforce children for babbling that approximates the form of real words, such as *da*, which, in English, resembles *dog* or *daddy*. Children, in fact, do increase their babbling when it results in adults smiling at them, stroking them, and talking back to them. As the first year progresses, children babble the sounds of their native tongues with increasing frequency; foreign sounds tend to drop out. The behaviorist explains this pattern of changing

syntax the rules in a language for placing words in order to form sentences.

models in learning theory, those whose behaviors are imitated by others.

Hurst Photo/Shutterstock.com

frequencies in terms of reinforcement of the sounds of the adults' language and **extinction** of foreign sounds. Another (nonbehavioral) explanation is that children actively attend to the sounds in their linguistic environments and are intrinsically motivated to utter them.

From Skinner's perspective, children acquire their early vocabularies through **shaping**. That is, parents require that children's utterances be progressively closer to actual words before they are reinforced. In support of Skinner's position, research has shown that reinforcement can accelerate the growth of vocabulary in children (Kroeger & Nelson, 2006; Waxman & Goswami, 2012).

But recall Ben's refusal to be shaped into correct syntax. If the reinforcement explanation of language development were sufficient, parents' reinforcement would facilitate children's learning of syntax and pronunciation. However, parents are more likely to reinforce their children for the accuracy, or "truth value," of their utterances than for their grammatical correctness (Brown, 1973). The child who points down and says "The grass is purple" is not likely to be reinforced, despite correct syntax. But the enthusiastic child who shows her empty plate and blurts out "I eated it all up" is likely to be reinforced, despite the grammatical incorrectness of "eated" (Morgenstern et al., 2013).

Selective reinforcement of children's pronunciation can also backfire. Children whose parents reward proper pronunciation but correct poor pronunciation develop vocabulary more slowly than children whose parents are more tolerant about pronunciation (Nelson, 1973).

Learning theory also cannot account for the invariant sequences of language development and for children's spurts in acquisition. The types of questions used, passive versus active sentences and so on, all emerge in the same order.

On the other hand, aspects of the child's language environment do influence the development of language. Studies show that language growth in young children is enhanced when adults (Tamis-LeMonda et al., 2014):

- Use "motherese" (technically termed infant-directed speech; see the nearby feature on motherese).
- Use questions that engage the child in conversation.
- Respond to the child's expressive language efforts in a way that is "attuned"; for example, adults relate their speech to the child's utterance by saying "Yes, your doll is pretty" in response to the child's statement "My doll."
- Join the child in paying attention to a particular activity or toy.
- Gesture to help the child understand what they are saying.
- Describe aspects of the environment occupying the infant's current focus of attention.
- Read to the child.
- Talk to the child a great deal.

5-4f VIEWS THAT EMPHASIZE NATURE

The nativist view of language development holds that inborn factors cause children to attend to and acquire language in certain ways. From this perspective, children bring an inborn tendency in the form of neurological "prewiring" to language learning. According to Steven Pinker (2007), the structures that enable humans to perceive and produce language evolved in bits and pieces. Those individuals who possessed these "bits" and "pieces" were more likely to reach maturity and transmit their genes from generation to generation because communication ability increased their chances of survival.

FICTION

T (F) You can advance children's development of pronunciation by correcting their errors.

It is not necessarily true that you can advance children's development of pronunciation by correcting their errors. Their vocabulary may not develop as rapidly if you focus on pronunciation.

extinction decrease in frequency of a response due to absence of reinforcement.

shaping gradual building of complex behavior through reinforcement of successive approximations to the target behavior.

> "Since all normal humans talk but no house pets or house plants do, no matter how pampered, heredity must be involved in language. But since a child growing up in Japan speaks Japanese whereas the same child brought up in California would speak English, the environment is also crucial. Thus, there is no question about whether heredity or environment is involved in language, or even whether one or the other is "more important." Instead, . . . our best hope [might be] finding out how they interact."
>
> —Steven Pinker

Devesh Mistry / Alamy Stock Photo

PSYCHOLINGUISTIC THEORY According to **psycholinguistic theory**, language acquisition involves an interaction between environmental influences—such as exposure to parental speech and reinforcement—and an inborn tendency to acquire language. Noam Chomsky (1988, 1990) labeled this innate tendency a **language acquisition device (LAD)**. Evidence for an inborn tendency is found in the universality of human language abilities; in the regularity of the early production of sounds, even among deaf children; and in the invariant sequences of language development among all languages (Pinker, 2007).

The inborn tendency primes the nervous system to learn grammar. On the surface, languages differ much in vocabulary and grammar. Chomsky labels these elements the **surface structure** of language. However, Chomsky believes that the LAD serves children all over the world because languages share a "universal grammar"—an underlying **deep structure** or set of rules for transforming ideas into sentences. From Chomsky's perspective, children are genetically prewired to attend to language and deduce the rules for constructing sentences from ideas. That is, it appears that children are prewired to listen to language in such a way that they come to understand rules of grammar.

TRUTH

 F Children are "prewired" to listen to language in such a way that they come to understand rules of grammar.

It is apparently true that children are "prewired" to listen to language in such a way that they come to understand rules of grammar. There is clearly an inborn biological component to language acquisition.

BRAIN STRUCTURES INVOLVED IN LANGUAGE

Many parts of the brain are involved in language development; however, some of the key biological structures that may provide the basis for the functions of the LAD are based in the left hemisphere of the cerebral cortex for nearly all right-handed people and for two out of three left-handed people (Hoff, 2014). In the left hemisphere, the two areas most involved in speech are Broca's area and Wernicke's area (see Figure 5.6 on page 106). Damage to either area is likely to cause an **aphasia**—a disruption in the ability to understand or produce language.

Broca's area is located near the section of the motor cortex that controls the muscles of the tongue and throat and other areas of the face that are used in speech. When Broca's area is damaged, people speak laboriously in a pattern termed **Broca's aphasia**. But they can readily understand speech.

psycholinguistic theory the view that language learning involves an interaction between environmental influences and an inborn tendency to acquire language.

language acquisition device (LAD) neural "prewiring" that eases the child's learning of grammar.

surface structure the superficial grammatical construction of a sentence.

deep structure the underlying meaning of a sentence.

aphasia a disruption in the ability to understand or produce language.

Broca's aphasia an aphasia caused by damage to Broca's area and characterized by difficulty speaking.

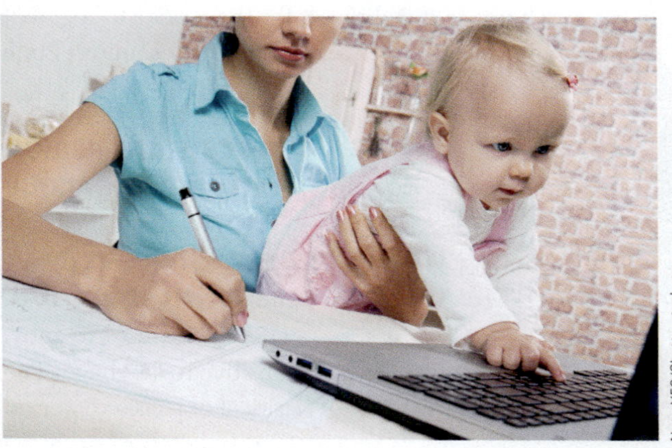

NotarYES/Shutterstock.com

FIG.5.6 BROCA'S AND WERNICKE'S AREAS OF THE CEREBRAL CORTEX

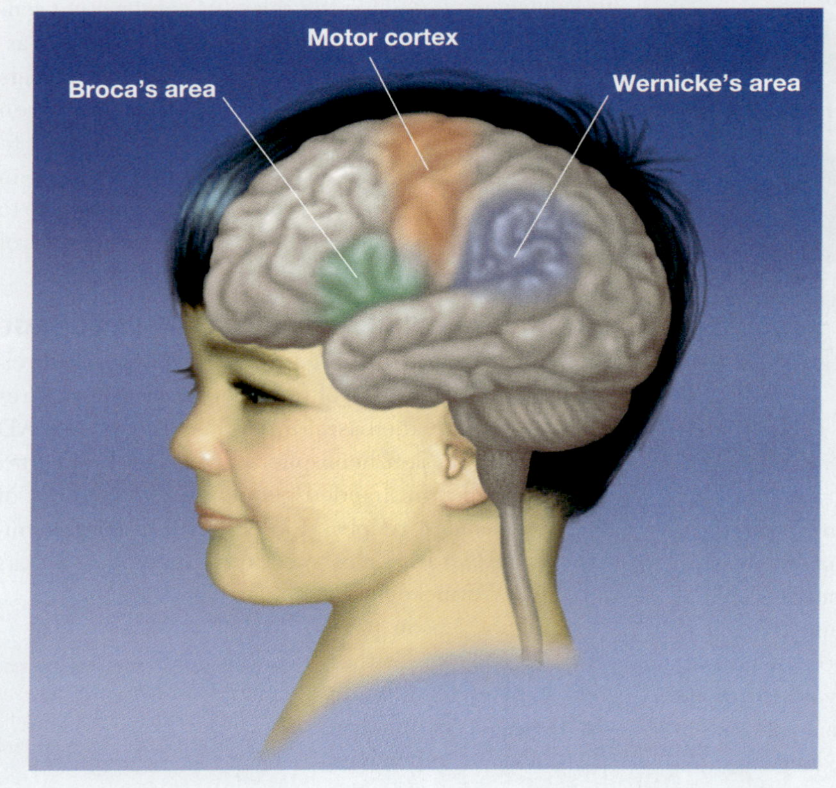

Wernicke's area lies near the auditory cortex and is connected to Broca's area by nerves. People with damage to Wernicke's area may show **Wernicke's aphasia**, in which they speak freely and with proper syntax but have trouble understanding speech and finding the words to express themselves.

A part of the brain called the angular gyrus lies between the visual cortex and Wernicke's area. The angular gyrus "translates" visual information, such as written words, into auditory information (sounds) and sends it on to Wernicke's area. Problems in the angular gyrus can cause problems in reading because it is difficult for the reader to segment words into sounds (Pugh et al., 2013).

wernicke's aphasia an aphasia caused by damage to Wernicke's area and characterized by impaired comprehension of speech and difficulty producing the right word.

critical period the period from about 18 months to puberty when the brain is especially capable of learning language. Also called the *sensitive period.*

THE CRITICAL PERIOD FOR LANGUAGE ACQUISITION Language learning is most efficient during the **critical period**, when children are most sensitive to language. The critical or sensitive period begins at about 18 to 24 months and lasts until puberty (Bedny et al., 2012; Werker & Hensch, 2015). During this period, neural development provides plasticity of the brain.

Evidence for a critical period is found in recovery from brain injuries in some people. Injuries to the hemisphere that controls language (usually the left hemisphere) can impair or destroy the ability to speak. But before puberty, children suffering left-hemisphere injuries frequently recover a good deal of speaking ability. In young children, left-hemisphere damage may encourage the development of language functions in the right hemisphere. But adaptation ability wanes in adolescence, when brain tissue has reached adult levels of differentiation (Snow, 2006; Garvain, 2015).

The best way to determine whether people are capable of acquiring language once they have passed puberty would be to run an experiment in which one or more children were reared in such severe isolation that they were not exposed to language until puberty. Of course, such an experiment could not be run for ethical reasons. However, the disturbing case history of Genie offers insights into whether there is a critical period for language development (Friedmann & Rusou, 2015).

Genie's father locked her in a small room at the age of 20 months and kept her there until she was 13 years old. Her social contacts during this period were limited to her mother, who entered the room only to feed Genie, and to beatings by her father. When Genie was rescued, she weighed only about 60 pounds, did not speak, was not toilet trained, and could barely stand. She was placed in a foster home, and thereafter her language development followed the normal sequence of much younger children in a number of ways. Five years after her liberation, however, Genie's language remained largely telegraphic. She still showed significant problems with syntax, such as failing to reverse subjects and verbs to phrase questions.

Genie's language development provides support for the critical-period hypothesis, although her language problems might also be partly attributed to her years of malnutrition and abuse. Her efforts to acquire English after puberty were laborious, and the results

"Motherese"—Of "Yummy-Yummy" and "Kitty Cats"

One way that adults attempt to prompt the language development of young children is through the use of baby talk, or "motherese," referred to more technically as *infant-directed speech (IDS)* (Meltzoff et al., 2013; Singh et al., 2009). *Motherese* is a limiting term because grandparents, fathers, siblings, and unrelated people have also been observed using IDS (Braarud & Stormark, 2008). Moreover, women (but usually not men) often talk to their pets as if they were infants (Xu et al., 2013). Infant-directed speech is used in languages as diverse as Arabic, English, Comanche, Italian, French, German, Xhosa (an African tongue), Japanese, Mandarin Chinese, and even a Thai sign language (Lee et al., 2010). Researchers have found that IDS has the following characteristics (McMurray et al., 2013; Meltzoff & Brooks, 2009):

- **It is spoken more slowly and at a higher pitch than speech addressed to adults. There are distinct pauses between ideas.**
- **Sentences are brief, and adults try to speak in a grammatically correct manner.**
- **Sentences are simple in syntax. The focus is on nouns, verbs, and just a few modifiers.**
- **Key words are placed at the ends of sentences and spoken in a higher and louder voice.**
- **The diminutive morpheme y is frequently added to nouns. *Dad* becomes *Daddy*, and *horse* becomes *horsey*.**
- **Adults repeat sentences several times, sometimes using minor variations, as in "Show me your nose." "Where is your nose?" "Can you touch your nose?" Adults also rephrase children's utterances to expand children's awareness of their expressive opportunities. If the child says, "Baby shoe," the mother may reply, "Yes, that's your shoe. Shall Mommy put the shoe on baby's foot?"**
- **It includes duplication. *Yummy* becomes *yummy-yummy*. *Daddy* may alternate with *Da-da*.**
- **Much IDS focuses on naming objects. Vocabulary is concrete and refers to the child's environment. For example, stuffed lions may be called "kitties."**
- **Objects may be overdescribed with compound labels. Rabbits may become "bunny rabbits," and cats may become "kitty cats." Users of IDS try to ensure that they are using at least one label that the child will recognize.**
- **Parents speak for the children, as in "Is baby tired?" "Oh, we're so tired." "We want to take our nap now, don't we?" Parents seem to be helping children express themselves by offering them models of sentences they can use.**

Does IDS encourage communication and foster language development? Research supports its use. Infants as young as two days old prefer IDS to adult talk (N. A. Smith & Trainor, 2008). The short, simple sentences and high pitch are more likely to produce a response from the child and enhance vocabulary development than complex sentences and those spoken in a lower pitch (Singh et al., 2009). Repetition of children's vocalizations appears to encourage vocalizing.

© Rubberball

were substandard compared even with the language of many two- and three-year-olds.

In sum, the development of language in infancy represents the interaction of environmental and biological factors. The child brings a built-in readiness to the task of language acquisition, whereas houseplants and other organisms do not. The child must also have the opportunity to hear spoken language and to interact verbally with others. In the next chapter, we see how interaction with others affects social development.

STUDY TOOLS

5

READY TO STUDY?

In the book, you can:

- ☐ Check your understanding of what you've read with the quizzes below.
- ☐ Rip out the chapter review card at the back of the book to have a summary of the chapter and the key terms handy.

ONLINE AT CENGAGEBRAIN.COM YOU CAN:

- ☐ Watch a video showing Piaget's four major stages of cognitive development.
- ☐ Prepare for tests with quizzes.
- ☐ Review the key terms with Flash Cards.
- ☐ Play games to master concepts.

SELF-ASSESSMENTS

Fill-Ins

Answers can be found in the back of the book.

1. According to Piaget, children try to use ____________ to absorb new events into existing schemes.
2. In the sensorimotor substage of ____________ circular reactions, activity is repeated because of its effect on the environment.
3. By the age of two months, an infant may show some surprise if a toy duck is placed behind a screen and then taken away so that when the screen is lifted, it is absent. But the infant will not look for it because she has not yet developed ____________ permanence.
4. The presence of ____________ imitation suggests that children have mentally represented behavior patterns.
5. ____________ is the first vocalizing that has the sound of human speech.
6. The use of visual ____________ memory to assess infants' cognitive development is based on habituation.
7. The ability of the infant to transfer an object from one hand to the other during play is typical of the ____________ month of cognitive development.
8. A certain class of neurons, called ____________ neurons, makes it possible for newborns to imitate an adult who is sticking out his tongue.
9. At 10 to 12 months, infants tend to repeat syllables, showing what linguists refer to as ____________.
10. At first a child uses a word such as *mooi* to refer to the moon. Then she uses the word to refer to round objects in general. This is an example of ____________.

Multiple Choice

1. In the fourth substage of the sensorimotor period, infants coordinate schemes to attain goals; that is, they begin to show intentional, goal-directed behavior. This substage lasts approximately from

a. 4 to 8 months of age.
b. 8 to 12 months of age.
c. 12 to 18 months of age.
d. 18 to 24 months of age.

2. All of the following are prelinguistic vocalizations, with the exception of

a. holophrases.
b. crying.
c. cooing.
d. babbling.

3. Infants typically say words beginning at about the age of

a. 6 months.
b. 12 months.
c. 18 months.
d. 24 months.

4. Which of the following is accurate about the Bayley Scales of Infant Development?

a. Most infants are not yet ready to take them.
b. Infants can be tested for motor skills but not for mental skills.
c. The scales predict long-term cognitive development, but are not reliable from testing to testing.
d. The scales do not predict school grades or IQ scores among school children.

5. Infants do not use their tongues when they

a. babble.
b. cry.
c. coo.
d. imitate words.

6. What is the relationship between a child's receptive vocabulary development and her expressive vocabulary development?

a. Receptive vocabulary develops more rapidly than expressive vocabulary.
b. Expressive vocabulary develops more rapidly than receptive vocabulary.
c. Receptive vocabulary and expressive vocabulary develop at the same pace.
d. There is so much individual variation that it is not possible to generalize about the relationship between receptive vocabulary and expressive vocabulary.

7. A child spontaneously creates two-word sentences sometime between the ages of

a. 4 and 8 months.
b. 8 and 12 months.
c. 12 and 18 months.
d. 18 and 24 months.

8. For the first couple of years, a child's vocabulary is mainly made of

a. verbs.
b. adjectives.
c. adverbs.
d. nouns.

9. In the study in which two-year-old "Ben" and an adult have a conversation about candy,

a. Ben extends the meaning of the word *candy* to include animals.
b. Ben uses his own understanding of syntax to produce his own language.
c. Ben imitates a model but does not understand why he is doing so.
d. Ben imitates the model and his language development is accelerated.

10. Infant-directed speech ("motherese") is characterized by all of the following *except*

a. brief sentences.
b. the diminutive morpheme y is frequently added to nouns.
c. speaking slowly and with a higher pitch than normal.
d. correcting children when their vocabulary or syntax is incorrect.

6 Infancy: Social and Emotional Development

Lisa Wikstrand/Maskot/Getty Images

LEARNING OUTCOMES

After studying this chapter, you will be able to . . .

6-1 Describe the development of attachment in infancy and theoretical views of how it occurs

6-2 Discuss the relationships between social deprivation, child abuse and neglect, autism spectrum disorders, and attachment

6-3 Discuss the effects of day care on attachment

6-4 Describe the emotional development of the infant

6-5 Describe the personality development of the infant, focusing on the self-concept, temperament, and gender differences

After you finish this chapter, go to **PAGE 128** for **STUDY TOOLS**

When she was two years old, one of my daughters almost succeeded at preventing publication of a book I was writing. When I locked myself into my study, she positioned herself outside the door and called, "Daddy, oh Daddy." At other times she would bang on the door or cry. When I would give in (several times a day) and open the door, she would run in and say, "I want you to pick up me," hold out her arms or climb into my lap. How would I finish the book? One solution was to write outside the home, but this solution had the drawback of distancing me from my family. Another solution was to ignore her and let her cry, but I didn't want to discourage her efforts to get to me. **Attachment**, you see, is a two-way street. The third solution was to fit in working when I could, which is how that book got written.

> Babies have behavior patterns—crying, smiling, clinging—that stimulate caregiving from adults.

6-1 ATTACHMENT: BONDS THAT ENDURE

Attachment is what most people refer to as affection or love. Mary Ainsworth (1989), a preeminent researcher on attachment, defines attachment as an enduring emotional bond between one animal or person and another. John Bowlby adds that attachment is essential to the survival of the infant (Bowlby, 1988). He notes that babies are born with behaviors—crying, smiling, clinging—that stimulate caregiving from adults.

Infants try to maintain contact with caregivers to whom they are attached. They engage in eye contact, pull and tug at them, and ask to be picked up. When they cannot maintain contact, they show **separation anxiety**—thrash about, fuss, cry, screech, or whine.

attachment an affectional bond characterized by seeking closeness with another and distress upon separation.

separation anxiety fear of separation from a target of attachment.

secure attachment a type of attachment characterized by mild distress at leave-takings and being readily soothed by reunion.

insecure attachment attachment behavior characterized by avoiding caregiver, excessive clinging, or inconsistency.

avoidant attachment a type of insecure attachment characterized by apparent indifference to leave-takings by and reunions with an attachment figure.

ambivalent/resistant attachment a type of insecure attachment characterized by severe distress at leave-takings and ambivalent behavior at reunions.

6-1a PATTERNS OF ATTACHMENT

Ainsworth and her colleagues (1978) identified various patterns of attachment. Broadly, infants show **secure attachment** or **insecure attachment**. Most infants in the United States are securely attached (Beebe et al., 2010; Zeanah et al., 2011).

Ainsworth developed the *Strange Situation method* as a way of measuring the development of attachment (see Figure 6.1 on page 112). In this method, an infant is exposed to a series of separations and reunions with a caregiver (usually the mother) and a stranger who is a confederate of the researchers. In the test, secure infants mildly protest their mother's departure, seek interaction upon reunion, and are readily comforted by her.

There are two major types of insecurity, or "insecure attachment": **avoidant attachment** and **ambivalent/resistant attachment**. Infants who

TRUTH OR FICTION?

T	F	Autistic children may respond to people as though they were pieces of furniture.
T	F	Autism can be caused by vaccines.
T	F	Children placed in day care are more aggressive than children who are cared for in the home.
T	F	Fear of strangers is abnormal among infants.
T	F	All children are born with the same temperament. Treatment by caregivers determines whether they are difficult or easygoing.
T	F	Girls may prefer dolls and toy animals, and boys may prefer toy trucks and sports equipment, but these preferences emerge only after they have become aware of the gender roles assigned to them by society.

FIG.6.1 THE STRANGE SITUATION

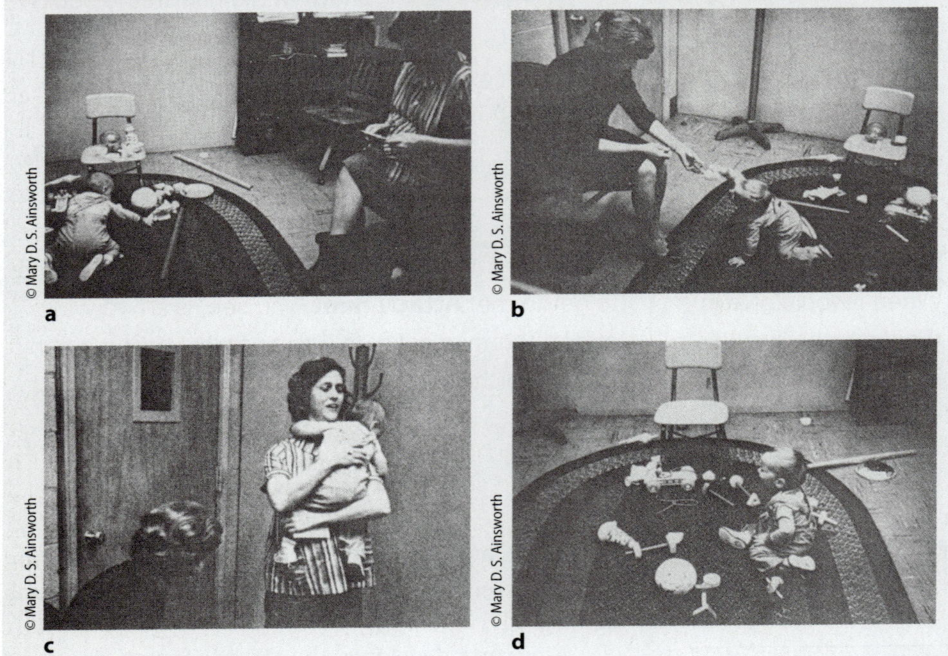

These historic photos show a 12-month-old child in the Strange Situation. In (a), the child plays with toys, glancing occasionally at mother. In (b), the stranger approaches with a toy. While the child is distracted, mother leaves the room. In (c), mother returns after a brief absence. The child crawls to her quickly and clings to her when picked up. In (d), the child cries when mother again leaves the room.

© Mary D. S. Ainsworth

show avoidant attachment are least distressed by their mothers' departure. They play without fuss when alone and ignore their mothers upon reunion. Ambivalent/resistant babies are the most emotional. They show severe signs of distress when their mothers leave and show ambivalence upon reunion by alternately clinging to their mothers and pushing them away. Additional categories of insecure attachment have been proposed, including **disorganized–disoriented attachment**. Babies showing this pattern seem dazed, confused, or disoriented. They may show contradictory behaviors, such as moving toward the mother while looking away from her.

Secure infants and toddlers are happier, more sociable, and more cooperative with caregivers. At ages five and six, they get along better with peers and are better adjusted in school than insecure children (Borelli et al., 2010; George et al., 2010). Insecure attachment in infancy predicts psychological disorders during adolescence (Milan et al., 2013).

disorganized–disoriented attachment a type of insecure attachment characterized by dazed and contradictory behaviors toward an attachment figure.

6-1b ESTABLISHING ATTACHMENT

Attachment is related to the quality of infant care (Oliveira et al., 2015; Sullivan et al., 2011). The parents of secure infants are more affectionate, cooperative, and predictable than parents of insecure infants. They respond more sensitively to their infants' smiles and cries (Bigelow et al., 2010; Xue et al., 2010).

Researchers have found evidence for the "intergenerational transmission of attachment" (Berzenski et al., 2014; Miljkovich et al., 2012). The children of secure mothers show the most secure patterns of attachment themselves (Cicchetti et al., 2006). Siblings may form quite different attachment relationships with their mother (O'Connor et al., 2011). Siblings of the same gender are more likely than girl–boy pairs to form similar attachment relationships with their mother.

Security is also connected with the infant's temperament (Lickenbrock et al., 2013; Solmeyer & Feinberg, 2011). The mothers of "difficult" children are less responsive to them and report feeling more distant from them (Lickenbrock et al., 2013; Wang et al., 2015).

INVOLVEMENT OF FATHERS How involved is the average father with his children? The brief answer, in developed nations, is more so than in the past (Grossmann et al., 2002). But mothers engage in more interactions with their infants. Most fathers are more likely to play with their children than to feed or clean them (Lucassen et al., 2011). Fathers more often than mothers engage in rough-and-tumble play, whereas mothers are more likely to play games involving toys, and patty-cake and peek-a-boo (Lucassen et al., 2011).

How strongly, then, do infants become attached to their fathers? The more sensitive the father is to the infant's needs, the stronger the attachment (Fuertes et al., 2016).

6-1c STABILITY OF ATTACHMENT

Patterns of attachment tend to persist when caregiving conditions remain constant (Beebe et al., 2010; Stupica et al., 2011). Byron Egeland and Alan Sroufe (1981) followed infants who were severely neglected and others who received high-quality care from 12 to 18 months of age. Attachment patterns remained stable (secure) for infants receiving fine care. But many insecure neglected infants became securely attached over the six-month period, either because of a relationship with a supportive family member or because home life grew less tense. Children can also become less securely attached to caregivers when home life deteriorates (Levendosky et al., 2011). On the positive side, children adopted at various ages can become securely attached to adoptive parents (Niemann & Weiss, 2011; Raby et al., 2013; Schoenmaker et al., 2014).

PHASES OF ATTACHMENT

Mary Ainsworth and her colleagues identified three phases of attachment in infants:

1. **Initial-preattachment**
2. **Attachment-in-the-making**
3. **Clear-cut attachment**

Mary Ainsworth (1913–1999)

6-1d STAGES OF ATTACHMENT

Cross-cultural studies have led to a theory of stages of attachment. In one study, Ainsworth tracked the behavior of Ugandan infants. Over a nine-month period, she noted their efforts to maintain contact with the mother, their protests when separated, and their use of the mother as a base for exploring the environment. At first, the Ugandan infants showed **indiscriminate attachment**—no particular preferences for a familiar caregiver. Specific attachment to the mother, as evidenced by separation anxiety and other behavior, began to develop at about four months of age and grew intense by about seven months. Fear of strangers developed one or two months later.

In another study, shown in Figure 6.2, Scottish infants showed indiscriminate attachment during the first six months or so after birth (Schaffer & Emerson, 1964). Then, indiscriminate attachment waned. Specific attachments to the mother and other familiar caregivers intensified, as demonstrated by the appearance of separation anxiety, and remained at high levels through the age of 18 months. Fear of strangers occurred a month or so after the intensity of specific attachments began to mushroom. In both this and the Ugandan study, fear of strangers followed separation anxiety and the development of specific attachments by weeks.

From such studies, Ainsworth and her colleagues (1978) identified the following three phases of attachment:

1. The **initial-preattachment phase** lasts from birth to about three months and is characterized by indiscriminate attachment.
2. The **attachment-in-the-making phase** occurs at about three or four months and is characterized by preference for familiar figures.

FIG.6.2 DEVELOPMENT OF ATTACHMENT

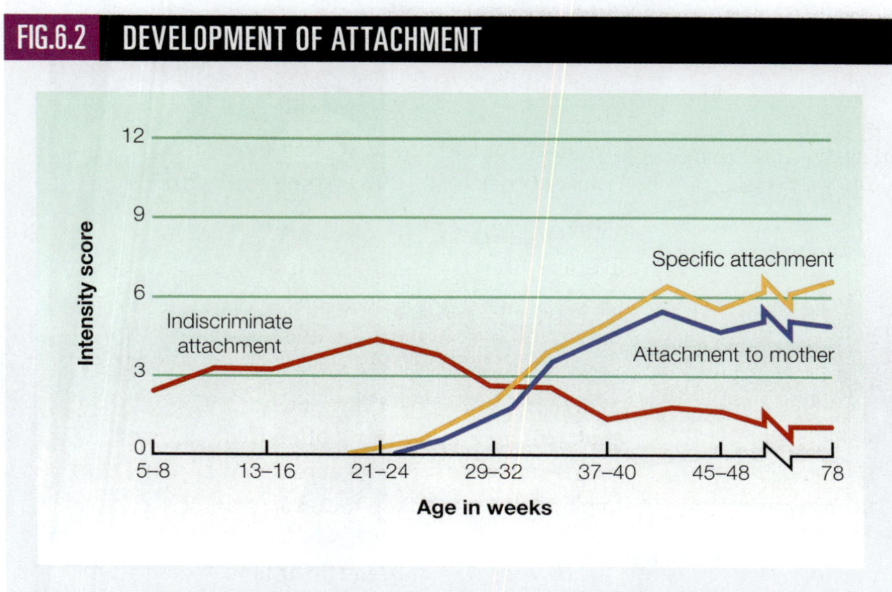

During the first six months, infants tend to show indiscriminate attachment, which wanes as specific attachments intensify.

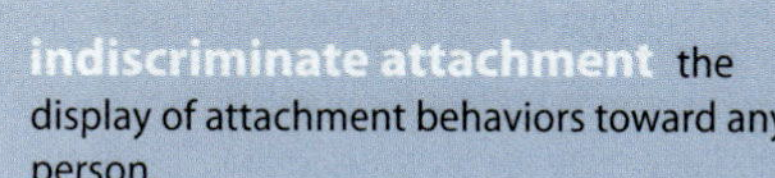

indiscriminate attachment the display of attachment behaviors toward any person.

initial-preattachment phase the first phase in development of attachment, characterized by indiscriminate attachment.

attachment-in-the-making phase the second phase in development of attachment, characterized by preference for familiar figures.

3. The **clear-cut-attachment phase** occurs at about six or seven months and is characterized by intensified dependence on the primary caregiver, usually the mother.

But most infants have more than one adult caregiver and are likely to form multiple attachments: to the father, day-care providers, grandparents, and other caregivers, as well as the mother.

6-1e THEORIES OF ATTACHMENT

There are several theories of the development of attachment.

COGNITIVE VIEW OF ATTACHMENT The cognitive view suggests that an infant must develop the concept of object permanence before specific attachment becomes possible. If caregivers are to be missed when absent, the infant must perceive that they continue to exist. We have seen that infants tend to develop specific attachments at about the age of six to seven months. Basic object permanence concerning objects develops somewhat earlier (see Chapter 5).

BEHAVIORAL VIEW OF ATTACHMENT Early in the 20th century, behaviorists argued that attachment behaviors are conditioned. Caregivers feed their infants and tend to their other physiological needs. Thus, infants associate their caregivers with gratification and learn to approach them to meet their needs. From this perspective, a caregiver becomes a conditioned reinforcer.

PSYCHOANALYTIC VIEWS OF ATTACHMENT According to psychoanalytic theorists, the caregiver, usually the mother, becomes not just a "reinforcer" but also a love object who forms the basis for all later attachments. Sigmund Freud emphasized the importance of oral activities, such as eating, in the first year. Freud believed that the infant becomes emotionally attached to the mother during this time because she is the primary satisfier of the infant's needs for food and sucking.

Erik Erikson characterized the first year of life as the stage of *trust vs. mistrust*. Erikson believed that the first year is critical for developing a sense of trust in the mother, which fosters attachment. The mother's general sensitivity to the child's needs, not just the need for food, fosters the development of trust and attachment.

THE CAREGIVER AS A SOURCE OF CONTACT COMFORT Harry and Margaret Harlow conducted classic experiments to demonstrate that feeding is not as critical to the attachment process as Freud suggested (Harlow & Harlow, 1966). In one study, the Harlows placed rhesus monkey infants in cages with two surrogate mothers (see Figure 6.3). One "mother" was made from wire mesh from which a baby bottle was extended. The other surrogate mother was made of soft, cuddly terry cloth. Infant monkeys spent most of their time clinging to the cloth mother, even though she did not offer food. The Harlows concluded that monkeys—and presumably humans—have a built-in need for **contact comfort**.

ETHOLOGICAL VIEW OF ATTACHMENT **Ethologists** note that for many animals, attachment is an inborn or instinctive response to a specific stimulus. Some researchers theorize that a baby's cry stimulates caregiving in women. By two to three months of age, the human

clear-cut-attachment phase the third phase in development of attachment, characterized by intensified dependence on the primary caregiver.

contact comfort the pleasure derived from physical contact with another.

ethologist a scientist who studies the behavior patterns characteristic of various species.

FIG.6.3 CONTACT COMFORT

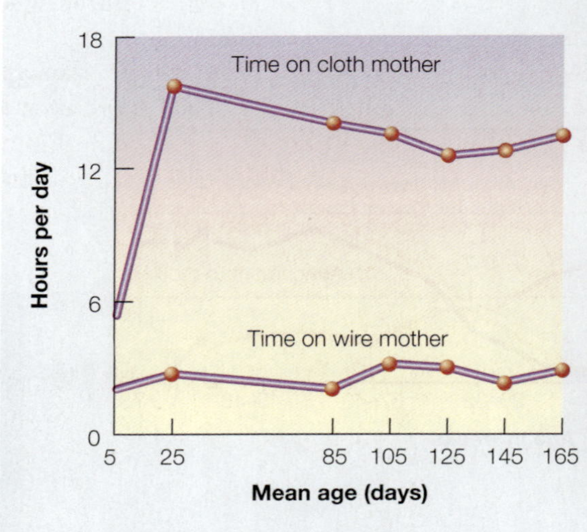

Although this rhesus monkey infant is fed by the "wire-mesh mother," it spends most of its time clinging to a soft, cuddly, "terry-cloth mother."

face begins to elicit a **social smile** in infants, helping to ensure survival by eliciting affection (Ainsworth & Bowlby, 1991; Bowlby, 1988). In circular fashion, the mother's social response to her infant's face can reliably produce infant smiling by eight months of age (Jones & Hong, 2005). The pattern contributes to a mutual attachment.

In many nonhumans, attachment occurs during a **critical period** of life. Waterfowl become attached during this period to the first moving object they encounter. Because the image of the moving object seems to become "imprinted" on the young animal, the process is termed **imprinting**.

Ethologist Konrad Lorenz (1962, 1981) became well known when pictures of his "family" of goslings were made public. Lorenz acquired his "following" by being present when the goslings hatched and allowing them to follow him. The critical period for geese and ducks begins when they first engage in locomotion and ends when they develop fear of strangers. The goslings followed Lorenz persistently, ran to him when frightened, honked with distress at his departure, and tried to overcome barriers placed between them. If you substitute crying for honking, it sounds quite human.

ETHOLOGY, AINSWORTH, AND BOWLBY Let us return to Ainsworth and Bowlby (1991). They wrote that "the distinguishing characteristic of the theory of attachment that we have jointly developed is that it is an ethological approach" (p. 333). But their ethological approach differs from Lorenz's in a number of ways. For example, Ainsworth and Bowlby write that caregiving in humans is largely learned and not inborn. Ainsworth and Bowlby also note that the critical period for attachment in humans (if one exists), as opposed to attachment periods for lower mammals, extends to months or years (Ainsworth & Bowlby, 1991; Takamura et al., 2016). Caregiving itself and infant responsiveness, such as smiling, also promote attachment.

6-2 WHEN ATTACHMENT FAILS

What happens when children are reared with little or no contact with caregivers? When parents neglect or abuse their children? In the case of autism spectrum disorders?

6-2a SOCIAL DEPRIVATION

Studies of children reared in institutions where they receive little social stimulation from caregivers are limited in that they are correlational. In other words, family factors that led to the children's placement in institutions may also have contributed to their developmental problems. Ethical considerations prevent us from conducting experiments in which we randomly assign children to social deprivation. However, experiments of this kind have been undertaken with rhesus monkeys, and the results are consistent with those of the correlational studies of children.

EXPERIMENTS WITH MONKEYS The Harlows and their colleagues conducted studies of rhesus monkeys that were "reared by" wire-mesh and terry-cloth surrogate mothers. In later studies, rhesus monkeys were reared without even this questionable "social" support—without seeing any other animal, monkey or human (Harlow et al., 1971).

The Harlows found that rhesus infants reared in this most solitary confinement later avoided other monkeys. Instead, they cowered in the presence of others. Nor did they try to fend off attacks by other monkeys. Rather, they sat in the corner, clutching themselves, and rocking back and forth. Females who later bore children ignored or abused them.

Can the damage from social deprivation be overcome? When monkeys deprived for six months or

social smile a smile that occurs in response to a human voice or face.

critical period a period during which imprinting can occur.

imprinting the process by which waterfowl become attached to the first moving object they follow.

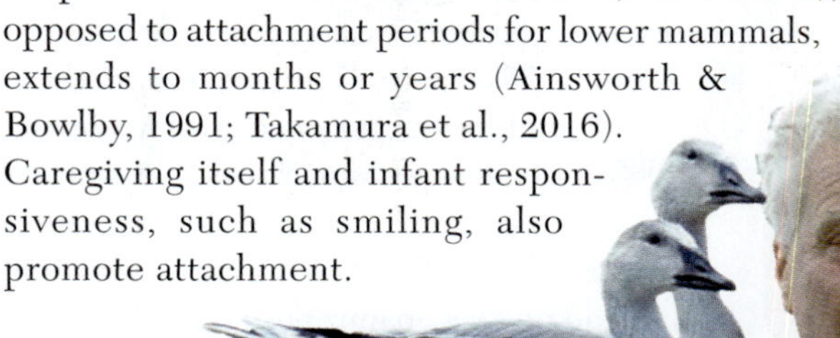

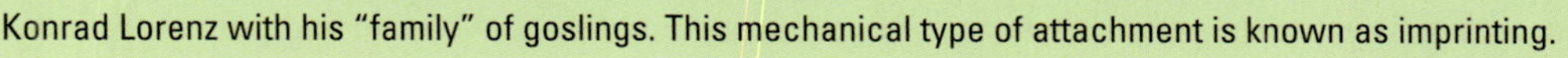

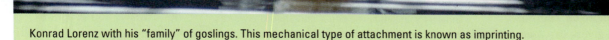

Konrad Lorenz with his "family" of goslings. This mechanical type of attachment is known as imprinting.

Nina Leen/Time & Life Pictures/Getty Images

more are placed with younger, three- to four-month-old females for a couple of hours a day, the younger monkeys attempt to interact with their deprived elders. Many of the deprived monkeys begin to play with the youngsters after a few weeks, and many eventually expand their social contacts to older monkeys (Suomi et al., 1972). Socially withdrawn children can similarly make gains in their social and emotional development when provided with younger playmates (Kumsta et al., 2010; Rubin & Coplan, 2010).

STUDIES WITH CHILDREN Institutionalized children whose material needs are met but who receive little social stimulation from caregivers encounter problems in all areas of development (Johnson & Gunnar, 2011; Koss et al., 2014). René A. Spitz (1965) found that many institutionalized children show withdrawal and depression. In one institution, infants were maintained in separate cubicles for most of their first year to ward off infectious diseases (Provence & Lipton, 1962).

Adults tended to them only to feed them and change their diapers. As a rule, baby bottles were propped up in their cribs. Attendants rarely responded to their cries; they were rarely played with or spoken to. By the age of four months, the infants showed little interest in adults. A few months later, some of them sat withdrawn in their cribs and rocked back and forth, almost like the Harlows' monkeys. None were speaking at 12 months.

Why do children whose material needs are met show such dramatic deficiencies? The answer may depend, in part, on the age of the child. Classic research by Leon Yarrow and his colleagues (Yarrow et al., 1971; Yarrow & Goodwin, 1973) suggests that deficiencies in sensory stimulation and social interaction may cause more problems than lack of love in infants who are too young to have developed specific attachments. But once infants have developed specific attachments, separation from their primary caregivers can lead to problems.

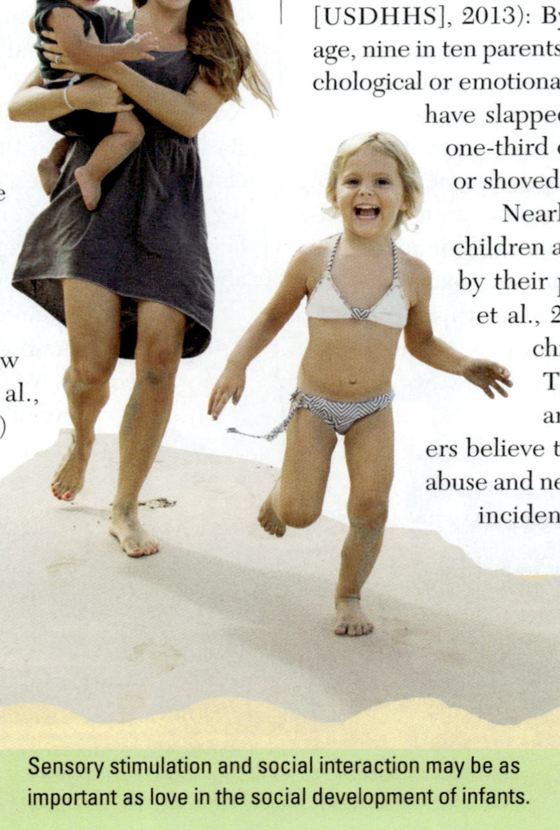

Jessica Peterson/Brand X Pictures/Getty Images

Sensory stimulation and social interaction may be as important as love in the social development of infants.

THE CAPACITY TO RECOVER FROM SOCIAL DEPRIVATION Infants also have powerful capacities to recover from deprivation. One study showed how many children may be able to recover fully from 13 or 14 months of deprivation (Kagan & Klein, 1973). The natives in an isolated Guatemalan village believe that fresh air and sunshine will sicken children. Children are thus kept in windowless huts until they can walk and are played with infrequently. During their isolation, the infants behave apathetically. They are physically and socially delayed when they start to walk. But by 11 years of age they are as alert and active as their age-mates in the United States.

A classic longitudinal study of orphanage children also offers evidence of the ability of children to recover from social deprivation (Skeels, 1966). In this study, a group of 19-month-old apparently intellectually disabled children were placed in the care of older institutionalized girls. The girls spent a great deal of time playing with and nurturing them. Four years after being placed with the girls, the "disabled" children made dramatic gains in IQ scores, whereas children who did not receive this stimulation showed declines in IQ.

6-2b CHILD ABUSE AND NEGLECT

Consider the following statistics from national surveys (U.S. Department of Health and Human Services [USDHHS], 2013): By the time a child is two years of age, nine in ten parents have engaged in some sort of psychological or emotional abuse; more than half of parents have slapped or spanked their children; and one-third of parents have pushed, grabbed, or shoved their children.

Nearly two-fifths (37.3%) of American children are neglected or abused each year by their parents or caregivers (Finkelhor et al., 2015). About one in ten of these children experiences serious injury. Thousands die. More than 150,000 are sexually abused. But researchers believe that 50% to 60% of cases of child abuse and neglect go unreported, so the actual incidences are likely to be significantly higher (USDHHS, 2013).

The U.S. Department of Health and Human Services recognizes several types of maltreatment of children (USDHHS, 2013):

- Physical abuse: actions causing pain and physical injury

Radius Images/Corbis

Abused children are at greater risk for delinquency, risky sexual behavior, and substance abuse.

- Sexual abuse: sexual molestation, exploitation, and intercourse
- Emotional abuse: actions that impair the child's emotional, social, or intellectual functioning
- Physical neglect: failure to provide adequate food, shelter, clothing, or medical care
- Emotional neglect: failure to provide adequate nurturance and emotional support
- Educational neglect: for example, permitting or forcing the child to be truant

Although blatant abuse is more horrifying, more injuries, illnesses, and deaths result from neglect (USDHHS, 2013). Table 6.1 shows examples of the three types of neglect.

Why do more than half the cases of abuse and neglect go unreported? One answer is that it can be difficult, especially for abusers, to draw the line between "normal discipline" and abuse. Other reasons include fear of embarrassing a family; fear of legal consequences; and, sometimes, a mother's fear that she will be victimized by the abuser if she reports the crime. In any event, child neglect is responsible for more injuries and deaths than abuse (USDHHS, 2013).

Although most sexually abused children are girls, one-quarter to one-third are boys (USDHHS, 2013). When we sample the population at large rather than rely on cases of abuse that are reported to authorities, it appears that the prevalence of sexual abuse among children is about 2% each year, but the rate for girls aged 14 to 17 is above 10% in a given year (Finkelhor et al., 2015). This chapter is about infants, but many boys in middle childhood and adolescence have been sexually abused by religious leaders and by athletic coaches—as made all too clear in news reports in recent years.

EFFECTS OF CHILD ABUSE Abused children show a high incidence of personal and social problems and psychological disorders (Sousa et al., 2011). In general, abused children are less securely attached to their parents. They are less intimate with peers and more aggressive, angry, and noncompliant than other children (Blow, 2014: Moylan et al., 2010). They have lower self-esteem and perform more poorly in school. Later on, abused children are at greater risk for delinquency, risky sexual behavior, substance abuse, and abusing their own children (Sousa et al., 2011; Sperry & Widom, 2013). When they reach adulthood, they are also more likely to act aggressively toward their intimate partners (Gomez, 2011).

CAUSES OF CHILD ABUSE Various factors contribute to child abuse, including stress, a history of child abuse in at least one parent's family of origin, lack of adequate coping and child-rearing skills, unrealistic expectations of

TABLE 6.1 THE THREE FORMS OF CHILD NEGLECT—EXAMPLES

Physical Neglect	Educational Neglect	Emotional Neglect
A 2-year-old who was found wandering in the street late at night, naked and alone	An 11-year-old and a 13-year-old who were chronically truant	Siblings who were subjected to repeated incidents of family violence between their mother and father
An infant who had to be hospitalized for near-drowning after being left alone in a bathtub	A 12-year-old whose parents permitted him to decide whether to go to school, how long to stay there, and in which activities to participate	A 12-year-old whose parents permitted him to drink and use drugs
Children who were living in a home contaminated with animal feces and rotting food	A special education student whose mother refused to believe he needed help in school	A child whose mother helped him shoot out the windows of a neighbor's house

Source: From Mash/Wolfe, *Abnormal Child Psychology, 5E.* © 2013 Cengage Learning.

FIG.6.4 TRENDS IN ATTITUDE TOWARD SPANKING AMONG U.S. ADULTS

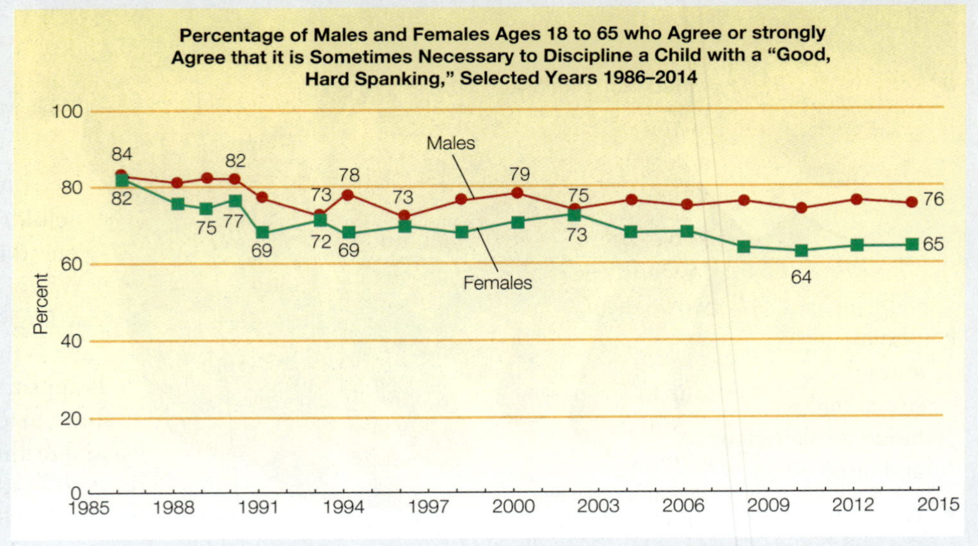

Although there have been slight declines in U.S. adults who support "a good, hard spanking" over the last three decades, about three in four males and two in three females continue to agree with the practice.

children, and substance abuse (Wolfe, 2011). Stress has many sources, including divorce, loss of a job, moving, and birth of a new family member (Wolfe, 2011). Much of the problem is also cultural: The great majority of Americans, male and female, agree with the statement that "It is sometimes necessary to discipline a child with a 'good hard spanking'" (Child Trends Data Bank; see Figure 6.4).

Ironically, infants who are already in pain of some kind and difficult to soothe are more likely to be abused (Stupica et al., 2011). Abusive parents may find the cries of their infants particularly aversive, so infants' crying may precipitate abuse (Schuetze et al., 2003). Children who are irritable, disobedient, inappropriate, or unresponsive are also at greater risk (Wolfe, 2011).

WHAT TO DO Many states require helping professionals such as psychologists and physicians to report any suspicion of child abuse. Some legally require *anyone* who suspects child abuse to report it to authorities.

A number of techniques have been developed to help prevent child abuse. One approach focuses on strengthening parenting skills among the general population (Bugental et al., 2010). Another approach targets groups at high risk for abuse, such as poor, single, teen mothers (Robling et al., 2016). In some programs, home visitors help new parents develop skills in caregiving and home management (Bugental et al., 2010).

A third technique focuses on presenting information about abuse and providing support to families. For instance, many locales have child abuse hotlines. Readers who suspect child abuse may call for advice. Parents having difficulty controlling aggressive impulses toward their children are also encouraged to call.

6-2c AUTISM SPECTRUM DISORDERS

Autism spectrum disorders (ASDs) are characterized by impairment in communication skills and social interaction, and by repetitive, stereotyped behavior (see Table 6.2). ASDs tend to become evident by the age of three and sometimes before the end of the first year. A Centers for Disease Control and Prevention study of 407,578 children from 14 parts of the United States identified 1 in every 152 children as having an ASD (Rice et al., 2007). Other researchers place the number as high as 1 in 68 children (Bhat et al., 2014; Moyal et al., 2013).

autism spectrum disorders (ASDs) developmental disorders characterized by impairment in communication and social skills, and by repetitive, stereotyped behavior.

TABLE 6.2 CHARACTERISTICS OF AUTISM SPECTRUM DISORDERS (ASDS)

Key Indicators	Other Indicators
Does not babble, point, or make meaningful gestures by 1 year of age	Poor eye contact
Does not speak one word by 16 months	Doesn't seem to know how to play with toys
Does not combine two words by 2 years	Excessively lines up toys or other objects
Does not respond to being called by his or her name	Is attached to one particular toy or object
Loses language or social skills	Doesn't smile
	At times seems to be hearing impaired

Source: American Psychiatric Association (2013).

There are several variations of ASDs, but autism is the major type. Other forms of ASDs include:

- *Asperger's disorder*. Characterized by social deficits and stereotyped behavior but without the significant cognitive or language delays associated with autism.
- *Rett's disorder*. Characterized by a range of physical, behavioral, motor, and cognitive abnormalities that begin after a few months of normal development.
- *Childhood disintegrative disorder*. Abnormal functioning and loss of previously acquired skills that begins after about two years of apparently normal development.

AUTISM **Autism** is four to five times more common among boys than girls. Autistic children do not show interest in social interaction and may avoid eye contact. Attachment to others is weak or absent.

Other features of autism include communication problems, intolerance of change, and ritualistic or stereotypical behavior (Georgiades et al., 2010). Parents of autistic children often say they were "good babies," which usually means they made few demands. But as autistic children develop, they tend to shun affectionate contacts such as hugging, cuddling, and kissing.

Development of speech lags. There is little babbling and communicative gesturing during the first year. Autistic children may show **mutism**, **echolalia**, and pronoun reversal, referring to themselves as "you" or "he." About half use language by middle childhood, but their speech is unusual and troubled.

Autistic children become bound by ritual (Overskeid, 2016). Even slight changes in routines or the environment may cause distress. The teacher of a five-year-old autistic girl would greet her each morning with, "Good morning, Lily, I am very, very glad to see you." Lily would ignore the greeting, but she would shriek if the teacher omitted even one of the *verys*. This feature of autism is termed "preservation of sameness." When familiar objects are moved from their usual places, children with autism may throw tantrums or cry until they are restored. They may insist on eating the same food every day. Autistic children show deficits in peer play, imaginative play, imitation, and emotional expression. Many sleep less than their age-mates (Georgiades et al., 2010).

Some autistic children mutilate themselves, even as they cry out in pain. They may bang their heads, slap their faces, bite their hands and shoulders, or pull out their hair.

TRUTH

(T) F Autistic children may respond to people as though they were pieces of furniture.

It is true that autistic children may respond to people as though they were pieces of furniture. They may ignore other people—for example, walking around them as if they are objects and not persons.

CAUSES OF AUTISM Contrary to what some theorists say or some of the public believe, scientific evidence shows that there is no connection between the development of autism and use of vaccines or deficiencies in child rearing (Archer, 2013; Dixon & Clarke, 2013).

Various lines of evidence suggest a key role for biological factors in autism (Bhat et al., 2014). Possible prenatal factors include exposure to lead, alcohol, mercury, misoprostol, and maternal rubella. Very low birth weight and advanced maternal age may heighten the risk of autism. There is also apparently a role for genetic mechanisms in autism (Vorstman & Burbach, 2014). The concordance (agreement) rates for autism are about 60% among pairs of identical (MZ) twins, who fully share their genetic heritage, compared with about 10% for pairs of fraternal (DZ) twins, whose genetic codes overlap by half (Kendler, 2010; Plomin et al., 1994).

Autistic children tend to shun affectionate contacts, such as hugging, cuddling, and kissing.

BSIP SA/Alamy Stock Photo

autism a disorder characterized by extreme aloneness, communication problems, preservation of sameness, and ritualistic behavior.

mutism refusal to speak.

echolalia automatic repetition of sounds or words.

FICTION

T (F) Autism can be caused by vaccines.

It is not true that autism can be caused by vaccines. There is no scientific evidence to support this claim.

Biological factors focus on neurological involvement. Many children with autism have abnormal brain wave patterns or seizures (Miyawaki et al., 2016). Other researchers have found that the brains of children with autism have abnormal sensitivities to neurotransmitters such as serotonin, dopamine, acetylcholine, and norepinephrine (Ye et al., 2014). Other researchers note unusual activity in the motor region of the cerebral cortex and less activity in some other areas of the brain (Eilam-Stock et al., 2014.

TREATMENT OF AUTISM Treatment for autism is mainly based on principles of learning, although investigation of biological approaches is also under way (Strock, 2004). Behavior modification has been used to increase the child's ability to attend to others, to play with other children, and to discourage self-mutilation. Brief bursts of physically painful but supposedly nondamaging electric shock rapidly eliminate self-mutilation (Lovaas, 1977). The use of electric shock raises serious moral, ethical, and legal concerns, but O. Ivar Lovaas countered that failure to eliminate self-injurious behavior places the child at yet greater risk.

Because children with autism show behavioral deficits, behavior modification is used to help them develop new behavior. Though autistic children often relate to people as if they were furniture, many can be taught to accept people as reinforcers, rather than objects, by pairing praise with food treats (Chezan & Drasgow, 2010). The most effective treatment programs focus on individualized instruction (Rapin, 1997). In a classic study conducted by Lovaas (Lovaas et al., 1989), autistic children received more than 40 hours of one-to-one behavior modification a week for at least two years. Significant intellectual and educational gains were reported for 9 of 19 children (47%) in the program (Stahmer et al., 2004).

Biological approaches for the treatment of autism are under study. Evidence is mixed as to whether drugs that enhance serotonin activity (selective serotonin reuptake inhibitors, or SSRIs) help prevent self-injury, aggressive outbursts, depression, anxiety, and repetitive behavior (Reiersen & Handen, 2011). Drugs that are usually used to treat schizophrenia—so-called "major tranquilizers"—are helpful with stereotyped behavior, hyperactivity, and self-injury, but not with cognitive and language problems (Moyal et al., 2013; Reiersen & Handen, 2011).

Autistic behavior generally continues into adulthood to one degree or another. Nevertheless, about half of adults who had been diagnosed with autism spectrum disorder in childhood go on to function independently (Eaves & Ho, 2008).

6-3 DAY CARE

Looking for a phrase that can strike fear in the hearts of millions of caregivers? Try *day care*. Most American parents, including mothers with infants, are in the workforce, including 64% of mothers with children under the age of six, and 57% of mothers with infants (O'Brien et al., 2014). As a result, of children under the age of four, 24% are cared for in center-based care, including day care, nursery school, preschool, or Head Start.

Many parents wonder whether day care will affect their children's attachment to them. Some studies have found that the amount of time infants spend in day care is associated with insecure attachment with their parents (Quan et al., 2013). Some researchers suggest that a mother who works full time puts her infant at risk for developing emotional insecurity. Others note that infants whose mothers work may simply become less distressed by her departure and less likely to seek her out when she returns as time goes on, thus providing the appearance of being less attached. However, the likelihood of insecure attachment is not much greater in infants placed in day care than in those cared for in the home. Most infants in both groups are securely attached (O'Brien et al., 2014).

Some studies report that infants with day-care experience are more peer oriented and play at higher developmental levels than do home-reared infants. Children in high-quality day care are more likely to share their toys. They are more independent, self-confident, outgoing, and affectionate as well as more helpful and cooperative with peers and adults (Bekkhus et al., 2011; O'Brien et al., 2014). Participation in day care is also linked with better academic performance in elementary school (Belsky, 2006b).

A study funded by the National Institute on Child Health and Human Development (NICHD) agrees that "high-quality" day care can result in scores on tests of cognitive skills that rival or exceed those of the children

Finding Day Care You (and Your Child) Can Live With

It is normal to be anxious. You are thinking about selecting a day-care center and there are risks. Despite anxiety, you can go about the task with a checklist that can guide your considerations. Above all: Don't be afraid to ask questions. If the day-care provider does not like questions or answer them satisfactorily, you want your child someplace else. Things to think about:

RubberBall /SuperStock

1. **Does the day-care center have a license?**
2. **How many children are cared for at the center? How many caregivers are there? It is important for caregivers not to be overburdened by too many children, especially infants.**
3. **How were the caregivers hired? How were they trained? Do caregivers engage children in activities and educational experiences, or are they inactive unless a child cries or screams?**
4. **Is the environment childproof and secure? Can children stick their fingers in electric sockets? Are toys and outdoor equipment in good condition? Are sharp objects within children's reach? Can anybody walk in off the street? What do meals consist of? Will your child find them appetizing or go hungry?**
5. **Is it possible for you to meet the caregivers who will be taking care of your child? If not, why not?**
6. **Does the center seem to have an enriching environment? Do you see books, toys, games, and educational objects strewn about?**
7. **Are there facilities and objects such as swings and tricycles that will enhance your child's physical and motor development? Are children supervised when they play with these things?**
8. **Does the center's schedule meet your needs?**
9. **Is the center located conveniently for you?**
10. **Are parents permitted to visit unannounced?**
11. **Do you like the overall environment and feel of the center? Listen to your "gut."**

reared in the home by their mothers (Belsky et al., 2007). The quality of the day care was defined in terms of the richness of the learning environment (availability of toys, books, and other materials), the ratio of caregivers to children (high quality meant more caregivers), the amount of individual attention received by the child, and the extent to which caregivers talked to the children and asked them questions.

However, the researchers also found that children placed in day care may be more aggressive toward peers and adults than children who are reared in the home. The more time spent away from their mothers, the more likely these children were to be rated as defiant, aggressive, and disobedient once they got to kindergarten.

Teacher ratings found that once children who were in day care are in school, they are significantly more likely than children cared for in the home to interrupt in class and tease or bully other children (Belsky et al., 2007). The degree of disturbance generally remained "within normal limits." That is, the children who had been in day care could not be labeled criminals and were not being expelled. *The quality of the day-care center made no difference*. Children from high-quality day-care centers were also more likely to be disruptive than children cared for in the home. Moreover, the behavioral difference persisted through the sixth grade.

TRUTH

(T) F Children placed in day care are more aggressive than children who are cared for in the home.

It is true that children placed in day care are more aggressive than children who are cared for in the home. On the other hand, the great majority of the time professional observers place their higher level of aggressive behavior as being "within normal limits."

There are some limitations of the NICHD study. Although the differences in disruptive behavior between children in full-time day care and those cared for in the home are statistically significant—meaning that they are unlikely to be due to chance—they are small. The study implies that day care *causes* the disruptive behavior of concern later on, but there is no control group. Children are *not* assigned at random to day care or care in the home. Therefore, it may be that children placed in day care are those whose caregivers are most stressed by work through their children's primary school years. Also, we do not know whether the so-called disruptive children become less productive and successful adults. Perhaps they actually become "assertive and entrepreneurial," especially since their cognitive skills and other social skills are intact.

In any case, reality intrudes. Millions of parents do not have the option of deciding whether to place their children in day care; their only choice is where. And some parents, given their financial and geographic circumstances, might not even have that choice.

6-4 EMOTIONAL DEVELOPMENT

An emotion is a state of feeling with physiological, situational, and cognitive components. Physiologically, when emotions are strong, our hearts may beat more rapidly and our muscles may tense. Situationally, we may feel anger when frustrated or pleasure or relief when we are being held by a loved one. Cognitively, anger may be triggered by the idea that someone is purposefully withholding something we need.

It is unclear how many emotions babies have, and they cannot tell us what they are feeling. We can only observe how they behave, including their facial expressions. Facial expressions appear to be universal in that they are recognized in different cultures around the world, so they are considered a reliable index of emotion.

Researchers have long debated whether the emotional expression of newborns begins in an undifferentiated state of diffuse excitement or whether several emotions are present (Camras & Shuster, 2013; Soussignan & Schaal, 2005). They have asked whether the newborn baby's crying is nothing more than a reflex in response to discomfort. They have even asked whether the facial expressions of infants, which many researchers claim to express emotions such as anger, joy, fear, and excitement within a few months after birth, actually reflect internal states of feeling. It seems clear enough that as infants develop through the first year, their cognitive appraisal of events, including their interaction with their caregivers, becomes a key part of their emotional life and their emotional expression (Camras et al., 2007; Soussignan & Schaal, 2005).

Infants' initial emotional expressions appear to comprise two basic states of emotional arousal: a positive attraction to pleasant stimulation, such as the caregiver's voice or being held, and withdrawal from aversive stimulation, such as a sudden loud noise. By the age of two to three months, social smiling has replaced reflexive smiling. Social smiling is usually highly endearing to caregivers. At three to five months, infants laugh at active stimuli, such as repetitively touching their bellies or playing "Ah, boop!"

In sum, researchers agree that infants show only a few emotions during the first few months. They agree that emotional development is linked to cognitive development and social experience. They do not necessarily agree on exactly when specific emotions are first shown or whether discrete emotions are present at birth.

6-4a EMOTIONAL DEVELOPMENT AND PATTERNS OF ATTACHMENT

Emotional development has been linked with various histories of attachment. In a longitudinal study of 112 children at ages 9, 14, 22, and 33 months, Kochanska (2001) studied the development of fear, anger, and joy by using laboratory situations designed to evoke these emotions. Patterns of attachment were assessed using the Strange Situation method. Differences in emotional development could first be related to attachment at the age of 14 months. Resistant children were most fearful and they frequently responded with distress even in episodes designed to evoke joy. When they were assessed repeatedly over time, it became apparent that securely attached children were becoming significantly less angry. By contrast, the negative emotions of insecurely attached children rose: Avoidant children grew more fearful, and resistant children became less joyful. At 33 months of age, securely attached children were less likely to show fear and anger, even when they were exposed to situations designed to elicit these emotions.

6-4b FEAR OF STRANGERS

When another daughter was one year old, her mother and I needed a nanny for a few hours a day so that we could teach, write, breathe, and engage in other life activities. We hired a graduate social work student who had a mild, engaging way about her. She nurtured my daughter and played with her for about four months, during which time my daughter came to somewhat grudgingly accept her, most of the time. Even so, my daughter was never completely comfortable with her and often let out a yowl as if buildings were collapsing around her, although the nanny did nothing except calmly try to soothe her.

Unfortunately, my daughter met the nanny during the period when she had developed fear of strangers. The fear would eventually subside, as these fears do, but during her entire encounter with the nanny, the nanny wondered what she was doing wrong. The answer was simple: She was existing, within sight of my daughter.

Fear of strangers—also called *stranger anxiety*—is normal. Most infants develop it. Stranger anxiety appears at about six to nine months of age (Brooker et al., 2013. By four or five months of age, infants may compare the faces of strangers and their mothers, looking back and forth. Somewhat older infants show distress by crying, whimpering, gazing fearfully, and crawling away. Fear of strangers often peaks at 9 to 12 months and declines in the second year.

FICTION

T (F) Fear of strangers is abnormal among infants.

It is not true that fear of strangers is abnormal among infants. Most infants develop some form of stranger anxiety at around six to nine months of age.

Children with fear of strangers show less anxiety when their mothers are present (Rapee, 2011). Children also are less fearful when they are in familiar surroundings, such as their homes, rather than in the laboratory (Brooker et al., 2013).

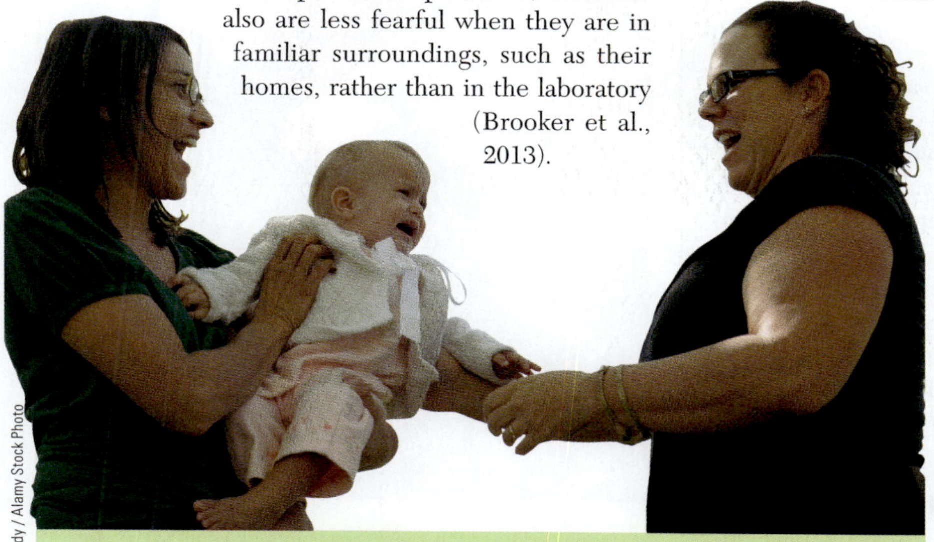

Christina Kennedy / Alamy Stock Photo

Stranger anxiety—also called fear of strangers—tends to emerge at about six to nine months of age. It is common but by no means universal.

6-4c SOCIAL REFERENCING: WHAT SHOULD I DO NOW?

Social referencing is the seeking out of another person's perception of a situation to help us form our own view of it. Leslie Carver and Brenda Vaccaro (2007) suggest that social referencing requires three components: (1) looking at another, usually older individual in a novel, ambiguous situation; (2) associating that individual's emotional response with the unfamiliar situation; and (3) regulating their own emotional response in accord with the response of the older individual.

Infants also display social referencing, as early as six months of age. They use caregivers' facial expressions or tone of voice as clues on how to respond (Schmitow & Stenberg, 2013). In one study, eight-month-old infants were friendlier to a stranger when their mothers exhibited a friendly facial expression in the stranger's presence than when she looked worried (Boccia & Campos, 1989).

EMOTIONAL REGULATION: KEEPING ON AN EVEN KEEL **Emotional regulation** refers to the ways in which young children control their own emotions. Even infants display certain behaviors to control unpleasant emotional states. They may look away from a disturbing event or suck their thumbs (Lewis, 2013; Rothbart & Sheese, 2007). Caregivers help infants learn to regulate their emotions. A two-way communication system develops in which the infant signals the caregiver that help is needed and the caregiver responds. Claire Kopp (1989, p. 347) provides an example of such a system:

> *A 13-month-old, playing with a large plastic bottle, attempted to unscrew the cover, but could not. Fretting for a short time, she initiated eye contact with her mother and held out the jar. As her mother took it to unscrew the cover, the infant ceased fretting.*

Research evidence suggests that the children of secure mothers are not only likely to be securely attached themselves but also are

social referencing using another person's reaction to a situation to form one's own response.

emotional regulation techniques for controlling one's emotional states.

Stuart Pearce/AGE Fotostock

The infant in the high chair seems to be regulating his emotions better than his parents are regulating theirs.

likely to regulate their own emotions in a positive manner (Lewis, 2013; Thompson & Meyer, 2007). A German longitudinal study (Zimmermann et al., 2001) related emotional regulation in adolescence with patterns of attachment during infancy, as assessed using the Strange Situation method. Forty-one adolescents, aged 16 and 17, were placed in complex problem-solving situations with friends. Those adolescents who were secure as infants were most capable of regulating their emotions to interact cooperatively with their friends.

6-5 PERSONALITY DEVELOPMENT

In this section, we look at the emergence of the self-concept. We then turn to a discussion of temperament. Finally, we consider gender differences in behavior.

6-5a THE SELF-CONCEPT

At birth, we may find the world to be a confusing blur of sights, sounds, and inner sensations—yet the "we" may be missing, at least for a while. When our hands first come into view, there is little evidence we realize that the hands "belong" to us and that we are separate and distinct from the world outside.

The self-concept appears to emerge gradually during infancy. At some point, infants understand that the hands they are moving in and out of sight are "their" hands. At some point, they understand that their own bodies extend only so far and then external objects and the bodies of others begin.

DEVELOPMENT OF THE SELF-CONCEPT Psychologists have devised ingenious methods to assess the development of the self-concept among infants. One of these is the *mirror technique*, which involves the use of a mirror and a dot of rouge. Before the experiment begins, the researcher observes the infant for baseline data on how frequently the infant touches his or her nose. Then the mother places rouge on the infant's nose, and the infant is placed before a mirror. Not until about the age of 18 months do infants begin to touch their own noses upon looking in the mirror (Keller et al., 2005; Taumoepeau & Reese, 2014).

Nose touching suggests that children recognize themselves and that they perceive that the dot of rouge is an abnormality. Most two-year-olds can point to pictures of themselves, and they begin to use "I" or their own name spontaneously (Smiley & Johnson, 2006).

Self-awareness affects the infant's social and emotional development (Foley, 2006). Knowledge

Voisin / Phanie / SuperStock

In the middle of the second year, infants begin to develop self-awareness, which has a powerful effect on social and emotional development.

of the self permits the infant and child to develop notions of sharing and cooperation. In one study, two-year-olds with a better developed sense of self were more likely to cooperate with other children (Brownell & Carriger, 1990).

Self-awareness also facilitates the development of "self-conscious" emotions such as embarrassment, envy, empathy, pride, guilt, and shame (Foley, 2006). In another study, Deborah Stipek and her colleagues (1992) found that children older than 21 months often seek their mother's attention and approval when they have successfully completed a task, whereas younger toddlers do not.

FICTION

T (F) All children are born with the same temperament. Treatment by caregivers determines whether they are difficult or easygoing.

It is not true that all children are "born" with the same temperament. Tendencies to be easygoing, difficult, or slow to warm up can apparently be inborn, although they can be modified by experience.

6-5b TEMPERAMENT: EASY, DIFFICULT, OR SLOW TO WARM UP?

Each child has a characteristic **temperament**, a stable way of reacting and adapting to the world that is present early in life. Many researchers believe that temperament involves a genetic component (Shiner & DeYoung, 2013; Zuckerman, 2011). The child's temperament includes many aspects of behavior, including activity level, smiling and laughter, regularity in eating and sleep habits, approach or withdrawal, adaptability to new situations, intensity of responsiveness, general cheerfulness or unpleasantness, distractibility or persistence, and soothability (Thomas & Chess, 1989).

TYPES OF TEMPERAMENT Thomas and Chess (1989) found that from the first days of life, many of the children in their study (65%) could be classified into one of three types of temperament: "easy" (40% of their sample), "difficult" (10%), and "slow to warm up" (15%). Some of the differences among these three types of children are shown in Table 6.3. The easy child has regular sleep and feeding schedules, approaches new situations (such as a new food or a new school) with enthusiasm and adapts to them easily, and is generally cheerful. Some children are more inconsistent and show a mixture of temperament traits. For example, a toddler may have a pleasant disposition but be frightened of new situations.

The difficult child, on the other hand, has irregular sleep and feeding schedules, is slow to accept new people and situations, takes a long time to adjust to new routines, and responds to frustrations with tantrums and crying. The slow-to-warm-up child falls between the other two.

STABILITY OF TEMPERAMENT Though not all children are born with the same temperament, as Thomas and Chess found, there is at least moderate consistency in the development of temperament from infancy onward (Shiner et al., 2012; Zuckerman, 2011). The infant who is highly active and cries in novel situations often becomes a fearful toddler. Difficult children in general are at greater risk for developing psychological disorders and adjustment problems later in life (Bales et al., 2013; Sayal et al., 2013). A longitudinal study tracked the progress of infants with a difficult temperament from 1½ through 12 years of age (Guerin et al., 1997). A difficult temperament correlated with parental reports of behavioral problems from ages 3 to 12, and teachers' reports of problems with attention span and aggression.

GOODNESS OF FIT: THE ROLE OF THE ENVIRONMENT

Our daughter was a difficult infant, but we weathered the storm. At the age of 15, she was climbing out the second-story bedroom window at 2 a.m. to be with friends. When we discovered it, she sarcastically asked if we disapproved. "Yes," we said. "Use the front

TABLE 6.3 TYPES OF TEMPERAMENT

Temperament Category	Easy	Difficult	Slow to Warm Up
Regularity of biological functioning	Regular	Irregular	Somewhat irregular
Response to new stimuli	Positive approach	Negative withdrawal	Negative withdrawal
Adaptability to new situations	Adapts readily	Adapts slowly or not at all	Adapts slowly
Intensity of reaction	Mild or moderate	Intense	Mild
Quality of mood	Positive	Negative	Initially negative; gradually more positive

Sources: Chess & Thomas (1991) and Thomas & Chess (1989).

temperament individual difference in style of reaction that is present early in life.

door; you're less likely to get hurt." She graduated college with honors. She has occasional outbursts, but that's her boyfriend's problem. And they love her on the job. She's a hard worker and the most creative thing they've ever seen.

The environment also affects the development of temperament. An initial biological predisposition to a certain temperament may be strengthened or weakened by the parents' reaction to the child. Parents may react to a difficult child by imposing rigid caregiving schedules, which in turn can cause the child to become even more difficult (Laxman et al., 2013). This example illustrates a poor fit between the child's behavior style and the parents' response.

On the other hand, parents may try to modify a child's initial temperament in a more positive direction to achieve a **goodness of fit** between child and parent. Realization that their youngster's behavior does not mean that the child is weak or deliberately disobedient, or that they are bad parents, helps parents modify their attitudes and behavior toward the child, whose behavior may then improve (Bird et al., 2006; Laxman et al., 2013).

goodness of fit agreement between the parents' expectations of a child and the child's temperament.

6-5c GENDER DIFFERENCES

All cultures distinguish between females and males and have expectations about how they ought to behave. For this reason, a child's gender is a key factor in society's efforts to shape her or his personality and behavior.

BEHAVIOR OF INFANT GIRLS AND BOYS Girls tend to advance more rapidly in their motor development in infancy: They sit, crawl, and walk earlier than boys (Hines, 2013; Zelazo, 2013). Although a few studies have found that infant boys are more active and irritable than girls, others have not (Hines, 2013; Zelazo, 2013). Girls and boys are similar in their social behaviors. They are equally likely to smile at people's faces, for example, and they do not differ in their dependency on adults (Hines, 2013; Zelazo, 2013). Girls and boys do begin to differ early in their preference for certain toys and play activities. By 12 to 18 months of age, girls prefer to play with dolls, doll furniture, dishes, and toy animals; boys prefer transportation toys (trucks, cars, airplanes, and the like), tools, and sports equipment as early as 9 to 18 months of age (Berenbaum et al., 2008; Leaper & Bigler, 2011). Gender differences that show up later,

zhang bo/E+/Getty Images

Do mothers and fathers relate differently to their infants?

such as differences in spatial relations skills, are not necessarily evident in infancy (Örnkloo & von Hofsten, 2007). By 24 months, both girls and boys appear to be aware of which behaviors are considered appropriate or inappropriate for their gender, according to cultural stereotypes (Hill & Flom, 2007). Thus it appears girls and boys may show a preference for gender stereotypical toys before they have been socialized and possibly before they understand their own sex.

FICTION

T (F) Girls may prefer dolls and toy animals, and boys may prefer toy trucks and sports equipment, but these preferences emerge only after they have become aware of the gender roles assigned to them by society.

It is not true that children prefer stereotypically gender-related toys only *after* they have become aware of the gender roles assigned to them by society. Recent research suggests that children may show a preference for gender stereotypical toys before they have been socialized, and possibly even before they understand which gender they are.

ADULTS' BEHAVIOR TOWARD INFANTS Despite any possible inborn tendencies, research shows that most adults interact differently with girls and boys. Researchers have presented American adults with an unfamiliar infant who is dressed in boy's clothes and has a boy's name or an infant who is dressed in girl's clothing and has a girl's name. (In reality, it is the same baby who simply is given different names and clothing.) When adults believe they are playing with a girl, they are more likely to offer "her" a doll; when they think the child is a boy, they are more likely to offer a football or a hammer. "Boys" also are encouraged to engage in more physical activity than "girls" (Worell & Goodheart, 2006).

Parents, especially fathers, are more likely to encourage rough-and-tumble play in sons than daughters (John et al., 2013; Paquette & Dumont, 2013). On the other hand, parents talk more to infant daughters than infant sons. They smile more at daughters and are more emotionally expressive toward them (Powlishta et al., 2001).

Infant girls are likely to be decked out in a pink or yellow dress and embellished with ruffles and lace, whereas infant boys wear blue or red (Eccles et al., 2000; Powlishta et al., 2001). Parents provide baby girls and boys with different bedroom decorations and toys. Examination of the contents of rooms of children from five months to six years of age found that boys' rooms were often decorated with animal themes and with blue bedding and curtains. Girls' rooms featured flowers, lace, ruffles, and pastels. Girls owned more dolls; boys had more vehicles, military toys, and sports equipment.

Parents react favorably when their infant daughters play with "girls' toys" and their sons play with "boys' toys." Adults, especially fathers, show more negative reactions when girls play with boys' toys and boys play with girls' toys (Martin et al., 2002; Worell & Goodheart, 2006). Parents thus try to shape their children's behavior during infancy and lay the foundation for development in early childhood. In the following chapter, we examine physical and cognitive developments of early childhood.

Antonio_Diaz/Getty Images

Is it just as easy to imagine the boy's mother in this picture as the father? Why or why not?

STUDY TOOLS 6

READY TO STUDY?

In the book, you can:

- ☐ Rip out the chapter review card at the back of the book for a handy summary of the chapter and key terms.
- ☐ Check your understanding of what you've read with the quizzes that follow.

ONLINE AT CENGAGEBRAIN.COM YOU CAN:

- ☐ Collect StudyBits while you read and study the chapter.
- ☐ Quiz yourself on key concepts.
- ☐ Find videos for further exploration.
- ☐ Prepare for tests with HDEV5 Flash Cards as well as those you create.

SELF-ASSESSMENTS

Fill-Ins

Answers can be found in the back of the book.

1. There are two major types of insecure attachment: avoidant attachment and ____________/____________ attachment.
2. The first phase of attachment is the initial-____________ phase.
3. Harry and Margaret ____________ conducted classic experiments to demonstrate that contact comfort is critical to the attachment process.
4. According to Lorenz, attachment can occur only during a ____________ period.
5. ____________ disorder is characterized by social deficits and stereotyped behavior but without significant cognitive or language delays.
6. About ____________% of American children under the age of five are cared for in center-based care.
7. Infants display social ____________ by using caregivers' facial expressions or tone of voice as clues on how to respond to a situation.
8. Researchers have studied development of the self-concept by placing ____________ on the noses of infants.
9. The three basic types of temperament are easy, ____________, and slow to warm up.
10. Parents may try to modify a child's initial temperament to achieve a(n) ____________ of fit between child and parent.

Multiple Choice

1. **Which kind of attachment is used to describe babies who seem confused and may move toward the mother while looking away from her?**
   a. disorganized–disoriented
   b. secure
   c. avoidant
   d. ambivalent/resistant

2. **Sroufe found that insecure attachment at the age of one year predicts psychological disorders at the age of**
   a. 7.
   b. 17.
   c. 27.
   d. 37.

3. **According to Ainsworth, the clear-cut attachment phase occurs at about what age?**
   a. 6 to 7 months
   b. 10 to 12 months
   c. 16 to 18 months
   d. 24 to 36 months

4. **Which of the following views of attachment proposes that there is a critical period for developing attachment?**
   a. behavioral
   b. psychoanalytic
   c. cognitive
   d. ethological

5. **The natives in one Guatemalan village keep their children in a windowless hut and play with them only rarely until they can walk. By what age do the children act as alert and active as children who have been reared normally?**
   a. Actually, they never show any behavioral delays.
   b. 2
   c. 5
   d. 11

6. **By the time a child is two years of age, nine out of ten parents have**
   a. engaged in some sort of psychological or emotional abuse.
   b. spanked their children.
   c. pushed or shoved their children.
   d. sexually abused their children.

7. **All of the following are symptoms of autism spectrum disorders *except***
   a. losing language or social skills.
   b. failing to respond to being called by name.
   c. developing fear of strangers.
   d. not seeming to know how to play with toys.

8. **What does research evidence show about autism?**
   a. Autism is caused by the vaccine for measles, mumps, and rubella.
   b. Autism is a result of poor child rearing.
   c. Autism runs in families to some degree.
   d. All of the above are true.

9. **If someone asked you whether or not day care were a good idea for her three-year-old, which of the following answers would be based on research evidence?**
   a. Some children in day care learn to be more cooperative than they were.
   b. Some children in day care become somewhat more aggressive than they were.
   c. Children in high-quality day care seem to fare better in some ways than children in poor-quality day care.
   d. All of the above.

10. **Brunhilda's son is eight months old and has suddenly begun to cry hysterically and cling to her when strangers come over in the supermarket to say how cute he is. Knowing you are a psychology student, she asks you what you think. Which of the following would reflect what you learned reading this chapter?**
    a. Brunhilda has probably abused her son.
    b. A stranger has threatened or abused her son.
    c. Her son has an overly reactive nervous system.
    d. Her son is behaving normally.

7 Early Childhood: Physical and Cognitive Development

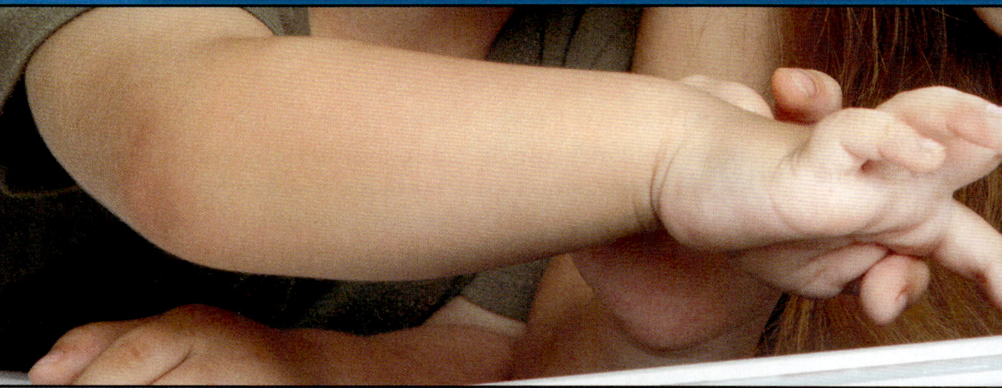

Joakim Leroy/E+/Getty Images

LEARNING OUTCOMES

After studying this chapter, you will be able to . . .

- 7-1 Describe trends in physical development in early childhood
- 7-2 Describe motor development in early childhood
- 7-3 Describe trends in health and illness in early childhood
- 7-4 Describe sleep patterns in early childhood
- 7-5 Discuss the elimination disorders
- 7-6 Describe Piaget's preoperational stage
- 7-7 Discuss influences on cognitive development in early childhood
- 7-8 Explain how "theory of mind" affects cognitive development
- 7-9 Describe memory development in early childhood
- 7-10 Describe language development in early childhood

After you finish this chapter, go to **PAGE 151** for **STUDY TOOLS**

The years from two to six are referred to as early childhood or the preschool years. During early childhood, physical growth is slower than in infancy. Children become taller and leaner, and by the end of early childhood they look more like adults than infants. Motor skills develop dramatically. Children become stronger, faster, and better coordinated.

During the preschool years, physical and motor development proceeds, literally, by leaps and bounds.

Language improves enormously, and children come to carry on conversations with others. As cognitive skills develop, a new world of make-believe or "pretend" play emerges. Most preschoolers are curious and eager to learn. Increased physical and cognitive capabilities enable children to emerge from total dependence on caregivers to become part of the broader world outside the family.

7-1 GROWTH PATTERNS

During the preschool years, physical and motor development proceeds, literally, by leaps and bounds.

7-1a HEIGHT AND WEIGHT

Following the dramatic gains in height in a child's first two years, the growth rate slows during the preschool years (Kuczmarski et al., 2000). Girls and boys tend to gain about two to three inches in height per year, and weight gains remain fairly even at about four to six pounds per year (see Figure 7.1). Children become increasingly slender as they gain in height and shed some "baby fat." Boys as a group become slightly taller and heavier than girls (see Figure 7.1). Noticeable variations in growth occur from child to child. (For a discussion of childhood obesity, see Chapter 9.)

7-1b DEVELOPMENT OF THE BRAIN

The brain develops more quickly than any other organ in early childhood. At two years of age, the brain already has attained 75% of its adult weight. By the age of five, the brain has reached 90% of its adult weight, even though the body weight of the five-year-old is barely one-third of what it will be as an adult.

The increase in brain size is due in part to the continuing myelination of nerve fibers. Completion of myelination of the neural pathways that link the cerebellum to the cerebral cortex facilitates development of fine motor skills, balance, and coordination (Fletcher, 2011; Rilling, 2013).

BRAIN DEVELOPMENT AND VISUAL SKILLS Brain development also improves processing of visual information (Seiler et al., 2011), facilitating learning to read. The parts of the brain that enable the child to sustain attention and screen out distractions become increasingly myelinated between the ages of about four and seven (Otero & Barker, 2014), enabling most children to focus on schoolwork. The speed of processing visual information improves throughout childhood, reaching adult levels at the onset of adolescence (Otero & Barker, 2014; Y. Wang et al., 2016).

RIGHT BRAIN, LEFT BRAIN? We often hear people described as being "right-brained" or "left-brained." The notion is that the hemispheres of the brain are involved in different kinds of intellectual and emotional activities. Research does suggest that in right-handed individuals, the left hemisphere is relatively more involved

TRUTH OR FICTION?

T F Some children are left-brained, and others are right-brained.

T F Some diseases are normal during childhood.

T F Competent parents toilet train their children by their second birthday.

T F A preschooler's having imaginary companions is a sign of loneliness or psychological problems.

T F Two-year-olds tend to assume that their parents are aware of everything that is happening to them, even when their parents are not present.

T F "Because Mommy wants me to" may be a perfectly good explanation—for a three-year-old.

FIG.7.1 GROWTH CURVES FOR HEIGHT AND WEIGHT, AGES TWO TO SIX YEARS

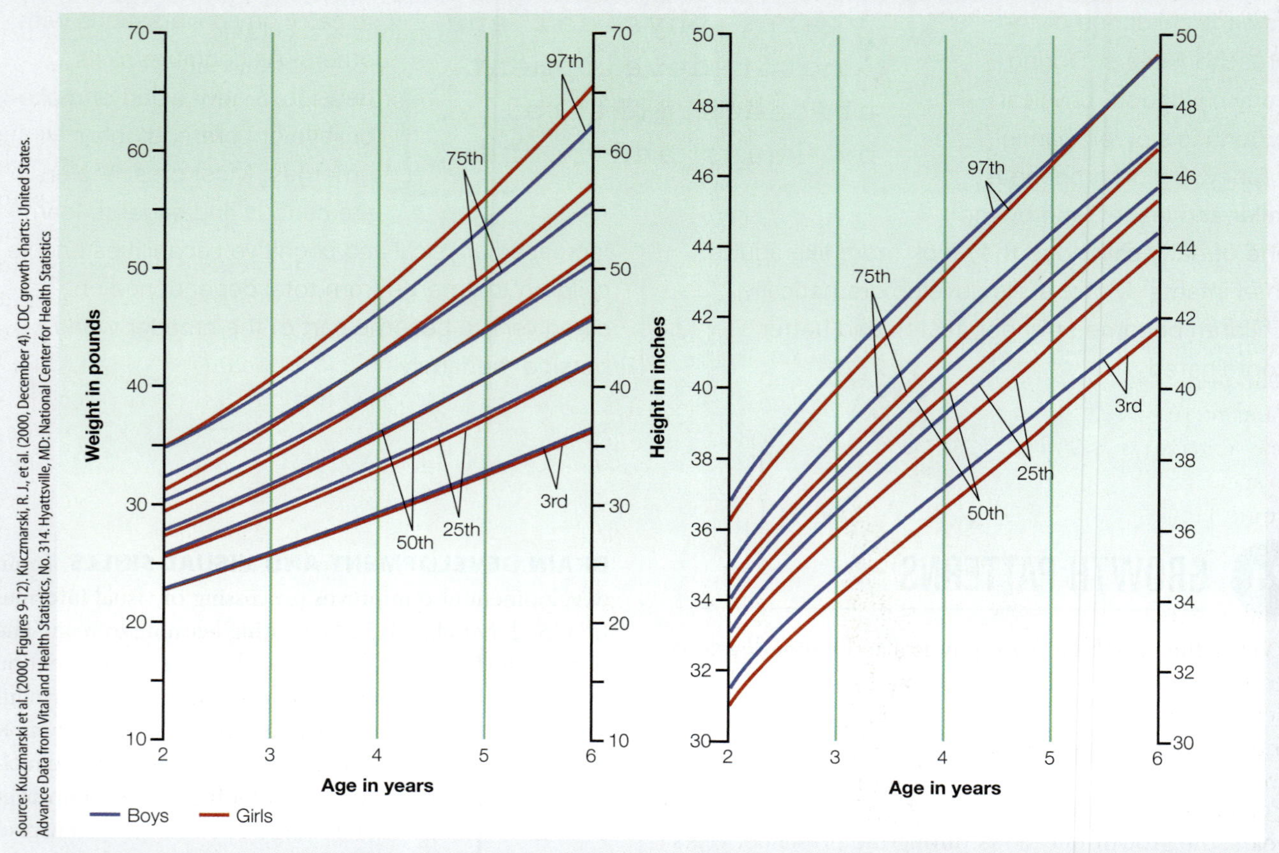

The numbers on the curves indicate the percentiles for height and weight at different ages. The growth rate slows during early childhood. As in infancy, boys are only slightly taller and heavier than girls.

in intellectual undertakings that require logical analysis and problem-solving, language, and computation (Scull, 2010). The other hemisphere (the right hemisphere) is usually superior in visual–spatial functions (such as piecing puzzles together), aesthetic and emotional responses, and understanding metaphors.

But it is not true that some children are left-brained and others are right-brained. The functions of the left and right hemispheres overlap, and the hemispheres respond simultaneously when we focus on one thing or another (Franklin, 2013). They are aided in "cooperation" by the myelination of the **corpus callosum**, a thick bundle of nerve fibers that connects the hemispheres (Luders et al., 2010). This process is largely complete by the age of eight, enabling the integration of logical and emotional functioning.

corpus callosum the thick bundle of nerve fibers that connects the left and right hemispheres of the brain.

plasticity the tendency of new parts of the brain to take up the functions of injured parts.

FICTION

T (F) Some children are left-brained, and others are right-brained.

It is not true that some children are left-brained and others are right-brained. The statement is too all-inclusive to be true. The functions of the two brain hemispheres overlap.

PLASTICITY OF THE BRAIN Many parts of the brain have specialized functions, allowing our behavior to be more complex. But it also means that injuries to certain parts of the brain can result in loss of these functions. However, the brain also shows **plasticity**, or the ability to compensate for injuries to particular areas. Plasticity is greatest at about one to two years of age and then gradually declines (Lohmann & Kessels, 2014; Skoe et al., 2013). When we as adults suffer damage to the areas of the brain that control language, we may lose the ability to speak or understand language. However, other areas of the brain may assume these functions in preschoolers who suffer such damage. As a result, they may regain the ability to speak or comprehend language. Neurological factors that enable plasticity include the growth of new dendrites ("sprouting") and the redundancy of neural connections (Lohmann & Kessels, 2014; Skoe et al., 2013).

Tom Merton/OJO Images/Jupiter Images

7-2 MOTOR DEVELOPMENT

The preschool years witness an explosion of motor skills, as children's nervous systems mature and their movements become more precise and coordinated.

7-2a GROSS MOTOR SKILLS

Gross motor skills involve the large muscles used in locomotion (see Table 7.1). At about the age of three, children can balance on one foot. By age three or four, they can walk up stairs as adults do, by placing a foot on each step. By age four or five, they can skip and pedal a tricycle (Allen et al., 2011). Older preschoolers are better able to coordinate two tasks, such as singing and running at the same time. In general, preschoolers appear to acquire motor skills by teaching themselves and observing other children. Imitating other children seems more important than adult instruction at this age.

Throughout early childhood, girls and boys are similar in motor skills. Girls are somewhat better at balance and precision. Boys show some advantage in throwing and kicking (Haywood & Getchel, 2014; Veldman et al., 2016).

Individual differences are larger than gender differences throughout early and middle childhood. Some children are genetically predisposed to developing better coordination or more strength. Motivation and practice also are important. Motor experiences in infancy may affect the development of motor skills in early childhood. For example, children with early crawling experience perform better than those who do not on tests of motor skills (Haywood & Getchell, 2014).

gross motor skills skills employing the large muscles used in locomotion.

TABLE 7.1 DEVELOPMENT OF GROSS MOTOR SKILLS IN EARLY CHILDHOOD

2 Years (24–35 Months)	3 Years (36–47 Months)	4 Years (48–59 Months)	5 Years (60–71 Months)
• Runs well straight ahead • Walks up stairs, two feet to a step • Kicks a large ball • Jumps a distance of 4–14 inches • Throws a small ball without falling • Pushes and pulls large toys • Hops on one foot, two or more hops • Tries to stand on one foot • Climbs on furniture to look out of window	• Goes around obstacles while running • Walks up stairs, one foot to a step • Kicks a large ball easily • Jumps from the bottom step • Catches a bounced ball, using torso and arms to form a basket • Goes around obstacles while pushing and pulling toys • Hops on one foot, up to three hops • Stands on one foot • Climbs nursery-school apparatus	• Turns sharp corners while running • Walks down stairs, one foot to a step • Jumps from a height of 12 inches • Throws a ball overhand • Turns sharp corners while pushing and pulling toys • Hops on one foot, four to six hops • Stands on one foot for 3–8 seconds • Climbs ladders • Skips on one foot • Rides a tricycle well	• Runs lightly on toes • Jumps a distance of 3 feet • Catches a small ball, using hands only • Hops 2 to 3 yards forward on each foot • Stands on one foot for 8–10 seconds • Climbs actively and skillfully • Skips on alternate feet • Rides a bicycle with training wheels

Note: The ages are averages; there are individual variations.

7-2b PHYSICAL ACTIVITY

Preschoolers spend an average of more than 25 hours a week in large muscle activity (Haywood & Getchell, 2014). Younger preschoolers are more likely than older preschoolers to engage in physically oriented play, such as grasping, banging, and mouthing objects (Haywood & Getchell, 2014; Hanson, 2013).

Motor activity level begins to decline after two or three years of age. Children become less restless and are able to sit still longer. Between the ages of two and four, children show an increase in sustained, focused attention.

Horizon/Horizon International Images Limited/Alamy Stock Photo

Aggression or normal rough-and-tumble play?

ROUGH-AND-TUMBLE PLAY Rough-and-tumble play consists of running, chasing, fleeing, wrestling, hitting with an open hand, laughing, and making faces. Rough-and-tumble play, which is more common among boys than among girls, is not the same as aggressive behavior, which involves hitting, pushing, taking, grabbing, and angry looks. Rough-and-tumble play helps develop physical and social skills (Cillessen & Bellmore, 2011; Van Gils, 2014).

INDIVIDUAL DIFFERENCES IN ACTIVITY LEVEL Physically active parents are likely to have physically active children. In a study of four- to seven-year-olds, children of active mothers were twice as likely to be active as children of inactive mothers (Monroe et al., 1991). Children of active fathers were 3½ times as likely to be active.

Several reasons may explain this relationship. First, active parents may serve as role models for activity. Second, sharing of activities by family members may be responsible. Active parents may also encourage their child's participation in physical activity. Twin studies also suggest there is a genetic tendency for activity level (Herring et al., 2014; Saudino, 2011).

fine motor skills skills employing the small muscles used in manipulation, such as those in the fingers.

7-2c FINE MOTOR SKILLS

Fine motor skills involve the small muscles used in manipulation and coordination. These skills develop gradually, a bit more slowly than gross motor skills (Haywood & Getchell, 2014). Control over the wrists and fingers enables children to hold a pencil properly, dress themselves, and stack blocks (see Table 7.2). Preschoolers can labor endlessly in attempting to tie their shoelaces and get their jackets zipped.

TABLE 7.2 DEVELOPMENT OF FINE MOTOR SKILLS IN EARLY CHILDHOOD			
2 Years (24–35 Months)	**3 Years (36–47 Months)**	**4 Years (48–59 Months)**	**5 Years (60–71 Months)**
• Builds tower of 6 cubes • Copies vertical and horizontal lines • Imitates folding of paper • Prints on easel with a brush • Places simple shapes in correct holes	• Builds tower of 9 cubes • Copies circle and cross • Copies letters • Holds crayons with fingers, not fist • Strings four beads using a large needle	• Builds tower of 10 or more cubes • Copies square • Prints simple words • Imitates folding paper three times • Uses pencil with correct hand grip • Strings 10 beads	• Builds 3 steps from 6 blocks, using a model • Copies triangle and star • Prints first name and numbers • Imitates folding of piece of square paper into a triangle • Traces around a diamond drawn on paper • Laces shoes

Note: The ages are averages; there are individual variations.

7-2d CHILDREN'S ARTISTIC DEVELOPMENT

Children's artistic development is linked to the development of motor and cognitive skills. Children first begin to scribble during the second year of life. Initially, they seem to make marks for the sheer joy of it (Jolley, 2010). Rhoda Kellogg (1959, 1970) found a meaningful pattern in the scribbles. She identified 20 basic scribbles that she considered the building blocks of art (see Figure 7.2).

Children progress through four stages from making scribbles to drawing pictures: the *placement, shape, design*, and *pictorial stages* (see Figure 7.3). Two-year-olds scribble in various locations on the page (e.g., in the middle of the page or near one of the borders). By age three, children are starting to draw basic shapes: circles, squares, triangles, crosses, X's, and odd shapes. As soon as they can draw shapes, children begin to combine them in the design stage. Between ages four and five, children reach the pictorial stage, in which designs begin to resemble recognizable objects.

Children's early drawings tend to be symbolic of broad categories rather than specific. A child might draw the same simple building whether asked to draw a school or a house (Tallandini & Valentini, 1991). Children between three and five usually do not set out to draw a particular thing. They are more likely to see what they have drawn, then name it. As motor and cognitive skills develop beyond the age of five, children become able to draw an object they have in mind. The ability to copy figures also improves (Daglioglu et al., 2010; Rübeling et al., 2011).

7-2e HANDEDNESS

Some infants show no hand preference during infancy (Nelson et al., 2013), but by the age of two to three months, in most cases a rattle placed in an infant's hand is held longer with the right hand than the left (Fitzgerald et al., 1991). By four months of age, most infants show a clear-cut right-hand preference in exploring objects (Streri, 2002). Preferring to grasp with one hand or the other increases markedly between 6 and 14 months (Ferre et al., 2010). Handedness becomes more strongly established during early childhood. Most people are right-handed, although studies vary as to how many are left-handed.

The origins of handedness apparently have a genetic component (Hopkins et al., 2015; Michel, 2013; Willems et al., 2014). If both of your parents are right-handed,

FIG.7.2 THE 20 BASIC SCRIBBLES

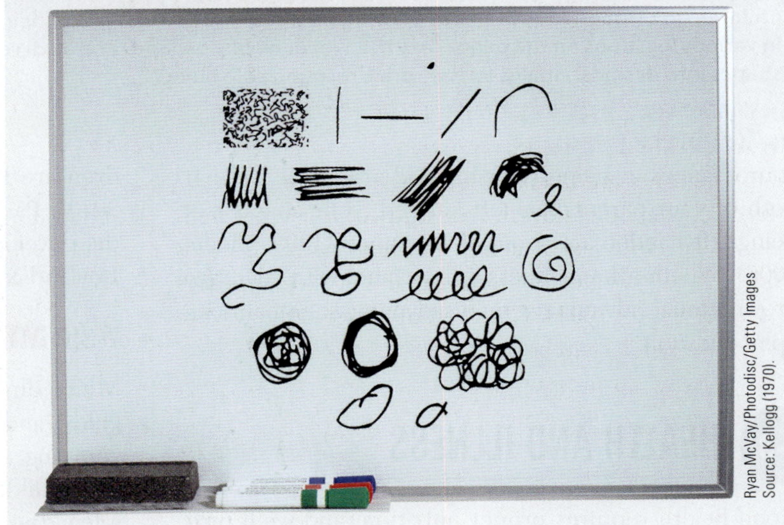

Ryan McVay/Photodisc/Getty Images
Source: Kellogg (1970).

By the age of two, children can scribble. Rhoda Kellogg has identified these 20 basic scribbles as the building blocks of children's drawings.

FIG.7.3 FOUR STAGES IN CHILDREN'S DRAWING

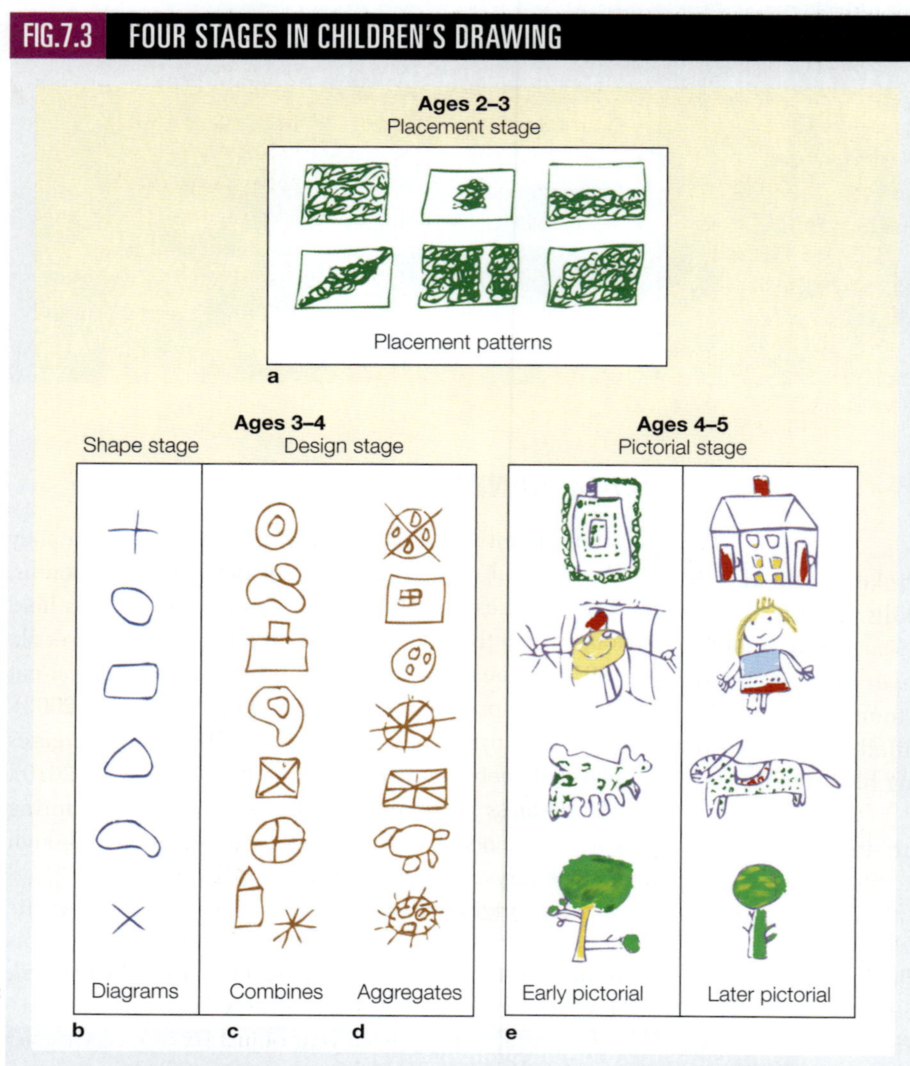

Children go through four stages in drawing pictures. (a) They first place their scribbles in various locations on the page. They then (b) draw basic shapes and (c, d) combine shapes into designs. Finally, (e) they draw recognizable objects.

your chances of being right-handed are about 92%. If both of your parents are left-handed, your chances of being left-handed are about 50% (Annett, 1999; Clode, 2006). Whether handedness is associated with cognitive or emotional advantages or disadvantages remains an open question.

7-3 HEALTH AND ILLNESS

Good health requires proper nutrition, and we'll provide some guidelines for helping young children obtain what they need. Nevertheless, regardless of how well they eat, nearly all children get ill now and then. Some seem to be ill every other week or so. Most illnesses are minor, and children seem to eventually outgrow many of them. Fortunately, we can prevent or cure many others.

7-3a NUTRITION

Between the ages of two and three, a child needs 1000–1,400 calories of food per day, and between the ages of four and eight, a child requires some 1,200–2,000 calories a day, depending on growth and activity level (Mayo Clinic, 2014). This is a very wide range, so an absolute prescription for a given child is not advisable. The Mayo Clinic advises eating a balanced diet of protein sources (e.g., seafood, lean meats, nuts), fruits, vegetables, grains, and dairy products. During the second and third years, a child's appetite typically becomes erratic, but because the child is growing more slowly than in infancy, he or she needs fewer calories. Children who eat little at one meal may compensate by eating more at another (Cooke et al., 2003).

Infants seem to be born liking the taste of sugar, although they are fairly indifferent to salt. But preference for sweet and salty foods increases if children are repeatedly exposed to them (Bouhlal et al., 2013). Parents and television advertising also influence the development of food preferences (Bost et al., 2014; Boyland & Halford, 2013).

7-3b MINOR ILLNESSES

Minor illnesses refer to respiratory infections, such as colds, and to gastrointestinal upsets, such as nausea, vomiting, and diarrhea. These diseases are normal in that most children come down with them. They typically last a few days or less and are not life threatening. Although diarrheal illness in the United States is usually mild, it is a leading killer of children in developing countries (Save the Children, 2015).

TRUTH

T F Some diseases are normal during childhood.

It is true that some diseases are normal in childhood. Minor illnesses, referred to by some as "the stuff going around," are statistically normal, meaning that many or even most children contract them.

American children between the ages of one and three average eight to nine minor illnesses a year. Between the ages of 4 and 10, the average drops to four to six. Childhood illnesses can lead to the creation of antibodies that may prevent children from coming down with the same illnesses in adulthood when they can do more harm.

Don Mason/Blend Images/Jupiter Images

7-3c MAJOR ILLNESSES

Advances in immunization along with the development of antibiotics and other medications have dramatically reduced the incidence and effects of serious childhood diseases. Because most preschoolers and schoolchildren have been inoculated against major childhood illnesses such as rubella (German measles), measles, tetanus, mumps, whooping cough, diphtheria, and polio, these diseases no longer pose the threat they once did.

Nearly one-third of children in the United States younger than 18 years of age suffer from a chronic illness (Agency for Healthcare Research and Quality, 2004). These illnesses include arthritis, diabetes, cerebral palsy, and cystic fibrosis.

Although many major childhood diseases have been largely eradicated in the United States and other industrialized nations, they remain fearsome killers of children in developing countries. Around the world, eight to nine million children die each year of just six diseases: pneumonia, diarrhea, measles, tetanus, whooping cough, and tuberculosis (Save the Children, 2015). Air pollution from the combustion of fossil fuels for heating and cooking causes many respiratory infections, which are responsible for nearly one death in five among children who are younger than five years of age (Save the Children, 2015). Diarrhea kills nearly two million children under the age of five each year. Diarrheal diseases are mostly related to unsafe drinking water and poor sanitation and hygiene (Save the Children, 2015).

Many youngsters are exposed to lead in early childhood, often by eating chips of lead paint from their homes or by breathing in dust from the paint.

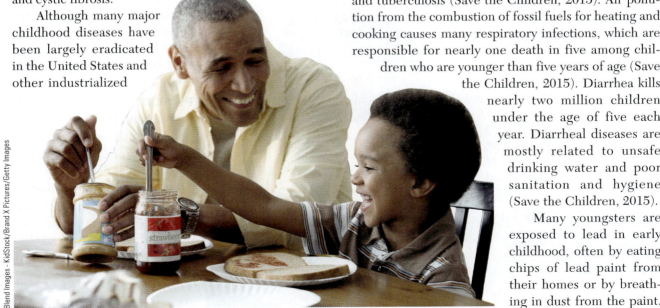

Blend Images - KidStock/Brand X Pictures/Getty Images

Infants fed formula made with tap water may be at risk of lead poisoning, because water pipes sometimes contain lead (Centers for Disease Control and Prevention, 2013b). Lead causes neurological damage and may result in lowered cognitive functioning and other delays.

7-3d ACCIDENTS

Accidents cause more deaths in early childhood than the next six most frequent causes combined (Johnson et al., 2014; Leading Causes of Death, 2016). The single most common cause of death in early childhood is motor vehicle accidents. Boys are more likely than girls to incur accidental injuries at all ages and in all socioeconomic groups. Poor children are five times as likely to die from fires and more than twice as likely to die in motor vehicle accidents than other children (Leading Causes of Death, 2016). The high accident rate of low-income children may result partly from living in dangerous housing and neighborhoods.

7-4 SLEEP

Preschoolers do not need as much sleep as infants. The National Sleep Foundation (2015) recommends 11 to 13 hours of sleep in a 24-hour period for preschoolers (see Table 7.3). A common pattern includes nine to ten hours at night and a nap of one to two hours. Many children resist going to bed or going to sleep (Freeman et al., 2012). Getting to sleep late can be a problem, because preschoolers tend not to make up fully for lost sleep (National Sleep Foundation, 2015). Many young children take a so-called "transitional object"—such as a favored blanket or a stuffed animal—to bed with them.

7-4a SLEEP DISORDERS

Not all children get the sleep they need. In this section, we focus on the sleep disorders of sleep terrors, nightmares, and sleepwalking.

sleep terrors frightening dreamlike experiences that occur during the deepest stage of non-REM sleep, shortly after the child has gone to sleep.

somnambulism sleepwalking.

Denise Hager/Catchlight Visual Services/Alamy Stock Photo

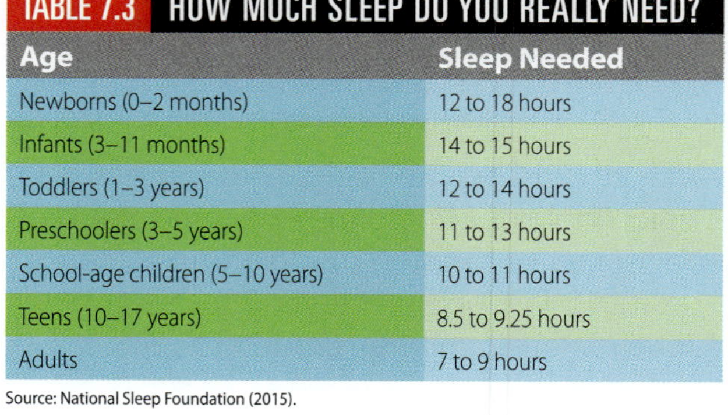

TABLE 7.3 HOW MUCH SLEEP DO YOU REALLY NEED?

Age	Sleep Needed
Newborns (0–2 months)	12 to 18 hours
Infants (3–11 months)	14 to 15 hours
Toddlers (1–3 years)	12 to 14 hours
Preschoolers (3–5 years)	11 to 13 hours
School-age children (5–10 years)	10 to 11 hours
Teens (10–17 years)	8.5 to 9.25 hours
Adults	7 to 9 hours

Source: National Sleep Foundation (2015).

SLEEP TERRORS AND NIGHTMARES **Sleep terrors** are more severe than the anxiety dreams we refer to as nightmares (National Sleep Foundation, 2015). Sleep terrors usually occur during deep sleep. Nightmares take place during lighter rapid-eye-movement (REM) sleep, when about 80% of normal dreams occur.

Sleep terrors usually begin in childhood or early adolescence and are outgrown by late adolescence. They are sometimes associated with stress, as in moving to a new neighborhood, beginning school, adjusting to parental divorce, or being in a war zone. Children with sleep terrors may wake suddenly with a surge in heart and respiration rates, talk incoherently, and thrash about. Children may then fall back into more restful sleep. The incidence of sleep terrors wanes as children develop.

Children who have frequent nightmares or sleep terrors may come to fear going to sleep. They may show distress at bedtime, refuse to get into their pajamas, and insist that the lights be kept on. As a result, they can develop insomnia. Children with frequent nightmares or sleep terrors need caregivers' understanding and affection. They also profit from a regular routine in which they are expected to get to sleep at the same time each night (Freeman et al., 2012).

SLEEPWALKING Sleepwalking, or **somnambulism**, is more common among children than adults. As with sleep terrors, sleepwalking tends to occur during deep sleep (National Sleep Foundation, 2015). Onset is usually between the ages of three and eight.

When children sleepwalk, they may rearrange toys, go to the bathroom, or go to the refrigerator and have a glass of milk. They then return to their rooms and go back to bed. There are myths about sleepwalking, for instance that sleepwalkers' eyes are closed, that they will avoid harm, and that they will become violently agitated if they are awakened during an episode. All these notions are false.

Sleepwalking in children is assumed to reflect immaturity of the nervous system. As with sleep terrors, the incidence of sleepwalking drops as children develop. It may help to discuss a child's persistent sleep terrors or sleepwalking with a health professional.

7-5 ELIMINATION DISORDERS

The elimination of waste products occurs reflexively in neonates. As children develop, they learn to inhibit the reflexes that govern urination and bowel movements. The process by which parents teach their children to inhibit these reflexes is referred to as toilet training.

In toilet training, maturation plays a crucial role. During the first year, only an exceptional child can be toilet trained. Most American children are toilet trained between the ages of three and four (American Psychiatric Association, 2013). They may have nighttime "accidents" for another year or so. Children who do not become toilet trained within reasonable time frames may be diagnosed with enuresis, encopresis, or both.

FICTION

T (F) Competent parents toilet train their children by their second birthday.

It is not true that competent parents toilet train their children by their second birthday. Most American children are actually toilet trained between the ages of three and four.

7-5a ENURESIS

Enuresis is failure to control the bladder (urination) once the "normal" age for achieving bladder control has been reached. The American Psychiatric Association (2013) places the cutoff age at five years and does not consider "accidents" to represent enuresis unless they occur at least twice a month for five- and six-year-olds.

A nighttime "accident" is termed **bed-wetting**. Nighttime control is more difficult to achieve than daytime control. At night, children must first wake up when their bladders are full. Only then can they go to the bathroom. Overall, 8% to 10% of American children wet their beds (Lucas et al., 2015), with the problem about twice as common among boys. Bed-wetting tends to occur during the deepest stage of sleep. That is also the stage when sleep terrors and sleepwalking take place.

It is believed that enuresis might have organic causes, most often immaturity of the motor cortex of the brain (Lucas et al., 2015). Just as children outgrow sleep terrors and sleepwalking, they tend to outgrow bed-wetting (Lucas et al., 2015).

7-5b ENCOPRESIS

Soiling, or **encopresis**, is lack of control over the bowels. Soiling, like enuresis, is more common among boys. About 1% to 2% of children at the ages of seven and eight have continuing problems controlling their bowels (Lucas et al., 2015). Soiling, in contrast to enuresis, is more likely to occur during the day. Thus, it can be embarrassing to the child, especially in school.

Encopresis stems from both physical causes, such as chronic constipation, and psychological factors (Mellon, 2012; von Gontard, 2011). Soiling may follow harsh punishment of toileting accidents, especially in children who are already anxious or under stress (Lucas et al., 2015). Punishment may cause the child to tense up on the toilet, when moving one's bowels requires that one relax the anal sphincter muscles. Soiling, punishment, and anxiety can become a vicious cycle.

7-6 JEAN PIAGET'S PREOPERATIONAL STAGE

According to Piaget, the **preoperational stage** of cognitive development lasts from about age two to age seven. Be warned: Any resemblance between the logic of a preschooler and your own may be purely coincidental. *Operations* are mental manipulations of information, and at this stage, young children's logic is at best "under construction."

enuresis failure to control the bladder (urination) once the normal age for control has been reached.

bed-wetting failure to control the bladder during the night.

encopresis failure to control the bowels once the normal age for bowel control has been reached. Also called soiling.

preoperational stage the second stage in Piaget's scheme, characterized by inflexible and irreversible mental manipulation of symbols.

7-6a SYMBOLIC THOUGHT

Preoperational thought is characterized by the use of symbols to represent objects and relationships among them. Perhaps the most important kind of symbolic activity of young children is language, but children's early use of language leaves something to be desired in the realm of logic. According to Piaget, preschoolers' drawings are symbols of objects, people, and events in children's lives. Symbolism is also expressed as symbolic or pretend play.

7-6b SYMBOLIC OR PRETEND PLAY

Children's **symbolic play**—the "let's pretend" type of play—may seem immature to busy adults meeting the realistic demands of the business world, but it requires cognitive sophistication (Hoff, 2013; Taylor, 2013).

Piaget ([1946] 1962) wrote that pretend play usually begins in the second year, when the child begins to symbolize objects. The ability to engage in pretend play is based on the use and recollection of symbols, that is, on mental representations of things children have experienced or heard about.

Children first engage in pretend play at about 12 or 13 months. They make believe that they are performing familiar activities, such as sleeping or feeding themselves. By 15 to 20 months, they can shift their focus from themselves to others. A child may pretend to feed her doll. By 30 months, she or he can make believe that the other object takes an active role. The child may pretend that the doll is feeding itself (Paavola et al., 2006).

symbolic play play in which children make believe that objects and toys are other than what they are. Also called pretend play.

egocentrism putting oneself at the center of things such that one is unable to perceive the world from another person's point of view.

The quality of preschoolers' pretend play has implications for subsequent development. For example, preschoolers who engage in violent pretend play are less empathic, less likely to help other children, and more likely to engage in antisocial behavior later on (Dunn & Hughes, 2001). The quality of pretend play is connected with preschoolers' academic performance later on, their creativity, and their social skills (Taylor, 2013).

Imaginary companions—also known as *virtual characters* (Aguiar & Taylor, 2015)—are one example of pretend play. It is estimated that between 10% and 50% of preschoolers have imaginary companions (Davis et al., 2013). Imaginary companions are most commonly found among firstborn and only children (Gleason, 2013; Hoff, 2013). Having an imaginary playmate does not mean that the child has problems with real relationships (Gleason, 2013; Hoff, 2005). In fact, children with imaginary companions are less aggressive, more cooperative, and more creative than other children (Gleason, 2013; Hoff, 2013). They have more real friends, show greater ability to concentrate, and are more advanced in language development (Aguilar & Taylor, 2015).

glenda/Shutterstock.com

FICTION

T (F) A preschooler's having imaginary companions is a sign of loneliness or psychological problems.

It is not true that having imaginary companions is a sign of loneliness or psychological problems. Having imaginary companions is a normal—though not universal—aspect of development.

7-6c EGOCENTRISM: IT'S ALL ABOUT ME

Sometimes the attitude "It's all about me" is a sign of early childhood, not of selfishness. One consequence of one-dimensional thinking is **egocentrism**. Egocentrism, in Piaget's use of the term, means that preoperational children do not understand that other people may have different perspectives on the world. Two-year-olds may, in fact, assume that their parents are aware of everything that is happening to them, even when their parents are not present. When I asked a daughter aged 2½ to tell me about a trip to the store with her mother, she answered, "You tell me." It did not occur to her that I could not see the world through her eyes.

TRUTH

T F Two-year-olds tend to assume that their parents are aware of everything that is happening to them, even when their parents are not present.

It is true that two-year-olds do tend to assume that their parents are aware of everything that is happening to them, even when their parents are not present. This erroneous (but adorable) assumption reflects their egocentrism and their inability to focus on multiple aspects of a situation simultaneously.

Piaget used the "three-mountains test" (see Figure 7.4) to show that egocentrism prevents young children from taking the viewpoints of others. In this demonstration, the child faces a table before a model of three mountains. One has a house on it, and another has a cross at the summit.

FIG.7.4 THE THREE MOUNTAINS TEST

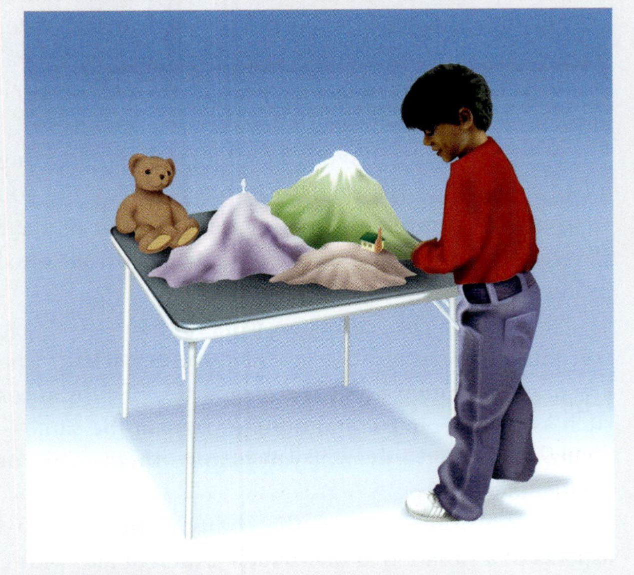

What does the teddy bear see? You might know the answer, but what might the young boy say? Piaget used the three-mountains test to learn whether children at certain ages are egocentric or can take the viewpoints of others.

Piaget then placed a doll elsewhere on the table and asked the child what the doll sees. The language abilities of very young children do not permit them to provide verbal descriptions of what can be seen from where the doll is situated, so they can answer in one of two ways. They can either select a photograph taken from the proper vantage point, or they can construct another model of the mountains as they would be seen by the doll. The results of a classic experiment with the three-mountains test suggest that five- and six-year-olds usually select photos or build models that correspond to their own viewpoints (Laurendeau & Pinard, 1970).

7-6d CAUSALITY: WHY? BECAUSE.

Preoperational children's responses to questions such as "Why does the sun shine?" show other facets of egocentrism. At the age of two or so, they may answer that they do not know or change the subject. Three-year-olds may report themselves as doing things because they want to do them or "Because Mommy wants me to." In egocentric fashion, this explanation of behavior is extended to inanimate objects. The sun may be thought of as shining because it wants to shine or someone wants it to shine.

TRUTH

 **F** "Because Mommy wants me to" may be a perfectly good explanation—for a three-year-old.

It is true that "Because Mommy wants me to" may be a perfectly good explanation—for a three-year-old. This line of "reasoning" is another reflection of early childhood egocentrism.

Piaget labels this structuring of cause and effect **precausal**. Preoperational children believe that things happen for reasons and not by accident (Sobel & Legare, 2014). Unless preoperational children know the natural causes of an event, their reasons are likely to have an egocentric flavor and not be based on science. Consider the question, "Why does it get dark outside?" The preoperational child usually does not have knowledge of Earth's rotation and is likely to answer something like, "So I can go to sleep."

precausal a type of thought in which natural cause-and-effect relationships are attributed to will and other preoperational concepts.

In **transductive reasoning**, children reason by going from one specific isolated event to another. For example, a three-year-old may argue that she should go on her swings in the backyard *because* it is light outside or that she should go to sleep *because* it is dark outside. That is, separate events, daylight and going on the swings (or being awake), are thought of as having cause-and-effect relationships.

Preoperational children also show **animism** and **artificialism** in their attributions of causality. In animistic thinking, they attribute life and intentions to inanimate objects, such as the sun and the moon. ("Why is the moon gone during the day?" "It is afraid of the sun.") Artificialism assumes that environmental features such as rain and thunder have been designed and made by people.

7-6e CONFUSION OF MENTAL AND PHYSICAL EVENTS

What would you do if someone asked you to pretend you were a galaprock? Chances are, you might inquire what a galaprock is and how it behaves. So might a five-year-old child. But a three-year-old might not think that such information is necessary (Gottfried et al., 2003).

According to Piaget, the preoperational child has difficulty making distinctions between mental and physical events. Children between the ages of two and four show confusion between symbols and the things they represent. Egocentrism contributes to the assumption that their thoughts exactly reflect external reality. They do not recognize that words are arbitrary and that people can use different words to refer to things. In *Play, Dreams, and Imitation in Childhood*, Piaget ([1946] 1962) asked a four-year-old child, "Could you call this table a cup and that cup a table?" "No," the child responded. "Why not?" "Because," explained the child, "you can't drink out of a table!" Another example of the preoperational child's confusion of the mental and the physical is the tendency of many four-year-olds to believe that dreams are real, but begin to understand that they are not real at about the age of seven (Honig & Nealis, 2012). Young boys, by the way, are more likely than girls to dream about fighting, chasing, and power; girls are more likely to dream about family members and joyful experiences (Honig & Nealis, 2012).

7-6f FOCUS ON ONE DIMENSION AT A TIME

To gain further insight into preoperational thinking, consider these two problems. Consider the first problem presented in Figure 7.5. Imagine that you pour the water from one of the low, wide beakers in part (a) into the tall, thin beaker in part (b). Now, as in part (c), consider whether the tall, thin beaker contains more water than, less water than, or the same amount of water as the low, wide beaker. We won't keep you in suspense. If you said the same amount, you were correct.

Next consider the second problem. Imagine taking a ball of clay and flattening it into a pancake. Do you wind up with more, less, or the same amount of clay? If you said the same amount, you were correct once more.

To arrive at the correct answers to these questions, you must understand the law of **conservation**. The law of conservation holds that properties of substances such as volume, mass, and number remain the same—or are conserved—even if you change their shape or arrangement.

Conservation requires the ability to focus on two aspects of a situation at once, such as height and width. A preoperational child focuses or centers on only one dimension at a time, a characteristic of thought that Piaget called **centration**. First, the child is shown two squat glasses or beakers of water and agrees that they have the same amount of water (as in Figure 7.5).

transductive reasoning reasoning from the specific to the specific.

animism the attribution of life and intentionality to inanimate objects.

artificialism the belief that environmental features were made by people.

conservation in cognitive psychology, the principle that properties of substances such as weight and mass remain the same (are conserved) when superficial characteristics such as their shapes or arrangement are changed.

centration focusing on an aspect or characteristic of a situation or problem.

FIG.7.5 CONSERVATION

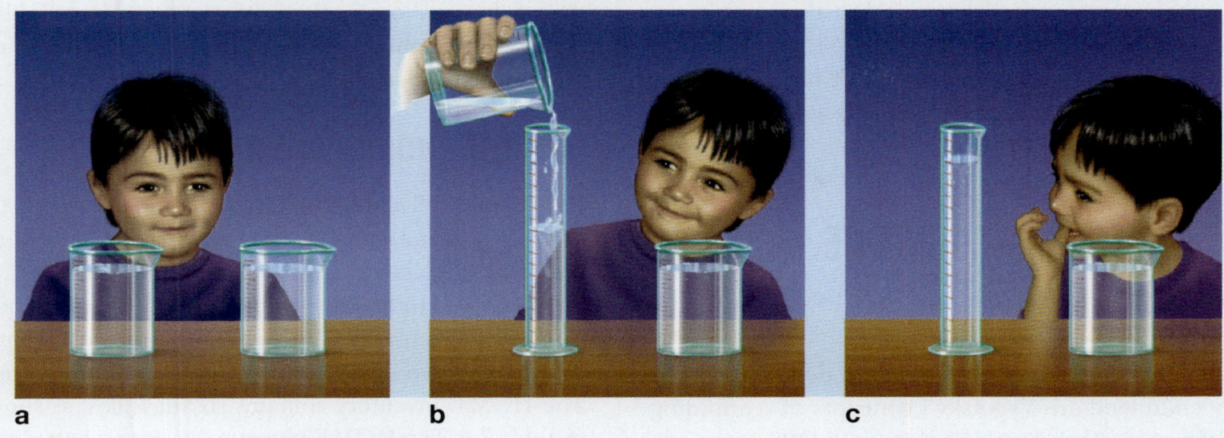
a
b
c

(a) The preoperational boy agrees that the amounts of water in the two containers is the same. (b) He watches as the water from one container is poured into a taller, thinner container. (c) When asked whether the tall and the squat containers now contain the same amount of water, he says no. Why?

Then, as he watches, water is poured from one squat glass into a tall, thin glass. Asked which glass has more water, he points to the tall glass. Why? When he looks at the glasses, he is swayed by the fact that the thinner glass is taller.

The preoperational child's failure to show conservation also comes about because of *irreversibility*. In the case of the water, the child does not realize that pouring water from the wide glass to the tall glass can be reversed, restoring things to their original condition.

After you have tried the experiment with the water, try this experiment on conservation of number. Make two rows with four pennies in each. As a four-year-old child watches, move the pennies in the second row to about an inch apart, as in Figure 7.6. Then ask the child which row has more pennies. What do you think the child will say? Why?

CLASS INCLUSION **Class inclusion**, as we are using it here, means including new objects or categories in broader mental classes or categories. Class inclusion also requires children to focus on two aspects of a situation at once. In one of Piaget's class-inclusion tasks, the child is shown several pictures from two subclasses of a larger class, for example, four cats and six dogs. She is asked whether there are more dogs or more animals. What do you think she will say? Preoperational children typically answer that there are more dogs than animals (Piaget, [1936] 1963).

FIG.7.6 CONSERVATION OF NUMBER

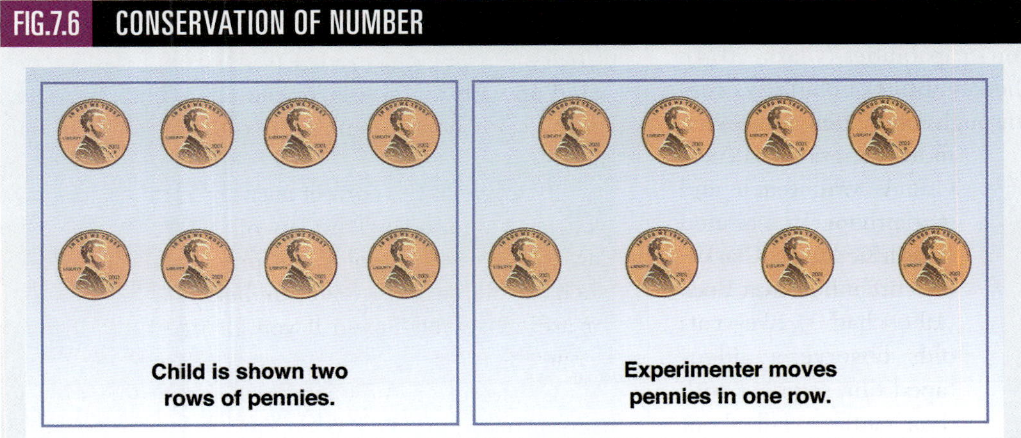
Child is shown two rows of pennies.
Experimenter moves pennies in one row.

We begin with two rows of pennies, spread out equally, as on the left. The child agrees that both rows have the same number of pennies. While a four-year-old child watches, we spread out the lower row of pennies so that it becomes wider. We then ask the child, "Do the two rows still have the same number of pennies?" What do you think the child will say? Why

class inclusion
categorizing a new object or concept as belonging to a broader group of objects or concepts.

Why do preoperational children make this error? According to Piaget, they cannot think about the two subclasses and the larger class at the same time. Therefore, they cannot easily compare them. Children view dogs as dogs, or as animals, but find it difficult to see them as both dogs and animals at once (Muller et al., 2015).

7-7 FACTORS IN COGNITIVE DEVELOPMENT

Two factors that influence cognitive development in early childhood are Vygotsky's concepts of scaffolding and the zone of proximal development. Others include the home environment, preschool education, and television.

7-7a SCAFFOLDING AND THE ZONE OF PROXIMAL DEVELOPMENT

Parental responsiveness and interaction with children are key ingredients in children's cognitive development. One component of this interaction is **scaffolding** (see Chapter 1). Cognitive scaffolding refers to temporary support provided by a parent or teacher to learning children. The guidance provided by adults decreases as children become capable of carrying out the task on their own (Clark, 2014).

A related concept is Vygotsky's **zone of proximal development (ZPD)**. The zone refers to the area in which children develop new cognitive skills as a function of working with more skilled people. Adults or older children can best guide children through this zone by gearing their assistance to children's capabilities (Clark, 2014). Researchers assert that the key forms of children's cognitive activities develop through interaction with older, more experienced individuals who teach and guide them. In a related study, K. Alison Clarke-Stewart and Robert Beck (1999) had 31 five-year-olds observe a videotaped film segment with their mothers, talk about it with their mothers, and then retell the story to an experimenter. Children whose mothers focused the children's attention on the tape, asked their children to talk about it, and discussed the feelings of the characters told better stories than children whose mothers did not use such scaffolding strategies and children in a control group who did not discuss the story at all.

scaffolding Vygotsky's term for temporary cognitive structures or methods of solving problems that help the child as he or she learns to function independently.

zone of proximal development (ZPD) Vygotsky's term for the situation in which a child carries out tasks with the help of someone who is more skilled, frequently an adult who represents the culture in which the child develops.

7-7b THE "HOME" ENVIRONMENT

Bettye Caldwell and her colleagues (Bradley et al., 2003) developed a measure for evaluating children's home environments labeled, appropriately enough, HOME, an acronym for Home Observation for the Measurement of the Environment. With this method, researchers directly observe parent–child interaction in the home. The HOME inventory contains six subscales, as shown in Table 7.4. The HOME inventory items are better predictors of young children's later IQ scores than social class, mother's IQ, or infant IQ scores (Bradley, 2006). Longitudinal research also shows that a stimulating home environment is connected with occupational success as an adult (Huesmann et al., 2006). On the other hand, harsh home environments have been linked with poor academic outcomes in school (Schwartz et al., 2013).

TABLE 7.4 SCALES OF THE HOME INVENTORY

Scale	Sample Items
Parental emotional and verbal responsiveness	The parent spontaneously vocalizes to the child during the visit. The parent responds to the child's vocalizations with vocal or other verbal responses.
Avoidance of restriction and punishment	The parent does not shout at the child. The parent does not interfere with the child's actions or restrict the child's movements more than three times during the visit.
Organization of the physical environment	The child's play environment seems to be safe and free from hazards.
Provision of appropriate play materials	The child has a push or a pull toy. The child has one or more toys or pieces of equipment that promote muscle activity. The family provides appropriate equipment to foster learning.
Parental involvement with child	The parent structures the child's play periods. The parent tends to keep the child within her or his visual range and looks at the child frequently.
Opportunities for variety in daily stimulation	The child gets out of the house at least four times a week. The parent reads stories to the child at least three times a week.

7-7c EFFECTS OF EARLY CHILDHOOD EDUCATION

How important are academic experiences in early childhood? Do they facilitate cognitive development? Research suggests that preschool education enables children to get an early start on achievement in school.

Children reared in poverty generally perform less well on standardized intelligence tests than children of higher socioeconomic status, and they are at greater risk for school failure (Robbins et al., 2012). As a result, preschool programs were begun in the 1960s to enhance their cognitive development and readiness for elementary school. Children in these programs typically are exposed to letters and words, numbers, books, exercises in drawing, pegs and pegboards, puzzles, and toy animals and dolls—materials and activities that middle-class children usually take for granted.

Studies of Head Start and other intervention programs show that environmental enrichment can enhance the cognitive development of economically disadvantaged children (Bierman et al., 2014). In the Milwaukee Project, poor children of low-IQ mothers were provided with enriched day care from the age of six months. By the late preschool years, the children's IQ scores averaged about 121, compared with an average of 95 for peers who did not receive day care (Garber, 1988).

7-7d TELEVISION

American children spend more time watching television than they do in school. By the time he or she turns three, the average child already watches two to three hours of television a day (Palmer, 2003). Television has great potential for teaching a variety of cognitive skills, social behaviors, and attitudes.

Sesame Street is the most successful children's educational TV program. The goal of *Sesame Street* is to promote the intellectual growth of preschoolers, particularly those of lower socioeconomic status. Large-scale evaluations of the effects of the program have concluded that regular viewing increases children's learning of numbers, letters, and cognitive skills such as sorting and classification (Mares & Pan, 2013). Preschoolers are often unable to tell the difference between commercials and program content (Chambers et al., 2015; Lillard et al., 2015). Children who are heavy TV viewers are more likely to believe commercial claims.

Then there is the "couch potato" effect. Research in the United States, England, and even China shows that among preschool children, the number of hours watching television is a stronger predictor of being overweight than diet (Borghese et al., 2015; Chen & Wang, 2015)!

7-8 THEORY OF MIND

Adults appear to have a commonsense understanding of how the mind works—that is, a **theory of mind**. We understand that we can gain knowledge through our senses or through hearsay. We know the distinction between actual and mental events and between how things appear and how they really are. We can infer the perceptions, thoughts, and feelings of others. We understand that mental states affect behavior.

Piaget might have predicted that preoperational children are too egocentric and too focused on misleading external appearances to have a theory of mind, but research has shown that even preschoolers can accurately predict and explain human action and emotion in terms of mental states (Wellman et al., 2006).

7-8a FALSE BELIEFS: WHERE ARE THOSE CRAYONS?

One indication of preschoolers' understanding that mental states affect behavior is the ability to understand false beliefs. This concept involves children's ability to separate their beliefs from those of another person who has false knowledge of a situation. It is illustrated in a study of three-year-olds by Louis Moses and John Flavell (1990). The children were shown a videotape in which a girl named Cathy found some crayons in a bag. When Cathy left the room briefly, a clown entered the room. The clown removed the crayons from the bag, hid them in a drawer, and put rocks in the bag instead. When Cathy returned, the children were asked whether Cathy thought there would be rocks or crayons in the bag. Most of the three-year-olds incorrectly answered "rocks," demonstrating their difficulty in understanding that the other person's belief would be different from their own. But by the age of four to five years, children do not have trouble with this concept and correctly answer "crayons" (Flavell, 1993).

7-8b ORIGINS OF KNOWLEDGE

Another aspect of theory of mind is how we acquire knowledge. By age three, most children begin to realize that people gain knowledge about something by looking at it (Lecce et al., 2015). By age four, children understand that particular senses provide information about only certain qualities of an object; for example, we come to know an

theory of mind a commonsense understanding of how the mind works.

object's color through our eyes, but we learn about its weight by feeling it (O'Neill & Chong, 2001). In a study by Daniela O'Neill and Alison Gopnik (1991), three-, four-, and five-year-olds learned about the contents of a toy tunnel in three different ways: They saw the contents, were told about them, or felt them. The children were then asked to state what was in the tunnel and how they knew. Although four- and five-year-olds had no trouble identifying the sources of their knowledge, the three-year-olds did. For example, after feeling but not seeing a ball in the tunnel, a number of three-year-olds told the experimenter that they could tell it was a blue ball. The children did not realize they could not learn the ball's color by feeling it.

7-8c THE APPEARANCE–REALITY DISTINCTION

Children must acquire an understanding of the difference between real events, on the one hand, and mental events, fantasies, and misleading appearances, on the other hand. This understanding is known as the **appearance–reality distinction**.

Piaget's view was that children do not differentiate reality from appearances or mental events until the age of seven or eight. In a study by Marjorie Taylor and Barbara Hort (1990), children age three to five were shown objects that had misleading appearances, such as an eraser that looked like a cookie. The children initially reported that the eraser looked like a cookie. However, once they learned that it was actually an eraser, they tended to report that it looked like an eraser. Apparently, the children could not mentally represent the eraser as both being an eraser and looking like a cookie.

Three-year-olds also apparently cannot understand changes in their mental states. In one study (Gopnik & Slaughter, 1991), three-year-olds were shown a crayon box with candles inside. Before it was opened, they consistently said they thought crayons were inside. When asked what they had thought was in the box before it was opened, the children now said "candles."

7-9 DEVELOPMENT OF MEMORY

Children, like adults, often remember what they want to remember (Crisp & Turner, 2011). By the age of four, children can remember events that occurred at least 1½ years earlier (Bauer & Fivush, 2010, 2013). Katherine Nelson (1990, 1993) interviewed children aged two to five to study their memory for recurring events in their lives, such as having dinner, playing with friends, and going to birthday parties. She found that three-year-olds can present coherent, orderly accounts of familiar events. Furthermore, young children seem to form **scripts**, which are abstract, generalized accounts of these repeated events. For example, in describing what happens during a birthday party, a child might say, "You play games, open presents, and eat cake" (Fivush, 2002). However, an unusual experience, such as a hurricane, may be remembered in detail for years (Bauer & Fivush, 2013).

Even though children as young as one and two years of age can remember events, these memories seldom last into adulthood. This memory of specific events—known as **autobiographical memory** or *episodic memory*—is facilitated by children talking about the memories with others (Bauer & Fivush, 2013).

RomillyLockyer/The Image Bank/Getty images

The appearance-reality distinction. Older children understand that many things are not what they seem. Preoperational children might not make this distinction.

appearance–reality distinction the difference between real events on the one hand and mental events, fantasies, and misleading appearances on the other hand.

scripts abstract, generalized accounts of familiar repeated events.

autobiographical memory the memory of specific episodes or events.

7-9a FACTORS INFLUENCING MEMORY

Factors that affect memory include what the child is asked to remember, the interest level of the child, the availability of retrieval cues or reminders, and what memory measure we are using. First, children find it easier to remember events that follow a fixed and logical order than events that do not. For instance, three- and five-year-olds have a better memory for the activities involved in making pretend cookies out of Play-Doh (you put the ingredients in the bowl, then mix the ingredients, then roll out the dough, and so on) than they do for the activities involved in sand play, which can occur in any order (Bauer & Fivush, 2013). Research consistently shows that (most) preschool boys are more interested in playing with toys such as cars and weapons, whereas (most) preschool girls are more interested in playing with dolls, dishes, and teddy bears. Later, the children typically show better recognition and recall for the toys in which they were interested (Goble et al., 2012).

Although young children can remember a great deal, they depend more than older children do on cues provided by others to help them retrieve their memories. Elaborating on the child's experiences and asking questions that encourage the child to contribute information to the narrative generally help children remember an episode (Bauer & Fivush, 2013).

Children's memory can often be measured or assessed by asking them to say what they remember. But verbal reports, especially from preschoolers, appear to underestimate children's memory (Bauer & Fivush, 2013). In one longitudinal study, children's memory for certain events was tested at age two and a half and again at age four. Most of the information recalled at age four had not been mentioned at age two and a half, indicating that when they were younger, the children remembered more than they reported (Fivush & Hammond, 1990). Another study found that when young children were allowed to use dolls to reenact an event, their recall was better than when they gave a verbal report (Schneider, 2010).

7-9b MEMORY STRATEGIES: REMEMBERING TO REMEMBER

Adults and older children use strategies to help them remember things. One strategy is mental repetition, or **rehearsal**. If you are trying to remember a new friend's phone number, for example, you might repeat it several times. Another strategy is to organize things to be remembered into categories. Most preschoolers do not engage in spontaneous rehearsal until about five years of age (Bebko et al., 2014). They also rarely group objects into related categories to help them remember. By about age five, many children have learned to verbalize information silently to themselves by counting mentally, for example, rather than aloud.

Having preschoolers sort objects into categories enhances memory (Howe, 2006; Lange & Pierce, 1992). Even three- and four-year-olds will use rehearsal and labeling if they are asked to try to remember something.

7-10 LANGUAGE DEVELOPMENT: WHY "DADDY GOED AWAY"

Children's language skills mushroom during the preschool years. By the fourth year, children are asking adults and each other questions, taking turns talking, and engaging in lengthy conversations (Hoover et al., 2011).

7-10a DEVELOPMENT OF VOCABULARY

The development of vocabulary proceeds at an extraordinary pace. Preschoolers learn an average of nine new words per day (Tamis-LeMonda et al., 2006, 2014). But how can that be possible when each new word has so many potential meanings? Consider the following example. A toddler observes a small, black dog running through the park. His older sister points to the animal and says, "Doggy." The word *doggy* could mean this particular dog, or all dogs, or all animals. It could refer to one part of the dog (e.g., its tail) or to its behavior (running, barking) or to its characteristics (small, black) (Waxman & Goswami, 2012). Does the child consider all these possibilities before determining what *doggy* actually means?

Word learning, in fact, does not occur gradually but is better characterized as a **fast-mapping** process in which the child quickly attaches a new word to its appropriate concept (Waxman & Goswami, 2012). Children apparently have early cognitive biases or constraints that lead them to prefer certain meanings over others (Waxman & Goswami, 2012).

Children also assume that words refer to whole objects and not to their component parts or their characteristics, such as color, size, or texture (Bloom, 2002). This bias

rehearsal repetition.

fast mapping a process of quickly determining a word's meaning, which facilitates children's vocabulary development.

is called the **whole-object assumption**. Therefore, the young child would assume that the word *doggy* refers to the dog rather than to its tail, its color, or its barking.

Children also seem to assume that objects have only one label. Therefore, novel terms must refer to unfamiliar objects and not to familiar objects that already have labels. This concept is the **contrast assumption**, which is also known as the mutual exclusivity assumption. Suppose that a child is shown two objects, one of which has a known label ("doggy") and one of which is unknown. Let's further suppose that an adult now says, "Look at the lemur." If the child assumes that "doggy" and "lemur" each can refer to only one object, the child would correctly figure out that "lemur" refers to the other object and is not just another name for "doggy" (Waxman & Goswami, 2012).

7-10b DEVELOPMENT OF GRAMMAR

There is a "grammar explosion" during the third year (Tamis-LeMonda et al., 2014). Children's sentence structure expands to include the words missing in telegraphic speech. Children usually add to their vocabulary an impressive array of articles (*a, an, the*), conjunctions (*and, but, or*), possessive adjectives (*your, her*), pronouns (*she, him, one*), and prepositions (*in, on, over, around, under, through*). Usually between the ages of three and four, children show knowledge of rules for combining phrases and clauses into complex sentences, as in "You goed and Mommy goed, too."

OVERREGULARIZATION The apparent basis of one of the more intriguing language developments—**overregularization**—is that children acquire grammatical rules as they learn language. At young ages they tend to apply these rules rather strictly, even in cases that call for exceptions (Ambridge et al., 2013). Consider the formation of the past tense and plurals in English. We add *d* or *ed* to regular verbs and *s* to regular nouns. Thus, *walk* becomes *walked* and *doggy* becomes *doggies*. But then there are irregular verbs and irregular nouns. For example, *sit* becomes *sat* and *go* becomes *went*. *Sheep* remains *sheep* (plural) and *child* becomes *children*.

As children become aware of the syntactic rules for forming the past tense and plurals in English, they often misapply them to irregular words. As a result, they tend to make charming errors (Ambridge et al., 2013). Some three- to five-year-olds are more likely to say "Mommy sitted down" than "Mommy sat down" or talk about the "sheeps" they "seed" on the farm and about all the "childs" they ran into at the playground.

Some parents recognize that their children at first were forming the past tense of irregular verbs correctly but that they then began to make errors. Some of these parents become concerned that their children are "slipping" in their language development and attempt to correct them. However, overregularization reflects accurate knowledge of grammar, not faulty language development. In another year or two, *mouses* will be boringly transformed into *mice*, and Mommy will no longer have sitted down. Parents might as well enjoy overregularization while they can.

Walter Lockwood/Flame/Corbis

ASKING QUESTIONS Children's first questions are telegraphic and characterized by a rising pitch (which signifies a question mark in English) at the end. Depending on the context, "More milky?" can be translated into "May I have more milk?" "Would you like more milk?" or "Is there more milk?" It is usually toward the latter part of the third year that the *wh* questions appear. Consistent with the child's general cognitive development, certain *wh* questions (*what, who,* and *where*) appear earlier than others (*why, when, which,* and *how*) (Tamis-LeMonda et al., 2006).

whole-object assumption the assumption that words refer to whole objects and not to their component parts or characteristics.

contrast assumption the assumption that objects have only one label.

overregularization the application of regular grammatical rules for forming inflections to irregular verbs and nouns.

Why is usually too philosophical for a two-year-old, and *how* is too involved. Two-year-olds are also likely to be now-oriented, so *when* is of less than immediate concern. By the fourth year, most children are spontaneously producing *why, when,* and *how* questions. These *wh* words are initially tacked on to the beginnings of sentences. "Where Mommy go?" can stand for "Where is Mommy going?" "Where did Mommy go?" or "Where will Mommy go?" and its meaning must be derived from context. Later on, the child will add the auxiliary verbs *is, did,* and *will* to indicate whether the question concerns the present, past, or future.

Serhiy Kobyakov/Alamy Stock Photo

PASSIVE SENTENCES Passive sentences, such as "The food is eaten by the dog," are difficult for two- and three-year-olds to understand, and so young preschoolers almost never produce them. In a study of children's comprehension (Strohner & Nelson, 1974), two- to five-year-olds used puppets and toys to act out sentences that were read to them. Two- and three-year-olds made errors in acting out passive sentences (e.g., "The car was hit by the truck") 70% of the time. Older children had less difficulty interpreting the meanings of passive sentences correctly. However, most children usually do not produce passive sentences spontaneously even at the ages of five and six.

7-10c PRAGMATICS

Pragmatics refers to the practical aspects of communication. Children show pragmatism when they adjust their speech to fit the social situation (Nelson, 2006). For example, children show greater formality in their choice of words and syntax when they are role-playing high-status figures, such as teachers or physicians, in their games. They say "please" more often when making requests of high-status people, or when they use "Motherese" in talking to an infant.

Preschoolers tend to be egocentric; therefore, a two-year-old telling another child "Gimme my book," without specifying which book, may assume that the other child knows what she herself knows. Once children can perceive the world through the eyes of others, they advance in their abilities to make themselves understood. Now the child recognizes that the other child will require a description of the book or of its location to carry out the request.

7-10d LANGUAGE AND COGNITION

Language and cognitive development are interwoven (Waxman & Goswami, 2012). For example, the child gradually gains the capacity to discriminate between animals on the basis of distinct features, such as size, patterns of movement,

pragmatics the practical aspects of communication, such as adaptation of language to fit the social situation.

Which Comes First?

Piaget believed that cognitive development precedes language development.

?

Many theorists claim that children create cognitive classes to understand things that are labeled by words.

and the sounds they make. At the same time, the child also is acquiring words that represent broader categories, such as mammal and animal.

But which comes first? Does the child first develop concepts and then acquire the language to describe them, or does the child's increasing language ability lead to the development of new concepts?

DOES COGNITIVE DEVELOPMENT PRECEDE LANGUAGE DEVELOPMENT? Piaget (1976) believed that cognitive development precedes language development. He argued that children must understand concepts before they use words to describe them. From Piaget's perspective, children learn words to describe classes or categories that they have already created (Nelson, 2005). Children can learn the word *kitty* because they have perceived the characteristics that distinguish cats from other things.

Some studies support the notion that cognitive concepts may precede language. For example, the vocabulary explosion that occurs at about 18 months of age is related to the child's ability to group a set of objects into two categories, such as "dolls" and "cars" (Gopnik & Meltzoff, 1992). Other research suggests that young children need to experience an action themselves or by observation to learn the meaning of a verb (Pulverman et al., 2006).

DOES LANGUAGE DEVELOPMENT PRECEDE COGNITIVE DEVELOPMENT? Although many theorists argue that cognitive development precedes language development, others reverse the causal relationship and claim that children create cognitive classes to understand things that are labeled by words (Clark, 1983). When children hear the word *dog*, they try to understand it by searching for characteristics that separate dogs from other things.

inner speech Vygotsky's concept of the ultimate binding of language and thought. Inner speech originates in vocalizations that may regulate the child's behavior and become internalized by age six or seven.

THE INTERACTIONIST VIEW: OUTER SPEECH AND INNER SPEECH Today, most investigators find something of value in each of these cognitive views (Waxman & Goswami, 2012). In the early stages of language development, concepts often precede words, and many of the infant's words describe classes that have already developed. But later language influences thought.

Vygotsky believed that during most of the first year, vocalizations and thought are separate. But during the second year, thought and speech combine forces. Children discover that objects have labels. Learning labels becomes more self-directed. Children ask what new words mean. Learning new words fosters creation of new categories, and new categories become filled with labels for new things.

Vygotsky's concept of **inner speech** is a key feature of his position. At first children's thoughts are spoken aloud. You can hear the three-year-old instructing herself as she plays with toys. At this age, her vocalizations serve to regulate her behavior, but they gradually become internalized. What was spoken aloud at four and five becomes an internal dialogue by six or seven. Inner speech is the ultimate binding of language and thought. It is involved in the development of planning and self-regulation, and facilitates learning.

In the next chapter, we'll continue our exploration of early childhood, looking at the social and emotional development that take place.

STUDY TOOLS 7

READY TO STUDY?

In the book, you can:

- ☐ Rip out the chapter review card at the back of the book for a handy summary of the chapter and key terms.
- ☐ Check your understanding of what you've read with the quizzes that follow.

ONLINE AT CENGAGEBRAIN.COM YOU CAN:

- ☐ Collect StudyBits while you read and study the chapter.
- ☐ Quiz yourself on key concepts.
- ☐ Find videos for further exploration.
- ☐ Prepare for tests with HDEV5 Flash Cards as well as those you create.

SELF-ASSESSMENTS

Fill-Ins

Answers can be found in the back of the book.

1. There is a debate as to whether language development follows or precedes ____________ development.
2. In the United States, about one child in ____________ suffers from a major chronic illness.
3. Sleep terrors differ from nightmares in that they typically occur during ____________ sleep.
4. We would expect a child to be able to catch a small ball, using the hands only, by the age of ____________.
5. According the Kellogg, the final stage in children's drawings is the ____________ stage.
6. According to the text, if both of a child's parents are left-handed, the child's probability of becoming left-handed is about ____________%.
7. A three-year-old may argue that she should go on the swings because it is light outside. Her logic is an example of ____________ reasoning.
8. Most children do not engage in spontaneous ____________ to remember things until they are about five years of age.
9. Piaget believed that children usually begin to engage in pretend play in the second year, when they have developed the ability to ____________ objects.
10. The average four- to eight-year-old needs about ____________ calories a day.

Multiple Choice

1. **What happens to the rate of growth between the ages of two and six, when compared to the growth rate during infancy?**
   a. It speeds up.
   b. It slows down.
   c. It remains the same.
   d. There is too much individual variation to make any generalizations.

2. **Plasticity of the brain is greatest**
   a. at about one to two years of age.
   b. during the preschool years of two to five.
   c. during adolescence.
   d. during adulthood.

3. **How many hours of sleep does the National Sleep Foundation recommend that three- to five-year-olds obtain in a 24-hour period?**
   a. 12 to 18
   b. 14 to 15
   c. 12 to 14
   d. 11 to 13

4. **We would expect a child to first be able to build a tower of six cubes at the age of**
   a. two years.
   b. three years.
   c. four years.
   d. five years.

5. **Which of the following is true about enuresis?**
   a. Enuresis is a sign that the child is angry or disappointed with his or her parents.
   b. Enuresis is a sign of poor parenting.
   c. Enuresis is more common among girls.
   d. Enuresis is usually outgrown.

6. **Most preschoolers cannot conserve volume, mass, or number because they**
   a. are lacking in intelligence.
   b. do not understand what the word *conservation* means.
   c. focus on one dimension of a situation at a time.
   d. have not been taught mathematics in an elementary school setting.

7. **Piaget used the three-mountains test to study __________ in children.**
   a. morality
   b. theory of mind
   c. confusion of mental and physical events
   d. egocentrism

8. **All of the following are scales of the HOME Inventory *except***
   a. parental verbal and emotional responsiveness.
   b. parental use of scaffolding and the zone of proximal development.
   c. parental provision of appropriate play materials.
   d. parental avoidance of restriction and punishment.

9. **Studies of Head Start show that it has been effective at**
   a. preventing children from developing major illnesses.
   b. decreasing aggressiveness in the home environment.
   c. helping children understand the appearance–reality distinction.
   d. enhancing the cognitive development of economically deprived children.

10. **Preschoolers' learning of grammatical rules has led to**
    a. vocabulary development.
    b. overregularization.
    c. development of the whole-object assumption.
    d. use of pragmatics.

8 Early Childhood: Social and Emotional Development

Steve Murray / Alamy Stock Photo

LEARNING OUTCOMES

After studying this chapter, you will be able to . . .

- 8-1 Describe the dimensions of child rearing and styles of parenting
- 8-2 Explain how siblings, birth order, peers, and other factors affect social development during early childhood
- 8-3 Discuss personality and emotional development during early childhood, focusing on the self, Erikson's views, and fears
- 8-4 Discuss the development of gender roles and gender differences

After you finish this chapter, go to **PAGE 169** for **STUDY TOOLS**

Parents decide how restrictive they will be. How will they respond when children make excessive noise, play with dangerous objects, damage property, mess up their rooms, hurt others, or masturbate?

Preschoolers usually spend most of their time with the family. Most parents want preschoolers to develop a sense of responsibility and develop into well-adjusted individuals. They want them to acquire social skills. How do parents try to achieve these goals? What role do siblings play? How do children's peers influence social and emotional development?

8-1 DIMENSIONS OF CHILD REARING

Parents have different approaches to rearing their children. Investigators of parental patterns of child rearing have found it useful to classify them according to two broad dimensions: warmth–coldness and restrictiveness–permissiveness (Baumrind, 1989, 2013).

Warm parents are affectionate toward their children. They tend to hug and kiss them and smile at them frequently. Warm parents are caring and supportive. They communicate their enjoyment in being with their children. Warm parents are less likely than cold parents to use physical discipline (Holden et al., 2011).

Cold parents may not enjoy their children and may have few feelings of affection for them. They are likely to complain about their children's behavior, saying they are naughty or have "minds of their own."

It requires no stretch of the imagination to conclude that it is better to be warm than cold toward children (Laible et al., 2015). The children of parents who are warm and accepting are more likely to develop internal standards of conduct—a moral sense or conscience (Gauvain et al., 2013). Parental warmth also is related to the child's social and emotional well-being.

Where does parental warmth come from? Some of it reflects parental beliefs about how best to rear children, and some reflects parents' tendencies to imitate the behavior of their own parents. But research by Hetherington and her colleagues (Feinberg et al., 2001) suggests that genetic factors may be involved as well.

Parents decide how restrictive they will be. How will they respond when children make excessive noise, play with dangerous objects, damage property, mess up their rooms, hurt others, or masturbate? Parents who are restrictive tend to impose rules and to watch their children closely.

Consistent control and firm enforcement of rules can have positive consequences for the child, particularly when combined with strong support and affection (Grusec & Sherman, 2011). This parenting style is termed the *authoritative style* (Baumrind, 2013). On the other hand, if "restrictiveness" means physical punishment, interference, or intrusiveness, it can give rise to disobedience, rebelliousness, and lower levels of cognitive development (Larzelere et al., 2013).

Permissive parents supervise their children less closely than restrictive parents do. Permissive parents allow their children to do what is "natural," such as make noise, treat toys carelessly, and experiment with their bodies. They may also allow their children to show some aggression, intervening only when another child is in danger.

TRUTH OR FICTION?

T	F	Parents who demand mature behavior wind up with rebellious children, not mature children.
T	F	First-born children are more highly motivated to achieve than later-born children.
T	F	Children who are physically punished are more likely to be aggressive than children who are not.
T	F	There is no scientific evidence that violence in the media contributes to aggression.
T	F	The most common fear among preschoolers is fear of social disapproval.
T	F	A 2½-year-old may know that he is a boy, but still think that he can grow up to be a mommy.

8-1a HOW PARENTS ENFORCE RESTRICTIONS

Regardless of their general approaches to child rearing, most parents are restrictive now and then, even if only when they are teaching their children not to run into the street or to touch a hot stove. Parents tend to use the methods of induction, power assertion, and withdrawal of love.

Loisjoy Thurstun/Bubbles Photolibrary / Alamy Stock Photo

Consistent enforcement of reasonable rules, combined with warmth and support, usually have positive consequences for children.

Inductive methods aim to teach knowledge that will enable children to generate desirable behavior on their own. The main inductive technique is "reasoning," or explaining why one kind of behavior is good and another is not. Reasoning with a one- or two-year-old can be basic. "Don't do that—it hurts!" qualifies as reasoning with toddlers. "It hurts!" is an explanation, though brief. The inductive approach helps the child understand moral behavior and fosters prosocial behavior such as helping and sharing (Grusec, 2014; Grusec & Sherman, 2011).

Power-assertive methods include physical punishment and denial of privileges. Parents often justify physical punishment with sayings such as "Spare the rod, spoil the child." Parents may insist that power assertion is necessary because their children are noncompliant. However, use of power-assertion is related to parental authoritarianism as well as children's behavior (Larzelere et al., 2013). Parental power assertion is associated with lower acceptance by peers, poorer grades, and more antisocial behavior in children. The more parents use power-assertive techniques, the less children appear to develop internal standards of conduct. Parental punishment and rejection are often linked with aggression and delinquency.

Some parents control children by threatening withdrawal of love. They isolate or ignore misbehaving children. Because most children need parental approval and contact, loss of love can be more threatening than physical punishment. Withdrawal of love may foster compliance but also instill guilt and anxiety (Grusec, 2014; Grusec & Sherman, 2011).

authoritative a child-rearing style in which parents are restrictive and demanding yet communicative and warm.

Preschoolers more readily comply when asked to do something than when asked to *stop* doing something (Kochanska et al., 2001). One way to manage children who are doing something wrong or bad is to involve them in something else.

8-1b PARENTING STYLES: HOW PARENTS TRANSMIT VALUES AND STANDARDS

Diana Baumrind (2013) focused on the relationship between parenting styles and the development of competent behavior in young children. She used the dimensions of warmth–coldness and restrictiveness–permissiveness to develop a grid of four parenting styles based on whether parents are high or low in each dimension (see Table 8.1).

The parents of the most capable children are rated high in both dimensions (see Table 8.1). They are highly restrictive and make strong demands for maturity. However, they also reason with their children and show strong support and feelings of love. Baumrind (2013) applies the label **authoritative** to these parents; they know what they want their children to do but also respect their children and are warm toward them. Compared with other children, the children of authoritative parents tend to show self-reliance and independence, high self-esteem, high levels of activity and exploratory behavior, and social competence. They are highly motivated to achieve and do well in school (Grusec, 2014; Grusec & Sherman, 2011).

FICTION

T (F) Parents who demand mature behavior wind up with rebellious children, not mature children.

It is not true that parents who are restrictive and demand mature behavior wind up with rebellious, immature children. As long as parents are not severe with the children, consistent control and firm enforcement of rules can have positive consequences for their children.

TABLE 8.1 BAUMRIND'S PATTERNS OF PARENTING

Parental Style	Parental Behavior Patterns	
	Restrictiveness and Control	Warmth and Responsiveness
Authoritative	High	High
Authoritarian	High	Low
Permissive–Indulgent	Low	High
Rejecting–Neglecting	Low	Low

"Because I say so" could be the motto of parents that Baumrind labels as **authoritarian**. Authoritarians value obedience for its own sake. They have strict guidelines for right and wrong and demand that their children accept them without question. Like authoritative parents, they are controlling. But unlike authoritative parents, their enforcement methods rely on force. Moreover, authoritarian parents do not communicate well with their children or respect their children's viewpoints. Most researchers find them to be generally cold and rejecting (Larzelere et al., 2013).

C Squared Studios/Photodisc/Getty Images

HELLO
my name is
Because I say so!

Baumrind found the sons of authoritarian parents to be relatively hostile and defiant and the daughters to be low in independence and dominance (Baumrind, 2013). Other researchers have found that the children of authoritarian parents are less competent socially and academically than those of authoritative parents. They are anxious, irritable, and restrained in their social interactions. As adolescents, they may be conforming and obedient but have low self-reliance and self-esteem.

Baumrind found two types of parents who are permissive as opposed to restrictive. One is permissive–indulgent and the other rejecting–neglecting. **Permissive–indulgent** parents are low in their attempts to control their children and in their demands for mature behavior. They are easygoing and unconventional. Their brand of permissiveness is accompanied by high nurturance (warmth and support).

Rejecting–neglecting parents are also low in their demands for mature behavior and attempts to control their children. Unlike indulgent parents, they are low in support and responsiveness. The children of neglectful parents are the least competent, responsible, and mature. The children of permissive–indulgent parents, like those of neglectful parents, are less competent in school and show more misconduct and substance abuse than children of more restrictive, controlling parents. But children from permissive–indulgent homes, unlike those from neglectful homes, are fairly high in social competence and self-confidence (Baumrind, 1991).

8-1c EFFECTS OF THE SITUATION AND THE CHILD ON PARENTING STYLES

Parenting styles are not merely a one-way street, from parent to child. Parenting styles also depend partly on the situation and partly on the characteristics of the child (Grusec, 2014; Grusec & Sherman, 2011). For example, parents are most likely to use power-assertive techniques when dealing with aggressive behavior (Larzalere et al., 2013). Parents prefer power assertion to induction when they believe that children understand the rules they have violated and are capable of acting appropriately. Stress also contributes to use of power.

Baumrind's research suggests that we can make an effort to avoid some of the pitfalls of being authoritarian or overly permissive. Some recommended techniques that parents can use to help control and guide their children's behavior are listed in Table 8.2.

authoritarian a child-rearing style in which parents demand submission and obedience.

permissive–indulgent a child-rearing style in which parents are warm and not restrictive.

rejecting–neglecting a child-rearing style in which parents are neither restrictive and controlling nor supportive and responsive.

TABLE 8.2 ADVICE FOR PARENTS IN GUIDING YOUNG CHILDREN'S BEHAVIOR

Do ...	Don't ...
• Reward good behavior with praise, smiles, and hugs. • Give clear, simple, realistic rules appropriate to the child's age. • Enforce rules with reasonable consequences. • Ignore annoying behavior such as whining and tantrums. • Childproof the house, putting dangerous and breakable items out of reach. • Then establish limits. • Be consistent.	• Pay attention only to a child's misbehavior. • Issue too many rules or enforce them haphazardly. • Try to control behavior solely in the child's domain, such as thumb sucking, which can lead to frustrating power struggles. • Nag, lecture, shame, or induce guilt. • Yell or spank. • Be overly permissive.

8-2 SOCIAL BEHAVIORS

During early childhood, children make tremendous advances in social skills and behavior (Underwood & Rosen, 2011). Their play increasingly involves other children. They learn how to share, cooperate, and comfort others. But young children, like adults, can be aggressive as well as loving and helpful.

8-2a INFLUENCE OF SIBLINGS

Siblings serve many functions, including giving physical care, providing emotional support and nurturance, offering advice, serving as role models, providing social interaction that helps develop social skills, making demands, and imposing restrictions (Holden et al., 2011).

In early childhood, siblings' interactions have positive aspects (cooperation, teaching, nurturance) and negative aspects (conflict, control, competition) (Parke & Buriel, 2006). Older siblings tend to be more caring but also more dominating than younger siblings. Younger siblings are more likely to imitate older siblings and accept their direction.

In many cultures, older girls care for younger siblings (Clark, 2005). Parents often urge their children to stop fighting among themselves, and there are times when these conflicts look deadly (and occasionally they are). But garden-variety sibling conflict can enhance their social competence, their development of self-identity (who they are and what they stand for), and their ability to rear their own children (Ross et al., 2006).

There is more conflict between siblings when the parents play favorites (Scharf et al., 2005). Conflict between siblings is also greater when the relationships between the parents or between the parents and children are troubled (Kim et al., 2006).

ADJUSTING TO THE BIRTH OF A SIBLING The birth of a sister or brother is often a source of stress for preschoolers because of changes in family relationships. When a new baby comes into the home, the mother pays relatively more attention to that child and spends less time with the older child, and the older child may feel displaced and resentful.

Children show a mixture of negative and positive reactions to the birth of a sibling. They include **regression** to baby-like behaviors, such as increased clinging, crying, and toilet accidents. Anger and naughtiness may increase. But the same children may also show increased independence and maturity, insisting on feeding or dressing themselves and helping to care for the baby (Underwood & Rosen, 2011). Parents can help a young child cope with the arrival of a baby by explaining in advance what is to come.

regression a return to behavior characteristic of earlier stages of development.

8-2b BIRTH ORDER

Differences in personality and achievement have been linked to birth order. First-born children, as a group, are somewhat more highly motivated to achieve than later-born children (Carette et al., 2011). First-born and only children appear to perform better academically and are more cooperative (Damian & Roberts, 2015). They obtain higher standardized test scores, including IQ and SAT scores (Damian & Roberts, 2015; Sulloway, 2011).

Before discussing differences in personality between first-born and later-born children, let us note that a recent analysis of research in the area charges that most studies have been flawed (Damian & Roberts, 2015). Nevertheless, as a group, several studies have strongly suggested that first-born children are more adult-oriented and less aggressive than later-born children (Beck et al., 2006; Zajonc, 2001). On the negative side, first-born and only children show somewhat greater anxiety levels and are somewhat less self-reliant than later-born children.

TRUTH

(T) F First-born children are more highly motivated to achieve than later-born children.

Research shows that first-born children are more highly motivated to achieve than later-born children. However, the difference is a group difference and does not apply to all first-born or later-born children.

Later-born children may learn to act aggressively to compete for the attention of their parents and older siblings (Carey, 2007b). Their self-concepts tend to be lower than those of first-born or only children, but the social skills later-born children acquire from dealing with their family position seem to translate into greater popularity with peers (Carey, 2007b). They also tend to be somewhat more rebellious and liberal than first-born children (Beck et al., 2006).

By and large, parents are more relaxed and flexible with later-born children. Many parents see that the first-born child is turning out well and perhaps they assume that later-born children will also turn out well.

iloveimages/Veer

The addition of a new baby to the family is often stressful for older siblings.

8-2c PEER RELATIONSHIPS

Peer interactions foster social skills—sharing, helping, taking turns, and dealing with conflict (Wentzel & Ramani, 2016). Groups teach children how to lead and how to follow. Physical and cognitive skills develop through peer interactions. Peers also provide emotional support (Bukowski et al., 2011).

By about two years of age, children imitate one another's play and engage in social games such as follow the leader (Bukowski et al., 2011). Also by this age, children show preferences for particular playmates—an early sign of friendship (Wentzel & Ramani, 2016). Friendship is characterized by shared positive experiences and feelings of attachment (Grusec & Sherman, 2011). Even early friendships can be fairly stable (Rubin et al., 2006).

When preschoolers are asked what they like about their friends, they typically mention the toys and activities they share (Holder & Coleman, 2015). Primary schoolchildren usually report that their friends are the children with whom they do things and have fun (Holder & Coleman, 2015). Not until late childhood and adolescence do friends' traits and notions of trust, communication, and intimacy become important.

8-2d PLAY–CHILD'S PLAY, THAT IS

Children's play is meaningful, pleasurable, and internally motivated. Play is fun but also serves important functions in the child. Play helps children develop motor skills and coordination (Burghardt, 2015). It contributes to social development because children learn to share play materials, take turns, and try on new roles through **dramatic play**. It supports the development of such cognitive qualities as curiosity, exploration, symbolic thinking, and problem solving (Bergen, 2015; Christie & Roskos, 2015). Play may even help children learn to control impulses (Bergen, 2015).

PLAY AND COGNITIVE DEVELOPMENT Play contributes to and expresses milestones in cognitive development. Jean Piaget ([1946] 1962) identified kinds of play, each characterized by increasing cognitive complexity (De Lisi et al., 2015):

- *Functional play.* Beginning in the sensorimotor stage, the first kind of play involves repetitive motor activity, such as rolling a ball or running and laughing.
- *Symbolic play.* Also called pretend play, imaginative play, or dramatic play, symbolic play emerges toward the end of the sensorimotor stage and increases during early childhood. In symbolic play, children create settings, characters, and scripts (Mottweiler & Taylor, 2014).
- *Constructive play.* Children use objects or materials to draw something or make something, such as a tower of blocks.
- *Formal games.* Games with rules include board games, which are sometimes enhanced or invented by children, and games involving motor skills, such as marbles and hopscotch, ball games involving sides or teams, and video games.

PARTEN'S TYPES OF PLAY In classic research on children's play, Mildred Parten observed the development of six types of play among two- to five-year-old nursery schoolchildren: unoccupied play, solitary play, onlooker play, parallel play, associative play, and cooperative play (see Table 8.3) (Dyson, 2015; Henricks, 2015). Solitary play and onlooker play are considered **nonsocial play**, that is, play in which children do not

dramatic play play in which children enact social roles.

nonsocial play solitary forms of play.

TABLE 8.3 PARTEN'S CATEGORIES OF PLAY

Category	Nonsocial or Social?	Description
Unoccupied play	Nonsocial	Children do not appear to be playing. They may engage in random movements that seem to be without a goal. Unoccupied play appears to be the least frequent kind of play in nursery schools.
Solitary play	Nonsocial	Children play with toys by themselves, independently of the children around them. Solitary players do not appear to be influenced by children around them. They make no effort to approach them.
Onlooker play	Nonsocial	Children observe other children who are at play. Onlookers frequently talk to the children they are observing and may make suggestions, but they do not overtly join in.
Parallel play	Social	Children play with toys similar to those of surrounding children. However, they treat the toys as they choose and do not directly interact with other children.
Associative play	Social	Children interact and share toys. However, they do not seem to share group goals. Although they interact, individuals still treat toys as they choose. The association with the other children appears to be more important than the nature of the activity. They seem to enjoy each other's company.
Cooperative play	Social	Children interact to achieve common, group goals. The play of each child is subordinated to the purposes of the group. One or two group members direct the activities of others. There is also a division of labor, with different children taking different roles. Children may pretend to be members of a family, animals, space monsters, and all sorts of creatures.

interact socially. Nonsocial play occurs more often in two- and three-year-olds than in older preschoolers. Parallel play, associative play, and cooperative play are considered **social play**; in each case, children are influenced by other children as they play. Parten found that associative play and cooperative play become common by age five. These types of play are more likely to be found among older and more experienced preschoolers (Bukowski et al., 2011). Girls are somewhat more likely than boys to engage in social play (Underwood & Rosen, 2011).

There are exceptions. Nonsocial play can involve educational activities that foster cognitive development. In fact, many four- and five-year-olds spend a good deal of time in parallel constructive play. For instance, they may work on puzzles or build with blocks near other children. Two-year-olds with older siblings or with group experience may engage in advanced social play (Dunn, 2015).

GENDER DIFFERENCES IN PLAY Research shows that infants show visual preferences for gender-stereotyped toys as early as three to eight months of age (Alexander et al., 2009). Although preferences for gender-typed toys are well developed by the ages of 15 to 36 months, girls are more likely to stray from the stereotypes (Underwood & Rosen, 2011). Girls ask for and play with "boys' toys" such as cars and trucks more often than boys choose dolls and other "girls' toys."

Girls and boys differ not only in toy preferences but also in their choice of play environments and activities. During the preschool and early elementary school years, boys prefer vigorous physical outdoor activities such as climbing, playing with large vehicles, and rough-and-tumble play (Underwood & Rosen, 2011). In middle childhood, boys spend more time than girls in play groups of five or more children and in competitive play. Girls are more

social play play in which children interact with and are influenced by others.

likely than boys to engage in arts and crafts and domestic play. Girls' activities are more closely directed and structured by adults (A. Campbell et al., 2002).

Why do children show these early preferences for gender-stereotyped toys and activities? Biological factors may play a role, for example, boys' slightly greater strength and activity levels and girls' slightly greater physical maturity and coordination. But adults treat girls and boys differently. They provide gender-stereotyped toys and room furnishings and encourage gender typing in play and household chores (Leaper, 2011). Children, moreover, tend to seek out information on which kinds of toys and play are "masculine" or "feminine" and then to conform to the label (Martin & Ruble, 2004).

Some studies find that children who "cross the line" by showing interest in toys or activities considered appropriate for the other gender are often teased, ridiculed, rejected, or ignored by their parents, teachers, other adults, and peers. Boys are more likely than girls to be criticized (Zosuls et al., 2011).

Another well-documented finding is that children begin to prefer playmates of the same gender by the age of two. Girls develop this preference somewhat earlier than boys (Hay et al., 2004). The tendency strengthens during middle childhood.

Two factors may be involved in the choice of the gender of playmates in early childhood. One is that boys' play is more oriented toward dominance, aggression, and rough play (Hines, 2011). The second is that boys are not very responsive to girls' polite suggestions. Boys may avoid girls because they see them as inferior (Caplan & Larkin, 1991).

8-2e PROSOCIAL BEHAVIOR

Prosocial behavior, also known as *altruism*, is intended to benefit another without expectation of reward. Prosocial behavior includes sharing, cooperating, and helping and comforting others in distress. It is shown by the preschool and early school years and is linked to the development of empathy and perspective taking (Grusec & Sherman, 2011).

EMPATHY Empathy is sensitivity to the feelings of others and is connected with sharing and cooperation. Infants frequently begin to cry when they hear other children crying, although this early agitated response may be largely reflexive (Roberts et al., 2014). Empathy promotes prosocial behavior and decreases aggressive behavior, and these links are evident by the second year (Hastings et al., 2000). During the second year, many children approach other children and adults who are in distress and try to help them. They may hug a crying child or tell the child not to cry. Toddlers who are rated as emotionally unresponsive to the feelings of others are more likely to behave aggressively throughout the school years (Olson et al., 2000).

Girls show more empathy than boys (Roberts et al., 2014). It is unclear whether this gender difference reflects socialization of girls to be attuned to the emotions of others or genetic factors, although some researchers argue that prenatal exposure to testosterone has a suppressive effect on empathy (Durdiakova et al., 2015; Zilioli et al., 2014).

Brand X Pictures/Jupiterimages

PERSPECTIVE TAKING According to Piaget, preoperational children tend to be egocentric. They tend not to be able to see things from the vantage points of others. It turns out that various cognitive abilities, such as being able to take another person's perspective, are related to knowing when someone is in need or distress. Perspective-taking skills improve with age, and so do prosocial skills. Among children of the same age, those with better developed perspective-taking ability also show more prosocial behavior and less aggressive behavior (Hastings et al., 2000).

INFLUENCES ON PROSOCIAL BEHAVIOR Although altruistic behavior is defined as prosocial behavior that occurs in the absence of rewards or the expectations of rewards, it is influenced by rewards and punishments. The peers of nursery schoolchildren who are cooperative, friendly, and generous respond more positively to them than they do to children whose behavior is self-centered

prosocial behavior behavior that benefits other people, generally without expectation of reward.

(Grusec & Davidov, 2015; Grusec & Hastings, 2015). Children who are rewarded for acting prosocially are likely to continue these behaviors (Grusec & Davidov, 2015).

Parents foster prosocial behavior when they use inductive techniques such as explaining how behavior affects others ("You made Josh cry. It's not nice to hit."). Parents of prosocial children are more likely to expect mature behavior from their children. They are less likely to use power-assertive techniques of discipline (Roberts et al., 2014).

8-2f DEVELOPMENT OF AGGRESSION

Children, like adults, not only can be loving and altruistic, but they also can be aggressive. Some children, of course, are more aggressive than others. Aggression refers to behavior intended to hurt or injure another person.

Aggressive behavior, as other social behavior, seems to follow developmental patterns. The aggression of preschoolers is frequently instrumental or possession oriented (Persson, 2005). Younger preschoolers tend to use aggression to obtain the toys and situations they want, such as a favored seat at the table or in the car. Older preschoolers are more likely to resolve conflicts over toys by sharing rather than fighting (Underwood, 2011). Anger and aggression in preschoolers usually cause other preschoolers to reject them (Gower et al., 2014; Walter & LaFreniere, 2000).

By age six or seven, aggression becomes hostile and person oriented. Children taunt and criticize one another and call one another names; they also attack one another physically.

Aggressive behavior appears to be generally stable and predictive of social and emotional problems later on, especially among boys (Nagin & Tremblay, 2001; Tapper & Boulton, 2004). Toddlers who are perceived as difficult and defiant are more likely to behave aggressively throughout the school years (Olson et al., 2000). A longitudinal study of more than 600 children found that aggressive eight-year-olds tended to remain more aggressive than their peers 22 years later, at age 30 (Kokko et al., 2014). Aggressive children of both genders are more likely to have criminal convictions as adults, to abuse their spouses, and to drive while drunk.

8-2g THEORIES OF AGGRESSION

What causes some children to be more aggressive than others? Aggression in childhood appears to result from a complex interplay of biological factors and environmental factors such as reinforcement and modeling.

Evidence suggests that genetic factors may be involved in aggressive behavior, including criminal and antisocial behavior (Bezdjian et al., 2011). There is a greater concordance (agreement) rate for criminal behavior between monozygotic (MZ) twins, who fully share their genetic code, than dizygotic (DZ) twins, who, like other brothers and sisters, share only half of their genetic code (Tehrani & Mednick, 2000). If genetics is involved in aggression, genes may do their work at least in part through the male sex hormone testosterone. Testosterone is apparently connected with feelings of self-confidence, high activity levels, and—the negative side—aggressiveness (Carre & Olmstead, 2015; Platje et al., 2015).

Cognitive research with primary schoolchildren finds that children who believe in the legitimacy of aggression are more likely to behave aggressively when they are presented with social provocations (Yaros et al., 2014). Aggressive children are also often found to be lacking in empathy and the ability to see things from the perspective of other people (Gini et al., 2014; Underwood & Rosen, 2011). They fail to conceptualize the experiences of their victims and are thus less likely to inhibit aggressive impulses.

Social cognitive explanations of aggression focus on environmental factors such as reinforcement and observational learning. When children repeatedly push, shove, and hit to grab toys or break into line, other children usually let them have their way (Kempes et al., 2005). Children who are thus rewarded for acting aggressively are likely to continue to use aggressive means, especially if they do not have alternative means to achieve their ends. Aggressive children may also associate with peers who value and encourage aggression (Stauffacher & DeHart, 2006).

Children who are physically punished are more likely to be aggressive themselves than children who are not physically punished (Patterson, 2005). Physically aggressive parents serve as models for aggression and also stoke their children's anger.

TRUTH

(T) F Children who are physically punished are more likely to be aggressive than children who are not.

It is true that children who are physically punished are more likely to be aggressive than children who are not. Perhaps punitive parents model punitive behavior and instill hostility in their children.

MEDIA INFLUENCES A classic experiment by Bandura, Ross, and Ross (1963) suggests the powerful influence of televised models on children's aggressive behavior. One group of preschool children observed a film of an adult model hitting and kicking an inflated Bobo doll, while a control group saw an aggression-free film. The experimental and control children were then left alone in a room with the same doll as hidden observers recorded their behavior. The children who had observed the aggressive model showed significantly more aggressive behavior toward the doll themselves (see Figure 8.1). Many children imitated bizarre attack behaviors devised for the model in this experiment—behaviors that they would not have thought up themselves.

Photodisc/Getty Images

Do we fully understand the effects of television on young children?

Television is a fertile source of aggressive models, and most organizations of health professionals agree that media violence contributes to aggression in children (Huesmann et al., 2003; 2013). This relationship has been found for girls and boys of different ages, social classes, ethnic groups, and cultures (Huesmann et al., 2013). Consider a number of ways that depictions of violence make their contribution (Anderson et al., 2015; Huesmann et al., 2013):

- *Observational learning.* Children learn from observation. TV violence supplies models of aggressive "skills," which children may acquire.
- *Disinhibition.* Punishment inhibits behavior. Conversely, media violence may **disinhibit** aggressive behavior, especially when characters "get away" with it.

disinhibit to encourage a response that has been previously suppressed.

FIG.8.1 BANDURA'S STUDY OF THE IMITATION OF AGGRESSION

© Albert Bandura/Dept. of Psychology, Stanford University

The top row of photos shows an adult striking a Bobo doll. The second and third rows show a boy and a girl who observed the adult imitating the aggressive behavior.

- *Increased arousal.* Media violence and aggressive video games increase viewers' level of arousal. We are more likely to be aggressive under high levels of arousal.
- *Priming of aggressive thoughts and memories.* Media violence "primes" or arouses aggressive ideas and memories.
- *Habituation.* We become used to repeated stimuli. Children exposed to violence are more likely to assume that violence is acceptable or normal and become desensitized to it.

FICTION

T (F) There is no scientific evidence that violence in the media contributes to aggression.

It is not true that scientific evidence is lacking on whether media violence contributes to aggression. Studies going back half a century show that children imitate violence they observe in the media.

Violent video games may create the greatest risk of violence because they require audience participation (DeLisi et al., 2013; Lin, 2013). Players don't just watch; they participate (Dubow et al., 2010). Playing violent video games increases aggressive thoughts and behavior in the laboratory (Anderson et al., 2015). Males are relatively more likely than females to act aggressively after playing violent video games and are more likely to see the world as a hostile place. However, students of both genders who obtain higher grades are less likely than students of lower achievement to behave aggressively following exposure to violent video games. Thus, cultural stereotyping of males and females, possible biological gender differences, and moderating variables like academic achievement also figure into the effects of media violence. There is no simple one-to-one connection between media violence and violence in real life. There seems to be a circular relationship between exposure to media violence and aggressive behavior (Anderson et al., 2015). Yes, TV violence and violent video games contribute to aggressive behavior, but aggressive youngsters are also more likely to seek out this kind of "entertainment." Figure 8.2 explores the possible connections between TV violence and aggressive behavior among viewers.

self-concept one's self-description and self-evaluation according to various categories, such as child, adolescent, or adult, one's gender, and one's skills.

categorical self definitions of the self that refer to external traits.

FIG.8.2 WHAT ARE THE CONNECTIONS BETWEEN MEDIA VIOLENCE AND AGGRESSIVE BEHAVIOR?

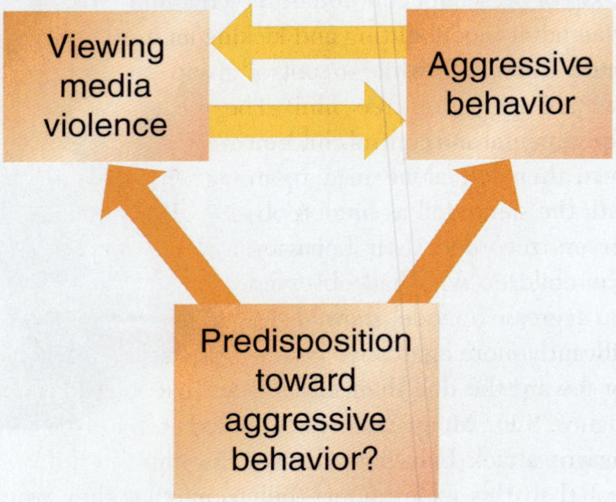

Does media violence cause aggressive behavior? Do aggressive children prefer to view violent TV shows or play violent video games? Or do other factors, such as personality traits, create a predisposition toward both seeking media violence and behaving aggressively?

8-3 PERSONALITY AND EMOTIONAL DEVELOPMENT

In early childhood, children's sense of self—who they are and how they feel about themselves—develops and grows more complex. They begin to acquire a sense of their own abilities and their increasing mastery of the environment. As they move out into the world, they also face new experiences that may cause them to feel fearful and anxious.

8-3a THE SELF

The sense of self, or the **self-concept**, emerges gradually during infancy. Infants and toddlers visually begin to recognize themselves and differentiate themselves from other individuals such as their parents.

In the preschool years, children continue to develop their sense of self. Almost as soon as they begin to speak, they describe themselves in terms of certain categories, such as age groupings (baby, child, adult) and gender (girl, boy). Self-definitions that refer to concrete external traits have been called the **categorical self**.

Children as young as three years are able to describe themselves in terms of behaviors and internal states that occur often and are fairly stable over time (Rosen & Patterson, 2011). For example, in response to the question "How do you feel when you're scared?" young children frequently respond, "Usually like running away" (Eder, 1989). In answer to the question "How do you usually act around grown-ups?" a typical response might be, "I mostly been good with grown-ups."

One aspect of the self-concept is self-esteem. Children with high self-esteem are more likely to be securely attached and have parents who are attentive to their needs (Roisman & Groh, 2011). They also are more likely to show prosocial behavior (Grusec & Davidov, 2015).

Preschool children begin to make evaluative judgments about two different aspects of themselves by the age of four (Underwood & Rosen, 2011). One is their cognitive and physical competence (e.g., being good at puzzles, counting, swinging, tying shoes), and the second is their social acceptance by peers and parents (e.g., having lots of friends, being read to by Mom). But preschoolers do not yet clearly distinguish between different areas of competence. A preschooler is not likely to report being good in school but poor in physical skills. One is either "good at doing things" or one is not (MacDonald & Leary, 2011; Piek et al., 2006).

Children also become increasingly capable of self-regulation in early childhood. They become more and more capable of controlling their eliminatory processes, of controlling aggressive behavior, of engaging in play with other children, and of focusing on cognitive tasks such as learning to count and to sound out letters. Self-regulatory abilities are connected with maturation of the brain and the rearing practices of caregivers.

8-3b INITIATIVE VERSUS GUILT

As preschoolers continue to develop a separate sense of themselves, they increasingly move out into the world and take the initiative in learning new skills. Erik Erikson (1963) refers to these early childhood years as the stage of *initiative versus guilt*.

Children in this stage strive to achieve independence from their parents and master adult behaviors. They are curious, try new things, and test themselves. Children learn that not all their plans, dreams, and fantasies can be realized. Adults prohibit children from doing certain things, and children begin to internalize adult rules. Fear of violating the rules may cause the child to feel guilty and may curtail efforts to master new skills. Parents can help children develop and maintain a healthy sense of initiative by encouraging their attempts to learn and explore and by not being unduly critical and punitive.

8-3c FEARS: THE HORRORS OF EARLY CHILDHOOD

In Erikson's view, fear of violating parental prohibitions can be a powerful force in the life of a young child. Children's fears change as they move from infancy into the preschool years. The number of fears seems to peak between two and a half and four years and then taper off (Muris & Field, 2011). The preschool period is marked by a decline in fears of loud noises, falling, sudden movement, and strangers. Fear of social disapproval is not the most common fear among preschoolers. Preschoolers are most likely to fear animals, imaginary creatures, the dark, and personal danger (Muris & Field, 2011). The fantasies of young children frequently involve stories they are told and media imagery (Pearce & Field, 2016). Frightening images of imaginary creatures can persist. Many preschoolers are reluctant to have the lights turned off at night for fear that such creatures may assault them. Real objects and situations also cause many preschoolers to fear for their personal safety—lightning, thunder and other loud noises, high places, sharp objects and being cut, blood, unfamiliar people, strange people, and stinging and crawling insects.

Michael Blann/Stone/Getty Images

FICTION

T (F) The most common fear among preschoolers is fear of social disapproval.

Actually, preschoolers are more likely to fear animals, imaginary creatures, the dark, and personal danger than social disapproval.

During middle childhood, children become less fearful of imaginary creatures, but fears of bodily harm and injury remain common. Children grow more fearful of failure and criticism in school and in social relationships (Underwood & Rosen, 2011). Girls report more fears and higher levels of anxiety than boys.

8-4 DEVELOPMENT OF GENDER ROLES AND GENDER DIFFERENCES

These lyrics are from the song "I Am Woman" by Helen Reddy and Ray Burton. They caught attention because they counter the **stereotype** of a vulnerable woman who needs the protection of a man. The stereotype of the vulnerable woman is a fixed, oversimplified, and conventional idea. So is the stereotype of the chivalrous, protective man. Unfortunately, these stereotypes create demands and limit opportunities for both genders.

Cultural stereotypes of males and females are broad expectations of behavior that we call **gender roles** (Leaper & Farkas, 2015). Researchers who investigate perceptions of gender differences in personality have found that people in our culture agree on certain groups of "masculine" and "feminine" traits, such as those in Table 8.4.

Gender-role stereotypes develop in stages. First, children learn to label the genders. At about 2 to 2½ years of age, they can identify pictures of girls and boys (Alexander et al., 2009). By age three, they display knowledge of gender stereotypes for toys, clothing, work, and activities (Campbell et al., 2004). Children of this age generally agree that boys play with cars and trucks, help their fathers, and tend to hit others. They agree that girls play with dolls, help their mothers, and do not hit others (Cherney et al., 2006). One study found that preschool boys but not girls were rejected by their peers when they showed distress (Walter & LaFreniere, 2000).

Children become increasingly traditional in their stereotyping of activities, jobs, and personality traits between the ages of three and nine or ten (Hilliard & Liben, 2010). For example, traits such as "cruel" and "repairs broken things" are viewed as masculine, and traits such as "often is afraid" and "cooks and bakes" are seen as feminine.

Children and adolescents perceive their own gender in a somewhat better light. For example, girls perceive other girls as nicer, more hardworking, and less selfish than boys. Boys, on the other hand, think that they are nicer, more hardworking, and less selfish than girls (Hilliard & Liben, 2010; Martin & Dinella, 2011).

stereotype a fixed, conventional idea about a group.

gender role a cluster of traits and behaviors that are considered stereotypical of females and males.

TABLE 8.4 CULTURAL STEREOTYPES OF "MASCULINE" AND "FEMININE" TRAITS. ARE THEY ACCURATE?

Masculine	Feminine
Adventurous	Affectionate
Aggressive	Agreeable
Assertive	Appreciative
Capable	Artistic
Coarse	Cautious
Confident	Dependent
Courageous	Emotional
Determined	Fearful
Disorderly	Fickle
Enterprising	Gentle
Hardheaded	Kind
Independent	Nurturing
Intelligent	Patient
Pleasure-seeking	Prudish
Quick	Sensitive
Rational	Sentimental
Realistic	Shy
Reckless	Softhearted
Scientific	Submissive
Sensation-seeking	Suggestible
Stern	Talkative
Tough	Unambitious

8-4a GENDER DIFFERENCES

Clearly, females and males are anatomically different. And according to gender-role stereotypes, people believe that females and males also differ in their behaviors, personality characteristics, and abilities (Maccoby, 2015). Gender differences in infancy are small and rather inconsistent. Preschoolers display some differences in their choices of toys and play activities. Boys engage in more rough-and-tumble play and are more aggressive. Girls tend to show more empathy and to report more fears. Girls show somewhat greater verbal ability than boys, whereas boys show somewhat greater visual–spatial ability than girls.

8-4b THEORIES OF THE DEVELOPMENT OF GENDER DIFFERENCES

Why is it that little girls (often) grow up to behave according to the cultural stereotypes of what it means to be female? Why is it that little boys (often) grow up to behave like male stereotypes?

THE ROLES OF EVOLUTION AND HEREDITY According to evolutionary psychologists, gender differences were fashioned by natural selection in response to problems in adaptation that were repeatedly encountered by humans over thousands of generations (Buss & Hawley, 2011; Bugental et al., 2015). Men, who have generally been the hunters, breadwinners, and warriors, are more likely to be seen as adventurous, aggressive, and assertive (see Table 8.4). Women, who have more often been the homemakers and caretakers, are more likely to be seen as affectionate, agreeable, and emotional. The story of the survival of our ancient ancestors is etched in our genes. Genes that bestow attributes that increase an organism's chances of surviving to produce viable offspring are most likely to be transmitted to future generations. We thus possess the genetic codes for traits that helped our ancestors survive and reproduce. These traits include structural gender differences, such as those found in the brain, and differences in body chemistry, such as hormones. The question is whether evolution has also etched social and psychological gender differences into our genes.

Does this woman's dress and behavior fit the traditional feminine gender-role stereotype? Why or why not?

PhotoStock-Israel / Alamy Stock Photo

ORGANIZATION OF THE BRAIN The organization of the brain is largely genetically determined. The hemispheres of the brain are specialized to perform certain functions, as noted in Chapter 7. Both males and females have a left hemisphere and a right hemisphere, but the question is whether they use them in quite the same way. Consider the hippocampus, a brain structure that is involved in the formation of memories and the relay of incoming sensory information to other parts of the brain. Matthias Riepe and his colleagues (Grön et al., 2000) have studied the ways in which humans and rats use the hippocampus when they are navigating mazes. Males use the hippocampus in both hemispheres when they are navigating (Grön et al., 2000). Women, however, rely on the hippocampus in the right hemisphere along with the right prefrontal cortex, an area of the brain that evaluates information and makes plans. Riepe and his colleagues wonder whether different patterns of brain activities might contribute to preference for using landmarks or maps.

Heide Benser/Corbis

Are there such things as "boys' toys"? As "girls' toys"? Where do such ideas come from?

SEX HORMONES Researchers suggest that the development of gender differences in personality, along with the development of anatomical gender differences, may be related to prenatal levels of sex hormones (Avinum & Knafo-Noam, 2015). Although the results of many studies attempting to correlate prenatal sex hormone levels with subsequent gender-typed play have been mixed, a study of 212 pregnant women conducted by Bonnie Auyeung and her colleagues (2009) found that higher-than-normal levels of testosterone in the fetal environment, due to maternal stress, were related to more masculine-typed play among girls at the age of eight and a half years. Emily Barrett and her colleagues (2014) found that exposure to the prenatal environments of stressed mothers can boost masculine-typed play in girls and decrease it in boys. Other studies have shown that children display gender-typed preferences—with boys preferring transportation toys and girls preferring dolls—as early as the age of 13 months (Knickmeyer et al., 2005). Another study investigated the gender-typed visual preferences of 30 human infants at the early ages of three to eight months (Alexander et al., 2009). The researchers assessed interest in a toy truck and a doll by using eye-tracking technology to indicate the direction of visual attention. Girls showed a visual preference for the doll over the truck (i.e., they made a greater number of visual fixations on the doll), and boys showed a visual preference for the truck.

SOCIAL COGNITIVE THEORY Social cognitive theorists consider both the roles of rewards and punishments (reinforcement) in gender typing and the ways in which children learn from observing others and decide which behaviors are appropriate for them. Children learn much about what society considers "masculine" or "feminine" by observing and imitating models of the same gender. These models may be their parents, other adults, other children, even characters in electronic media such as TV and video games.

Socialization also plays a role (Maccoby, 2015). Parents, teachers, other adults—even other children—provide children with information about the gender-typed behaviors expected of them (Leaper & Farkas, 2015). Children are rewarded with smiles and respect and companionship when they display "gender-appropriate" behavior. Children are punished with frowns and loss of friends when they display "inappropriate" behavior.

Boys are encouraged to be independent, whereas girls are more likely to be restricted. Boys are allowed to roam farther from home at an earlier age and are more likely to be left unsupervised after school (Miller et al., 2006).

Primary schoolchildren show less stereotyping if their mothers frequently engage in traditionally "masculine" tasks such as washing the car, taking children to ball games, or assembling toys (Leaper & Farkas, 2015). Maternal employment is associated with less polarized gender-role concepts for girls and boys (Leaper & Farkas, 2015).

COGNITIVE-DEVELOPMENTAL THEORY Lawrence Kohlberg (1966) proposed a cognitive-developmental view of gender typing. According to this perspective, children form concepts about gender and then fit their behavior to the concepts (Zosuls et al., 2011). These developments occur in stages and are entwined with general cognitive development.

According to Kohlberg, gender typing involves the emergence of three concepts: gender identity, gender stability, and gender constancy. The first step in gender typing is attaining **gender identity**. Gender identity is the knowledge that one is male or female. At two years, most children can say whether they are boys or girls. By the age of three, many children can discriminate anatomic gender differences (Campbell et al., 2004; Zosuls et al., 2011).

At around age four or five, most children develop the concept of **gender stability**, according to Kohlberg. They recognize that people retain their gender for a lifetime. Girls no longer believe that they can grow up to be daddies, and boys no longer think that they can become mommies.

TRUTH

T F A 2½-year-old may know that he is a boy, but still think that he can grow up to be a mommy.

Yes, a 2½-year-old will likely have developed gender identity but not yet gender stability.

By the age of five to seven years, Kohlberg believes that most children develop the more sophisticated concept of **gender constancy** and recognize that people's gender does not change, even if they change their dress or behavior. A woman who cuts her hair short remains a woman. A man who dons an apron and cooks remains a man. Once children have established concepts of gender stability and constancy, they seek to behave in ways that are consistent with their gender (Liben et al., 2014; Zosuls et al., 2011).

Sylvie Villeger/Science Source

gender identity knowledge that one is female or male.

gender stability the concept that one's gender is unchanging.

gender constancy the concept that one's gender remains the same despite changes in appearance or behavior.

Cross-cultural studies in the United States, Samoa, Nepal, Belize, and Kenya have found that the concepts of gender identity, gender stability, and gender constancy emerge in the order predicted by Kohlberg (Leonard & Archer, 1989; Munroe et al., 1984). But research shows that gender-typed play emerges earlier than gender identity. Girls show preferences for dolls and soft toys and boys for hard transportation toys under the age of a year, but they are not fitting it to their concept of gender identity, which is yet to emerge (Alexander et al., 2009).

GENDER-SCHEMA THEORY **Gender-schema theory** proposes that children use gender as one way of organizing their perceptions of the world (Leaper, 2013; Martin & Ruble, 2004). A gender schema is a cluster of concepts about male and female physical traits, personality traits, and behaviors. According to gender-schema theory, once children come to see themselves as female or male, they begin to seek information concerning gender-typed traits and try to live up to them (Liben et al., 2014; Tenenbaum et al. 2010). Jack will retaliate when provoked because boys are expected to do so. Jill will be "sugary and sweet" if such is expected of little girls.

Today, most scholars would agree that both biology and social cognition interact to affect most areas of behavior and mental processes—including the complex processes involved in gender typing.

Rob Marmion/Shutterstock.com

gender-schema theory the view that one's knowledge of the gender schema in one's society guides one's assumption of gender-typed preferences and behavior patterns.

STUDY TOOLS 8

READY TO STUDY?

In the book, you can:

- ☐ Rip out the chapter review card at the back of the book for a handy summary of the chapter and key terms.
- ☐ Check your understanding of what you've read with the quizzes that follow.

ONLINE AT CENGAGEBRAIN.COM YOU CAN:

- ☐ Collect StudyBits while you read and study the chapter.
- ☐ Quiz yourself on key concepts.
- ☐ Find videos for further exploration.
- ☐ Prepare for tests with HDEV5 Flash Cards as well as those you create.

SELF-ASSESSMENTS

Fill-Ins

Answers can be found in the back of the book.

1. Research shows that children tend to distort their ____________ to conform to their gender schemas.
2. According to Erikson, early childhood is the stage of ____________ versus guilt.
3. Self-definitions that refer to concrete external traits have been called the ____________ self.
4. Research shows that the hormone ____________ is connected with feelings of self-confidence, high activity levels, and aggressiveness.
5. The children of ____________ parents tend to show self-reliance and independence, high self-esteem, high levels of activity and exploratory behavior, and social competence.
6. According to Piaget, the first type of play is ____________ play.
7. ____________ behavior is also known as altruism.
8. Anger and aggression in preschoolers usually cause other preschoolers to ____________ them.
9. Children try on new roles through ____________ play.
10. The classic study of aggression by ____________ and his colleagues (1963) showed people attacking Bobo doll.

Multiple Choice

1. **Which of the following is part of the feminine gender-role stereotype?**
   a. patient
   b. independent
   c. realistic
   d. disorderly

2. **Which of the following are children in early childhood least likely to fear?**
   a. lightning
   b. stinging and crawling insects
   c. strange people
   d. social disapproval

3. **All of the following are listed as reasons that viewing violent media can contribute to aggressive behavior, *except***
   a. disinhibition of aggressive impulses.
   b. explaining that media violence is not real.
   c. priming of aggressive thoughts and memories.
   d. observational learning.

4. **Which of the following statements best describes the relationship between empathy and gender?**
   a. Girls show more empathy than boys do.
   b. Boys show more empathy than girls do.
   c. Girls and boys show equal amounts of empathy.
   d. The research literature on the subject is inconclusive.

5. **Children first show visual preferences for stereotypical "boys' toys" or "girls' toys"**
   a. before the first birthday.
   b. between the ages of one to two years.
   c. between the ages of two to five years.
   d. between the ages of five to eight years.

6. **Which of the following, according to Parten's types, is a form of nonsocial play?**
   a. cooperative play
   b. associative play
   c. onlooker play
   d. parallel play

7. **When preschoolers are asked what they like about friends, they are most likely to report that**
   a. they and their friends can share their innermost thoughts.
   b. their friends are the people they can trust.
   c. they and their friends share toys and activities.
   d. their friends are of the same gender and ethnic background.

8. **Compared to later-born children, first-born children are**
   a. less anxious.
   b. more self-reliant.
   c. more adult-oriented.
   d. more aggressive.

9. **Baumrind found the sons of ____________ parents to be hostile and defiant and the daughters to be low in independence and social dominance.**
   a. authoritative
   b. authoritarian
   c. permissive–indulgent
   d. rejecting–neglecting

10. **Children who are physically punished**
    a. are more likely to be motivated to succeed.
    b. are less intelligent than other children.
    c. do not understand why they are being disciplined.
    d. are more likely to be aggressive than other children.

9 Middle Childhood: Physical and Cognitive Development

PhotoAlto/Laurence Mouton/Brand X Pictures/Getty Images

LEARNING OUTCOMES

After studying this chapter, you will be able to...

- 9-1 Describe trends in physical development in middle childhood
- 9-2 Describe changes in motor development in middle childhood
- 9-3 Discuss attention deficit hyperactivity disorder and learning disabilities
- 9-4 Describe Piaget's concrete-operational stage
- 9-5 Discuss Piaget's and Kohlberg's theories of moral development
- 9-6 Describe developments in information processing in middle childhood
- 9-7 Describe intellectual development in middle childhood, focusing on theories of intelligence
- 9-8 Describe language development in middle childhood, including reading and bilingualism

After you finish this chapter, go to **PAGE 196** for **STUDY TOOLS**

In middle childhood, children show the beginnings of adult logic.

GROWTH PATTERNS

Middle childhood is typically defined as the ages from 6 to 12, beginning with the school years and bound at the upper end by the beginning of the adolescent **growth spurt** at about the age of 12. Following the growth trends of early childhood, boys and girls continue to gain a little over two inches in height per year until the spurt begins (see Figure 9.1). The average gain in weight during middle childhood is five to seven pounds a year, but children grow less stocky and more slender (Kuczmarski et al., 2000).

9-1a NUTRITION AND GROWTH

In middle childhood, the average child's body weight doubles. Children also spend a good deal of energy in physical activity and play. To fuel this growth and activity, schoolchildren eat more than preschoolers. The average four- to six-year-old needs 1,400 to 1,800 calories per day, but the average seven- to ten-year-old requires 2,000 calories.

Nutrition involves more than calories. It is healthful to eat fruits and vegetables, fish, poultry (without skin), and whole grains, and to limit intake of fats, sugar, and starches. However, most foods in school cafeterias and elsewhere are heavy in sugar, animal fats, and salt (Bray & Bouchard, 2014).

GENDER SIMILARITIES AND DIFFERENCES IN PHYSICAL GROWTH Boys are slightly heavier and taller than girls through the age of nine or ten (see Figure 9.1). Girls then begin their adolescent growth spurt and surpass boys in height and weight until about 13 or 14. Then boys spurt and grow taller and heavier than girls. The steady gains in height and weight in middle childhood are paralleled by increased muscle strength in both genders. Beginning at about age 11, boys develop relatively more muscle, and girls develop relatively more fat.

growth spurt a period during which growth advances at a dramatically rapid rate compared with other periods.

9-1b WEIGHT

Between 16% and 25% of children and adolescents in the United States are overweight or obese (see Figure 9.2). Consider some facts about childhood overweight and obesity (Bray & Bouchard, 2014; Ogden et al., 2014):

- Over the past 20 years the prevalence of obesity among children has doubled.
- Latin American boys are significantly more likely than European American boys to be overweight.
- African American girls are significantly more likely than European American girls to be overweight.
- Children who are obese are more likely to develop high blood pressure and high cholesterol—as children!
- Children who are obese are more likely to develop diabetes.

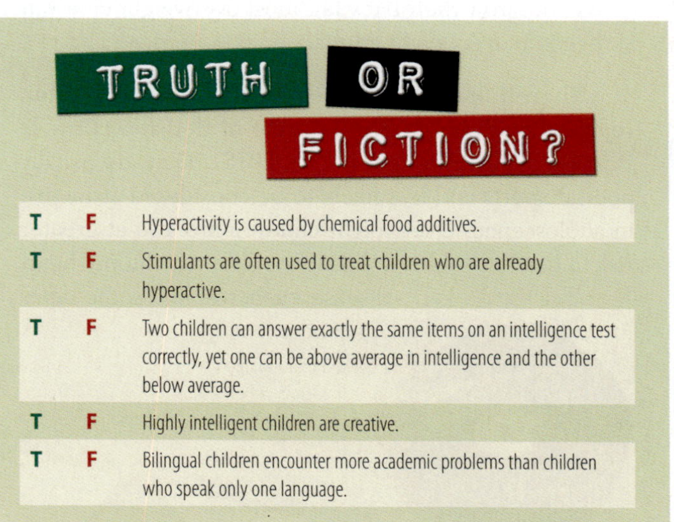

TRUTH OR FICTION?
T F Hyperactivity is caused by chemical food additives.
T F Stimulants are often used to treat children who are already hyperactive.
T F Two children can answer exactly the same items on an intelligence test correctly, yet one can be above average in intelligence and the other below average.
T F Highly intelligent children are creative.
T F Bilingual children encounter more academic problems than children who speak only one language.

FIG.9.1 GROWTH CURVES FOR WEIGHT AND HEIGHT

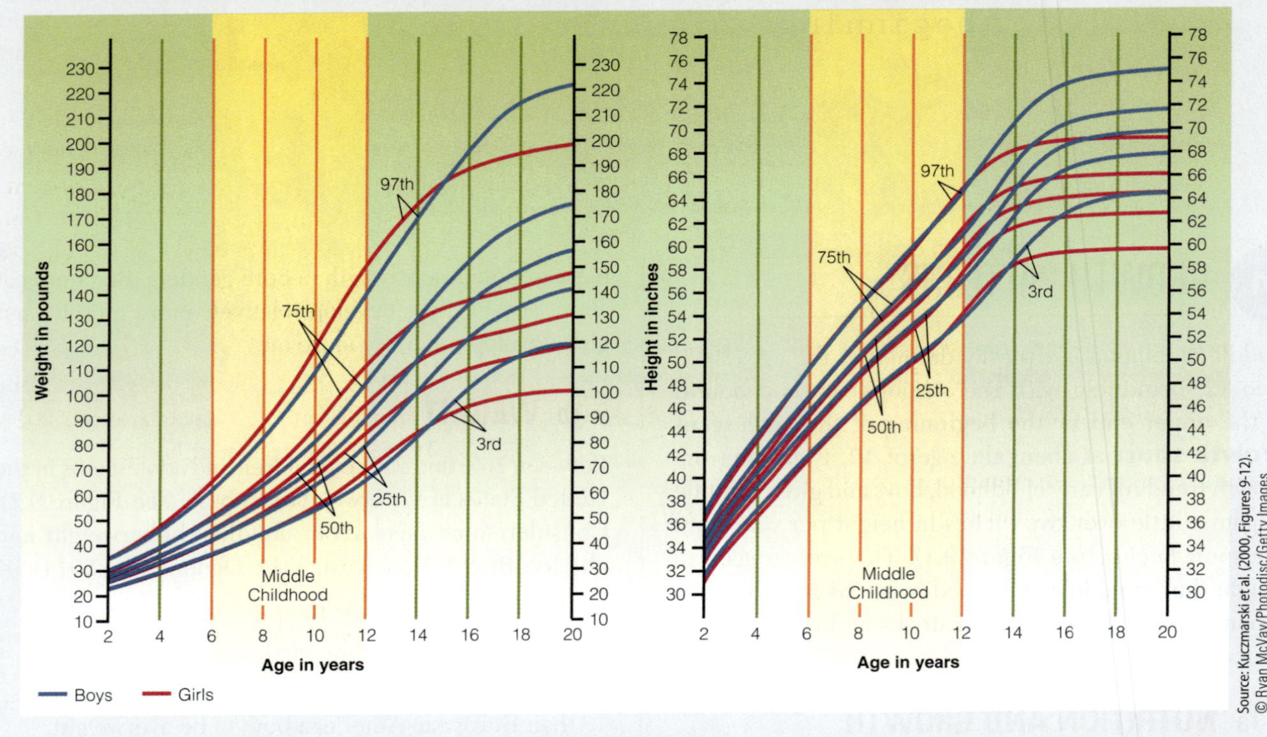

Gains in height and weight are fairly steady during middle childhood.

- Obese children are more likely to develop breathing problems and asthma, joint problems, fatty liver disease, gallstones, and acid reflux—all in childhood.
- Although parents often assume that heavy children will outgrow their baby fat, most overweight children become overweight adults.

There's more: Overweight children are often rejected by peers or are a source of derision (Bray & Bouchard, 2014; Williams et al., 2013). They are usually poor at sports and less likely to be considered attractive in adolescence. Overweight children are also at greater risk of health problems throughout life—including heart disease, diabetes, and some types of cancer.

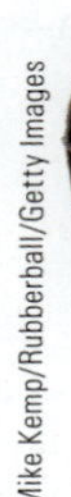

CAUSES OF BEING OVERWEIGHT Evidence from kinship studies, including twin studies, and adoption studies shows that heredity plays a role in being overweight (den Hoed & Loos, 2014; Perusse et al., 2014). Some people inherit a tendency to burn up extra calories, whereas others inherit a tendency to turn extra calories into fat.

Except in rare cases of gene therapy, there is nothing one can do about one's heredity. Other factors that contribute to child overweight and obesity include consumption of sugary drinks and less healthful food at schools and child-care centers, the advertising of fattening foods, lack of regular physical activity (and for low-income children, lack of community places in which to play or exercise), limited access to healthful affordable foods, availability of "high energy" (translation: high sugar) drinks, large portion sizes (supersizing), lack of breast-feeding, and TV and other media (couch-potato syndrome) (Leech et al., 2014; Berge et al., 2015). Overweight

FIG.9.2 OVERWEIGHT CHILDREN IN THE UNITED STATES

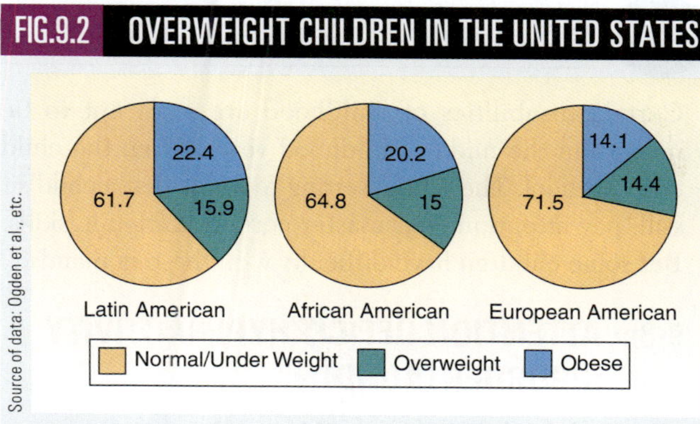

Percentage of children (ages 6–11) and adolescents (ages 12–19) who are overweight, according to the American Heart Association (AHA).

parents may serve as examples of poor exercise habits, encourage overeating, and keep unhealthful foods in the home (Berge et al., 2015).

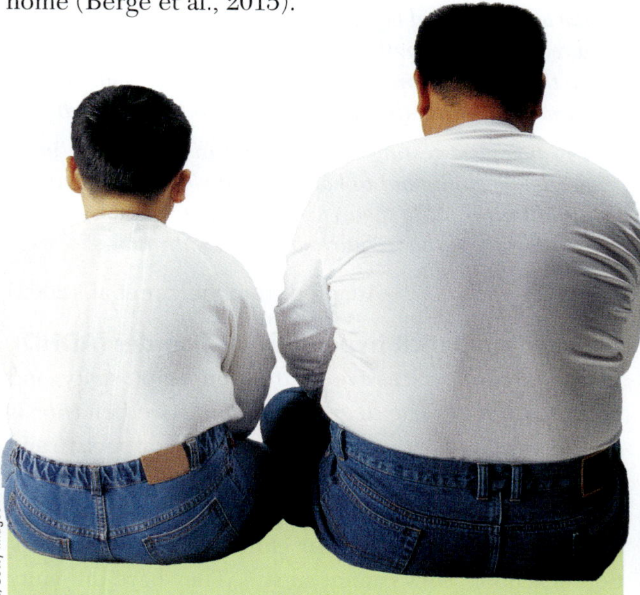

We know that being overweight runs in families, but we don't know exactly why. Heredity plays a role, but so do environmental factors.

9-2 MOTOR DEVELOPMENT

The school years are marked by increases in the child's speed, strength, agility, and balance. These developments lead to more skillful motor activities.

9-2a GROSS MOTOR SKILLS

Throughout middle childhood, children show steady improvement in their ability to perform gross motor skills. Children are hopping, jumping, and climbing by age six or so; by age six or seven, they are usually capable of pedaling and balancing on a bicycle. By the ages of eight to ten, children are showing the balance, coordination, and strength that allow them to engage in gymnastics and team sports.

During these years, muscles grow stronger, and neural pathways that connect the cerebellum to the cortex become more myelinated. Experience refines sensorimotor abilities, but there are also inborn differences. Some people have better visual acuity, depth perception, or coordination than others.

Reaction time is basic to the child's timing a swing of the bat or hitting a tennis ball. It gradually improves (decreases) from early childhood to about age 18, but there are individual differences (Swartz et al., 2014). Reaction time increases again in adulthood.

9-2b FINE MOTOR SKILLS

By the age of six to seven, children can usually tie their shoelaces and hold pencils as adults do. Their abilities to fasten buttons, zip zippers, brush their teeth, wash themselves, coordinate a knife and fork, and use chopsticks all develop during the early school years and improve during childhood (Beilei et al., 2002; Gaul & Issartel, 2016).

9-2c GENDER DIFFERENCES

Throughout middle childhood, boys and girls perform similarly in most motor activities. Boys show slightly greater strength, especially more forearm strength, which aids them in swinging a bat or throwing a ball (Hay et al., 2011). Girls show somewhat greater limb coordination and overall flexibility, which is valuable in dancing, balancing, and gymnastics (Bruton et al., 2013).

At puberty, gender differences favoring boys increase. But prior to that, boys are more likely than girls to receive encouragement and opportunities in sports (White, 2016). Between middle childhood and adolescence, physical activities become increasingly stereotyped by children as being masculine (e.g., football) or feminine (e.g., dance) (Boiche et al., 2014).

9-2d EXERCISE AND FITNESS

Exercise reduces the risk of heart disease, stroke, diabetes, and certain forms of cancer (Trost et al., 2014). Physically active children also have a better self-image and coping skills than those who are inactive (Noordstar et al., 2016). Yet most children in the United States are not physically fit (Pate et al., 2013).

reaction time the amount of time required to respond to a stimulus.

How Can Parents Prevent or Reverse Childhood Overweight and Obesity?

Parents can't give their children new genes, but they can take measures including the following (Bray & Bouchard, 2014; Conrad, 2016):

- **Follow the advice of the American Academy of Pediatrics and limit media time for kids to no more than one to two hours of playing handheld video games or watching television per day whether at home, school, or child care.**
- **Visit the child-care centers to see if they serve healthy foods and drinks, and limit TV and video time.**
- **Work with schools to limit foods and drinks with added sugar, fat, and salt that can be purchased outside the school lunch program.**
- **Provide plenty of fruits and vegetables, limit foods high in fat and sugar, and prepare healthy foods at family meals.**
- **Serve your family water rather than sugar drinks. (Ask your doctor about drinks with sugar substitutes.)**
- **Make sure your child gets physical activity every day. (The Centers for Disease Control and Prevention recommend 60 minutes a day. It doesn't all have to be brisk activity or weight training! Fast walking is excellent. Jump-rope and sit-ups and push-ups, with pauses in-between, are all good. Or simply encourage being on the playground for an hour a day. If an hour a day is unrealistic for you, try a half hour. Some is better than none.)**

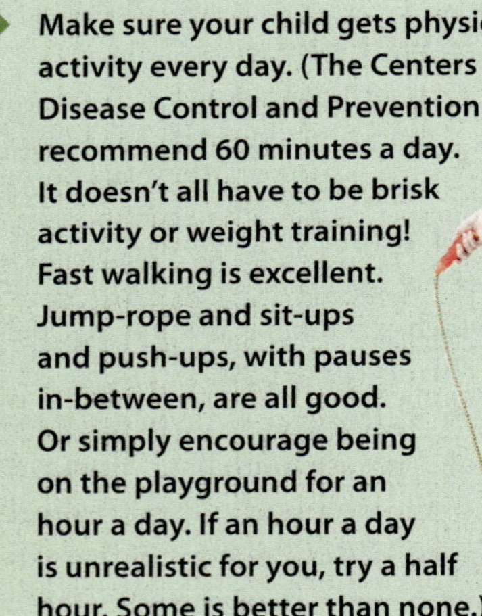

Rubberball/Mike Kemp/Getty Images

Cardiac and muscular fitness is developed by participation in aerobic exercises such as running, walking quickly, swimming laps, bicycling, or jumping rope for several minutes at a time. However, schools and parents tend to focus on sports such as baseball and football, which are less apt to promote fitness.

attention deficit hyperactivity disorder (ADHD) a disorder characterized by excessive inattention, impulsiveness, and hyperactivity.

hyperactivity excessive restlessness and overactivity; a characteristic of ADHD.

9-3 DISORDERS THAT AFFECT LEARNING

Certain disabilities of childhood are most apt to be noticed in the middle childhood years, when the child enters school. The school setting requires that a child sit still, pay attention, and master certain academic skills. But some children have difficulty with these demands.

9-3a ATTENTION DEFICIT HYPERACTIVITY DISORDER (ADHD)

Nine-year-old Eddie is a problem in class. His teacher complains that he is so restless and fidgety that the rest of the class cannot concentrate on their work. He . . . is in constant motion, roaming the classroom, talking to other children while they are working. He has been suspended repeatedly for outrageous behavior, most recently swinging from a fluorescent light fixture. . . . He has never needed much sleep and always awakened before anyone else in the family, . . . wrecking things in the living room and kitchen. Once, at the age of four, he unlocked the front door and wandered into traffic, but was rescued by a passerby.

Psychological testing shows Eddie to be average in academic ability but to have a "virtually nonexistent" attention span. He shows no interest in television or in games or toys that require some concentration.

—Adapted from Spitzer et al. (2002)

In **attention deficit hyperactivity disorder (ADHD)**, the child shows excessive inattention, impulsivity, and **hyperactivity**. The degree of hyperactive behavior is crucial, because many normal children are overactive and fidgety from time to time.

ADHD typically occurs by age seven. The hyperactivity and restlessness impair children's ability to function in school. They cannot sit still. They have difficulty getting along with others. ADHD is diagnosed in about 1% to 5% of school-age children and is many times more common in boys than girls.

ADHD is sometimes overdiagnosed (Gordon et al., 2016; Schwartz & Cohen, 2013). Some children who misbehave in school are diagnosed with ADHD and medicated to encourage more acceptable behavior.

CAUSES OF ADHD There may be a genetic component to ADHD involving the brain chemical dopamine (Martel et al., 2011). Studies in brain imaging have found differences in the brain chemistry of children with ADHD.

In the 1970s, it was widely believed that food coloring and preservatives caused ADHD, but research has shown that this view is incorrect (Nigg & Holton, 2014); Rytter, et al. 2015). Researchers suggest that

FICTION

T (F) Hyperactivity is caused by chemical food additives.

It is not true that hyperactivity is caused by food additives. This view was popular in the 1970s, but researchers now generally agree that food coloring and preservatives do not cause ADHD.

ADHD reflects lack of executive control of the brain over motor and more primitive functions (Hale et al., 2011).

TREATMENT AND OUTCOME **Stimulants** such as Ritalin are the most widespread treatment for ADHD, promoting the activity of the brain chemicals dopamine and noradrenaline, which stimulate the "executive center" of the brain to control more primitive areas of the brain. Stimulants increase children's attention spans and improve their academic performance (Pearson & Crowley, 2012). Most children with ADHD continue to have problems in attention, conduct, or learning in adolescence and adulthood (Martel et al., 2012).

TRUTH

 **F** Stimulants are often used to treat children who are already hyperactive.

It is true that stimulants are often used to treat children who are already hyperactive. The stimulants help children obtain cortical control over lower brain centers (which may fire overactivity).

9-3b LEARNING DISABILITIES

Some children who are intelligent and provided with enriched home environments cannot learn how to read (**dyslexia**) or do simple math problems (Armstrong et al., 2013). Many such children have **learning disabilities**. Learning-disabled children may show problems in math, writing, or reading. Some have difficulties in articulating the sounds of speech or in understanding spoken language. Others have problems in motor coordination. Children are usually diagnosed with a learning disability when they are performing below the level expected for their age and intelligence, and when there is no evidence of other handicaps such as vision or hearing problems, intellectual disability, or socioeconomic disadvantage (Ferrer et al., 2010). Learning disabilities may persist through life, but with early recognition and remediation, many children can learn to compensate for their disability.

It has been estimated that dyslexia affects anywhere from 5% to 17.5% of American children (Shaywitz & Shaywitz, 2013). Most studies show that dyslexia is much more common in boys than in girls. Figure 9.3 shows a writing sample from a dyslexic child.

FIG.9.3 WRITING SAMPLE OF A DYSLEXIC CHILD

Will & Deni McIntyre / Science Source

Dyslexic children may perceive letters as upside down (confusing *w* with *m*) or reversed (confusing *b* with *d*), leading to rotations or reversals in writing, as shown here.

ORIGINS OF DYSLEXIA Theories of dyslexia focus on the ways in which sensory and neurological problems may contribute to the reading problems we find in dyslexic individuals. Genetic factors appear to be involved; from 25% to 65% of children who have one dyslexic parent are dyslexic themselves (Plomin et al., 2013a). About 40% of the siblings of children with dyslexia are dyslexic.

Genetic factors may give rise to neurological problems or circulation problems in the left hemisphere of the brain (Shaywitz & Shaywitz, 2013). The circulation problems would result in oxygen deficiency. The part of the brain called the angular gyrus "translates" visual information, such as written words, into auditory information (sounds). Problems in the angular gyrus may give rise to reading problems by making it difficult for the reader to associate letters with sounds (Shaywitz & Shaywitz, 2013).

stimulants drugs that increase the activity of the nervous system.

dyslexia a reading disorder characterized by letter reversals, mirror reading, slow reading, and reduced comprehension.

learning disabilities disorders characterized by inadequate development of specific academic, language, and speech skills.

Most researchers also focus on *phonological processing*. That is, dyslexic children may not discriminate sounds as accurately as other children do (Tanaka et al., 2011). As a result, *b*'s and *d*'s and *p*'s may be hard to tell apart, creating confusion that impairs reading ability (Shaywitz & Shaywitz, 2013).

EDUCATING CHILDREN WITH DISABILITIES In childhood, treatment of dyslexia focuses on remediation (Bakker, 2006). Children are given highly structured exercises to help them become aware of how to blend sounds to form words, such as identifying word pairs that rhyme and do not rhyme. Later in life, the focus tends to be on accommodation rather than on remediation. For example, college students with dyslexia may be given extra time to do the reading involved in taking tests.

Evidence is mixed on whether placing disabled children in separate classes can also stigmatize them and segregate them from other children. In **mainstreaming**, disabled children are placed in regular classrooms that have been adapted to their needs. Most students with mild learning disabilities spend most of the school day in regular classrooms (Fergusson, 2007).

9-4 COGNITIVE DEVELOPMENT

Did you hear the one about the judge who pounded her gavel and yelled, "Order! Order in the court!"? "A hamburger and french fries, Your Honor," responded the defendant. Such children's jokes are based on ambiguities in the meanings of words and phrases. Most seven-year-olds will find the joke about order in the court funny because they recognize that the word *order* has more than one meaning. At about the age of 11, children can understand ambiguities in grammatical structure. Children make enormous strides in their cognitive development during middle childhood as their thought processes and language become more logical and complex.

9-4a PIAGET: THE CONCRETE-OPERATIONAL STAGE

According to Jean Piaget, the typical child is entering the stage of **concrete operations** by the age of seven. In this stage, which lasts until about 12, children show the beginnings of adult logic but generally focus on tangible objects rather than abstract ideas, which is why they are "concrete."

Concrete-operational thought is reversible and flexible. Adding the numbers two and three to get five is an operation. Subtracting two from five to get three reverses the operation. Subtracting three from five to get two demonstrates flexibility.

Concrete-operational children are less egocentric than preoperational children. They recognize that people see things in different ways because of different situations and values. Concrete-operational children also engage in **decentration**. They can focus on multiple parts of a problem at once.

CONSERVATION Concrete-operational children show understanding of the laws of conservation. A seven-year-old child would say that the flattened ball of clay from the example in Chapter 7 still has the same amount of clay as the round one "because you can roll it up again." The concrete-operational child knows that objects can have several properties or dimensions. By attending to both the height and the width of the clay, the child recognizes that the loss in height compensates for the gain in width.

TRANSITIVITY If your parents are older than you are and you are older than your children, are your parents older than your children? The answer, of course, is yes. But how did you arrive at this answer? If you said yes simply on the basis of knowing that your parents are older than your children (e.g., 58 and 56 compared with 5 and 3), your answer did not require concrete-operational thought. One aspect of such thought is the principle of **transitivity**: If A exceeds B in some property (say, age or height) and if B exceeds C, then A must also exceed C.

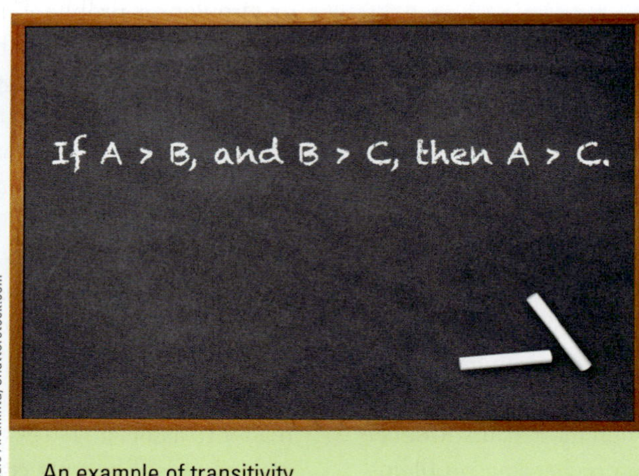

© Studio Araminta/Shutterstock.com

An example of transitivity.

mainstreaming placing disabled children in classrooms with nondisabled children.

concrete operations the third stage in Piaget's scheme, characterized by flexible, reversible thought concerning tangible objects and events.

decentration simultaneous focusing on more than one aspect or dimension of a problem or situation.

transitivity the principle that if A > B and B > C, then A > C.

Researchers can assess whether children understand the principle of transitivity by asking them to place objects in a series, or order, according to some property, such as lining up one's family members according to age, height, or weight. Placing objects in a series is termed **seriation**. Consider some examples with preoperational and concrete-operational children.

Piaget assessed children's abilities at seriation by asking them to place ten sticks in order of size. Children who are four to five usually place the sticks in a random sequence, or in small groups, as in small, medium, or large. But consider the approach of seven- and eight-year-olds who are capable of concrete operations. They look over the array, then select either the longest or shortest and place it at the point from which they will begin. Then they select the next longest (or shortest) and continue until the task is complete.

FIG.9.4 A DEMONSTRATION OF SERIATION

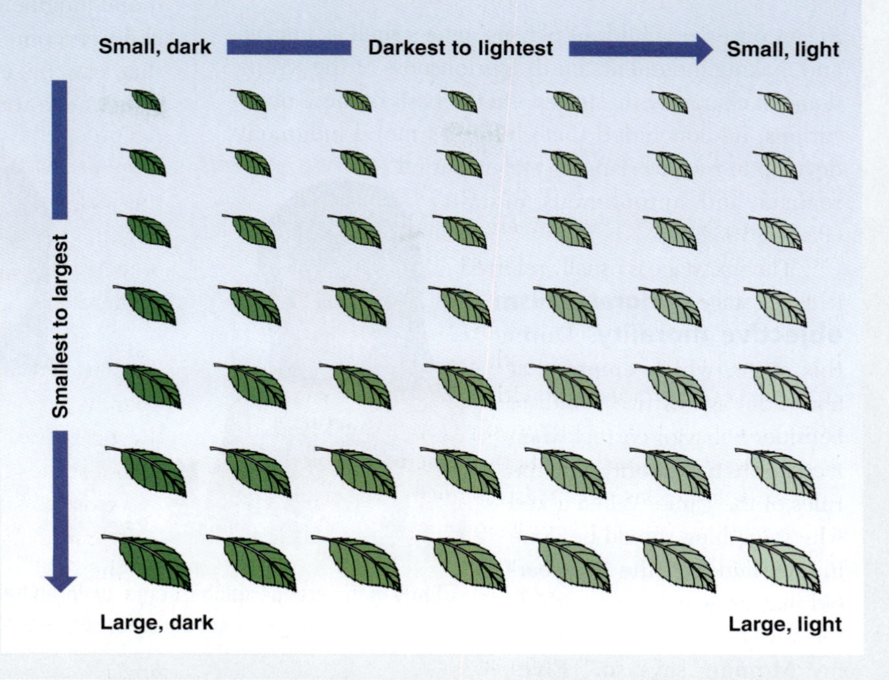

To classify these leaves, children must focus on two dimensions at once: size and lightness. They must also understand the principle of transitivity—that if A > B and B > C, then A > C.

Concrete-operational children also have the decentration capacity to allow them to seriate in two dimensions at once, unlike preoperational children. Consider a seriation task used by Piaget and his longtime colleague, Barbel Inhelder (Inhelder & Piaget, 1959). In this test, children are given 49 leaves and asked to classify them according to size and brightness (from small to large and from dark to light) (see Figure 9.4). As the grid is completed from left to right, the leaves become lighter. As it is filled in from top to bottom, the leaves become larger.

CLASS INCLUSION Imagine a four-year old being shown pictures of four cats and six dogs. When asked whether there are more dogs or more animals, she replies more dogs. The preoperational child apparently cannot focus on the two subclasses (dogs, cats) and the larger subclass (animals) at the same time. But concrete-operational children can do so. Therefore, they are more likely to answer the question about the dogs and the animals correctly.

APPLICATIONS OF PIAGET'S THEORY TO EDUCATION Piaget believed that learning involves active discovery. Also, instruction should be geared to the child's level of development. When teaching a concrete-operational child about fractions, for example, the teacher should not only lecture but should also allow the child to divide concrete objects into parts. Third, Piaget believed that learning to take into account the perspectives of others is a key ingredient in the development of both cognition and morality.

9-5 MORAL DEVELOPMENT: THE CHILD AS JUDGE

On a cognitive level, moral development concerns the basis on which children make judgments that an act is right or wrong. Jean Piaget and Lawrence Kohlberg believed that moral reasoning undergoes the same cognitive-developmental pattern around the world. The moral considerations that children weigh at a given age may be influenced by the values of the cultural settings in which they are reared, but also reflect the unfolding of cognitive processes (Nucci et al., 2014). Moral reasoning is related to the child's overall cognitive development.

seriation placing objects in an order or series according to a property or trait.

9-5a PIAGET'S THEORY OF MORAL DEVELOPMENT

Piaget observed children playing games such as marbles and making judgments on the seriousness of the wrongdoing of characters in stories. On the basis of these observations, he concluded that children's moral judgments develop in two overlapping stages: moral realism and autonomous morality (Piaget, 1932).

The first stage is usually referred to as the stage of **moral realism**, or **objective morality**. During this stage, which emerges at about the age of five, children consider behavior correct when it conforms to authority or to the rules of the game. When asked why something should be done in a certain way, the five-year-old may answer "Because that's the way to do it" or "Because my Mommy says so." Five-year-olds perceive rules as embedded in the structure of things. Rules, to them, reflect ultimate reality, hence the term *moral realism*. Rules and right and wrong are seen as absolute, not as deriving from people to meet social needs.

Another consequence of viewing rules as embedded in the fabric of the world is **immanent justice**, or automatic retribution. This involves thinking that negative experiences are punishment for prior misdeeds, even when realistic causal links are absent.

Preoperational children tend to focus on only one dimension at a time. Therefore, they judge the wrongness of an act only in terms of the amount of damage done, not in terms of the intentions of the wrongdoer. Consider children's response to Piaget's story about the broken cups. Piaget told children a story in which one child breaks 15 cups accidentally and another child breaks one cup deliberately. Children in the stage of moral realism typically say that the child who did the most damage is the naughtiest and should be punished most (Piaget, 1932).

moral realism the judgment of acts as moral when they conform to authority or to the rules of the game.

objective morality the perception of morality as objective, that is, as existing outside the cognitive functioning of people.

immanent justice the view that retribution for wrongdoing is a direct consequence of the wrongdoing.

autonomous morality the second stage in Piaget's cognitive-developmental theory of moral development, in which children base moral judgments on the intentions of the wrongdoer and on the amount of damage done.

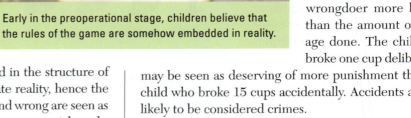

UpperCut Images Photography/Jupiter Images

Early in the preoperational stage, children believe that the rules of the game are somehow embedded in reality.

Piaget found that when children reach the ages of 9 to 11, they begin to show **autonomous morality**. Their moral judgments tend to become more self-governed, as children come to view social rules as social agreements that can be changed. Children realize that circumstances can warrant breaking rules. Children who show autonomous morality can focus simultaneously on multiple dimensions, so they consider social rules and the motives of the wrongdoer.

Children in this stage also show a greater capacity to take the point of view of others, to empathize with them. Decentration and increased empathy prompt children to weigh the intentions of the wrongdoer more heavily than the amount of damage done. The child who broke one cup deliberately may be seen as deserving of more punishment than the child who broke 15 cups accidentally. Accidents are less likely to be considered crimes.

9-5b KOHLBERG'S THEORY OF MORAL DEVELOPMENT

Kohlberg (1981, 1985) advanced the cognitive-developmental theory of moral development by elaborating on the kinds of information children use and on the complexities of moral reasoning. Before we discuss Kohlberg's views, read the tale that Kohlberg used in his research and answer the questions that follow.

> *In Europe, a woman was near death from a special kind of cancer. There was one drug that the doctors thought might save her. It was a form of radium that a druggist in the same town had recently discovered. The drug was expensive to make, but the druggist was charging 10 times what the drug cost him to make. He paid $200 for the radium and charged $2,000 for a small dose of the drug. The sick woman's husband, Heinz, went to everyone he knew to borrow the money, but he could only get together about $1,000, which was half of what it cost. He told the druggist that his wife was dying and asked him to sell it cheaper or let him pay later. But the druggist said: "No, I discovered the drug and I'm going to make money from it." So Heinz got desperate and broke into the man's store to steal the drug for his wife.*
>
> —Kohlberg (1969)

Why do some children cheat, while others do their own work?

Alloy Photography/Veer Images

Kohlberg emphasized the importance of being able to view the moral world from the perspective of another person. Look at the situation from Heinz's perspective. What do you think? Should Heinz have tried to steal the drug? Was he right or wrong? As you can see from Table 9.1, the issue is more complicated than a simple yes or no. Heinz is caught in a moral dilemma in which legal or social rules (in this case, laws against stealing) are pitted against a strong human need (Heinz's desire to save his wife). According to Kohlberg's theory, children and adults arrive at yes or no answers for different reasons. These reasons can be classified according to the level of moral development they reflect.

Children (and adults) are faced with many moral dilemmas. Consider cheating in school. When children fear failing a test, they may be tempted to cheat. Different children may decide not to cheat for different reasons. One child may fear getting caught. Another may decide that it is more important to live up to her moral principles than to get the highest possible grade. In each case, the child's decision is not to cheat. However, the decisions reflect different levels of reasoning.

Kohlberg argued that the developmental stages of moral reasoning follow the same sequence in all children. Children progress at different rates—not everyone reaches the highest stage. But children must experience Stage 1 before Stage 2, and so on. Kohlberg theorizes three levels of moral development and two stages within each level.

TABLE 9.1 KOHLBERG'S LEVELS AND STAGES OF MORAL DEVELOPMENT

Stage of Development	Examples of Moral Reasoning That Support Heinz's Stealing the Drug	Examples of Moral Reasoning That Oppose Heinz's Stealing the Drug
Level I: Preconventional—Typically Begins in Early Childhood[a]		
Stage 1: Judgments guided by obedience and the prospect of punishment (the consequences of the behavior)	It is not wrong to take the drug. Heinz did try to pay the druggist for it, and it is only worth $200, not $2,000.	Taking things without paying is wrong because it is against the law. Heinz will get caught and go to jail.
Stage 2: Naively egoistic, instrumental orientation (things are right when they satisfy people's needs)	Heinz ought to take the drug because his wife really needs it. He can always pay the druggist back.	Heinz should not take the drug. If he gets caught and winds up in jail, it won't do his wife any good.
Level II: Conventional—Typically Begins in Middle Childhood		
Stage 3: Good-boy/good-girl orientation (moral behavior helps others and is socially approved)	Stealing is a crime, so it is bad, but Heinz should take the drug to save his wife or else people would blame him for letting her die.	Stealing is a crime. Heinz should not just take the drug because his family will be dishonored and they will blame him.
Stage 4: Law-and-order orientation (moral behavior is doing one's duty and showing respect for authority)	Heinz must take the drug to do his duty to save his wife. Eventually, he has to pay the druggist for it, however.	If we all took the law into our own hands, civilization would fall apart, so Heinz should not steal the drug.
Level III: Postconventional—Typically Begins in Adolescence[b]		
Stage 5: Contractual, legalistic orientation (one must weigh pressing human needs against society's need to maintain social order)	This thing is complicated because society has a right to maintain law and order, but Heinz has to take the drug to save his wife.	I can see why Heinz feels he has to take the drug, but laws exist for the benefit of society as a whole and cannot simply be cast aside.
Stage 6: Universal ethical principles orientation (people must follow universal ethical principles and their own consciences, even if it means breaking the law)	In this case, the law comes into conflict with the principle of the sanctity of human life. Heinz must take the drug because his wife's life is more important than the law.	If Heinz truly believes that stealing the drug is worse than letting his wife die, he should not take it. People have to make sacrifices to do what they think is right.

[a] Tends to be used less often in middle childhood
[b] May not develop at all

THE PRECONVENTIONAL LEVEL At the **preconventional level**, children base their moral judgments on the consequences of their behavior. Stage 1 is oriented toward obedience and punishment. Good behavior means being obedient so one can avoid punishment. In Stage 2, good behavior allows people to satisfy their own needs and, perhaps, the needs of others. In a study of U.S. children aged 7 through 16, Kohlberg (1963) found that Stage 1 and 2 types of moral judgments were offered most frequently by seven- to ten-year-olds. Stage 1 and 2 judgments fell off steeply after age ten.

THE CONVENTIONAL LEVEL At the **conventional level** of moral reasoning, right and wrong are judged by conformity to conventional (family, religious, societal) standards of right and wrong. According to the Stage 3 "good-boy/good-girl orientation," it is good to meet the needs and expectations of others. Moral behavior is what is "normal," what the majority does. In Stage 4, moral judgments are based on rules that maintain the social order. Showing respect for authority and duty is valued highly. Many people do not develop beyond the conventional level. Kohlberg (1963) found that Stage 3 and 4 types of judgments emerge during middle childhood. They are all but absent among seven-year-olds. However, they are reported by about 20% of ten-year-olds and by higher percentages of adolescents.

THE POSTCONVENTIONAL LEVEL At the **postconventional level**, moral reasoning is based on the person's own moral standards (Snarey & Samuelson, 2014). If this level of reasoning develops at all, it is found among adolescents and adults.

preconventional level according to Kohlberg, a period during which moral judgments are based largely on expectations of rewards or punishments.

conventional level according to Kohlberg, a period during which moral judgments largely reflect social rules and conventions.

postconventional level according to Kohlberg, a period during which moral judgments are derived from moral principles, and people look to themselves to set moral standards.

9-6 INFORMATION PROCESSING: LEARNING, REMEMBERING, PROBLEM SOLVING

Key elements in children's information processing include the following:

- Development of selective attention
- Development of the capacity of memory and of children's understanding of the processes of memory
- Development of the ability to solve problems as, for example, by finding the correct formula and applying it

9-6a DEVELOPMENT OF SELECTIVE ATTENTION

The ability to focus one's attention and screen out distractions advances steadily through middle childhood (Lim et al., 2015). Preoperational children engaged in problem solving tend to focus (or center) their attention on one element of the problem at a time, which is a major reason they lack conservation. Concrete-operational children can attend to multiple aspects of the problem at once, permitting them to conserve number and volume.

A classic experiment illustrates how selective attention and the ability to ignore distraction develop during middle childhood. The researchers (Strutt et al., 1975) asked children between 6 and 12 years of age to sort a deck of cards as quickly as possible on the basis of the figures depicted on each card (e.g., circle versus square). In one condition, only the relevant dimension (i.e., form) was shown on each card. In another condition, a dimension not relevant to the sorting also was present (e.g., a horizontal or vertical line in the figure). In a third condition, two irrelevant dimensions were present (e.g., a star above or below the figure, in addition to a horizontal or vertical line in the figure). As seen in Figure 9.5, the irrelevant information interfered with sorting ability for all age groups, but older children were much less affected than younger children.

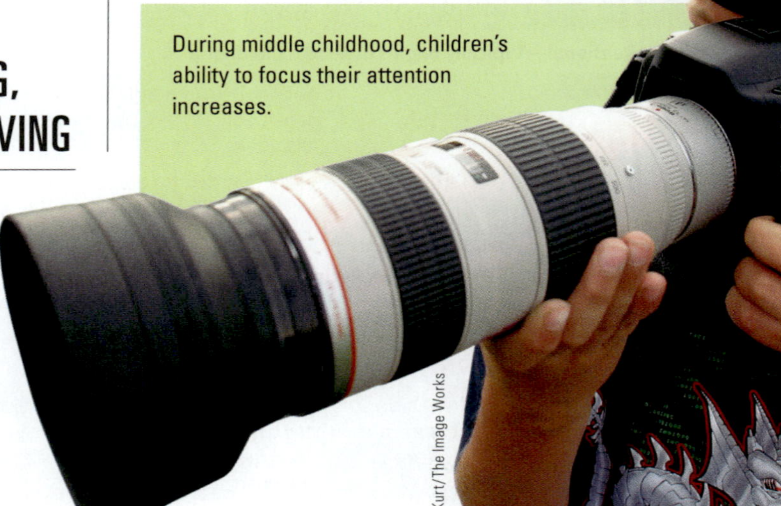

During middle childhood, children's ability to focus their attention increases.

Jack Kurt/The Image Works

FIG.9.5 DEVELOPMENT OF THE ABILITY TO IGNORE DISTRACTIONS

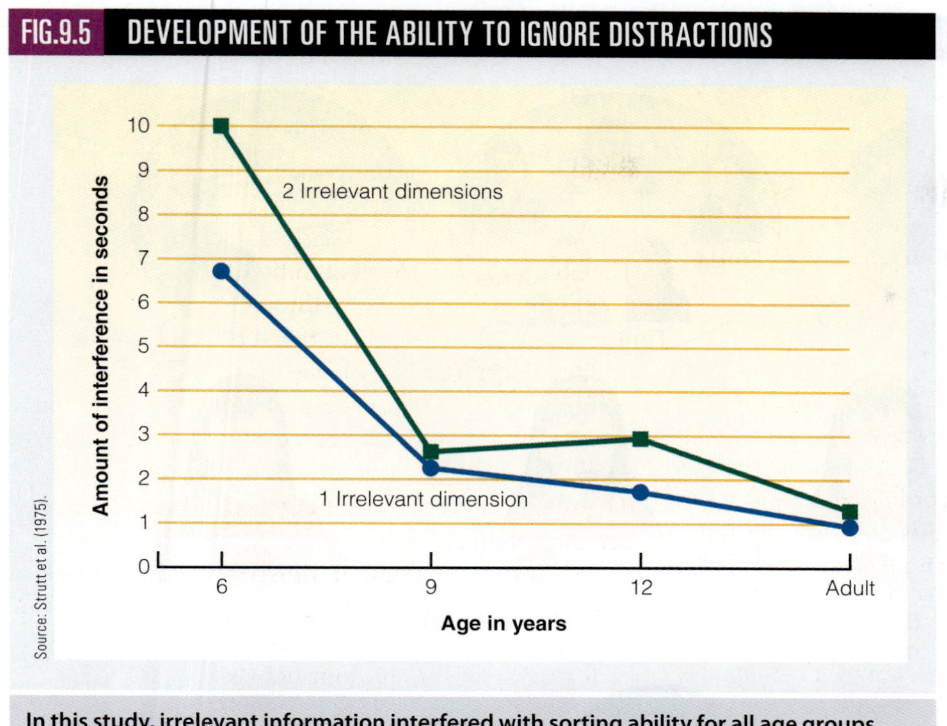

In this study, irrelevant information interfered with sorting ability for all age groups, but older children were less affected than younger ones.

9-6b DEVELOPMENTS IN THE STORAGE AND RETRIEVAL OF INFORMATION

Psychologists use the term *memory* to refer to the processes of storing and retrieving information. Many psychologists divide memory functioning into three major processes or structures: sensory memory, working memory, and long-term memory (see Figure 9.6).

SENSORY MEMORY When we look at an object and then blink our eyes, the visual impression of the object lasts for a fraction of a second in what is called **sensory memory**, or the **sensory register**. Then the "trace" of the stimulus decays. The concept of sensory memory applies to all the senses. For example, when we are introduced to somebody, the trace of the sound of the name also decays, but we can remember the name by focusing on it.

WORKING MEMORY (SHORT-TERM MEMORY) When children focus on a stimulus in the sensory register, it tends to be retained in **working memory** (also called *short-term memory*) for up to 30 seconds after the trace of the stimulus decays. Ability to maintain information in short-term memory depends on cognitive strategies and on capacity to continue to perceive a vanished stimulus. Memory function in middle childhood seems largely adult-like in organization and strategies and shows only quantitative improvement through early adolescence (Alloway & Alloway, 2013).

Auditory stimuli can be maintained longer in short-term memory than can visual stimuli. For this reason, one strategy for promoting memory is to **encode** visual stimuli as sounds. Then the sounds can be repeated out loud or mentally. In Figure 9.6, mentally repeating or **rehearsing** the sound of Linda's name helps the other girl remember it.

LONG-TERM MEMORY Think of **long-term memory** as a vast storehouse of information containing names, dates, places, what Johnny did to you in second grade, what Alyssa said about you when you were 12. Long-term memories may last days, years, or, for practical purposes, a lifetime.

There is no known limit to the amount of information that can be stored in long-term memory. From time to time, it may seem that we have forgotten, or lost, a long-term memory, such as the names of elementary or high school classmates. But it is more likely that we cannot find the right cues to retrieve it. It is "lost" in the same way we misplace an object but know it is still in the house.

Older children are more likely than younger children to use rote rehearsal, or repetition, to try to remember information (Camos & Barrouillet, 2011). A more effective method than rote rehearsal is to purposefully relate new material to well-known information, making it meaningful. Relating new material to known

sensory memory the structure of memory first encountered by sensory input. Information is maintained in sensory memory for only a fraction of a second.

sensory register another term for sensory memory.

working memory the structure of memory that can hold a sensory stimulus for up to 30 seconds after the trace decays.

encode to transform sensory input into a form that is more readily processed.

rehearsing repeat—in this case, mentally.

long-term memory the memory structure capable of relatively permanent storage of information.

FIG.9.6 THE STRUCTURE OF MEMORY

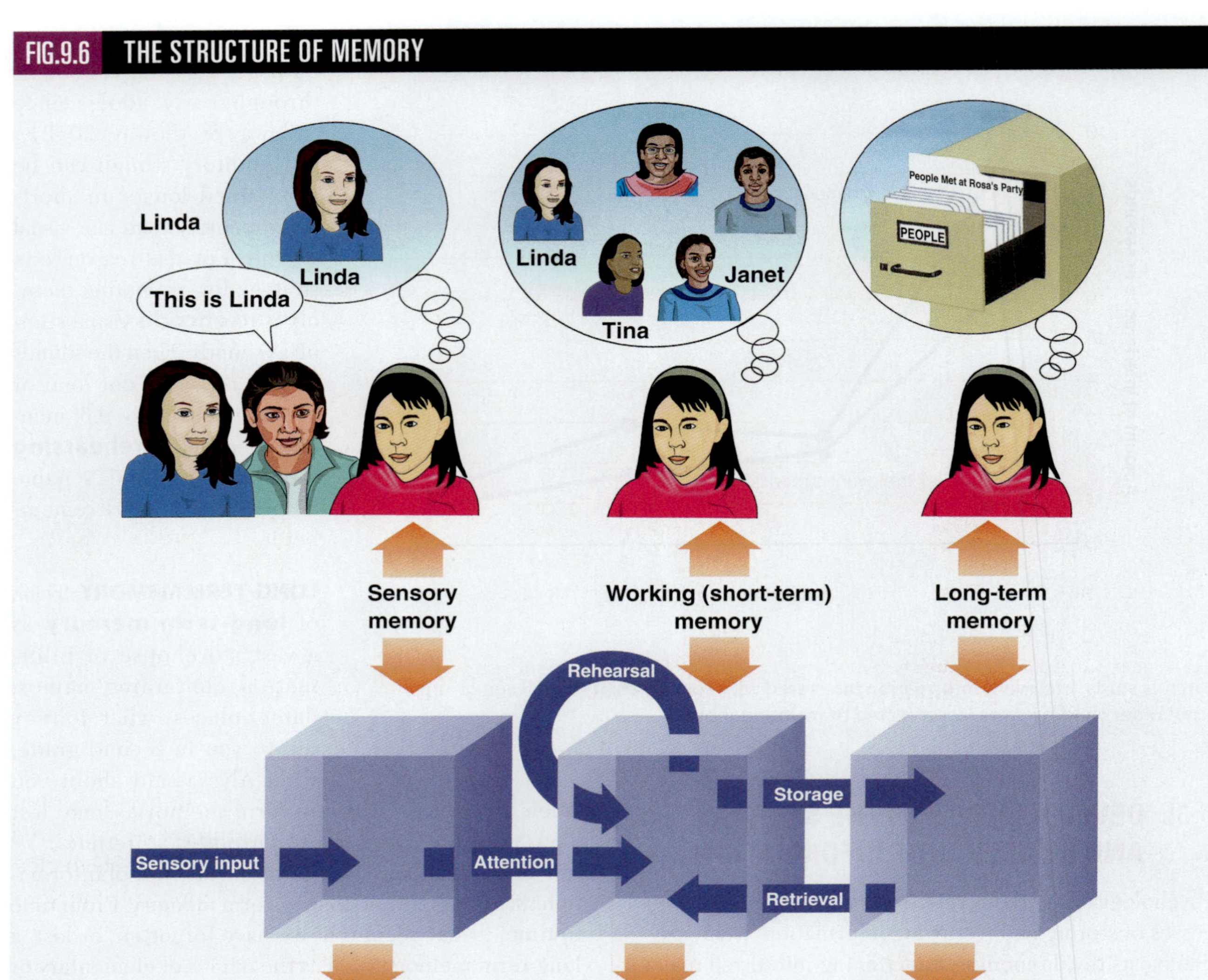

Many psychologists divide memory into three processes or "structures." Sensory information enters (1) sensory memory, where memory traces are held briefly before decaying. If we attend to the information, much of it is transferred to (2) working memory (also called *short-term memory*), where it may decay or be displaced if it is not transferred to long-term memory. We may use rehearsal (repetition) or elaborative strategies to transfer memories to (3) long-term memory, from which memories can be retrieved with the correct cues.

material is called an **elaborative strategy**. English teachers use an elaborative strategy when they have children use new words in sentences to help remember them.

ORGANIZATION IN LONG-TERM MEMORY As children's knowledge of concepts advances, the storehouse of their long-term memory becomes organized according to categories. Preschoolers tend to organize their memories by grouping objects that share the same function (Towse, 2003). "Toast" may be grouped with "peanut butter sandwich," because both are edible. In middle childhood toast and peanut butter are likely to be joined as foods.

elaborative strategy a method for increasing retention of new information by relating it to well-known information.

When items are correctly categorized in long-term memory, children are more likely to recall accurate information about them (see Figure 9.7). For instance, do you "remember" whether whales breathe underwater? If you did not know that whales are mammals or if you knew nothing about mammals, a correct answer might depend on an instance of rote learning.

FIG.9.7 THE CATEGORICAL STRUCTURE OF LONG-TERM MEMORY

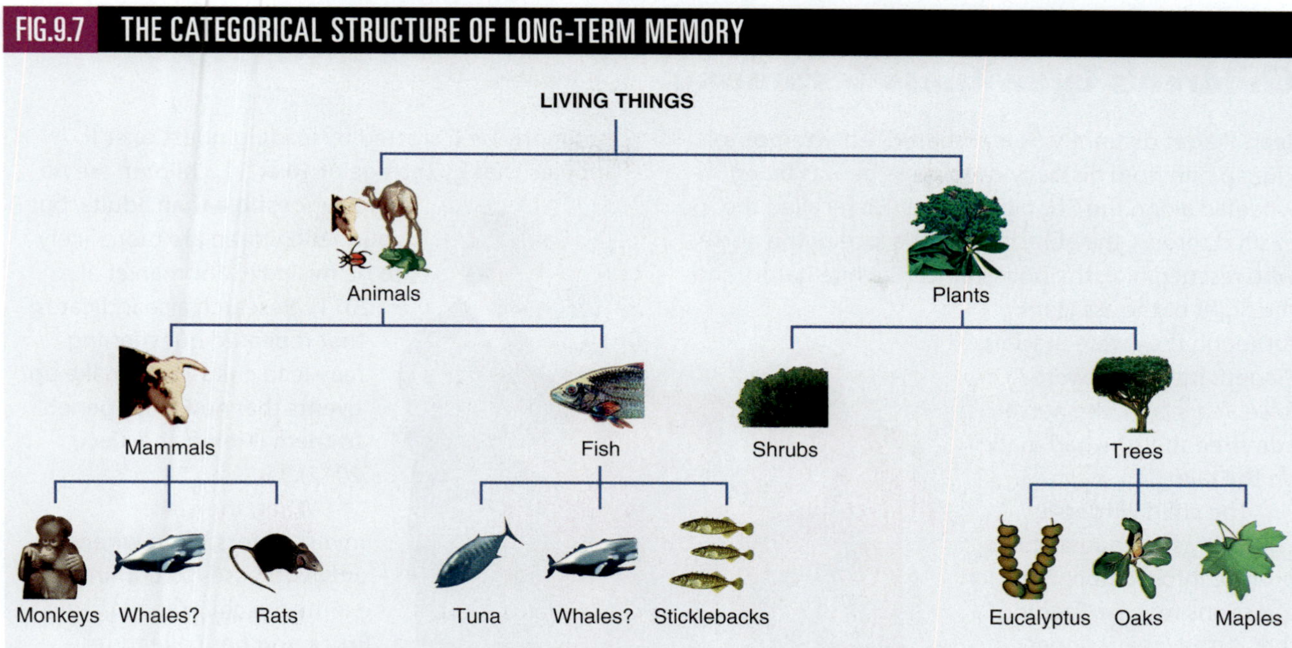

Where are whales filed in the cabinets of your memory? Do whales breathe underwater? Are they warm-blooded? Do they nurse their young? Your classification of the "whale" concept will provide your answers to these questions.

If children have incorrectly classified whales as fish, they might search their "memories" and construct the wrong answer.

Knowledge in a particular area increases the capacity to store and retrieve related information. Chess experts are superior to amateurs at remembering where chess pieces have been placed on the board (Gobet & Simon, 2000). In these studies, the experts were 8- to 12-year-old children and the amateurs were adults!

9-6c DEVELOPMENT OF RECALL MEMORY

Children's memory is a good overall indicator of their cognitive ability (Alloway & Alloway, 2013; Gignac & Weisse, 2015). In an experiment on categorization and memory, researchers placed objects that fell into four categories (furniture, clothing, tools, fruit) on a table before second- and fourth-graders (Hasselhorn, 1992). The children were allowed three minutes to arrange the pictures as they wished and to remember as many as they could. Fourth-graders were more likely to categorize and recall the pictures than second-graders.

9-6d DEVELOPMENT OF METACOGNITION AND METAMEMORY

Children's knowledge and control of their cognitive abilities is termed **metacognition**. The development of metacognition is shown by the ability to formulate problems, awareness of the processes required to solve a problem, activation of cognitive strategies, maintaining focus on the problem, and checking answers.

As a sixth-grader decides which homework assignments to do first, memorizes the state capitals for tomorrow's test, and then tests herself to see which she needs to study more, she is displaying metacognition. **Metamemory** is an aspect of metacognition that refers to children's awareness of the functioning memory. Older students are more likely to accurately assess their knowledge. So, older children store and retrieve information more effectively (Daugherty & Ofen, 2015).

Older children also show more knowledge of strategies that can be used to facilitate memory. Preschoolers will usually use rehearsal if someone suggests they do, but not until about the age of six or seven do children use it on their own (Camos & Barrouillet, 2011). As children develop, they are more likely to use selective rehearsal to remember important information.

metacognition awareness of and control of one's cognitive abilities.

metamemory knowledge of the functions and processes involved in one's storage and retrieval of information.

Children's Eyewitness Testimony

Jean Piaget distinctly "remembered" an attempt to kidnap him from his baby carriage as he was being wheeled along the Champs Élysées. He recalled the excited throng, the abrasions on the face of the nurse who rescued him, the police officer's white baton, and the flight of the assailant. Although they were graphic, Piaget's memories were false. Years later, the nurse admitted that she had made up the tale.

The child witness is typically asked questions to prompt information. But such questions may be "leading," that is, they may suggest an answer. For example, "What happened at school?" is not a leading question, but "Did your teacher touch you?" is. Can children's testimony be distorted by leading questions? It appears that by the age of 10 or 11, children are no more suggestible than adults, but younger children are more likely to be misled (Goodman et al., 2011). Research also indicates that repeated questioning may lead children to make up events that never happened to them (Klemfuss & Ceci, 2012).

Rob Crandall/SCPhotos/Alamy Stock Photo

What, then, are investigators to do when the only witnesses to criminal events are children? Maggie Bruck and her colleagues (2006) recommend that interviewers avoid leading or suggestive questions to minimize influencing the child's response.

9-7 INTELLECTUAL DEVELOPMENT, CREATIVITY, AND ACHIEVEMENT

At an early age, we gain impressions of how intelligent we are compared with other family members and schoolmates. We associate **intelligence** with academic success, advancement on the job, and appropriate social behavior (Mayer, 2011). Despite our sense of familiarity with the concept of intelligence, intelligence cannot be seen, touched, or measured physically. For this reason, intelligence is subject to various interpretations.

Intelligence is usually perceived as a child's underlying competence or *learning ability*, whereas **achievement** involves a child's acquired competencies or *performance*. Most psychologists also would agree that many of the competencies underlying intelligence are seen during middle childhood, when most children are first exposed to formal schooling.

intelligence a general mental capability that involves the ability to reason, plan, solve problems, think abstractly, comprehend complex ideas, learn quickly, and learn from experience

achievement that which is attained by one's efforts and presumed to be made possible by one's abilities.

9-7a THEORIES OF INTELLIGENCE

Let's consider some theoretical approaches to intelligence. Then we will see how researchers and practitioners assess intellectual functioning.

FACTOR THEORIES Many investigators view intelligence as consisting of one or more major mental abilities, or factors (Willis et al., 2011). In 1904, Charles Spearman suggested that the behaviors we consider intelligent have a common underlying g factor, or general intelligence, which represents broad reasoning and problem-solving abilities, and that specific capacities, or s factors, account for certain individual abilities, like music or poetry.

Psychologist Louis Thurstone (1938) believed that intelligence consists of several specific factors, or *primary mental abilities*, such as the ability to learn the meaning of words and visual–spatial abilities. Thurstone's research suggested that these factors were somewhat independent.

STERNBERG'S THEORY OF INTELLIGENCE Psychologist Robert Sternberg (Sternberg, 2015) constructed a three-part, or "triarchic," theory of intelligence. The parts are *analytical intelligence*, *creative intelligence*,

FIG.9.8 STERNBERG'S TRIARCHIC THEORY OF INTELLIGENCE

Analytical intelligence
(academic ability)
Abilities to solve problems, compare and contrast, judge, evaluate, and criticize

Creative intelligence
(creativity and insight)
Abilities to invent, discover, suppose, and theorize

Practical intelligence
("street smarts")
Abilities to adapt to the demands of one's environment and apply knowledge in practical situations

Robert Sternberg views intelligence as having three parts: academic ability, creativity, and "street smarts."

and *practical intelligence* (see Figure 9.8). Analytical intelligence is academic ability. Creative intelligence is defined by the abilities to invent solutions to problems and cope with novel situations. Practical intelligence, or "street smarts," enables people to adapt to the demands of their environment, including the social environment.

GARDNER'S THEORY OF MULTIPLE INTELLIGENCES

Psychologist Howard Gardner (1983; Sternberg, 2015), like Sternberg, believes that intelligence—or intelligences—reflect more than academic ability. Gardner refers to each kind of intelligence in his theory as "an intelligence" because each differs in quality (see Figure 9.9).

Three of Gardner's intelligences are verbal (linguistic) ability, logical–mathematical reasoning, and spatial intelligence (visual–spatial skills). Others include bodily–kinesthetic intelligence (as shown by dancers and gymnasts), musical intelligence, interpersonal intelligence (as shown by empathy and ability to relate to others), and personal knowledge (self-insight). Individuals may show great "intelligence" in one area without notable abilities in others. Critics agree that many people have special talents, as in music, but they question whether such talents are "intelligences" (Neisser et al., 1996).

FIG.9.9 GARDNER'S THEORY OF MULTIPLE INTELLIGENCES

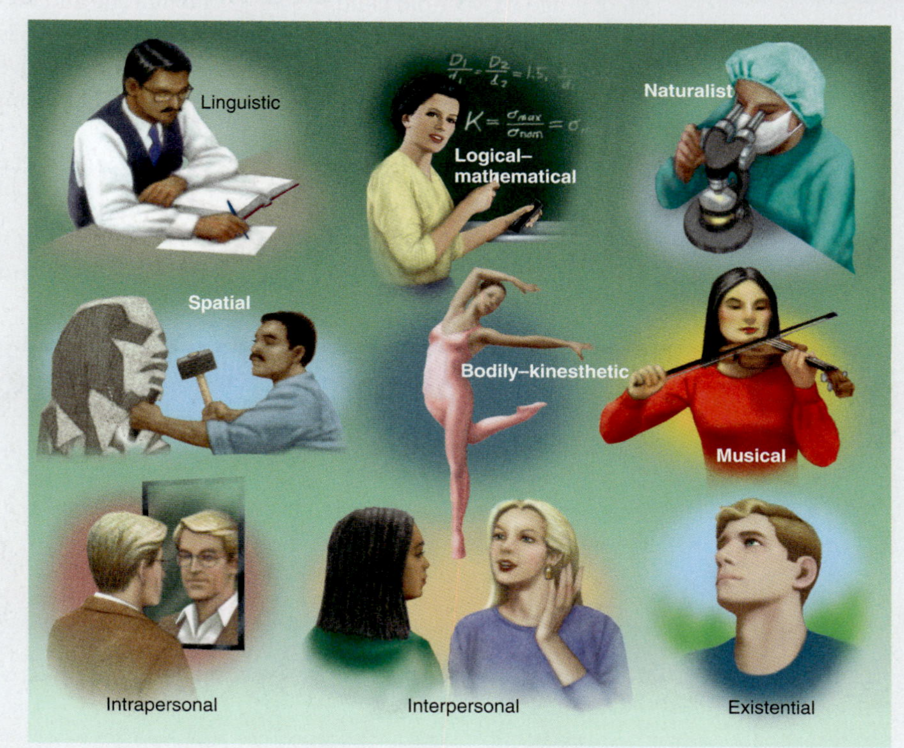

Gardner asserts that there are many "intelligences," not just one, and that each is based in different areas of the brain.

9-7b MEASUREMENT OF INTELLECTUAL DEVELOPMENT

There may be disagreements about the nature of intelligence, but thousands of intelligence tests are administered by psychologists and educators every day (Urbina, 2011).

The Stanford–Binet Intelligence Scale (SBIS) and the Wechsler scales for children and adults are the most widely used and well respected intelligence tests. The SBIS and Wechsler scales yield scores called **intelligence quotients (IQs)**. The concept of intelligence per se is more difficult to define. The SBIS and Wechsler scales have been carefully developed and revised over the years. Each of them has been used to make vital educational decisions about children. In many cases, children whose test scores fall below or above certain scores are placed in special classes for intellectually disabled or gifted children.

THE STANFORD–BINET INTELLIGENCE SCALE

The SBIS originated in the work of Frenchmen Alfred Binet and Theodore Simon about a century ago for the French public school system. Binet assumed that intelligence increased with age. Therefore, older children should get more items right. Thus, Binet arranged a series of questions in order of difficulty, from easier to harder. It has since undergone revision and refinement.

The Binet–Simon scale yielded a score called a **mental age (MA)**. The MA shows the intellectual level at which a child is functioning. A child with an MA of 6 is functioning, intellectually, like the average six-year-old child.

Louis Terman adapted the Binet–Simon scale for use with American children in 1916. Because Terman carried out his work at Stanford University, it is now named the Stanford–Binet Intelligence Scale.

intelligence quotient (IQ) (1) a ratio obtained by dividing a child's mental age on an intelligence test by his or her chronological age; (2) a score on an intelligence test.

mental age (MA) the intellectual level at which a child is functions, based on the typical performance of a child of a certain age.

chronological age (CA) a person's age.

SSPL / The Image Works

In 1905 Alfred Binet and Theodore Simon in France introduced the idea of measuring intelligence. This version of the test was produced in 1937 by Lewis Terman and Maude Merrill in the United States and was specifically designed for younger children.

The SBIS yielded an intelligence quotient, or IQ, rather than an MA. The SBIS today can be used with children from the age of two up to adults. Table 9.2 shows the kinds of items given at various ages.

The IQ states the relationship between a child's mental age and his or her actual or **chronological age (CA)**. An MA of 8 is an above-average score for a six-year-old but a below-average score for a ten-year-old.

The IQ is computed by the following formula:

$$\text{IQ} = \frac{\text{Mental Age (MA)}}{\text{Chronological Age (CA)}} \times 100$$

According to this formula, a child with an MA of 6 and a CA of 6 would have an IQ of 100. Furthermore,

TABLE 9.2 ITEMS SIMILAR TO THOSE ON THE STANFORD–BINET INTELLIGENCE SCALE

Age	Item
2 years	1. Children show knowledge of basic vocabulary words by identifying parts of a doll, such as the mouth, ears, and hair. 2. Children show counting and spatial skills along with visual–motor coordination by building a tower of four blocks to match a model.
4 years	1. Children show word fluency and categorical thinking by filling in the missing words when they are asked questions such as "Father is a man; mother is a __________?" and "Hamburgers are hot; ice cream is __________?" 2. Children show comprehension by answering correctly when they are asked questions such as "Why do people have automobiles?" and "Why do people have medicine?"
9 years	1. Children can point out verbal absurdities, as in this question: "In an old cemetery, scientists unearthed a skull which they think was that of George Washington when he was only 5 years of age. What is silly about that?" 2. Children display fluency with words, as shown by answering questions such as "Can you tell me a number that rhymes with snore?" and "Can you tell me a color that rhymes with glue?"
Adult	1. Adults show knowledge of the meanings of words and conceptual thinking by correctly explaining the differences between word pairs such as "sickness and misery," "house and home," and "integrity and prestige." 2. Adults show spatial skills by correctly answering questions such as "If a car turned to the right to head north, in what direction was it heading before it turned?"

because of the factor of chronological age in the formula, children of different ages might answer the same items on a test the same but end up receiving different IQ scores.

TRUTH

F Two children can answer exactly the same items on an intelligence test correctly, yet one can be above average in intelligence and the other below average.

It is true that two children can answer exactly the same items on an intelligence test correctly, yet one can be above average in intelligence and the other below average. The younger child would have the higher IQ score, because his or her performance is compared to those of others in his or her age group.

Today, IQ scores on the SBIS are derived by comparing children's and adults' performances with those of other people of the same age. People who get more items correct than average attain IQ scores above 100, and people who answer fewer items correctly attain scores below 100.

THE WECHSLER SCALES David Wechsler (1975) developed a series of scales for use with school-age children (Wechsler Intelligence Scale for Children; WISC), younger children (Wechsler Preschool and Primary Scale of Intelligence; WPPSI), and adults (Wechsler Adult Intelligence Scale; WAIS).

The Wechsler scales group test questions into subtests (such as those shown in Table 9.3) that measure different intellectual tasks. For this reason, subtests compare a person's performance on one type of task (such as defining words) with another (such as using blocks to construct geometric designs). The Wechsler scales thus suggest children's strengths and weaknesses as well as provide overall measures of intellectual functioning.

Wechsler described some subtests as measuring verbal tasks and others as assessing performance tasks. In general, verbal subtests require knowledge of verbal concepts, whereas performance subtests (see Figure 9.10 on page 190) require familiarity with spatial-relations concepts. Wechsler's scales permit the computation of verbal and performance IQs.

Figure 9.11 on page 190 indicates the labels that Wechsler assigned to various IQ scores and the approximate percentages of the population who attain IQ scores at those levels. Most children's IQ scores cluster around the average. Only about 5% of the population have IQ scores above 130 or below 70.

THE TESTING CONTROVERSY Most psychologists and educational specialists consider intelligence tests to be at least somewhat biased against African Americans and members of lower social classes (Daley & Onwuegbuzie, 2011; Saklofske et al., 2015). If scoring well on intelligence tests requires a certain type of cultural experience, the tests are said to have a **cultural bias**. For this reason, psychologists have tried to construct **culture-free** or culture-fair intelligence tests.

Some tests do not rely on expressive language at all. For example, Raymond Cattell's (1949) Culture-Fair Intelligence Test evaluates reasoning

cultural bias a factor hypothesized to be present in intelligence tests that provides an advantage for test takers from certain cultural backgrounds.

culture-free descriptive of a test in which cultural biases have been removed.

TABLE 9.3 KINDS OF ITEMS FOUND ON WECHSLER'S INTELLIGENCE SCALES

Verbal Items	Nonverbal-Performance Items
• Information: "What is the capital of the United States?" "Who was Shakespeare?" • Comprehension: "Why do we have ZIP codes?" "What does 'A stitch in time saves 9' mean?" • Arithmetic: "If 3 candy bars cost 25 cents, how much will 18 candy bars cost?" • Similarities: "How are good and bad alike?" "How are peanut butter and jelly alike?" • Vocabulary: "What does canal mean?" • Digit span: Repeating a series of numbers, presented by the examiner, forward and backward.	• Picture completion: Pointing to the missing part of a picture. • Picture arrangement: Arranging cartoon pictures in sequence so that they tell a meaningful story. • Block design: Copying pictures of geometric designs using multicolored blocks. • Object assembly: Putting pieces of a puzzle together so that they form a meaningful object. • Coding: Rapid scanning and drawing of symbols that are associated with numbers. • Mazes: Using a pencil to trace the correct route from a starting point to home.

FIG.9.10 PERFORMANCE ITEMS ON AN INTELLIGENCE TEST

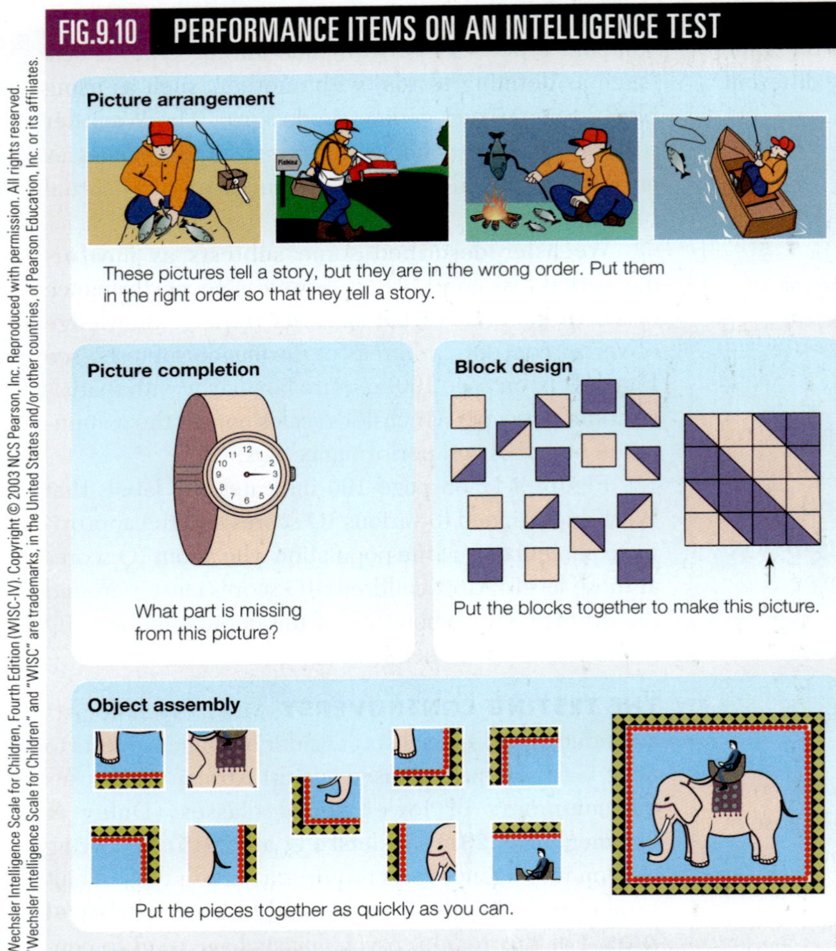

Picture arrangement
These pictures tell a story, but they are in the wrong order. Put them in the right order so that they tell a story.
Picture completion
What part is missing from this picture?
Block design
Put the blocks together to make this picture.
Object assembly
Put the pieces together as quickly as you can.

This figure shows items that resemble those found on the performance subtest of the Wechsler Intelligence Scale for Children (WISC).

ability through the child's comprehension of the rules that govern a progression of geometric designs, as shown in Figure 9.12.

But culture-free tests have not lived up to their promise. First, middle-class children still outperform lower-class children on them (Daley & Onwuegbuzie, 2011; Saklofske et al., 2015). Middle-class children, for example, are more likely to have basic familiarity with materials used in the testing such as blocks and pencils and paper. They are more likely to have played with blocks (a practice relevant to the Cattell test). Second, culture-free tests do not predict academic success as well as other intelligence tests, and scholastic aptitude remains the central concern of educators (Daley & Onwuegbuzie, 2011; Saklofske et al., 2015).

9-7b PATTERNS OF INTELLECTUAL DEVELOPMENT

Intellectual growth seems to occur in at least two major spurts. The first occurs at about the age of six. It coincides with entry into school and also with the shift from preoperational to concrete- operational thought (Rose & Fischer, 2011). School may help crystallize intellectual functioning at this time. The second spurt occurs at about age 10 or 11.

But once they reach middle childhood, children appear to undergo relatively more stable patterns of gains in intellectual functioning, although there are still spurts (Rose & Fischer, 2011). As a result, intelligence tests gain greater predictive power. In a classic study by Marjorie Honzik and her colleagues (1948), intelligence test scores taken at the age of nine

FIG.9.11 IDEALIZED DISTRIBUTION OF IQ SCORES

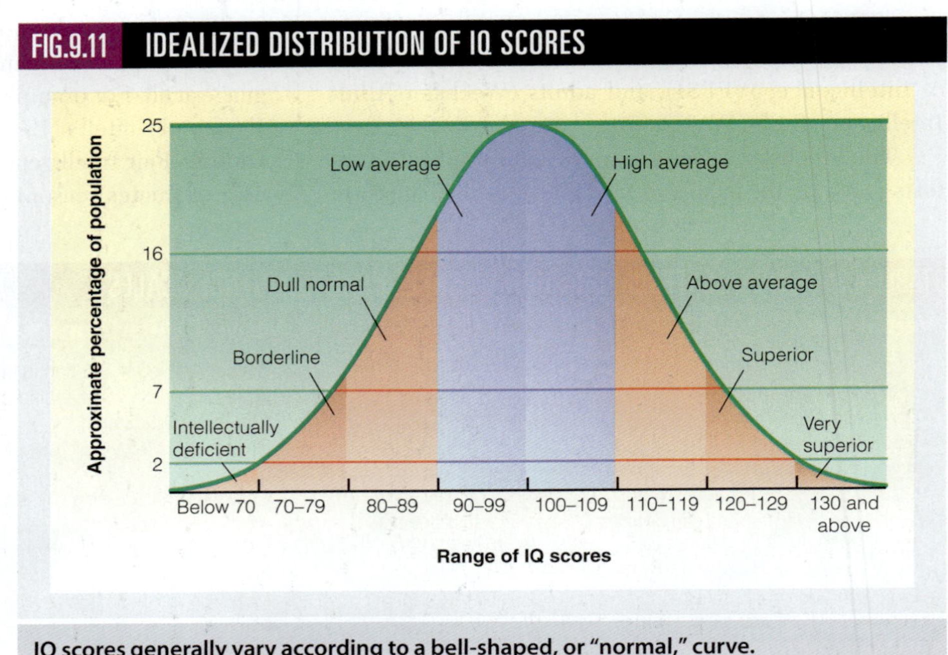

IQ scores generally vary according to a bell-shaped, or "normal," curve.

FIG.9.12 SAMPLE ITEMS FROM CATTELL'S CULTURE-FAIR INTELLIGENCE TEST

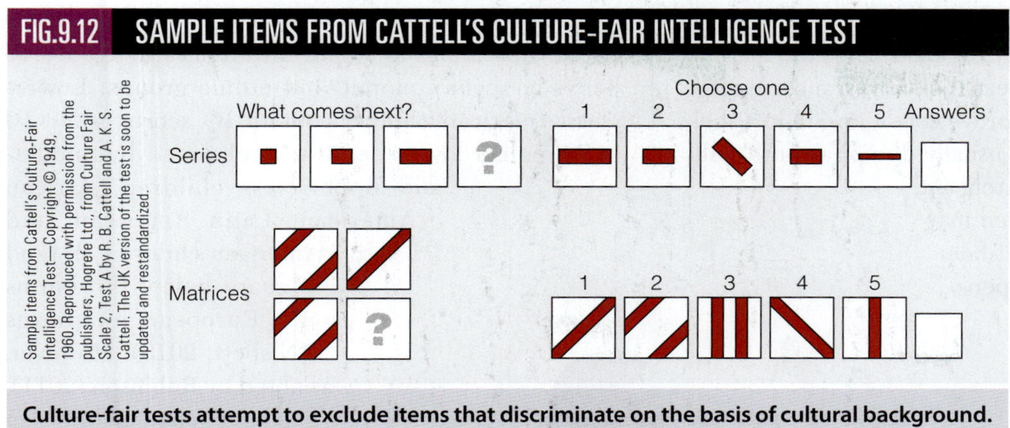

Sample items from Cattell's Culture-Fair Intelligence Test—Copyright © 1949, 1960. Reproduced with permission from the publishers, Hogrefe Ltd., from Culture Fair Scale 2, Test A by R. B. Cattell and A. K. S. Cattell. The UK version of the test is soon to be updated and restandardized.

Culture-fair tests attempt to exclude items that discriminate on the basis of cultural background.

correlated strongly (+0.90) with scores at the age of ten and more moderately (+0.76) with scores at the age of 18. Testing at age 11 even shows a moderate to high relationship with scores at the age of 77 (Deary et al., 2004).

Despite the increased predictive power of intelligence tests during middle childhood, individual differences exist. In the classic Fels Longitudinal Study (see Figure 9.13), two groups of children (Groups 1 and 3) made reasonably consistent gains in intelligence test scores between the ages of 10 and 17, whereas three groups declined. Group 4, children who had shown the most intellectual promise at age ten, went on to show the most precipitous decline, although they still wound up in the highest 2% to 3% of the population (McCall et al., 1973). Many factors influence changes in IQ scores, including changes in the home, socioeconomic circumstances, and education (Rose & Fischer, 2011).

FIG.9.13 FIVE PATTERNS OF CHANGE IN IQ SCORES FOR CHILDREN IN THE FELS LONGITUDINAL STUDY

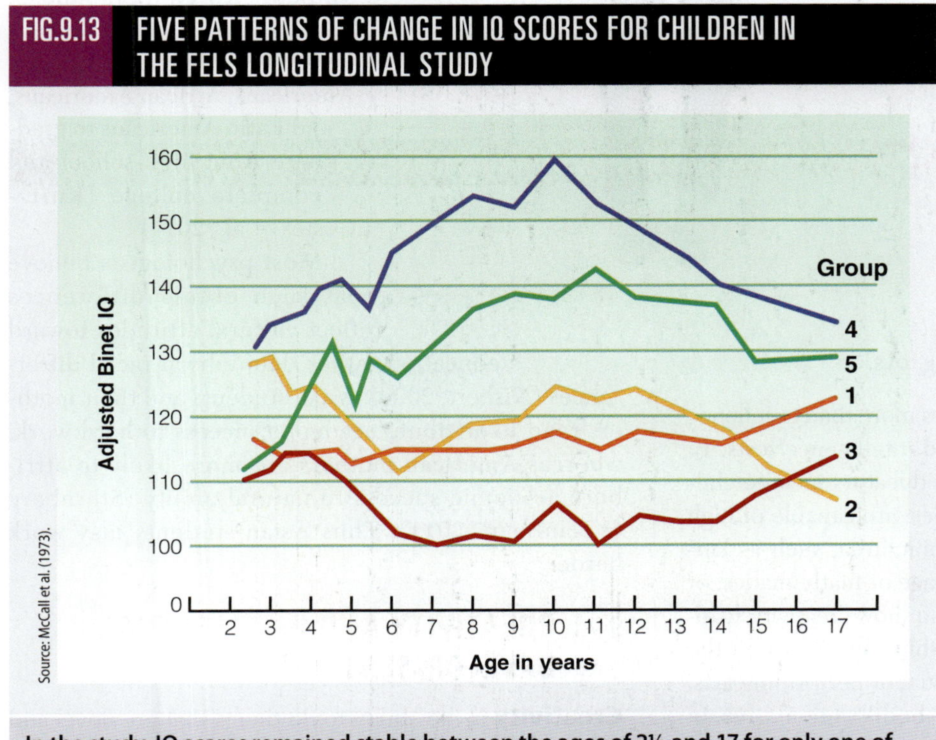

Source: McCall et al. (1973).

In the study, IQ scores remained stable between the ages of 2½ and 17 for only one of five groups, Group 1.

9-7c DIFFERENCES IN INTELLECTUAL DEVELOPMENT

The average IQ score in the United States is close to 100. About half the children in the United States attain IQ scores in the broad average range from 90 to 110. Nearly 95% attain scores between 70 and 130. Children who attain IQ scores below 70 are generally labeled "intellectually disabled." Children who attain scores of 130 or above are usually labeled "gifted."

INTELLECTUAL DISABILITY According to the American Association on Intellectual and Developmental Disabilities (AAIDD, 2016), "Intellectual disability is . . . characterized by significant limitations both in intellectual functioning and in adaptive behavior, which covers many everyday social and practical skills. This disability originates before the age of 18." Intellectual disability involves an IQ score of no more than 70 to 75.

Most of the children (more than 80%) who are intellectually disabled are mildly disabled. Mildly disabled children are the most capable of adjusting to the demands of educational institutions and to society at large (Hodapp et al., 2011). Many mildly disabled children are mainstreamed in regular classrooms rather than placed in special-needs classes.

Children with Down's syndrome are most likely to be moderately intellectually disabled. They can learn to speak; to dress, feed, and clean themselves; and to engage in useful work under supportive conditions, as in a sheltered workshop, but they usually do not acquire skills in reading and math. Severely and profoundly disabled children may not acquire speech and self-help skills and may remain dependent on others for survival.

Some causes of intellectual disability are biological (Carlier & Roubertoux, 2014). Intellectual disability can stem from chromosomal abnormalities, such as Down's syndrome; genetic disorders such as phenylketonuria (PKU); and brain damage (Haier, 2011; Hodapp et al., 2011). Brain damage can have many origins, including childhood accidents and problems during pregnancy. For example, maternal alcohol abuse, malnutrition, or diseases can damage the fetus. In **cultural–familial disability**, children are biologically normal but do not develop age-appropriate behavior at the normal pace because of an impoverished home environment (Carlier & Roubertoux, 2014). They may have little opportunity to interact with adults or play with stimulating toys.

© wong yu liang/Shutterstock.com

GIFTEDNESS Giftedness involves more than excellence on the tasks provided by standard intelligence tests. In determining who is gifted, most educators include children who have outstanding abilities; are capable of high performance in a specific academic area, such as language or mathematics; or who show creativity, leadership, distinction in the visual or performing arts, or bodily talents, as in gymnastics and dancing (Reis & Renzulli, 2011).

cultural–familial disability substandard intellectual performance stemming from lack of opportunity to acquire knowledge and skills.

creativity a trait characterized by flexibility, ingenuity, and originality.

SOCIOECONOMIC AND ETHNIC DIFFERENCES IN IQ Research has found differences in IQ scores between socioeconomic and ethnic groups. Lower-class American children obtain IQ scores some 10 to 15 points lower than those obtained by middle- and upper-class children. African American, Latin American, and Native American children all tend to score below the norms for European Americans (Nisbett, 2013). However, as noted by Robinson (2011), "a gap has opened up between an educated middle-class Black America and a poor, undereducated Black America." In other words, we cannot lump all African Americans together. Youth of Asian descent frequently outscore youth of European backgrounds on achievement tests in math and science, including the math portion of the SAT (Suzuki et al., 2011). In addition, people of Asian Indian, Korean, Japanese, Filipino, and Chinese descent are more likely than European Americans, African Americans, and Latin Americans to graduate from high school and complete college (Kurtz-Costes et al., 2014).

Most psychologists believe that such ethnic differences reflect cultural attitudes toward education rather than inborn racial differences (Nisbett, 2009). Asian students and their mothers tend to attribute academic success to hard work, whereas American mothers are more likely to attribute academic success to natural ability (Sternberg & Kaufman, 2011). Thus Asian students may work harder.

9-7d CREATIVITY AND INTELLECTUAL DEVELOPMENT

Creativity is the ability to do things that are novel and useful (Plucker et al., 2015). Creative children and adults can solve problems to which there are no preexisting solutions, no tried and tested formulas. Creative children take chances (Kaufman & Plucker, 2011): They refuse to accept limitations. They appreciate art and music. They challenge social norms. They examine ideas that other people accept at face value.

Some scientists argue that creativity and innovation require high levels of general intelligence, but the tests we use to measure intelligence and creativity tend to show only a moderate relationship between IQ scores and measures of creativity (Sternberg et al., 2012). Some children who obtain average IQ scores excel in creative areas such as music or art.

FICTION

T (F) Highly intelligent children are creative.

It is not necessarily true that highly intelligent children are creative—unless, of course, one considers creativity to be an aspect of intelligence, as in Robert Sternberg's triarchic theory of intelligence.

Children mainly use convergent thinking to arrive at the correct answers on intelligence tests. In **convergent thinking**, thought is limited to present facts; the problem solver narrows his or her thinking to find the best solution. A child uses convergent thinking to arrive at the right answer to a multiple-choice question or to a question on an intelligence test.

Creative thinking tends to be divergent rather than convergent (Plucker et al., 2015). In **divergent thinking**, the child associates freely to the elements of the problem. (We use divergent thinking when we are trying to generate ideas to answer an essay question or to find keywords to search on the Internet.) Tests of creativity determine how flexible, fluent, and original a person's thinking is. A measure of creativity might ask you how many ways you can classify the following group of names:

Martha Paul Jeffry Sally Pablo Joan

Other measures of creativity include suggesting improvements or unusual uses for a familiar toy or object, naming things that belong in the same class, producing words similar in meaning, and writing different endings for a story.

9-7e DETERMINANTS OF INTELLECTUAL DEVELOPMENT

If heredity is involved in human intelligence, closely related people ought to have more similar IQs than distantly related or unrelated people, even when they are reared separately (Bouchard, 2013). Figure 9.14 on page 194 shows the averaged results of more than 100 studies of IQ and heredity (McGue et al., 1993; Plomin et al., 2013b). The IQ scores of identical (monozygotic; MZ) twins are more alike than the scores for any other pairs, even when the twins have been reared apart. The average correlation for MZ twins reared together is +0.85; for those reared apart, it is +0.67. Correlations between the IQ scores of fraternal (dizygotic; DZ) twins, siblings, and parents and children are generally comparable, as is their degree of genetic relationship. The correlations tend to vary from about +0.40 to +0.59.

Overall, studies suggest that the **heritability** of intelligence is between 40% and 60% (Plomin et al., 2013b; Wadsworth et al., 2014). About half of the difference between your IQ score and those of other people can be explained in terms of genetic factors.

Let's return to Figure 9.14. Genetic pairs (such as MZ twins) reared together show higher correlations between IQ scores than similar genetic pairs (such as other MZ twins) who were reared apart. This finding holds for MZ twins, siblings, parents, children, and unrelated people. For this reason, the same group of studies that suggests that heredity plays a role in determining IQ scores also suggests that the environment plays a role.

Classic projects involving adopted children in Colorado, Texas, and Minnesota (Plomin et al., 2013a; Scarr, 1993; Sternberg & Kaufman, 2011) have found a stronger relationship between the IQ scores of adopted children and their biological parents than between the IQ scores of adopted children and their adoptive parents.

Studies of environmental influences on IQ use several research strategies, including discovering situational factors that affect IQ scores, exploring children's abilities to rebound from early deprivation, and exploring the effects of positive early environments. Children whose parents are responsive and provide appropriate play materials and varied experiences during the early years attain

convergent thinking a thought process that attempts to focus on the single best solution to a problem.

divergent thinking free and fluent association to the elements of a problem.

heritability the degree to which the variations in a trait from one person to another can be attributed to genetic factors.

higher IQ and achievement test scores (Bradley, 2006). Graduates of Head Start and other preschool programs also show significant gains in IQ and other test scores (Bierman et al., 2014).

Many psychologists believe that heredity and environment interact to influence intelligence (Daley & Onwuegbuzie, 2011; Haier, 2011). An impoverished environment may prevent some children from living up to their potential. An enriched environment may encourage others to realize their potential.

9-8 LANGUAGE DEVELOPMENT AND LITERACY

Children's language ability grows more sophisticated in middle childhood. Children learn to read as well. Many children are exposed to a variety of linguistic experiences, and these experiences affect cognitive development.

9-8a VOCABULARY AND GRAMMAR

By the age of six, the child's vocabulary has expanded to nearly 10,000 words. By seven to nine years of age, most children realize that words can have different meanings, and they become entertained by riddles and jokes that require semantic sophistication. (Remember the joke at the beginning of the section on cognitive development.) By the age of eight or nine, children are able to form "tag questions," in which the question is tagged on to the end of a declarative sentence, such as "You want more ice cream, don't you?" and "You're sick, aren't you?" (Weckerly et al., 2004).

Children make subtle advances in articulation and in the capacity to use complex grammar. Preschoolers have difficulty understanding passive sentences such as "The truck was hit by the car," but children in the middle years have less difficulty interpreting them (Aschermann et al., 2004).

During these years, children develop the ability to use connectives, as illustrated by the sentence "I'll eat

FIG.9.14 FINDINGS OF STUDIES OF THE RELATIONSHIP BETWEEN IQ SCORES AND HEREDITY

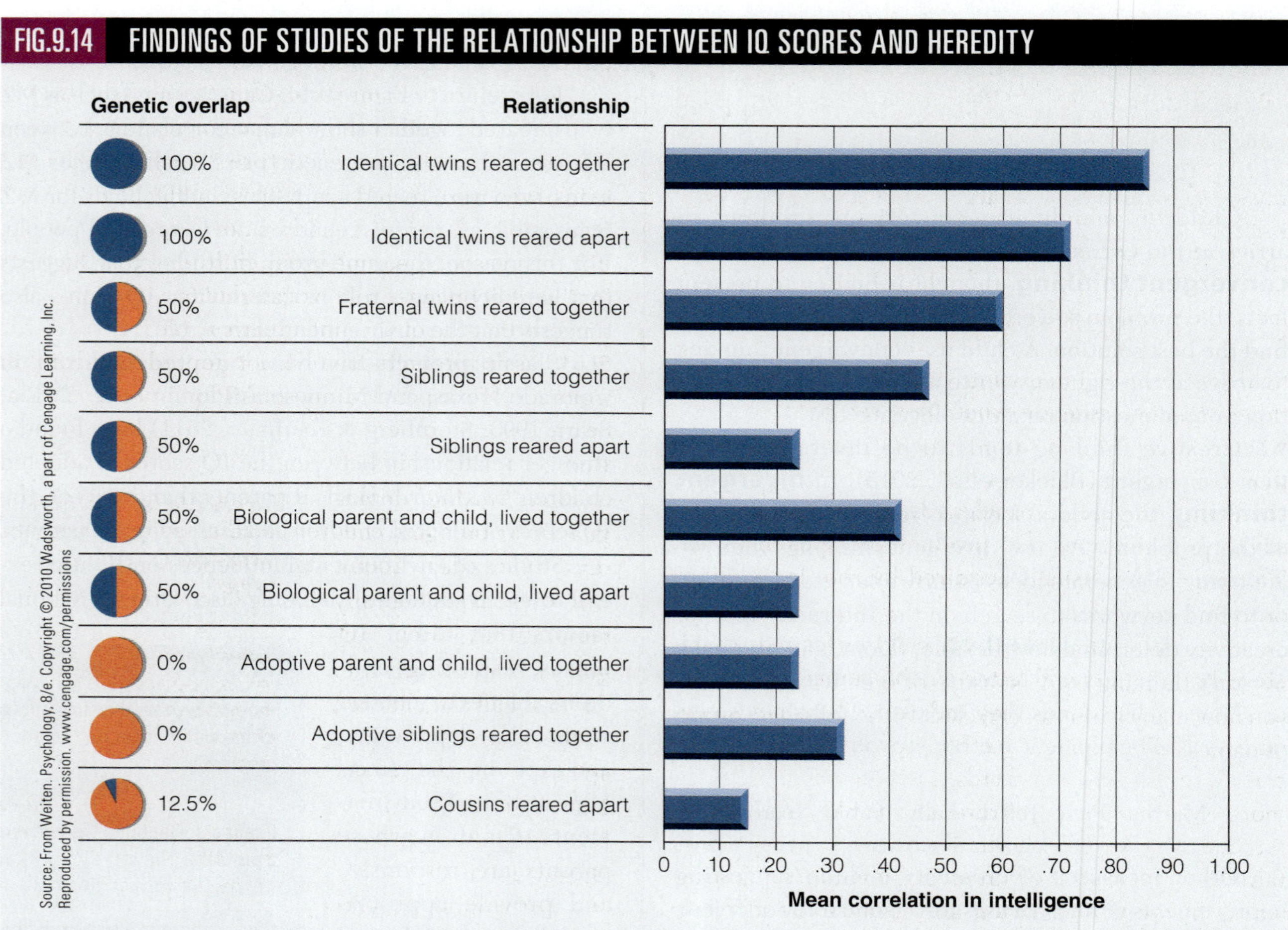

Correlations are stronger for persons who are more closely related and for persons who are reared together or living together, thus supporting both genetic and environmental hypotheses of the origins of intelligence.

FIG.9.15 NUMBER OF LANGUAGES SPOKEN IN THE 15 LARGEST METRO AREAS

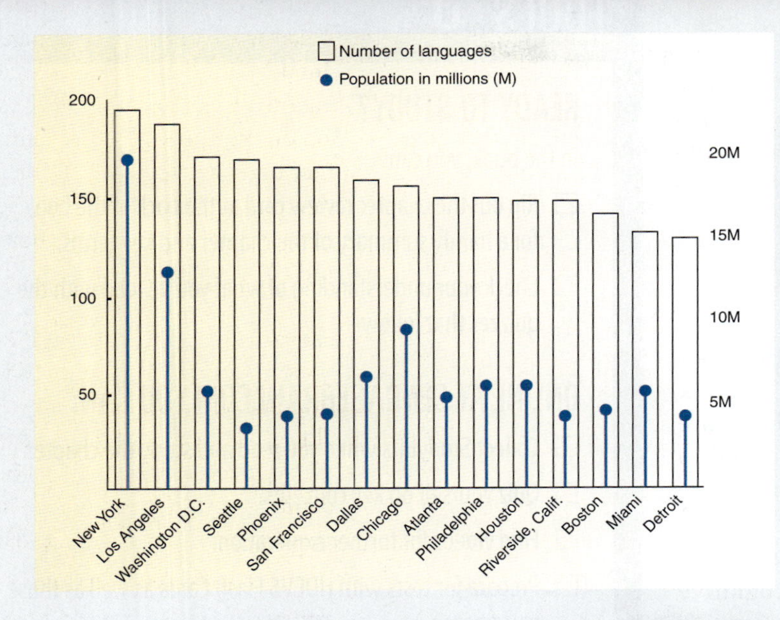

United States Census Bureau, https://www.census.gov/content/dam/Census/newsroom/releases/2015/cb15-185_graphic.jpg

my spinach, but I don't want to." They also learn to form indirect object–direct object constructions. (e.g., "She showed her sister the toy.")

9-8b METHODS OF TEACHING READING

Children read by integrating visual and auditory information (they associate what they see with sounds), whether they use the word-recognition method or the phonetic method. The **word-recognition method** associates visual stimuli such as *cat* and *Robert* with the sound combinations that produce the spoken words. This capacity is usually acquired by rote learning, or extensive repetition.

In the **phonetic method**, children learn to associate written letters and letter combinations (such as *ph* or *sh*) with the sounds they indicate. Then they sound out words. The phonetic method provides skills children can use to decode new words, but some children learn more rapidly at early ages through the word-recognition method. The phonetic method can slow them down with familiar words. Most children and adults read familiar words by word recognition and make some effort to sound out new words.

Some English words can be read only by recognition, as with *one* and *two*. This method is useful when it comes to words such as *danger*, *stop*, *poison*, and a child's name, because it provides children with a basic **sight vocabulary**. But decoding skills help children read new words on their own.

9-8c BILINGUALISM: LINGUISTIC PERSPECTIVES ON THE WORLD

In 2015, 50 to 60 million Americans spoke a language other than English at home (U.S. Census Bureau, 2015). Thirty-five to forty million people speak Spanish, and more than a million each speak Chinese, French, Vietnamese, German, and Korean. Figure 9.15 estimates the number of languages spoken in major metropolitan areas of the United States.

A century ago it was widely believed that children reared in **bilingual** homes were delayed in their cognitive development. The theory was that mental capacity is limited, so people who store two linguistic systems are crowding their mental abilities (Barac & Bialystok, 2011). Bilingual children do show some differences with monolingual children, but this may largely be because the vocabularies used at home and in the school are not identical (Bialystok et al., 2010). Bilingual children do not generally encounter more academic problems than children who speak only one language (Barac & Bialystok, 2011). There is some "mixing" of languages by bilingual children (Gonzalez, 2005), but they can generally separate the two languages from an early age. At least half the children in the United States who speak Spanish in the home are proficient in both languages (Shin & Bruno, 2003).

Today most linguists consider it advantageous for children to be bilingual because knowledge

word-recognition method a method for learning to read in which children come to recognize words through repeated exposure to them.

phonetic method a method for learning to read in which children decode the sounds of words based on their knowledge of the sounds of letters and letter combinations.

sight vocabulary words that are immediately recognized on the basis of familiarity with their overall shapes, rather than decoded.

bilingual using or capable of using two languages with nearly equal or equal facility.

FICTION

T (F) Bilingual children encounter more academic problems than children who speak only one language.

It is not true that bilingual children encounter more academic problems than children who speak only one language.

of more than one language contributes to the complexity of the child's cognitive processes (Barac & Bialystok, 2011). For example, bilingual children are more likely to understand that the symbols used in language are arbitrary. Monolingual children are more likely to think erroneously that the word *dog* is somehow intertwined with the nature of the beast. Bilingual children therefore have somewhat more cognitive flexibility.

STUDY TOOLS 9

READY TO STUDY?

In the book, you can:

- ☐ Rip out the chapter review card at the back of the book for a handy summary of the chapter and key terms.
- ☐ Check your understanding of what you've read with the quizzes that follow.

ONLINE AT CENGAGEBRAIN.COM YOU CAN:

- ☐ Collect StudyBits while you read and study the chapter.
- ☐ Quiz yourself on key concepts.
- ☐ Find videos for further exploration.
- ☐ Prepare for tests with HDEV5 Flash Cards as well as those you create.

SELF-ASSESSMENTS

Fill-Ins

Answers can be found in the back of the book.

1. The good-boy/good-girl orientation is characteristic of the ____________ level of moral development.
2. In ____________ memory, forgetting occurs through decay.
3. The Binet–Simon IQ score is computed by dividing ____________ age by chronological age and then multiplying the result by 100.
4. The Wechsler Intelligence Scales have both verbal items and ____________ items.
5. In the United States, the language other than English most likely to be spoken in the home is ____________.
6. In the ____________ method of teaching reading, teachers associate visual stimuli such as *dog* and *John* with the sound combinations that produce the spoken word.
7. Spearman suggested that the behaviors we consider intelligent have a common underlying factor, which he labeled ____________.
8. Children who realize that if A exceeds B and B exceeds C, then A exceeds C, are showing understanding of the principle of ____________.
9. Children who cannot learn to read, even though they are old enough and have enriched home environments, are diagnosed with ____________.
10. According to Piaget, children who judge right and wrong only in terms of the amount of harm done are said to be in the stage of ____________ morality.

Multiple Choice

1. **The ability to ignore distractions increases most dramatically between**
   a. 6 and 9 years of age.
   b. 9 and 12 years of age.
   c. 12 and 16 years of age.
   d. early adulthood and late adulthood.

2. **Children are said to be intellectually disabled when they obtain IQ scores of no more than**
   a. 70–75.
   b. 80–85.
   c. 90–95.
   d. 100.

3. **The group most likely to show similarity in IQ scores is**
   a. children and their adoptive parents.
   b. children and their biological parents.
   c. fraternal twins reared together.
   d. identical twins reared apart.

4. **Which of the following theorists considers bodily–kinesthetic ability to be an intelligence?**
   a. Sternberg
   b. Wechsler
   c. Gardner
   d. Terman

5. **Childhood obesity is caused by**
   a. heredity/genetics.
   b. fast foods and other environmental contributors.
   c. a combination of heredity and environmental factors.
   d. factors that have not yet been determined.

6. **The best way to keep information in working memory is by**
   a. sensory input.
   b. rehearsal.
   c. hierarchical organization.
   d. decay.

7. **At the preconventional level of moral development, children judge what is right and wrong on the basis of**
   a. universal abstract principles.
   b. weighing human needs against social needs.
   c. obedience and the prospect of punishment.
   d. one's duty to others, as set down in the law.

8. **The most common treatment for attention-deficit/hyperactivity disorder is the use of**
   a. behavior therapy.
   b. time out.
   c. depressants.
   d. stimulants.

9. **Over the past 20 years, the prevalence of obesity among children has**
   a. decreased.
   b. increased by about 20%.
   c. increased by 50%.
   d. doubled.

10. **Which of the following statements about attention deficit hyperactivity disorder (ADHD) is *not* supported by scientific research?**
    a. ADHD is caused by chemical food additives.
    b. There may be a genetic component to development of ADHD.
    c. ADHD appears to be connected with the brain chemical dopamine.
    d. ADHD involves lack of executive control over motor and more primitive functions.

10 Middle Childhood: Social and Emotional Development

Mat Hayward/Shutterstock.com

LEARNING OUTCOMES

After studying this chapter, you will be able to . . .

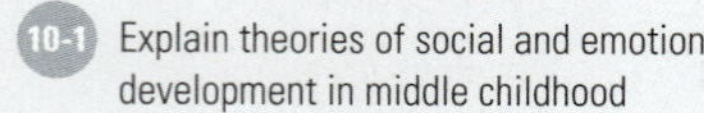

- **10-1** Explain theories of social and emotional development in middle childhood
- **10-2** Discuss the influences of the family on social development in middle childhood
- **10-3** Discuss the influences of peers on social development in middle childhood
- **10-4** Describe the influence of the school on social development in middle childhood
- **10-5** Discuss social and emotional problems that tend to develop in middle childhood

After you finish this chapter, go to **PAGE 215** for **STUDY TOOLS**

In the years between 6 and 12, peers take on greater importance and friendships deepen.

People are social creatures, and social relationships, which begin in infancy between the infant and one or two central caregivers, widen to emphasize the role of peers. Entry into school exposes the child to the influence of teachers. Relationships with parents change as children develop greater independence.

10-1 THEORIES OF SOCIAL AND EMOTIONAL DEVELOPMENT IN MIDDLE CHILDHOOD

The major theories of personality have had less to say about this age group than about the other periods of childhood and adolescence. Nevertheless, some common threads emerge.

10-1a PSYCHOANALYTIC THEORY

According to Freud, children in the middle years are in the **latency stage**. Freud believed that sexual feelings remain repressed (unconscious) during this period. Children use this period to focus on developing intellectual, social, and other culturally valued skills.

Erik Erikson, like Freud, saw the major developmental task of middle childhood as the acquisition of cognitive and social skills. Erikson labeled this stage **industry versus inferiority**. Children who are able to master the challenges of the middle years develop a sense of industry or competence. Children who have difficulties in school or with peer relationships may develop a sense of inferiority.

latency stage in psychoanalytic theory, the fourth stage of psychosexual development, characterized by repression of sexual impulses and development of skills.

industry versus inferiority a stage of psychosocial development in Erikson's theory occurring in middle childhood. Mastery of tasks leads to a sense of industry, whereas failure produces feelings of inferiority.

social cognition development of children's understanding of the relationship between the self and others.

10-1b SOCIAL COGNITIVE THEORY

Social cognitive theory focuses on the importance of rewards and modeling in middle childhood. During these years, children depend less on external rewards and punishments and increasingly regulate their own behavior. Children are exposed to an increasing variety of models. Not only parents but also teachers, other adults, peers, and symbolic models (such as TV characters or the heroine in a story) serve as influential models (Grusec, 2015; Richert et al., 2011).

10-1c COGNITIVE-DEVELOPMENTAL THEORY AND SOCIAL COGNITION

According to Piaget, middle childhood coincides with the stage of concrete operations and is partly characterized by a decline in egocentrism and an expansion of the capacity to view the world and oneself from other people's perspectives. This cognitive advance affects the child's social relationships (Slaughter, 2011).

Social cognition refers to perception of the social world, and our concern is the development of children's perspective-taking skills (Bengtsson & Arvidsson, 2011). Robert Selman and his colleagues (Kwok & Selman, 2013) studied the development of these skills by presenting children with a social dilemma such as the following:

> *Holly is an eight-year-old girl who likes to climb trees. She is the best tree climber in the neighborhood. One day while climbing down from a tall*

TRUTH OR FICTION?

T	F	Children's self-esteem tends to rise in middle childhood.
T	F	The daughters of employed women are more achievement-oriented and set higher career goals for themselves than the daughters of unemployed women.
T	F	In middle childhood, popular children tend to be attractive and relatively mature for their age.
T	F	Some children blame themselves for all the problems in their lives, whether they deserve the blame or not.
T	F	It is better for children with school phobia to remain at home until the origins of the problem are uncovered and resolved.

tree, she falls off the bottom branch but does not hurt herself. Her father sees her fall. He is upset and asks her to promise not to climb trees any more. Holly promises. Later that day, Holly and her friends meet Sean. Sean's kitten is caught up in a tree and can't get down. Something has to be done right away, or the kitten may fall. Holly is the only one who climbs trees well enough to reach the kitten and get it down, but she remembers her promise to her father.

—Selman, (1980, p. 36)

Radius Images/Getty Images

The children then were asked questions such as "How will Holly's father feel if he finds out she climbed the tree?" Based on the children's responses, Selman (1976) described five levels of perspective-taking skills in childhood (see Table 10.1). Children with better perspective-taking skills tend to have better peer relationships (Abrams et al., 2014; Smith & Rose, 2011).

10-1d DEVELOPMENT OF THE SELF-CONCEPT IN MIDDLE CHILDHOOD

In early childhood, children's self-concepts focus on concrete external traits, such as appearance, activities, and living situations. But as children undergo the cognitive developments of middle childhood, more abstract internal traits, or personality traits, begin to play a role. Social relationships and group memberships take on significance (Bukowski & Veronneau, 2014; Rosen & Patterson, 2011).

An investigative method called the Twenty Statements Test bears out this progression. Children are given a sheet of paper with the question "Who am I?" and 20 spaces in which to write answers. Consider the answers of a 9-year-old boy and an 11-year-old girl:

The nine-year-old boy: My name is Bruce C. I have brown eyes. I have brown hair. I have brown eyebrows. I'm nine years old. I LOVE? sports. I have seven people in my family. I have great? eye site. I have lots! of friends. I live on 1923 Pinecrest Drive. I'm going on ten in September. I'm a boy. I have a uncle that is almost seven feet tall. My school is Pinecrest. My teacher is Mrs. V. I play hockey! I'm also the smartest boy in the class. I LOVE! food. I love fresh air. I LOVE school.

The 11-year-old girl: My name is A. I'm a human being. I'm a girl. I'm a truthful person. I'm not pretty. I do so-so in my studies. I'm a very good

TABLE 10.1 LEVELS OF PERSPECTIVE TAKING

Level	Approximate Age (Years)	What Happens
0	3–6	Children are egocentric and do not realize that other people have perspectives different from their own. A child of this age will typically say that Holly will save the kitten because she likes kittens and that her father will be happy because he likes kittens too. The child assumes that everyone feels as she does.
1	5–9*	Children understand that people in different situations may have different perspectives. The child still assumes that only one perspective is "right." A child might say that Holly's father would be angry if he did not know why she climbed the tree. But if she told him why, he would understand. The child recognizes that the father's perspective may differ from Holly's because of lack of information. But once he has the information, he will assume the "right" (i.e., Holly's) perspective.
2	7–12*	The child understands that people may think or feel differently because they have different values or ideas. The child also recognizes that others are capable of understanding the child's own perspective. Therefore, the child is better able to anticipate reactions of others. The typical child of this age might say that Holly knows that her father will understand why she climbed the tree and that he therefore will not punish her.
3	10–15*	The child finally realizes that both she and another person can consider each other's point of view at the same time. The child may say something similar to this reasoning: Holly's father will think that Holly shouldn't have climbed the tree. But now that he has heard her side of the story, he would feel that she was doing what she thought was right. Holly realizes that her father will consider how she felt.
4	12 and above*	The child realizes that mutual perspective taking does not always lead to agreement. The perspectives of the larger social group also must be considered. A child of this age might say that society expects children to obey their parents and therefore that Holly should realize why her father might punish her.

*Ages may overlap.
Source: Selman (1976).

cellist. I'm a very good pianist. I'm a little bit tall for my age. I like several boys. I like several girls. . . . I play tennis. I am a very good musician. . . . I'm always ready to be friends with anybody. Mostly I'm good, but I lose my temper. I'm not well liked by some girls and boys. I don't know if boys like me or not. Montemayor, R., & Eisen, M. (1977).

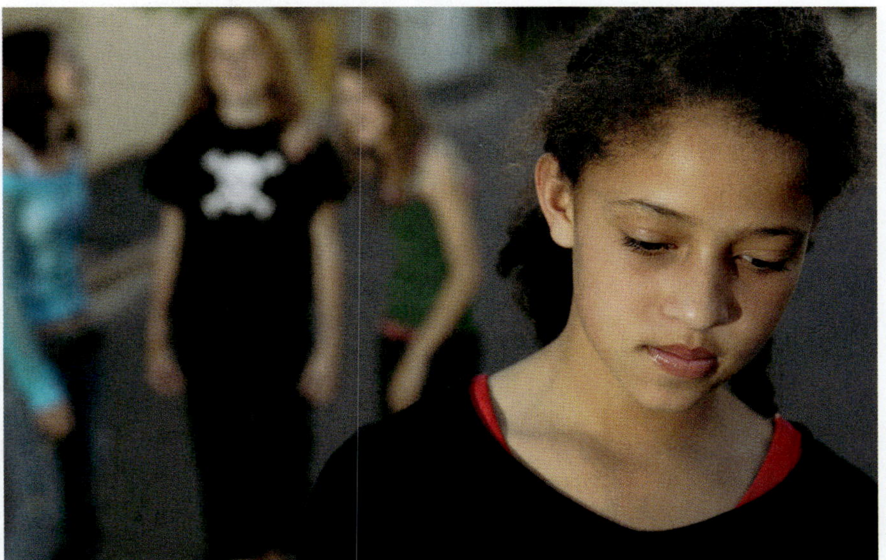

Lou Cypher/Fancy/Corbis

Children's self-esteem tends to decline during middle childhood, in part because they come to evaluate their physical appearance and their performance in academic and social domains more realistically.

Only the nine-year-old lists his age and address, discusses his family, and focuses on physical traits, such as eye color, in his self-definition. The nine-year-old mentions his likes, which can be considered rudimentary psychological traits, but they are tied to the concrete, as would be expected of a concrete-operational child. The 9- and 11-year-olds list their competencies. The 11-year-old's struggle to bolster her self-esteem—her insistence on her musical abilities despite her qualms about her attractiveness—shows a greater concern with psychological traits and social relationships.

SELF-ESTEEM As children enter middle childhood, they evaluate their self-worth in many different areas (Rosen & Patterson, 2011). Preschoolers tend to see themselves as generally "good at doing things" or not. But by five to seven years of age, children are able to judge their performance in seven different areas: physical ability, physical appearance, peer relationships, parent relationships, reading, math, and general school performance. They also report a general self-concept (Harter, 2012).

Children's self-esteem declines throughout middle childhood, reaching a low ebb at 12 or 13. Then it increases during adolescence (Harter, 2012). What accounts for the decline? Because preschoolers are egocentric, their self-concepts may be unrealistic. By middle childhood, children can compare themselves with other children and arrive at a more honest and critical self-appraisal. Girls tend to have more positive self-concepts regarding reading, general academics, and helping others than boys. Boys tend to have more positive self-concepts in math, physical ability, and physical appearance (Tobin et al., 2010; Underwood & Rosen, 2011).

FICTION

T (F) Children's self-esteem tends to rise in middle childhood.

It is not true that children's self-esteem rises during middle childhood. In fact, it tends to decline, reaching a low ebb at 12 or 13, as children confront more realistic evaluations of their strengths and shortcomings.

Authoritative parenting apparently contributes to children's self-esteem (Chan & Koo, 2011; Scales, 2014). Children with a favorable self-image tend to have parents who are restrictive, involved, and loving. Children with low self-esteem are more likely to have authoritarian or rejecting–neglecting parents.

Social acceptance by peers is related to self-perceived competence in academic, social, and athletic domains (Cillessen & Bellmore, 2011). Parents and classmates have an equally strong effect on children's self-esteem in middle childhood. Friends and teachers have relatively less influence but also matter (Harter, 2012).

LEARNED HELPLESSNESS One outcome of low self-esteem in academics is known as **learned helplessness**. Learned helplessness is the acquired belief that one is unable to obtain the rewards that one seeks. "Helpless" children tend to quit following failure, whereas children who believe in their own ability tend to persist or change their strategies (Steca et al., 2014). One reason for this difference is that "helpless" children believe that success is due more to ability than effort and that they have little ability in a particular area. Consequently, persistence seems futile. Helpless children typically obtain lower grades and lower scores on IQ and achievement tests (Burnette et al., 2013; Dweck, 2015).

A gender difference emerges in mathematics (Else-Quest et al., 2013; Hyde, 2014). Researchers have found that even when girls are performing as well as boys in math and science, they have less confidence in their ability (Hall, 2012). Why? Many parents hold the stereotype that girls have less math ability than boys despite their daughters' demonstrated skills.

10-2 THE FAMILY

In middle childhood, the family continues to play a key role in socializing the child, although peers, teachers, and other outsiders begin to play a greater role (Dunn, 2015; Grusec & Davidov, 2015).

10-2a PARENT–CHILD RELATIONSHIPS

Parent–child interactions focus on some new concerns during middle childhood. They include school-related matters, assignment of chores, and peer activities (Grusec & Davidov, 2015). Parents do less monitoring of children's activities and provide less direct feedback than they did in the preschool years. Control is gradually transferred from parent to child in a process known as **coregulation** (Maughan, 2011). Children begin to internalize the standards of their parents.

Children and parents spend less time together in middle childhood than in the preschool years. Children spend more time with their mothers than with their fathers. Mothers' interactions with school-age children continue to revolve around caregiving; fathers are relatively more involved in recreation (Keown & Palmer, 2014; Demby et al., 2015).

Because of their developing cognitive ability, 10- to 12-year-olds evaluate their parents more harshly than they did in early childhood (Grusec & Davidov, 2015). But throughout middle childhood, children rate their parents as their best source of emotional support (Grusec, 2015).

10-2b LESBIAN AND GAY PARENTS

"Where did you get that beautiful necklace?" I asked the little girl in the pediatrician's office. "From my Moms," she answered. It turned out that her family consisted of two women, each of whom had a biological child, one girl and one boy.

Research on lesbian and gay parenting has fallen into two general categories: the general adjustment of children and whether the children of lesbian and gay parents are more likely than other children to be lesbian or gay themselves. Research by Charlotte Patterson and her colleagues (e.g., Farr & Patterson, 2013) has generally found that the psychological adjustment of children of lesbian and gay parents is comparable to that of children of heterosexual parents. Despite the stigma attached to homosexuality, lesbians and gay men are as likely to sustain positive family relationships (Tasker & Granville, 2011).

Mahdees Mahjoob / Alamy Stock Photo

Being reared by lesbian or gay parents has not been shown to influence children's adjustment or their sexual orientation. But LGBT families, as lesbian, gay, or transgender individuals, fare better in supportive communities.

learned helplessness an acquired (hence, learned) belief that one is unable to control one's environment.

coregulation a gradual transferring of control from parent to child, beginning in middle childhood.

However, we must also note that the psychological adjustment of lesbian and gay couples and their children is superior in communities in which there is social support for lesbian and gay families in the area (Lick et al., 2012; Oswald et al., 2013). Locales in which there is greater density of lesbian and gay populations—such as major metropolitan areas—generally offer more support.

What of the sexual orientation of the children of lesbian and gay parents? Green (1978) observed 37 children and young adults, age 3 to 20, who were being reared—or had been reared—by lesbian or **transgender** parents. All but one of the children reported or recalled preferences for toys, clothing, and friends (male or female) that were typical for their gender and age. All the 13 older children who reported sexual fantasies or sexual behavior were heterosexually oriented.

10-2c GENERATION X OR GENERATION EX? WHAT HAPPENS TO CHILDREN WHOSE PARENTS GET DIVORCED?

Is this the time of "Generation Ex"—a generation characterized by ex-wives and ex-husbands? More than one million American children each year experience the divorce of their parents. Nearly 40% of European American children and 75% of African American children in the United States who are born to married parents will spend at least part of their childhoods in single-parent families as a result of divorce (U.S. Bureau of the Census, 2015).

Superstock / Alamy Stock Photo

Divorce may be tough on parents; it can be even tougher on children (Kim, 2011; Moon, 2011). No longer do children eat with both parents. No longer do they go to ball games, movies, or Disneyland with both of them. The parents are now often supporting two households, resulting in fewer resources for the children. Many children who live with their mothers scrape by—or fail to scrape by—in poverty. The mother who was once available may become an occasional visitor, spending more time at work and placing the kids in day care for extended periods.

Most children live with their mothers after a divorce. Some fathers remain devoted to their children despite the split, but others tend to spend less time with their children as time goes on. Not only does the drop-off in paternal attention deprive children of activities and social interactions, but it also saps their self-esteem: "Why doesn't Daddy love me anymore? What's wrong with me?"

The children of divorce are more likely to have conduct disorders, to abuse drugs, and to have poor grades in school (Amato & Anthony, 2014; Hicks et al., 2013). Their physical health may decline (Brockmann, 2013). By and large, the fallout for children is worst during the first year after the breakup. Children tend to rebound after a couple of years (Malone et al., 2004).

LIFE IN STEPFAMILIES: HIS, HERS, THEIRS, AND . . . Most divorced people remarry, usually while the children are young. More than one in three American children will spend part of his or her childhood in a stepfamily (U.S. Bureau of the Census, 2015).

The rule of thumb about the effects of living in stepfamilies is that there is no rule of thumb (Harvey & Fine, 2011). Many stepparents treat stepchildren as though they were biologically their own (Marsiglio, 2004), but there are also some risks to living in stepfamilies, such as the greater risk of being physically abused by stepparents than by biological parents (Adler-Baeder, 2006). There is also a significantly higher incidence—by a factor of eight—of sexual abuse by stepparents than natural parents.

Why do we find these risks in stepfamilies? According to evolutionary psychologists, people often behave as though they want their genes to flourish in the next generation. Thus, it could be that stepparents are less devoted to rearing other people's children.

SHOULD WE REMAIN MARRIED "FOR THE SAKE OF THE CHILDREN"? Many people believe—for moral reasons—that marriage and family life must be permanent, no matter what. People must consider the moral aspects of divorce in the light of their own value systems. But—from a purely psychological perspective—what should bickering parents do? The answer

transgender referring to people who feel as though they are persons of the other sex who are 'trapped' in the body of the wrong sex. Some transgender individuals (also called 'trans') are content to adopt the clothing and cosmetic appearance of people of the other sex; others undergo hormone treatments and surgery to achieve the body shape and external physical traits of persons of the other sex.

Talking to Children About Divorce

Talking to children about a divorce is difficult. The following tips can help both the child and parents with the challenge and stress of these conversations:

- **Do not keep it a secret or wait until the last minute.**
- **Tell your children together with your spouse.**
- **Keep things simple and straightforward.**
- **Tell them the divorce is not their fault.**
- **Admit that this will be sad and upsetting for everyone.**
- **Reassure your children that you both still love them and will always be their parents.**
- **Do not discuss each other's faults or problems with the children.**

Source: American Academy of Child & Adolescent Psychiatry (2008).

seems to depend largely on how they behave in front of the children. Research shows that severe parental bickering is linked to the same kinds of problems that children experience when their parents get separated or divorced (Troxel & Holt-Lunstad, 2013). When children are exposed to adult or marital conflict, they display a biological "alarm reaction": their heart rate, blood pressure, and sweating rise sharply (El-Sheikh, 2007). Therefore, a number of researchers acknowledge that some children tend to fare better after parents who fight continually parents get divorced (Amato & Anthony, 2014)

10-2e THE EFFECTS OF MATERNAL EMPLOYMENT

Why is this section labeled "The Effects of Maternal Employment"? Why not "Parental Employment" or "Paternal Employment"? Perhaps because of the traditional role of women as homemakers. A half-century ago, most women remained in the home, but today, nearly three out of four married mothers of children under age 18 are employed, as are four out of five divorced, separated, or widowed mothers (O'Brien et al., 2014).

Many commentators have been concerned about the effects of maternal employment on children. In part, this has been based on more traditional values that argue that the mother ought to remain in the home. Research results are mixed. Some studies suggest that maternal employment can have negative effects on children (Belsky, 2006b). Other studies suggest that employed mothers provide greater learning opportunities for their children (Buehler et al., 2014).

One common belief is that Mom's being in the workforce rather than in the home leads to delinquency. Researchers using data on 707 adolescents, ages 12 to 14, from the National Longitudinal Survey of Youth examined whether the occupational status of a mother was connected with delinquent behavior (Vander Ven & Cullen, 2004). They found that maternal employment per se made no difference, but delinquency was connected with lack of supervision. Similar results have been found in the European Union (Cabrera et al., 2014).

There are benefits for maternal employment. Daughters of employed women are more achievement-oriented and set higher career goals for themselves than daughters of nonworking women (Greene et al., 2013). Children of working mothers tend to be more prosocial, less anxious, and flexible in their gender role stereotypes (Goldberg et al., 2012; Greene et al., 2013).

TRUTH

F The daughters of employed women are more achievement-oriented and set higher career goals for themselves than the daughters of unemployed women.

It is true that the daughters of employed women are more achievement-oriented and set higher career goals for themselves than the daughters of unemployed women. One possible explanation is that the mothers serve as role models for their daughters.

10-3 PEER RELATIONSHIPS

Families exert the most powerful influence on a child during his or her first few years (Carr, 2011; Grusec, 2015). But as children move into middle childhood, peers take on more importance (Wentzel & Muenks, 2016).

10-3a PEERS AS SOCIALIZATION INFLUENCES

Parents can provide children only with experience relating to adults. Children profit from experience with peers because peers have interests and skills that reflect the child's generation (Eivers et al., 2012; Gauvain, 2016).

Peers afford practice in cooperating, relating to leaders, and coping with aggressive impulses, including their own. Peers can be important confidants (Dunn, 2015; Wentzel, 2014). Peers, like parents, help children learn what types of impulses—affectionate, aggressive, and so on—they can safely express. Children who are at odds with their parents can turn to peers as sounding boards. They can compare feelings and experiences. When children share troubling ideas and experiences with peers, they realize they are normal and not alone (Wentzel, 2014).

10-3b PEER ACCEPTANCE AND REJECTION

Acceptance or rejection by peers is important in childhood because problems with peers affect adjustment later on (Dunn, 2015; Wentzel, 2014). Popular children tend to be attractive, mature for their age, and successful in sports or academics, although attractiveness seems to be more important for girls than boys (Rennels & Langlois, 2014). Socially speaking, popular children are friendly, nurturant, cooperative, helpful, and socially skillful (Rodkin et al., 2013; Xie et al., 2006). They also have high self-esteem.

TRUTH

T F In middle childhood, popular children tend to be attractive and relatively mature for their age.

It is true that popular children tend to be attractive and relatively mature for their age—although, in the case of attractiveness, the statement applies more to girls than to boys.

Children who are aggressive and disrupt group activities are sometimes rejected by peers (Boivin et al., 2005). However, some aggressive children are popular; there is apparently no general rule (Ojanen & Findley-Van Nostrand, 2014; Troop-Gordon & Ranney, 2014).

10-3c DEVELOPMENT OF FRIENDSHIPS

In the preschool years and early years of middle childhood, friendships are based on geographic closeness or proximity. Friendships are superficial; quickly formed, easily broken. What matters are shared activities and who has the swing set or sandbox (Berndt, 2004; MacEvoy et al., 2016).

Between 8 and 11, children recognize the importance of friends meeting each other's needs and possessing desirable traits (Lansford et al., 2014). They are more likely to say that friends are nice and share their interests. They increasingly pick friends who are similar in behavior and personality. Trustworthiness, mutual understanding, and a willingness to disclose personal information characterize friendships in middle childhood and beyond (Lansford et al., 2014). Girls tend to develop closer friendships than boys, to seek confidants (Zarbatany et al., 2000).

Robert Selman (1980) described five stages in children's changing concepts of friendship (see Table 10.2). The stages correspond to the levels of perspective-taking skills discussed earlier.

Friends behave differently with each other than with other children. School-age friends are more verbal, attentive, relaxed, and responsive to each other during play than are mere acquaintances (Saldarriage et al. (2015)). Conflicts can occur among friends, but when they do, they tend to be less intense and get resolved in positive ways (Bowker et al., 2011).

TABLE 10.2 STAGES IN CHILDREN'S CONCEPTS OF FRIENDSHIP

Stage	Name	Approximate Age (Years)	What Happens
0	Momentary physical interaction	3–6	Children remain egocentric. Their concept of a friend is one who likes to play with the same things and lives nearby.
1	One-way assistance	5–9*	Children are less egocentric but view a friend as someone who does what they want.
2	Fair-weather cooperation	7–12*	Friends are viewed as doing things for one another, but the focus remains on self-interest.
3	Intimate and mutual sharing	10–15*	The focus is on the relationship rather than on the individuals separately. Friendship is viewed as providing mutual support over a long period of time.
4	Autonomous interdependence	12 and above*	Children (adolescents, and adults) understand that friendships grow and change as people change and that they may need different friends to satisfy different needs.

*Ages can overlap
Source: Selman (1980).

Bullying: An Epidemic of Pain

> I was called really horrible, profane names very loudly in front of huge crowds of people, and my schoolwork suffered at one point. . . . I didn't want to go to class. And I was a straight-A student, so there was a certain point in my high school years where I just couldn't even focus on class because I was so embarrassed all the time. I was so ashamed of who I was.
>
> —Lady Gaga[1]

Eleven-year-old Michael Wilson committed suicide in 2011. His family found him with a plastic bag tied around his head (Nurwisah, 2011). Michael had had muscular dystrophy. He used a walker to get by in school. At school, a 12-year-old mugged him for his iPhone. A few months before his death, Michael said, "If I have to go back to that school, I'll kill myself." And he did.

Twelve-year-old Rebecca killed herself by climbing a platform at an abandoned cement plant and jumping off. She had received a continuous stream of threatening and taunting text messages and cellphone photo-sharing—aspects of all too common **cyberbullying** (Alvarez, 2013).

Bullying has devastating effects on the school atmosphere. It transforms the perception of school from a safe place into a violent place (Lorenzo-Blanco et al., 2016). Nine-year-old Stephanie had gotten into a disagreement with Susan, and Susan had told her she would beat her mercilessly if she showed up at school again. To highlight her warning, Susan had shoved Stephanie across the hall. Stephanie did not know it, but, ironically, Susan was also bullied from time to time by a couple of other girls at school. Stephanie's response was to refuse to go to school, not suicide.

Was there something unusual about Michael, Rebecca, and Stephanie's situations? Sadly, no. Bullying is everywhere and there are all too many suicides from victims who are bullied on Facebook and in other ways on the Internet (Kowalski et al., 2014). Suicide is especially common among middle schoolers who have not yet developed a strong sense of who they are and where they are going in life (Henry et al., 2014).

cyberbullying the use of electronic devices such as cellphones, computers, and tablets to transmit threatening and taunting messages.

Lady Gaga may be a superstar now, but bullying led her to have serious self-doubts in school.

Jason Laveris/FilmMagic/Getty Images

Boys are more likely than girls to be bullies, but many girls engage in bullying (Juvonen & Graham, 2014). All in all, at least half of middle school students in the United States have been exposed to bullying (Baly et al., 2014).

Many bullies have things in common. Their achievement tends to be lower than average, such that peer approval or deference might be more important to them than academics (Espelage & Colbert, 2016; Leiner et al., 2104). Bullies are more likely to come from homes of lower socioeconomic status with parental violence (Perren & Alsaker, 2006). Bullying is also associated with more frequent diagnoses of conduct disorder, oppositional defiant disorder, and attention deficit hyperactivity disorder (ADHD) (Leiner et al., 2014). Victims of bullies, like Michael, Rebecca, and Stephanie, are commonly anxious and depressed, and they often find other peers avoiding them, so that the others can avoid getting involved (Howard et al., 2014).

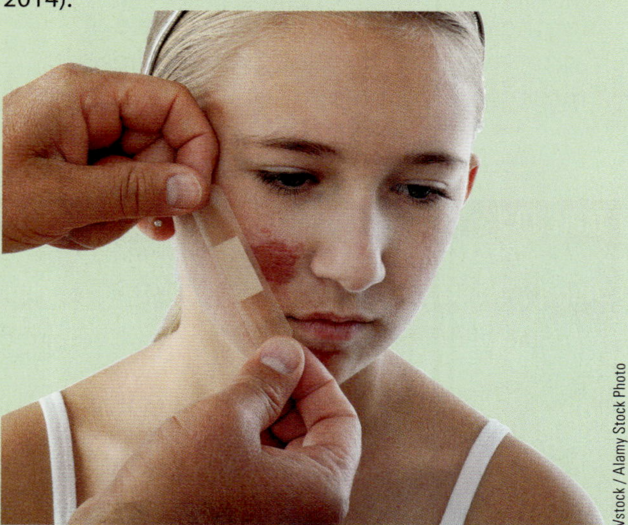

Vstock / Alamy Stock Photo

[1]In Nicholas D. Kristof. (2012, March 1). Born to not get bullied. *The New York Times*, p. A31.

Children in middle childhood will typically say they have more than one "best" friend (Berndt et al., 1989; Bowker et al., 2011). Nine-year-olds report an average of four best friends. Best friends tend to be more alike than other friends. In middle childhood, boys tend to play in larger groups than girls. Children's friendships are almost exclusively with others of the same gender, continuing the trend of gender segregation.

10-4 THE SCHOOL

The school exerts a powerful influence on many aspects of the child's development. Schools, like parents, set limits on behavior, make demands for mature behavior, attempt to communicate, and are oriented toward nurturing positive physical, social, and cognitive development. Schools influence children's IQ scores, achievement motivation, and career aspirations (Kaplan & Owings, 2015; Woolfolk, 2013). Schools also influence social and moral development (Kaplan & Owings, 2015).

Schools are also competitive environments, and children who do too well—as well as students who do not do well enough—may incur the resentment or ridicule of others.

10-4a ENTRY INTO SCHOOL

Children must master many new tasks when they start school—new academic challenges, new school and teacher expectations, fitting into a new peer group, coping with extended separation from parents, and developing increased self-control and self-help skills.

How well prepared are children to enter school? School readiness involves at least three critical factors:

1. The diversity and inequity of children's early life experiences
2. Individual differences in young children's development and learning
3. The degree to which schools establish reasonable and appropriate expectations of children's capabilities when they enter school

Some children enter school less well prepared than others. Kindergarten teachers report that many students begin school unprepared to learn (Kaplan & Owings, 2015; Woolfolk, 2013). Most teachers say that children often lack the language skills needed to succeed. Poor health care and nutrition, and lack of adequate parental stimulation and support, place many children at risk for academic failure before they enter school.

10-4b THE SCHOOL ENVIRONMENT: SETTING THE STAGE FOR SUCCESS OR . . .

Research summaries (Kaplan & Owings, 2015; Patrick et al., 2016) indicate that an effective school has the following characteristics:

- An active, energetic principal
- An orderly but not oppressive atmosphere
- Empowerment of teachers; that is, teachers participating in decision making
- Teachers with high expectations that children will learn
- A curriculum that emphasizes academics
- Frequent assessment of student performance
- Empowerment of students; that is, students participating in setting goals, making decisions, and engaging in cooperative learning activities

Certain aspects of the school environment are important as well. One key factor is class size. Smaller classes permit students to receive more individual attention and are particularly useful in teaching the "basics"—reading, writing, and arithmetic—to students at risk for academic failure (Kaplan & Owings, 2015; Wentzel & Ramani, 2016).

10-4b TEACHERS

Teachers, like parents, set limits, make demands, communicate values, and foster development. They are powerful role models and dispensers of reinforcement. After all, children spend several hours each weekday with teachers.

TEACHER INFLUENCES ON STUDENT PERFORMANCE Achievement is enhanced when teachers expect students to master the curriculum, allocate most of the available time to academic activities, and manage the classroom effectively. Students learn more in classes when they are actively instructed or supervised by teachers than when they are working on their own. The most effective teachers ask questions, give personalized feedback, and provide opportunities for drill and practice (Kaplan & Owings, 2015; Fox & Dinsmore, 2016).

Student achievement also is linked to the emotional climate of the classroom (Meyer, 2016; Woolfolk, 2013). Students do not do as well when teachers rely heavily on criticism, ridicule, threats, or punishment. Achievement is high in classrooms with a pleasant, friendly—but not overly warm—atmosphere.

The Value of Good Teaching

Is it possible to determine what makes a good teacher? Is it possible to measure "good teaching" objectively? A team of economists—not educators—tried to do precisely that, and they did it in terms of money—what students earned over the years. Raj Chetty and his colleagues (2012) tracked elementary and high school students over a period of 20 years and found that "good teachers"—defined for the sake of the study as teachers who raise students' scores on standardized achievement texts—contribute to lasting academic and financial gains for the students. The research team labeled such teaching "value added" teaching, and, as you see in Figure 10.1, there is a strong correlation between value-added teaching and financial outcome at age 28. (The relatively low dollar amounts reflect the times during which data was gathered.) Value-added teaching even lowered the risk of unwanted teenage pregnancy. One commentator summarized the data as showing that "having a good fourth-grade teacher" increases the likelihood that a student will go on to college by 25%, lowers the risk of teen pregnancy by 25%, and boosts the student's lifetime income by an average of $25,000 (Kristof, 2012).

FIG.10.1 THE LONG-TERM IMPACT OF GOOD TEACHING

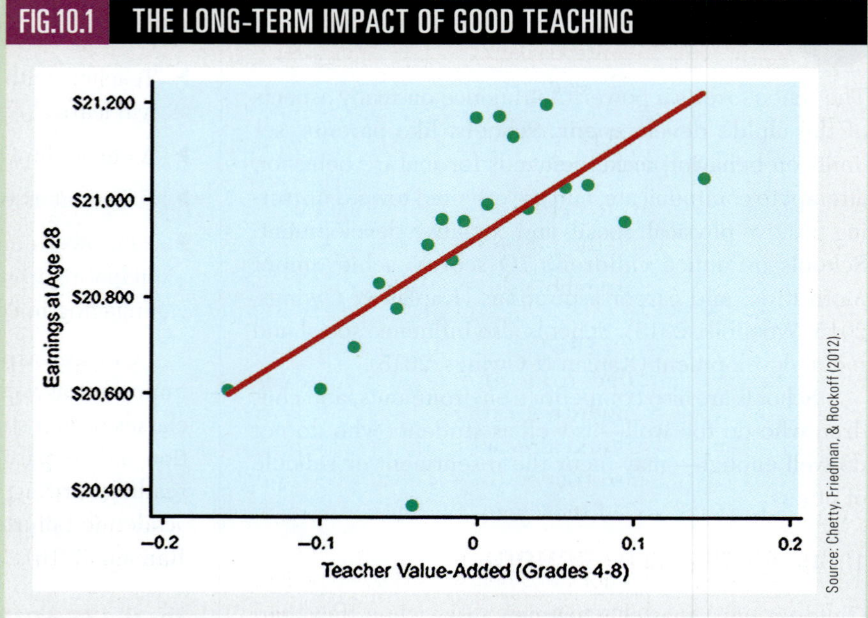

Teaching that raises students' standardized achievement test scores also raises their income potential and lowers the risk of teenage pregnancy.

TEACHER EXPECTATIONS There is a saying that "You find what you're looking for." Consider the so-called **Pygmalion effect** in education. In Greek mythology, the amorous sculptor Pygmalion breathed life into a beautiful statue he had carved. Teachers also try to bring out positive traits they believe dwell within their students. A classic experiment by Robert Rosenthal and Lenore Jacobson (1968) suggested that teacher expectations can become **self-fulfilling prophecies**. Rosenthal and Jacobson (1968) first gave students a battery of psychological tests. Then they informed teachers that a handful of the students, although average in performance to date, were about to blossom forth intellectually in the current school year.

Pygmalion effect a positive self-fulfilling prophecy in which an individual comes to display improved performance because of the positive expectation of the people with whom he or she interacts.

self-fulfilling prophecy an event that occurs because of the behavior of those who expect it to occur.

In fact, the tests indicated nothing about the chosen children. These children had been selected at random. The purpose of the experiment was to determine whether enhancing teacher expectations could affect student performance. It did; the identified children made significant gains in IQ scores.

In subsequent research, however, results have been mixed. Some studies have found support for the Pygmalion effect (Madon et al., 2001; Sarrazin et al., 2005a, 2005b). Others have not. But these findings have serious implications for children from ethnic minority and low-income families because there is some indication that teachers expect less from children in these groups (Kaplan & Owings, 2015; Woolfolk, 2013). Teachers who expect less may spend less time encouraging and working with children.

What are some of the ways that teachers can help motivate all students to do their best? Here are some suggestions (Gehlbach & Robinson, 2016; Wubbels et al., 2016):

- Make the classroom and the lesson interesting and inviting.
- Ensure that students can profit from social interaction.
- Make the classroom a safe and pleasant place.
- Recognize that students' backgrounds can give rise to diverse patterns of needs.
- Help students take appropriate responsibility for their successes and failures.
- Encourage students to perceive the links between their own efforts and their achievements.
- Help students set attainable short-term goals.

SEXISM IN THE CLASSROOM Although girls were systematically excluded from formal education for centuries, today we might not expect to find **sexism** among teachers. Teachers, after all, are generally well educated. They are also trained to be fair minded and sensitive to the needs of their young charges in today's changing society.

However, we may not have heard the last of sexism in our schools. According to a classic review of more than 1,000 research publications about girls and education, girls are treated unequally by their teachers, their male peers, and the school curriculum (Sadker & Silber, 2007). The reviewers concluded:

- Many teachers pay less attention to girls than boys, especially in math, science, and technology classes.
- Many girls are subjected to **sexual harassment**—unwelcome verbal or physical conduct of a sexual nature—from male classmates, and many teachers ignore it.
- Some textbooks still stereotype or ignore women, portraying males as the movers and shakers in the world.

In a widely cited study, Myra Sadker and David Sadker (Sadker & Silber, 2007) observed students in fourth-, sixth-, and eighth-grade classes in four states and in the District of Columbia. Teachers and students were European American and African American, urban, suburban, and rural. In almost all cases, the findings were depressingly similar. Boys generally dominated classroom communication, whether the subject was math (a traditionally "masculine" area) or language arts (a traditionally "feminine" area). Despite the stereotype that girls are more likely to talk or even chatter, boys were eight times more likely than girls to call out answers without raising their hands. So far, it could be said, we have evidence of a gender difference, but not of sexism. However, teachers were less than impartial in responding to boys and girls when they called out. Teachers, male and female, were more likely to accept calling out from boys. Girls were more likely to be reminded that they should raise their hands and wait to be called on. Boys, it appears, are expected to be impetuous, but girls are reprimanded for "unladylike behavior." Until they saw videotapes of themselves, the teachers were largely unaware they were treating girls and boys differently.

sexism discrimination or bias against people based on their gender.

sexual harassment unwelcome verbal or physical conduct of a sexual nature.

Cheryl Casey/Shutterstock.com

10-5 SOCIAL AND EMOTIONAL PROBLEMS

Millions of children in the United States suffer from emotional or behavioral problems and could profit from professional treatment, but most of them are unlikely to receive it (Cicchetti, 2013). Here, we focus on conduct disorders, depression, and anxiety.

10-5a CONDUCT DISORDERS

David is a 16-year-old high school dropout. He has just been arrested for the third time in two years for stealing video equipment and computers from people's homes. Acting alone, David was caught in each case when he tried to sell the stolen items. In describing his actions in each crime, David expressed defiance and showed a lack of remorse. In fact, he bragged about how often he had gotten away with similar crimes.

—Adapted from Halgin & Whitbourne (1993, p. 335)

David has a **conduct disorder**. Children with conduct disorders persistently break rules or violate the rights of others. They exhibit behaviors such as lying, stealing, fire setting, truancy, cruelty to animals, and fighting (American Psychiatric Association, 2013). Conduct disorders typically emerge by eight years of age and are much more common in boys than girls (American Psychiatric Association, 2013; Seguin & Tremblay, 2013).

Children with conduct disorders are often involved in sexual activity before puberty and smoke, drink, and abuse other substances. They have a low tolerance for frustration and may have temper flare-ups. They tend to blame other people for their scrapes. Academic achievement is usually below grade level, but intelligence is usually at least average. Many children with conduct disorders also are diagnosed with ADHD (American Psychiatric Association, 2013).

ORIGINS OF CONDUCT DISORDERS Conduct disorders may have a genetic component (Kendler et al., 2013). Other contributors include antisocial family members, deviant peers, inconsistent discipline, parental insensitivity to the child's behavior, physical punishment, and family stress (Wu et al., 2015).

conduct disorder disorder marked by persistent breaking of the rules and violations of the rights of others.

TREATMENT OF CONDUCT DISORDERS The treatment of conduct disorders is challenging, but it seems that cognitive-behavioral techniques involving parent training hold promise (Graham & Reynolds, 2013). Children profit from interventions in which there are consequences (such as time-outs) for unacceptable behavior and positive social behavior is rewarded.

One method teaches children social skills and problem-solving skills to manage interpersonal conflicts (Burke & Loeber, 2016). Social skills include asking other children to stop annoying behavior rather than hitting them. Children are also taught to "stop and think" before engaging in aggressive behavior.

10-5b CHILDHOOD DEPRESSION

Kristin, age 11, feels "nothing is working out for me." For the past year, she has been failing in school, although she previously had been a B student. She has trouble sleeping, feels tired all the time, and has started refusing to go to school. She cries easily and thinks her peers are making fun of her because she is "ugly and stupid." Her mother recently found a note written by Kristin that said she wanted to jump in front of a car "to end my misery."

—Adapted from Weller & Weller (1991, p. 655)

Many children, like Kristin, are depressed. Depressed children may feel sad, blue, down in the dumps. They may show poor appetite, insomnia, lack of energy and inactivity,

Ocean Photography/Veer Images

Childhood depression can have many origins, including feelings of failure and helplessness, losses, self-blame for problems that are not of one's own making—and, possibly, genetic factors.

loss of self-esteem, difficulty concentrating, loss of interest in people and activities they usually enjoy, crying, feelings of hopelessness and helplessness, and thoughts of suicide (American Psychiatric Association, 2013).

But many children do not recognize depression in themselves until the age of seven or so. When children cannot report their feelings, depression is inferred from behavior, such as withdrawal from social activity. In some cases, childhood depression is "masked" by conduct disorders, physical complaints, academic problems, and anxiety.

It has been estimated that between 5% and 9% of children are seriously depressed in any given year. Childhood depression occurs equally often in girls and boys.

ORIGINS OF DEPRESSION The origins of depression are complex and varied. Psychological and biological explanations have been proposed.

Some social cognitive theorists explain depression in terms of relationships between competencies (knowledge and skills) and feelings of self-esteem. Children who gain academic, social, and other competencies usually have high self-esteem. Perceived low levels of competence are linked to helplessness, low self-esteem, and depression. Longitudinal studies have found that problems in academics, socializing, physical appearance, and sports can predict feelings of depression (Peterson, 2013). Some competent children might not credit themselves because of excessive parental expectations. Or children may be perfectionistic themselves. Perfectionistic children may be depressed because they cannot meet their own standards.

A tendency to blame oneself (an internal attribution) or others (an external attribution) is called a child's **attributional style**. Certain attributional styles can contribute to helplessness and hopelessness and hence to depression (Cohen et al., 2011). Research shows that children who are depressed are more likely to attribute the causes of their failures to internal, stable, and global factors, factors they are relatively helpless to change (Cohen et al., 2011; Schleider et al., 2014). Helplessness triggers depression. Consider the case of two children who do poorly on a math test. John thinks, "I'm a jerk! I'm just no good in math! I'll never learn." Jim thinks, "That test was tougher than I thought it would be. I'll have to work harder next time." John is perceiving the problem as global (he's "a jerk") and stable (he'll "never learn"). Jim perceives the problem as specific rather than global (related to the type of math test the teacher makes up) and as unstable rather than stable (he can change the results by working harder). In effect, John thinks, "It's me" (an internal attribution). By contrast, Jim thinks, "It's the test" (an external attribution).

TRUTH

(T) F Some children blame themselves for all the problems in their lives, whether they deserve the blame or not.

It is true that some children blame themselves for all the problems in their lives, whether they deserve the blame or not. (So do some adults!) Children who are depressed are more likely to attribute the causes of their failures to factors that they are helpless to change.

There is also evidence of genetic factors in depression (Kendler et al., 2011). A Norwegian study of 2,794 twins estimated that the heritability of depression in females was 49% and 25% in males (Orstavik et al., 2007). On a neurological level, evidence suggests that depressed children (and adults) "underutilize" the neurotransmitter **serotonin** (Rice, 2014; Hankin, 2015).

TREATMENT OF DEPRESSION Parents and teachers can do a good deal to alleviate relatively mild feelings of depression among children—involve them in enjoyable activities, encourage them to develop skills, praise them when appropriate, and point out when they are being too hard on themselves. But if feelings of depression persist, treatment is called for.

Psychotherapy for depression tends to be cognitive-behavioral today. Children (and adolescents) are encouraged to do enjoyable things and build social skills. They are made aware of their tendencies to minimize their accomplishments, exaggerate their problems, and overly blame themselves for shortcomings.

Because depressed children may underutilize serotonin, drugs that increase the action of serotonin in the brain (selective serotonin reuptake inhibitors, or SSRIs, such as Luvox, Prozac, and Zoloft) are sometimes used to treat childhood depression. Although SSRIs are often effective, the Food and Drug Administration has warned that there may be a link between their use and suicidal thinking in children (Gupta et al., 2015).

attributional style the way in which one is disposed toward interpreting outcomes (successes or failures), as in tending to place blame or responsibility on oneself or on external factors.

serotonin a neurotransmitter that is involved in mood disorders such as depression.

10-5c CHILDHOOD ANXIETY

Children show many kinds of anxiety disorders, and they are accompanied by depression in 50% to 60% of children (Cummings et al., 2014; Rice, 2014). Yet many children show anxiety disorders, such as **generalized anxiety disorder (GAD)**, in the absence of depression (Vallance & Garralda, 2011). Other anxiety disorders shown by children include **phobias**, such as **separation anxiety disorder (SAD)**, and stage fright.

Jake Wyman/Photolibrary/Getty Images

SEPARATION ANXIETY DISORDER It is normal for children to show anxiety when they are separated from their caregivers. Separation anxiety is normal and begins during the first year. But the sense of security that is usually provided by bonds of attachment encourages children to explore their environment and become progressively independent.

Separation anxiety disorder affects an estimated 4% to 5% of children and young adolescents (American Psychiatric Association, 2013). It occurs more often in girls and is often associated with school refusal (Vallance & Garralda, 2011). The disorder may persist into adulthood, leading to an exaggerated concern about the wellbeing of one's children and spouse and difficulty tolerating separation from them.

SAD is diagnosed when separation anxiety is persistent and excessive, when it is inappropriate for the child's developmental level, and when it interferes with activities or development tasks, such as attending school. Six-year-olds ought to be able to enter first grade without nausea and vomiting and without dread that they or their parents will come to harm. Children with SAD tend to cling to their parents and follow them around the house. They may voice concerns about death and dying and insist that someone stay with them at bedtime. They may complain of nightmares and have stomachaches on school days. They may throw tantrums or plead with their parents not to leave the house.

SAD may occur before middle childhood, preventing adjustment to day care or nursery school. SAD usually becomes a significant problem in middle childhood because that is when children are expected to adjust to school.

SEPARATION ANXIETY DISORDER, SCHOOL PHOBIA, AND SCHOOL REFUSAL SAD is an extreme form of separation anxiety. It is characterized by anxiety about separating from parents and may be expressed as **school phobia**—fear of school—or of refusal to go to school (which can be based on fear or other factors). Separation anxiety is not behind all instances of school refusal. Some children refuse school because they perceive it as unpleasant, unsatisfying, or hostile, and it may be—as in the case of bullying. Some children are concerned about doing poorly in school or being asked questions in class (in which case, they may have stage fright). High parental expectations may heighten concern, as may problems with classmates.

TREATMENT OF SCHOOL PHOBIA OR SCHOOL REFUSAL Except for extreme cases, such as the threatening and taunting of severe bullying, it is usually not better for children with school phobia to remain at home. In cases of bullying and other forms of harsh treatment, the parents should work with the school to resolve the issue

generalized anxiety disorder (GAD) an anxiety disorder in which anxiety appears to be present continuously and is unrelated to the situation.

phobia an irrational, excessive fear that interferes with one's functioning.

separation anxiety disorder (SAD) an extreme form of otherwise normal separation anxiety that is characterized by anxiety about separating from parents; SAD often takes the form of refusal to go to school.

school phobia fear of attending school, marked by extreme anxiety at leaving parents.

Alison—A Case of Separation Anxiety Disorder

SAD frequently develops after a stressful life event, such as illness, the death of a relative or pet, or a change of schools or homes. Alison's problems followed the death of her grandmother:

Alison's grandmother died when Alison was seven years old. Her parents decided to permit her request to view her grandmother in the open coffin. Alison took a tentative glance from her father's arms across the room, then asked to be taken out of the room. Her five-year-old sister took a leisurely close-up look, with no apparent distress.

Alison had been concerned about death for two or three years by this time, but her grandmother's passing brought on a new flurry of questions: "Will I die?" "Does everybody die?" and so on. Her parents tried to reassure her by saying, "Grandma was very, very old, and she also had a heart condition. You are very young and in perfect health. You have many, many years before you have to start thinking about death."

Alison also could not be alone in any room in her house. She pulled one of her parents or her sister along with her everywhere she went. She also reported nightmares about her grandmother and, within a couple of days, insisted on sleeping in the same room with her parents. Fortunately, Alison's fears did not extend to school. Her teacher reported that Alison spent some time talking about her grandmother, but her academic performance was apparently unimpaired.

Alison's parents decided to allow Alison time to "get over" the loss. Alison gradually talked less and less about death, and by the time three months had passed, she was able to go into any room in her house by herself. She wanted to continue to sleep in her parents' bedroom, however. So her parents "made a deal" with her. They would put off the return to her own bedroom until the school year had ended (a month away), if Alison would agree to return to her own bed at that time. As a further incentive, a parent would remain with her until she fell asleep for the first month. Alison overcame the anxiety problem in this fashion with no additional delays.

Author's files

before the child returns. But if there is no actual threat to the child, most professionals agree that the first rule in the treatment of most cases of school phobia is: Get the child back into school. The second rule is: Get the child back into school. And the third rule . . . you get the idea. The disorder often disappears once the child is back in school on a regular basis.

FICTION

T (F) It is better for children with school phobia to remain at home until the origins of the problem are uncovered and resolved.

When a child is in danger at school, as in being threatened by bullies, it may be better to keep the child at home until the problem is resolved. But in most cases it is better to get the child back in school.

There is nothing wrong with trying to understand why a child refuses to attend school. Knowledge of the reasons for refusal can help parents and educators devise strategies for assisting the child. But perhaps such understanding—again with certain exceptions—need not always precede insistence that the child return to school.

Antidepressant medication has been used with school phobia with some success (Mohatt et al., 2013; Warnke, 2014). However, drugs do not teach children how to cope. Many psychologists and educators suggest that drugs are best used only when psychological treatments, such as challenging irrational ideas as to why the child should be remaining out of school, have proven to be ineffective (Maric et al., 2013; Walter et al., 2014).

It seems unfortunate to depart middle childhood following a discussion of social and emotional problems. Most children in developed nations come through middle childhood quite well, in good shape for the challenges and dramas of adolescence.

Getting a Phobic Child Back into School

There is nothing wrong with trying to understand why a child refuses to attend school. Knowledge of the reasons for refusal can help parents and educators devise strategies for helping the child adjust. But should such understanding precede insistence that the child return to school? Again, depending on the apparent causes of school refusal, insisting on an early return to school might be the best course of action. Here are some things parents can do to get a child back into school:

- **Do not give in to the child's demands to stay home. If the child complains of being tired or ill, tell the child that he or she may feel better at school and can rest there if necessary.**
- **Discuss the problem with the child's teacher, principal, and school nurse. (Gain the cooperation of school professionals.)**
- **If there is a specific school-related problem, such as an overly strict teacher, help the child find ways to handle the situation. (Finding ways to handle such problems can be accomplished while the child is in school. Not all such problems need to be ironed out before the child returns to school.)**
- **Reward the child for attending school. (Yes, parents shouldn't "have to" reward children for "normal" behavior, but do you want the child in school or not?)**

What if these measures don't work? Can professionals help? A variety of therapeutic approaches have been tried, and it appears that cognitive-behavioral approaches are the most effective (Chu et al., 2014; James et al., 2015). One cognitive-behavioral method involves gradually requiring the child to spend more and more time in school to reduce his or her fear step by step. In this gradual method, the child may also attend some after-school activities with friends or work individually with teachers for a while. In systematic desensitization, the child might be shown photos or videos of the school while remaining in supportive surroundings. In cognitive restructuring, the child might be encouraged to talk about why school is "awful," and parents or therapists can counter the child's arguments in constructive ways. In the technique of "flooding," which needs to be handled very carefully, the child is simply thrust back into the school and presumably learns, as terrible things do not happen, that the school is not as awful as anticipated. But keep in mind that other students are likely to notice and react to a child who has been absent for a while and is now trembling at his or her desk.

Antidepressant medication has been used—often in conjunction with cognitive-behavioral methods—with a good deal of success (Mohatt et al., 2013; Warnke, 2014). Antidepressants can have side effects, however, such as abdominal discomfort. Moreover, some health professionals fear that antidepressants can trigger suicidal thoughts in children. However, drugs in themselves do not teach children how to cope with situations. Many health professionals suggest that the drugs—in this case, antidepressants—are best used only when psychological treatments, such as challenging irrational ideas as to why the child should remain out of school, have proven to be ineffective (Maric et al., 2013; Walter et al., 2014).

Cultura RM / Alamy Stock Photo

STUDY TOOLS 10

READY TO STUDY?

In the book, you can:

- ☐ Rip out the chapter review card at the back of the book for a handy summary of the chapter and key terms.
- ☐ Check your understanding of what you've read with the quizzes that follow.

ONLINE AT CENGAGEBRAIN.COM YOU CAN:

- ☐ Collect StudyBits while you read and study the chapter.
- ☐ Quiz yourself on key concepts.
- ☐ Find videos for further exploration.
- ☐ Prepare for tests with HDEV5 Flash Cards as well as those you create

SELF-ASSESSMENTS

Fill-Ins

Answers can be found in the back of the book.

1. According to psychoanalytic theory, children in middle childhood are in the ____________ stage of psychosexual development.
2. Erik Erikson labeled the life crisis of middle childhood as ____________ versus inferiority.
3. Selman described five levels of ____________-taking in childhood.
4. During middle childhood, control is gradually transferred from parent to child in a process known as ____________.
5. Selective serotonin reuptake inhibitors are most likely to be prescribed for childhood ____________.
6. Teachers who expect more from students often get more. This is an example of a(n) ____________ prophecy.
7. Children with ____________ disorders persistently break rules or violate the rights of others.
8. Children who are depressed are more likely than other children to attribute their failures and shortcomings to internal, stable, and ____________ factors.
9. In middle childhood, mothers' interactions with children continue to revolve around ____________, whereas fathers' interactions are relatively more involved in recreational activities.
10. In their self-concepts, children in middle childhood are more likely to focus on ____________ traits than are children in early childhood.

Multiple Choice

1. What happens to children's self-esteem in middle childhood?

a. It rises.
b. It declines.
c. It remains the same.
d. It rises, then declines.

2. What kind of parenting contributes to high self-esteem in a child?

a. authoritarian
b. authoritative
c. rejecting–neglecting
d. permissive

3. How do 10- to 12-year-olds evaluate their parents in middle childhood as compared to how they evaluated them in early childhood?

a. The same
b. Less harshly
c. More harshly
d. There is no evidence on this matter.

4. What is the likelihood that the children of lesbian or gay parents will have a lesbian or gay sexual orientation?

a. About 50-50 (half)
b. Somewhat more than children raised by heterosexual parents
c. About the same as children raised by heterosexual parents
d. Less than that of children raised by heterosexual parents

5. According to the text, the research about whether parents in conflict should remain together for the sake of the children shows that

a. they should stay together if their religion forbids divorce.
b. even fighting parents provide a better environment for children than do single parents or stepfamilies.
c. they should get a divorce.
d. it depends on how the parents behave in front of and toward their children.

6. According to evolutionary theory, stepparents may be less devoted to rearing stepchildren because

a. they do not have enough resources.
b. they have not had the experience of how to get along with stepchildren for the same amount of time as with their own children.
c. the stepchildren do not care for them as much as they care for their biological parents.
d. people often behave as if they want their own genes to flourish in the next generation.

7. All of the following are helpful ideas about talking to children about a divorce *except*

a. reassuring the children that you both love them and will always be their parents.
b. waiting until the last minute.
c. admitting that the divorce will be sad and upsetting for everyone.
d. telling the children that the divorce is not their fault.

8. Does maternal employment increase the likelihood that children will become delinquent?

a. No
b. Yes—almost always
c. Yes, but only if maternal employment is connected with lack of supervision
d. Yes, for girls but not for boys

9. Between the ages of 7 and 12, children see friends as

a. doing things for one another, with a focus on self-interest.
b. doing what they want.
c. providing mutual support over a long period of time.
d. changing as people change and develop new goals for friendships.

10. Which of the following is accurate about bullies?

a. They are less likely than other children to have attention deficit hyperactivity disorder.
b. They are likely to come from homes with higher socioeconomic status.
c. Their school achievement is the same as other children's.
d. They are more likely to have conduct disorders.

HDEV
ONLINE

REVIEW FLASHCARDS ANYTIME, ANYWHERE!

Create Flashcards from Your StudyBits

Review Key Term Flashcards Already Loaded on the StudyBoard

Access HDEV ONLINE at www.cengagebrain.com

11 Adolescence: Physical and Cognitive Development

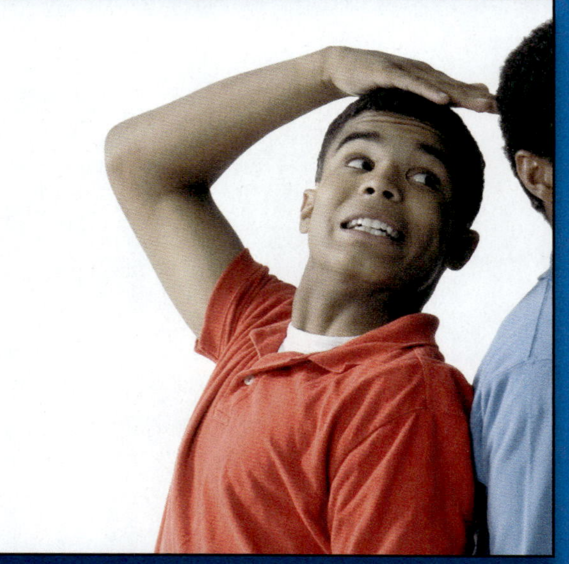

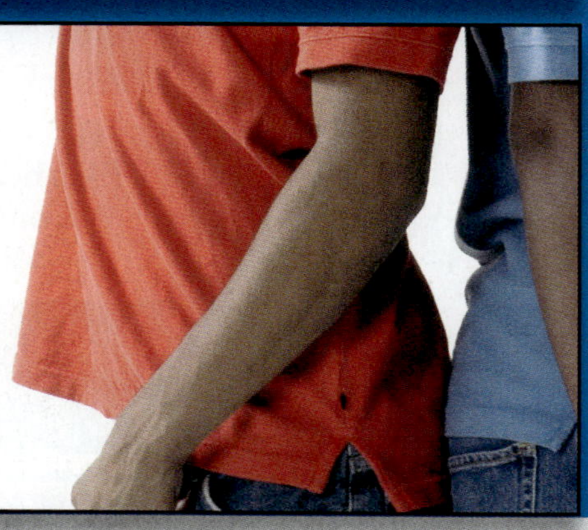

rubberball/Getty Images

LEARNING OUTCOMES

After studying this chapter, you will be able to . . .

11-1 Describe the key events of puberty and their relationship to social development

11-2 Discuss health issues in adolescence, focusing on the causes of death, on eating disorders, and on substance use

11-3 Discuss adolescent cognitive development and the key events of Piaget's stage of formal operations

11-4 Describe gender differences in cognitive abilities

11-5 Discuss Kohlberg's theory of moral development in adolescence

11-6 Discuss the roles of the school in adolescence, focusing on dropping out

11-7 Discuss work experience during adolescence

After you finish this chapter, go to **PAGE 236** for **STUDY TOOLS**

Perhaps no other period of life is as exciting—and bewildering—as adolescence, bounded at the lower end by the ages of 11 or 12 and at the upper end by the ages of 18 or 19. Except for infancy, more changes occur during adolescence than any other time of life. In our society, adolescents are "neither fish nor fowl," as the saying goes, neither children nor adults. Adolescents may be old enough to reproduce and be as large as their parents, yet they may not be allowed to get drivers' licenses until they are 16 or 17, and they cannot attend R-rated films unless accompanied by an adult. Given the restrictions placed on them, their growing yearning for independence, and a sex drive heightened by high levels of sex hormones, it is not surprising that adolescents are occasionally in conflict with their parents.

> The reasonably stable patterns of growth and development that occurred in early and middle adulthood end abruptly in adolescence. What are the psychological effects of dramatic physical change?

The idea that adolescence is an important and separate developmental stage was proposed by G. Stanley Hall (1904). Hall believed that adolescence is marked by turmoil and used the German phrase *Sturm und Drang* ("storm and stress") to refer to the conflicts of adolescence. Contemporary theorists no longer see adolescent storm and stress as inevitable (Hollenstein & Lougheed, 2013; Smetana, 2011). Instead, they see adolescence as a period when biological changes drive certain kinds of behavior but are shaped by environmental influences and adolescents' ability to regulate their emotions and behavior (Hollenstein & Lougheed, 2013). In any case, adolescents need to adapt to biological changes and social expectations.

11-1 PUBERTY: THE BIOLOGICAL ERUPTION

Puberty is a stage of development characterized by reaching sexual maturity and the ability to reproduce. The onset of adolescence coincides with the advent of puberty. Puberty is controlled by a **feedback loop** involving the hypothalamus, pituitary gland, the gonads—the ovaries in females and the testes in males—and hormones. The hypothalamus signals the pituitary gland, which, in turn, releases hormones that control physical growth and the gonads. The gonads respond to pituitary hormones by increasing their production of sex hormones (androgens and estrogens). The sex hormones further stimulate the hypothalamus, perpetuating the feedback loop.

The sex hormones also trigger the development of primary and secondary sex characteristics. The **primary sex characteristics** are the structures that make reproduction possible. In girls, these are the ovaries, vagina, uterus, and fallopian tubes. In boys, they are the penis, testes, prostate gland, and seminal vesicles. The **secondary sex characteristics** are physical

puberty the biological stage of development characterized by changes that lead to reproductive capacity.

feedback loop a system in which glands regulate each other's functioning through a series of hormonal messages.

primary sex characteristics the structures that make reproduction possible.

secondary sex characteristics physical indicators of sexual maturation—such as changes to the voice and growth of bodily hair—that do not directly involve reproductive structures.

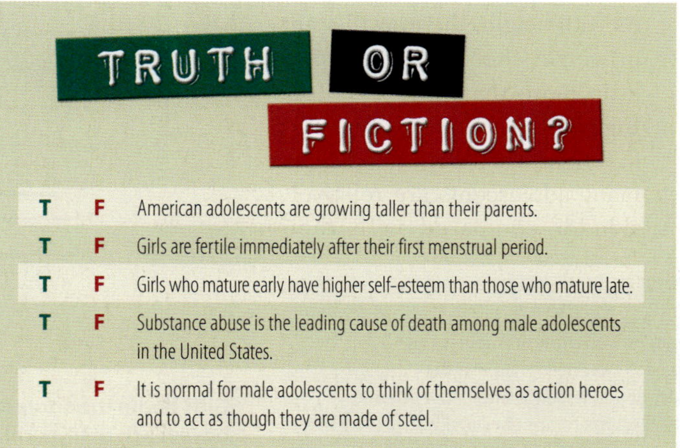

TRUTH OR FICTION?
T F American adolescents are growing taller than their parents.
T F Girls are fertile immediately after their first menstrual period.
T F Girls who mature early have higher self-esteem than those who mature late.
T F Substance abuse is the leading cause of death among male adolescents in the United States.
T F It is normal for male adolescents to think of themselves as action heroes and to act as though they are made of steel.

indicators of sexual maturation that are not directly involved in reproduction. They include breast development, deepening of the voice, and the appearance of facial, pubic, and underarm hair.

Is adolescence a period of *Sturm und Drang* (storm and stress)?

Indexstock Imagery/Ju

11-1a THE ADOLESCENT GROWTH SPURT

The stable growth patterns in height and weight that characterize early and middle childhood end abruptly with the adolescent growth spurt. Girls start to spurt in height sooner than boys, at an average age of a little more than ten. Boys start to spurt about two years later. Girls and boys reach their peak growth in height about two years after the growth spurt begins, at about 12 and 14 years, respectively (see Figure 11.1). The spurt in height for both girls and boys continues for about another two years at a gradually declining pace. Boys add nearly four inches per year during the fastest year of the spurt compared with slightly more than three inches per year for girls. Overall, boys add an average of 14½ inches during the spurt and girls add a little more than 13 inches (Hills & Byrne, 2011; Tanner et al., 1991a).

Adolescents begin to spurt in weight about half a year after they begin to spurt in height. The period of peak growth in weight occurs about a year and a half after the onset of the spurt. As with height, the growth spurt in weight then continues for a little more than two years (see Figure 11.2). Because the spurt in weight lags the spurt in height, many adolescents are relatively slender compared with their preadolescent stature. However, adolescents tend to eat enormous quantities of food to fuel their growth spurts. Active 14- and 15-year-old boys may consume 3,000 to 4,000 calories a day without becoming obese.

Girls' and boys' body shapes begin to differ in adolescence. Girls develop relatively broader hips compared with their shoulders, whereas the opposite is true for boys. A girl's body shape is more rounded than a boy's because girls gain almost twice as much fatty tissue as boys. Boys gain twice as much muscle tissue as girls.

ASYNCHRONOUS GROWTH Adolescents may be awkward and gawky due to **asynchronous growth**; different parts of the body grow at different rates. The hands and feet mature before the arms and legs do. As a consequence, adolescent girls and boys may complain of big hands or feet. Legs reach their peak growth before

asynchronous growth
unbalanced growth, such as the growth that occurs during the early part of adolescence and causes many adolescents to appear gawky.

FIG.11.1 SPURTS IN GROWTH

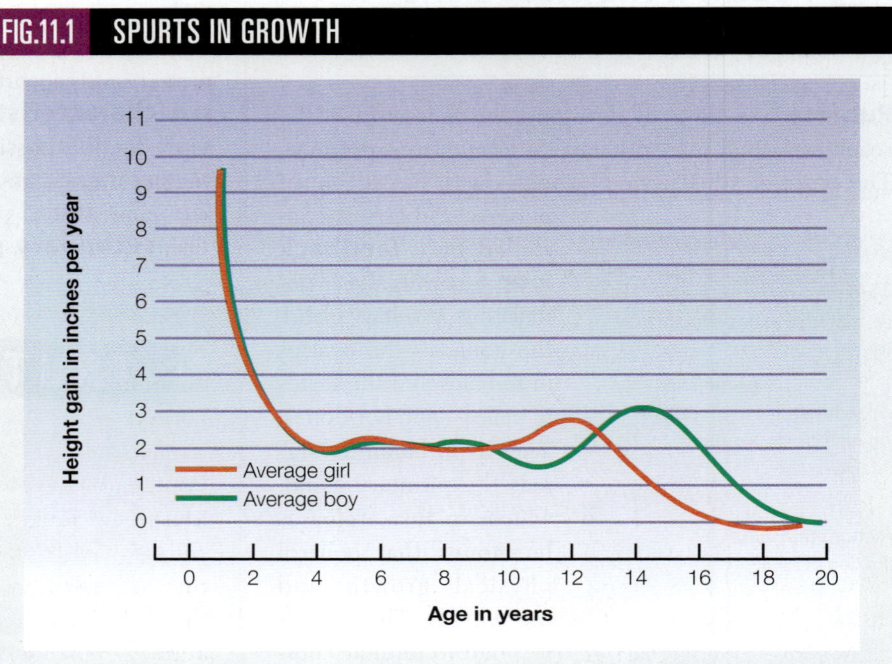

Girls begin the adolescent growth spurt about two years earlier than boys. Girls and boys reach their periods of peak growth about two years after the spurt begins.

FIG.11.2 GROWTH CURVES FOR WEIGHT AND HEIGHT

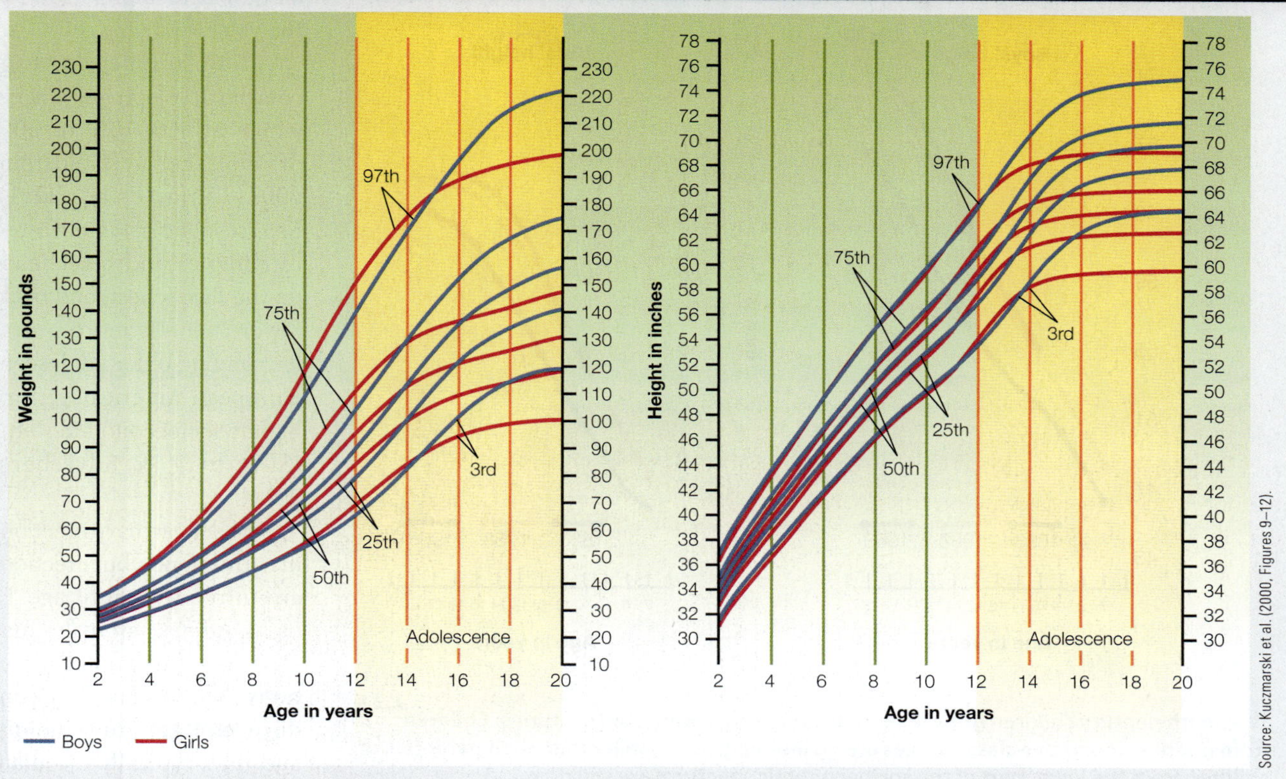

Girls are taller and heavier than boys from about age 9 or 10 until about age 13 because their growth spurt occurs earlier. Once boys begin their spurt, they catch up with girls and eventually become taller and heavier.

the shoulders and chest. Boys stop growing out of their pants about a year before they stop growing out of their jackets (Tanner, 1989).

THE SECULAR TREND During the 20th century, children in the Western world grew dramatically more rapidly and wound up taller than children from earlier times (Johnson et al., 2013; Ulijaszek, 2010). This historical trend toward increasing adult height was also accompanied by an earlier onset of puberty, and is known as the **secular trend**. Figure 11.3 shows that Swedish boys and girls grew more rapidly in 1938 and 1968 than they did in 1883 and ended up several inches taller. At the age of 15, boys were more than six inches taller and girls were more than three inches taller, on average, than their counterparts from the previous century (Tanner, 1989). The occurrence of a secular trend in height and weight has been documented in nearly all European countries and the United States.

However, children from middle- and upper-class families in developed nations, including the United States, no longer grow taller, whereas their poorer counterparts continue to gain in height from generation to generation. Although it is clear that heredity is the major contributor to adult height, nutrition and general health also play key roles (NCD-RisC, 2016).

FICTION

T (F) American adolescents are growing taller than their parents.

The statement that adolescents are growing taller than their parents is too general to be considered true. The average height for adults is greater than it was 100 years ago, but the upward trend seems to have stopped for middle- and upper-class children. It does seem to remain true for children of lower socioeconomic status.

secular trend a historical trend toward increasing adult height and earlier puberty.

FIG.11.3 ARE WE STILL GROWING TALLER THAN OUR PARENTS?

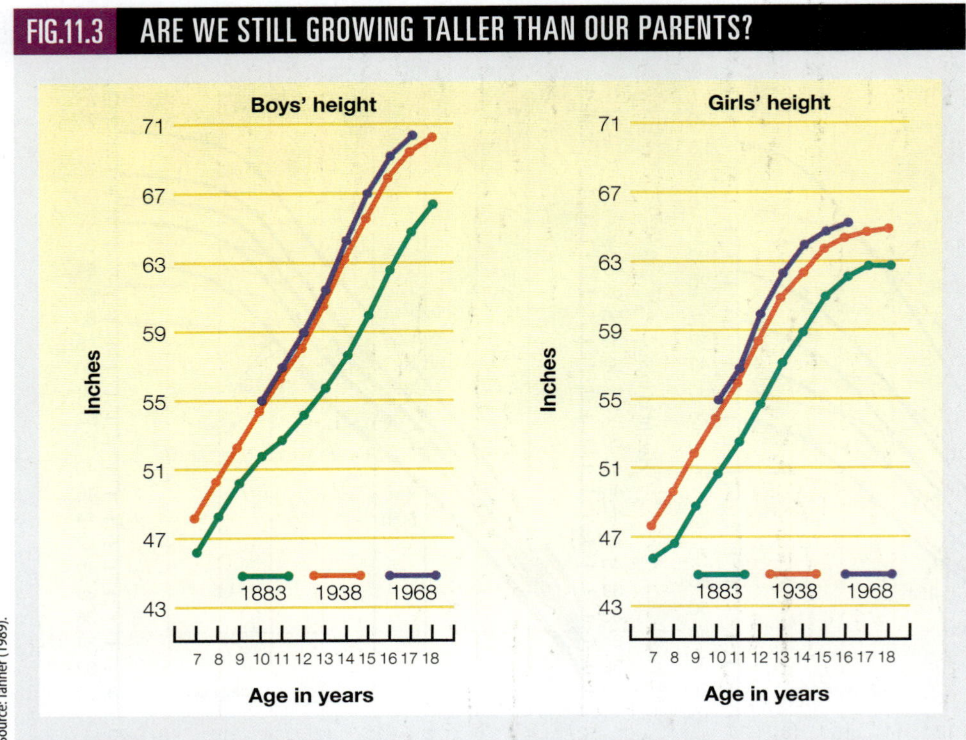

Twentieth-century children grew taller than children in preceding centuries. Children from middle- and upper-class families are no longer growing taller than their parents, but children from the lower part of the socioeconomic spectrum are still doing so.

11-1b CHANGES IN BOYS

At puberty, the pituitary gland stimulates the testes to increase their output of testosterone, leading to further development of the male genitals. The first visible sign of puberty is accelerated growth of the testes, which begins at an average age of about 11½ plus or minus 2 years. Testicular growth further accelerates testosterone production and other pubertal changes. The penis growth spurt begins about a year later, and still later, pubic hair develops.

Underarm and facial hair appears at about age 15. Only half of American boys shave (of necessity) by 17. At 14 or 15, the voice deepens because of growth of the "voice box," or larynx, and the lengthening of the vocal cords. The process is gradual, and adolescent boys sometimes encounter an embarrassing cracking of the voice.

Testosterone also triggers the development of acne, which afflicts 75% to 90% of adolescents (Goldstein, 2004; Taylor et al., 2011). Severe acne is manifested by pimples and blackheads on the face, chest, and back. Severe acne is more prevalent among older adolescent European American girls of higher socioeconomic status (Silverberg & Silverberg, 2014).

Males can have erections in early infancy, but erections are infrequent until age 13 or 14. Adolescent males may experience unwanted erections. The organs that produce **semen** grow rapidly, and boys typically ejaculate seminal fluid by age 13 or 14. About a year later they begin to have **nocturnal emissions**, also called "wet dreams" because of the false myth that emissions necessarily accompany erotic dreams. Mature sperm are found in ejaculatory emissions by about the age of 15.

Nearly half of all boys experience enlargement of the breasts, or **gynecomastia**, which usually declines in a year or two. Gynecomastia stems from the small amount of female sex hormones secreted by the testes.

At age 20 or 21, men stop growing taller because testosterone causes **epiphyseal closure**, which prevents the long bones from making further gains in length. Puberty for males draws to a close.

semen the fluid that contains sperm and substances that nourish and help transport sperm.

nocturnal emission emission of seminal fluid while asleep.

gynecomastia enlargement of breast tissue in males.

epiphyseal closure the process by which the cartilage that separates the long end of a bone from the main part of the bone turns to bone.

menarche the onset of menstruation.

11-1c CHANGES IN GIRLS

In girls, the pituitary gland signals the ovaries to boost estrogen production at puberty. Estrogen may stimulate the growth of breast tissue ("breast buds") as early as the age of eight or nine, but the breasts usually begin to enlarge during the tenth year. The development of fatty tissue and ducts elevates the areas of the breasts surrounding the nipples and causes the nipples to protrude. The breasts typically reach full size in about three years, but the *mammary glands* do not mature fully until a woman has a baby. Estrogen also promotes the growth of the fatty and supporting tissue in the hips and buttocks, which, along with the widening of the pelvis, causes the hips to round. Beginning at about age 11, girls develop pubic and underarm hair.

Estrogen causes the *labia*, vagina, and uterus to develop during puberty, and androgens cause the *clitoris* to develop. The vaginal lining varies in thickness according to the amount of estrogen in the bloodstream. Estrogen typically brakes the female growth spurt some years before testosterone brakes that of males.

FIG.11.4 THE DECLINE IN AGE AT MENARCHE

Age in years (12.0–16.0) by Year of menarche (1860–1980): Finland, Sweden, Norway, Italy (North), U.K. (South), U.S.A. (Middle class)

Source: Tanner (1989).

The age at menarche has been declining since the mid-1800s among girls in Western nations, apparently because of improved nutrition and health care.

MENARCHE The current mean age for **menarche** (first menstruation) in the United States is the thirteenth year (with, for example, 12.8 years the average for European Americans and 12.2 years the average for African Americans) (Cabrera et al., 2014). During the past 150 years, menarche has occurred at progressively earlier ages in Western nations, another example of the secular trend (see Figure 11.4).

What accounts for the earlier age of puberty? One hypothesis is that girls must reach a certain body weight to trigger pubertal changes such as menarche. Body fat could trigger the changes because fat cells secrete a protein that signals the brain to secrete hormones that raise estrogen levels. Menarche comes later to girls who have a lower percentage of body fat, such as those with eating disorders or athletes (Crocker et al., 2014; Terasawa et al., 2012). The average body weight for triggering menarche depends on the girl's height (Novotny et al., 2011). Today's girls are larger than those of the early 20th century because of improved nutrition and health care.

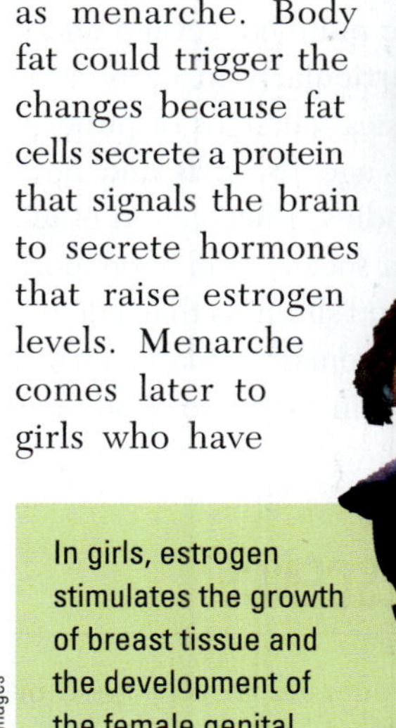

In girls, estrogen stimulates the growth of breast tissue and the development of the female genital organs.

Purestock/Jupiterimages

REGULATION OF THE MENSTRUAL CYCLE Testosterone levels remain fairly stable in boys throughout adulthood, but estrogen and progesterone levels in girls vary markedly and regulate the menstrual cycle. Following menstruation—the sloughing off of the endometrium—estrogen levels increase, leading once more to the growth of endometrial tissue. Girls usually begin to ovulate 12 to 18 months after menarche. After the ovum is released, if it is not fertilized, estrogen and progesterone levels drop suddenly, triggering menstruation once again.

The average menstrual cycle is 28 days, but variations are common. Girls' cycles are often irregular for a few years after menarche but later become more regular. Most cycles during the first 12 to 18 months after menarche occur without ovulation.

FICTION

T (F) Girls are fertile immediately after their first menstrual period.

It is not true that girls are fertile immediately after their first menstrual period. Girls usually begin to ovulate 12 to 18 months after menarche.

11-1d EARLY VERSUS LATE MATURERS

Early-maturing boys tend to be more popular than their late-maturing peers and more likely to be leaders in school (Teunissen et al., 2011). They are more poised, relaxed, and good-natured. Their edge in sports and the admiration of their peers heighten their sense of worth. On the negative side, early maturation is associated with greater risks of aggression and delinquency (Dimler & Natsuaki, 2015) and abuse of alcohol and other drugs (Modecki et al., 2014). Coaches may expect too much of them in sports, and peers may want them to fight their battles. Sexual opportunities may create demands before they know how to respond (James et al., 2012).

Late maturers have the "advantage" of not being rushed into maturity. On the other hand, late-maturing boys often feel dominated by early-maturing boys. They have been found to be more dependent and insecure and may be more likely to get involved in substance abuse (Vroman, 2010).

Although boys who mature early usually have higher self-esteem than those who mature late, the research evidence is somewhat mixed for girls. Early-maturing girls may be popular in that boys like them and they "have" what late-maturing girls would like to develop. However, they may feel awkward, because they are among the first of their peers to begin the physical changes of puberty (Teunissen et al., 2011). They become conspicuous with their height and their developing breasts. Tall girls of dating age frequently find that shorter boys are reluctant to approach them or be seen with them. All in all, early-maturing girls are at greater risk for psychological problems and substance abuse than girls who mature later on (Graber, 2013; Mrug et al., 2014). Many girls who mature early obtain lower grades in school and initiate sexual activity earlier (Mrug et al., 2014). For reasons such as these, the parents of early-maturing girls may increase their vigilance and restrictiveness, leading to new child–parent conflicts.

FICTION

T (F) Girls who mature early have higher self-esteem than those who mature late.

It is true that boys who mature early often have higher self-esteem than boys who mature late, but it seems to work in the opposite way for girls. That is, late-maturing girls appear to have higher self-esteem than early-maturing girls.

BODY IMAGE Adolescents are quite concerned about their physical appearance, particularly in early adolescence during the rapid physical changes of puberty (Bucchianeri et al., 2013). By age 18, girls and boys are more satisfied with their bodies (Bucchianeri et al., 2013). Adolescent females in our society tend to be more preoccupied with body weight and slimness than adolescent males (Tiggeman, 2014; Tiggeman, & Slater, 2013). Many adolescent males want to gain weight to build their muscle mass (Field et al., 2014).

11-2 HEALTH IN ADOLESCENCE

Around five of six U.S. adolescents are in very good or excellent health (Adolescent Health, 2014). Few are chronically ill or miss school. Injuries tend to heal quickly. Only 1% to 2% are in fair or poor health (Adolescent Health, 2014).

11-2a CAUSES OF DEATH

Death rates are low in adolescence, but they are nearly twice as great for male adolescents as female adolescents. A major reason for this discrepancy is that males take more risks that end in death as a result of accidents, homicide, or suicide (see Figure 11.5). These three causes of death account for most adolescent deaths (Heron, 2016). Nearly 80% of adolescent deaths are due to injuries, and motor vehicle and firearm injuries account for more than half of them. Firearms account for 80% of homicides and nearly 50% of suicides.

FICTION

T (F) Substance abuse is the leading cause of death among male adolescents in the United States.

It is not true that substance abuse is the leading cause of death among male adolescents in the United States. Accidents, homicide, and suicide all account for larger numbers of deaths.

11-2b NUTRITION

Physical growth occurs more rapidly in the adolescent years than at any other time after birth, with the exception of the first year of infancy. To fuel the adolescent growth spurt, the average girl needs 1,800 to 2,400 calories per day, and the average boy needs 2,200 to 3,200 calories (Nutrition Facts, 2013). The nutritional needs of adolescents vary according to their activity level and stage of pubertal development. At the peak of the growth spurt, adolescents use twice as much calcium, iron, zinc, magnesium, and nitrogen as during other years of adolescence (Nutrition Facts, 2013). Calcium intake is particularly important for females to build bone density and help prevent **osteoporosis** later in life, but most teenagers do not consume enough calcium. Adolescents are also likely to obtain less vitamin A, thiamine, and iron but more fat, sugar, and sodium than recommended (Nutrition Facts, 2013).

One reason for adolescents' nutritional deficits is irregular eating patterns. Breakfast is often skipped, especially by dieters (Wennberg et al., 2014). Teenagers may rely on fast food and junk food, which is high in fat and calories. Junk food is connected with being overweight, and being overweight in adolescence can lead to chronic illness and premature death in adulthood (Wennberg et al., 2014).

11-2c EATING DISORDERS

The American ideal has slimmed down to where most American females of normal weight are dissatisfied with the size and shape of their bodies (Tiggeman, 2014; Prendergast et al., 2015). In the section on

osteoporosis a condition involving progressive loss of bone tissue.

FIG.11.5 LEADING CAUSES OF DEATH AMONG 15- TO 19-YEAR-OLDS IN THE UNITED STATES

MALES:	FEMALE:
Accidents	Accidents
Suicide	Suicide
Homicide	Cancer
Cancer	Homicide
Heart disease	Heart disease
Congenital health problems	Congenital health problems
Influenza and pneumonia	Problems related to pregnancy and childbirth
Chronic respiratory diseases	Influenza and pneumonia
Diabetes	Stroke
Stroke	Chronic respiratory diseases

Golden Pixels LLC/Alamy Stock Photo

Sources: Minino, Xu, & Kochanek (2010); National Center for Health Statistics, Health (2009), United States, 2008 with Chartbook, Hyattsville, MD, Table 31.

The great majority of U.S. 15- to 19-year-olds are in good or excellent health, which is why the leading causes of death for this age group are accidents and suicide.

cognitive development, we will see that adolescents also tend to think that others are paying a great deal of attention to their appearance. Because of cultural emphasis on slimness and the psychology of the adolescent, they are highly vulnerable to eating disorders, which are characterized by gross disturbances in patterns of eating.

James Worrell/Photodisc/Getty Images

ANOREXIA NERVOSA **Anorexia nervosa** is a life-threatening eating disorder characterized by extreme fear of being heavy, dramatic weight loss, a distorted body image, and resistance to eating enough to maintain a healthful weight. Anorexia nervosa afflicts males as well as females, but most studies put the female-to-male ratio at ten to one or greater (Stice et al., 2013a). By and large, anorexia nervosa afflicts females during adolescence and young adulthood (Stice et al., 2013a). The typical person with anorexia is a young European American female of higher socioeconomic status (Striegel-Moore et al., 2003). Affluent females are more likely to read the magazines that idealize slender bodies and shop in the boutiques that cater to females with svelte figures (Tiggeman, 2014). Female athletes are also at risk. The *female athlete triad* describes women who have low availability of energy (as from eating poorly), menstrual problems, and lessened bone density, which usually afflicts people in late adulthood (House et al., 2013; Mountjoy & Goolsby, 2015).

Females with anorexia nervosa can drop 25% or more of their weight within a year. Severe weight loss triggers abnormalities in the endocrine system (i.e., with hormones) that prevent ovulation (Mehler & Brown, 2015). General health declines. Problems arise in the respiratory system and the cardiovascular system (Mehler & Brown, 2015). The mortality rate for anorexic females is about 4% to 5%.

Girls often develop anorexia nervosa to lose weight after gains from menarche (Shroff et al., 2006). Dieting and exercise continue well after the weight has been lost, and even after others say things are going too far. Denial is a major factor of anorexia nervosa. Distortion of the body image is also a major feature of the disorder (Harrison, 2013).

BULIMIA NERVOSA **Bulimia nervosa** is characterized by recurrent cycles of binge eating and purging. Binge eating often follows on the heels of dieting (Martire et al., 2015). There are various methods of purging. Vomiting is common. Other avenues include strict dieting or fasting, laxatives, and demanding exercise regimes. Individuals with eating disorders will not settle for less than their idealized body shape and weight (Chang et al., 2013; Wade et al., 2015). Bulimia, like anorexia, is connected with irregular menstrual cycles (Mendelsohn & Warren, 2010) and tends to afflict females during adolescence and young adulthood (Bravender et al., 2010). Eating disorders are upsetting and dangerous in themselves, but are also connected with depression (Erikson et al., 2014; Stice et al., 2013b).

PERSPECTIVES ON EATING DISORDERS Psychoanalytic theory suggests that anorexia nervosa may help young women cope with sexual fears, especially fear of pregnancy. Their breasts and hips flatten, and perhaps, in adolescents' fantasies, they remain asexual children. Anorexia prevents some adolescents from separating from their families and assuming adult responsibilities.

anorexia nervosa an eating disorder characterized by irrational fear of weight gain, distorted body image, and severe weight loss.

bulimia nervosa an eating disorder characterized by cycles of binge eating and purging as a means of controlling weight gain.

Do these catwalk models have the ideal figure of the 2010's? Unfortunately, too many teenage U.S. girls attempt to emulate them.

Bulimia Nervosa: The Case of Nicole

Nicole awakens in her cold dark room and already wishes it was time to go back to bed. She dreads the thought of going through this day, which will be like so many others in her recent past. She asks herself the question every morning, "Will I be able to make it through the day without being totally obsessed by thoughts of food, or will I blow it again and spend the day [binge eating]?" She tells herself that today she will begin a new life, today she will start to live like a normal human being. However, she is not at all convinced that the choice is hers.

—Boskind-White & White (1983, p. 29)

David J. Green - Lifestyle / Alamy Stock Photo

A particularly disturbing risk factor for eating disorders in adolescent females is a history of child abuse, particularly sexual abuse, although the numbers of eating disorders that are reported as attributable to abuse and neglect are variable (Dworkin et al., 2014; Mitchell & Bulik, 2013). Certainly young women have a very slender social ideal set before them in women such as runway models. As the cultural ideal slenderizes, women with normal body weight, according to health charts, feel fat, and heavy women feel huge (Harrison, 2013; Tiggeman, 2014). Eating disorders tend to run in families, which raises the possibility of genetic involvement. Genetic factors would not directly cause eating disorders, but might involve obsessionistic and perfectionistic personality traits (Dodge & Simic, 2015; Halmi et al., 2014).

11-2d SUBSTANCE USE AND SUBSTANCE USE DISORDERS

The United States is flooded with drugs that can distort your perceptions and change your mood—drugs that can pull you up, let you down, and move you across town. Some of these drugs are legal, others illegal. Some are used recreationally, others medically. Some are safe if used correctly and dangerous if they are not. Some adolescents use drugs because their friends do or because their parents tell them not to. Some are seeking pleasure; others are seeking escape.

Adolescents often become involved with drugs that impair their ability to learn at school and are connected with reckless behavior (Pani et al., 2010). Alcohol is the most popular drug on high school (and college) campuses (see Table 11.1; Johnston et al., 2016). Nearly half of high school 12th graders have smoked marijuana (Johnston et al., 2016). Two in five have tried cigarettes. Some use amphetamines or other stimulants, and of these, some use stimulants to help them focus on their studying. Cocaine was once a toy of the well-to-do, but price breaks have brought it into the lockers of high school students.

Alcohol and cigarettes are the most widely used substances by adolescents. Likelihood of use increases from 8th grade through 12th grade (see Table 11.1). Why? One reason is simply that 12th graders have had more years of opportunity to use drugs. But note that the researchers asked whether students had ever used the drug. Therefore, many yes answers reflect an incident or two of experimentation, and not regular use. Other drugs, like heroin, may be in the news, but

TABLE 11.1 HAVE YOU USED _____ IN YOUR _____?

Percent saying "Yes"

	Lifetime	Last year	Last 30 days
Alcohol	45.2	39.9	21.8
Amphetamines	9.1	6.2	2.7
Cigarettes	21.1	N/A	7.0
E-cigarettes	N/A	N/A	13.2
Cocaine	2.7	1.7	0.8
Ecstasy	3.5	2.2	0.8
Heroin	0.7	0.4	0.2
LSD	2.8	1.9	0.7
Marijuana	30.0	23.7	14.0

Source: Johnston, L. D., O'Malley, P. M., Miech, R. A., Bachman, J. G., & Schulenberg, J. E. (2016). Monitoring the Future national survey results on drug use, 1975–2015: Overview, key findings on adolescent drug use. Ann Arbor: Institute for Social Research, The University of Michigan.

Notes: Drug use increases from the 8th grade through the 12th grade. Use of e-cigarettes has surpassed use of tobacco cigarettes among adolescents. Finally, results reflect usage only among adolescents in school; dropouts are not included.

they have been used by only about 1% of high schoolers. Johnston and his colleagues (2016) note that parental and societal warnings may be getting through to adolescents because their substance use declined steadily over the past generation. Marijuana is one of the few drugs that has seen an increase in popularity.

Where does substance use end and a **substance use disorder** begin? Most psychologists use the *Diagnostic and Statistical Manual of Mental Disorders* of the American Psychiatric Association (5th edition, 2013) in defining substance use disorders. Substance use disorders may develop with repeated use of a substance, according to the manual, leading to changes in "brain circuitry" that are connected with impaired control over use of the substance, social problems, risky behavior (such as reckless driving or "unprotected" sex), and biological factors suggestive of addiction. Some substances can lead to physical addiction, so that when the dosage is lowered, withdrawal symptoms, also known as **abstinence syndrome**, occur. When addicted individuals lower their intake of alcohol, for example, they may experience symptoms such as tremors (shakes), high blood pressure, rapid heart and pulse rate, anxiety, restlessness, and weakness. Three of the most common types of abused substances are depressants, stimulants, and hallucinogens.

DEPRESSANTS Depressants slow the activity of the nervous system. Depressants include alcohol, narcotics derived from the opium poppy (such as heroin, morphine, and codeine), and sedatives (such as barbiturates and methaqualone).

Alcohol lessens inhibitions so that drinkers may do things when drinking that they might otherwise resist (Winograd & Sher, 2015). Alcohol is also an intoxicant: It distorts perceptions, impairs concentration, hinders coordination, and slurs the speech. Alcohol use is most prevalent among 21- to 34-year-olds. More than one million students between the ages of 18 and 24 are accidentally injured each year while under the influence, assaulted by other students who have been drinking, or raped by college men who have been drinking.

The major medical use of heroin, morphine, and other opioids is relief from pain. But they also can provide a euphoric "rush." Heroin is addictive, and regular users develop tolerance. *Barbiturates* are depressants with various legitimate medical uses, such as relief from pain, anxiety, and tension, but people can become rapidly dependent on them.

substance use disorder a persistent pattern of use of a substance characterized by frequent intoxication; impairment of physical, social, or emotional well-being; and possible physical addiction.

abstinence syndrome a characteristic cluster of symptoms that results from a sudden decrease in the level of usage of a substance.

Do You Have a Problem with Alcohol?

How can you tell whether you may have a drinking problem? Answering the following four questions can help you find out (NIAAA, 2005):

Yes	No	Have you ever felt you should cut down on your drinking?
Yes	No	Have people annoyed you by criticizing your drinking?
Yes	No	Have you ever felt bad or guilty about your drinking?
Yes	No	Have you ever had a drink first thing in the morning (as an "eye opener") to steady your nerves or get rid of a hangover?

Just one "yes" answer suggests a possible alcohol problem. Two or more yeses make it highly likely that a problem exists. In either case, it is advisable to discuss your answers with your doctor or another health care provider.

STIMULANTS Stimulants speed up the heartbeat and other bodily functions. Nicotine, cocaine, and amphetamines are the most common stimulants. Nicotine is the addictive chemical in tobacco (Brody, 2014). Nearly 450,000 Americans die from smoking-related problems each year (American Lung Association, 2014). Cigarette smoke contains carbon monoxide, which causes shortness of breath, and hydrocarbons ("tars"). Smoking is responsible for most respiratory diseases and lung cancer. E-cigarettes contain nicotine, but not the hydrocarbons (Brody, 2014).

Cocaine accelerates the heart rate, spikes the blood pressure, constricts the arteries of the heart, and thickens the blood, a combination that can cause cardiovascular and respiratory collapse (Liaudet et al., 2014). Overdoses can cause restlessness, insomnia, tremors, and even death. Amphetamines can keep users awake for long periods and reduce their appetites. Tolerance for amphetamines develops rapidly. The powerful amphetamine called methamphetamine is apparently physically addictive (Shoptaw, 2014). Methamphetamine abuse can cause brain damage, leading to problems in learning and memory.

HALLUCINOGENICS Hallucinogenics give rise to perceptual distortions called hallucinations, which sometimes can be so strong as to be confused with reality. Marijuana, Ecstasy, LSD, and PCP are hallucinogenic drugs. Marijuana, which is typically smoked, helps users relax, elevates their mood, increases sensory awareness, and can induce visual hallucinations, for example, time seeming to slow down. Marijuana carries health risks such as impairing the perceptual–motor coordination and short-term memory (Ratzan, 2014). Regular users may experience withdrawal, which is a sign of addiction (American Psychiatric Association, 2013).

Ecstasy, a popular "party" drug, provides the boost of a stimulant and mild hallucinogenic effects. The combination appears to free users from inhibitions and awareness of the consequences of risky behavior, such as unprotected sex. Ecstasy can also impair working memory, increase anxiety, and lead to depression (Lamers et al., 2006). LSD is the acronym for lysergic acid diethylamide, another hallucinogenic drug. High doses of hallucinogenics can impair coordination and judgment (driving while using hallucinogenic drugs poses grave risks), change the mood, and cause paranoid delusions.

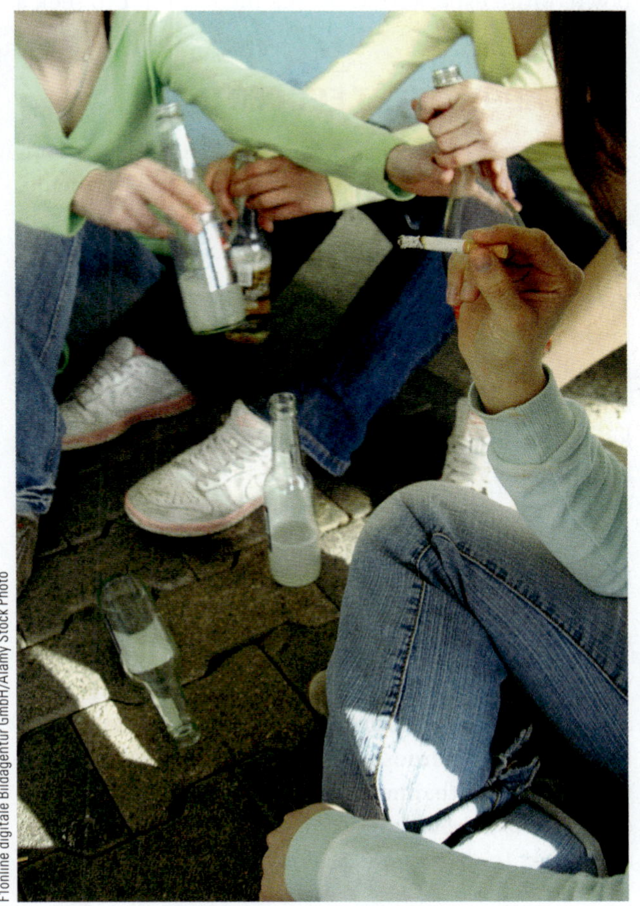
F1online digitale Bildagentur GmbH/Alamy Stock Photo

11-3 COGNITIVE DEVELOPMENT: PIAGET'S STAGE OF FORMAL OPERATIONS

I am a college student of extremely modest means. Some crazy psychologist interested in something called "formal operational thought" has just promised to pay me $20 if I can make a coherent logical argument for the proposition that the federal government should under no circumstances ever give or lend more to needy college students. Now what could people who believe that possibly say by way of supporting that argument? Well, I suppose they could offer this line of reasoning ...

—Flavell et al. (2002)

This "college student of extremely modest means" is thinking like an adolescent. Concrete-operational children are bound by the facts as they are, but the adolescent, as the adult, can ponder abstract ideas and see the world as it could be. Our college student recognizes that a person can find arguments for causes in which he or she does not believe.

The stage of **formal operations** is the top level in Jean Piaget's theory. Adolescents in this stage have reached cognitive maturity, even if rough edges remain. For many children in developed nations, the stage of formal operations can begin at about the time of puberty, 11 or 12 years old. But some reach this stage somewhat later, and some not at all. Piaget describes the accomplishments of the stage of formal operations in terms of the individual's increased ability to classify objects and ideas, engage in logical thought, and hypothesize, just as

iStockPhoto.com/mipan

In the formal-operational stage, adolescents are capable of sophisticated use of symbols, such as those found in geometry.

hallucinogenics drugs that give rise to hallucinations.

formal operations the fourth stage in Piaget's cognitive-developmental theory, characterized by the capacity for flexible, reversible operations concerning abstract ideas and concepts, such as symbols, statements, and theories.

researchers make hypotheses in their investigations. The adolescent can group and classify symbols, statements, and even theories. Adolescents can follow and formulate arguments from premise to conclusion and back once more, even if they do not believe in them. Hypothetical thinking, the use of symbols to represent other symbols, and deductive reasoning allow the adolescent to more fully comprehend the real world and to play with the world that dwells within the mind alone.

11-3a HYPOTHETICAL THINKING

In formal-operational thought, adolescents discover the concept of "what might be." Adolescents can project themselves into situations that transcend their immediate experience and become wrapped up in fantasies. Adolescents can think ahead, systematically trying out various possibilities in their minds. They "conduct research" to see whether their hypotheses about themselves and their friends and teachers are correct, for example, "trying on" different clothes and attitudes to see which work best for them.

In terms of career decisions, the wealth of possible directions leads some adolescents to experience anxiety about whether they will pick the career that is the best fit for them and to experience a sense of loss because they may be able to choose only one.

11-3b SOPHISTICATED USE OF SYMBOLS

Children in elementary school can understand what is meant by abstract symbols such as 1 and 2. They can also perform operations in which numbers are added, subtracted, and so on. But consider x, the primary algebraic symbol for variables. Children up to the age of 11 or 12 or so usually cannot fully understand the symbolic meaning of this concept, even if they can be taught the mechanics of solving for x in simple equations. But formal-operational children can grasp intuitively what is meant by x. Formal-operational children, or adolescents, can perform mental operations with symbols that stand for nothing in their own experience.

These symbols include those used in geometry. Adolescents work with points that have no dimensions, lines that have no width and are infinite in length, and circles that are perfectly round, even though such things are not found in nature. The ability to manipulate these symbols will permit them to work in theoretical physics or math or to obtain jobs in engineering or architecture.

Formal-operational individuals can understand, appreciate, and sometimes produce metaphors—figures of speech in which words or phrases that ordinarily signify one thing are applied to another. We find metaphors in literature, but consider how everyday figures of speech enhance our experience: *squeezing* out a living, *basking in the sunshine* of fame or glory, *hanging by a thread*, or *jumping* to conclusions.

Enhanced cognitive abilities can backfire when adolescents adamantly advance their religious, political, and social ideas without recognition of the subtleties and practical issues that might give pause to adults. For example, let's begin with the premise, "Industries should not be allowed to pollute the environment." If Industry A pollutes the environment, an adolescent may argue to shut down Industry A, at least until it stops polluting. The logic is reasonable and the goal is noble, but Industry A may be indispensable to the nation, or many thousands of people may be put out of work if it is shut down. More experienced people might prefer to seek a compromise.

11-3c ADOLESCENT EGOCENTRISM

Adolescents show a new egocentrism in which they comprehend the ideas of other people, but have difficulty sorting out those things that concern other people from the things that concern themselves.

THE IMAGINARY AUDIENCE Many adolescents fantasize about becoming rock stars or movie stars adored by millions. The concept of the **imaginary audience** achieves part of that fantasy, in a way. It places the adolescent on stage, but surrounded by critics more than by admirers. Adolescents assume that other people are concerned with their appearance and behavior, more so than they really are (Martin & Soko, 2011). The self-perception of adolescents as being on stage may account for their intense desire for privacy and their preoccupation with their appearance.

THE PERSONAL FABLE Spider-Man and Batman, stand aside! Because of the **personal fable**, many adolescents become action heroes, at least in their own minds. In the personal fable, one believes that one's thoughts and emotions are special and unique (Hill et al., 2011). It also refers to the common adolescent belief that one is invulnerable.

imaginary audience the belief that others around us are as concerned with our thoughts and behaviors as we are; one aspect of adolescent egocentrism.

personal fable the belief that our feelings and ideas are special and unique and that we are invulnerable; one aspect of adolescent egocentrism.

TRUTH

(T) F It is normal for male adolescents to think of themselves as action heroes and to act as though they are made of steel.

It is true that it is normal for male adolescents to think of themselves as action heroes and to act as though they are made of steel. These are examples of the "personal fable" at work. The fable in males is grounded in high levels of testosterone and immaturity of the part of the brain involved in judgment.

The personal fable is connected with such behaviors as showing off and risk taking (Smith et al., 2014). Many adolescents assume that they can smoke with impunity (Morrell et al., 2015). Cancer? "It can't happen to me," or, "I've got years and years to think about that." They may drive recklessly. They often engage in spontaneous, unprotected sexual activity, allowing the biological drive to rule them and possibly assuming that sexually transmitted infections (STIs) and unwanted pregnancies happen to other people, not to them.

Many adolescents believe that their parents and other adults—even their peers—could never feel what they are feeling or know the depth of their passions. "You just don't understand me!" claims the adolescent. But, at least often enough, we do.

Adolescents may spend a great deal of time seeking imperfections—or admiring themselves—in the mirror. The concept of the imaginary audience places them on stage, but surrounded more by critics than admirers.

Thomas Northcut/Stone/Getty Images

11-4 GENDER DIFFERENCES IN COGNITIVE ABILITIES

Although females and males do not differ noticeably in overall intelligence, beginning in childhood (Miller & Halpern, 2014), gender differences appear in certain cognitive abilities. Females are somewhat superior to males in verbal ability. Males seem somewhat superior in visual–spatial skills. The picture for mathematics is more complex, with females excelling in some areas and males in others.

11-4a VERBAL ABILITY

Verbal abilities include reading, spelling, grammar, oral comprehension, and word fluency. As a group, females surpass males in verbal ability throughout their lives (Halpern, 2012). These differences show up early. Girls seem to acquire language faster than boys. They make more prelinguistic vocalizations, utter their first word sooner, and develop larger vocabularies. Boys in the United States are more likely than girls to have reading problems (Brun et al., 2009).

Why do females excel in verbal abilities? Biological factors such as the organization of the brain may play a role, but do not discount cultural factors—whether a culture stamps a skill as gender-neutral, masculine, or feminine (Goldstein, 2005). In Nigeria and England, reading is looked on as a masculine activity, and boys traditionally surpass girls in reading ability. But in the United States and Canada, reading tends to be stereotyped as feminine, and girls tend to excel.

11-4b VISUAL–SPATIAL ABILITY

Visual–spatial ability refers to the ability to visualize objects or shapes and to mentally manipulate and rotate them. This ability is important in such fields as

FIG.11.6 EXAMPLES OF TESTS USED TO MEASURE VISUAL–SPATIAL ABILITY

Mental-rotation test. If you mentally rotate the figure on the left, which of the five figures on the right would you obtain?

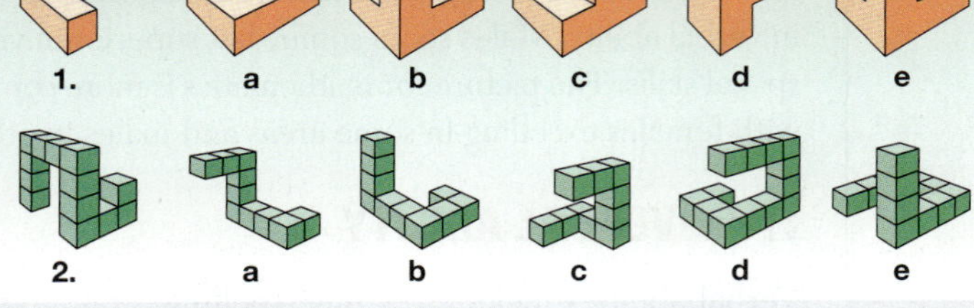

No gender differences are found on the spatial visualization tasks. The gender difference is greatest on the mental rotation tasks. What are some possible reasons for these differences?

art, architecture, and engineering. Boys begin to outperform girls on many types of visual–spatial tasks starting at age eight or nine, and the difference persists into adulthood (Halpern, 2012; Sneider et al., 2015). The gender difference is particularly notable on tasks that require imagining how objects will look if they are rotated in space (see Figure 11.6).

Some researchers link visual–spatial performance to evolutionary theory and sex hormones. It may be related to a genetic tendency to create and defend a territory (Lawton, 2010). An environmental theory is that gender stereotypes influence the spatial experiences of children. Gender-stereotyped "boys' toys," such as blocks, Legos, and Erector sets, provide more practice with spatial skills than gender-stereotyped "girls' toys." Boys are also more likely to engage in sports, which involve moving balls and other objects through space (Hoffman et al., 2011).

Image Source /Jupiter Images

postconventional level according to Kohlberg, a period during which moral judgments are derived from moral principles and people look to themselves to set moral standards.

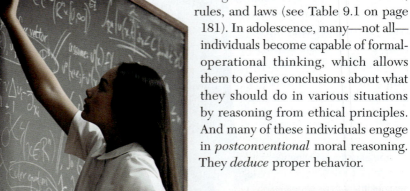

11-4c MATHEMATICAL ABILITY

For half a century or more, it has been believed that male adolescents generally outperform females in mathematics, and research has tended to support that belief (Else-Quest et al., 2013; Miller & Halpern, 2014). But a study by Hyde and her colleagues (2008) of some 7 million second- through eleventh-graders found no mean gender differences for performance in mathematics on standardized tests, although boys were somewhat more represented at the extremes—extreme high and low scores. The complexity of the test items apparently made no difference. Although girls may be generally as capable as boys in math, most Americans have different expectations for them, and these expectations may still discourage girls from entering "STEM fields" (i.e., fields in science, technology, engineering, and math) (Else-Quest et al., 2013).

11-5 MORAL DEVELOPMENT

Children in early childhood tend to view right and wrong in terms of rewards and punishments. Lawrence Kohlberg referred to such judgments as *preconventional*. In middle childhood, *conventional* thought tends to emerge, and children usually begin to judge right and wrong in terms of social conventions, rules, and laws (see Table 9.1 on page 181). In adolescence, many—not all—individuals become capable of formal-operational thinking, which allows them to derive conclusions about what they should do in various situations by reasoning from ethical principles. And many of these individuals engage in *postconventional* moral reasoning. They *deduce* proper behavior.

11-5a THE POSTCONVENTIONAL LEVEL

In the **postconventional level**, moral reasoning is based on the person's own moral standards. Consider once more the case of Heinz that was introduced in Chapter 9. Moral

TABLE 11.2 KOHLBERG'S POSTCONVENTIONAL LEVEL OF MORAL DEVELOPMENT

Stage	Examples of Moral Reasoning That Support Heinz's Stealing the Drug	Examples of Moral Reasoning That Oppose Heinz's Stealing the Drug
Stage 5: Contractual, legalistic orientation: One must weigh pressing human needs against society's need to maintain social order.	This thing is complicated because society has a right to maintain law and order, but Heinz has to take the drug to save his wife.	I can see why Heinz feels he has to take the drug, but laws exist for the benefit of society as a whole and cannot simply be cast aside.
Stage 6: Universal ethical principles orientation: People must follow universal ethical principles and their own consciences, even if it means breaking the law.	In this case, the law comes into conflict with the principle of the sanctity of human life. Heinz must take the drug because his wife's life is more important than the law.	If Heinz truly believes that stealing the drug is worse than letting his wife die, he should not take it. People have to make sacrifices to do what they think is right.

judgments are derived from personal values, not from conventional standards or authority figures. In the contractual, legalistic orientation of Stage 5, it is recognized that laws stem from agreed-on procedures and that many rights have great value and should not be violated (see Table 11.2). But under exceptional circumstances, such as in the case of Heinz, laws cannot bind the individual. A Stage 5 reason for stealing the drug might be that it is the right thing to do, even though it is illegal. Conversely, it could be argued that if everyone in need broke the law, the legal system and the social contract would be destroyed.

Stage 6 thinking relies on supposed universal ethical principles, such as those of human life, individual dignity, justice, and *reciprocity*. Behavior that is consistent with these principles is considered right. If a law is seen as unjust or contradicts the right of the individual, it is wrong to obey it.

In the case of Heinz, it could be argued from the perspective of Stage 6 that the principle of preserving life takes precedence over laws prohibiting stealing. Therefore, it is morally necessary for Heinz to steal the drug, even if he must go to jail. It could also be asserted, from the principled orientation, that if Heinz finds the social contract or the law to be the highest principle, he must remain within the law, despite the consequences.

Stage 5 and 6 moral judgments were virtually absent among the seven- and ten-year-olds in Kohlberg's (1963) sample of American children. They increased in frequency during the early and middle teens. By age 16, Stage 5 reasoning was shown by about 20% of adolescents and Stage 6 reasoning was demonstrated by about 5% of adolescents. However, Stage 3 and 4 judgments were made more frequently at all ages—7 through 16—studied by Kohlberg and other investigators (Commons et al., 2006; Rest, 1983) (see Figure 11.7).

11-5b MORAL BEHAVIOR AND MORAL REASONING

Are individuals whose moral judgments are more mature more likely to engage in moral behavior? The answer seems to be yes (Bazerman & Tenbrunsel, 2011; Cheng, 2014).

FIG.11.7 AGE AND TYPE OF MORAL JUDGMENT

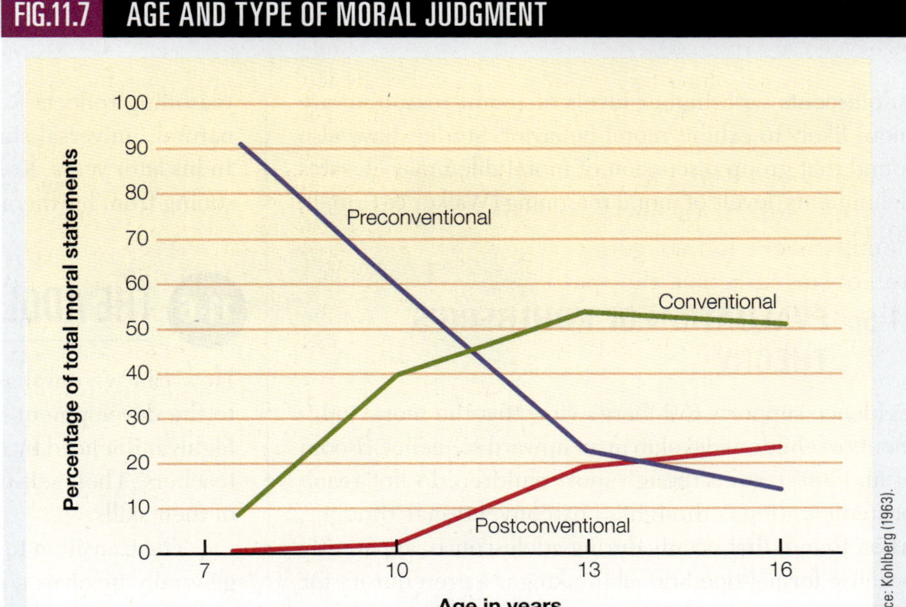

The incidence of preconventional reasoning declines from more than 90% of moral statements at age 7 to less than 20% of statements at age 16. Conventional moral statements increase with age between the ages of 7 and 13 but then level off to account for 50% to 60% of statements at ages 13 and 16. Postconventional moral statements are all but absent at ages 7 and 10 but account for about 20% to 25% of statements at ages 13 and 16.

Gender Differences in Moral Development

Do males reason at higher levels of moral development than females? Kohlberg and Kramer (1969) reported that the average stage of moral development for men was Stage 4, which emphasizes justice, law, and order. The average stage for women was reported to be Stage 3, which emphasizes caring and concern for others.

Carol Gilligan (Gilligan, 1982) argues that this gender difference reflects patterns of socialization: 11-year-old Jake views Heinz's dilemma as a math problem. He sets up an equation showing that life has greater value than property. Heinz should thus steal the drug. But 11-year-old Amy notes that stealing the drug and letting Heinz's wife die are both wrong. She searches for alternatives, such as getting a loan, saying that it wouldn't be wise for Heinz to go to jail and no longer be around to help his wife.

rubberball/Getty Images

Although Gilligan sees Amy's reasoning as being as sophisticated as Jake's, it could be said to show a lower level of moral development according to Kohlberg's system. Yet Gilligan and other researchers note that Amy, like other girls, has been socialized into being sensitive to the needs of others and foregoing simplistic judgments of right and wrong (You et al., 2011). They consider girls therefore to be more morally sensitive, that is, to be more likely to base their moral judgments and behavior on empathy (Loewenthal, 2016). To Jake, clear-cut conclusions are to be derived from a set of premises, but it is questionable whether his methodology suggests a higher level of moral development.

Adolescents with higher levels of moral reasoning are more likely to exhibit moral behavior. Studies have also found that group discussion of moral dilemmas elevates delinquents' levels of moral reasoning (Walker & Frimer, 2011).

11-5c EVALUATION OF KOHLBERG'S THEORY

Evidence supports Kohlberg's view that the moral judgments of children develop in an upward sequence (Boom et al., 2007), even though most children do not reach postconventional thought. Postconventional thought, when found, first occurs during adolescence, apparently because formal-operational thinking is a prerequisite for it (Patenaude et al., 2003).

Kohlberg believed that the stages of moral development follow the unfolding of innate sequences and are therefore universal. But he may have underestimated the influence of social, cultural, and educational institutions (Dawson, 2002).

Postconventional thinking is all but absent in developing societies (Snarey, 1994). Perhaps postconventional reasoning reflects Kohlberg's personal ideals and not a natural, universal stage of development (Gibbs, 2014). In his later years, Kohlberg (1985) dropped Stage 6 reasoning from his theory in recognition of this possibility.

11-6 THE ADOLESCENT IN SCHOOL

How can we emphasize the importance of the school to the development of the adolescent? Adolescents are highly influenced by the opinions of their peers and their teachers. Their self-esteem rises or falls with the pillars of their skills.

The transition to middle, junior high, or high school generally involves a shift from a smaller neighborhood elementary school to a larger, more impersonal setting with more students and different teachers for different classes. These changes may not fit the developmental needs of early adolescents. For example, adolescents express a desire for increased autonomy, yet teachers in junior high typically allow less student input and exert more control than teachers in elementary school (Tobbell, 2003).

The transition to the new school setting is often accompanied by a decline in grades and participation in school activities. Students may also experience a drop in self-esteem and an increase in stress (Rudolph & Flynn, 2007).

The transition from elementary school appears to be more difficult for girls than boys. Girls are more likely to be undergoing puberty and to earn the attention of boys in higher grades, whereas younger boys are not likely to be of interest to older girls. Girls experience major life changes, and children who experience many life changes at once find it more difficult to adjust (Tobbell, 2003).

But the transition need not be that stressful (Rudolph et al., 2001). Elementary and middle schools can help ease the transition. Some middle schools create a more intimate, caring atmosphere by establishing smaller schools within the school building. Others have "bridge programs" during the summer that introduce students to the new school culture and strengthen their academic skills.

11-6a DROPPING OUT

Completing high school is a critical developmental task. The consequences of dropping out can be grim. Dropouts are more likely to be unemployed or have low incomes (Catterall, 2011). Dropouts are more likely to develop delinquency, criminal behavior, and substance abuse (Catterall, 2011).

Excessive school absence and reading below grade level are two predictors of school dropout (Lever et al., 2004). Other risk factors include low grades, low self-esteem, problems with teachers, substance abuse, being old for one's grade level, and being male (Chapman et al., 2012). Adolescents who adopt adult roles early, especially marrying at a young age or becoming a parent, are also more likely to drop out (Chapman et al., 2012). Students from low-income households or large urban areas are also at greater risk (Chapman et al., 2012).

PREVENTING DROPPING OUT Many programs have been developed to prevent dropping out of school. Successful programs have some common characteristics (Bost & Riccomini, 2006; Reschly & Christenson, 2006): early preschool interventions (such as Head Start); identification and monitoring of high-risk students; small class size, individualized instruction, and counseling; vocational components that link learning and community work experiences; involvement of families or community organizations; and clear and reasonable educational goals.

Unfortunately, most intervention efforts are usually not introduced until students are on the verge of dropping out—when it is usually too late.

11-7 ADOLESCENTS IN THE WORKFORCE

Life experiences help shape vocational development. One life experience that is common among American teenagers is holding a job.

11-7a PREVALENCE OF ADOLESCENT EMPLOYMENT

About half of all high school sophomores, two-thirds of juniors, and almost three-fourths of seniors have a job during the school year (Bachman et al., 2013). European Americans are more likely than minority students to work (Bachman et al., 2013). Girls and boys are equally likely to be employed, but boys work more hours (Staff et al., 2004).

Jim West/The Image Works

Although millions of adolescents between the ages of 14 and 18 are legally employed, another two to three million work illegally (Holloway, 2004). Others work too many hours, work late hours on school nights, or hold hazardous jobs. Middle-class teenagers are twice as likely to be employed as lower-income teenagers, but employed lower-income adolescents work longer hours (Bachman et al., 2003).

11-7b PROS AND CONS OF ADOLESCENT EMPLOYMENT

The potential benefits of adolescent employment include developing a sense of responsibility, self-reliance, and discipline; learning to appreciate the value of money and education; acquiring positive work habits and values; and enhancing occupational aspirations (Rosenbaum et al., 2014). Disadvantaged adolescent female African Americans are more likely to graduate from high school and avoid coercive romantic relationships, yet they are more likely to use illicit substances and alcohol (Rosenbaum et al., 2014). Working apparently provides more of an opportunity to access various substances. Other researchers not that students who work lengthy hours—more than 11 to 13 hours per week—report lower grades, higher rates of drug and alcohol use, more delinquent behavior, lower self-esteem, and higher levels of psychological problems than students who do not work or who work only a few hours (Brandstätter & Farthofer, 2003). Ironically, adolescents whose grade point averages are most negatively affected by school-year employment are European Americans and Asian Americans with the most highly educated parents (Bachman et al., 2013). Parents and educators apparently need to consider the number of hours adolescents should be working during the school year.

11-7c CAREER CHOICES

Children may say they want to be rock stars or astronauts, but they become increasingly realistic—and often more conventional—as they mature and gain experience. In adolescence, ideas about the kind of work one wants to do tend to become more firmly established, but some people do not choose a particular occupation until the college years or afterward (Creed & Wamelink, 2015).

self-efficacy expectations beliefs that we will be able to successfully meet the requirements of our situations

From a social-cognitive perspective, the factors that influence adolescents' career choices include the following (Creed & Wamelink, 2015; Garcia et al., 2015):

- Competencies—the adolescent's knowledge or skills
- An adolescent's way of viewing a career, or himself or herself in relation to a career
- The adolescent's expectancies—his or her expectations about what will happen in a given career, including **self-efficacy expectations**; that is, his or her beliefs that he or she will be able to handle the tasks in a given career

Sometimes we plan our careers on the basis of our perceived abilities and personality traits (Garcia et al., 2015). Sometimes our early work experiences point us in certain directions (Creed & Wamelink, 2015). Most adolescents actually choose from a relatively small range of occupations on the basis of their personalities, experiences, and opportunities (Sawitri & Creed, 2015). And many sort of fall into jobs that are offered to them or follow career paths that are blazed by parents or role models in the community (Kaziboni & Uys, 2015; Sawitri & Creed, 2015).

STUDY TOOLS 11

READY TO STUDY?

In the book, you can:

- ☐ Rip out the chapter review card at the back of the book for a handy summary of the chapter and key terms.
- ☐ Check your understanding of what you've read with the quizzes that follow.

ONLINE AT CENGAGEBRAIN.COM YOU CAN:

- ☐ Collect StudyBits while you read and study the chapter.
- ☐ Quiz yourself on key concepts.
- ☐ Find videos for further exploration.
- ☐ Prepare for tests with HDEV5 Flash Cards as well as those you create.

SELF-ASSESSMENTS

Fill-Ins

Answers can be found in the back of the book.

1. ____________ triggers the development of acne, which afflicts 75% to 90% of adolescents.
2. Menstruation is the sloughing off of the ____________.
3. The major cause of death for adolescents is ____________.
4. A disturbing risk factor for eating disorders in adolescent females is a history of ____________ abuse.
5. Adolescents may be awkward and gawky due to ____________ growth.
6. The stage of ____________ operations is the top level in Jean Piaget's theory.
7. ____________ emissions are also known as "wet dreams."
8. On a cognitive level, research evidence shows that adolescent males tend to outperform adolescent females on tasks requiring ____________ ability.
9. Two predictors of school dropout are reading below grade level and excessive school ____________.
10. The historical trend toward increasing adult height was accompanied by an earlier onset of puberty, and is known as the ____________ trend.

Multiple Choice

1. **All of the following are risk factors for adolescents dropping out of school *except***
   a. living in a rural area.
   b. excessive school absence.
   c. reading below grade level.
   d. becoming a parent as a teenager.

2. **Adolescents who have reached Piaget's stage of formal operations differ from children who are still at Piaget's stage of concrete operations in that they are capable of**
   a. seriating a distribution of numbers.
   b. conserving volume.
   c. object permanence.
   d. hypothetical thinking.

3. **In terms of Kohlberg's theory of moral development, Stage 6 moral reasoning is least likely to be based on**
   a. the concept of reciprocity.
   b. seeking revenge for insults.
   c. universal ethical principles.
   d. belief in human dignity.

4. **We would probably find that, as a group, adolescent females tend to be somewhat better than boys in**
   a. studying maps.
   b. imagining how objects will look if they are rotated in space.
   c. learning algebra.
   d. reading.

5. **Government statistics show that firearms account for about ____________% of adolescent suicides.**
   a. 10
   b. 25
   c. 50
   d. 75

6. **According to the text, perfectionistic and obsessionistic personality traits play a role in**
   a. dropping out of school.
   b. committing suicide.
   c. achieving Stage 6 of Kohlberg's levels and stages of moral development.
   d. eating disorders.

7. **Gynecomastia stems from the small amount of female sex hormones secreted by the**
   a. testes.
   b. endometrium.
   c. epiphyses.
   d. uterus.

8. **Of the following, the least likely cause of death for an adolescent is**
   a. homicide.
   b. pneumonia.
   c. cancer.
   d. suicide.

9. **Which of the following is true about early- and late-maturing adolescents?**
   a. Early-maturing boys are more likely to be agitated and ill-natured.
   b. Early-maturing boys are often dominated by late-maturing boys.
   c. Early-maturing girls become conspicuous with their height and development of their breasts.
   d. Early-maturing girls are at less risk for psychological problems and substance abuse.

10. **Many adolescents believe that their parents and other adults—even other adolescents—could never understand what they are feeling or the depth of their passions. This way of thinking reflects**
    a. the imaginary audience.
    b. the personal fable.
    c. sophisticated use of symbols.
    d. hypothetical thinking.

TEACH 3
NOW WITH TEACH ONLINE

HIST 4

BCOM 8
NOW WITH BCOM ONLINE

SPEAK 3
NOW WITH SPEAK ONLINE

ORGB 5
NOW WITH ORGB ONLINE

GLOBAL 3
NOW WITH GLOBAL ONLINE

IPC 3
NOW WITH IPC ONLINE

COMM 4

GOVT 9
NOW WITH GOVT ONLINE

CJ 4
NOW WITH CJ ONLINE

PSYCH 5
NOW WITH PSYCH ONLINE

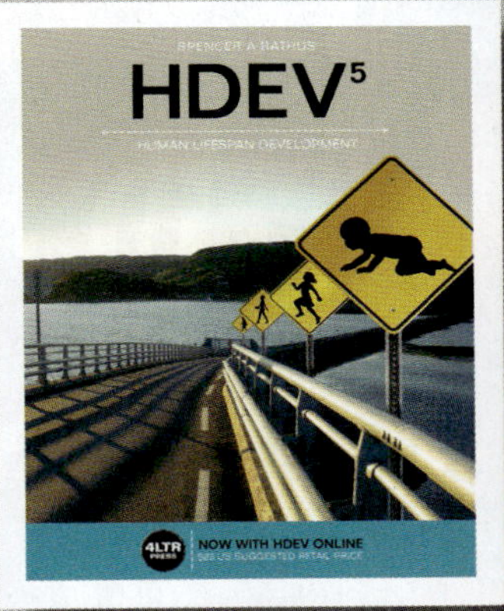
HDEV 5
NOW WITH HDEV ONLINE

CFIN 5
NOW WITH CFIN ONLINE

BUSN 9
NOW WITH BUSN ONLINE

SELL 5
NOW WITH SELL ONLINE

MGMT 9
NOW WITH MGMT ONLINE

12 Adolescence: Social and Emotional Development

Blend Images / Alamy Stock Photo

LEARNING OUTCOMES

After studying this chapter, you will be able to . . .

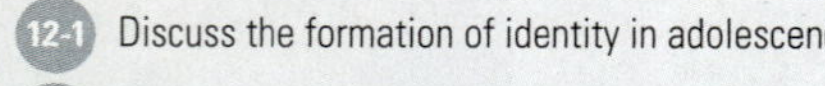

- **12-1** Discuss the formation of identity in adolescence
- **12-2** Describe relationships with parents and peers during adolescence
- **12-3** Discuss sexuality during adolescence, focusing on sexual orientation, sexual behavior, and teenage pregnancy
- **12-4** Discuss the characteristics of juvenile delinquents
- **12-5** Discuss risk factors in adolescent suicide

After you finish this chapter, go to **PAGE 254** for **STUDY TOOLS**

What am I like as a person? Complicated! I'm sensitive, friendly and outgoing, though I can also be shy, self-conscious, and even obnoxious. . . . I'm responsible, even studious every now and then, but on the other hand I'm a goof-off too, because if you're too studious, you won't be popular. . . . Sometimes I feel phony, especially around boys. . . . I'll be flirtatious and fun-loving. And then everybody else is looking at me . . . Then I get self-conscious and embarrassed and become radically introverted, and I don't know who I really am! I can be my true self with my close friends. I can't be my real self with my parents. They don't understand me. They treat me like I'm still a kid. That gets confusing, though. I mean, which am I, a kid or an adult?[1]

These thoughts of a 15-year-old girl illustrate a key aspect of adolescence: the search for an answer to the question "Who am I?" She is struggling to reconcile contradictory traits and behaviors to determine the "real me." Adolescents are preoccupied not only with their present selves but also with what they want to become.

12-1 DEVELOPMENT OF IDENTITY: "WHO AM I?"

In this chapter, we explore social and emotional development in adolescence. We begin with the formation of identity.

12-1a ERIKSON AND IDENTITY DEVELOPMENT

ego identity vs. role diffusion Erikson's fifth life crisis, during which adolescents develop a firm sense of who they are and what they stand for (ego identity), or they do not develop a sense of who they are and tend to be subject to the whims of others.

psychological moratorium a period when adolescents experiment with different roles, values, beliefs, and relationships.

Erik Erikson's fifth stage of psychosocial development is called **ego identity versus role diffusion**. The primary task is for adolescents to develop ego identity: a sense of who they are and what they stand for. They are faced with choices about their future occupations, political and religious beliefs, gender roles, and more. Because of formal-operational thinking, adolescents can weigh options they have not experienced (Moshman, 2013).

One aspect of identity development is a **psychological moratorium** during which adolescents experiment with different roles, values, beliefs, and relationships (Erikson, 1968). During this time, adolescents

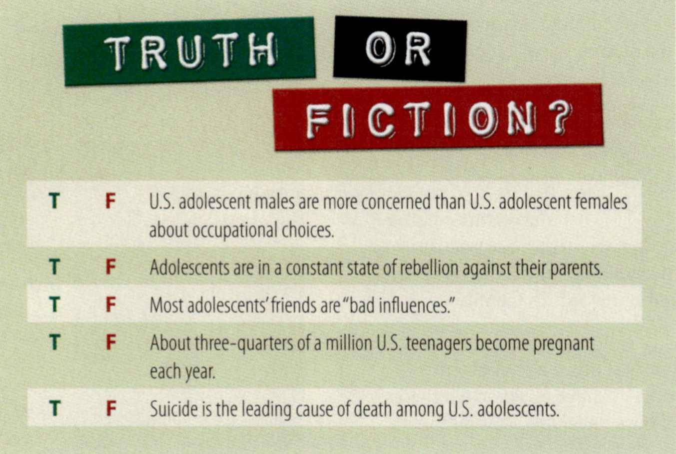

T	F	U.S. adolescent males are more concerned than U.S. adolescent females about occupational choices.
T	F	Adolescents are in a constant state of rebellion against their parents.
T	F	Most adolescents' friends are "bad influences."
T	F	About three-quarters of a million U.S. teenagers become pregnant each year.
T	F	Suicide is the leading cause of death among U.S. adolescents.

[1]Adapted from Harter (1990, pp. 352–353).

undergo an **identity crisis** in which they examine their values and make decisions about their life roles. Should they attend college? What career should they pursue? Should they become sexually active? With whom?

In their search for identity, many—not all—adolescents join "in" groups, slavishly imitating their peers' clothing, speech, hairstyles, and ideals (Erikson, 1963). Those who successfully resolve their identity crises develop a strong sense of who they are and what they stand for. Those who do not may be intolerant of people who are different and blindly follow people who adhere to convention.

12-1b IDENTITY STATUSES

Building on Erikson's approach, James Marcia (2010) theorized four *identity statuses* that represent the four possible combinations of the dimensions of exploration and commitment that Erikson believed were critical to the development of identity (Kroger & Marcia, 2011; Marcia, 2010) (see Table 12.1). *Exploration* involves active questioning and searching among alternatives to establish goals, values, or beliefs. *Commitment* is a stable investment in one's goals, values, or beliefs.

Identity diffusion is the least advanced status and includes adolescents who neither have commitments nor are trying to form them. This stage is characteristic of younger adolescents and of older adolescents who drift through life or become alienated and rebellious.

In the **foreclosure** status, individuals make commitments without considering alternatives. These commitments are usually established early in life and are often based on identification with parents, teachers, or religious leaders who have made a strong impression.

identity crisis a turning point in development during which one examines one's values and makes decisions about life roles.

identity diffusion an identity status that characterizes those who have no commitments and who are not in the process of exploring alternatives.

foreclosure an identity status that characterizes those who have made commitments without considering alternatives.

moratorium an identity status that characterizes those who are actively exploring alternatives in an attempt to form an identity.

identity achievement an identity status that characterizes those who have explored alternatives and have developed commitments.

The **moratorium** status refers to a person who is actively exploring alternatives in an attempt to make choices. Such individuals are often anxious and intense.

Identity achievement refers to those who have explored alternatives and developed relatively firm commitments. They generally have high self-esteem and self-acceptance.

DEVELOPMENT OF IDENTITY STATUSES Before high school, children show little interest in questions of identity. Most are either in identity diffusion or foreclosure statuses. During the high school and college years, adolescents increasingly move from the diffusion and foreclosure statuses to the moratorium and achievement statuses (Marcia, 2014; Moshman, 2013). The greatest gains in identity formation occur in college (Bartoszuk & Pittman, 2010; Berzonsky, 2011). College students are exposed to a variety of lifestyles, beliefs, and career choices, which spur consideration of identity issues. Are you a student who has changed majors once or twice (or more)? If so, you have most likely experienced the moratorium identity status, which is common among college students. College seniors have a stronger sense of identity than first-year students as a result of resolving identity crises (Meeus, 2011), and a sense of identity is associated with higher self-esteem and grades (Perez et al., 2014; Ryeng et al., 2013).

12-1c ETHNICITY AND DEVELOPMENT OF IDENTITY

The development of self-identity is a key task for all adolescents (Kunnen & Metz, 2015). The task is more complex for adolescents who are members of ethnic minority groups (Azmitia, 2015; Worrell, 2015; Umana-Taylor, 2016). Adolescents who belong to the

TABLE 12.1 THE FOUR IDENTITY STATUSES OF JAMES MARCIA

		Exploration	
		Yes	**No**
Commitment	**Yes**	**Identity Achievement** • Most developed in terms of identity • Has experienced a period of exploration • Has developed commitments • Has a sense of personal well-being, high self-esteem, and self-acceptance • Cognitively flexible • Sets goals and works toward achieving them	**Foreclosure** • Makes commitments without considering alternatives • Commitments based on identification with parents, teachers, or other authority figures • Often authoritarian and inflexible
	No	**Moratorium** • Actively exploring alternatives • Attempting to make choices with regard to occupation, ideological beliefs, and so on • Often anxious and intense • Ambivalent feelings toward parents and authority figures	**Identity Diffusion** • Least developed in terms of identity • Lacks commitments • Not trying to form commitments • May be carefree and uninvolved or unhappy and lonely • May be angry, alienated, rebellious

dominant culture—in this country, European Americans of Christian, especially Protestant, heritage—are usually faced with assimilating one set of cultural values into their identities. However, adolescents who belong to ethnic minority groups, such as African Americans and Islamic Americans, confront two sets of cultural values: the values of the dominant culture and those of their particular ethnic group. If the cultural values conflict, the adolescent needs to sort out the values that are most meaningful to him or her and incorporate them into his or her identity (Cooper et al., 2015). Some adolescents do it cafeteria style; they take a little bit of this and a little bit of that. For example, a young Catholic woman may decide to use artificial means of birth control even though doing so conflicts with her religion's teachings.

Geri Lavrov/Photographer's Choice/Getty Images

Who do I want to become?

Adolescents from ethnic minority groups also often experience prejudice and discrimination. Their cultural heroes may be ignored. A relative scarcity of successful role models can be a problem, particularly for youth who live in poverty. Identifying too strongly with the dominant culture may also lead to rejection by the minority group. On the other hand, rejecting the dominant culture's values for those of the minority group may limit opportunities for advancement in the larger society.

Some researchers hypothesize three stages in the development of **ethnic identity** (Phinney & Baldelomar, 2011). The first is **unexamined ethnic identity**. It is similar to Marcia's identity statuses of diffusion or foreclosure. In the second stage, the adolescent embarks on an **ethnic identity search**. This second stage, similar to Marcia's moratorium, may be based on some incident that makes the adolescent aware of his or her ethnicity. During this stage, the adolescent may explore his or her ethnic culture, participating in cultural events, reading, and discussion. In the third stage, individuals have an **achieved ethnic identity** that involves self-acceptance as a member of one's ethnic group and helps individuals withstand the stress that comes from societal discrimination (Romero et al., 2014).

Adolescents who belong to ethnic minority groups may need to sort out two sets of cultural values.

Alejandro Rivera/E+/Getty Images

12-1d GENDER AND DEVELOPMENT OF IDENTITY

Erikson believed that there were gender differences in the development of identity, and his views reflected the times in which he wrote. Identity development relates to relationships and occupational choice, among other matters. Erikson (1968, 1975) assumed that relationships were more important to women's development of identity, while occupational and ideological matters were relatively more important to men's. He believed that a young woman's identity was intimately bound up with her roles as wife and mother. Studies today show that both adolescent females and males are concerned about occupational choices, even though females are more likely to expect that they will have to balance the demands of a career and a

ethnic identity a sense of belonging to an ethnic group.

unexamined ethnic identity the first stage of ethnic identity development; similar to the diffusion or foreclosure identity statuses.

ethnic identity search the second stage of ethnic identity development; similar to the moratorium identity status.

achieved ethnic identity the final stage of ethnic identity development; similar to the identity achievement status.

family (Cinamon & Rich, 2014; Skorikov & Vondracek, 2011). Despite cultural lip service to gender equality, this gender difference has persisted because females continue to assume primary responsibility for child rearing, even though most women are employed outside the home.

FICTION

T (F) U.S. adolescent males are more concerned than U.S. adolescent females about occupational choices.

It is no longer true that U.S. adolescent males are more concerned than adolescent females about occupational choices. Even so, females continue to worry more about the integration of occupational and family plans.

12-1e DEVELOPMENT OF THE SELF-CONCEPT

Before adolescence, children describe themselves primarily in terms of their physical characteristics and their actions. As they approach adolescence, children begin to incorporate psychological characteristics and social relationships into their self-descriptions (Arnett, 2015).

Adolescents' self-perceptions become more complex than those of younger children (Arnett, 2015). According to Susan Harter's Self-Perception Profile of academically talented adolescents (see Table 12.2), many factors come into play. Adolescents may describe themselves as anxious or sarcastic with parents but as talkative and cheerful with friends. Such contradictions and conflicts in self-description reach their peak at about age 14 and then decline (Schwartz et al., 2011). The advanced formal-operational skills of older adolescents allow them to integrate contradictory aspects of the self. The older adolescent might say: "I'm very adaptable. When I'm around my friends, who think that what I say is important, I'm very talkative; but around my family, I'm quiet because they're not interested enough to really listen to me" (Damon, 1991, p. 988).

TABLE 12.2 FACTORS IN SUSAN HARTER'S SELF-PERCEPTION PROFILE FOR ADOLESCENTS

Harter's test contains items similar to these:
1. I'm good-looking. (factor: general attractiveness)
2. I get good grades. (scholastic competence)
3. I have a lot of friends. (peer support)
4. I do well at sports. (athletic competence)
5. I'm ready to do well in a job. (job competence)
6. I don't get into trouble. (conduct)
7. I date the people I'm attracted to. (romantic appeal)

Source: Worrell (1997).

12-1f SELF-ESTEEM

Self-esteem tends to decline as the child progresses from middle childhood to about the age of 12 or 13 (Harter & Whitesell, 2003). The growing cognitive maturity of young adolescents makes them increasingly aware of the disparity between their ideal selves and their real selves, especially in terms of physical appearance (Fourchard & Courtinat-Camps, 2013; Stieger et al., 2014). Boys might fantasize they would like to have the physiques of the warriors they see in video games or in the media. Most American girls want to be thin, thin, thin (Daniels & Gillen, 2015).

After hitting a low point at about age 12 or 13, self-esteem gradually improves (Harter & Whitesell, 2003). Perhaps adolescents adjust their ideal selves to better reflect reality. Also, as adolescents develop academic, physical, and social skills, they may grow less self-critical (Schwartz et al., 2011).

For most adolescents, low self-esteem produces temporary discomfort (Harter & Whitesell, 2003). For others, low self-esteem has serious consequences. For example, low self-esteem is often found in teenagers and adults who are depressed or suicidal (Stieger at al., 2014).

Emotional support from parents and peers is important in self-esteem. Adolescents who feel highly regarded by family and friends are more likely to feel positive about themselves (Boudreault-Bouchard et al., 2013; Smetana, 2011).

12-2 RELATIONSHIPS WITH PARENTS AND PEERS

Adolescents coping with the task of establishing a sense of identity and direction in their lives are heavily influenced both by parents and peers.

12-2a RELATIONSHIPS WITH PARENTS

Although most adolescents get along well with their parents, they spend less time with their parents than they did in childhood (Smetana, 2011). Adolescents continue to interact more with their mothers than their fathers.

Teenagers have more conflicts with their mothers, but they also view their mothers as being more supportive and knowing them better (Rote & Smetana, 2015; Smetana et al., 2013). Adverse relationships with fathers are often associated with depression in adolescents, but good relations with fathers contribute to psychological well-being (Rote & Smetana, 2015).

The decrease in time spent with family may reflect the adolescents' striving for independence (Smetana, 2011). A certain degree of distancing from parents may be adaptive as adolescents form relationships outside the family. However, adolescents continue to maintain love, loyalty, and respect for their parents (Collins & Laursen, 2006). And adolescents who feel close to their parents have more self-reliance and self-esteem, better school performance, and fewer adjustment problems (Costigan et al., 2007; Rote & Smetana, 2015).

The relationship between parents and teens is not always rosy, of course. Early adolescence, in particular, is characterized by increased bickering and a decrease in shared activities and expressions of affection (Smetana, 2011; van den Akker et al., 2010). Conflicts typically center on the everyday details of family life, such as chores, homework, curfews, personal appearance, finances, and dating—often because adolescents believe that they should manage matters that were previously controlled by parents (Costigan et al., 2007). But parents, especially mothers, continue to believe that they should retain control in most areas, for example, encouraging adolescents to do their homework and clean their rooms. As adolescents get older, they and their parents are more likely to compromise (Smetana, 2011, 2013). On the other hand, parents and adolescents are usually quite similar in their values and beliefs regarding social, political, religious, and economic issues (Collins & Laursen, 2006). Even though the notion of a generation gap between adolescents and their parents may persist as a stereotype, there is little evidence of one.

FICTION

T (F) Adolescents are in a constant state of rebellion against their parents.

It is not true that adolescents are in a constant state of rebellion against their parents. Parents and adolescents are usually quite similar in their values and beliefs regarding social, political, religious, and economic issues.

As adolescents grow older, parents are more likely to relax controls and less likely to use punishment (Smetana, 2011, 2013). Although parent–child relationships change, most adolescents feel that they are close to and get along with their parents, even though they may develop a less idealized view of them (Collins & Laursen, 2006).

PARENTING STYLES Differences in parenting styles continue to influence the development of adolescents (Kenney et al., 2015; Vermeulen-Smit et al., 2015). Adolescents from authoritative homes—whose parents are willing to exert control and explain the reasons for doing so—show the most competent behavior. They are more self-reliant, do better in school, have better mental health, and show the lowest incidence of psychological problems and misconduct, including drug use.

Phanie / Alamy Stock Photo

Adolescents are often in conflict with their parents over the desire for autonomy, but most adolescents and parents agree on political, religious, and economic issues.

12-2b RELATIONSHIPS WITH PEERS

The transition from childhood to adolescence is accompanied by a shift in the relative importance of parents and peers. Although relationships with parents generally remain positive, the role of peers as a source of activities, influence, and support increases. Parents are perceived as the most frequent providers of social and emotional support by fourth-graders—by seventh grade, friends of the same gender are seen to be as supportive as parents. By tenth grade, same-gender friends are viewed as providing more support than parents (Furman & Winkles, 2010; Laursen et al., 2010).

FRIENDSHIPS IN ADOLESCENCE Adolescents have more friends than younger children do (Laursen et al., 2010). Most adolescents have one or two "best friends" and several good friends. Teenagers see, text, or spend time with their friends on the phone or the Internet frequently, usually several hours a day. According to the Pew Research Center (A. Smith, 2014), Facebook is used by more than half (57%) of U.S. adults, and almost three out of four (73%) of U.S. adolescents aged 12–17. The four top dislikes of Facebook users (A. Smith, 2014) are:

- People share too much information about themselves (36%)
- Other people post information—including photos—about you without your permission (36%)
- Other people see comments or posts that you meant to keep private (27%)
- There is pressure to disclose too much information about yourself (24%)

Many adolescent Facebook users reported that they were concerned that more and more adults were using Facebook, that it was crucial that they manage their self-presentation carefully, the burden of "drama" (negative social interactions), and friends sharing too much information (Madden, 2013). An overwhelming percentage (94%!) of teenagers who are social media users have Facebook profiles, as compared with 26% who report having Twitter profiles or the 11% who report having Instagram profiles.

Adolescents and young adults report having more Facebook friends than all adults combined: whereas 15% of all adults report having more than 500 friends, nearly twice that amount (27%) of users aged 18–29 report having more than 500 friends. Sixty-five-year-olds also use Facebook, but nearly three in four of them (72%) have 100 friends or fewer. This finding is consistent with research that finds that older people have fewer (actual) friends than younger people have, but that their friends have more in common with them and are more deeply committed to them at advanced ages.

clique a group of five to ten individuals who hang around together and who share activities and confidences.

crowd a large, loosely organized group of people who may or may not spend much time together and who are identified by the activities of the group.

Friendships in adolescence differ from the friendships of childhood. Adolescents are more likely to stress acceptance, intimate self-disclosure, and mutual understanding (Hall, 2011). There are some gender differences. Adolescent girls are more likely to stress the importance of loyalty, intimacy, and companionship, but status—having friends on one's level of social dominance—was more important for males (Hall, 2011). One eighth-grade girl described her best friend this way: "I can tell her things and she helps me talk. And she doesn't laugh at me if I do something weird—she accepts me for who I am" (Berndt & Perry, 1990, p. 269).

Adolescents and their friends are similar in many respects. They typically are the same age and race. They almost always are the same gender. Even though romantic attachments increase during the teen years, most adolescents still choose members of their own gender as best friends (Field et al., 2014; Hartl et al., 2015). Friends are often alike in school attitudes, educational aspirations, and grades. Friends also tend to have similar attitudes about drinking, drug use, and sexual activity.

Friendship contributes to psychological adjustment. Adolescents who have a close friend have higher self-esteem than adolescents who do not (Brendgen et al., 2010).

Intimacy and closeness appear to be more central to the friendships of girls than of boys (Leaper, 2013). Adolescent and adult females also are generally more likely than males to disclose secrets, personal problems, thoughts, and feelings to their friends (Hall, 2011).

Friendship networks among girls are smaller and more exclusive than networks among boys (Leaper, 2013). Girls tend to have one or two close friends, whereas boys tend to congregate in larger, less intimate groups. The activities of girls' and boys' friendship networks differ as well. Girls are more likely to engage in unstructured activities such as talking and listening to music. Boys are more likely to engage in organized group activities, games, and sports.

PEER GROUPS Most adolescents belong to one or more peer groups: *cliques* and *crowds* (Brown, 2013). **Cliques** consist of five to ten individuals who hang around together, sharing activities and confidences. **Crowds** are larger groups who may or may not spend much time together and are identified by their activities or attitudes. Crowds are usually given labels by other adolescents— "jocks," "brains," "druggies," or "nerds." The most negatively labeled groups ("druggies," "rejects") show higher levels of alcohol and drug abuse, delinquency, and depression.

Adolescent peer groups function with less adult guidance or control than childhood peer groups (Staff et al., 2004). Adolescent peer groups may include members of the other gender, sharply contrasting with the gender segregation of childhood peer groups. Such associations may lead to dating and romantic relationships.

DATING AND ROMANTIC RELATIONSHIPS Romantic relationships usually begin during early and middle adolescence, and most adolescents start dating or going out by the time they graduate from high school (Florsheim, 2003). For heterosexuals, the development of dating typically takes the following sequence: putting oneself in situations where peers of the other gender probably will be present (e.g., hanging out at the mall), group activities including peers of the other gender (e.g., school dances or parties), group dating (e.g., joining a mixed-gender group at the movies), and then traditional two-person dating (Connolly et al., 2004; Kreager et al., 2015).

Dating serves a number of functions. First and foremost, people date to have fun. Dating, especially in early adolescence, also serves to enhance prestige with peers. Dating gives adolescents additional experiences in learning to relate to people. Finally, dating prepares adolescents for adult courtship (Florsheim, 2003).

Dating relationships tend to be casual and short-lived in early adolescence. In late adolescence, relationships tend to become more stable and committed (Connolly et al., 2000). Eighteen-year-olds are more likely than 15-year-olds to mention love, trust, and commitment when describing romantic relationships (Furman & Winkles, 2010; Hall, 2011).

PEER INFLUENCE Peer pressure is fairly weak in early adolescence. It peaks during mid-adolescence and declines after about age 17 (Reis & Youniss, 2004). Peer influence may increase during adolescence because peers provide a standard by which adolescents measure their own behavior as they develop independence from the family (Smetana, 2011). Peers also provide support in times of trouble (Smetana, 2011).

Parents often worry that their teenage children will fall in with the wrong crowd and be persuaded to engage in self-destructive behavior. Despite the widespread assumption that peer and parental influences will be in conflict, with peers exerting pressure on adolescents to engage in negative behaviors such as alcohol and drug abuse, research paints a more complex picture. Parents and peers are usually complementary rather than competing influences (Smetana et al., 2013).

Parents and peers also seem to exert influence in different domains. Adolescents are more likely to conform to peer standards in matters pertaining to style and taste, such as clothing, hairstyles, speech patterns, and music (Smetana, 2011). They are more likely to agree with their parents on moral principles and future educational and career goals (Smetana, 2011).

Adolescents influence each other positively and negatively. In many cases, peer pressure to finish high school and achieve academically can be stronger than pressures to engage in misconduct (Smetana et al., 2013). Yet many times adolescents discourage one another from doing well or from doing too well in school. Adolescents who smoke, drink, use drugs, and engage in sexual activity also often have friends who engage in these behaviors, but adolescents tend to choose friends and peers who are like them to begin with.

FICTION

T (F) Most adolescents' friends are "bad influences."

It is certainly not true that most adolescents' friends are "bad influences." Parents and peers are usually complementary rather than competing influences.

12-3 SEXUALITY

My first sexual experience occurred in a car after the high school junior prom. We were both virgins, very uncertain but very much in love. We had been going together since eighth grade. The experience was somewhat painful. I remember wondering if I would look different to my mother the next day. I guess I didn't because nothing was said.

Because of the flood of sex hormones, adolescents tend to experience a powerful sex drive. In addition, they are bombarded with sexual messages in the media, including scantily clad, hip-grinding, crotch-grabbing pop stars; print ads for barely-there underwear; and countless articles on "How to tell if your boyfriend has been [whatever]" and "The 10 things that will drive your girlfriend wild." Teenagers are strongly motivated to follow the crowd, yet they are also influenced by the views of their parents and teachers. So what is a teen to do?

What teens do takes various directions. In this section we first consider adolescent sexual behavior, including masturbation and male–female sexual behavior. As noted in Chapter 11, adolescents often take risks that adults might avoid–in this case, sex without adequate precautions. For that reason we consider teenage pregnancy. Not all adolescents desire members of the other sex as partners; some prefer members of their own sex. They are said to have a homosexual (gay male or lesbian) orientation, and we consider sexual orientation next. Although gay males and lesbians prefer members of the own sex for sexual activity; sexual orientation is not a matter of choice. As we'll see, gay males and lesbians—like those who prefer to have sex with members of the other sex—is biologically built in before birth.

Ammentorp Photography / Alamy Stock Photo

12-3a ADOLESCENT SEXUAL BEHAVIOR

MASTURBATION Masturbation, or sexual self-stimulation, is the most common sexual outlet in adolescence. Surveys indicate that most adolescents masturbate at some time and most educated adolescents and early adults see masturbation as beneficial. Although it has not been shown to be physically harmful, beliefs that masturbation is harmful and guilt about masturbating lessen the incidence of masturbation (Robbins et al., 2011).

About three-quarters of adolescent males and half of adolescent females masturbate (Robbins et al., 2011). Males who masturbate do so more often than females who masturbate. It is unclear whether this gender difference reflects a stronger sex drive in males, greater social constraints on females, or both, but young women are more likely than young men to struggle in coming to terms with the contradiction between social stigma and pleasure (Robbins et al., 2011; Hakim, 2015).

MALE–FEMALE SEXUAL BEHAVIOR Adolescents today start dating and going out earlier than in past generations. Teens who date earlier are more likely to engage in sexual activity during high school (Temple et al., 2014). Teens who initiate sexual activity earlier are also less likely to use contraception and more likely to become pregnant. But early dating does not always lead to early sex, and early sex does not always lead to unwanted pregnancies.

Petting is practically universal among U.S. adolescents and has been for many generations. Adolescents use petting to express affection, satisfy their curiosities, heighten their sexual arousal, and reach orgasm while avoiding pregnancy and maintaining virginity. Many adolescents do not see themselves as having sex if they stop short of vaginal intercourse (De Rosa et al., 2010). Girls are more likely than boys to be pushed into petting and to feel guilty about it (Slotboom et al., 2011).

Since the early 1990s, the percentage of high school students who have engaged in sexual intercourse has been gradually declining. The incidences of kissing, "making out," oral sex, and sexual intercourse all increase with age. Figure 12.1 summarizes some findings about teenage male–female sexual behavior with results from the National Survey of Family Growth (Martinez & Abma, 2015). There was a gradual decline in the incidence of sexual intercourse between 1988 and the first

FIG.12.1 NEVER-MARRIED TEENAGERS, AGED 15–19, WHO HAVE HAD SEXUAL INTERCOURSE

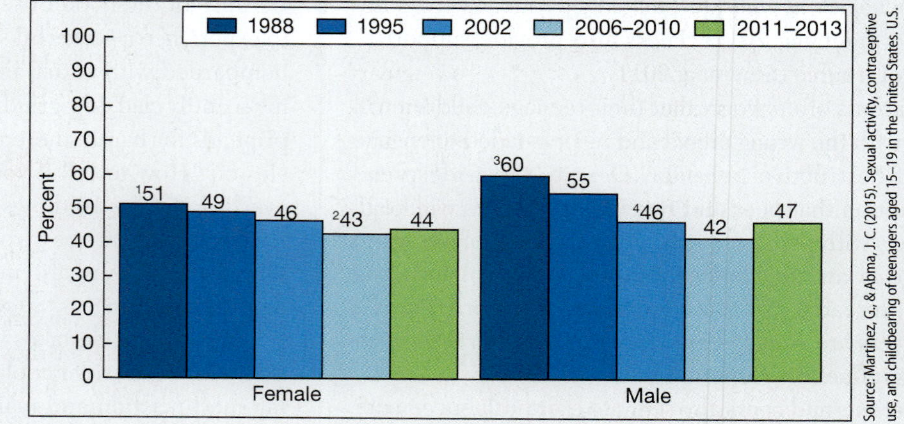

Source: Martinez, G., & Abma, J. C. (2015). Sexual activity, contraceptive use, and childbearing of teenagers aged 15–19 in the United States. U.S. Department of Health and Human Services, National Center for Health Statistics. NCHS Data Brief, No. 209, Figure 1.

masturbation sexual self-stimulation.

petting kissing and touching the breasts and genitals.

decade of the 21st century, but the incidence of never-married teenagers between the ages of 15 and 19 who have had sex has leveled off at about 44% for females and 47% for males. It should not be surprising that the probability of having had sex rises dramatically between the ages of 15 and 19. More than 90% of the girls aged 15–19 who have had sex have used a condom at one time or another, and majorities have used the withdrawal method of birth control (which is all but useless) or the birth-control pill.

EFFECTS OF PUBERTY The hormonal changes of puberty probably are partly responsible for the onset of sexual activity. In boys, levels of testosterone are associated with sexual behavior. In girls, however, testosterone levels are linked to sexual interests but not to sexual behavior. Social factors may therefore play a greater role in regulating sexual behavior in girls than boys (De Rosa et al., 2010).

The physical changes associated with puberty also may trigger the onset of sexual activity. For example, the development of secondary sex characteristics such as breasts in girls and muscles and deep voices in boys may make them more sexually attractive. Early-maturing girls are more likely to have older friends, who may draw them into sexual relationships.

PARENTAL INFLUENCES Teenagers who have close relationships with their parents are less likely to initiate sexual activity at an early age (Bynum, 2007). Adolescents who communicate well with their parents also delay the onset of sexual activity (Aspy et al., 2007). If these youngsters do have sexual intercourse, they are more likely to use birth control and have fewer partners.

PEER INFLUENCES A good predictor of sexual activity for adolescents is the sexual activity of their best friends. When teenagers are asked why they do not wait to have sex until they are older, the main reason reported is usually peer pressure (Ali & Dwyer, 2011). Peers, especially those of the same gender, also serve as a key source of sex education for adolescents. Adolescents report that they are somewhat more likely to receive information about sex from friends and media sources—TV shows, films, magazines, and the Internet—than from sex education classes or their parents (Kaiser Family Foundation et al., 2003).

SEXTING Sexting is short for *sex texting*, and refers to sending or receiving text messages with sexual content. Sexting can be used to titillate the recipient, to highlight the intimacy of one's relationship, to humiliate someone—or to ask or arrange for a sexual encounter (Walrave et al., 2015).

A survey of Texas high school students found that 28% said they had transmitted a nude photo of themselves in a text message or an email (Temple & Choi, 2014). Three in ten (31%) had requested a "sext" message, and more than half (57%) had asked someone else to send them a sexual text or email. Girls who had sexted were more likely to begin dating early and to engage in risky sexual behavior.

Baron Bratby / Alamy Stock Photo

What about you? Before pressing "send," consider:

- *Don't believe that what you sext will remain private.* Many teens say they have received a sext that was meant to be private.
- *Whatever you sext may never go away.* Potential employers, college recruiters, teachers and coaches, parents, friends, and total strangers may be able to access your posts, even if you delete them.
- *Resist pressure to sext. Many adolescent girls* say that "pressure from guys" is a reason they sext.
- *Consider the recipient's reaction before you press send.* A girl may send sexually suggestive content for a "joke," but guys may think that the girl will hook up in real life.
- *Nothing you post or send will necessarily remain anonymous.* People you meet online can often track you down on the basis of your screen name and other information you have provided.

12-3b TEENAGE PREGNANCY

In the United States today, the great majority of single adolescents who become pregnant do so accidentally and without committed partners (America's Children, 2013). Most young women in developed nations defer pregnancy until after they have completed some or all of their education. Many do so until they are well into their careers and in their late 20s, their 30s, even their 40s.

Why do single U.S. adolescents get pregnant? For one thing, adolescent girls typically get little advice in school or at home about how to deal with boys' sexual advances. Another reason is failure to use contraception. Some initiate sex at very early ages, when they are least likely to use contraception (Martin et al., 2015; Martinez & Abma, 2015). Many adolescent girls, especially younger adolescents, do not have access to contraceptive devices. Among those who do, fewer than half use them reliably.

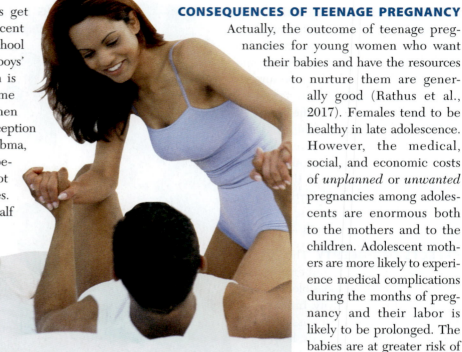

Fuse/Getty Images

About 700,000 U.S. teenagers become pregnant each year. Most of them do so accidentally, and without a committed partner.

Some teenage girls purposefully get pregnant to try to force their partners to make a commitment to them. Some are rebelling against their parents or the moral standards of their communities. But most girls are impregnated because they and their partners miscalculate the odds of getting pregnant (Guttmacher Institute, 2013).

For all these reasons, about 700,000 teenage girls in the United States are impregnated each year. The pregnancies result in about 400,000 births. However, large this number may sound, 10 to 20 years ago, about 1 million girls were getting pregnant each year. Researchers at the Centers for Disease Control and Prevention attribute the drop-off in careless sex to educational efforts by schools, the media, religious institutions, and communities (America's Children, 2013).

Nearly half of pregnant teenagers will have an abortion (Guttmacher Institute, 2016). Most others will become single mothers.

TRUTH

 F About three-quarters of a million U.S. teenagers become pregnant each year.

It is true that about three-quarters of a million single U.S. teenagers become pregnant each year, mostly because of miscalculation of the odds of getting pregnant.

CONSEQUENCES OF TEENAGE PREGNANCY Actually, the outcome of teenage pregnancies for young women who want their babies and have the resources to nurture them are generally good (Rathus et al., 2017). Females tend to be healthy in late adolescence. However, the medical, social, and economic costs of *unplanned* or *unwanted* pregnancies among adolescents are enormous both to the mothers and to the children. Adolescent mothers are more likely to experience medical complications during the months of pregnancy and their labor is likely to be prolonged. The babies are at greater risk of being premature and of low birth weight (Mathews & MacDorman, 2007). These medical problems are not necessarily because of the age of the mother, but rather because single teenage mothers—especially poor single teenage mothers—are less likely to have access to prenatal care or to obtain adequate nutrition.

The teenage mother is less likely than her peers to graduate from high school or move on the postsecondary education. Therefore, she will earn less and be in greater need of public assistance. Few teenage mothers obtain assistance from the babies' fathers. The fathers typically cannot support themselves, much less a family.

PREVENTING TEENAGE PREGNANCY The past several decades have seen a dramatic increase in programs to help prevent teenage pregnancies. Prevention efforts include educating teenagers about sexuality and contraception and providing family planning services. A majority of U.S. parents want their children to have sex education in the schools.

How successful are sex education programs? The better programs increase students' knowledge about sexuality. Despite fears that sex education will increase sexual activity in teenagers, some programs seem to delay the onset of sexual activity (Bennett & Assefi, 2005; Kirby, 2011). Among teenagers who already are sexually active, sex education is associated with the increased use of effective contraception.

12-3c SEXUAL ORIENTATION AND SEXUAL IDENTITY

Most people, including a majority of adolescents, have a heterosexual sexual orientation. They are sexually attracted to and interested in forming romantic relationships with people of the other gender. However, some people have a **homosexual** orientation. They are attracted to and interested in forming romantic relationships with people of their own gender. Males with a homosexual orientation are referred to as *gay males*. Females with a homosexual orientation are referred to as *lesbians*. However, males and females with a homosexual orientation are sometimes categorized together as "gay people," or "gays." **Bisexual** people are attracted to both females and males. **Transgender** individuals feel that they are actually members of the other gender, "trapped" in the body of the wrong gender. Collectively, lesbian, gay, bisexual, and transgender individuals are frequently referred to as **LGBT** people.

A person's **sexual identity** is the label that he or she adopts to inform others as to who they are as a sexual being, especially concerning sexual orientation. Most people's sexual identity is consistent with their sexual orientation. That is, most people who are attracted to members of the other gender identify themselves as "heterosexual" or "straight." Most people who are attracted to people of the same gender see themselves as being "lesbian" or "gay." However, some people's sexual orientation does not correspond to their sexual identity.

About 7% of U.S. women and men define themselves as being "other than heterosexual," but the behavior of the other 93% doesn't exactly match up with the way in which people label themselves. For example, nearly twice as many people—about 14%—say they have had oral sex with a person of the same gender (Herbenick et al., 2010a, 2010b, 2010c; Reece et al., 2010).

DEVELOPMENT OF SEXUAL ORIENTATION Theories of the origins of sexual orientation look both at nature and nurture—the biological makeup of the individual and environmental factors. Some theories bridge the two.

Social cognitive theorists look for the roles of factors such as reinforcement and observational learning. From this perspective, reinforcement of sexual behavior with members of one's own gender—as in reaching orgasm with them when members of the other gender are unavailable—might affect one's sexual orientation. Similarly, childhood sexual abuse by someone of the same gender could lead to a pattern of sexual activity with people of one's own gender and affect sexual orientation. Observation of others engaged in enjoyable male–male or female–female sexual encounters could also affect the development of sexual orientation. But critics point out that most individuals become aware of their sexual orientation before they experience sexual contacts with other people of either gender (Calzo et al., 2011; Savin-Williams, 2011). Moreover, in a society where many still frown upon the LGBT community, young people are unlikely to believe that an other-than-heterosexual orientation or identity will have positive effects for them.

There is evidence for genetic factors in sexual orientation or identity (Brakefield et al., 2014). About 52% of identical (MZ) twin pairs are concordant (in agreement) for a gay male sexual orientation compared with 22% for fraternal (DZ) twins and 11% for adoptive brothers (Dawood et al., 2009). Monozygotic (MZ) twins fully share their genetic heritage, whereas dizygotic (DZ) twins, like other pairs of siblings, overlap 50%.

It has been demonstrated repeatedly that sex hormones predispose lower animals toward stereotypical masculine or feminine mating patterns (Hines et al., 2015; Pradhan et al., 2015). But can sex hormones influence the developing human embryo and fetus (Garcia-Falgueras & Swaab, 2010)? Swedish neuroscientists Ivanka Savic and her colleagues (2011) report evidence that one's gender identity as being male or being female and one's sexual orientation (heterosexual, homosexual, bisexual, or transgender) can develop during the intrauterine period. They point out that sexual differentiation of the sex organs occurs during the first two months of pregnancy, whereas sexual differentiation of the brain begins later, during the second half of pregnancy. Sexual differentiation of the genitals and the brain both depend on surges of testosterone, but because they happen at different times, they can occur independently. Therefore, it is possible that an individual's sex organs can develop in one direction while the biological factors that may underlie one's sexual orientation develop in another direction.

homosexual referring to an erotic orientation toward members of one's own gender.

bisexual attracted to individuals of both genders.

transgendered psychologically belonging to the other gender—that is, the gender that is inconsistent with one's sexual anatomy.

LGBT acronym for *l*esbian, *g*ay, *b*isexual, and *t*ransgendered.

sexual identity the label a person uses to signal who she or he is as a sexual being, especially concerning her or his sexual orientation.

bilderlounge/bilderlounge/Getty Images

According to Ritch Savin-Williams (2011), the development of sexual orientation in gay males and lesbians involves several steps: attraction to members of the same gender, self-labeling as gay or lesbian, sexual contact with members of the same gender, and eventual disclosure of one's sexual orientation to other people. There is generally a gap of about ten years between initial attraction to members of the same gender, which tends to occur at about the age of eight or nine, and disclosure of one's orientation to other people, which usually occurs at about age 18. But some gay males and lesbians never disclose their sexual orientations to anyone or to certain people, such as their parents.

The process of "coming out"—that is, accepting one's sexual minority identity and declaring it to others—can be a long and painful struggle (Mustanski et al., 2014). Gay adolescents may be ostracized and rejected by family and friends. Depression and suicide rates are higher among gay youth than among heterosexual adolescents (Stone et al., 2014). About one in three LGBT adolescents has attempted suicide or engaged in self-harm (Liu & Mustanski, 2012). LGBT adolescents often engage in substance abuse, run away from home, and do poorly in school (Moskowitz et al., 2013; Dermody et al., 2016).

"Coming out to others" sometimes means an open declaration to the world. More often, an adolescent feels more comfortable telling a couple of close friends. Before they inform family members, gay adolescents often anticipate their family's negative reactions, including denial, anger, and rejection (Mustanski et al., 2014). Yet some families are more accepting.

juvenile delinquency conduct in a child or adolescent characterized by illegal activities.

12-4 JUVENILE DELINQUENCY

The term **juvenile delinquency** refers to children or adolescents who engage in illegal activities and come into contact with the criminal justice system. At the most extreme end, juvenile delinquency includes serious behaviors such as homicide, rape, and robbery. Less serious offenses, such as truancy, underage drinking, running away from home, and sexual promiscuity, are considered illegal only when performed by minors. Hence, these activities are termed *status offenses*.

Antisocial and criminal behaviors show a dramatic increase in many societies during adolescence and then taper off during adulthood. For example, about four in ten serious crimes in the United States are committed by individuals under the age of 21, and about three in ten are committed by adolescents under 18 (Snyder & Sickmund, 2006).

Many delinquent acts do not result in arrest or conviction. And when adolescents are arrested, their cases may be disposed of informally, as by referral to a mental health agency (Snyder & Sickmund, 2006).

Boys are much more likely than girls to engage in delinquent behavior, especially crimes of violence. On the other hand, girls are more likely to commit status offenses such as truancy or running away (Snyder & Sickmund, 2006).

12-5 SUICIDE: WHEN THE ADOLESCENT HAS NOTHING—EXCEPT EVERYTHING—TO LOSE

Adolescence is such an exciting time of life. For many, the future is filled with promise. Many count the days until they graduate high school, until they enter college. Many enjoy thrilling fantasies of what might be. And then there are those who take their own lives. Suicide is the second leading cause of death among adolescents (Heron, 2016). Since 1960, the suicide rate has more than tripled for young people aged 15 to 24. About 1 to 2 U.S. adolescents in 10,000 commit suicide each year. About 1 in 10 has attempted suicide at least once.

FICTION

T (F) Suicide is the leading cause of death among U.S. adolescents.

It is not true that suicide is the leading cause of death among U.S. adolescents. But it's close. Right behind accidents.

12-5a RISK FACTORS IN SUICIDE

Most suicides among adolescents and adults are linked to feelings of depression and hopelessness (Miranda & Shaffer, 2013). Suicidal adolescents experience four areas of psychological problems: (1) confusion about the self, (2) impulsiveness, (3) emotional instability, and (4) interpersonal problems (Rathus & Miller, 2002). Some suicidal teenagers are highly achieving, rigid perfectionists who have set impossibly high expectations for themselves. Many teenagers throw themselves into feelings of depression and hopelessness by comparing themselves negatively with others, even when the comparisons are inappropriate. ("Yes, you didn't get into Harvard, but you did get into the University of California at Irvine, and it's a great school.")

Adolescent suicide attempts are more common after stressful life events, especially events that entail loss of social support, as in the death of a parent or friend, breaking up with a boyfriend or girlfriend, or a family member's leaving home (Nock et al., 2013). Other contributors to suicidal behavior include concerns over sexuality, school grades, problems at home, and substance abuse (Nock et al., 2013). It is not always a stressful event itself that precipitates suicide, but the adolescent's anxiety or fear of being "found out" for something, such as failing a course or getting arrested.

Suicide tends to run in families (Centers for Disease Control and Prevention, 2013, 2014). Do genetic factors play a role, possibly leading to psychological problems, such as depression, that are connected with suicide?

Researchers have found the following warning signs of suicide among adolescents (May & Klonsky, 2011):

- Belief that it is acceptable to kill oneself
- Drug abuse and other kinds of delinquency
- Victimization by bullying
- Extensive body piercing
- Stress
- Hostility
- Depression and other psychological disorders
- Heavy smoking
- Low self-esteem
- Increasing age from 11 to 21

Why do you think that extensive body piercing is considered a warning sign of possible suicide among adolescents? Can you find teenagers in the news who have committed suicide because they were bullied? Why do you think that heavy smoking is a warning sign?

12-5b ETHNICITY, GENDER, AND SUICIDE

Rates of suicide and suicide attempts vary among different ethnic groups. Native American and Latin American teenagers have the highest suicide rates, in part because of the stresses to which they are exposed, in part because of their lack of access to health care (Centers for Disease Control and Prevention, 2014). European Americans are next. African American teens are least likely to attempt suicide or to think about it (Heron, 2016).

About three times as many adolescent females as males attempt suicide, but about four times as many males complete a suicide (Heron, 2016).

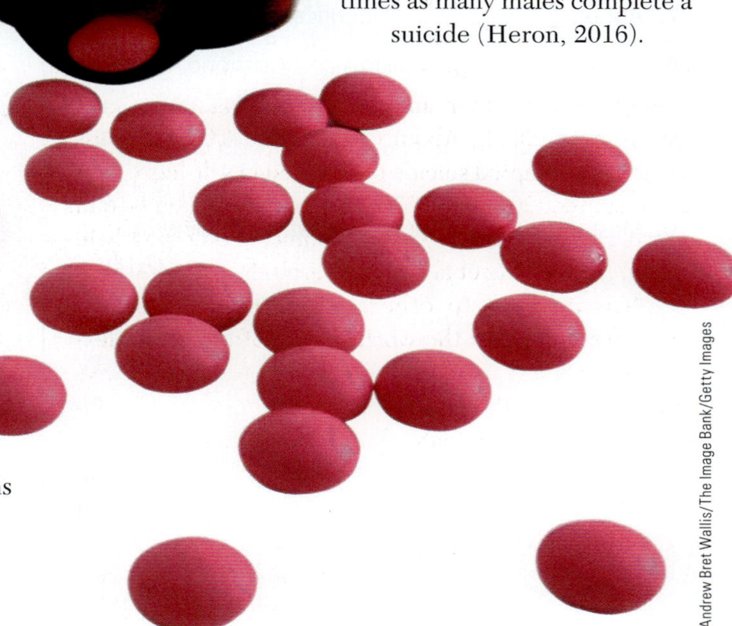

Andrew Bret Wallis/The Image Bank/Getty Images

STUDY TOOLS 12

READY TO STUDY?

In the book, you can:

- ☐ Rip out the chapter review card at the back of the book for a handy summary of the chapter and key terms.
- ☐ Check your understanding of what you've read with the quizzes that follow.

ONLINE AT CENGAGEBRAIN.COM YOU CAN:

- ☐ Collect StudyBits while you read and study the chapter.
- ☐ Quiz yourself on key concepts.
- ☐ Find videos for further exploration.
- ☐ Prepare for tests with HDEV5 Flash Cards as well as those you create.

SELF-ASSESSMENTS

Fill Ins

Answers can be found in the back of the book.

1. In terms of parenting styles, adolescents with ____________ parents show the most competent behavior.
2. ____________ appears to be more central to the friendships of girls than of boys.
3. Eighteen-year-olds are more likely than 15-year-olds to mention ____________ when describing romantic relationships.
4. Peer influence declines after about age ____________.
5. Because of the flood of sex hormones, adolescents tend to experience a powerful ____________ drive.
6. Most adolescents have a(n) ____________ sexual orientation.
7. About ____________ of identical (MZ) twins are concordant (in agreement) for a gay male sexual orientation.
8. According to Savin-Williams and Diamond, the first step in the development of sexual orientation in gay males and lesbians involves ____________.
9. When teenagers are asked why they do not wait to have sex until they are older, the main reason reported is usually ____________.
10. Most adolescent suicides are linked to feelings of ____________.

Multiple Choice

1. **Which of the following has not been shown to be a risk factor for adolescent suicide?**
   a. belief that it is unacceptable to kill oneself
   b. extensive body piercing
   c. depression
   d. increasing from age 11 to age 21

2. **About ____________% of serious crimes in the United States are committed by individuals under the age of 21.**
   a. 10
   b. 20
   c. 40
   d. 60

3. **Which of the following is true of sexual orientation?**
   a. Sexual orientation is a preference.
   b. The majority of people in the United States are lesbian, gay, or bisexual.
   c. Diet affects sexual orientation.
   d. More people engage in sexual behavior with people of the same gender than report that they are gay or lesbian.

4. **Which of the following is accurate about the incidences of kissing, petting, oral sex, and sexual intercourse?**
   a. There is no way of estimating the incidence of these behaviors.
   b. The incidence of these behaviors increases with age.
   c. The incidence of these behaviors among teenagers has been declining rapidly.
   d. Adolescents who engage in petting or oral sex are no longer virgins.

5. **Adolescents are likely to have attitudes similar to their parents concerning all of the following *except***
   a. career goals.
   b. religious preference.
   c. belief in the value of education.
   d. clothing and hair styles.

6. **Of teenagers who use social media, approximately ____________% report having Facebook profiles or accounts.**
   a. 34
   b. 54
   c. 74
   d. 94

7. **Which of the following is the most accurate statement about U.S. adolescents' relationships with their fathers?**
   a. The majority of adolescents live in a home without a father.
   b. Most adolescents are involved in constant bickering with their fathers.
   c. Male adolescents interact more with their fathers than their mothers.
   d. Good relations with fathers contribute to adolescents' well-being.

8. **Self-esteem tends to hit a low point at the age of**
   a. 10 or 11.
   b. 12 or 13.
   c. 14 or 15.
   d. 16 or 17.

9. **In terms of Marcia's identity statuses, the adolescent who is most developed in terms of identity has the status of**
   a. identity achievement.
   b. foreclosure.
   c. moratorium.
   d. identity diffusion.

10. **Which of the following statements about adolescents and their friends is *not* true?**
    a. Friends tend to be of the same race.
    b. Girls tend to have one or two close friends.
    c. Adolescents prefer friends of the other gender.
    d. Friendship contributes to psychological adjustment.

13 Early Adulthood: Physical and Cognitive Development

Mint Images Limited / Alamy Stock Photo

LEARNING OUTCOMES

After studying this chapter, you will be able to . . .

13-1 Discuss the (theoretical) stage of emerging adulthood

13-2 Describe trends in physical development in early adulthood

13-3 Discuss health in early adulthood, focusing on causes of death, diet, exercise, and substance use and abuse

13-4 Discuss sexuality in early adulthood, focusing on sexually transmitted infections, menstrual problems, and sexual coercion

13-5 Discuss cognitive development in early adulthood, focusing on "postformal" developments and effects of college life

13-6 Describe career choice and development during early adulthood

After you finish this chapter, go to **PAGE 273** for **STUDY TOOLS**

Over the years, marriage has been a key standard for adulthood for developmentalists (Aurelle, 2013). Other criteria include holding a full-time job and living independently. Today, the transition to adulthood is mainly marked by adjustment issues such as settling on one's values and beliefs, accepting self-responsibility, becoming financially independent, and establishing an equal relationship with one's parents (Mortimer, 2012).

Adulthood is usually defined in terms of what people do rather than how old they are.

Adulthood itself has been divided into stages. The first of these, early adulthood, is usually considered to range from the ages of 20 to 40, although, as we will see, it can overlap with emerging adulthood.

Early adulthood is seen as the period when people focus on establishing careers or pathways in life. It has been acknowledged that the transition to adulthood can be rapid or piecemeal, with many individuals in their late teens and early 20s remaining dependent on parents and reluctant or unable to make enduring commitments in terms of identity formation or intimate relationships. The question is whether we can speak of the existence of another stage of development, one that bridges adolescence and early adulthood. A number of developmental theorists, including Jeffrey Arnett (2014), who terms this stage emerging adulthood, believe that we can.

13-1 EMERGING ADULTHOOD

> *When our mothers were our age, they were engaged. They at least had some idea what they were going to do with their lives. I, on the other hand, will have a dual degree in majors that are ambiguous at best and impractical at worst (English and political science), no ring on my finger and no idea who I am, much less what I want to do. Under duress, I will admit that this is a pretty exciting time. Sometimes, when I look out across the wide expanse that is my future, I can see beyond the void. I realize that having nothing ahead to count on means I now have to count on myself; that having no direction means forging one of my own.*
>
> —Kristen, age 22 (Page, 1999, pp. 18, 20)

Well, Kristen has some work to do: She needs to forge her own direction. Kristen is accumulating information about herself and the world outside. In earlier days, adolescents made a transition directly into adulthood. Now many of them in affluent nations with abundant opportunities spend time in what some theorists consider a new period of development roughly spanning the ages of 18 to 25: **emerging adulthood**.

Sandwiched between the stages of adolescence, which precedes it, and young adulthood, which follows it, emerging adulthood is theorized to be a distinct period of development that is found in societies that allow young people an extended opportunity to explore their roles in life. Some parents in the United States are often affluent enough to continue to support their children through college and graduate school. When parents cannot do the job, the government may step in to help, as through student loans. These supports allow many young people the luxury of sorting out identity issues and creating meaningful life plans. But even in the United States, of course, many, perhaps most, young people cannot afford the luxury of sojourning in emerging adulthood.

emerging adulthood a theoretical period of development, spanning the ages of 18 to 25, in which young people in developed nations engage in extended role exploration.

TRUTH OR FICTION?

T	F	HIV/AIDS is the leading cause of death of young adults in the United States today.
T	F	Menstrual discomfort is abnormal.
T	F	The majority of rapes are committed by strangers in deserted neighborhoods or darkened alleyways.
T	F	Piaget proposed a fifth stage of cognitive development, the postformal stage.
T	F	Million-dollar lottery winners often feel aimless and dissatisfied if they quit their jobs after striking it rich.

Jeffrey Arnett (2012, 2016) hypothesizes that five features distinguish the stage of emerging adulthood: identity exploration, instability, self-focus, feeling in-between, and a sense of the possibilities.

13-1a THE AGE OF IDENTITY EXPLORATION

Many people age 18 or 20 to about 25 or 30 are on the path to making vital choices in terms of their love lives and their career lives. They are experimenting with romantic partners and career possibilities.

13-1b THE AGE OF INSTABILITY

In times gone by, many adolescents obtained jobs fresh out of high school—if they completed high school—and kept them for many years, sometimes a lifetime. Today, Arnett notes, Americans have on average about seven different jobs during the years between 20 and 29. Over this period they frequently change their romantic partners—sometimes by choice, sometimes because the partner decided to move on. They frequently switch their living arrangements, often moving from place to place with little if any furniture, and change educational directions—finding what they like, finding what they can actually do, and finding what is available to them.

Bill Varie / Alamy Stock Photo

Emerging adults in our society tend to be self-focused, meaning that they are responding to the fact that they are freer to make decisions than they were as children and will be as adults.

13-1c THE AGE OF SELF-FOCUS

People are exceptionally self-focused during emerging adulthood (Paulsen et al., 2016). This does not mean that they are egocentric as in childhood or adolescence (Arnett, 2016), or selfish. It means, simply, that they are freer to make decisions than they were as children or adolescents. They are more mature and more independent from parental influences; they usually have more resources than they did before, but are not yet encumbered by the constraints of trying to mesh their lives with those of life partners.

13-1d THE AGE OF FEELING IN-BETWEEN

Emerging adults are similar to adolescents in one way: Whereas adolescents may feel that they exist somewhere between childhood and adulthood, emerging adults are likely to think that they are swimming between adolescence and "real" adulthood. They are likely to be out of school—that is, high school or undergraduate college—but obtaining further training or education. They are beyond the sometimes silly flirtations of adolescence but not yet in a long-term, or at least permanent, relationship. They may not be completely dependent on caregivers, but they are just as unlikely to be self-supporting. They may be between roommates or apartments.

Where are they? In transit. Emerging adults seem to be well aware of the issues involved in defining the transition from adolescence to adulthood. Arnett (2000) reported what people say when they are asked whether they think they have become adults. The most common answer of 18- to 25-year-olds was something like, "In some respects yes and in other respects no" (see Figure 13.1). Many think that they have developed beyond the conflicts and exploratory voyages of adolescence, but they may not yet have the ability—or desire—to assume the financial and interpersonal responsibilities they associate with adulthood. Recent college graduates, for example, have an average of $23,300 in loans tol pay back (Martin & Lehren, 2012).

FIG.13.1 SUBJECTIVE CONCEPTIONS OF ADULT STATUS IN RESPONSE TO THE QUESTION, "DO YOU FEEL THAT YOU HAVE REACHED ADULTHOOD?"

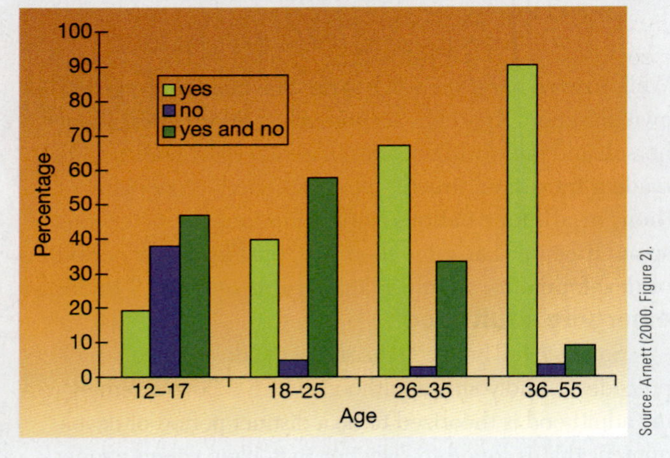

13-1e THE AGE OF POSSIBILITIES

Emerging adults typically feel that the world lies open before them. Like the majority of adults, they have an optimistic bias (Arnett, 2016). They believe that things will work out.

In this age of possibilities, emerging adults have the feeling that they have the opportunity to make dramatic changes in their lives. Unlike children and adolescents, they are, to a large degree, independent of their parents. Many of them leave home for good; others return home for financial reasons. Some have a "revolving door" existence: leaving home and then coming back, according to the ebb and flow of financial and emotional resources.

13-2 PHYSICAL DEVELOPMENT

Physical development peaks in early adulthood. Most people are at their heights of sensory sharpness, strength, reaction time, and cardiovascular fitness. Young adults are at their tallest, and height remains stable through middle adulthood, declining somewhat in late adulthood. A higher percentage of men's body mass is made of muscle, and men are normally stronger than women. Physical strength in both men and women peaks in the 20s and early 30s, then slowly declines (Markham, 2006).

Sensory sharpness also peaks in the early 20s (Fozard & Gordon-Salant, 2001; Naveh-Benjamin & Kilb, 2014). Visual acuity remains stable until middle adulthood, when a gradual decline leads to farsightedness and, in many people, a need for reading glasses. Hearing tends to decline once people reach their late 20s and early 30s, particularly for tones that are high in pitch.

The changes of aging in the cardiovascular, respiratory, and immune systems begin in early adulthood, but they are gradual. The heart muscle becomes more rigid, decreasing the maximum heart rate and reducing the ability of the heart to pump enough blood to provide oxygen for stressful exercise. But regular exercise increases cardiovascular and respiratory capacity from what they would otherwise be at any age. As people age, the immune system produces fewer white blood cells and the disease-fighting ability of those that remain declines.

Fertility in both genders declines as early adulthood progresses and, after age 35, women are usually advised to have their fetuses checked for Down's syndrome and other chromosomal abnormalities. Older men may also contribute to chromosomal abnormalities. A major problem in women is the reduced quality and quantity of ova (egg cells). But because of advances in reproductive technology, today it is not unusual for women to have healthy children, including their first children, in their 30s and 40s.

Both genders may find their hair thinning and graying by the end of early adulthood. Toward the end of early adulthood, and almost certainly in middle adulthood, the skin begins to loosen, grow less elastic, and wrinkle, more so in women than in men.

13-3 HEALTH AND FITNESS

As a group, young adults tend to be healthy. Their immune systems are generally functioning well. Table 13.1 shows the leading causes of death for 15- to 44-year-olds. The National Center for Health Statistics, which accumulated the data, did not distinguish between 15- to 19-year-olds, who are late adolescents, and 20- to 24-year-olds, who are early adults (and possibly, according to our definition, emerging adults). The leading cause of death for late teenagers and early adults in the United States was clearly accidents. Because 15- to 24-year-olds tend to be healthy, the next two leading causes of death were

Physical strength and sensory sharpness usually peak in the 20s, then undergo a gradual decline.

SM/AIUEO/Stone/Getty Images

TABLE 13.1 LEADING CAUSES OF DEATH FOR 15- TO 44-YEAR-OLDS	
15 – 24	**25 – 44**
Accidents	Accidents
Suicide	Suicide
Homicide	Homicide
Cancer	Cancer
Heart disease	Heart disease
Congenital problems	Liver disease
Influenza & pneumonia	Diabetes
Diabetes	HIV/AIDS
Respiratory disease	Stroke
Stroke	Influenza & pneumonia

Source: National Vital Statistics System, National Center for Health Statistics, CDC. 10 Leading Causes of Death by Age Group, United States–2014. Produced by: National Center for Injury Prevention and Control, CDC.

also by violence—self-inflicted (suicide) and by others (homicide). Homicide does not disappear as one of the top 10 leading causes of death until middle age (which is bounded by the ages of 40–45 at the lower end and 60–65 at the upper end). Cancer and heart disease take fourth and fifth place. HIV/ AIDS becomes a much more prominent cause of death among 25- to 44-year-olds because it takes many years for the condition to overwhelm the body's immune system, even if the infection occurred during the teenage years or early 20s.

FICTION

T (F) HIV/AIDS is the leading cause of death of young adults in the United States today.

It is not true that HIV/AIDS is the leading cause of death of young adults in the United States today. Accidents are the most prominent cause of death for young men and women.

Given that so many young adults are in excellent or good health, it is ironic that many are careless about their health or put it on the "back burner." Many are concerned about their careers or college or their social lives and think of health issues—diet, smoking, sedentary lives, excessive drinking—as something they can get to later on.

Consider the results of a poll by the Centers for Disease Control and Prevention (CDC) that reported on the health-related behavior patterns of a nationally representative sample of more than 18,000 young adults aged 18–24 (McCracken et al., 2007). Forty-three percent reported either no or insufficient physical activity. More than one in four (29%) were smokers, and 30% reported binge drinking—having five drinks in a row on single occasions. About one respondent in four (26%) was *overweight* (having a body mass index [BMI] of 25.0–29.9; see Figure 13.2), and another 14% were *obese* (having a BMI of 30.0 or above). Other CDC polls show that only 13% of Americans eat the recommended amounts of fruit, and only 9% eat the recommended amount of vegetables (MMWR, 2015).

13-3a DIET AND WEIGHT

The "good news" in the CDC survey (McCracken et al., 2007) is that the 40% of 18- to 24-year-olds reported as being overweight or obese is lower than the more than

The Skinny on Weight Control

The most effective and healthful weight-control programs involve improving nutritional knowledge, decreasing calorie intake, exercising, and changing eating habits by reducing portion sizes and eating less saturated fat and cholesterol. Most health professionals believe that people in the United States eat too much animal fat and not enough fruits and vegetables (see www.choosemyplate.gov). Dieting plus exercise is more effective than dieting alone. Exercise burns calories and builds muscle tissue, which metabolizes more calories than fatty tissue does.

Cognitive-behavioral methods such as the following also help:

- **Establish calorie-intake goals and keep track of whether you are meeting them.**
- **Eat preplanned low-calorie snacks.**
- **Take a five-minute break between helpings. Ask yourself, "Am I still hungry?" If not, stop eating.**
- **Avoid temptations. Plan your meal before entering a restaurant. Shop from a list.**
- **Reward yourself for meeting calorie goals (not with food).**
- **Mentally rehearse solutions to problems. Plan what you will do when cake is handed out at the office party or when you visit relatives who try to stuff you with food.**
- **If you binge, don't give up. Resume dieting the next day.**

two in three adults reported in the general adult population (Bray & Bouchard, 2014; Ogden et al., 2014). Overweight and obese young women are more likely than young men to report dieting. The gender difference in dieting is found among the entire adult population (Bish et al., 2005).

Why are so many young adults overweight and obese? Many biological and psychological factors are involved. Being overweight runs in families, and it is widely accepted that heredity plays a role in overweight in humans (Albuquerque et al., 2016; Perusse et al., 2014). Efforts by overweight and obese people to maintain a slender profile may be sabotaged by a mechanism that would help preserve life in times of famine—**adaptive thermogenesis** (Browning, 2016; Schutz & Dullou, 2014). This mechanism causes the body to produce less energy (burn fewer calories) when someone goes on a diet. This does not mean that overweight people will not lose weight by dieting; it means that it may take longer than expected.

adaptive thermogenesis the process by which the body converts food energy (calories) to heat at a lower rate when a person eats less, because of, for example, famine or dieting.

Fatty tissue in the body also metabolizes (burns) food more slowly than muscle. For this reason, a person with a high fat-to-muscle ratio metabolizes food more slowly than

Antonio Guillem Fernández / Alamy Stock Photo

FIG.13.2 BODY MASS INDEX

Height	Body Mass Index (BMI)															
	19	20	21	22	23	24	25	26	27	28	29	30	31	32	33	34
58″	91	96	100	105	110	115	119	124	129	134	138	143	148	153	158	162
59″	94	99	104	109	114	119	124	128	133	138	143	148	153	158	163	168
60″	97	102	107	112	118	123	128	133	138	143	148	153	158	163	168	174
61″	100	106	111	116	122	127	132	137	143	148	153	158	164	169	174	160
62″	104	109	115	120	126	131	136	142	147	153	158	164	169	175	180	186
63″	107	113	118	124	130	135	141	146	152	158	163	169	175	180	186	191
64″	110	116	122	128	134	140	145	151	157	163	169	174	180	186	192	197
65″	114	120	126	132	138	144	150	156	162	168	174	180	186	192	198	204
66″	118	124	130	136	142	148	155	161	167	173	179	186	192	198	204	210
67″	121	127	134	140	146	153	159	166	172	178	185	191	198	204	211	217
68″	125	131	138	144	151	158	164	171	177	184	190	197	203	210	216	223
69″	128	135	142	149	155	162	169	176	182	189	196	203	209	216	223	230
70″	132	139	146	153	160	167	174	181	188	195	202	209	216	222	229	236
71″	136	143	150	157	165	172	179	186	193	200	208	215	222	229	236	243
72″	140	147	154	162	169	177	184	191	199	206	213	221	228	235	242	250
73″	144	151	159	166	174	182	189	197	204	212	219	227	235	242	250	257
74″	148	155	163	171	179	186	194	202	210	218	225	233	241	249	256	264
75″	152	160	168	176	184	192	200	208	216	224	232	240	248	256	264	272
76″	156	164	172	180	189	197	205	213	221	230	238	246	254	263	271	279
	Body Weight (pounds)															

Your BMI is based on your height and weight. You can locate your own BMI by finding your height in inches and then running your finger from left to right until you find your weight. Then look at the top of the chart to find your BMI. Health professionals consider a BMI of 25 to 29 to be overweight, and 30 or above to be obese.

a person of the same weight with more muscle (Langin & Lafontan, 2014). Family celebrations, watching television, arguments, and tension at work can all lead to overeating or going off a diet. Efforts to diet may also be impeded by negative emotions such as depression and anxiety, which can lead to binge eating (Rosenbaum & White, 2013).

13-3b EXERCISE

According to the CDC (*Physical Activity for Everyone*, 2011), adults 18 and older need at least 30 minutes of vigorous physical activity five days a week. Significant benefits can be reaped from a moderate amount of activity, such as 30 minutes of brisk walking or raking leaves, 15 minutes of running, or 45 minutes of volleyball. You can break 30 to 60 minutes of physical activity into smaller segments of 10 or 15 minutes through the day. The CDC recommends the combinations of activities shown in Figure 13.3.

This amount of activity can substantially reduce the risk of developing or dying from cardiovascular disease, type 2 diabetes, and certain cancers, such as colon cancer. Exercise also benefits the brain and cognitive performance (Hollas et al., 2014; P. J. Smith et al., 2010). Exercise may even help with psychological disorders such as anxiety and depression (Herring et al., 2012a, 2012b). The "trick" for most young adults is to integrate exercise into their daily routines, perhaps by means of moderately vigorous activities for 15 minutes two times a day or for 10 minutes three times a day.

In general, mankind, since the improvement of cookery, eats twice as much as nature requires.

HELLO my name is Benjamin Franklin

C Squared Studios/Photodisc/Getty Images; ClassicStock/Alamy Stock Photo

13-3c SUBSTANCE USE AND ABUSE IN EARLY ADULTHOOD

According to the Monitoring the Future study (Johnston et al., 2013), Americans in early adulthood (ages 19–28) are most likely to use alcohol. As you can see in Table 13.2, more than 80% of young adults have "ever used" alcohol, as compared with 68% of 12th graders (see Table 11.1 on page 227). The percentages increase for at least two reasons: One is that young adults are more likely to be emancipated from parental and school rules than high school students. Second, young adults have simply had several years of greater opportunity to experiment with and use drugs.

FIG.13.3 PHYSICAL ACTIVITY RECOMMENDATIONS FROM THE CDC

It is recommended that adults obtain:

5 hours (300 minutes) each week of *moderate-intensity aerobic activity* and

muscle-strengthening activities on 2 or more days a week that work all major muscle groups (legs, hips, back, abdomen, chest, shoulders, and arms)

2 hours and 30 minutes (150 minutes) each week of *vigorous-intensity aerobic activity* and

muscle-strengthening activities on 2 or more days a week that work all major muscle groups (legs, hips, back, abdomen, chest, shoulders, and arms).

An equivalent mix of moderate- and vigorous-intensity *aerobic activity* and

muscle-strengthening activities on 2 or more days a week that work all major muscle groups (legs, hips, back, abdomen, chest, shoulders, and arms).

Source of data: Physical Activity for Everyone (2011).

The story is different for marijuana. A larger percentage of 12th graders than young adults have used marijuana (compare Tables 11.1 and 13.2). How is this possible? One answer is that there is apparently a cohort effect (Johnston et al., 2015). That is, today's 12th graders may be more drawn to marijuana than today's young adults were at the same age. Marijuana may also be easier to get for them. Then, too, today's 12th graders are a bit less likely (39%) than young adults (42–44%) to believe that smoking marijuana regularly is a great risk. Table 13.2 also shows that college students are somewhat more likely (34.4%) than young adults in general (31.6%) to have used marijuana in the past year. College students may experience more peer pressure to use marijuana. Moreover, fewer than half of young adults say that smoking marijuana regularly is a great risk (see Table 13.3).

The perils of cigarette smoking have been so broadly publicized that eight to nine of ten young adults say that smoking one or more packs a day is a great risk, which is a major reason that only two to three college students and young adults out of ten have smoked in the past year. But only one in five or six young adults say smoking e-cigarettes is a great risk. The great majority of college students and young adults also believe that trying cocaine and heroin are great risks, largely because they suspect that trying these substances may well lead to regular use. Interestingly, only one young adult in 20 sees a great risk in trying a drink or two, and one in five or six sees harm in having a drink or two a day, which is presumably why so many use it.

LSC Youth/LatinStock Collection / Alamy Stock Photo

Having tried or experimented with a drug is very different from continuing or regular use of the drug. The Monitoring the Future group found that four out of five young adults have used alcohol in the last year (Table 13.2), but 68.4% have used it in the past 30 days (Table 13.4). Only 1.3 percent have used it recently (in the past 30 days). One in five young adults has smoked marijuana in the last 30 days. Table 13.4 also reveals that over the past 20 years use of alcohol has remained stable, use of cigarettes has declined, and use of marijuana has increased. Recreational use of marijuana was illegal throughout the 50 states of the United States when young adults were surveyed in 2012, but is now legal in a number of states.

TABLE 13.2 HAVE YOU USED __________ IN THE PAST YEAR?

Percent of college students and young adults (aged 19–28) saying "yes":

	College students	Young Adults
Alcohol	76.1	82.3
Amphetamines	10.1	8.0
Cigarettes	22.6	27.0
Cocaine	4.4	5.0
Ecstasy	5.0	4.8
Heroin	0.0	0.4
Narcotics other than heroin*	4.8	6.3
LSD	2.2	2.2
Marijuana	34.4	31.6

*e.g., OxyContin, Vicodin

Source: Johnston, L. D., O'Malley, P. M., Bachman, J. G., Schulenberg, J. E. & Miech, R. A. (2015). Monitoring the Future national survey results on drug use, 1975–2014: Volume 2, College students and adults ages 19–55. Ann Arbor: Institute for Social Research, The University of Michigan.

TABLE 13.3 PERCEIVED HARMFULNESS IF PEOPLE . . .

Percent of people aged 19–30 who say the following drug use is a "great risk":

Drug use	Percent saying "great risk"
Try marijuana once or twice	8.8 – 9.6
Smoke marijuana regularly	34.5 – 35.3
Try LSD once or twice	40.1 – 45.6
Take LSD regularly	74.7 – 80.3
Try ecstasy once or twice	50.7 – 56.5
Take ecstasy occasionally	71.6 – 77.7
Try cocaine once or twice	50.1 – 57.3
Take cocaine regularly	88.7 – 92.4
Try heroin once or twice	66.1 – 71.7
Take heroin regularly	94.0 – 96.2
Try amphetamines once or twice	30.4 – 37.4
Take amphetamines regularly	65.3 – 68.5
Try one or two drinks of an alcoholic beverage	3.8 – 5.7
Take one or two drinks nearly every day	16.5 – 22.4
Take four or five drinks nearly every day	67.8 – 72.6
Smoke one or two packs of cigarettes a day	82.8 – 83.9
Use e-cigarettes regularly	16.8 – 21.7

Source: Data adapted from Table 6.1 in Johnston, L. D., O'Malley, P. M., Bachman, J. G., Schulenberg, J. E. & Miech, R. A. (2015). Monitoring the Future national survey results on drug use, 1975–2014: Volume 2, College students and adults ages 19–55. Ann Arbor: Institute for Social Research, The University of Michigan.

TABLE 13.4 TRENDS IN USE OF DRUGS IN THE PAST 30 DAYS AMONG YOUNG ADULTS AGES 19–28

Drug	1994	2014
Alcohol	67.7	68.4
Amphetamines	1.7	3.5
Cigarettes	28.0	17.5
Cocaine	1.3	1.3
Ecstasy	0.2	1.3
E-cigarettes	—	10.0
Heroin	0.1	0.2
LSD	1.1	0.4
Marijuana	14.1	19.2

Source: Table 2.3 in in Johnston, L. D., O'Malley, P. M., Bachman, J. G., Schulenberg, J. E. & Miech, R. A. (2015). Monitoring the Future national survey results on drug use, 1975–2014: Volume 2, College students and adults ages 19–55. Ann Arbor: Institute for Social Research, The University of Michigan.

13-3d STRESS AND HEALTH

According to a national poll taken by the American Psychological Association (2012), one-third of Americans report that they are living with "extreme stress." Stress has a negative impact on people's psychological and physical health, with 46% of 18- to 32-year-olds reporting that they have lain awake at night because of stress, 38% saying that they overate or ate unhealthful foods due to stress, and 31% reporting that they missed a meal due to stress (American Psychological Association, 2012). Significant percentages of 18- to 32-year-olds reported experiencing the following sources of stress:

Money	80%
Work	72%
Housing costs	49%
The economy	54%
Relationships	63%

As you can see in Figure 13.4, overall, 18- to 32-year-olds were the age group most likely (52%) to report that the amount of stress they experience increased over the past five years. They were also least likely to say that their stress had decreased (19%).

Stress Management Tips

Here are some suggestions for managing stress more effectively (American Psychological Association, 2014):

1. **Get in touch with the ways in which you experience stress.**
2. **Identify the situations and people that are stressing you out.**
3. **Get in touch with how you handle—or don't handle—stress.**
4. **Develop better ways to cope with stress.**
5. **Take care of your health.**
6. **Obtain social support.**

13-4 SEXUALITY

Sexual activity with a partner usually peaks in the 20s. The results reported in Figure 13.5 represent the percentage of men and women in a nationally representative survey who said that they had sex at least a few times or more often each month.

FIG.13.4 STRESS OVER PAST 5 YEARS

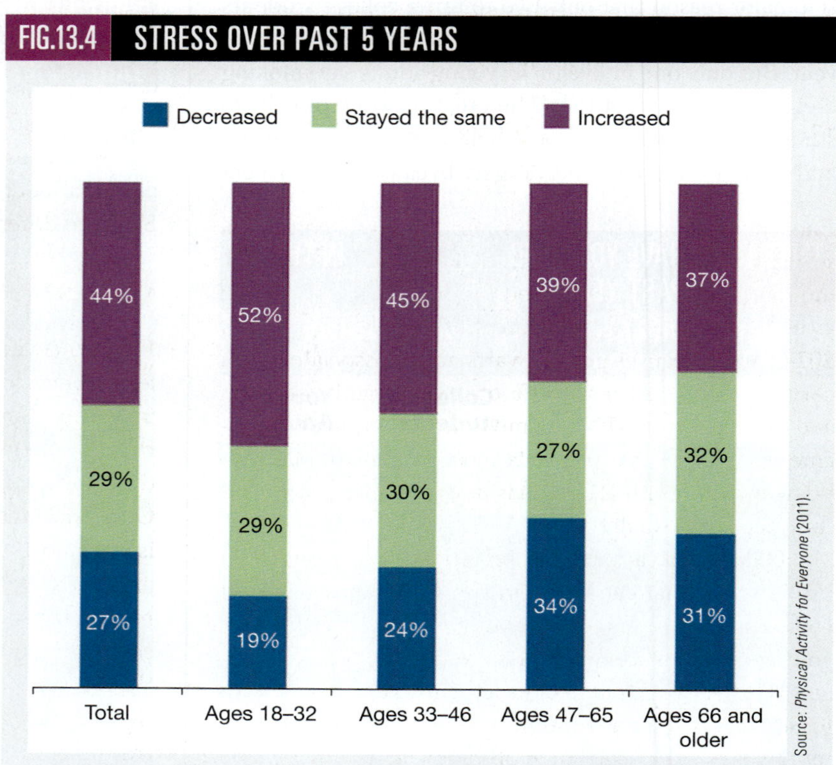

Young adults aged 18–32 were most likely to report that their stress had increased over the past 5 years.

FIG.13.5 FREQUENCY OF SEX BY AGE

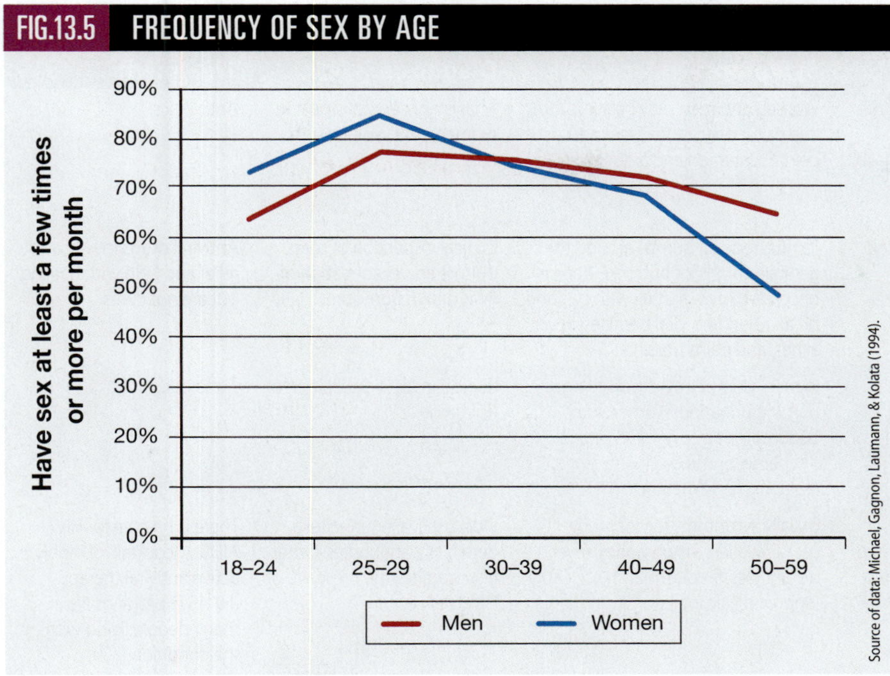

Why does this age group have sex most frequently? The answer is a combination of youth and opportunity. Men and women in this age group are still to some degree experiencing the flood of sex hormones that affected them as adolescents. Now, however, they are of an age at which they are likely to be in sexual relationships.

13-4a SEXUALLY TRANSMITTED INFECTIONS (STIs)

Each year millions of young American adults contract a sexually transmitted infection (STI), including about six million new infections caused by the human papilloma virus (HPV) (Genital HPV Infection—CDC Fact Sheet, 2014), which causes genital warts and is associated with cervical cancer. At least 50% of sexually active women and men contract HPV at some time in their lives. A vaccine is available that prevents most young women from being infected with HPV and is best administered before they become sexually active.

Chlamydia, a bacterial infection of the vagina or urinary tract that can result in sterility, is the next most commonly occurring STI in young adults, followed by gonorrhea, HPV/genital warts, genital herpes, syphilis, and HIV/AIDS. Because of its lethality, HIV/AIDS tends to capture most of the headlines. However, other STIs are more widespread, and some of them can also be deadly.

Nearly 2.8 million new chlamydia infections occur each year (Chlamydia—CDC Fact Sheet, 2014). The incidence of chlamydia is especially high among college students. Chlamydia is a major cause of pelvic inflammatory disease (PID), which can lead to infertility.

HIV/AIDS HIV/AIDS is the most devastating STI. If left untreated, it is lethal, and the long-term prospects of those who do receive treatment remain unknown. HIV—the virus that causes AIDS—has spread rapidly around the world and some 37 million people are living with HIV/AIDS, of which 2.5 million are children under the age of 15 (World Health Organization, 2015). More than 1.1 million Americans are living with HIV/AIDS, and about one in six people are unaware of it (HIV in the United States, 2015). The primary mode of HIV transmission worldwide is male–female intercourse, but anal intercourse is the primary mode of HIV transmission in the United States (HIV/AIDS—CDC Fact Sheet, 2014). Injecting drugs is another way in which HIV is spread because sharing needles with infected individuals can transmit HIV. Other major risk factors include having sex with multiple partners, failing to use condoms, and abusing drugs and alcohol (HIV in the United States, 2015).

The causes, methods of transmission, symptoms, and treatment—where it exists—of HIV/AIDS and other STIs are described in Table 13.5.

13-4b MENSTRUAL PROBLEMS

Fifty to seventy-five percent of women experience at least some discomfort prior to or during menstruation, including dysmenorrhea, menstrual migraines, amenorrhea, premenstrual syndrome (PMS), and premenstrual dysphoric disorder (PMDD) (American College of Obstetricians and Gynecologists, 2011). **Dysmenorrhea** is the most common menstrual problem, and pelvic cramps are the most common symptom. Cramps are most often brought about by high amounts of hormones called **prostaglandins** that cause muscles in the uterine wall to contract, as during labor. Fluid retention in the pelvic region may cause bloating.

dysmenorrhea painful menstruation.

prostaglandins hormones that cause muscles in the uterine wall to contract, as during labor.

TABLE 13.5 OVERVIEW OF SEXUALLY TRANSMITTED INFECTIONS (STIs)

Sti and Cause	Transmission	Symptoms	Diagnosis	Treatment
Chlamydia and nongonococcal urethritis: caused by *Chlamydia trachomatous* bacterium in women	Vaginal, oral, or anal sex. To newborns passing through the birth canal of an infected mother.	Women and men may be symptom-free or experience frequent and painful urination and a discharge.	Analysis of cervical smear in women. Analysis of penile fluid in men.	Antibiotics.
Genital herpes: caused by Herpes simplex virus-type 2 (HSV-2)	Vaginal, oral, or anal sex.	Painful, reddish bumps around the genitals, thighs, or buttocks. Bumps become blisters that fill with pus and break, shedding viral particles. Fever, aches, and pains possible.	Clinical inspection of sores. Culture and examination of fluid drawn from sore.	Antiviral drugs may provide relief and help with healing but are not cures.
Gonorrhea ("clap," "drip"): Gonococcus bacterium (*Neisseria gonorrhoeae*)	Vaginal, oral, or anal sex. To newborns passing through the birth canal of an infected mother.	In men, yellowish, thick discharge, burning urination. Women may be symptom-free or have vaginal discharge, burning urination, or irregular menstruation.	Clinical inspection. Culture of discharge.	Antibiotics.
HIV/AIDS: Acronym for human immunodeficiency virus, the cause of acquired immunodeficiency syndrome	Vaginal or anal sex. Infusion of contaminated blood by needle sharing or from mother to baby during childbirth or breast-feeding.	Usually symptom-free for many years. Swollen lymph nodes, fever, weight loss, fatigue, diarrhea. Deadly "opportunistic infections."	Blood, saliva, or urine tests detect HIV antibodies. Other tests confirm the presence of HIV itself.	There is no cure for HIV/AIDS. A "cocktail" of highly active antiviral therapy (HAART) prolongs life in many people living with the condition.
HPV/Genital warts: caused by human papilloma virus (HPV)	Sexual contact. Contact with infected towels or clothing.	Painless warts resembling cauliflowers on the genitals or anus or in the rectum. Associated with cervical cancer.	Clinical inspection.	A vaccine can prevent infection in most young people. Warts may be removed by freezing, topical drugs, burning, and surgery.
Pubic lice ("crabs"): *Pthirus pubis* (an insect, not a crab)	Sexual contact. Contact with an infested towel, sheet, or toilet seat.	Intense itching in pubic area and other hairy regions to which lice can attach.	Clinical inspection.	Topical drugs containing pyrethrins or piperonal butoxide.
Syphilis: *Treponema pallidum*	Vaginal, oral, or anal sex. Touching an infectious chancre.	Hard, painless chancre appears at site of infection within 2–4 weeks. May progress through additional stages if untreated.	Clinical inspection or examination of fluid from a chancre. Blood test.	Antibiotics.

FICTION

Menstrual discomfort is abnormal.

It is not true that menstrual discomfort is abnormal. Statistically speaking, some degree of menstrual discomfort is the norm.

amenorrhea the absence of menstruation.

premenstrual syndrome (PMS) the discomforting symptoms that affect many women during the 4–6 day interval preceding their periods.

premenstrual dysphoric disorder (PMDD) a condition similar to but more severe than PMS.

Amenorrhea is the absence of menstruation and a sign of infertility. **Premenstrual syndrome (PMS)** describes the combination of biological and psychological symptoms that may affect women during the four- to six-day interval that precedes their menses each month. **Premenstrual dysphoric disorder (PMDD)** is more severe than PMS and a technical term used as a diagnostic category by the American Psychiatric Association (2013). According to the American Psychiatric Association, the diagnosis of PMDD requires that several of the following symptoms be present most of the time during the week before the period and ending within a few days after the period begins: tension, mood changes, irritability and anger, difficulty concentrating, fatigue, changes in appetite, sleeping too much or too little, feeling overwhelmed, and physical discomfort.

The most common premenstrual symptoms are minor psychological discomfort, muscular tension, and aches or pains, but only a small minority of women report symptoms severe enough to impair their social, academic, or occupational functioning. The causes of PMS may involve the body's responses to changing levels of sex hormones. PMS also appears to be linked with imbalances in neurotransmitters such as serotonin and GABA, which are connected with the appetite, anxiety, and mood changes (Eriksson, 2014; MacKenzie & Maguire, 2014). There are many treatment options for PMS: exercise, dietary control, hormone treatments, and medications that reduce anxiety or increase the activity of serotonin in the nervous system.

13-4c RAPE: THE MOST INTIMATE CRIME OF VIOLENCE

According to a poll conducted by the *Washington Post* (2015), 20% of female respondents aged 17 to 26 reported they had been sexually assaulted in college. So did 5% of the men. The women told the interviewers things like "We were kind of wrestling around. Things turned more sexual. I told him to stop. He thought I was joking. I froze." "There was no question about consent. I said 'no' and he didn't care."

Rape has its sexual aspects, but it is also the subjugation of women by men (Malamuth et al., 2005). The definition of rape varies from state to state, but is usually defined as sex with a nonconsenting person by the use of force or the threat of force (Urbina, 2014). Penile–vaginal penetration is usually not necessary to fit the definition. Most states permit the prosecution of husbands who rape their wives.

About 5% of rape victims are men, and their assailants are also generally men. But about two-thirds of victims do not report rapes because of concern that they will be humiliated by the criminal justice system, or else they fear reprisal from their families or the rapist (U.S. Department of Justice, 2011).

FICTION

T (F) The majority of rapes are committed by strangers in deserted neighborhoods or darkened alleyways.

It is not the case that the majority of rapes are committed by strangers in deserted neighborhoods or darkened alleyways. The great majority of rapes are committed by an acquaintance of the victim.

TYPES OF RAPE According to the U.S. Department of Justice (2011), more than 90% of rapes are committed by acquaintances of the victim, including classmates, coworkers, dates, or family friends. Acquaintance rapes are less likely than stranger rapes to be reported to the police, because rape survivors may not perceive sexual assaults by acquaintances as rapes. Even when acquaintance rapes are reported to police, they may be treated as "misunderstandings" or lovers' quarrels rather than crimes (Campbell, 2006). Date rape is a form of acquaintance rape. Date rape is more likely to occur when the couple has too much to drink and then parks in the man's car or goes to his residence (Paul et al., 2013).

SOCIAL ATTITUDES, MYTHS, AND CULTURAL FACTORS THAT ENCOURAGE RAPE Many people believe a number of myths about rape, such as "Women say no when they mean yes" and "The way women dress, they are just asking to be raped" (Moullso & Calhoun, 2013). Yet another myth is that deep down inside, women want to be overpowered and forced into sex by men. These myths have the effect of justifying rape in assailants' and the public's minds.

Males are also often reinforced from childhood for aggressive and competitive behavior, as in sports. Gender typing may lead men to reject "feminine" traits such as tenderness and empathy that might restrain aggression (Flood, 2014).

13-4d SEXUAL HARASSMENT

Sexual harassment occurs everywhere: in colleges, in the workplace, in the military, and online. It victimizes 40% to 60% of working women and similar percentages of female students in colleges and universities (Foote & Goodman-Delahunty, 2005).

For legal purposes, sexual harassment in the workplace is usually defined as deliberate or repeated unwanted comments, gestures, or physical contact. Sexual harassment makes the workplace or other setting a hostile place. Examples range from unwelcome sexual jokes, suggestive comments, verbal abuse, leering at or ogling a person's body, unwelcome physical contact, outright sexual assault, or demands for sex accompanied by threats concerning one's job or student status.

Charges of sexual harassment are often ignored or trivialized by coworkers and employers. The victim may hear, "Why make a big deal out of it? It's not like you were attacked in the street." Yet evidence shows that people who are sexually harassed suffer from it. Some become physically ill (Diehl et al., 2014). Some suffer posttraumatic stress disorder

sexual harassment deliberate or repeated unwanted comments, gestures, or physical contact.

FIG.13.6

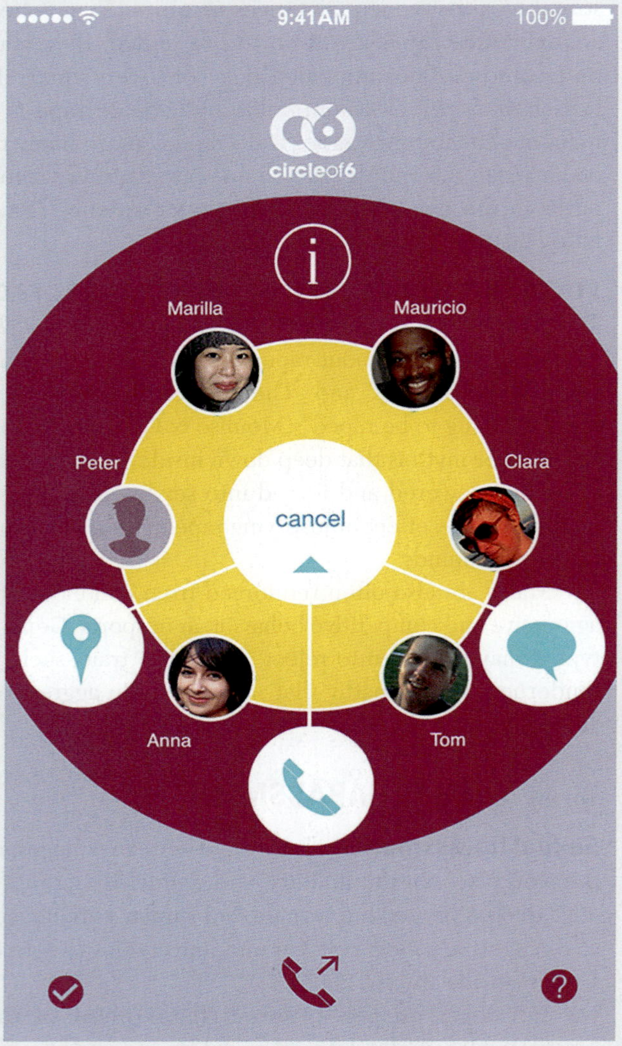

Circle of 6 is a free rape-prevention App, hailed by the White House as an excellent method for preventing abuse. Use it to have your friends use GPS to pick you up or to call you *right now.*

(Larsen & Fitzgerald, 2011). Some find harassment on the job so unbearable that they resign (Diehl et al., 2014). College women have dropped courses and switched majors, and medical residents have even left their programs to avoid it (Diehl et al., 2014).

One reason that sexual harassment is so stressful is that blame tends to fall on the victim. Some harassers argue that charges of harassment were exaggerated. In our society, women are often demonized if they assert themselves, but they remain victimized if they don't (Klein et al., 2011; Schwartz & Hunt, 2011).

Sexual harassment sometimes has more to do with the abuse of power than sexual desire (Burns et al., 2014). This is especially so in work settings that are traditional male preserves, such as the firehouse, the construction site, or the military academy (Burns et al., 2014). The U.S. Supreme Court recognized sexual harassment as a form of sex discrimination and holds that employers are accountable if harassment creates a hostile or abusive work environment.

crystallized intelligence one's intellectual attainments, as shown, for example, by vocabulary and accumulated knowledge.

fluid intelligence mental flexibility; the ability to process information rapidly.

13-5 COGNITIVE DEVELOPMENT

As with physical development, people are at the height of their cognitive powers during early adulthood. Some aspects of cognitive development, such as memory, show a general decline as people age, yet people typically retain their verbal skills and may even show improvement in vocabulary and general knowledge. Performance on tasks that require reasoning or problem-solving speed and visual–spatial skills, such as piecing puzzles together, tends to decline in middle and late adulthood (Haasz et al., 2013).

Consider the difference between **crystallized intelligence** and **fluid intelligence**. Crystallized intelligence represents one's lifetime of intellectual attainments, generally increasing with age. Fluid intelligence—the ability to process information, such as solving a math problem, rapidly—is more susceptible to the effects of aging (Murray et al., 2011).

How then should we think of cognitive development in relation to early adulthood? Piaget did not propose a fifth stage of cognitive development, beyond formal-operational thought, and postconventional thought, the final stage in Kohlberg's theory of moral development, often develops in adolescence.

In terms of brain development, it may very well be that most verbal and quantitative capacities of the sort measured by the SATs and the ACT have developed by late adolescence and early adulthood. However, adolescence carries with it a certain egocentrism that can impair judgment, problem solving, and other areas of cognition. Certain experiences of early adulthood can lead to further cognitive developments, but these experiences are not universal, and many people become set in their cognitive ways long before the arrival of early adulthood.

FICTION

T (F) Piaget proposed a fifth stage of cognitive development, the postformal stage.

It is not true that Piaget proposed a fifth stage of cognitive development—a postformal stage, or any other. Piaget's theory of cognitive development ended with formal-operational thinking. Having said that, some followers of Piaget have proposed a postformal stage.

13-5a COGNITION ACROSS AGE GROUPS AND GENDER

K. Walter Schaie sought to separate the effects of age-related changes within the individual from cohort effects (similarities among peers due to group members being about the same age). To do so, he introduced a developmental model that elevated the study of age-related changes above simple longitudinal and cross- sectional studies (Bergeman & Boker, 2006). He used successive repeated and independent sampling of age cohorts across the decades of a longitudinal study. The resulting data permitted many comparisons within and across age groups and birth cohorts.

Using his method, Schaie (2002; Schaie & Zanjani, 2006) found that late adolescents are likely to have the broadest general knowledge of the sciences, but young adults become more focused in their use of scientific expertise than adolescents are. Many adolescents acquire general scientific knowledge in biology, chemistry, and physics during high school. And now, more than ever, girls remain with boys and keep pace with them in these classes. The same is generally true in algebra, geometry, precalculus, and calculus.

Aristotle

13-5b EPISTEMIC COGNITION

The concept of **epistemic cognition** concerns our ideas about how we arrive at our beliefs, 'facts,' and ideas (Greene et al., 2016; Perry 1970 [1998], 1981). Young adults may wonder why their beliefs differ from others' and may seek to justify or revise their thinking and their conclusions. College students' views on what they know and how they come to know what they know become more complex as they are exposed to the complexities of college thought (Patton et al., 2016). Cognitive development in college life rests not only on exposure to "great books"; it is also fostered by being challenged by students from different backgrounds and by professors who have views that differ from those of students (Moshman, 2013).

Students often enter college or adult life assuming that there are right and wrong answers for everything, and that the world can be divided easily into black versus white, good versus bad, and us versus them. This type of thinking is termed **dualistic thinking**. After a while, in a multicultural society or on a college campus, students may realize that judgments of good or bad are often made from a certain belief system, such as a religion or a cultural background, so that such judgments actually represent **relativistic thinking** rather than absolute judgments (Moshman, 2013). For example, some world cultures may believe that they put women "on pedestals" by restricting their activities outside the home. The newly "relativistic" college student may be hard-pressed to take issue with this argument, but as thought deepens, adults may become capable of *commitment within relativistic thinking*. That is, the more cognitively mature person can say, "Yes, I understand where you're coming from when you say you're putting women on pedestals by preventing them from going outdoors unless they are chaperoned, but my bottom line is that you're treating them like second-class citizens and would never allow them to do the same to you."

epistemic cognition thought processes directed at considering how we arrive at our beliefs, facts, and ideas

dualistic thinking dividing the cognitive world into opposites, such as good and bad, or us versus them.

relativistic thinking recognition that judgments are often not absolute but made from a certain belief system or cultural background.

13-5c PRAGMATIC THOUGHT

Gisella Labouvie-Vief's (2006) theory of **pragmatic thought** notes that adults must typically narrow possibilities into choices, whether these are choices about careers or graduate school or life partners. The "cognitively healthy" adult is more willing than the egocentric adolescent to compromise and cope within the world as it is, not the world as she or he would like it to be (Labouvie-Vief et al., 2014). In order to deal with the real world, adults need to be able to accept living with mixed feelings about their goals. As people mature, Labouvie-Vief found that they tend to develop a **cognitive–affective complexity** that enables them to harbor both positive and negative feelings about their career choices ("I may never get rich, but when I wake up in the morning, I'll look forward to what I'm doing that day") and their partners ("Okay, he may not be a hunk, but he's stable and kind"). Adults function best when they accept reality but choose goals that allow them to experience positive feelings (Labouvie-Vief et al., 2014).

13-5d POSTFORMAL THINKING

Most developmentalists agree that the cognitive processes of young adults are in many ways more advanced than the cognitive processes of adolescents—at least in our cultural setting (Kallio, 2011). Young adults maintain most of the benefits of their general secondary educations, and some may have gathered specialized knowledge and skills through opportunities in higher education. Many have gained knowledge and expertise in the career world as well.

The thinking of young adults tends to be *less* egocentric than that of adolescents. Young adults are less likely to see the world in black and white. They are more relativistic, but ideally capable of making commitments in their relativistic worlds. For example, an adolescent viewing an environmentally damaging oil spill in the Gulf of Mexico may want to immediately stop all oil drilling and lock up the oil company's executives for life—or worse. A 25-year-old may have similar feelings of outrage but opt instead to heavily fine the oil company and, given the country's need for oil, focus on ways to improve the safety of drilling until the country is less dependent on oil.

What developmentalists do not agree on is whether they should consider the cognitive abilities of young adults to be a fifth stage of cognitive development, perhaps called a *postformal* stage, that would extend beyond Piaget's stage of formal operations.

pragmatic thought decision making characterized by willingness to accept reality and compromise.

cognitive–affective complexity a mature form of thinking that permits people to harbor positive and negative feelings about their career choices and other matters.

13-5e COLLEGE AND COGNITIVE DEVELOPMENT

Emily, 22, was in her senior year at a college in Massachusetts, and she was describing her semester abroad in South Africa. Her face lit up as she painted a picture—not at all rosy—of her experiences working on HIV/AIDS education programs. She discussed the conditions of the South African poor and the "insanely deplorable" treatment of workers in the diamond mines. Little if any of Emily's experiences would improve her scores on standardized tests, and they would have little impact on graduate admissions exams like the Law School Admissions Test (LSAT). Nonetheless, it is safe to say that these experiences had a major impact on Emily's cognitive development.

Numerous studies show that college and university life encourage such cognitive developments through broadened experience, both at the community college and four-year college levels (Patton, L. D., et al., 2016). Recent research also suggests that men and women are about equal overall in math ability, yet higher percentages of men enter so-called STEM fields (science, technology, engineering, and mathematics) than women do (Hyde, 2014). Why? According to psychologists Stephen Ceci, Wendy Williams, and Susan Barnett (2009), who have studied the issue extensively, the reasons are likely as follows: (1) Women who are proficient in math are more likely than math-proficient men to prefer careers that do not require skills in math; (2) more males than females obtain extremely high scores on the SAT math test and the quantitative reasoning sections of the Graduate Record Exam; (3) women who are proficient in math are more likely than men with this proficiency to have high verbal competence as well, which encourages many such women to choose other careers.

THE DIVERSE CULTURE OF COLLEGE In her semester abroad, Emily took full advantage of the diversity students can experience in college. Some students attend colleges that are close to home, culturally if not necessarily geographically. Others attend colleges that are more diverse. Diversity speaks to the differences we find among groups of people: ethnic and cultural diversity (race, religion, country of origin, language), socioeconomic level, gender, age, and sexual orientation. Many students find more kinds of people on campus than they "dreamt of" before they began college. They meet people from other backgrounds, places, and walks of life—among them, their professors.

Here are some ideas adapted from the Association of American Colleges and Universities (Dey et al., 2010; National Task Force on Civic Learning and Democratic Engagement, 2012) on how you can benefit from diversity on your campus to achieve cognitive growth:

- Recognize that your way of looking at the world is not universal.
- Embrace opportunities for encountering people who are different.
- Recognize that your initial reaction to cultural difference may be defensive.
- Understand what makes other people's cultural views and traits valuable to them.
- Listen carefully to others' descriptions of cultural differences and concerns.
- Immerse yourself in a different culture (as Emily did) for an extended period of time.
- Commit yourself to understanding a given situation from another point of view.

13-6 CAREER DEVELOPMENT

Work is a major part of life, and early adulthood is the time when most of us become established in our careers. We will consider how this happens, but before this, let's ask, "What motivates people to work in the first place?"

The first reason people work is obvious: Earning a living, fringe benefits, and ensuring future security all inspire people to pursue careers and employment. These external benefits of working are called *extrinsic motives*; however, extrinsic motives alone do not explain why people work. Work can also satisfy many internal or *intrinsic motives*, including the opportunities to engage in stimulating and satisfying activities and to develop one's talents (Ryan & Deci, 2000). Many million-dollar lottery winners who quit their jobs encounter feelings of aimlessness and dissatisfaction afterward (Corliss, 2003). Moreover, within a year of cashing their checks, lottery winners generally report happiness (or unhappiness) levels corresponding to their pre-winning levels (Corliss, 2003). Despite folk wisdom, money does not always buy happiness; many people seek more in life than extrinsic rewards such as a paycheck and financial security. They also want the intrinsic rewards gained through engaging in challenging activities, broadening their social contacts, and filling their days with meaningful activity.

TRUTH

(T) F Million-dollar lottery winners often feel aimless and dissatisfied if they quit their jobs after striking it rich.

It is true that million-dollar lottery winners often feel aimless and dissatisfied if they quit their jobs after striking it rich. Work can have social, emotional, and cognitive rewards, not simply financial rewards.

Intrinsic reasons for working include (Chow et al., 2014):

- *The work ethic*. The view that we are morally obligated to avoid idleness.
- *Self-identity*. Our occupational identity can become intertwined with our self-identity.
- *Self-fulfillment*. We often express our personal needs and interests through our work.
- *Self-worth*. Recognition and respect for a job well done contribute to self-esteem.
- *Socialization*. The workplace extends our social contacts.
- *Public roles*. Work roles help define our functions in the community.

Why are women less likely than men to enter STEM fields—that is, fields in science, technology, engineering, and math?

DCPhoto / Alamy Stock Photo

13-6a CHOOSING A CAREER AND STAGES OF CAREER DEVELOPMENT

For most of us, career development has a number of stages. Our discussion is informed by psychologist Donald Super's theory of career development, but we have made some changes to reflect contemporary realities.

The first or *fantasy stage* involves the child's unrealistic conception of self-potential and of the world of work, which dominates from early childhood until about age 11. Young children focus on glamour professions, such as acting, medicine, sports, and law enforcement (Patton & McMahon, 2014). They show little regard for the fit between these occupations and their abilities. During the second or *tentative choice stage*, from about 11 through high school, children base their choices on their interests, abilities, and limitations, as well as glamour.

Beyond age 17 or so, in the *realistic choice stage*, choices become narrowed as students weigh job requirements and rewards against their interests, abilities, and values (Patton & McMahon, 2014). They may direct their educational plans to ensure they obtain the knowledge and skills they need to enter their intended occupations. Some follow the paths of role models such as parents or respected members of the community (Patton & McMahon, 2014). Many "fall into" careers not because of particular skills and interests, but because of what is available at the time, family pressures, or the lure of high income or a certain lifestyle. Others may "job hop" through several different career paths before finally finding one that fits well.

During the *maintenance stage*, we begin "settling" into our career roles, which often happens in the second half of our thirties. Although we may change positions within a company or within a career, as in moving from marketing to management, there is often a sense of our careers continuing to develop, a feeling of forward motion. Of course, people can also get "trapped" into dead-end jobs during this stage (Savickas, 2012).

Here is where we diverge from the traditional view of career development. Because of corporate downsizing, mergers, and acquisitions, many employees no longer feel the loyalty to their employers that workers once did (Carless & Amup, 2011). Thus they are more likely to "job hop" when the opportunity arises. People are also living longer, healthier lives in rapidly changing times. They are staying in school longer and returning to school for education, training, and retraining. It has become the norm, rather than the exception, for people

Masterfile

to switch jobs more than once (Carless & Amup, 2011). That said, vocational interests tend to be stable over the life course (Rottinghaus et al., 2007). Though people may switch jobs, they generally seek jobs that reflect stable interests.

The final stage in Super's scheme is the *retirement stage*, during which the individual severs bonds with the workplace. In the chapters on late adulthood, we will see that retirement today is far from final. Retirees often become restless and undertake second or third careers.

STUDY TOOLS 13

READY TO STUDY?

In the book, you can:

- ☐ Rip out the chapter review card at the back of the book for a handy summary of the chapter and key terms.
- ☐ Check your understanding of what you've read with the quizzes that follow.

ONLINE AT CENGAGEBRAIN.COM YOU CAN:

- ☐ Collect StudyBits while you read and study the chapter.
- ☐ Quiz yourself on key concepts.
- ☐ Find videos for further exploration.
- ☐ Prepare for tests with HDEV5 Flash Cards as well as those you create.

SELF-ASSESSMENTS

Fill Ins

Answers can be found in the back of the book.

1. The source of stress most commonly reported by 18- to 32-year-olds is ____________.
2. Arnett considers ____________ adulthood to be an age of instability.
3. Efforts to diet may be sabotaged by a bodily mechanism called adaptive ____________, which slows the body's metabolic rate.
4. According to Perry, assuming that the world can be easily divided into black and white, good versus bad, or us versus them, is termed ____________ thinking.
5. The leading cause of death among young adults is ____________
6. After age ____________, women who become pregnant are usually advised to have their fetuses checked for Down's syndrome and other chromosomal abnormalities.
7. Among 25- to 44-year-olds, the leading cause of death is ____________.
8. As people mature, Labouvie-Vief found that they tend to develop a ____________ complexity that enables them to harbor both positive and negative feelings about their career choices.
9. The CDC recommends that adults engage in at least ____________ minutes of vigorous physical activity five days a week.
10. In a multicultural society or on a college campus, students may realize that judgments of good or bad are often made from a certain belief system, such as a religion or a cultural background, so that such judgments actually represent ____________ thinking rather than absolute judgments.

Multiple Choice

1. Piaget's final stage of cognitive development is the

a. postformal stage.
b. stage of cognitive-affective complexity.
c. formal operational stage.
d. stage of pragmatic thought.

2. The most common sexually transmitted infection in the United States is

a. chlamydia.
b. HIV/AIDS.
c. gonorrhea.
d. HPV.

3. Which of the following cannot be treated successfully with antibiotics?

a. genital herpes
b. chlamydia
c. gonorrhea
d. syphilis

4. Which age group is most likely to report that the amount of stress they are experiencing has increased over the past five years?

a. 18- to 32-year-olds
b. 33- to 46-year-olds
c. 47- to 65-year-olds
d. people aged 66 and above

5. Which of the following substances is most likely to accelerate the heart rate and constrict the arteries?

a. alcohol
b. marijuana
c. cocaine
d. heroin

6. All of the following are recommended by the text as ways of helping overweight people lose weight, *except*

a. eating preplanned low-calorie snacks.
b. exposing oneself to temptations and saying "No!"
c. establishing calorie-intake goals and keeping track of whether one is meeting them.
d. mentally rehearsing solutions to possible problems.

7. In the Arnett survey, when 18- to 25-year-olds were asked "Do you feel that you have reached adulthood?", the largest number said,

a. Yes.
b. No.
c. In some ways yes, and in other ways no.
d. Not sure.

8. By the end of early adulthood, the skin begins to do all of the following except

a. develop acne.
b. grow less elastic.
c. wrinkle.
d. loosen.

9. By the ages of 25 to 44, which of the following replaces homicide as the second leading cause of death?

a. suicide
b. HIV/AIDS
c. influenza and pneumonia
d. cancer

10. According to the Centers for Disease Control and Prevention, approximately ____________% of 18- to 24-year-olds are either overweight or obese.

a. 20
b. 40
c. 60
d. 80

YOUR FEEDBACK MATTERS.

www.cengage.com/4ltrpress

14 Early Adulthood: Social and Emotional Development

Tim Robbins/ Mint Images Limited / Alamy Stock photo

LEARNING OUTCOMES

After studying this chapter, you will be able to . . .

14-1 Examine the issues involved in early adulthood separation

14-2 Describe the conflict between intimacy and isolation

14-3 Discuss the seasons of life experienced during early adulthood

14-4 Examine the emotional forces of attraction and love

14-5 Explain why people get lonely and what they do in response

14-6 Discuss the lifestyle of being single

14-7 Describe the practice of cohabitation

14-8 Describe the practice of marriage

14-9 Discuss the state of parenthood

14-10 Discuss divorce and its repercussions

After you finish this chapter, go to **PAGE 299** for **STUDY TOOLS**

Early adulthood spans the decades from ages 20 to 40. Some theorists mark the start of this stage at 17 or 18, however, and others extend the period to age 44 or 45. The traditional view of development in early adulthood was laid down by developmental psychologist Robert Havighurst (1972) more than 40 years ago. He believed that each stage of development involved accomplishing certain "tasks," and the tasks he describes for early adulthood include the following:

- ☑ 1. Getting started in an occupation
- ☑ 2. Selecting and courting a mate
- ☑ 3. Learning to live contentedly with one's partner
- ☑ 4. Starting a family and becoming a parent
- ☑ 5. Assuming the responsibilities of managing a home
- ☑ 6. Assuming civic responsibilities
- ☑ 7. Finding a congenial social group

Erik Erikson saw the establishment of intimate relationships as the key "crisis" of early adulthood.

Many modern young adults will laugh at this list of tasks. Others will think that it doesn't sound too bad at all. I bring it to your attention because it is a traditional view of young adulthood of past generations that ignores some realities of human diversity and contemporary life. For example, many young adults (and older adults) remain single today. Many never assume civic responsibilities. Many married couples choose not to have children; some others are infertile. Gays and lesbians may have partners, and in most states can have spouses, but many do not become parents—and Havighurst was certainly not including them. Nor did Havighurst list *separation* from one's family of origin as a task involved in young adulthood. Yet most developmentalists see it as a crucial "task."

14-1 SEPARATION

Young adults leave home at different ages and for different reasons, and some never had a traditional home life to begin with. The typical developmental milestones seem distant to young adults who have spent years in orphanages, bounced about from one foster home to another, or spent time in detention or in the homes of grandparents or other relatives because their parents could not provide a home (Minkler & Fuller-Thomson, 2005).

Young adults who enter the job market out of high school, or without completing high school, may live at home for a while to save some money before venturing out on their own. When they do, they may move in with roommates or to a poorer neighborhood than that of their parents so that they can afford independent living. Even so, parents may contribute cash.

Other young adults may leave home to go to college or to join the military. If students are attending a local college, they may stay at home or move in with roommates so they can afford it. Young adults who attend college away from home do leave, but very often a room is kept for them at home and is relatively untouched. Psychologically, the "nest" remains if and when they need it. Highly traditional or insecure parents may find a son's or daughter's leaving for college to be so stressful that departure damages the parent–child relationship (Kins et al., 2011; Sax & Weintraub, 2014). The departure tends to be more stressful when the child is

TRUTH OR FICTION?

T	F	People are considered to be more attractive when they are smiling.
T	F	"Opposites attract."
T	F	Couples can remain in love after passion fades.
T	F	Jealousy can lessen feelings of affection and heighten feelings of insecurity and depression, leading to a breakup.
T	F	Many people remain lonely because they fear being rejected by others.
T	F	Being single has become a more common U.S. lifestyle over the past few decades.
T	F	Cohabitation has become a normal stage of courtship for many U.S. couples.
T	F	Having a child is a way to help save a marriage that is in trouble.

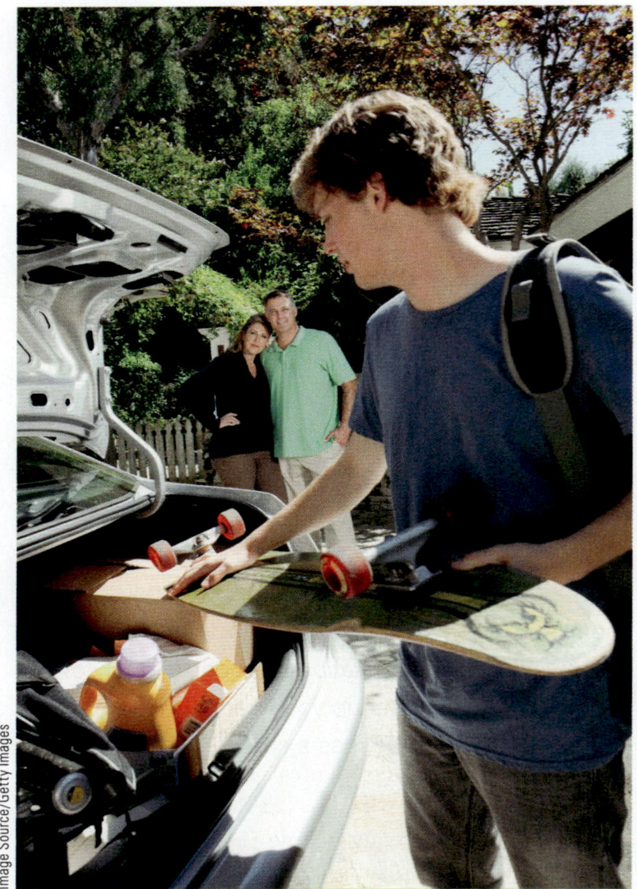

Image Source/Getty Images

Breaking up can be somewhat overwhelming, especially when one is "breaking up" with the home life of nearly two decades.

a daughter, perhaps because women appear to be more vulnerable than men are "out there" in the "real" world. Mothers also report significantly higher degrees of separation anxiety than fathers (Miller-Ott et al., 2014).

Those who join the military have their housing needs taken care of. Their rupture from home and neighborhood is sudden and complete, although they can return when they are on leave or their service is finished.

individuation the young adult's process of becoming an individual by means of integrating his or her own values and beliefs with those of his or her parents and society at large.

If young adults are working within commuting distance of their homes of origin, even after graduating college, they may return home to live for financial reasons (Selingo, 2016). They have been referred to as the "boomerang generation"; that is, they are tossed out into the world and then they come back. Entry-level jobs often do not pay well, or the young adult may want to try to save enough to place a down payment on a house or apartment or accumulate rent in advance. It is not uncommon for young adults to get married and then move in with a set of parents. Today, even couples who are living together without being married may move in with parents.

14-1a SEPARATION–INDIVIDUATION

Whether or not young adults leave the nest, it is time for them to separate from their parents psychologically. Psychologists and educators refer to the relevant processes as *separation* and **individuation**—that is, becoming an individual by means of integrating one's own values and beliefs with those of one's parents and one's society.

Most men in our society consider separation and individuation to be key goals of personality development in early adulthood (Blazina et al., 2007). But many psychologists argue that things are somewhat different for women—that for women, the establishment and maintenance of social relationships are also of primary importance (Ziv & Hermel, 2011). Nevertheless, many young women work on becoming their own persons in the sense of separating their values and patterns of behavior from those of their mothers (Sax & Weintraub, 2014). When young men's views differ from those of their parents, they are more likely to engage in an active struggle or a fight for independence (Sax & Weintraub, 2014).

The transition to college or to the workplace can play a role in separation and individuation. Employment and financial independence can lessen feelings of connectedness with parents, whereas college or university can maintain these feelings (Sax & Weintraub, 2014). Feelings of connectedness are related to the amount of financial and emotional support students receive from parents (Selingo, 2016).

Masterfile

Employment and financial independence can help early adults make the transition from the home to life in the outside world.

14-2 INTIMACY VERSUS ISOLATION

Erik Erikson was aware that young adults often have problems separating from their parents. He was a psychoanalyst, and many of the young women who opened their hearts to him complained of difficulties in disappointing mothers whose values were different and usually more traditional than their own. However, Erikson focused on one central conflict for each stage of life, and the core conflict he identified for early adulthood was **intimacy versus isolation**.

Erikson (1963) saw the establishment of intimate relationships as the key "crisis" of early adulthood. Young adults who have evolved a firm sense of identity during adolescence are now ready to "fuse" their identities with those of other people through marriage and abiding friendships. Erikson's clinical experience led him to believe that young adults who had not achieved ego identity—a firm sense of who they are and what they stand for—may not be ready to commit themselves to others. They may not be able to gauge the extent to which their developing values may conflict with those of a potential intimate partner. He suggested that in our society, which values compatibility in relationships, an absent or fluctuating ego identity is connected with the high divorce rate in teenage marriages. Once passion fades a bit, conflicting ways of looking at the world may be too abrasive to bear. Erikson argued that young adults who do not reach out to develop intimate relationships risk retreating into isolation and loneliness.

Erikson, like Havighurst, has been criticized for suggesting that young adults who choose to remain celibate or single are not developing normally (Hayslip et al., 2006). Erikson believed that it was normal, and psychologically healthy, for people to develop intimate relationships and bear children within a generally stable and nurturing environment during early adulthood.

14-3 SEASONS OF LIFE

Psychologist Daniel Levinson, who had worked with Erik Erikson at Harvard University, and his colleagues published an influential book on development called *Seasons of a Man's Life* (1978). Levinson (1996) followed it with *Seasons of a Woman's Life*. These books explained Levinson's view, compatible with Erikson's, that adults go through certain periods of life, which Levinson dubbed *seasons*, in which their progress and psychological well-being are shaped by common social and physical demands and crises—the development of relationships, rearing children, establishing and developing a career, and coming to terms with successes and failures. At any given moment, the underlying pattern of a person's life is his or her **life structure**. One's religion, race, and socioeconomic status also influence his or her life structure and life satisfaction. Many young adults also adopt what Levinson calls "**the dream**"—the drive to become someone, to leave one's mark on history—which serves as a tentative blueprint for life. Levinson (1996) found that women undergo somewhat similar developments, but experience more social constraints, both from their families of origin and society in general. Thus it may take women longer to leave home, and there may be more pressure on them to go from one home (their parents') to another (their husbands').

Levinson labeled the ages of 28 to 33 the *age-30 transition*. For men and women, he found that the late 20s and early 30s are commonly characterized by reassessment: "Where is my life going?" "Why am I doing this?"

Levinson and his colleagues also found that the later 30s are often characterized by settling down or planting roots. At this time, many people feel a need to make a financial and emotional investment in their homes. Their concerns become focused on promotion or tenure, career advancement, mortgages, and, in many or most cases, raising their own families.

Today, Levinson's views sound rather archaic, at least when they are applied to young women (Hayslip et al., 2006). It has become more acceptable and widespread for women to lead independent, single lives, for as long as they wish. And, truth be told, the great majority of career women in sizeable American cities simply would not care what anyone thinks about their marital status or living arrangements. Given the mobility young adults have in the United States today, many will choose not to live in places where people would frown upon their styles of life.

intimacy versus isolation according to Erik Erikson, the central conflict or life crisis of early adulthood, in which a person develops an intimate relationship with a significant other or risks heading down a path toward social isolation.

life structure in Levinson's theory, the underlying pattern of a person's life at a given stage, as defined by relationships, career, race, religion, economic status, and the like.

the dream according to Daniel Levinson and his colleagues, the drive to become someone, to leave one's mark on history, which serves as a tentative blueprint for the young adult.

14-4 ATTRACTION AND LOVE: FORCES THAT BIND?

Young adults separate from their families of origin and (often, not always) join with others. In developed nations, they are free to choose the people with whom they will associate and develop friendships and romantic relationships. The emotional forces that fuel these associations are *attraction* and *love*.

14-4a ATTRACTION

We might like to think of ourselves as so sophisticated that physical attractiveness does not move us. We might like to claim that sensitivity, warmth, and intelligence are more important to us. However, we may never learn about other people's personalities if they do not meet our minimal standards for physical attractiveness. Research for many decades has shown—and keeps on showing—that physical attractiveness is a major determinant of interpersonal and sexual attraction (Meltzer et al., 2014). The power of Tinder—in which people express interest in others on the basis of their photo alone—also testifies to the importance of physical appearance in consideration of partners for dates, sex, and long-term relationships.

Men appear to be more responsive to visual stimuli than women, although women are also clearly attuned to appealing eyefuls. Evolutionary psychologists note that it would make sense for males and females to be more attracted to one another when the woman is ovulating: that is, capable of conceiving a child. It would be likely that women might act somewhat differently or that men would pick up on certain cues—perhaps unconsciously—that would communicate a woman's phase of the menstrual cycle (Haselton & Gildersleeve, 2015). Interestingly, women tend to dress and ornament themselves in more appealing ways when they are in the fertile phase of their ovulatory cycle (Starratt & Alesia, 2014).

Although physical appeal is important in sexual attraction, other factors matter and may even challenge the equation that good looks = sexual attractiveness. For example, there is the issue of whether or not it seems that an individual would be able to provide a high-quality relationship (Eastwick & Hunt, 2014). And because men are somewhat more attuned to the visual than women, we would expect women to be somewhat more flexible in mate choice in that they may be more willing to trade

What features contribute to facial attractiveness?

Are our standards of beauty subjective, or is there broad agreement on what is attractive? As shown in Figure 14.1, there are some common views on features that contribute to an attractive face—at least in England and Japan.

FIG.14.1 IS BEAUTY IN THE EYE OF THE BEHOLDER?

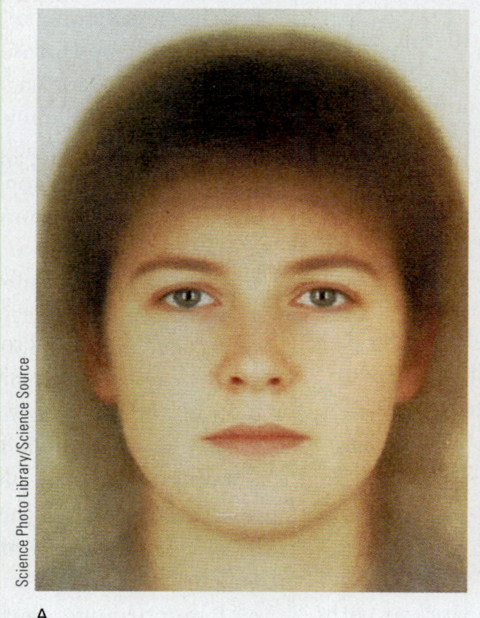

A.

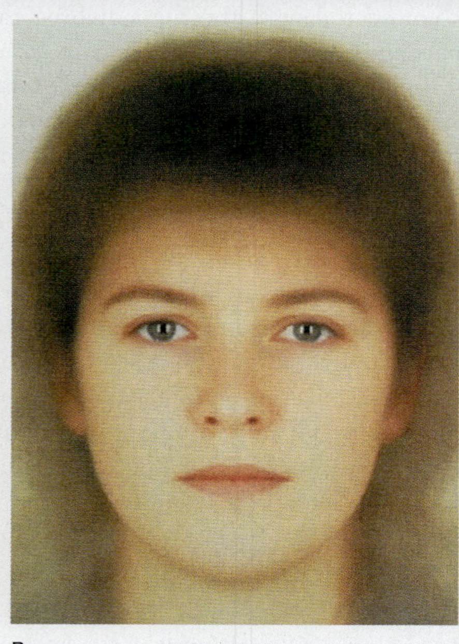

B.

In both England and Japan, features such as large eyes, high cheekbones, and narrow jaws contribute to perceptions of the appeal of women. Part A shows a composite of the faces of 15 women rated as the most attractive of a group of 60. Part B is a composite in which the features of these 15 women are exaggerated—that is, developed further in the direction that separates them from the average of the entire 60. Part B, which shows higher cheekbones and a narrower jaw than part A, was rated as the more attractive image.

(some) good looks for a good relationship. Evolutionary theory proposes that women on some level recognize that they are more likely than men to be reproductively successful if they can rear their children in high-quality relationships.

Generally speaking, taller men are considered to be more attractive by women (Sohn, 2015). Height plays a key role in choice of a mate because it suggests social dominance, status, access to resources, protection, and a positive heritable trait (Meston & Buss, 2009). Undergraduate women prefer their dates to be about 6 inches taller than they are. Undergraduate men, on the average, prefer women who are about 4 to 5 inches shorter (Furnham, 2009). Consistent with stereotypical gender roles, tall women are not viewed so positively as tall men are.

"Thin is in" today (Milhausen et al., 2015). Both females and males find slenderness (though not anorexic thinness) attractive. In a survey of 22,815 U.S. adults, it was found that men and women both said that it is desirable or essential for potential partners to be good-looking (92% of men and 84% of women) and slender (80% of men and 58% of women) (Fales et al., 2016). Women were relatively more likely to desire men who had a steady income (74% versus 97%) and made a lot of money (47% versus 69%). These findings are all consistent with evolutionary theory: women are relatively more concerned with a partner's ability to help provide an environment conducive to successful child rearing.

The dominant culture also prefers the hourglass figure. Studies find that women of average weight with a waist-to-hip ratio of 0.7 to 0.8 are rated as most attractive and desirable for relationships (Dural et al., 2015). Neither gaunt nor obese women are found to be as attractive.

FIG.14.2 WHY DID THEY DECK HER OUT IN RED?

Fancy/Veer/Corbis/Getty Images

Cultural conditioning and the human biological heritage provide two good answers.

THE ALLURE OF THE COLOR RED When you go to buy a box of Valentine's Day candy, what color will the box be? Green? Blue? The answer, of course, is red. What is the most popular color of women's lipstick? Yellow? Brown? Again, the answer is red (Elliot, 2015). Red has been the most popular lipstick color since the hot days that saw the construction of the pyramids in ancient Egypt (Elliot, 2015). Red is similarly the most popular color for women's lingerie.

Why is the color red associated with feelings of attraction? Could the answer be the history of the use of red coloration—that is, cultural conditioning? Or may the link between red and physical attraction also be rooted in our biological heritage? Many nonhuman female primates, including baboons, chimpanzees, gorillas, and rhesus monkeys, show reddened genital regions and sometimes reddened chests and faces when they are nearing ovulation—the time of the month when they are fertile (Elliot, 2015; Elliot et al., 2013). Reddening of the skin is caused by elevated estrogen levels (relative to progesterone), which increase the flow of blood under the surface of the skin. It is widely believed that reddish skin tones are a sexual signal that attracts mates. Research has found that male primates are in fact especially attracted to females when they display red, as shown by attempts at sexual relations. For men, as with other male primates, the reddening of a woman's skin at the time of ovulation may be a sexual signal.

Andrew Elliot and Daniela Niesta (2008) ran a series of experiments in which men did, indeed, rate the same woman as more attractive when her photograph was shown against a red background compared with a variety of other background colors. One experiment revealed that the red-related difference in attractiveness was found in male raters but not in female raters. Men found women more attractive when they were shown with red backgrounds as opposed to white. Women also rate photos of men as being more attractive when the photos are bordered in red or the men are wearing red clothing. With men as with women, red coloration can also be an indicator of health, because highly oxygenated blood levels can be maintained only by organisms in good health (Elliot, 2015).

ARE PREFERENCES CONCERNING ATTRACTIVENESS INBORN? On the surface, gender differences in perceptions of attractiveness seem unbearably sexist—and perhaps they are. But some evolutionary psychologists believe that evolutionary forces favor the continuation of gender differences in preferences for mates because they may provide reproductive advantages (Conroy-Beam et al., 2015; Fales et al., 2016). Physical features such as cleanliness, good complexion, clear eyes, good teeth, good hair, firm muscle tone, and a steady gait, are universally appealing to both females and males. Perhaps they are markers of reproductive potential. Age and health may be relatively more important to a woman's appeal, because these characteristics tend to be associated with her reproductive capacity (the "biological clock" limits her reproductive potential). Physical characteristics associated with a woman's youthfulness, such as smooth skin, firm muscle tone, and lustrous hair, may thus have become more closely linked to her appeal. A man's reproductive value, however, may depend more on how well he can provide for his family than on his age or physical appeal. The value of men as reproducers, therefore, is more intertwined with factors that contribute to a stable environment for childrearing—such as economic status and reliability (Fales et al., 2016).

NONPHYSICAL TRAITS AFFECT PERCEPTIONS OF ATTRACTIVENESS Although there are physical standards for beauty in our culture, nonphysical traits also affect our perceptions. For example, the attractiveness of a partner is likely to be enhanced by traits such as familiarity, liking, respect, and sharing of values and goals (Weekes-Shackelford & Shackelford, 2014). People also rate the attractiveness of faces higher when they are smiling than when they are not smiling (O'Doherty et al., 2003).

TRUTH

(T) F People are considered to be more attractive when they are smiling.

It is true that people are considered to be more attractive when they are smiling. (So put on "a happy face"?)

GENDER DIFFERENCES IN PERCEPTIONS OF ATTRACTIVENESS Gender-role expectations may affect perceptions of attractiveness. For example, women are more likely to be attracted to socially dominant men than men are to be attracted to socially dominant women (Weekes-Shackelford & Shackelford, 2014). Women who viewed videos of prospective dates found men who acted outgoing and self-expressive more appealing than men who were passive (Riggio & Woll, 1984). Yet men who viewed videos in the Riggio and Woll (1984) study were put off by outgoing, self-expressive behavior in women.

A Pew Research Center Survey conducted in 2014 provided additional information about what women and men feel to be "very important" to them in choosing a spouse or partner (Wang & Parker, 2014; see Figure 14.3). The quest for economic security showed the greatest gender difference, with 78% of women respondents saying that it was very important to them that a spouse or partner be holding a steady job, as compared to 46% of men who held the same view. Both men (62%) and women (70%) found it very important that the couple share similar beliefs about having and rearing children. Only a small minority of men (7%) and women (10%) said that it was very important to them that their partner or spouse share their racial or ethnic background.

FIG.14.3 WHAT NEVER-MARRIED PEOPLE ARE LOOKING FOR IN A SPOUSE

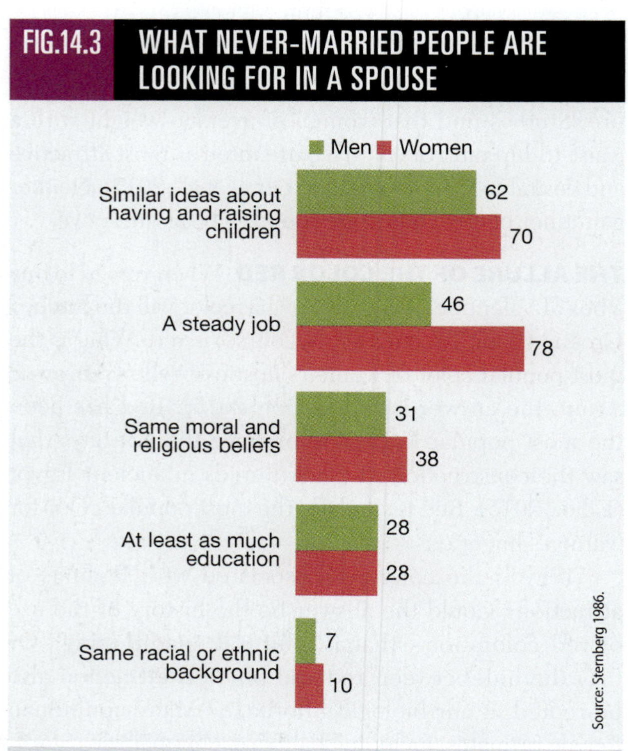

Percentage of never-married adults who say that ______ would be "very important" to them in choosing a spouse or partner

THE ATTRACTION–SIMILARITY HYPOTHESIS: DO "OPPOSITES ATTRACT" OR "DO BIRDS OF A FEATHER FLOCK TOGETHER"? Do not despair if you are less than exquisite in appearance, along with most of us mere mortals. You may be saved from permanently blending in with the wallpaper by the effects of the **attraction–similarity hypothesis**. This hypothesis holds that people tend to develop romantic relationships with people who are similar to themselves in attractiveness and other traits (Morry et al., 2011; Reis et al., 2011).

Researchers have found that people who are involved in committed relationships are most likely to be similar to their partners in their attitudes and cultural attributes (Montoya et al., 2013). Our partners tend to be like us in race and ethnicity, age, level of education, and religion.

FICTION

T (F) "Opposites attract."

The cultural maxim that "opposites attract" does not appear to be borne out by research evidence. People who are similar in physical attractiveness and attitudes are usually more likely to be attracted to one another.

RECIPROCITY: IF YOU LIKE ME, YOU MUST HAVE EXCELLENT JUDGMENT Has anyone told you that you are good-looking, brilliant, and emotionally mature to boot? That your taste is elegant? Ah, what superb judgment! When we feel admired and complimented, we tend to return these feelings and behaviors. This is called **reciprocity**. Although reciprocity can contribute to feelings of attraction (Sprecher et al., 2008), some research also suggests that women are sometimes more attracted to men whose feelings toward them are uncertain (Dai et al., 2014). Yet the power of reciprocity has apparently enabled many couples to become happy with one another and reasonably well adjusted. When someone confesses his or her feelings of attraction, the recipient of the feelings is certainly likely to pay more attention to the other person.

Attraction can lead to feelings of love. Let us now turn to that most fascinating topic.

14-4b LOVE

The experience of **romantic love**, as opposed to attachment or sexual arousal, occurs within a cultural context in which the concept is idealized (Berscheid, 2010; Graham, 2011). Western culture has a long tradition of idealizing the concept of romantic love, as represented, for instance, by romantic fairy tales that have been passed down through the generations. In fact, our exposure to the concept of romantic love may begin with hearing those fairy tales, and later, perhaps, continue to blossom through exposure to romantic novels, television and film scripts, and the heady tales of friends and relatives.

Researchers have also found that love is a complex concept, involving many areas of experience (Graham, 2011). Let us consider two psychological perspectives on love, both of which involve emotional arousal.

LOVE AS APPRAISAL OF AROUSAL Social psychologists Ellen Berscheid and Elaine Hatfield (Berscheid, 2010; Hatfield & Rapson, 2002) define romantic love in terms of a state of intense

attraction–similarity hypothesis the view that people tend to develop romantic relationships with people who are similar to themselves in physical attractiveness and other traits.

reciprocity the tendency to respond in kind when we feel admired and complimented.

romantic love a form of love fueled by passion and feelings of intimacy.

Blend Images Photography/Veer

Romantic love is a complex concept, involving passion and intimacy.

physiological arousal and the cognitive appraisal of that arousal as love. The arousal may be experienced as a pounding heart, sweaty palms, and butterflies in the stomach when one is in the presence of, or thinking about, one's love interest. Cognitive appraisal of the arousal means attributing the arousal to some cause, such as fear or love. The perception that one has fallen in love is thus derived from: (1) a state of intense arousal that is connected with an appropriate love object (that is, a person, not an event like a rock concert), (2) a cultural setting that idealizes romantic love, and (3) the attribution of the arousal to feelings of love for the person.

intimacy the experience of warmth toward another person that arises from feelings of closeness and connectedness.

passion intense romantic or sexual desire for another person.

commitment the decision to devote oneself to a cause or another person.

STERNBERG'S TRIANGULAR THEORY OF LOVE

Robert Sternberg's (2006a, 2014) "triangular theory" of love includes three building blocks, or components, of loving experiences:

1. **Intimacy**: The experience of warmth toward another person that arises from feelings of closeness and connectedness, and the desire to share one's innermost thoughts.
2. **Passion**: Intense romantic or sexual desire, accompanied by physiological arousal.
3. **Commitment**: Commitment to maintain the relationship through good times and bad.

Sternberg's model is triangular in that various kinds of love can be conceptualized in terms of a triangle in which each vertex represents one of the building blocks (see Figure 14.4). In Sternberg's model, couples are well matched if they possess corresponding levels of passion,

FIG.14.4 STERNBERG'S TRIANGULAR THEORY OF LOVE

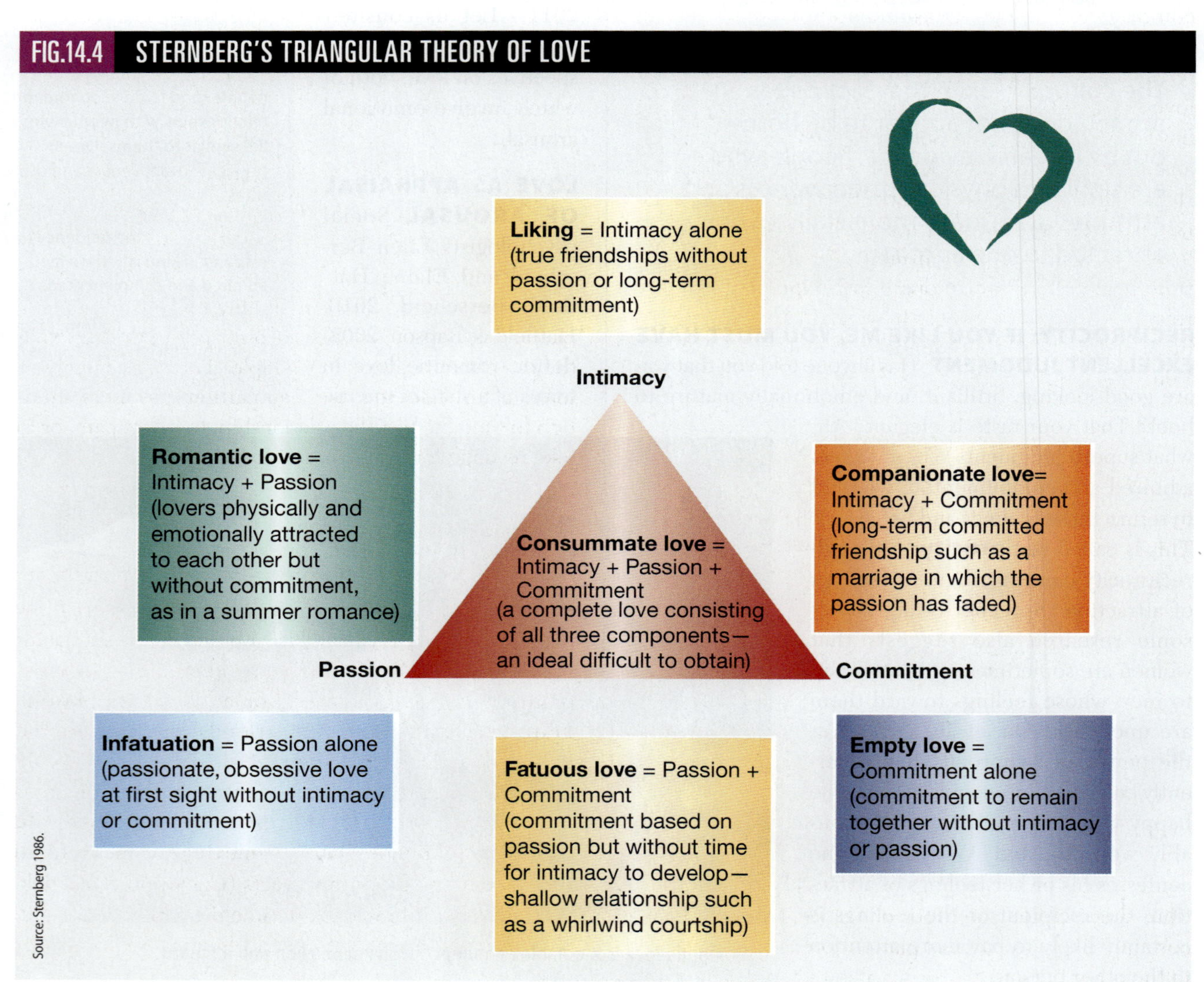

Liking = Intimacy alone (true friendships without passion or long-term commitment)
Intimacy
Romantic love = Intimacy + Passion (lovers physically and emotionally attracted to each other but without commitment, as in a summer romance)
Consummate love = Intimacy + Passion + Commitment (a complete love consisting of all three components—an ideal difficult to obtain)
Companionate love= Intimacy + Commitment (long-term committed friendship such as a marriage in which the passion has faded)
Passion
Commitment
Infatuation = Passion alone (passionate, obsessive love at first sight without intimacy or commitment)
Fatuous love = Passion + Commitment (commitment based on passion but without time for intimacy to develop—shallow relationship such as a whirlwind courtship)
Empty love = Commitment alone (commitment to remain together without intimacy or passion)

Source: Sternberg 1986.

intimacy, and commitment. According to the model, various combinations of the building blocks of love characterize different types of love relationships. For example, infatuation (passionate love) is typified by sexual desire but not by intimacy and commitment.

"Being in love" can refer to states of passion or infatuation, whereas friendship is usually based on shared interests, liking, and respect. Friendship and passionate love do not necessarily overlap. There is nothing that prevents people in love from becoming good friends, however—perhaps even the best of friends. Sternberg's model recognizes that the intimacy we find in true friendships and the passion we find in love are blended in two forms of love—romantic love and consummate love. These love types differ along the dimension of commitment, however.

Romantic love has both passion and intimacy but lacks commitment. Romantic love may burn brightly and then flicker out. Or it may develop into a more complete love, called consummate love, in which all three components flower. Consummate love is an ideal toward which many Westerners strive. Sometimes a love relationship has both passion and commitment but lacks intimacy. Sternberg calls this *fatuous* (foolish) *love*. Fatuous love is associated with whirlwind courtships that burn brightly but briefly as the partners realize that they are not well matched. In companionate love, intimacy and commitment are strong, but passion is lacking. Companionate love typifies long-term relationships and marriages in which passion has ebbed but a deep and abiding friendship remains (Sprecher & Fehr, 2011).

TRUTH

 **F** Couples can remain in love after passion fades.

It is true that couples can remain "in love" after passion fades, assuming that they have developed companionate love.

JEALOUSY

O! beware, my lord, of jealousy;
It is the green-ey'd monster . . .

—William Shakespeare, *Othello*

Thus was Othello, the Moor of Venice, warned of jealousy in the Shakespearean play that bears his name. Yet Othello could not control his feelings and wound up killing his beloved (and innocent) wife, Desdemona. Partners can become jealous, for example, when others show sexual interest in their partners or when their partners show interest in others.

Jealousy can lead to loss of feelings of affection, feelings of insecurity and rejection, anxiety, loss of self-esteem, and feelings of mistrust. Jealousy, therefore, can be one reason that relationships fail. In extreme cases jealousy can cause depression or give rise to spouse abuse, suicide, or, as with Othello, murder (Kerr & Capaldi, 2010; Weizmann-Henelius et al., 2011).

TRUTH

 **F** Jealousy can lessen feelings of affection and heighten feelings of insecurity and depression, leading to a breakup.

It is true that jealousy can lessen feelings of affection and heighten feelings of insecurity and depression, leading to a breakup. Yet in a milder form, jealousy may have the effect of reinforcing how much one cares for one's partner.

Some young adults—including college students—play jealousy games. They let their partners know that they are attracted to other people. They flirt openly or manufacture tales to make their partners pay more attention to them, to test the relationship, to inflict pain, or to take revenge for a partner's disloyalty.

14-5 LONELINESS

Loneliness increases from childhood to adolescence, when peer relationships are beginning to supplant family ties and individuals are becoming—often—painfully aware of how other adolescents may be more successful at making friends and earning the admiration of others (Adam et al., 2011). But young adults are also likely to encounter feelings of loneliness because of life changes such as entrance into college or graduate school, or moving to a new city to take advantage of job prospects (Cacioppo & Patrick, 2008). They often leave behind childhood friends and neighbors with whom they had lengthy relationships (Kagan, 2009).

TRUTH

 F Many people remain lonely because they fear being rejected by others.

It is true that many people remain lonely because they fear being rejected by others.

Some young adults feel lonely even when they are in relationships. A study of 101 dating couples with a mean age of 21 found that poor relationships contributed to feelings of loneliness and depression—even though the individuals had partners (Segrin et al., 2003). Loneliness also means that the individual feels that she or he is lacking in social support. Stress can lead to a host of health problems such as obesity and high blood pressure, and social support helps people cope with stress (Adam et al., 2011). Therefore, it is not surprising that feelings of loneliness are connected with such health problems as well as depression.

The causes of loneliness are many and complex. Lonely people tend to have several of the following characteristics: lack of social skills, lack of interest in other people, and lack of empathy (Montesi et al., 2013). The fear of rejection is often connected with self-criticism of social skills and expectations of failure in relating to others (Montesi et al., 2013). Lonely people also fail to disclose personal information to potential friends (Valkenburg et al., 2011), are cynical about human nature (for example, seeing people as only out for themselves), and demand too much too soon.

14-6 THE SINGLE LIFE

Being single, not married, is the most common lifestyle of people in their early 20s. The percentage of men and women aged 25 and above has more than doubled in the past two generations: from 8% of women in 1960 to 17% of women in 2012, and from 10% of men in 1960 to 23% of men in 2012 (Wang & Parker, 2014). Several factors contribute to the increased proportion of singles. The three main reasons people reported for remaining single in a 2014 Pew Research Center survey is that they have not met the right person (30%), they do not have sufficient financial stability (27%), and that they are not ready to settle down (22%) (Wang & Parker, 2014). Couples now are more likely to enter into sexual activity or sexual relationships without being married, and, often, without having a meaningful relationship. More young adults are postponing marriage to pursue educational and career goals. As we will discuss in a bit, many are also deciding to "live together" (cohabit), at least for a while, rather than get married. People are also getting married later, as shown in Figure 14.5. The median age for first marriage for men is currently 29–30; for women, it is 27.

Single-mother families have doubled to more than one-quarter of all families as compared with three decades ago (Wilcox & Marquardt, 2011). Some of these women started their families as single mothers, but the increased prevalence of divorce also swells their ranks.

Single people encounter less social stigma today. They are less likely today to be perceived as socially inadequate or as failures. On the other hand, many young adults do

Coping With Loneliness

What can you do to deal with loneliness in your own life? Here are some suggestions:

1. **Challenge your feelings of pessimism. Adopt the attitude that things happen when you make them happen.**
2. **Challenge your cynicism about human nature. Yes, lots of people are selfish and not worth knowing, but your task is to find people who possess the qualities you value.**
3. **Challenge the idea that failure in social relationships is unbearable and is therefore a valid reason for giving up on them. We must all learn to live with some rejection. Keep looking for the people who possess the qualities you value and who will find things of value in you.**
4. **Get out among people. Sit down at a table with people in the cafeteria, not off in a corner by yourself. Smile and say "hi" to people who interest you.**
5. **Make numerous social contacts. Join committees, intramural sports, social-action groups, the photography club, or the ski club.**
6. **Become a good listener. Ask people for opinions and actually listen to what they have to say. Tolerate diverse opinions.**
7. **Give people the chance to know you. Seek common ground by exchanging opinions and talking about your interests.**
8. **Remember that you're worthy of friends—warts and all. None of us is perfect.**
9. **Use your college counseling center. You might even ask whether there's a group at the center for students seeking to improve their dating or social skills.**

not choose to be single. Some have not yet found Mr. or Ms. Right. But many young adults see being single as an alternative, open-ended way of life—not a temporary stage that precedes marriage. As career options for women have expanded, they are not as financially dependent on men as their mothers and grandmothers were.

Being single is not without its problems. Many single people are lonely (Soons & Liefbroer, 2008). Some singles would like to have a steady, meaningful relationship. Others, usually women, worry about their physical safety. Some young adults who are living alone find it difficult to satisfy their needs for intimacy, companionship, and sex. Despite these concerns, most singles are well adjusted.

FIG.14.5 MEDIAN AGE AT FIRST MARRIAGE: 1950 TO THE PRESENT

30
28
26
24
22
20
18

Men
Women

1950 1960 1970 1980 1990 2000 2010 2014

Source: Current Population Survey, Annual Social and Economic Supplements, 1947 to 2014. https://www.census.gov/hhes/families/files/graphics/MS-2.pdf

TRUTH

(T) F Being single has become a more common U.S. lifestyle over the past few decades.

Yes, it is true that being single has become a more common U.S. lifestyle over the past few decades. There is less stigma connected with remaining single.

There is no single "singles scene." Single people differ in their sexual interests and lifestyles. Many achieve emotional and psychological security through a network of intimate relationships with friends. Many are sexually active and practice **serial monogamy** (Kulick, 2006). Others have a primary sexual relationship with one steady partner but occasional flings. A few pursue casual sexual encounters. By contrast, some singles remain celibate, either by choice or lack of opportunity. Some choose **celibacy** for religious reasons, to focus on work or another cause, because they find sex unalluring, or because of fear of STIs.

serial monogamy a series of exclusive sexual relationships.

celibacy abstention from sexual activity, whether from choice or lack of opportunity.

There is no single "singles scene." Young singles have different sexual interests and lead different lifestyles.

Jeff Greenberg 2 of 6 / Alamy Stock Photo

Swiping Right to Hook Up

"Has Tinder replaced dating with hookup culture?" asks CNN commentator Mel Robbins (2015). She refers to magazine article which referred to a "dating apocalypse," in which all the 20-somethings at a Manhattan sports bar are drinking, focusing on their screens, and swiping left or right, looking for people with whom they might hook up. Young investment bankers from the Ivy League are making dates, sometimes two or three, because something better might come along from the endless supply of what they call "Tinderellas."

Cyberstock/Alamy Stock Photo

"Guys view everything as a competition," one of the men says. "Who's slept with the best, hottest girls?" With dating apps, "you're always sort of prowling. You could talk to two or three girls at a bar and pick the best one, or you can swipe a couple hundred people a day . . . It's setting up two or three Tinder dates a week and, chances are, sleeping with all of them, so you could rack up 100 girls you've slept with in a year" (in Sales, 2015).

Women, relatively speaking, are more interested in having sex within relationships than men are (Gorelik & Shackelford, 2014). Based on research with 1,372 college students, men more often have short-term goals for having sex, such as pleasure, enjoying the physical desirability of their partners, reducing stress, and boosting their self-esteem and social status (Kennair et al., 2015). If Tinder-type dating then "sucks for women," as Robbins puts it, it's because they allow themselves to enter the world of hooking up online. Women who use Tinder and similar apps may be fooling themselves if they think that they are auditioning for long-term relationships.

Having noted these issues with Tinder and like-minded Apps, Finkel (2015) rises to the defense of Tinder. He acknowledges that the "old" or standard way to find an enduring relationship online is to use an App like Match.com or eHarmony, which use elaborate algorithms to examine your profile and the profiles of potential partners and to enable communication between you and your possible match. But Finkel believes that the kinds of information required to determine whether someone is a good match for you only comes to light after you have actually met. Tinder expands the dating pool. How you use it is up to you.

14-7 COHABITATION: DARLING, WOULD YOU BE MY POSSLQ?

> There is nothing I would not do If you would be my POSSLQ
>
> —*Charles Osgood*

POSSLQ? POSSLQ is the unromantic abbreviation used by the U.S. Bureau of the Census to refer to **cohabitation**. It stands for People of Opposite Sex Sharing Living Quarters and applies to unmarried heterosexual couples who live together (that is, cohabit) and have sexual relationships. Yet, cohabiting couples may also be of the same sex.

cohabitation living together with a romantic partner without being married.

Cohabitation has become largely accepted as a mainstream style of life (Wilcox & Marquardt, 2011). We rarely hear cohabitation referred to as "living in sin" as we once did. People today are more likely to refer to cohabitation with value-free expressions such as "living together." A Pew Research Center survey cited above found that only 46% of adults now say that people and society at large will be better off if marriage and children are a priority in people's lives. A somewhat higher percentage (50%) say that society will be just as well off if people have other priorities (Wang & Parker, 2014). Twenty-four percent of never-married adults aged 25 to 29 are currently cohabiting (Wang & Parker, 2014).

The numbers of households consisting of cohabiting male–female couples in the United States has increased more than tenfold since 1960, from fewer than half a million couples to around 8 million couples today

FIG.14.6 NUMBER OF COHABITING, UNMARRIED ADULT COUPLES OF THE OPPOSITE SEX, BY YEAR, UNITED STATES

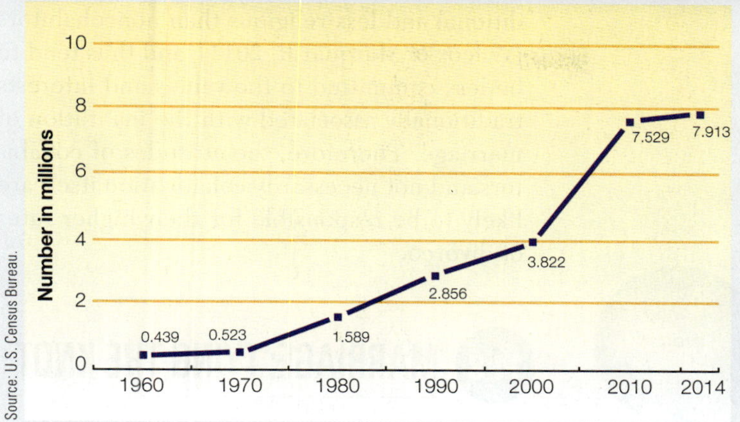

Source: U.S. Census Bureau.

FIG.14.7 THOUGHTS OF HIGH SCHOOL SENIORS ON LIVING TOGETHER

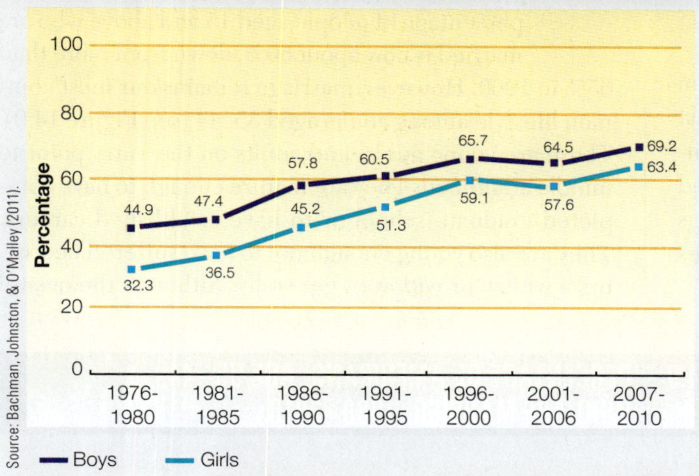

Source: Bachman, Johnston, & O'Malley (2011).

Percentage of U.S. high school seniors who agreed or mostly agreed with the statement: "It is usually a good idea for a couple to live together before getting married in order to find out whether they really get along," by time period.

(see Figure 14.6). More than half a million additional households consist of cohabiting same-sex couples.

More than half of today's marriages are preceded by the couple living together (Daniels et al., 2015). There is a 58% probability that a cohabiting American woman will marry her partner if the couple cohabit for three years (Copen et al., 2013). Some social scientists see cohabitation as a new stage of courtship. As you can see in Figure 14.7, more than half of today's high school seniors believe that it is a good idea for couples to live together before getting married to test their compatibility. Even so, about 40% of these couples get divorced later on, so "trial marriages" may not provide couples with accurate information.

Nearly half of divorced people who are cohabiting with new partners have children in the household (Copen et al., 2013). At least one out of three households with never-married cohabiting couples also has children (Copen et al., 2013).

Young adults cohabit for many reasons. Cohabitation, like marriage, is an alternative to living alone. Romantic partners may have deep feelings for each other but are not ready to get married. Some couples prefer cohabitation because it provides an abiding relationship without the legal entanglements of marriage (Wilcox & Marquardt, 2011). The couple may also be testing the compatibility and endurance of the relationship prior to tying the knot (Wang & Parker, 2014).

Willingness to cohabit is related to less traditional views of marriage and gender roles (Wilcox & Marquardt, 2011). For example, divorced people are more likely than people who have never been married to cohabit. Perhaps the experience of divorce leaves some people more willing to share their lives than their bank accounts. Cohabitants are also less likely than noncohabitants to say that religion is very important to them (Wilcox & Marquardt, 2011). Tradition aside, many cohabitants are simply less committed to their relationships than married people are (Wilcox & Marquardt, 2011). It is more often the man

TRUTH

(T) F Cohabitation has become a normal stage of courtship for many U.S. couples.

Yes, a majority of Americans in 2015 (55%) did report that they favor same-sex marriage. The number of people supporting same-sex marriage has risen throughout the century, and younger people are more likely than older people to favor same-sex marriage. Thus the numbers supporting same-sex marriage may continue to increase.

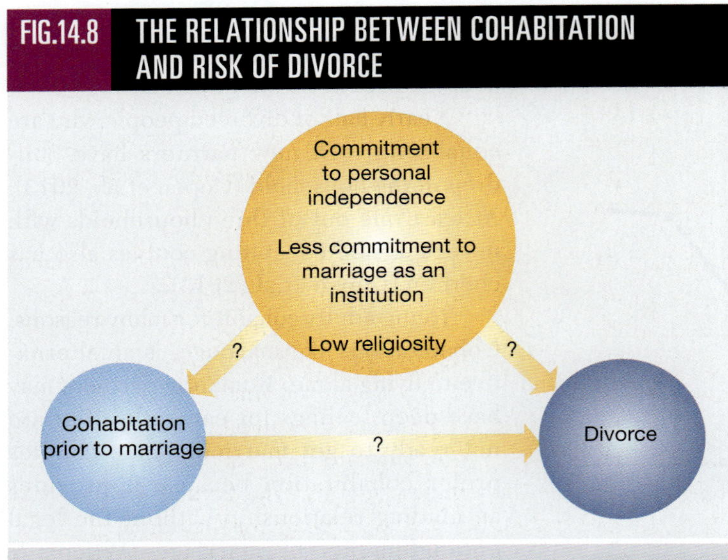

Does living together before marriage heighten the risk of divorce later on, or do factors that encourage cohabitation also heighten the risk of divorce?

who is unwilling to make a commitment, because men are typically more interested in sexual variety, at least in the short term (Schmitt, 2014; Shackelford & Hansen, 2015). In the long term, however, both men and women may seek to invest in a relationship, feelings of love, companionship, and a sharing of resources (Njus & Bane, 2009).

Economic factors also come into play. Young adults may decide to cohabit because of the economic advantages of sharing household expenses. Cohabiting individuals who receive public assistance risk losing support if they get married (Wilcox & Marquardt, 2011). College students may cohabit secretly to maintain parental support that they might lose if they were to reveal their living arrangements.

Cohabiting couples may believe that cohabitation will strengthen eventual marriage by helping them iron out the kinks in their relationship. Yet, some studies suggest that the likelihood of divorce within ten years of marriage is nearly twice as great among married couples who cohabited before marriage. Why?

We cannot conclude that cohabitation necessarily causes divorce. We must be cautious about drawing causal conclusions from correlational data. Selection factors—the factors that led some couples to cohabit and others not to cohabit—may explain the results (see Figure 14.8). For example, as noted earlier, cohabitors tend to be less traditional and less religious than noncohabitors (Wilcox & Marquardt, 2011), and thus tend to be less committed to the values and interests traditionally associated with the institution of marriage. Therefore, the attitudes of cohabitors and not necessarily cohabitation itself are likely to be responsible for their higher rates of divorce.

14-8 MARRIAGE: TYING THE KNOT

The percentage of Americans who are married has been decreasing sharply over the past 50 years (see Figure 14.9). At first it might seem as though marriage is in jeopardy since the total percentage of people aged 15 and above who are married is now about 50%, down from more than 65% in 1960. However, marriage remains our most common lifestyle among adults aged 35–44 (see Figure 14.9). These are young adults and adults on the entry point to middle adulthood. They are mature enough to have completed graduate school or to have established careers. They are also young enough not to have suffered becoming a widow or widower, generally. Although the overall

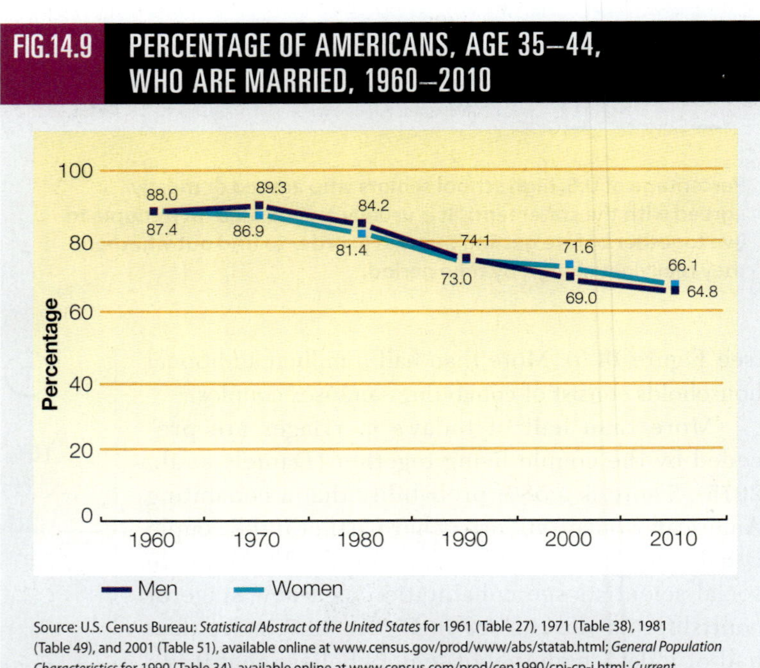

Source: U.S. Census Bureau: *Statistical Abstract of the United States* for 1961 (Table 27), 1971 (Table 38), 1981 (Table 49), and 2001 (Table 51), available online at www.census.gov/prod/www/abs/statab.html; *General Population Characteristics* for 1990 (Table 34), available online at www.census.com/prod/cen1990/cpi-cp-i.html; *Current Population Reports*, "America's Families and Living Arrangements" for 2010 (Table UC3), available online at http://www.census.com/population.www.socdemo.hh-gam.cps202.html.

percentage of American households made up of married couples has been decreasing, 60% to 70% of American men and women aged 35 to 44 are married.

14-8a WHY DO PEOPLE GET MARRIED?

Even in this era of serial monogamy and cohabitation, people get married. Marriage meets many personal and cultural needs. For traditionalists, marriage legitimizes sexual relations. Marriage provides an institution in which children can be supported and socialized. Marriage (theoretically) restricts sexual relations so that a man can be assured—or assume—that his wife's children are his. Unless one has signed a prenuptial agreement to the contrary, marriage permits the orderly transmission of wealth from one family to another and one generation to another.

Today, because more people believe that premarital sex is acceptable between two people who feel affectionate toward each other, the desire for sex is less likely to motivate marriage. But marriage provides a sense of security and opportunities to share feelings, experiences, and ideas with someone with whom one forms a special attachment. Most young adults agree that marriage is important for people who plan to spend the rest of their lives together (Jayson, 2008).

Broadly speaking, many people in the United States today want to get married because they believe that they will be happier. The National Marriage Project suggests that most of them are correct (see Figure 14.10), even if the percentages of those reporting that their marriages are "very happy" have declined since the 1970s.

14-8b TYPES OF MARRIAGE

Among male and female couples, we have two types of marriage: monogamy and polygamy. In **monogamy**, one person is married to one other person. In **polygamy**, a person has more than one spouse and is permitted sexual access to each of them.

ARRANGED MARRIAGE In the Broadway musical *Fiddler on the Roof*, Tevye, the Jewish father of three girls of marriageable age in 19th-century Russia, demands that his daughters marry Jewish men to perpetuate their families' religious and cultural traditions. Today, traditional societies such as those of India (Myers et al., 2005) and Pakistan (Zaidi & Shuraydi, 2002) frequently use arranged marriages, in which the families of the bride and groom more or less arrange for the union.

As in *Fiddler*, one of the purposes of arranged marriage is to make certain that the bride and groom share similar backgrounds so that they will carry on family traditions. Supporters of arranged marriage also argue that it is wiser to follow family wisdom than one's own heart, especially since the attraction couples feel is often infatuation and not a deep, abiding love. Proponents also claim a lower divorce rate for arranged marriages than for "self-arranged marriages" (but it must be noted that couples who enter arranged marriages are generally more traditional to begin with). In Hong Kong, for example, as arranged marriage declines and couples marry whom they wish, the divorce rate is increasing (Fan & Lui, 2008).

FIG.14.10 HAPPY MARRIAGES

Source: Wilcox & Marquardt (2011, Figure 4).

Percentage of married persons age 18 and older who said their marriages were "very happy"

SAME-SEX MARRIAGE

[T]he right to marry is a fundamental right inherent in the liberty of the person, and under the Due Process and Equal Protection Clauses of the Fourteenth Amendment couples of the same-sex may not be deprived of that right and that liberty. The Court now holds that same-sex couples may exercise the fundamental right to marry. No longer may this liberty be denied to them.

Supreme Court Justice
Anthony Kennedy, 2015, p. 33

monogamy marriage between one person and one other person.

polygamy marriage in which a person has more than one spouse and is permitted sexual access to each of them.

With a single decision in 2015, the U.S. Supreme Court cut through thousands of years of history, decades of debate, and piecemeal state-by-state advances toward the legalization of same-sex marriage in the United States. At the time, some 30 of the 50 states had already recognized gay marriage, and it was recognized in many countries including our next-door neighbors Canada and Mexico; The Netherlands, Sweden, and Norway in Europe; and Israel and South Africa, to name a few.

Although the Supreme Court decision was handed down overnight, the struggle to obtain the right to marry people of one's own anatomic sex was fought for decades. The Fifth Amendment of the U.S. Constitution requires that the federal government not deprive people of life, liberty, or property without "due process of the law" and guarantees that all individuals will receive "equal protection" under the law. Section 1 of the Fourteenth Amendment further prohibits states from depriving individuals of rights, again on the basis of due process and equal protection.

Many Americans had been instructed by the Bible: "If a man lies with a man as with a woman, both of them have committed an abomination; they shall be put to death, their blood is upon them" (Leviticus 20:13). The U.S. Supreme Court in effect upheld the separation of church and state; the Court agreed that the United States is a nation of laws and not a theocracy. Justice Kennedy recognized, as we see in his following statement, that people may disagree with the Court ruling on religious grounds, but, he asserts, states may not "bar same-sex couples from marriage":

> *[It] must be emphasized that religions, and those who adhere to religious doctrines, may continue to advocate with utmost, sincere conviction that, by divine precepts, same-sex marriage should not be condoned. . . . The Constitution, however, does not permit the State to bar same-sex couples from marriage on the same terms as accorded to couples of the opposite sex.*
>
> Supreme Court Justice
> Anthony Kennedy, 2015, p. 32

A generation ago, the great majority of Americans were opposed to same-sex marriage (Leubsdorf & Nelson, 2015). As recently as 2001, only one American in three (35%) favored same-sex marriage, but in 2015 the majority (55%) favored same-sex marriage (see Figure 14.11).

14-8c WHOM DO WE MARRY: ARE MARRIAGES MADE IN HEAVEN OR IN THE NEIGHBORHOOD?

Although the selection of a mate is (officially) free in our society, factors such as race, social class, and religion often determine the categories of people within which we seek mates (Laumann et al., 2007). Young adults tend to marry others from the same area and social class. Since

FIG.14.11 PERCENT OF AMERICANS WHO SUPPORT AND OPPOSE SAME-SEX MARRIAGE

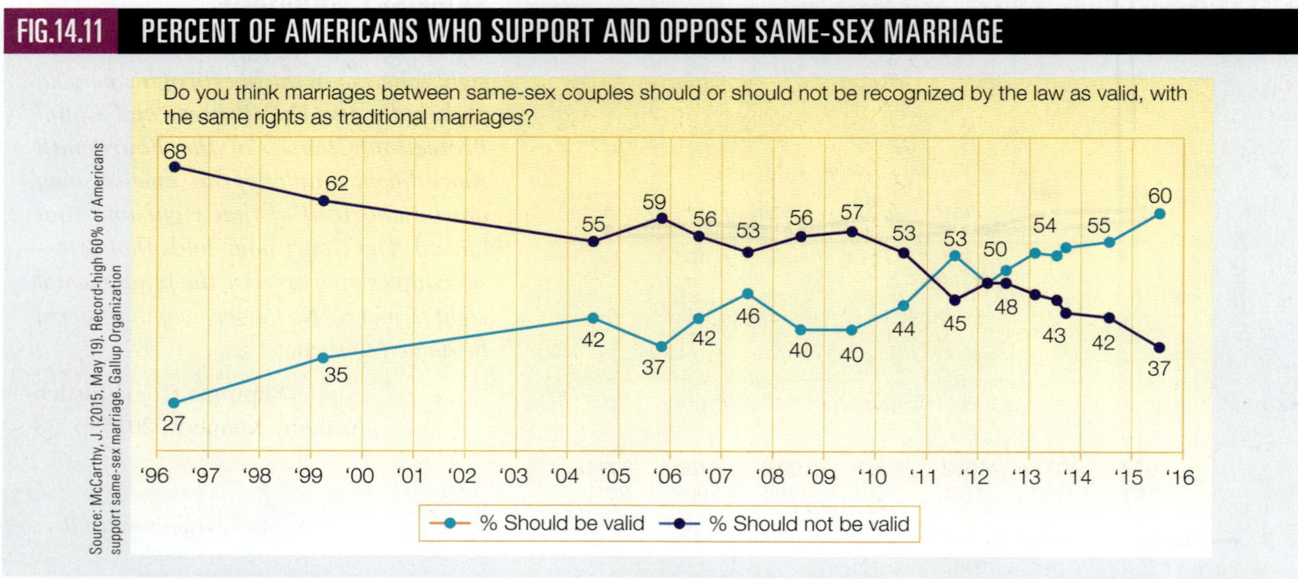

In 2001 57% of Americns opposed same-sex marriage and 35% approved of it. By 2016 those numbers had been in effect reversed, so that 60% of Americans approve of same-sex marriage and 37% are opposed.

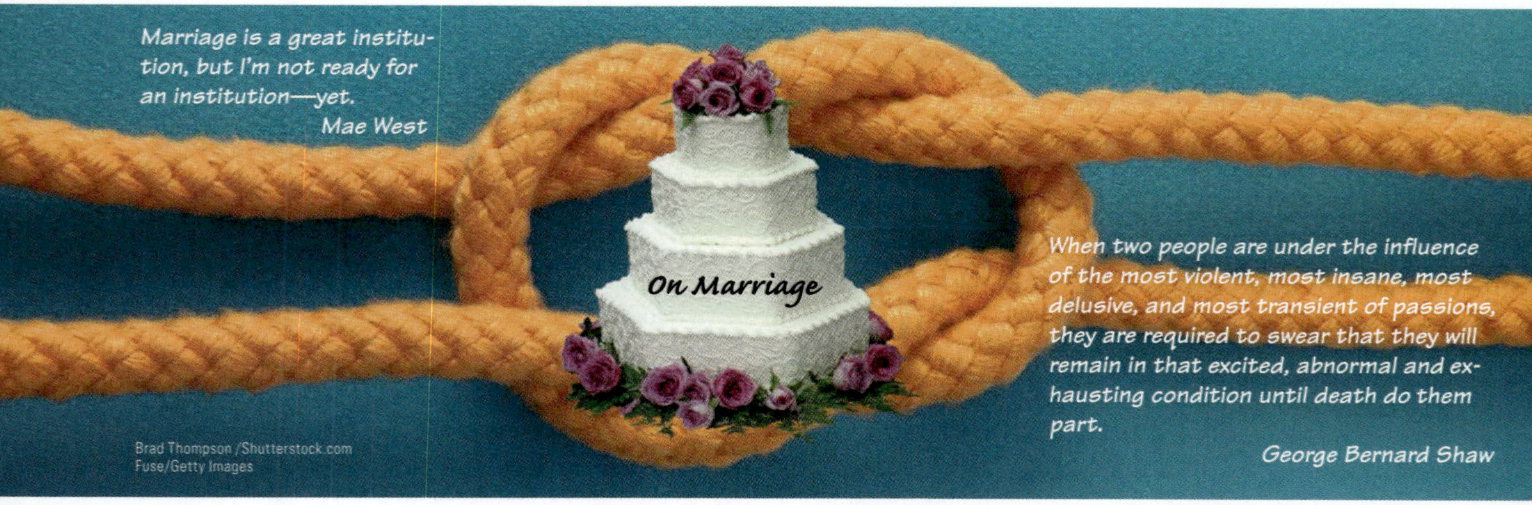

neighborhoods are often made up of people from a similar social class, storybook marriages like Cinderella's are the exception to the rule.

Marriage is a great institution, but I'm not ready for an institution—yet.
Mae West
On Marriage
When two people are under the influence of the most violent, most insane, most delusive, and most transient of passions, they are required to swear that they will remain in that excited, abnormal and exhausting condition until death do them part.
George Bernard Shaw
Brad Thompson /Shutterstock.com
Fuse/Getty Images

Young adults tend to marry people who are similar in physical attractiveness, attitudes, background, and interests (Blackwell & Lichter, 2004). Young adults are more often than not similar to their mates in height, weight, personality traits, intelligence, educational level, religion, and even in use of alcohol and tobacco (DeCuyper et al., 2012; Kandler & Riemann, 2013; van Straaten et al., 2009). Nearly 95% of marriages and 80% to 90% of cohabiting unions were between partners of the same race at the time of the 2010 U.S. census (U.S. Census Bureau, 2011). The concept of "like marrying like" is termed **homogamy**. Research shows that marriages between people from similar backgrounds tend to be more stable (DeCuyper et al., 2012), perhaps because partners are more likely to share values and attitudes (Eeckhaut et al., 2013).

homogamy the practice of people getting married to people who are similar to them.

LUIS ACOSTA/AFP/Getty Images

Jeremy Woodhouse/SuperStock/Getty Images

Even in the same country—in this case, Mexico—people get married in various ways. The couple on the left are taking part in a civil wedding ceremony on Valentine's Day with many other couples. The couple on the right have had a traditional church wedding, and now photographers take their pictures near the church steps while a mariachi ensemble serenades them to celebrate their union.

Most people also tend to follow *age homogamy*—to select a partner who falls in their own age range, with husbands two to five years older than wives (Burrows, 2013). But age homogamy reflects the tendency to marry in early adulthood. Persons who marry late or who remarry tend not to select partners so close in age because they are "out in the world"—rather than in school or fresh out of school—and tend to work with or otherwise meet people from different age groups (Shafer, 2013).

14-8d MARITAL SATISFACTION

The nature of romantic relationships and the satisfaction of the partners strongly affect the well-being of each member of the couple at various stages throughout adulthood (Boerner et al., 2014). A meta-analysis of gender differences in marital satisfaction found that wives were more likely than husbands to report that their marriages were unhappy and that they had considered divorce, but the difference was not large (Jackson et al., 2014). An Italian study of married couples found that the partners' confidence in their abilities to influence their relationship for the better contributed to the quality of the marriage (Bertoni et al., 2007). In turn, the quality of the marital relationship appeared to positively affect individuals' physical and psychological health (Boerner et al., 2014). Another study found that intimacy, which is fueled by trust, honesty, and the sharing of innermost feelings, is strongly connected with marital satisfaction (Patrick et al., 2007). So is the psychological support of one's spouse.

Satisfaction with one's career is positively correlated with marital satisfaction, and both of them are related to general life satisfaction (Dyrbye et al., 2014). Perhaps general tendencies toward happiness (or depression) manifest themselves in various walks of life, including one's vocational life and one's romantic relationships. Or perhaps doing very well in one arena can cast a positive glow on other parts of life.

When one marital partner is a heavy drinker and the other is not, marital satisfaction declines over time (Homish & Leonard, 2007). It doesn't matter which one is the heavy drinker, the man or the woman; in either case, satisfaction declines. Another study followed 172 newlywed couples over four years and found that physical aggression preceded sharp declines in marital satisfaction (Lawrence & Bradbury, 2007).

Researchers in one study investigated the effects of infants' sleep patterns and crying on marital satisfaction in 107 first-time parent couples during the first year following birth. In general, marital satisfaction decreased as the year wore on, and the baby's crying was apparently the main source of the problem (Meijer & van den Wittenboer, 2007). Parental loss of sleep compounded the difficulties.

Satisfaction in the Relationships of Heterosexual and Same-Sex Couples

Numerous researchers have studied the factors that predict satisfaction in a relationship or the deterioration and ending of a relationship. Much of this research has sought to determine whether there are differences in the factors that satisfy heterosexual and same-sex couples, and the interesting finding is that we are hard pressed to find differences. Both heterosexual and same-sex couples are more satisfied when they receive social support from their partners, when there is sharing of power in the relationship, when they fight fair, and when they perceive their partners to be committed to the relationship (Lennon et al., 2013; Markey et al., 2014). One difference that stands out favors the stability of same-sex couples: They tend to distribute household chores evenly and not in terms of gender-role stereotypes (Kurdek, 2005, 2006). But there are a couple of differences that favor stability in the relationships of the heterosexual couples: They are more likely to have the support of their families and less likely to be stigmatized by society at large.

Masterfile

14-9 PARENTHOOD

Just as people are getting married in their later 20s in the United States today, so are they delaying parenthood (Arnett, 2012; Wilcox & Marquardt, 2011). The median age for a woman's first birth is 26.3 (Births and Natality, 2016). But bearing children in developed nations is generally seen as something that ideally occurs in early adulthood, although a few hundred thousand teenage girls bear children in the United States each year. Becoming a parent is a major life event that requires changes in nearly every sphere of life: personal, social, and financial (Redshaw & van den Akker, 2007). In fact, many individuals and couples in contemporary developed nations no longer think of parenthood as a necessary part of marriage or a relationship (Doherty et al., 2007). In developed nations the decision not to have children or to have only one child is becoming more common. The average American woman is having about two children today, down from between three and four (3.65) 50 years ago. The average woman needs to have 2.11 children for a couple to be at "replacement level," because some children will not survive to reproduce. If this fertility rate were to remain the same and there were no immigration, the population of the United States would decline.

Why do people have children? Reflect on the fact that reliable birth-control methods have separated sex acts from reproduction. Except for women living under the most "traditional" circumstances, or for couples who accidentally get pregnant, or for women who are victims of sexual assault, becoming pregnant is a choice. In developed nations, most couples report that they choose to have children for personal happiness or well-being (Dyer, 2007). In more traditional societies people report having children to strengthen marital bonds, provide social security, assist with labor (as in having more farmhands), provide social status, maintain the family name and lineage, secure property rights and inheritance, and in some places, improve the odds of—yes—reincarnation (Dyer, 2007). Of these reasons, having children to care for one in one's old age ("social security") looms large. In the United States, the federal Social Security program helps support older people, but how many middle-aged people (typically daughters) are running in one direction to rear their children and in another direction to provide emotional and other support for elderly parents and other relatives?

It is actually unlikely that having a child will save a marriage. Numerous studies show that with the added stress of caring for a new baby, the quality of a couple's adjustment often declines significantly throughout the year following delivery (Pollmann-Schult, 2014).

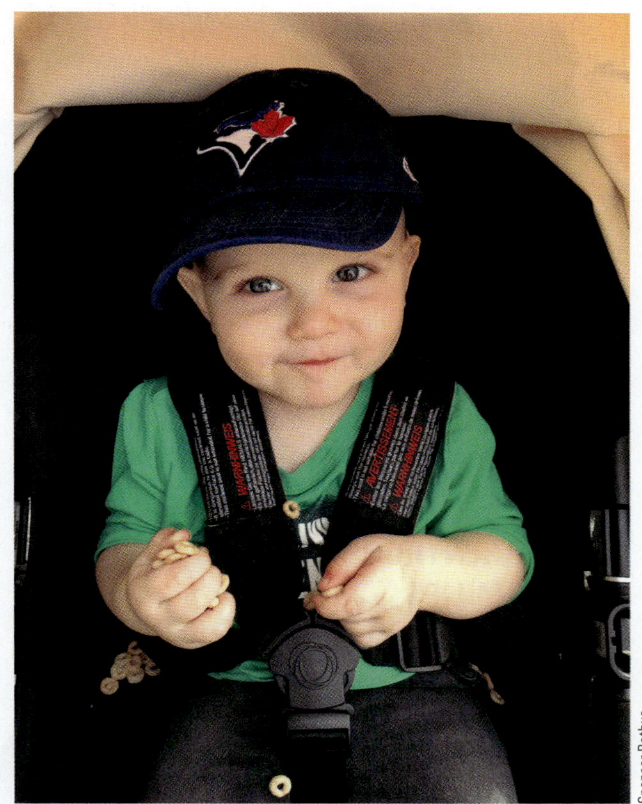

Spencer Rathus

FICTION

T (F) Having a child is a way to help save a marriage that is in trouble.

It is not true that having a child is a way to help save a marriage that is in trouble. The resultant environment is not conducive to the adjustment of the child or the parents.

14-9a PARENTHOOD AND ROLE OVERLOAD

Some research has focused on the effects of newborns entering the lives of working-class families, especially when the mother must return to work shortly after the birth (Rholes et al., 2014). In such cases, the parents are frequently depressed, and conflict often emerges. Although fathers in such cases may give lip service to helping with the baby and do a few things to help out here and there, the mother is almost always the primary caregiver (Rholes et al., 2014) and thus encounters role overload. That is, the mother suffers from playing roles as both primary caregiver and, in our demanding economy, one of two primary breadwinners.

Yet a longitudinal study of 45 couples expecting their first child showed that family life does not have to be this stressful (McHale & Rotman, 2007). The couples were assessed during pregnancy and from infancy through toddlerhood—at 3, 12, and 30 months after birth. When the parents generally agreed on their beliefs about parenting, and who should do what, their postnatal adjustment was largely solid and remained stable. In other words, if each member of the couple believed they should share caregiving equally and they lived up to it, their adjustment was good. If they believed that one parent should be primarily responsible for caregiving and abided by that scenario, adjustment was also good. Consistency between their expressed beliefs and their behavior predicted adjustment.

14-9b PARENTHOOD IN DUAL-EARNER FAMILIES

The financial realities of contemporary life, and the women's movement, have made the move of women into the workplace the norm in American society. Thus young married or cohabiting adults with children more often than not are dual-earner families.

European and American studies find that the mothers in dual-earner families encounter more stress than the fathers do (Schneewind & Kupsch, 2007; Wall, 2007). Evidence of a powerful gender difference in dual-earner families is also found in analysis of longitudinal survey data on 884 dual-earner couples (Chesley & Moen, 2006). Caring for children was connected with declines in well-being for dual-earner women, but, ironically, with increases in well-being for dual-earner men. Perhaps the men were relieved of much stress by the second income. Dual-earner women with flexible work schedules encountered less stress than women with fixed schedules, apparently because they were more capable of managing their role overload.

What happens in the workplace doesn't necessarily stay in the workplace. A study of 113 dual-earner couples found that problems in the workplace contributed to tension in the couples, health problems, and dissatisfaction with the relationship (Matthews et al., 2006).

Because of problems balancing work and family life, it is usually the mother and not the father who cuts back on work or drops out of the workforce altogether when dual-earner families can no longer afford to have a parent out of the home (Wall, 2007). Because of experience with dual-earner families around them, a sample

Jade Brookbank/Taxi/Getty Images

It may be Halloween, but still . . . in the text, we posed the question, "Why do people have children?" Perhaps we could also ask, "Why do children have parents?"

of 194 adolescents from dual-earner families generally expected that they (if they were female) or their partners (if they were male) would be the ones to cut back or quit work in the future, at least temporarily, if the couple had a child (Weinshenker, 2006). The responses showed little insight into the problems raised by interrupting careers. On the other hand, the fact that their mothers work did encourage the adolescents—female and male—to say they believed in gender egalitarianism.

14-10 DIVORCE: BREAKING BONDS

Some 40% to 50% of the marriages in the United States end in divorce (Wilcox & Marquardt, 2011). The divorce rate in the United States rose steadily through much of the 20th century before leveling off in the 1980s. Divorced women outnumber divorced men, in part because men are more likely to remarry.

Fuse/Getty Images

American studies find that the mothers in dual-earner families encounter more stress than the fathers do.

Why the increase in divorce? Until the mid-1960s, adultery was the only legal grounds for divorce in most states. But no-fault divorce laws have been enacted in nearly every state, allowing a divorce to be granted without a finding of marital misconduct. The increased economic independence of women has also contributed to the divorce rate. More women today have the economic means of breaking away from a troubled marriage. Also, today more people consider marriage an alterable condition than in prior generations.

Americans today also want more from marriage than did their grandparents. They expect marriage to be personally fulfilling as well as an institution for family life and rearing children. The most common reasons given for a divorce today are problems in communication and a lack of understanding. Key complaints include a husband's criticism, defensiveness, contempt, and stonewalling—not lack of financial support (Theiss & Leustek, 2016; Wilcox & Marquardt, 2011). A British study notes that violence, infidelity, and lack of commitment to a specific partner also play prominent roles in divorce (Lampard, 2014).

14-10a THE COST OF DIVORCE

Divorce is usually connected with financial and emotional problems. When a household splits, the resources often cannot maintain the earlier standard of living for each partner. Divorce hits women in the pocketbook harder than men. Women who have not pursued a career may have to struggle to compete with younger, more experienced workers. Divorced mothers often face the combined stress of the sole responsibility for child rearing and the need to increase their incomes. Divorced fathers may find it difficult to pay alimony and child support while establishing a new lifestyle.

Divorce can also prompt feelings of failure as a spouse and parent, loneliness and uncertainty about the future, and depression. Married people appear to be better able to cope with the stresses and strains of life, perhaps because they can lend each other emotional support. Divorced and separated people have the highest rates of physical and mental illness (Lorenz et al., 2006; Perry, 2014). They also have high rates of suicide (Batterham et al., 2014). As noted in the chapter on social and emotional development in middle childhood, children are often the biggest losers when parents get a divorce, yet chronic marital conflict is also connected with psychological distress in children (Amato, 2006; Amato & Anthony, 2014). Researchers attribute children's problems following divorce not only to the divorce itself but also to a consequent decline in the quality of parenting. Children's adjustment is enhanced when both parents maintain parenting responsibilities and set aside their differences long enough to agree on child-rearing practices (Hetherington, 2006). Children of divorce also benefit when their parents avoid saying negative things about each other in the children's presence (Hetherington, 2006).

Despite the difficulties in adjustment, most divorced people eventually bounce back. Most remarry. Indeed, divorce may permit personal growth and renewal and the opportunity to take stock of oneself and establish a new, more rewarding life. Most children whose parents have divorced also bounce back, although recovery may take a year or two (Arkowitz & Lilienfeld, 2013).

As we see in the following chapters, middle adulthood presents challenges that continue from early adulthood, as well as a number of new challenges. Issues of parenting continue, and sometimes they move in two directions—toward children and toward one's own parents.

Image Source/Getty Images

Image Source/Getty Images

My wife and I were considering a divorce, but after pricing lawyers we decided to buy a new car instead.
—*Henny Youngman*

Whenever I date a guy, I think, is this the man I want my children to spend their weekends with?
—*Rita Rudner*

STUDY TOOLS 14

READY TO STUDY?

In the book, you can:

- ☐ Rip out the chapter review card at the back of the book for a handy summary of the chapter and key terms.
- ☐ Check your understanding of what you've read with the quizzes that follow.

ONLINE AT CENGAGEBRAIN.COM YOU CAN:

- ☐ Collect StudyBits while you read and study the chapter.
- ☐ Quiz yourself on key concepts.
- ☐ Find videos for further exploration.
- ☐ Prepare for tests with HDEV5 Flash Cards as well as those you create.

SELF-ASSESSMENTS

Fill Ins

Answers can be found in the back of the book.

1. According to Erik Erikson, the life crisis of early adulthood is intimacy versus ____________.
2. Daniel Levinson refers to the young adult's drive to leave his or her mark on history as the ____________.
3. Men appear to be more attracted to women who are shown against ____________-colored backgrounds.
4. ____________ psychologists believe that gender differences in preferences for mates persist because they have been connected with reproductive advantages.
5. According to Sternberg, people who experience nothing but passion for one another are experiencing the kind of love relationship that he terms ____________.
6. Young adults who leave home and then return because of financial need have been referred to as the ____________ generation.
7. In the practice of serial ____________, a single person has consecutive exclusive sexual relationships.
8. The concept of like marrying like is termed ____________.
9. ____________ is the most common lifestyle for Americans in their early 20s.
10. "The green-eyed monster" is ____________.

Multiple Choice

1. **Individuation is the process of becoming an individual by**
   a. rebelling against one's family of origin.
   b. placing friendships at college or work ahead of relationships with relatives.
   c. entering a moratorium.
   d. integrating one's own values with those of parents and society.

2. **Erikson and Havighurst have both been criticized for their view that**
   a. money is everything to young adults.
   b. young adults are too critical of their parents and of society at large.
   c. some individuals are not "ready" to go to college.
   d. young adults who remain celibate or single are not developing normally.

3. **Daniel Levinson and his colleagues believed that the later 30s are characterized by**
   a. settling down or planting roots.
   b. ripping up the life that one struggled to build in the 20s.
   c. becoming more politically liberal.
   d. turning away from dualistic thinking.

4. **According to Sprecher and her colleagues, _________ is the key factor in consideration of partners for dates, sex, and long-term relationships.**
   a. intelligence
   b. reliability and social position
   c. physical appearance
   d. a sense of humor

5. **What is the relationship between cohabitation and subsequent divorce?**
   a. Cohabitation is a cause of divorce.
   b. Unstable people cohabit.
   c. There is no link between cohabitation and divorce.
   d. There is a positive correlation between cohabitation and divorce

6. **According to a Pew Research Center survey, more than three never-married women in four are likely to consider _____________ very important in choosing a spouse or a partner.**
   a. attitudes toward having children and child-rearing
   b. age
   c. having a steady job
   d. religion

7. **According to Sternberg's theory of love, love can have all of the following components *except***
   a. jealousy.
   b. passion.
   c. commitment.
   d. intimacy.

8. **People who are lonely have been shown to have all of the following characteristics *except***
   a. fear of rejection.
   b. an inadequate standard of living.
   c. lack of social skills.
   d. lack of interest in other people.

9. **About ___________ million male–female couples are cohabiting in the United States today.**
   a. 2.5
   b. 5.0
   c. 8
   d. 15.0

10. **A factor that aids in the stability of same-sex couples is that they**
    a. are more likely than heterosexual couples to have the support of their families.
    b. tend to distribute household chores more evenly than heterosexual couples do.
    c. are less likely than heterosexual couples to be stigmatized by society.
    d. tend to live in large cities.

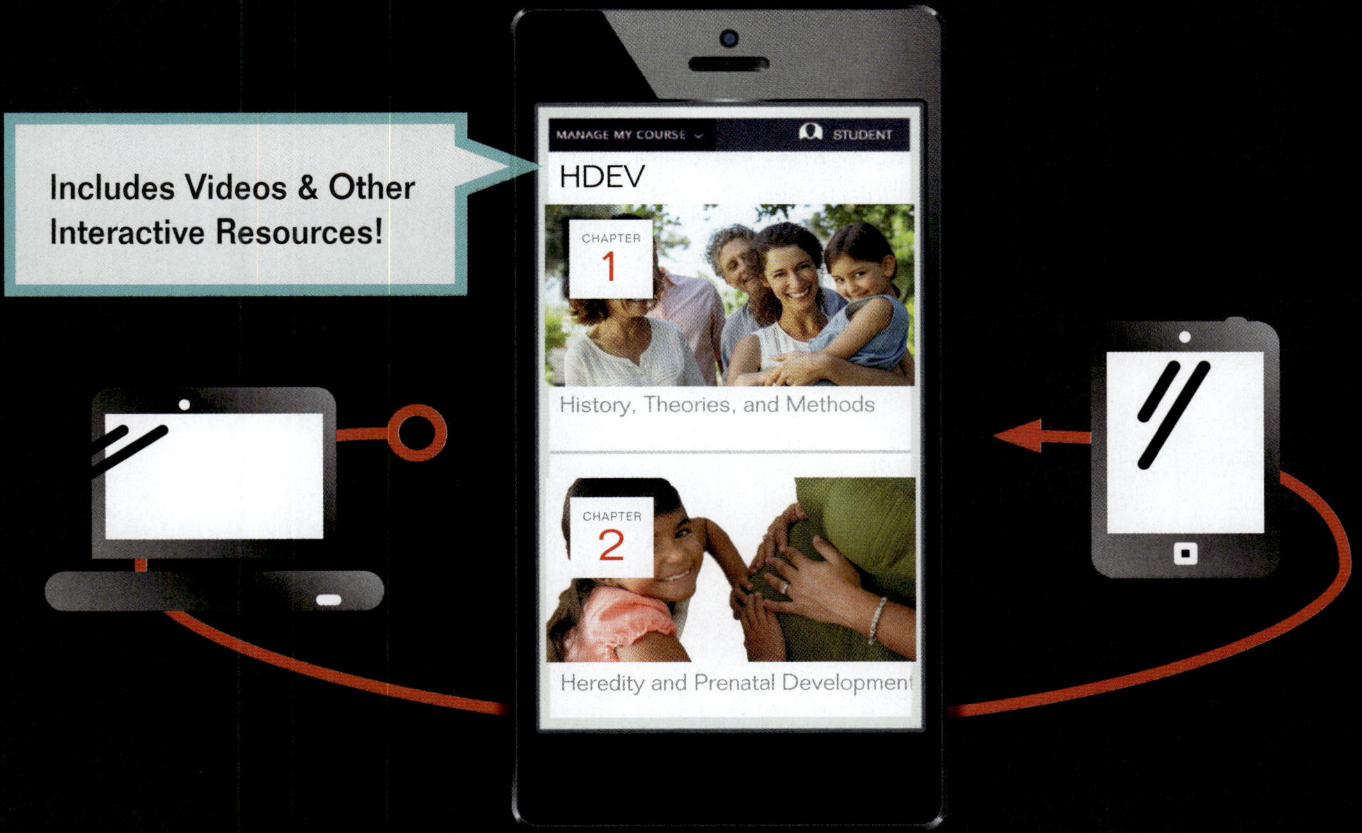

15 Middle Adulthood: Physical and Cognitive Development

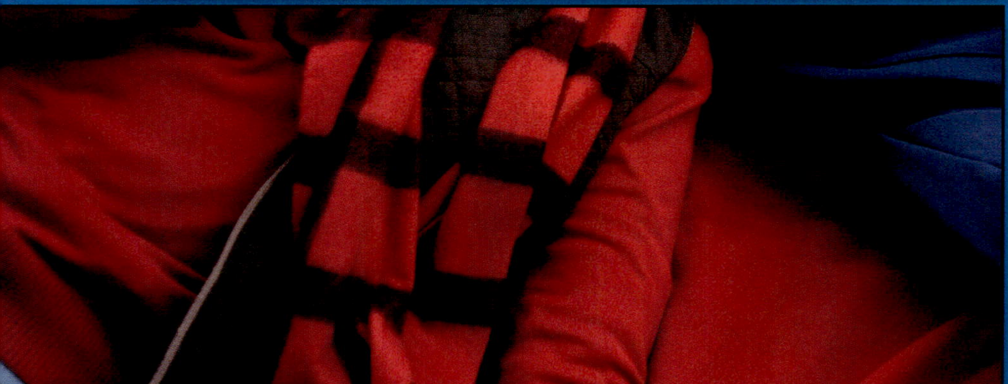

Don Mason/Blend Images/Getty Images

LEARNING OUTCOMES

After studying this chapter, you will be able to . . .

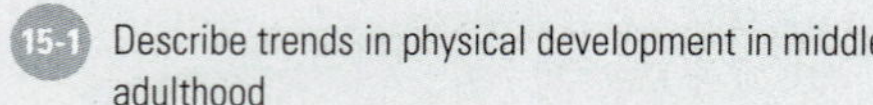

- 15-1 Describe trends in physical development in middle adulthood
- 15-2 Discuss the major health concerns of middle adulthood, including cancer and heart disease
- 15-3 Discuss the functioning of the immune system
- 15-4 Discuss sexuality in middle adulthood, focusing on menopause and sexual dysfunctions
- 15-5 Describe cognitive development in middle adulthood, distinguishing between crystallized and fluid intelligence
- 15-6 Discuss opportunities for exercising creativity and continuing education in middle adulthood

After you finish this chapter, go to **PAGE 318** for **STUDY TOOLS**

Some years back, the American Board of Family Practice asked 1,200 Americans when middle age begins; 46% answered that middle age began when you realize you don't know who the new music groups are (Beck, 1992). If they had been polled today, perhaps they would have said that middle age begins when you don't know who won *The Voice* or *Dancing with the Stars*. In chronological terms, most theorists consider **middle adulthood** to span the years from 40 to 65, with 60 to 65 as a transition period to late adulthood. But we might also note that some theorists are beginning to assert that we are truly becoming only as old as we feel, that 65 is the new 55, and so on.

Some theorists view middle age as a time of peak performance, and others have portrayed it as a time of crisis or decline. Physically speaking, we are at a peak in early adulthood, but in general those who eat right and exercise will in many ways undergo only a gradual and relatively minor physical decline in middle adulthood. As people age, they become more vulnerable to a variety of illnesses, but they also become less prone to irresponsible behavior that may result in injury or death. On the other hand, some sensory and sexual changes might well become major issues. Cognitively speaking, we are at our peak in many intellectual functions in middle adulthood, but there may be some loss of processing speed and some lapses in memory. Even so, these are often counterbalanced by expertise.

> Some theorists view middle age as a time of peak performance, and others portray it as a time of crisis or decline.

15-1 PHYSICAL DEVELOPMENT

No two people age in the same way or at the same rate. This phenomenon is called **interindividual variability**. But whatever individual differences may exist, physiological aging is defined by changes in the body's integumentary system (the body's system of skin, hair, and nails), senses, reaction time, and lung capacity. These changes may well be unavoidable. Changes in metabolism, muscle mass, strength, bone density, aerobic capacity, blood-sugar tolerance, and ability to regulate body temperature may be moderated and sometimes reversed through exercise and diet.

SKIN AND HAIR Hair usually begins to gray in middle adulthood as the production of *melanin*, the pigment responsible for hair color, decreases. Hair loss also accelerates with aging, especially in men. Much wrinkling associated with aging is actually caused by exposure to ultraviolet (UV) rays.

Beginning gradually in early adulthood, the body produces fewer proteins that give the skin its elasticity. The body also produces fewer *keratinocytes*—the cells in the outer layer of the skin that are regularly shed and renewed, leaving the skin dryer and more brittle.

SENSORY FUNCTIONING Normal age-related changes in vision begin to appear by the mid-30s and assert themselves as significant problems in middle adulthood.

middle adulthood the stage of adulthood between early adulthood and late adulthood, beginning at 40 to 45 and ending at 60 to 65.

interindividual variability the fact that people do not age in the same way or at the same rate.

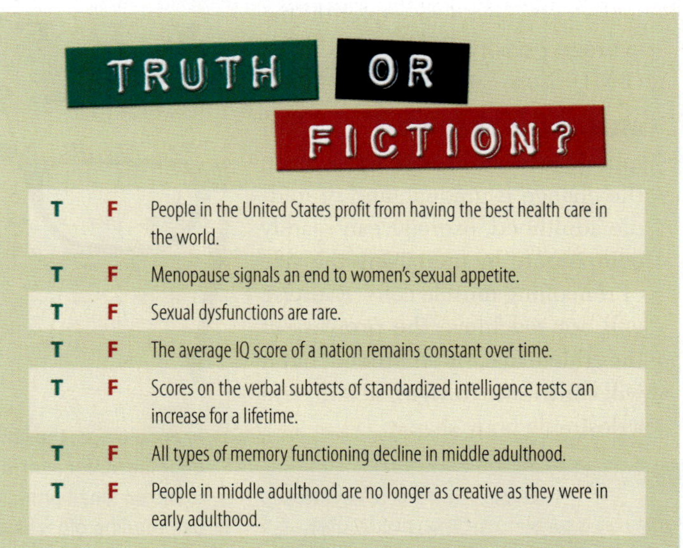

TRUTH OR FICTION?
T F People in the United States profit from having the best health care in the world.
T F Menopause signals an end to women's sexual appetite.
T F Sexual dysfunctions are rare.
T F The average IQ score of a nation remains constant over time.
T F Scores on the verbal subtests of standardized intelligence tests can increase for a lifetime.
T F All types of memory functioning decline in middle adulthood.
T F People in middle adulthood are no longer as creative as they were in early adulthood.

Presbyopia (Latin for "old vision") refers to loss of elasticity in the lens that makes it harder to focus on, or accommodate to, nearby objects or fine print. Cataracts, glaucoma, and hearing loss are usually problems of late adulthood.

REACTION TIME Reaction time—the amount of time it takes to respond to a stimulus—increases with age, mainly because of changes in the nervous system. Beginning at around age 25, we begin to lose neurons, which are responsible for sensing signals such as sights and sounds and those involved in coordinating muscular responses to them.

Ron Chapple Stock / Alamy Stock Photo

Hair grays in middle age and there is some decline in physical processes, but healthful diet, exercise, and screening for health problems can make middle adulthood joyful and productive.

LUNG CAPACITY Lung tissue stiffens with age, diminishing capacity to expand, such that breathing capacity may decline by half between early and late adulthood. Regular exercise can offset much of this loss, and beginning to exercise regularly in middle adulthood can expand breathing capacity beyond what it was earlier in life.

LEAN-BODY MASS AND BODY FAT Beginning at age 20, we lose nearly seven pounds of lean-body mass with each decade. The rate of loss accelerates after the age of 45. Fat replaces lean-body mass, which includes muscle. Consequently, the average person's body mass index (BMI) rises.

MUSCLE STRENGTH Loss of muscle lessens strength. However, the change is gradual, and in middle adulthood, exercise can readily compensate by increasing the size of remaining muscle cells. Exercise will not reachieve the prowess of the athlete in early adulthood, but it will contribute to vigor, health, and a desirable body shape.

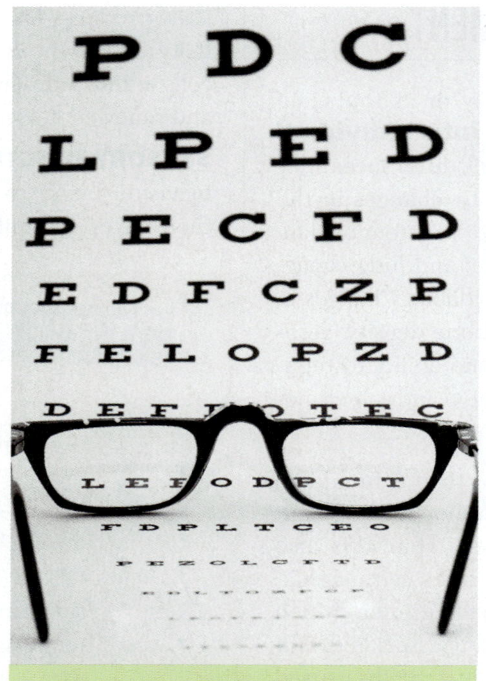

Diane Macdonald/Photographer's Choice RF/Getty Images

In middle age, the lenses of the eyes become stiffer, making it more difficult to focus on small print. Many people begin to use reading glasses during this stage of life.

presbyopia loss of elasticity in the eye lens that makes it harder to focus on nearby objects.

METABOLISM Metabolism is the rate at which the body processes or "burns" food to produce energy. The resting metabolic rate—also called the *basal metabolic rate (BMR)*—declines as we age. Fatty tissue burns fewer calories than muscle, and the decline in BMR is largely attributable to the loss of muscle tissue and the corresponding increase in fatty tissue. Since we require fewer calories to maintain our weight as we age, middle-aged people (and older adults) are likely to gain weight if they eat as much as they did as young adults.

BONE DENSITY Bone, which consists largely of calcium, begins to lose density and strength at around the age of 40. As bones lose density, they become more brittle and prone to fracture. Bones in the spine, hip, thigh (femur), and forearm lose the most density as we age. We discuss osteoporosis, a disorder affecting the strength of bones, in Chapter 17.

AEROBIC CAPACITY As we age, the cardiovascular system becomes less efficient. Heart and lung muscles shrink. Aerobic capacity declines as less oxygen is taken into the lungs and the heart pumps less blood. The maximum heart rate declines, but exercise expands aerobic capacity at *any* age.

BLOOD SUGAR TOLERANCE Blood sugar, or glucose, is the basic fuel and energy source for cells. The energy from glucose supports cell activities and maintains body temperature. Glucose circulates in the bloodstream and enters cells with the help of insulin, a hormone secreted by the pancreas.

As we age, the tissues in our body become less capable of taking up glucose from the bloodstream. Body tissues lose their sensitivity to insulin; the pancreas must thus produce more of it to achieve the same effect. Therefore, blood sugar levels rise, increasing the risk of adult-onset diabetes.

15-2 HEALTH

The health of people aged 40 to 65 in developed nations such as ours is better than it has ever been. Nearly everyone has been vaccinated for preventable diseases. Many, perhaps the majority, practice preventive health care. Once people reach 40, they are advised to have annual physical checkups. More is known today about curing or treating illnesses than we have ever known.

Yet there are racial, ethnic, and gender differences in the incidence and treatment of various diseases. People from certain groups appear to be more likely to develop certain chronic conditions such as hypertension and specific types of cancer. The statement that people in the United States profit from having the best health care in the world is too broad to be considered true. The "best" health care has not reached everyone. Some racial and ethnic minority groups lack access to health care, and men, more so than women, often resist seeking health care when symptoms arise.

As we consider the health of people in middle adulthood, we focus on many things that can go wrong. But for most of us, things go quite right if we get regular medical checkups, pay attention to our diets, get some exercise, avoid smoking, drink in moderation if at all, regulate stress, and—we hope—have some supportive relationships.

FICTION

T (F) People in the United States profit from having the best health care in the world.

It is false to say that people in the United States in general profit from having the best health care in the world. The fact is that many, perhaps most, Americans do not have access to "the best." Even those who are insured may not to be able to choose doctors who are "outside" their plans.

15-2a LEADING CAUSES OF DEATH

In early adulthood, the three leading causes of death screamed out their preventability: accidents, homicide, and suicide. In middle adulthood (see Table 15.1), diseases come to the fore. Cancer and heart disease are numbers one and two, and accidents now show up in third place. Cancer and heart disease are also preventable to some degree, of course. According to the National Cancer Institute (2015), men should begin being screen for prostate cancer at about the age of 50. African Americans are at greater risk of developing

Comstock Images/Stockbyte/Getty Images

There is a gradual loss of muscle strength in middle age, but couch potatoes who start working out can significantly increase their muscle mass.

TABLE 15.1 LEADING CAUSES OF DEATH IN MIDDLE ADULTHOOD, UNITED STATES

45–54	55–64
Cancer	Cancer
Heart disease	Heart disease
Accidents	Accidents
Suicide	Respiratory disease
Liver disease	Diabetes
Diabetes	Liver disease
Stroke	Stroke
Respiratory disease	Suicide
Influenza & pneumonia	Blood poisoning
Blood poisoning	Influenza & pneumonia

Source: National Vital Statistics System, National Center for Health Statistics, CDC. Produced by National Center for Injury Control and Prevention, CDC using WISQARS.

prostate cancer and are advised to begin screening at 40 or 45. Most men should obtain digital rectal exams in which the doctor feels the prostate gland with a gloved finger. The value of blood tests for prostate specific antigen (PSA) has come under question for most men, and readers should check with their physicians. Women are advised to begin screening for breast cancer with mammograms at age 40. Baseline electrocardiograms (EKGs) are typically used to measure heart health at age 50 and then repeated every two to three years.

15-2b CANCER

Although heart disease becomes the nation's number-one cause of death among people aged 65 and above (women have a sharply increased incidence of death due to heart disease following menopause), cancer is the overall leading cause of death in middle adulthood. Cancer eventually causes nearly one of every four deaths in the United States. Yet, in many cases, cancer can be controlled or cured, especially when detected early.

Cancer is a chronic, noncommunicable disease characterized by uncontrolled growth of cells, forming masses of excess tissue called *tumors*. Tumors can be *benign* (noncancerous) or *malignant* (cancerous). Benign tumors do not spread and rarely pose a threat to life. Malignant tumors invade and destroy surrounding tissue. Cancerous cells in malignant tumors may also break away from the primary tumor and travel through the bloodstream or lymphatic system to form new tumors, called **metastases**, elsewhere in the body. Metastases damage vital body organs and systems and in many cases lead to death. Table 15.2 shows the lifetime risk of being diagnosed with various kinds of cancer.

metastasis the movement of malignant or cancerous cells into parts of the body other than where they originated.

Cancer begins when a cell's DNA, its genetic material, changes such that the cell divides indefinitely. The change is triggered by mutations in the DNA, which can be caused by internal or external factors. Internal factors include heredity, problems in the immune system, and hormonal factors. External agents are called carcinogens and include some viruses, chemical compounds in tobacco and elsewhere, and ultraviolet (UV) solar radiation.

About one man in two and one woman in three in the United States will eventually develop cancer if they live long enough (American Cancer Society, 2012b; see Table 15.2). The incidence of death from cancer almost triples in the decade of ages 55 to 64 as compared with the decade of ages 45t to 54.

Although cancer cuts across all racial and ethnic groups, African Americans have higher than average colorectal cancer incidence and death rates from that disease (American Cancer Society, 2016a). African Americans have twice the average death rate from prostate cancer. The incidence of cervical cancer in Latina

TABLE 15.2 LIFETIME RISK OF DEVELOPING CANCER

Site	Men	Women
All sites	1 in 2	1 in 3
Bladder	1 in 26	1 in 87
Breast	1 in 769	1 in 8
Cervix	—	1 in 147
Colon and rectum	1 in 19	1 in 20
Esophagus	1 in 127	1 in 417
Hodgkin disease	1 in 400	1 in 476
Kidney	1 in 51	1 in 84
Larynx (voice box)	1 in 167	1 in 714
Leukemia	1 in 64	1 in 88
Liver and bile duct	1 in 88	1 in 204
Lung and bronchus	1 in 13	1 in 16
Melanoma	1 in 41	1 in 64
Oral cavity and pharynx	1 in 69	1 in 149
Ovary	—	1 in 71
Pancreas	1 in 69	1 in 69
Prostate	1 in 6	—
Stomach	1 in 91	1 in 149
Testicles	1 in 270	—
Thyroid	1 in 200	1 in 69
Uterus	—	1 in 38

Sources: American Cancer Society (2012); National Cancer Institute (2011a, 2011b).

iStockPhoto.com/wragg

A little common sense will help prevent the development of skin cancer.

American women is higher than that of other demographic groups. Only about half of American Indian and Alaska Native women age 40 years and over have had a recent mammogram. American Indian and Alaska Natives have the poorest survival rate from cancer.

Much of the difference in mortality rates can be attributed to lack of early detection and treatment (American Cancer Society, 2016b). One reason for late diagnosis is that many minority groups lack health insurance or access to health care facilities. Many members of minority groups also avoid screening by the health care system, which they see as impersonal, insensitive, and racist.

Though there are many causes of cancer (see Figure 15.1) and risk factors vary among population groups, two out of three cancer deaths in the United States are the result of two controllable factors: smoking and diet (American Cancer Society, 2016b). Cigarette smoking causes 87% of lung cancer deaths in the United States and is responsible for most cancers of the mouth, larynx, pharynx, esophagus, and bladder. Secondhand smoking also accounts for several thousand cancer deaths per year. Diet may account for about 30% of all cancers in Western cultures. However, many cases of cancer also involve family history, or heredity (American Cancer Society, 2016b).

Traditional methods for treating cancer are surgery (surgical removal of cancerous tissue), radiation (high-dose x-rays or other sources of high-energy radiation to kill cancerous cells and shrink tumors), chemotherapy (drugs that kill cancer cells or shrink tumors), and hormonal therapy (hormones that stop tumor growth). These methods have their limitations. Anticancer drugs and radiation kill healthy tissue as well as malignant tissue. They also have side effects such as nausea, vomiting, loss of appetite, loss of hair, and weakening of the immune system.

FIG.15.1 RISK FACTORS IN CANCER

CANCER

Biological:

Family history

Physiological conditions: Obesity

Psychological (personality and behavior):

Patterns of consumption:
Smoking
Drinking alcohol (especially in women)

Eating animal fats
Sunbathing (skin cancer)
Prolonged depression
Prolonged stress may increase vulnerability to cancer by depressing activity of the immune system.

Sociocultural:

Socioeconomic status
Access to health care
Timing of diagnosis and treatment
Higher death rates are found in nations with higher rates of fat intake.

Goodshoot/Jupiterimages

15-2c HEART DISEASE

In 2014, the leading causes of death of males and females of all ages were heart disease and cancer. In heart disease, the flow of blood to the heart is insufficient to supply the heart with the oxygen it needs. Heart disease most commonly results from **arteriosclerosis** or *hardening of the arteries*, which impairs circulation and increases the risk of a blood clot (thrombus). The most common form of arteriosclerosis is **atherosclerosis**—the buildup of fatty deposits called *plaque* in the lining of arteries (see Figure 15.2). Plaque results in the heart receiving insufficient blood and can cause a heart attack.

The risk factors for heart disease are shown in Figure 15.3. Several of them are beyond the control of the individual (such as age and race/ethnicity), but people can have some control over other risk factors (smoking, exercise, diet, and getting medical checkups).

SIGNS OF A HEART ATTACK Heart attacks are medical emergencies that require immediate attention. The first minutes and hours are critical to survival, as most people who die of heart attacks succumb within two hours. Yet many people minimize their symptoms or attribute them to more benign causes, like indigestion or heartburn.

arteriosclerosis hardening of the arteries.

atherosclerosis the buildup of fatty deposits (plaque) on the lining of arteries.

FIG.15.2 ATHEROSCLEROSIS

Fatty deposits and cellular debris

a b c

Goodshoot/Jupiterimages

In atherosclerosis, fatty deposits called *plaque* build up along artery walls. As arteries narrow, blood flow becomes constricted, setting the stage for heart attacks or strokes. In this figure, (a) shows a fully open artery, (b) shows moderate buildup of plaque, and (c) shows dangerous buildup of plaque.

FIG.15.3 RISK FACTORS IN HEART DISEASE

HEART DISEASE
Biological:
Family history
Physiological conditions: Obesity
High serum cholesterol
Hypertension
Psychological (personality and behavior): Type A behavior
Hostility and holding in feelings of anger
Job strain
Chronic fatigue, stress, anxiety, depression, and emotional strain
Patterns of consumption:
Heavy drinking (but a drink a day may be helpful with heart disease)
Smoking
Overeating
Sudden stressors
Physical inactivity
Sociocultural:
African Americans are more prone to hypertension and heart disease than European Americans are.
Access to health care
Timing of diagnosis and treatment
Goodshoot/Jupiterimages

Whether or not one survives a heart attack depends on the extent of damage to heart tissue and to the electrical system that controls the heart rhythm. Death rates from heart disease have declined steadily during the past 50 years, in part because fewer people are smoking (smoking is a major risk factor) and because of improvements in treatment.

Becoming aware of the signs of a heart attack can save a life, perhaps your own. Though not all of the following symptoms need be present, the signs of a heart attack may include:

- Intense, prolonged chest pain, described as crushing, not sharp, which may be experienced as a feeling of heavy pressure or tightness in the chest. Some describe a squeezing sensation in the chest, or a sensation like a giant fist enclosing the heart. Yet some people have heart attacks without chest pain.
- Pain extending beyond the chest to the left shoulder and arm, the back, even into the jaws and gums.
- Prolonged pain in the upper abdomen.
- Shortness of breath.
- Fainting or weakness.
- Heavy perspiration, nausea, or vomiting.
- Anxiety and fear.

If you experience the signs of a heart attack or are with someone who does, seek medical attention immediately. Call 911 or your local emergency operator and follow their instructions.

15-3 THE IMMUNE SYSTEM

The immune system is the body's defense against infections and some other sources of disease. It combats disease in several ways. One is the production of white blood cells, which engulf and kill pathogens such as bacteria, fungi, and viruses, and worn-out and cancerous body cells. The technical term for white blood cells is **leukocytes**.

leukocyte white blood cell.

Leukocytes recognize foreign substances by their shapes. The foreign substances are termed *antigens* because the body reacts to them by generating specialized proteins, or *antibodies*. Antibodies attach themselves to the foreign substances, deactivating them and marking them for destruction. The immune system "remembers" how to battle antigens by maintaining their antibodies in the bloodstream, often for years.

Inflammation is another function of the immune system. When injury occurs, blood vessels in the area first contract (to stem bleeding) and then dilate. Dilation increases the flow of blood, cells, and natural chemicals to the damaged area, causing redness, swelling, and warmth. The increased blood supply floods the region with white blood cells to combat invading microscopic life forms such as bacteria, which otherwise might use the local damage as a port of entry into the body.

15-3a STRESS AND THE IMMUNE SYSTEM

Short-term stress may boost the functioning of the immune system, as flooring the gas pedal kicks a car into rapid acceleration. But prolonged stress—like burning all your gas—suppresses the functioning of the immune system, as measured by substances in the blood that make up the immune system (Adamo, 2014). Stress thus leaves us more vulnerable to infections such as the common cold (Christian & Glaser, 2012).

John Lund/Heather Hryciw/Blend Images/Getty Images

The stress hormones connected with anger—steroids, epinephrine, and norepinephrine—can constrict the blood vessels to the heart, leading to a heart attack in people who are vulnerable (Adamo, 2014). The stress of chronic hostility and anger is connected with higher cholesterol levels and a greater risk of heart disease (Fernandez & Smith, 2015).

15-4 SEXUALITY

Most people in middle adulthood are capable of leading rich sex lives (Nappi et al., 2014). Table 15.3 compares the frequency of sex in early adulthood with that in middle adulthood. Generally, the frequency of sexual activity tends to decline in middle adulthood but the decline is gradual. Note that a significant percentage of 50- to 59-year-old women become sexually inactive. This drop-off may in part reflect lack of opportunity. Women in this age group are increasingly likely to be widowed, and as divorced women grow older, they are also increasingly less likely to get remarried.

In the latter part of middle adulthood, ages 50 and above, the majority of women are sexually active and more than three women out of five in partnered relationships report being sexually satisfied (Gass et al., 2011). But sexual problems are often working their way into relationships. The most common problems among women are lack of sexual desire and difficulty becoming sexually aroused (Kingsberg & Woodard, 2015). The most common problem among men is erectile dysfunction.

Researchers find that sexual daydreaming, sex drive, and sexual activity may decline with age, but, as noted, people do not lose their sexuality as they age (Connaughton & McCabe, 2015). Most people in middle adulthood report that they like (or love!) sex, and a majority report that orgasm is important to their sexual fulfillment. Sexual fulfillment also involves psychological well-being, feelings of intimacy, and cultural expectations.

TABLE 15.3 FREQUENCY OF SEX IN THE PAST 12 MONTHS ACCORDING TO AGE (PERCENTS)

Age	Not at All	A Few Times a Year	A Few Times per Month	2 or 3 Times a Week	4 or More Times a Week
Men					
25–29	7	15	31	36	11
30–39	8	15	37	33	6
40–49	9	18	40	27	6
50–59	11	22	43	20	3
Women					
25–29	5	10	38	37	10
30–39	9	16	36	33	6
40–49	15	16	44	20	5
50–59	30	22	35	12	2

Note: Percentages for 18- to 24-year-olds are excluded because they are likely to reflect sexual opportunity as well as sexual interest and biological factors.

Source: Robert T. Michael, John H. Gagnon, Edward O. Laumann, & Gina Kolata (1994). *Sex in America: A definitive survey*. New York, NY: Warner Books, Table 8, p. 117.

15-4a MENOPAUSE, PERIMENOPAUSE, AND THE CLIMACTERIC

Menopause, or the "change of life," is the cessation of menstruation. Menopause is a normal process that most commonly occurs between the ages of 46 and 50 and lasts for about two years. **Perimenopause** refers to the beginning of menopause and is usually characterized by 3 to 11 months of amenorrhea (lack of menstruation) or irregular periods.

Menopause is a specific event in a longer-term process known as the **climacteric** ("critical period"), which is the gradual decline in the reproductive capacity of the ovaries due to a decline in production of estrogen. The climacteric generally lasts about 15 years, from about 45 to 60. After 35 or so, the menstrual cycles of many women shorten, from an average of 28 days to 25 days at age 40 and to 23 days by the mid-40s. By the end of her 40s, a woman's cycles may become erratic, with some periods shortened and others missed.

The estrogen deficit may lead to unpleasant perimenopausal sensations, such as night sweats and hot flashes (suddenly feeling hot) and hot flushes (suddenly reddened skin). Hot flashes and flushes may alternate with cold sweats, in which a woman feels suddenly cold and clammy. All of these sensations reflect *vasomotor instability*, disruptions in the body mechanisms that dilate or constrict the blood vessels to maintain an even body temperature. Additional signs of estrogen deficiency include dizziness, headaches, joint pain, tingling in the hands or feet, burning or itchy skin, and heart palpitations. The skin usually becomes drier. There is some loss of breast tissue and decreased vaginal lubrication during sexual arousal. However, menopause does not signal an end to women's sexual appetite.

Long-term estrogen deficiency has been linked to brittleness and porosity of the bones—osteoporosis. Osteoporosis can be handicapping, even life threatening. The brittleness of the bones increases the risk of serious fractures, especially of the hip, and many older women never recover from them (Kanis et al., 2014). Estrogen deficiency also can impair cognitive functioning and feelings of psychological well-being (Engler-Chiurazzi et al., 2016; Koyama et al., 2016).

HORMONE REPLACEMENT THERAPY Some women with severe physical symptoms have been helped by hormone replacement therapy (HRT), which typically consists of synthetic estrogen and progesterone. HRT may reduce the hot flushes and other symptoms brought about by hormonal deficiencies. Estrogen replacement also lowers the risks of osteoporosis and colon cancer (Sturdee et al., 2011; Giannini et al., 2016).

Yet HRT is controversial. The Women's Health Initiative study of some 16,600 postmenopausal women aged 50 to 79 found that exposure to a combination of estrogen and progestin appears to significantly increase the risk of breast cancer, strokes, and blood clots (Chlebowski et al., 2003).

Because of the Chlebowski study and studies with similar findings, the number of women using HRT has dropped significantly over the past few years (Rabin, 2007), and many women are considering alternatives. Progestin alone—that is, the use of progestin without estrogen—prevents or lessens hot flashes in many women (Shams et al., 2014). Selective serotonin reuptake inhibitors (SSRIs) may also be of help (Shams et al., 2014).

15-4b GENDER DIFFERENCES IN SEX HORMONES AND FERTILITY

For women, menopause is a time of relatively distinct age-related declines in sex hormones and fertility. In men, the decline in the production of male sex hormones and fertility is more gradual. It is therefore not surprising to find a man in his 70s or older fathering a child. However, many men in their 50s experience problems in achieving and maintaining erections, which may reflect circulatory problems, hormone deficiencies, or other factors (McCabe et al., 2016).

To help with these symptoms, physicians in the United States write more than one million prescriptions for testosterone and related drugs each year, but the benefits are not fully proven, and the risks, including heightened risks of prostate cancer and heart disease, should inspire caution.

menopause the cessation of menstruation.

perimenopause the beginning of menopause, usually characterized by 3 to 11 months of amenorrhea or irregular periods.

climacteric the gradual decline in reproductive capacity of the ovaries, generally lasting about 15 years.

FICTION

T (F) Menopause signals an end to women's sexual appetite.

It is not true that menopause signals an end to women's sexual appetite. Some women actually feel sexually liberated because of the separation of sex from reproduction.

15-4c SEXUAL DYSFUNCTIONS

Sexual dysfunctions are persistent or recurrent problems in becoming sexually aroused or reaching orgasm. Many of us have sexual problems on occasion, but sexual dysfunctions are chronic and cause significant distress.

We do not have precise figures on the occurrence of sexual dysfunctions. The most accurate information may be based on the report by Ronald Lewis and his colleagues (2010), which summarizes data from surveys around the world (see Table 15.4). Although there is wide variation in the figures gleaned from the surveys, we can make some generalizations:

- Women report a higher prevalence of sexual dysfunctions than men do.
- The prevalence of every sexual dysfunction except premature ejaculation increases with age.
- The most prevalent sexual problems in women are low sexual desire and difficulty reaching orgasm.
- Despite the stereotype that men are "always ready" to engage in sexual activity, many men report having low sexual desire.

Repeated erectile problems, characterized by persistent difficulty in achieving or maintaining an erection during the course of sexual activity, may make men anxious when sexual opportunities arise because they expect failure rather than pleasure. As a result, they may avoid sex. Their partners may also avoid sexual contact because of their own frustration.

FICTION

T (F) Sexual dysfunctions are rare.

It is not true that sexual dysfunctions are rare. Surveys around that world show that sexual dysfunctions are actually quite common, especially as people age.

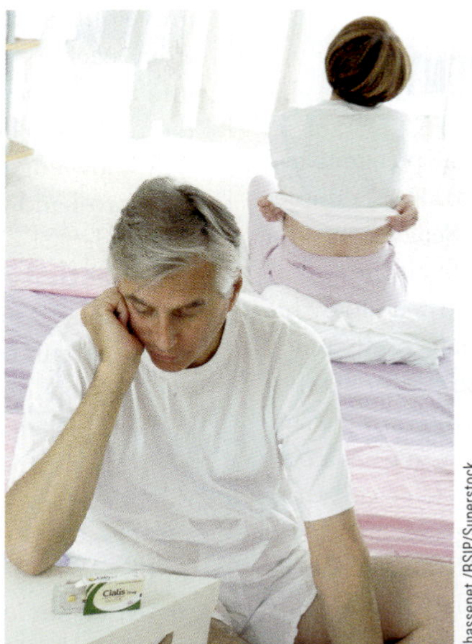

Chassenet /BSIP/Superstock

Sexual dysfunctions become more prevalent as people reach middle age, and they can be exceptionally frustrating. Drugs such as Cialis and Viagra help many—but not all!—men with erectile dysfunction.

The reduction in testosterone levels that occurs in middle and later adulthood may in part explain a gradual loss of sexual desire in men—along with some loss of muscle mass and strength (McCabe et al., 2016). But women's sexual desire may also decline with age because of physical and psychological changes (McCabe et al., 2016). Some medications, especially those used to control anxiety, depression, or hypertension, may also reduce desire.

Fatigue may lead to erectile disorder in men, and to inadequate lubrication and, consequently, painful sex in women. But these will be isolated incidents unless the person attaches too much meaning to them and becomes concerned about future performances. Painful sex, however, can also reflect underlying infections or medical conditions.

TABLE 15.4 PREVALENCE OF SEXUAL DYSFUNCTIONS BASED ON STUDIES AROUND THE WORLD

	Women	Men
At least one sexual dysfunction	40–45%	20–30%
Low sexual desire	17–55%	8–25%
Arousal and lubrication problems; erectile dysfunction (ED) in males	8–28%	1–40%*
Orgasmic dysfunction**	16–25%**	12–19%
Premature ejaculation****		8–30%
Sexual pain disorders	1–27%	1–6%

Source: Lewis, et al. (2010). Definitions/epidemiology/risk factors for sexual dysfunction. *Journal of Sexual Medicine, 7*, 1598–1607.

*The prevalence may double from the 40s to the 60s and again from the 60s to the 70s

**Difficulty reaching orgasm

***Some studies put the percentage as high as 80% for older women

****Ejaculating before the man or his partner wishes it

Biological causes of erectile disorder affect the flow of blood to and through the penis, a problem that becomes more common as men age or experience damage to nerves involved in erection. Erectile problems can arise when clogged or narrow arteries leading to the penis deprive the penis of blood and oxygen.

Similarly, aging can affect the sexual response of women. Perimenopausal and postmenopausal women usually produce less vaginal lubrication than younger women and the vaginal walls thin, which can render sex painful and create anxiety about engaging in sexual activity. Artificial lubrication can supplement the woman's own production, and estrogen replacement may halt or reverse some

sexual dysfunction a persistent or recurrent problem in becoming sexually aroused or reaching orgasm.

of the sexual changes of aging (McCabe et al., 2016). But partners also need to have realistic expectations and consider what kinds of sexual activities they can engage in without discomfort or high demands.

Middle-aged and older men might try weight control and regular exercise, measures which may ward off erectile dysfunction. Exercise seems to lessen clogging of arteries, keeping them clear for the flow of blood into the penis. Oral medications—Viagra, Levitra, and Cialis—are commonly used to treat erectile disorder.

15-5 COGNITIVE DEVELOPMENT

Though middle adults do continue to develop cognitively, they do so in various ways (Schaie, 2013). For example, the overall Wechsler Adult Intelligence Scale score of a 53-year-old farmer in Kansas decreases from the age of 27. His "verbal intelligence," as measured mainly by his knowledge of the meaning of words, remains pretty much the same, but his "performance subtest" scores, or his ability to perform on timed spatially related subtests, declines. A woman in her mid-40s, who had been "all-business" through her mid-20s in college, moved to Chicago at the age of 29 and is now extremely knowledgeable in art history and opera. She had known absolutely nothing about these areas as an undergraduate, when her math ability was at its height. A 55-year-old family practitioner is "lost" when he tries to understand the science behind a new medical test presented at a professional meeting in San Francisco; nevertheless, he learns how to interpret a report based on results from the test and he discovers, to his relief, that most of his peers are in the same boat. A 47-year-old woman returns to college to complete her B.A. At first she is fearful of competing with the "kids," but she finds out quickly enough that her sense of purpose more than compensates for what she thinks of as any "loss in brainpower."

15-5a CHANGES IN INTELLECTUAL ABILITIES

Intellectual development in adulthood shows multidirectionality, interindividual variability, and plasticity. The concept of **multidirectionality** underscores the finding that some aspects of intellectual functioning may improve while others remain stable or decline. Rather than being something measured strictly by degrees, intellectual functioning reflects the interaction of heredity and environmental factors—and, as we have discussed, personal choice to engage in further study to increase one's facility in certain intellectual areas.

multidirectionality in the context of cognitive development, the fact that some aspects of intellectual functioning may improve while others remain stable or decline.

plasticity the fact that intellectual abilities are not absolutely fixed but can be modified.

We discussed *interindividual variability* in terms of physical development, and we find it in cognitive development as well. People mature in different cultural settings. Some still frown on education for women. Some areas have better schools than others. Some youth find themselves in subcultures in which their peers disapprove of them if they earn high grades or seek approval from teachers. We also find interindividual variability in middle adulthood. Some people find themselves or allow themselves to be in "ruts" in which they gain little if any new knowledge. Others are hungry for the new and read and travel and visit museums in any spare moment they can find.

Plasticity refers to the fact that people's intellectual abilities are not absolutely fixed but can be modified under certain conditions at almost any time in life. The ideal period for language learning may be childhood, but you can pick up a new language in your 40s, 50s, or even later. You learn the meanings of new words for a lifetime (unless you lock yourself in a closet).

Consider the so-called *Flynn Effect*. Philosopher and researcher John Flynn (2003) found that IQ scores increased some 18 points in the United States between the years of 1947 and 2002. Psychologist Richard Nisbett (2009) argues that our genetic codes could not possibly have changed enough in half a century to account for this enormous difference; he concludes that social and cultural factors such as the penetration of better educational systems and mass media must be the reasons for the change.

FICTION

T (F) The average IQ score of a nation remains constant over time.

It is not true that the average IQ score of a nation remains constant. IQ scores in the United States have actually risen over the past couple of generations, in part because of schooling, in part because of the information explosion in the media.

COHORT EFFECTS The people who were middle-aged in 1947 and those who were middle-aged in 2002 belong to different cohorts. Figure 15.4 shows some cohort

FIG.15.4 DIFFERENCES IN INTELLECTUAL ABILITIES ACROSS COHORTS

Total change in performance based on standard scores

15
10
5
0
−5
−10

1924 1931 1938 1945 1952 1959 1966

Cohort

Verbal Meaning
Spatial Orientation
Inductive Reasoning
Numeric Ability
Word Fluency

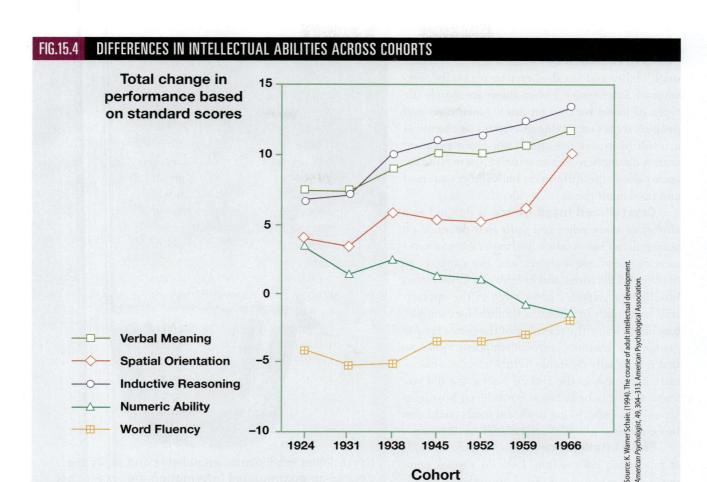

Source: K. Warner Schaie. (1994). The course of adult intellectual development. *American Psychologist*, 49, 304–313. American Psychological Association.

More recently born cohorts in the Seattle Longitudinal Study show greater intellectual abilities in all areas except for numeric abilities. What technological factors might contribute to a decrease in numerical skills among people today?

effects from the Seattle Longitudinal Study, begun in 1956 by K. Warner Schaie. Participants were tested every seven years, and Schaie and his colleagues were able to assess cohort effects as well as longitudinal effects on intellectual functioning. The figure shows that groups of adults born more recently were superior to those born at earlier times in four of five mental abilities assessed: inductive reasoning, verbal meaning, spatial orientation, and word fluency (Schaie, 1994). The cohorts born earlier performed better in numeric ability. Schaie notes that the intellectual functioning of the members of a society reflects their education and the technology of the day (Charness & Schaie, 2003). This also indicates that the younger cohorts were actually exposed to a better educational system—one that encouraged them to think abstractly (*inductive reasoning*), learn the meaning of words (*verbal meaning, word fluency*), and interact with geometric figures (*spatial orientation*).

Keeping mentally active tends to help stave off decline in mental functioning in middle age.

Flynn Larsen/Cultura RM / Alamy Stock Photo

CRYSTALLIZED INTELLIGENCE VERSUS FLUID INTELLIGENCE Some might ask whether math ability and vocabulary size are really measures of "intelligence," when these are merely the types of items we find on intelligence tests and people's scores on intelligence tests can change as a result of experience. But John Horn came up with a distinction that may be of some use. He spoke about the difference between crystallized and fluid intelligence.

Crystallized intelligence is defined as a cluster of knowledge and skills that depends on accumulated information and experience, awareness of social conventions, and the capacity to make good decisions and judgments. Crystallized intelligence includes knowledge of the specialized vocabulary in a field; in English, for example, one might know the meaning of the terms *iambic pentameter*, *rhetoric*, and *onomatopoeia*. We know that it is socially desirable to look a business associate in the eye in the United States, but did you know that this behavior is considered hostile in Japan? Choosing to eat healthful foods could also be considered a sign of crystallized intelligence.

Fluid intelligence: skills at processing information
Crystallized intelligence: knowledge and skills that depend on accumulated information and experience

Ray Massey/The Image Bank/Getty Images

Crystallized intelligence versus fluid intelligence

Fluid intelligence involves a person's skills at processing information. Let's do a quick comparison to a computer. Your crystallized intelligence is like the amount of information you have in storage. Your fluid intelligence is more like the sizes of your processor and your memory (meaning *working memory*—how much you can keep in mind at once), which work together to access and manipulate information and arrive at answers quickly and accurately. Whereas researchers suggest a powerful role for environmental factors in the genesis of crystallized intelligence, they theorize a relatively stronger role for neurological factors in fluid intelligence (Salthouse, 2011).

Studies show that crystallized intelligence tends to increase with age through middle adulthood. In the absence of senile dementias, crystallized intelligence commonly increases throughout the life span, along with the verbal subtest scores of standardized intelligence tests. The same studies that indicate that crystallized intelligence tends to increase throughout adulthood tend to show a decline for fluid intelligence (Salthouse, 2011). K. Warner Schaie's (1994) longitudinal data (see Figure 15.5) shows that the intellectual factor of perceptual speed, which is most strongly related to fluid intelligence, is also the one that drops off most dramatically from early adulthood to late adulthood. Spatial orientation and numeric ability, both related to fluid intelligence, also decline dramatically in late adulthood. Verbal ability and inductive reasoning are more related to crystallized intelligence, and these show gains through middle adulthood and hold up in late adulthood.

crystallized intelligence a cluster of knowledge and skills that depends on accumulated information and experience, awareness of social conventions, and good judgment.

fluid intelligence a person's skills at processing information. Skills at processing information.

TRUTH

 **F** Scores on the verbal subtests of standardized intelligence tests can increase for a lifetime.

It is true that verbal subtest scores of standardized intelligence tests can increase for a lifetime. These scores tend to reflect crystalized intelligence.

Figure 15.5 reveals group trends; there are interindividual variations. Schaie and his colleagues (2004) found that circumstances such as the following tend to stem cognitive decline in advanced late adulthood:

- Good physical health
- Favorable environmental conditions, such as decent housing
- Remaining intellectually active through reading and keeping up with current events
- Being open to new ideas and new styles of life
- Living with a partner who is intellectually active
- Being satisfied with one's achievements

When these factors are present, they help individuals maximize their potential at any age.

15-5b INFORMATION PROCESSING

One of the interesting things about aging is that it can become more difficult to keep new information in working memory ("in one ear and out the other") even when long-term memory remains relatively intact.

SPEED OF INFORMATION PROCESSING There are several ways to measure the speed of information processing. One is simply physical: *reaction time*. That is the amount of time it takes to respond to a stimulus. If you touch a hot stove, how long does it take you to pull your hand away? In one assessment of reaction time, people push a button when a light is flashed. People in middle adulthood respond to the light more slowly—their reaction time is greater—than young adults do (Hartley, 2006). The difference in reaction time is only a fraction of a second, but it is enough to keep the typical middle-aged adult out of the firing line in the military and on the sidelines of professional sports (Salthouse, 2010, 2014; Thompson et al., 2014). It can also make a difference when trying to avoid getting into a collision on the freeway.

Reaction time is only one aspect of processing speed. There is also the broad cognitive aspect of perceptual speed, which is intertwined with fluid intelligence. As with reaction time, the changes in middle adulthood are not that dramatic, but they are measurable. Because of continuous experience with reading and writing, an educated person in middle adulthood may be better than

FIG.15.5 LONGITUDINAL CHANGES IN SIX INTELLECTUAL ABILITIES, AGES 25–88

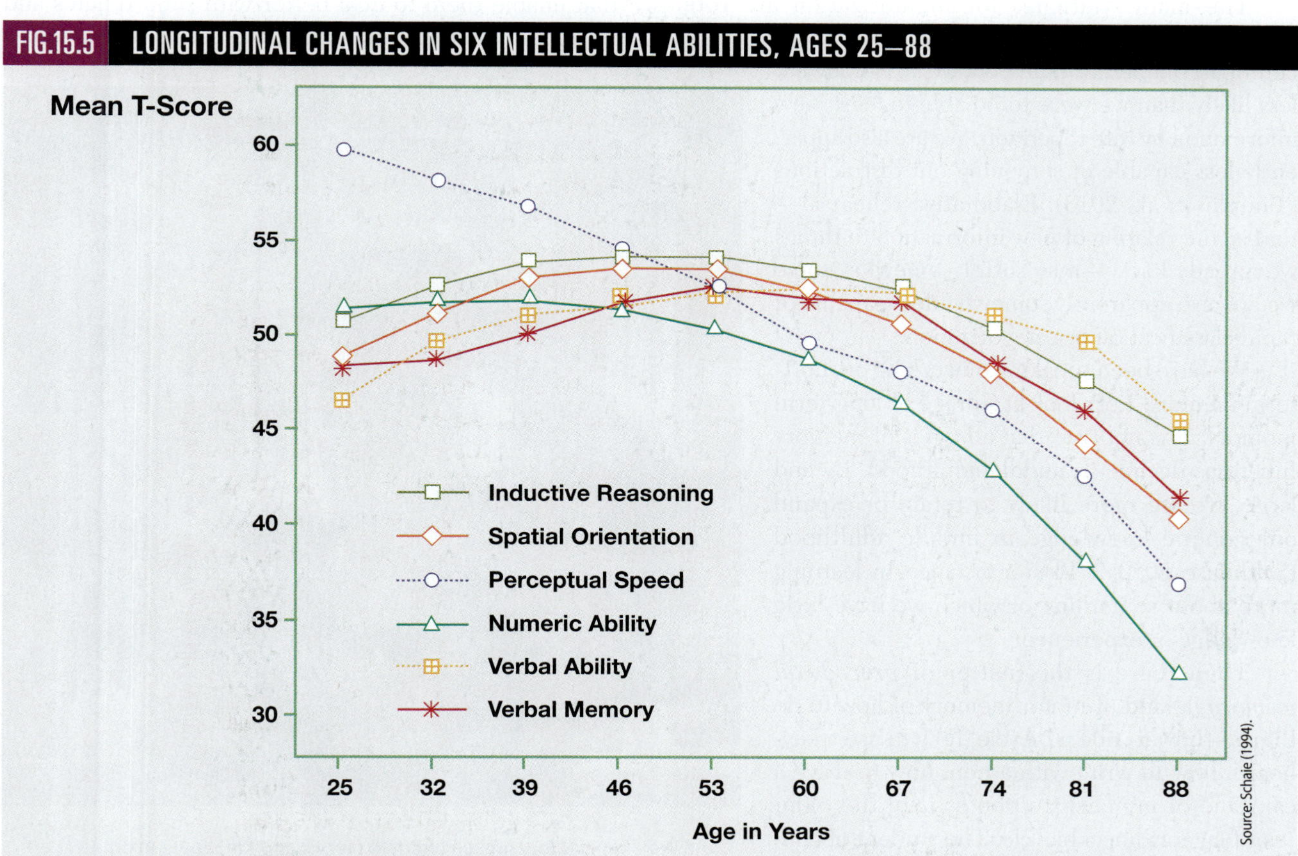

Most intellectual abilities show gains or remain largely stable from early adulthood through middle adulthood. Numeric ability shows a modest decline throughout middle adulthood, and perceptual speed shows a more dramatic drop-off.

ever at doing crossword puzzles (largely dependent on crystallized intelligence), but she might find it somewhat more difficult to navigate new cities than she did in early adulthood (largely dependent on fluid intelligence) (Salthouse, 2011).

Most researchers believe that the decline in processing speed reflects changes in the integrity of the nervous system. Having said that, hypotheses run rampant, from the death of neurons in the brain to changes in specific parts of the brain and changes in the secretion of neurotransmitters (Hartley, 2006).

MEMORY K. Warner Schaie's (2013) longitudinal research found that memory is one of the intellectual factors that showed improvement through most of the years of middle adulthood and stability from 53 to 60. Not all researchers agree. Researchers use several kinds of memory tasks, and they do not necessarily find the same results with all of them (Salthouse, 2010, 2014). By and large, despite Schaie's results, most researchers conclude that people in middle adulthood and late adulthood perform less well than young adults at memorizing lists of words, numbers, or passages of prose (Salthouse, 2010, 2014).

The main strategies for memorization are rote rehearsal and elaborative rehearsal. Once we are in the latter part of middle adulthood, we are somewhat less likely than we were to be able to learn new information by rote repetition. We are also apparently less capable of screening out distractions (Tamplin et al., 2013). Elaborative rehearsal—that is, the relating of new information to things we already know—may suffer somewhat since we are also apparently somewhat less capable of rapid classification or categorization.

We have been speaking of working or short-term memory. Let's look at storage or long-term memory. It is not true that all types of memory functions decline in middle adulthood. By and large, we are more likely to retain or expand our general knowledge in middle adulthood (Salthouse, 2010, 2014), for instance, by learning more about something of which we have little knowledge or experience.

Then there is the matter of *procedural memory*, a kind of motor memory of how to do things—how to ride a bicycle, how to use a keyboard, how to write with a pen, how to drive a car. One of my favorite photos is of the older Jean Piaget riding a bicycle. The student of children looks childlike, but the message for the student of psychology or education is that we can maintain procedural memories for a lifetime.

FICTION

T (F) All types of memory functioning decline in middle adulthood.

It is not true that all types of memory functioning decline in middle adulthood. Long-term memory and general knowledge often improve with age.

EXPERTISE AND PRACTICAL PROBLEM SOLVING

Any employer with some knowledge of human development would want to hire someone in middle adulthood. Middle-aged people have the verbal abilities of younger people and perhaps some more, have lost very little in the way of fluid intelligence, and have a greater store of expertise and practical problem-solving skills (Hess & Queen, 2014; Verhaeghen & Hertzog, 2014). Although, again, there is always interindividual variation, as a group the middle-aged show it every day in every way.

Over the years, they have also acquired social skills that enable them to deal better with subordinates and with supervisors. They have a better feel for other people's

Siri Stafford/Getty images

As we age, memory lapses become more common. Some middle-aged and older people find that written memos, such as Post-its, help remind them of things they had intended to do.

limitations and potentials, and they have a better understanding of how to motivate them. They may also have experience that will help them be calmer in stressful situations.

The parent who was so distraught when the first child cried may now be relaxed when the grandchildren cry. Part of the difference may be the "distance"—the generation of removal. But part of it is also the years of learning that the children will survive and develop into normal human beings (whatever that means) whether or not they cry as children.

In terms of vocations, the initial training or education of middle-aged people has now had the benefits of years of experience. People in middle adulthood have learned what works and what does not work for them. In the cases of the professions, for instance, "book learning" and perhaps internships have been supplemented by years of experience in the real world. Pianist Arthur Rubinstein became so accomplished as the years wore on that he often practiced " mentally"—he needed the physical keyboard only intermittently. Although he lost some speed when playing rapid passages, he compensated by slowing before entering them, and he created drama when he escalated his pacing.

Olga Besnard/Shutterstock.com

Author Toni Morrison wrote the Pulitzer-Prize-winning novel *Beloved* at the age of 57.

15-6 CREATIVITY AND LEARNING

Middle adulthood offers numerous opportunities for exercising creativity, expanding knowledge, and gaining intellectual experience.

15-6a CREATIVITY

People in middle adulthood can be creative and, in fact, many middle adults are at the height of their creativity. Artist Pablo Picasso painted *Guernica*, which protested the Spanish civil war and is one of the best-known images in art, at the age of 56. Author Toni Morrison wrote the Pulitzer-Prize-winning novel *Beloved* at the age of 57. Inventor Thomas Edison built the kinetoscope, an early peephole method for watching films, at the age of 44. Yet, researchers have found some differences in creativity among young adults and middle-aged people. Aspects of creativity that are relatively more likely to be found among young adults include creativity in music, mathematics, and physics (Norton et al., 2005; Simonton, 2006b). Wolfgang Amadeus Mozart, considered by many critics to be the greatest composer in history, died at the age of 35. Albert Einstein published his general theory of relativity at the age of 36.

Writers and visual artists often continue to improve into middle adulthood, although their most emotional and fervent works may be produced at younger ages. The most emotionally charged works of poets tend to be penned in early adulthood (Simonton, 2007).

FICTION

T (F) People in middle adulthood are no longer as creative as they were in early adulthood.

It is too general a statement to say that people in middle adulthood are no longer as creative as they were in early adulthood. Many are as creative. Pablo Picasso, Toni Morrison, and Thomas Edison all had great creative achievements during middle age.

15-6b MATURE LEARNERS

For most adults, learning is a perpetual process. We learn when a new store opens in the neighborhood or when we watch or listen to the media. We learn when we hear what is happening with a family member, or observe a pet. But when psychologists and educators use the term "adult learning," they are usually speaking of learning as it occurs within some formal educational setting.

Even when we limit our discussion to educational settings, we find vast diversity and interindividual variation. But research on mature learners suggests that they are likely to have some things in common: They are apt to be highly motivated, and they are more likely than younger learners to find the subject matter interesting for its own sake (Salthouse, 2010, 2011).

> Research on mature learners suggests that they are apt to be highly motivated, and they are more likely than younger learners to find the subject matter interesting for its own sake.

Women make up more than three of every five postsecondary students aged 35 and above in the United States (U.S. Department of Education, 2015). Among those with families, you might assume that those who returned to college would be the ones with the least exacting combinations of family and work demands. Actually, it's the other way around (Hostetler et al., 2007). Women with the greatest demands on them from family and work are the ones most likely to return to school. But once they're back, their major source of stress is time constraints; those who receive the emotional support of their families and employers experience the least stress and do best (Kirby et al., 2004).

The percentage of returning students in postsecondary institutions has increased markedly since 1970, from about 10% to 17% of the student population (U.S. Department of Education, 2005). When returning students come to campus, they often feel a bit on the periphery of things because rules, regulations, and activities are generally designed for younger students (Morgan, 2013). They are often not sure as to whether or not they should share their thoughts or perspectives with the class; perhaps, they may think, their ideas will be out of date. Then again, some returning students achieved commanding positions at work or in social roles and it may be difficult for them to accept their subordinate status in the teacher–student relationship. However, all in all, research suggests that both younger and returning students, and instructors, benefit from the mix of views in a classroom that includes returning students (Morgan, 2013). In the next chapter, we'll continue our exploration into middle adulthood by looking at the social and emotional development that takes place during this time.

STUDY TOOLS 15

READY TO STUDY?

In the book, you can:

- ☐ Rip out the chapter review card at the back of the book for a handy summary of the chapter and key terms.
- ☐ Check your understanding of what you've read with the quizzes that follow.

ONLINE AT CENGAGEBRAIN.COM YOU CAN:

- ☐ Collect StudyBits while you read and study the chapter.
- ☐ Quiz yourself on key concepts.
- ☐ Find videos for further exploration.
- ☐ Prepare for tests with HDEV5 Flash Cards as well as those you create.

SELF-ASSESSMENTS

Fill Ins

Answers can be found in the back of the book.

1. The body's system of skin, hair, and nails is called the __________ system.
2. In middle age, the hair grays because of lessened production of __________.
3. Presbyopia refers to loss of __________ in the eye lens.
4. In middle age, __________ normally replaces lean body mass, so that the BMI rises.

5. Between the ages of 45 and 64, __________ is the leading cause of death.

6. Two out of three cancer deaths in the United States are attributable to two controllable factors: smoking and __________.

7. Heart disease most commonly results from __________.

8. The term __________ refers to the fact that people's intellectual abilities are not absolutely fixed but can be modified under certain conditions at almost any time in life.

9. The fact that Jean Piaget rode a bicycle at a very advanced age suggests that people can maintain __________ memories for a lifetime.

10. The __________ Effect refers to the research finding that IQ scores in the United States increased an average of 18 points between 1947 and 2002.

Multiple Choice

1. Of the following, the most common type of cancer is

a. bladder cancer.

b. kidney cancer.

c. lung and bronchus cancer.

d. thyroid cancer.

2. A woman's lifetime risk of developing cancer at any or all sites is 1 in

a. 2.

b. 3.

c. 5.

d. 10.

3. ____________ Americans have higher than average rates of colorectal cancer and deaths from that disease.

a. African

b. Asian

c. European

d. Native

4. Cigarette smoking causes ____________% of lung cancer deaths in the United States.

a. 27

b. 47

c. 67

d. 87

5. Which of the following risk factors for heart disease is controllable?

a. gender

b. age

c. smoking

d. family history

6. Which of the following statements about stress is accurate?

a. Stress causes cancer.

b. Stress suppresses the immune system.

c. Stress is a completely controllable factor.

d. Stress hormones connected with anger dilate the blood vessels to the heart.

7. An estrogen deficit in a woman may lead to any of the following symptoms *except*

a. some impairment of cognitive functioning.

b. hot flashes and flushes.

c. increased risk of heart disease.

d. increased fertility.

8. Which of the following is accurate about the prevalence of sexual dysfunctions?

a. Estimates of their prevalence vary widely.

b. Men are more likely than women to have difficulty reaching orgasm.

c. Young men are more likely than older men to have erectile dysfunction.

d. Men are more likely than women to experience pain during sexual intercourse.

9. Throughout adulthood, a person's ____________ is most likely to remain stable.

a. numeric ability

b. perceptual speed

c. verbal ability

d. spatial orientation

10. Which of the following cognitive facilities is most likely to increase or expand in middle adulthood?

a. general knowledge

b. navigating new cities

c. fluid intelligence

d. mathematical problem-solving ability

16 Middle Adulthood: Social and Emotional Development

David Burch/UpperCut Images/Getty Images

LEARNING OUTCOMES

After studying this chapter, you will be able to . . .

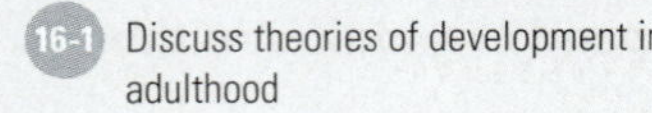

16-1 Discuss theories of development in middle adulthood

16-2 Discuss stability and change in social and emotional development in middle adulthood

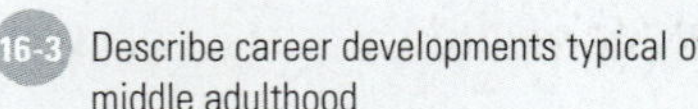

16-3 Describe career developments typical of middle adulthood

16-4 Discuss trends in relationships in middle adulthood, focusing on grandparenting and on being in the "sandwich generation"

After you finish this chapter, go to **PAGE 335** for **STUDY TOOLS**

There was once a TV sitcom called *Father Knows Best* (really), with upright Jim Anderson as the title character. He was an insurance agent who was apparently born in a suit and wore it 24 hours a day. His wife was apparently born in an apron and wore it proudly all day long. The series caught them in middle age, with three children, presumably because they could not have the average two and a fraction children. The older two, teenagers, were called Bud and Princess. They lived in a spacious, clean, suburban house and had a spacious, clean, suburban car. It was with the vision, perhaps, of such a "fine," "typical" American family in mind that Robert Havighurst proposed his "developmental tasks" of middle adulthood in the 1970s (see Figure 16.1).

There is no room in Havighurst's vision of normalcy for gays and lesbians, for people who cannot have or choose not to have children, for people who choose the single life, and for people who do not undertake "meaningful" social and civic responsibilities—nor for racial nor ethnic minorities. Having said that, Havighurst did arrive at a list of issues that affect many of us at midlife, issues we will be discussing in this chapter.

> Many of us "launch" our children into the outside world during middle adulthood and help them establish themselves.

Many of us do "launch" our children into the outside world during our middle adulthood, and we do help them establish themselves—although establishment in modern times often takes much longer than we had anticipated. We may find that our preferences in leisure activities have changed over the years, or we may be continuing them—athletic, cultural, social, what have you. Some of us are establishing deeper relationships with life partners, but the fact is that some are living alone, some were never partnered or are divorced, and some are living with stepfamilies and struggling along. Some of us are involved in social or civic activities, but some of us are loners, and, as we will see, going it alone can have negative consequences for our mental and physical well-being.

Havighurst sounds pessimistic about work—keeping our performance at a satisfactory level. But the fact is that today many of us are reaching

FIG.16.1 ROBERT HAVIGHURST'S DEVELOPMENTAL TASKS OF MIDDLE ADULTHOOD

This is a traditional 40-year-old view of tasks of middle adulthood that few of us envision as ideal these days. Many of us do not have lifepartners or children. Many of us do not have jobs; others do not have time for leisure activities.

- ☑ ***Helping our children establish themselves in the outside world***
- ☑ ***Developing a range of enjoyable leisure activities***
- ☑ ***Establishing a deeper relationship with our life partner***
- ☑ ***Becoming involved in meaningful social and civic responsibilities***
- ☑ ***Keeping our performance at work at a satisfactory level***
- ☑ ***Adjusting to the physical changes that accompany aging through the midlife period***
- ☑ ***Adjusting to the demands and responsibilities of caring for aging parents***

TRUTH OR FICTION?

T	F	Most people experience a midlife crisis in middle adulthood.
T	F	Mothers experience an "empty nest syndrome" when the last child leaves home.
T	F	The events of middle adulthood tend to cause major shifts in personality.
T	F	College-educated women experience increased personal distress as they advance from middle adulthood to late adulthood.
T	F	Job satisfaction increases throughout middle adulthood.
T	F	Middle-aged people tend to have fewer friends than young adults do.

peak performance or first coming into our own in middle adulthood. We have gained expertise, and our abilities remain generally intact. And then some of us, unfortunately, have lost our jobs in middle age and may wind up in work for which we are overqualified, or not be able to join the work force again.

There may be issues in adjusting to physical aging. We may encounter health problems we really weren't thinking about during young adulthood. We may indeed have to come to the aid of aging parents. On the other hand, we may also find new rewards in our relationships with our parents once we are both quite "grown up."

16-1 THEORIES OF DEVELOPMENT IN MIDDLE ADULTHOOD

Theories of development in middle adulthood largely deal with the issue of whether or not we can consider middle adulthood to be a distinct stage or phase of life. According to Erikson's theory of psychosocial development, middle adulthood is characterized by a particular life crisis. Daniel Levinson spoke of a specific midlife transition and a midlife crisis.

16-1a ERIK ERIKSON'S THEORY OF PSYCHOSOCIAL DEVELOPMENT

Erikson believed that the major psychological challenge of the middle years is **generativity versus stagnation**. Generativity is the ability to generate or produce. Erikson (1980) saw psychosocial generativity as based in an instinctual drive toward procreativity—that is, bearing and rearing children. To him, the negative counterpart of generativity meant rejection or suppression of this natural drive and would lead to stagnation. He did recognize that some people could not have children of their own or that social or interpersonal conditions made it difficult for some people to bear children. Under such circumstances, substitutes might work for the individual. For example, a person or couple without children (or even with children) might contribute to the teaching or welfare of other people's children, or might make things of lasting value such as objects of art, or might contribute to charity or to civic works.

generativity versus stagnation Erikson's seventh stage of psychosocial development, in which the life crisis is the dichotomy between generativity (as in rearing children or contributing to society) and stagnation (a state characterized by lack of development, growth, or advancement).

Jeffrey Coolidge/Jupiterimages

Erikson and others (e.g., Hebblethwaite & Norris, 2011; Hayslip, 2015). also note that grandparenthood provides additional opportunities for generativity. Generativity not only contributes to future generations; it also enhances one's self-esteem and sense of meaning in life (Zeigler-Hill, 2013).

Erikson argued that people who do not engage in generative behavior risk stagnating and falling into routines that can strip their lives of meaning and purpose. This particular point remains murky. For example, Van Hiel and colleagues (2006) administered a battery of psychological tests to nearly 200 middle-aged adults, many of whom were identified as high in generativity and many of whom were identified as high in stagnation. The more generative group scored significantly higher in the personality variable of conscientiousness, and the more stagnating group scored significantly higher on the personality variable of neuroticism. Neuroticism, as measured by the NEO Personality Inventory, is defined as emotional instability—an enduring tendency to experience negative feelings such as

Heide Benser/Getty Images

anxiety, anger, guilt, and depression. So the first question we might ask is whether some people stagnate "because of" less generative behavior or whether their lower generativity is related to personality traits such as neuroticism. The Van Hiel group also found, with a group of 457 middle-aged adults, that generativity and stagnation are independent dimensions rather than opposites. In other words, middle-aged people can be low in generativity and also be low in stagnation.

16-1b DANIEL LEVINSON'S SEASONS

According to Daniel Levinson and his colleagues (1978), the years from 40 to 45 comprise a **midlife transition**—a psychological shift into middle adulthood that is often accompanied by a crisis during which people fear they have more to look back upon than forward to. Erikson and Levinson both termed this crisis the **midlife crisis**, and it is defined as a time of anxiety and self-doubt during which people sense the passing of youth and become preoccupied with their mortality (Allison & Setterberg, 2016). Levinson believed that marker events such as menopause, the death of a parent or a friend, or a child's leaving "the nest" could trigger the crisis.

Once beset by the crisis, there may be attempts to deny of aging, such as an extramarital affair to prove that we remain attractive, buying a sports car (red, of course), or shifting careers. Yet many people view the years from age 45 onward as a second adulthood, filled with opportunities for new directions and fulfillment.

For many people today, the so-called midlife crisis is imposed from the outside in the form of a career crash resulting from corporate and government *downsizing*—the thinning of the ranks of employees. But people who are flexible enough to make the transition to other careers may find increased satisfaction.

FICTION

T (F) Most people experience a midlife crisis in middle adulthood.

According to research evidence, it is not true that "most people" experience a midlife crisis in middle adulthood. A midlife crisis may be more the exception than the rule. However, some people certainly do have them.

The 50s are often more relaxed and productive than the 40s. Yet many people in their 50s need to adjust to the children leaving home (the "empty nest"), the effects of aging, and competition from younger workers. On the other hand, the last child's leaving home is often seen as a positive event.

16-1c ENTERING MIDLIFE: CRISIS, TURNING POINT, OR PRIME OF LIFE?

Theorists have made much of turning 35 or 40, or of entering midlife. I mention the age of 35 because it is the age at which women who become pregnant are advised to check for chromosomal abnormalities in their fetuses (Norton et al., 2014; see Figure 16.2). Women are also sometimes advised to discontinue using birth control pills after age 35, to switch pills, or to use "the pill" under greater supervision (Russo & Nelson, 2016; Shoupe, 2016). At this age, women have also traditionally become more aware that their "biological clocks" are ticking. Today, of course, we could say that 40 or 45 is the new 30 or 35, and that most women at 35 can still safely use birth control pills. And many women do become pregnant in their late 30s and early 40s (Li et al., 2014). However, careful monitoring of the fetus is usually recommended for women who become pregnant at 35 or later.

With people now more likely to live into their late 70s and 80s, 40 has become a much more realistic halfway point, or turning point, than 35 (Zhu et al., 2011). It turns out, for example, that the sperm count and "swimming ability" of sperm begin to decline markedly at age 40 (Zhu et al., 2011). Daniel Levinson and his colleagues (1978) considered the transition to midlife at about the age of 40 a crisis, a midlife crisis, characterized by recognition that one has fallen short of one's dream or dreams. The once promising ballerina has never danced *The Nutcracker* at Lincoln Center. The Wharton business major never became a Fortune 500 company vice president. The Naval Academy graduate at the top of her class never made admiral. Thus, argues Becker (2006), many people who did not need psychotherapy earlier in life seek it now.

These portraits are negative, to say the least. Evidence is actually mixed as to whether adults experience such losses and

midlife transition a psychological shift into middle adulthood that is theorized to occur between the ages of 40 and 45 as people begin to believe they have more to look back upon than forward to.

midlife crisis a time of dramatic self-doubt and anxiety during which people sense the passing of their youth and become concerned with their own aging and mortality.

low points at midlife (Cheng et al., 2014; Jeste & Oswald, 2014). While some theorists present portraits of middle-aged people suddenly focusing on tragedy, loss, or doom, others find people to be in or entering the "prime of life" (Graham & Lachman, 2012; Seeman et al., 2011). People can develop certain illnesses at almost any time of life, but as described in Chapter 15, most people in middle adulthood suffer little loss of physical prowess. However professionals who rely on peak performance, such as athletes and dancers, will find the loss compelling enough to shuttle them in new life directions. Intellectually, moreover, there is little if any loss in fluid intelligence, and crystallized intelligence is growing—especially among professionals who are still developing skills in their fields.

Middle-aged adults, especially professionals, are also often earning more money than young adults. They are more likely to be settled geographically and vocationally, although midlife career changes and relocation are certainly possibilities. By now one may have built systems of social support, be involved in enduring romantic and social relationships, and have children. The flip side of all this may be overwhelming responsibility, such as caring for children, a spouse, aging parents, and remaining in the workplace all at once—quite a juggling act! But many in middle adulthood are at the height of their productivity and resilience, despite the challenges.

LIFE EVENTS OF MIDDLE ADULTHOOD

- **Possible loss of a parent**
- **Divorce or separation**
- **Change in health status**
- **The need to care for one's parents**
- **Change in relationship with one's children or friends**
- **Financial difficulties**
- **Change in appearance**
- **Loss of a job or change in job responsibilities**

16-1d THE LIFE-EVENTS APPROACH

The life-events approach to middle age focuses on the particular challenges and changes that people are likely to face at this time rather than on phases or stages of life. The most stressful life events of middle adulthood include the death of a spouse or a child; the death of a parent or a sibling; marital divorce or separation, or separation from a cohabitant; hospitalization or change in the health status of oneself, one's child, one's parent, or sibling; the need to care for one's parents; a change in the relationship with one's children; financial difficulties; concern about one's appearance, weight, or aging; moving; change or loss of employment; a change in a relationship with an important friend; or a change in responsibilities at work (Mechanic & McAlpine, 2011; Stegenga et al., 2011).

One common change in middle adulthood takes place when the last child leaves home. It was once assumed that women without children in the home would experience a painful "**empty nest syndrome**,"

empty nest syndrome a feeling of loneliness or loss of purpose that parents, and especially the mother, are theorized to experience when the youngest child leaves home.

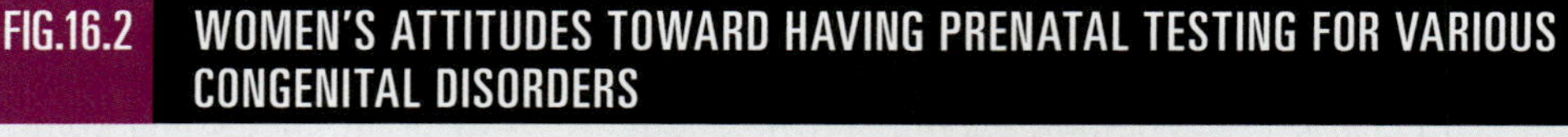
FIG.16.2 WOMEN'S ATTITUDES TOWARD HAVING PRENATAL TESTING FOR VARIOUS CONGENITAL DISORDERS

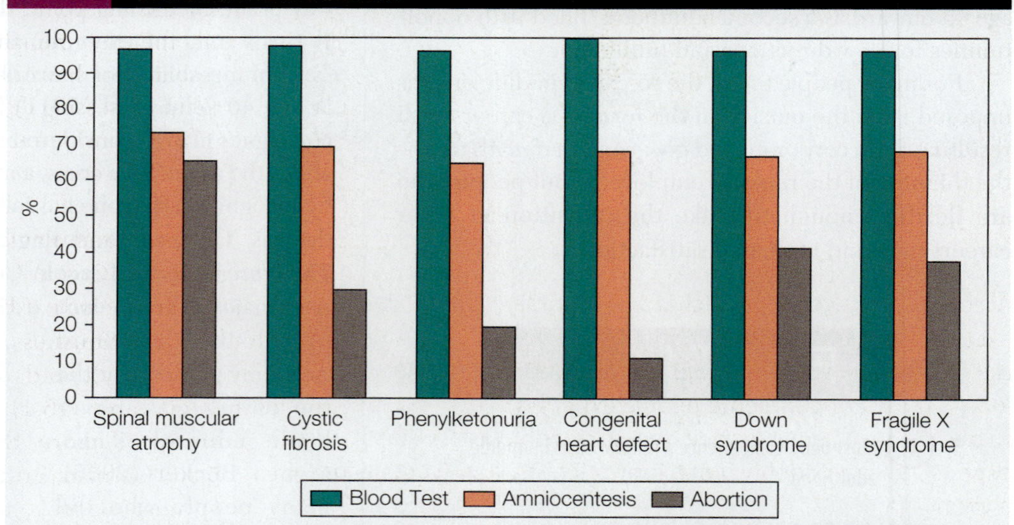

Source: Norton, M. E., Nakagawa, S., & Kuppermann, M. (2014). Women's attitudes regarding prenatal testing for a range of congenital disorders of varying severity. *Journal of Clinical Medicine*, 3, 144–152. Figure 1.

Proportion of women who say they would have a blood test to screen for various fetal health problems, who would have an amniocentesis to test for the problem, and who would have an abortion if the problem were found. Note that the women were more willing to have (less-obtrusive) blood tests than amniocenteses. Moreover, most women said they would not abort a fetus that was shown to have one of these problems.

but this transition is often a positive event (Aronsson, 2014; Mitchell, 2016). Today, many middle-aged women in developed nations can keep themselves "as young as they feel." Most of them are in the workforce and find life satisfaction in activities other than child rearing and homemaking. Moreover, some children fail to leave home by 18 or 21, or—in a syndrome that has been referred to as *failure to launch*—even by age 30. Other adult children, because of financial problems or just for convenience, are in and out of their parents' home in what has been dubbed the *revolving-door syndrome*. Or, as part of the *boomerang generation*, they return home for prolonged periods.

As sources of stress, negative life events, including physical illness and depression, have been shown to be harmful to people's health in middle adulthood (Sutin et al., 2010). Some stressed people resort to a host of medicines, both prescribed and over-the-counter. Middle-aged people's situations—such as having understanding and helpful family members or friends—and attitudes can have moderating effects on stressors (Aronsson, 2014). A sense of control has been shown to mitigate the effects of stress and foster feelings of well-being among midlife adults (Jopp & Schmitt, 2010).

FICTION

T (F) Mothers experience an "empty nest syndrome" when the last child leaves home.

It is not (universally) true that mothers experience an "empty nest syndrome" when the last child leaves home. Many middle-aged women have mixed feelings about the youngest taking wing, and some breathe a sign of relief.

Who's Having a Crisis?

Peathegee Inc / Blend Images / Superstock

According to psychiatrist Richard A. Friedman (2008), one excuse for messing up is "my dog ate my homework." Another is "I'm going through a midlife crisis." As mortality begins to loom on the horizon, some people experience the impulse to do things in denial of their age, such as buy a new, fast, expensive car; suddenly quit a job; or leave a loyal spouse for a younger person.

Friedman reports on the experiences of middle-aged men who cheated on their wives, attributing their indiscretions to midlife crises. They may say that they love their wives and don't know what got into them, but they're usually seeking novelty and risking too much for a few moments of fun. Being bored with routine is not what is meant by the term midlife crisis.

16-2 STABILITY AND CHANGE IN MIDDLE ADULTHOOD

It's easy enough to measure changes in height or in weight, but how would one measure whether people change in personality or whether they remain the same? A number of researchers have been answering this question by assessing differences over the decades in paper-and-pencil tests of five basic factors of personality—dubbed the **"big five" personality traits**—isolated by Robert McCrae and Paul Costa Jr. and their colleagues (Costa & McCrae, 2010). These factors include extraversion, agreeableness, conscientiousness, neuroticism (emotional instability), and openness to experience (see Table 16.1). A study of more than 5,000 German, British, Spanish, Czech, and Turkish people suggests that the factors are related to people's basic temperaments, which are considered to be largely inborn (McCrae et al., 2000).

"big five" personality traits basic personality traits derived from contemporary statistical methods: extraversion, agreeableness, conscientiousness, neuroticism (emotional instability), and openness to experience.

Factor	Name	Traits
I	Extraversion	Contrasts talkativeness, assertiveness, and activity with silence, passivity, and reserve
II	Agreeableness	Contrasts kindness, trust, and warmth with hostility, selfishness, and distrust
III	Conscientiousness	Contrasts organization, thoroughness, and reliability with carelessness, negligence, and unreliability
IV	Neuroticism	Contrasts nervousness, moodiness, and sensitivity to negative stimuli with coping ability
V	Openness to experience	Contrasts imagination, curiosity, and creativity with shallowness and lack of perceptiveness

TABLE 16.1 THE "BIG FIVE": THE FIVE-FACTOR MODEL OF PERSONALITY

The researchers interpret the results to suggest that our personalities tend to mature rather than be shaped by environmental conditions, although the expression of personality traits is certainly affected by culture. (For example, a person who is "basically" open to new experience is likely to behave less openly in a traditional, fundamentalist society than in an open society.)

16-2a ARE THERE SUDDEN SHIFTS IN PERSONALITY?

The notions of crises or turning points in emotional development also suggest that people undergo rather sudden changes or shifts in personality. As pointed out by Robert McCrae and Paul Costa Jr. (2006), it has also been widely assumed that adult life events such as getting married, working one's way up in a vocation, and having and rearing children would deeply affect people's personality. However, at least by middle adulthood, and during middle adulthood, research finds that the "big five" personality traits remain reasonably stable (Lucas & Donnellan, 2011; see Figure 16.3). As you see in Figure 16.3, extraversion shows a mild gradual decline across the years of adulthood. Agreeableness tends to increase during the later years. Conscientiousness increases dramatically from early adulthood and peaks during middle adulthood, followed by a decline during late adulthood. Neuroticism—emotional instability—increases slightly and gradually during middle adulthood, but then levels off and declines somewhat in later adulthood. The most dramatic changes appear to be in openness to experience, which would appear to be in the province of the young. It declines strongly from young adulthood but then, like other traits, remains reasonably stable through middle adulthood until it falls off precipitously during the later years. Regardless of whether or not middle adulthood is the "prime of life," it may well be the most stable period of life.

FICTION

T (F) The events of middle adulthood tend to cause major shifts in personality.

Interestingly, it is not true that the events of middle adulthood—and the passage of the years—tend to cause major shifts in personality. The "big five" personality traits show a good deal of stability during middle adulthood.

Stuart McClymont/Stone/Getty Images

What will their personalities be like in 20 years?

FIG.16.3 CHANGES IN "BIG FIVE" PERSONALITY TRAITS THROUGHOUT ADULTHOOD

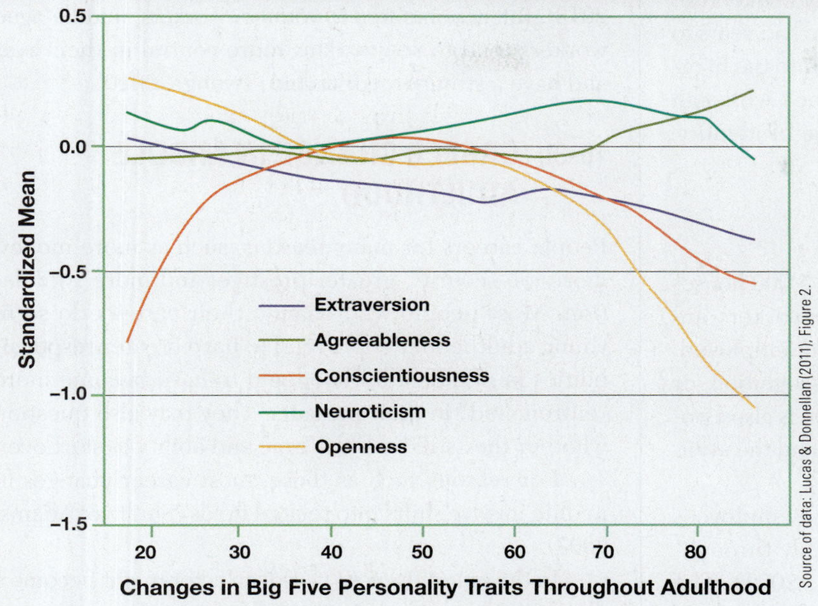

Research shows that middle adulthood—the period between 40 and 60 or 65—is a relatively stable period of life in terms of the personality factors of extraversion, agreeableness, and conscientiousness. Neuroticism—emotional instability—shows a gradual increase throughout middle adulthood. Openness to experience shows stability and then a very gradual decline throughout middle adulthood, followed by a more precipitous decline during late adulthood.

FICTION

T (F) College-educated women experience increased personal distress as they advance from middle adulthood to late adulthood.

It is not true that college-educated women experience increased personal distress as they advance from middle adulthood to late adulthood—aside from increased concern with aging itself. Many women become more authoritative as they approach middle age.

16-2b PERSONALITY THEMES AMONG COLLEGE-EDUCATED WOMEN

Abigail Stewart, Joan Ostrove, and Ravenna Helson (2001) developed scales to assess a number of personality themes among women:

- identity certainly (knowing who one is and what one stands for),
- confident power (self confidence),
- concern with aging,
- generativity, and
- personal distress.

Alyssa Zucker and her colleagues (2002) administered these scales to three cohorts of college-educated women: women in their 20s, 40s, and 60s. As you can see in Figure 16.4, scores on three of the scales were higher for women in their 40s than women in their 20s, and then higher again for women in their 60s: identity certainty, confident power, and concern about aging. Generativity was higher in the 40s than in the 20s, but the generativity of the cohort in their 60s was much the same as for those in their 40s. Despite increasing concern with aging, personal distress was lower among older women, suggesting, perhaps, that older women are more settled. Remember, however, that these samples are of college-educated women, so they may be less likely than the general population to incur certain financial and health problems in late adulthood.

FIG.16.4 MEAN SCORES OF COLLEGE-EDUCATED WOMEN OF DIFFERENT AGES ACCORDING TO FIVE PERSONALITY THEMES

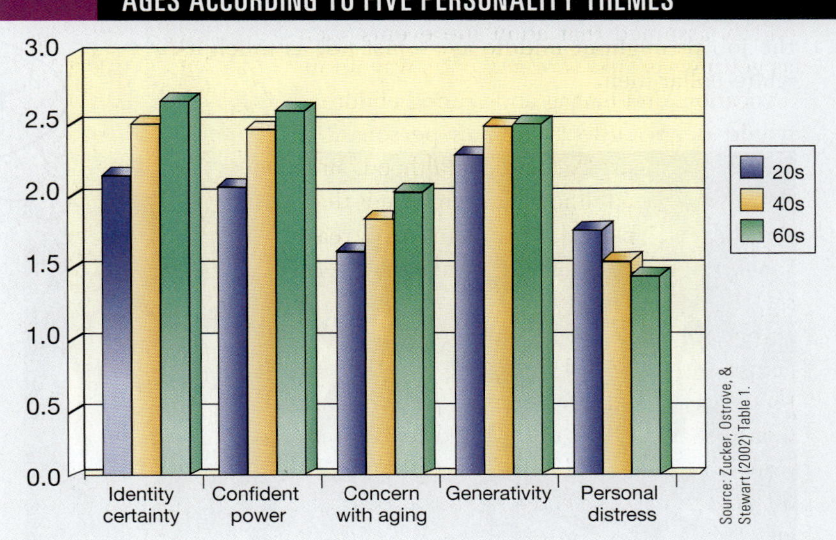

16-3 WORK IN MIDDLE ADULTHOOD

As suggested by Erikson and Levinson, many workers are at their peak in middle adulthood. They have had years to "learn the ropes," and many have advanced into the highest ranks of their trades or professions. One's work can continue to provide social benefits, a sense of identity, and self-esteem.

16-3a JOB SATISFACTION

A Conference Board (2010) survey of some 5,000 households found that only 45% of American workers are satisfied with their jobs. Some 10% were unemployed, but others were unhappy with their pay, recognition, or health or retirement benefits. Job satisfaction is also associated with such factors as interesting work and the availability of child-care facilities (Russell, 2008).

A study of more than 2,000 university employees found that job satisfaction increased steadily throughout middle adulthood (Hochwarter et al., 2001). The gains were greatest for men, and especially for men who were white-collar workers, for example, professors. Some workers—particularly blue-collar workers—reported feelings of alienation and dissatisfaction. Some complained that supervisors treated them with disrespect and failed to ask them how to improve working conditions and productivity (Judge & Klinger, 2008). These feelings are particularly painful for middle-aged workers when their supervisors are younger than they are. Women are often balancing the demands of the workplace and a family, and they may still experience a "glass ceiling" on the job (Lyness & Judiesch, 2014). They may be sought out in the hiring process but find it difficult advance. Still, most women and blue-collar workers also reported more satisfaction on the job throughout middle age—just not as much as white-collar men.

On the other hand, many middle-aged workers feel threatened by changes in the workplace brought about by increased automation and outsourcing (Krumm et al., 2013). But as compared to younger workers, middle-aged workers tend to see work as more central in their lives and have a stronger work ethic (Twenge, 2010).

16-3b CAREER CHANGE IN MIDDLE ADULTHOOD

People careers for many reasons, such as more money, more job security, greater prestige, and more stimulation. Most people who change their careers do so in young adulthood. People tend to have greater responsibilities in middle adulthood and to have become more "entrenched" in their pursuits. They may also question whether they still have the time and ability to start over.

For reasons such as these, most career changes in midlife involve shifts into related fields (Shultz & Adams, 2007).

In the entertainment world, an actor might become a director or a producer. In the field of education, a teacher or professor might move into educational administration. A laboratory chemist who has spent 20 years working for a pharmaceuticals company might decide she wishes to work with people and have more time for herself, so she might move into teaching high school chemistry and travel during the summers.

These are all voluntary, planned changes. When middle-aged people switch jobs voluntarily and obtain better working conditions or benefits, there tend to be corresponding positive changes in their mental health (Strazdins et al., 2011). But some middle-aged people change careers following a personal crisis such as a divorce, conflict with coworkers, or being fired. In such cases, middle-aged people may pick up whatever work they can to sustain themselves—and pay a price in psychological well-being (Strazdins et al., 2011).

"I guess we've learned the ropes..."

Kay Lee Davies/Photodisc/Getty Images

16-3c UNEMPLOYMENT

My friend lost her executive position in her late 40s when her company was bought out and a new management team came in. She knew she was in a vulnerable position because the company taking over usually "chops off the head" of the acquired company; still, she thought she might be low enough on the totem pole to escape notice. Not so. New management cut in half the number of professionals at her level. At first she focused on the fact that her severance package was good. She thought she would take a month off to relax and then use the headhunting firm hired by the company to relocate. However, she soon found that hers was a relatively small industry and that there were few openings that approximated her level. Former work friends clustered around her at first but began to drift away. After four months she had sunk into a deep clinical depression.

Research shows that people who are involuntarily unemployed have lower physical and psychological well-being than employed subjects, and unemployed middle-aged subjects have lower well-being than unemployed young adults (van der Noordt et al., 2014). Within the samples of unemployed middle-aged adults, those for whom work was more important, who had fewer financial resources and less social support, and who tended to blame themselves for losing their jobs fare worst. Those who had emotional and financial resources and social support, who could structure their time, and who had realistic strategies for job hunting or finding substitutes for jobs fare best.

TRUTH

T **F** Job satisfaction increases throughout middle adulthood.

It is true that job satisfaction tends to increase throughout middle adulthood. But we are talking about samples of the population at large. Obviously, many are less satisfied as time goes on, and some are out of work.

Among unemployed women, we find age differences in the intensity of their search for employment and their willingness to accept certain kinds of jobs. In a study of married women in four age groups, post-adolescents (up to age 21) spent more time trying to find employment than did women aged 22 to 35, 36 to 49, or 50 to 62 (Kulik, 2000). The women aged 50–62 were most likely to accept jobs low in pay, as long as they liked the work, and those aged 22 to 49 were most likely to reject jobs because they conflicted with family life or because of work conditions. The older women in the study were more likely to experience declines in their well-being following the loss of employment. On the other hand, the older women were least likely to suffer financial strain.

Merie W. Wallace/Warner Brothers/Photofest

After working for more than 15 years as a television and film actor, Clint Eastwood made his directorial debut with *The Beguiled* in 1971, at the age of 41. He has continued to make Oscar-nominated and Oscar-winning films through the 2000s and 2010s.

16-4 RELATIONSHIPS IN MIDDLE ADULTHOOD

The term *middle adulthood* is a convenient way of describing people whose ages lie between young adulthood and late adulthood. In terms of their family relationships, their generation is in the middle in another way—often, as we will see, "sandwiched" in between their own children (and grandchildren) and their parents.

16-4a EVOLVING PARENT–CHILD RELATIONSHIPS

Infants are completely dependent on their parents. Children are also dependent. Adolescents strive for independence, and, as they mature and gain experience, parents generally begin to share control with them. As a matter of fact, it is stressful for parents when adolescents do not exert self-control, and when parents must direct

Tom Merton/OJO Images/Getty Images
David Papazian/Stockbyte/Getty Images

them in many areas of life—getting them up for school, urging them to maintain personal hygiene, fighting with them over their choice of clothing, and coaxing them to complete their homework.

Once their children become emerging adults or young adults, most parents in the United States are content to "launch" their children to live on their own or with roommates. In many cases, the children remain at least partly financially dependent, sometimes for several years (Kins et al., 2014). If they have been close to their parents, they may also remain somewhat emotionally dependent once they are out on their own as well—or at the very least, it may hurt when their parents disapprove of their personal choices.

Parents are usually satisfied with their children living apart if they call or e-mail regularly and drop by (or allow the parents to drop by) with some sort of reasonable frequency. Parents often try to find a balance between staying in touch and "interfering," especially once their children have partners or children of their own.

In some traditional societies, young adults do not usually leave the home of origin until they are married or some other key event takes place. Alessandra Rusconi (2004) compared Germany and Italy and found that Germans normally left home to set up independent homes prior to marriage. In Italy, however, the picture was mixed. In large industrial cities, young adults tended to follow the German model, whereas more rural and southern Italians tended to remain in the home until they got married. Similarly, parents in some traditional societies assume that their adult children will live nearby; moving to another part of the country is not only painful but also something of an embarrassment for them among their extended family and community.

When the children of middle-aged adults take partners or get married, new challenges can emerge. First of all, it may seem that nobody can be "good enough" for their child, but, sometimes, their child does apparently make a poor choice—or at least a poor match. The parents must then deal with the issues of whether, and how, they express their feelings about it. Regardless of the partner or spouse chosen by their child, there are also in-laws and the extended family of the in-laws. Sometimes there is a good match between the families of both partners, but more often the families would not have chosen each other as friends. Still, for the sake of the children, the parents may try to act friendly when they get together. But the new relationships can be another source of stress.

And then the children may have children.

16-4b GRANDPARENTING

Let's begin this section by selecting one of the following two statements. Which of them will you live by (or damage your relationship with your child by)?

- As a grandparent, you have the right to tell your son or daughter how to raise your grandchild.
- As a grandparent, you have to keep your mouth tightly shut when you see your son-in-law or daughter-in-law doing the wrong thing with your grandchild.

As you can see, one of the most challenging jobs of the newly minted grandparent is to navigate carefully between the treacherous rocks of reckless interference and painful neglect.

Young adulthood is the time of life when most of those who will bear children do so, and middle adulthood is the time of life when most of us who will become grandparents begin that role. Having and relating to grandchildren, like having and relating to one's children, has its pluses and its minuses. But research generally finds that the balance is more positive in the case of having grandchildren. For example, a study of grandparenting conducted in China, Greece, and Poland found that having grandchildren was viewed as an overwhelmingly positive event in each culture and that it was beneficial to grandparents both socially and psychologically (Filus, 2006). The study also found that grandparents, like parents, participated in the care of grandchildren and in their recreational and educational activities. But the balance differed, as it does in the

Lesbians and Bisexual Women as Grandparents

One study that relied on extensive interviews of lesbian and bisexual grandmothers found that the experiences of these women were in some ways similar to those of heterosexual people, and in other ways quite different (Orel, 2006). Like most heterosexual grandparents, the lesbian and bisexual grandmothers believed that they were important sources of emotional support for their grandchildren. They also reported that their children either helped (facilitated) or hindered (discouraged) their relationships with their grandchildren, and that the pattern might shift from time to time. On the other hand, the grandmothers in the study were concerned about whether or not they should disclose their sexual orientations to their grandchildren and just how they should go about it.

United States. Parents spend a higher proportion of their time taking care of their children, whereas grandparents spend relatively more time in recreational and educational activities. We are speaking, of course, of situations in which the grandparents do not live in the same household with the grandchildren.

Cross-cultural studies also find gender differences in grandchildren's relationships with their grandparents that tend to parallel their relationships with their parents. Studies in the United States, Poland, Greece, Germany, and China all find that grandchildren through adolescence spend more time in activities with their grandmothers than their grandfathers (Mann et al., 2013). Grandchildren are also relatively more involved with their mother's parents than their father's. The gender of the grandchild has little effect on these overall findings. Even male grandchildren, who would toss the football back and forth with the grandfather and not the grandmother, tend to generally gravitate more toward contacts with grandmothers than with grandfathers. Despite the greater involvement with grandmothers, grandchildren say they value their grandfathers just as highly.

One of the "hyped" advantages of being a grandparent is that one is able to play with one's grandchildren but then go home, leaving the "work" to the children's parents. In many cases, however, this

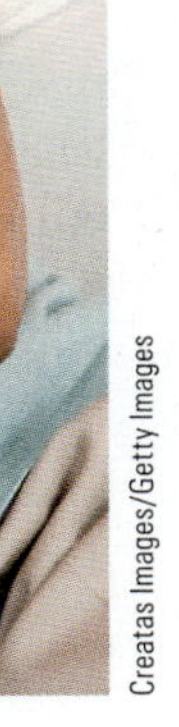

Creatas Images/Getty Images

mind-set assumes plentiful sources of money and leisure time. It hardly addresses all the complications of family separations or divorce, or loss of identity as a family unit, which are so common today (Bridges et al., 2007; Soliz, 2007). It doesn't address the fact that some grandparents hardly get to see—or never get to see—their grandchildren because of geographical separation or because of harsh feelings following family conflict.

> Most grandparents enjoy their roles in their grandchildren's lives. Their grandchildren tend to value them deeply, even when they do not see them as often as they might wish.

The notion of grandparents enjoying the best of the grandchild while escaping responsibility also ignores the fact that in thousands of cases grandparents bear the primary responsibility for rearing grandchildren (Goodman, 2007a; Hayslip & Kaminski, 2006).

GRANDPARENTS IN CHARGE In most cases, one or two biological parents determine the course of childrearing of grandchildren. But sometimes grandparents play a major role—or *the* major role (Yankura, 2013). For example, an Israeli study of immigrants from Ethiopia and Eastern European countries found that grandparents who lived with single parents and their grandchildren had a strong influence on their grandchildren and contributed to the overall adjustment of the family (Doron & Markovitzky, 2007). Among Native Hawaiians, it is customary for grandparents to rear the grandchildren (Yancura, 2013).

Many studies (e.g., Doron & Markovitzky, 2007; Goodman, 2007b) show that grandparents have less influence when they live with couples and their grandchildren; under these circumstances, they are less likely to contribute to the adjustment of the family. Rather than "filling a hole," they frequently become a source of discord between their son or daughter and their son- or daughter-in-law.

In some cases grandparents are the sole caregivers of their grandchildren. These arrangements typically begin when the grandchild has a single parent (Hayslip et al., 2013; Park & Greenberg, 2007). Now and then that single parent dies. The single parent may be in the military and be sent on a tour of duty. The parent may place the child with grandparents while she or he "tries" living in another location, with or without a new job, and the time extends. The parent may run off, perhaps involved with drugs or prostitution.

Regardless of the reasons that grandparents—usually grandmothers—assume the responsibility for parenting grandchildren, becoming a parent, again, in middle adulthood, can be stressful as well as rewarding (Hayslip et al., 2014). Do they attend school meetings with young parents and continually make explanations? If they are at the height of their careers, where do they find the time for all the chores? Do they have to become current with the new crop of children's TV programs? It's a far cry from playing with the grandchildren, or taking them to a museum, and then going home—leaving the "work" to the parents!

But most grandparents do enjoy their roles in their grandchildren's lives. Their grandchildren value them deeply, even when they do not see them as often as they might wish (Bridges et al., 2007). The greater fund of child-rearing experience of grandparents often allows them to relate to their grandchildren in a more relaxed way than parents can.

16-4c MIDDLE-AGED CHILDREN AND AGING PARENTS

Because of increasing life expectancy, more than half of the middle-aged people in developed nations have at least one living parent, and they frequently go on to experience late adulthood together (Callahan, 2007; U.S. Bureau of the Census, 2008). In Far Eastern nations such as China, Japan, and Korea, older parents tend to live with their children and their grandchildren, but not so in the United States (Kwok, 2006).

You might think that most aging American parents move to Sunbelt locations such as Florida and Arizona, but it isn't so. Nearly two-thirds of them have a residence near a child (U.S. Bureau of the Census, 2010), and there are frequent visits and phone calls. The relationships between middle-aged and older parents can grow quite close, especially as tensions and expectations from earlier years tend to slip into history. If an older mother had been disappointed in her now middle-aged daughter's choice of a husband, now the marriage may have ended or worked out, or there might be grandchildren to focus on. The years and other events place things in perspective.

michaeljung/iStock/360/ Getty images

Many middle-aged people feel sandwiched between the needs of their teenaged children and their aging parents. This is why they are sometimes said to belong to the "sandwich generation."

If the aging parents require assistance, in the United States and Canada the task usually falls to a middle-aged daughter, who then becomes what has been dubbed part of the **sandwich generation** (Do et al., 2014). She is "sandwiched" between several generations, caring for or contributing to the support of her own children at the same time she is caring for one or two parents (Seltzer & Bianchi, 2013; Cravey & Mitra, 2011). She may also be helping out with grandchildren. If she is fortunate, there is a sibling living in the vicinity to share the task. Given that she is also likely to be in the workforce, her role overload is multiplied (Chassin et al., 2010).

In other societies, such as that of Hong Kong in China, however, where aging parents usually live with a son's family, it is more often than not the son who assumes the major responsibility for caring for his parents, emotionally and financially (Kwok, 2006). In this patriarchal society, the son's priorities often run like this: first, his own children; second, his parents; third, his wife.

16-4d SIBLINGS

Sibling relationships continue into late adulthood for most adults in the United States. The majority of people in middle adulthood have at least one living brother or sister. Most adult sibling relationships are close, but they tend to reflect the nature of sibling relationships in childhood. Then, too, sisters tend to have more intimate relationships than brothers (Bedford & Avioli, 2006). Yet now and then sibling relationships that were antagonistic or competitive in childhood or adolescence grow closer in middle adulthood if the siblings cooperate in caring for a disabled parent. Conversely, a sibling relationship that had been close can grow distant if one sibling allows another to do all the work in caring for a parent.

16-4e FRIENDS

Adolescents are often parts of cliques and crowds, and young adults often have large numbers of friends. In middle adulthood, the number of friends tends to dwindle, and couples and individuals tend to place more value on the friends they keep (Blieszner, 2014). In midlife, people become less willing to spend their time with "just anybody"; therefore, their remaining friends are more likely to be "close matches" in terms of interests, activities, and, often, years of mutual experience. For this reason, the loss of a friend is felt more deeply. But as in earlier years, there are gender differences. Male friends are more likely to be competitive and less likely to be intimate than female friends (Blieszner, 2014).

Toni Antonucci and Kira Burditt (2004) report that men are more likely than women not to have friends or other close social relationships, and that social isolation is connected with poorer physical and psychological health and with mortality. In a survey of 1,421 Detroit men ranging in age from 20 to 93, they found that men without close social ties were significantly more depressed than men with relationships.

In the next chapter, we'll turn our attention to the physical and cognitive developments that occur in late adulthood.

sandwich generation the term given to middle-aged people who need to meet the demands of their own children and of aging parents.

TRUTH

F Middle-aged people tend to have fewer friends than young adults do.

It is true that middle-aged people tend to have fewer friends than young adults do; however, they have more in common with the friends who remain.

Middle Adulthood: Life Reimagined?

Midlife crisis? As noted by *New York Times* columnist David Brooks, When we use the word "midlife," we almost automatically think, "Midlife . . . crisis. It's the stage in the middle of the journey when people feel youth vanishing, their prospects narrowing and death approaching. So they become undone. The red Corvette pops up in the driveway [if you've got the cash!]. Stupidity reigns."[1]

However, according to Barbara Bradley Hagety's book, *Life Reimagined*,[2] the midlife crisis is one of the clichés about middle adulthood that may sound right, but for which there is little or no research evidence.

Hagerty writes that "the forties, fifties, and sixties are the least understood and, in some ways, the most critical phase of life. Midlife is not flyover territory. Midlife is . . . a bustling hub where the decisions you make today largely determine the rest of your journey on this planet" (Hagerty, pp. 4–5). In her book *Passages*, written in the 1970s, Gail Sheehy had slandered the decades of middle adulthood with terms like the "forlorn 40s" and the "resigned 50s." Research suggests that people are likely to reflect on where they have been and where they are going in middle adulthood, but that the search can be uplifting rather than frightening—neither forlorn nor resigned. Even Sheehy had allowed that the 50s could be "refreshed" as well as "resigned," and a positive shift can make life exciting in middle adulthood for those who do not spend the period of life on autopilot. Autopilot is the resignation Sheehy wrote about. Resignation means believing that one's path has been made and that deviation is not possible. Yet many, perhaps most of us remain vital if not completely youthful in middle adulthood. As Brooks writes, people today tend to be "healthy and energetic longer. [In 2016 we had] presidential candidates running for their first term in office at age 68, 69 and 74." So there is clearly nothing wrong with thinking about what can be the "next big thing" in one's life in one's 40s, 50s, and 60s.

We already saw that many people aged approximately 18–25 can be thought of as being in a new stage of development: emerging adulthood. Brooks refers to these years as the "Odyssey years," years of discovery, when people are taking more time "to try on new career options, new cities and new partners." But the shape of middle adulthood has also changed. According to Brooks, "What could have been considered the beginning of a descent is now a potential turning point—the turning point you are most equipped to take full advantage of. It is the moment when you can look back on your life so far and see it with different eyes. Hopefully you've built up some wisdom, which . . . means seeing the world with more compassion, grasping opposing ideas at the same time, tolerating ambiguity and reacting with equanimity to the small setbacks of life."

Sergio Azenha / Alamy Stock Photo

What may emerge is a new sense of meaning and purpose. People in middle adulthood may "dive fully into existing commitments, or embrace new ones. . . . Either way, with a little maturity, they're less likely by middle age to be blinded by ego, more likely to know what it is they actually desire, more likely to get out of their own way, and maybe a little less likely, given all the judgments that have been made, to care about what other people think" (Brooks, p. A25).

[1]Brooks, D. (2016, March 22). The Middle-Age Surge. *The New York Times*, p. A25.

[2]Hagerty, B. B. (2016) *Life reimagined: The science, art, and opportunity of midlife.* New York: Riverhead Books.

STUDY TOOLS 16

READY TO STUDY?

In the book, you can:

- ☐ Rip out the chapter review card at the back of the book for a handy summary of the chapter and key terms.
- ☐ Check your understanding of what you've read with the quizzes that follow.

ONLINE AT CENGAGEBRAIN.COM YOU CAN:

- ☐ Collect StudyBits while you read and study the chapter.
- ☐ Quiz yourself on key concepts.
- ☐ Find videos for further exploration.
- ☐ Prepare for tests with HDEV5 Flash Cards as well as those you create.

SELF-ASSESSMENTS

Fill Ins

Answers can be found in the back of the book.

1. It was once assumed that women whose youngest children have left home would experience a painful ____________ syndrome.
2. In the "big five" personality model, emotional instability is termed ____________.
3. The trait of ____________ increases dramatically from early adulthood and peaks during middle adulthood, followed by a decline during late adulthood.
4. In the "big five" personality model, as people develop from middle age to late adulthood, they tend to show a rise in the trait of ____________.
5. According to Abigail Stewart and her colleagues, believing that one will seize opportunities and be of a clear mind about what one can accomplish are aspects of ____________ certainty.
6. According to Erik Erikson, the life crisis of middle adulthood is generativity versus ____________.
7. According to Daniel Levinson, the years of 40 to 45 comprise a midlife ____________.
8. In a study of women aged 22 to 35, 36 to 49, or 50 to 62 who were seeking employment, the women aged ____________ were most likely to accept jobs low in pay, as long as they liked the work.
9. Middle-aged adults who care for aging parents and their own children are sometimes said to belong to the ____________ generation.
10. A survey of Detroit men ranging in age from 20 to 93 found that men without close social ties were significantly more ____________ than men with relationships.

Multiple Choice

1. **When Van Hiel and colleagues looked into generativity and stagnation, they found that**
   a. people high in generativity are also high in anxiety and depression.
   b. it is not possible to put stagnation into a form that is measurable.
   c. the more generative one is, the less stagnant one is.
   d. generativity and stagnation are independent dimensions.

2. **Research into Levinson's concept of the midlife crisis has found that**
   a. women are more likely than men to experience a midlife crisis.
   b. men are more likely than women to experience a midlife crisis.
   c. grandparents are less likely than people without grandchildren to experience a midlife crisis.
   d. there may not be such a thing as a midlife crisis as Levinson envisioned it.

3. **Research into middle-aged people has found that they**
   a. encounter little decline in physical prowess.
   b. are no longer capable of reaching orgasm.
   c. are extremely upset when the youngest child leaves home.
   d. tend to lose interest in work.

4. **All of the following are factors in the "big five" personality model *except***
   a. openness to experience.
   b. conscientiousness.
   c. intelligence.
   d. agreeableness.

5. **Research by Alyssa Zucker and her colleagues found that as women develop from their 20s to their 60s, they experience a decline in**
   a. confident power.
   b. identity certainty.
   c. concern with aging.
   d. personal distress.

6. **Alexandra Rusconi compared Germany and Italy and found that**
   a. Germans normally set up independent homes prior to marriage.
   b. Italians normally set up independent homes prior to marriage.
   c. Germans were more likely to become grandparents.
   d. Italians were more likely to become grandparents.

7. **In middle adulthood, most sibling relationships**
   a. are stressed.
   b. are close.
   c. are emotionally without feeling.
   d. vary too much to make any generalizations.

8. **When we compare friendships in middle adulthood to those during early adulthood we find that those in middle adulthood**
   a. have more friends.
   b. are more interested in what they can get from friendships rather than what they can give.
   c. are more similar to their friends than early adults are.
   d. add and drop friends rather quickly and easily.

9. **About how many aging parents live near a child?**
   a. one in ten
   b. 25%
   c. half
   d. two-thirds

10. **Most developmentalists believe that midlife begins between the ages of**
    a. 30 and 35.
    b. 35 and 40.
    c. 40 and 45.
    d. 45 and 50.

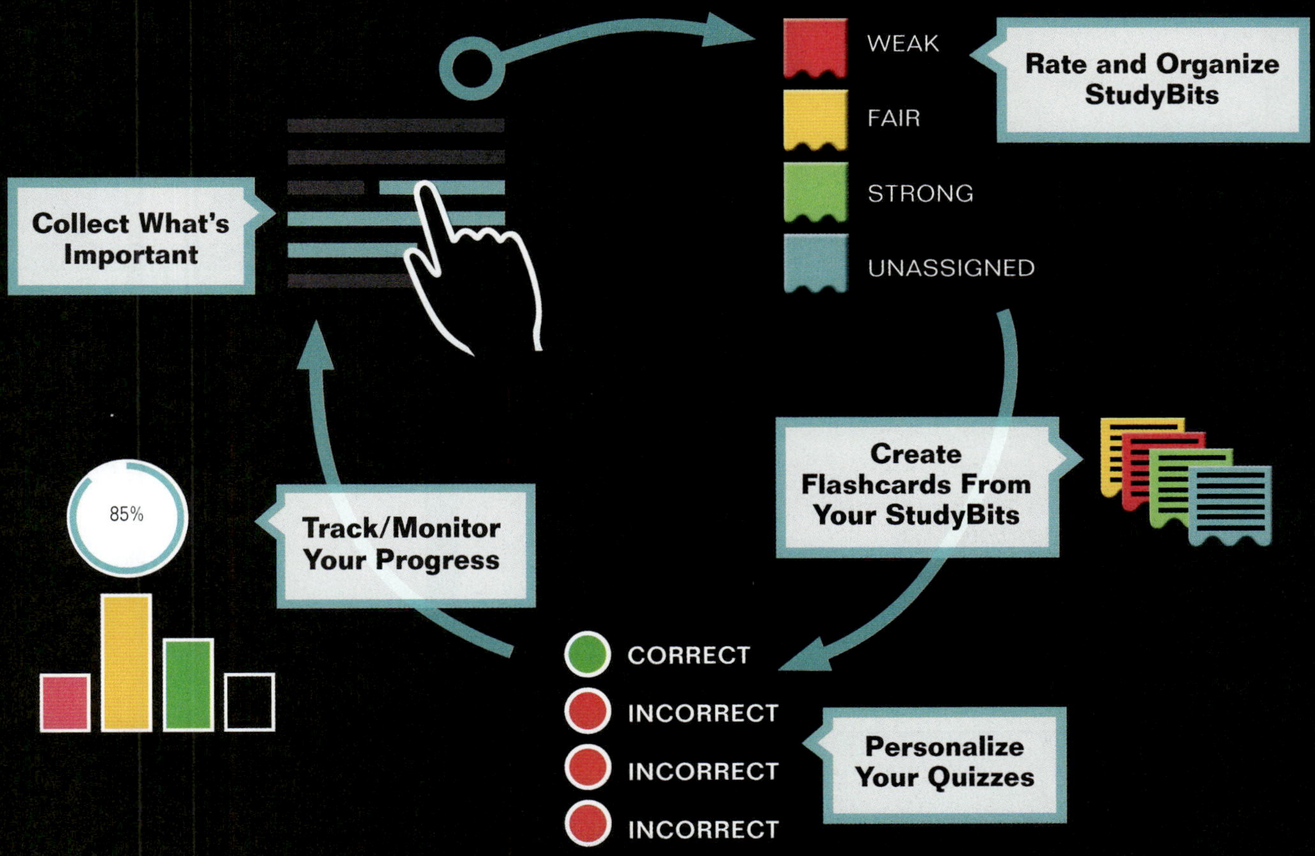

17 Late Adulthood: Physical and Cognitive Development

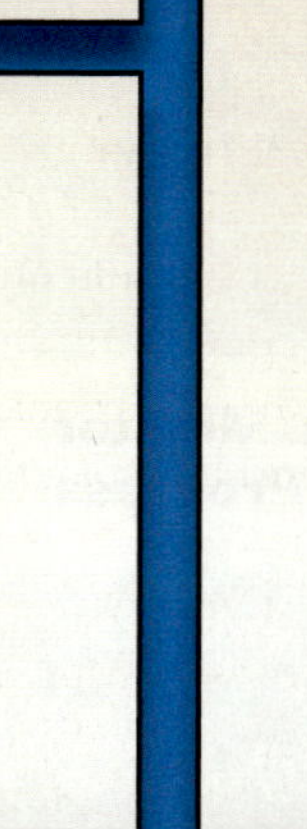

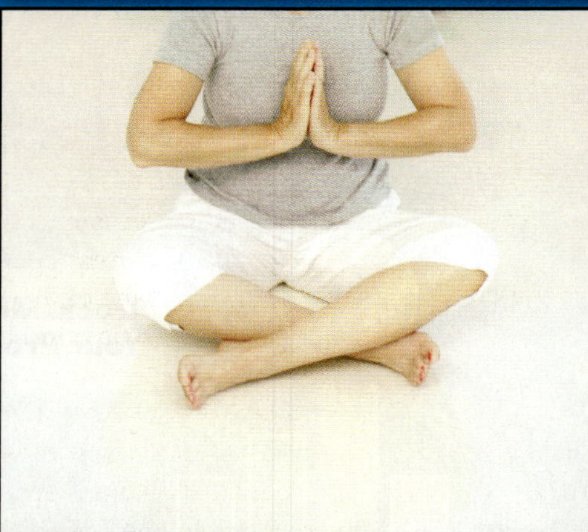

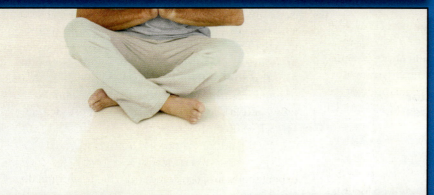

Tomas Rodriguez/Getty Images

LEARNING OUTCOMES

After studying this chapter, you will be able to . . .

 17-1 Discuss physical development in late adulthood

 17-2 Compare programmed and cellular damage theories of aging

 17-3 Identify common health concerns associated with late adulthood

 17-4 Discuss cognitive development in late adulthood

After you finish this chapter, go to **PAGE 357** for **STUDY TOOLS**

People age 65 and above are the most rapidly growing segment of the American population.

An *Agequake Is Coming*. People age 65 and above—those who are in **late adulthood**—are the most rapidly growing segment of the American population. So many people are living longer that we are in the midst of a "graying of America," an aging of the population that is having significant effects on many aspects of society.

17-1 PHYSICAL DEVELOPMENT

In 1900, only 1 person in 25 was over the age of 65. Today, that figure has more than tripled, to 1 in 8. By midcentury, more than 1 in 5 Americans will be 65 years of age or older. By the year 2050, we expect to see the percentage of Americans over the age of 75 to double (Population Estimates and Projections, 2010). To put these numbers in historical context, consider that through virtually all of human history, until the beginning of the 19th century, only a small fraction of humans lived to the age of 50.

17-1a LONGEVITY AND LIFE EXPECTANCY

One's **life span**, or **longevity**, is the length of time one can live under the best of circumstances. The life span of a species, including humans, depends on its genetic programming. With the right genes and environment, and with the good fortune to avoid serious injuries or illnesses, people have a maximum life span of about 115 years.

One's **life expectancy** refers to the number of years a person in a given population group can actually expect to live. The average European American child born 100 years ago in the United States could expect to live 47 years. The average African American at that time could expect a shorter life of 35.5 years (Andersen & Taylor, 2009). Great strides have been made in increasing life expectancy. High infant mortality rates due to diseases such as German measles, smallpox, polio, and diphtheria contributed to the lower life-expectancy rates of a century ago. These diseases have been brought under control or eradicated. Other major killers, including bacterial infections such as tuberculosis, are now largely controlled by antibiotics. Other factors that contribute to longevity include public health measures such as safer water supplies, improved dietary habits, and health care. Table 17.1 shows the life expectancy of males and females born in 2015 in various regions and countries of the world.

late adulthood the final stage of development, beginning at age 65.

life span (longevity) the maximum amount of time a person can live under optimal conditions.

life expectancy the amount of time a person can actually be expected to live in a given setting.

LIFE EXPECTANCY IN THE UNITED STATES Today, the average American newborn female can expect to live about 82 years, and the average American newborn male can expect to live about 77 years. However, there are important differences in life expectancy according to gender, race, geographic location, and health-related behavior patterns (National Center for Health Statistics, 2013). For example, the life expectancy for an Asian American woman living in an upscale county is in the upper 80s. The life expectancy for a male living in an urban environment with a high risk of homicide is in the 60s. In the case of groups that run a high risk of homicide, the ages at death of those who die in their teens and 20s are averaged in with those who live into their 70s, 80s, or 90s, bringing down the overall average for the group. As possibly expected, Americans who have greater access to health care live longer. Lower life expectancies are also commonly due to chronic illnesses

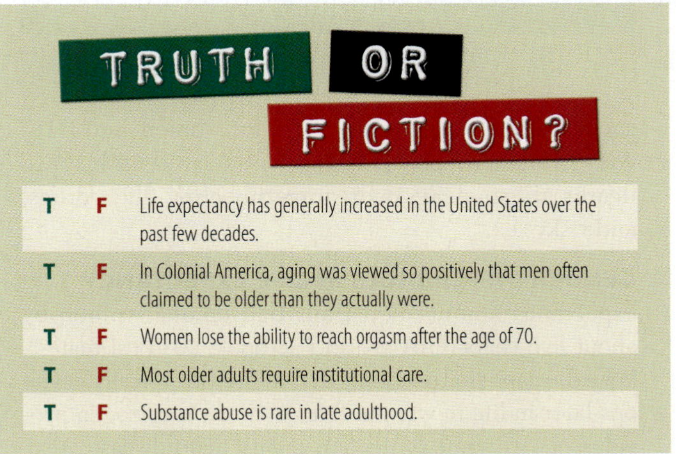

T	F	Life expectancy has generally increased in the United States over the past few decades.
T	F	In Colonial America, aging was viewed so positively that men often claimed to be older than they actually were.
T	F	Women lose the ability to reach orgasm after the age of 70.
T	F	Most older adults require institutional care.
T	F	Substance abuse is rare in late adulthood.

TABLE 17.1 LIFE EXPECTANCY AT BIRTH BY REGION, COUNTRY, AND GENDER	Males	Females
Africa		
Egypt	71	76
Kenya	62	65
Libya	74	78
South Africa	61	64
Asia		
Afghanistan	50	52
China	73	78
India	67	69
Iran	70	73
Israel	80	84
Japan	81	88
Korea, South	77	83
Pakistan	65	69
Latin America		
Argentina	74	81
Brazil	70	77
Cuba	76	81
Dominican Republic	76	80
Haiti	62	65
Jamaica	72	75
Mexico	73	79
Europe		
France	79	85
Germany	78	83
Greece	78	83
Ireland	78	83
Italy	79	85
Poland	74	88
Russia	65	77
Spain	79	85
Sweden	80	84
United Kingdom	78	83
North America		
Canada	79	85
United States	77	82

Source: CIA World Factbook (2015 Estimates).

such as diabetes and lung cancer for women, and HIV/AIDS for men. The behaviors associated with these deaths are smoking, overeating, injecting illicit drugs, and risky sex.

GENDER DIFFERENCES IN LIFE EXPECTANCY Life expectancy among men trails that among women by about five years (CIA World Factbook, 2014 estimates). Why the gap? For one thing, heart disease typically develops later in life in women than in men, as estrogen provides women some protection against heart disease. Also, men are more likely to die from accidents, cirrhosis of the liver, strokes, suicide, homicide, HIV/AIDS, and some forms of cancer. Many of these causes of death reflect unhealthful habits that are more typical of men, such as drinking, reckless behavior, and smoking.

Many men are also reluctant to have regular physical examinations or to talk over health problems with their doctors (Hartocollis, 2014). Many men avoid medical attention until problems that could have been easily prevented or treated become serious or life threatening. For example, women are more likely to examine themselves for signs of breast cancer than men are to examine their testicles for unusual lumps.

A newborn can expect to live to about the age of 79 in the United States today. Table 17.2 shows the a person's life expectancy at different ages in late adulthood. One could almost say, the older you are the longer you are likely to live. For example a 65-year-old can expect to live another 19.3 years, until about the age of 84. A 75-year-old can expect to live another 12.2 years, until about the age of 87. The reason for these extended periods is that only healthier individuals reach advanced ages to begin with.

TRUTH

(T) F Life expectancy has generally increased in the United States over the past few decades.

It is true that life expectancy has generally increased in the United States over the past few decades. However, geographic location, life style, and access to health care are all associated with dramatic differences in life expectancy.

TABLE 17.2 LIFE EXPECTANCY AT DIFFERENT AGES IN LATE ADULTHOOD

Age	Projected Years to Live
65 – 70	19.3
70 – 75	15.6
75 – 80	12.2
85 – 90	6.6
90 – 95	4.6
95 – 100	3.2
100 and over	2.3

Source: Abridged life table for the total population. (2016, February 16). *National Vital Statistics Report, 64*(2).

17-1b PHYSICAL AND SOCIAL CHANGES

After we reach our physical peak in our 20s, our biological functions begin a gradual decline. Aging also involves adapting to changing physical and social realities. "Young Turks" in the workplace become the "old guard." One-time newlyweds come to celebrate their silver and golden anniversaries. Yet aging can involve more than adjustment; it can bring about personal growth and exciting changes in direction as well. Even advanced age can bring greater harmony and integration to our personalities. However, we must learn to adapt to changes in our mental skills and abilities. Though older people's memories and fluid intelligence may not be as keen as they once were, maturity and experience frequently make them founts of wisdom.

Aging also has social aspects. Our self-concepts and behavior as "young," "middle-aged," or "old" stem in large measure from cultural beliefs. In Colonial times, "mature" people had great prestige, and men routinely claimed to be older than they were. Women, among whom reproductive capacity was valued, did not do so. By contrast, the modern era has been marked by **ageism**—prejudice against people because of their age. Stereotypes that paint older people as crotchety, sluggish, forgetful, and fixed in their ways shape the way people respond to older people and may impair their performance (Avers et al., 2011; T. D. Nelson, 2011).

TRUTH

(T) F In Colonial America, aging was viewed so positively that men often claimed to be older than they actually were.

It is true that in Colonial America, aging was viewed so positively that men often claimed to be older than they actually were. Maturity was considered a mark of prestige.

In Chapter 15, we reviewed a number of physical changes that occur as people advance from early adulthood to middle adulthood and, in a number of cases, to late adulthood (changes in the skin, hair, and nails; senses; reaction time; lung capacity; metabolism; muscle strength; bone density; aerobic capacity; blood-sugar tolerance; and ability to regulate body temperature). Here we revisit and highlight changes in sensory functioning and bone density as they apply to late adulthood.

Image Source/Getty Images

After we reach our physical peak in our 20s, our biological functions begin a gradual decline. An exception would be the previous couch potato who decides to begin aerobic activities of strength training in middle or late adulthood.

CHANGES IN SENSORY FUNCTIONING

Beginning in middle age, the lenses of the eyes become stiffer, leading to presbyopia, as discussed in Chapter 15. Chemical changes of aging can lead to vision disorders such as **cataracts** and **glaucoma**. Cataracts cloud the lenses of the eyes, reducing vision. Today, outpatient surgery for correcting cataracts is routine. If performed before the condition progresses too far, the outcome for regained sight is excellent. Glaucoma is a buildup of fluid pressure inside the eyeball. Glaucoma can lead to tunnel vision (lack of peripheral vision) or blindness. Glaucoma rarely occurs before age 40, and affects about 1 in 250 people over the age of 40, and 1 in 25

ageism prejudice against people because of their age.

cataract a condition characterized by clouding of the lens of the eye.

glaucoma a condition involving abnormally high fluid pressure in the eye.

people over 80. Rates are higher among African Americans than European Americans, and among diabetics than non-diabetics. Glaucoma is treated with medication or surgery.

The sense of hearing, especially the ability to hear higher frequencies, also declines with age. **Presbycusis** is age-related hearing loss that affects about 1 person in 3 over the age of 65 (Parham et al., 2011). Hearing ability tends to decline more quickly in men than in women. Hearing aids magnify sound and can compensate for hearing loss. The NIDCD's Ten Ways to Recognize Hearing Loss questionnaire in Figure 17.1 provides ways of recognizing hearing loss.

Taste and smell become less acute as we age. Our sense of smell decreases almost ninefold from youth to advanced late adulthood. We also lose taste buds in the tongue with aging. As a result, foods must be more strongly spiced to yield the same flavor.

BONE DENSITY Bones begin to lose density in middle adulthood, becoming more brittle and vulnerable to fracture. Bones in the spine, hip, thigh, and forearm lose the most density as we age. **Osteoporosis** is a disorder in which bones lose so much calcium that they become dangerously prone to breakage. An estimated ten million people in the United States over the age of 50 have osteoporosis of the hip (USDHHS, 2005). Osteoporosis results in more than one million bone fractures a year in the United States, the most serious of which are hip fractures (that is, breaks in the thigh bone, just below the hip joint).

presbycusis loss of acuteness of hearing due to age-related degenerative changes in the ear.

osteoporosis a disorder in which bones become more porous, brittle, and subject to fracture, due to loss of calcium and other minerals.

FIG.17.1 TEN WAYS TO RECOGNIZE HEARING LOSS

The following questions from the NIDCD* will help you determine if you need to have your hearing evaluated by a medical professional:

Yes	No	
Y	N	Do you have a problem hearing over the telephone?
Y	N	Do you have trouble following the conversation when two or more people are talking at the same time?
Y	N	Do people complain that you turn the TV volume up too high?
Y	N	Do you have to strain to understand a conversation?
Y	N	Do you have trouble hearing in a noisy background?
Y	N	Do you find yourself asking people to repeat themselves?
Y	N	Do people you talk to seem to mumble (or not speak clearly)?
Y	N	Do you misunderstand what others are saying and respond inappropriately?
Y	N	Do you have trouble understanding the speech of women and children?
Y	N	Do people get annoyed because you misunderstand what they say?

If you answered "yes" to three or more of these questions, you may want to see an ear, nose, and throat specialist or an audiologist for a hearing evaluation.

*NIDCD (National Institute on Deafness and Other Communication Disorders; Accessed August 12, 2016).

Preventing Osteoporosis: Messages from the National Osteoporosis Foundation

There is much that you can do over the course of your lifetime to promote your bone health. These same behaviors also contribute to overall health and vitality.

- **Eating a well-balanced diet, including foods such as fish, fruits and green, leafy vegetables, beans, and wheat bran.**
- **Getting enough calcium. Eating dairy products (preferably low-fat) each day, combined with the calcium from the rest of a normal diet, is enough for most individuals.**
- **Getting vitamin D. If one cannot get enough vitamin D from sunshine, fortified foods, and vitamin supplements can help make up the difference.**
- **Engaging in regular exercise. In addition to meeting recommended guidelines of at least 30 minutes a day of physical activity, strength and weight-bearing activities help build and maintain bone mass.**
- **Avoiding smoking and limiting alcohol intake. (Keep in mind, however, that most health professionals agree that a drink a day can be good for adults.)**

Source: Adapted from *Learn about Osteoporosis. National Osteoporosis Foundation*. Retrieved May 3, 2014 from http://nof.org/learn/prevention.

FIG.17.2 THE RELENTLESS MARCH OF TIME

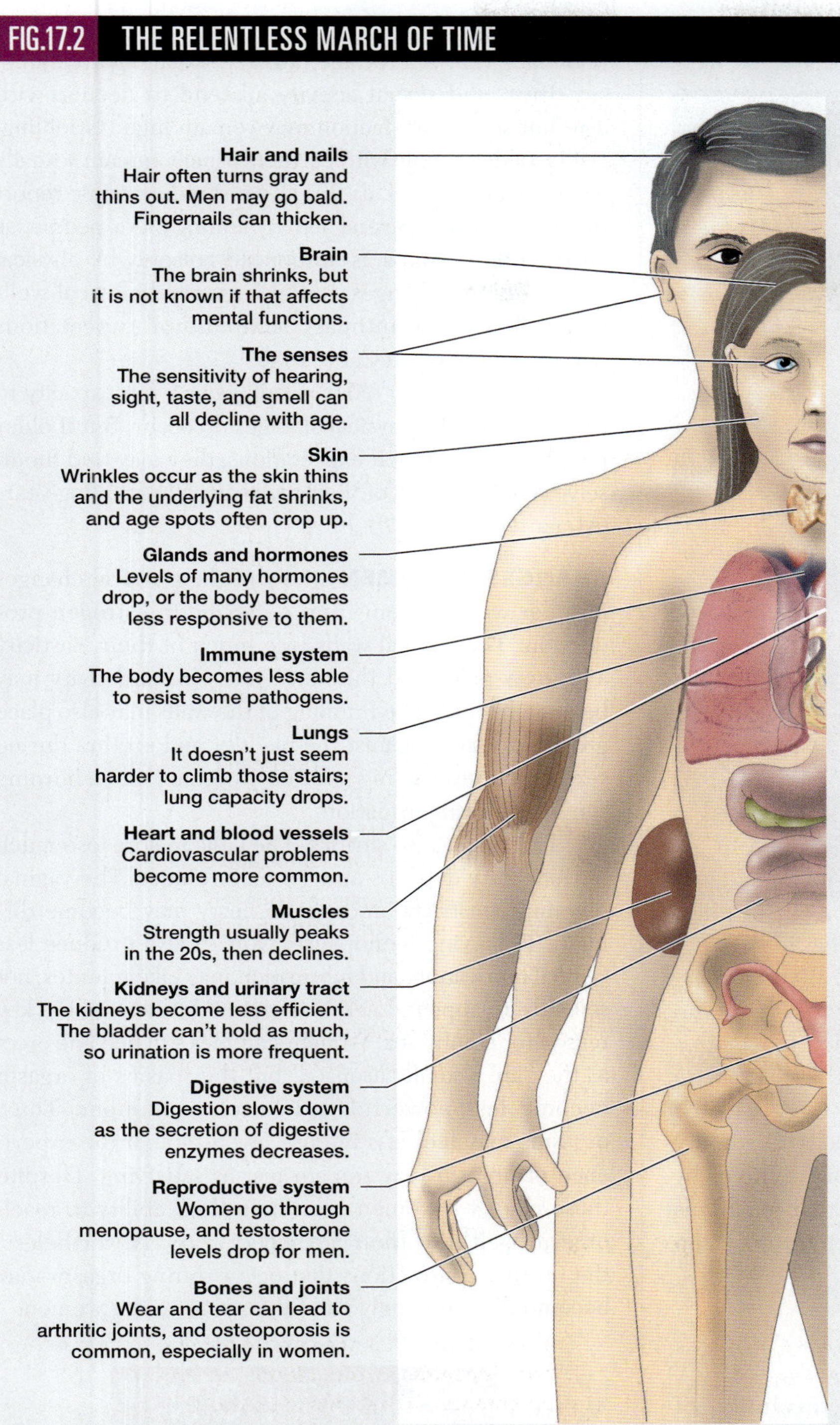

Hair and nails
Hair often turns gray and thins out. Men may go bald. Fingernails can thicken.
Brain
The brain shrinks, but it is not known if that affects mental functions.
The senses
The sensitivity of hearing, sight, taste, and smell can all decline with age.
Skin
Wrinkles occur as the skin thins and the underlying fat shrinks, and age spots often crop up.
Glands and hormones
Levels of many hormones drop, or the body becomes less responsive to them.
Immune system
The body becomes less able to resist some pathogens.
Lungs
It doesn't just seem harder to climb those stairs; lung capacity drops.
Heart and blood vessels
Cardiovascular problems become more common.
Muscles
Strength usually peaks in the 20s, then declines.
Kidneys and urinary tract
The kidneys become less efficient. The bladder can't hold as much, so urination is more frequent.
Digestive system
Digestion slows down as the secretion of digestive enzymes decreases.
Reproductive system
Women go through menopause, and testosterone levels drop for men.
Bones and joints
Wear and tear can lead to arthritic joints, and osteoporosis is common, especially in women.

Hip fractures often result in hospitalization, loss of mobility, and, in people in advanced late adulthood, even death from complications. Fifteen to 20 percent of the people who sustain a hip fracture die within a year (Brunner et al., 2003).

Osteoporosis can shorten one's stature by inches and deform one's posture, causing the curvature in the spine known as "dowager's hump." Both men and women are at risk of osteoporosis, but it poses a greater threat to women. Men typically have a larger bone mass, which provides them with more protection against the disorder. Following the decline in bone density that women experience after menopause, women stand about twice the risk of hip fractures and about eight times the risk of spine fractures that men do. But older women who engage in walking as a form of regular exercise are less likely than their sedentary counterparts to suffer hip fractures (National Osteoporosis Foundation, 2014).

17-1c SLEEP

Older people need about seven hours of sleep per night, yet sleep disorders such as insomnia and **sleep apnea** become more common in later adulthood (Wickwire et al., 2008). Sleep apnea sufferers stop breathing repeatedly during the night, causing awakenings. Apnea may be more than a sleep problem. For reasons that are not entirely clear, it is linked to increased risk of heart attacks and strokes.

Sleep problems in late adulthood may involve physical changes that bring discomfort. Sometimes they symptomize psychological disorders such as depression, anxiety, or dementia. Men with enlarged prostate glands commonly need to urinate during the night, causing awakening. Other contributing factors include loneliness, especially after the death of a close friend, spouse, or life partner.

Sleep medications are the most common treatment for insomnia (Wickwire et al., 2008). Alternatives may include keeping a regular sleep schedule, challenging exaggerated worries about the consequences of remaining awake, using relaxation techniques,

sleep apnea temporary suspension of breathing while asleep.

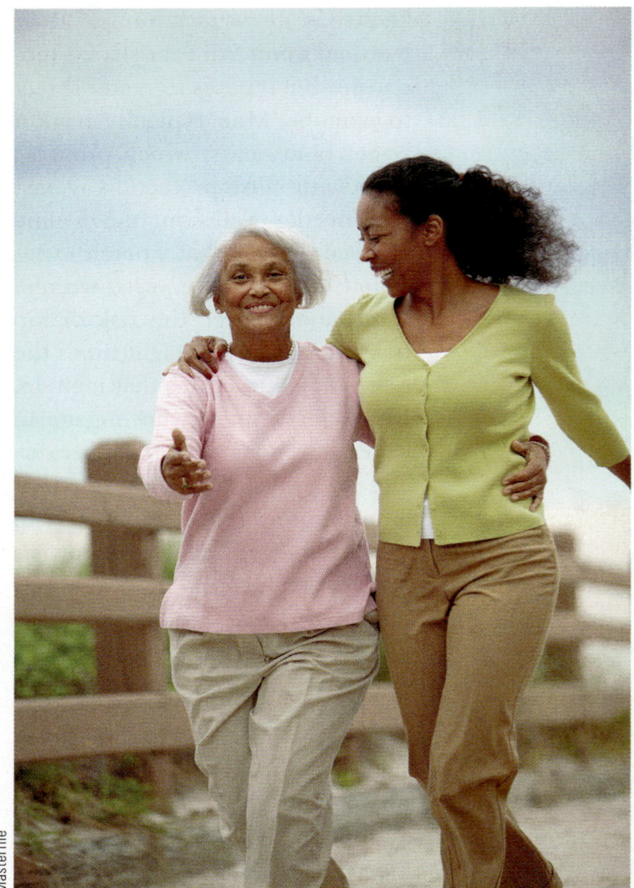

Masterfile

Exercise can increase bone density. Therefore, older women (and men) who engage in walking as regular exercise are less likely than their sedentary peers to suffer hip fractures.

and exercise. Sleep apnea may be treated with surgery to widen the upper airways that block breathing or by the use of devices such as a nose mask that maintains air pressure to keep airway passages open during sleep (Wickwire et al., 2008).

17-1d SEXUALITY

Even in the aftermath of the sexual revolution of the 1960s, many people still tie sex to reproduction. Therefore, they assume that sex is appropriate only for the young. Unfounded cultural myths suggest that older people are sexless and that older men with sexual interests are "dirty old men." If older people believe these myths, they may renounce sex or feel guilty if they remain sexually active. Older women are handicapped by a double standard of greater tolerance of continued sexuality among men.

People do not lose their sexuality as they age (Connaughton & McCabe, 2015). Sexual daydreaming, sex drive, and sexual activity all tend to decline with age, but sexual satisfaction may remain high (Griebling, 2011). Older people with partners usually remain sexually active (Thompson et al., 2011). Most older people report that they like sex. Sexual activity among older people, as among other groups, is influenced not only by physical structures and changes, but also by psychological well-being, feelings of intimacy, and cultural expectations (Connaughton & McCabe, 2015).

Although many older people retain the capacity to respond sexually, physical changes do occur. But if older people fine-tune their expectations, they may find themselves leading some of their most sexually fulfilling years (Menard et al., 2015).

CHANGES IN WOMEN Many of the physical changes in older women stem from a decline in estrogen production. The vaginal walls lose much of their elasticity and grow paler and thinner. Thus, sexual activity may become painful. The thinning of the walls may also place greater pressure against the bladder and urethra during sex, sometimes leading to urinary urgency and a burning sensation during urination.

The vagina also shrinks. The labia majora lose much of their fatty deposits and become thinner. The vaginal opening constricts, and penile entry may become difficult. Following menopause, women also produce less vaginal lubrication, and lubrication may take minutes, not seconds, to appear. Lack of adequate lubrication is a key reason for painful sex. Women's nipples still become erect as they are sexually aroused, but the spasms of orgasm become less powerful and fewer in number. Thus, orgasms may feel less intense, even though the experience of orgasm may remain just as satisfying. Despite these changes, women can retain their ability to reach orgasm well into their advanced years. Nevertheless, the uterine contractions that occur during orgasm may become discouragingly painful for some older women.

FICTION

T (F) Women lose the ability to reach orgasm after the age of 70.

It is not true that women lose the ability to reach orgasm after the age of 70. Unless women have a health problem, they can reach orgasm at any age.

CHANGES IN MEN Age-related changes tend to occur more gradually in men than in women and are not clearly connected with any one biological event. Male adolescents may achieve erection in seconds. After about age 50, men take progressively longer to achieve erection. Erections become less firm, perhaps because of lowered testosterone levels (Besiroglu et al., 2015; Luo et al., 2015).

Testosterone production usually declines gradually from about age 40 to age 60 and then begins to level off. However, the decline is not inevitable and may be related to a man's general health. Sperm production tends to decline, but viable sperm may be produced by men in their 70s, 80s, and 90s.

Nocturnal erections diminish in intensity, duration, and frequency as men age, but they do not normally disappear altogether (Besiroglu et al., 2015; Luo et al., 2015). An adolescent may require but a few minutes to regain erection and ejaculate again after a first orgasm, whereas a man in his 30s may require half an hour. Past age 50, regaining erection may require several hours.

Older men produce less ejaculate, and the contractions of orgasm become weaker and fewer. Still, an older male may enjoy orgasm as thoroughly as he did at a younger age. Following orgasm, erection subsides more rapidly than in a younger man.

PATTERNS OF SEXUAL ACTIVITY Despite decline in physical functions, older people can lead fulfilling sex lives. Years of sexual experience may more than compensate for any lessening of physical response (McCarthy & Pierpaoli, 2015; Menard et al., 2015). Frequency of sexual activity tends to decline with age because of hormonal changes, physical problems, boredom, and cultural attitudes. Yet sexuality among older people is variable. Many older people engage in sexual activity as often as or more often than when younger; some develop an aversion to sex; others lose interest.

Couples may adapt to the physical changes of aging by broadening their sexual repertoire to include more diverse forms of stimulation. The availability of a sexually interested and supportive partner may be the most important determinant of continued sexual activity (McCarthy & Pierpaoli, 2015; Menard et al., 2015).

Couples may accommodate to the physical changes of aging by broadening their sexual repertoire to include more diverse forms of stimulation. Many older people report using petting, oral–genital stimulation, sexual fantasy, pornography, anal stimulation, vibrators, and other techniques to offset problems in achieving lubrication or erection. Sexual satisfaction may be derived from manual or oral stimulation, cuddling, caressing, petting, and tenderness—all of which have been summarized as "good enough sex, or GES" (McCarthy & Pierpaoli, 2015)—as well as intercourse to orgasm. The availability of a sexually interested and supportive partner may be the most important determinant of continued sexual activity (Menard et al., 2015).

17-2 THEORIES OF AGING

So far, everyone who has lived has aged—which may not be a bad fate, considering the alternative. Although we can make lengthy lists of the things that happen as we age, we don't know exactly why they happen. Theories of aging fall into two broad categories:

- *Programmed theories* see aging as the result of genetic instructions.
- *Cellular damage theories* propose that aging results from damage to cells.

Dougal Waters/Digital Vision/Getty Images

Despite decline in physical functions, older people can have fulfilling sex lives. The nature of the general relationship, open communication, and reasonable expectations are all-important.

17-2a PROGRAMMED THEORIES OF AGING

Programmed theories of aging propose that aging and longevity are determined by a biological clock that ticks at a rate governed by genes. That is, the seeds of our own demise are carried in our genes. Evidence supporting a genetic link to aging comes in part from studies showing that longevity tends to run in families (Montesanto et al., 2011). For example, the siblings of centenarians are more likely than members of the general population to live to be 100 themselves (Barzilai & Atzmon, 2014).

But why should organisms carry "suicidal" genes? Programmed aging theorists believe that it would be adaptive for species to survive long enough to reproduce and transmit their genes to future generations. From the evolutionary perspective, there would be no advantage to the species (and probably a disadvantage given limited food supplies) to repair cell machinery and body tissues to maintain life indefinitely.

One theory focuses on the built-in limits of cell division. After dividing about 50 times, human cells cease dividing and eventually die (Goldsmith, 2016). Researchers find clues to the limits of cell division in **telomeres**, the protective segments of DNA at the tips of chromosomes. Telomeres shrink each time cells divide. When the loss of telomeres reaches a critical point after a number of cell divisions, the cell may no longer be able to function. The length of the telomeres for a species may determine the number of times a cell can divide and survive.

Another theory focuses on the endocrine system, which releases hormones into the bloodstream. Hormonal changes foster age-related changes such as puberty and menopause. As we age, stress hormones, including corticosteroids and adrenaline, are left at elevated levels following illnesses, making the body more vulnerable to chronic conditions such as diabetes, osteoporosis, and heart disease (Banks et al., 2010). The changes in production of stress hormones over time may be preprogrammed by genes.

Immunological theory holds that the immune system is preset to decline by an internal biological clock (Jin, 2010). For example, the production of antibodies declines with age, rendering the body less able to fight off infections. Age-related changes in the immune system also increase the risk of cancer and may contribute to general deterioration.

programmed theories of aging views of aging based on the concept that the processes of aging are governed, at least in part, by genetic factors.

telomeres protective segments of DNA located at the tips of chromosomes.

immunological theory a theory of aging that holds that the immune system is preset to decline by an internal biological clock.

cellular damage theories of aging views of aging based on the concept that internal bodily changes and external environmental insults, such as carcinogens and poisons, cause cells and organ systems to malfunction, leading to death.

wear-and-tear theory a theory of aging that suggests that over time our bodies become less capable of repairing themselves.

free-radical theory a theory of aging that attributes aging to damage caused by the accumulation of unstable molecules called free radicals.

cross-linking theory a theory of aging that holds that the stiffening of body proteins eventually breaks down bodily processes, leading to aging.

17-2b CELLULAR DAMAGE THEORIES OF AGING

Programmed theories assume that internal bodily processes are preset to age by genes. **Cellular damage theories of aging** propose that internal bodily changes and external environmental assaults (such as carcinogens and toxins) cause cells and organ systems to malfunction, leading to death (Velarde et al., 2012). For example, the **wear-and-tear theory** suggests that over the years our bodies—as machines that wear out through use—become less capable of repairing themselves.

The **free-radical theory** attributes aging to damage caused by the accumulation of unstable molecules called *free radicals*. Free radicals are produced during metabolism by oxidation, possibly damaging cell proteins, membranes, and DNA. Most free radicals are naturally disarmed by nutrients and enzymes called *antioxidants*. Most antioxidants are either made by the body or found in food. As we age, our bodies produce fewer antioxidants. People whose diets are rich in antioxidants may be less likely to develop heart disease and some cancers (Labat-Robert & Robert, 2014).

As we age, cell proteins bind to one another in a process called *cross-linking*, thereby toughening tissues. Cross-linking stiffens collagen—the connective tissue supporting tendons, ligaments, cartilage, and bone. One result is coarse, dry skin. (Flavored animal collagen, or gelatin, is better known by the brand name *Jell-O*.) **Cross-linking theory** holds that the stiffening of body proteins accelerates and eventually breaks down bodily processes, leading to some of the effects of aging (Saito & Marumo, 2010). The immune system combats cross-linking, but becomes less able to do so as we age.

In considering the many theories of aging, we should note that aging is an extremely complex biological process that may not be explained by any single theory or cause. Aging may involve a combination of these and other factors.

Tim Pannell/Corbis/VCG/Getty Images

One cellular damage theory of aging attributes aging to the accumulation of molecules called free radicals. Free radicals may also be produced by exposure to environmental agents such as ultraviolet light, extreme heat, pesticides, and air pollution. Should we hide indoors? No, sunlight also provides essential vitamin D. As the philosopher said: "Moderation in all things."

The population of nursing homes is made up largely of people age 80 and older. Yet if older adults live long enough, nearly half will eventually require some form of nursing or home health care.

It is also untrue that most older Americans spend their later years in a retirement community. The majority of older adults remain in their own communities after retirement. Moreover, despite beliefs that most older people are impoverished, Americans aged 65 and above are actually less likely than the general population to live under the poverty level. The institution of the Social Security and Medicare programs was of great benefit to older Americans.

17-3 HEALTH CONCERNS AND AGING

Though aging takes a toll on our bodies, many gerontologists believe that disease is not inevitable. They distinguish between *normal aging* and *pathological aging*. In **normal aging**, physiological processes decline slowly with age and the person is able to enjoy many years of health and vitality into late adulthood. In **pathological aging**, chronic diseases or degenerative processes, such as heart disease, diabetes, and cancer, lead to disability or premature death. Older persons typically need more health care than younger persons. Though people over the age of 65 make up about 12% of the population, they occupy 25% of the hospital beds. As the numbers of older people increase in the 21st century, so will the cost of health care.

Medicare, a federally controlled health insurance program for older Americans and the disabled, only partially subsidizes the healthcare needs of these groups. Another government program, *Medicaid*, covers a portion of the healthcare costs of people of all ages who are otherwise unable to afford coverage. Many older adults use both programs.

It is not true that most older adults require institutional care, such as nursing homes or residential care facilities. More than two of three adults age 65 and older live in their own homes. Less than 10% of older adults live in nursing homes or other long-term care facilities.

FICTION

T (F) Most older adults require institutional care.

It is not true that most older adults require institutional care. More than two-thirds of adults over the age of 65 live in their own homes.

In 1900, older people were more likely to die from infectious diseases such as influenza and pneumonia than they are today. Today, older people are at greater risk of dying from chronic diseases such as heart disease and cancer. More than four out of five people over the age of 65 have at least one chronic health problem (Heron, 2007). Some, like varicose veins, are minor. Others, like heart disease, pose serious health risks. Figure 17.3 shows the percentages of people age 65 and older who are affected by common chronic health conditions. While longevity is increasing, so too are the number of years older persons are living with one or more chronic health problems.

normal aging processes of aging that represent a gradual decline of systems and body functions, enabling people to enjoy health and vitality well into late adulthood.

pathological aging aging in which chronic diseases or degenerative processes, such as heart disease, diabetes, and cancer, lead to disability or premature death.

FIG.17.3 CHRONIC HEALTH CONDITIONS AMONG PEOPLE AGE 65 AND OVER

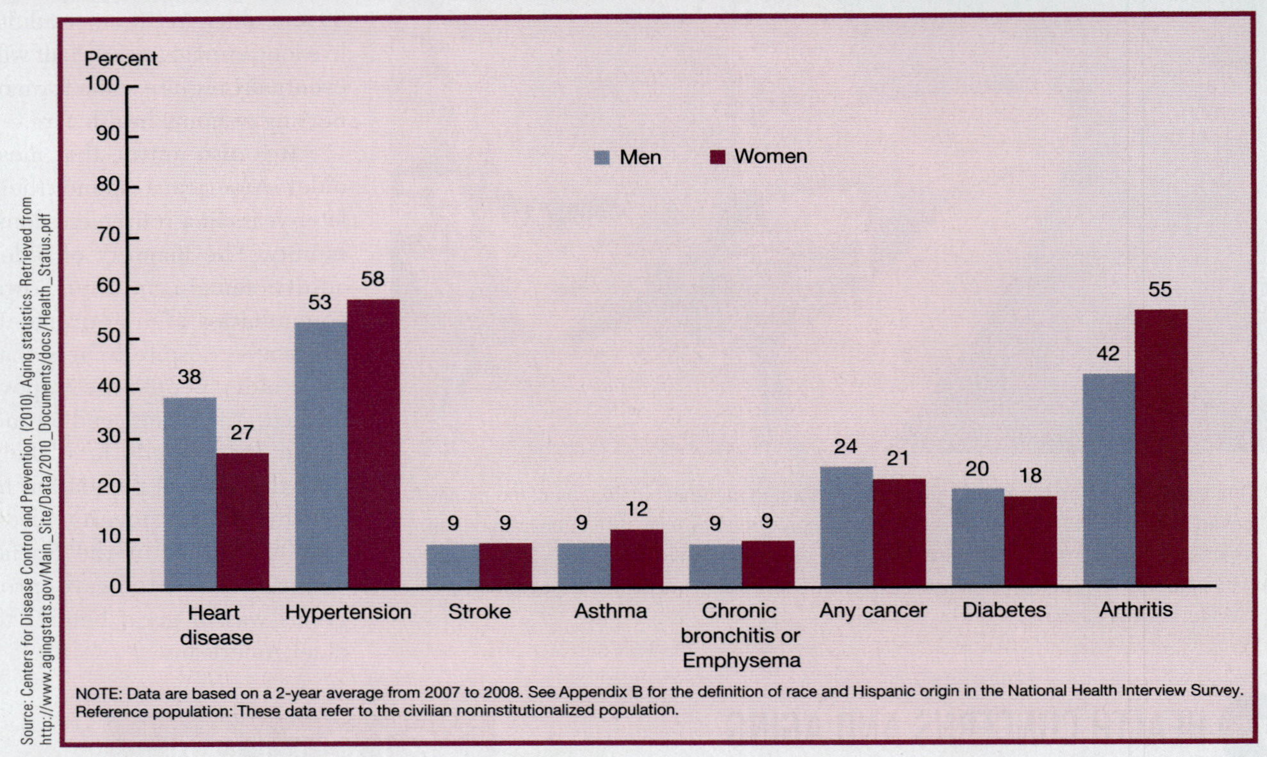

Six of the seven leading causes of death among older Americans are chronic conditions.

17-3a HEART DISEASE, CANCER, AND STROKE

The three major causes of death of Americans age 65 and older are heart disease, cancer, and respiratory diseases (see Figure 17.4). Cancer is the leading cause of death in women between the ages of 40 and 79, and men between the ages of 60 and 79, but heart disease is the nation's leading cause of death among both men and women beyond the age of 80.

FIG.17.4 LEADING CAUSES OF DEATH AMONG U.S. ADULTS, MEN AND WOMEN, 65 YEARS AND OVER

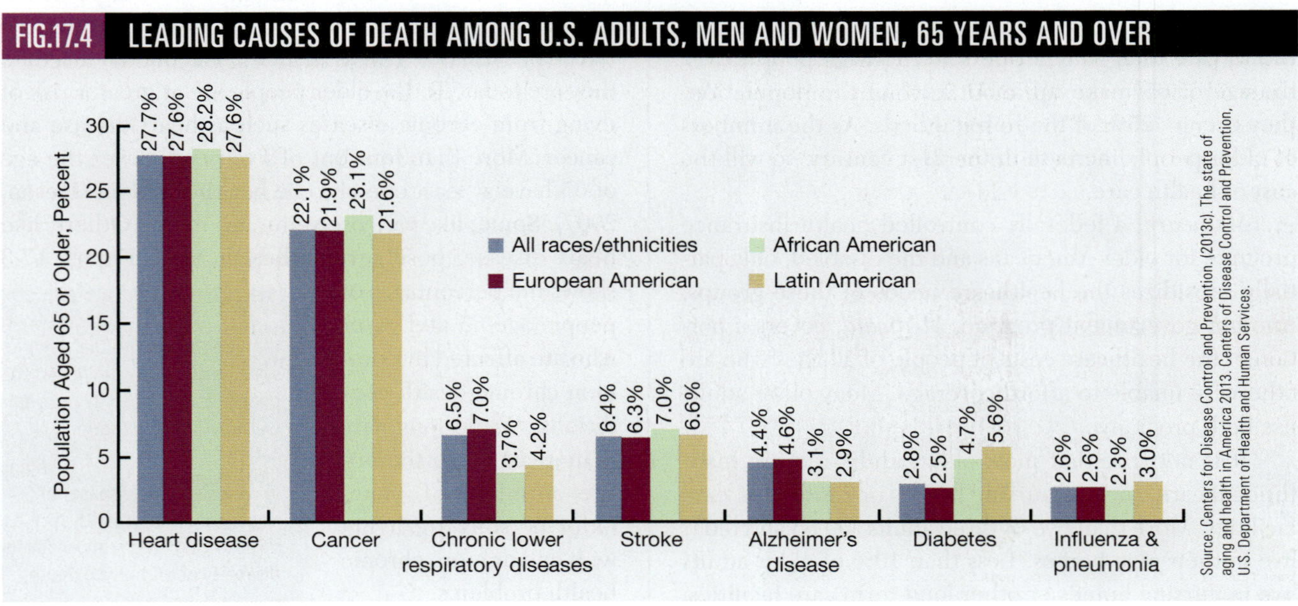

Is Calorie Restriction the Fountain of Youth?

Image Source/Getty Images

Restricting calories by approximately 30% may trigger antiaging responses that evolved to increase the chances of survival when food is scarce. For example, calorie restriction in humans, nonhuman primates, and other mammals lowers blood pressure, cholesterol, and blood-sugar and insulin levels. It strengthens the immune system and lowers the fat mass (Everitt et al., 2010). Calorie restriction also fends off Alzheimer-like symptoms in rhesus monkeys.

In laboratory experiments, mice were fed a diet that was 30% to 40% lower in calories than normal but contained all necessary nutrients. The development of chronic diseases and cancers was retarded, and the mice lived 50% beyond their normal life spans.

Raising levels of the hormone DHEAS (dehydroepiandrosterone sulfate) may be one way that calorie restriction reduces the risk of cancer and improves immune system functioning. DHEAS production usually begins to decline after approximately age 30, dipping to as low as 5% to 15% of peak levels by age 60. DHEAS levels are higher than normal in long-lived men and in rhesus monkeys with calorie-restricted diets.

It remains to be seen whether, and by how much, calorie restriction extends the life span of people who have access to modern health care. Moreover, it is difficult enough for many people to keep their weight within normal limits. How willing would we be to lower our calorie intake further? Researchers are therefore also seeking alternate ways of triggering the antiaging responses caused by calorie restriction.

Recent findings show that hypertension (high blood pressure) is the one chronic health condition shared by well over half of U.S. women and men. The percents in Table 17.3 are higher than those in Figure 17.3 because they include people whose blood pressure readings are normal due to taking blood pressure medication.

TABLE 17.3 PERCENT OF PERSONS WITH HYPERTENSION (HIGH BLOOD PRESSURE) AND WHO ARE TAKING MEDICATION FOR THE CONDITION

Ages	Women	Men
65 – 74	66.7%	61.7%
75 and over	79.3%	75.1%

Source: Older Persons' Health. (2016). National Center for Health Statistics. http://www.cdc.gov/nchs/fastats/older-american-health.htm#

The risk of most cancers rises as we age because the immune system becomes less able to rid the body of precancerous and cancerous cells. Many older people are not adequately screened or treated for cancer or heart disease. One reason for the gap in diagnosis and treatment is discrimination against the elderly on the part of some health professionals (Goodheart, 2012; Sabbadini et al., 2012).

17-3b ARTHRITIS

Arthritis is joint inflammation that results from conditions affecting the structures inside and surrounding the joints. Symptoms progress from swelling, pain, and stiffness to loss of function. Children can also be affected by arthritis, but it is more common with advancing age. Arthritis is more common in women than men and in African Americans than European Americans. Osteoarthritis and rheumatoid arthritis are the two most common forms of arthritis.

Osteoarthritis is a painful, degenerative disease characterized by wear and tear on joints. By the age of 60, more than half of Americans show some signs of the disease. Among people over the age of 65, two of three have the disease. The joints most commonly affected are in the knees, hips, fingers, neck, and lower back. Osteoarthritis is caused by erosion of cartilage, the pads of fibrous tissue that cushion the ends of bones. As cartilage wears down, bones grind together, causing pain. Osteoarthritis is more common among obese people because excess weight adds to the load on the hip and knee joints. Health professionals use over-the-counter anti-inflammatory drugs (aspirin, acetaminophen, ibuprofen, naproxen) and prescription anti-inflammatory drugs to help relieve pain and discomfort. In severe cases, joint replacement surgery may be needed. Specific exercises are also sometimes prescribed.

arthritis inflammation of the joints.

osteoarthritis a painful, degenerative disease characterized by wear and tear on joints.

Rheumatoid arthritis is characterized by chronic inflammation of the membranes that line the joints because the body's immune system attacks its own tissues. The condition affects the entire body. It can produce unrelenting pain and eventually lead to severe disability. Bones and cartilage may also be affected. Onset of the disease usually occurs between the ages of 40 and 60. Anti-inflammatory drugs are used to treat it.

FICTION

T (F) Substance abuse is rare in late adulthood.

It is not true that substance abuse is rare in late adulthood, but the motives for use among older adults differ from those we find among teenagers and early adults.

17-3c SUBSTANCE ABUSE

Abuse or misuse of medication (prescription and over-the-counter drugs), much of which is unintentional, poses a serious health threat to older Americans. Forty percent of prescription drugs in the United States are taken by people age 60 and older, and more than half of them take two to five medications daily (Johnson-Greene & Inscore, 2005). Among the most commonly used drugs are blood pressure medication, tranquilizers, sleeping pills, and antidepressants. Taken correctly, prescription drugs can be of help. If used incorrectly, they can be harmful.

Millions of older adults are addicted to, or risk becoming addicted to, prescription drugs, especially tranquilizers. About a quarter of a million older adults are hospitalized each year because of adverse drug reactions. Reasons include the following (Coffey et al., 2011):

1. *The dosage of drugs is too high.* Because bodily functions slow with age (such as the ability of the liver and kidneys to clear drugs out of the body), the same amount of drug can have stronger effects and last longer in older people.
2. *Some people may misunderstand directions or be unable to keep track of their usage.*
3. *Many older persons have more than one doctor, and treatment plans may not be coordinated.*

rheumatoid arthritis a painful, degenerative disease characterized by chronic inflammation of the membranes that line the joints.

Sean Murphy/Getty Images

What not to do! Older people who fall, especially women, frequently fracture their hips and die within a year or so.

Although alcohol consumption is lower overall among older people compared to younger adults, many older adults suffer from long-term alcoholism. However, the health risks of alcohol abuse increase with age. The slowdown in the metabolic rate reduces the body's ability to metabolize alcohol, increasing the likelihood of intoxication. The combination of alcohol and other drugs, including prescription drugs, can be dangerous or even lethal. Alcohol can also lessen or intensify the effects of prescription drugs.

17-3d ACCIDENTS

Though accidents can occur at any age, older people face greater risks of unintentional injuries from falls, motor vehicle accidents, residential fires, and nonfatal poisoning. Accidents are the ninth leading cause of death among older Americans. Falls are especially dangerous for older adults with osteoporosis because of the increased risks of fractures ("Falls among Older Adults," 2013).

Many accidents involving older adults could be prevented by equipping the home with safety features such as railings and nonskid floors. Wearing proper glasses and using hearing aids can reduce the risk of accidents resulting from vision or hearing problems, including many motor vehicle accidents. Adherence to safe driving speeds is especially important among older drivers because they have slower reaction times than do younger drivers.

17-3e DEMENTIA AND ALZHEIMER'S DISEASE

Dementia is a condition characterized by dramatic deterioration of mental abilities involving thinking, memory, judgment, and reasoning. Dementia is not a consequence of normal aging, but of disease processes that damage brain tissue. Some causes of dementia include brain infections, such as meningitis, HIV, and encephalitis; chronic alcoholism, strokes, and tumors (see Figure 17.5). The most common cause of dementia is **Alzheimer's disease (AD)**, a progressive brain disease affecting four to five million Americans.

The risk of AD increases dramatically with age, and it is expected that the 21st century will see a rapid rise in the prevalence of Alzheimer's disease in the United States (see Figure 17.6). About 1 in 10 Americans over the age of 65 has AD, jumping to more than 1 in 2 among those 75 to 84 years old. AD is rare in people under the age of 65 (Alzheimer's Disease Statistics, 2011). Although some dementias may be reversible, especially those caused by tumors and treatable infections and those that result from depression or substance abuse, the dementia resulting from AD is progressive and irreversible.

FIG.17.6 PROJECTION OF THE NUMBER OF CASES OF ALZHEIMER'S DISEASE IN THE UNITED STATES BY AGE GROUP

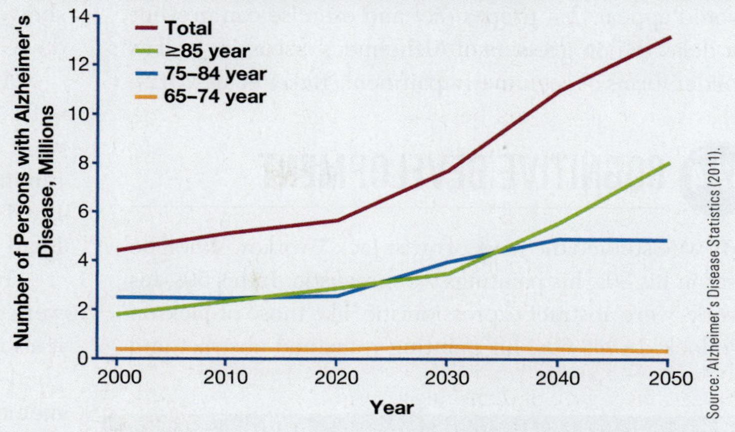

The number of people afflicted with Alzheimer's disease is expected to mushroom in coming decades.

AD is the fifth leading killer of older Americans. It progresses in several stages. At first there are subtle cognitive and personality changes in which people with AD have trouble managing finances and recalling recent events. As AD progresses, people find it harder to manage daily tasks, select clothes, recall names and addresses, and drive. Later, they have trouble using the bathroom and maintaining hygiene. They no longer recognize family and friends or speak in full sentences. They may become restless, agitated, confused, and aggressive. They may get lost in stores, parking lots, even their own homes. They may experience hallucinations or paranoid delusions, believing that others are attempting to harm them. People with AD may eventually become unable to walk or communicate and become completely dependent on others.

Although the cause or causes of AD remain a mystery, researchers believe that both environmental and genetic factors are involved (Hiltunen et al., 2011). It is possible that the accumulation of plaque causes the memory loss and other symptoms of AD, but experiments with nonhumans suggest that memory deficits may also precede the formation of plaque (Jacobsen et al., 2006).

Medicines may help improve memory functions in people with AD, but their effects are modest at best. Researchers are investigating whether regular use of anti-inflammatory drugs and antioxidants may lower the risk of developing AD by preventing the brain inflammation associated with AD (Vina et al., 2011).

FIG.17.5 CAUSES OF DEMENTIA

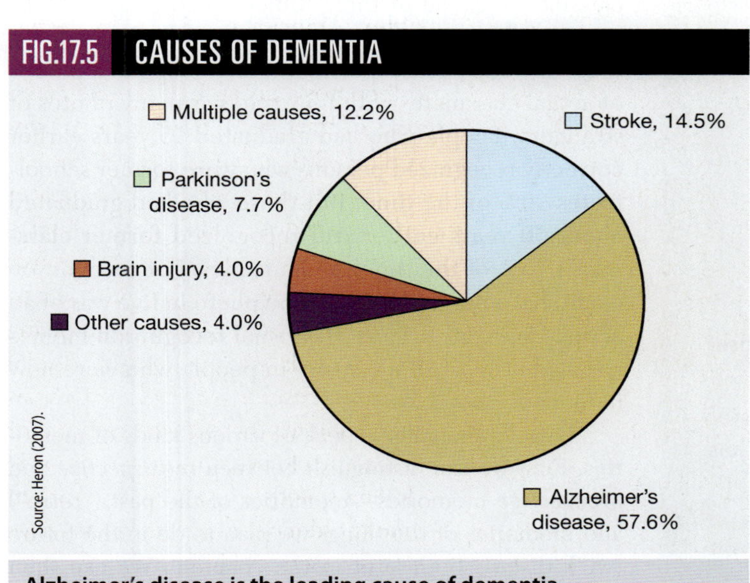

Alzheimer's disease is the leading cause of dementia.

dementia a condition characterized by deterioration of cognitive functioning.

Alzheimer's disease (AD) a severe form of dementia characterized by memory lapses, confusion, emotional instability, and progressive loss of cognitive functioning.

Fish (or omega-3 fatty acid food supplements) may help prevent or delay the progress of AD (Hooijmans et al., 2012). As in so many other chronic health conditions, it would appear that proper diet and exercise can prevent or delay the progression of Alzheimer's disease as well as milder forms of cognitive impairment (Baker et al., 2012).

17-4 COGNITIVE DEVELOPMENT

My wife studied the work of artist Jack Tworkov. When he was in his 30s, his paintings were realistic. In his 50s, his works were abstract expressionistic, like those of Jackson Pollock. In his 60s, his painting remained abstract and became hard-edged with geometric precision. At the age of 79, two years before his death, he was experimenting with a loosely flowing calligraphic style that he never showed to the public. It was in the early stages of development.

Although Tworkov's body was in decline, he told my wife, "Every morning I go to the easel in a fever." He wore a T-shirt and blue jeans, and something about him reminded me of the self I had projected as a teenager. But Tworkov seemed more at ease in his attire at 79 than I had been at 16.

Tworkov was fortunate in that his cognitive processes were clear. Given the scores of new works he showed us, it also appeared that his processing speed had remained good—or at least good enough. His visual and motor memory and his capacity to rivet his attention to a task all remained superb. All these skills are part of what we labeled *fluid intelligence* in Chapter 15, and they are most vulnerable to decline in late adulthood (Salthouse, 2011). We had no personal way of comparing these skills to what they were 20 or 40 years earlier, but based simply on what we saw, we were stunned at his ability.

Crystallized intelligence can continue to improve throughout much of late adulthood (Salthouse, 2011). However, all cognitive skills, on average, tend to decline in advanced age.

How Do I Know If It's Alzheimer's Disease?

Some change in memory is normal as we grow older, but the warning signs of Alzheimer's disease are more than simple memory lapses. According to the National Institute on Aging, someone with Alzheimer's disease may experience one or more of the following signs:

- **Has difficulty with new learning and making new memories.**
- **Has trouble finding words—may substitute or make up words that sound like or mean something like the forgotten word.**
- **Loses spark or zest for life—does not start anything.**
- **Loses memory for recent events.**
- **Loses judgment about money.**
- **Has shorter attention span and less motivation to stay with an activity.**
- **Easily loses way going to familiar places.**
- **Resists change or new things.**
- **Has trouble organizing and thinking logically.**
- **Asks repetitive questions.**
- **Withdraws, loses interest, is irritable and not as sensitive to others' feelings, is uncharacteristically angry when frustrated or tired.**
- **Takes longer to do routine chores and becomes upset if rushed or if something unexpected happens.**

If someone has several or even most of the signs listed above, it does not necessarily mean that he or she has Alzheimer's disease. Consult a health professional.

Source: National Institutes of Health's National Institute on Aging, *About Alzheimer's Disease: Symptoms*. Retrieved from http://www.nia.nih.gov/alzheimers/topics/symptoms

17-4a MEMORY: REMEMBRANCE OF THINGS PAST—AND FUTURE

In a classic study of memory, Harry Bahrick and his colleagues (1975) sought to find out how well high school graduates would recognize photographs of their classmates. Some of their subjects had graduated 15 years earlier, and others had been out of school for some 50 years. The experimenters interspersed photos of actual classmates with four times as many photos of strangers. People who had graduated 15 years earlier correctly recognized persons who were former schoolmates 90% of the time. But those who had graduated about 50 years earlier still recognized former classmates 75% of the time. A chance level of recognition would have been only 20% (one photo in five was of an actual classmate). Thus, the visual recognition memories had lasted half a century in people who were now in late adulthood.

Developmentalists speak of various kinds of memories. First we can distinguish between *retrospective* and *prospective* memories—memories of the past ("retro") and memories of the things we plan to do in the future (we'll discuss both later in the chapter). We can then divide retrospective memories into explicit and implicit

"Do we remember who is the author of the play *Hamlet?* That is the question."

AlgolOnline / Alamy Stock Photo

memories. **Explicit memories** are of specific information, such as things we did or things that happened to us (called episodic or autobiographical memories) and general knowledge, such as the author of *Hamlet* (semantic memory). **Implicit memories** are more automatic and recall the performance of tasks such as reciting the alphabet or multiplication tables, riding a bicycle, or using a doorknob.

Older adults often complain that they struggle to remember the names of people they know, even people they know very well. They are frustrated by the awareness that they knew the name yesterday, perhaps even a half hour ago, but "now" it is gone. When they do recall it, or another person reminds them of the name, they think, "Of course!" and perhaps belittle themselves for forgetting. An experiment with young adults and adults in their 70s found that the older adults did have a disproportionate difficulty naming pictures of public figures, but not of uncommon objects (Rendell et al., 2005). It seems that the working memories of older adults hold less information simultaneously than the working memories of young adults. Perhaps, then, when they are picturing the person whose name they forget, or thinking about that person engaged in some activity, the picture or activity momentarily displaces the name (Braver & West, 2008).

The temporal memory of older adults—that is, their recall of the order in which events have occurred—may become confused (Blachstein et al., 2012). Older adults may have difficulty discriminating actual events from illusory events (M. K. Johnson et al., 2012).

Older adults usually do not fare as well as younger adults in tasks that measure explicit memory, but they tend to do as well, or nearly as well, in tasks that assess implicit memory (Mitchell & Bruss, 2003). Implicit memory tasks tend to be automatic and do not require any conscious effort. They may reflect years of learning and repetition. Examples include one's memory of multiplication tables or the alphabet. I could ask you which letter comes after p or to recite the alphabet. The second task would be easier because that is the way in which you learned, and overlearned, the 26 letters of the alphabet.

It is said that you never forget how to ride a bicycle or to use a keyboard; these are also implicit memories—in these cases, sensorimotor habits.

Daniel Schacter (1992) illustrates implicit memory with the story of a woman with amnesia who was found wandering the streets. The police picked her up and found that she could not remember who she was or anything else about her life, and she had no identification. After extensive fruitless questioning, the police hit on the idea of asking her to dial phone numbers—any number at all. Although the woman did not "know" what she was doing, she dialed her mother's number. She could not make her mother's number explicit, but dialing it was a habit, and she remembered it *implicitly*.

ASSOCIATIVE MEMORY We use associative learning, and associative memory, to remember that the written letter A has the sound of an A. We also use associative memory to develop a sight vocabulary; that is, we associate the written word *the* with the sound of the word; we do not decode it as we read. In these cases we usually learn by rote rehearsal, or repetition. But we also often use elaborative rehearsal, which is a more complex strategy that makes learning meaningful, to retrieve the associated spellings for spoken words. For example, we may remember to recall the rule "*i* before *e* except after *c*" to retrieve the correct spelling of *retrieve*.

It turns out that aging has a more detrimental effect on associative memory than on memory for single items (Naveh-Benjamin et al., 2007). For example, older adults have greater difficulty discriminating between new and already experienced combinations of items on an associative recognition task—that is, recognizing pairs of words that have been presented before—than between new and already experienced single items on an item recognition task (Light et al., 2004). Various possibilities have been hypothesized to explain the age-related

explicit memory memory for specific information, including autobiographical information, such as what you had for breakfast, and general knowledge, such as state capitals.

implicit memory automatic memories based on repetition and apparently not requiring any conscious effort to retrieve.

deficit in associative memory. One is an impairment in the initial binding or learning phase of individual pieces of information when the individual is attempting to encode them (Naveh-Benjamin et al., 2003). According to the binding hypothesis, older adults are impaired primarily in associating items with one another, but not in remembering individual items (Cohn et al., 2008). A second hypothesis states that the specific impairment is in recollection when the individual attempts to retrieve the information (Yonelinas, 2002), which may reflect poor binding during encoding, poor use of strategic processes during retrieval, or both.

Research by Melanie Cohn and her colleagues (2008) suggests that impairments in associative memory among older adults represent problems in binding information, recollection, and use of effective strategies for retrieval (such as creating sentences that use both members of a pair of words as they are presented). For example, if one member of a pair is "man" and another is "cigarette," an elaborative strategy for recollecting the pair could be to rapidly construct the sentence, "The man refuses to smoke a cigarette." Cohn and her colleagues believe that these cognitive developments "are consistent with neurobiological models" of memory that focus on the frontal and medial temporal lobes of the brain. The frontal regions—the executive center of the brain—are involved in directing one's attention and organizing information and strategic processes. The medial temporal lobe binds elements to form memory traces, recovers information in response to use of proper memory cues, and is therefore a key to recollection. Neurological research shows that deterioration is evident in aging in the frontal lobes and to a lesser degree in the medial temporal lobe, thus logically impairing binding, recollection, and the use of effective strategies for the retrieval of information.

LONG-TERM MEMORY

Long-term memory has no known inherent limits. Memories may reside there for a lifetime, to be recalled with the proper cues. But long-term memories are also subject to distortion, bias, and even decay.

Harry Bahrick and his colleagues (2008) administered questionnaires to 267 alumni of Ohio Wesleyan University, who had graduated anywhere from 1 to 50 years earlier. Subjects thus ranged in age from early adulthood to late adulthood. They were asked to recall their college grades, and their recollections were checked against their actual grades. Of 3,967 grades, 3,025 were recalled correctly. Figure 17.7 relates correct responses to the age of the respondent. The number of correct recollections fell off with the age of the respondent, due, generally, to errors of omission—that is, leaving items blank rather than entering the wrong grade. As a matter of fact, graduates who were out of school more than 40 years entered no more wrong grades, on average, than those who were out of school eight years or so. The researchers found a grade-inflation bias: 81% of entries of the wrong grade inflated the true grade.

In typical studies of long-term memory, researchers present older adults with timelines that list ages from early childhood to the present day and ask them to fill in key events and to indicate how old they were at the time. Using this technique, people seem to recall events from the second and third decades of life in greatest detail and with the most emotional intensity (Glück & Bluck, 2007). These include early romances (or their

FIG.17.7 MEMORY FOR COLLEGE GRADES, 1 TO 50 YEARS LATER

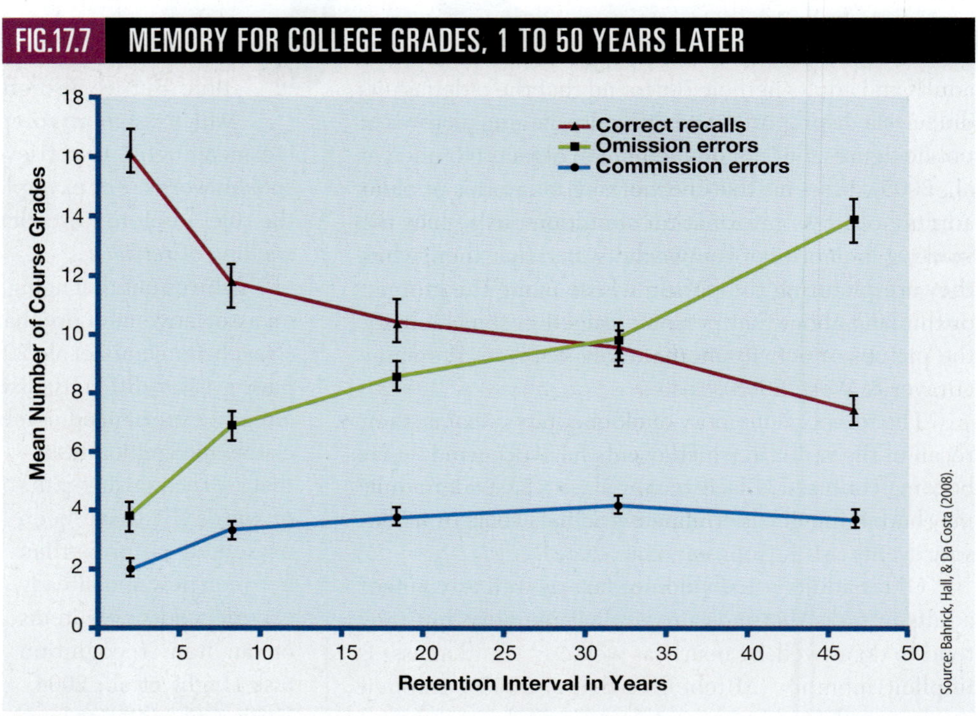

Mean number of correctly recalled grades, omission errors, and commission errors as a function of retention interval.

absence), high school days, music groups and public figures, sports heroes, "life dreams," and early disappointments. Many psychologists look to psychological explanations for these findings, and, considering "coming of age" and the development of "identity" are common characteristics of the second and third decades of life, they may be correct in their pursuit. But note that sex hormones also have their strongest effects in adolescence and early adulthood, and the secretion of these hormones is connected with the release of neurotransmitters that are involved in memory formation (Lupien et al., 2007).

PROSPECTIVE MEMORY Why do we need electronic organizers, desk calendars, and shopping lists? To help us remember the things we have planned to do. **Retrospective memory** helps us retrieve information from the past. **Prospective memory** aids us in remembering things we have planned to do in the future, despite the passage of time and despite the occurrence of interfering events. In order for prospective memory to succeed, we need to have foolproof strategies, such as alarm reminders on our cell phones, or we need to focus our attention and keep it focused. Distractibility will prevent us from reaching the goal.

A Swiss study examined the relationships between processing speed, working memory (the amount of information a person can keep in mind at once), prospective memory, and retrospective memory among 361 people between the ages of 65 and 80 (Zeintl et al., 2007). It was found that age-related declines in processing speed and working memory—aspects of fluid intelligence—had important effects on retrospective memory. However, there were age-related declines in prospective memory that appeared to be independent of processing speed and working memory. In other words, even if fluid intelligence remained intact, prospective memory might decline, suggestive of powerful roles for attention and distractibility.

Another study found that the age-related decline in prospective memory is greatest when the task to be completed is not crucial and the cues used to jog the memory are not very prominent (Kliegel et al., 2008). When the task is important and older adults use conspicuous cues to remind them, age-related declines in prospective memory tend to disappear. However, the adults have to be cognitively intact enough to plan the strategy.

17-4b LANGUAGE DEVELOPMENT

People aged 75 and above tend to show a decline in reading comprehension that is related to a decrease in the scope of working memory (De Beni et al., 2007). Because of the decline in working memory and because of impairments in hearing, many older adults find it more difficult to understand the spoken language (Salthouse & Mandell, 2013). However, when the speaker slows down and articulates more clearly, comprehension increases (Gordon-Salant, 2014).

Older adults may also show deficiencies in language production. Although they may retain their receptive vocabularies, they often show a gradual decline in their expressive vocabularies—that is, the number of words they produce (Hough, 2007). It appears that declines in associative memory and working memory decrease the likelihood that words will "be there" when older people try to summon up ideas (Salthouse & Mandell, 2013). Similarly, older people are more likely to experience the frustrating "tip-of-the-tongue" phenomenon, in which they are certain that they know a word but temporarily cannot produce it (Salthouse & Mandell, 2013).

17-4c PROBLEM SOLVING

Figure 17.8 shows the so-called Duncker Candle Problem, which is sometimes used to challenge problem-solving skills. The goal is to attach the candle to the wall, using

retrospective memory memory of past events and general knowledge.

prospective memory memory of things one has planned for the future.

FIG.17.8 THE DUNCKER CANDLE PROBLEM

Can you use the objects shown on the table to attach the candle to the wall of the room so that it will burn properly? You can find the answer in Figure 17.9 on the next page.

only the objects shown, so that it will burn properly. Rather than be concerned about whether or not you solve the problem, notice the types of thoughts you have already had as you have surveyed the objects in the figure. Even if you haven't arrived at a solution yet, you have probably used mental trial and error to visualize what might work. (You will find the answer to the Duncker Candle Problem in Figure 17.9.)

FIG.17.9 ANSWER TO THE DUNCKER CANDLE PROBLEM

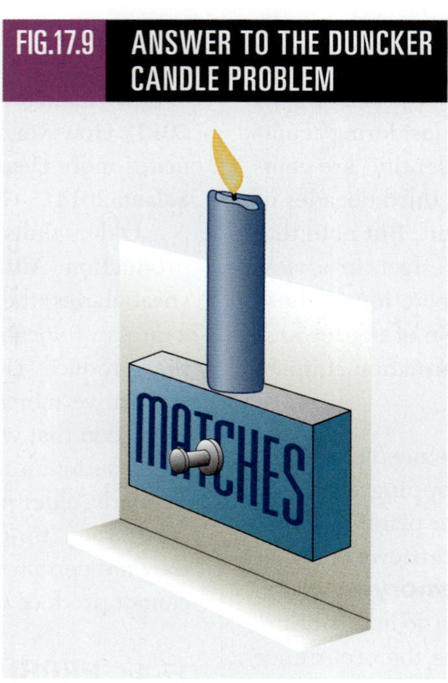

These standard problem-solving methods require executive functioning to select strategies, working memory to hold the elements of the problem in mind, and processing speed to accomplish the task while the elements remain in mind, all of which have fluid components that tend to decline with age (Hassing & Johanssom, 2005). Experiments with young and older adults consistently show that the older adults use fewer strategies and display slower processing speed in solving complex math problems (Allain et al., 2007; Lemaire & Arnaud, 2008).

How important, you might wonder, is it for older people to solve complex math problems or "teasers" like the Duncker Candle Problem? The answer depends on what people are attempting to accomplish in life. However, research suggests that for the vast majority of older adults, abstract problem-solving ability, as in complex math problems, is not related to their quality of life. Real-world or everyday problem-solving skills are usually of greater concern (Gilhooly et al., 2007).

Moreover, when older adults encounter interpersonal conflicts, they tend to regulate their emotional responses differently from young and middle-aged adults. Whereas the younger groups are relatively more likely to express feelings of anger or frustration, to seek support from other people, or to solve interpersonal problems, the older adults are more likely to focus on remaining calm and unperturbed (Coats & Blanchard-Fields, 2008). The difference appears to be partially due to older adults' decreased tendency to express anger and increased priority on regulating emotion. Perhaps the older adults do not wish to be jarred, but it also sounds a bit like wisdom.

17-4d WISDOM

We may seek athletes who are in their 20s, but we prefer older coaches. It may be desirable to hire high school teachers and college professors who have recently graduated, but we seek high school principals and department chairpersons who are somewhat older. It is helpful to have 18-year-olds who are bursting with energy knocking on doors to get out the vote, but we want our presidential candidates to be older. Why? Because we associate age with *wisdom*.

Among the numerous cognitive hazards of aging, older people tend to be more distractible than young adults. Developmental psychologist Lynn Hasher (2008) suggests that distractibility can enable older adults to take a broader view of various situations: Shifting one's attention from item to item "may enable older adults to ultimately know more about a situation and...what's going on than their younger peers....[This] characteristic may play a significant role in why we think of older people as wiser."

Kunzmann and Baltes (2005) note that wise people approach life's problems in a way that addresses the meaning of life. They consider not only the present, but also the past and the future, as well as the contexts in which the problems arise. They tend to be tolerant of other people's value systems and to acknowledge that there are uncertainties in life and that one can only attempt to find workable solutions in an imperfect world. Ardelt (2008a, 2008b) adds emotional and philosophical dimensions to the definition of wisdom. She suggests that wise people tend to possess an unselfish love for others and tend to be less afraid of death. In the following chapter, we explore social and emotional developments of late adulthood. We see that most senior citizens can continue to lead rich, satisfying lives.

STUDY TOOLS 17

READY TO STUDY?

In the book, you can:

- ☐ Rip out the chapter review card at the back of the book for a handy summary of the chapter and key terms.
- ☐ Check your understanding of what you've read with the quizzes that follow.

ONLINE AT CENGAGEBRAIN.COM YOU CAN:

- ☐ Collect StudyBits while you read and study the chapter.
- ☐ Quiz yourself on key concepts.
- ☐ Find videos for further exploration.
- ☐ Prepare for tests with HDEV5 Flash Cards as well as those you create.

SELF-ASSESSMENTS

Fill-Ins

Answers can be found in the back of the book.

1. Your life ____________ refers to the number of years you can look forward to living in your population group and under your life circumstances.
2. Cataracts cloud the ____________ of the eyes, reducing vision.
3. "Dowager's hump" is a result of ____________.
4. Researchers investigating DNA have found that the length of the ____________ for a species may determine the number of times a cell can divide and survive.
5. Researchers investigating the immune system have found that the production of ____________ declines with age, rendering the body less able to fight off infections.
6. Research suggests that it might be possible to ward off the ill effects of ____________ radicals with antioxidants.
7. Arthritis is an inflammation of the ____________.
8. ____________ memories are automatic and recall the performance of tasks such as reciting the alphabet or multiplication tables, riding a bicycle, or using a doorknob.
9. ____________ memory has no known limits.
10. Alzheimer's disease is the most common cause of a broader category of cognitive impairments termed ____________.

Multiple Choice

1. **People who live in which of the following countries have the greatest life expectancy?**
   a. India
   b. North Korea
   c. South Africa
   d. Cuba

2. **Men in the United States are likely to die earlier than women in the United States for all of the following reasons *except* that men**
   a. have a lower income.
   b. are less willing to go to the doctor for regular examinations.
   c. are more likely to drink and smoke.
   d. typically develop heart disease earlier in life.

3. **The most serious fracture that results from osteoporosis is fracture of the**
   a. skull.
   b. hip.
   c. elbow.
   d. leg.

4. **All of the following sexual changes tend to occur in men in late adulthood *except***
   a. production of less ejaculate.
   b. decrease in the intensity of nocturnal erections.
   c. increased amount of time to regain an erection after an orgasm.
   d. termination of sexual fantasies.

5. **The most accurate statement about sexuality in couples in late adulthood is that**
   a. it is variable.
   b. it is painful.
   c. frequency increases.
   d. intensity of orgasm increases.

6. **The most common chronic health condition among people in late adulthood is**
   a. arthritis.
   b. diabetes.
   c. heart disease.
   d. hypertension.

7. **Alzheimer's disease is characterized by**
   a. high blood pressure.
   b. memory loss.
   c. muscular weakness.
   d. proliferation of cancerous cells.

8. **Alzheimer's disease is the ____________ leading killer of older Americans.**
   a. first
   b. third
   c. fifth
   d. eighth

9. **Older adults tend to do about as well as younger adults in performing cognitive tasks that measure ____________ memory.**
   a. associative
   b. implicit
   c. short-term
   d. explicit

10. **Which of the following is a programmed theory of aging?**
    a. immunological theory
    b. wear-and-tear theory
    c. free radical theory
    d. cross-linking theory

18 Late Adulthood: Social and Emotional Development

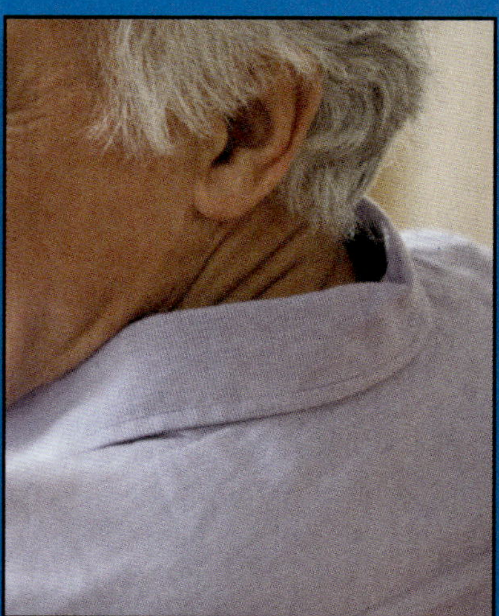
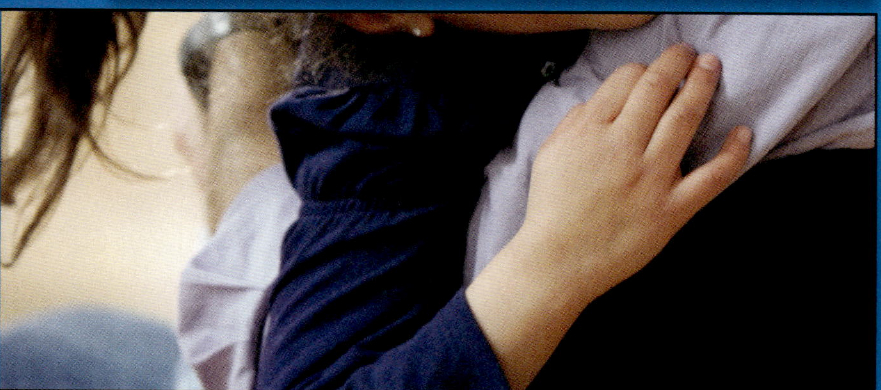
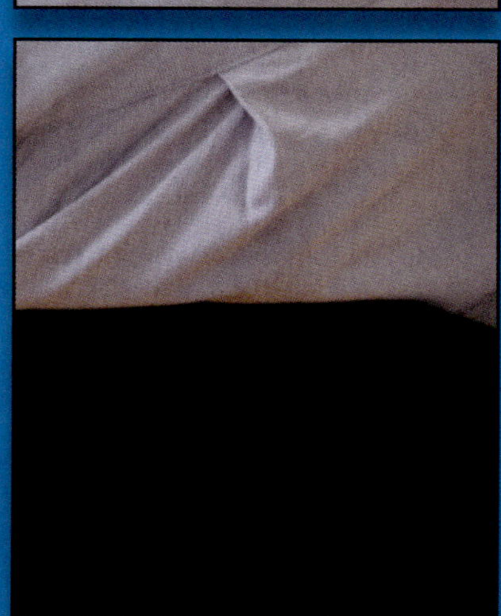

Masterfile

LEARNING OUTCOMES

After studying this chapter, you will be able to . . .

- **18-1** Evaluate various theories of social and emotional development in late adulthood
- **18-2** Discuss psychological development in late adulthood, focusing on self-esteem and maintaining independence
- **18-3** Discuss the social contexts in which people age, focusing on housing, religion, and family
- **18-4** Describe factors that contribute to adjustment to retirement
- **18-5** Discuss factors in "successful aging"

After you finish this chapter, go to **PAGE 377** for **STUDY TOOLS**

For many people, the later years are the best years—especially when they are filled with meaningful activity. The stresses involved in building and maintaining a career, selecting a mate, and rearing children may have receded. Questions of identity may have become settled.

> For many people, the later years are the best years—especially when they are filled with meaningful activity.

Troubling emotions such as depression and anxiety tend to decline as we age, whereas positive emotions remain fairly steady (Charles & Carstensen, 2010). On the whole, older Americans are at least as happy as younger people, and the majority of people 65 and older consider themselves to be in good overall health when compared with other people of their age (Charles & Carstensen, 2010).

Yet, as we will see, aging has its challenges. Older people are more likely to be bereaved by the loss of spouses and close friends. Older people may need to cope with declining health, retirement, and relocation.

18-1 THEORIES OF SOCIAL AND EMOTIONAL DEVELOPMENT IN LATE ADULTHOOD

Late adulthood differs from the phases of life that come before it. Previous phases or stages focus on growth and gains, or at least on stability, in most areas. In late adulthood, we must now cope with decline and death. Theories of development in late adulthood deal with the ways in which we can approach our relationships with our changing bodies, our mental capacities, transitions in intimate relationships, our families, society at large, and voluntary and involuntary relocations (Lange & Grossman, 2010).

18-1a ERIK ERIKSON'S PSYCHOSOCIAL THEORY AND OFFSHOOTS

Erikson labeled his eighth or final stage of life the stage of **ego integrity versus despair**. As a perennial optimist, Erikson believed that people who achieved positive outcomes to earlier life crises—for example, generativity rather than stagnation in middle adulthood—would be more likely to obtain ego integrity than despair in late adulthood.

ego integrity versus despair Erikson's eighth life crisis, defined by maintenance of the belief that life is meaningful and worthwhile despite physical decline and the inevitability of death versus depression and hopelessness.

EGO INTEGRITY VERSUS DESPAIR The basic challenge in the crisis of ego integrity versus despair is to maintain the belief that life is meaningful and worthwhile despite physical decline and the inevitability of death. Ego integrity derives from wisdom, as well as from the acceptance of one's life span being limited and occurring at a certain point in the sweep of history. We spend most of our lives accumulating things and relationships, and Erikson also argues that adjustment in the later years requires the wisdom to let go.

TRUTH OR FICTION?

T	F	The majority of people aged 65 and older consider themselves to be in good or excellent health compared to other people of their age.
T	F	It is normal for older people to be depressed when their friends and partners are dying.
T	F	People aged 80 and older are more likely to be victimized by crime than people in any other age group.
T	F	African Americans who attend church more than once a week live more than 13 years longer than African Americans who never attend.
T	F	Older married couples argue more than younger married couples do.
T	F	The key to successful retirement is doing as little as possible.

TRUTH

T F The majority of people aged 65 and older consider themselves to be in good or excellent health compared to other people of their age.

It is true that the majority of people aged 65 and older consider themselves to be in good or excellent health compared to other people of their age. (Do some people look at themselves through rose-colored glasses?)

ROBERT PECK'S DEVELOPMENTAL TASKS Robert Peck (1968) amplified Erikson's stage of ego integrity versus despair by outlining three developmental tasks that people face in late adulthood:

- *Ego differentiation versus work-role preoccupation.* After retirement, people need to find new ways of defining their self-worth outside of their achievements in the workplace, perhaps in terms of roles in the community, activities with friends and family, or spiritual undertakings.
- *Body transcendence versus body preoccupation.* At some point in late adulthood, people face inevitable physical decline, and it is in their best interests to come to terms with it by placing more value on cognitive activities and social relationships. Some people, of course, run into chronic illnesses or disabilities years earlier and must face the need to transcend body preoccupation prior to late adulthood.
- *Ego transcendence versus ego preoccupation.* Ego transcendence means preparing in some way to go beyond the physical limitations of one's own life span. As death comes nearer, some prepare to transcend death by helping secure the futures of their children or grandchildren. Others work more broadly to benefit a church, synagogue, or mosque, or to leave planet Earth in "better shape" than they found it.

Many people become more aware of their bodies and their bodies' limitations as they age, which, for some, may lead to ego transcendence (Thomas & Wardle, 2014). Based on extensive interviews with small samples, Monika Ardelt and Michel Ferrari (2014) write that ego transcendence is characterized by a concern for the well-being of humankind in general, not only for the self and close loved ones.

life review looking back on the events of one's life in late adulthood, often in an effort to construct a meaningful narrative.

disengagement theory the view that older adults and society withdraw from one another as older adults approach death.

Robert Peck's Three Developmental Tasks

- Ego differentiation versus work-role preoccupation
- Body transcendence versus body preoccupation
- Ego transcendence versus ego preoccupation

THE LIFE REVIEW Daniel Levinson theorized that one aspect of the "midlife crisis" was that people realized they had more to look back on than forward to. In Chapter 16, we saw that the existence of the midlife crisis is in dispute; however, no one can argue that people in late adulthood have more to look back on than forward to. In fact, one of the complaints younger people sometimes level at older relatives is that they too often engage in reminiscence— that is, relating stories from the distant past. At times, it may seem that some older people live in the past, possibly in denial of current decline and the approach of death.

Reminiscence was once considered a symptom of dementia, but contemporary researchers consider it to be a normal aspect of aging (Achenbaum, 2014). In working with healthy older volunteers as individuals and in groups, Robert Butler (2002) found that **life reviews** can be complex and nuanced, incoherent and self-contradictory, or even replete with irony, tragedy, and comedy. Butler believes that older people engage in life reviews to attempt to make life meaningful, to move on with new relationships as contemporaries pass on, and to help them find ego integrity and accept the end of life (Achenbaum, 2014).

Butler (2002) also argues that health care professionals rely far too much on drugs to ease the discomforts of older adults. Pilot programs suggest that therapists may be able to relieve depression and other psychological problems in older adults by helping them reminisce about their lives (Hyams & Scogin, 2015.)

18-1b DISENGAGEMENT THEORY

According to **disengagement theory**, older people and society mutually withdraw from one another as older people approach death (Brown, 2016). People in late adulthood focus more on their inner lives, preparing for the inevitable. Because of retirement, government or industry now supports them through pensions or charity rather than vice versa. Family members expect less from older people.

How accurate is this theory? Probably not very. It seems that well-being among older adults generally increases when they pursue goals rather than withdraw from society (Carstensen, 2010; Johnson & Mutchler, 2014). Goals might have to be adjusted so that they are consistent with the person's physical and cognitive abilities, but disengagement does not appear to be the path to adjustment. Moreover, relationships between children and parents change as parents travel the years of late adulthood, but children—who are now middle-aged—often maintain close, supportive ties with aging parents, and despite some diminished capacities, aging parents may become founts of wisdom.

18-1c ACTIVITY THEORY

Activity theory states, in contrast to disengagement theory, that older adults are better adjusted when they are more active and involved in physical and social activities. Activity theory places many of the barriers to such activity in social attitudes such as beliefs that older people should "take it easy," and in structural matters such as forced retirement, without regard to the desires of the individual.

Research shows that physical activity is associated with a lower mortality rate in late adulthood (Haber, 2010; Lin et al., 2011). Leisure and informal social activities contribute to life satisfaction among retired people (Wang & Shi, 2014). An Israeli study found particular benefits for life satisfaction in activities involving the next generation, the visual and performing arts, and spiritual and religious matters (Nimrod, 2007). However, there was also value in independent activities in the home.

18-1d SOCIOEMOTIONAL SELECTIVITY THEORY

Socioemotional selectivity theory addresses the development of older adults' social networks. Laura Carstensen (Charles & Carstensen, 2010) hypothesizes that increasing emphasis is placed on emotional experience as we age. As a result, we are more focused on emotionally fulfilling experiences. Figure 18.1 shows on page 364 the results of an experiment by Carstensen and her colleagues (1999) in which research participants aged 20 to 83 read two pages from a popular novel. Then the subjects spent an hour on meaningless activities before being asked to recall everything they could about the pages they had read. Their recollections were classified as emotional or nonemotional. The proportion of emotional material recalled increased with the age group, showing a greater emotional response of the older subjects.

In order to regulate their emotional lives as they grow older, people limit their social contacts to a few individuals who are of major importance to them (English & Carstensen, 2014; Wrzus et al., 2013). By the time older adults reach their 80s, they are likely to have whittled their social networks down to a few family members and friends. This does not mean that older adults are antisocial. It means, rather, that they see themselves as having

David Burton / Alamy stock Photo

According to activity theory, senior citizens are better adjusted when they are more active and involved in social activities.

activity theory the view that older adults fare better when they engage in physical and social activities.

socioemotional selectivity theory the view that we place increasing emphasis on emotional experience as we age but limit our social contacts to regulate our emotions.

FIG.18.1 MEAN PROPORTION OF EMOTIONAL MATERIAL RECALLED IN FOUR ADULT AGE GROUPS

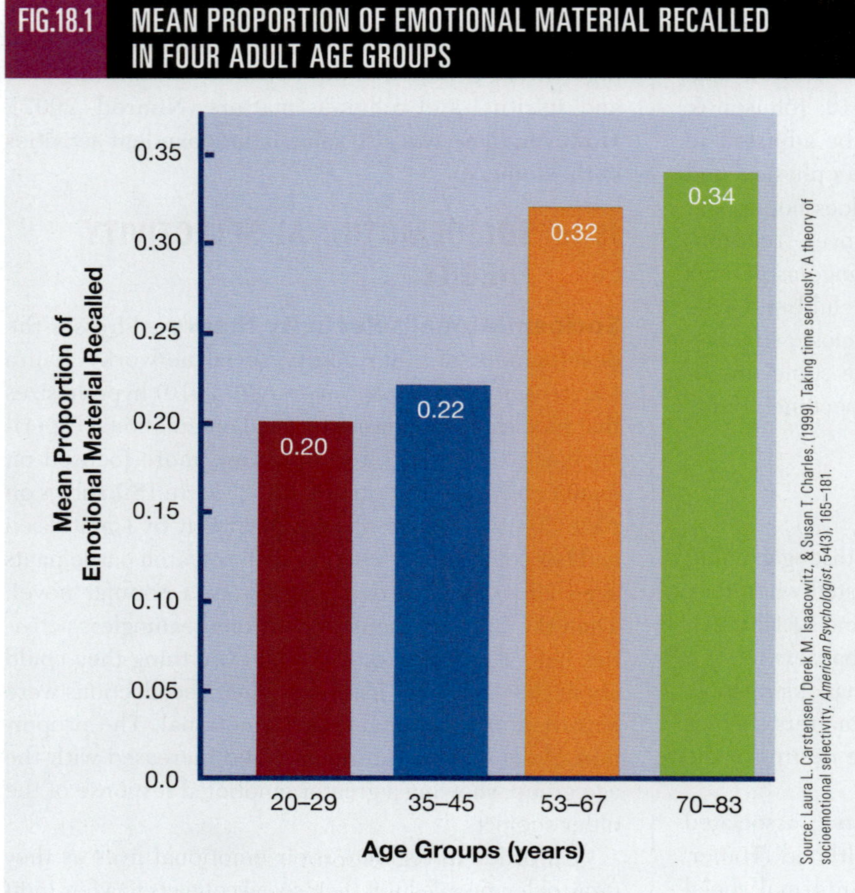

less time to waste and that they are more risk-averse; that is, they do not want to involve themselves in painful social interactions.

Laura Carstensen and her colleagues (Ersner-Hershfield et al., 2013) also note that older people's perceived limitation on future time increases their appreciation for life, which brings about positive emotions. On the other hand, the same constraints on future time heighten awareness that such positive experiences will be drawing to a close, thus giving rise to mixed emotional states that have a poignant quality.

18-2 PSYCHOLOGICAL DEVELOPMENT

Various psychological issues affect older adults, including self-esteem and the factors that contribute to self-esteem in late adulthood. Self-esteem, as we will see, is tied into independence and dependence. Also, the psychological problems of depression and anxiety can affect us at any age, but they warrant special focus in late adulthood.

18-2a SELF-ESTEEM

To study the life-span development of self-esteem, Richard Robins and his colleagues (2002) recruited more than 300,000 individuals to complete an online questionnaire that provided demographic information (age, gender, ethnic background, and so forth) and measures of self-esteem. Two-thirds of the respondents were from the United States, and 57% were female. Results are shown in Figure 18.2. Generally, the self-esteem of males was higher than that of females. Self-esteem was high in childhood (likely an inflated estimate) and dipped precipitously with entry into adolescence, a finding that is consistent with studies reported in Chapter 12. Self-esteem then rose gradually throughout middle adulthood and declined in late adulthood, with most of the decline occurring between the ages of 70 and 85. However, this is all relative. Even for people in their 80s, self-esteem levels were above the midpoint of the questionnaire.

Researchers suggest a couple of possible reasons for the drop in self-esteem they found among people in their 70s and 80s (Shaw et al., 2010). The first is that life changes such as retirement, loss of a spouse or partner, lessened social support, declining health, and downward movement in socioeconomic status account for the drop in self-esteem. The other hypothesis is more optimistic, namely that older people are wiser and more content. Erikson (1968) and other theorists suggest the possibility that ego transcendence occurs in this stage of life, meaning that people come to accept themselves as they are, "warts and all," and no longer need to inflate their self-esteem.

As the years wear on in late adulthood, people express progressively less "body esteem"—that is, pride in the appearance and functioning of their bodies. There is also a gender difference, with older men expressing less body esteem than older women do (Rocha & Terra, 2013). Men are more likely to accumulate fat around the middle, whereas women are more likely to accumulate fat in the hips. On the other hand, older men seem to be more accepting of the shortcomings of their bodies than young men are (Rocha & Terra, 2013).

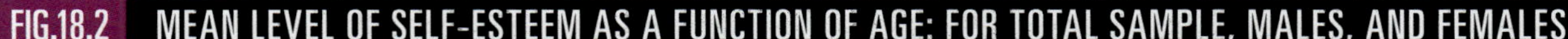

FIG.18.2 MEAN LEVEL OF SELF-ESTEEM AS A FUNCTION OF AGE: FOR TOTAL SAMPLE, MALES, AND FEMALES

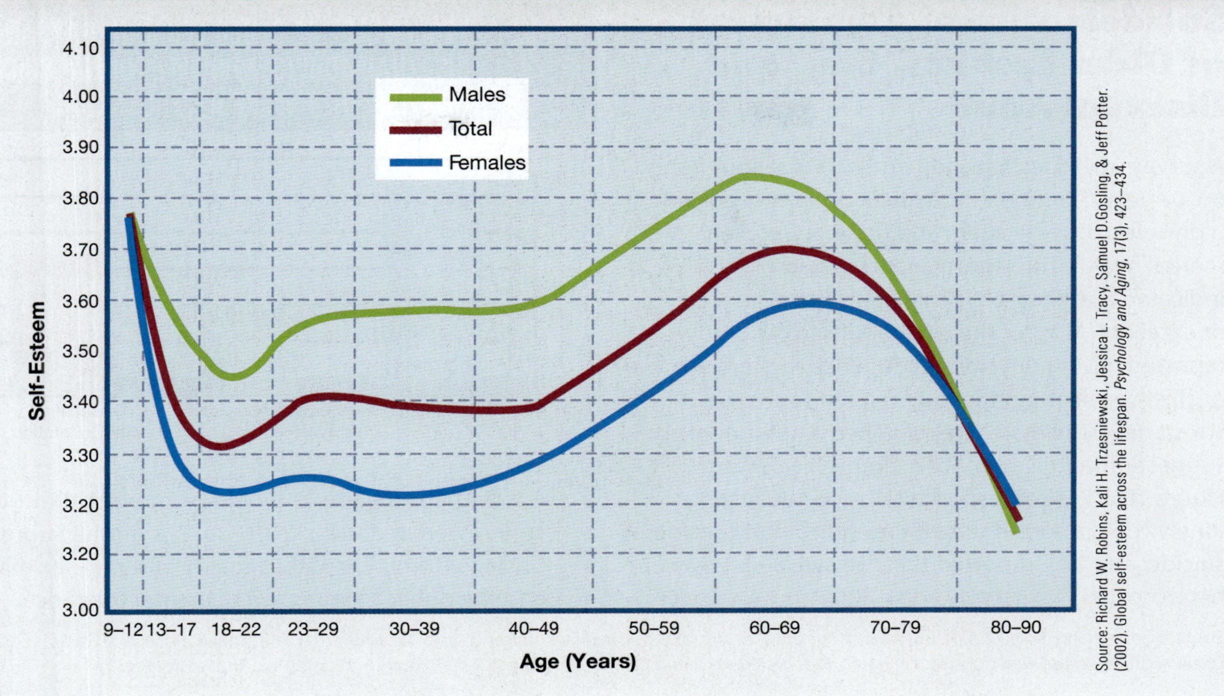

Source: Richard W. Robins, Kali H. Trzesniewski, Jessica L. Tracy, Samuel D Gosling, & Jeff Potter. (2002). Global self-esteem across the lifespan. *Psychology and Aging, 17*(3), 423–434.

18-2b INDEPENDENCE VERSUS DEPENDENCE

Being able to care for oneself would appear to be a core condition of successful aging. Older people who are independent tend to think of themselves as leading a "normal life," whereas those who are dependent on others, even if they are only slightly dependent, tend to worry more about aging and encountering physical disabilities and stress (Krieger-Blake, 2010). A study of 441 healthy people aged 65 to 95 found that dependence on others to carry out the activities of daily living increased with age (Perrig-Chiello et al., 2006). A particularly sensitive independence issue is toileting, as found in a study of stroke victims (Clark & Rugg, 2005). Interviews found that independence in toileting is especially important in enabling older people to avoid slippage in self-esteem.

18-2c PSYCHOLOGICAL PROBLEMS

Problems in coping with aging are associated with psychological problems, including depression and anxiety.

DEPRESSION Depression affects some 10% of people ages 65–80, and affects some 20% of the population aged 81 and above (Solhaug et al., 2012). Depression in older people can be a continuation of depression from earlier periods of life, or it can be a new development (Casey, 2012). Depression can be connected with the personality factor of neuroticism (Grav et al., 2012), possible structural changes in the brain (Casey, 2012), and a possible genetic predisposition to imbalances of the neurotransmitter norepinephrine (Cohen-Woods et al., 2013). Researchers are also investigating links between depression and physical illnesses such as Alzheimer's disease, heart disease, stroke, Parkinson's disease, and cancer. Depression is also connected with the loss of friends and loved ones, but depression is a mental disorder that goes beyond sadness or bereavement. The loss of companions and friends will cause profound sadness, but mentally healthy people bounce back within approximately a year and find new sources of pleasure and support. Inability to bounce back is a symptom of depression.

Depression goes undetected and untreated in older people much of the time (Hansson et al., 2012). Depression may be overlooked because its symptoms are masked by physical complaints such as low energy, loss of appetite, and insomnia, and because health care providers tend to focus more on older people's physical health than their mental health. Many older people are reluctant to admit to depression because psychological problems carried more of a stigma when they were young. Depression is also connected with memory lapses and other cognitive impairment, such as difficulty concentrating (Hertzog & Pearman, 2014), so some cases of depression are attributed

Socioemotional Adjustment of Older Lesbian, Gay, and Bisexual Adults

A survey of 416 lesbian, gay, and bisexual adults aged 60–91 years found that the great majority reported high levels of self-esteem and good or excellent mental health. Three participants in four (75%) indicated that their physical health was also good or excellent. Most of the older adults in the study reported having developed resilience to prejudice against sexual minorities and related sources of stress; nevertheless, there remained a number of suggestions of distress. For example, as shown in Figure 18.3, 27% of respondents reported feeling lonely; 10% reported that at times they had considered suicide; and 17% reported that they wished they were heterosexual.

FIG.18.3 PERCENTAGE OF OLDER LESBIAN, GAY, AND BISEXUAL ADULTS WHO FEEL LONELY, SUICIDAL, OR WISH THEY WERE HETEROSEXUAL

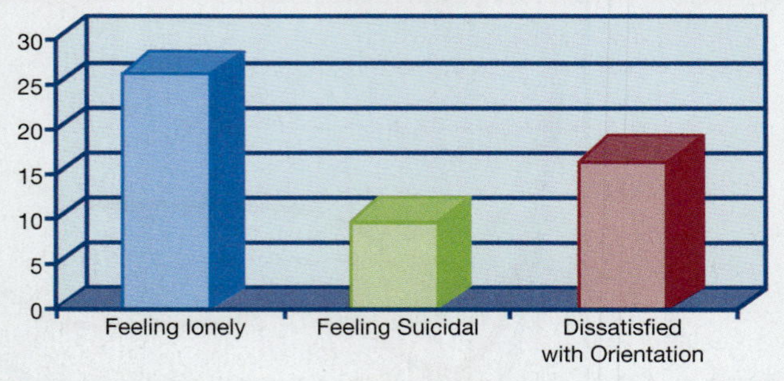

Perhaps the results would be more optimistic if the survey were redone in 2016-2017, after the Supreme Court's affirmation of the legality of same–sex marriage and the public's expression of greater tolerance.

Source: Grossmann, A. H. (2006). Physical and mental health of older, lesbian, gay, and bisexual adults. In D. Kimmel, T. Rose, & S. David. (Eds.) *Lesbian, gay, bisexual, and transgender aging: Research and clinical perspectives*. (pp. 53–69). New York: Columbia University Press.

simply to the effects of aging or are misdiagnosed as dementia or Alzheimer's disease. Depression in older people can usually be treated successfully with the same means that work in younger people, such as antidepressant drugs and cognitive-behavioral psychotherapy (Hansson et al., 2012). Then again, feelings of depression sometimes pass on their own (Hansson et al., 2012).

Untreated depression can lead to suicide, which is most common among older people. The highest rates of suicide are found among older men who have lost their wives or partners, lost their social networks, or fear the consequences of physical illnesses and loss of freedom (Fässberg et al., 2012). Though fewer older adults suffer from depression than younger adults, suicide is more frequent among older adults, especially European American men (Szanto et al., 2012).

ANXIETY DISORDERS Anxiety disorders affect at least 3% of people aged 65 and older, but coexist with depression in about 8% to 9% of older adults (Kvaal et al., 2008). Older women are approximately twice as likely to be affected than older men. The most common anxiety disorders among older adults are **generalized anxiety disorder** and **phobic disorders**. **Panic disorder** is rare. Most cases of **agoraphobia** affecting older adults tend to be of recent origin and may involve the loss of social support systems due to the death of a spouse or close friends. Then again, some older individuals who are frail may have realistic fears of falling on the street and may be misdiagnosed as agoraphobic if they refuse to leave the house alone. Generalized anxiety disorder may arise from the perception that one lacks control over one's life.

Anxiety disorders can be harmful to older people's physical health. When older adults with anxiety disorders are subjected to stress, their levels of cortisol (a stress hormone) rise, and it takes a good deal of time for them to subside (Chaudieu et al., 2008). Cortisol suppresses the functioning of the immune system, making people more vulnerable to illness.

generalized anxiety disorder general feelings of dread and foreboding.

phobic disorder irrational, exaggerated fear of an object or situation.

panic disorder recurrent experiencing of attacks of extreme anxiety in the absence of external stimuli that usually evoke anxiety.

agoraphobia fear of open, crowded places.

FICTION

T (F) It is normal for older people to be depressed when their friends and partners are dying.

It is not normal for older people to be *depressed* when their friends and partners are dying. It is normal to be *sad* when we suffer a loss. Depression is usually defined as a mental disorder.

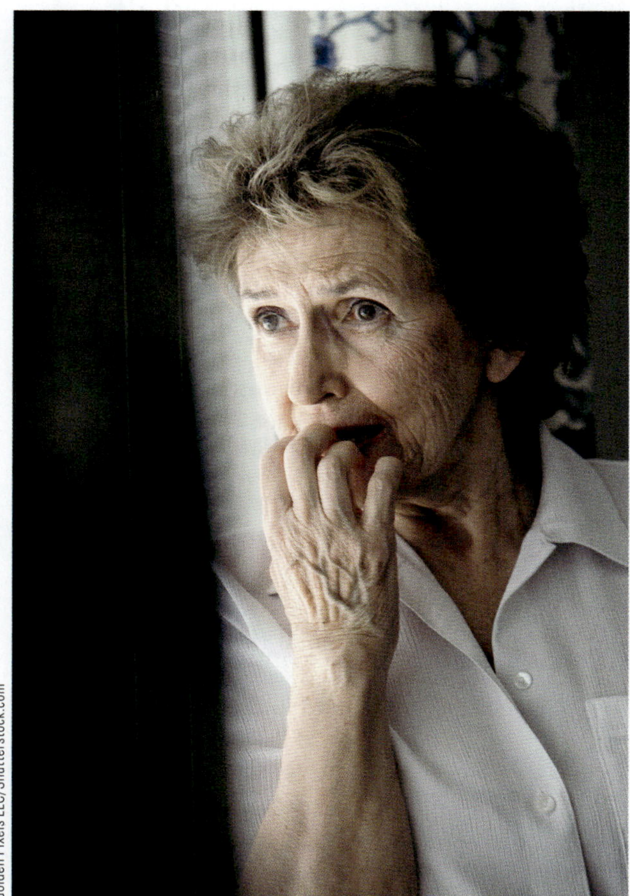
Golden Pixels LLC/Shutterstock.com

Older women are twice as likely to be affected by anxiety as older men, especially when they live alone.

Mild tranquilizers (Valium is one) are commonly used to quell anxiety in older adults. Psychological interventions, such as cognitive-behavior therapy, have proven beneficial and do not carry the risk of side effects or potential dependence (Casey, 2012).

18-3 SOCIAL CONTEXTS OF AGING

People do not age within a vacuum, but within social and communal contexts, including their living arrangements, facilities and services within their communities, religious affiliations, and family and social relationships.

18-3a COMMUNITIES AND HOUSING FOR OLDER PEOPLE

There's no place like home. According to surveys, older Americans consistently report that they prefer to remain in their homes as long as their physical and mental conditions allow them to do so (Scharlach, 2012). Older people with plentiful financial resources, large amounts of equity in their homes, and strong ties to their communities are more likely to remain in their homes. Conversely, older people with declining health conditions, changes in their family composition, and significant increases in property taxes and costs of utilities are likely to need to consider residing elsewhere (Ferreira, 2010). In many suburban communities, for example, property taxes have been skyrocketing to keep pace with the costs of public education. Older people no longer have children in the schools or—most crucially—sufficient income to pay the increased taxes, and so they often sell their homes.

Older people who live in urban areas (especially inner cities) are often highly concerned about exposure to crime, particularly crimes of violence. Ironically, people aged 80 and older are significantly less likely to be victimized than people in other age groups (Beaulieu et al., 2008). Social support helps older people cope with their concerns about victimization (Beaulieu et al., 2008). For example, if they are victimized, social support helps them avoid some of the problems that characterize post-traumatic stress disorder, such as intrusive thoughts and nightmares (Sexton, 2008).

FICTION

T (F) People aged 80 and older are more likely to be victimized by crime than people in any other age group.

It is not true that people aged 80 and older are more likely to be victimized by crime than people in any other age group. Despite experiencing heightened concern about exposure to crime, older people are generally at lower risk.

When older people can no longer manage living on their own, they may consider utilizing the services of home health aides and visiting nurses to help them remain in the home. More affluent older people can afford to hire live-in help. Others may move in with adult children. Still others may move into assisted living residences, in which they have their own apartments, community dining rooms, 24-hour nursing aid, and on-call physician care.

Blend Images - Hill Street Studios/Walter Jimenez/Getty Images

In addition to their cognitive and spiritual values, religion and religious activities provide older adults with an arena for social networking.

When older adults relocate to residences for the elderly, whether or not they have facilities for assisted living, existing social networks tend to be disrupted and they are challenged to find new friends and create new networks (Bekhet, 2016). It is valuable for such residences to have communal dining facilities and organized activities, including transportation to nearby shopping and entertainment. Residents typically take time in engaging other people socially and are selective in forming new relationships (Bekhet, 2016).

Older adults may be reluctant to relocate to nursing homes because nursing homes signify the loss of independence.

Older adults may be reluctant to relocate to nursing homes because nursing homes signify the loss of independence. Surveys indicate that older adults are relatively more willing to enter nursing homes when they perceive themselves to be in poor health and when one or more close family members live near the nursing home (Bekhet, 2016).

There are frightening stories of what happens in nursing homes, and there are heartening stories. Occasionally, cases of **elder abuse** occur, with staff acting harshly toward residents, sometimes in response to cognitively impaired residents acting aggressively toward the staff (Holroyd-Leduc & Reddy, 2012). However, a well-selected and well-trained staff can deal well with impaired residents, many of whom are disoriented and frightened (Bekhet, 2016).

elder abuse the abuse or neglect of senior citizens, particularly in nursing homes.

18-3b RELIGION

Religion involves beliefs and practices centered on claims about the nature of reality and moral behavior, usually codified as rituals, religious laws, and prayers. Religions also usually encompass cultural traditions and myths, faith, spiritual experience, and communal as well as private worship. Nearly half the people in the world identify with one of the "Abrahamic" religions: Judaism, Christianity, and Islam. These religions, and many others, teach that there is a life after death, and that moral living will enable one to experience the benefits of the afterlife.

We discuss religion as part of the social context in which older adults (and others) dwell, because religion often involves participating in the social, educational, and charitable activities of a congregation, as well as worshiping. Therefore, religion and religious activities provide older adults a vast arena for social networking.

Religion also has a special allure as people approach the end of life. As people undergo physical decline, religion asks them to focus, instead, on moral conduct and spiritual "substance" such as the soul. People who experience physical suffering in this world are advised to look forward to relief in the next.

Therefore, it is not surprising that studies find that religious involvement in late adulthood is usually associated with less depression and more life satisfaction (Blazer, 2012). Frequent churchgoing has also been shown to be associated with fewer problems in the activities of daily living among older people (Miller et al., 2012). Here, of course, we can assume that there are benefits for social networking as well as for church attendance per se.

Consider some of the benefits related to regular church attendance found in studies of older African Americans. Older African Americans who attend services more than once a week live 13.7 years longer, on average, than their counterparts who *never* attend church (Marks et al., 2005). In-depth interviews with the churchgoers found several reasons for their relative longevity, including avoidance of negative coping methods such as aggressive behavior and drinking alcohol, success in evading victimization by violence, a sense of hopefulness, and social support.

TRUTH

F African Americans who attend church more than once a week live more than 13 years longer than African Americans who never attend.

It is true that African Americans who attend church more than once a week live more than 13 years longer, on average, than African Americans who never attend. Of course we have to consider whether a "selection factor" is involved. In other words, does church "cause" the difference, or do people who choose to attend church regularly differ to begin with from those who do not?

18-3c FAMILY AND SOCIAL RELATIONSHIPS

Family and social relationships provide some of the most obvious—and most important—elements in the social lives of older adults.

MARRIAGE While approximately half the marriages in the United States end in divorce, it is important to note that 20% to 25% of them last half a century or more, ending only with the death of one of the spouses (Määtta & Uusiautti, 2012). Married people face very different life tasks as young adults, middle-aged adults, and older adults, and the qualities in relationships that help them fulfill these tasks may also vary from stage to stage. Core issues in early adulthood are the selection of a partner, the development of a shared life, and emotional intimacy. Given these needs, similarity in personality may foster feelings of attachment and intimacy and provide a sense of equity in contributing to the relationship (Shiota & Levenson, 2007).

By middle adulthood, the partners' concerns appear to shift toward meeting shared and individual responsibilities (Musick & Bumpass, 2012). The partnership needs to handle tasks such as finances, household chores, and parenting. Conflicts may easily arise over a division of labor unless the couple can divide the tasks readily (Claxton et al., 2012). At this stage, similarity in personality may work against the couple, with each partner competing to handle or avoid the same task. For example, as found by Shiota and Levenson (2007) in a study of the "big five" personality factors in middle-aged and older adults and marital satisfaction, *difference rather than similarity* in conscientiousness and extraversion predicts marital satisfaction in the decade of the 40s, whereas similarity does just as well in the decade of the 60s.

Shiota and Levenson (2007) suggest that conscientious people want to get things done, but by middle adulthood they have their own way of doing things. When two people in close quarters each want a task completed in her or his own way, there is likely to be conflict. It is better for the relationship if one partner is detail-oriented while the other is more easygoing. It is also useful if one partner is the workaholic and the other partner is the "people person" or social butterfly. They each then have their domains of expertise and are unlikely to clash.

TRUTH

F Older married couples argue more than younger married couples do.

It is true that older married couples argue more than younger married couples do. Older couples spend more time together, so friction may develop more readily. Women from cohorts in which they were reared to take a back seat to men may also grow more self-assertive with time.

When couples reach their 60s, many midlife responsibilities such as childrearing and work have declined, allowing the partners to spend more time together, and intimacy becomes a central issue once more. In this stage, couples report less disagreement over finances, household chores, and parenting (or grandparenting), but may have concerns about emotional expression and companionship (Hatch & Bulcroft, 2004). As compared with couples in midlife, older couples show more affectionate behavior when they discuss conflicts, and they disagree with one another less in general (Driscoll & Driscoll, 2012). Similarity in personality is less of a contributor to conflict than it is in midlife, consistent with the finding that similarity in conscientiousness and extraversion is no longer strongly associated with marital dissatisfaction.

On the other hand, older couples may complain that they spend too much time together, especially women whose husbands have just retired (Shiota & Levenson, 2007). If similarity in personality is a problem in this stage of life, perhaps it is because highly similar spouses are getting bored with one another (Amato & Previti, 2003).

In a study of 120 older Israeli couples, Kulik (2004) found that sharing power in the relationship and dividing household tasks contributed to satisfaction in the relationships. Past assistance from one's spouse in a time of need also affected the quality of the marriage and life satisfaction for both partners in the relationship.

DIVORCE, COHABITATION, AND REMARRIAGE Having worked out most of the problems in their relationships and having learned to live with those that remain, older adults are less likely than younger adults to seek divorce. The ideal of lifelong marriage retains its strength (Amato et al., 2007). Because of fear of loss of assets, family disruption, and relocation, older adults do not undertake divorce lightly. When they do, it is often because one of the partners has taken up a relationship with an outsider (Bengtson et al., 2005).

Older people are increasingly likely to cohabit today, making up about 4% of the unmarried population (Brown et al., 2006). Nearly 90% of older people who cohabit have been married, and they are less likely than younger people to wish to remarry (Mahay & Lewin, 2007). Although they are less likely than younger cohabiters to marry their partners, older cohabiters report being in more intimate, stable relationships (King & Scott, 2005). Whereas younger cohabiters often see their lifestyle as a prelude to marriage, older cohabiters are more likely to see their relationship as an alternate lifestyle. They cite reasons for avoiding remarriage such as concern about ramifications for pensions and disapproval of adult children, who may be concerned about their inheritance (King & Scott, 2005). Yet when older partners do remarry, as when they decide to cohabit, they usually make a strong commitment to one another and form a stable relationship (Kemp & Kemp, 2002).

GAY AND LESBIAN RELATIONSHIPS Most of the research on gay men and lesbians has focused on adolescents and young adults. However, a growing body of information about older gay men and lesbians has shown that, as with heterosexuals, gay men and lesbians in long-term partnerships tend to enjoy higher self-esteem, less

F1online digitale Bildagentur GmbH / Alamy Stock Photo

Senior citizens are increasingly likely to cohabit today, and divorced seniors are less likely to remarry than younger people are. Even so, older cohabitors are more likely than their younger counterparts to report that they have stable relationships.

depression, fewer suicidal urges, and less alcohol and drug abuse (Grossman et al., 2013). Gay men in long-term partnerships are also less likely to incur sexually transmitted infections (Wierzalis et al., 2006).

An interesting pattern has emerged in which gay men or lesbians sometimes form long-term intimate relationships with straight people of the other gender (Muraco, 2006). These relationships do not involve sexual activity, but the couples consider themselves to be "family" and are confidants.

WIDOWHOOD Losing one's spouse in late adulthood is certainly one of the most traumatic—if not the most traumatic—experiences of one's life. The couple may have been together for half a century or more, and most of the rough edges of the relationship will likely have been smoothed. Men in their 70s seem to have the most difficulty coping, especially when they have retired and have been expecting to spend more time with their wives during the coming years (Lund & Caserta, 2001; Lee et al., 2016). In contrast, middle-aged widowers are relatively more capable of dealing with their loss (Lund & Caserta, 2001).

> The involuntary nature of being widowed is much more likely than marital separation to lead to social isolation.

Once widowed, men and women both need to engage in the activities of daily living by taking care of their personal hygiene, assuming the responsibilities that had been handled by their spouse, and remaining connected to the larger social community, whether that community mostly involves kin, friends, or people at a place of worship (Caserta & Lund, 2007). Yet the involuntary nature of being widowed is much more likely to lead to social isolation than marital separation (Stafford et al., 2013). The reasons for isolation are physical, cognitive, and emotional. Widowhood is also associated with increased levels of stress hormones, leading to a decline in physical and mental health, including increased mortality and deterioration in memory functioning (Stafford et al., 2013). Loss of a spouse also heightens the risks of depression and suicide among older adults, and more so among men than women (Ajdacic-Gross et al., 2008).

Men who are widowed are more likely than women to remarry, or at least to form new relationships with people of the other gender. One reason is simply that women tend to outlive men, so there are more older women who are available. Another is that women, more so than men, make use of the web of kinship relations and close friendships available to them. Men may also be less adept than women at various aspects of self and household care, and therefore seek that help from a new partner.

SINGLES AND OLDER PEOPLE WITHOUT CHILDREN Single, never-married—and noncohabiting—adults without children make up a small minority of the adult American population. According to data from the United States, Japan, Europe, Australia, and Israel, single older adults without children are just as likely as people who have had children—married or not—to be socially active and involved in volunteer work (Wenger et al., 2007). They also tend to maintain close relationships with siblings and longtime friends. Advanced-age (mean age = 93) mothers and women who have not had children report equally positive levels of well-being (Hoppmann & Smith, 2007).

On the other hand, married older men without children appear to be especially dependent on their spouses (Wenger et al., 2007). Parents also seem to be more likely than people without children to have the sort of social network that permits them to avoid nursing homes or other residential care upon physical decline (Wenger et al., 2007).

SIBLINGS By and large, older sibling pairs tend to shore each other up with emotional support (Taylor et al., 2008; Merz & Gierveld, 2016). This is especially true among sisters (as women are more likely than men to talk about feelings) who are close in age and geographically near one another. Siblings (and children) of the widowed tend to ramp up their social contacts and emotional support (Guiaux et al., 2007). A widowed person's sibling, especially a sister, often takes the place of the spouse as a confidant (Wenger & Jerrome, 1999; Merz & Gierveld, 2016).

A life-span developmental study of twin relationships found that, compared with other sibling relationships, the twin relationships were more intense in terms of frequency of contacts, intimacy, conflict, and emotional support (Neyer, 2002). Frequency of contact and emotional closeness declined from early to middle adulthood, but increased again in late adulthood (mean age at time of study = 71.5 years).

FRIENDSHIPS You can't pick your relatives—at least not your blood relatives—but you can choose your friends. Older people have often narrowed their friendships to friends who are most like them and enjoy the same kinds of activities (English & Carstensen, 2014). As a way of regulating their emotions, they tend to avoid "friends" with whom they have had conflict over the years. Friends serve many functions in the lives of older adults, including providing social networks, acting as confidants, and offering emotional closeness and support, especially when a family member or another friend dies.

ADULT CHILDREN AND GRANDCHILDREN It is in late adulthood when one's grandchildren also typically reach adulthood. The generation of removal that grandparents had from their grandchildren in middle adulthood continues to provide a perspective on the behavior and achievements of their grandchildren that they might not have had with their own children. Although there is great variation in grandparent–adult grandchild relationships, research suggests that both cohorts view each other in a positive light and see their ties as deep and meaningful (Kemp, 2005). They conceptualize their relationships as distinct family connections that involve unconditional love, emotional support, obligation, and respect. Grandparents and adult grandchildren often act as friends and confidants. As they experience life events together, their relationships can seem precious and capable of being cut short at any time.

18-4 RETIREMENT

The very concept of retirement, or of a period of retirement, is rather new to the human condition (Shultz & Wang, 2011). Historically speaking, people worked until they became physically or mentally incapable of doing so. But the industrial revolution, company and government pensions, and extended life expectancies have worked together to create a situation in which many or most people expect that they will spend their "golden years" tucked safely away from the demands of the workplace, perhaps in some sort of idyllic setting involving sunshine and pleasant leisure activities.

Also, in days when it was assumed that work was by definition mind-numbing, it was assumed that people retired as soon as they could afford to do so, usually at age 65. But according to the *National Vital Statistics Reports* (Arias, 2011), the average person has nearly two decades of life in front of him or her at the age of 65 (see Table 18.1). That number has been increasing and is likely to continue to increase. Moreover, with medical advances, that person is more and more likely to be robust. Therefore, many people, especially professionals, are working well beyond the age of 65.

But many people retire "on schedule," and most people retire at some time. Let's look at some of the issues they deal with, beginning with retirement planning.

Purestock/Getty Images

You can't pick your relatives, but you can choose your friends. As people age, their numbers of friends tend to winnow, but they have more in common with the friends who remain.

TABLE 18.1 LIFE EXPECTANCY BY AGE AND GENDER, BEGINNING WITH MIDDLE ADULTHOOD		
Age	**Male**	**Female**
40	38.53	42.43
45	33.98	37.73
50	29.58	33.16
55	25.41	28.74
60	21.48	24.46
65	17.75	20.32
70	14.24	16.43
75	11.03	12.83
80	8.20	9.64
85	5.84	6.92
90	4.03	4.80
95	2.82	3.34
100	2.12	2.45

Source: Arias, E. (2015, September 22). United States Life Tables, 2011. *National Vital Statistics Reports*, 64 (11), 1–62.

18-4a RETIREMENT PLANNING

One of the keys to a successful retirement is planning (Adams & Rau, 2011). According to psychologists Gary Adams and Barbara Rau (2011), and Daniel Feldman and Terry Beehr (2011), retirement planning involves dealing with some questions:

- What will I do? A majority of people retiring these days plan some sort of "bridge employment," in which they continue to work for the same employer with a reduced workload or obtain new employment, possibly part-time. About half plan to do volunteer work. Most expect to devote more time to hobbies or special interests. Most people in one way or another maintain—or strive to maintain—their identities and self-concepts (Wang et al., 2011). They see retirement as an opportunity to continue the desired aspects of their lifestyle and essential social relationships.
- How will I afford it? Adequate finances are strongly related to satisfaction with retirement (Wang et al., 2011). Most people plan—or attempt—to save for retirement, by putting money away, building equity in a home, and so on. They expect, or hope, that with pensions and government support (e.g., Social Security) kicking in, they will be all right. In recent years, pensions have been shrinking, layoffs have been looming, and property values have been falling, so many older employees have had to postpone their plans for retirement.
- Where will I live? The great majority of retirees stay put. They don't sell their homes or hop to the Sunbelt. However, as time goes on and they become less physically independent, many live in assisted facilities or with children.
- With whom will I share my retirement years? If life partners are not in agreement about retirement activities and residences, the stresses of an unwanted living situation can provide a continuous source of stress.
- How will I decide? There are many phases of retirement decision making: imagining the possibility of retirement, deciding whether and when it is time to let go of a long-held job, and when and how to put concrete plans to retire into action (Feldman & Beehr, 2011).

Retirement planning may include regularly putting money aside in plans such as IRAs, Keoghs, and various pension plans in the workplace; investing in stocks, bonds, or a second home; and, perhaps, investigating the kinds of health care and cultural activities that are available in other geographic areas of interest. People who are thinking of another area will also be interested in learning about the weather (including effects on allergies) and crime statistics.

People who live alone may do their retirement planning as individuals. However, couples—including married and cohabiting heterosexuals and gay and lesbian

Three Phases of Retirement Decision Making

1. Imagining the possibility of retirement
2. Deciding when to let go of one's job
3. Deciding how and when to put concrete retirement plans into action

ImagesBazaar / Alamy Stock Photo

couples—usually make their retirement plans collaboratively (Adams & Rau, 2011; Shultz & Wang, 2011). By and large, the closer the relationship, the more likely partners are to make retirement plans jointly (Feldman & Beehr, 2011). Phyllis Moen and her colleagues (2006) found that in married couples, husbands more often than wives tended to be in control of the plans, although control was also related to the partner's workload and income level. Men in same-gender couples are more likely than women in same-gender couples to do retirement planning, but women who do such planning are more likely to do it collaboratively.

FICTION

T (F) The key to successful retirement is doing as little as possible.

It is not true that doing as little as possible is the key to successful retirement. Research shows that the best-adjusted older adults are involved in a variety of activities.

18-4b ADJUSTMENT TO RETIREMENT

Let's begin this section with two questions: Is the key to retirement doing as little as possible? Does adjustment to retirement begin with retirement? The answer to both questions is no.

Research has consistently shown that older adults who are best adjusted to retirement are highly involved in a variety of activities, such as community activities and organizations (Wang et al., 2011). In the case of community activities, the experience and devotion of retirees renders their participation an important asset for the community, and the activities promote the adjustment of older adults into retirement.

Pinquart and Schindler (2007) found in a retirement study that retirees could be broken down into three groups, according to their satisfaction with retirement and various other factors. The group that was most satisfied with retirement maintained leisure and other nonwork-related activities as sources of life satisfaction, or replaced work with more satisfying activities. They retired at a typical retirement age and had a wealth of resources to compensate for the loss of work: They were married, in good health, and of high socioeconomic status. The majority of the second group retired at a later age and tended to be female; the majority of the third group retired at a younger age and tended to be male. The second and third groups were not as satisfied with retirement. They were in poorer health, less likely to be married, and lower in socioeconomic status than the first group. The third group had a spotty employment record. Another way to look at this data is to suggest that retirement per se didn't change these people's lives in major ways.

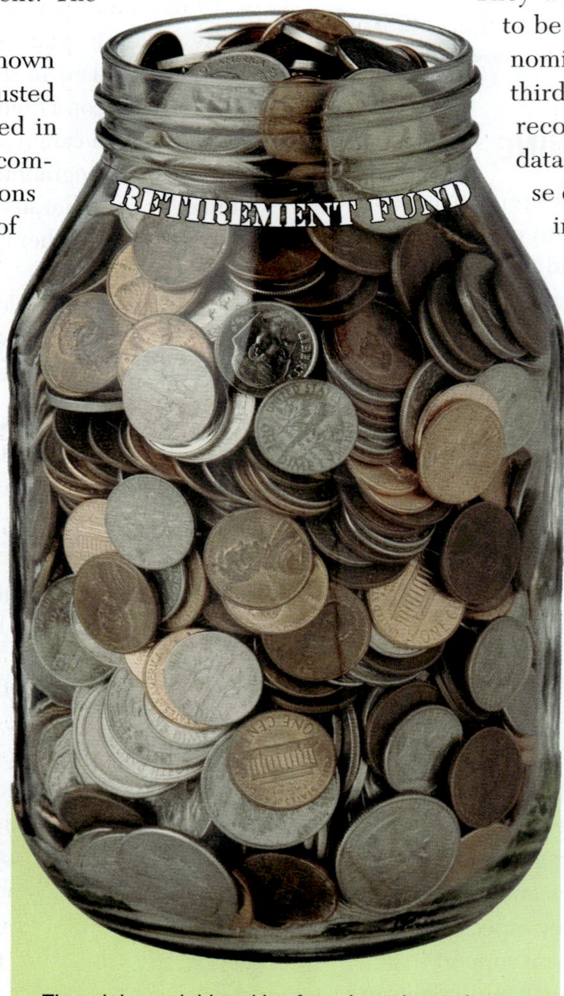

shippee/Shutterstock.com

Though late adulthood is often viewed as a time to sit back and rest, it is an excellent opportunity to engage in new challenges and activities, such as going back to school.

A two-year longitudinal study found that the adjustment of older retirees was affected by their pre-retirement work identities (Reitzes & Mutran, 2006). For example, upscale professional workers continued to be well adjusted and had high self-esteem. They weren't simply "retirees"; they were retired professors or retired doctors or retired lawyers and the like. On the other hand, hourly wage earners and other blue-collar workers had somewhat lower self-esteem and were more likely to think of themselves as simply "retirees."

Data from Dutch and American retirees found that the following factors impeded adjustment to retirement: a lengthy attachment to work, lack of control over the transition to retirement (e.g., forced retirement at age 65), worrying prior to retirement about what retirement would bring, and lack of self-confidence (Reitzes & Mutran, 2004; van Solinge & Henkens, 2005). Nevertheless, a wide range of feelings about giving up work surface just before retirement. Some people are relieved; others are worried—about finances, about surrendering their work roles, or both. Even so, most retirees report that their well-being has increased a year after they have retired, and that much of the stress they felt before retiring has diminished (Nuttman-Shwartz, 2007).

TABLE 18.2 FACTOR ANALYSIS OF LEISURE ACTIVITIES OF RETIREES

Factor #	Name	Items
I	Athletic–Competitive–Outdoors	Adventure sports, team sports, hunting & fishing, individual sports, camping & outdoors, building & repair, cards & games, computer activities, collecting
II	Artistic–Cultural–Self-Expressive	Shopping, arts & crafts, entertaining & culinary arts, cultural arts, dancing, literature & writing, socializing, gardening & nature, community involvement, travel
III	Social	Partying

Source: Hansen, Dik, & Zhou (2008).

18-4c LEISURE ACTIVITIES AND RETIREMENT

Once people retire, they have the opportunity to fill most of their days with leisure activities. Research has shown that engaging in leisure activities is essential for retirees' physical and psychological health (Hansen et al., 2008). Engaging in leisure activities is especially helpful with the cognitive aspects of aging. Kohncke and her colleagues (2016) studied a sample of people over the age of 80, without dementia, and found that leisure activities were associated with superior perceptual speed. The researchers also used a form of brain imaging and found that leisure activities delayed declines in white matter microstructure (myelin).

Shared leisure activities also contribute to the satisfaction of marital and other intimate partners and to family well-being (Ton & Hansen, 2001). They reduce stress (Melamed et al., 1995) and help retirees avert boredom (Sonnentag, 2003). Contributing to civic activities or volunteering at hospitals and the like also enhances retirees' self-esteem and fosters feelings of self-efficacy (Siegrist et al., 2004).

Leisure takes on special importance after retirement and may become central to the retiree's identity and self-acceptance. If the retiree's health remains robust, leisure activities tend to carry over from working days and may ease the transition to retirement. On the other hand, the physical aspects of aging and the death of companions can force changes in the choice of activities and diminish the level of satisfaction gotten from them.

A British study of adults with an average age of 72 reported that nearly three in four (73%) engaged in leisure activities (Ball et al., 2007); of these, 23% engaged in "active leisure" (sailing, walking); 18%, "passive leisure" (listening to music, watching television); 24%, social activities; 20%, hobbies; and 15%, other activities. The key motives for leisure activity were pleasure and relaxation.

Jo-Ida Hansen and her colleagues (Hansen et al., 2008) administered a questionnaire about leisure activities to 194 retirees, also with an average age of 72, who had been employed at a Midwestern university. They mathematically correlated the respondents' self-reported leisure activities and found that they fell into three clusters or factors, as shown in Table 18.2. Factor I included athletic, competitive, and outdoor activities. Factor II involved artistic, cultural, and self-expressive activities. Partying was the sole activity that defined Factor III. Partying isn't just for youngsters.

18-5 SUCCESSFUL AGING

The concept of *successful aging* in some ways addresses aging from a very different perspective. Whereas Erikson focused on letting go and accepting one's place in the sweep of history, successful aging focuses on maximizing one's life experiences at any age. Researchers who study successful aging focus on factors such as overall good physical health, including the absence or control of chronic diseases such as arthritis and diabetes, engaging in physical activity, social networking, and the absence of serious cognitive impairment and depression (Baltes & Rudolph, 2013). Sexual activity remains desirable, even if some aspects of performance are not what they were (Brown, 2016). According to researchers Margaret Baltes and Laura Carstensen, successful agers tend to seek emotional fulfillment by reshaping their lives to concentrate on what they find to be important and meaningful (Baltes & Rudolph, 2013; English & Carstensen, 2014).

Successful agers form emotional goals that bring them satisfaction (English & Carstensen, 2014). They may no longer compete in certain athletic or business activities. Instead, they focus on matters that allow

Participating in Activities You Enjoy—More Than Just Fun and Games

Tips from the National Institute on Aging

There are many things you can do to help yourself age will: exercise and be physically active, make healthy food choices, and don't smoke. But did you know that participating in activities you enjoy may also support healthy aging?

MITO images / Alamy stock Photo

Activities to Consider

Would you like to get more involved in your community or be more socially active? There are plenty of places to look for opportunities, depending on your interests. Here are some ideas:

Get out and about

- **Join a senior center and take part in its events and activities**
- **Play cards or other games with friends**
- **Go to the theater, a movie, or a sporting event**
- **Travel with a group of older adults, such as a retiree group**

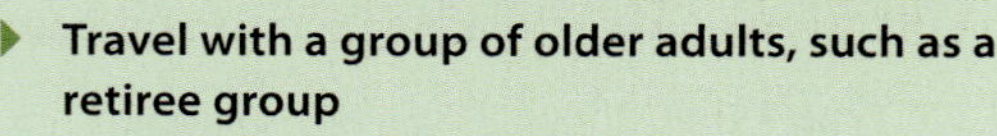

- **Visit friends and family**
- **Try different restaurants**
- **Join a group interested in a hobby like knitting, hiking, painting, or wood carving**

Learn something new

- **Take a cooking, art, or computer class**
- **Form or join a book club**
- **Try yoga, tai chi, or another new physical activity**
- **Learn (or relearn) how to play a musical instrument**

Tony Tallec / Alamy stock Photo

Become more active in your community

- **Severe meals or organize clothing donations at a place for homeless people**
- **Help an organization send care packages to soldiers stationed overseas**
- **Care for dogs and cats at an animal shelter**
- **Volunteer to run errands for people with disabilities**
- **Join a committee or volunteer for an activity at your place of worship**
- **Volunteer at a school, library, or hospital**
- **Help with gardening at a community garden or park**
- **Organize a park clean-up through your local recreation center or community association**
- **Sing in a community choral group, or play in a local band or orchestra**
- **Take part in a local theater troupe**
- **Get a part-time job**

Adapted from USDHHS National Institute on Aging. "Participating in activities you enjoy—More than just fun and games." NIH PUBLICATION NO. 15-7411 (2015, April 15). https://d2cauhfh6h4x0p.cloudfront.net/s3fs-public/participating-in-activities-you-enjoy_0.pdf (Accessed April 18, 2016).

them to maintain a sense of control over their own lives. Retaining social contacts and building new ones also contributes to a positive outlook, as does continuing with one's athletic activities, when possible, and one's artistic and cultural activities.

18-5a SELECTIVE OPTIMIZATION WITH COMPENSATION

A different view of successful aging is being advanced by researchers who focus on the processes by which individuals attempt to provide better person–environment fits to the changing physical, cognitive, and social circumstances of late adulthood (e.g., Sims et al., 2015). From this point of view, often referred to as **selective optimization with compensation**, older people manage to maximize their gains while minimizing their losses.

Successful agers also tend to be optimistic. Such an outlook may be derived from transcendence of the ego, from spirituality, or sometimes from one's genetic heritage. (Yes, there is a genetic component to happiness [Lykken & Csikszentmihalyi, 2001].) However, retaining social contacts and building new ones also contributes to a positive outlook, as does continuing with one's athletic activities, when possible, and one's, artistic and cultural activities.

The stereotype is that retirees look forward to late adulthood as a time when they can rest from life's challenges. But sitting back and allowing the world to pass by is a prescription for depression, not for living life to its fullest. In one experiment, Sandman and Crinella (1995) randomly assigned people (average age = 72) either to a foster grandparent program with neurologically impaired children or to a control group. They followed both groups for ten years. The foster grandparents carried out physical challenges, such as walking a few miles each day, and also engaged in new kinds of social interactions. Those in the control group did not engage in these activities. After ten years, the foster grandparents showed superior overall cognitive functioning, including memory functioning, and better sleep patterns, as compared with the controls.

In the more normal course of events, many successful agers challenge themselves by taking up new pursuits such as painting, photography, or writing. Some travel to new destinations. Others return to school, taking special courses for older students, sitting in on regular college classes, or participating in seminars on special topics of interest. "Get away from that computer for a while!" demands an author's spouse. "Look at this weather. Let's go biking along the river."

Although senior citizens are living longer and leading richer lives than they did in past generations, in one way or another life does draw to a close, as we see in Chapter 19.

selective optimization with compensation reshaping of one's life to concentrate on what one finds to be important and meaningful in the face of physical decline and possible cognitive impairment.

STUDY TOOLS 18

READY TO STUDY?

In the book, you can:

- ☐ Rip out the chapter review card at the back of the book for a handy summary of the chapter and key terms.
- ☐ Check your understanding of what you've read with the quizzes that follow.

ONLINE AT CENGAGEBRAIN.COM YOU CAN:

- ☐ Collect StudyBits while you read and study the chapter.
- ☐ Quiz yourself on key concepts.
- ☐ Find videos for further exploration.
- ☐ Prepare for tests with HDEV5 Flash Cards as well as those you create.

SELF-ASSESSMENTS

Fill Ins

Answers can be found in the back of the book.

1. According to Erik Erikson, late adulthood is characterized by the stage of ego integrity versus ____________.
2. The average person retiring at age 65 has about ____________ of life to look forward to.
3. Older adults may be reluctant to relocate to nursing homes because nursing homes signify the loss of ____________.
4. According to ____________ theory, we would expect that people who are better adjusted to retirement will be doing many things rather than "taking it easy."
5. Inability to bounce back from a loss is a sign of ____________.
6. As compared with couples in midlife, older couples show more affectionate behavior when they discuss conflicts, and they disagree with one another (more/ less).
7. In keeping with ____________ theory, people who age successfully tend to seek emotional fulfillment by reshaping their lives to concentrate on what they find to be important and meaningful.
8. Ego ____________ means preparing in some way to go beyond the physical limitations of one's own life span.
9. According to ____________ theory, older people and society mutually withdraw from one another as older people approach death.
10. Depression can be connected with the "big five" factor of ____________.

Multiple Choice

1. Which of the following is *not* one of Robert Peck's developmental tasks for late adulthood?

a. ego differentiation versus work-role preoccupation
b. retirement versus work-role preoccupation
c. body transcendence versus body preoccupation
d. ego transcendence versus ego preoccupation

2. Which of the following is true of the life review?

a. It is usually a sign of dementia.
b. It is filled with important "holes" because of decay of long-term memory.
c. It is egotistical and selfish.
d. It is a normal aspect of aging.

3. Socioemotional selectivity theory proposes that people

a. place more emphasis on emotional experience as they age.
b. filter out emotions that lead to recollection of unpleasant experiences.
c. disengage from society as they reach late adulthood.
d. can choose their emotional responses to situations.

4. Which is true of "body esteem" in late adulthood?

a. Men lose interest in the bodies of potential sex partners as they advance through late adulthood.
b. Body esteem increases as people progress through late adulthood.
c. Older men express lower body esteem than older women do.
d. Men and women express equal amounts of body esteem in late adulthood.

5. What percentage of lesbian, gay, and bisexual adults aged 60–91 reported good or excellent mental health in a research study?

a. 10%
b. 25%
c. 50%
d. 75%

6. Which of the following is *not* true about depression in late adulthood?

a. Depression and sadness are pretty much the same thing in late adulthood.
b. Depression in older people can be a continuation of depression from earlier periods of life.
c. Depression can be connected with the personality factor of neuroticism.
d. Depression may reflect a genetic predisposition to imbalances in the neurotransmitter norepinephrine.

7. Older people typically report preferring to live

a. in assisted living arrangements.
b. in their own homes.
c. with children.
d. in rural areas.

8. A study found that African Americans who attend church regularly live an average of 13 years longer than African Americans who never attend. As a skeptical scientist, you recognize that this study may show that

a. church attendance causes longevity.
b. people who do not attend church are too sick to attend.
c. people who do not attend church get into trouble and develop health problems.
d. people who choose to attend church may differ from those who do not.

9. Which of the following life issues tends to increase in importance as couples reach their 60s?

a. finances
b. intimacy
c. child rearing
d. political differences

10. Which of the following does *not* describe or characterize gay men or lesbians in long-term intimate relationships?

a. more alcohol and drug abuse
b. higher self-esteem
c. fewer suicidal urges
d. less depression

19 Life's Final Chapter

Millennium Images/Superstock

LEARNING OUTCOMES

After studying this chapter, you will be able to . . .

- 19-1 Define death and dying, and evaluate views on stages of dying
- 19-2 Identify settings in which people die, distinguishing between hospitals and hospices
- 19-3 Discuss various kinds of euthanasia and controversies about them
- 19-4 Discuss people's perspectives on death at various stages of development
- 19-5 Discuss coping with death, focusing on the funeral and possible stages of grieving

After you finish this chapter, go to **PAGE 398** for **STUDY TOOLS**

When we are young and our bodies are supple and strong, it may seem that we will live forever. All we have to do is eat right and exercise, and avoid smoking, reckless driving, and hanging around with the wrong people in the wrong neighborhoods. We may have but a dim awareness of our own mortality. We parcel thoughts about death and dying into a mental file cabinet to be opened later in life, along with items like retirement, Social Security, and varicose veins. But death can occur at any age—by accident, violence, or illness. Death can also affect us deeply at any stage of life through the loss of others.

> "Do not go gentle into that good night, Old age should burn and rave at close of day; Rage, rage against the dying of the light."
>
> —Dylan Thomas

The denial of death is deeply embedded in our culture. Many people prefer not to think about death or plan ahead for their eventual demise, as though thinking about it or planning for it might magically bring it about sooner. Elisabeth Kübler-Ross (1969) wrote that "We use euphemisms, we make the dead look as if they were asleep, we ship the children off to protect them from the anxiety and turmoil around the house if the [person] is fortunate enough to die at home, [and] we don't allow children to visit their dying parents in the hospitals." When we consider death and dying, a number of questions arise:

- How do we know when a person has died?
- Are there stages of dying as there are stages of development?
- What is meant by the "right to die"? Do people have a right to die?
- What is a living will?
- Is there a proper way to mourn? Are there stages of grieving?

This chapter addresses these questions and more.

19-1 UNDERSTANDING DEATH AND DYING

Death is commonly defined as the cessation of life. Many people think of death as a part of life, but death is the termination of life and not a part of life. **Dying**, though, is a part of life. It is the end stage of life in which bodily processes decline, leading to death. Yet, life can still hold significance and meaning even in the face of impending death.

19-1a CHARTING THE BOUNDARIES BETWEEN LIFE AND DEATH

death the irreversible cessation of vital life functions.

dying the end stage of life in which bodily processes decline, leading to death.

brain death cessation of activity of the cerebral cortex.

How do we know that a person has died? Is it the stop-page of the heart? Of breathing? Of brain activity?

Medical and legal professionals generally use **brain death** as the standard for determining that a person has died (Ave & Bernat, 2016). The most widely used criteria for establishing brain death include absence of activity of the cerebral cortex, as shown by a flat EEG recording. When there

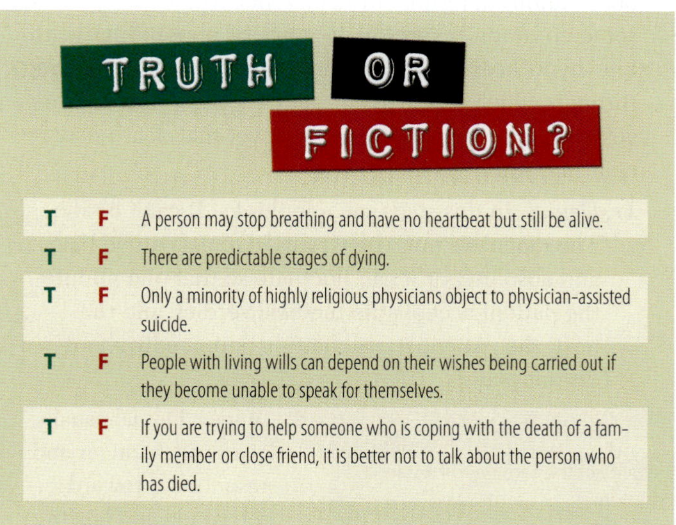

T	F	A person may stop breathing and have no heartbeat but still be alive.
T	F	There are predictable stages of dying.
T	F	Only a minority of highly religious physicians object to physician-assisted suicide.
T	F	People with living wills can depend on their wishes being carried out if they become unable to speak for themselves.
T	F	If you are trying to help someone who is coping with the death of a family member or close friend, it is better not to talk about the person who has died.

is no activity in the cortex, consciousness—the sense of self and all psychological functioning—has ceased. The broader concept of **whole brain death** includes death of the brain stem, which is responsible for certain automatic functions, such as reflexes like breathing (G. Miller, 2011; Wijdicks, 2011). Thus, a person who is "brain dead" can continue to breathe. On the other hand, in some cases people have been kept "alive," even though they were whole-brain dead, by life-support equipment that took over their breathing and circulation.

Death is also a legal matter. Most states rely on some combination of these criteria in establishing the legal standard of death. In most states, a person is considered legally dead if there is an irreversible cessation of breathing and circulation or if there is an irreversible cessation of brain activity, including activity in the brain stem, which controls breathing (Ave & Bernat, 2016).

TRUTH

(T) F A person may stop breathing and have no heartbeat but still be alive.

It is true that a person may stop breathing and have no heartbeat but still be alive. People whose hearts and lungs have ceased functioning are sometimes revived by cardiopulmonary resuscitation (CPR).

19-1b ARE THERE STAGES OF DYING?

Our overview of the process of dying has been influenced by the work of Elisabeth Kübler-Ross (1969). From her observations of terminally ill patients, Kübler-Ross found some common responses to news of impending death. She hypothesized that there are five stages of dying through which many dying patients pass. She has suggested that older people who suspect that death may be near may undergo similar responses:

1. *Denial*. In this stage, people think, "It can't be me. The diagnosis must be wrong." Denial can be flat and absolute, or it can fluctuate so that one minute the patient accepts the medical verdict, and the next, the patient starts chatting animatedly about distant plans.
2. *Anger*. Denial usually gives way to anger and resentment toward the young and healthy, and, sometimes, toward the medical establishment: "It's unfair. Why me?" or "They didn't catch it in time."
3. *Bargaining*. People may bargain with God to postpone death, promising, for example, to do good deeds if they are given another six months, or another year.
4. *Depression*. With depression come feelings of grief, loss, and hopelessness—grief at the prospect of leaving loved ones and life itself.
5. *Final acceptance*. Ultimately, inner peace may come as a quiet acceptance of the inevitable. This "peace" is not contentment; it is nearly devoid of feeling. The patient may still fear death, but comes to accept it with a sense of peace and dignity.

whole brain death cessation of activity of the cerebral cortex and brain stem.

Some current "death education" methods suggest that hospital staff and family members can support dying people by understanding the stages they are going through, by not imposing their own expectations on patients, and by helping patients achieve final acceptance when patients are ready to do so. But critics note that staff may be imposing Kübler-Ross's expectations on dying patients. At the worst, some medical students and physicians attempt to have terminally ill patients experience a "good death" by breaking through denial of what is happening to them (Borgstrom et al., 2013). Denial of impending death, to these professionals, seems to be a disease-like thing that they need to diagnose and treat.

There are other critiques of the views of Kübler-Ross. For example, (Dennis, 2015; Retsinas, 1988) Kübler-Ross's stages are limited to cases in which people receive a diagnosis of a terminal illness. Retsinas points out that most people die because of advanced

FICTION

T (F) There are predictable stages of dying.

Are there predictable stages of dying? Probably not. Though Kübler-Ross identified five stages that dying individuals commonly experience, other researchers have found that these feelings are not necessarily universal, and that even those who experience them do not necessarily do so in the predicted order.

The Case of Terri Schiavo

Marka/Superstock

Terri Schiavo collapsed from cardiac arrest, at the age of 26 and suffered brain damage due to stopping breathing. Although tests showed that her brain was largely inactive due to lack of oxygen, she began breathing on her own and was sustained in a hospital by a feeding tube for more than a decade. Following court battles between her husband, who wanted the tube removed, and her parents, who did not, the husband was finally allowed to remove the tube, resulting in the end of all life functions. The case set off numerous religious conflicts and arguments over the definition of death.

Twenty-six-year-old Terri Schiavo collapsed from cardiac arrest, stopped breathing, and suffered brain damage due to lack of oxygen. An electroencephalogram (EEG) showed that her cerebral cortex, the seat of consciousness, was largely inactive. After the collapse, Terri began breathing on her own again, but she was sustained by a feeding tube. Fifteen years later, Terri's doctors removed the feeding tube, following a protracted court battle between her husband, who had custody and wanted the tube removed, and her parents, who wanted the tube to remain in place. The battle reached state and federal courts, and even led to Congress passing a special law involving only Terri. Nevertheless, the tube was removed, and within two weeks, all of Terri's life functions ceased. Many issues were involved in Terri's case: medical, psychological, legal, religious, and philosophical (Johnson, 2016).

- **Medical (Majority Opinion): Terri's state was "persistently vegetative" (Annas, 2010; Quill, 2005), offering her no chance of regaining consciousness. Terri had experienced brain death but not whole-brain death.**
- **Medical (Minority Opinion): Terri might be suffering from a "minimally conscious state," offering her a small possibility of recovery.**
- **Psychological: Terri's EEG argued in favor of the vegetative state. Her continued breathing could be explained by the functioning of lower parts of her brain.**
- **Legal (Terri's Husband): According to state and federal courts, Terri's husband had legal custody. He argued that Terri would not have wanted to remain indefinitely in such a state.**
- **Religious (Terri's Parents/Catholic Church): Every human life is precious and sacred, regardless of how disabled.**
- **Philosophical (Aristotelian): No person's existence should ever be violated (Leland, 2005).**
- **Philosophical (Terri's Husband/Cartesian): Psychological self-awareness or consciousness is more important than biological functioning by itself, such as we might find in a plant.**

Which of these points of view makes the most sense to you?

years with no specific terminal diagnosis, and Kübler-Ross's approach may not be of much use in helping us understand reactions under circumstances other than terminal illness.

Edwin Shneidman (2008) acknowledges the presence of feelings such as those described by Kübler-Ross in dying people, but his research shows that individuals behave in dying more or less as they behaved during earlier periods when they experienced stress, failure, and threat. A gamut of emotional responses and psychological defenses emerges, especially denial; they can be observed in every death. However, the process of dying does not necessarily follow any progression of stages, as suggested by Kübler-Ross. The key factors that appear to affect the adjustment of the dying individual include the nature and extent of possible biological cognitive impairment, pain and weakness, the time or phase of the person's life, the person's philosophy of life (and death), and prior experiences with crises.

19-2 WHERE PEOPLE DIE

A hundred years ago, most people died in their homes, surrounded by family members. Today, only a small minority of Americans—typically those who are in advanced old age or who are gravely or terminally ill—die in their own homes. The growing exception, as we will see, concerns those terminally ill patients who receive hospice care at home. According to the National Hospice and Palliative Care Organization (NHPCO, 2013), two-thirds of hospice patients die in their own home or a relative's home, a nursing home, or another residential facility (see Figure 19.1). Many people, of course, die suddenly wherever they happen to be at the time, either because of accidents, heart attacks, or other unanticipated events.

19-2a IN THE HOSPITAL

Today, about half of the deaths that occur in the United States do so in hospitals, and another one in five occur in nursing homes (NHPCO, 2013). Yet, hospitals can be impersonal places. Hospitals function to treat diseases, not to help prepare patients and their families for death. Instead of dying in familiar surroundings, comforted by family and friends, patients in hospitals often face death alone, cut off from their usual supports. On the other hand, patients and their families may assume that going to the hospital gives them the best chance of averting death.

19-2b HOSPICE CARE

Increasing numbers of dying people and their families are turning to **hospice** care to help make their final days as meaningful and pain-free as possible. More than one and one half million Americans receive hospice care each year, and the number has been growing (NHPCO, 2013; see Figure 19.2). More than one-third of hospice patients are dying of cancer, and the next largest group of patients is suffering from heart disease (NHPCO, 2013). The word "hospice" derives from the Latin *hospitium*, meaning "hospitality," the same root of the words *hospital* and *hospitable*. The derivation is fitting, as hospice centers provide a homelike atmosphere to help terminally ill patients approach death with a maximum of dignity and a minimum of pain and discomfort. When necessary, hospice services can provide care in inpatient settings such as hospitals, nursing facilities, or hospice centers, but most hospice care is provided in the patient's home.

Hospice workers typically work in teams that include physicians, nurses, social workers, mental health or pastoral

FIG.19.1 LOCATION OF DEATH OF HOSPICE PATIENTS

Location of Death	2014	2011
Patient's place of residence	58.9%	66.6%
Private residence	35.7%	41.7%
Nursing home	14.5%	17.9%
Residential facility	8.7%	7.0%
Hospice inpatient facility	31.8%	26.4%
Acute care hospital	9.3%	7.0%

Source: Corbis

FIG.19.2 TOTAL HOSPICE PATIENTS SERVED, BY YEAR

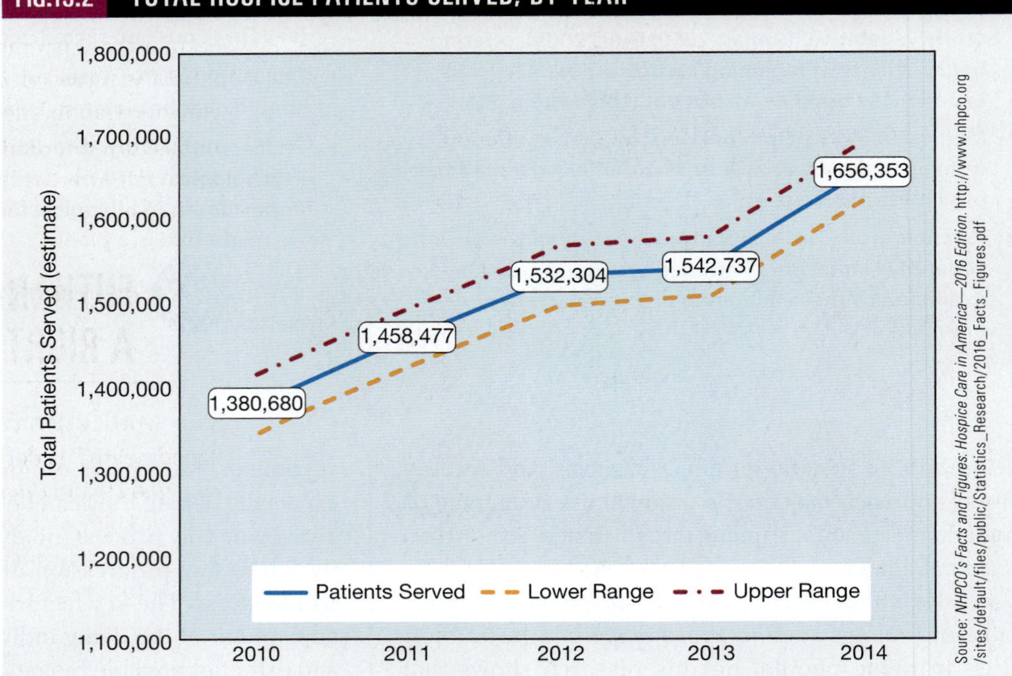

The broken lines show the probable boundaries for the actual numbers. Hospice patients comprise about half of all dying individuals today.

hospice an organization that treats dying patients by focusing on palliative care rather than curative treatment.

counselors, and home health aides (see Figure 19.3). Team members provide physical, medical, spiritual, and emotional support to the entire family, not just the patient. Bereavement specialists assist the family to prepare for the loss and help them through grieving after the death. In contrast to hospitals, hospices provide the patient and family with as much control over decision making as possible. The patient's wishes not to be resuscitated or kept alive on life-support equipment are honored. Patients are given ample amounts of pain-killing narcotics to alleviate suffering.

Hospices not only provide a more supportive environment for the patient and family, but they are less costly than hospital treatment, especially home-based care. Though the patient may be required to pay some of the costs, most of the costs are borne by insurance plans.

Hospice care has the following characteristics:

- Hospices offer **palliative care**, rather than curative treatment. They control pain and symptoms to enable the patient to live as fully and comfortably as possible.
- Hospices treat the person, not the disease. The hospice team addresses the medical, emotional, psychological, and spiritual needs of patients, family, and friends.
- Hospices emphasize quality, rather than length, of life, neither hastening nor postponing death.
- The hospice considers the entire family, not just the patient, to be the unit of care.
- Bereavement counseling is provided after the death.
- Help and support is available to the patient and family around the clock.

FIG.19.3 THE INTERDISCIPLINARY TEAM OF HOSPICE WORKERS

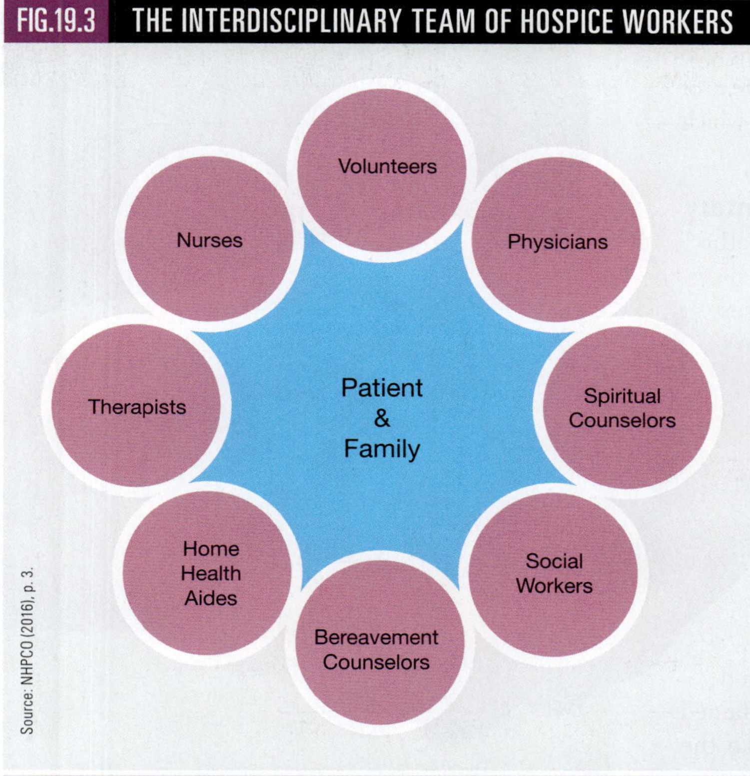

Hospice workers attempt to include the patient and the family as part of the team that will try to ease the passing of the patient.

19-2c SUPPORTING A DYING PERSON

Hospice workers are trained in what to do to help people who are dying. Following are some things you can do. First of all, you must be there for the person. Put yourself at the same eye level and don't withhold touching. Be available to listen, to talk, and to share experiences. Give the person the opportunity to talk about death and to grieve, but don't be afraid to also talk about the ongoing lives of mutual acquaintances. People who are dying often need to focus on things other than impending death, and some enjoy humorous events. They may be comforted to hear about your life experiences—your concerns and worries as well as your joys, hopes, and dreams. But be aware of the person's emotional state on any given day. Some days are better than others. Don't attempt to minimize the person's emotional pain or need to grieve by changing the subject or refusing to acknowledge it. Be sensitive to the person's feelings, and offer consolation and support. People with cognitive impairment may repeat certain thoughts many times (Cipriani et al., 2013); you can go with it or gently guide the conversation in another direction. They may repeatedly ask whether certain tasks have been taken care of, and a simple yes may do each time (Kelly et al., 2009).

19-3 EUTHANASIA: IS THERE A RIGHT TO DIE?

The word **euthanasia**, literally meaning "good death," is derived from the Greek roots *eu* ("good") and *thanatos* ("death"). Also called "mercy killing," it refers to the purposeful taking of a person's life through gentle or painless means to relieve pain or suffering.

palliative care treatment focused on the relief of pain and suffering rather than cure.

euthanasia the purposeful taking of life to relieve suffering.

19-3a ACTIVE EUTHANASIA: MERCY KILLING OR MURDER?

In **active euthanasia**, a lethal treatment (usually a drug) is administered to cause a quick and painless death. Usually a spouse or family member administers it.

VOLUNTARY ACTIVE EUTHANASIA When euthanasia is carried out with the patient's consent, it is called **voluntary active euthanasia**. Voluntary active euthanasia remains illegal throughout most of the United States, although legal challenges to state laws are working their way through the courts. It is not illegal in some other countries, such as the Netherlands.

PHYSICIAN-ASSISTED SUICIDE In some cases of active voluntary euthanasia, physicians have assisted patients with terminal or incapacitating illnesses who wished to die by providing them with lethal doses of drugs or sometimes by administering the drugs when the patients were too ill to administer them themselves. The best-known cases of such physician-assisted suicides have involved Dr. Jack Kevorkian, a retired pathologist dubbed "Dr. Death" by the press for having assisted in more than 35 patient suicides. Following an assisted suicide that was aired on *60 Minutes* in 1998, Kevorkian was convicted of second-degree homicide in Michigan and served eight years in prison. Unlike Kevorkian, an activist for the legalization of euthanasia who sought publicity to promote his cause, most physicians who assist in patient suicides avoid public scrutiny for fear of legal prosecution and sanctions by medical societies, which remain ethically opposed to the practice.

INVOLUNTARY ACTIVE EUTHANASIA **Involuntary active euthanasia** stands on shakier moral, ethical, and legal ground than voluntary euthanasia. In involuntary active euthanasia, a person causes the death of another person without that person's informed consent. Cases of involuntary euthanasia usually involve patients who are comatose or otherwise incapacitated and whose guardians believe they would have wanted to die if they had retained the capacity to make the decision. Still, in the eyes of the law, it is considered homicide.

active euthanasia the administration of a lethal treatment (usually a drug) to cause a quick and painless death.

voluntary active euthanasia the intentional administration of lethal drugs or other means of producing a painless death with the person's informed consent.

involuntary active euthanasia the intentional administration of lethal drugs or other means of producing a painless death without the person's informed consent.

TERMINAL SEDATION Terminal sedation is an alternative to euthanasia. It is the practice of relieving distress in a terminally ill patient in the last hours or days of his or her life, usually by means of a continuous intravenous infusion of a sedative drug, such as a tranquilizer. Terminal sedation is supposedly not intended to hasten death, although there is some debate as to whether it has that effect.

ATTITUDES TOWARD PHYSICIAN-ASSISTED SUICIDE The issue of physician-assisted suicide continues to be debated among physicians and in the lay community, even though the American Medical Association and a majority of physicians oppose it (Hains & Hubert-Williams, 2013; McCormack et al., 2012). Physicians themselves are split on the question of whether this form of active euthanasia is ever justified. Physicians opposing assisted suicides often cite the belief that it goes against thousands of years of medical tradition of treating patients.

Euthanasia is legal in the Netherlands, but that does not mean that it is undertaken lightly. For example,

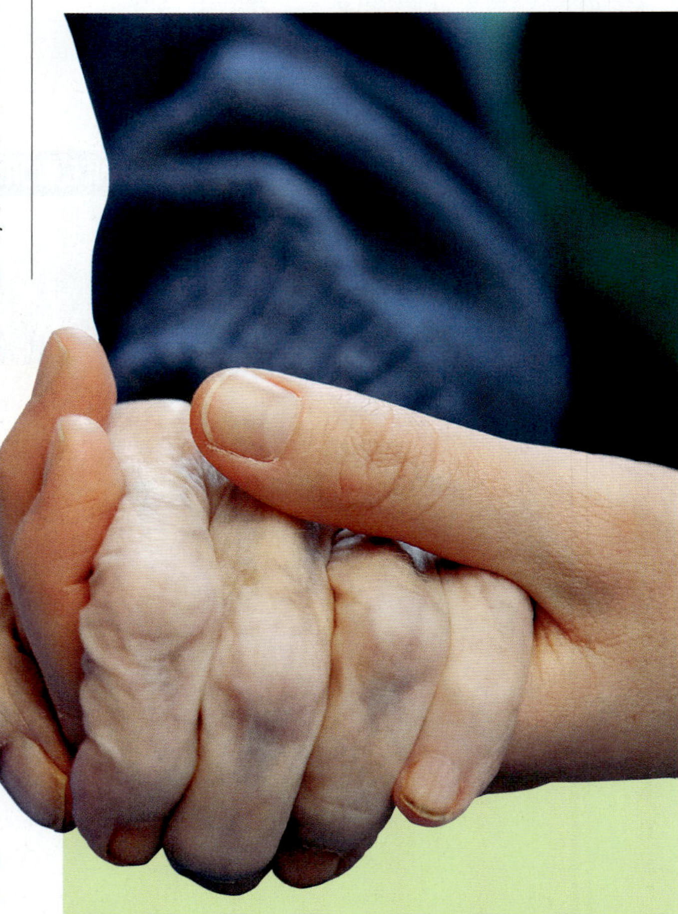

Letting go of someone who is terminally ill and in great pain can be a devastating experience.

iStock.com/leaf

An Emperor of Rome Meditates on Death

Marcus Aurelius, who lived from 121 to 180 CE, occupies a unique place in history as a Roman soldier, emperor, and philosopher. He wrote his best-known work, *Meditations*, while on one of the military campaigns that occurred during his reign, which lasted from 170 CE to 180 CE. (One such campaign is portrayed at the beginning of the Russell Crowe movie *Gladiator*.) *Meditations* is a spiritual guide to self-improvement by a man who saw a great deal of death, and he offered words of comfort:

> *We live for an instant [but to be swallowed in] complete forgetfulness and the void of infinite time. . . . Of the life of man, the duration is but a point, its substance streaming away, its perception dim, the fabric of the entire body prone to decay, and the soul a vortex, fortune incalculable and fame uncertain. In a word, all things of the body are as a river, and the things of the soul as a dream and a vapor. [It matters not how long one lives], for look at the yawning gulf of time behind thee and before thee at another infinity to come. In this eternity the life of a baby of three days and [a span] of three centuries are of one.*

Christian Handl/imageBROKER/Alamy stock Photo

Statue of Marcus Aurelius, Capitoline Museums, Rome

when a patient or a patient's family requests euthanasia to relieve a terminally ill patient's suffering, about half of the physicians try to avoid the issue because their values oppose it or it is emotionally burdensome (Georges et al., 2008). Many of these physicians suggest that it is often possible to lessen patients' suffering without hastening their death (Rietjens et al., 2008). Physicians who were open to euthanasia explained that patients' suffering sometimes could not be lessened with medicine.

A nationally representative survey of American physicians found that 69% object to physician-assisted suicide, 18% object to terminal sedation, but only 5% object to withdrawal of artificial life support (Curlin et al., 2008).

FICTION

T (F) Only a minority of highly religious physicians object to physician-assisted suicide.

It is not true that only a minority of highly religious physicians object to physician-assisted suicide. A recent study found that the great majority of highly religious physicians object to physician-assisted suicide.

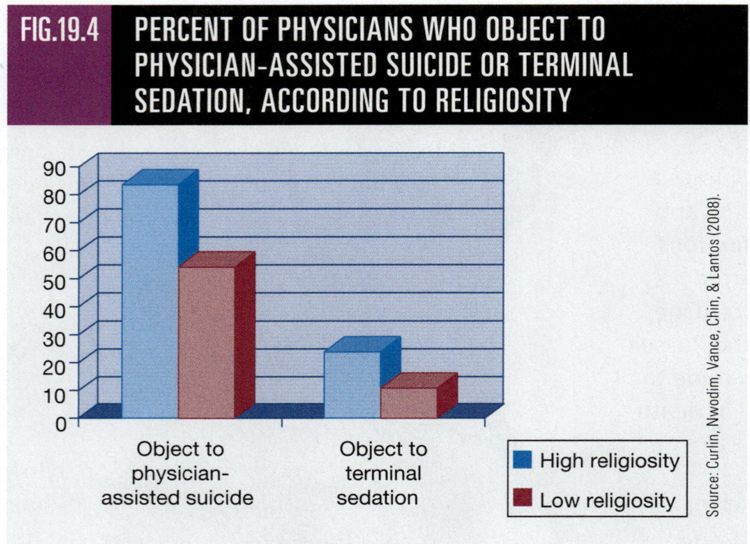

FIG.19.4 PERCENT OF PHYSICIANS WHO OBJECT TO PHYSICIAN-ASSISTED SUICIDE OR TERMINAL SEDATION, ACCORDING TO RELIGIOSITY

Religion played a role in the physicians' attitudes, as is illustrated in Figure 19.4: 84% of highly religious physicians objected to physician-assisted suicide, as compared with 55% of physicians who were not particularly religious; 25% of highly religious physicians objected to terminal sedation, as compared with 12% of less religious physicians.

A survey of 988 terminally ill patients found that 60.2% said they supported euthanasia or physician-assisted suicide in general, but only 10.6% reported seriously considering it for themselves (Emanuel et al., 2000). Patients who were 65 and older and who felt more appreciated by others were less likely to consider euthanasia and suicide. Not surprisingly, depression, pain, and substantial caregiving needs all contributed to consideration of suicide.

Euthanasia, defined as performance of the death-inducing act by another person (such as a physician), is illegal nearly everywhere in the United States. Oregon and Washington enacted Death with Dignity Acts (in 1997 and 2008, respectively). Death with Dignity Acts are being signed into law elsewhere as well. These acts in Oregon and Washington enable terminally ill patients to ask physicians to prescribe lethal doses of medication. The medication is then administered by patients themselves. In 2014, Brittany Maynard, a woman with brain cancer, moved to Oregon so she could terminate her life with medication (Nursing Management, 2014).

passive euthanasia the withholding or withdrawal of life-sustaining treatment to hasten death.

living will a document prepared when a person is well, directing medical care providers to terminate life-sustaining treatment in the event he or she becomes incapacitated and unable to speak.

19-3b PASSIVE EUTHANASIA

Passive euthanasia involves actions that hasten death by means of withholding potentially life-saving treatments, such as failing to resuscitate a terminally ill patient who stops breathing, or withdrawing medicine, food, or life-support equipment (such as a respirator) from a comatose patient. The legal status of passive euthanasia varies with the circumstances. One form of passive euthanasia that is legal throughout the United States and Canada is the withholding or withdrawing of life- sustaining equipment or techniques from terminally ill people who clearly specify their wish not to be kept alive by aggressive or heroic treatment. The declaration of these wishes may be in the form of a *living will* (discussed next), which specifies the conditions under which the person desires to have life-sustaining treatment withdrawn or withheld.

19-3c THE LIVING WILL

Carlos suffers a tragic accident that leaves him in an irreversible coma and dependent on artificial life support—a respirator to maintain his breathing and feeding tubes to supply his body with nutrients. Would Carlos want his life to be maintained by whatever means were at the disposal of modern medicine, or would he prefer doctors to withdraw life support, allowing him to die naturally?

Keisha has been in pain day after day. She suffers from a terminal disease and her heart suddenly stops due to cardiac arrest. Would she want the doctors to resuscitate her by whatever means necessary in order to prolong her life for another few days or weeks? Who is to decide when it is time for her to die—Keisha or the doctors managing her care?

In 1990, the U.S. Supreme Court ruled that individuals have a right to end life-sustaining treatment. The decision provided the legal basis for the **living will**, a legal document that people usually draft before their terminal illness that directs health-care workers not to use aggressive medical procedures or life-support equipment to prolong vegetative functioning in the event they became permanently incapacitated and unable to communicate their wishes. Terminally ill patients can insist, for example, that "Do not resuscitate" orders be included in their charts, directing doctors not to use CPR in the event they suffer cardiac arrest.

The withdrawal of life-sustaining treatment is a form of passive euthanasia. Unlike active euthanasia, death is

iStockPhoto.com/doublediamondphoto/John Cooke

The U.S. Supreme Court has ruled that a living will, signed by the patient before death, allows the patient to specify that he or she does not want to be kept alive by indefinitely by life-sustaining medical equipment if he or she has no chance of recovery and is incapable of verbally communicating his or her preferences at the end.

not induced by administering a drug or assisting in the patient's suicide. More than 90% of the American public approve of living wills.

Living wills must be drafted in accordance with state laws. The living will only takes effect if people are unable to speak for themselves. For this reason, living wills usually identify a proxy such as the next of kin to make decisions in the event that the signer cannot communicate.

Still, many living wills are ignored. Some are disregarded by proxies, often because they don't judge the patient's wishes accurately, or if they do, because they can't bear the emotional burden of "pulling the plug." Physicians, too, may not comply with advance directives, perhaps because they weren't available when needed or they weren't clear. Physicians are more likely to follow specific advance directives (e.g., "Do not resuscitate") than general guidelines.

FICTION

T (F) People with living wills can depend on their wishes being carried out if they become unable to speak for themselves.

It is not always the case that people with living wills can depend on their wishes being carried out if they become unable to speak for themselves. There are many reasons that a living will may not be carried out, but specific advance directives have a better chance of being carried out than general guidelines.

19-4 LIFE-SPAN PERSPECTIVES ON DEATH

Psychologists have found interesting developments in people's understanding of and reactions to death. Children, for example, seem to follow something of a Piagetian route in their cognitive development although reversibility is reversed—in other words, they begin by thinking of death as reversible and, by about the time they enter school, they see it as irreversible (Poltorak & Glazer, 2006). People who truly understand what death is appear to take some reasonable steps to avert it, even "risk-taking" adolescents (Mills et al., 2008).

Without taking sides in what we might think of as a religious debate, we can note that many people at most ages assume, or are encouraged to assume, a form of spiritual reversibility in their thinking about death (Balk et al., 2007; Lattanzi-Licht, 2007). Religious traditions inform them that the soul of the person who has passed on will dwell in heaven or in Paradise forever, or that it will be reincarnated on Earth.

19-4a CHILDREN

Many young children lack the cognitive ability to understand the permanent nature of death (Christ, 2010; Nader & Salloum, 2011). Preschoolers may think that death is reversible or temporary, a belief reinforced by cartoon characters that die and come back to life again (Corr, 2010). Nevertheless, their thinking becomes increasingly realistic as they progress through the ages of four through seven (Corr & Balk, 2010; Gaab et al., 2013). It appears that children's understanding of death is increased as they learn about the biology of the human body and how various organs contribute to the processes of life (McGuire et al., 2013).

Loss is often most difficult to bear for children, especially when it involves the loss of a parent (Christ,

2010). Death of a loved one strikes at the core of a child's sense of security and well-being. Older children may feel guilty because of the mistaken belief that they brought about the death by once wishing for the person to die. The loss of security may lead to anger, which may be directed toward surviving family or expressed in aggressive play. They also may show regressive or infantile behaviors, such as talking "baby talk" or becoming more demanding of food or attention. Some children may persist for several weeks in maintaining the belief that the deceased person is still alive. Though child psychiatrists believe this is normal, prolonged denial can be a harbinger of the development of more severe problems (Corr & Balk, 2010).

When children learn about death, it is normal for them to fear it. But children in various cultures are also taught that it is possible to survive death, either through reincarnation, as in some Eastern religions, or as in the transcendence of the soul, as in Christianity. Children in the United States are sometimes told things like "Your father is now in heaven and you will see him there again. Meanwhile, he is watching over you." The concept of surviving death renders death less permanent and less frightening to many children—and adults (Moore & Moore, 2010).

Organ Donation: The Gift of Life

Donating your organs for transplant surgery after your death keeps a part of you alive while helping someone else in need (Hyde & White, 2014). Living donors—usually family members— can be used for some transplants. For most procedures, such as those involving liver, heart, lung, and corneal transplants, organs must be taken from donors shortly after death. Only organs that were healthy at the time of death and remain intact after death are suitable for transplantation. The donor must also be free of infectious diseases.

Medical advances have greatly improved the chances of success of organ transplantation. To minimize the risk of rejection of the transplanted organ by the body's immune system, the recipient may require lifelong immunosuppressive drugs.

There is a shortage of donor organs (Hyde & White, 2014). Many patients anxiously await word that an organ is available. The federal government helps ensure an equitable distribution of donated organs by requiring hospitals to inform relatives of donors about the United Network for Organ Sharing (www.unos.org). Many people indicate their organ donor status on their driver's licenses. However, because the status list on the license is not legally binding, prospective donors are advised to discuss their wishes with their family members.

Aphp-St Antoine-Garo / Phanie

How can you help a child cope with grief? First of all, don't force a frightened child to attend a funeral. Another kind of service or observance may be more appropriate for them, such as lighting a candle, saying a prayer, or visiting a grave site at another time. Many helping professionals suggest avoiding the use of euphemisms that deny the reality the children face—euphemisms such as "Aunt Jane is sleeping comfortably now" (Moore & Moore, 2010). They also suggest responding to children's questions and worries as honestly and openly as possible, but in a way that reassures them that you are available to help them cope with their loss. But here, of course, we again run into the issue of what the reality of death is; the person who believes in an afterlife, the agnostic, and the atheist all have different versions.

It is generally advised to let children know that they can express their feelings openly and freely without fear of criticism (Moore & Moore, 2010). Spend time with them, providing emotional support and reassurance. Also, be aware of danger signals—such as loss of sleep or

Peter Casolino / Alamy Stock Photo

Children generally experience death differently from adults. They may fear it but not quite understand what has happened. They tend to take their cues for responding from their elders and their peers. After they had been running around their grandfather's coffin in the funeral home, and were about to leave for the ceremony at the church, your author heard one young child ask another, "What was your favorite part?"

appetite, depressed mood for several weeks, the development of excessive fears (such as fear of being alone), withdrawal from friends, a sharp decline in school performance, or refusal to attend school—that indicate the child may need professional help.

There has been debate as to whether it is best to encourage children to let go of their ties to the person who has died, reach some sort of "closure," and "move on" with their own lives (Corr & Balk, 2010). Research suggests that it is possible for children to maintain their bond with the deceased person even while they continue to grieve, invest in other relationships and new activities, and learn to live under the changed circumstances (Sasaki, 2007).

19-4b ADOLESCENTS

Adolescents are "in between" in many ways. They know full well that when life functions come to an end in a particular body, they cannot be restored, yet they are not beyond constructing magical, spiritual, or pseudoscientific theories as to how some form of life or thought might survive (Corr & Balk, 2010; Nader & Salloum, 2011). Adolescents also speak of death in terms of concepts such as light, darkness, transition, and nothingness (Corr & Balk, 2010).

As compared with young children, adolescents also become increasingly exposed to death among older family members such as grandparents, and even among fellow adolescents, some of whom have died of illness but others from accidents, suicide, or foul play. Adolescents are more likely than young children to attend funerals, including funerals with open caskets. These experiences challenge the adolescent sense of immortality that is connected with the personal fable (see Chapter 11; Corr & Balk, 2010). Even though adolescents come to recognize that the concept of death applies to them, they continue to engage in riskier behavior than adults do.

Although older children and adolescents may be prey to some cognitive distortions about death, they can also be remarkably insightful. When asked for advice on how to communicate with loved ones who are dying, a group of 49 children and adolescents suggested the following (Keeley & Generous, 2014):

- Confirm your deep relationship with the person who is dying,
- Try to remain as positive as possible, and
- Seek support from external networks—people beyond the family.

19-4c ADULTS

Most young adults in developed nations need not spend much time thinking about the possibility of their deaths. The leading causes of death in early adulthood are accidents, suicide, and homicide. Except for those living in high-risk environments such as war zones, some inner cities, or, in the case of women, places where there are high rates of maternal death during pregnancy and childbirth, young adults do not often die. Heart disease, cancer, HIV/AIDS, and, for women, complications of pregnancy, remain less common causes of death in the United States.

In middle adulthood, heart disease and cancer have become the leading causes of death. People are advised to become proactive by screening for cardiovascular problems and several kinds of cancer. There are some gender differences with kinds of cancer, but educated women and men become aware that age is a risk factor for both heart disease and cancer, and they are likely to become aware of middle-aged people who died "untimely" deaths from these diseases.

Heart disease and cancer remain the leading causes of death in late adulthood. As people move into advanced old age, many should no longer be driving due to loss of sensory acuity and slowed reaction time. They are also more prone to falls. Alzheimer's disease and other dementias increase greatly. Some older people come to fear disability and discomfort nearly as much as death.

Theorists of social and emotional development in late adulthood suggest that ego transcendence, or concern for the well-being of humankind in general, enables some people to begin to face death with an inner calm (Ardelt & Ferrari, 2014). On the other hand, continuing with physical, leisure, and informal social activities are all associated with greater life satisfaction among older, retired people (Joung & Miller, 2007; Talbot et al., 2007). There is no single formula for coping with physical decline and the approach of death.

19-5 COPING WITH DEATH

For most of us, coping with death is at best complicated, and at worst painful and disorienting. Losing a spouse or life partner is generally considered to be the most stressful life change we can endure.

19-5a WHAT TO DO WHEN SOMEONE DIES

If you are present at someone's death, call the family doctor, the police, or 911. A doctor is needed to complete the death certificate and indicate the cause of death. If the cause of death cannot be readily determined, a coroner or medical examiner may become involved to determine the cause of death. Once the person's body has been examined by the doctor and the death certificate has been completed, a funeral director may be contacted to remove the body from the home or the hospital, and arrangements may be made for burial, cremation, or placement in a mausoleum. If death occurs unexpectedly or foul play is involved or suspected, an autopsy may be performed to determine the cause and circumstances of death. Sometimes an autopsy is performed, with the family's consent, if the knowledge gained from the procedure could benefit medical science.

FUNERAL ARRANGEMENTS Funerals provide an organized way of responding to death that is tied to religious custom and cultural tradition. They offer family and community a ritual that allows them to grieve publicly and say farewell to the person who died. Funerals grant a kind of closure that can help observers begin to move on with their lives.

Family members of the deceased decide how simple or elaborate they prefer the funeral to be, whether they want embalming (treating a dead body with chemicals in order to preserve it), and whether the deceased's body should be buried or cremated (reducing a dead body to ashes, by burning, usually as a funeral rite). Sometimes these matters are spelled out by religious or family custom. Sometimes family members fight over them.

After their homes, automobiles, and children's educations, funerals may be American families' next largest expense. Consider these guidelines to arrange a funeral that meets your needs and remains in your budget.

1. Have a good friend go with you to arrange the funeral. Bring someone who will be able to make decisions based on reason and good sense, rather than emotions or guilt.
2. If a funeral home has not yet been selected, shop around; you can and should ask about services and costs.
3. Be aware that some cemeteries offer the plot for free but then make their profits from charging exorbitant maintenance fees, opening and closing fees, charges for monuments, and other fees.
4. Veterans are entitled to a free burial plot in a national cemetery, but the family will incur the costs of transporting the body.
5. Caskets are often the major burial expense and can range from $500 to $50,000 or more! Recognize that the type of casket you choose makes no difference to the deceased person, and tell the funeral director to show you models that fall within the price range that you are comfortable paying.

LEGAL AND FINANCIAL MATTERS Many legal and financial matters usually require attention following a death. There may be issues concerning estates, inheritance, outstanding debts, insurance, and amounts owed for funeral expenses. It can be difficult for family members to focus on these matters during a time of grief. They should seek legal counsel if they have questions concerning how to handle the deceased person's affairs and to protect their own financial interests. Usually an attorney will be needed to settle the estate, especially if the estate is sizeable or if complex matters arise in sorting through the deceased person's affairs.

Coping with loss requires time and the ability to come to terms with the loss and move ahead with one's life. Having a supportive social network also helps.

19-5b GRIEF AND BEREAVEMENT

The death of a close friend or family member can be a traumatic experience. It typically leads to a state of **bereavement**, an emotional state of longing and deprivation that is characterized by feelings of **grief** and a deep sense of loss. **Mourning** is synonymous with grief over the death of a person, but also describes culturally prescribed ways of displaying grief. Different cultures prescribe different periods of mourning and different rituals for expressing grief. The tradition of wearing unadorned black clothing for mourning dates at least to the Roman Empire. In rural parts of Mexico, Italy, and Greece, widows are often still expected to wear black for the remainder of their lives. In England and the United States, the wearing of black is on the decline.

Coping with loss requires time and the ability to come to terms with the loss and move ahead with one's life. Having a supportive social network also helps.

GRIEVING There is neither one right way to grieve nor a fixed period of time for which grief should last. In some cases, especially for parents who have lost a child, grief never ends, although it does tend to lessen over time. People grieve in different ways (Nseir & Larkey, 2013). Some grieve more publicly, while others reveal their feelings only in private. You may not always know when someone is grieving.

Grief usually involves a combination of emotions, especially depression, loneliness, feelings of emptiness, disbelief and numbness, apprehension about the future ("What will I do now?"), guilt ("I could have done something"), even anger ("They could have handled this better"). Grief may also be punctuated by relief that the deceased person is no longer suffering intense pain and by a heightened awareness of one's own mortality. Grief may also compromise the immune system, leaving the person more vulnerable to disease. Researchers also find that the death of a loved one puts one at greater risk of committing suicide, especially during the first week following the loss (Pitman et al., 2016).

19-5c ARE THERE STAGES OF GRIEVING?

John Bowlby (1961), the attachment theorist, was the first to propose a stage theory of grief for coping with bereavement. It included four stages: shock-numbness, yearning-searching, disorganization-despair, and reorganization. Elisabeth Kübler-Ross (1969) adapted Bowlby's stage theory to describe her five-stage reaction of terminally ill patients to knowledge of their own impending death: denial-isolation, anger, bargaining, depression, and acceptance. The stage theory of grief has become generally accepted when applied to various kinds of losses, including children's responses to parental separation, adults' responses to marital separation (Gray et al., 1991), and hospital staffs' responses to the death of an inpatient. There is currently heavy reliance in medical education on the Kübler-Ross (Kübler-Ross & Kessler, 2005) model of grief (Maciejewski et al., 2007).

Jacobs (1993) modified the stage theory of grief to include the following stages: numbness-disbelief, separation distress (yearning-anger-anxiety), depression-mourning, and recovery. Jacobs' stage theory, like those that have come before, is largely based on anecdotes and case studies.

In order to test Jacobs' theory, Paul Maciejewski and his colleagues (2007) administered five items measuring disbelief, yearning, anger, depression, and acceptance of death to 233 bereaved individuals from 1 to 24 months following their losses. The results are shown visually in Figure 19.5. A number of findings are clear. Disbelief was highest just after the loss and gradually waned over the course of two years. Acceptance of the loss shows the opposite course, being nonexistent at the outset, growing gradually, and peaking two years later. Yearning, anger, and depression rise suddenly in the predicted order and then each wanes gradually.

bereavement the state of deprivation brought about by the death of a family member or close friend.

grief emotional suffering resulting from a death.

mourning customary methods of expressing grief.

FIG.19.5 INDICATORS OF GRIEF AMONG BEREAVED PEOPLE

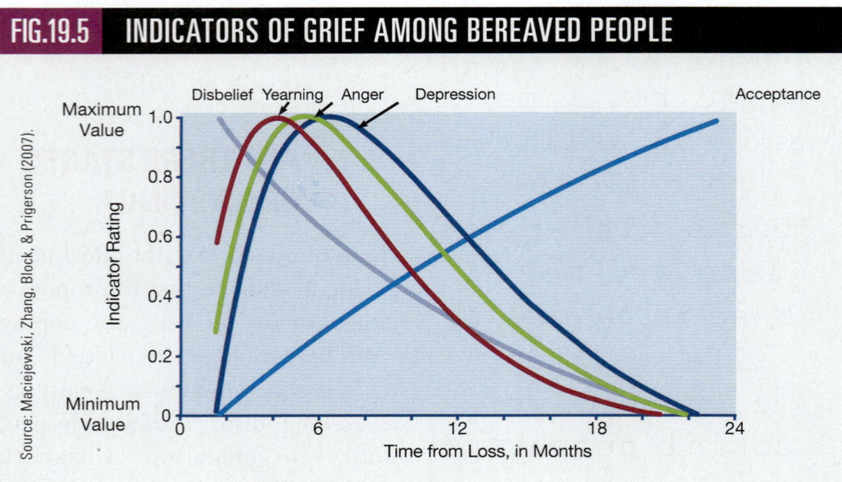

grieving. When you feel the time is right, turning to a trusted friend or a counselor may help you get in touch with your feelings.

Don't reject offers of help from friends and family. If they don't know how they can help, tell them what you need.

Don't command yourself to get over it. Give yourself time. There is no fixed timetable for grief to run its course. Don't let other people push you into moving on "to the next stage" unless you are prepared to do so.

19-5d THE DUAL PROCESS MODEL OF GRIEVING

Rather than theorizing about stages of grieving, the **dual process model** captures the ways in which the bereaved individual is torn between focusing on the loss and focusing on reengaging his or her own life (Neimeyer & Harris, 2016; Strobe & Schut, 2010). If we think of how each view can inform professionals who help grieving people, stage theory might suggest helping people move through the stages, leading to final acceptance. Dual process theory would suggest helping people fully appreciate and try to come to terms with the loss while also thinking about who and what remains and how to move forward with life (Neimeyer, 2016).

19-5e ADVICE FOR COPING

What can you do if you are faced with the death of someone who is close to you? Consider some combination of the following: First, take care of yourself. People who are grieving can become so absorbed with their loss that they fail to attend to their own personal needs. They may not eat or bathe. They may feel guilty doing things for themselves and avoid any pleasurable experiences. One can grieve without withdrawing from life.

Allow yourself to feel your loss. Some people prefer to bottle up their feelings, but covering up feelings or trying to erase them with tranquilizers may prolong

dual process model the view that people who have suffered the loss of a loved one vacillate between focusing on the death and focusing on reengaging with their own lives.

David Harry Stewart/The Image Bank/Getty Images

According to the dual process model of grieving, people who have suffered a loss tend to be torn between focusing on the death and reengaging their own lives. How can psychotherapy help grieving individuals?

The Widow Who Wasn't a Bride

What do you call a widow who isn't a widow? Part of the problem, according to Shatz (2006), is that there is no word for a woman who has cohabited with a man who has died, even if she has been with him for decades. In her doctoral dissertation, Shatz describes the experiences of nine women who experienced "disenfranchised grief" following the loss of their partners. The bereaved women felt marginalized by society and cut off from their partners' biological children. Not only had their partners taken care of their children in their wills, to the exclusion of their cohabitants, but they had arranged to be buried next to their late spouses at some time in the past and never made a change. Apparently, their partners did not want to be thought of badly by their biological children.

Andrew Bret Wallis/Photolibrary/Getty Images

Where does she belong? She mourns but was not related to her deceased partner. They cohabited for a decade but did not get married after her partner was divorced from his first wife. Often there is no formal place for such women; they are frequently at odds with the partner's children, and the man's grave may be in a plot he will someday share with the woman from whom he was divorced.

Join a bereavement support group. You will find that you are not alone in your suffering. Sharing experiences can help you cope better and work through your grief in a supportive environment (Clark et al., 2011; Damlanakis & Marzlall, 2012; Nseir & Larkey, 2013).

ADVICE FOR HELPING A BEREAVED FRIEND OR RELATIVE COPE When someone you know has lost a loved one, it is natural to want to reach out to her or him. Yet you may not know how to help, or you may fear that you'll say the wrong thing. *Don't worry about*

FICTION

T (F) If you are trying to help someone who is coping with the death of a family member or close friend, it is better not to talk about the person who has died.

It is not necessarily true that you should avoid talking about the person who has died when you are trying to help someone who is coping with the death of a family member or close friend.

what to say. Just spending time with the bereaved person can help. Nor should you expect to have all the answers; sometimes there are no answers. Sometimes what matters is simply being a good listener. Don't be afraid to talk about the deceased person. Take your cue from the bereaved person. Not talking about the departed person brings down a curtain of silence that can make it more difficult for the bereaved person to work through feelings of grief. By the same token, don't force bereaved people to talk about their feelings. Keep in touch regularly, but don't assume that because you don't get a call, the person doesn't want to talk. The bereaved person may be too depressed or lack the energy to reach out. Offer to help with chores like shopping, running errands, and babysitting (Benkel et al., 2009; Brown et al., 2008).

Don't minimize the loss, and avoid clichés like, "You're young, you can have more children," or "It was for the best."

19-5f "LYING DOWN TO PLEASANT DREAMS . . ."

The American poet William Cullen Bryant is best known for his poem "Thanatopsis," which he composed at the age of 18. "Thanatopsis" expresses Erik Erikson's goal of ego integrity—optimism that we can maintain a sense of trust through life. By meeting squarely the challenges of our adult lives, perhaps we can take our leave with dignity. When our time comes to "join the innumerable caravan"—the billions who have died before us—perhaps we can depart life with integrity.

Bryant died at age 85. At that advanced age, his feelings—and his verse—might have differed from those of the young man who wrote "Thanatopsis." But literature and poetry, unlike science, need not reflect reality. They can serve to inspire and warm us.

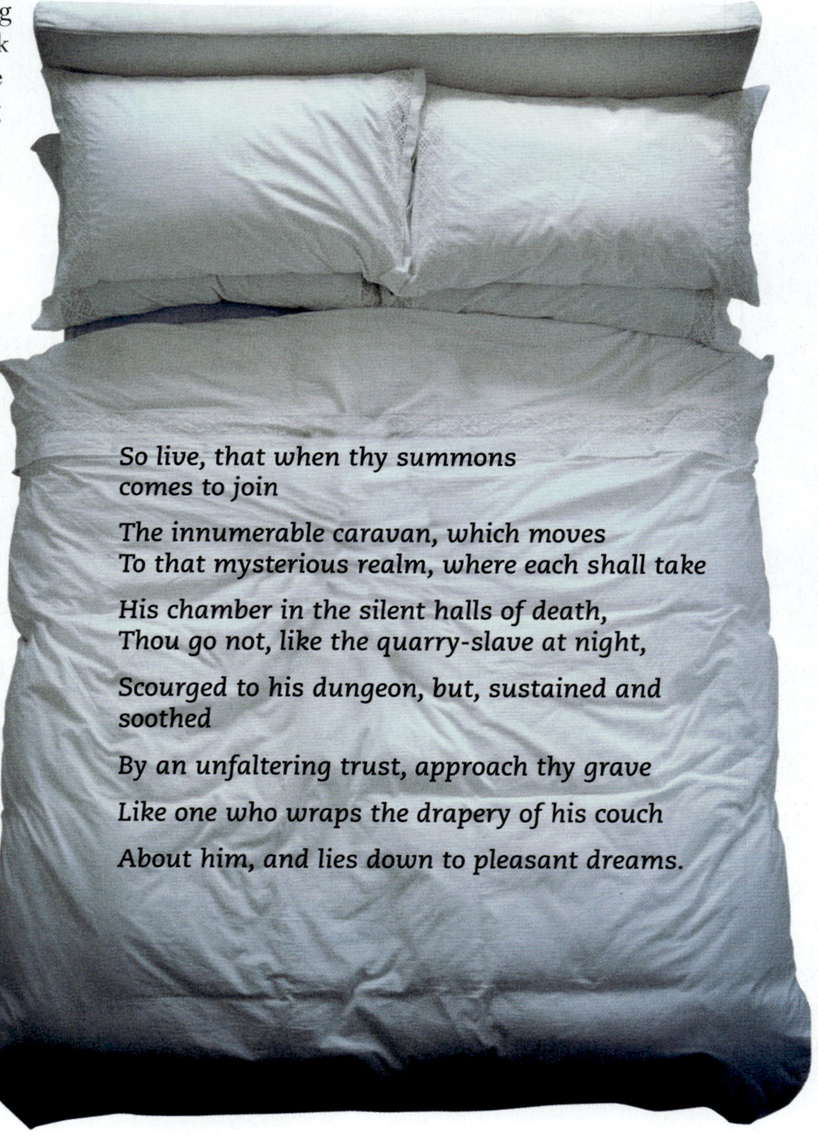

So live, that when thy summons comes to join
The innumerable caravan, which moves
To that mysterious realm, where each shall take
His chamber in the silent halls of death,
Thou go not, like the quarry-slave at night,
Scourged to his dungeon, but, sustained and soothed
By an unfaltering trust, approach thy grave
Like one who wraps the drapery of his couch
About him, and lies down to pleasant dreams.

Corbis/VCG/Getty Images

Festivals for the Dead

Around the globe, there are those who depart the world and those who are left behind to remember them and, often, to celebrate them. Many cultures have festivals or holidays during which they celebrate the dead:

- **In Latin America, people build altars to the departed on the Day of the Dead (*Dia de los Muertos*), using skulls made of sugar, marigolds, and the favorite foods of the deceased.**
- **In many other European countries, Roman Catholics take off from work on All Saints Day and All Souls Day, visit cemeteries with flowers and candles, and shower children with candy and toys.**
- **In Japan, Buddhists celebrate the Bon Festival to honor the departed spirits of their ancestors. Bon is a time for visiting one's hometown, reuniting with family, cleaning graves, and—yes—dancing.**
- **On the holiday of Chuseok, Koreans visit shrines for the spirits of their more distant ancestors and worship them. They bring offerings of food and drink to the graves of their more immediate ancestors.**
- **Chinese who follow the traditional Ching Ming Festival tend the graves of their departed in the spring. The seventh month of the Chinese calendar is Ghost Month, when many Chinese believe that the spirits of the dead visit the Earth from the underworld.**
- **During the Philippines holiday of *Araw ng mga Patay* (Day of the Dead), bereaved families may camp out near grave sites for a night or two, bringing flowers, repairing tombs, and lighting candles. Families eat, drink, sing and dance, and play cards.**

Craig Lovell / Eagle Visions Photography / Alamy Stock Photo

Chocolate skulls are sold during the Day of the Dead in Guanajuato, Mexico.

John & Lisa Merrill/The Image Bank/Getty Images

Selling special *pan de muertos* (bread of the dead) as offerings during the Day of the Dead in Mexico.

The *Dia de los Muertos* celebrations in Mexico and among Mexican Americans can be traced back 2,500–3,000 years, to the cultures that dwelled in Mexico prior to colonization by Europeans. Archeological evidence suggests that the Aztecs and others kept the skulls of their ancestors and displayed them during rituals that symbolized life and death.

On the *Dia de los Muertos*, Mexicans visit cemeteries to communicate with the souls of the dead. They build altars and offer food, drink—tequila, mescal, pulque, and the like—and photographs to encourage the souls to visit. These are not necessarily somber occasions. Laughter can be heard as celebrants recount humorous stories about the departed. Celebrants may provide pillows and blankets to allow the deceased to rest after their tiring journeys from the underworld.

The celebrants at the *Dia de los Muertos* and at similar festivals around the world believe that some kind of spiritual work is being done—that there is some kind of special communion taking place between the living and their departed ancestors. They expect, perhaps, that when they themselves depart, the younger generations will also keep their spirits in touch with the world and their own descendants. At the very least, these festivals provide comfort for the bereaved and enable them to channel their own concerns about the end of life into cultural festivals with joyous elements.

STUDY TOOLS 19

READY TO STUDY?

In the book, you can:

- ☐ Rip out the chapter review card at the back of the book for a handy summary of the chapter and key terms.
- ☐ Check your understanding of what you've read with the quizzes that follow.

ONLINE AT CENGAGEBRAIN.COM YOU CAN:

- ☐ Collect StudyBits while you read and study the chapter.
- ☐ Quiz yourself on key concepts.
- ☐ Find videos for further exploration.
- ☐ Prepare for tests with HDEV5 Flash Cards as well as those you create.

SELF-ASSESSMENTS

Fill-Ins

Answers can be found in the back of the book.

1. Medical and legal professionals generally use ____________ death as the standard for determining that a person has died.
2. Elisabeth Kübler-Ross claimed that there are ____________ stages of dying.
3. Medical opinion asserted that Terri Schiavo's state was persistently ____________ as she lay sustained by a feeding tube.
4. Terminal ____________ is the practice of relieving distress in a terminally ill patient in the last hours or days of his or her life, usually by means of a continuous intravenous infusion of a sedative drug.
5. Jack Kevorkian was found guilty of second-degree homicide for his practicing of physician-assisted ____________.
6. Maciejewski and his colleagues studied stages of grieving and found that ____________ is highest just after the loss and gradually lessens over the course of two years.
7. The ____________ will is a legal document that people typically draft before a terminal illness that directs health-care workers not to use aggressive medical procedures or life-support equipment to prolong vegetative functioning in the event they became permanently incapacitated and unable to communicate their wishes.
8. Hospices provide ____________ care, treatment focused on the relief of pain and suffering.
9. The term ____________ is synonymous with grief over the death of a person, but also describes culturally prescribed ways of displaying grief.
10. ____________ was the first researcher to propose a stage theory of grief.

Multiple Choice

1. **The concept of whole brain death refers to death of the brain and the**
   a. corpus callosum.
   b. executive center of the brain.
   c. myelin sheath.
   d. brain stem.

2. **The last stage in Kübler-Ross's stages of dying is**
   a. depression.
   c. final acceptance.
   b. grieving.
   d. anger.

3. **Kübler-Ross carried out her research with**
   a. people younger than age 40.
   b. terminally ill patients.
   c. people who had recovered from serious illnesses.
   d. nonhuman mammalian species.

4. **Actions that hasten death by means of withholding potentially life-saving treatments are known as**
   a. physician-assisted suicide.
   b. passive euthanasia.
   c. involuntary active euthanasia.
   d. voluntary active euthanasia.

5. **The location of death for the greatest number of hospice patients is a**
   a. hospital.
   b. hospice inpatient facility.
   c. nursing home.
   d. private residence.

6. **In the years 2008 through 2010, an estimated ______ people received hospice care each year.**
   a. 50,000
   c. 750,000
   b. 250,000
   d. 1,500,000

7. **When supporting a dying person, all of the following are helpful suggestions *except***
   a. putting yourself at the same eye level.
   b. encouraging the person to go through the stages of dying in order.
   c. giving the person the opportunity to talk about death and to grieve.
   d. discussing the ongoing lives of mutual acquaintances.

8. **Children are more likely than adults to believe that death is**
   a. reversible.
   b. painful.
   c. the doorway to an afterlife.
   d. punishment for wrongdoing.

9. **Experience with a death challenges the adolescent sense of immortality that is connected with**
   a. intellectual deficiency.
   b. the personal fable.
   c. formal operations.
   d. dualistic thinking.

10. **Which of the following is an emotional state of longing and deprivation that is characterized by a deep sense of loss?**
    a. mourning
    b. depression
    c. bereavement
    d. denial

ANSWERS TO STUDY TOOLS QUESTIONS

Chapter 1

FILL-INS

1. Locke
2. superego
3. psychosocial
4. bladder
5. assimilation
6. species
7. exosystem
8. Terman
9. positive
10. sequential

MULTIPLE CHOICE

1. b
2. d
3. a
4. d
5. b
6. a
7. a
8. c
9. d
10. c

Chapter 2

FILL-INS

1. Genes
2. 50
3. XYY
4. Sickle
5. calcium
6. endometriosis
7. trophoblast
8. placenta
9. Preeclampsia
10. oxygen

MULTIPLE CHOICE

1. d
2. b
3. a
4. a
5. c
6. d
7. c
8. b
9. a
10. b

Chapter 3

FILL-INS

1. Braxton-Hicks
2. epidural
3. vernix
4. Europe
5. hormones
6. bonding
7. Apgar
8. rooting
9. underarm
10. postpartum psychosis

MULTIPLE CHOICE

1. c
2. a
3. d
4. c
5. c
6. b
7. a
8. c
9. d
10. b

Chapter 4

FILL-INS

1. critical
2. second
3. cradle board
4. canalization
5. antibodies
6. multiple sclerosis
7. neurons
8. visual cortex
9. toddler
10. face

MULTIPLE CHOICE

1. c
2. a
3. a
4. d
5. c
6. a
7. c
8. d
9. c
10. c

Chapter 5

FILL-INS

1. assimilation
2. secondary
3. object
4. deferred
5. Babbling
6. recognition
7. fifth
8. mirror
9. echolalia
10. overextension

MULTIPLE CHOICE

1. b
2. a
3. b
4. d
5. b
6. a
7. d
8. d
9. b
10. d

Chapter 6

FILL-INS

1. ambivalent/resistant
2. preattachment
3. Harlow
4. critical
5. Asperger's
6. 24
7. referencing
8. rouge
9. difficult
10. goodness

MULTIPLE CHOICE

1. a
2. b
3. a
4. d
5. d
6. a
7. c
8. c
9. d
10. d

Chapter 7

FILL-INS

1. cognitive
2. three
3. deep
4. 5 years, or any answer between 60–71 months
5. pictoral
6. 50
7. transductive
8. rehearsal
9. symbolize
10. 1,400

MULTIPLE CHOICE

1. b
2. a
3. d
4. a
5. d
6. c
7. d
8. b
9. d
10. b

Chapter 8

FILL-INS

1. memories
2. initiative
3. categorical
4. testosterone
5. authoritative
6. functional
7. Prosocial
8. reject
9. dramatic
10. Bandura

MULTIPLE CHOICE

1. a
2. d
3. b
4. a
5. a
6. c
7. c
8. c
9. b
10. d

Chapter 9

FILL-INS

1. conventional
2. sensory
3. mental
4. performance
5. Spanish
6. word-recognition
7. g factor or general intelligence
8. transitivity
9. dyslexia
10. objective

MULTIPLE CHOICE

1. a
2. a
3. d
4. c
5. c
6. b
7. c
8. d
9. d
10. a

Chapter 10

FILL-INS

1. latency
2. industry
3. perspective
4. coregulation
5. depression
6. self-fulfilling
7. conduct
8. global
9. caregiving
10. inner, personality, psychological

MULTIPLE CHOICE

1. b
2. b
3. c
4. c
5. d
6. d
7. b
8. c
9. a
10. d

Chapter 11

FILL-INS

1. Testosterone
2. endometrium
3. accidents, injuries
4. child, sexual
5. asynchronous
6. formal
7. Nocturnal
8. visual–spatial
9. absence
10. secular

MULTIPLE CHOICE

1. a
2. d
3. b
4. d
5. c
6. d
7. a
8. b
9. c
10. b

Chapter 12

FILL-INS

1. authoritative
2. Intimacy, Closeness, Self-disclosure
3. love, trust, commitment
4. 17
5. sex
6. heterosexual
7. half, 50%, 52%
8. attraction to members of the same gender
9. peer pressure
10. depression, hopelessness, low self-esteem

MULTIPLE CHOICE

1. a
2. c
3. d
4. b
5. d
6. d
7. d
8. b
9. a
10. c

Chapter 13

FILL-INS

1. money
2. emerging
3. thermogenesis
4. dualistic
5. accidents
6. 35
7. accidents, injuries
8. cognitive–affective
9. 30
10. relativistic

MULTIPLE CHOICE

1. c
2. d
3. a
4. a
5. c
6. b
7. c
8. a
9. d
10. b

Chapter 14

FILL-INS

1. isolation
2. dream
3. red
4. Evolutionary
5. infatuation
6. Boomerang
7. monogamy
8. homogamy
9. Being single, Singlehood
10. jealousy

MULTIPLE CHOICE

1. d
2. d
3. a
4. c
5. d
6. c
7. a
8. b
9. c
10. b

Chapter 15

FILL-INS

1. integumentary
2. melanin
3. elasticity
4. fat
5. cancer
6. diet
7. arteriosclerosis, atherosclerosis
8. plasticity
9. procedural
10. Flynn

MULTIPLE CHOICE

1. c
2. b
3. a
4. d
5. c
6. b
7. d
8. a
9. c
10. a

Chapter 16

FILL-INS

1. empty nest
2. neuroticism
3. conscientiousness
4. agreeableness
5. identity
6. stagnation
7. transition
8. 50–62
9. sandwich
10. depressed

MULTIPLE CHOICE

1. d
2. d
3. a
4. c
5. d
6. a
7. b
8. c
9. d
10. b

Chapter 17

FILL-INS

1. expectancy
2. lenses
3. osteoporosis
4. telomeres
5. antibodies
6. free
7. joints
8. Implicit
9. Long-term
10. dementia

MULTIPLE CHOICE

1. d
2. a
3. b
4. d
5. a
6. d
7. b
8. c
9. b
10. a

Chapter 18

FILL-INS

1. despair
2. 20 years, two decades
3. independence
4. activity
5. depression
6. less
7. socioemotional selectivity
8. transcendence
9. disengagement
10. neuroticism

MULTIPLE CHOICE

1. b
2. d
3. a
4. c
5. d
6. a
7. b
8. d
9. b
10. a

Chapter 19

FILL-INS

1. brain
2. five
3. vegetative
4. sedation
5. suicide
6. disbelief
7. living
8. palliative
9. mourning
10. John Bowlby

MULTIPLE CHOICE

1. d
2. c
3. b
4. b
5. d
6. d
7. b
8. a
9. b
10. c

REFERENCES

AAIDD. (2012). *What is the AAIDD definition of intellectual disability?* Retrieved from http://www.aaidd.org/intellectualdisabilitybook/content_7473.cfm?navID5366

Aartsen, M. J., et al. (2005). Does widowhood affect memory performance of older persons? *Psychological Medicine, 35*(2), 217–226.

Abdelaziz, Y. E., Harb, A. H., & Hisham, N. (2001). *Textbook of Clinical Pediatrics*. Philadelphia, PA: Lippincott Williams & Wilkins.

Aber, J. L., Bishop-Josef, S. J., Jones, S. M., McLearn, K. T., & Phillips, D. A. (Eds.). (2007). *Child development and social policy: Knowledge for action. APA Decade of Behavior volumes*. Washington, DC: American Psychological Association.

Abravanel, E., & DeYong, N. G. (1991). Does object modeling elicit imitative-like gestures from young infants? *Journal of Experimental Child Psychology, 52*, 22–40.

Adam, E. K., et al. (2011). Adverse adolescent relationship histories and young adult health: Cumulative effects of loneliness, low parental support, relationship instability, intimate partner violence, and loss. *Journal of Adolescent Health, 49*(3), 278–286.

Adams, G. A., & Rau, B. L. (2011). Putting off tomorrow to do what you want today. *American Psychologist, 66*(3), 180–192.

Adams, R. G., & Ueno, K. (2006). Middle-aged and older adult men's friendships. In V. H. Bedford & B. Formaniak Turner (Eds.), *Men in relationships: A new look from a life course perspective* (pp. 103–124). New York, NY: Springer.

Adler-Baeder, F. (2006). What do we know about the physical abuse of stepchildren? A review of the literature. *Journal of Divorce & Remarriage, 44*(3–4), 67–81.

Adolescent Health. (2014). Summary health statistics: National Health Interview Survey, 2014. Table C-5a. Centers for Disease Control and Prevention. http://ftp.cdc.gov/pub/Health_Statistics/NCHS/NHIS/SHS/2014_SHS_Table_C-5.pdf.

Adolph, K. E., & Berger, S. E. (2005). Physical and motor development. In M. H. Bornstein & M. E. Lamb (Eds.), *Developmental science: An advanced textbook* (5th ed., pp. 223–281). Hillsdale, NJ: Erlbaum.

Adolph, K. E., Berger, S. E., & Leo, A. J. (2011). Developmental continuity? Crawling, cruising, and walking. *Developmental Science, 14*(2), 306–318.

Adolph, K. E., & Robinson, S. R. (2015). Motor development, vol. 2: Cognitive processes. *Handbook of Child Psychology and Developmental Sciences*, DOI: 10.1002/9781118963418.childpsy204

Agency for Healthcare Research and Quality. (2004, April). Chronic illnesses. In *Child Health Research Findings*. (Program Brief, AHRQ Publication 04-P011). Rockville, MD: Author. Retrieved from http://www.ahrq.gov/research/childfind/chfchrn.htm

Aguiar, N. R., & Taylor, M. (2015). Children's concepts of the social affordances of a virtual dog and a stuffed dog. *Cognitive Development, 34*, 16–27.

Ainsworth, M. D. S. (1989). Attachments beyond infancy. *American Psychologist, 44*, 709–716.

Ainsworth, M. D. S., & Bowlby, J. (1991). An ethological approach to personality development. *American Psychologist, 46*(4), 333–341.

Ainsworth, M. D. S., Blehar, M. C., Waters, E., & Wall, S. (1978). *Patterns of attachment: A psychological study of the Strange Situation*. Hillsdale, NJ: Erlbaum.

Ajdacic-Gross, V., et al. (2008). Suicide after bereavement. *Psychological Medicine, 38*(5), 673–676.

Albuquerque, D., Manco, L., & Nobrega, C. (2016). Genetics of human obesity. In S. I. Ahmad, & S. K. Imam (Eds.). *Obesity* (pp. 87–106). Switzerland: Springer.

Alexander, G. M., Wilcox, T., & Woods, R. (2009). Sex differences in infants' visual interest in toys. *Archives of Sexual Behavior, 38*(3), 427–433.

Alfirevic, Z., Sundberg, K., & Brigham, S. (2003). Amniocentesis and chorionic villus sampling for prenatal diagnosis. *Cochrane Database of Systematic Reviews*. doi:10.1002/14651858.CD003252

Ali, M. M., & Dwyer, D. S. (2011). Estimating peer effects in sexual behavior among adolescents. *Journal of Adolescence, 34*(1), 183–190.

Allain, P., Kauffmann, M., Dubas, F., Berrut, G., & Le Gall, D. (2007). Executive functioning and normal aging: A study of arithmetic word-problem-solving. *Psychologie & NeuroPsychiatrie Du Vieillissement, 5*(4), 315–325.

Allen, G., et al. (2011). Functional neuroanatomy of the cerebellum. In A. S. Davis (Ed.), *Handbook of pediatric neuropsychology* (pp. 147–160). New York, NY: Springer.

Allison, S. T., & Setterberg, G. C. (2016). *Suffering and sacrifice: Individual and collective benefits, and implications for leadership*. http://works.bepress.com/scott_allison/29/.

Alloway, R. G., & Alloway, T. P. (2013). Working memory in development. In T. P. Alloway, & R. G. Alloway (Eds.). *Working memory: The connected intelligence* (pp. 63–82). New York: Psychology Press.

Alloway, T. P., Gathercole, S. E., Willis, C., & Adams, A. (2004). A structural analysis of working memory and related cognitive skills in young children. *Journal of Experimental Child Psychology, 87*(2), 85–106.

Alzheimer's disease statistics. (2011). Centers for Disease Control and Prevention. Retrieved from http://www.cdc.gov/mentalhealth/data_stats/alzheimers.htm

Amanatullah, E. T., & Morris, M. W. (2010). Negotiating gender roles: Gender differences in assertive negotiating are mediated by women's fear of backlash and attenuated when negotiating on behalf of others. *Journal of Personality and Social Psychology, 98*(2), 256–267.

Amato, P. R. (2006). Marital discord, divorce, and children's well-being: Results from a 20-year longitudinal study of two generations. In A. Clarke-Stewart & J. Dunn (Eds.), *Families count: Effects on child and adolescent development. The Jacobs Foundation series on adolescence* (pp. 179–202). New York, NY: Cambridge University Press.

Amato, P. R., & Cheadle, J. E. (2008). Parental divorce, marital conflict and children's behavior problems: A comparison of adopted and biological children. *Social Forces, 86*(3), 1139–1161.

Amato, P. R., & Previti, D. (2003). People's reasons for divorcing. *Journal of Family Issues, 24*, 602–626.

Amato, P. R., Booth, A., Johnson, D. R., & Rogers, S. J. (2007). *Alone together: How marriage in America is changing*. Cambridge, MA: Harvard University Press.

Amato, P. R., & Anthony, C. J. (2014). Estimating the effects of parental divorce and death with fixed effects models. *Journal of Marriage and Family, 76*(2), 370–386.

America's Children. (2007). Centers for Disease Control and Prevention. National Center for Health Statistics. Childstats.gov. *America's children: Key national indicators of well-being*, 2007. Adolescent births. Indicator Fam6: Birth Rates for Females Ages 15–17 by Race and Hispanic Origin, 1980–2005. Retrieved from http://www.childstats.gov/americaschildren/famsoc6.asp

American Academy of Child & Adolescent Psychiatry. (2008). *Children and divorce*. Retrieved from http://www.aacap.org/cs/root/facts_for_families/children_and_divorce

American Academy of Family Physicians. (2006, November 1). Nutrition in toddlers. *American Family Physician, 74*(9). Retrieved from http://www.aafp.org/afp/20061101/1527.html

American Academy of Pediatrics. (2011). SIDS and other sleep-related infant deaths: Expansion of recommendations for a safe infant sleeping environment. *Pediatrics, 128*(5), e1341–e1367.

American Cancer Society. (2012a). *Cancer facts & figures 2012.* Atlanta, GA: Author. Retrieved from http://www.cancer.org/acs/groups/content/@epidemiologysurveilance/documents/document/acspc-031941.pdf

American Cancer Society. (2012b). *Lifetime risk of developing or dying from cancer.* Retrieved from http://www.cancer.org/Cancer/CancerBasics/lifetime-probability-of-developing-or-dying-from-cancer

American Cancer Society. (2012c). *Cancer facts & figures for African Americans.* Retrieved from http://www.cancer.org/Research/CancerFactsFigures/

American Cancer Society. (2016a). *Colorectal cancer facts and figures.* http://www.cancer.org/research/cancerfactsstatistics/colorectal-cancer-facts-figures.

American Cancer Society. (2016b). *Cancer basics.* http://www.cancer.org/cancer/cancerbasics/index.

American College of Obstetricians and Gynecologists. (2011). *Dysmenorrhea.* Retrieved from http://www.acog.org/~/media/for%20patients/faq046.ashx

American Fertility Association. (2010). *Fertility drugs: Clomiphene citrate.* Retrieved from http://www.theafa.org/article/fertility-drugs-clomiphene-citrate

American Fertility Association. (2012). *Infertility: Causes and treatments.* Retrieved from http://www.theafa.org/family-building/infertility-causes-treatments

American Heart Association. (2007). *Overweight in children.* Retrieved from http://www.americanheart.org/presenter.jhtml?identifier=4670

American Lung Association. (2007). Various fact sheets. Retrieved from http://www.lungusa.org

American Psychiatric Association. (2000). *Diagnostic and statistical manual of mental disorders (DSM–IV–TR).* Washington, DC: Author.

American Psychological Association. (2007). *Stress in America: Mind/body health: For a healthy mind and body, talk to a psychologist.* Washington, DC: Author.

American Psychological Association. (2012). *Stress tip sheet.* American Psychological Association Help Center Media Room, Page A, Item 42.

American Psychological Association. (2012). *Stress in America: Our health at risk.* Washington, DC: Author. Retrieved from http://www.apa.org/news/press/releases/stress/2011/final-2011.pdf

Amodio, D. M., & Showers, C. J. (2005). "Similarity breeds liking" revisited: The moderating role of commitment. *Journal of Social and Personal Relationships, 22*(6), 817–836.

Andersen, A. E., & Ryan, G. L. (2009). Eating disorders in the obstetric and gynecologic patient population. *Obstetrics and Gynecology, 114*(6), 1353–1367.

Andersen, M. L., & Taylor, H. H. (2009). *Sociology: The essentials* (5th ed.). Belmont, CA: Wadsworth.

Anderson, B. J. (2011). Plasticity of gray matter volume: The cellular and synaptic plasticity that underlies volumetric change. *Developmental Psychobiology, 53*(5), 456–465.

Anderson, C. A., et al. (2010). Violent video game effects on aggression, empathy, and prosocial behavior in Eastern and Western countries: A meta-analytic review. *Psychological Bulletin, 136*(2), 151–173.

Anderson, C. A. (2015). Consensus on media violence effects: Comment on Bushman, Gollwitzer, and Cruz. *Psychology of Popular Media Culture, 4*(3), 215–221.

Anderson, P. J., & Leuzzi, V. (2010). White matter pathology in phenylketonuria. *Molecular Genetics and Metabolism, 99*(Suppl.), S3–S9.

Ando, M., et al. (2011). Factors that influence the efficacy of bereavement life review therapy for spiritual well-being: A qualitative analysis. *Supportive Care in Cancer, 19*(2), 309–314.

Andreano, J. M., & Cahill, L. (2009). Sex influences on the neurobiology of learning and memory. *Learning and Memory, 16*, 248–266.

Andrews, G., Clark, M., & Luszcz, M. (2002). Successful aging in the Australian longitudinal study of aging: Applying the MacArthur Model cross-nationally. *Journal of Social Issues, 58*, 749–765.

Annas, G. J. (2005, April 4). "Culture of life" politics at the bedside—The case of Terri Schiavo. *New England Journal of Medicine.* Retrieved from http://www.nejm.org

Annett, M. (1999). Left-handedness as a function of sex, maternal versus paternal inheritance, and report bias. *Behavior Genetics, 29*(2), 103–114.

Ansell, E. B., et al. (2010). The prevalence and structure of obsessive-compulsive personality disorder in Hispanic psychiatric outpatients. *Journal of Behavior Therapy and Experimental Psychiatry, 41*(3), 275–281.

Antonucci, T. C., & Birditt, K. S. (2004). *Lack of close relationships and well-being across the life span.* Paper presented to the American Psychological Association.

Aquilino, W. S. (2005). Impact of family structure on parental attitudes toward the economic support of adult children over the transition to adulthood. *Journal of Family Issues, 26*(2), 143–167.

Arai, A., et al. (2007). Association between lifestyle activity and depressed mood among home-dwelling older people. *Aging & Mental Health, 11*(5), 547–555.

Arbib, M. A. (2015). Language evolution: An emergentist perspective. In B. MacWinney, & W. O'Grady (Eds.). *The handbook of language emergence* (pp. 600–623). West Sussex, UK: Wiley.

Ardelt, M. (2008a). Wisdom, religiosity, purpose in life, and death attitudes of aging adults. In A. Tomer, G. T. Eliason, T. Grafton, & P. T. P. Wong (Eds.), *Existential and spiritual issues in death attitudes* (pp. 139–158). Mahwah, NJ: Erlbaum.

Ardelt, M. (2008b). Self-development through selflessness: The paradoxical process of growing wiser. In H. A. Wayment, & J. J. Bauer (Eds.), *Transcending self-interest: Psychological explorations of the quiet ego. Decade of behavior* (pp. 221–233). Washington, DC: American Psychological Association.

Arias, E. (2011, September 28). *National Vital Statistics Reports, 59*(9). Table B. Retrieved from http://www.cdc.gov/nchs/data/nvsr/nvsr59/nvsr59_09.pdf

Arnett, J. J. (2007). Socialization in emerging adulthood: From the family to the wider world, from socialization to self-socialization. In J. E. Grusec & P. D. Hastings (Eds.), *Handbook of socialization: Theory and research* (pp. 208–231). New York, NY: Guilford.

Arnett, J. J. (2012). New horizons in research on emerging and young adulthood. *National Symposium on Family Issues, 2*(5), 231–244.

Arnett, J. J. (2016). Emerging adulthood theory and research: Where we are and where we should go. *Oxford handbook on emerging adulthood* (pp. 1–10). New York: Oxford University Press.

Arterberry, M. E., & Kellman, P. J. (2016). *Development of perception in infancy.* New York: Oxford University Press.

Aschermann, E., Gülzow, I., & Wendt, D. (2004). Differences in the comprehension of passive voice in German-and English-speaking children. *Swiss Journal of Psychology, 63*(4), 235–245.

Aslin, R. N. (2012). Infant eyes: A window on cognitive development. *Infancy: Special Issue: Advances in Eye Tracking in Infancy Research, 17*(1), 126–140.

Aspy, C. B., et al. (2007). Parental communication and youth sexual behaviour. *Journal of Adolescence, 30*(3), 449–466.

Atkinson, G., & Davenne, D. (2007). Relationships between sleep, physical activity and human health. *Physiology & Behavior, 90*(2–3), 229–235.

Auger, R. W., Blackhurst, A. E., & Wahl, K. H. (2005). The development of elementary-aged children's career aspirations and expectations. *Professional School Counseling, 8*(4), 322–329.

August, D., Carlo, M., Dressler, C., & Snow, C. (2005). The critical role of vocabulary development for English language learners. *Learning Disabilities Research & Practice, 20*(1), 50–57.

Auyeung, B., et al. (2009). Fetal testosterone predicts sexually differentiated childhood behavior in girls and in boys. *Psychological Science, 20*(2), 144–148.

Ave, A. L. D., & Bernat, J. L. (2016). Using the brain criterion in organ donation after the circulatory determination of death. *Journal, of Critical Care*, DOI: 10.1016/jcrc.2016.01.005.

Avers, D., et al. (2011). Use of the term "elderly." *Journal of Geriatric Physical Therapy*, *34*(4), 153–154.

Avinum, R., & Knafo-Noam, A. (2015). Socialization, genetics, and their interplay in development. In J. E. Grusec & P. D. Hastings (Eds.). *Handbook of socialization: Theory and Research* (pp. 347–371). New York. Guilford.

Aviv, A., & Bogden, J. D. (2010). Telomeres and the arithmetic of human longevity. *The Future of Aging, Part 2*, 573–586.

Awasaki, T., & Ito, K. (2016). Neurodevelopment: Regeneration is a gas. *Nature*, *531*, 182–183.

Azmitia, M. (2015). Reflections on the cultural lenses of identity development. In K. C. McLean, & M. Syed (Eds.). *The Oxford handbook of identity development* (pp. 286–298). New York: Oxford University Press.

B

Bachman, J. G., Johnston, L. D., & O'Malley, P. M. (2011). *Monitoring the future: Questionnaire responses from the nation's high school seniors 2010*. Survey Research Center, Institute for Social Research. Ann Arbor, MI: The University of Michigan.

Bachman, J. G., Safron, D. J., Sy, S. R., & Schulenberg, J. E. (2003). Wishing to work: New perspectives on how adolescents' part-time work intensity is linked to educational disengagement, substance use, and other problem behaviours. *International Journal of Behavioral Development*, *27*(4), 301–315.

Bäckström T., et al. (2003). The role of hormones and hormonal treatments in premenstrual syndrome. *CNS Drugs*, *17*(5), 325–342.

Bada, H. S., et al. (2011). Preadolescent behavior problems after prenatal cocaine exposure: Relationship between teacher and caretaker ratings (Maternal Lifestyle Study). *Neurotoxicology and Taratology*, *33*(1), 78–87.

Badious, S., et al. (2016). Association between breast milk and HIV-1 transmission through breastfeeding. Prostaglandins, Leukotrienes, and *Essential Fatty Acids (PLEFA)*, *105*, 35–42.

Bagley, C., & D'Augelli, A. R. (2000). Suicidal behaviour in gay, lesbian, and bisexual youth. *British Medical Journal*, *320*, 1617–1618.

Bahrick, H. P., Bahrick, P. O., & Wittlinger, R. P. (1975). Fifty years of memory for names and faces: A cross-sectional approach. *Journal of Experimental Psychology: General*, *104*(1), 54–75.

Bahrick, H. P., Hall, L. K., & Da Costa, L.A. (2008). Fifty years of memory of college grades: Accuracy and distortions. *Emotion*, *8*(1), 13–22.

Baker, L. D., et al. (2012). High-intensity physical activity modulates diet effects on cerebrospinal amyloid-b levels in normal aging and mild cognitive impairment. *Journal of Alzheimer's Disease*, *28*(1), 137–146.

Bakker, D. J. (2006). Treatment of developmental dyslexia: A review. *Pediatric Rehabilitation*, *9*(1), 3–13.

Bakker, R., et al. (2010). Maternal caffeine intake from coffee and tea, fetal growth, and the risks of adverse birth outcomes: The Generation R Study. *The American Journal of Clinical Nutrition*, *91*(6), 1691–1698.

Baldry, A. C. (2003). Bullying in schools and exposure to domestic violence. *Child Abuse and Neglect*, *27*(7), 713–732.

Balk, D., Wogrin, C., Thornton, G., & Meagher, D. (2007). *Handbook of thanatology*. New York, NY: Routledge/ Taylor & Francis Group.

Ball, V., Corr, S., Knight, J., & Lowis, M. J. (2007). An investigation into the leisure occupations of older adults. *British Journal of Occupational Therapy*, *70*(9), 393–400.

Ballmaier, M., et al. (2008). Hippocampal morphology and distinguishing lateonset from early-onset elderly depression. *American Journal of Psychiatry*, *165*(2), 229–237.

Baltes, M., & Carstensen, L. L. (2003). The process of successful aging: Selection, optimization and compensation. In U. M. Staudinger & U. Lindenberger (Eds.), *Understanding human development: Dialogues with lifespan psychology* (pp. 81–104). Dordrecht, Netherlands: Kluwer Academic Publishers.

Bandura, A. (1986). *Social foundations of thought and action: A social-cognitive theory*. Englewood Cliffs, NJ: Prentice Hall.

Bandura, A. (2011). The social and policy impact of social cognitive theory. In M. M. Mark, S. I. Donaldson, & B. Campbell (Eds.), *Social psychology and evaluation* (pp. 33–71). New York, NY: Guilford.

Bandura, A., Ross, S. A., & Ross, D. (1963). Imitation of film-mediated aggressive models. *Journal of Abnormal and Social Psychology*, *66*, 3–11.

Bangal, V. B., Giri, P. A., & Mahajan, A. S. (2012). Maternal and foetal outcome in pregnancy induced hypertension: A study from rural tertiary care teaching hospital in India. *International Journal of Biomedical Research*, *2*(12), 595–599.

Banks, W. A., et al. (2010). Effects of a growth hormone-releasing hormone antagonist on telomerase activity, oxidative stress, longevity, and aging in mice. *Proceedings of the National Academy of Sciences*, *107*(51), 22272–22277.

Barac, R., & Bialystok, E. (2011). Cognitive development in bilingual children. *Language Teaching*, *44*, 36–54.

Barelli, C., Heistermann, M., Boesch, C., & Reichard, U. H. (2008). Mating patterns and sexual swellings in pair-living and multiple groups of wild whitehanded gibbons, *Hylobates lar. Animal Behaviour*, *75*(3), 991–1001.

Barr, R. G., Paterson, J. A., MacMartin, L. M., Lehtonen, L., & Young, S. N. (2005). Prolonged and unsoothable crying bouts in infants with and without colic. *Journal of Developmental & Behavioral Pediatrics*, *26*(1), 14–23.

Barr, R., Rovee-Collier, C., & Learmonth, A. (2011). Potentiation in young infants. *Memory & Cognition*, *39*(4), 625–636.

Barry, C. M., & Wentzel, K. R. (2006). Friend influence on prosocial behavior: The role of motivational factors and friendship characteristics. *Developmental Psychology*, *42*(1), 153–163.

Bartoszuk, K., & Pittman, J. F. (2010). Profiles of identity exploration and commitment across domains. *Journal of Child and Family Studies*, *19*(4), 444–450.

Bartzokis, G., et al. (2010). Lifespan trajectory of myelin integrity and maximum motor speed. *Neurobiology of Aging*, *31*(9), 1554–1562.

Bauer, P. J., & Fivush, R. (2010). Context and consequences of autobiographical memory development. *Cognitive Development*, *25*(4), 303–308.

Bauer, P., San Souci, P., & Pathman, T. (2010). Infant memory. *Wiley Interdisciplinary Reviews: Cognitive Science*, *1*, 267–277.

Baum, N., Weidberg, Z., Osher, Y., & Kohelet, D. (2011). No longer pregnant, not yet a mother: Giving birth prematurely to a very low birth weight baby. *Qualitative Health Research*, *22*(6). doi:10.1177/1049732311422899

Bauman, M. L., Anderson, G., Perry, E., & Ray, M. (2006). Neuroanatomical and neurochemical studies of the autistic brain: Current thought and future directions. In S. O. Moldin & J. L. R. Rubenstein (Eds.), *Understanding autism: From basic neuroscience to treatment* (pp. 303–322). Boca Raton, FL: CRC Press.

Baumgartner, S. E., Valkenburg, P. M., & Peter, J. (2010). Unwanted online sexual solicitation and risky sexual behavior across the lifespan. *Journal of Applied Developmental Psychology*, *31*(6), 439–447.

Baumrind, D. (1989). Rearing competent children. In W. Damon (Ed.), *Child development today and tomorrow*. San Francisco, CA: Jossey-Bass.

Baumrind, D. (1991a). The influence of parenting style on adolescent competence and substance use. *Journal of Early Adolescence*, *11*, 56–95.

Baumrind, D. (2005). Taking a stand in a morally pluralistic society: Constructive obedience and responsible dissent in moral/character education. In L. Nucci (Ed.), *Conflict, contradiction, and contrarian elements in moral development and education* (pp. 21–50). Mahwah, NJ: Erlbaum.

Bazerman, M. H., & Tenbrunsel, A. A. (2011). *Blind spots: Why we fail to do what's right and what to do about it*. Princeton, NJ: Princeton University Press.

Beauchamp, G. K., & Mennella, J. A. (2011). Flavor perception in human infants: Development and functional significance. *Digestion*, *83*(Suppl. 1), 1–6.

Beaulieu, M-D., et al. (2008). When is knowledge ripe for primary care? *Evaluation & the Health Professions*, *31*(1), 22–42.

Bebko, J. M., McMorris, C. A., Metcalfe, A., Ricciuti, C., & Goldstein, G. (2014). Language proficiency and metacognition as predictors of spontaneous rehearsal in children. *Canadian Journal of Experimental Psychology, 68*(1), 46–58.

Beck, E., Burnet, K. L., & Vosper, J. (2006). Birth-order effects on facets of extraversion. *Personality and Individual Differences, 40*(5), 953–959.

Beck, M. (1992, December 7). The new middle age. *Newsweek*, 50–56.

Becker, D. (2006). Therapy for the middleaged: The relevance of existential issues. *American Journal of Psychotherapy, 60*(1), 87–99.

Becquet, R., & Dabis, F. (2013). Turning the tide on HIV in women and children: Preventing breast-milk HIV transmission while increasing maternal life expectancy. *Clinical Infectious Diseases, 56*(1), 140–142.

Bedford, V. H., & Avioli, P. S. (2006). "Shooting the bull": Cohort comparisons of fraternal intimacy in midlife and old age. In V. H. Bedford & B. Formaniak Turner (Eds.), *Men in relationships: A new look from a life course perspective* (pp. 81–101). New York, NY: Springer.

Bedny, M., Pascual-Leone, A., Dravida, S., & Saxe, R. (2011). A sensitive period for language in the visual cortex: Distinct patterns of plasticity in congenitally versus late blind adults. *Brain and Language*, in press.

Beebe, B., et al. (2010). The origins of 12-month attachment: A microanalysis of 4-month mother-infant interaction. *Attachment & Human Development, 12*(1–2), 3–141.

Beilei, L., Lei, L., Qi, D., & von Hofsten, C. (2002). The development of fine motor skills and their relations to children's academic achievement. *Acta Psychologica Sinica, 34*(5), 494–499.

Bekhet, A. K. (2016). Relocation adjustment in older adults. *The encyclopedia of adulthood and aging*. Hoboken, NJ: Wiley.

Bekkhus, M., Rutter, M., Maughan, B., & Borge, A. I. H. (2011). The effects of group daycare in the context of paid maternal leave and high-quality provision. *European Journal of Developmental Psychology, 8*(6), 681–696.

Bell, M. A. (2011). A psychobiological perspective on working memory performance at 8 months of age. *Child Development. 83*(1), 251–265. doi:10.1111/j.1467-8624.2011.01684.x

Belmonte, M. K., & Carper, R. A. (2006). Monozygotic twins with Asperger syndrome: Differences in behaviour reflect variations in brain structure and function. *Brain and Cognition, 61*(1), 110–121.

Belsky, J. (2006a). Determinants and consequences of infant–parent attachment. In L. Balter & C. S. Tamis-LeMonda (Eds.), *Child psychology: A handbook of contemporary issues* (2nd ed., pp. 53–77). New York, NY: Psychology Press.

Belsky, J. (2006b). Early child care and early child development: Major findings of the NICHD Study of Early Child Care. *European Journal of Developmental Psychology, 3*(1), 95–110.

Belsky, J., et al. (2007). Are there long-term effects of early child care? *Child Development, 78*(2), 681–701.

Bender, H. L., et al. (2007). Use of harsh physical discipline and developmental outcomes in adolescence. *Development and Psychopathology, 19*(1), 227–242.

Bengtson, V. L., et al. (Eds.). (2005). *Sourcebook of family theory and research*. Thousand Oaks, CA: Sage.

Bengtsson, H., & Arvidsson, A. (2011). The impact of developing social perspective-taking skills on emotionality in middle and late childhood. *Social Development, 20*(2), 353–375.

Benkel, I., Wijk, H., & Molander, U. (2009). Managing grief and relationship roles influence which forms of social support the bereaved needs. *American Journal of Hospice and Palliative Medicine, 26*. doi:10.1177/1049909108330034

Bennett, S. E., & Assefi, N. P. (2005). School-based teenage pregnancy prevention programs: A systematic review of randomized controlled trials. *Journal of Adolescent Health, 36*(1), 72–81.

Berenbaum, S. A., Martin, C. L., Hanish, L. D., Briggs, P. T., & Fabes, R. A. (2008). Sex differences in children's play. In J. B. Becker et al. (Eds.), *Sex differences in the brain* (pp. 275–290). New York, NY: Oxford University Press.

Bergeman, C. S., & Boker, S. M. (Eds.) (2006). *Methodological issues in aging research. Notre Dame series on quantitative methods*. Mahwah, NJ: Erlbaum.

Berge, J. M., et al. (2015). All in the family: Correlations between parents' and adolescent siblings' weight and weight-related behaviors. *Obesity, 23*(4), 833–839.

Bergen, D. (2015). Psychological approaches to the study of play. In J. E. Johnson et al. (Eds.). *The handbook of the study of play, Vol. 2* (pp. 51–70). Lanham, MD: Rowman & Littlefield.

Berndt, T. J. (2004). Friendship and three A's (aggression, adjustment, and attachment). *Journal of Experimental Child Psychology, 88*(1), 1–4.

Berndt, T. J., & Perry, T. B. (1990). Distinctive features and effects of early adolescent friendships. In R. Montemayor, G. R. Adams, & T. P. Gullotta (Eds.), *From childhood to adolescence: A transitional period?* Newbury Park, CA: Sage.

Berndt, T. J., Miller, K. E., & Park, K. E. (1989). Adolescents' perceptions of friends and parents' influence on aspects of their school adjustment. *Journal of Early Adolescence, 9*, 419–435.

Bernstein, I. M., et al. (2005). Maternal smoking and its association with birth weight. *Obstetrics & Gynecology, 106*, 986–991.

Berscheid, E. (2010). Love in the fourth dimension. *Annual Review of Psychology, 61*, 1–25.

Bertoni, A., et al. (2007). Stress communication, dyadic coping and couple satisfaction: A cross-sectional and cross-cultural study. *Età Evolutiva, 86*, 58–66.

Berzonsky, M. D. (2011). A social-cognitive perspective on identity construction. In S. J. Schwartz et al. (Eds.), *Handbook of identity theory and research* (Part 1, pp. 55–76). New York, NY: Springer.

Besiroglu, H., Otunctemur, A., & Ozbek, E. (2015). The relationship between metabolic syndrome, its components, and erectile dysfunction: A systematic review and a meta-analysis of observational studies. *The Journal of Sexual Medicine, 12*(6), 1309–1318.

Bezdjian, S., Tuvblad, C., Raine, A., & Baker, L. A. (2011). The genetic and environmental covariation among psychopathic personality traits, and reactive and proactive aggression in children. *Child Development, 82*(4), 1267–1281.

Bialystok, E., & Senman, L. (2004). Executive processes in appearance–reality tasks: The role of inhibition of attention and symbolic representation. *Child Development, 75*(2), 562–579.

Bialystok, E., Luk, G., Peets, K. F., & Yang, S. (2010). Receptive vocabulary differences in monolingual and bilingual children. *Bilingualism: Language and Cognition, 13*, 525–531.

Bianchi, S. M., & Spain, D. (1997). Women, work and family in America. Population Reference Bureau.

Bierman, K. L., et al. (2014). Effects of Head Start REDI on children's outcomes 1 year later in different kindergarten contexts. *Child Development, 85*(1), 140–159.

Bigelow, A. E., et al. (2010). Maternal sensitivity throughout infancy: Continuity and relation to attachment security. *Infant Behavior and Development, 33*(1), 50–60.

Bigsby, R., et al. (2011). Prenatal cocaine exposure and motor performance at 4 months. *The American Journal of Occupational Therapy, 65*(5), e60–e68.

Bird, A., Reese, E., & Tripp, G. (2006). Parent–child talk about past emotional events: Associations with child temperament and goodness-of-fit. *Journal of Cognition and Development, 7*(2), 189–210.

Births and Natality. (2016). National Center for Health Statistics. http://www.cdc.gov/nchs/fastats/births.htm.

Bish, C. L., et al. (2005). Diet and physical activity behaviors among Americans trying to lose weight. *Obesity Research, 13*(3), 596–607.

Bishop, D. M. (2005). The role of race and ethnicity in juvenile justice processing. In D. F. Hawkins & K. Kempf-Leonard (Eds.), *Our children, their children: Confronting racial and ethnic differences in American juvenile justice* (pp. 23–82). The John D. and Catherine T. MacArthur foundation series on mental health and development. Research network on adolescent development and juvenile justice. Chicago, IL: University of Chicago Press.

Blachstein, H., Greenstein, Y., & Vakil, E. (2012). Aging and temporal order memory: A comparison of direct and indirect measures. *Journal of Clinical and Experimental Neuropsychology, 34*(1), 107–112.

Black, D. W. (2007). Antisocial personality disorder, conduct disorder, and psychopathy. In J. E. Grant, & M. N. Potenza. (Eds.), *Textbook of men's mental health* (pp. 143–170). Washington, DC: American Psychiatric Publishing.

Blackwell, D. L., & Lichter, D. T. (2004). Homogamy among dating, cohabiting, and married couples. *Sociological Quarterly, 45*(4), 719–737.

Blazer, D. (2012). Religion/spirituality and depression: What can we learn from empirical studies? *The American Journal of Psychiatry, 169*(1), 10–12.

Blazina, C., Eddins, R., Burridge, A., & Settle, A. G. (2007). The relationship between masculinity ideology, loneliness, and separation-individuation difficulties. *The Journal of Men's Studies, 15*(1), 101–109.

Bloom, B., Cohen, R. A., & Freeman, G. (2011). Summary health statistics for U.S. children: National Health Interview Survey, 2010. National Center for Health Statistics. *Vital Health Statistics 10*(250).

Bloom, B., Dey, A. N., & Freeman, G. (2006). Summary health statistics for U.S. children: National Health Interview Survey, 2005. *National Center for Health Statistics, Vital Health Statistics 10*(231).

Bloom, P. (2002). Mind reading, communication, and the learning of names for things. *Mind and Language, 17*(1–2), 37–54.

Blum, K., et al. (2009). *Genes and happiness. Gene Therapy and Molecular Biology, 13*, 91–129.

Blumberg, M. S., & Seelke, A. M. H. (2010). The form and function of infant sleep: From muscle to neocortex. In M. S. Blumberg, J. H. Freeman, & S. R. Robinson (Eds.), *Oxford Handbook of Developmental Behavioral Neuroscience* (pp. 391–423). New York, NY: Oxford University Press.

Blumenthal, H., et al. (2011). Elevated social anxiety among early maturing girls. *Developmental Psychology, 47*(4), 1133–1140.

Boccia, M., & Campos, J. J. (1989). Maternal emotional signals, social referencing, and infants' reactions to strangers. In N. Eisenberg (Ed.), *New directions for child development* (No. 44): *Empathy and related emotional responses*. San Francisco, CA: Jossey-Bass.

Bohon, C., Garber, J., & Horowitz, J. L. (2007). Predicting school dropout and adolescent sexual behavior in offspring of depressed and nondepressed mothers. *Journal of the American Academy of Child & Adolescent Psychiatry, 46*(1), 15–24.

Boivin, M., Vitaro, F., & Poulin, F. (2005). Peer relationships and the development of aggressive behavior in early childhood. In R. E. Tremblay, W. W. Hartup, & J. Archer (Eds.), *Developmental origins of aggression* (pp. 376–397). New York, NY: Guilford.

Boom, J., Wouters, H., & Keller, M. (2007). A cross-cultural validation of stage development: A Rasch re-analysis of longitudinal socio-moral reasoning data. *Cognitive Development, 22*(2), 213–229.

Borelli, J., et al. (2010). Attachment and emotion in school-aged children. *Emotion, 10*(4), 475–485.

Borghese, M. M., et al. (2015). Television viewing and food intake during television viewing in normal-weight, overweight and obese 9- to 11-year-old Canadian children: a cross-sectional analysis. *Journal of Nutritional Science, 4*, DOI: http://dx.doi.org/10.1017/jns.2014.72.

Bosi, M. L. & de Oliveira, F. P. (2006). Bulimic behavior in adolescent athletes. In P. I. Swain (Ed.), *New developments in eating disorders research* (pp. 123–133). Hauppauge, NY: Nova Science Publishers.

Bost, L. W., & Riccomini, P. J (2006). Effective instruction: An inconspicuous strategy for dropout prevention. *Remedial and Special Education, 27*(5), 301–311.

Bouchard, C. (2010). Defining the genetic architecture of the predisposition to obesity: A challenging but not insurmountable task. *American Journal of Clinical Nutrition, 91*(1), 5–6.

Bouchard, T. J., Jr., & Loehlin, J. C. (2001). Genes, evolution, and personality. *Behavior Genetics, 31*(3), 243–273.

Bouchard, T. J., Jr., Lykken, D. T., McGue, M., Segal, N. L., & Tellegen, A. (1990). Sources of human psychological differences: The Minnesota study of twins reared apart. *Science, 250*, 223–228.

Bowker, J. C., Thomas, K. K., Norman, K. E., & Spencer, S. V. (2011). Mutual best friend involvement. *Journal of Youth and Adolescence, 40*(5), 545–555.

Bowlby, J. (1961). Processes of mourning. *International Journal of Psychoanalysis, 42*, 317–339.

Bowlby, J. (1988). *A secure base*. New York, NY: Basic Books.

Bowman, N. A. (2010). College diversity experiences and cognitive development: A meta-analysis. *Review of Educational Research, 80*(1), 4–33.

Bozionelos, N., & Wang, L. (2006). The relationship of mentoring and network resources with career success in the Chinese organizational environment. *International Journal of Human Resource Management, 17*(9), 1531–1546.

Braarud, H. C., & Stormark, K. M. (2008). EJ814142—Prosodic modification and vocal adjustments in mothers' speech during face-to-face interaction with their two- to four-month-old infants: A double video study. *Social Development, 17*(4), 1074–1084.

Braddick, O., & Atkinson, J. (2011). Development of human visual function. *Vision Research, 51*(13), 1588–1609.

Bradley, R. H. (2006). The home environment. In N. F. Watt et al. (Eds.), *The crisis in youth mental health: Critical issues and effective programs* (Vol. 4): *Early intervention programs and policies, Child psychology and mental health* (pp. 89–120). Westport, CT: Praeger/Greenwood.

Bradley, R. H., Caldwell, B. M., & Corwyn, R. F. (2003). The child care HOME inventories: Assessing the quality of family child care homes. *Early Childhood Research Quarterly, 18*(3), 294–309.

Brady, E. M. (2007). Review of adulthood: New terrain. *Educational Gerontology, 33*(1), 85–86.

Bramlett, M. D., & Mosher, Mosher (2002). Cohabitation, marriage, divorce, and remarriage. National Center for Health Statistics, *Vital Health Statistics, 23* (22). Retrieved from http://www.cdc.gov/nchs/data/series/sr_23/sr23_022.pdf

Branco, J. C., & Lourenço, O. (2004). Cognitive and linguistic aspects in 5- to 6-year-olds' class-inclusion reasoning. *Psicologia Educação Cultura, 8*(2), 427–445.

Brandstätter, H., & Farthofer, A. (2003). Influence of part-time work on university students' academic performance. *Zeitschrift für Arbeits-und Organisationspsychologie, 47*(3), 134–145s.

Brandtjen, H., & Verny, T. (2001). Short and long term effects on infants and toddlers in full time daycare centers. *Journal of Prenatal & Perinatal Psychology & Health, 15*(4), 239–286.

Bravender, T., et al. (2010). Classification of eating disturbance in children and adolescents: Proposed changes for the *DSM-V. European Eating Disorders Review, 18*(2), 79–89.

Braver, T. S., & West, R. (2008). Working memory, executive control, and aging. In F. I. M. Craik & T. A. Salthouse (Eds.), *The handbook of aging and cognition* (3rd ed., pp. 311–372). New York, NY: Psychology Press.

Bray, G., & Bouchard, C. (2014). *Handbook of obesity: Epidemiology, etiology, and physiopathology* (4th ed.). CRC Press.

Bray, S., Dunkin, B., Hong, D. S., & Reiss, A. L. (2011). Reduced functional connectivity during working memory in Turner syndrome. *Cerebral Cortex, 21*(11), 2471–2481.

Brendgen, M., et al. (2010). Link between friendship relations and early adolescents' trajectories of depressed mood. *Developmental Psychology, 46*(2), 491–501.

Bridges, A. J. (2007). Successful living as a (single) woman. *Psychology of Women Quarterly, 31*(3), 327–328.

Bridges, L. J., Roe, A. E. C., Dunn, J., & O'Connor, T. G. (2007). Children's perspectives on their relationships with grandparents following parental separation: A longitudinal study. *Social Development, 16*(3), 539–554.

Brigham, N. B., Yoder, P. J., Jarzynka, M. A., & Tapp, J. (2011). The sequential relationship between parent attentional cues and attention to objects in young children with autism. *Journal of Autism and Developmental Disorders, 40*(2), 200–208.

Brockington, I. (2011). Maternal rejection of the young child: Present status of the clinical syndrome. *Psychopathology, 44*(5), 329–336.

Brockman, D. D. (2003). *From late adolescence to young adulthood*. Madison, CT: International Universities Press.

Bronfenbrenner, U., & Morris, P. A. (2006). The bioecological model of human development. In R. M. Lerner & W. Damon (Eds.), *Handbook of child psychology* (6th ed., Vol. 1), *Theoretical models of human development* (pp. 793–828). Hoboken, NJ: Wiley.

Brooker, R. J., et al. (2011). The association between infants' attention control and social inhibition is moderated by genetic and environmental risk for anxiety. *Infancy, 16*(5), 490–507.

Brown, C. A. (2016). Successful aging. In *The encyclopedia of adulthood and aging*. Hoboken, NJ: Wiley.

Brown, R. (1973). *A first language: The early stages*. Cambridge, MA: Harvard University Press.

Brown, R. (1977). Introduction. In C. A. Snow & C. Ferguson (Eds.), *Talking to children*. New York, NY: Cambridge University Press.

Brown, S. D., & Lent, R. W. (2016). Vocational psychology: Agency, equity, and well-being. *Annual Review of Psychology*, *67*, 541–565.

Brown, S. L., Brown, R. M., House, J. S., & Smith, D. M. (2008). Coping with spousal loss: Potential buffering effects of self-reported helping behavior. *Personality and Social Psychology Bulletin, 34*. doi:10.1177/0146167208314972

Brown, S. L., Lee, G. R., & Bulanda, J. R. (2006). Cohabitation among older adults. *Journals of Gerontology: Series B: Psychological Sciences and Social Sciences*, *61*B(2), S71–S79.

Brownell, C. A., & Carriger, M. S. (1990). Changes in cooperation and self-other differentiation during the second year. *Child Development*, 61, 1164–1174.

Browning, M. G. (2016). Methodological considerations in the evaluation of adaptive thermogenesis. *The American Journal of Clinical Nutrition, 103*(3), 952–953.

Bruchmüller, K., Margraf, J., & Schneider, S. (2011). Is ADHD diagnosed in accord with diagnostic criteria? Overdiagnosis and influence of client gender on diagnosis. *Journal of Consulting and Clinical Psychology*. doi:10.1037/a0026582

Bruck, M., Ceci, S. J., & Principe, G. F. (2006). The child and the law. In K. Renninger, I. E. Sigel, W. Damon, & R. M. Lerner (Eds.), *Handbook of child psychology* (6th ed., Vol. 4), *Child psychology in practice* (pp. 776–816). Hoboken, NJ: Wiley.

Brucker, B., et al. (2015). Watching corresponding gestures facilitates learning with animations by activating human mirror-neurons: An fNIRS study. *Learning and Instruction*, *36*001), 27–37.

Brummelte, S., & Galea, L. A. M. (2010). Depression during pregnancy and postpartum: Contribution of stress and ovarian hormones. *Progress in Neuro-Psychopharmacology and Biological Psychiatry*, *34*(5), 766–776.

Brun, C. C., et al. (2009). Sex differences in brain structure in auditory and cingulate regions. *NeuroReport: For Rapid Communication of Neuroscience Research*, *20*(10), 930.

Brunner, L. C., Eshilian-Oates, L., & Kuo, T. Y. (2003, February 1). Hip fractures in adults. *American Family Physician*, *67*(3):537–542.

Brydon, L., et al. (2011). Hostility and cellular aging in men from the Whitehall II cohort. *Biological Psychiatry*. Retrieved from http://dx.doi.org/10.1016/j.biopsych.2011.08.020

Bucholz, E. M., Desai, M. M., & Rosenthal, M. S. (2011). Dietary intake in Head Start vs non-Head Start preschool-aged children: Results from the 1999–2004 National Health and Nutrition Examination Survey. *Journal of the American Dietetic Association*, *111*(7), 1021–1030.

Budney, A. J., Vandrey, R. G., Hughes, J. R., Moore, B. A., & Bahrenburg, B. (2007). Oral delta-9-tetrahydrocannabinol suppresses cannabis withdrawal symptoms. *Drug and Alcohol Dependence*, *86*(1), 22–29.

Buehler, C., O'Brien, M., Swartout, K. M., & Zhou, N. (2014). Maternal employment and parenting through middle childhood: Contextualizing factors. *Journal of Marriage and Family*, *76*(5), 1025–1046.

Bugental, D. B., & Happaney, K. (2004). Predicting infant maltreatment in low-income families: The interactive effects of maternal attributions and child status at birth. *Developmental Psychology*, *40*(2), 234–243.

Bugental, D. B., et al. (2010). A cognitive approach to child abuse prevention. *Psychology of Violence*, 1(Suppl.), 84–106.

Bugental, D. B., Corpuz, R., & Beaulieu, D. A. (2015). An evolutionary approach to socialization. In J. E. Grusec & P. D. Hastings (Eds.). *Handbook of socialization: Theory and Research* (pp. 325–346). New York. Guilford.

Buhl, H. M., Wittmann, S., & Noack, P. (2003). Child–parent relationship of university students and young employed adults. *Zeitschrift für Entwicklungspsychologie und Pädagogische Psychologie*, *35*(3), 144–152.

Bukowski, W. M., Buhrmeister, D., & Underwood, M. K. (2011). Peer relations as a developmental context. In M. K. Underwood & L. H. Rosen (Eds.), *Social development: Relationships in infancy, childhood, and adolescence* (pp. 153–179). New York, NY: Guilford.

Bukvic, D., Fanelli, M., Ginerva, G., & Bukvic, N. (2011). Justifiability of amniocentesis on the basis of positive findings of triple test, ultrasound scan and advanced maternal age. *Acta Medica Academica*, *40*(1), 10–16.

Buratovic, S., et al. (2016). Developmental effects of fractionated low-dose exposure to gamma radiation on behaviour and susceptibility of the cholinergic system in mice. *International Journal of Radiation Biology*, *92*(7), DOI: 10.3109/09553002.2016.1164911.

Burgaleta, M., et al. (2016). Bilingualism at the core of the brain. Structural differences between bilinguals and monolinguals revealed by subcortical shape analysis. *NeuroImage*, *125*, 437–445.

Burghardt, G. M. (2015). Integrative approaches to the biological study of play. In J. E. Johnson et al. (Eds.). *The handbook of the study of play, Vol. 2* (pp. 21–40). Lanham, MD: Rowman & Littlefield.

Burke, C. M., Schipper, A. M., & Wijdicks, E. F. M. (2011). Brain death and the courts. *Neurology*, *76*(9), 837–841.

Burke, D. M., & Shafto, M. A. (2008). Language and aging. In F. I. M. Craik, & T. A. Salthouse (Eds.), *The handbook of aging and cognition* (3rd ed., pp. 373–443). New York, NY: Psychology Press.

Burke, J. D., & Loeber, R. (2016). Mechanisms of behavioral and affective treatment outcomes in a cognitive behavioral intervention for boys. *Journal of Abnormal Child Psychology*, *44*(1), 179–189.

Burke, J. D., & Loeber, R. (2016). Mechanisms of behavioral and affective treatment outcomes in a cognitive behavioral intervention for boys. *Journal of Abnormal Child Psychology*, *44*(1), 179–189.

Burnham, D., & Matlock, K. (2010). Auditory development. In J. G. Bremner & T. D. Wachs (Eds.), *The Wiley-Blackwell handbook of infant development* (2nd ed., Vol. 1, pp. 81–119). Oxford, UK: Wiley-Blackwell.doi:10.1002/9781444327564.ch3

Bushman, B. J., & Anderson, C. A. (2007). Measuring the strength of the effect of violent media on aggression. *American Psychologist*, *62*(3), 253–254.

Bushnell, E. W. (1993, June). *A dualprocessing approach to cross-modal matching: Implications for development*. Paper presented at the Society for Research in Child Development, New Orleans, LA.

Bushnell, I. W. R. (2001). Mother's face recognition in newborn infants: Learning and memory. *Infant and Child Development*, *10*(1–2), 67–74.

Buss, D. M. (1994). *The evolution of desire: Strategies of human mating*. New York, NY: Basic Books.

Buss, D. M. (2009) How can evolutionary psychology successfully explain personality and individual differences? *Perspectives on Psychological Science*, *4*(4), 359–366.

Buss, D. M. (Ed.). (2005). *The handbook of evolutionary psychology*. Hoboken, NJ: John Wiley & Sons.

Buston, K., Williamson, L., & Hart, G. (2007). Young women under 16 years with experience of sexual intercourse: Who becomes pregnant? *Journal of Epidemiology & Community Health*, *61*(3) 221–225.

Butler, R. N. (2002). The life review. *Journal of Geriatric Psychology*, *35*(1), 7–10.

Buunk, B. P., et al. (2002). Age and gender differences in mate selection criteria for various involvement levels. *Personal Relationships*, *9*(3), 271–278.

Bynum, M. S. (2007). African American mother–daughter communication about sex and daughters' sexual behavior: Does college racial composition make a difference? *Cultural Diversity & Ethnic Minority Psychology*, *13*(2), 151–160.

C

Cacioppo, J. T., & Patrick, W. (2008). *Loneliness: Human nature and the need for social connection*. New York, NY: W. W. Norton & Co.

Callahan, J. J. (2007). Sandwich anyone? *Gerontologist*, *47*(4), 569–571.

Callahan, R., et al. (2015). Pregnancy and contraceptive use among women participating in the FEM-PrEP Trial. *Journal of Acquired Immune Deficiency Syndrome, 68*(2), 196–203.

Calvert, S. L., & Kotler, J. A. (2003). Lessons from children's television: The impact of the Children's Television Act on children's learning. *Journal of Applied Developmental Psychology*, *24*(3), 275–335.

Campanella, J., & Rovee-Collier, C. (2005). Latent learning and deferred imitation at 3 months. *Infancy*, *7*(3), 243–262.

Campbell, A., Shirley, L., & Caygill, L. (2002). Sex-typed preferences in three domains: Do two-year-olds need cognitive variables? *British Journal of Psychology*, *93*(2), 203–217.

Campbell, D. A., Lake, M. F. Falk, M., & Backstrand, J. R. (2006). A randomized control trial of continuous support in labor by a lay doula. *Journal of Obstetric, Gynecologic, and Neonatal Nursing*, *35*(4), 456–464.

Campbell, D. W., Eaton, W. O., & McKeen, N. A. (2002). Motor activity level and behavioural control in young children. *International Journal of Behavioral Development*, *26*(4), 289–296.

Campbell, R., & Wasco, S. M. (2005). Understanding rape and sexual assault. *Journal of Interpersonal Violence*, *20*(1), 127–131.

Campbell, S. B., et al. (2004). The course of maternal depressive symptoms and maternal sensitivity as predictors of attachment security at 36 months. *Development and Psychopathology*, *16*(2), 231–252.

Campos, J. J., Hiatt, S., Ramsey, D., Henderson, C., & Svejda, M. (1978). The emergence of fear on the visual cliff. In M. Lewis & L. Rosenblum (Eds.), *The origins of affect*. New York, NY: Plenum.

Campos, J. J., Langer, A., & Krowitz, A. (1970). Cardiac responses on the visual cliff in prelocomotor human infants. *Science*, *170*, 196–197.

Camras, L. A., et al. (2007). Do infants show distinct negative facial expressions for fear and anger? Emotional expression in 11-month-old European American, Chinese, and Japanese Infants. *Infancy*, *11*(2), 131–155.

Caplan, P. J., & Larkin, J. (1991). The anatomy of dominance and self-protection. *American Psychologist*, *46*, 536.

Capron, C., Thérond, C., & Duyme, M. (2007). Brief report: Effect of menarcheal status and family structure on depressive symptoms and emotional/behavioural problems in young adolescent girls. *Journal of Adolescence*, *30*(1), 175–179.

Carey, B. (2007b, June 22). Research finds firstborns gain the higher I.Q. *The New York Times online*.

Carlson, J. S., Tiret, H. B., Bender, S. L., & Benson, L. (2011). The influence of group training in the Incredible Years Teacher Classroom Management Program on preschool teachers' classroom management strategies. *Journal of Applied School Psychology*, *27*(2), 134–154.

Carr, A. (2011). Social and emotional development in middle childhood. In D. Skuse, H. Bruce, L. Dowdney, & D. Mrazek (Eds.), *Child psychology and psychiatry: Frameworks for practice* (2nd ed., pp. 56–61). Hoboken, NJ: Wiley.

Carre, J. M., & Olmstead, N. A. (2015). Social neuroendocrinology of human aggression: Examining the role of competition-induced testosterone dynamics. *Neuroscience*, *286*, 171–186.

Carrère, S., Buehlman, K. T., Gottman, J. M., Coan, J. A., & Ruckstuhl, L. (2000). Predicting marital stability and divorce in newlywed couples. *Journal of Family Psychology*, 14(1), 42–58.

Carroll, J. S., et al. (2007). So close, yet so far away: The impact of varying marital horizons on emerging adulthood. *Journal of Adolescent Research*, *22*(3), 219–247.

Carstensen, L. (2010). Social and emotional aging. *Annual Review of Psychology*, *61*, 383–409.

Carstensen, L. L., Isaacowitz, D. M., & Charles, S. T. (1999). Taking time seriously: A theory of socioemotional selectivity. *American Psychologist*, *54*(3), 165–181.

Carver, L. J., & Vaccaro, B. G. (2007). 12-month-old infants allocate increased neural resources to stimuli associated with negative adult emotion. *Developmental Psychology*, *43*(1), 54–69.

Casas, J. F., et al. (2006). Early parenting and children's relational and physical aggression in the preschool and home contexts. *Journal of Applied Developmental Psychology*, *27*(3), 209–227.

Cascio, C. J. (2010). Somatosensory processing in neurodevelopmental disorders. *Journal of Neurodevelopmental Disorders*, 2(2), 62–69.

Caserta, M. S., & Lund, D. A. (2007). Toward the development of an Inventory of Daily Widowed Life (IDWL). *Death Studies*, *31*(6), 505–534.

Casey, D. A. (2012). Depression in the elderly: A review and update. *Asia–Pacific Psychiatry*, DOI: 10.1111/j.1758-5872.2012.00191.x

Casini, A., & Sanchez-Mazas, M. (2005). "This job is not for me!": The impact of the gender norm and the organizational culture on professional upward mobility. *Cahiers Internationaux de Psychologie Sociale, Sep-Dec* (Vol. 67–68), 101–112.

Cassia, V. M., Simion, F., & Umilta, C. (2001). Face preference at birth: The role of an orienting mechanism. *Developmental Science*, *4*(1), 101–108.

Cattaneo, L., Sandrini, M., & Schwarzbach, J. (2010). State-dependent TMS reveals a hierarchical representation of observed acts in the temporal, parietal, and premotor cortices. *Cerebral Cortex*, *20*(9), 2252–2258.

Cattell, R. B. (1949). *The culture-fair intelligence test*. Champaign, IL: Institute for Personality and Ability Testing.

Caudle, D. D., et al. (2007). Cognitive errors, symptom severity, and response to cognitive behavior therapy in older adults with generalized anxiety disorder. *American Journal of Geriatric Psychiatry*, *15*(8), 680–689.

Cavallini, A., et al. (2002). Visual acuity in the first two years of life in healthy term newborns: An experience with the Teller Acuity Cards. *Functional Neurology: New Trends in Adaptive and Behavioral Disorders*, *17*(2), 87–92.

Cavell, T. A. (2001). Updating our approach to parent training. I. The case against targeting noncompliance. *Clinical Psychology: Science and Practice*, *8*(3), 299–318.

Ceci, S. J., Williams, W. M., & Barnett, S. M. (2009). Women's underrepresentation in science. *Psychological Bulletin*, *135*(2), 218–261.

Centers for Disease Control and Prevention. (2006). *HIV/AIDS surveillance report, 2005, Vol. 17*. Atlanta, GA: U.S. Department of Health and Human Services, Centers for Disease Control and Prevention. Retrieved from http://www.cdc.gov/hiv/topics/surveillance/resources/reports

Centers for Disease Control and Prevention. (2010a). *Breastfeeding FAQs*. Retrieved from http://www.cdc.gov/breastfeeding/faq

Centers for Disease Control and Prevention. (2011a). *Basics about childhood obesity*. Retrieved from http://www.cdc.gov/obesity/childhood/basics.html

Centers for Disease Control and Prevention. (2011b). *Overweight and obesity*. Retrieved from http://www.cdc.gov/obesity/childhood/problem.html

Centers for Disease Control and Prevention. (2011c). *Strategies and solutions*. Retrieved from http://www.cdc.gov/obesity/childhood/solutions.html

Centers for Disease Control and Prevention. National Center for Health Statistics. (2009). Early release of selected estimates based on data from the 2008 National Health Interview Survey. Retrieved from http://www.cdc.gov/nchs/nhis/released200906.htm

Centers for Disease Control. (2012). *National Vital Statistics Reports*, *60*(1). Retrieved from http://www.cdc.gov/nchs/products/nvsr.htm

Cernoch, J., & Porter, R. (1985). Recognition of maternal axillary odors by infants. *Child Development*, *56*, 1593–1598.

Chan, T. W., & Koo, A. (2011). Parenting style and youth outcomes in the UK. *European Sociological Review*, *27*(3), 385–399.

Chambers, S. A., Freeman, R., Anderson, A. S., & MacGillivray, S. (2015). Reducing the volume, exposure and negative impacts of advertising for foods high in fat, sugar and salt to children: A systematic review of the evidence from statutory and self-regulatory actions and educational measures. *Preventive Medicine*. http://www.sciencedirect.com/science/article/pii/S0091743515000626; and Lillard, A. S., Li, H., & Boguszewski, K. (2015). Chapter 7–Television and children's executive function. *Advances in Child Development and Behavior*, *48*, 219–248.

Chao, J.-K., et al. (2011). Relationship among sexual desire, sexual satisfaction, and quality of life in middle-aged and older adults. *Journal of Sex & Marital Therapy*, *37*(5), 386–403. doi:1 0.1080/0092623X.2011.607051

Charles, S. T., & Carstensen, L. L. (2007). Emotion regulation and aging. In J. J. Gross (Ed.), *Handbook of emotion regulation* (pp. 307–327). New York, NY: Guilford Press.

Charles, S. T., Reynolds, C. A., & Gatz, M. (2001). Age-related differences and change in positive and negative affect over 23 years. *Journal of Personality and Social Psychology*, *80*, 136–151.

Charness, N., & Schaie, K. W. (2003). *Impact of technology on successful aging*. New York, NY: Springer.

Chassin, L., et al. (2010). The association between membership in the sandwich generation and health behaviors: A longitudinal study. *Journal of Applied Developmental Psychology*, *31*(1), 38–46.

Chaudieu, I., et al. (2008). Abnormal reactions to environmental stress in elderly persons with anxiety disorders. *Journal of Affective Disorders*, 106(3), 307–313.

Chen, Z., & Hancock, J. E. (2011). Cognitive development. In A. Davis (Ed.), *Handbook of pediatric neuropsychology*. New York, NY: Springer.

Chen, H., & Wang, Y. (2015). Do weight status and television viewing influence children's subsequent dietary changes? A National Longitudinal Study in the United States. *International Journal of Obesity*, DOI: 10.1038/ijo. 2015.16.

Cheng, E. R., et al. (2016). Postnatal depressive symptoms among mothers and fathers of infants born preterm: Prevalence and impacts on children's early cognitive function. *Journal of Developmental and Behavioral Pediatrics*, *37*(1), 33–42.

Cheng, S.-T., & Chan, A. C. M. (2007). Multiple pathways from stress to suicidality and the protective effect of social support in Hong Kong adolescents. *Suicide and Life-Threatening Behavior*, *37*(2), 187–196.

Cherney, I. D., Harper, H. J., & Winter, J. A. (2006). Nouveaux jouets: Ce que les enfants identifient comme "jouets de garcons" et "jouets de filles." *Enfance*, *58*(3), 266–282.

Chesley, N., & Moen, P. (2006). When workers care: Dual-earner couples' caregiving strategies, benefit use, and psychological well-being. *American Behavioral Scientist*, *49*(9), 1248–1269.

Chetty, R., Friedman, J. N., & Rockoff, J. E. (2012). *The long-term impacts of teachers: Teacher value-added and student outcomes in adulthood*. Retrieved from http://obs.rc.fas.harvard.edu/chetty/value_added.pdf

Chezan, L. C., & Drasgow, E. (2010). Pairing vocalizations with preferred edibles and toys may produce a modest increase in the frequency of vocalizations in three young children with autism. *Evidence-Based Communication Assessment and Intervention*, *4*(2), 101–104.

Childstats.gov. (2011). *America's children: Key national indicators of well-being, 2011–family and social environment*. Retrieved from http://www.childstats.gov/americaschildren/famsoc3.asp

Chlamydia—CDC Fact Sheet. (2011). Centers for Disease Control and Prevention. Retrieved from http://www.cdc.gov/std/Chlamydia/STDFact-Chlamydia.htm

Chlebowski, R. T., et al. (2003). Influence of estrogen plus progestin on breast cancer and mammography in healthy postmenopausal women: The Women's Health Initiative Randomized Trial. *Journal of the American Medical Association*, *289*, 3243–3253.

Chomsky, N. (1988). *Language and problems of knowledge*. Cambridge, MA: MIT Press.

Chomsky, N. (1990). On the nature, use, and acquisition of language. In W. G. Lycan (Ed.), *Mind and cognition*. (pp. 627–646.) Oxford, UK: Blackwell.

Chonchaiya, W., et al. (2011). Increased prevalence of seizures in boys who were probands with the fMRI premutation and co-morbid autism spectrum disorder. *Human Genetics*. doi:10.1007/s00439–011-1106-6

Chou, T.-L., et al. (2006). Developmental and skill effects on the neural correlates of semantic processing to visually presented words. *Human Brain Mapping*, *27*(11), 915–924.

Christ, G. H. (2010). Children bereaved by the death of a parent. In C. A. Corr & D. E. Balk (Eds.), *Children's encounters with death, bereavement, and coping* (pp. 169–189). New York, NY: Springer.

Christian, L. M., & Glaser, R. (2012). The impact of everyday stressors on the immune system and health. *Stress Challenges and Immunity in Space*, Part 2, 31–43. doi:10.1007/978-3-642-22272-6_4

Christophersen, E. R., & Mortweet, S. L. (2003). Establishing bedtime. In E. R. Christophersen & S. L. Mortweet (Eds.), *Parenting that works: Building skills that last a lifetime* (pp. 209–228). Washington, DC: American Psychological Association.

Christie, J. F., & Roskos, K. A. (2015). How does play contribute to literacy? In J. E. Johnson et al. (Eds.). *The handbook of the study of play, Vol. 2* (pp. 417–424). Lanham, MD: Rowman & Littlefield.

Chronis, A. M., et al. (2007). Maternal depression and early positive parenting predict future conduct problems in young children with attention-deficit/hyperactivity disorder. *Developmental Psychology*, *43*(1), 70–82.

CIA World Factbook. (2012). *Life expectancy at birth*. Retrieved from https://www.cia.gov/library/publications/the-world-factbook/fields/2102.html

Cicchetti, D., Rogosch, F. A., & Toth, S. L. (2006). Fostering secure attachment in infants in maltreating families through preventive interventions. *Development and Psychopathology*, *18*(3), 623–649.

Cillessen, A. H. N., & Bellmore, A. D. (2011). Social skills and social competence in interactions with peers. In P. K. Smith & C. H. Hart (Eds.), *The Wiley-Blackwell handbook of childhood social development* (2nd ed.) (pp. 393–412). Oxford, UK: Wiley-Blackwell. doi:10.1002/9781444390933.ch21

Clark, E. V. (1973). What's in a word? On the child's acquisition of semantics in his first language. In E. Moore (Ed.), *Cognitive development and the acquisition of language*. (pp. 65–110.) New York, NY: Academic Press.

Clark, E. V. (1975). Knowledge, context, and strategy in the acquisition of meaning. In D. P. Date (Ed.), *Georgetown University roundtable on language and linguistics*. (pp. 77–98.) Washington, DC: Georgetown University Press.

Clark, J. (2005). Sibling relationships: Theory and issues for practice. *Child & Family Social Work*, *10*(1), 90–91.

Clark, J. C. (2014). Towards a cultural historical theory of knowledge mapping: Collaboration and activity in the zone of proximal development. In D. Ifenthaler, & R. Hanewld (Eds.). *Digital knowledge maps in education* (pp. 161–174). New York: Springer Science + Business Media

Clark, J. J. (2010). Life as a source of theory: Erik Erikson's contributions, boundaries, and marginalities. In T. W. Miller (Ed.), *Handbook of stressful transitions across the lifespan* (Part 1, pp. 59–83). New York, NY: Springer Science + Business Media.

Clark, J., & Rugg, S. (2005). The importance of independence in toileting. *British Journal of Occupational Therapy*, *68*(4), 165–171.

Clark, P. G., Brethwaite, D. S., & Gnesdiloff, S. (2011). Providing support at time of death for cancer: Results of a 5-year post-bereavement group study. *Journal of Social Work in End-of-Life & Palliative Care*, *7*(2–3), 195–215.

Clark, R. (1983). *Family life and school achievement: Why poor black children succeed or fail*. Chicago, IL: University of Chicago Press.

Clarke-Stewart, K. A., & Beck, R. J. (1999). Maternal scaffolding and children's narrative retelling of a movie story. *Early Childhood Research Quarterly*, *14*(3), 409–434.

Claxton, A., et al. (2012). Personality traits and marital satisfaction within enduring relationships: An intra-couple discrepancy approach. *Journal of Social and Personal Relationships*, *29*(3), 375–396.

Cleary, D. J., Ray, G. E., LoBello, S. G., & Zachar, P. (2002). Children's perceptions of close peer relationships: Quality, congruence and meta-perceptions. *Child Study Journal*, *32*(3), 179–192.

Clode, D. (2006). Review of A left-hand turn around the world: Chasing the mystery and meaning of all things southpaw. *Laterality: Asymmetries of Body, Brain and Cognition*, *11*(6) 580–581.

Coats, A. H., & Blanchard-Fields, F. (2008). Emotion regulation in interpersonal problems: The role of cognitive-emotional complexity, emotion regulation goals, and expressivity. *Psychology and Aging*, *23*(1), 39–51.

Coffey, C. E., Cummings, J. L., George, M. S., & Weintraub. (2011). *Textbook of geriatric psychiatry* (3rd ed.). Arlington, VA: American Psychiatric Association.

Cohen, D. L., & Belsky, J. (2008). Individual differences in female mate preferences as a function of attachment and hypothetical ecological conditions. *Journal of Evolutionary Psychology*, *6*(1), 25–42.

Cohen, J. R., Young, J. F., & Abela, J. R. Z. (2011). Cognitive vulnerability to depression in children. *Cognitive Therapy and Research*. doi:10.1007/s10608-011-9431-6

Cohen, L. S., et al. (2006). Relapse of major depression during pregnancy in women who maintain or discontinue antidepressant treatment. *Journal of the American Medical Association*, *295*(5), 499–507.

Cole, D. A., et al. (2011). A longitudinal study of cognitive risks for depressive symptoms in children and young adolescents. *The Journal of Early Adolescence*, *3*(6), 782–816.

Cole, T. B. (2006). Rape at U.S. colleges often fueled by alcohol. JAMA: *Journal of the American Medical Association*, *296*(5), 504–505.

Collaer, M. L., & Hill, E. M. (2006). Large sex difference in adolescents on a timed line judgment task: Attentional contributors and task relationship to mathematics. *Perception*, *35*(4), 561–572.

Colombo, J. (1993). *Infant cognition*. Newbury Park, CA: Sage.

Commons, M. L., Galaz-Fontes, J. F., & Morse, S. J. (2006). Leadership, crosscultural contact, socio-economic status, and formal operational reasoning about moral dilemmas among Mexican nonliterate adults and high school students. *Journal of Moral Education*, *35*(2), 247–267

Conel, J. L. (1959). *The postnatal development of the human cerebral cortex*, *5*. Cambridge, MA: Harvard University Press.

The Conference Board. (2010). U.S. job satisfaction at lowest level in two decades. http://www.conference-board.org/utilities/pressDetail.cfm?press_ID53820.

Connaughton, C., & McCabe, M. (2015). Sexuality and aging. In N. A. Pachana (Ed.). *Encyclopedia of geropsychology* (pp. 1–10). Singapore: Springer Science + Business Media.

Conner, K. R., & Goldston, D. B. (2007). Rates of suicide among males increase steadily from age 11 to 21: Developmental framework and outline for prevention. *Aggression and Violent Behavior*, *12*(2), 193–207.

Conniff, J., & Evensen, A. (2016). Preexposure prophylaxis (PrEP) for HIV prevention: The primary care perspective. *Journal of the American Board of Family Medicine*, *29*(1), 143-151.

Connolly, J., Craig, W., Goldberg, A., & Pepler, D. (2004). Mixed-gender groups, dating, and romantic relationships in early adolescence. *Journal of Research on Adolescence*, *14*(2), 185–207.

Connolly, J., Furman, W., & Konarski, R. (2000). The role of peers in the emergence of heterosexual romantic relationships in adolescence. *Child Development*, *71*(5), 1395–1408.

Connor, P. D., Sampson, P. D., Streissguth, A. P., Bookstein, F. L., & Barr, H. M. (2006). Effects of prenatal alcohol exposure on fine motor coordination and balance: A study of two adult samples. *Neuropsychologia*, *44*(5), 744–751.

Conrad, D. (2016). The Stanford Sorts to Prevent Obesity Randomized Trial (SPORT). In D. Conrad & A. White (Eds.). *Sports-based health interventions* (pp. 261–267). New York: Springer Science + Business Media.

Conrad, N. J., Walsh, J. A., Allen, J. M., & Tsang, C. D. (2011). Examining infants' preferences for tempo in lullabies and playsongs. *Canadian Journal of Experimental Psychology/Revue canadienne de psychologie expérimentale*, *65*(3), 168–172.

Conrad, P. (2007). *The medicalization of society: On the transformation of human conditions into treatable disorders*. Baltimore, MD: Johns Hopkins University Press.

Cooke, B. M., & Shukla, D. (2011). Double helix: Reciprocity between juvenile play and brain development. *Developmental Cognitive Neuroscience*, *1*(4), 459–470.

Cooke, B. M., Breedlove, S. M., & Jordan, C. L. (2003). Both estrogen receptors and androgen receptors contribute to testosterone-induced changes in the morphology of the medial amygdala and sexual arousal in male rats. *Hormones & Behavior*, *43*(2), 336–346.

Cooper, J., Appleby, L., & Amos, T. (2002). Life events preceding suicide by young people. *Social Psychiatry and Psychiatric Epidemiology*, *37*(6), 271–275.

Coovadia, H. (2004). Antiretroviral agents: How best to protect infants from HIV and save their mothers from AIDS. *New England Journal of Medicine*, *351*(3), 289–292.

Copeland, W., et al. (2010). Do the negative effects of early pubertal timing on adolescent girls continue into young adulthood? *American Journal of Psychiatry*, *167*(10), 1218–1225.

Corballis, M. C. (2010). Mirror neurons and the evolution of language. *Brain and Language*, *112*(1), 25–35.

Corliss, R. (2003, August 12). Bollywood: Frequently questioned answers. *Time Magazine*. Retrieved from http://www.time.com/time/coloumnist/corliss/article/0,9565,475407,00.html

Corona, G., et al. (2010). Age-related changes in general and sexual health in middle-aged and older men: Results from the European Male Ageing Study. *The Journal of Sexual Medicine*, *7*(4), 1362–1380.

Corr, C. A. (2010). Children, development, and encounters with death, bereavement, and coping. In C. A. Corr & D. E. Balk (Eds.), *Children's encounters with death, bereavement, and coping* (pp. 3–20). New York, NY: Springer.

Corr, C. A., & Balk, D. E. (2010). *Children's encounters with death, bereavement, and coping*. New York, NY: Springer.

Costa, P. T., Jr., & McCrae, R. R. (2010). The five-factor model, five-factor theory, and interpersonal psychology. In L. M. Horowitz & S. Strack (Eds.), *Handbook of interpersonal psychology: Theory, research, assessment, and therapeutic interventions*. Hoboken, NJ: Wiley.

Costello, E. J., Sung, M., Worthman, C., & Angold, A. (2007). Pubertal maturation and the development of alcohol use and abuse. *Drug and Alcohol Dependence*, *88*, S50–S59.

Costigan, C. L., Cauce, A. M., & Etchison, K. (2007). Changes in African American mother–daughter relationships during adolescence: Conflict, autonomy, and warmth. In B. J. R. Leadbeater & N. Way (Eds.), *Urban girls revisited: Building strengths* (pp. 177–201). New York, NY: New York University Press.

Courage, M. L., Howe, M. L., & Squires, S. E. (2004). Individual differences in 3.5-month olds' visual attention: What do they predict at 1 year? *Infant Behavior and Development*, *27*(1), 19–30.

Couzens, D., Cuskelly, M., & Haynes, M. (2011). Cognitive development and Down syndrome: Age-related change on the Stanford-Binet Test (Fourth Edition). *American Journal on Intellectual and Developmental Disabilities*, *116*(3), 181–204.

Cramer, D. (2003). Facilitativeness, conflict, demand for approval, self-esteem, and satisfaction with romantic relationships. *Journal of Psychology*, *137*(1), 85–98.

Cozolino, L. (2014). *The neuroscience of human relationships* (2nd Ed.). New York: W. W. Norton.

Cramm, J. M., Strating, M. M. H., de Vreede, P. L., Steverink, N., & Nieboer, A. P. (2012). Validation of the selfmanagement ability scale and development of a shorter scale among older patients shortly after hospitalization. *Health and Quality of Life Outcomes*, *10*(9). doi:10.1186/1477-7525-10-9

Cravey, T., & Mitra, A. (2011). Demographics of the sandwich generation by race and ethnicity in the United States. *Journal of Socio-Economics*, *40*(3), 306–311.

Crisp, R. J., & Turner, R. N. (2011). Cognitive adaptation to the experience of social and cultural diversity. *Psychological Bulletin*, *137*(2), 242–266.

Crook, C. K., & Lipsitt, L. P. (1976). Neonatal nutritive sucking: Effects of taste stimulation upon sucking rhythm and heart rate. *Child Development*, *47*, 518–522.

Cruz, N. V., & Bahna, S. L. (2006). Do foods or additives cause behavior disorders? *Psychiatric Annals*, *36*(10), 724–732.

Cuellar, J., & Curry, T. R. (2007). The prevalence and comorbidity between delinquency, drug abuse, suicide attempts, physical and sexual abuse, and self-mutilation among delinquent Hispanic females. *Hispanic Journal of Behavioral Sciences*, *29*(1), 68–82.

Cuevas, K., & Bell, M. A. (2010). Developmental progression of looking and reaching performance on the A-not-B task. *Developmental Psychology*, *46*(5), 1363–1371.

Cumming, S. P., Eisenmann, J. C., Smoll, F. L., Smith, R. E., & Malina, R. M. (2005). Body size and perceptions of coaching behaviors by adolescent female athletes. *Psychology of Sport and Exercise*, *6*(6), 693–705.

Cunningham, F. G., et al. (2011). National Institutes of Health Consensus Development Conference Statement: Vaginal birth after cesarean section: New insights, March 8–10, 2010. *Obstetric Anesthesia Digest*, *31*(3), 140–142.

Cummings, C. M., Caporino, N. E., & Kendall, P. C. (2014). Comorbidity of anxiety and depression in children and adolescents: 20 years after. *Psychological Bulletin*, *140*(3), 816–845.

Curlin, F. A., Nwodim, C., Vance, J. L., Chin, M. H., & Lantos, J. D. (2008). To die, to sleep: U.S. physicians' religious and other objections to physician-assisted suicide, terminal sedation, and withdrawal of life support. *American Journal of Hospice and Palliative Medicine*, *25*(2), 112–120.

Cystic Fibrosis Foundation. (2012). *About CF*. Retrieved from http://www.cff.org/AboutCF

D

D'Augelli, A. R., Grossman, A. H., Hershberger, S. L., & O' Connell, T. S. (2001). Aspects of mental health among older lesbian, gay, and bisexual adults. *Aging & Mental Health*, *5*(2), 149–158.

Daglioglu, H. E., Calisandemir, F., Alemdar, M., & Bencik Kangal, S. (2010). Examination of human figure drawings by gifted and normally developed children at preschool period. *Elementary Education Online*, *9*(1), 31–43.

Daley, C. E., & Onwuegbuzie, A. J. (2011). Race and intelligence. In R. J. Sternberg & S. J. Kaufman (Eds.), *The Cambridge handbook of intelligence* (pp. 293–308). New York, NY: Cambridge University Press.

Damlanakis, T., & Marzlall, E. (2012). Older adults' response to the loss of a spouse. *Aging & Mental Health*, *16*(1), 57–66.

Damian, R. I., & Roberts, B. W. (2015). Settling the debate on birth order and personality. *Proceedings of the National Academy of Sciences of the United States of America*, *112*(46), 14119–14120.

Damon, W. (1991). Adolescent self-concept. In R. M. Lerner, A. C. Petersen, & J. Brooks-Gunn (Eds.), *Encyclopedia of adolescence*. New York, NY: Garland.

Datta, S., Kodali, B. S., & Segal, S. (2010). Non-pharmacological methods for relief of labor pain. *Obstetric Anesthesia Handbook*, 85–93.

Daniels, E. A.,& Gillen, M. M. (2015). Body image and identity: A call for new research. In S. J. Schwatrz, K. Luyckx, & V. L. Vignoles (Eds.). *Handbook of identity theory and research* (pp. 406–422). New York: Springer Science + Business Media.

Daniels, K., Martinez, G., & Copen, C. (2015). Using the National Surb=vey of Family Growth. Workshop presented at the 2015 NCHS National Conference on Health Statistics. North Bethesda, MD. http://www.cdc.gov/nchs/data/nsfg/Using_the_NSFG_from_2015_NCHS_conference.pdf.

Daryanani, I., Hamilton, J. L., Abramson, L. Y., & Alloy, L. B. (2016). Single mother parenting and adolescent psychopathology. *Journal of Abnormal Child Psychology*, 1–13. DOI: 10.1007/s10802-016-0128-x

Daugherty, A. M., & Ofen, N. (2015). That's a good one! Belief in efficacy of mnemonic strategies contributes to age-related increase in associative memory. *Journal of Experimental Child Psychology*, *136*, 17–29.

Daum, M. M., Prinz, W., & Aschersleben, G. (2010). Perception and production of object-related grasping in 6-month olds. *Journal of Experimental Child Psychology*, *108*(4), 810–818.

Davis, K., Christodoulou, J., Seider, S., & Gardner, H. (2011). The theory of multiple intelligences. In R. J. Sternberg & S. J. Kaufman (Eds.), *The Cambridge handbook of intelligence* (pp. 485–503). New York, NY: Cambridge University Press.

Dawood, K., Bailey, J. M., & Martin, N. G. (2009). Genetic and environmental influences on sexual orientation. In Y.-K. Kim (Ed.), *Handbook of behavior genetics* (pp. 269–279). New York, NY: Springer.

Dawson, C., et al. (2011). Dietary treatment of phenylketonuria: The effect of phenylalanine on reaction time. *Journal of Inherited Metabolic Disease*, *34*(2), 449–454.

Dawson, T. L. (2002). New tools, new insights: Kohlberg's moral judgement stages revisited. *International Journal of Behavioral Development*, *26*(2), 154–166.

De Beni, R., Borella, E., & Carretti, B. (2007). Reading comprehension in aging: The role of working memory and metacomprehension. *Aging, Neuropsychology, and Cognition*, *14*(2), 189–212.

De Haan, M., & Groen, M. (2006). Neural bases of infants' processing of social information in faces. In P. J. Marshall & N. A. Fox (Eds.), *The development of social engagement: Neurobiological perspectives. Series in affective science* (pp. 46–80). New York, NY: Oxford University Press.

De Rosa, C. J., et al. (2010). Sexual intercourse and oral sex among public middle school students: Prevalence and correlates. *Perspectives on Sexual and Reproductive Health*, *42*(3), 197–205.

De Lisi, R. (2015). Piaget's sympathetic but unromantic account of children's play. In J. E. Johnson et al. (Eds.). *The handbook of the study of play, Vol. 2* (pp. 227–238). Lanham, MD: Rowman & Littlefield.

de Souza, A. S., Fernandes, F. S., & do Carmo, M. (2011). Effects of maternal malnutrition and postnatal nutritional rehabilitation on brain fatty acids,learning, and memory. *Nutrition Reviews*, *69*(3), 132–144.

Deary, I. J., Whiteman, M. C., Starr, J. M., Whalley, L. J., & Fox, H. C. (2004). The impact of childhood intelligence on later life: Following up the Scottish mental surveys of 1932 and 1947. *Journal of Personality and Social Psychology*, *86*(1), 130–147.

DeCasper, A. J., & Fifer, W. P. (1980). Of human bonding: Newborns prefer their mothers' voices. *Science*, *208*, 1174–1176.

DeCasper, A. J., & Prescott, P. A. (1984). Human newborns' perception of male voices: Preference, discrimination, and reinforcing value. *Developmental Psychobiology*, *17*, 481–491.

DeCasper, A. J., & Spence, M. J. (1991). Auditorially mediated behavior during the perinatal period: A cognitive view. In M. J. Weiss & P. R. Zelazo (Eds.), *Infant attention* (pp. 142–176). Norwood, NJ: Ablex.

DeCuyper, M., de Bolle, M., & de Fruyt, F. (2012). Personality similarity, perceptual accuracy, and relationship satisfaction in dating and married couples. *Personal Relationships*, *19*(1), 128–145.

Deep, A. L., et al. (1999). Sexual abuse in eating disorder subtypes and control women: The role of comorbid substance dependence in bulimia nervosa. *International Journal of Eating Disorders*, *25*(1), 1–10.

Dennis, W. (1960). Causes of retardation among institutional children: Iran. *Journal of Genetic Psychology*, *96*, 47–59.

Demby, K. P., Riggs, S. A., & Kaminski, P. L. (2015). Attachment and family processes in children's psychological adjustment in middle childhood. *Family Process*, DOI: 10.1111/famp.12145.

Dennis, T. (2016). The grief river. In R. A. Neimeyer (Ed.). *Techniques of grief therapy: Assessment and intervention* (pp. 105–108). New York: Routledge.

Dennis, W., & Dennis, M. G. (1940). The effect of cradling practices upon the onset of walking in Hopi children. *Journal of Genetic Psychology*, *56*, 77–86.

Depp, C. A., & Jeste, D. V. (2006). Definitions and predictors of successful aging: A comprehensive review of larger quantitative studies. *American Journal of Geriatric Psychiatry*, *14*, 6–20.

DeRogalis, L. R., & Burnett, A. L. (2008). The epidemiology of sexual dysfunctions. *The Journal of Sexual Medicine*, *5*(2), 289–300.

Dermody, S. S., Marchal, M. P., Burton, C. M., & Chisolm, D. J. (2016). Risk of heavy drinking among sexual minority adolescents: Indirect pathways through sexual orientation-related victimization and affiliation with substance-using peers. *Addiction*, DOI: 10.1111/add.13409.

Dey, E. L., et al. (2010). *Engaging diverse viewpoints: What is the campus climate for perspective-taking?* Washington, DC: Association of American Colleges and Universities.

Dettmer, A. M., et al. (2016). Neonatal face-to-face interactions promote social behaviour in infant rhesus monkeys. *Nature Communications*, DOI: 10.1038/ncomms11940.

Dezoete, J. A., MacArthur, B. A., & Tuck, B. (2003). Prediction of Bayley and Stanford–Binet scores with a group of very low birthweight children. *Child: Care, Health and Development*, *29*(5), 367–372.

DiPietro, J. A. (2010). Psychological and psychophysiological considerations regarding the maternal–fetal relationship. *Infant and Child Development*, *19*(1), 27–38.

Dimler, L. M., & Natsuaki, M. N. (2015). The effects of pubertal timing on externalizing behaviors in adolescence and early adulthood. *Journal of Adolescence*, *45*, 160–170.

Dishion, T. J., & Stormshak, E. A. (2007). Family and peer social interaction. In T. J. Dishion & E. A. Stormshak. (Eds.), *Intervening in children's lives: An ecological, family-centered approach to mental health care* (pp. 31–48). Washington, DC: American Psychological Association.

Doherty, W. J., Carroll, J. S., & Waite, L. J. (2007). Supporting the institution of marriage: Ideological, research, and ecological perspectives. In A. S. Loveless & T. B. Holman (Eds.), *The family in the new millennium: World voices supporting the "natural" clan* (*Vol. 2: Marriage and human dignity*, pp. 21–51). Praeger perspectives. Westport, CT: Praeger Publishers/ Greenwood Publishing Group.

Dodge, E., & Simic, M. (2015). Anorexia runs in families: does this make the families responsible? A commentary on "Anorexia runs in families: is this due to genes or the family environment?" (Dring, 2014). *Journal of Family Therapy*, *37*(1), 93–102

Donald, M., et al. (2006). Risk and protective factors for medically serious suicide attempts. *Australian and New Zealand Journal of Psychiatry*, *40*(1), 87–96.

Donovan, D. M., & Wells, E. A. (2007). "Tweaking 12-Step": The potential role of 12-Step self-help group involvement in methamphetamine recovery. *Addiction*, *102*(Suppl. 1), 121–129.

Doron, H., & Markovitzky, G. (2007). Family structure and patterns and psychological adjustment to immigration in Israel. *Journal of Ethnic & Cultural Diversity in Social Work*, *15*(1–2), 215–235.

Douglas, P. S., & Hill, P. S. (2011). The crying baby: What approach? *Current Opinion in Pediatrics*, *23*(5), 523–529.

Dowda, M. et al. (2011). Parental and environmental correlates of physical activity of children attending preschool. *Archives of Pediatrics and Adolescent Medicine*, *165*(10), 939–944.

Drasgow, E., Halle, J. W., & Phillips, B. (2001). Effects of different social partners on the discriminated requesting of a young child with autism and severe language delays. *Research in Developmental Disabilities*, *22*(2), 125–139.

Driscoll, M., & Driscoll, G. (2012). *Real marriage: The truth about sex, friendship, and life together*. Nashville, TN: Thomas Nelson.

Duarté-Vélez, Y. M., & Bernal, G. (2007). Suicide behavior among Latino and Latina adolescents: Conceptual and methodological issues. *Death Studies*, *31*(5) 425–455.

Duberstein, P. R., Pálsson, S. P., Waern, M., & Skoog, I. (2008). Personality and risk for depression in a birth cohort of 70-year-olds followed for 15 years. *Psychological Medicine*, *38*(5), 663–671.

Dubow, E. F., et al. (2010). Exposure to conflict and violence across contexts: Relations to adjustment among Palestinian children. *Journal of Clinical Child and Adolescent Psychology*, *39*(1), 103–116.

Duenwald, M. (2002, July 16). Hormone therapy: One size, clearly, no longer fits all. *The New York Times*.

Duffy, R. D., & Sedlacek, W. E. (2007). What is most important to students' long-term career choices. *Journal of Career Development*, *34*(2), 149–163.

Dunn, J., & Hughes, C. (2001). "I got some swords and you're dead!": Violent fantasy, antisocial behavior, friendship, and moral sensibility in young children. *Child Development*, *72*(2), 491–505.

Dunn, J., Davies, L. C., O'Connor, T. G., & Sturgess, W. (2001). Family lives and friendships: The perspectives of children in step-, single-parent, and nonstep families. *Journal of Family Psychology*, *15*(2), 272–287.

Duplassie, D., & Daniluk, J. C. (2007). Sexuality: Young and middle adulthood. In M S. Tepper & A. F. Owens (Eds.), *Sexual health Vol. 1: Psychological foundations* (pp. 263–289). *Praeger perspectives: Sex, love, and psychology*. Westport, CT: Praeger Publishers/Greenwood Publishing Group.

Dunn, J. (2015). Siblings. In J. E. Grusec, & P. D. Hastings (Eds.). *Handbook of socialization: Theory and research,* 2nd ed. New York. Guilford.

Dunn, J., (2015). Siblings. In J. E. Grusec & P. D. Hastings (Eds.). *Handbook of socialization: Theory and Research* (pp. 182–201). New York: Guilford.

Dupuis-Blanchard, S. M. (2008). Social engagement in relocated older adults. *Dissertation Abstracts International: Section B: The Sciences and Engineering*. *68*(7-B), 4387.

Durkin, S. J., Paxton, S. J., & Sorbello, M. (2007). An integrative model of the impact of exposure to idealized female images on adolescent girls' body satisfaction. *Journal of Applied Social Psychology*, *37*(5), 1092–1117.

Durdiakova, J., et al. (2015). Differences in salivary testosterone, digit ratio and empathy between intellectually gifted and control boys. *Intelligence*, *48*, 76–84.

Dweck, C. S. (2015). The secret to raising smart kids. *Scientific American*, *23*, 76–83.

Dworkin, E., Javdani, S., Verona, E., & Campbell, R. (2014). Child sexual abuse and disordered eating: The mediating role of impulsive and compulsive tendencies. *Psychology of Violence*, *4*(1), 21–36.

Dyer, S. J. (2007). The value of children in African countries—Insights from studies on infertility. *Journal of Psychosomatic Obstetrics & Gynecology*, *28*(2), 69–77.

Dykman, R. A., Casey, P. H., Ackerman, P. T., & McPherson, W. B. (2001). Behavioral and cognitive status in school-aged children with a history of failure to thrive during early childhood. *Clinical Pediatrics*, *40*(2), 63–70.

Dyson, J. C. (2015). Play in America: A historical overview. In J. E. Johnson et al. (Eds.). *The handbook of the study of play, Vol. 2* (pp. 41–50). Lanham, MD: Rowman & Littlefield.

E

Eaves, L. C., & Ho, H. H. (2008). Young adult outcome of autism spectrum disorder. *Journal of Autism and Developmental Disorders*, *38*(4), 739–747.

Ebstein, R., Israel, S., Chew, S., Zhong, S., & Knafo, A. (2010). Genetics of human social behavior. *Neuron*, *65*(6), 831–844.

Eccles, J. S., et al. (2000). Gender-role socialization in the family: A longitudinal approach. In T. Eckes & H. M. Trautner (Eds.), *The developmental social psychology of gender* (pp. 333–360). Mahwah, NJ: Erlbaum.

Ecuyer-Dab, I., & Robert, M. (2004). Spatial ability and home-range size: Examining the relationship in Western men and women *(Homo sapiens)*. *Journal of Comparative Psychology*, *118*(2), 217–231.

Eder, R. A. (1989). The emergent personologist: The structure and content of 3½-, 5½-, and 7½-year-olds' concepts of themselves and other persons. *Child Development*, *60*, 1218–1228.

Edwards, J., et al. (2011). Developmental coordination disorder in school-aged children born very preterm and/or at very low birth weight: A systematic review. *Journal of Developmental Behavioral Pediatrics*, *32*(9), 678–687.

Edwards, V. J., Holden, G. W., Felitti, V. J., & Anda, R. F. (2003). Relationship between multiple forms of childhood maltreatment and adult mental health in community respondents: Results from the Adverse Childhood Experiences study. *American Journal of Psychiatry*, *160*(8), 1453–1460.

Egeland, B., & Sroufe, L. A. (1981). Attachment and early maltreatment. *Child Development*, *52*, 44–52.

Egerton, A., Allison, C., Brett, R. R., & Pratt, J. A. (2006). Cannabinoids and prefrontal cortical function: Insights from preclinical studies. *Neuroscience & Biobehavioral Reviews*, *30*(5), 680–695.

Eimas, P. D., Sigueland, E. R., Juscyk, P., & Vigorito, J. (1971). Speech perception in infants. *Science*, *171*, 303–306.

Eisenberg, M. E., Neumark-Sztainer, D., & Paxton, S. J. (2006). Five-year change in body satisfaction among adolescents. *Journal of Psychosomatic Research*, *61*(4), 521–527.

Eisenberg, N., Eggum, N. D., & Edwards, A. (2010). Emotions, aggression, and morality in children. In W. F. Arsenio, & E. A. Lemerise (Eds.), *Emotions, aggression, and morality in children: Bridging development and psychopathology* (pp. 115–135). Washington, DC: American Psychological Association.

Eivers, A. R., Brendgen, M., Vitaro, F., & Borge, A. I. H. (2012). Concurrent and longitudinal links between children's and their friends' antisocial and prosocial behavior in preschool. *Early Childhood Research Quarterly*, *27*(1), 137–146.

Elkind, D. (2007). *The power of play: How spontaneous imaginative activities lead to happier, healthier children*. Cambridge, MA: Da Capo Press.

Elliot, A. J., & Niesta, D. (2008). Romantic red: Red enhances men's attraction to women. *Journal of Personality and Social Psychology*, *95*(5), 1150–1164.

Elliot, A. J., Kayser D. N., Greitemeyer T., Lichtenfeld S., Gramzow R. H., Maier M. A., & Liu H. (2010). Red, rank, and romance in women viewing men. *Journal of Experimental Psychology: General*, *139*(3), 399–417.

Elliot, A. J., & Thrash, T. M. (2010). Approach and avoidance temperament as basic dimensions of personality. *Journal of Personality*, *78*(3), 865–906.

El-Sheikh, M. (2007). Children's skin conductance level and reactivity: Are these measures stable over time and across tasks? *Developmental Psychobiology*, *49*(2), 180–186.

Emanuel, E. J., Fairclough, D. L., & Emanuel, L. L. (2000). Attitudes and desires related to euthanasia and physician-assisted suicide among terminally ill patients and their caregivers. *JAMA: Journal of the American Medical Association*, *284*(19), 2460–2468.

Emler, N., Tarry, H., & St. James, A. (2007). Post-conventional moral reasoning and reputation. *Journal of Research in Personality*, *41*(1), 76–89.

Erikson, E. H. (1963). *Childhood and society*. New York, NY: Norton.

Engler-Chiurazzi, E. B., et al. (2016). Estrogens as neuroprotectants: Estrogenic actions in the context of cognitive aging and brain injury. *Progress in Neurobiology*, DOI: 10.1016/j.pneurobio.2015.12.008; Koyama, A. K., et al. (2016). Endogenous sex hormones and cognitive function in older women. *Alzheimer's & Dementia*, DOI: 10.1016/j.jalz.2015.12.010.

Erikson, E. H. (1968). *Identity: Youth and crisis*. New York, NY: Norton.

Erikson, E. H. (1975). *Life history and the historical moment*. New York, NY: Norton.

Eron, L. D., Huesmann, L. R., & Zelli, A. (1991). The role of parental variables in the learning of aggression. In D. J. Pepler & K. H. Rubin (Eds.), *The development and treatment of childhood aggression*. Hillsdale, NJ: Erlbaum.

Ersner-Hershfield, H., Mikels, J. A., Sullivan, S. J., & Carstensen, L. L. (2008). Poignancy: Mixed emotional experience in the face of meaningful endings. *Journal of Personality and Social Psychology*, *94*(1) 158–167.

Estes, A., et al. (2011). Basal ganglia morphometry and repetitive behavior in young children with autism spectrum disorder. *Autism Research*, *4*(3), 212–220.

Espelage, D. L., & Colbert, C. L. (2016). In K. R. Wentzel, & G. B. Ramani (Eds.). *Handbook of social influences in school contexts: Social-emotional, motivation, and cognitive outcomes* (pp. 405–422). New York: Routledge.

Etaugh, C. A., & Bridges, J. S. (2006). Midlife transitions. In J. Worell & C. D. Goodheart (Eds.), *Handbook of girls' and women's psychological health: Gender and well-being across the lifespan* (pp. 359–367). *Oxford series in clinical psychology*. New York, NY: Oxford University Press.

Everitt, A. V., Rattan, S. I. S., Le Couteur, D. G., & de Cabo, R. (2010). Calorie restriction, aging, and longevity. Sydney, Australia: The University of Sydney.

Ezzati M., Friedman, A. B., Kulkarni, S. C., & Murray, C. J. L. (2008, April 22). The reversal of fortunes: Trends in county mortality and cross-county mortality disparities in the United States. *PLoS Medicine*, 5(4), e66.

F

Facts about falling (2008, January 28). *The Washington Post*.

Facts about the Death with Dignity Act. (2007, September 22). Oregon Office of Disease Prevention and Epidemiology. Retrieved from http://www.oregon.gov/DHS/ph/pas/faqs.shtml

Fagot, B. I., Rodgers, C. S., & Leinbach, M. D. (2000). Theories of gender socialization. In T. Eckes & H. M. Trautner (Eds.), *The developmental social psychology of gender* (pp. 65–89). Mahwah, NJ: Erlbaum.

Fair, R. C. (2007). Estimated age effects in athletic events and chess. *Experimental Aging Research*, *33*(1), 37–57.

Fan, C. S., & Lui, H.-K. (2008). Extramarital affairs, marital satisfaction, and divorce: Evidence from Hong Kong. *Contemporary Economic Policy*, *22*(4), 442–452.

Fancy, S. P. J., et al. (2010). Overcoming remyelination failure in multiple sclerosis and other myelin disorders. *Experimental Neurology*, *225*(1), 18–23.

Fantz, R. L. (1961). The origin of form perception. *Scientific American*, *204*, 66–72.

Fantz, R. L., Fagan, J. F., III, & Miranda, S. B. (1975). Early visual selectivity. In L. B. Cohen & P. Salapatek (Eds.), *Infant perception: From sensation to cognition* (Vol. 1). New York, NY: Academic Press.

Fässberg, M. M. et al. (2012). A systematic review of social factors and suicidal behavior in older adulthood. *International Journal of Environmental Research and Public Health*, *9*(3), 722–745.

Farr, R. H., & Patterson, C. J. (2013). Lesbian and gay adoptive parents and their children. In A. E Goldberg, & K. R. Allen (Eds.). *LGBT-parent families: Innovations in research and implications for practice* (pp. 39–55). New York: Springer Science + Business Media.

Feig, S. A., Segel, G. B., & Morimoto, K. (2011). Sickle cell anemia. In S. Yazdani, S. A. McGhee, & E. R. Stiehm (Eds.), *Chronic complex diseases of childhood* (pp. 235–240). Boca Raton, FL: Brown Walker Press.

Feijó, L., et al. (2006). Mothers' depressed mood and anxiety levels are reduced after massaging their preterm infants. *Infant Behavior & Development*, *29*(3), 476–480.

Feinberg, M. E., Neiderhiser, J. M., Howe, G., & Hetherington, E. M. (2001). Adolescent, parent, and observer perceptions of parenting: Genetic and environmental influences on shared and distinct perceptions. *Child Development*, *72*(4), 1266–1284.

Feldman, D. C., & Beehr, T. A. (2011). A three-phase model of retirement decision making. *American Psychologist*, *66*(3), 193–203.

Feldman, R., & Masalha, S. (2007). The role of culture in moderating the links between early ecological risk and young children's adaptation. *Development and Psychopathology*, *19*(1), 1–21.

Feldman, R., Rosenthal, Z., & Eidelman, A. I. (2014). Maternal-preterm skin-to-skin contact enhances child physiologic organization and cognitive control across the first 10 years of life. *Biological Psychiatry*, *75*(1), 56–64.

Fergusson, A. (2007). What successful teachers do in inclusive classrooms: Research-based teaching strategies that help special learners succeed. *European Journal of Special Needs Education*, 22(1), 108–110.

Fernandes, A., Campbell-Yeo, M., & Johnston, C. C. (2011). Procedural pain management for neonates using nonpharmacological strategies: Part 1: Sensorial interventions. *Advances in Neonatal Care*, *11*(4), 235–241s.

Fernandez, E., & Smith, T. W. (2015). Anger, hostility and cardiovascular disease in the context of interpersonal relationships. In M. Alvarenga & D. Byrne (Eds.). *Handbook of psychocardiology* (pp. 1–19). Singapore: Springer Science + Business Media.

Féron, J., Gentaz, E., & Streri, A. (2006). Evidence of amodal representation of small numbers across visuo-tactile modalities in 5-month-old infants. *Cognitive Development*, *21*(2), 81–92.

Ferre, C. L., Babik, I., & Michel, G. F. (2010). Development of infant prehension handedness: A longitudinal analysis during the 6- to 14-month age period. *Infant Behavior and Development*, *33*(4), 492–502.

Ferreira, F. (2010). You can take it with you: Proposition 13 tax benefits, residential mobility, and willingness to pay for housing amenities. *Journal of Public Economics*, *94*(9–10), 661–673.

Ferrer, E., et al. (2010). Uncoupling of reading and IQ over time. *Psychological Science*, 21(1), 93–101.

Field, A. P. (2006). The behavioral inhibition system and the verbal information pathway to children's fears. *Journal of Abnormal Psychology*, *115*(4), 742–752.

Field, T. (1999). Sucking and massage therapy reduce stress during infancy. In M. Lewis & D. Ramsay (Eds.), *Soothing and stress* (pp. 157–169). Hillsdale, NJ: Erlbaum.

Field, T., Orozco, A., Corbin, J., Dominguez, G., & Frost, P. (2014). Face-to-face interaction behaviors of preadolescent same-sex and opposite-sex friends and acquaintances. *Journal of Child and Adolescent Behavior*, DOI: 10.4172/jcalb.1000134

Filus, A. (2006). Being a grandparent in China, Greece and Poland. *Studia Psychologiczne*, *44*(1), 35–46.

Finkelhor, D., Turner, H. A., Shattuck, A., & Hamby, S. L. (2015). Prevalence of childhood exposure to violence, crime, and abuse: Results from the National Survey of Children's Exposure to Violence. *JAMA Pediatrics*, *169*(8), 746–754.

Finkelman, J. M. (2005). Sexual harassment. In A. Barnes (Ed.), *The handbook of women, psychology, and the law* (pp. 64–78). Hoboken, NJ: Wiley.

Fisch, S. M. (2004). *Children's learning from educational television: Sesame Street and beyond*. Mahwah, NJ: Erlbaum.

Fiske, A. (2006). The nature of depression in later life. In S. H. Qualls & B. G. Knight (Eds.), *Psychotherapy for depression in older adults* (pp. 29–44). Hoboken, NJ: John Wiley & Sons.

Fitzgerald, H. E., et al. (1991). The organization of lateralized behavior during infancy. In H. E. Fitzgerald, B. M. Lester, & M. W. Yogman (Eds.), *Theory and research in behavioral pediatrics*. New York, NY: Plenum.

Fivush, R. (2002). Scripts, schemas, and memory of trauma. In N. L. Stein et al. (Eds.), *Representation, memory, and development: Essays in honor of Jean Mandler* (pp. 53–74). Mahwah, NJ: Erlbaum.

Fivush, R., & Hammond, N. R. (1990). Autobiographical memory across the preschool years: Toward reconceptualizing childhood amnesia. In R. Fivush & J. A. Hudson (Eds.), *Knowing and remembering in young children*. Cambridge, UK: Cambridge University Press.

Flavell, J. H. (1993). Young children's understanding of thinking and consciousness. *Current Directions in Psychological Science*, 2, 40–43.

Flavell, J. H., Miller, P. H., & Miller, S. A. (2002). *Cognitive development* (4th ed.). Upper Saddle River, NJ: Prentice Hall.

Flegal, K. M., Carroll, M. D., Ogden, C. L., & Curtin, L. R. (2010). Prevalence and trends in obesity among U.S. adults, 1999–2008. *Journal of the American Medical Association*, *303*(3), 235–241.

Fletcher, K. L. (2011). Neuropsychology of early childhood (3 to 5 years old). In A. S. Davis (Ed.), *Handbook of pediatric neuropsychology*. New York, NY: Springer.

Florsheim, P. (Ed.). (2003). *Adolescent romantic relations and sexual behavior: Theory, research, and practical implications*. Mahwah, NJ: Erlbaum.

Flynn, J. R. (2003). Movies about intelligence: The limitations of g. *Current Directions in Psychological Science*, *12*(3), 95–99.

Foley, G. M. (2006). Self and social–emotional development in infancy: A descriptive synthesis. In G. M. Foley & J. D. Hochman (Eds.), *Mental health in early intervention: Achieving unity in principles and practice* (pp. 139–173). Baltimore: Paul H. Brookes.

Fogassi, L., & Rizzolatti, G. (2013). The mirror mechanism as neurophysiological basis for action and intention understanding. In A. Suarez, & P. Adams (Eds.). *Is science compatible with free will?* (pp. 117–134). New York: Springer.

Foote, W. E., & Goodman-Delahunty, J. (2005). *Evaluating sexual harassment*. Washington, DC: American Psychological Association.

Forbush, K., Heatherton, T. F., & Keel, P. K. (2007). Relationships between perfectionism and specific disordered eating behaviors. *International Journal of Eating Disorders*, *40*(1), 37–41.

Fournier, K. A., Hass, C. J., Naik, S. K., Lodha, N., & Cauraugh, J. H. (2010). Motor coordination in autism spectrum disorder: A synthesis and meta-analysis. *Journal of Autism and Developmental Disorders*, *40*(10), 1227–1240.

Fox, E., & Dinsmore, D. L. (2016). Teacher influences on the development of students' personal interest in academic domains. In K. R. Wentzel, & G. B. Ramani (Eds.). *Handbook of social influences in school contexts: Social-emotional, motivation, and cognitive outcomes* (pp. 143–157). New York: Routledge.

Fozard, J. L., & Gordon-Salant, S. (2001). Changes in vision and hearing with aging. In J. E. Birren, & K. W. Schaie (Eds.), *Handbook of psychology of aging* (5th ed., pp. 241–266). San Diego, CA: Academic Press.

Freedenthal, S. (2007). Racial disparities in mental health service use by adolescents who thought about or attempted suicide. *Suicide and Life-Threatening Behavior*, *37*(1), 22–34.

Freeman, M. S., Spence, M. J., and Oliphant, C. M. (1993, June). *Newborns prefer their mothers' low-pass filtered voices over other female filtered voices*. Paper presented at the meeting of the American Psychological Society, Chicago.

Friedman, R. A. (2008, January 15). Crisis? Maybe he's a narcissistic jerk. *The New York Times online*.

Friedmann, N., & Rusou, D. (2015). Critical period for first language: The crucial role of language input during the first year of life. *Current Opinion in Neurobiology*, *35*, 27–34.

Frühmesser, A., & Kotzot, D. (2011). Chromosomal variants in Klinefelter syndrome. *Sexual Development*, *5*(3), 109–123.

Fry, D. P. (2005). Rough-and-tumble social play in humans. In A. D. Pellegrini & P. K. Smith (Eds.), *The nature of play: Great apes and humans* (pp. 54–85). New York, NY: Guilford Press.

Fucile, S., & Gisel, E. G. (2010). Sensorimotor interventions improve growth and motor function in preterm infants. Neonatal Network: *The Journal of Neonatal Nursing*, *29*(6), 359–366.

Fuertes, M., Faria, A., Beeghly, M., & Lopes-dos-Santos, P. (2016). The effects of parental sensitivity and involvement in caregiving on mother-infant and father-infant attachment in a Portuguese sample. *Journal of Family Psychology*, *30*(1), 147–156.

Fuller, T. (2011). Is scientific theory change similar to early cognitive development? Gopnik on science and childhood. *Philosophical Psychology*. doi:10.1080/09515089.2011.625114

Furman, W., & Winkles, J. K. (2010). Predicting romantic involvement, relationship cognitions, and relationship qualities from physical appearance, perceived norms, and relational styles regarding friends and parents. *Journal of Adolescence, 33*(6), 827–836.

Furman, W., Rahe, D., & Hartup, W. W. (1979). Social rehabilitation of lowinteractive preschool children by peer intervention. *Child Development*, *50*, 915–922.

Furnham, A. (2009). Sex differences in mate selection preferences. *Personality and Individual Differences*, *47*(4), 262–267.

G

Gallese, V., Fadiga, L., Fogassi, L., & Rizzolatti, G. (1996). Action recognition in the premotor cortex. *Brain*, *119*(2), 593–609.

Garber, H. L. (1988). *The Milwaukee Project: Preventing mental retardation in children at risk*. Washington, DC: American Association on Mental Retardation.

Garcia-Falgueras, A., & Swaab, D. F. (2010). Sex hormones and the brain: An essential alliance for sexual identity and sexual orientation. In S. Loche et al. (Eds.), *Pediatric neuroendocrinology* (Vol. 17, pp. 22–35). Basel, Switzerland: Karger.

Gardenghi, G. G., et al. (2009). Respiratory function in patients with stable anorexia nervosa. *Chest*, *136*(5), 1356–1363.

Gardner, H. (1983). *Frames of mind: The theory of multiple intelligences*. New York, NY: Basic Books.

Garvain, J. (2015). Plasticity in early language acquisition: The effects of prenatal and early childhood experience. *Current Opinion in Neurobiology*, *35*, 13–20.

Gass, M. L. S., et al. (2011). Patterns and predictors of sexual activity in the hormone therapy trials of the Women's Health Initiative. *Menopause*, *18*(11), 1160–1171.

Gathercole, S. E., Pickering, S. J., Ambridge, B., & Wearing, H. (2004a). The structure of working memory from 4 to 15 years of age. *Developmental Psychology*, *40*(2), 177–190.

Gathercole, S. E., Pickering, S. J., Knight, C., & Stegmann, Z. (2004b). Working memory skills and educational attainment: Evidence from national curriculum assessments at 7 and 14 years of age. *Applied Cognitive Psychology*, *18*(1), 1–16.

Gavin, N. I., et al. (2005). Perinatal depression: A systematic review of prevalence and incidence. *Obstetrics & Gynecology*, *106*, 1071–1083.

Gaul, D., & Issartel, J. (2016). Fine motor skill proficiency in typically developing children: On or off the maturation track? *Human Movement Science*, *46*, 78–85.

Gauvain, M. (2016). Peer contributions to cognitive development. In K. R. Wentzel, & G. B. Ramani (Eds.). *Handbook of social influences in school contexts: Social-emotional, motivation, and cognitive outcomes* (pp. 80–95). New York: Routledge.

Ge, X., et al. (2003). It's about timing and change: Pubertal transition effects on symptoms of major depression among African American youths. *Developmental Psychology*, *39*(3), 430–439.

Gee, R. E., Wood, S. F., & Schubert, K. G. (2014). Women's health, pregnancy, and the U.S. Food and Drug Administration. *Obstetrics & Gynecology*, *123*(1), 161–165.

Gehlbach, H., & Robinson, C. D. (2016). Commentary: The foundational role of teacher-student relationships. In K. R. Wentzel, & G. B. Ramani (Eds.). *Handbook of social influences in school contexts: Social-emotional, motivation, and cognitive outcomes* (pp. 230–238). New York: Routledge.

Genital HPV Infection—Fact Sheet. (2011). Centers for Disease Control and Prevention. Retrieved from http://www.cdc.gov/std/HPV/STDFact-HPV.htm

George, M. R. W., Koss, K. J., McCoy, K. P., Cummings, E. M., & Davies, P. T. (2010). Examining the family context and relations with attitudes to school and scholastic competence. *Advances in School Mental Health Promotion*, *3*(4), 51–62.

Georges, J.-J., The, A. M., Onwuteaka-Philipsen, B. D., & van der Wal, G. (2008). Dealing with requests for euthanasia. *Journal of Medical Ethics*, *34*(3), 150–155.

Georgiades, S., et al. (2010). Phenotypic overlap between core diagnostic features and emotional/behavioral problems in preschool children with autism spectrum disorder. *Journal of Autism and Developmental Disorders*, *41*(10), 1321–1329.

Gerard, J. M., Landry-Meyer, L., & Roe, J. G. (2006). Grandparents raising grandchildren: The role of social support in coping with caregiving challenges. *International Journal of Ageing & Human Development*, *62*(4), 359–383.

Gervain, J., Berent, I., & Werker, J. F. (2011). Binding at birth: The newborn brain detects identity relations and sequential position in speech. *Journal of Cognitive Neuroscience*, *24*(3), 564–574.

Gesell, A. (1928). *Infancy and human growth*. New York, NY: Macmillan.

Gesell, A. (1929). Maturation and infant behavior patterns. *Psychological Review*, *36*, 307–319.

Giannini, A., Genazzani, A. R., & Simoncini, T. (2016). Management of symptoms during the menopausal transition. In A. R. Genazzani, & B. C. Tarlatzis (Eds.). *Frontiers in Gynecological Endocrinology* (pp. 161–168). New York: Springer International Publishing.

Gibson, E. J. (1969). *Principles of perceptual learning and development*. New York, NY: Appleton-Century-Crofts.

Gibson, E. J. (1991). *An odyssey in learning and perception*. Cambridge, MA: MIT Press.

Gibson, E. J., & Walk, R. D. (1960). The visual cliff. *Scientific American*, *202*, 64–71.

Gignac, G. E., & Weiss, L. G. (2015). Digit span is (mostly) related linearly to general intelligence: Every extra bit of span counts. *Psychological Assessment*, *27*(4), 1312–1323.

Giles, A., & Rovee-Collier, C. (2011). Infant long-term memory for associations formed during mere exposure. *Infant Behavior and Development*, *34*(2), 327–338.

Gilhooly, M. L., et al. (2007). Real-world problem solving and quality of life in older people. *British Journal of Health Psychology*, *12*(4), 587–600.

Gilligan, C. (1982). *In a different voice*. Cambridge, MA: Harvard University Press.

Gima, H., Ohgi, S., Fujiwara, T., & Abe, K. (2010). Stress behavior in premature infants with periventricular leukomalacia. *Journal of Physical Therapy Science*, *22*(2), 109–115.

Giussani, D. A. (2011). The vulnerable developing brain. *Proceedings of the National Academy of Sciences*, *108*(7), 2641–2642.

Glaser, K., Tomassini, C., Racioppi, F., & Stuchbury, R. (2006). Marital disruptions and loss of support in later life. *European Journal of Ageing*, *3*(4), 207–216

Glasser, C. L., Robnett, B., & Feliciano, C. (2009). Internet daters' body type preferences: Race–ethnic and gender differences. *Sex Roles*, *61*(1–2), 14–33.

Gleason, T. R. (2002). Social provisions of real and imaginary relationships in early childhood. *Developmental Psychology*, *38*(6), 979–992.

Gleason, T. R. (2004). Imaginary companions and peer acceptance. *International Journal of Behavioral Development*, *28*(3), 204–209.

Gleason, T. R., & Hohmann, L. M. (2006). Concepts of real and imaginary friendships in early childhood. *Social Development*, *15*(1), 128–144.

Gleason, T. R., Gower, A. L., Hohmann, L. M., & Gleason, T. C. (2005). Temperament and friendship in preschool-aged children. *International Journal of Behavioral Development*, *29*(4), 336–344.

Gleason, T. R., Sebanc, A. M., & Hartup, W. W. (2003). Imaginary companions of preschool children. In M. E. Hertzig & E. A. Farber (Eds.), *Annual progress in child psychiatry and child development: 2000–2001* (pp. 101–121). New York, NY: Brunner-Routledge.

Glück, J., & Bluck, S. (2007). Looking back across the life span: A life story account of the reminiscence bump. *Memory & Cognition*, *35*(8), 1928–1939.

Gobet, F., & Simon, H. A. (2000). Five seconds or sixty? Presentation time in expert memory. *Cognitive Science*, *24*(4), 651–682.

Goble, P., Martin, C. L., Hanish, L. D., & Fabes, R. A. (2012). Children's gender-typed activity choices across preschool social contexts. *Sex Roles*, *67*(7-8), 435–451.

Godfrey, E. M., Chin, N. P., Fielding, S. L., Fiscella, K., & Dozier, A. (2011). Contraceptive methods and use by women aged 35 and over: A qualitative study of perspectives. *BMC Women's Health*, *11*(5). Retrieved from http://www.biomedcentral.com/1472-6874/11/5

Goldberg, W. A., et al. (2012). The more things change, the more they stay the same: Gender, culture, and college students' views about work and family. *Journal of Social Issues*, *68*(4), 814–837.

Goldschmidt, L., Day, N. L., & Richardson, G. A. (2000). Effects of prenatal marijuana exposure on child behavior problems at age 10. *Neurotoxicology and Teratology*, *22*(3), 325–336.

Goldsmith, T. C. (2016). Emerging programmed aging mechanisms and their medical implications. *Medical Hypotheses*, *86*, 92–96.

Goldstein, E. B. (2005). *Cognitive psychology: Connecting mind, research, and everyday experience*. Belmont, CA: Wadsworth.

Goldstein, H. (2004). International comparisons of student attainment. *Assessment in Education: Principles, Policy & Practice*, *11*(3), 319–330.

Goldstein, I., & Alexander, J. L. (2005). Practical aspects in the management of vaginal atrophy and sexual dysfunction in perimenopausal and postmenopausal women. *Journal of Sexual Medicine*, *2*(Suppl. 3), 154–165.

Goldstein, I., Meston, C., Davis, S., & Traish, A. (Eds.). (2006). *Female sexual dysfunction*. New York, NY: Parthenon.

Goldstein, S., & Brooks, R. B. (2005). *Handbook of resilience in children*. New York, NY: Kluwer Academic/Plenum.

Gomez, A. M. (2011). Testing the cycle of violence hypothesis: Child abuse and adolescent dating violence as predictors of intimate partner violence in young adulthood. *Youth & Society*, *43*(1), 171–192.

Goodheart, C. D. (2012). The impact of health disparities on cancer caregivers. *Cancer Caregiving in the United States*, Part 1, 63–77.

Goodman, C. G. (2007a). Intergenerational triads in skipped-generation grandfamilies. *International Journal of Ageing & Human Development*, *65*(3), 231–258.

Goodman, C. G. (2007b). Family dynamics in three-generation grandfamilies. *Journal of Family Issues*, *28*(3), 355–379.

Goodman, G. S., Pipe, M-E., & McWilliams, K. (2011). Children's eyewitness testimony: Methodological issues. In B. Rosenfeld & S. D. Penrod (Eds.), *Research methods on forensic psychology* (pp. 257–282). Hoboken, NJ: Wiley.

Goodman, G. S., Rudy, L., Bottoms, B. L., & Aman, C. (1990). Children's concerns and memory: Issues of ecological validity in the study of children's eyewitness testimony. In R. Fivush & J. A. Hudson (Eds.), *Knowing and remembering in young children*. Cambridge, UK: Cambridge University Press.

Gopnik, A., & Meltzoff, A. N. (1992). Categorization and naming: Basic-level sorting in eighteen-month-olds and its relation to language. *Child Development*, *63*, 1091–1103.

Gopnik, A., & Slaughter, V. (1991). Young children's understanding of changes in their mental states. *Child Development*, *62*, 98–110.

Gordon, M. K., et al. (2016). Comparison of performance on ADHD quality of care indicators. *Journal of Attention Disorders*, DOI: 10.1177/1087054715624227.

Gordon-Salant, S., Fitzgibbons, P. J., & Friedman, S. A. (2007). Recognition of time-compressed and natural speech with selective temporal enhancements by young and elderly listeners. *Journal of Speech, Language, and Hearing Research*, *50*(5), 1181–1193.

Gottfried, G. M., Hickling, A. K., Totten, L. R., Mkroyan, A., & Reisz, A. (2003). To be or not to be a galaprock: Preschoolers' intuitions about the importance of knowledge and action for pretending. *British Journal of Developmental Psychology*, *21*(3), 397–414.

Gottlieb, B. H., Still, E., & Newby-Clark, I. R. (2007). Types and precipitants of growth and decline in emerging adulthood. *Journal of Adolescent Research*, *22*(2), 132–155.

Graber, J. A. (2013). Pubertal timing and the development of psychopathology in adolescence and beyond. *Hormones and Behavior*, *64*(2), 262–269.

Grace, D. M., David, B. J., & Ryan, M. K. (2008). Investigating preschoolers' categorical thinking about gender through imitation, attention, and the use of self-categories. *Child Development*, *79*(6), 1928–1941.

Graham, E. K., & Lachman, M. E. (2012). Personality and aging. In S. K. Whitbourne & M. Sliwinski (Eds.), *The Wiley-Blackwell handbook of adulthood and aging*. Chichester, West Sussex, UK: Wiley-Blackwell.

Graham, J. M. (2011). Measuring love in romantic relationships: A meta-analysis. *Journal of Social and Personal Relationships*, *28*(6), 748–771.

Gray, C., Koopman, E., & Hunt, J. (1991). The emotional phases of marital separation: An empirical investigation. *American Journal of Orthopsychiatry*, *1991*(61), 138–143.

The great prostate cancer debate. (2012). *Scientific American*, *306*, 38–43.

Greco, C., Rovee-Collier, C., Hayne, H., Griesler, P., & Early, L. (1986). Ontogeny of early event memory: II. Encoding and retrieval by 2- and 3-month-olds. *Infant Behavior and Development*, *9*, 461–472.

Greene, F. J., Han, L., & Marlow, S. (2013). Like mother, like daughter? Analyzing maternal influences upon women's entrepreneurial propensity. *Entrepreneurship: Theory and Practice*, *37*(4), 687–711.

Green, R. (1978). Sexual identity of 37 children raised by homosexual or transsexual parents. *American Journal of Psychiatry*, *135*, 692–697.

Greene, J. A., Sandoval, W. A., & Braten, I. (Eds.). (2016). *Handbook of epistemic cognition*. New York.

Greenough, W. T., Black, J. E., & Wallace, C. S. (2002). Experience and brain development. In M. H. Johnson, Y. Munakata, & R. O. Gilmore (Eds.), *Brain development and cognition: A reader* (2nd ed., pp. 186–216). Malden, MA: Blackwell.

Griebling, T. L. (2011). Sexual activities, sexual and life satisfaction, and successful aging in women. *The Journal of Urology*, *185*(6), 2276–2277.

Grigorenko, E. L. (2007). Triangulating developmental dyslexia: Behavior, brain, and genes. In D. Coch, G. Dawson, & K. W. Fischer (Eds.), *Human behavior, learning, and the developing brain: Atypical development*. (pp. 117–144). New York, NY: Guilford.

Grolnick, W. S., McMenamy, J. M., & Kurowski, C. O. (2006). Emotional self-regulation in infancy and toddlerhood. In L. Balter & C. S. Tamis-LeMonda (Eds.), *Child psychology: A handbook of contemporary issues* (2nd ed., pp. 3–25). New York, NY: Psychology Press.

Grön, G., Wunderlich, A. P., Spitzer, M., Tomczak, R., & Riepe, M. W. (2000). Brain activation during human navigation: Gender-different neural networks as substrate of performance. *Nature Neuroscience*, *3*(4), 404–408.

Gross, L. (2006). Evolution of neonatal imitation. *PLoS BIol*, *4*(9), e311. doi:10.1371/journal.pbio.0040311

Grossmann, A. H., D'Augelli, A. R., & O'Connell, T. S. (2003). Being lesbian, gay, bisexual, and sixty or older in North America. In L. D. Garnets & D. C. Kimmel (Eds.), *Psychological perspectives on lesbian, gay, and bisexual experiences* (2nd ed., pp. 629–645). New York, NY: Columbia University Press.

Grossmann, K., et al. (2002). The uniqueness of the child–father attachment relationship: Fathers' sensitive and challenging play as a pivotal variable in a 16-year longitudinal study. *Social Development*, *11*(3), 307–331.

Grusec, J. E. (2002). Parenting socialization and children's acquisition of values. In M. H. Bornstein (Ed.), *Handbook of parenting* (2nd ed.), *Vol. 5, Practical issues in parenting* (pp. 143–167). Mahwah, NJ: Erlbaum.

Grusec, J. E. (2006). The development of moral behavior and conscience from a socialization perspective. In M. Killen & J. G. Smetana (Eds.), *Handbook of moral development* (pp. 243–265). Mahwah, NJ: Erlbaum

Grusec, J. E. (2011). Socialization processes in the family: Social and emotional development. *Annual Review of Psychology*, *62*, 243–269.

Grusec, J. E., & Sherman, A. (2011). Prosocial behavior. In M. K. Underwood & L. H. Rosen (Eds.), *Social development: Relationships in infancy, childhood, and adolescence* (pp. 263–288). New York, NY: Guilford.

Grusec, J. E. (2015). Family relationships and development. *Emerging Trends in the Social and Behavioral Sciences*, DOI: 10.1002/9781118900772.etrds0130.

Grusec, J. E., & Davidov, M. (2015). Analyzing socialization from a domain-specific perspective. In J. E. Grusec, & P. D. Hastings (Eds.). *Handbook of socialization: Theory and research* (pp. 158–181). New York Guilford.

Grusec, J. E., & Davidov, M. (2015). Analyzing socialization from a domain-specific perspective. In J. E. Grusec, & P. D. Hastings (Eds.). *Handbook of socialization: Theory and research*, 2nd ed. (pp. 158–181). New York. Guilford.

Grusec, J. E. (2015). Family relationships and development. *Emerging Trends in the Social and Behavioral Sciences*, DOI: 10.1002/9781118900772.etrds0130.

Grusec, J. E., & Hastings, P. D. (2015). *Handbook of socialization: Theory and research*. New York: Guilford.

Gudmundsson, G. (2010). Infantile colic: Is a pain syndrome. *Medical Hypotheses*, *75*(6), 528–529.

Guerin, D. W., Gottfried, A. W., & Thomas, C. W. (1997). Difficult temperament and behaviour problems: A longitudinal study from 1.5 to 12 years. *International Journal of Behavioral Development*, *21*(1), 71–90.

Guerrini, I., Thomson, A. D., & Gurling, H. D. (2007). The importance of alcohol misuse, malnutrition and genetic susceptibility on brain growth and plasticity. *Neuroscience & Biobehavioral Reviews*, *31*(2), 212–220

Guiaux, M., van Tilburg, T., & van Groenou, M. B. (2007). Changes in contact and support exchange in personal networks after widowhood. *Personal Relationships*, *14*(3), 457–473.

Gupta, N. D., & Simonsen, M. (2010). Non-cognitive child outcomes and universal high-quality child care. *Journal of Public Economics*, *94*(1–2), 30–43.

Gupta, S., Gersing, K. R., Erkanli, A., & Burt, T. (2015). Antidepressant regulatory warnings, prescription patterns, suicidality and other aggressive behavirs in major depressive disorder and anxiety disorder. *Psychiatric Quarterly*, 1–14, DOI: 10.1007/s11126-015-9389-8.

Guttmacher Institute. (2007, June 8). Retrieved from http://www.guttmacher.org

Guttmacher Institute. (2016). *Teen pregnancy*. https://www.guttmacher.org/united-states/teens/teen-pregnancy (Accessed April 3, 2016).

Guzzetti, B. J. (2010). Feminist perspectives on the new literacies. In E. A. Baker & D. J. Leu (Eds.), *The new literacies* (pp. 242–264). New York, NY Guilford Press.

H

Haber, D. (2010). Promoting healthy aging. In K. L. Mauk (Ed.), *Gerontological nursing: Competencies for care* (pp. 328–353). Sudbury, MA: Jones and Bartlett.

Haier, R. J. (2011). Biological basis of intelligence. In R. J. Sternberg & S. J. Kaufman (Eds.), *The Cambridge handbook of intelligence* (pp. 351–370). New York, NY: Cambridge University Press.

Haith, M. M. (1979). Visual cognition in early infancy. In R. B. Kearsly & I. E. Sigel (Eds.), *Infants at risk: Assessment of cognitive functioning*. Hillsdale, NJ: Erlbaum.

Hakim, C. (2015). The male sexual deficit: A social fact of the 21st century. *International Sociology*, *30*(3), 314–335.

Hale, J. B., et al. (2011). Executive impairment determines ADHD medication response. *Journal of Learning Disabilities*, *44*(2), 196–212.

Haley, D. W., Grunau, R. E., Weinberg, J., Keidar, A., & Oberlander, T. F. (2010). *Infant Behavior and Development*, *33*(2), 219–234.

Halgin, R. P., & Whitbourne, S. K. (1993). *Abnormal psychology*. Fort Worth, TX: Harcourt Brace Jovanovich.

Hall, D. T. (2004). The protean career: A quarter-century journey. *Journal of Vocational Behavior*, *65*(1), 1–13.

Hall, G. S. (1904). *Adolescence: Its psychology and its relations to physiology, anthropology, sociology sex, crime, religion and education* (Vol. II). New York: D Appleton & Company.

Hall, J. (2012). Gender issues in mathematics. *Journal of Teaching and Learning*, *8*(1), 59–72.

Hall, J. A. (2011). Sex differences in friendship expectations: A meta-analysis. *Journal of Social and Personal Relationships*, *28*(6), 723–747.

Halmi, K. A., et al. (2014). Perfectionism in anorexia nervosa: Variation by clinical subtype, obsessionality, and pathological eating behavior. *The American Journal of Psychiatry*, *157*(11), 1799–1805.

Hamm, J. V. (2000). Do birds of a feather flock together? The variable bases for African American, Asian American, and European American adolescents' selection of similar friends. *Developmental Psychology*, *36*(2), 209–219.

Hangal, S., & Aminabhavi, V. A. (2007). Self-concept, emotional maturity, and achievement motivation of the adolescent children of employed mothers and homemakers. *Journal of the Indian Academy of Applied Psychology*, *33*(1), 103–110.

Hankin, B. L. (2015). Depression from childhood through adolescence: Risk mechanisms across multiple systems and levels of analysis. *Current Opinion in Psychology*, *4*, 13–20.

Hanlon, T. E., Bateman, R. W., Simon, B. D., O'Grady, K. E., & Carswell, S. B. (2004). Antecedents and correlates of deviant activity in urban youth manifesting behavioral problems. *Journal of Primary Prevention*, *24*(3), 285–309.

Hannon, P., Bowen, D. J., Moinpour, C. M., & McLerran, D. F. (2003). Correlations in perceived food use between the family food preparer and their spouses and children. *Appetite*, *40*(1), 77–83.

Hansen, J. C., Dik, B. J., & Zhou, S. (2008). An examination of the structure of leisure interests of college students, working-age adults, and retirees. *Journal of Counseling Psychology*, *55*(2), 133–145.

Hansson, M., Chotai, J., & Bodlund, O. (2012). What made me feel better? Patients' own explanations for the improvement of their depression. *Nordic Journal of Psychiatry*. doi:10.3109/080 39488.2011.644807

Harlow, H. F., & Harlow, M. K. (1966). Learning to love. *American Scientist*, *54*, 244–272.

Harlow, H. F., Harlow, M. K., & Suomi, S. J. (1971). From thought to therapy: Lessons from a primate laboratory. *American Scientist*, *59*, 538–549.

Harris, G. (2004, September 14). *FDA links drugs to being suicidal*. Retrieved from http://www.nytimes.com.

Harris, S. R., Megens, A. M., Backman, C. L., & Hayes, V. E. (2005). Stability of the Bayley II Scales of Infant Development in a sample of low-risk and high-risk infants. *Developmental Medicine & Child Neurology*, *47*(12), 820–823.

Harter, S. (1990). Self and identity development. In S. S. Feldman & G. R. Elliott (Eds.), *At the threshold: The developing adolescent*. Cambridge, MA: Harvard University Press.

Harter, S. (2006). The Self. In K. A. Renninger, I. E. Sigel, W. Damon, & R. M. Lerner (Eds.), *Handbook of child psychology* (6th ed., Vol. 4), *Child psychology in practice* (pp. 505–570). Hoboken, NJ: Wiley.

Harter, S., & Whitesell, N. R. (2003). Beyond the debate: Why some adolescents report stable self-worth over time and situation, whereas others report changes in self-worth. *Journal of Personality*, *71*(6), 1027–1058.

Harter, S. (2012). *The construction of the self: Developmental and Sociocultural Foundations,* 2nd ed. New York: Guilford.

Hartl, A. C., Laursen, B., & Cillessen, A. H. N. (2015). A survival analysis of adolescent friendships: The downside of dissimilarity. *Psychological Science*, *26*(8), 1304–1315.

Hartley, A. (2006). Changing role of the speed of processing construct in the cognitive psychology of human aging. In J. E. Birren & K. W. Schaie (Eds.), *Handbook of the psychology of aging* (6th ed., pp. 183–207). Amsterdam, Netherlands: Elsevier.

Harvey, J. H., & Fine, M. A. (2011). *Children of divorce*. New York, NY: Routledge, Taylor & Francis Group.

Hasher, L. (2008, May 20). Cited in Reistad-Long, S. Older brain, wiser brain. *The New York Times online*.

Hasselhorn, M. (1992). Task dependency and the role of typicality and metamemory in the development of an organizational strategy. *Child Development*, *63*, 202–214.

Hassing, L. B., & Johanssom. B. (2005). Aging and cognition. *Nordisk Psykologi*, *57*(1), 4–20.

Hastings, P. D., Zahn-Waxler, C., Robinson, J., Usher, B., & Bridges, D. (2000). The development of concern for others in children with behavior problems. *Developmental Psychology*, *36*(5), 531–546.

Hatch, L. R., & Bulcroft, K. (2004). Does long-term marriage bring less frequent disagreements? *Journal of Family Issues*, *25*, 465–495.

Hatfield, E., & Rapson, R. L. (2002). Passionate love and sexual desire: Cultural and historical perspectives. In A. L. Vangelisti, H. T. Reis, et al. (Eds.), *Stability and change in relationships. Advances in personal relationships* (pp. 306–324). New York, NY: Cambridge University Press.

Hauck, F. R., Thompson, J. M., Tanabe, K., Moon, R., Vennemann, M. (2011). Breastfeeding and reduced risk of sudden infant death syndrome: A meta-analysis. *Pediatrics*, *128*(1), 103–110.

Hautamäki, A., Hautamäki, L., Neuvonen, L., Maliniemi-Piispanen, S. (2010). Transmission of attachment across three generations. *European Journal of Developmental Psychology*, *7*(5), 618–634.

Havighurst, R. (1972). *Robert Havighurst: Developmental theorist*. Retrieved from http://faculty.mdc.edu/jmcnair/EDF3214. Topic.Outline/Robert.Havighurst. htm

Haworth, C. M. A., et al. (2009). A twin study of the genetics of high cognitive ability selected from 11,000 twin pairs in six studies from four countries. *Behavior Genetics*, *39*(4), 359–370.

Hay, D. F., Payne, A., & Chadwick, A. (2004). Peer relations in childhood. *Journal of Child Psychology and Psychiatry*. *45*(1), 84–108.

Hayes, R., & Dennerstein, L. (2005). The impact of aging on sexual function and sexual dysfunction in women: A review of population-based studies. *Journal of Sexual Medicine*, *2*(3), 317–330.

Hayne, H., & Fagen, J. W. (Eds.). (2003). *Progress in infancy research* (Vol. 3). Mahwah, NJ: Erlbaum.

Hayslip, B., Jr., & Kaminski, P. L. (2006). Custodial grandchildren. In G. G. Bear & K. M. Minke (Eds.), *Children's needs III: Development, prevention, and intervention* (pp. 771–782). Washington, DC: National Association of School Psychologists.

Healy, M. D., & Ellis, B. J. (2007). Birth order, conscientiousness, and openness to experience Tests of the family-niche model of personality using a within-family methodology. *Evolution and Human Behavior*, *28*(1), 55–59.

Hayslip, B., Jr. (2015). Bringing the generations closer. *Journal of Intergenerational Relationships*, *13*(2), 99–103.

Haywood, K. M., & Getchell, N. (2014). *Life span motor development* (6th ed.). Champaign, IL: Human Kinetics.

Heard, E., & Turner, J. (2011). Function of the sex chromosomes in mammalian fertility. *Cold Spring Harbor Perspectives in Biology*. *3*(10), a002675.

Hebblethwaite, S., & Norris, J. (2011). Expressions of generativity through family leisure: Experiences of grandparents and adult grandchildren. *Family Relations*, *60*(1), 121–133.

Heilman, K. M., Nadeau, S. E., & Beversdorf, D. O. (2003). Creative innovation: Possible brain mechanisms. *Neurocase*, *9*(5), 369–379.

Heimann, M., et al. (2006). Exploring the relation between memory, gestural communication, and the emergence of language in infancy: A longitudinal study. *Infant and Child Development*, *15*(3), 233–249.

Heindel, J. J., & Lawler, C. (2006) Role of exposure to environmental chemicals in developmental origins of health and disease. In P. Gluckman & M. Hanson (Eds.), *Developmental origins of health and disease* (pp. 82–97). New York, NY Cambridge University Press.

Heineman, K. R., Middelburg, K. J., & Hadders-Algra, M. (2010). Development of adaptive motor behavior in typically developing infants. *Acta Paediatrica*, *99*(4), 618–624.

Heinonen, K., et al. (2011). Trajectories of growth and symptoms of attention-deficit/hyperactivity disorder in children: A longitudinal study. *BMC Pediatrics*, *11*(84). doi:10.1186/1471-2431-11-84

Helwig, C. C. (2006). Rights, civil liberties, and democracy across cultures. In M. Killen & J. G. Smetana (Eds.), *Handbook of moral development* (pp. 185–210). Mahwah, NJ: Erlbaum.

Henricks, T. S. (2015). Classic theories of play. In J. E. Johnson et al. (Eds.). *The handbook of the study of play, Vol. 2* (pp. 163–180). Lanham, MD: Rowman & Littlefield.

Henry, D., et al. (2000). Normative influences on aggression in urban elementary school classrooms. *American Journal of Community Psychology*, *28*(1) 59–81.

Henzi, S. P., et al. (2007). Look who's talking: Developmental trends in the size of conversational cliques. *Evolution and Human Behavior*, *28*(1), 66–74.

Herbenick, D., et al. (2010a). Sexual behavior in the United States: Results from a national probability sample of males and females ages 14 to 94. *Journal of Sexual Medicine*, *7*(Suppl. 5), 255–265.

Herbenick, D., et al. (2010b). Sexual behaviors, relationships, and perceived health among adult women in the United States: Results from a national probability sample. *Journal of Sexual Medicine*, *7*(Suppl. 5), 277–290.

Herbenick, D., et al. (2010c). An event-level analysis of the sexual characteristics and composition among adults ages 18 to 59: Results from a national probability sample in the United States. *Journal of Sexual Medicine*, *7*(Suppl. 5), 346–361.

Hergenhahn, B. R., & Henley, T. (2014). *An introduction to the history of psychology* (7th ed.). San Francisco: Cengage Learning.

Heron, M. (2016). Deaths: Leading causes for 2013. *National Vital Statistics Reports*, *65*(2).

Heron, M. P. (2007). *National Vital Statistics Reports*, *56*(5). Centers for Disease Control and Prevention. Retrieved from http://www.cdc.gov/nchs/data/nvsr/nvsr56/nvsr56_05

Herring, M. P., et al. (2012a). Feasibility of exercise training for the short-term treatment of generalized anxiety disorder: A randomized controlled trial. *Psychotherapy and Psychosomatics*, *81*(1), 21–28.

Herring, M. P., et al. (2012b). Effects of exercise training on depressive symptoms among patients with a chronic illness: Systematic review and meta-analysis of randomized controlled trials. *Archives of Internal Medicine*, *172*(2), 101–111.

Hershberger, S. L., & D'Augelli, A. R. (2000). Issues in counseling lesbian, gay, and bisexual adolescents. In R. M. Perez, K. A. De-Bord, & K. J. Bieschke (Eds.), *Handbook of counseling and psychotherapy with lesbian, gay, and bisexual clients* (pp. 225–247). Washington, DC: American Psychological Association.

Hertenstein, M. J., & Campos, J. J. (2004). The retention effects of an adult's emotional displays on infant behavior. *Child Development*, *75*(2), 595–613.

Hetherington, E. M. (1989). Coping with family transition: Winners, losers, and survivors. *Child Development*, *60*, 1–14.

Hetherington, E. M. (2006). The effects of marital discord, divorce, and parental psychopathology. *New Directions for Child and Adolescent Development*, *1984*(24), 6–33.

Hill, P. L., Duggan, P. M., & Lapsley, D. K. (2011). Subjective invulnerability, risk behavior, and adjustment in early adolescence. *The Journal of Early Adolescence*. doi:10.1177/0272431611400304

Hill, S. E., & Flom, R. (2007). 18- and 24-month-olds' discrimination of gender-consistent and inconsistent activities. *Infant Behavior & Development*, *30*(1) 168–173.

Hillerer, K. M., Neumann, I. D., & Slattery, D. A. (2011). Exposure to chronic pregnancy stress reverses peripartum-associated adaptations: Implications for postpartum anxiety and mood disorders. *Endocrinology*, *152*(10), 3930–3940.

Hilliard, L. J., & Liben, L. S. (2010). Differing levels of gender salience in preschool classrooms: Effects on children's gender attitudes and intergroup bias. *Child Development*, *81*(6), 1787–1798.

Hills, A. P., & Byrne, N. M. (2011). An overview of physical growth and maturation. In J. Jurimae, A. P. Hills, & T. Jurimae (Eds.), Cytokines, growth mediators and physical activity in children during puberty (pp. 1–13). Basel, Switzerland: S. Karger.

Hiltunen, M., Bertram, L., & Saunders, A. J. (2011). Genetic risk factors: Their function and comorbidities in Alzheimer's disease. *International Journal of Alzheimer's Disease*. doi:10.4061/2011/925362

Hines, M. (2011). Gender development and the human brain. *Annual Review of Neuroscience*, *34*, 69–88.

Hines, M. (2011). Prenatal endocrine influences on sexual orientation and on sexually differentiated childhood behavior. *Frontiers in Neuroendocrinology*, *32*(2), 170–182.

Hines, M., Constantinescu, M., & Spencer, D. (2015). Early androgen exposure and human gender development. *Biology of Sex Differences*, *6*(3), DOI: 10.1186/s13293–015-0022–1.

Hochwarter, W. A., Ferris, G. R., Perrewé, P. L., Witt, L. A., & Kiewitz, C. (2001). A note on the nonlinearity of the age-job-satisfaction relationship. *Journal of Applied Social Psychology*, *31*(6), 1223–1237.

Hodapp, R. M., Griffin, M. M., Burke, M. M., & Fisher, M. H. (2011). Intellectual disabilities. In R. J. Sternberg & S. J. Kaufman (Eds.), *The Cambridge handbook of intelligence* (pp. 193–209). New York, NY: Cambridge University Press.

Hoff, E. (2006). Language experience and language milestones during early childhood. In K. McCartney & D. Phillips (Eds.), *Blackwell handbook of early childhood development., Blackwell handbooks of developmental psychology* (pp. 233–251). Malden, MA: Blackwell.

Hoff, E. (2014). *Language development* (5th Ed.). San Francisco: Cengage Learning. Tamis-LeMonda, C. S., et al. (2014). Children's vocabulary growth in English and Spanish across early development and associations with school readiness skills. *Developmental Neuropsychology*, *39*(2), 69–87.

Hoff, E. V. (2005). A friend living inside me—The forms and functions of imaginary companions. *Imagination, Cognition and Personality*, *24*(2), 151–189.

Hoffman, M., Gneezy, U., & List, J. A. (2011). Nurture affects gender differences in spatial abilities. *Proceedings of the National Academy of Sciences*, *108*(36), 14786–14788.

Holden, G. W., Vittrup, B., & Rosen, L. H. (2011). Families, parenting and discipline. In M. K. Underwood & L. H. Rosen (Eds.), *Social development: Relationships in infancy, childhood, and adolescence* (pp. 127–152). New York, NY Guilford.

Holder, M. D., & Coleman, B. (2015). Children's friendships and positive well-being. In M. Demir (Ed.) *Friendship and happiness* (pp. 81–97). Dordrecht, Netherlands: Springer Science + Business Media.

Holloway, J. H. (2004). *Part-time work and student achievement*. Alexandria VA: Association for Supervision and Curriculum Development. Retrieved from http://www.ascd.org/publications/ed_ lead/200104/holloway.html

Holroyd-Leduc, J., & Reddy, M. (Eds.). (2012). *Evidence-based geriatric medicine*. Chichester, West Sussex, UK Wiley-Blackwell.

Holsti, L. (2010). A preventive care program for very preterm infants improves infant behavioural outcomes and decreases anxiety and depression in caregivers. *Journal of Physiotherapy*, *56*(4), 277.

Homae, F., Watanabe, H., Nakano, T., & Taga, G. (2012). Functional development in the human brain for auditory pitch processing. *Human Brain Mapping*. *33*(3), 596–608.

Homer, B. D., & Nelson, K. (2005). Seeing objects as symbols and symbols as objects: Language and the development of dual representation. In B. D. Homer & C. S. Tamis-LeMonda (Eds.), *The development of social cognition and communication* (pp. 29–52). Mahwah, NJ: Erlbaum.

Homish, G. G., & Leonard, K. E. (2007). The drinking partnership and marital satisfaction: The longitudinal influence of discrepant drinking. *Journal of Consulting and Clinical Psychology*, *75*(1) 43–51.

Hong, D. S., Dunkin, B., & Reiss, A. L. (2011). Psychosocial functioning and social cognitive processing in girls with Turner syndrome. *Journal of Developmental & Behavioral Pediatrics*, *32*(7), 512–520.

Honig, A. S., & Nealis, A. L. (2012). What do young children dream about? *Early Child Development and Care*, *182*(6), 771–795.

Honzik, M. P., Macfarlane, J. W., & Allen, L. (1948). The stability of mental test performance between two and eighteen years. *Journal of Experimental Education*, *17*, 309–324.

Hooijmans, C. R., et al. (2012). The effects of long-term omega-3 fatty acid supplementation on cognition and Alzheimer's pathology in animal models of Alzheimer's disease: A systematic review and meta-analysis. *Journal of Alzheimer's Disease*, *28*(1), 191–209.

Hoover, J. R., Sterling, A. M., & Storkel, H. L. (2011). Speech and language development. In A. S. Davis (Ed.), *Handbook of pediatric neuropsychology*. New York, NY: Springer.

Höpflinger, F., & Hummel, C. (2006). Heranwachsende Enkelkinder und ihre Großeltern: Im Geschlechtervergleich. *Zeitschrift für. Gerontologie und Geriatrie*, *39*(1), 33–40.

Hopkins, W. D., Reamer, L., Mareno, M. C., & Schapiro, S. J. (2015). Genetic basis in motor skill and hand preference for tool use in chimpanzees (Pan troglodytes). *Proceedings of the Royal Society B*, *282*(1800), DOI: 10.1098/rspb.2014.1223.

Hoppmann, C., & Smith, J. (2007). Life-history related differences in possible selves in very old age. *International Journal of Aging & Human Development*, *64*(2), 109–127.

Hossain, M., Chetana, M., & Devi, P. U. (2005). Late effect of prenatal irradiation on the hippocampal histology and brain weight in adult mice. *International Journal of Developmental Neuroscience*, *23*(4), 307–313.

Hostetler, A. J., Sweet, S., & Moen, P. (2007). Gendered career paths: A life course perspective on returning to school. *Sex Roles*, *56*(1–2), 85–103.

Hough, M. S. (2007). Adult age differences in word fluency for common and goal-directed categories. *Advances in Speech Language Pathology*, *9*(2), 154–161.

Howe, M. L. (2006). Developmentally invariant dissociations in children's true and false memories: Not all relatedness is created equal. *Child Development*, *77*(4), 1112–1123.

Huesmann, L. R., Dubow, E. F., Eron, L. D., & Boxer, P. (2006). Middle childhood family contextual factors as predictors of adult outcomes. In A. C. Huston & M. N. Ripke (Eds.), *Middle Childhood: Contexts of Development*. Cambridge, UK: Cambridge University Press.

Huesmann, L. R., Moise-Titus, J., Podolski, C., & Eron, L. D. (2003). Longitudinal relations between children's exposure to TV violence and their aggressive and violent behavior in young adulthood: 1977–1992. *Developmental Psychology*, *39*(2), 201–221.

Huizink, A. C., & Mulder, E. J. H. (2006). Maternal smoking, drinking or cannabis use during pregnancy and neurobehavioral and cognitive functioning in human offspring. *Neuroscience & Biobehavioral Reviews*, *30*(1), 24–41.

Hur, Y. (2005). Genetic and environmental influences on self-concept in female preadolescent twins: Comparison of Minnesota and Seoul data. *Twin Research and Human Genetics*, *8*(4), 291–299.

Hyams, A., & Scogin, F. (2015). Reminiscence/life review therapy. In *The encyclopedia of clinical psychology*. Hoboken, NJ: Wiley.

Hyde, J. S. & Mertz, J. E. (2009). Gender, culture, and mathematics performance. *Proceedings of the National Academy of Sciences*, *106*(22), 8801–8807.

Hyde, J. S., Lindberg, S. M., Linn, M. C., Ellis, A. B., & Williams, C. C. (2008). Gender similarities characterize math performance. *Science*, *321*, 494–495.

I

International Human Genome Sequencing Consortium (2006). A global map of p53 transcription-factor binding sites in the human genome. *Cell*, *124*(1), 207–219.

Inhelder, B., & Piaget, J. (1959). *The early growth of logic in the child: Classification and seriation*. New York: Harper & Row.

J

Jacobs, S. (1993). *Pathologic grief: Maladaptation to loss*. Washington, DC: American Psychiatric Press.

Jacobsen, J. S., et al. (2006). Early-onset behavioral and synaptic deficits in a mouse model of Alzheimer's disease. *Proceedings of the National Academy of Sciences*, *103*, 5161–5166.

Jacobson, J. L., Jacobson, S. W., Padgett, R. J., Brumitt, G. A., & Billings, R. L. (1992). Effects of prenatal PCB exposure on cognitive processing efficiency and sustained attention. *Developmental Psychology*, *28*, 297–306.

Jacobson, P. F., & Schwartz, R. G. (2005). English past tense use in bilingual children with language impairment. *American Journal of Speech-Language Pathology*, *14*(4), 313–323.

Jaffe, A. C. (2011). Failure to thrive: Current clinical concepts. *Pediatrics in Review*, *32*(3), 100–108.

James, D. K. (2010). Fetal learning: A critical review. *Infant and Child Development*, *19*(1), 45–54.

Jang, Y., Kim, G., Chiriboga, D. A., & Cho, S. (2008). Willingness to use a nursing home. *Journal of Applied Gerontology*, *27*(1), 110–117.

Janssen, E. (Ed). (2006). *The psychophysiology of sex*. Bloomington, IN: Indiana University Press.

Jayson, S. (2008, June 8). More view cohabitation as acceptable choice. *USA Today*. Retrieved from http://www.usatoday.com/news/nation/2008-06-08-cohabitation-study_N.htm

Jecker, N. S. (2012). Applying ethical reasoning: Philosophical, clinical, and cultural challenges. In N. S. Jecker et al. (Eds.), *Bioethics* (3rd ed., pp. 127–139). Sudbury, MA: Jones & Bartlett.

Jeng, S.-F., Yau, K.-I. T., Liao, H.-F., Chen, L.-C., & Chen, P.-S. (2000). Prognostic factors for walking attainment in very low-birthweight preterm infants. *Early Human Development*, *59*(3), 159–173.

Jenkins, L. N., Floress, M. T., & Reinke, W. (2015). Rates and types of teacher praise: A review and future directions. *Psychology in the Schools*, *52*(5), 463–476.

Jin, K. (2010). Modern biological theories of aging. *Aging and Disease*, *1*(2), 72–74.

Johnson, D. A., & Gunnar, M. R. (2011). Growth failure in institutionalized children. *Monographs of the Society for Research in Child Development*, *76*(4), 92–126.

Johnson, L. S. M. (2016). Moving beyond end of life: The ethics of disorders of consciousness in an age of discovery and uncertainty. In M. M. Monti, & W. G. Sannita (Eds.). *Brain function and responsiveness in disorders of consciousness* (pp. 185–194). Switzerland: Springer International Publishing.

Johnson, M. H. (2011). *Developmental cognitive neuroscience* (3rd ed.). Chichester, West Sussex, UK: Wiley-Blackwell.

Johnson, M. K., et al. (2012). The cognitive neuroscience of true and false memories. True and false recovered memories. *Nebraska Symposium on Motivation*, *58*, 15–52.

Johnson, S. P. (2011). Development of visual perception. *WIREs Cognitive Science*, *2*, 515–528. doi:10.1002/wcs.128

Johnson, W., McGue, M., Krueger, R. F., & Bouchard, T. J., Jr. (2004). Marriage and personality: A genetic analysis. *Journal of Personality and Social Psychology*, *86*(2), 285–294.

Johnson, E. K. (2016). Constructing a proto-lexicon: An integrative view of infant language development. *Annual Review of Linguistics*, *2*, 391–412.

Johnson-Greene, D., & Inscore, A. B. (2005). Substance abuse in older adults. In S. S. Bush & T. A. Martin (Eds.), Geriatric neuropsychology: Practice essentials (pp. 429–451). *Studies on Neuropsychology, Neurology and Cognition*. Philadelphia, PA: Taylor & Francis.

Johnson, N. B., et al. (2014). CDC National Health Report: Leading causes of morbidity and mortality and associated risk and protective factors–United States, 2005 – 2013. *Centers for Disease Control and Prevention*, http://www.cdc.gov/mmwr/preview/mmwrhtml/su6304a2.htm; Leading Causes of Death. (2016, February 26). Centers for Disease Control and Prevention. http://www.cdc.gov/nchs/fastats/leading-causes-of-death.htm

Johnston, C. C., Campbell-Yeo, M., & Fillon, F. (2011). Paternal vs maternal kangaroo care for procedural pain in preterm neonates: A randomized crossover trial. *Archives of Pediatrics and Adolescent Medicine*, *165*(9), 792–796.

Johnston, L. D., O'Malley, P. M., Miech, R. A., Bachman, J. G., & Schulenberg, J. E. (2016). Monitoring the Future national survey results on drug use, 1975–2015: Overview, key findings on adolescent drug use. Ann Arbor: Institute for Social Research, The University of Michigan.

Jolley, R. P. (2010). Children and pictures: Drawing and understanding. Chichester, West Sussex, UK: Wiley-Blackwell.

Jones, D. C., & Crawford, J. K. (2006). The peer appearance culture during adolescence: Gender and body mass variations. *Journal of Youth and Adolescence*, *35*(2), 257–269.

Jones, S. S., & Hong, H.-W. (2005). How some infant smiles get made. *Infant Behavior & Development*, *28*(2), 194–205.

Jonkman, S. (2006). Sensitization facilitates habit formation: Implications for addiction. *Journal of Neuroscience*, *26*(28), 7319–7320.

Jopp, D. A., & Schmitt, M. (2010). Dealing with negative life events: Differential effects of personal resources, coping strategies, and control beliefs. *European Journal of Ageing*, *7*(3), 167–180.

Joshi, P. T., Salpekar, J. A., & Daniolos, P. T. (2006). Physical and sexual abuse of children. In M. K. Dulcan & J. M. Wiener (Eds.), *Essentials of child and adolescent psychiatry* (pp. 595–620). Washington, DC: American Psychiatric Publishing.

Judge, T. A., & Klinger, R. (2008). Job satisfaction: Subjective well-being at work. In M. Eid & R. J. Larsen (Eds.), *The science of subjective well-being* (pp. 393–413). New York, NY: Guilford Press.

K

K. R. Wentzel, & G. B. Ramani (Eds.). *Handbook of social influences in school contexts: Social-emotional, motivation, and cognitive outcomes*. New York: Routledge.

Kaestle, C. E., & Allen, K. R. (2011). The role of masturbation in healthy sexual development: Perceptions of young adults. *Archives of Sexual Behavior*, *40*(5), 983–994.

Kagan, J. (2009). Review of loneliness: Human nature and the need for social connection. *The American Journal of Psychiatry*, *166*(3), 375–376.

Kagan, J., & Klein, R. E. (1973). Cross-cultural perspectives on early development. *American Psychologist*, *28*, 947–961.

Kaiser Family Foundation, Holt, T., Greene, L., & Davis, J. (2003). National Survey of Adolescents and Young Adults: Sexual health knowledge, attitudes, and experiences. Menlo Park, CA: Author.

Käll, A., & Lagercrantz, H. (2012). Highlights in this issue. *Acta Paediatrica*, *101*(1), 1. doi:10.1111/j.1651-2227.2011.02524.x

Kallio, E. (2011). Integrative thinking is the key: An evaluation of current research into the development of thinking in adults. *Theory & Psychology*. *21*(6), 785–801.

Kaminski, P. L., & Hayslip, B., Jr. (2006). Gender differences in body esteem among older adults. *Journal of Women & Aging*, *18*(3), 19–35.

Kaminski, R. A., & Stormshak, E. A. (2007). Project STAR: Early intervention with preschool children and families for the prevention of substance abuse. In P. Tolan, J. Szapocznik, & S. Sambrano (Eds.), *Preventing youth substance abuse: Science-based programs for children and adolescents* (pp. 89–109). Washington, DC: American Psychological Association.

Karasahin, K. E. (2016). The emotional storms of breast feeding and points to remember. *Midwifery*, *35*, 1–2.

Karatekin, C., Marcus, D. J., & White, T. (2007). Oculomotor and manual indexes of incidental and intentional spatial sequence learning during middle childhood and adolescence. *Journal of Experimental Child Psychology*, *96*(2), 107–130.

Kaufman, J. C., & Plucker, J. A. (2011). Intelligence and creativity. In R. J. Sternberg & S. J. Kaufman (Eds.), *The Cambridge Handbook of Intelligence* (pp. 771–783). New York, NY: Cambridge University Press.

Kavšek, M., Yonas, A., & Granrud, C. E. (2012). Infants' sensitivity to pictorial depth cues: A review and meta-analysis of looking studies. *Infant Behavior and Development*, *35*(1), 109–128.

Kaye, D. A., & Shah, R. V. (2015). *Case studies in pain management*. Cambridge, UK: Cambridge University Press.

Kazdin, A. E. (2000). Treatments for aggressive and antisocial children. *Child and Adolescent Psychiatric Clinics of North America*, *9*(4), 841–858.

Kazui, H., et al. (2008). Association between quality of life of demented patients and professional knowledge of care workers. *Journal of Geriatric Psychiatry and Neurology*, *21*(1), 72–78.

Kazui, M., Endo, T., Tanaka, A., Sakagami, H., & Suganuma, M. (2000). Intergenerational transmission of attachment: Japanese mother–child dyads. *Japanese Journal of Educational Psychology*, *48*(3), 323–332.

Keen, D., Rodger, S., Doussin, K., & Braithwaite, M. (2007). A pilot study of the effects of a social-pragmatic intervention on the communication and symbolic play of children with autism. *Autism*, *11*(1), 63–71.

Keller, H., Kärtner, J., Borke, J., Yovsi, R., & Kleis, A. (2005). Parenting styles and the development of the categorical self: A longitudinal study on mirror self-recognition in Cameroonian Nso and German families. *International Journal of Behavioral Development*, *29*(6), 496–504.

Kellman, P. J., & Arterberry, M. E. (2006). Infant visual perception. In D. Kuhn et al. (Eds.), *Handbook of child psychology: Vol. 2, Cognition, perception, and language* (6th ed., pp. 109–160). Hoboken, NJ: Wiley.

Kellogg, R. (1959). *What children scribble and why*. Oxford, UK: National Press.

Kellogg, R. (1970). Understanding children's art. In P. Cramer (Ed.), *Readings in developmental psychology today*. Del Mar, CA: CRM.

Kelly, L., et al. (2009) Palliative care of First Nations people. *Canadian Family Physician*, *55*(4), 394–395.

Kemp, C. L. (2005). Dimensions of grandparent–adult grandchild relationships: From family ties to intergenerational friendships. *Canadian Journal on Aging*, *24*(2), 161–178.

Kemp, E. A., & Kemp, J. E. (2002). *Older couples: New romances: Finding & keeping love in later life*. Berkeley, CA: Celestial Arts.

Kempes, M., Matthys, W., de Vries, H., & van Engeland, H. (2005). Reactive and proactive aggression in children: A review of theory, findings and the relevance for child and adolescent psychiatry. *European Child & Adolescent Psychiatry*, *14*(1), 11–19.

Kendler, K. S. (2010). Advances in our understanding of genetic risk factors for autism spectrum disorders. *American Journal of Psychiatry*, *167*(11), 1291–1293.

Kendler, K. S., et al. (2011). The impact of environmental experiences on symptoms of anxiety and depression across the life span. *Psychological Science*, *22*(1), 1343–1352.

Kendler, K. S., Gardner, C. O., Gatz, M., & Pedersen, N. L. (2007). The sources of co-morbidity between major depression and generalized anxiety disorder in a Swedish national twin sample. *Psychological Medicine*, *37*(3), 453–462.

Kenney, S. R., et al. (2015). Pathways of parenting style on adolescents' college adjustment, academic achievement, and alcohol risk. *Journal of College Student Retention: Research, Theory & Practice*, *17*(2), 186–203.

Kerr, D. C. R., & Capaldi, D. M. (2010, June 14). Young men's intimate partner violence and relationship functioning. *Psychological Medicine*, pp. 1–14.

Kibbe, M. M., & Leslie, A. M. (2011). What do infants remember when they forget? Location and identity in 6-month-olds' memory for objects. *Psychological Science*, *22*(12), 1500–1505.

Killen, M., & Smetana, J. G. (Eds.). (2006). *Handbook of moral development*. Mahwah, NJ: Erlbaum.

Kim, H. S. (2011). Consequences of parental divorce for child development. *American Sociological Review*, *76*(3), 487–511.

Kim, J.-Y., McHale, S. M., Osgood, D. W., & Crouter, A. C. (2006). Longitudinal course and family correlates of sibling relationships from childhood through adolescence. *Child Development*, *77*(6), 1746–1761.

Kimura, et al. (2010). Infants' recognition of objects using canonical color. *Journal of Experimental Child Psychology*, *105*(3), 256–263.

King, V., & Scott, M. E. (2005). A comparison of cohabiting relationships among older and younger adults. *Journal of Marriage and Family*, *67*(2), 271–285.

Kingsberg, S. A., & Woodard, T. (2015). Female sexual dysfunction: Focus on low desire. *Obstetrics & Gynecology*, *125*(2), 477–486.

Kingsberg, S. A.,& Woodard, T. (2015). Female sexual dysfunction: Focus on low desire. *Obstetrics & Gynecology*, *125*(2), 477–486.

Kins, E., Soenens, B., & Beyers, W. (2011). "Why do they have to grow up so fast?" Parental separation anxiety and emerging adults' pathology of separation-individuation. *Journal of Clinical Psychology, 67*(7), 647–664.

Kinsey, A. C., Pomeroy, W. B., & Martin, C. E. (1948). *Sexual behavior in the human* male. Philadelphia: W. B. Saunders.

Kinsey, A. C., Pomeroy, W. B., Martin, C. E., & Gebhard, P. H. (1953). *Sexual behavior in the human female*. Philadelphia, PA: W. B. Saunders.

Kirby, P. G., Biever, J. L., Martinez, I. G., & Gómez, J. P. (2004). Adults returning to school: The impact on family and work. *Journal of Psychology: Interdisciplinary and Applied, 138*(1), 65–76.

Kirkcaldy, B. D., Shephard, R. J., & Siefen, R. G. (2002). The relationship between physical activity and self-image and problem behaviour among adolescents. *Social Psychiatry and Psychiatric Epidemiology, 37*(11), 544–550.

Kistner, J. (2006). Children's peer acceptance, perceived acceptance, and risk for depression. In T. E. Joiner, J. S. Brown, & J. Kistner (Eds.), *The interpersonal, cognitive, and social nature of depression* (pp. 1–21). Mahwah, NJ: Erlbaum.

Kjelsås, E., Bjornstrom, C., & Götestam, K. G. (2004). Prevalence of eating disorders in female and male adolescents (14–15 years). *Eating Behaviors, 5*(1), 13–25.

Klaus, M. H., & Kennell, J. H. (1978). Parent-to-infant attachment. In J. H. Stevens Jr. & M. Mathews (Eds.), *Mother/child, father/child relationships*. Washington, DC: National Association for the Education of Young Children.

Klee, T., & Stokes, S. F. (2011). Language development. In D. Skuse et al. (Eds.), *Child psychology and psychiatry: frameworks for practice* (2nd ed.) (pp. 45–50). Chichester, UK: John Wiley & Sons. doi:10.1002/9781119993971.ch8

Kleiber, D. A., & Kelly, J. R. (1980). Leisure, socialization, and the life cycle. In S. E. Iso-Ahola (Ed.), *Social psychological perspectives on leisure and recreation* (pp. 91–137). Springfield, IL: Charles C. Thomas.

Klein, K. M., Apple, K. J., & Kahn, A. S. (2011). Attributions of blame and responsibility in sexual harassment. *Law and Human Behavior, 35*(2), 92–103.

Klein, P. J., & Meltzoff, A. N. (1999). Long-term memory, forgetting and deferred imitation in 12-month-old infants. *Developmental Science, 2*(1), 102–113.

Kliegel, M., Jäger, T., & Phillips, L. H. (2008). Adult age differences in event-based prospective memory: A meta-analysis on the role of focal versus nonfocal cues. *Psychology and Aging, 23*(1), 203–208.

Klier, C. M. (2006). Mother–infant bonding disorders in patients with postnatal depression: The Postpartum Bonding Questionnaire in clinical practice. *Archives of Women's Mental Health, 9*(5), 289–291.

Knickmeyer, R., et al. (2005). Gender-typed play and amniotic testosterone. *Developmental Psychology, 41*, 517–528.

Kniffin, K. M., & Wilson, D. S. (2004). The effect of nonphysical traits on the perception of physical attractiveness: Three naturalistic studies. *Evolution and Human Behavior, 25*(2), 88–101.

Kochanek, K. D., et al. (2011). Deaths: Preliminary data for 2009. Centers for Disease Control and Prevention. *National Vital Statistics Reports, 59*(4).

Kochanska, G. (2001). Emotional development in children with different attachment histories: The first three years. *Child Development, 72*(2), 474–490.

Kochanska, G., Coy, K. C., Murray, K. T. (2001). The development of self-regulation in the first four years of life. *Child Development, 72*(4), 1091–1111.

Kohlberg, L. (1963). Moral development and identification. In H. W. Stevenson (Ed.), *Child psychology: 62nd yearbook of the National Society for the Study of Education* (pp. 277–332). Chicago, IL: University of Chicago Press.

Kohlberg, L. (1966). Cognitive stages and preschool education. *Human Development, 9*, 5–17.

Kohlberg, L. (1969). Stage and sequence: The cognitive-developmental approach to socialization. In D. A. Goslin (Ed.), *Handbook of socialization theory and research* (pp. 347–480). Chicago, IL: Rand McNally.

Kohlberg, L. (1981). *The meaning and measurement of moral development*. Worcester, MA: Clark University Press.

Kohlberg, L. (1985). *The psychology of moral development*. San Francisco, CA Harper & Row.

Kohlberg, L., & Kramer, R. (1969). Continuities and discontinuities in childhood and adult moral development. *Human Development, 12*, 93–120.

Kohncke, Y., et al. (2016). Three-year changes in leisure activities are associated with concurrent changes in white matter microstructure and perceptual speed in individuals aged 80 years and older. *Neurobiology of Aging, 41*, 173–186.

Kohyama, J., Shiiki, T., Ohinata-Sugimoto, J., & Hasegawa, T. (2002). Potentially harmful sleep habits of 3-year-old children in Japan. *Journal of Developmental and Behavioral Pediatrics, 23*(2), 67–70.

Kokko, K., et al. (2014). Country, sex, and parent occupational status: Moderators of the continuity of aggression from childhood to adulthood. *Aggressive Behavior, 40*(6), 552–567.

Kolb, B., & Gibb, R. (2007). Brain plasticity and recovery from early cortical injury. *Developmental Psychobiology, 49*(2), 107–118.

Kooistra, L., Crawford, S., Gibbard, B., Ramage, B., & Kaplan, B. (2010). Differentiating attention deficit in child with fetal alcohol spectrum disorder or attention-deficit-hyperactivity disorder. *Developmental Medicine & Child Neurology, 52*(2), 205–211.

Kopp, C. B. (1989). Regulation of distress and negative emotions: A developmental view. *Developmental Psychology, 25*, 343–354.

Korja, R., Latva, R., & Lhtonen, L. (2011). The effects of preterm birth on mother-infant interaction and attachment during the infant's first two years. *ACTA Obstetrica et Gynecologica Scandinavica, 91*(2), 164–173. doi:10.1111/j.1600–0412.2011.01304.x

Kreager, D. A., Molloy, L. E., Moody, J., & Feinberg, M. E. (2015). Friends first? The peer network origins of adolescent dating. *Journal of Research on Adolescence*, DOI: 10.1111/jora.12189.

Krebs, D. L., & Denton, K. (2005). Toward a more pragmatic approach to morality: A critical evaluation of Kohlberg's model. *Psychological Review, 112*(3), 629–649.

Krieger-Blake, L. S. (2010). Promoting independence in later life. In K. L. Mauk (Ed.), *Gerontological nursing: Competencies for care* (pp. 300–326). Sudbury, MA: Jones and Bartlett.

Kristensen, P., & Bjerkedal, T. (2007). Explaining the relation between birth order and intelligence. *Science, 313*(5832), 1717.

Kristof, N. D. (2012, January 11). The value of teachers. *The New York Times*, p. A7.

Kristof, N. D. (2012, March 1). Born to not get bullied. *The New York Times*, p. A31.

Kroeger, K. A., & Nelson, W. M., III. (2006). A language programme to increase the verbal production of a child dually diagnosed with Down syndrome and autism. *Journal of Intellectual Disability Research, 50*(2), 101–108.

Kroger, J., & Marcia, J. E. (2011). The identity statuses: Origins, meanings, and interpretations. In S. J. identifier="DPLV QNT0R6YK7MJBU038">Schwartz et al. (Eds.), *Handbook of identity theory and research* (Part 1, pp. 31–53). New York, NY Springer.

Krumm, S., Grube, A., & Hertel, G. (2013). No time for compromise: Age as a moderator of the relationship between needs-supply fit and job satisfaction. *European Journal of Work and Organizational Psychology, 22*(5), 547–562.

Kübler-Ross, E. (1969). *On death and dying*. New York, NY: Macmillan.

Kübler-Ross, E., & Kessler, D. (2005). *On grief and grieving*. New York, NY Scribner.

Kuczaj, S. A., II. (1982). On the nature of syntactic development. In S. A. Kuczaj II (Ed.), *Language development, Vol. 1: Syntax and semantics*. Hillsdale, NJ: Erlbaum.

Kuczmarski, R. J., et al. (2000, December 4). CDC growth charts: United States. *Advance Data from Vital and Health Statistics, No. 314*. Hyattsville, MD: National Center for Health Statistics.

Kuhl, P. K., et al. (1997). Cross-language analysis of phonetic units in language addressed to infants. *Science, 277*(5326), 684–686.

Kuhl, P. K., et al. (2006). Infants show a facilitation effect for native language phonetic perception between 6 and 12 months. *Developmental Science, 9*(2) F13–F21.

Kulick, D. (2006). Regulating sex: The politics of intimacy and identity. *Sexualities, 9*(1), 122–124.

Kulik, L. (2000). Women face unemployment: A comparative analysis of age groups. *Journal of Career Development*, *27*(1), 15–33.

Kulik, L. (2004). Perceived equality in spousal relations, martial quality, and life satisfaction. *Families in Society*, *85*(2), 243–250.

Kunz, J. A. (2007). The life story matrix. In J. A. Kunz & F. G. Soltys (Eds.), *Transformational reminiscence: Life story work* (pp. 1–16). New York, NY: Springer Publishing Co.

Kunzmann, U., & Baltes, P. B. (2005). The psychology of wisdom: Theoretical and empirical challenges. In R. J. Sternberg & J. Jordan (Eds.), *A handbook of wisdom: Psychological perspectives* (pp. 110–135). New York, NY: Cambridge University Press.

Kurdek, L. A. (2005). What do we know about gay and lesbian couples? *Current Directions in Psychological Science*, *14*(5), 251.

Kurdek, L. A. (2006). Differences between partners from heterosexual, gay, and lesbian cohabiting couples. *Journal of Marriage and the Family*, *68*(2), 509–528.

Kurosawa, K., Masuno, M., & Kuroki, Y. (2012). Trends in occurrence of twin births in Japan. *American Journal of Medical Genetics*, *158*A(1), 75–77.

Kvaal, K., et al. (2008). Co-occurrence of anxiety and depressive disorders in a community sample of older people. *International Journal of Geriatric Psychiatry*, *23*(3) 229–237.

Kwok, H.-K. (2006). A study of the sandwich generation in Hong Kong. *Current Sociology*, *54*(2), 257–272.

L

Labouvie-Vief, G. (2006). Emerging structures of adult thought. In J. J. Arnett & J. L. Tanner (Eds.), *Emerging adults in America*. (pp. 59–84). Washington, DC: American Psychological Association.

Labouvie-Vief, G., & González, M. M. (2004). Dynamic integration: Affect optimization and differentiation in development. In D. Y. Dai & R. J. Sternberg (Eds.), *Motivation, emotion, and cognition* (pp. 237–272). Mahwah, NJ: Erlbaum.

Labrell, F., & Ubersfeld, G. (2004). Parental verbal strategies and children's capacities at 3 and 5 years during a memory task. *European Journal of Psychology of Education*, *19*(2), 189–202.

Lagercrantz, H. (2010). Basic consciousness of a newborn. *Seminars in Perinatology*, *34*(3), 201–206.

Laible, D., Thompson, R. A., & Froimson, J. (2015). Early socialization: The influence of close relationships. In J. E. Grusec & P. D. Hastings (Eds.). *Handbook of socialization: Theory and Research* (pp. 35–59). New York: Guilford.

Lam, K. S. L., Aman, M. G., & Arnold, L. E. (2006). Neurochemical correlates of autistic disorder: A review of the literature. *Research in Developmental Disabilities*, *27*(3), 254–289.

Lam, T. H., Shi, H. J., Ho, L. M., Stewart, S. M., & Fan, S. (2002). Timing of pubertal maturation and heterosexual behavior among Hong Kong Chinese adolescents. *Archives of Sexual Behavior*, *31*(4), 359–366.

Lampl, M., Veldhuis, J. D., & Johnson, M. L. (1992). Saltation and stasis: A model of human growth. *Science*, *258*, 801–803.

Landau, R., & Yentis, S. (2011). Maternal–fetal conflicts: Cesarean delivery on maternal request. In G. A. V. Norman et al. (Eds.), *Clinical Ethics in Anesthesiology* (pp. 49–54). New York, NY: Cambridge University Press.

Landolt, A. S., & Milling, L. S. (2011). The efficacy of hypnosis as an intervention for labor and delivery pain: A comprehensive methodological review. *Clinical Psychology Review*, *31*(6), 1022–1031.

Landrigan, P. J. (2010). What causes autism? Exploring the environmental contribution. *Current Opinion in Pediatrics*, *22*(2), 219–225.

Lange, G., & Pierce, S. H. (1992). Memory-strategy learning and maintenance in preschool children. *Developmental Psychology*, *28*, 453–462.

Lange, J., & Grossman, S. (2010). Theories of aging. In K. L. Mauk (Ed.), *Gerontological nursing: Competencies for care* (pp. 50–74). Sudbury, MA: Jones and Bartlett.

Lantolf, J. P., & Thorne, S. L. (2007). Sociocultural theory and second language learning. In B. VanPatten & J. Williams (Eds.), *Theories in second language acquisition: An introduction* (pp. 201–224). Mahwah, NJ: Erlbaum.

LaPointe, L. L. (Ed.). (2005). Feral children. *Journal of Medical Speech-Language Pathology*, *13*(1), vii–ix.

Lapsley, D. K. (2006). Moral stage theory. In K. Killen & J. G. Smetana (Eds.), *Handbook of moral development* (pp. 37–66). Mahwah, NJ: Erlbaum.

Larsen, S. E., & Fitzgerald, L. F. (2011). PTSD symptoms and sexual harassment: The role of attributions and perceived control. *Journal of Interpersonal Violence*, *26*(13), 2555–2567.

Larsson, I., & Svedin, C. (2002). Experiences in childhood: Young adults' recollections. *Archives of Sexual Behavior*, *31*(3), 263–273.

Latham, G. P., & Budworth, M.-H. (2007). The study of work motivation in the 20th century. In L. L. Koppes, (Ed.), *Historical perspectives in industrial and organizational psychology* (pp. 353– 381). Mahwah, NJ: Erlbaum.

Lattanzi-Licht, Marcia. (2007). Religion, spirituality, and dying. In D. Balk et al. (Eds.), *Handbook of thanatology* (pp. 11–17). New York, NY: Routledge/ Taylor & Francis Group.

Lau, A. S., Litrownik, A. J., Newton, R. R., Black, M. M., & Everson, M. D. (2006). Factors affecting the link between physical discipline and child externalizing problems in Black and White families. *Journal of Community Psychology*, *34*(1), 89–103.

Laumann, E. O., Mahay, J., & Youm, Y. (2007). Sex, intimacy, and family life in the United States. In M. Kimmel (Ed.), *The sexual self: The construction of sexual scripts* (pp. 165–190). Nashville, TN: Vanderbilt University Press.

Laurendeau, M., & Pinard, A. (1970). The development of the concept of space in the child. New York, NY: International Universities Press.

Laursen, B., DeLay, D., & Adams, R. E. (2010). Trajectories of perceived support in mother–adolescent relationships. *Developmental Psychology*, *46*(6), 1792–1798.

Lawrence, E. B., & Bradbury, T. N. (2007). Trajectories of change in physical aggression and marital satisfaction. *Journal of Family Psychology*, *21*(2), 236–247.

Lawrence, E., Nylen, K., & Cobb, R. J. (2007). Prenatal expectations and marital satisfaction over the transition to parenthood. *Journal of Family Psychology*, *21*(2), 155–164.

Leaper, C. (2011). More similarities than differences in contemporary theories of social development? A plea for theory bridging. *Advances in Child Development and Behavior*, *40*, 337–378.

Leaper, C., & Bigler, R. S. (2011). Gender. In M. K. Underwood & L. H. Rosen (Eds.), *Social development: Relationships in infancy, childhood, and adolescence* (pp. 289–315). New York, NY: Guilford.

Leaper, C., & Farkas, T. (2015). The socialization of gender during childhood and adolescence. In J. E. Grusec & P. D. Hastings (Eds.). *Handbook of socialization: Theory and Research* (pp. 541–565). New York: Guilford.

Lecanuet, J. P., Graniere-Deferre, C., Jacquet, A.-Y., & DeCasper, A. J. (2000). Fetal discrimination of low-pitched musical notes. *Developmental Psychobiology*, *36*(1), 29–39.

Lecce, S., Demicheli, P., Zocchi, A., & Palladino, P. (2015). The origins of children's metamemory: The role of theory of mind. *Journal of Experimental Child Psychology*, *131*, 56–72.

Leclerc, C. M., & Hess, T. M. (2007). Age differences in the bases for social judgments: Tests of a social expertise perspective. *Experimental Aging Research*, *33*(1), 95–120.

Leder, S., Grinstead, L. N., & Torres, E. (2007). Grandparents raising grandchildren: Stressors, social support, and health outcomes. *Journal of Family Nursing*, *13*(3), 333–352.

Lee, A. C., He, J., & Ma, M. (2011). Olfactory marker protein is crucial for functional maturation of olfactory sensory neurons and development of mother preference. *The Journal of Neuroscience*, *31*(8), 2974–2982.

Lee, H. J., et al. (2016). Sex differences in depressive effects of experiencing spousal bereavement. *Geriatrics & Gerontology*, DOI: 10.1111/ggi.12712.

Lee, N. R., Lopez, K. C., Adeyemi, E. I., & Giedd, J. N. (2011). Sex chromosome aneuploidies: A window for examining the effects of the X and Y chromosomes on speech, language, and social development. In D. J. Fidler (Ed.), *Early development in neurogenetic disorders* (pp. 141–171). New York, NY Elsevier.

Lee, S. A. S., & Davis, B. L. (2010). Segmental distribution patterns of English infant-and adult-directed speech. *Journal of Child Language, 37*, 767–791.

Lejeune, C., et al. (2006). Prospective multicenter observational study of 260 infants born to 259 opiate-dependent mothers on methadone or high-dose buprenophine substitution. *Drug and Alcohol Dependence, 82*(3), 250–257.

Leland, J. (2005, March 27). The Schiavo case: Final moments. *The New York Times online*.

Lemaire, P., & Arnaud, L. (2008). Young and older adults' strategies in complex arithmetic. *American Journal of Psychology, 121*(1), 1–16.

Lengua, L., J., Honorado, E., & Bush, N. R. (2007). Contextual risk and parenting as predictors of effortful control and social competence in preschool children. *Journal of Applied Developmental Psychology, 28*(1), 40–55.

Lenneberg, E. H. (1967). *Biological foundations of language*. New York, NY: Wiley.

Leonard, S. P., & Archer, J. (1989). A naturalistic investigation of gender constancy in three- to four-year-old children. *British Journal of Developmental Psychology, 7*, 341–346.

Leonardo, E. D., & Hen, R. (2006). Genetics of affective and anxiety disorders. *Annual Review of Psychology*. *57*, 117–137.

Leung, P., Curtis, R. L., Jr., & Mapp, S. C. (2010). Incidences of sexual contacts of children: Impacts of family characteristics and family structure from a national sample. *Children and Youth Services Review, 32*(5), 650–656.

Levendosky, A. A., Bogat, G. A., Huth-Bocks, A. C., Rosenblum, K., & von Eye, A. (2011). *Journal of Clinical Child & Adolescent Psychology, 40*(3), 398–410.

Lever, N., et al. (2004). A drop-out prevention program for high-risk inner-city youth. *Behavior Modification, 28*(4), 513–527.

Levinson, D. J. (1996). *The seasons of a woman's life*. New York, NY: Knopf.

Levinson, D. J., Darrow, C. N, & Klein, E. B. (1978). *Seasons of a man's life*. New York, NY: Knopf.

Levpušcek, M. P. (2006). Adolescent individuation in relation to parents and friends: Age and gender differences. *European Journal of Developmental Psychology, 3*(3), 238–264.

Lewis, B. A., et al. (2004). Four-year language outcomes of children exposed to cocaine in utero. *Neurotoxicology and Teratology, 26*(5), 617–627.

Lewis, S. (2011). Development: Pruning the dendritic tree. *Nature Reviews Neuroscience, 12*, 493. doi:10.1038/nrn3099

Lick, D. J., Tornello, S. L., Riskind, R. G., Schmidt, K. M., & Patterson, C. J. (2012). Social climate for sexual minorities predicts well-being among heterosexual offspring of lesbian and gay parents. *Sexuality Research and Social Policy, 9*(2), 99–112.

Li, Q. (2007). New bottle but old wine: A research of cyberbullying in schools. *Computers in Human Behavior, 23*(4), 1777–1791.

Light, L. L., Patterson, M. M., Chung, C., & Healy, M. R. (2004). Effects of repetition and response deadline on associative recognition in young and older adults. *Memory & Cognition, 32*, 1182–1193.

Lim, L., et al. (2015). Disorder-specific grey matter deficits in attention deficit hyperactivity disorder relative to autism spectrum disorder. *Psychological Medicine, 45*(5), 965–976.

Lin, Y.-P., et al. (2011). Non-leisure time physical activity is an independent predictor of longevity for a Taiwanese elderly population: An eight-year follow-up study. *BioMed Central Public Health, 11*, 428.

Lipman, E. L., et al. (2006). Testing effectiveness of a community-based aggression management program for children 7 to 11 years old and their families. *Journal of the American Academy of Child & Adolescent Psychiatry, 45*(9), 1085–1093.

Lippa, R. A. (2010). Sex differences in personality traits and gender-related occupational preferences across 53 nations: Testing evolutionary and social-environmental theories. *Archives of Sexual Behavior, 39*(3), 619–636.

Lipsitt, L. P. (2002). Early experience and behavior in the baby of the twenty-first century. In J. Gomes-Pedro et al. (Eds.), *The infant and family in the twentyfirst century* (pp. 55–78). London: Brunner-Routledge.

Lipsitt, L. P. (2003). Crib death: A biobehavioral phenomenon? *Current Directions in Psychological Science, 12*(5), 164–170.

Liu, W., et al. (2011). Protective effects of hydrogen on fetal brain injury during maternal hypoxia. *Intracerebral Hemorrhage Research, 111*(3), 307–311.

Loayza, I. M., Sola, I., & Prats, C. J. (2011). *Biofeedback for pain management during labor*. John Wiley & Sons: The Cochrane Library. doi:10.1002/14651858.CD006168 . pub2.

Locke, B. D., & Mahalik, J. R. (2005). Examining masculinity norms, problem drinking, and athletic involvement as predictors of sexual aggression in college men. *Journal of Counseling Psychology, 52*(3), 279–283.

Löckenhoff, C. E., & Carstensen, L. L. (2004). Socioemotional selectivity theory, aging, and health: The increasingly delicate balance between regulating emotions and making tough choices. *Journal of Personality, 72*(6), 1395–1424.

Loeb, S., et al. (2011). Baseline prostate-specific antigen testing at a young age. *European Urology, 61*(1), 1ff.

Loewenthal, K. M. (2016). Psychological views of conscience. In D. A. Leeming (Ed.). *Encyclopedia of psychology and religion* (pp. 1–4). Berlin Heidelberg: Springer-Verlag Berlin Heidelberg.

Lohman, D. F., & Lakin, J. M. (2009). Consistencies in sex differences on the Cognitive Abilities Test across countries, grades, test forms, and cohorts. *British Journal of Educational Psychology, 79*(2), 389–407.

Lokuge, S., Frey, B. N., Foster, J. A., Soares, C. N., & Steiner, M. (2011). Depression in women: Windows of vulnerability and new insights into the link between estrogen and serotonin. *Journal of Clinical Psychiatry, 72*(11), e156–e1569.

Lomanowska, A. M., & Melo, A. I. (2016). Deconstructing the function of maternal stimulation in offspring development: Insights from the artificial rearing model in rats. *Hormones and Behavior, 77*, 224–236.

Lonstein, J. S., & Auger, A. P. (2009). Perinatal gonadal hormone influences on neurobehavioral development. In M. S. Blumberg, J. H. Freeman, & S. R. Robinson (Eds.), *Oxford handbook of developmental behavioral neuroscience* (pp. 424–453). New York, NY: Oxford University Press.

Lorant, V., et al. (2005). A European comparative study of marital status and socio-economic inequalities in suicide. *Social Science & Medicine, 60*(11), 2431–2441.

Lorenz, F. O., Wickrama, K. A. S., Conger, R. D., & Elder Jr., G. H. (2006). The short-term and decade-long effects of divorce on women's midlife health. *Journal of Health and Social Behavior, 47*(2), 111–125.

Lorenz, K. (1962). *King Solomon's ring*. London: Methuen.

Lorenz, K. (1981). *The foundations of ethology*. New York, NY: Springer-Verlag.

Lorenzo-Blanco, E. I., et al. (2016). Profiles of bullying victimization, discrimination, social support, and school safety: Links with Latino/a youth acculturation, gender, depressive symptoms, and cigarette use. *American Journal of Orthopsychiatry, 86*(1), 37–48.

Lothian, J. A. (2011). Lamaze breathing. *The Journal of Perinatal Education, 20*(2), 118–120.

Lovaas, O. I. (1977). *The autistic child: Language development through behavior modification*. New York, NY: Halstead Press.

Lovaas, O. I., Smith, T., & McEachin, J. J. (1989). Clarifying comments on the young autism study: Reply to Schapler, Short, and Mesibov. *Journal of Consulting and Clinical Psychology, 57*, 165–167.

Lucas, C. P., Hazen, E. P., & Shaffer, D. (2015). Childhood elimination disorders. In A. Tasman et al. (Eds.). *Psychiatry*, 4th ed. (pp. 1250ff). Hoboken, NJ: Wiley.

Lucas, R. E., & Donnellan, M. B. (2011). Personality development across the life span: Longitudinal analyses with a national sample from Germany. *Journal of Personality and Social Psychology, 101*(4), 847–861.

Lucassen, N., et al. (2011). The association between paternal sensitivity and infant–father attachment security: A meta-analysis of three decades of research. *Journal of Family Psychology*, *25*(6), 986–992.

Luciano, M., Kirk, K. M., Heath, A. C., & Martin, N. G. (2005). The genetics of tea and coffee drinking and preference for source of caffeine in a large community sample of Australian twins. *Addiction*, *100*(10), 1510–1517.

Luders, E., Thompson, P. M., & Toga, A. W. (2010). The development of the corpus callosum in the healthy human brain. *The Journal of Neuroscience*, *30*(33), 10985–10990.

Ludwick, R., & Silva, M. C. (2003, December 19). Ethical challenges in the care of elderly persons. *The Online Journal of Issues in Nursing*. Retrieved from http://nursingworld.org/ojin

Ludwig, F. M., Hattjar, B., Russell, R. L., & Winston, K. (2007). How caregiving for grandchildren affects grandmothers' meaningful occupations. *Journal of Occupational Science*, *14*(1), 40–51.

Lund, D. A., & Caserta, M. S. (2001). When the unexpected happens: Husbands coping with the deaths of their wives. In D. A. Lund (Ed.), *Men coping with grief* (pp. 147–167). Amityville, NY: Baywood Publishing.

Luo, Y., et al. (2015). Sex hormones predict the incidence of erectile dysfunction: From a population-based prospective cohort study (FAMHES).

Lupien, S. J., Maheu, F., Tu, M., Fiocco, A., & Schramek, T. E. (2007). The effects of stress and stress hormones on human cognition: Implications for the field of brain and cognition. *Brain and Cognition*, *65*(3), 209–237.

Lustgarden, M., Muller, F. L., & Van Remmen, H. (2010). An objective appraisal of the free radical theory of aging. In E. J. Masoro & S. N. Austad (Eds.), *Handbook of the biology of aging* (7th ed., pp. 177–202). London: Academic Press.

Lustig, S. L. (2010). Chaos and its influence on children's development: An ecological perspective. In G. W. Evans & T. D. Wachs (Eds.), *Decade of behavior (science conference)* (pp. 239–251). Washington, DC: American Psychological Association.

Lykken, D. T. (2006b). The mechanism of emergenesis. *Genes, Brain & Behavior*, *5*(4), 306–310.

Lykken, D. T., & Csikszentmihalyi, M. (2001). Happiness—stuck with what you've got? *Psychologist*, *14*(9), 470–472.

Lynch, J. B., et al. (2011). The breadth and potency of passively acquired human immunodeficiency virus Type 1-specific neutralizing antibodies do not correlate with the risk of infant infection. *Journal of Virology*, *85*(11), 5252–5261.

Lynne, S. D., Graber, J. A., Nichols, T. R., Brooks-Gunn, J., & Botvin, G. J. (2007). Links between pubertal timing, peer influences, and externalizing behaviors among urban students followed through middle school. *Journal of Adolescent Health*, *40*(2), 181.e7–181.e13.

M

Maatta, K., & Uusiautti, S. (2012). Loves does not retire—Not even after a half century of marriage. *Journal of Educational and Social Research*, *2*(1). doi:10.5901/jesr.2012.02.01.23

Maccoby, E. E., & Jacklin, C. N. (1974). *The psychology of sex differences*. Stanford, CA: Stanford University Press.

Maccoby, E. E. (2015). Historical overview of socialization research and theory. In J. E. Grusec & P. D. Hastings (Eds.). *Handbook of socialization: Theory and Research* (pp. 3–34). New York: Guilford.

MacDonald, G., & Leary, M. R. (2011). Individual differences in self-esteem. In M. R. Leary, & J. P. Tangney (Eds.). *Handbook of Self and Identity*, second edition (pp. 354–377). New York: Guilford Press.

MacEvoy, J. P., Papadakis, A. A., Fedigan, S. K., & Ash, S. E. (2016). Friendship expectations and children's friendship-related behavior and adjustment. *Merrill-Palmer Quarterly*, *62*(1), 74–104.

Macfarlane, A. (1975). Olfaction in the development of social preferences in the human neonate. In M. A. Hofer (Ed.), *Parent–infant interaction* (pp. 103–117). Amsterdam: Elsevier.

Macfarlane, A. (1977). *The psychology of childbirth*. Cambridge, MA: Harvard University Press.

Maciejewski, P. K., Zhang, B., Block, S. D., & Prigerson H. G. (2007). An empirical examination of the stage theory of grief. *Journal of the American Medical Association*, *297*, 716–723.

Madon, S., et al. (2001). Am I as you see me or do you see me as I am? Self-fulfilling prophecies and self-verification. *Personality and Social Psychology Bulletin*, *27*(9), 1214–1224.

Mahay, J., & Lewin, A. C. (2007). Age and the desire to marry. *Journal of Family Issues*, *28*(5), 706–723.

Malamuth, N. M., Huppin, M., & Paul, B. (2005). Sexual coercion. In D. M. Buss (Ed.), *The handbook of evolutionary psychology* (pp. 394–418). Hoboken, NJ: John Wiley & Sons.

Malone, P. S., et al. (2004). Divorce and child behavior problems: Applying latent change score models to life event data. *Structural Equation Modeling*, *11*(3), 401–423.

Maratsos, M. P. (2007). Commentary. *Monographs of the Society for Research in Child Development*, *72*(1), 121–126.

Marcia, J. E. (2010). Life transitions and stress in the context of psychosocial development. In T. W. Miller (Ed.), *Handbook of stressful transitions across the lifespan* (Part 1, pp. 19–34). New York, NY: Springer Science + Business Media.

Marcia, J. E. (2014). From industry to integrity. Identity: *An International Journal of Theory and Research*, *14*(3), 165–176.

Marean, G. C., Werner, L. A., & Kuhl, P. K. (1992). Vowel categorization by very young infants. *Developmental Psychology*, *28*, 396–405.

Markham, B. (2006). Older women and security. In J. Worell & C. D. Goodheart (Eds.), *Handbook of girls' and women's psychological health: Gender and wellbeing across the lifespan* (pp. 388–396). *Oxford series in clinical psychology*. New York, NY: Oxford University Press.

Marks, L., Nesteruk, O., Swanson, M., Garrison, B., & Davis, T. (*2005*). Religion and health among African Americans. *Research on Aging*, *27*(4), 447–474.

Markus, H. R. (2016). What moves people to action? Culture and motivation. *Current Opinion in Psychology*, *8*, 161–166.

Marquis, C. (2003, March 16). Living in sin. *The New York Times*, p. WK2.

Marsiglio, W. (2004). When stepfathers claim stepchildren: A conceptual analysis. *Journal of Marriage and Family*, *66*(1), 22–39.

Martel, M. M., et al. (2011). The dopamine receptor D4 gene (DRD4) moderates family environmental effects on ADHD. (2011). *Journal of Abnormal Child Psychology*, *39*(1), 1–10.

Martel, M. M., von Eye, A., & Nigg, J. (2012). Developmental differences in structure of attention-deficit/hyperactivity disorder (ADHD) between childhood and adulthood. *International Journal of Behavioral Development*, *36*(4), 279–292.

Martin, C. L., & Dinella, L. M. (2011). Congruence between gender stereotypes and activity preference in self-identified tomboys and non-tomboys. *Archives of Sexual Behavior*. doi: 10.1007/s10508–011-9786–5

Martin, A., & Lehren, A. W. (2012, May 12). A generation hobbled by the soaring cost of college. *The New York Times*, p. A1.

Martin, C. L., & Ruble, D. (2004). Children's search for gender cues: Cognitive perspectives on gender development. *Current Directions in Psychological Science*, *13*(2), 67–70.

Martin, C. L., Ruble, D. N., & Szkrybalo, J. (2002). Cognitive theories of early gender development. *Psychological Bulletin*, *128*(6), 903–933.

Martin, J., & Soko, B. (2011). Generalized others and imaginary audiences: A neo-Meadian approach to adolescent egocentrism. *New Ideas in Psychology*, *29*(3), 364–375.

Martin, J. A., Hamilton, B. E., Osterman, M. J. K., Curtin, S. C., & Mathews, T. J. (2015). Births: Final data for 2013. National Vital Statistics Reports. *64*(1).

Martinez, G. M., & Abma, J. C. (2015). Sexual activity, contraceptive use, and childbearing of teenagers aged 15–19 in the United States. NCHS data brief, no 209. Hyattsville, MD: National Center for Health Statistics.

Martire, S. I., Westbrook, R. F., & Morris, M. J. (2015). Effects of long-term cycling between palatable cafeteria diet and regular chow on intake, eating patterns, and response to saccharin and sucrose. *Physiology & Behavior*, *139*, 80–88.

Marwick, C. (2000). Consensus panel considers osteoporosis. *Journal of the American Medical Association online*, *283*(16).

Mash, E. J., & Wolfe, D. A. (2013). *Abnormal child psychology* (5th ed.). Belmont, CA: Cengage Learning.

Masi, G., Mucci, M., & Millepiedi, S. (2001). Separation anxiety disorder in children and adolescents: Epidemiology, diagnosis, and management. *CNS Drugs, 15*(2), 93–104.

Mathews, T.J., & MacDorman, M.F. (2007). Infant mortality statistics from the 2004 period linked birth/infant death data set. *National Vital Statistics Reports, 55* (14). Hyattsville, MD: National Center for Health Statistics.

Matlin, M. W. (2008). *The psychology of women* (8th ed.). Belmont, CA: Thomson/Wadsworth.

Mattanah, J. F., Lopez, F. G., & Govern, J. M. (2011). The contribution of parental attachment bonds to college student development and adjustment: A meta-analytic review. *Journal of Counseling Psychology, 58*(4), 565–596.

Matthews, A. K., Hughes, T. L., & Tartaro, J. (2006). Sexual behavior and sexual dysfunction in a community sample of lesbian and heterosexual women. In A. M. Omoto & H. S. Kurtzman (Eds.), *Sexual orientation and mental health*. (pp. 185–205). Washington, DC: American Psychological Association.

Maughan, B. (2011). Family and systemic influences. In D. Skuse, H. Bruce, L. Dowdney, & D. Mrazek (Eds.), *Child psychology and psychiatry: Frameworks for practice* (2nd ed., pp. 1–7). Hoboken, NJ: Wiley.

Maxwell, C. D., Robinson, A. L., & Post, L. A. (2003). The nature and predictors of sexual victimization and offending among adolescents. *Journal of Youth & Adolescence, 32*(6) 465–477.

May, A., & Klonsky, E. D. (2011). Validity of suicidality items from the Youth Risk Behavior Survey in a high school sample. *Assessment, 18*(3), 379–381.

Mayer, R. E. (2011). Intelligence and achievement. In R. J. Sternberg & S. J. Kaufman (Eds.), *The Cambridge handbook of intelligence* (pp. 738–747). New York, NY: Cambridge University Press.

Mayor, J., & Plunkett, K. (2010). A neurocomputational account of taxonomic responding and fast mapping in early word learning. *Psychological Review, 117*(1), 1–31.

McCabe, M. P., et al. (2016). Risk factors for sexual dysfunction among women and men: A consensus statement from the Fourth International Consultation on Sexual Medicine 2015. *The Journal of Sexual Medicine, 13*(2), 153–167.

McCall, R. B., Applebaum, M. I., & Hogarty, P. S. (1973). *Developmental changes in mental performance. Monographs of the Society for Research in Child Development, 38*(3, ser. 150).

McCardle, P., Colombo, J., & Freud, L. (2009). Measuring language in infancy. In J. Colombo, P. McCardle, & L. Freud (Eds.), *Infant pathways to language: Methods, models, and research disorders* (pp. 1–12). New York, NY: Psychology Press.

McCarthy, B., & Pierpaoli, C. (2015). Sexual challenges with aging: Integrating the GES approach in an elderly couple. *Sex & Marital Therapy, 41*(1), 72–82.

McClellan, J. M., & Werry, J. S. (2003). Evidence-based treatments in child and adolescent psychiatry: An inventory. *Journal of the American Academy of Child and Adolescent Psychiatry, 42*(12), 1388–1400.

McCracken, M., Jiles, R., & Blanck, H. M. (2007). Health behaviors of the young adult U.S. population: Behavioral risk factor surveillance system, 2003. *Preventing Chronic Disease, 4*(2), A25.

McCrae, R. R., & Costa, P. T., Jr. (2006). Cross-cultural perspectives on adult personality trait development. In D. K. Mroczek, & T. D Little (Eds.), *Handbook of personality development* (pp. 129–145). Mahwah, NJ: Lawrence Erlbaum Associates Publishers.

McCrae, R. R., et al. (2000). Nature over nurture: Temperament, personality, and life span development. *Journal of Personality and Social Psychology, 78*(1), 173–186.

McEwan, M. H., Dihoff, R. E., & Brosvic, G. M. (1991). Early infant crawling experience is reflected in later motor skill development. *Perceptual and Motor Skills, 72*, 75–79.

McGlaughlin, A., & Grayson, A. (2001). Crying in the first year of infancy: Patterns and prevalence. *Journal of Reproductive and Infant Psychology, 19*(1), 47–59.

McGue, M., Bouchard, T. J., Jr., Iacono, W. G., & Lykken, D. T. (1993). Behavioral genetics of cognitive ability: A life-span perspective. In R. Plomin & G. E. McClearn (Eds.), *Nature, nurture & psychology* (pp. 59–76). Washington, DC: American Psychological Association.

McGuire, S. L., McCarthy, L. S., & Modrcin, M. A. (2013). An ongoing concern: Helping children understand death. *Open Nursing Journal, 3*(3), 307–313.

McHale, J. P., & Rotman, T. (2007). Is seeing believing? Expectant parents' outlooks on coparenting and later coparenting solidarity. *Infant Behavior & Development, 30*(1), 63–81.

McKee-Ryan, F., Song, Z., Wanberg, C. R., & Kinicki, A. J. (2005). Psychological and physical well-being during unemployment: A meta-analytic study. *Journal of Applied Psychology, 90*(1), 53–76.

McLeod, J. D., & Knight, S. (2010). The association of socioemotional problems with early sexual initiation. *Perspectives on Sexual and Reproductive Health, 42*(2), 93–101.

Meaney, K. S., Dornier, L. A., & Owens, M. S. (2002). Sex-role stereotyping for selected sport and physical activities across age groups. *Perceptual and Motor Skills, 94*(3), 743–749s.

Mechanic, D., & McAlpine, D. D. (2011). Mental health and aging: A life-course perspective. In R. A. Settersten & J. L. Angel (Eds.), *Handbook of sociology of aging*. New York, NY: Springer.

Medland, S. E., et al. (2009). Genetic influences on handedness: Data from 25,732 Australian and Dutch twin families. *Neuropsychologia, 47*, 330–337.

Meek, J. Y. (Ed.). (2011). *American Academy of Pediatrics new mother's guide to breastfeeding* (2nd ed.). New York, NY: Bantam Books.

Meeus, W. (2011). The study of adolescent identity formation 2000–2010: A review of longitudinal research. *Journal of Research on Adolescence, 21*(1), 75–94.

Mehler, P. S., & Brown, C. (2015). Anorexia nervosa—Medical complications. *Journal of Eating Disorders, 3*(11). DOI 10.1186/s40337-015-0040-8.

Meijer, A. M., & van den Wittenboer, G. L. H. (2007). Contribution of infants' sleep and crying to marital relationship of first-time parent couples in the first year after childbirth. *Journal of Family Psychology, 21*(1) 49–57.

Melamed, S., Meir, E. I., & Samson, A. (1995). The benefits of personality-leisure congruence. *Journal of Leisure Research, 27*, 25–40.

Mellon, M. W. (2006). Enuresis and encopresis. In G. Bea & K. M. Minke (Eds.), *Children's needs III: Development, prevention, and intervention* (pp. 1041–1053). Washington, DC: National Association of School Psychologists.

Mellon, M. W., & Houts, A. C. (2006). Nocturnal enuresis. In J. E. Fisher & W. T. O'Donohue (Eds.), *Practitioner's guide to evidence-based psychotherapy* (pp. 432–441). New York, NY: Springer Science + Business Media.

Meltzoff, A. N. (1988). Infant imitation and memory: Nine-month-olds in immediate and deferred tests. *Child Development, 59*, 217–225.

Meltzoff, A. N., & Brooks, R. (2009). Social cognition and language: The role of gaze following in early word learning. In J. Colombo, P. McCardle, & L. Freund (Eds.), *Infant pathways to language: Methods, models, and research disorders* (pp. 169–194). New York, NY: Psychology Press.

Meltzoff, A. N., & Moore, M. K. (1977). Imitation of facial and manual gestures by human neonates. *Science, 198*, 75–78.

Meltzoff, A. N., & Prinz, W. (Eds.). (2002). *The imitative mind: Development, evolution, and brain bases*. New York, NY: Cambridge University Press.

Menard, A. D., et al. (2015). Individual and relationship contributors to optimal sexual experiences in older men and women. *Sexual and Relationship Therapy, 30*(1), 78–93.

Mendelsohn, F., & Warren, M. (2010). Anorexia, bulimia, and the female athlete triad: Evaluation and management. *Endocrinology and Metabolism Clinics of North America, 39*(1), 155–167.

Mendle, J., et al. (2006). Family structure and age at menarche: A children-of-twins approach. *Developmental Psychology, 42*(3), 533–542.

Merz, E., & Gierveld, J. D. (2016). Childhood memories, family ties, sibling support and loneliness in ever-widowed older adults: Quantitative and qualitative results. *Ageing and Society*, *36*(3), 534–561.

Meyer, D. K. (2016). Emotion regulation in K-12 classrooms. In K. R. Wentzel, & G. B. Ramani (Eds.). *Handbook of social influences in school contexts: Social-emotional, motivation, and cognitive outcomes* (pp. 192–207). New York: Routledge.

Meyer, S., & Shore, C. (2001). Children's understanding of dreams as mental states. *Dreaming*, *11*(4), 179–194.

Michael, R., Gagnon, J., Laumann, E., & Kolata, G. (1994). *Sex in America: A definitive survey*. Boston, MA: Little Brown.

Miller, A. L., Wyman, S. E., Huppert, J. D., Glassman, S. L., & Rathus, J. H. (2000). Analysis of behavioral skills utilized by suicidal adolescents receiving dialectical behavior therapy. *Cognitive and Behavioral Practice*, *7*(2), 183–187.

Miller, C. F., Trautner, H. M., & Ruble, D. N. (2006). The role of gender stereotypes in children's preferences and behavior. In L. Balter & C. S. Tamis-LeMonda (Eds.), *Child psychology: A handbook of contemporary issues* (2nd ed., pp. 293–323). New York, NY: Psychology Press.

Miller, G. (2011). The determination of death. In. D. S. Diekema, M. R. Mercurio, & M. B. Adam. (Eds.), *Clinical ethics in pediatrics: A case-based textbook* (pp. 118–122). New York, NY: Cambridge University Press.

Miller, L., et al. (2012). Religiosity and major depression in adults at high risk: A ten-year prospective study. *American Journal of Psychiatry*, *169*(1), 89–94.

Mills, B., Reyna, V. F., & Estrada, S. (2008). Explaining contradictory relations between risk perception and risk taking. *Psychological Science*, *19*(5), 429–433.

Miniño, A. M. (2011). *Death in the United States* (NCHS data brief, No. 64). Hyattsville, MD: National Center for Health Statistics. Retrieved from http://www.cdc.gov/nchs/data/databriefs/db64.htm

Minino, A. M., Xu, J., & Kochanek, K. D. (2010). *Deaths: National Vital Statistics Reports*, *59*(2).

Minkler, M., & Fuller-Thomson, E. (2005). African American grandparents raising grandchildren: A national study using the Census 2000 *American Community Survey. Journals of Gerontology: Series B: Psychological Sciences and Social Sciences*, 60B(2), S82–S92.

Minnes, S., Lang, A., & Singer, L. (2011). Prenatal tobacco, marijuana, stimulant, and opiate exposure: Outcomes and practice implications. *Addiction Science & Clinical Practice*, *6*(1), 57–70.

Miscarriage. (2007, January 11). Retrieved from http://www.nlm.nih.gov/medlineplus/ency/article/001488.htm

Miscarriage. (2016). Mayo Clinic. http://www.mayoclinic.org/diseases-conditions/pregnancy-loss-miscarriage/home/ovc-20213664 (Accessed August 1, 2016).

Misra, D. P., Caldwell, C., Young, A. A., & Abelson, S. (2010). Do fathers matter? Paternal contributions to birth outcomes and racial disparities. *American Journal of Obstetrics & Gynecology*, *202*(2), 99–100.

Mitchell, A. L. (2006). Medical consequences of cocaine. *Journal of Addictions Nursing*, *17(4)*, 249.

Mitchell, A. L. (2006). Medical consequences of cocaine. *Journal of Addictions Nursing*, *17*(4), 249.

Mitchell, B. A. (2016). Empty nest. In C. L. Shehan (Ed.). *The Wiley Blackwell Encyclopedia of Family Studies*, DOI: 10.1002/9781119085621.wbefs008.

Mitchell, D. D., & Bruss, P. J. (2003). Age differences in implicit memory: Conceptual, perceptual, or methodological? *Psychology and Aging*, *18*(4), 807–822.

Miyake, Y., et al. (2010). Neural processing of negative word stimuli concerning body image in patients with eating disorders: An fMRI study. *NeuroImage*, *50*(3), 1333–1339.

Miyawaki, D., et al. (2016). Psychogenic nonepileptic seizures as a manifestation of psychological distress associated with undiagnosed autism spectrum disorder. *Neuropyschiatric Disease and Treatment*, *12*, 185–189.

MMWR (Morbidity and Mortality Weekly Report), 2015, July 10. Adults meeting fruit and vegetable recommendations–United States, 2013. *MMWR*, *64*(26), 709–713.

Moberg, C. A., Weber, S. M., & Curtin, J. J. (2011). Alcohol dose effects on stress response to cued threat vary by threat intensity. *Psychopharmacology*, *218*(1), 217–227.

Moen, P., Huang, Q., Plassmann, V., & Dentinger, E. (2006). Deciding the future. *American Behavioral Scientist*, *49*(10), 1422–1443.

Montemayor, R., & Eisen, M. (1977). The development of self-conceptions from childhood to adolescence. *Developmental Psychology*, *13*, 314–319.

Montesanto, A., et al. (2011). The genetic component of human longevity. *European Journal of Human Genetics*, *19*, 882–886.

Montoya, R. M., Horton, R. S., & Kirchner, J. (2008). Is actual similarity necessary for attraction? A meta-analysis of actual and perceived similarity. *Journal of Social and Personal Relationships*, *25*(6), 889–922.

Moon, M. (2011). The effects of divorce on children: Married and divorced parents' perspectives. *Journal of Divorce & Remarriage*, *52*(5), 344–349.

Moon, R. Y., Tanabe, K.O., Yang, D.C., Young, H.A., Hauck, F.R. (2011). Pacifier use and SIDS: Evidence for a consistently reduced risk. *Maternal and Child Health Journal*, *128*(1), 103–110.

Moore, J., & Moore, C. (2010). Talking to children about death-related issues. In C. A. Corr & D. E. Balk (Eds.), *Children's encounters with death, bereavement, and coping* (pp. 277–292). New York, NY: Springer.

Moore, M. K., & Meltzoff, A. N. (2008). Factors affecting infants' manual search for occluded objects and the genesis of object permanence. *Infant Behavior and Development*, *31*(2), 168–180.

Moreno-Briseño, P., et al. (2010). Sex-related differences in motor learning and performance. *Brain and Behavioral Functions*, *6*, 74.

Morgenstern, A., Leroy-Collombel, M., & Caet, S. (2013). Self-and other-repairs in child-adult interaction at the intersection of pragmatic abilities and language acquisition. *Journal of Pragmatics*, *56*, 151–167.

Morrell, J., & Steele, H. (2003). The role of attachment security, temperament, maternal perception, and care-giving behavior in persistent infant sleeping problems. *Infant Mental Health Journal*, *24*(5), 447–468.

Morrell, H. E. R., Lapsley, D. K., & Halpern-Felsher, B. L. (2015). Subjective invulnerability and perceptions of tobacco-related benefits predict adolescent smoking behavior. *The Journal of Early Adolescence*, DOI: 10.1177/0272431615578274.

Morry, M. M., Kito, M., & Ortiz, L. (2011). The attraction–similarity model and dating couples. *Personal Relationships*, *18*(1), 125–143.

Moses, L. J., & Flavell, J. H. (1990). Inferring false beliefs from actions and reactions. *Child Development*, *61*, 929–945.

Mosher, W. D., Chandra, A., & Jones, J. (2005). *Sexual behavior and selected health measures: men and women 15– 44 years of age, United States, 2002. Advance data from vital and health statistics*. Centers for Disease Control and Prevention. National Center for Health Statistics, Number 362, Figures 2 and 3.

Moshman, D. (2005). *Adolescent psychological development* (2nd ed.). Mahwah, NJ: Erlbaum.

Moshman, D. (2011). *Adolescent rationality and development* (3rd ed.). New York, NY: Psychology Press.

Moshman, D. (2013). Epistemic cognition and development. In P. Barrouillet, & C. Gauffroy (Eds.). *The development of thinking and reasoning* (pp. 13–33). New York: Psychology Press.

Most, S. B., Sorber, A. V., & Cunningham, J. G. (2007). Auditory Stroop reveals implicit gender association in adults and children. *Journal of Experimental Social Psychology*, *43*(2), 287–294.

Mountjoy, M. L., & Goolsby, M. (2015). Female athlete triad. *Handbook of sports medicine and science: The female athlete*. Hoboken, NJ: Wiley.

Moylan, C. A., et al. (2010). The effects of child abuse and exposure to domestic violence on adolescent internalizing and externalizing behavior problems. *Journal of Family Violence*, *25*(1), 53–63.

Muhlbauer, V., & Chrisler, J. C. (Eds.). (2007). *Women over 50: Psychological perspectives*. New York, NY: Springer Science + Business Media.

Muller, U., Ten Eycke, K., & Baker, L. (2015). Piaget's theory of intelligence. In S. Goldstein, D. Princiotta, & J. A. Naglieri (Eds.). *Handbook of intelligence* (pp. 137–151). New York: Springer Science + Business Media.

Munck, P., et al. (2010). Cognitive outcome at 2 years of age in Finnish infants with very low birth weight born between 2001 and 2006. *Acta Paediatrica*, *99*(3), 359–366.

Munroe, R. H., Shimmin, H. S., & Munroe, R. L. (1984). Gender role understanding and sex role preference in four cultures. *Developmental Psychology*, *20*, 673–682.

Muraco, A. (2006). Intentional families: Fictive kin ties between cross-gender, different sexual orientation friends. *Journal of Marriage and Family*, *68*(5), 1313–1325.

Muris, P., Bodden, D., Merckelbach, H., Ollendick, T. H., & King, N. (2003). Fear of the beast: A prospective study on the effects of negative information on childhood fear. *Behaviour Research and Therapy*, *41*(2), 195–208.

Muris, P., & Field, A. P. (2011). The "normal" development of fear. In W. K. Silverman, & A. P. Field (Eds.), *Anxiety disorders in children and adolescents* (pp. 76–89). New York: Cambridge University Press.

Murphy, K. E., et al. (2011). Maternal side-effects after multiple courses of antenatal corticosteroids (MACS): The three-month follow-up of women in the Randomized Controlled Trial of MACS for Preterm Birth Study. *Journal of Obstetrics and Gynecology, Canada*, *33*(9), 909–921.

Murray, A. D., et al. (2011). Brain lesions, hypertension, and cognitive ageing in the 1921 and 1936 Aberdeen birth cohorts. *Age*, *34*(2), 451–459.

Murray, C. J. L., et al. (2006). Eight Americas: Investigating mortality disparities across races, counties, and race-counties in the United States. *PLoS Med 3*(9): e260. doi:10.1371/journal. pmed.0030260

Musick, K., & Bumpass, L. (2012). Reexamining the case for marriage: Union formation and changes in well-being. *Journal of Marriage and the Family*, *74*(1), 1–18.

Myers, J. E., Madathil, J., & Tingle, L. R. (2005). Marriage satisfaction and wellness in India and the United States: A preliminary comparison of arranged marriages and marriages of choice. *Journal of Counseling & Development*, *83*(2), 183–190.

N

Nadeau, L., et al. (2003). Extremely premature and very low birthweight infants: A double hazard population? *Social Development*, *12*(2), 235–248.

Nader, K., & Salloum, A. (2011). Complicated grief reactions in children and adolescents. *Journal of Child & Adolescent Trauma*, *4*(3), 233–257.

Nagin, D. S., & Tremblay, R. E. (2001). Parental and early childhood predictors of persistent physical aggression in boys from kindergarten to high school. *Archives of General Psychiatry*, *58*(4), 389–394.

Namiiro, F. B., Mugalu, J., McAdams, R. M., & Ndeezi, G. (2012). Poor birth weight recovery among low birth weight/preterm infants following hospital discharge in Kampala, Uganda. *BMC Pregnancy and Childbirth*, *12*(1). doi:10.1186/1471-2393-12-1

National Cancer Institute. (2011a). *SEER cancer statistics review* 1975–2008. Lifetime Risk (Percent) of Being Diagnosed with Cancer by Site and Race/Ethnicity: Males, 17 SEER Areas, 2006–2008 (Table 1.15) and Females, 17 SEER Areas, 2006–2008 (Table 1.16).

National Cancer Institute. (2011b). *SEER cancer statistics review* 1975–2008. Lifetime Risk (Percent) of Dying from Cancer by Site and Race/Ethnicity: Males, Total US, 2006–2008 (Table 1.18) and Females, Total US, 2006– 2008 (Table 1.19).

National Cancer Institute. (2012). *Screening and testing to detect cancer*. Retrieved from http://cancer.gov/cancertopics/screening

National Cancer Institute. (2015, March 24). Screening tests. http://www.cancer.gov/about-cancer/screening/screening-tests.

National Center for Children in Poverty. (2004). Low-income children in the United States. Retrieved from http://cpmcnet.columbia.edu/dept/nccp

National Center for Education Statistics. (2007, June). Dropout rates in the United States: 2005. Retrieved from http://nces.ed.gov/pubs2007/dropout05

National Center for Health Statistics. (2010). *Health, United States, 2009: With special feature on medical technology*. Hyattsville, MD: Author. Table 29.

National Center for Injury Prevention and Control. (2007b, July 11). *Suicide: Fact sheet*. Retrieved from http://www.cdc.gov/ncipc/factsheets/suifacts.htm

National Guideline Clearinghouse. (2007). *Use of clomiphene citrate in women*. Retrieved from http://www.guideline.gov/summary/summary.aspx?ss515&doc_id54843&nbr53484

National Institute on Deafness and Other Communication Disorders (NIDCD). (2011). *Ten ways to recognize hearing loss*. Retrieved from http://www.nidcd.nih.gov/health/hearing/10ways.asp

National Sleep Foundation. (2012). *How much sleep to we really need?* Retrieved from http://www.sleepfoundation.org/article/how-sleep-works/how-much-sleep-do-we-really-need

National Sleep Foundation. (2015). Children and sleep. http://sleepfoundation.org/sleep-topics/children-and-sleep

National Task Force on Civic Learning and Democratic Engagement. (2012). *A crucible moment: College learning and democracy's future*. Washington, DC: Association of American Colleges and Universities.

Nauta, M. M. (2007). Career interests, self-efficacy, and personality as antecedents of career exploration. *Journal of Career Assessment*, *15*(2), 162–180.

Naveh-Benjamin, M., Brav, T. K., & Levy, O. (2007). The associative memory deficit of older adults: The role of strategy utilization. *Psychology and Aging*, *22*, 202–208.

Naveh-Benjamin, M., Hussain, Z., Guez, J., & Bar-On, M. (2003). Adult age differences in episodic memory: Further support for an associative-deficit hypothesis. *Journal of Experimental Psychology: Learning, Memory, and Cognition*, *29*, 826–837.

NCD Risk Factor Collaboration (NCD-RisC). eLife 2016;5:e13410. DOI: 10.7554/eLife.13410

Nduati, R., et al. (2000). Effect of breast-feeding and formula feeding on transmission of HIV-1. *Journal of the American Medical Association*, *283*, 1167–1174.

Needlman, R. (2011). Chaos and its influence on children's development: An ecological perspective. *Journal of Developmental Behavioral Pediatrics*, *32*(3), 275.

Neisser, U., et al. (1996). Intelligence: Knowns and unknowns. *American Psychologist*, *51*, 77–101.

Nelson, C. A., & Luciana, M. (Eds.). (2001). *Handbook of developmental cognitive neuroscience*. Cambridge, MA: MIT Press.

Nelson, C. A., de Haan, M., & Thomas, K. M. (2006). *Neuroscience of cognitive development: The role of experience and the developing brain*. Hoboken, NJ: Wiley.

Nelson, K. (1973). Structure and strategy in learning to talk. *Monographs for the Society for Research in Child Development*, 38(1–2, ser. 149).

Nelson, K. (1990). Remembering, forgetting, and childhood amnesia. In R. Fivush & J. A. Hudson (Eds.), *Knowing and remembering in young children*. Cambridge, UK: Cambridge University Press.

Nelson, K. (1993). Events, narratives, memory: What develops? In C. A. Nelson (Ed.), *Minnesota symposia on child psychology, Vol. 26: Memory and affect in development*. Hillsdale, NJ: Erlbaum.

Nelson, K. (2005). Cognitive functions of language in early childhood. In B. D. Homer & C. S. Tamis-LeMonda (Eds.), *The development of social cognition and communication* (pp. 7–28). Mahwah, NJ: Erlbaum.

Nelson, K. (2006). Advances in pragmatic developmental theory: The case of language acquisition. *Human Development*, *49*(3), 184–188.

Nelson, K., & Fivush, R. (2004). The emergence of autobiographical memory: A social cultural developmental theory. *Psychological Review*, *111*(2), 486–511.

Nelson, T. D. (2011). Ageism: The strange case of prejudice against the elder you. *Disability and Aging Discrimination, Part 1*, 37–47.

Newburn-Cook, C. V., et al. (2002). Where and to what extent is prevention of low birth weight possible? *Western Journal of Nursing Research*, *24*(8), 887–904.

Newman, R., Ratner, N. B., Jusczyk, A. M., Jusczyk, P. W., & Dow, K. A. (2006). Infants' early ability to segment the conversational speech signal predicts later language development: A retrospective analysis. *Developmental Psychology*, *42*(4), 643–655.

Newport, F. (2011, May 20). *For first time, majority of Americans favor legal gay marriage*. Gallup's May 5–8 Values and Beliefs Poll. Princeton, NJ. Retrieved from http://www.gallup.com/poll/147662/first-time-majority-americans-favor-legal-gay-marriage.aspx

The New York Times/CBS News Poll, April 22–26, 2009. (2009, April 27). Retrieved from http://graphics8.nytimes.com/packages/images/nytint/docs/newyork-times-cbs-news-poll-obamas-100th-day-in-office/original.pdf

Neyer, F. J. (2002). Twin relationships in old age. *Journal of Social and Personal Relationships*, *19*(2), 155–177.

Nguyen, T., et al. A testosterone-related structural brain phenotype predicts aggressive behavior from childhood to adulthood. *Psychoneuroendocrinology*, *63*, 109–118.

(NHPCO) National Hospice and Palliative Care Organization. (2012). *NHPCO facts and figures: Hospice care in America*. Retrieved from http://www.nhpco.org/files/public/Statistics_Research/2011_Facts_Figures.pdf

NHS Choices. (2011). *Do twins run in families?* Retrieved from http://www.nhs.uk/chq/pages/2550.aspx

NIAAA (National Institute on Alcohol Abuse and Alcoholism). (2005). Cage questionnaire. Retrieved from http://pubs.niaaa.nih.gov/publications/Assesing%20Alcohol/InstrumentPDFs/16_CAGE.pdf

Niemann, S., & Weiss, S. (2011). Attachment behavior and children adopted internationally at six months post adoption. *Adoption Quarterly*, *14*(4), 246–267.

Niemeier, H. M., Raynor, H. A., Lloyd-Richardson, E. E., Rogers, M. L., & Wing, R. R. (2006). Fast food consumption and breakfast skipping: Predictors of weight gain from adolescence to adulthood in a nationally representative sample. *Journal of Adolescent Health*, *39*(6), 842–849.

Nigg, J. T., Goldsmith, H. H., & Sachek, J. (2004). Temperament and attention deficit hyperactivity disorder: The development of a multiple pathway model. *Journal of Clinical Child and Adolescent Psychology*, *33*(1), 42–53.

Nigg, J. T. & Holton, K. (2014). Restriction and elimination diets in ADHD treatment. *Child and Adolescent Psychiatric Clinics of North America*, *23*(4), 937–953.

Nimrod, G. (2007). Retirees' leisure. *Leisure Studies*, *26*(1), 65–80.

Nisbett, R. E. (2009). *Intelligence and how to get it: Why schools and cultures count*. New York, NY: W. W. Norton.

Nisbett, R. E. (2013, Spring). Schooling makes you smarter. *American Educator*, 10–39.

Nisbett, R. E. (2016). Think big, bigger . . . and smaller. In M. Scherer (Ed.). *On poverty and learning: Readings from educational leadership* (pp. 94–103). Alexandria, VA: ASCD.

Nixon, A. E., et al. (2011). Can work make you sick: A meta-analysis of the relationships between job stressors and physical symptoms. *Work & Stress*, *25*(1), 1–22.

Njus, D. M., & Bane, C. M. H. (2009). Religious identification as a moderator of evolved sexual strategies of men and women. *Journal of Sex Research*, *46*(6), 546–557.

Nock, M. K., Kazdin, A. E., Hiripi, E., & Kessler, R. C. (2006). Prevalence, subtypes, and correlates of DSM-IV conduct disorder in the National Comorbidity Survey Replication. *Psychological Medicine*, *36*, 699–710.

Nomaguchi, K. M. (2006). Maternal employment, nonparental care, mother-child interactions, and child outcomes during preschool years. *Journal of Marriage and Family*, *68*(5), 1341–1369.

Nonaka, A. M. (2004). The forgotten endangered languages: Lessons on the importance of remembering from Thailand's Ban Khor Sign Language. *Language in Society*, *33*(5), 737–767.

Nonnemaker, J. M., & Homsi, G. (2007). Measurement properties of the Fagerström Test for nicotine dependence adapted for use in an adolescent sample. *Addictive Behaviors*, *32*(1), 181–186.

Noordstar, J. J., et al. (2016). Global self-esteem, perceived athletic competence, and physical activity in children: A longitudinal cohort study. *Psychology of Sport and Exercise*, *22*, 83–90.

Nordhov, S. M., et al. (2010). Early intervention improves cognitive outcomes for preterm infants: Randomized controlled trial. *Pediatrics*, *126*(5), e1088–e1094.

Nordhov, S. M., et al. (2012). Early intervention improves behavioral outcomes for preterm infants: Randomized controlled trial. *Pediatrics*, *129*(1), e9–e16.

Norman, G. A. V., et al. (Eds.). (2011). *Clinical ethics in Anesthesiology* (pp. 49–54). New York, NY: Cambridge University Press.

Norton, A., et al. (2005). Are there pre-existing neural, cognitive, or motoric markers for musical ability? *Brain and Cognition*, *59*(2), 124–134.

Novotny, R., et al. (2011). Puberty, body fat, and breast density in girls of several ethnic groups. *American Journal of Human Biology*, *23*(3), 359–365.

Nurwisah, R. (2011, September 29). Mitchell Wilson suicide: Disabled boy's death raises bullying concerns. *The Huffington Post Canada*.

Nutrition Facts. (2012). Centers for Disease Control and Prevention. Retrieved from http://www.cdc.gov/healthyyouth/nutrition/facts.htm

Nuttman-Shwartz, O. (2007). Is there life without work? *International Journal of Aging & Human Development*, *64*(2) 129–147.

O'Connor, K. A., et al. (2011). The puzzle of sibling attachment non-concordance. *Psychology Presentations*, Paper 32. Retrieved from http://ir.lib.uwo.ca/psychologypres/32

O'Doherty, J., et al. (2003). Beauty in a smile: The role of medial orbitofrontal cortex in facial attractiveness. *Neuropsychologia*, *41*(2), 147–155.

Ogden, C. L., et al. (2014). Prevalence of childhood and adult obesity in the United States, 2011–2012. *Journal of the American Medical Association*, *311*(8), 806–814.

Ojanen, T., & Findley-Van Nostrand, D. (2014). Social, goals, aggression, peer preference, and popularity: Longitudinal links during middle school. *Developmental Psychology*, *50*(8), 2134–2143.

O'Leary, C. M., et al. (2010). Prenatal alcohol exposure and risk of birth defects. *Pediatrics*, *126*(4), e843-e850.

O'Neill, D. K., & Chong, S. C. F. (2001). Preschool children's difficulty understanding the types of information obtained through the five senses. *Child Development*, *72*(3), 803–815.

O'Neill, D. K., & Gopnik, A. (1991). Young children's ability to identify the sources of their beliefs. *Developmental Psychology*, *27*, 390–397.

Oliveira, P. S., Fearon, R. M. P., Belsky, J., Fachada, I., & Soares, I. (2015). Quality of institutional care and early childhood development. *International Journal of Behavioral Development*, *39*(2), 161–170.

Olson, S. D., Fauci, L. J., & Suarez, S. S. (2011). Mathematical modeling of calcium signaling during sperm hyperactivation. *Molecular Human Reproduction*, *17*(8), 500–510.

Olson, S. L., Bates, J. E., Sandy, J. M., & Lanthier, R. (2000). Early developmental precursors of externalizing behavior in middle childhood and adolescence. *Journal of Abnormal Child Psychology*, *28*(2), 119–133.

Orel, N. (2006). Lesbian and bisexual women as grandparents: The centrality of sexual orientation in the grandparent–grandchild relationship. In D. Kimmel, T. Rose, & S. David (Eds.), *Lesbian, gay, bisexual, and transgender ageing: Research and clinical perspectives* (pp. 175–194). New York, NY: Columbia University Press.

Örnkloo, H., & von Hofsten, C. (2007). Fitting objects into holes: On the development of spatial cognition skills. *Developmental Psychology*, *43*(2), 404–416.

Orstavik, R. E., Kendler, K. S., Czajkowski, N., Tambs, K., & Reichborn-Kjennerud, T. (2007). Genetic and environmental contributions to depressive personality disorder in a population-based sample of Norwegian twins. *Journal of Affective Disorders*, *99*(1–3), 181–189.

Oswald, R. F., et al. (2013). LGB families in community context. In A. E Goldberg, & K. R. Allen (Eds.). *LGBT-parent families: Innovations in research and implications for practice* (pp. 193–208). New York: Springer Science + Business Media.

Out, D., Pieper, S., Bakermans-Kranenburg, M., Zeskind, P., van Ijzendoorn, M. (2010). Intended sensitive and harsh caregiving responses to infant crying: The role of cry pitch and perceived urgency in an adult twin sample. *Child Abuse & Neglect*, *34*(11), 863–873.

Oversekeid, G. (2016). Systematizing in autism: The case for an emotional mechanism. *New Ideas in Psychology, 41*, 18–22.

P

Paavola, L., Kemppinen, K., Kumpulainen, K., Moilanen, I., & Ebeling, H. (2006). Maternal sensitivity, infant co-operation and early linguistic development: Some predictive relations. *European Journal of Developmental Psychology*, *3*(1), 13–30.

Pace, C. S., & Zavattini, G. C. (2011). "Adoption and attachment theory": The attachment models of adoptive mothers and the revision of attachment patterns of their late-adopted children. *Child: Care, Health and Development*, *37*(1), 82–88.

Page, K. (1999, May 16). The graduate. *Washington Post Magazine*, *152*, 18, 20.

Palmer, E. L. (2003). Realities and challenges in the rapidly changing televisual media landscape. In E. L. Palmer & B. M. Young (Eds.), *The faces of televisual media: Teaching, violence, selling to children* (2nd ed., pp. 361–377). Mahwah, NJ: Erlbaum.

Papadopoulos, F. C., Ekbom, A., Brandt, L., & Ekselius, L. (2009). Excess mortality, causes of death and prognostic factors in anorexia nervosa. *British Journal of Psychiatry*, *194*, 10–17.

Parham, K., McKinnon, B. J., Eibling, D., & Gates, G. A. (2011). Challenges and opportunities in presbycusis. *Otolaryngology—Head and Neck Surgery*, *144*(4), 491–495.

Park, H.-O. H., & Greenberg, J. S. (2007). Parenting grandchildren. In J. Blackburn & C. N. Dulmus (Eds.), *Handbook of gerontology: Evidence-based approaches to theory, practice, and policy* (pp. 397–425). Hoboken, NJ: John Wiley & Sons.

Park, Y., Kwon, J. Y., Kim, Y. H., Kim, M., & Shin, J. C. (2010). Maternal age-specific rates of fetal chromosomal abnormalities at 16–20 weeks' gestation in Korean pregnant women greater than or equal to 35 years of age. *Fetal Diagnosis and Therapy*, *27*(4), 214–221.

Parke, R. D., & Buriel, R. (2006). Socialization in the family: Ethnic and ecological perspectives. In N. Eisenberg, W. Damon, & R. M. Lerner (Eds.), *Handbook of child psychology, Vol. 3: Social, emotional, and personality development* (6th ed., pp. 429–504). Hoboken, NJ: Wiley.

Parsons, H. G., George, M. A., & Innis, S. M. (2011). Growth assessment in clinical practice: Whose growth curve? *Current Gastroenterology Reports*, *13*(3), 286–292.

Parten, M. B. (1932). Social participation among preschool children. *Journal of Abnormal and Social Psychology*, *27*, 243–269.

Patenaude, J., Niyonsenga, T., & Fafard, D. (2003). Changes in students' moral development during medical school: A cohort study. *Canadian Medical Association Journal*, *168*(7), 840–844.

Paterson, D. S., et al. (2006). Multiple serotonergic brainstem abnormalities in sudden infant death syndrome. *Journal of the American Medical Association*, *296*, 2124–2132.

Patrick, H., Turner, J. C., & Strati, A. D. (2016). Classroom and school influences on student motivation. In K. R. Wentzel, & G. B. Ramani (Eds.). *Handbook of social influences in school contexts: Social-emotional, motivation, and cognitive outcomes* (pp. 241–257). New York: Routledge.

Patrick, H., Turner, J. C., & Strati, A. D. (2016). Classroom and school influences on student motivation. In K. R. Wentzel, & G. B. Ramani (Eds.). *Handbook of social influences in school contexts: Social-emotional, motivation, and cognitive outcomes* (pp. 241–257). New York: Routledge.

Patrick, S., Sells, J. N., Giordano, F. G., & Tollerud, T. R. (2007). Intimacy, differentiation, and personality variables as predictors of marital satisfaction. *The Family Journal*, *15*(4), 359–367.

Patterson, C. J. (2006). Children of lesbian and gay parents. *Current Directions in Psychological Science*, *15*(5), 241–244.

Patterson, G. R. (2005). The next generation of PMTO models. *The Behavior Therapist*, *28*(2), 27–33.

Patton, L. D., Renn, K. A., Guido, F. M., & Quaye, S. J. (2016). *Student development in college*. San Francisco: Jossey-Bass.

Pauli-Pott, U., Mertesacker, B., & Beckmann, D. (2003). Ein Fragebogen zur Erfassung des fruhkindlichen Temperaments im Elternurteil. *Zeitschrift für Kinder-und Jugendpsy-chiatrie und Psychotherapie*, *31*(2), 99–110.

Paulsen, J. A., Syed, M., Trzesniewski, K. H., & Donnellan, M. B. (2016). Generational perspectives on emerging adulthood: A focus on narcissism. In J. J. Arnett (Ed.). *The Oxford handbook on emerging adulthood* (pp. 26–46). New York: Oxford University Press.

Paulussen-Hoogeboom, M. C., Stams, G. J. J. M., Hermanns, J. M. A., & Peetsma, T. T. D. (2007). Child negative emotionality and parenting from infancy to preschool: A meta-analytic review. *Developmental Psychology*, *43*(2), 438–453.

Pearce, L. J., & Field, A. P. (2016). The impact of "scary" TV and film on children's internalizing emotions: A meta-analysis. *Human Communication Research*, *42*(1), 98–121.

Pearson, G. S., & Crowley, A. A. (2012). Attention deficit hyperactivity disorder. In E. L. Yearwood, G. S. Pearson, & J. A. Newland (Eds.), *Child and adolescent behavioral health* (pp. 139–152). Chichester, West Sussex, UK: Wiley-Blackwell.

Peat, C. M., Peyerl, N. L., Ferraro, F., & Butler, M. (2011). Age and body image in Caucasian men. *Psychology of Men & Masculinity*, *12*(2), 195–200.

Peck, R. C. (1968). Psychological developments in the second half of life. In B. L. Neugarten (Ed.), *Middle age and aging* (pp. 88–92). Chicago, IL: University of Chicago Press.

Pelphrey, K. A., et al. (2004). Development of visuospatial short-term memory in the second half of the first year. *Developmental Psychology*, *40*(5), 836–851.

Penn, H. E. (2006). Neurobiological correlates of autism: A review of recent research. *Child Neuropsychology*, *12*(1), 57–79.

Pereira, B., Mendonça, D., Neto, C., Valente, L., & Smith, P. K. (2004). Bullying in Portuguese schools. *School Psychology International*, *25*(2), 241–254.

Peres, J. (2012). New PSA guidelines discourage overscreening. *Journal of the National Cancer Institute*, *104*(1), 8–9.

Perrig-Chiello, P., Perrig, W. J., Uebelbacher, A., & Stähelin, H. B. (2006). Impact of physical and psychological resources on functional autonomy in old age. *Psychology, Health & Medicine*, *11*(4), 470–482.

Perrone, K. M., Webb, L. K., & Jackson, Z. V. (2007). Relationships between parental attachment, work and family roles, and life satisfaction. *The Career Development Quarterly*, *55*(3), 237–248.

Perry, J. E., Churchill, L. R., & Kirshner, H. S. (2012). Withholding and withdrawing medical treatment: The Terri Schiavo case. In N. S. Jecker et al. (Eds.), *Bioethics* (3rd ed., pp. 457–464). Sudbury, MA: Jones & Bartlett.

Perry, W. G. (1970/1998). *Forms of intellectual and ethical development in the college years: A scheme*. New York, NY: Holt, Rinehart and Winston.

Perry, W. G. (1981). Cognitive and ethical growth: The making of meaning. In A. W. Chickering & Assoc. (Eds.), The modern American college (pp. 76–116). San Francisco, CA: Jossey-Bass.

Perry-Jenkins, M., Goldberg, A. E., Pierce, C. P., & Sayer, A. G. (2007). Shift work, role overload, and the transition to parenthood. *Journal of Marriage and Family*, *69*(1), 123–138.

Persson, G. E. B. (2005). Developmental perspectives on prosocial and aggressive motives in preschoolers' peer interactions. *International Journal of Behavioral Development*, *29*(1), 80–91.

Philip, J., et al. (2004). Late first-trimester invasive prenatal diagnostic results of an international randomized trial. *Obstetrics & Gynecology*, *103*(6), 1164–1173.

Phillips, D. A., & Styfco, S. J. (2007). Child development research and public policy: Triumphs and setbacks on the way to maturity. In J. L. Aber et al. (Eds.), *Child development and social policy: Knowledge for action. APA Decade of Behavior volumes* (pp. 11–27). Washington, DC: American Psychological Association.

Phinney, J. S., & Baldelomar, O. A. (2011). Identity development in multiple cultural contexts. In L. A. Jensen (Ed.), *Bridging cultural and developmental approaches to psychology* (pp. 161–186). New York, NY: Oxford University Press.

Physical activity for everyone. (2011). Centers for Disease Control and Prevention. Retrieved from http://www.cdc.gov/physicalactivity/everyone/guidelines/adults.html

Piaget, J. (1932). *The moral judgment of the child*. London: Kegan Paul.

Piaget, J. (1962). *Play, dreams, and imitation in childhood*. New York, NY: Norton. (Originally published in 1946.)

Piaget, J. (1963). *The origins of intelligence in children*. New York, NY: Norton. (Originally published in 1936.)

Piaget, J. (1976). *The grasp of consciousness: Action and concept in the young child*. Cambridge, MA: Harvard University Press.

Pickren, W. E., Marsella, A. J., Leong, F. T. L., & Leach, M. M. (2012). Playing our part: Crafting a vision for a psychology curriculum marked by multiplicity. In F. T. L. Leong, W. E. Pickren, M. M. Leach, & A. J. Marsella (Eds.), *Internationalizing the psychology curriculum in the United States* (pp. 307–322). New York, NY: Springer.

Piek, J. P., Baynam, G. B., & Barrett, N. C. (2006). The relationship between fine and gross motor ability, self-perceptions and self-worth in children and adolescents. *Human Movement Science*, *25*(1), 65–75.

Pine, D. S., et al. (2001). Fluvoxamine for the treatment of anxiety disorders in children and adolescents. *New England Journal of Medicine*, *344*(17), 1279–1285.

Pinker, S. (2007). *The stuff of thought: Language as a window into human nature*. New York, NY: Penguin Books.

Pinquart, M., & Schindler, I. (2007). Changes of life satisfaction in the transition to retirement. *Psychology and Aging*, *22*(3), 442–455.

Pitman, A. L., Osborn, D. P. J., Rantell, K., & King, M. B. (2016). Bereavement by suicide as a risk factor for suicide attempt: A cross-sectional national UK-wide study of 3432 bereaved adults. *British Medical Journal Open*, *6*, DOI: 10.1136/bmjopen-2015–009948.

Platje, E., et al. (2015). Testosterone and cortisol in relation to a nonclinical sample of boys and girls. *Aggressive Behavior*, DOI: 10.1002/ab.21585.

Plomin, R. (Ed.). (2002). *Behavioral genetics in the postgenomic era*. Washington, DC: American Psychological Association.

Plomin, R., & Asbury, K. (2005). Nature and nurture: Genetic and environmental influences on behavior. *The Annals of the American Academy of Political and Social Science*, *600*(1), 86–98.

Plomin, R., & Haworth, C. M. A. (2009). Genetics of high cognitive abilities. *Behavior Genetics*, *39*(4), 347–349.

Plomin, R., & Spinath, F. M. (2004). Intelligence: Genetics, genes, and genomics. *Journal of Personality and Social Psychology*, *86*(1), 112–129.

Plomin, R., & Walker, S. O. (2003). Genetics and educational psychology. *British Journal of Educational Psychology*, *73*(1), 3–14.

Plomin, R., DeFries, J. C., McClearn, G. E., & McGuffin, P. (2008). *Behavioral genetics*. New York, NY: Worth.

Plomin, R., DeFries, J. C., McClearn, G. E., & McGuffin, P. (2008). *Behavioral genetics*. New York, NY: Worth Publishers.

Plomin, R., Owen, M. J., & McGuffin, P. (1994). The genetic basis of complex human behaviors. *Science*, *264*, 1733–1739.

Pluchino, N., Bucci, F., Cela, V., Cubeddu, A., & Genazzani, A. R. (2011). Menopause and mental well-being: Timing of symptoms and timing of hormone treatment. *Women's Health*, *7*(1), 71–80.

Plucker, J. A., Esping, A., Kaufman, J. C., & Avitia, M. J. (2015). Creativity and intelligence. In S. Goldstein, D. Princiotta, & J. A. Naglieri (Eds.). *Handbook of intelligence: Evolutionary theory, historical perspective, and current concepts* (pp. 283–291). New York: Springer Science + Business Media.

Plunkett, J., et al. (2011). An evolutionary genomic approach to identify genes involved in human birth timing. *PLoS Genetics*, *7*(4): e1001365. doi:10.1371/journal.pgen.1001365

Polivy, J., Herman, C. P., & Boivin, M. (2005). Eating disorders. In J. E. Maddux & B. A. Winstead (Eds.), *Psychopathology: Foundations for a contemporary understanding* (pp. 229–254). Mahwah, NJ: Erlbaum.

Pollack, D. (2008). Organ donation and transplants. *International Social Work*, *51*(1), 103–109.

Poltorak, D. Y., & Glazer, J. P. (2006). The development of children's understanding of death. *Child and Adolescent Psychiatric Clinics of North America*, *15*(3), 567–573.

Population Estimates and Projections. (2010). *The next four decades: The older population in the United States: 2010–2050*. U.S. Census Bureau. Retrieved from http://www.census.gov/prod/2010pubs/p25-1138.pdf

Porfeli, E. J. (2007). Work values system development during adolescence. *Journal of Vocational Behavior*, *70*(1), 42–60.

Porter, R. H., Makin, J. W., Davis, L. B., & Christensen, K. M. (1992). Breast-fed infants respond to olfactory cues from their own mother and unfamiliar lactating females. *Infant Behavior and Development*, *15*, 85–93.

Posner, M. I., & Rothbart, M. K. (2007). *Relating brain and mind. Educating the human brain*. Washington, DC: American Psychological Association.

Potter, D. (2010). Psychosocial well-being and the relationship between divorce and children's academic achievement. *Journal of Marriage and the Family*, *72*(4), 933–946.

Powlishta, K. K. (2004). Gender as a social category: Intergroup processes and gender-role development. In M. Bennett & F. Sani (Eds.), *The development of the social self* (pp. 103–133). New York, NY: Psychology Press.

Powlishta, K. K., Sen, M. G., Serbin, L. A., Poulin-Dubois, D., & Eichstedt, J. A. (2001). From infancy through middle childhood: The role of cognitive and social factors in becoming gendered. In R. K. Unger (Ed.), *Handbook of the psychology of women and gender* (pp. 116–132). New York, NY: Wiley.

Powrie, R. O., et al. (2010) Special concerns for parents with advanced maternal age. In *de Swiet's medical disorders in obstetric practice* (5th ed.). Hoboken, NJ: Wiley.

Pradhan, D. S., Solomon-Lane, T. K., & Grober, M. S. (2015). Contextual modulation of social and endocrine correlates of fitness: Insights from the life history of a sex changing fish. *Frontiers in Neuroscience*, *9*(8), DOI: 10.3389/fnins.2015.00008.

Prato-Previde, E., Fallani, G., & Valsecchi, P. (2006). Gender differences in owners interacting with pet dogs: An observational study. *Ethology*, *112*(1), 64–73.

Pratt, C., & Bryant, P. (1990). Young children understand that looking leads to knowing (so long as they are looking into a single barrel). *Child Development*, *61*, 973–982.

Prendergast, G., West, D. C., & Yan, L. K. (2015). Eating disorders: The role of advertising and editorial. In H. E. Spotts (Ed.). *Developments in marketing science: Proceedings of the Academy of Marketing Science* (pp. 175–178). New York: Springer International Publishing.

Provence, S., & Lipton, R. C. (1962). *Infants in institutions*. New York, NY: International Universities Press.

Pugh, K. R., et al. (2000). The angular gyrus in developmental dyslexia: Task-specific differences in functional connectivity within posterior cortex. *Psychological Science*, *11*(1), 51–56.

Pulverman, R., Hirsh-Pasek, K., Golinkoff, R. M., Pruden, S., & Salkind, S. J. (2006). Conceptual foundations for verb learning: Celebrating the event. In K. Hirsh-Pasek & R. M. Golinkoff (Eds.), *Action meets word: How children learn verbs* (pp. 134–159). New York, NY: Oxford University Press.

Q

Quigley, N. R., & Tymon, Jr., W. G. (2006). Toward an integrated model of intrinsic motivation and career self-management. *Career Development International*, *11*(6), 522–543.

Quill, T. E. (2005, April 4). Terri Schiavo—A tragedy compounded. *New England Journal of Medicine*. Available at http://www.nejm.org. Accessed October 5, 2010.

Quinsey, V. L., et al. (2006). Sex offenders. In V. L. Quinsey et al. (Eds.), *Violent offenders: Appraising and managing risk* (2nd ed., pp. 131–151). Washington, DC: American Psychological Association.

R

Rabin, R. C. (2007, August 28). For a low-dose hormone, take your pick. *The New York Times online*.

Radvansky, G. A., Zacks, R. T., & Hasher, L. (2005). Age and inhibition: The retrieval of situation models. *Journals of Gerontology: Series B: Psychological Sciences and Social Sciences*, *60B*(5), P276–P278.

Ramagopalan, S. V., et al. (2010). A genome-wide scan of male sexual orientation. *Journal of Human Genetics*, *55*, 131–132.

Ramey, C. T., Campbell, F. A., & Ramey, S. L. (1999). Early intervention: Successful pathways to improving intellectual development. *Developmental Neuropsychology*, *16*(3) 385–392.

Randel, B., Stevenson, H. W., & Witruk, E. (2000). Attitudes, beliefs, and mathematics achievement of German and Japanese high school students. *International Journal of Behavioral Development*, *24*(2), 190–198.

Rapee, R. M. (2011). Family factors in the development and management of anxiety disorders. *Clinical Child and Family Psychology Review*. doi:10.1007/s10567-011-0106-3

Rapin, I. (1997). Autism. *New England Journal of Medicine*, *337*, 97–104.

Rathus, J. H., & Miller, A. L. (2002). Dialectical Behavior Therapy adapted for suicidal adolescents. *Suicide and Life-Threatening Behavior*, *32*(2), 146–157.

Rathus, S. A., Nevid, J. S., & Fichner-Rathus, L. (2011). *Human sexuality in a world of diversity*. Boston: Allyn & Bacon.

Rathus, S. A. et al. (2017). *Human sexuality in a changing world*. Hoboken, NJ: Pearson.

Raynes-Greenough, C. H., Gordon, A., Li, Q., & Hyett, J. A. (2013). A cross-sectional study of maternal perception of fetal movements and antenatal advice in a general pregnant population, using a qualitative framework. *BMC Pregnancy and Childbirth*, *13*, 32.

Redshaw, M., & van den Akker, O. (2007). Editorial. *Journal of Reproductive and Infant Psychology*, *25*(2), 103–105.

Reece, M., et al. (2010). Sexual behaviors, relationships, and perceived health among adult men in the United States: Results from a national probability sample. *Journal of Sexual Medicine*, *7*(Suppl. 5), 291–304.

Reiersen, A. M., & Handen, B. (2011). Commentary on "Selective serotonin reuptake inhibitors (SSRIs) for autism spectrum disorders (ASD)." *Evidence-Based Child Health: A Cochrane Review Journal*, *6*, 1082–1085.

Reis, H. T., Maniaci, M. R., Caprariello, P. A., Eastwick, P. W., & Finkel, E. L. (2011). Familiarity does indeed promote attraction in live interaction. *Journal of Personality and Social Psychology*, *101*(3), 557–570.

Reis, O., & Youniss, J. (2004). Patterns in identity change and development in relationships with mothers and friends. *Journal of Adolescent Research*, *19*(1), 31–44.

Reis, S. M., & Renzulli, J. S. (2011). Intellectual giftedness. In R. J. Sternberg & S. J. Kaufman (Eds.), *The Cambridge handbook of intelligence* (pp. 235–252). New York, NY: Cambridge University Press.

Reitzes, D. C., & Mutran, E. J. (2004). The transition to retirement. *International Journal of Aging & Human Development*, *59*(1), 63–84.

Reitzes, D. C., & Mutran, E. J. (2006). Lingering identities in retirement. *Sociological Quarterly*, *47*(2), 333–359.

Rendell, P. G., Castel, A. D., & Craik, F. I. M. (2005). Memory for proper names in old age: A disproportionate impairment? *The Quarterly Journal of Experimental Psychology A: Human Experimental Psychology*, 58A(1), 54–71.

Rennie, J., & Rosenbloom, L. (2011). How long have we got to get the baby out? A review of the effects of acute and profound intrapartum hypoxia and ischaemia. *The Obstetrician and Gynecologist*, *13*(3), 169–174.

Reschly, A., & Christenson, S. L. (2006). School completion. In G. G. Bear & K. M. Minke (Eds.), *Children's needs III: Development, prevention, and intervention* (pp. 103–113). Washington, DC: National Association of School Psychologists.

Rest, J. R. (1983). Morality. In P. H. Mussen (Ed.), *Handbook of child psychology, Vol. 3: Cognitive development* (pp. 556–629). New York, NY: Wiley.

Retsinas, J. (1988). A theoretical reassessment of the applicability of Kübler-Ross's stages of dying. *Death Studies*, *12*(3), 207–216.

Reynolds, C. A., Barlow, T., & Pedersen, N. L. (2006). Alcohol, tobacco and caffeine use: Spouse similarity processes. *Behavior Genetics*, *36*(2), 201–215.

Reynolds, G. D., & Romano, A. C. (2016). The development of attention systems and working memory in infancy. *Frontiers in Systems Neuroscience*, *10*, DOI: 10.3389/fnsys.2016.00015

Rice, C. E., et al. (2007). A public health collaboration for the surveillance of autism spectrum disorders. *Paediatric and Perinatal Epidemiology*, *21*(2), 179–190.

Richert, R. A., Robb, M. B., & Smith, E. I. (2011). Media as social partners: The social nature of young children's learning from screen media. *Child Development*, *82*(1), 82–95.

Rickards, H., et al. (2011). Factor analysis of behavioural symptoms in Huntington's disease. *Journal of Neurology, Neurosurgery, & Psychiatry*, *82*(4), 411–412.

Rietjens, J., et al. (2008). Continuous deep sedation for patients nearing death in the Netherlands: Descriptive study. *British Medical Journal*, *336*(7648), 810–813.

Riggio, R. E., & Woll, S. B. (1984). The role of nonverbal cues and physical attractiveness in the selection of dating partners. *Journal of Social and Personal Relationships*, *1*(3), 347–357.

Rizzolati, G., & Fabbri-Destro, M. (2011). Mirror neurons: From discovery to autism. *Experimental Brain Research*, *200*(3–4), 223–237.

Rizzolatti, G., & Craighero, L. (2004). The mirror-neuron system. *Annual Review of Neuroscience*, *27*, 169–172.

Rizzolatti, G., Fadiga, L., Fogassi, L., & Gallese, V. (2002). From mirror neurons to imitation: Facts and speculations. In A. N. Meltzoff & W. Prinz (Eds.), *The imitative mind: Development, evolution, and brain bases*. New York, NY: Cambridge University Press.

Roberts, W., Strayer, J., & Denham, S. (2014). Empathy, anger, guilt: Emotions and prosocial behavior. *Canadian Journal of Behavioural Science*, *46*(4), 465–474.

Robins, R. W., Trzesniewski, K. H., Tracy, J. L., Gosling, S. D., & Potter, J. (2002). Global self-esteem across the lifespan. *Psychology and Aging*, *17*(3), 423–434.

Robling, M., et al. (2016). Effectiveness of a nurse-led intensive home-visitation programme for first-time teenage mothers (Building Blocks). *The Lancet*, *387*(10014), 146–155.

Roberts, C. L., et al. (2015). Association of prelabor cesarean delivery with reduced mortality in twins born near term. *Obstetrics & Gynecology*, *125*(1), 103–110.

Roffwarg, H. P., Muzio, J. N., & Dement, W. C. (1966). Ontogenetic development of the human sleep–dream cycle. *Science*, *152*, 604–619.

Roisman, G. I., & Groh, A. M. (2011). Attachment theory and research in developmental psychology: An overview and appreciative critique. In M. K. Underwood & L. H. Rosen (Eds.), *Social development: Relationships in infancy, childhood, and adolescence* (pp. 101–126). New York, NY: Guilford.

Ronald, A., et al. (2006). Genetic heterogeneity between the three components of the autism spectrum: A twin study. *Journal of the American Academy of Child & Adolescent Psychiatry*, *45*(6), 691–699.

Roopnarine, J. L., Krishnakumar, A., Metindogan, A., & Evans, M. (2006). Links between parenting styles, parent–child academic interaction, parent–school interaction, and early academic skills and social behaviors in young children of English-speaking Caribbean immigrants. *Early Childhood Research Quarterly*, *21*(2), 238–252.

Rose, A. J., Swenson, L. P., & Carlson, W. (2004). Friendships of aggressive youth: Considering the influences of being disliked and of being perceived as popular. *Journal of Experimental Child Psychology*, *88*(1), 25–45.

Rose, L. Y., & Fischer, K. W. (2011). Intelligence in childhood. In R. J. Sternberg & S. J. Kaufman (Eds.), *The Cambridge handbook of intelligence* (pp. 144–173). New York, NY: Cambridge University Press.

Rose, S. A., Feldman, J. F., & Jankowski, J. J. (2001). Visual short-term memory in the first year of life: Capacity and recency effects. *Developmental Psychology*, *37*(4), 539–549.

Rose, S. A., Feldman, J. F., & Jankowski, J. J. (2004). Infant visual recognition memory. *Developmental Review*, *24*(1), 74–100.

Rose, S. A., Feldman, J. F., & Wallace, I. F. (1992). Infant information processing in relation to six-year cognitive outcomes. *Child Development*, *63*, 1126–1141.

Rose, S. A., Feldman, J. F., Jankowski, J. J., & van Rossem, R. (2011). The structure of memory in infants and toddlers: An SEM study with full-terms and preterms. *Developmental Science*, *14*(1), 83–91.

Rose, S. A., Feldman, J. F., & Jankowski, J. J. (2015). Pathways from toddler information processing to adolescent lexical proficiency. *Child Development*, *86*(6), 1935–1947.

Rosen, L. H., & Patterson, M. M. (2011). The self and identity. In M. K. Underwood & L. H. Rosen (Eds.), *Social development: Relationships in infancy, childhood, and adolescence* (pp. 73–100). New York, NY: Guilford.

Rosenbaum, M., & Leibel, R. L. (2010). Adaptive thermogenesis in humans. *International Journal of Obesity*, *34*, S47–S55.

Rosenstein, D., & Oster, H. (1988). Differential facial responses to four basic tastes. *Child Development*, *59*, 1555–1568.

Rosenthal, R., & Jacobson, L. (1968). *Pygmalion in the classroom*. New York, NY: Holt, Rinehart & Winston.

Rospenda, K. M., et al. (2005). Is workplace harassment hazardous to your health? *Journal of Business and Psychology*, *20*(1), 95–110.

Ross, H., Ross, M., Stein, N., & Trabasso, T. (2006). How siblings resolve their conflicts: The importance of first offers, planning, and limited opposition. *Child Development*. 77(6) 1730–1745.

Rote, W. M., & Smetana, J. G. (2015). Parenting, adolescent-parent relationships, and social domain theory: Implications for identity development. In S. J. Schwatrz, K. Luyckx, & V. L. Vignoles (Eds.). *Handbook of identity theory and research* (pp. 437–453). New York: Springer Science + Business Media.

Rotenberg, K. J., et al. (2004). Cross-sectional and longitudinal relations among peer-reported trustworthiness, social relationships, and psychological adjustment in children and early adolescents from the United Kingdom and Canada. *Journal of Experimental Child Psychology*, *88*(1), 46–67.

Rothbart, M. K., & Sheese, B. E. (2007). Temperament and emotion regulation. In J. J. Gross (Ed.), *Handbook of emotion regulation* (pp. 331–350). New York, NY: Guilford.

Rothbart, M. K., Ellis, L. K., & Posner, M. I. (2004). Temperament and self-regulation. In R. F. Baumeister & K. D. Vohs (Eds.), *Handbook of self-regulation: Research, theory, and applications* (pp. 283–300). New York, NY: Guilford.

Rottinghaus, P. J., Coon, K. L., Gaffey, A. R., & Zytowski, D. G. (2007). Thirty-year stability and predictive validity of vocational interests. *Journal of Career Assessment*, *15*(1), 5–22.

Rovee-Collier, C. (1993). The capacity for long-term memory in infancy. *Current Directions in Psychological Science*, *2*, 130–135.

Rübeling, H., Schwarzer, S., Keller, H., & Lenk, M. (2011). Young children's nonfigurative drawings of themselves and their families in two different cultures. *Journal of Cognitive Education and Psychology*, *10*(1), 63–76.

Rubia, K., et al. (2006). Progressive increase of frontostriatal brain activation from childhood to adulthood during event-related tasks of cognitive control. *Human Brain Mapping*, *27*(12), 973–993.

Rubin, K. H., & Coplan, R. J. (Eds.). (2010). *The development of shyness and social withdrawal*. New York, NY: Guilford.

Rubin, K. H., Bukowski, W. M., & Parker, J. G. (2006). Peer interactions, relationships, and groups. In N. Eisenberg, W. Damon, & R. M. Lerner (Eds.), *Handbook of child psychology* (6th ed.), *Vol. 3: Social, emotional, and personality development* (pp. 571–645). Hoboken, NJ: Wiley.

Ruble, D. N., Martin, C. L., & Berenbaum, S. A. (2006). Gender development. In N. Eisenberg, W. Damon, & R. M. Lerner (Eds.), *Handbook of child psychology* (6th ed.), *Vol. 3: Social, emotional, and personality development* (pp. 858– 932). Hoboken, NJ: Wiley.

Rudolph, K. D., & Flynn, M. (2007). Childhood adversity and youth depression: Influence of gender and pubertal status. *Development and Psychopathology*, *19*(2), 497–521.

Rudolph, K. D., Lambert, S. F., Clark, A. G., & Kurlakowsky, K. D. (2001). Negotiating the transition to middle school: The role of self-regulatory processes. *Child Development*, *72*(3), 929–946.

Rudy, D., & Grusec, J. E. (2006). Authoritarian parenting in individualist and collectivist groups: Associations with maternal emotion and cognition and children's self-esteem. *Journal of Family Psychology*, *20*(1), 68–78.

Rusconi, A. (2004). Different pathways out of the parental Home: A comparison of West Germany and Italy. *Journal of Comparative Family Studies*, *35*(4), 627–649.

Russ, S. W. (2006). Pretend play, affect, and creativity. In P. Locher, C. Martindale, & L. Dorfman (Eds.), *New directions in aesthetics, creativity and the arts, Foundations and frontiers in aesthetics* (pp. 239–250). Amityville, NY: Baywood.

Russell, J. E. A. (2008). Promoting subjective well-being at work. *Journal of Career Assessment*, *16*(1), 117–131.

Russell, S. T. (2006). Substance use and abuse and mental health among sexual-minority youths: Evidence from add health. In A. M. Omoto & H. S. Kurtzman (Eds.), *Sexual orientation and mental health: Examining identity and development in lesbian, gay, and bisexual people* (pp. 13–35). Washington, DC: American Psychological Association.

Russo, N. F., Pirlott, A. G., & Cohen, A. B. (2012). The psychology of women and gender in international perspective: Issues and challenges. In F. T. L. Leong, W. E. Pickren, M. M. Leach, & A. J. Marsella (Eds.), *Internationalizing the psychology curriculum in the United States* (pp. 157–178). New York, NY: Springer.

Russo, J., & Nelson, A. L. (2016) Contraception for women with medical conditions. In D. Shoupe, & D. R. Mishell, Jr. (Eds.). *The handbook of contraception* (pp. 43–60). Switzerland: Springer International Publishing.

Rutter, M. (2006). The psychological effects of early institutional rearing. In P. J. Marshall & N. A. Fox (Eds.), *The development of social engagement: Neurobiological perspectives. Series in affective science* (pp. 355–391). New York, NY: Oxford University Press.

Ryan, R. M., & Deci, E. L. (2000). Self-determination theory and the facilitation of intrinsic motivation, social development, and well-being. *American Psychologist*, *55*(1), 68–78.

Rytter,m M. J. H., et al. (2015). Diet in the treatment of ADHD in children—A systematic review of the literature. *Nordic Journal of Psychiatry*, *69*(1), 1–18.

S

Sabattini, L., & Leaper, C. (2004). The relation between mothers' and fathers' parenting styles and their division of labor in the home: Young adults' retrospective reports. *Sex Roles*, *50*(3–4), 217–225.

Sabbadini, G., Travan, L., & Toigo, G. (2012). Elderly women with heart failure: Unseen, unheard, or simply forgotten? *Aging Health*, *8*(2), 191–204.

Sadker, D. M., & Silber, E. S. (Eds.) (2007). *Gender in the classroom: Foundations, skills, methods, and strategies across the curriculum*. Mahwah, NJ: Erlbaum.

Sadler, T. W. (Ed.). (2005). Abstracts of papers presented at the thirty-fifth annual meeting the Japanese Teratology Society, Tokyo, Japan. *Teratology*, *52*(4), b1–b51.

Saito, M., & Marumo, K. (2010). Collagen cross-links as a determinant of bone quality: A possible explanation for bone fragility in aging, osteoporosis, and diabetes mellitus. *Osteoporosis International*, *21*(2), 195–214.

Saklofske, D. H., van de Vijver, F. J. R., Oakland, T., Mpofu, E., & Suzuki, L. A. (2015). Intelligence and culture: History and assessment. In S. Goldstein, D. Princiotta, & J. A. Naglieri (Eds.). *Handbook of intelligence: Evolutionary theory, historical perspective, and current concepts* (pp. 341–365). New York: Springer Science + Business Media.

Salami, M. (2010). Change in visual experience impairs rat's spatial learning in Morris water maze. *Journal of Isfahan Medical School*, 28(111).

Salapatek, P. (1975). Pattern perception in early infancy. In L. B. Cohen & P. Salapatek (Eds.), *Infant perception: From sensation to cognition* (pp. 133–248). New York, NY: Academic Press.

Saldarriage, L. M., Bukowski, W. M., & Greco, C. (2015). Friendship and happiness: A bidirectional dynamic process. In Demir, M. *Friendship and happiness: Across the life-span and cultures* (pp. 59–78). Netherlands: Springer Science + Media.

Salihu, H. M. (2011). Maternal obesity and stillbirth. *Seminars in Perinatology*, *35*(6), 340–344.
Salthouse, T. (2010). *Major issues in cognitive aging*. New York, NY: Oxford University Press.
Salthouse, T. (2011). Consequences of age-related cognitive declines. *Annual Review of Psychology*, *63*, 5.1–5.6.
Salzarulo, P., & Ficca, G. (Eds.). (2002). *Awakening and sleep–wake cycle across development*. Amsterdam: John Benjamins.
Sandman, C., & Crinella, F. (1995). Cited in Margoshes, P. (1995). For many, old age is the prime of life. *APA Monitor*, *26*(5), 36–37.
Santelli, J. S., et al. (2003). Reproductive health in school-based health centers: Findings from the 1998–99 census of school-based health centers. *Journal of Adolescent Health*, *32*(6), 443–451.
Sarrazin, P., Trouilloud, D., & Bois, J. (2005a). Attentes du superviseur et performance sportive du pratiquant. Amplitude et fonctionnement de l'effet Pygmalion en contexte sportif. *Bulletin de Psychologie*, *58*(1), 63–68.
Sarrazin, P., Trouilloud, D., Tessier, D., Chanal, J., & Bois, J. (2005b). Attentes de motivation et comportements différenciés de l'enseignant d'éducation physique et sportive à l'égard de ses élèves: une étude en contexte naturel d'enseignement. *Revue Européenne de Psychologie Appliquée*, *55*(2), 111–120.
Sasaki, C. (2007). Grounded-theory study of therapists' perceptions of grieving process in bereaved children. *Dissertation Abstracts International: Section B: The Sciences and Engineering*, *68*(1-B), 635.
Saudino, K. J. (2011). Sources of continuity and change in activity level in early childhood. *Child Development*. *82*(6), 2138–2143.
Save the Children. (2015). *State of the World's Mothers*. Fairfield, CT: Save the Children.
Save the Children. (2011). *State of the world's mothers* 2011. Westport, CT: Author. Retrieved from http://www.savethechildren.org
Savic, I., Garcia-Falgueras, A., & Swaab, D. F. (2011). Sexual differentiation of the human brain in relation to gender identity and sexual orientation. In I. Savic (Ed.). *Sex differences in the human brain, Their underpinnings and implications: Progress in brain research*, *186* (pp. 41–64). New York: Elsevier.
Savickas, M. L. (2005). The theory and practice of career construction. In S. D. Brown & R. W. Lent (Eds.), *Career development and counseling* (pp. 42–70). Hoboken, NJ: Wiley.
Savikas, M. L. (2012). Life design: A paradigm for career intervention in the 21st century. *Journal of Counseling & Development*, *90*(1), 13–19.
Savin-Williams, R. C. (2007). Girl-on-girl sexuality. In B. J. R. Leadbeater & N. Way (Eds.), *Urban girls revisited: Building strengths* (pp. 301–318). New York, NY: New York University Press.
Savin-Williams, R. C., & Cohen, K. M. (2007). Development of same-sex attracted youth. In I. H. Meyer & M. E. Northridge (Eds.), *The health of sexual minorities: Public health perspectives on lesbian, gay, bisexual, and transgender populations* (pp. 27–47). New York, NY: Springer Science + Business Media.
Savin-Williams, R. C., & Diamond, L. M. (2004). Sex. In R. M. Lerner & L. Steinberg (Eds.), *Handbook of adolescent psychology* (2nd ed., pp. 189–231). Hoboken, NJ: Wiley.
Sayegh, Y., & Dennis, W. (1965). The effect of supplementary experiences upon the behavioral development of infants in institutions. *Child Development*, *36*(1), 81–90.
Scarr, S. (1993, March). *IQ correlations among members of transracial adoptive families*. Paper presented at the meeting of the Society for Research in Child Development, New Orleans, LA.
Schacter, D. I. (1992). Understanding implicit memory: A cognitive neuroscience approach. *American Psychologist*, *47*(4), 559–569.
Schaffer, H. R., & Emerson, P. E. (1964). The development of social attachments in infancy. *Monographs of the Society for Research in Child Development*, *29*(94).
Schaie, K. W. (1994). The course of adult intellectual development. *American Psychologist*, *49*, 304–313. Copyright © American Psychological Association.
Schaie, K. W. (2002). The impact of longitudinal studies on understanding development from young adulthood to old age. In. W. W. Hartup & R. K. Silbereisen (Eds.), *Growing points in developmental science* (pp. 307–328). New York, NY: Psychology Press.
Schaie, K. W. (2005). What can we learn from longitudinal studies of adult development? *Research in Human Development*, *2*(3), 133–158.
Schaie, K. W., & Zanjani, F. A. K. (2006). Intellectual development across adulthood. In C. Hoare (Ed.), *Handbook of adult development and learning* (pp. 99–122). New York, NY: Oxford University Press.
Schaie, K. W., Willis, S. L., & Caskie, G. I. L. (2004). The Seattle longitudinal study: Relationship between personality and cognition. *Aging, Neuropsychology, and Cognition*, *11*(2–3), 304–324.
Scharf, M., Shulman, S., & Avigad-Spitz, L. (2005). Sibling relationships in emerging adulthood and in adolescence. *Journal of Adolescent Research*, *20*(1), 64–90.
Scharlach, A. (2012). Creating aging-friendly communities in the United States. *Ageing International*, *37*(1), 25–38.
Scheithauer, H., Hayer, T., Petermann, F., & Jugert, G. (2006). Physical, verbal, and relational forms of bullying among German students: Age trends, gender differences, and correlates. *Aggressive Behavior*, *32*(3), 261–275.
Scheres, A., & Castellanos, F. X. (2003). Assessment and treatment of childhood problems, 2nd ed.: A clinician's guide. *Psychological Medicine*, *33*(8), 1487–1488.
Schick, V. R., Rima, B. N., & Calabrese, S. K. (2011). Evulvalution: The portrayal of women's external genitalia and physique across time and the current Barbie doll ideals. *Journal of Sex Research*, *48*(1), 74–81.
Schmitt, D. P. (2008). An evolutionary perspective on mate choice and relationship initiation. In S. Sprecher, A. Wenzel, & J. H. Harvey (Eds.), *Handbook of relationship initiation* (pp. 55–74). New York, NY: CRC Press.
Schneewind, K. A., & Kupsch, M. (2007). Patterns of neuroticism, work-family stress, and resources as determinants of personal distress: A cluster analysis of young, dual-earner families at the individual and couple level. *Journal of Individual Differences*, *28*(3), 150–160.
Schneider, W. (2010). Memory development in childhood. In U. Goswami (Ed.), *The Wiley-Blackwell handbook of childhood cognitive development*. (2nd ed.) (pp. 347–376). Chichester, West Sussex, UK: Wiley-Blackwell.
Schneider, W. (2015). Memory development during the infant and toddler years. *Motor development from early childhood through emerging adulthood* (pp. 39–74). Switzerland: Springer International Publishing.
Schoppe-Sullivan, S. J., Mangelsdorf, S. C., Brown, G. L., & Sokolowski, M. S. (2007). Goodness-of-fit in family context: Infant temperament, marital quality, and early coparenting behavior. *Infant Behavior & Development*, *30*(1), 82–96.
Schraf, M., & Hertz-Lazarowitz, R. (2003). Social networks in the school context: Effects of culture and gender. *Journal of Social and Personal Relationships*, *20*(6), 843–858.
Shubert, T. R., Sitaram, S., & Jadcherla, S. R. (2016). Effects of pacifier and taste on swallowing, esophageal motility, transit, and respiratory rhythm in human neonates. *Neurogastroenterology & Motility*, *28*(4), 532–542.
Schuetze, P., Zeskind, P. S., & Eiden, R. D. (2003). The perceptions of infant distress signals varying in pitch by cocaine-using mothers. *Infancy*, *4*(1), 65–83.
Schwartz, D., Lansford, J. E., Dodge, K. E., Pettit, G. S., & Bates, J. E. (2013). The link between harsh home environments and negative academic trajectories is exacerbated by victimization in the elementary school peer group. *Developmental Psychology*, *49*(2), 305–316.
Shultz, K. S., & Wang, M. (2011). Psychological perspectives on the changing nature of retirement. *American Psychologist*, *66*(3), 170–179.
Schultz, D. P., & Schultz, S. E. (2008). *A history of modern psychology* (9th ed.). Belmont, CA: Thomson/Wadsworth.
Schumacher, D., & Queen, J. A. (2007). *Overcoming obesity in childhood and adolescence: A guide for school leaders*. Thousand Oaks, CA: Corwin Press.
Schwartz, S. J., et al. (2011). Daily dynamics of personal identity and self-concept clarity. *European Journal of Personality*, *25*(5), 373–385.

Schwartz, S. L., & Hunt, J. S. (2011). Considering her circumstances. *Behavioral Sciences and the Law*, *29*(3), 419–438.

Schwartz, A., & Cohen, S. (2013, March 31). ADHD seen in 11% of U.S. children as diagnoses rise. *The New York Times*. http://www.nytimes.com/2013/04/01/health/more-diagnoses-of-hyperactivity-causing-concern.html?pagewanted=all&_r=0.

Scourfield, J., Van den Bree, M., Martin, N., & McGuffin, P. (2004). Conduct problems in children and adolescents: A twin study. *Archives of General Psychiatry*, *61*, 489–496.

Scull, A. (2010). Left brain, right brain: One brain, two brains. *Brain*, *133*(10), 3153–3156.

Sebastiani, P., et al. (2010). Genetic signatures of exceptional longevity in humans. *Science Express*. doi:1/10.1126/science.1190532

Seeman, T. E., et al. (2011). Histories of social engagement and adult cognition: Midlife in the U.S. study. *The Journals of Gerontology, Series B*, *66B* (Suppl. 1), i141–i152.

Segrin, C., Powell, H. L., Givertz, M., & Brackin, A. (2003). Symptoms of depression, relational quality, and loneliness in dating relationships. *Personal Relationships*, *10*(1), 25–36.

Seidah, A., & Bouffard, T. (2007). Being proud of oneself as a person or being proud of one's physical appearance: What matters for feeling well in adolescence? *Social Behavior and Personality*, *35*(2), 255–268.

Seiler, C. B., Jones, K. E., Shera, D., & Armstrong, C. L. (2011). Brain region white matter associations with visual selective attention. *Brain Imaging and Behavior*, *5*(4), 262–273.

Selingo, J. J. (2016, April 10). College and the next big thing—Life. *The New York Times, Education*, 12–15.

Selman, R. L. (1976). Social-cognitive understanding. In T. Lickona (Ed.), *Moral development and behavior: Theory, research, and social issues*. New York, NY: Holt, Rinehart & Winston.

Selman, R. L. (1980). *The growth of interpersonal understanding: Developmental and clinical analysis*. New York, NY: Academic Press.

Selman, R. L., & Dray, A. J. (2006). Risk and prevention. In K. A. Renninger, I. E. Sigel, W. Damon, & R. M. Lerner (Eds.), *Handbook of child psychology* (6th ed.), *Vol. 4: Child psychology in practice* (pp. 378–419). Hoboken, NJ: Wiley.

Sexton, S. A. (2008). The influence of social support systems on the degree of PTSD symptoms in the elderly. *Dissertation Abstracts International: Section B: The Sciences and Engineering*, *68*(7-B), 2008, 4846.

Shafto, M. A., Burke, D. M., Stamatakis, E. A., Tam, P. P., & Tyler, L. K. (2007). On the tip-of-the-tongue: Neural correlates of increased word-finding failures in normal aging. *Journal of Cognitive Neuroscience*, *19*(12), 2060–2070.

Shamay-Tsoory, S. G. (2011). The neural bases for empathy. *The Neuroscientist*, *17*(1), 18–24.

Shatz, K. H. (2006). The widow who wasn't a bride. *Dissertation Abstracts International Section A: Humanities and Social Sciences*, *67*(2-A), 739.

Shaw, B. A., Liang, J., & Krause, N. (2010). Age and race differences in the trajectories of self-esteem. *Psychology and Aging*, *25*(1), 84–94.

Shaywitz, B. A., Lyon, G. R., & Shaywitz, S. E. (2006a). The role of functional magnetic resonance imaging in understanding reading and dyslexia. *Developmental Neuropsychology*, *30*(1), 613–632.

Shaywitz, S. E. (1998). Dyslexia. *New England Journal of Medicine*, *338*, 307–312.

Shaywitz, S. E., Mody, M., & Shaywitz, B. A. (2006b). Neural mechanisms in dyslexia. *Current Directions in Psychological Science*, *15*(6), 278–281.

Shear, K., Jin, R., Ruscio, A. M., Walters, E. E., & Kessler, R. C. (2006). Prevalence and correlates of estimated DSM-IV child and adult separation anxiety disorder in the National Comorbidity Survey Replication. *American Journal of Psychiatry 163*, 1074–1083.

Sherwin-White, S. (2006). The social toddler: Promoting positive behaviour. *Infant Observation*, *9*(1), 95–97.

Shin, H. B., & Bruno, R. (2003, October). *Language use and English speaking ability: 2000*. Washington, DC: U.S. Bureau of the Census.

Shiota, M. N., & Levenson, R. W. (2007). Birds of a feather don't always fly farthest. *Psychology and Aging*, *22*(4), 666–675.

Shirk, S., Burwell, R., & Harter, S. (2003). Strategies to modify low self-esteem in adolescents. In M. A. Reinecke et al. (Eds.), *Cognitive therapy with children and adolescents: A casebook for clinical practice* (2nd ed., pp. 189–213). New York, NY: Guilford.

Shneidman, E. S. (2008). *A commonsense book of death: Reflections at ninety of a lifelong thanatologist*. Latham, MD: Rowman & Littlefield.

Shoupe, D. (2016). Choosing the right contraceptive. In D. Shoupe, & D. R. Mishell, Jr. (Eds.). *The handbook of contraception* (pp. 17–41). Switzerland: Springer International Publishing.

Shroff, H., et al. (2006) Features associated with excessive exercise in women with eating disorders. *International Journal of Eating Disorders*, *39*(6), 454–461.

Shultz, K. S., & Adams, G. A. (Eds.). (2007). *Aging and work in the 21st century*. New York: Lawrence Erlbaum Associates.

Siegel, L. S. (1992). Infant motor, cognitive, and language behaviors as predictors of achievement at school age. In C. Rovee-Collier & L. P. Lipsitt (Eds.), *Advances in infancy research* (Vol. 7) (pp. 227–237). Norwood, NJ: Ablex.

Siegler, R., et al. (2016). Die fruhe kindheit–Sehen, denken und tun. In S. Pauen (Ed.). *Entwicklungspsychologie im kindes-und jugendalter* (pp. 155–196). Berlin Heidelberg: Springer-Verlag Berlin Heidelberg.

Siegler, R. S., & Alibali, M. W. (2005). *Children's thinking* (4th ed.). Upper Saddle River, NJ: Prentice Hall.

Siegrist, J., Von Dem Knesebeck, O., & Pollack, C. E. (2004). Social productivity and well-being of older people. *Social Theory & Health*, *2*(1), 1–17.

Signorello, L. B., & McLaughlin, J. K. (2004). Maternal caffeine consumption and spontaneous abortion: A review of the epidemiologic evidence. *Epidemiology*, *15*(2), 229–239.

Silk, T. J., & Wood, A. G. (2011). Lessons about neurodevelopment from anatomical magnetic resonance imaging. *Journal of Developmental Behavioral Pediatrics*, *32*(2), 158–168.

Silverberg, J. I., & Silverberg, N. B. (2014). Epidemiology and extracutaneous comorbidities of severe acne in adolescence: A U.S. population-based study. *British Journal of Dermatology*, *170*(5), 1136–1142.

Simion, F., Cassia, V. M., Turati, C., & Valenza, E. (2001). The origins of face perception: Specific versus nonspecific mechanisms. *Infant and Child Development*, *10*(1–2), 59–65.

Simonelli, A., Vizziello, G. F., Bighin, M., De Palo, F., & Petech, E. (2007). Transition to triadic relationships between parenthood and dyadic adjustment. *Età Evolutiva*, *86*, 92–99.

Simonton, D. K. (2007). Creative life cycles in literature: Poets versus novelists or conceptualists versus experimentalists? *Psychology of Aesthetics, Creativity, and the Arts*, *1*(3), 133–139.

Simpkins, S. D., Fredricks, J. A., Davis-Kean, P. E., & Eccles, J. S. (2006). Healthy mind, healthy habits: The influence of activity involvement in middle childhood. In A. C. Huston & M. N. Ripke (Eds.), *Developmental contexts in middle childhood: Bridges to adolescence and adulthood. Cambridge studies in social and emotional development* (pp. 283–302). New York, NY: Cambridge University Press.

Simpson, J. L., Bailey, L. B., Pietrzik, K., Shane, B., & Holzgreve. (2011). Micronutrients and women of reproductive potential: Required dietary intake and consequences of dietary deficiency or excess. Part II—Vitamin D, Vitamin A, iron, zinc, iodine, essential fatty acids. *Journal of Maternal–Fetal and Neonatal Medicine*, *24*(1), 1–24.

Sims, C. S., Drasgow, F., & Fitzgerald, L. F. (2005). The effects of sexual harassment on turnover in the military. *Journal of Applied Psychology*, *90*(6), 1141–1152.

Sims, T., Hogan, C. L., & Carstensen, L. L. (2015). Selectivity as an emotion regulation strategy: Lessons from older adults. *Current Opinion in Psychology*, *3*, 80–84.

Singh, L., Nestor, S., Parikh, C., & Yull, A. (2009). Influences of infant-directed speech on early word recognition. *Infancy*, *14*(6), 654–666.

Skeels, H. M. (1966). *Adult status of children with contrasting early life experiences: A follow-up study*. Monographs of the Society for Research in Child Development, 31(3, ser. 105).

Skinner, B. F. (1957). *Verbal behavior*. New York, NY: Appleton.

Skoczenski, A. M. (2002). Limitations on visual sensitivity during infancy: Contrast sensitivity, vernier acuity, and orientation processing. In J. W. Fagen & H. Hayne (Eds.), *Progress in infancy research* (Vol. 2). Mahwah, NJ: Erlbaum.

Skorikov, V. B., & Vondracek, F. W. (2011). Occupational identity. In S. J. Schwartz et al. (Eds.), *Handbook of identity theory and research* (Part 1, pp. 693–714). New York, NY: Springer.

Slater, A., & Tiggeman, M. (2010). Body image and disordered eating in adolescent girls and boys: A test of objectification theory. *Sex Roles*, *63*(1–2), 42–49.

Slater, A., et al. (2010). Visual perception. In J. G. Bremner & T. D. Wachs (Eds.), *The Wiley-Blackwell handbook of infant development* (2nd ed., Vol. 1, pp. 40–80). Oxford, UK: Wiley-Blackwell. doi:10.1002/9781444327564.ch2

Slaughter, V. (2011). Development of social cognition. In D. Skuse, H. Bruce, L. Dowdney, & D. Mrazek (Eds.), *Child psychology and psychiatry: Frameworks for practice* (2nd ed., pp. 51–55). Hoboken, NJ: Wiley.

Slaughter, V., & Griffiths, M. (2007). Death understanding and fear of death in young children. *Clinical Child Psychology and Psychiatry*, *12*(4), 525–535.

Slavin, R. E. (2012). *Educational psychology: Theory and practice* (10th ed.). Upper Saddle River, NJ: Pearson.

Slobin, D. I. (2001). Form/function relations: How do children find out what they are? In M. Tomasello & E. Bates (Eds.), *Language development: The essential readings* (pp. 267–290). Malden, MA: Blackwell.

Smetana, J. G. (2011). *Adolescents, families, and social development*. Chichester, West Sussex, UK: Wiley-Blackwell.

Smetana, J. G., Jambon, M., & Ball, C. (2013). The social domain approach to children's moral and social judgments. In M. Killen, & J. G. Smetana (Eds.). *Handbook of moral development*, 2nd ed. (pp. 23–45). New York: Psychology Press.

Smiley, P. A., & Johnson, R. S. (2006). Self-referring terms, event transitivity and development of self. *Cognitive Development*, *21*(3), 266–284.

Smith, N. A., & Trainor, L. J. (2008). Infant-directed speech is modulated by infant feedback. *Infancy*, *13*(4), 410–420.

Smith, P. J., et al. (2010). Aerobic exercise and neurocognitive performance: A meta-analytic review of randomized controlled trials. *Psychosomatic Medicine*, *72*(3), 239–252.

Smith, R. L., & Rose, A. J. (2011). The "cost of caring" in youths' friendships: Considering associations among social perspective taking, co-rumination, and empathetic distress. *Developmental Psychology*, *47*(6), 1792–1803.

Smith, A. R., Chein, J., & Steinberg, L. (2014). Peers increase adolescent risk taking even when the probabilities of negative outcomes are known. *Developmental Psychology*, *50*(5), 1564–1568.

Snarey, J. R. (1994). Cross-cultural universality of social-moral development: A critical review of Kohlbergian research. In B. Puka (Ed.), *New research in moral development* (pp. 268–298). New York, NY: Garland.

Snarey, J., & Samuelson, P. L. (2014). Lawrence Kohlberg's revolutionary ideas: Moral education in the cognitive-developmental tradition. In L. Nucci, T. Krettenauer, & D. Narvaez. *Handbook of moral and character education* (pp. 61–83). New York: Routledge.

Snegovskikh, V. V., et al. (2011). Surfactant protein-A (SP-A) selectively inhibits prostaglandin F2a (PGF2a) production in term decidua: Implications for the onset of labor. *The Journal of Clinical Endocrinology & Metabolism*, *96*,(4), E624-E632.

Sneider, J. T., et al. (2015). Sex differences in spatial navigation and perception in human adolescents and emerging adults. *Behavioural Processes*, *111*, 42–50.

Snow, C. (2006). Cross-cutting themes and future research directions. In D. August & T. Shanahan (Eds.), *Developing literacy in second-language learners: Report of the National Literacy Panel on Language-Minority Children and Youth* (pp. 631–651). Mahwah, NJ: Erlbaum.

Snyder, H. M., & Sickmund, M. (2006). *Juvenile offenders and victims: 2006 national report*. Washington, DC: U.S. Department of Justice, Office of Justice Programs, Office of Juvenile Justice and Delinquency Prevention.

Snyder, J., et al. (2011). The impact of brief teacher training in classroom management and child behavior in at-risk preschool settings: Mediators and treatment utility. *Journal of Applied Developmental Psychology*, *32*(6), 336–345.

Sobel, D. M., & Legare, C. H. (2014). Causal learning in children. *Wiley Interdisciplinary Reviews: Cognitive Science*, *5*(4), 423–427.

Soliz, J. (2007). Communicative predictors of a shared family identity: Comparison of grandchildren's perceptions of family-of-origin grandparents and step-grandparents. *Journal of Family Communication*, *7*(3), 177–194.

Solmeyer, A. R., & Feinberg, M. E. (2011). Mother and father adjustment during early parenthood: The roles of infant temperament and coparenting relationship quality. *Infant Behavior and Development*, *34*(4), 504–514.

Son, J., & Wilson, J. (2011). Generativity and volunteering. *Sociological Forum*, *26*(3), 644–667.

Sonnentag, S. (2003). Recovery, work engagement, and proactive behavior. *Journal of Applied Psychology*, *88*, 518–528.

Sontag, L. W., & Richards, T. W. (1938). *Studies in fetal behavior: Fetal heart rate as a behavioral indicator. Child Development Monographs*, *3*(4).

Soons, J. P. M., & Liefbroer. (2008). Together is better? Effects of relationship status and resources on young adults' well-being. *Journal of Social and Personal Relationships*, *25*(4), 603–624.

Sorce, J., Emde, R. N., Campos, J. J., Klinnert, M. D. (2000). Maternal emotional signaling: Its effect on the visual cliff behavior of 1-year-olds. In D. Muir & A. Slater, (Eds.), *Infant development: The essential readings. Essential readings in developmental psychology* (pp. 282–292). Malden, MA: Blackwell.

Sousa, C., et al. (2011). Longitudinal study of the effects of child abuse and children's exposure to domestic violence, parent-child attachments, and antisocial behavior in adolescence. *Journal of Interpersonal Violence*, *26*(1), 111–136.

Soussignan, R., & Schaal, B. (2005). Emotional processes in human newborns: a functionalist perspective. In J. Nadel & D. Muir (Eds.), *Emotional development: Recent research advances* (pp. 127–159). New York, NY: Oxford University Press.

South, S. J., Haynie, D. L., & Bose, S. (2007). Student mobility and school dropout. *Social Science Research*, *36*(1), 68–94.

Spelke, E. S., & Owsley, C. (1979). Intermodal exploration and knowledge in infancy. *Infant Behavior and Development*, *2*, 13–27.

Spittle, A. J., et al. (2010). Preventive care at home for very preterm infants improves infant and caregiver outcomes at 2 years. *Pediatrics*, *126*, e171–e178.

Spitz, R. A. (1965). *The first year of life: A psychoanalytic study of normal and deviant object relations*. New York, NY: International Universities Press.

Spitzer, R. L., Gibbon, M., Skodol, A. E., Williams, J. B. W., & First, M. B. (2002). *DSM–IV–TR casebook*. Washington, D.C.: American Psychiatric Press.

Sprecher, S., & Fehr, B. (2011). Dispositional attachment and relationship-specific attachment as predictors of compassionate love for a partner. *Journal of Social and Personal Relationships*, *28*(4), 558–574.

Sprecher, S., Sullivan, Q., & Hatfield, E., (1994). Mate selection preferences: Gender differences examined in a national sample. *Journal of Personality and Social Psychology*, *66*(6), 1074–1080.

Sprecher, S., Wenzel, A., & Harvey, J. (Eds.). (2008). *Handbook of relationship initiation*. New York, NY: Psychology Press.

Sroufe, L. A. (1998). Cited in S. Blakeslee (1998, August 4), Re-evaluating significance of baby's bond with mother, *New York Times*, pp. F1, F2.

Staff, J., Mortimer, J. T., & Uggen, C. (2004). Work and leisure in adolescence. In Lerner, R. M., & Steinberg, L. (Eds.), *Handbook of adolescent psychology* (2nd ed., pp. 429–450). Hoboken, NJ: Wiley.

Stagnitti, K., Unsworth, C., & Rodger, S. (2000). Development of an assessment to identify play behaviours that discriminate between the play of typical preschoolers and preschoolers with pre-academic problems. *Canadian Journal of Occupational Therapy*, *67*(5), 291–303.

Stahmer, A. C., Ingersoll, B., & Koegel, R. L. (2004). Inclusive programming for toddlers autism spectrum disorders: Outcomes from the Children's Toddler School. *Journal of Positive Behavior Interventions*, *6*(2), 67–82.

Stams, G. J. M., Juffer, F., & IJzendoorn, M. H. van (2002). Maternal sensitivity, infant attachment, and temperament in early childhood predict adjustment in middle childhood: The case of adopted children and their biologically unrelated parents. *Developmental Psychology*, *38*(5), 806–821.

Stanford, J. N., & McCabe, M. P. (2005). Sociocultural influences on adolescent boys' body image and body change strategies. *Body Image*, *2*(2), 105–113.

Stauffacher, K., & DeHart, G. B. (2006). Crossing social contexts: Relational aggression between siblings and friends during early and middle childhood. *Journal of Applied Developmental Psychology*, *27*(3), 228–240.

Ste. Croix, M. (2007). Advances in paediatric strength assessment: Changing our perspective on strength assessment. *Journal of Sports Science and Medicine*, *6*, 292–304.

Stearns, V., Beebe, K. L., Iyengar, M., & Dube, E. (2003). Paroxetine controlled release in the treatment of menopausal hot flashes. *Journal of the American Medical Association*, *289*, 2827–2834.

Steele, H. (2005a). Editorial. *Attachment & Human Development*, *7*(4), 345.

Steele, H. (2005b). Editorial: Romance, marriage, adolescent motherhood, leaving for college, plus shyness and attachment in the preschool years. *Attachment & Human Development*, *7*(2), 103–104.

Stegenga, B. T., et al. (2011). Recent life events pose greatest risk for onset of major depressive disorder during midlife. *Journal of Affective Disorders*. *136*(3), 505–513.

Sternberg, R. J. (2015). Multiple intelligences in the new age of thinking. In S. Goldstein, D. Princiotta, & J. A. Naglieri (Eds.). *Handbook of intelligence: Evolutionary theory, historical perspective, and current concepts* (pp. 229–241). New York: Springer Science + Business Media.

Stemberger, J. P. (2004). Phonological priming and irregular past. *Journal of Memory and Language*, *50*(1), 82–95.

Sternberg, R. J. (2006a). A duplex theory of love. In R. J. Sternberg, & K. Weis (Eds.), *The new psychology of love* (pp. 184–199). New Haven, CT: Yale University Press.

Sternberg, R. J. (2006b). The nature of creativity. *Creativity Research Journal*, *18*(1), 87–98.

Sternberg, R. J., & Kaufman, S. J. (Eds.). (2011). *The Cambridge handbook of intelligence*. New York, NY: Cambridge University Press.

Sternberg, Robert J. (1986, April). A triangular theory of love. *Psychological Review*, *93*(2), 119–135.

Stevens, B., et al. (2005). Consistent management of repeated procedural pain with sucrose in preterm neonates: Is it effective and safe for repeated use over time? *Clinical Journal of Pain*, *21*(6), 543–548.

Stewart, A. J., Ostrove, J. M., & Helson, R. (2001). Middle aging in women: Patterns of personality change from the 30s to the 50s. *Journal of Adult Development*, *8*, 23–37.

Stewart, J. Y., & Armet, E. (2000, April 3). Aging in America: Retirees reinvent the concept. *Los Angeles Times online*. Retrieved from http://articles.latimes.com/2000/apr/03/news/mn-15453

Stillbirth Collaborative Research Network Writing Group. (2011). *The Journal of the American Medical Association*, *306*(22), 2469–2479.

Stipek, D., & Hakuta, K. (2007). Strategies to ensure that no child starts from behind. In J. L. Aber et al. (Eds.), *Child development and social policy: Knowledge for action, APA Decade of Behavior volumes* (pp. 129–145). Washington, DC: American Psychological Association.

Stipek, D., Recchia, S., & McClintic, S. (1992). *Self-evaluation in young children*. Monographs of the Society for Research in Child Development, 57(1, ser. 226).

Stores, G., & Wiggs, L. (Eds.). (2001). *Sleep disturbance in children and adolescents with disorders of development: Its significance and management*. New York, NY: Cambridge University Press.

Strassberg, D. S., & Holty, S. (2003). An experimental study of women's Internet personal ads. *Archives of Sexual Behavior*, *32*(3), 253–260.

Stratton, T. D., et al. (2005). Does students' exposure to gender discrimination and sexual harassment in medical school affect specialty choice and residency program selection? *Academic Medicine*, *80*(4), 400–408.

Strayer, J., & Roberts, W. (2004). Children's anger, emotional expressiveness, and empathy: Relations with parents' empathy, emotional expressiveness, and parenting practices. *Social Development*, *13*(2), 229–254.

Strazdins, L., et al. (2011). Could better jobs improve mental health? A prospective study of change in work conditions and mental health in mid-aged adults. *Journal of Epidemiology and Community Health*, *65*, 529–534.

Streri, A. (2002). Hand preference in 4-month-old infants: Global or local processing of objects in the haptic mode. *Current Psychology Letters: Behaviour, Brain and Cognition*, *7*, 39–50.

Striegel-Moore, R. H., et al. (2003). Eating disorders in White and Black women. *American Journal of Psychiatry*, *160*(7), 1326–1331.

Stright, A. D., Neitzel, C., Sears, K. G., & Hoke-Sinex, L. (2001). Instruction begins in the home: Relations between parental instruction and children's self-regulation in the classroom. *Journal of Educational Psychology*, *93*(3), 456–466.

Strock, M. (2004). *Autism spectrum disorders (pervasive developmental disorders)*. NIH Publication NIH-04-5511. Bethesda, MD: National Institute of Mental Health, National Institutes of Health, U.S. Department of Health and Human Services. Retrieved from http://www.nimh.nih.gov/publicat/autism.cfm

Strohner, H., & Nelson, K. E. (1974). The young child's development of sentence comprehension: Influence of event probability, nonverbal context, syntactic form, and strategies. *Child Development*, *45*, 567–576.

Strunk, T., Simmer, K., & Burgner, D. (2012). Prematurity and mortality in childhood and early adulthood. *Journal of the American Medical Association*, *307*(1). doi:10.1001/jama.2011.1952

Strutt, G. F., Anderson, D. R., & Well, A. D. (1975). A developmental study of the effects of irrelevant information on speeded classification. *Journal of Experimental Child Psychology*, *20*, 127–135.

Stupica, B., Sherman, L. J., & Cassidy, J. (2011). Newborn irritability moderates the association between infant attachment security and toddler exploration and sociability. *Child Development*, *82*(5), 1381–1389.

Sturdee, D. W., et al. (2011). Updated IMS recommendations on postmenopausal hormone therapy and preventive strategies for midlife health. *Climacteric*, *14*, 302–320.

Sukhodolsky, D. G., Golub, A., Stone, E. C., & Orban, L. (2005). Dismantling anger control training for children: A randomized pilot study of social problem-solving versus social skills training components. *Behavior Therapy*, *36*, 15–23.

Sullivan, R., et al. (2011). Infant bonding and attachment to the caregiver: Insights from basic and clinical science. *Clinics in Perinatology*, *38*(4), 643–655.

Sulloway, F. J. (2007). Birth order and intelligence. *Science*, *316*(5832), 1711–1712.

Suomi, S. J., Harlow, H. F., & McKinney, W. T. (1972). Monkey psychiatrists. *American Journal of Psychiatry*, *128*, 927–932.

Supple, A. J., & Small, S. A. (2006). The influence of parental support, knowledge, and authoritative parenting on Hmong and European American adolescent development. *Journal of Family Issues*, *27*(9), 1214–1232.

Sutin, A. R., Costa, P. T., Wethington, E., & Eaton, W. (2010). *Psychology and Aging*, *25*(3), 524–533.

Suzuki, L. A., Short, E. L., & Lee, C. S. (2011). Racial and ethnic group differences in intelligence in the United States. In R. J. Sternberg & S. J. Kaufman (Eds.), *The Cambridge handbook of intelligence* (pp. 273–292). New York, NY: Cambridge University Press.

Swaggart, K. A., Pavlicev, M., & Muglia, L. J. (2015). Genomics of preterm birth. *Coldspring Harbor Perspectives in Medicine*, DOI:10.1101/cshperspect.a023127

Syed, E. C. J., Sharott, A., Moll, C. K., Engel, A. K., Kral, A. (2010). Effect of sensory stimulation in rat barrel cortex, dorsolateral striatum and on corticostriatal functional connectivity. *European Journal of Neuroscience*, *33*(3), 461–470.

Sylva, K., et al. (2007). Curricular quality and day-to-day learning activities in pre-school. *International Journal of Early Years Education*, *15*(1), 49–65.

Szaflarski, J. P., et al. (2006). A longitudinal functional magnetic resonance imaging study of language development in children 5 to 11 years old. *Annals of Neurology*, *59*(5), 796–807.

Szanto, K., et al. (2012). Social emotion recognition, social functioning, and attempted suicide in late-life depression. *The American Journal of Geriatric Psychiatry*, *20*(3), 257–265.

T

Takamura, T., Nishitani, S., Doi, Hirokazu, & Shinohara, K. (2016). Possible neural correlates of young child attachment to mother in 4 to 5 year olds. *Acta Medica Nagasakiensia*, *60*(2), 45–51.

Talbot, L. A., Morrell, C. H., Fleg, J. L., & Metter, E. J. (2007). Changes in leisure time physical activity and risk of all-cause mortality in men and women. *Preventive Medicine: An International Journal Devoted to Practice and Theory*, *45*(2–3), 169–176.

Tallandini, M. A., & Valentini, P. (1991). Symbolic prototypes in children's drawings of schools. *Journal of Genetic Psychology*, *152*, 179–190.

Tamis-LeMonda, C. S., Cristofaro, T. N., Rodriguez, E. T., & Bornstein, M. H. (2006). Early language development: Social influences in the first years of life. In L. Balter & C. S. Tamis-LeMonda (Eds.), *Child psychology: A handbook of contemporary issues* (2nd ed., pp. 79–108). New York, NY: Psychology Press.

Tanaka, H., et al. (2011). The brain basis of the phonological deficit in dyslexia is independent of IQ. *Psychological Science*, *22*(11), 1442–1451.

Tanner, J. L., & Arnett, J. J. (2011). Presenting "emerging adulthood": What makes it developmentally distinctive? In J. J. Arnett, M. Kloep, L. B. Hendry, & J. L. Tanner (Eds.), *Debating emerging adulthood: Stage or process?* (pp. 13–30). New York, NY: Oxford University Press.

Tanner, J. M. (1989). *Fetus into man: Physical growth from conception to maturity*. Cambridge, MA: Harvard University Press.

Tanner, J. M. (1991a). Adolescent growth spurt, I. In R. M. Lerner, A. C. Petersen, & J. Brooks-Gunn (Eds.), *Encyclopedia of adolescence*. New York, NY: Garland.

Tapper, K., & Boulton, M. J. (2004). Sex differences in levels of physical, verbal, and indirect aggression amongst primary school children and their associations with beliefs about aggression. *Aggressive Behavior*, *30*(2), 123–145.

Tasker, F., & Granville, J. (2011). Children's views of family relationships in lesbian-led families. *Journal of GLBT Studies*, *7*(1–2), 182–199.

Taylor, M. (1999). *Imaginary companions and the children who create them*. London: Oxford University Press.

Taylor, M. F., Clark, N., & Newton, E. (2008). Counselling Australian baby boomers. *British Journal of Guidance & Counselling*, *36*(2), 189–204.

Taylor, M., & Hort, B. (1990). Can children be trained in making the distinction between appearance and reality? *Cognitive Devlopment 5*, 89–99.

Taylor, M., Gonzalez, M., & Porter, R. (2011). Pathways to inflammation: Acne pathophysiology. *European Journal of Dermatology*, *21*(3), 323–333.

Teen Pregnancy Prevention and U.S. Students. (2011). Centers for Disease Control and Prevention. Retrieved from http://www.cdc.gov/healthyyouth/yrbs/pdf/us_pregnancy_combo.pdf

Tehrani, J. A., & Mednick, S. A. (2000). Genetic factors and criminal behavior. *Federal Probation*, *64*(2), 24–27.

Tenenbaum, H. R., et al. (2010). "It's a boy because he's painting a picture." Age differences in children's conventional and unconventional gender schemas. *British Journal of Psychology*, *101*(1), 137–154.

Tennant, P. W. G., Rankin, J., & Bell, R. (2011). Impact of maternal obesity on stillbirth and infant death: Absolute risk and temporal trends. *Journal of Epidemiology and Community Health*, 65. doi:10.1136/jech.2011.142976a.79

Teunissen, H. A., et al. (2011). The interaction between pubertal timing and peer popularity for boys and girls. *Journal of Abnormal Child Psychology*, 39(3), 413–423.

Tharner, A., et al. (2012). Maternal lifetime history of depression and depressive symptoms in the prenatal and early postnatal period do not predict infant–mother attachment quality in a large, population-based Dutch cohort study. *Attachment & Human Development*, *14*(1), 63–81.

Theiss, J. A., & Leustek, J. (2016). Marital conflict. The Wiley Blackwell encyclopedia of family studies, DOI:10.1002/9781119085621.wbefs378.

Thomas, A., & Chess, S. (1989). Temperament and personality. In G. A. Kohnstamm, J. E. Bates, & M. K. Rothbart (Eds.), *Temperament in childhood* (pp. 249–261). Chichester, UK: Wiley.

Thompson, A. M., Baxter-Jones, A. D. G., Mirwald, R. L., & Bailey, D. A. (2003). Comparison of physical activity in male and female children: Does maturation matter? *Medicine and Science in Sports and Exercise*. *35*(10), 1684–1690.

Thompson, R. A., & Meyer, S. (2007). Socialization of emotion regulation in the family. In J. J. Gross (Ed.), *Handbook of emotion regulation* (pp. 249–268). New York, NY: Guilford.

Thompson, R. B., Foster, B. J., & Kapinos, J. R. (2016). Poverty, affluence, and the Socratic method: Parents' questions versus statements within collaborative problem-solving. *Language & Communication*, *47*, 23–29.

Thompson, W. K., et al. (2011). Association between higher levels of sexual function, activity, and satisfaction and selfrated successful aging in older postmenopausal women. *Journal of the American Geriatrics Society*, *59*(8), 1503–1508.

Thurstone, L. L. (1938). *Primary mental abilities*. Psychometric Monographs, 1.

Timmerman, L. M. (2006). Family care versus day care: Effects on children. In B. M. Gayle et al. (Eds.), *Classroom communication and instructional processes: Advances through meta-analysis* (pp. 245–260). Mahwah, NJ: Erlbaum.

Tisdale, S. (2011). Linking social environments with the well-being of adolescents in dual-earner and single working parent families. *Youth & Society*. *44*(1), 118–140.

Tobbell, J. (2003). Students' experiences of the transition from primary to secondary school. *Educational and Child Psychology*, *20*(4), 4–14.

Tobin, D. D., et al. (2010). The intrapsychics of gender: A model of self-socialization. *Psychological Review*, *117*(2), 601–622.

Togsverd, M., et al. (2008). Association of a dopamine beta-hydroxylase gene variant with depression in elderly women possibly reflecting noradrenergic dysfunction. *Journal of Affective Disorders*, *106*(1–2), 169–172.

Ton, M., & Hansen, J. C. (2001). Using a person-environment fit framework to predict satisfaction and motivation in work and marital roles. *Journal of Career Assessment*, *9*, 315–331.

Torpy, J. M., Lynm, C., & Golub, R. M. (2011). Local anesthesia. *Journal of the American Medical Association*, *306*(12), 1395.

Towse, J. (2003). Lifespan development of human memory. *Quarterly Journal of Experimental Psychology: Human Experimental Psychology*, *56*A(7), 1244–1246.

Towse, J., & Cowan, N. (2005). Working memory and its relevance for cognitive development. In W. Schneider, R. Schumann-Hengsteler, & B. Sodian (Eds.), *Young children's cognitive development: Interrelationships among executive functioning, working memory, verbal ability, and theory of mind* (pp. 9–37). Mahwah, NJ: Erlbaum.

Troop-Gordon, W., & Ranney, J. D. (2014). Popularity among same-sex and cross-sex peers: A process-oriented examination of links to aggressive behaviors and depressive affect. *Developmental Psychology*, *50*(6), 1721–1733.

Turkheimer, E. (1991). Individual and group differences in adoption studies of IQ. *Psychological Bulletin*, *110*, 392–405.

Twenge, J. M. (2010). A review of empirical evidence on generational differences in work attitudes. *Journal of Business and Psychology*, *25*(2), 201–210.

Twist, M. (2005). Review of Relationship therapy with same-sex couples. *Journal of Marital & Family Therapy*, *31*(4), 413–417.

Tzuriel, D., & Egozi, G. (2010). Gender differences in spatial ability of young children: The effects of training and processing strategies. *Child Development*, *81*(5), 1417–1430.

U

U.S. Bureau of the Census. (2007). *Statistical abstract of the United States* (127th ed.). Washington, DC: U.S. Government Printing Office.

U.S. Bureau of the Census. (2008). Statistical abstract of the United States (128th ed.). Washington, DC: U.S. Government Printing Office.

U.S. Bureau of the Census. (2010). 2010 Census data. Retrieved from http://2010.census.gov/2010census/data

U.S. Bureau of the Census. (2010). America's families and living arrangements for 2010. (Current Population Reports, Table UC3). Retrieved from www.census.gov/population/www/socdemo/hh-fam/cps2010.html

U.S. Bureau of the Census. (2011). Families and living arrangements. Retrieved from http://www.census.gov/population/www/socdemo/hh-fam.html

U.S. Bureau of the Census. (2012). *Languages spoken at home*. Retrieved from http://www.census.gov/compendia/statab/2012/tables/12s0053.pdf

U.S. Bureau of the Census. (2015). America's families and living arrangements: 2015. http://www.census.gov/hhes/families/.

U.S. Bureau of Census. (2015). QuickFacts, United States. http://www.census.gov/quickfacts/table/PST045215/00

U.S. Census Bureau. (2015, November 3). Census Bureau reports at least 350 languages spoken in U.S. homes. Release Number: CB15–185. https://www.census.gov/newsroom/press-releases/2015/cb15-185.html.

U.S. Department of Education, National Center for Education Statistics. (2005). *Projections of Education Statistics to 2014* (23rd ed.), Table 11. Retrieved from http://nces.ed.gov/pubs2005/2005074.pdf

U.S. Department of Education. (2015). Characteristics of postsecondary students. http://nces.ed.gov/programs/coe/indicator_csb.asp.

U.S. Department of Health & Human Services. (2011). Childhood obesity. Retrieved from http://aspe.hhs.gov/health/reports/child_obesity/

U.S. Department of Health and Human Services. (2010). *Child maltreatment 2010*. Administration for Children and Families—Administration on Children, Youth and Families, Children's Bureau. Retrieved from http://www.acf.hhs.gov/programs/cb/stats_research/index.htm#can

U.S. Department of Justice. (2011). *Criminal victimization, 2010*. National Crime Victimization Survey. Retrieved from http://bjs.ojp.usdoj.gov/content/pub/pdf/cv10.pdf

Ulijaszek, S. J. (2010). Variation in human growth patterns due to environmental factors. In M. P. Muehlenbein (Ed.), *Human evolutionary biology* (pp. 396–404). New York, NY: Cambridge University Press.

Umana-Taylor, A. J. (2016). Ethnic-racial identity: Conceptualization, development, and youth adjustment. (pp. 305–328). In L. Balter & C. S. Tamis-LeMonda (Eds.). *Child psychology: A handbook of contemporary issues*, 3rd ed. New York: Routledge.

UNAIDS. (2010). *UNAIDS report on the global AIDS epidemic 2010*. Retrieved from http://www.slideshare.net/UNAIDS/unaids-report-on-the-global-aids-epidemic-2010

Underwood, M. K. (2011). Aggression. In M. K. Underwood & L. H. Rosen (Eds.), *Social development: Relationships in infancy, childhood, and adolescence* (pp. 207–234). New York, NY: Guilford.

Underwood, M. K., & Rosen, L. H. (Eds.). (2011). *Social development: Relationships in infancy, childhood, and adolescence* (pp. 289–315). New York, NY: Guilford.

UNICEF. (2006). The state of the world's children: 2007. New York, NY: United Nations.

UNICEF. (2012). HIV and infant feeding. Retrieved from http://www.unicef.org/programme/breastfeeding/hiv.htm

U.S. Department of Agriculture. (2011). Food and Nutrition Information Center. Retrieved from http://fnic.nal.usda.gov

U.S. Department of Health and Human Services. (2010). Breastfeeding. Womenshealth. gov. Retrieved from http://www.womenshealth.gov/Breastfeeding/index.cfm?page5home

Upton, K. J., & Sullivan, R. M. (2010). Defining age limits of the sensitive period for attachment learning in rat pups. *Developmental Psychobiology*, *52*(5), 453–464.

Urbina, S. (2011). Tests of intelligence. In R. J. Sternberg & S. J. Kaufman (Eds.), *The Cambridge handbook of intelligence* (pp. 20–38). New York, NY: Cambridge University Press.

USDHHS. (2005, January 10). *Bone health and osteoporosis: A report of the Surgeon General*. Retrieved from http://www.surgeongeneral.gov/library/bonehealth

Uylings, H. B. M. (2006). Development of the human cortex and the concept of "critical" or "sensitive" periods. *Language Learning*, *56*(Suppl. 1), 59–90.

V

Valenzuela, S., Park, N., & Kee, K. F. (2009). Is there social capital in a social network site? Facebook use and college students' life satisfaction, trust, and participation. *Journal of Computer-Mediated Communication*, *14*(4), 875–901.

Valkenburg, P. M., Sumter, S. R., & Peter, J. (2011). Gender differences in online and offline self-disclosure in preadolescence and adolescence. *British Journal of Developmental Psychology*, *29*(2), 253–269.

Vallance, A., & Garralda, E. (2011). Anxiety disorders in children and adolescents. In D. Skuse, H. Bruce, L. Dowdney, & D. Mrazek (Eds.), *Child psychology and psychiatry: Frameworks for practice* (2nd ed., pp. 169–174). Hoboken, NJ: Wiley.

van den Akker, A. L., Dekovic, M., & Prinzie, P. (2010). Transitioning to adolescence: How changes in child personality and overreactive parenting predict adolescent adjustment problems. *Development and Psychopathology*, *22*, 151–163.

Van Hiel, A., Mervielde, I., & De Fruyt, F. (2006). Stagnation and generativity: Structure, validity, and differential relationships with adaptive and maladaptive personality. *Journal of Personality*, *74*(2), 543–574.

van IJzendoorn, M. H., & Hubbard, F. O. A. (2000). Are infant crying and maternal responsiveness during the first year related to infant–mother attachment at 15 months? *Attachment and Human Development*, *2*(3), 371–391.

van Solinge, H., & Henkens, K. (2005). Couples' adjustment to retirement: A Multi-Actor Panel Study. *Journals of Gerontology: Series B: Psychological Sciences and Social Sciences*, *60*B(1), S11–S20.

van Straaten, I., Engels, R. C. M. E., Finkenauer, C., & Holland, R. W. (2009). Meeting your match: How attractiveness similarity affects approach behavior in mixed-sex dyads. *Personality and Social Psychology Bulletin*, *35*(6), 685–697.

Van Zalk, M. H. W., et al. (2010). It takes three: Selection, influence, and de-selection processes of depression in adolescent friendship networks. *Developmental Psychology*, *46*(4), 927–938.

Vander Ven, T., & Cullen, F. T. (2004). The impact of maternal employment on serious youth crime: Does the quality of working conditions matter? *Crime & Delinquency*, *50*(2), 272–291.

Vares, T., Potts, A., Gavey, N., & Grace, V. M. (2007). Reconceptualizing cultural narratives of mature women's sexuality in the Viagra era. *Journal of Aging Studies*, *21*(2), 153–164.

Velarde, M. C., et al. (2012). Mitochondrial oxidative stress caused by Sod2 deficiency promotes cellular senescence and aging phenotypes in the skin. *Aging*, *4*(1), 1–10.

Veldman, S. L. C., Palmer, K. K., Okely, A. D., & Robinson, L. E. (2016). Promoting ball skills in preschool-age girls. *Journal of Science and Medicine in Sport*, DOI:10.1016/j.jsams.2016.04.009

Vélez, C. E., Wolchik, S. A., Tein, J-Y., & Sandler, I. (2011). Protecting children from the consequences of divorce: A longitudinal study of the effects of parenting on children's coping processes. *Child Development*, *82*(1), 244–257.

Vellutino, F. R., Fletcher, J. M., Snowling, M. J., & Scanlon, D. M. (2004). Specific reading disability (dyslexia): What have we learned in the past four decades? *Journal of Child Psychology and Psychiatry*, *45*(1), 2–40.

Verlohren, S., Stepan, H., & Dechend, R. (2012). Angiogenic growth factors in the diagnosis and prediction of pre-eclampsia. *Clinical Science*, *122*, 43–52.

Verloop, J., van Leeuwen, F., Helmerhorst, T., van Boven, H., & Rookus, M. (2010). Cancer risk in DES daughters. *Cancer Causes Control*, *21*(7), 999–1007.

Vermeulen-Smit, E., Verdurmen, J. E. E., Engels, R. C. M. E., & Vollebergh, W. A. M. (2015). The role of general parenting and cannabis-specific practices in adolescent cannabis and other illicit drug use. *Drug and Alcohol Dependence*, *147*, 222–228.

Vigod, S. N., Villegas, L., Dennis, C-L., & Ross, L. E. (2010). Prevalence and risk factors for postpartum depression among women with preterm and low-birth-weight infants: A systematic review. *BJOG: An International Journal of Obstetrics & Gynaecology*, *117*(5), 540–550.

Vina, J., et al. (2011). Antioxidant pathways in Alzheimer's disease: Possibilities of intervention. *Current Pharmaceutical Design*, *17*(35), 3861–3864.

Virji-Babul, N., Kerns, K., Zhou, E., Kapur, A., & Shiffrar, M. (2006). Perceptual-motor deficits in children with Down syndrome: Implications for intervention. *Down Syndrome: Research & Practice*, *10*(2), 74–82.

Vitiello, B. (Ed.). (2006). Guest editorial: Selective serotonin reuptake inhibitors (SSRIs) in children and adolescents. *Journal of Child and Adolescent Psychopharmacology*, *16*(1–2), 7–9.

Volkova, A., Trehub, S. E., & Schellenberg, E. G. (2006). Infants' memory for musical performances. *Developmental Science*, *9*(6), 583–589.

Volterra, M. C., Caselli, O., Capirci, E., & Pizzuto, E. (2004). Gesture and the emergence and development of language. In M. Tomasello & D. I. Slobin (Eds.), *Beyond nature–nurture* (pp. 3–40). Mahwah, NJ. Erlbaum.

Volz, J. (2000). Successful aging: The second 50. *Monitor on Psychology*, *31*(1), online.

Von Gontard, A., et al. (2011). Psychological and psychiatric issues in urinary and fecal incontinence. *The Journal of Urology*, *185*(4), 1432–1437.

Vorauer, J. D., Cameron, J. J., Holmes, J. G., & Pearce, D. G. (2003). Invisible overtures: Fears of rejection and the signal amplification bias. *Journal of Personality & Social Psychology*, *84*(4), 793–812.

Vukman, K. B. (2005). Developmental differences in metacognition and their connections with cognitive development in adulthood. *Journal of Adult Development*, *12*(4), 211–221.

Vuoksimaa, E., Koskenvuo, M., Rose, R. J., & Kaprio, J. (2009). Origins of handedness: A nationwide study of 30,161 adults. *Neuropsychologia*, *47*(5), 1294–1301.

Vygotsky, L. S. (1962). *Thought and language*. Cambridge, MA: MIT Press.

W

Wade, T. D., Wilksch, S. M., Paxton, S. J., Byrne, S. M., & Austin, S. B. (2015). How perfectionism and ineffectiveness influence growth of eating disorder risk in young adolescent girls. *Behaviour Research and Therapy*, *66*, 56–63.

Wald, J., & Losen, D. J. (2007). Out of sight: The journey through the school-to-prison pipeline. In S. Books (Ed.), *Invisible children in the society and its schools* (3rd ed., pp. 23–37). Mahwah, NJ: Erlbaum.

Walker, A. (2010). Breast milk as the gold standard for protective nutrients. *Journal of Pediatrics*, *156*(Suppl. 2), S3-S7.

Walker, D. W. (Ed.). (2016). *Prenatal and postnatal determinants of development. Neuromethods, Vol. 109*. New York: Springer Science + Business Media.

Walker, L. J., & Frimer, J. A. (2011). The science of moral development. In M. K. Underwood & L. H. Rosen (Eds.), *Social development* (pp. 235–263). New York, NY: Guilford.

Walkup, J. T., et al. (2001). Fluvoxamine for the treatment of anxiety disorders in children and adolescents. *New England Journal of Medicine*, *344*(17), 1279–1285.

Wall, A. (2007). Review of Integrating gender and culture in parenting. *The Family Journal*, *15*(2), 196–197.

Wall, G., & Arnold, S. (2007). How involved is involved fathering? *Gender & Society*, *21*(4), 508–527.

Wallerstein, J., Lewis, J., Blakeslee, S., Hetherington, E. M., & Kelly, J. (2005). Issue 17: Is divorce always detrimental to children? In R. P. Halgin (Ed.), *Taking sides: Clashing views on controversial issues in abnormal psychology* (3rd ed., pp. 298–321). New York: McGraw-Hill.

Walter, J. L., & LaFreniere, P. J. (2000). A naturalistic study of affective expression, social competence, and sociometric status in preschoolers. *Early Education and Development*, *11*(1), 109–122.

Wang, F., Cox, M. J.,, Mills-Koonce, R., & Snyder, P. (2015). Parental behaviors and beliefs, child temperament, and attachment disorganization. *Family Relations*, *64*(2), 191–204.

Wang, L. (2005). Correlations between self-esteem and life satisfaction in elementary school students. *Chinese Mental Health Journal*, *19*(11), 745–749.

Wang, M., Henkens, K., & van Solinge, H. (2011). Retirement adjustment: A review of theoretical and empirical advancements. *American Psychologist*, *66*(3), 204–213.

Wang, Y. et al. (2016). Development of tract-specific white matter pathways during early reading development in at-risk children and typical controls. *Cerebral Cortex*, DOI: 10.1093/cercor/bhw095

Washington Post-Kaiser Family Foundation poll. (2015). Washington Post-Kaiser Family Foundation Survey of College Students on Sexual Assault. http://apps.washingtonpost.com/g/page/national/washington-post-kaiser-family-foundation-survey-of-college-students-on-sexual-assault/1726/.

Wass, R., Harland, T., & Mercer, A. (2011). Scaffolding critical thinking in the zone of critical development. *Higher Education Research & Development*, *30*(3), 317–328.

Watson, H. J., et al. (2011). Mediators between perfectionism and eating disorder psychopathology: Shape and weight overvaluation and conditional goal-setting. *International Journal of Eating Disorders*, *44*(2), 142–149.

Waxman, S. R., & Lidz, J. L. (2006). Early word learning. In D. Kuhn, R. S. Siegler, W. Damon, & R. M. Lerner (Eds.), *Handbook of child psychology* (6th ed.), *Vol. 2: Cognition, perception, and language* (pp. 299–335). Hoboken, NJ: Wiley.

Weckerly, J., Wulfeck, B., & Reilly, J. (2004). The development of morphosyntactic ability in atypical populations: The acquisition of tag questions in children with early focal lesions and children with specific-language impairment. *Brain and Language*, *88*(2), 190–201.

Weinberger, D. R., & Levitt, P. (2011). Neurodevelopmental origins of schizophrenia. In D. R. Weinberger & P. J. Harrison (Eds.), *Schizophrenia* (pp. 393–412). Hoboken, NJ: Wiley.

Weinshenker, M. N. (2006). Adolescents' expectations about mothers' employment: Life course patterns and parental influence. *Sex Roles*, *54*(11–12), 845–857.

Weizmann-Henelius, G., et al. (2011). Gender-specific risk factors for intimate partner homicide. *Journal of Interpersonal Violence*. doi:10.1177/0886260511425793.

Welch, M. G., et al. (2016). Depression and anxiety symptoms of mothers of preterm infants are decreased at 4 months corrected age with Family Nurture Intervention in the NICU. *Archive of Women's Mental Health*, *19*(1), 51–61.

Weller, E. B., & Weller, R. A. (1991). Mood disorders. In M. Lewis (Ed.), *Child and adolescent psychiatry: A comprehensive textbook* (pp. 646–664). Baltimore, MD: Williams & Wilkins.

Wellman, H. M., Cross, D., & Bartsch, K. (1986). *Infant search and object permanence: A meta-analysis of the A-not-B error*. Monographs of the Society for Research in Child Development, 5(3, ser. 214).

Wellman, H. M., Fang, F., Liu, D., Zhu, L., & Liu, G. (2006). Scaling of theory-of-mind understandings in Chinese children. *Psychological Science*, *17*(12), 1075–1081.

Wenger, G. C., & Jerrome, D. (1999). Change and stability in confidant relationships. *Journal of Aging Studies*, *13*(3), 269–294.

Wennergren, A.-C., & Rönnerman, K. (2006). The relation between tools used in action research and the zone of proximal development. *Educational Action Research*, *14*(4), 547–568.

Wentworth, N., Benson, J. B., & Haith, M. M. (2000). The development of infants' reaches for stationary and moving targets. *Child Development*, *71*(3), 576–611.

Wentzel, K. R., Barry, C. M., & Caldwell, K. A. (2004). Friendships in middle school: Influences on motivation and school adjustment. *Journal of Educational Psychology*, *96*(2), 195–203.

Wentzel, K. R. (2014). Prosocial behavior and peer relations in adolescence. In L. M. Padilla-Walker, & G. Carlo (Eds.). *Prosocial development: A multidimensional approach* (pp. 178–200). New York: Oxford University Press.

Wentzel, K. R., & Muenks, K. (2016). Peer influence on students' motivation, academic achievement, and social behavior. In K. R. Wentzel, & G. B. Ramani (Eds.). *Handbook of social influences in school contexts: Social-emotional, motivation, and cognitive outcomes* (pp. 13–30). New York: Routledge.

Wentzel, K. R., & Ramani, G. B. (2016). *Handbook of social influences in school contexts*. New York: Routledge.

Werker, J. F. (1989). Becoming a native listener. *American Scientist, 77*, 54–59.

Werker, J. F., et al. (2007). Infant-directed speech supports phonetic category learning in English and Japanese. *Cognition, 103*(1), 147–162.

Werker, J. F., & Hensch, T. K. (2015). Critical periods in speech perception: New directions. *Annual Review of Psychology, 66*, 173–196.

Werner, E. E. (1988). A cross-cultural perspective on infancy. *Journal of Cross-Cultural Psychology, 19*, 96–113.

Werner, L. A., & Bernstein, I. L. (2001). Development of the auditory, gustatory, olfactory, and somatosensory systems. In E. B. Goldstein (Ed.), Blackwell handbook of perception., *Handbook of experimental psychology series* (pp. 669–708). Boston, MA: Blackwell.

White, A. (2016). Public health in sporting settings: A gender perspective. In D. Conrad, & A. White. (Eds.). *Sports-based health interventions* (pp. 61–76). New York: Springer Science + Business Media.

Whitehouse, E. M. (2006). Poverty. In G. G. Bear & K. M. Minke (Eds.), *Children's needs III: Development, prevention, and intervention* (pp. 835–845). Washington, DC: National Association of School Psychologists.

Wickwire Jr., E. M., Roland, M. M. S., Elkin, T. D., & Schumacher, J. A. (2008). Sleep disorders. In M. Hersen & D. Michel (Eds.), *Handbook of psychological assessment, case conceptualization, and treatment, Vol 2: Children and adolescents* (pp. 622–651). Hoboken, NJ: Wiley.

Wierzalis, E. A., Barret, B., Pope, M., & Rankins, M. (2006). Gay men and aging: Sex and intimacy. In D. Kimmel, T. Rose, & S. David (Eds.), *Lesbian, gay, bisexual, and transgender aging: Research and clinical perspectives* (pp. 91–109). New York, NY: Columbia University Press.

Wijdicks, E. F. M. (2011). The transatlantic divide over brain death determination and the debate. *Brain, 135*(4), 1321–1331.

Wilcox, W. B., & Marquardt, E. (Eds.). (2011). *The state of our unions: Marriage in America 2011*. Institute for American Values. Charlottesville, VA: University of Virginia: The National Marriage Project.

Willetts, M. C. (2006). Union quality comparisons between long-term heterosexual cohabitation and legal marriage. *Journal of Family Issues, 27*(1), 110–127.

Williams, M., El-Sheikh, A., Mallick, A., & Gardosi, J. (2011). Maternal age and risk of stillbirth. *Archives of Disease in Childhood Fetal & Neonatal Edition, 96*(Suppl. 1). doi:10.1136/adc.2011.300160.6.

Willis, J. O., Dumont, R., & Kaufman, A. S. (2011). Factor-analytic models of intelligence. In R. J. Sternberg & S. J. Kaufman (Eds.), *The Cambridge handbook of intelligence* (pp. 39–57). New York, NY: Cambridge University Press.

Willis, S. L., & Schaie, K. W. (2006). Cognitive functioning in the baby boomers: Longitudinal and cohort effects. In S. K. Whitbourne & S. L. Willis (Eds.), *The baby boomers grow up: Contemporary perspectives on midlife* (pp. 205–234). Mahwah, NJ: Lawrence Erlbaum Associates Publishers.

Wilson, E. O. (2004). *On Human Nature*. Cambridge, MA: Harvard University Press.

Wilson, G. T., Wilfley, D. E., Agras, W. S., & Bryson, S. W. (2010). Psychological treatments of binge eating disorder. *Archives of General Psychiatry, 67*(1), 94–101.

Wilson, P. (2004). A preliminary investigation of an early intervention program: Examining the intervention effectiveness of the Bracken Concept Development Program and the Bracken Basic Concept Scale–Revised with Head Start students. *Psychology in the Schools, 41*(3), 301–311.

Winograd, R. P., & Sher, K. J. (2015). *Binge drinking and alcohol misuse: Advances in psychotherapy*. Boston: The Hogrefe Group Publishing.

Witherington, D. C., Campos, J. J., Harriger, J. A., Bryan, C. and Margett, T. E. (2010) Emotion and its development in infancy. In J. G. Bremner & T. D. Wachs (Eds.), *The Wiley-Blackwell handbook of infant development* (2nd ed., Vol. 1, pp. 568–591). Oxford, UK: Wiley-Blackwell. doi:10.1002/9781444327564.ch19

Wolfe, D. A. (2011). Violence against women and children. In J. W. White, M. P. Koss, & A. E. Kazdin (Eds.), *Violence against women and children, Vol. 1: Mapping the terrain* (pp. 31–53). Washington, DC: American Psychological Association.

Wolfenden, L. E., & Holt, N. L. (2005). Talent development in elite junior tennis: Perceptions of players, parents, and coaches. *Journal of Applied Sport Psychology, 17*(2), 108–126.

Wong, F. Y., et al. (2011). Cerebral oxygenation is depressed during sleep in healthy term infants when they sleep prone. *Pediatrics, 127*(3), e558–e565.

Woolfolk, A. (2013). *Educational psychology* (12th ed.). Upper Saddle River, NJ: Pearson.

Worell, J., & Goodheart, C. D. (Eds.). (2006). *Handbook of girls' and women's psychological health: Gender and well-being across the lifespan*. New York, NY: Oxford University Press.

World Health Organization. (2015). HIV/AIDS. http://www.who.int/features/qa/71/en/.

Worrell, F. C. (1997). An exploratory factor analysis of Harter's Self-Perception Profile for Adolescents with academically talented students. *Educational and Psychological Measurement, 57*(6), 1016–1024.

Worrell, F. C. (2015) Culture as race/ethnicity. In K. C. McLean, & M. Syed (Eds.). *The Oxford handbook of identity development* (pp. 249–268). New York: Oxford University Press.

Worthman, C. M. (2010). The ecology of human development: Evolving models for cultural psychology. *Journal of Cross-Cultural Psychology, 41*(4), 563–577.

Wright, C., & Birks, E. (2000). Risk factors for failure to thrive: A population-based survey. *Child: Care, Health, and Development, 26*(1), 5–16.

Wright, D. W., & Young, R. (1998). The effects of family structure and maternal employment on the development of gender-related attitudes among men and women. *Journal of Family Issues, 19*(3), 300–314.

Wubbels, T., et al. (2016). Teacher-student relationships and student achievement. In K. R. Wentzel, & G. B. Ramani (Eds.). *Handbook of social influences in school contexts: Social-emotional, motivation, and cognitive outcomes* (pp. 127–142). New York: Routledge.

Wu, T., et al. (2015). Conduct disorder. In G. M. Kapalka (Ed.). *Treating disruptive disorders*. New York: Routledge.

Xie, H. L., Yan, B., Signe M., Hutchins, B. C., & Cairns, B. D. (2006). What makes a girl (or a boy) popular (or unpopular)? African American Children's perceptions and developmental differences. *Developmental Psychology, 42*(4), 599–612.

Xue, Y. F., Moran, G., Pederson, D. R., & Bento, S. (2010, March). *The continuity of attachment development from infancy to toddlerhood: The role of maternal sensitivity*. International Conference on Infant Studies, Baltimore, MD.

Yaros, A., Lochman, J. E., Rosenbaum, J., & Jimenez-Camargo, L. A. (2014). Real-time hostile attribution measurement and aggression in children. *Aggressive Behavior, 40*(5), 409–420.

Yarrow, L. J., & Goodwin, M. S. (1973). The immediate impact of separation: Reactions of infants to a change in mother figures. In L. J. Stone, H. T. Smith, & L. B. Murphy (Eds.), *The competent infant: Research and commentary*. New York, NY: Basic Books.

Yarrow, L. J., Goodwin, M. S., Manheimer, H., & Milowe, I. D. (1971, March). *Infant experiences and cognitive and personality development at ten years*. Paper presented at the meeting of the American Orthopsychiatric Association, Washington, DC.

Yazzie, A. (2010). Visual-spatial thinking and academic achievement: A concurrent and predictive validity study. *Dissertation Abstracts International: Section A, Humanities and Social Sciences, 70*(8-A), 2897.

Yermolayeva, Y., & Rakison, D. H. (2014). Connectionist modeling of developmental changes in Infancy: Approaches, challenges, and contributions. *Psychological Bulletin*, *140*(1), 224–255.

Yonelinas, A. P. (2002). The nature of recollection and familiarity: A review of 30 years of research. *Journal of Memory and Language*, *46*, 441–517.

Yost, M. R., & Zurbriggen, E. L. (2006). Gender differences in the enactment of sociosexuality. *Journal of Sex Research*, *43*(2), 163–173.

You, D., Maeda, Y., & Bebeau, M. J. (2011). Gender differences in moral sensitivity: A meta-analysis. *Ethics & Behavior*, *21*(4), 263–282.

Z

Zahran, S. (2011). Type of parental socialization across cultures. *Psychology*, *2*(5) 526–534.

Zaidi, A. U., & Shuraydi, M. (2002). Perceptions of arranged marriages by young Pakistani Muslim women living in a Western society. *Journal of Comparative Family Studies*, *33*(4), 495–514.

Zajonc, R. B. (2001). The family dynamics of intellectual development. *American Psychologist*, *56*(6/7), 490–496.

Zarbatany, L., McDougall, P., & Hymel, S. (2000). Gender-differentiated experience in the peer culture: Links to intimacy in preadolescence. *Social Development*, *9*(1), 62–79.

Zeanah, C. H., Berlin, L. J. & Boris, N. W. (2011). Practitioner review: Clinical applications of attachment theory and research for infants and young children. *The Journal of Child Psychology & Psychiatry*, *52*(8), 819–833.

Zeifman, D. M. (2004). Acoustic features of infant crying related to intended caregiving intervention. *Infant and Child Development*, *13*(2), 111–122.

Zeintl, M., Kliegel, M., & Hofer, S. M. (2007). The role of processing resources in age-related prospective and retrospective memory within old age. *Psychology and Aging*, *22*(4), 826–834.

Zelazo, P. D., & Müller, U. (2010) Executive function in typical and atypical development. In U. Goswami (Ed.), *The Wiley-Blackwell handbook of childhood cognitive development* (2nd ed., pp. 574–603). Oxford, UK: Wiley-Blackwell. doi:10.1002/9781444325485.ch22

Zhang, Y., et al. (2016). Quantitative susceptibility mapping and R2 measured changes during white matter lesion development in multiple sclerosis: Myelin breakdown, myelin debris degradation and removal, and iron accumulation. *American Journal of Neuroradiology*, DOI:10.3174/ajnr.A4825.

Zheng, L., Lippa, R. A., & Zheng, Y. (2011). Sex and sexual orientation differences in personality in China. *Archives of Sexual Behavior*, *40*(3), 533–541.

Zhiqi, L., Kun, Y., & Zhiwu, H. (2010). Tympanometry in infants with middle ear effusion having been identified using spiral computerized tomography. *American Journal of Otolaryngology*, *31*(2), 96–103.

Zhu, Q.-X., et al. (2011). Turning point of age for semen quality. *Fertility and Sterility*, *96*(3), 572–576.

Ziegler, M. G., Elayan, H., Milic, M., Sun, P., & Gharaibeh, M. (2011). Epinephrine and the metabolic syndrome. *Current Hypertension Reports*, *14*(1), 1–7.

Zilioli, S., Ponzi, D., Henry, A., & Maestripieri, D. (2014). Testosterone, cortisol, and empathy: Evidence for the dual-hormone hypothesis. *Adaptive Human Behavior and Physiology*, DOI:10.1007/s40750-014-0017-x.

Zimmerman, B. J. (2000). Self-efficacy: An essential motive to learn. *Contemporary Educational Psychology*, *25*(1), 82–91.

Zimmerman, F. J., & Bell, J. F. (2010). Association of television content type and obesity in children. *American Journal of Public Health*, *100*(2), 334–340.

Zimmermann, P., Maier, M. A., Winter, M., & Grossmann, K. E. (2001). Attachment and adolescents' emotion regulation during a joint problem-solving task with a friend. *International Journal of Behavioral Development*, *25*(4), 331–343.

Ziv, I., & Hermel, O. (2011). Birth order effects on the separation process in young adults: An evolutionary and dynamic approach. *The American Journal of Psychology*, *124*(3), 261–273.

Zosuls, K.M., et al. (2011). "It's not that we hate you": Understanding children's gender attitudes and expectancies about peer relationships. *British Journal of Developmental Psychology*, 29, 288–304.

Zosuls, K. M., Miller, C. F., Ruble, D. N., Martin, C. L., & Fabes, R. A. (2011). Gender development research in Sex Roles: Historic trends and future directions. *Sex Roles*, *64*(11–12), 826–842.

Zucker, A. N., Ostrove, J. M., & Stewart, A. J. (2002). College-educated women's personality development in adulthood: Perceptions and age differences. *Psychology and Aging*, *17*, 236–244.

Zuckerman, M. (2011). Personality science: Three approaches and their applications to the causes and treatment of depression. In M. Zuckerman (Ed.), *Three approaches and their applications to the causes and treatment of depression* (pp. 47–77). Washington, DC: American Psychological Association.

Zweigenhaft, R. L., & Von Ammon, J. (2000). Birth order and civil disobedience: A test of Sulloway's "born to rebel" hypothesis. *Journal of Social Psychology*, *140*(5), 624–627.

NAME INDEX

A

B

C

D

E

F

G

H

M

N

P

R

SUBJECT INDEX

Note: Italic page numbers indicate material in tables or figures

A

B

C

D

F

M

N

O

P

Q

R

S

T

U

V

W

Z

CHAPTER 1 LEARNING OUTCOMES / KEY TERMS

1-1 Relate the history of the study of human development. In centuries past, children often were viewed as innately evil, and discipline was harsh. The philosopher John Locke focused on the role of experience in development. Jean-Jacques Rousseau argued that children are good by nature, and if allowed to express their natural impulses, will develop into moral people. G. Stanley Hall founded child development as an academic discipline and brought scientific attention to focus on the period of adolescence. Alfred Binet developed the first standardized intelligence test. By the start of the 20th century, child development had emerged as a scientific field of study. Soon major theories about the developing child were proposed by theorists such as Arnold Gesell, Sigmund Freud, John B. Watson, and Jean Piaget.

Developmental psychology is the discipline that studies the physical, cognitive, social, and emotional development of humans. It focuses on the many influences on behavior, including the effects of the person's physical, social, and cultural environment and how these factors interact to influence the developments that occur over time. William Perry and Gisella Labouvie-Vief have studied the development of cognitive complexity from adolescence to late adulthood. K. Warner Schaie and others have studied trends in crystallized and fluid mental abilities throughout adulthood.

developmental psychology the discipline that studies the physical, cognitive, social, and emotional development of humans

life-span perspective perspective in which psychologists view human development as occurring throughout the individual's lifetime

1-2 Compare and contrast theories of human development. Psychoanalytic theory focuses on the roles of internal conflict. Sigmund Freud believed that children undergo five stages of psychosexual development. Erik Erikson focused on social relationships and included adulthood by extending Freud's five developmental stages to eight.

Learning theorists focus on how learning influences behavior. Behaviorists such as John B. Watson and B. F. Skinner stressed classical and operant conditioning. Social cognitive theorists, such as Albert Bandura, argue that much learning occurs by observation and that we choose whether to engage in learned behavior.

Jean Piaget's cognitive developmental theory hypothesizes that children's cognitive processes develop in an invariant series of stages, culminating with *formal operational* reasoning. Other cognitive theorists suggest that adults can experience *postformal* reasoning. Information-processing theory deals with the ways in which we encode information, manipulate it, place it in memory, and retrieve it.

The biological perspective refers to genetics and developments such as conception, health, gains in height and weight, puberty, and peak performance and decline in adulthood. Ethology involves instinctive behavior patterns. *Evolutionary psychology* is the branch of psychology that deals with the ways in which the history of human adaptation to the environment influences behavior and mental processes, with special focus on aggressive behavior and mating strategies.

Urie Bronfenbrenner's ecological theory explains development in terms of the *reciprocal interaction* between children and the settings in which development occurs. Lev Semenovich Vygotsky's sociocultural perspective has the key concepts of the *zone of proximal development (ZPD)* and *scaffolding*. The sociocultural perspective more broadly addresses the richness of diversity, as in the influences of ethnicity, gender, and socioeconomic status on development.

behaviorism Watson's view that science must study observable behavior only and investigate relationships between stimuli and responses

maturation the unfolding of genetically determined traits, structures, and functions

psychosexual development the process by which libidinal energy is expressed through different erogenous zones during different stages of development

stage theory a theory of development characterized by distinct periods of life

psychosocial development Erikson's theory, which emphasizes the importance of social relationships and conscious choice throughout eight stages of development

life crisis an internal conflict that attends each stage of psychosocial development

identity crisis according to Erikson, a period of inner conflict during which one examines one's values and makes decisions about one's life roles

classical conditioning a simple form of learning in which one stimulus comes to bring forth the response usually brought forth by a second stimulus by being paired repeatedly with the second stimulus

operant conditioning a simple form of learning in which an organism learns to engage in behavior that is reinforced

reinforcement the process of providing stimuli following responses that increase the frequency of the responses

positive reinforcer a reinforcer that, when applied, increases the frequency of a response

negative reinforcer a reinforcer that, when removed, increases the frequency of a response

extinction the cessation of a response that is performed in the absence of reinforcement

social cognitive theory a cognitively oriented learning theory that emphasizes observational learning

cognitive-developmental theory the stage theory that holds that the child's abilities to mentally represent the world and solve problems unfold as a result of the interaction of experience and the maturation of neurological structures

scheme an action pattern or mental structure that is involved in the acquisition and organization of knowledge

adaptation the interaction between the organism and the environment, consisting of assimilation and accommodation

assimilation the incorporation of new events or knowledge into existing schemes

accommodation the modification of existing schemes to permit the incorporation of new events or knowledge

equilibration the creation of an equilibrium, or balance, between assimilation and accommodation

ethology the study of behaviors that are specific to a species

(continues)

1 History, Theories, and Methods

(continued)

evolutionary psychology the branch of psychology that deals with the ways in which humans' historical adaptations to the environment influence behavior and mental processes, with special focus on aggressive behavior and mating strategies

fixed action pattern (FAP) a stereotyped pattern of behavior that is evoked by a "releasing stimulus"; an instinct

ecology the branch of biology that deals with the relationships between living organisms and their environment

ecological systems theory the view that explains child development in terms of the reciprocal influences between children and environmental settings

microsystem the immediate settings with which the child interacts, such as the home, the school, and peers

mesosystem the interlocking settings that influence the child, such as the interaction of the school and the larger community

exosystem community institutions and settings that indirectly influence the child, such as the school board and the parents' workplaces

macrosystem the basic institutions and ideologies that influence the child

chronosystem the environmental changes that occur over time and have an effect on the child

zone of proximal development (ZPD) Vygotsky's term for the situation in which a child carries out tasks with the help of someone who is more skilled

scaffolding Vygotsky's term for temporary cognitive structures or methods of solving problems that help the child as he or she learns to function independently

1-3 Enumerate key controversies in human development. The discussion about theories of development reveals that developmentalists can see things in very different ways. There are three major debates in the field.

nature the processes within an organism that guide it to develop according to its genetic code

nurture environmental factors that influence development

empirical based on observation and experimentation

1-4 Describe ways in which researchers study human development. Development is studied through gathering sound information and conducting research. Naturalistic observation is conducted in "the field"—the settings in which people develop. The case study is a carefully drawn account or biography of behavior. Correlational studies reveal relationships between variables but not cause and effect, as demonstrated in Figure 1.5. Experiments seek to determine cause and effect by exposing research participants to treatments and observing the results. Researchers have devised different strategies for comparing children of one age with children or adults of other ages. Longitudinal research studies the same people repeatedly over time. Cross-sectional research observes and compares people of different ages. A drawback to cross-sectional research is the cohort effect. Cross-sequential research combines the longitudinal and cross-sectional methods by breaking the span of the ideal longitudinal study down into convenient segments. Ethical standards require that researchers not use treatments that harm participants.

naturalistic-observation a scientific method in which organisms are observed in their natural environments

case study a carefully drawn biography of the life of an individual

standardized test a test in which an individual's score is compared to the scores of a group of similar individuals

correlation coefficient a number ranging from +1.00 to –1.00 that expresses the direction (positive or negative) and strength of the relationship between two variables

positive correlation a relationship between two variables in which one variable increases as the other increases

negative correlation a relationship between two variables in which one variable increases as the other decreases

experiment a method of scientific investigation that seeks to discover cause-and-effect relationships by introducing independent variables and observing their effects on dependent variables

hypothesis a proposition to be tested

independent variable a condition in a scientific study that is manipulated so that its effects can be observed

dependent variable a measure of an assumed effect of an independent variable

experimental group a group made up of subjects who receive a treatment in an experiment

control group a group made up of subjects in an experiment who do not receive the treatment but for whom all other conditions are comparable to those of subjects in the experimental group

longitudinal research the study of developmental processes by taking repeated measures of the same group of participants at various stages of development

cross-sectional research the study of developmental processes by taking measures of participants of different age groups at the same time

cohort effect similarities in behavior among a group of peers that stem from the fact that group members were born at the same time in history

cross-sequential research an approach that combines the longitudinal and cross-sectional methods by following individuals of different ages for abbreviated periods of time

time-lag the study of developmental processes by taking measures of participants of the same age group at different times

CHAPTER 2 LEARNING OUTCOMES / KEY TERMS

2-1 Describe the influences of heredity on development. Heredity is the biological transmission of traits from one generation to another. People normally have 46 strands of DNA called chromosomes, which are organized into 23 pairs (see Figure 2.3). Genes, which regulate the development of traits, are segments of chromosomes.

Sperm and ova are produced by meiosis and have 23 rather than 46 chromosomes. Monozygotic (MZ) or identical twins develop from a single fertilized ovum that splits in two. Dizygotic (DZ) or fraternal twins develop from two fertilized ova. Traits are determined by pairs of genes, either from "averaging" the genetic instructions, or by dominant genes. Carriers of a trait bear one dominant gene and one recessive gene for it.

Chromosomal abnormalities are more likely as parents age. Down syndrome is caused by an extra chromosome on the 21st pair. Sex-linked disorders include XYY males and single-X girls. Genetic disorders include phenylketonuria (PKU), Huntington's disease, sickle-cell anemia, Tay-Sachs disease, cystic fibrosis, and hemophilia. Prenatal blood tests, ultrasound, and amniocentesis can determine the presence of various genetic and chromosomal abnormalities.

FIG.2.3 THE 23 PAIRS OF HUMAN CHROMOSOMES

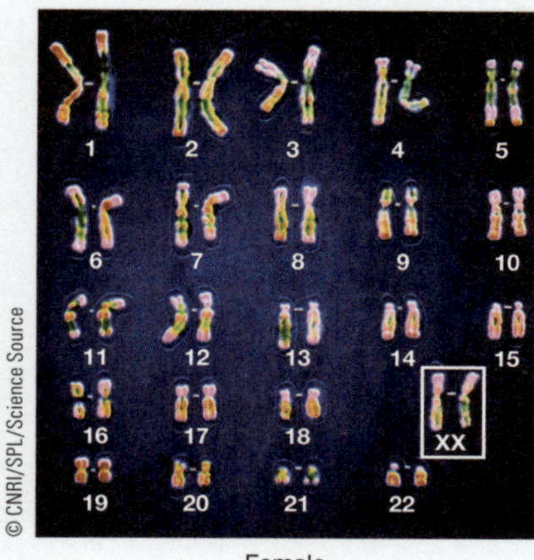

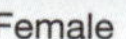

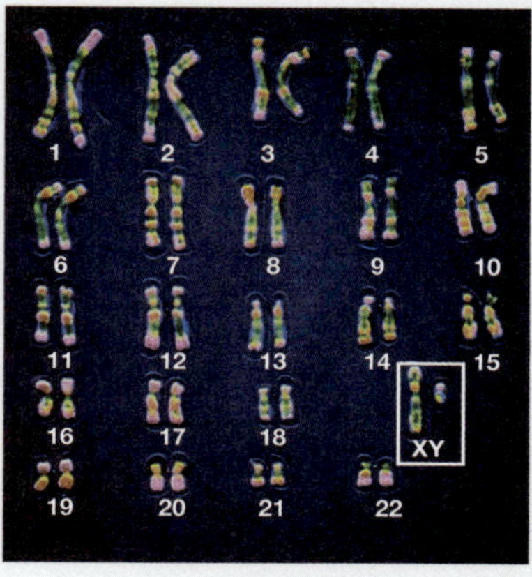

© CNRI/SPL/Science Source

People normally have 23 pairs of chromosomes. Females have two X chromosomes, whereas males have an X and a Y sex chromosome.

genetics the branch of biology that studies heredity

chromosomes rod-shaped structures composed of genes that are found within the nuclei of cells

gene the basic unit of heredity. Genes are composed of deoxyribonucleic acid (DNA)

polygenic resulting from many genes

deoxyribonucleic acid (DNA) genetic material that takes the form of a double helix composed of phosphates, sugars, and bases

mitosis the form of cell division in which each chromosome splits lengthwise to double in number. Half of each chromosome combines with chemicals to retake its original form and then moves to the new cell

mutation a sudden variation in a heritable characteristic, as by an accident that affects the composition of genes

meiosis the form of cell division in which each pair of chromosomes splits so that one member of each pair moves to the new cell. As a result, each new cell has 23 chromosomes

autosome a member of a pair of chromosomes (with the exception of sex chromosomes)

sex chromosome a chromosome in the shape of a Y (male) or X (female) that determines the anatomic sex of the child

monozygotic (MZ) twins twins that derive from a single zygote that has split into two; identical twins. Each MZ twin carries the same genetic code

dizygotic (DZ) twins twins that derive from two zygotes; fraternal twins

ovulation the releasing of an ovum from an ovary

allele a member of a pair of genes

homozygous having two identical alleles

heterozygous having two different alleles

dominant trait a trait that is expressed

recessive trait a trait that is not expressed when the gene or genes involved have been paired with dominant genes

carrier a person who carries and transmits characteristics but does not exhibit them

multifactorial problems problems that stem from the interaction of heredity and environmental factors

Down's syndrome a chromosomal abnormality characterized by intellectual disabilities and caused by an extra chromosome in the 21st pair

sex-linked chromosomal abnormalities abnormalities that are transmitted from generation to generation and carried by a sex chromosome

Klinefelter syndrome a chromosomal disorder found among males that is caused by an extra X sex chromosome and that is characterized by infertility and mild intellectual disabilities

testosterone a male sex hormone produced mainly by the testes

Turner syndrome a chromosomal disorder found among females that is caused by having a single X sex chromosome and is characterized by infertility

estrogen a female sex hormone produced mainly by the ovaries

phenylketonuria (PKU) a genetic abnormality in which phenylalanine builds up and causes intellectual disabilities

Huntington's disease (HD) a fatal genetic neurological disorder whose onset is in middle age

(continues)

(continued)

sickle-cell anemia a genetic disorder that decreases the blood's capacity to carry oxygen

Tay-Sachs disease a fatal genetic neurological disorder

cystic fibrosis a fatal genetic disorder in which mucus obstructs the lungs and pancreas

hemophilia a genetic disorder in which blood does not clot properly

sex-linked genetic abnormalities abnormalities resulting from genes that are found on the X sex chromosome. They are more likely to be shown by male offspring (who do not have an opposing gene from a second X chromosome) than by female offspring

muscular dystrophy a chronic disease characterized by a progressive wasting away of the muscles

genetic counselors health workers who compile information about a couple's genetic heritage to advise them as to whether their children might develop genetic abnormalities

prenatal before birth

amniocentesis a procedure for drawing and examining fetal cells sloughed off into amniotic fluid to determine the presence of various disorders

miscarriage the expulsion of an embryo or fetus before it can sustain life on its own, most often due to defective development

chorionic villus sampling (CVS) a method for the prenatal detection of genetic abnormalities that samples the membrane enveloping the amniotic sac and fetus

uterus the hollow organ within females in which the embryo and fetus develop

ultrasound sound waves too high in pitch to be sensed by the human ear

sonogram a procedure for using ultrasonic sound waves to create a picture of an embryo or fetus

alpha-fetoprotein (AFP) assay a blood test that assesses the mother's blood level of alpha-fetoprotein, a substance that is linked with fetal neural tube defects

2-2 **Describe the influences of the environment on development.** Our genotypes are the sets of traits that we inherit. But environmental conditions can vary their expression, resulting in our phenotypes. Researchers can study the heritability of a trait by observing its expression among relatives who differ in genetic closeness. Parents and children have a 50% overlap in genes, as do siblings, with the exception of monozygotic (MZ) twins, who have 100% overlap. MZ twins resemble each other more closely than dizygotic (DZ) twins on physical and psychological traits, even when reared apart. Expressed traits in adopted children that more closely resemble those of the natural parents are more likely to have a genetic basis.

genotype the genetic form or constitution of a person as determined by heredity

phenotype the actual form or constitution of a person as determined by heredity and environmental factors

autism a developmental disorder characterized by failure to relate to others, communication problems, intolerance of change, and ritualistic behavior

2-3 **Explain what happens in the process of conception.** Conception is the union of an ovum and a sperm cell and usually occurs in a fallopian tube (see Figure 2.7). More boys are conceived than girls, but they have a higher rate of miscarriage. Once a sperm cell has entered the ova, the chromosomes from the sperm cell line up across from the corresponding chromosomes in the egg cell. They form 23 new pairs with a unique set of genetic instructions.

The diagnosis of infertility usually is not applied until the couple has failed to conceive on their own for one year. A low sperm count—or lack of sperm—is the most common infertility problem in men. The most common problem in women is irregular ovulation or lack of ovulation; others include infections such as PID, endometriosis, and obstructions. Fertility drugs regulate ovulation. Other ways of conceiving include artificial insemination and in vitro fertilization (IVF). Preimplantation genetic diagnosis permits prenatal sex selection.

FIG.2.7 FEMALE REPRODUCTIVE ORGANS

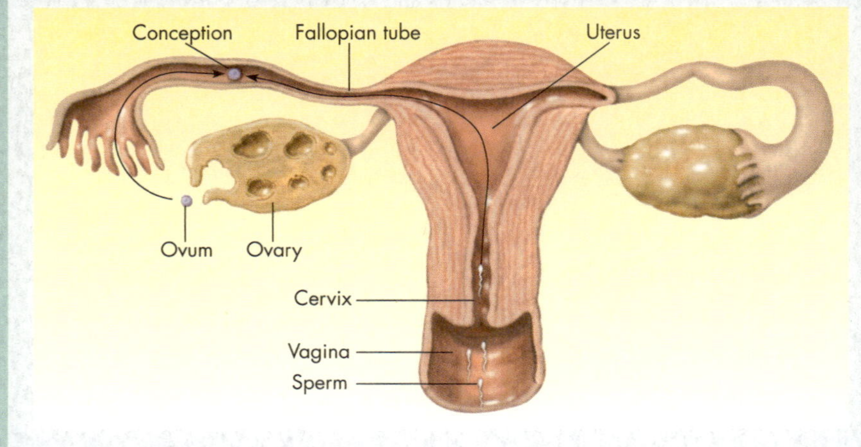

The ovaries release egg cells (ova), which find their ways into fallopian tubes—exactly how is not fully known. Fertilization normally takes place in a fallopian tube. The fertilized ovum begins to divide while it travels through the tube into the uterus, where it becomes implanted in the wall and grows to term.

CHAPTER 2 LEARNING OUTCOMES / KEY TERMS

conception the union of a sperm cell and an ovum that occurs when the chromosomes of each of these cells combine to form 23 new pairs

endometrium the inner lining of the uterus

motility self-propulsion

pelvic inflammatory disease (PID) an infection of the abdominal region that may have various causes and that may impair fertility

endometriosis inflammation of endometrial tissue sloughed off into the abdominal cavity rather than out of the body during menstruation; the condition is characterized by abdominal pain and sometimes infertility

artificial insemination injection of sperm into the uterus to fertilize an ovum

in vitro fertilization (IVF) fertilization of an ovum in a laboratory dish

donor IVF the transfer of a donor's ovum, fertilized in a laboratory dish, to the uterus of another woman

2-4 **Recount the major events of prenatal development.** During the germinal stage, the zygote divides repeatedly and travels through a fallopian tube to the uterus, where it implants. Before implantation, it is nourished by the yolk of the original egg cell. Once implanted in the uterine wall, it is nourished by the mother. The embryonic stage lasts from implantation until the eighth week of development, during which the major organ systems differentiate. Development follows cephalocaudal and proximodistal trends. The heart begins to beat during the fourth week. By the end of the second month, facial features are becoming distinct, teeth buds have formed, the kidneys are working, and the liver is producing red blood cells. Male sex hormones spur development of the male reproductive system. The embryo and fetus exchange nutrients and wastes with the mother through the placenta. Some disease organisms, such as those that cause syphilis and rubella, can pass through the placenta. Some drugs also pass through, including aspirin, narcotics, and alcohol.

The fetal stage is characterized by maturation of organs and gains in size. It lasts from the end of the embryonic stage until birth. The fetus begins to turn at the ninth or tenth week. It responds to sound waves by the 13th week of pregnancy. By the end of the second trimester, the fetus opens and shuts its eyes, sucks its thumb, and alternates between wakefulness and sleep. During the third trimester, it becomes increasingly capable of sustaining independent life.

FIG.2.9 A HUMAN EMBRYO AT 7 WEEKS

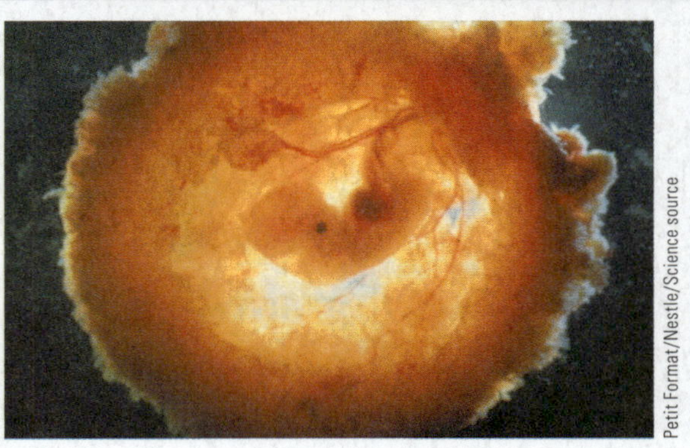

Petit Format/Nestle/Science source

By the time this photo was taken, the embryo's heart had already been beating for about a month. By another week, all the major organs systems will have formed, and the embryo will enter the fetal stage.

Maternal malnutrition is linked to low birth weight, prematurity, and cognitive and behavioral problems. Teratogens are most harmful during critical periods, when certain organs are developing. Women who contract rubella can bear children who suffer from deafness, mental retardation, heart disease, or cataracts. Syphilis can cause miscarriage or stillbirth. Toxemia is characterized by high blood pressure and is connected with preterm or small babies. In Rh incompatibility, the mother's antibodies cause brain damage or death. Environmental agents that can harm the embryo and fetus include thalidomide, tetracycline, DES, high doses of vitamins A and D, narcotics, marijuana, cocaine, alcohol (see Figure 2.11), cigarette smoke, heavy metals, PCBs, and radiation.

FIG.2.11 FETAL ALCOHOL SYNDROME (FAS)

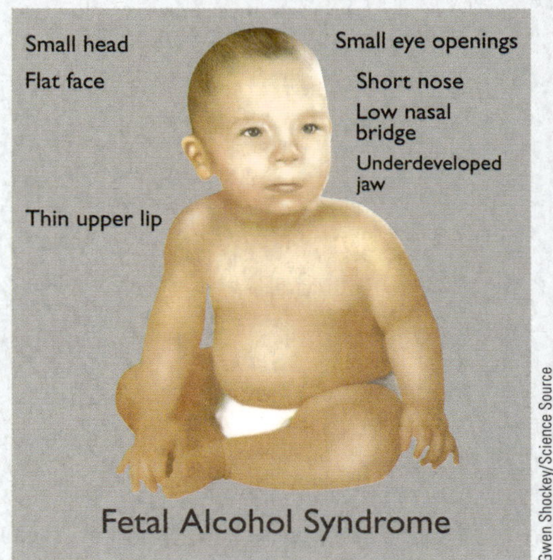

Gwen Shockey/Science Source

The children of many mothers who drank alcohol during pregnancy exhibit FAS. This syndrome is characterized by developmental lags and such facial features as an underdeveloped upper jaw, a flattened nose, and widely spaced eyes.

Teenage mothers have a higher incidence of infant mortality and children with low birth weight. Older parents run an increasing risk of chromosomal abnormalities and stillborn or preterm babies.

CHAPTER 2 LEARNING OUTCOMES / KEY TERMS

FIG.2.12 AUTISM RISK INCREASES WITH PATERNAL AGE

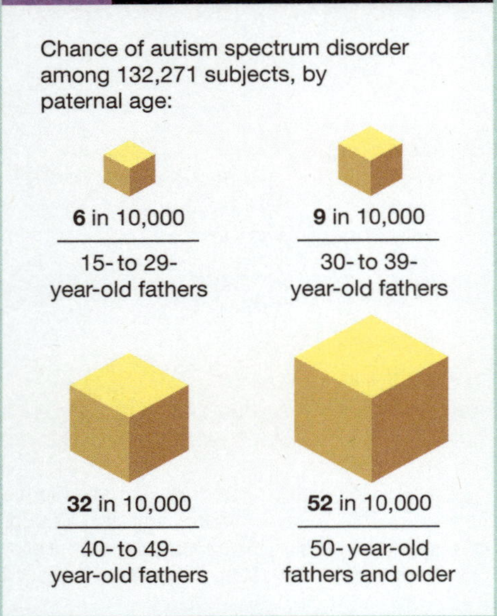

Chance of autism spectrum disorder among 132,271 subjects, by paternal age:

6 in 10,000	15- to 29-year-old fathers
9 in 10,000	30- to 39-year-old fathers
32 in 10,000	40- to 49-year-old fathers
52 in 10,000	50-year-old fathers and older

germinal stage the period of development between conception and the implantation of the embryo

blastocyst a stage within the germinal period of prenatal development in which the zygote has the form of a sphere of cells surrounding a cavity of fluid

embryonic disk the platelike inner part of the blastocyst that differentiates into the ectoderm, mesoderm, and endoderm of the embryo

trophoblast the outer part of the blastocyst from which the amniotic sac, placenta, and umbilical cord develop

umbilical cord a tube that connects the fetus to the placenta

placenta an organ connected to the uterine wall and to the fetus by the umbilical cord. The placenta serves as a relay station between mother and fetus for the exchange of nutrients and wastes

embryonic stage the stage of prenatal development that lasts from implantation through the eighth week of pregnancy; it is characterized by the development of the major organ systems

cephalocaudal from head to tail

proximodistal from the inner part (or axis) of the body outward

ectoderm the outermost cell layer of the newly formed embryo from which the skin and nervous system develop

neural tube a hollowed-out area in the blastocyst from which the nervous system develops

endoderm the inner layer of the embryo from which the lungs and digestive system develop

mesoderm the central layer of the embryo from which the bones and muscles develop

androgens male sex hormones

amniotic sac the sac containing the fetus

amniotic fluid fluid within the amniotic sac that suspends and protects the fetus

placenta the organ formed in the lining of the uterus that provides nourishment for the fetus and elimination of its waste products

fetal stage the stage that begins with the third month of pregnancy and ends with childbirth, during which organ systems mature and there are gains in size

stillbirth the birth of a dead fetus

teratogens environmental influences or agents that can damage the embryo or fetus

critical period in this usage, a period during which an embryo is particularly vulnerable to a certain teratogen

syphilis a sexually transmitted infection that, in advanced stages, can attack major organ systems

congenital present at birth and resulting from genetic or chromosomal abnormalities or from exposure to the prenatal environment

HIV/AIDS HIV stands for human immunodeficiency virus, which cripples the body's immune system. AIDS stands for acquired immunodeficiency syndrome, a condition in which the immune system is weakened such that it is vulnerable to diseases it would otherwise fight off

rubella a viral infection that can cause retardation and heart disease in the embryo. Also called German measles

preeclampsia (or **toxemia**) a life-threatening disease that can afflict pregnant women; it is characterized by high blood pressure

premature born before the full term of gestation. Also referred to as preterm

Rh incompatibility a condition in which antibodies produced by the mother are transmitted to the child, possibly causing brain damage or death

thalidomide a sedative used in the 1960s that has been linked to birth defects, especially deformed or absent limbs

Progestin a synthetic hormone used to maintain pregnancy that can cause masculinization of the fetus

DES diethylstilbestrol, an estrogen that has been linked to cancer in the reproductive organs of children of women who used the hormone when pregnant

fetal alcohol syndrome (FAS) a cluster of symptoms shown by children of women who drank heavily during pregnancy, including characteristic facial features and intellectual disabilities

CHAPTER 3 LEARNING OUTCOMES / KEY TERMS

3-1 Identify the stages of childbirth. The first uterine contractions are called Braxton-Hicks contractions, or "false labor" contractions. A day or so before labor begins, women might spot blood. About 1 woman in 10 has a rush of amniotic fluid. Maternal hormones stimulate contractions strong enough to expel the baby.

Childbirth begins with the onset of regular contractions of the uterus, which efface and dilate the cervix. The first stage may last from hours to more than a day. During transition, the head of the fetus moves into the vagina. The second stage begins when the baby appears at the opening of the birth canal and ends with birth of the baby. Mucus is suctioned from the baby's mouth so that breathing is not obstructed. The umbilical cord is severed. During the third stage, the placenta is expelled.

term the typical nine-month period from conception to childbirth

Braxton-Hicks contractions the first, usually painless, contractions of childbirth

cervix the narrow lower end of the uterus, through which a baby passes to reach the vagina

prostaglandins hormones that stimulate uterine contractions

oxytocin a hormone that stimulates labor contractions

efface to become thin

dilate to widen

episiotomy a surgical incision between the birth canal and anus that widens the vaginal opening

transition movement of the head of the fetus into the vagina

3-2 Examine different methods of childbirth. General anesthesia renders the woman unconscious, but it decreases the strength of uterine contractions and lowers the responsiveness of the neonate. Local anesthetics deaden pain in parts of the body. The Lamaze method teaches women to dissociate uterine contractions from pain and fear by associating responses such as relaxation with contractions. A coach aids the mother. A Cesarean section (C-section) delivers a baby surgically through the abdomen. C-sections are most likely when the baby is large or in distress. Herpes and HIV infections can be bypassed by C-section.

midwife an individual who helps women in childbirth

anesthetics agents that lessen pain

general anesthesia elimination of pain by putting a person to sleep

local anesthetic reduction of pain in an area of the body

neonate an infant from birth through the first four weeks of life

natural childbirth childbirth without anesthesia

Lamaze method a childbirth method in which women are educated about childbirth, breathe in patterns that lessen pain during birth, and have a coach present

cesarean section (C-section) delivery of a baby by abdominal surgery

3-3 Discuss potential problems with childbirth. Prenatal oxygen deprivation can be fatal or impair development of the nervous system. A baby is preterm when birth occurs at or before 37 weeks of gestation. A baby has a low birth weight when it weighs less than 5.5 pounds (about 2,500 grams). Risks of prematurity include infant mortality and delayed neurological and motor development. Preterm babies are relatively thin. Sucking may be weak, and they can show respiratory distress. Preterm babies usually remain in the hospital in incubators, but they profit from early stimulation.

anoxia absence of oxygen

hypoxia less oxygen than required

breech (bottom-first) presentation buttocks-first childbirth

preterm born prior to 37 weeks of gestation

small for gestational age descriptive of neonates who are small for their age

lanugo fine, downy hair on premature babies

vernix oily white substance on the skin of premature babies

respiratory distress syndrome weak and irregular breathing, typical of preterm babies

incubator a heated, protective container for premature infants

3-4 Describe the postpartum period. Women may encounter the "baby blues," postpartum depression, and postpartum psychosis (see Table 3-2). These problems probably reflect hormonal changes following birth, although stress can play a role.

Postpartum depression symptoms include:

- serious sadness
- feelings of hopelessness, helplessness, and worthlessness
- difficulty concentrating
- mood swings
- major changes in appetite (usually loss of appetite)
- abnormal sleep patterns (frequently insomnia)

Early infant bonding has not been shown to be critical, despite oft-cited research suggesting that the first few hours after birth present a maternal-sensitive period during which hormone levels dispose the mother to bonding.

postpartum period the period immediately following childbirth

major depression with perinatal onset serious maternal depression following delivery; characterized by sadness, apathy, and feelings of worthlessness

bonding formation of parent–infant attachment

3-5 **Examine the characteristics of a neonate.** The neonate's health is usually evaluated by the Apgar scale, displayed below. The Brazelton Neonatal Behavioral Assessment Scale also screens for behavioral and neurological problems. The neonate's rooting and sucking reflexes are basic to survival. Other key reflexes include the startle reflex, the grasping reflex, the stepping reflex, the Babinski reflex, and the tonic-neck reflex. Most reflexes disappear or are replaced by voluntary behavior within months. Neonates are nearsighted. They visually detect movement, and many track movement. Neonates are particularly responsive to the sounds and rhythms of speech. The nasal and taste preferences of neonates are similar to those of older children and adults. The sensations of skin against skin can contribute to attachment.

TABLE 3.2 THE APGAR SCALE

Points	0	1	2
Appearance: Color	Blue, pale	Body pink, extremities blue	Entirely pink
Pulse: Heart rate	Absent (not detectable)	Slow—below 100 beats/minute	Rapid—100–140 beats/minute
Grimace: Reflex irritability	No response	Grimace	Crying, coughing, sneezing
Activity level: Muscle tone	Completely flaccid, limp	Weak, inactive	Flexed arms and legs; resists extension
Respiratory effort: Breathing	Absent (infant is apneic)	Shallow, irregular, slow	Regular breathing; lusty crying

Neonates are capable of classical and operant conditioning. Neonates spend two-thirds of their time in sleep, distributing sleep through naps. Neonates spend about half their time sleeping in REM sleep, but as time goes on, REM sleep accounts for less of their sleep. REM sleep might be connected with brain development. Babies cry mainly because of pain and discomfort. Crying communicates hunger, anger, pain, and the presence of health problems.

SIDS is the most common cause of death in infants between the ages of one month and one year. SIDS is more common among babies who are put to sleep in the prone position, preterm and low-birth-weight infants, male infants, and infants whose mothers smoked during or after pregnancy.

Apgar scale a measure of a newborn's health that assesses appearance, pulse, grimace, activity level, and respiratory effort

Brazelton Neonatal Behavioral Assessment Scale a measure of a newborn's motor behavior, response to stress, adaptive behavior, and control over physiological state

reflexe an unlearned, stereotypical response to a stimulus

rooting reflex turning the mouth and head toward stroking of the cheek or the corner of the mouth

Moro reflex arching the back, flinging out the arms and legs, and drawing them back to the chest in response to a sudden noise or change in position

grasping reflex grasping objects that touch the palms

stepping reflex taking steps when held under the arms and leaned forward so the feet press the ground

Babinski reflex fanning the toes when the soles of the feet are stroked

tonic-neck reflex turning the head to one side, extending the arm and leg on that side, and flexing the limbs on the opposite side

visual accommodation automatic adjustments of the lenses to focus on objects

convergence inward movement of the eyes to focus on an object that is drawing nearer

amplitude loudness (of sound waves)

pitch highness or lowness (of a sound), as determined by the frequency of sound waves

rapid-eye-movement (REM) sleep a sleep period when dreams are likely, as suggested by rapid eye movements

non-rapid-eye-movement (non-REM) sleep a sleep period when dreams are unlikely

pacifier a device such as an artificial nipple or teething ring that soothes babies when sucked

sudden infant death syndrome (SIDS) the death, while sleeping, of apparently healthy babies who stop breathing

medulla a part of the brain stem that regulates vital and automatic functions such as breathing and the sleep–wake cycle

4-1 **Describe trends in the physical development of the infant.** Three key sequences of physical development are cephalocaudal development, proximodistal development, and differentiation. Infants usually double their birth weight in five months and triple it by their first birthday. Height increases by about half in the first year. Infants grow another 4 to 6 inches and gain another 4 to 7 pounds in the second year. The head diminishes in proportion to the rest of the body. Failure to thrive (FTT) impairs growth in infancy and early childhood. FTT can have organic causes or inorganic causes, possibly including deficiencies in caregiver-child interaction. Infants require breast milk or an iron-fortified formula. Introduction of solid foods is recommended at four to six months. Breast-feeding is connected with the mother's availability, knowledge of the advantages of breast-feeding, and availability of alternatives. Breast milk is tailored to human digestion, contains essential nutrients, contains the mothers' antibodies, helps protect against infant diarrhea, and is less likely than formula to cause allergies.

differentiation the processes by which behaviors and physical structures become specialized

failure to thrive (FTT) a disorder of infancy and early childhood characterized by variable eating and inadequate gains in weight

canalization the tendency of growth rates to return to normal after undergoing environmentally induced change

4-2 **Describe the physical development of the brain and the nervous system.** Neurons receive and transmit messages in the form of neurotransmitters. As the child matures, axons grow in length, dendrites and axon terminals proliferate, and many neurons become wrapped in myelin, making them more efficient. The brain triples in weight by the first birthday, reaching nearly 70% of its adult weight. There are two major prenatal growth spurts: Neurons proliferate during the first, and the second spurt is mainly from the proliferation of dendrites and axon terminals. Sensory and motor areas of the brain begin to develop because of maturation, but sensory stimulation and motor activity spur development. Malnutrition is connected with a smaller brain, fewer neurons, and less myelination.

FIG.4.4 STRUCTURES OF THE BRAIN

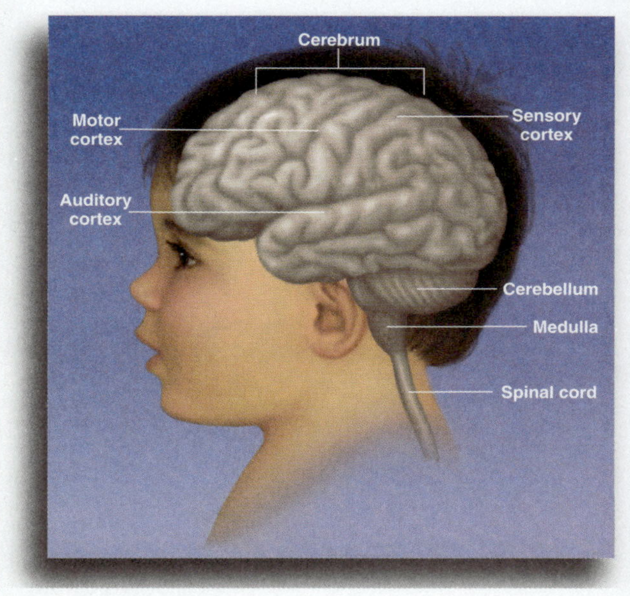

nerves bundles of axons from many neurons

neurons cells in the nervous system that transmit messages

dendrites rootlike parts of neurons that receive impulses from other neurons

axon a long, thin part of a neuron that transmits impulses to other neurons through branching structures called axon terminals

neurotransmitter a chemical that transmits a neural impulse across a synapse from one neuron to another

myelin sheath a fatty, whitish substance that encases and insulates axons

myelination the coating of axons with myelin

multiple sclerosis a disorder in which hard fibrous tissue replaces myelin, impeding neural transmission

medulla an area of the lower, back part of the brain involved in heartbeat and respiration

cerebellum the area of the lower, back part of the brain involved in coordination and balance

cerebrum the largest, rounded part of the brain, responsible for learning, thought, memory, and language

4-3 **Describe the key events in the motor development of the infant.** Motor development is connected with changes in posture, movement, and coordination. Children gain the ability to move their bodies through a sequence of activities that includes rolling over, sitting up, crawling, creeping, walking, and running. Although the sequence remains stable, some children skip a step. Both maturation (nature) and experience (nurture) play roles in motor development. Development of motor skills can be accelerated by training, but the effect is generally slight.

ulnar grasp grasping objects between the fingers and the palm

pincer grasp grasping objects between the fingers and the thumb

locomotion movement from one place to another

toddler a child who walks with short, uncertain steps

4-4 Describe patterns of sensory and perceptual development in infancy. Neonates are nearsighted and have poor peripheral vision. Acuity and peripheral vision approximate adult levels by the age of six months. Neonates attend longer to stripes than blobs, and by 8–12 weeks of age they prefer curved lines to straight ones. Two-month-old infants fixate longer on the human face than on other stimuli. Infants can discriminate the mother's face from a stranger's after about 8 hours of contact. Neonates direct their attention to the edges of objects, but two-month-olds scan objects from the edges inward.

Researchers use the visual cliff apparatus to study depth perception. Most infants refuse to venture out over the cliff by the time they can crawl. Perhaps infants need some experience crawling before they develop fear of heights. Size constancy appears to be present by 2½ to 3 months of age; shape constancy develops by age four to five months. Neonates reflexively orient their heads toward a sound.

FIG.4.8 EYE MOVEMENTS OF 1- AND 2-MONTH-OLDS

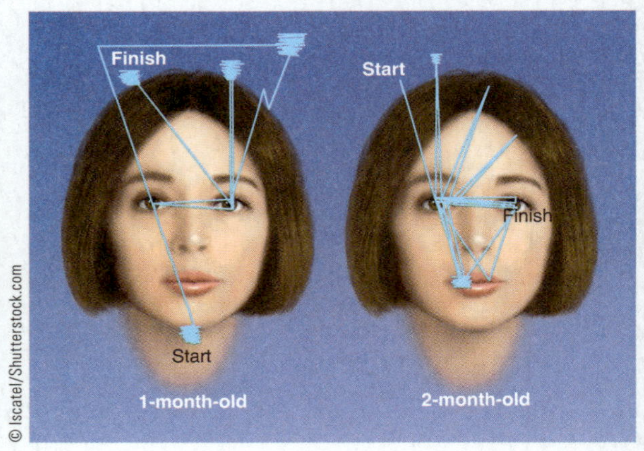

One-month-olds direct their attention to the edges of objects. Two-month-olds move in from the edge.

Infants discriminate caregivers' voices by 3½ months of age. Early infants can perceive most of the speech sounds used in the world's languages, but by 10–12 months of age, this ability lessens.

Neonates seem to be at the mercy of external stimuli but, later, intentional action replaces "capture." Systematic search replaces unsystematic search, attention becomes selective, and irrelevant information gets ignored. Sensory changes are linked to maturation of the nervous system (nature), but experience (nurture) also plays a crucial role. There are critical periods in the perceptual development of children and lower animals during which sensory experience is required to optimize—or maintain—sensory capacities.

FIG.4.10 DECLINING ABILITY TO DISCRIMINATE THE SOUNDS OF FOREIGN LANGUAGES

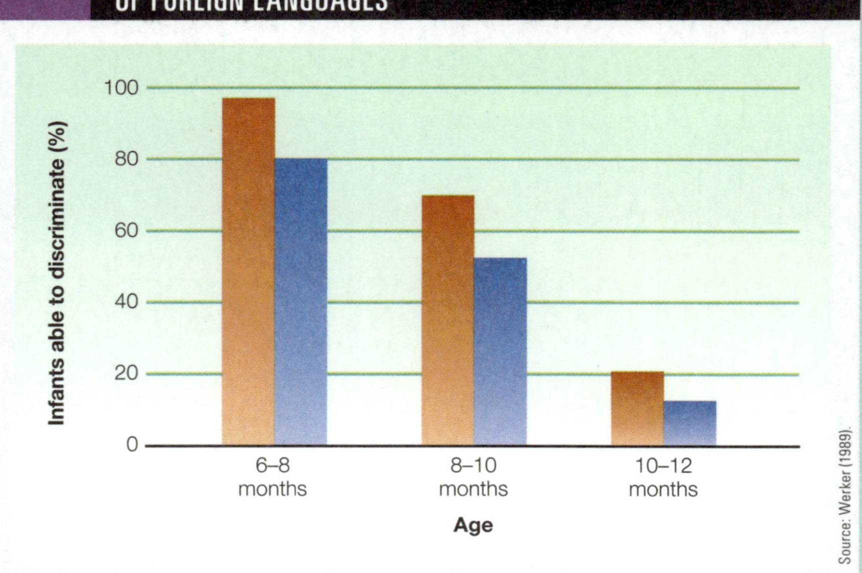

Infants show a decline in the ability to discriminate sounds not found in their native language. Before six months of age, infants from English-speaking families could discriminate sounds found in Hindi (red bars) and Salish, a Native American language (blue bars). By 10 to 12 months of age, they could no longer do so.

perceptual constancy perceiving objects as maintaining their identity although sensations from them change as their positions change

habituation becoming used to a stimulus and therefore paying less attention to it

5-1 **Examine Jean Piaget's studies of cognitive development.** Piaget hypothesized that cognitive processes develop in an orderly sequence of stages: sensorimotor, preoperational, concrete operational, and formal operational. The sensorimotor stage refers to the first two years of cognitive development and involves the progression from responding to events with reflexes to displaying goal-oriented behavior.

A critical milestone in the sensorimotor stage is the appearance of early signs of object permanence, or the ability of an infant to appreciate that an object continues to exist physically even when out of view.

Researchers who question the validity of Piaget's claims argue that

- development is not tied to discrete stages
- adult and peer influences play a role in cognitive development
- infants are more competent than Piaget estimated

sensorimotor stage Piaget's first stage of cognitive development, which lasts through infancy and is generally characterized by increasingly complex coordination of sensory experiences with motor activity

primary circular reactions the repetition of actions that first occurred by chance and that focus on the infant's own body

secondary circular reactions the repetition of actions that produce an effect on the environment

tertiary circular reactions the purposeful adaptation of established schemes to new situations

object permanence recognition that objects continue to exist when they are not in view

A-not-B error the error made when an infant selects a familiar hiding place (A) for an object rather than a new hiding place, even after the infant has seen it hidden in the new place

deferred imitation the imitation of people and events that occurred in the past

5-2 **Discuss the information-processing approach to cognitive development.** The information-processing approach focuses on how children manipulate or process information coming from the environment or already stored in the mind. Two primary tools used in this processing are memory and imitation. Even neonates demonstrate memory to stimuli, and between two and six months of age, infants' memory develops dramatically. Infant memory can be improved if infants receive a reminder before given a memory test. Researchers disagree about how early nonreflexive imitation is exhibited in infants. Deferred imitation occurs as early as six months of age.

information-processing approach the view of cognitive development that focuses on how children manipulate sensory information and/or information stored in memory

5-3 **Identify individual differences in intelligence among infants.** The Bayley Scales of Infant Development are one of the most important tests of intellectual development among infants. A total of 287 scale items tests for mental skills (verbal communication, perceptual skills, learning and memory, and problem-solving skills) and motor skills (gross and fine). Infant intelligence is tested to determine the presence of handicaps, and although the Bayley scales can identify gross lags in development and relative strengths and weaknesses, infant intelligence scores are generally poor predictors of intelligence scores taken more than a year later.

Assessing visual recognition memory is another way of studying infant intelligence. Longitudinal studies by Susan Rose and her colleagues showed that the capacity for visual recognition memory is stable and the trait shows predictive validity for broad cognitive abilities throughout childhood, including intelligence and language ability.

visual recognition memory the kind of memory shown in an infant's ability to discriminate previously seen objects from novel objects

5-4 **Examine language development in infants.** Children develop language according to an invariant sequence of steps or stages. The first stage involves prelinguistic vocalizations such as cooing, babbling, and echolalia. Once children can express themselves with words, they try to talk about more objects than they have words for. Just as first words are simple syllabic combinations, first sentences are often single words that on their own express simple but complete ideas. Developing language skills are marked by changes in the mean length of utterance (MLU). In early language acquisition, children use telegraphic speech to communicate full ideas.

Theories about language development are divided into those emphasizing nurture and those emphasizing nature. Proponents of nurture theories build on the work of B. F. Skinner and cite the roles of imitation and reinforcement in language development. Proponents of the nativist view, like Noam Chomsky, argue that the ability to acquire language is innate and therefore biological. The work of Steven Pinker, among others, shows, however, that language acquisition results from an interaction of environmental and biological factors (or, is a combination of nature and nurture).

FIG.5.5 MEAN LENGTH OF UTTERANCE FOR THREE CHILDREN

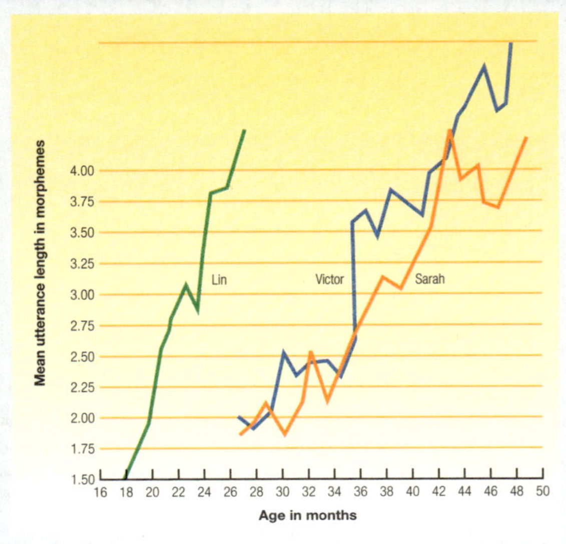

The mean length of utterance (MLU) increases rapidly once speech begins.

FIG.5.6 BROCA'S AND WERNICKE'S AREAS OF THE CEREBRAL CORTEX

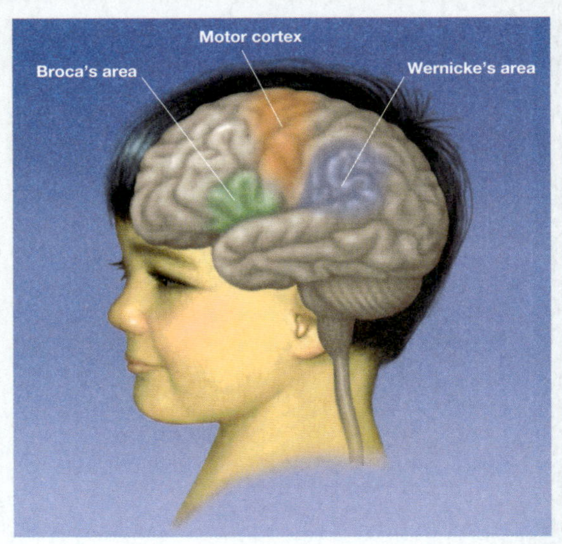

prelinguistic vocalizations made by the infant before the use of language

cooing prelinguistic vowel-like sounds that reflect feelings of positive excitement

babbling the child's first vocalizations that have the sounds of speech

echolalia the automatic repetition of sounds or words

intonation the use of pitches of varying levels to help communicate meaning

receptive vocabulary the number of words one understands

expressive vocabulary the number of words one can use in the production of language

overextension use of words in situations in which their meanings become extended

telegraphic speech type of speech in which only the essential words are used

mean length of utterance (MLU) the average number of morphemes used in an utterance

morpheme the smallest unit of meaning in a language

holophrase a single word that is used to express complex meanings

syntax the rules in a language for placing words in order to form sentences

models in learning theory, those whose behaviors are imitated by others

extinction decrease in frequency of a response due to absence of reinforcement

shaping gradual building of complex behavior through reinforcement of successive approximations to the target behavior

psycholinguistic theory the view that language learning involves an interaction between environmental influences and an inborn tendency to acquire language

language acquisition device (LAD) neural "prewiring" that eases the child's learning of grammar

surface structure the superficial grammatical construction of a sentence

deep structure the underlying meaning of a sentence

aphasia a disruption in the ability to understand or produce language

Broca's aphasia an aphasia caused by damage to Broca's area and characterized by difficulty speaking

Wernicke's aphasia an aphasia caused by damage to Wernicke's area and characterized by impaired comprehension of speech and difficulty producing the right word

critical period the period from about 18 months to puberty when the brain is especially capable of learning language. Also called the *sensitive period*

CHAPTER REVIEW

CHAPTER 6 LEARNING OUTCOMES / KEY TERMS

6-1 Describe the development of attachment in infancy and theoretical views of how it occurs. Most infants in the United States are securely attached. In the Strange Situation, secure infants mildly protest mother's departure and are readily comforted by her. The two major types of insecure attachment are avoidant attachment and ambivalent/resistant attachment. Secure infants are happier, more sociable, and more competent. They use the mother as a secure base from which to explore the environment. Parents of securely attached infants are more likely to be affectionate and sensitive to their needs.

According to Ainsworth's studies of the development of attachment, the initial-preattachment phase lasts from birth by about three months and is characterized by indiscriminate attachment. The attachment-in-the-making phase occurs by about three or four months and is characterized by preference for familiar figures. The clear-cut-attachment phase occurs at six or seven months and involves dependence on the primary caregiver.

Cognitive theorists suggest that an infant must develop object permanence before specific attachment is possible. Behaviorists suggest that infants become attached to caregivers because caregivers meet their physical needs. Psychoanalysts suggest that the primary caregiver becomes a love object. The Harlows' experiments with monkeys suggest that contact comfort is a key to attachment. Ethologists view attachment as an instinct (fixed action pattern) that occurs during a critical period.

FIG.6.2 DEVELOPMENT OF ATTACHMENT

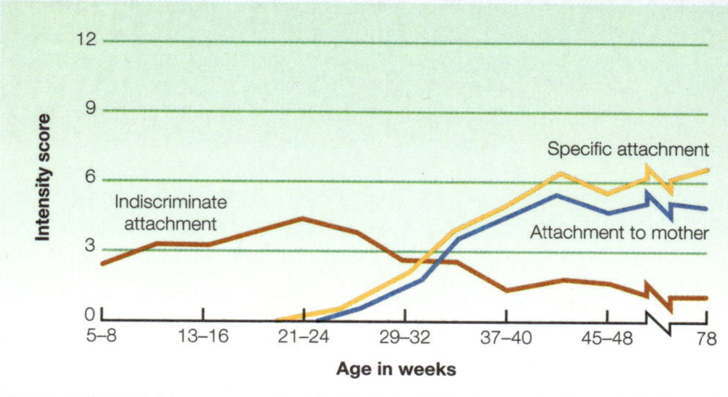

During the first six months, infants tend to show indiscriminate attachment, which wanes as specific attachments intensify.

FIG.6.3 CONTACT COMFORT

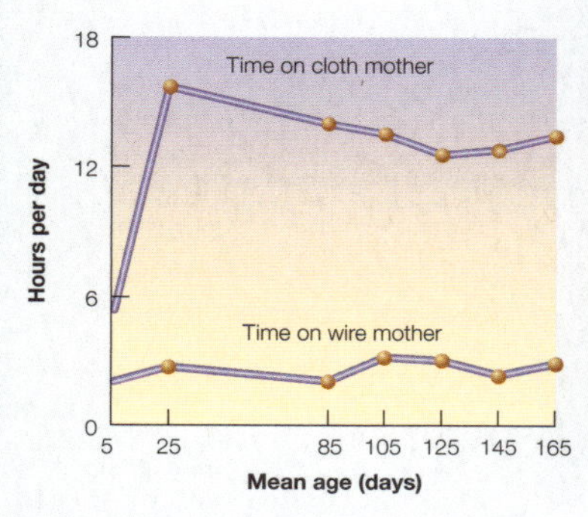

Nina Leen/Time Life Pictures/Getty Images

Although this rhesus monkey infant is fed by the "wire-mesh mother," it spends most of its time clinging to a soft, cuddly, "terry-cloth mother."

attachment an affectional bond characterized by seeking closeness with another and distress upon separation

separation anxiety fear of separation from a target of attachment

secure attachment a type of attachment characterized by mild distress at leave-takings and being readily soothed by reunion

insecure attachment attachment behavior characterized by avoiding caregiver, excessive clinging, or inconsistency

avoidant attachment a type of insecure attachment characterized by apparent indifference to leave-takings by and reunions with an attachment figure

ambivalent/resistant attachment a type of insecure attachment characterized by severe distress at leave-takings and ambivalent behavior at reunions

disorganized–disoriented attachment a type of insecure attachment characterized by dazed and contradictory behaviors toward an attachment figure

indiscriminate attachment the display of attachment behaviors toward any person

initial-preattachment phase the first phase in development of attachment, characterized by indiscriminate attachment

attachment-in-the-making phase the second phase in development of attachment, characterized by preference for familiar figures

clear-cut-attachment phase the third phase in development of attachment, characterized by intensified dependence on the primary caregiver

contact comfort the pleasure derived from physical contact with another

ethologist a scientist who studies the behavior patterns characteristic of various species

social smile a smile that occurs in response to a human voice or face

critical period a period during which imprinting can occur

imprinting the process by which waterfowl become attached to the first moving object they follow

6 Infancy: Social and Emotional Development

CHAPTER REVIEW

CHAPTER 6 LEARNING OUTCOMES / KEY TERMS

6-2 **Discuss the relationships between social deprivation, child abuse and neglect, autism spectrum disorders and attachment.** The Harlows found that rhesus infants reared in isolation later avoided contact with other monkeys. Females who later had offspring tended to neglect or abuse them. Many institutionalized children who receive little social stimulation develop withdrawal and depression. Mistreated children are less intimate with peers and are more aggressive, angry, and noncompliant than other children. Child abuse tends to run in families, perhaps because abusive parents serve as role models. Some parents rationalize that they are hurting their children "for their own good" to discourage bad behavior.

Autism spectrum disorders (ASDs) are characterized by impairment in communication skills and social interactions, and repetitive, stereotyped behavior. The most striking feature of autism is the child's aloneness. Other features include communication problems, intolerance of change, and self-mutilation. Twin studies suggest that autism involves heredity, and neurological impairment is also suspected. Behavior modification has been used to increase the child's attention to others and social play and to decrease self-mutilation. Researchers are studying the use of SSRIs and major tranquilizers.

autism spectrum disorders (ASDs) developmental disorders characterized by impairment in communication and social skills, and by repetitive, stereotyped behavior

autism a disorder characterized by extreme aloneness, communication problems, preservation of sameness, and ritualistic behavior

mutism refusal to speak

echolalia automatic repetition of sounds or words

6-3 **Discuss the effects of day care on attachment** Infants with day-care experience are more independent, self-confident, outgoing, affectionate, and more cooperative with peers and adults than infants who are not in day care. Children in high-quality day care outperform children who remain in the home in terms of cognitive development. Children in day care are more aggressive than other children, but some aggression may indicate independence, not maladjustment.

6-4 **Describe the emotional development of the infant.** Researchers debate whether the emotional expression of newborns begins in an undifferentiated state of diffuse excitement or whether several emotions are present. Infants' initial emotional expressions appear to comprise either a positive attraction to pleasant stimulation or withdrawal from aversive stimulation. By the age of two to three months, social smiling has replaced reflexive smiling. Most infants develop fear of strangers by about six to nine months.

Infants display social referencing as early as six months of age, when they use caregivers' facial expressions or tones of voice for information about how to respond in novel situations. Emotional regulation is emotional self-control. The children of secure mothers are more likely to regulate their emotions well.

social referencing using another person's reaction to a situation to form one's own response

emotional regulation techniques for controlling one's emotional states

6-5 **Describe the personality development of the infant, focusing on the self-concept, temperament, and gender differences.** Research using the mirror technique finds that the self-concept develops by about 18 months of age. Self-awareness enables the child to develop concepts of sharing and cooperation and emotions such as embarrassment, envy, empathy, pride, guilt, and shame.

An infant's temperament (see Table 6.2) involves activity level, regularity, approach or withdrawal, adaptability, response threshold, response intensity, quality of mood, distractibility, attention span, and persistence. Thomas and Chess found that most infants can be classified as having easy, difficult, or slow-to-warm-up temperaments. Temperament remains moderately consistent from infancy through young adulthood.

Female infants sit, crawl, and walk earlier than boys do. By 12 to 18 months of age, girls prefer to play with dolls and similar toys, whereas boys prefer sports equipment and transportation toys.

temperament individual difference in style of reaction that is present early in life

goodness of fit agreement between the parents' expectations of a child and the child's temperament

TABLE 6.3 TYPES OF TEMPERAMENT

Temperament Category	Easy	Difficult	Slow to Warm Up
Regularity of biological functioning	Regular	Irregular	Somewhat irregular
Response to new stimuli	Positive approach	Negative withdrawal	Negative withdrawal
Adaptability to new situations	Adapts readily	Adapts slowly or not at all	Adapts slowly
Intensity of reaction	Mild or moderate	Intense	Mild
Quality of mood	Positive	Negative	Initially negative; gradually more positive

Sources: Chess & Thomas (1991) and Thomas & Chess (1989).

7-1 Describe trends in physical development in early childhood. Children gain about 2 to 3 inches in height and 4 to 6 pounds in weight per year in early childhood. Boys are slightly larger than girls. The brain develops more quickly than any other organ in early childhood, in part because of myelination. The left hemisphere is relatively more involved in logical analysis, language, and computation. The right hemisphere is usually superior in visual–spatial functions, emotional responses, and creative mathematical reasoning. But the hemispheres work together. The brain shows plasticity in early childhood. Two factors involved in the brain's plasticity are the growth of new dendrites and the redundancy of neural connections.

corpus callosum the thick bundle of nerve fibers that connects the left and right hemispheres of the brain

plasticity the tendency of new parts of the brain to take up the functions of injured parts

7-2 Describe motor development in early childhood. Preschoolers make great strides in the development of gross motor skills. Girls are somewhat better in balance and precision; boys have some advantage in throwing and kicking. Physically active parents are likely to have physically active children. Fine motor skills develop gradually. Kellogg identified 20 scribbles that she considers the building blocks of art. Handedness emerges by six months. Left-handedness may be connected with some language and health problems, yet a disproportionately large number of artists, musicians, and mathematicians are left-handed.

gross motor skills skills employing the large muscles used in locomotion

fine motor skills skills employing the small muscles used in manipulation, such as those in the fingers

7-3 Describe trends in health and illness in early childhood. The incidence of minor illnesses, such as colds, nausea and vomiting, and diarrhea, is high. Diarrheal diseases are almost completely related to unsafe drinking water and lack of sanitation in developing countries and are a leading cause of death there. Immunization and antibiotics reduce the incidence of disease. Air pollution contributes to respiratory infections. Lead poisoning causes neurological damage. Accidents cause more deaths in early childhood than the next six most frequent causes combined.

7-4 Describe sleep patterns in early childhood. Most two- and three-year-olds sleep about 10 hours at night and nap during the day. Sleep terrors are more severe than nightmares. Sleep terrors and sleepwalking usually occur during deep sleep. Sleepwalkers' eyes are usually open; if awakened, they may show confusion but are unlikely to be violent.

sleep terrors frightening dreamlike experiences that occur during the deepest stage of non-REM sleep, shortly after the child has gone to sleep

somnambulism sleepwalking

7-5 Discuss the elimination disorders. Most U.S. children are toilet trained by 3 or 4 but continue to have "accidents." Enuresis is apparently connected with physical immaturity and stress. Encopresis can stem from constipation and stress.

enuresis failure to control the bladder (urination) once the normal age for control has been reached

bed-wetting failure to control the bladder during the night

encopresis failure to control the bowels once the normal age for bowel control has been reached. Also called soiling

7-6 Describe Piaget's preoperational stage. Piaget's preoperational stage lasts from about 2 to 7 and is characterized by the use of symbols. Preoperational thinking is characterized by pretend play, egocentrism, precausal thinking, confusion between mental and physical events, and ability to focus on only one dimension at a time. Conservation is lacking because it requires focusing on two aspects of a situation at once.

preoperational stage the second stage in Piaget's scheme, characterized by inflexible and irreversible mental manipulation of symbols

(continues)

FIG.7.5 CONSERVATION

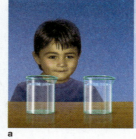

a

b

c

(a) The preoperational boy agrees that the amounts of water in the two containers is the same. (b) He watches as the water from one container is poured into a taller, thinner container. (c) When asked whether the tall and the squat containers now contain the same amount of water, he says no. Why?

7 Early Childhood: Physical and Cognitive Development

(continued)

symbolic play play in which children make believe that objects and toys are other than what they are. Also called pretend play

egocentrism putting oneself at the center of things such that one is unable to perceive the world from another person's point of view

precausal a type of thought in which natural cause-and-effect relationships are attributed to will and other preoperational concepts

transductive reasoning reasoning from the specific to the specific

animism the attribution of life and intentionality to inanimate objects

artificialism the belief that environmental features were made by people

conservation in cognitive psychology, the principle that properties of substances such as weight and mass remain the same (are conserved) when superficial characteristics such as their shapes or arrangement are changed

centration focusing on an aspect or characteristic of a situation or problem

class inclusion categorizing a new object or concept as belonging to a broader group of objects or concepts

7-7 **Discuss influences on cognitive development in early childhood.** Vygotsky envisions scaffolding and the zone of proximal development as two factors in cognitive development. The HOME scale was developed to evaluate children's home environments. The scale includes six factors that influence child development, including parental emotional and verbal responsiveness, avoidance of restriction and punishment, organization of the physical environment, provision of appropriate play materials, parental involvement with the child, and opportunities for variety in daily stimulation. The children of parents who provide appropriate play materials and stimulating experiences show gains in social and language development. Head Start programs enhance economically disadvantaged children's academic readiness and skills.

scaffolding Vygotsky's term for temporary cognitive structures or methods of solving problems that help the child as he or she learns to function independently

zone of proximal development (ZPD) Vygotsky's term for the situation in which a child carries out tasks with the help of someone who is more skilled, frequently an adult who represents the culture in which the child develops

7-8 **Explain how "theory of mind" affects cognitive development.** Children come to understand that there are distinctions between external and mental events and between appearances and realities. By age three, most children begin to realize that people gain knowledge through the senses, and by age four, they understand which senses provide certain kinds of information.

theory of mind a commonsense understanding of how the mind works

appearance–reality distinction the difference between real events on the one hand and mental events, fantasies, and misleading appearances on the other hand

7-9 **Describe memory development in early childhood.** Preschoolers recognize more items than they can recall. Autobiographical memory is linked to language skills. Factors affecting memory include what the child is asked to remember, interest level and motivation, the availability of retrieval cues, and the memory measure being used. Preschoolers engage in behavior such as looking, pointing, and touching when trying to remember. Preschoolers can be taught to use memory strategies such as rehearsal and grouping of items.

scripts abstract, generalized accounts of familiar repeated events

autobiographical memory the memory of specific episodes or events

rehearsal repetition

7-10 **Describe language development in early childhood.** Preschoolers acquire about nine new words per day, some of which occur because of fast mapping. During the third year, children usually add articles, conjunctions, possessive adjectives, pronouns, and prepositions. Between the ages of three and four, children combine phrases and clauses into complex sentences. Preschoolers overregularize irregular verbs and nouns as they learn grammar. Piaget believed that children learn words to describe classes they have created. Other theorists argue that children create classes to understand words. To Vygotsky, inner speech is the ultimate binding of language and thought.

fast mapping a process of quickly determining a word's meaning, which facilitates children's vocabulary development

whole-object assumption the assumption that words refer to whole objects and not to their component parts or characteristics

contrast assumption the assumption that objects have only one label

overregularization the application of regular grammatical rules for forming inflections to irregular verbs and nouns

pragmatics the practical aspects of communication, such as adaptation of language to fit the social situation

inner speech Vygotsky's concept of the ultimate binding of language and thought. Inner speech originates in vocalizations that may regulate the child's behavior and become internalized by age six or seven

8-1 **Describe the dimensions of child rearing and styles of parenting.** Approaches to child rearing can be classified according to two broad dimensions: warmth–coldness and restrictiveness–permissiveness. Consistent control and firm enforcement of rules can have positive consequences for the child. Parents tend to use inductive methods, power assertion, and withdrawal of love to enforce rules. Inductive methods use "reasoning," or explaining why one sort of behavior is good and another is not. Authoritative parents are restrictive but warm and tend to have the most competent and achievement-oriented children. Authoritarian parents are restrictive and cold. The sons of authoritarian parents tend to be hostile and defiant; daughters are low in independence. Children of neglectful parents show the least competence and maturity.

TABLE 8.1 BAUMRIND'S PATTERNS OF PARENTING

Parental Style	Parental Behavior Patterns: Restrictiveness and Control	Parental Behavior Patterns: Warmth and Responsiveness
Authoritative	High	High
Authoritarian	High	Low
Permissive–Indulgent	Low	High
Rejecting–Neglecting	Low	Low

authoritative a child-rearing style in which parents are restrictive and demanding yet communicative and warm

authoritarian a child-rearing style in which parents demand submission and obedience

permissive–indulgent a child-rearing style in which parents are warm and not restrictive

rejecting–neglecting a child-rearing style in which parents are neither restrictive and controlling nor supportive and responsive

8-2 **Explain how siblings, birth order, peers, and other factors affect social development during early childhood.** Siblings provide caregiving, emotional support, advice, role models, social interaction, restrictions, and cognitive stimulation. However, they are also sources of conflict, control, and competition. Younger siblings usually imitate older siblings. First-born and only children are generally more highly motivated to achieve, more cooperative, more helpful, more adult-oriented, and less aggressive, but later-born children tend to have greater social skills with peers. Children learn social skills—such as sharing, taking turns, and coping with conflict—from peers. Peers also provide emotional support. Preschoolers' friendships are characterized by shared activities and feelings of attachment.

FIG.8.1 BANDURA'S STUDY OF THE IMITATION OF AGGRESSION

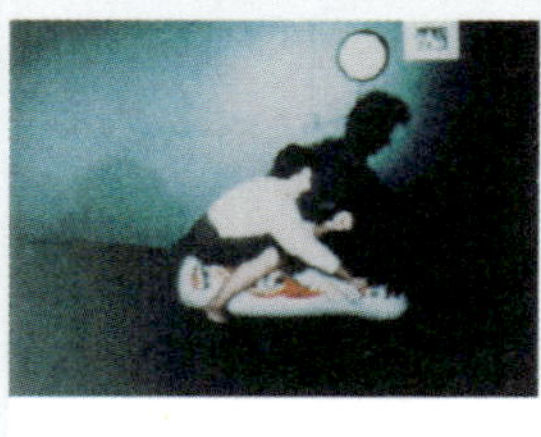

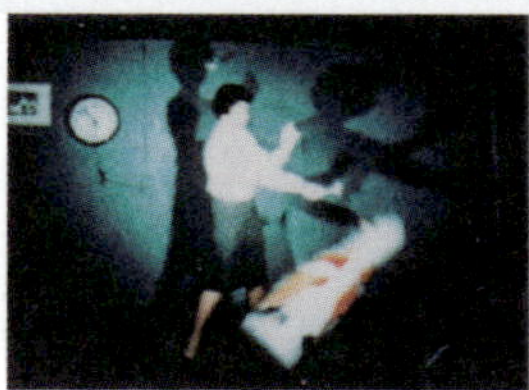

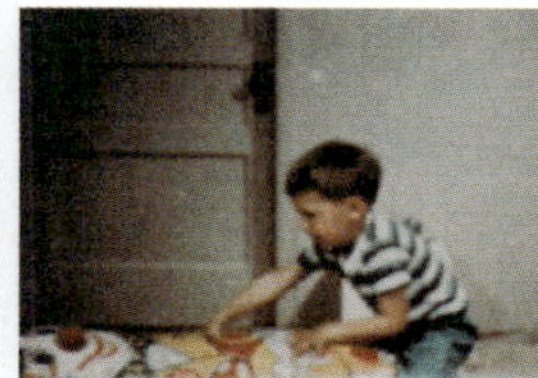

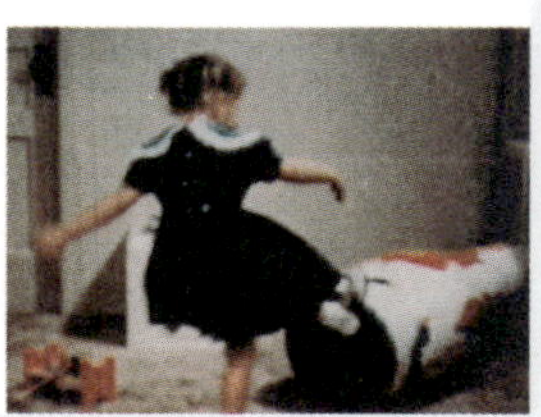

The top row of photos shows an adult striking a Bobo doll. The second and third rows show a boy and a girl who observed the adult imitating the aggressive behavior.

Play develops motor, social, and cognitive skills. Parten followed the development of six types of play among two- to five-year-olds: unoccupied play, solitary play, onlooker play, parallel play, associative play, and cooperative play. Children show preferences for gender-stereotyped toys by 15 to 30 months of age. Boys' toys commonly include transportation toys (cars and trucks) and weapons; girls' toys more often include dolls. Boys prefer vigorous outdoor activities and rough-and-tumble play. Girls are more likely to prefer arts and crafts. Preschool children generally prefer playmates of their own gender partly because of shared interest in activities. Boys' play is more oriented toward dominance, aggression, and rough play.

Prosocial behavior begins to develop in the first year, when children begin to share. Development of prosocial behavior is linked to the development of empathy and perspective taking. Girls show more empathy than boys do.

Preschool aggression is often instrumental. By age six or seven, aggression becomes hostile. Aggressive behavior appears to be stable and to predict problems in adulthood. Genetic factors may be involved in aggressive behavior, partly because of testosterone. Social cognitive theory suggests that children become aggressive as a result of frustration and observational learning. Aggressive children are often rejected by less aggressive peers. Children who are physically punished are more likely to behave aggressively. Observing aggressive behavior teaches aggressive skills, disinhibits the child, and habituates children to violence.

regression a return to behavior characteristic of earlier stages of development

dramatic play play in which children enact social roles

nonsocial play solitary form of play

social play play in which children interact with and are influenced by others

prosocial behavior behavior that benefits other people, generally without expectation of reward

disinhibit to encourage a response that has been previously suppressed

8-3 **Discuss personality and emotional development during early childhood, focusing on the self, Erikson's views, and fears.** Children as young as 3 can describe themselves in terms of behavior and internal states. Secure attachment and competence contribute to self-esteem. Preschoolers are most likely to fear animals, imaginary creatures, and the dark. Girls report more fears than boys do.

self-concept one's self-description and self-evaluation according to various categories, such as child, adolescent, or adult, one's gender, and one's skills

categorical self definitions of the self that refer to external traits

8-4 **Discuss the development of gender roles and gender differences.** Females are stereotyped as dependent, gentle, and home-oriented. Males are stereotyped as aggressive, self-confident, and independent. Cultural expectations of females and males are called gender roles. Males tend to excel in math and spatial-relations skills, whereas girls tend to excel in verbal skills. Stereotypical gender preferences for toys and play activities are in evidence at an early age. Males are more aggressive and more interested in sex than females. Testosterone may specialize the hemispheres of the brain more in males than females, explaining why females excel in verbal skills that require some spatial organization, such as reading. Social cognitive theorists explain the development of gender-typed behavior in terms of observational learning and socialization. According to Kohlberg's cognitive-developmental theory, gender-typing involves the emergence of gender identity, gender stability, and gender constancy. According to gender-schema theory, preschoolers attempt to conform to the cultural gender schema. Theorists differ as to whether it is beneficial to promote psychological androgyny.

stereotype a fixed, conventional idea about a group

gender role a cluster of traits and behaviors that are considered stereotypical of females and males

gender identity knowledge that one is female or male

gender stability the concept that one's gender is unchanging

gender constancy the concept that one's gender remains the same despite changes in appearance or behavior

gender-schema theory the view that one's knowledge of the gender schema in one's society guides one's assumption of gender-typed preferences and behavior patterns.

9-1 **Describe trends in physical development in middle childhood.** Children tend to gain a little more than 2 inches in height and 5 to 7 pounds in weight per year during middle childhood. Boys are slightly heavier and taller than girls through age 9 or 10, until girls begin their adolescent growth spurt. Overweight children usually do not outgrow baby fat. Heredity plays a role in weight. Sedentary habits also foster weight gain.

growth spurt a period during which growth advances at a dramatically rapid rate compared with other periods

9-2 **Describe changes in motor development in middle childhood.** Middle childhood is marked by increases in speed, strength, agility, and balance. Children improve in gross and fine motor skills as pathways that connect the cerebellum to the cortex become more myelinated. Reaction time decreases. Boys have slightly greater overall strength, whereas girls have better coordination and flexibility. Most U.S. children are not physically fit, in part because of the amount of time spent watching TV.

reaction time the amount of time required to respond to a stimulus

9-3 **Discuss ADHD and learning disabilities.** Attention-deficit/hyperactivity disorder (ADHD) runs in families, and brain damage might be involved. Children with ADHD are often treated with stimulants because they stimulate the cerebral cortex to inhibit more primitive areas of the brain. Dyslexia also runs in families. The double-deficit hypothesis suggests that dyslexic children have problems in phonological processing and naming speed. Some learning-disabled children profit from mainstream classrooms; others find them overwhelming.

attention deficit hyperactivity disorder (ADHD) a disorder characterized by excessive inattention, impulsiveness, and hyperactivity

hyperactivity excessive restlessness and overactivity; a characteristic of ADHD

stimulants drugs that increase the activity of the nervous system

dyslexia a reading disorder characterized by letter reversals, mirror reading, slow reading, and reduced comprehension

learning disabilities disorders characterized by inadequate development of specific academic, language, and speech skills

mainstreaming placing disabled children in classrooms with nondisabled children

9-4 **Describe Piaget's concrete-operational stage.** By the age of 11, many children begin to recognize ambiguities in grammar and their thought processes become more logical and complex. Piaget characterized children during this period as entering the concrete-operational stage, in which children begin to think in logical terms but focus on tangible objects rather than abstract ideas. Concrete-operational children are less egocentric, engage in decentration, and understand concepts such as conservation, transitivity, seriation, and class inclusion.

concrete operations the third stage in Piaget's scheme, characterized by flexible, reversible thought concerning tangible objects and events

decentration simultaneous focusing on more than one aspect or dimension of a problem or situation

transitivity the principle that if $A > B$ and $B > C$, then $A > C$

seriation placing objects in an order or series according to a property or trait

9-5 **Discuss Piaget's and Kohlberg's theories of moral development.** Piaget and Kohlberg both presumed that moral reasoning in children was related to overall cognitive development. Piaget proposed that children's moral judgments develop in two overlapping stages, which he termed moral realism and autonomous morality. Kohlberg's theory emphasized the importance of being able to view a situation from multiple perspectives, and the reasons on which people base their judgments reflect their level of moral development. At a preconventional level, moral judgments are based on the positive or negative consequences of one's actions. At the conventional level, moral judgments are based on conformity to conventional standards. At a postconventional level, moral judgments are based on personal moral standards.

moral realism the judgment of acts as moral when they conform to authority or to the rules of the game

objective morality the perception of morality as objective, that is, as existing outside the cognitive functioning of people

immanent justice the view that retribution for wrongdoing is a direct consequence of the wrongdoing

autonomous morality the second stage in Piaget's cognitive-developmental theory of moral development, in which children base moral judgments on the intentions of the wrongdoer and on the amount of damage done

preconventional level according to Kohlberg, a period during which moral judgments are based largely on expectations of rewards or punishments

conventional level according to Kohlberg, a period during which moral judgments largely reflect social rules and conventions

postconventional level according to Kohlberg, a period during which moral judgments are derived from moral principles, and people look to themselves to set moral standards

9-6 **Describe developments in information processing in middle childhood.** Key elements in children's information processing capabilities include development in selective attention; development in the storage and retrieval of sensory, short-term, and long-term memory; development of recall memory; and development of metacognition and metamemory.

sensory memory the structure of memory first encountered by sensory input. Information is maintained in sensory memory for only a fraction of a second

sensory register another term for sensory memory

working memory the structure of memory that can hold a sensory stimulus for up to 30 seconds after the trace decays

encode to transform sensory input into a form that is more readily processed

rehearsing repeat—in this case, mentally

long-term memory the memory structure capable of relatively permanent storage of information

elaborative strategy a method for increasing retention of new information by relating it to well-known information

metacognition awareness of and control of one's cognitive abilities

metamemory knowledge of the functions and processes involved in one's storage and retrieval of information

9-7 **Describe intellectual development in middle childhood, focusing on theories of intelligence.** Intelligence is usually perceived as a child's underlying competence or *learning ability*, whereas achievement involves a child's acquired competencies or *performance*. Factor theorists view intelligence as consisting of one or more major mental abilities. Sternberg proposed a three-part theory of intelligence (see Figure 9.7). Gardner theorized that intelligence reflected more than academic achievement, with nine different categories of intelligence, or "talents." The Wechsler and SBIS scales have been developed to measure intelligence. Many psychologists and educational specialists have developed culture-free tests to avoid cultural biases they feel are present in the Wechsler and SBIS. About half of children score between 90 and 110 on IQ tests. Those who score below 70 are labeled "intellectually deficient" and above 130 are labeled "gifted." Most tests indicate only a moderate relationship between IQ scores and creativity. Intelligence tests usually rely on convergent thinking, and creativity is generally based on divergent thinking.

intelligence a general mental capability that involves the ability to reason, plan, solve problems, think abstractly, comprehend complex ideas, learn quickly, and learn from experience

achievement that which is attained by one's efforts and presumed to be made possible by one's abilities

intelligence quotient (IQ) (1) a ratio obtained by dividing a child's mental age on an intelligence test by his or her chronological age; (2) a score on an intelligence test

mental age (MA) the intellectual level at which a child is functions, based on the typical performance of a child of a certain age

chronological age (CA) a person's age

cultural bias a factor hypothesized to be present in intelligence tests that provides an advantage for test takers from certain cultural backgrounds

culture-free descriptive of a test in which cultural biases have been removed

cultural–familial disability substandard intellectual performance stemming from lack of opportunity to acquire knowledge and skills

creativity a trait characterized by flexibility, ingenuity, and originality

convergent thinking a thought process that attempts to focus on the single best solution to a problem

divergent thinking free and fluent association to the elements of a problem

heritability the degree to which the variations in a trait from one person to another can be attributed to genetic factors

9-8 **Describe language development in middle childhood, including reading and bilingualism.** Children's language ability grows more sophisticated in middle childhood. Children learn to read as well. Table 9.4 illustrates literacy rates in various regions around the world. Approximately 47 million Americans live in homes where a language other than English is spoken.

word-recognition method a method for learning to read in which children come to recognize words through repeated exposure to them

phonetic method a method for learning to read in which children decode the sounds of words based on their knowledge of the sounds of letters and letter combinations

sight vocabulary words that are immediately recognized on the basis of familiarity with their overall shapes, rather than decoded

bilingual using or capable of using two languages with nearly equal or equal facility

CHAPTER 10 LEARNING OUTCOMES / KEY TERMS

10-1 **Explain theories of social and emotional development in middle childhood.** Freud viewed middle childhood as the latency stage; Erikson saw it as the stage of industry versus inferiority. Social cognitive theorists note that children now depend less on external rewards and punishments and increasingly regulate their own behavior. Cognitive-developmental theory notes that concrete operations enhance social development. In middle childhood, children become more capable of taking the role or perspective of another person. Selman theorizes that children move from egocentricity to seeing the world through the eyes of others in five stages.

In early childhood, children's self-concepts focus on external traits. In middle childhood, children begin to include abstract internal traits. Social relationships and group membership assume importance. In middle childhood, competence and social acceptance contribute to self-esteem, but self-esteem tends to decline because the self-concept becomes more realistic. Authoritative parenting fosters self-esteem. Children with "learned helplessness" tend not to persist in the face of failure.

latency stage in psychoanalytic theory, the fourth stage of psychosexual development, characterized by repression of sexual impulses and development of skills

industry versus inferiority a stage of psychosocial development in Erikson's theory occurring in middle childhood. Mastery of tasks leads to a sense of industry, whereas failure produces feelings of inferiority

social cognition development of children's understanding of the relationship between the self and others

learned helplessness an acquired (hence, learned) belief that one is unable to control one's environment

10-2 **Discuss the influences of the family on social development in middle childhood.** In middle childhood, the family continues to play a key role in socialization. Parent–child interactions focus on school-related issues, chores, and peers. Parents do less monitoring of children; "coregulation" develops. Children of lesbian and gay parents by and large develop as well as children of heterosexual parents. The sexual orientation of these children is generally heterosexual. Divorce disrupts children's lives and usually lowers the family's financial status. Children are likely to greet divorce with sadness, shock, and disbelief. Children of divorce fare better when parents cooperate on child rearing. Children appear to suffer as much from marital conflict as from divorce. Having both parents in the workforce can lead to lack of supervision, but there is little evidence that maternal employment per se harms children. Maternal employment fosters greater independence and flexibility in gender-role stereotypes.

coregulation a gradual transferring of control from parent to child, beginning in middle childhood

transgender referring to people who feel as though they are persons of the other sex who are 'trapped' in the body of the wrong sex. Some transgender individuals (also called 'trans') are content to adopt the clothing and cosmetic appearance of people of the other sex; others undergo hormone treatments and surgery to achieve the body shape and external physical traits of persons of the other sex

10-3 **Discuss the influences of peers on social development in middle childhood.** Peers take on increasing importance in middle childhood and exert pressure to conform. Peers afford practice in social skills, sharing, relating to leaders, and coping with aggressive impulses. Popular children tend to be attractive and mature for their age. Early in middle childhood, friendships are based on proximity. Between the ages of 8 and 11, children become more aware of the value of friends as meeting each other's needs and having traits such as loyalty. At this age, peers tend to discourage contact with members of the other sex.

cyberbullying the use of electronic devices such as cellphones, computers, and tablets to transmit threatening and taunting messages

TABLE 10.2 STAGES IN CHILDREN'S CONCEPTS OF FRIENDSHIP

Stage	Name	Approximate Age (Years)	What Happens
0	Momentary physical interaction	3–6	Children remain egocentric. Their concept of a friend is one who likes to play with the same things and lives nearby.
1	One-way assistance	5–9*	Children are less egocentric but view a friend as someone who does what they want.
2	Fair-weather cooperation	7–12*	Friends are viewed as doing things for one another, but the focus remains on self-interest.
3	Intimate and mutual sharing	10–15*	The focus is on the relationship rather than on the individuals separately. Friendship is viewed as providing mutual support over a long period of time.
4	Autonomous interdependence	12 and above*	Children (adolescents, and adults) understand that friendships grow and change as people change and that they may need different friends to satisfy different needs.

*Ages can overlap

Source: Selman (1980).

10 Middle Childhood: Social and Emotional Development

10-4 **Describe the influence of the school on social development in middle childhood.** Schools make demands for mature behavior and nurture positive physical, social, and cognitive development. Readiness for school is related to children's early life experiences, individual differences in development and learning, and the schools' expectations. An effective school has an orderly atmosphere, empowers teachers and students, holds high expectations of children, and has solid academics. Teachers' expectations can become self-fulfilling prophecies. Many girls suffer from sexism and sexual harassment in school. Math and science are still often stereotyped as masculine, and language arts as feminine.

Pygmalion effect a positive self-fulfilling prophecy in which an individual comes to display improved performance because of the positive expectation of the people with whom he or she interacts

self-fulfilling prophecy an event that occurs because of the behavior of those who expect it to occur

sexism discrimination or bias against people based on their gender

sexual harassment unwelcome verbal or physical conduct of a sexual nature

10-5 **Discuss social and emotional problems that tend to develop in middle childhood.** There may be a genetic component to conduct disorders, but sociopathic models in the family, deviant peers, and inconsistent discipline contribute. Depressed children tend to complain of poor appetite, insomnia, lack of energy, and feelings of worthlessness. They blame themselves excessively for shortcomings. Psychotherapy focuses on cognitive errors; antidepressants are sometimes helpful but controversial. Separation anxiety disorder (SAD) is diagnosed when separation anxiety is persistent and excessive and interferes with daily life. Children with SAD tend to cling to parents and might refuse to attend school. Children might also refuse school because they find it to be unpleasant or hostile. The central aspect of treatment of school refusal is to insist that the child attend school.

conduct disorder marked by persistent breaking of the rules and violations of the rights of others

attributional style the way in which one is disposed toward interpreting outcomes (successes or failures), as in tending to place blame or responsibility on oneself or on external factors

serotonin a neurotransmitter that is involved in mood disorders such as depression

generalized anxiety disorder (GAD) an anxiety disorder in which anxiety appears to be present continuously and is unrelated to the situation

phobia an irrational, excessive fear that interferes with one's functioning

separation anxiety disorder (SAD) an extreme form of otherwise normal separation anxiety that is characterized by anxiety about separating from parents; SAD often takes the form of refusal to go to school

school phobia fear of attending school, marked by extreme anxiety at leaving parents

CHAPTER REVIEW

CHAPTER 11 LEARNING OUTCOMES / KEY TERMS

11-1 **Describe the key events of puberty and their relationship to social development.** G. Stanley Hall believed that adolescence is marked by "storm and stress." Current views challenge the idea that storm and stress are normal or beneficial. Puberty is a stage of physical development that is characterized by reaching sexual maturity. Sex hormones trigger the development of primary and secondary sex characteristics. Girls undergo a growth spurt earlier than boys do. Boys tend to spurt up to 4 inches per year, and girls, up to 3 inches per year. During their growth spurts, boys catch up with girls and grow taller and heavier. Boys' shoulders become broader, and girls develop broader and rounder hips. More of a male's body weight is made of muscle. Adolescents may look gawky because of asynchronous growth. Boys typically ejaculate by age 13 or 14. Female sex hormones regulate the menstrual cycle.

The effects of early maturation are generally positive for boys and often negative for girls. Early-maturing boys tend to be more popular. Early-maturing girls become conspicuous, often leading to sexual approaches, deviant behavior, and a poor body image. Girls are generally more dissatisfied with their bodies than boys are. By age 18, dissatisfaction tends to decline.

FIG.11.1 SPURTS IN GROWTH

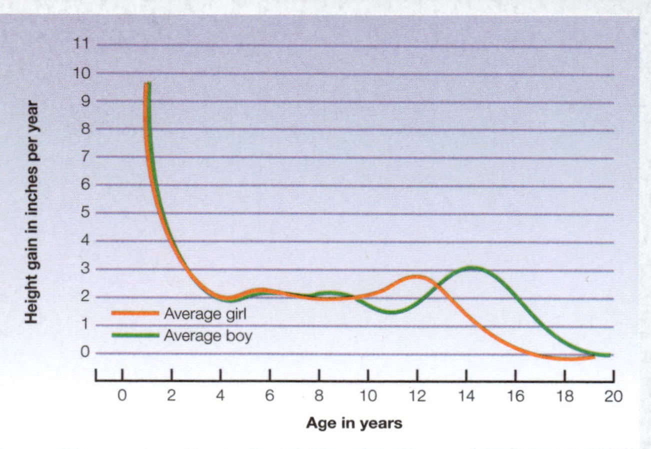

Girls begin the adolescent growth spurt about two years earlier than boys. Girls and boys reach their periods of peak growth about two years after the spurt begins.

FIG.11.4 THE DECLINE IN AGE AT MENARCHE

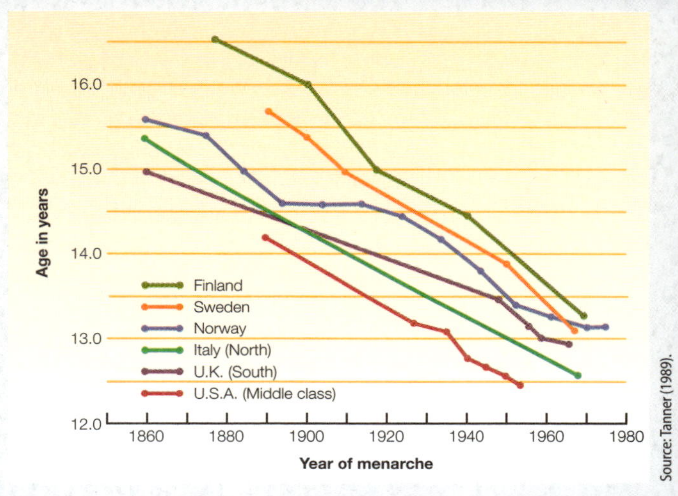

The age at menarche has been declining since the mid-1800s among girls in Western nations, apparently because of improved nutrition and health care.

puberty the biological stage of development characterized by changes that lead to reproductive capacity

feedback loop a system in which glands regulate each other's functioning through a series of hormonal messages

primary sex characteristics the structures that make reproduction possible

secondary sex characteristics physical indicators of sexual maturation—such as changes to the voice and growth of bodily hair—that do not directly involve reproductive structures

asynchronous growth unbalanced growth, such as the growth that occurs during the early part of adolescence and causes many adolescents to appear gawky

secular trend a historical trend toward increasing adult height and earlier puberty

semen the fluid that contains sperm and substances that nourish and help transport sperm

nocturnal emission emission of seminal fluid while asleep

gynecomastia enlargement of breast tissue in males

epiphyseal closure the process by which the cartilage that separates the long end of a bone from the main part of the bone turns to bone

menarche the onset of menstruation

11-2 **Discuss health issues in adolescence, focusing on the causes of death, on eating disorders, and on substance use.** Most adolescent health problems stem from their lifestyles. Accidents, suicide, and homicide account for aboutthree in four deaths among adolescents. To fuel the adolescent growth spurt, the average girl needs 1,800 to 2,400 calories per day, and the average boy needs 2,200 to 3,200 calories. Adolescents need high quantities of calcium, iron, zinc, magnesium, and nitrogen. Adolescents usually need more vitamins than they get from what they usually eat, but less sugar, fat, protein, and sodium.

Adolescence: Physical and Cognitive Development

Eating disorders include anorexia nervosa and bulimia nervosa. Eating disorders mainly afflict females. Some psychoanalysts suggest that anorexia represents efforts to remain prepubescent. One risk factor for eating disorders in adolescent females is a history of child abuse. Eating disorders might develop because of fear of gaining weight resulting from cultural idealization of the slim female. Genetic factors might connect eating disorders with perfectionistic personality styles.

TABLE 11.1 HAVE YOU USED ___ IN YOUR ___?

Percent saying "Yes"

	Lifetime	Last year	Last 30 days
Alcohol	45.2	39.9	21.8
Amphetamines	9.1	6.2	2.7
Cigarettes	21.1	N/A	7.0
E-cigarettes	N/A	N/A	13.2
Cocaine	2.7	1.7	0.8
Ecstasy	3.5	2.2	0.8
Heroin	0.7	0.4	0.2
LSD	2.8	1.9	0.7
Marijuana	30.0	23.7	14.0

Source: Johnston, L. D., O'Malley, P. M., Miech, R. A., Bachman, J. G., & Schulenberg, J. E. (2016). Monitoring the Future national survey results on drug use, 1975–2015: Overview, key findings on adolescent drug use. Ann Arbor: Institute for Social Research, The University of Michigan.

Notes: Drug use increases from the 8th grade through the 12th grade. Use of e-cigarettes has surpassed use of tobacco cigarettes among adolescents. Finally, results reflect usage only among adolescents in school; dropouts are not included.

osteoporosis a condition involving progressive loss of bone tissue

anorexia nervosa an eating disorder characterized by irrational fear of weight gain, distorted body image, and severe weight loss

bulimia nervosa an eating disorder characterized by cycles of binge eating and purging as a means of controlling weight gain

substance use disorder a persistent pattern of use of a substance characterized by frequent intoxication; impairment of physical, social, or emotional well-being; and possible physical addiction

abstinence syndrome a characteristic cluster of symptoms that results from a sudden decrease in the level of usage of a substance

hallucinogenics drugs that give rise to hallucinations

11-3 **Discuss adolescent cognitive development and the key events of Piaget's stage of formal operations.** In Western societies, formal operational thought begins at about the time of puberty. The major achievements of the stage involve classification, logical thought (deductive reasoning), and the ability to hypothesize. Adolescent egocentrism is shown in the concepts of the imaginary audience and the personal fable.

formal operations the fourth stage in Piaget's cognitive-developmental theory, characterized by the capacity for flexible, reversible operations concerning abstract ideas and concepts, such as symbols, statements, and theories

imaginary audience the belief that others around us are as concerned with our thoughts and behaviors as we are; one aspect of adolescent egocentrism

personal fable the belief that our feelings and ideas are special and unique and that we are invulnerable; one aspect of adolescent egocentrism

11-4 **Describe gender differences in cognitive abilities.** The stage of formal operations is Piaget's final stage of development. Many children reach this stage during adolescence, but not all. The formal operational stage is characterized by the individual's increased ability to classify objects and ideas, engage in logical thought, hypothesize, and demonstrate a sophisticated use of symbols. Adolescents show a new egocentrism in which they comprehend the ideas of other people, but have difficulty sorting out those things that concern other people from the things that concern themselves.

11-5 **Discuss Kohlberg's theory of moral development in adolescence.** Females tend to excel in verbal ability. Males tend to excel in visual–spatial ability. Females and males show equal ability in math. Boys are more likely than girls to have reading problems. Gender differences in cognitive abilities have been linked to biological factors and to gender stereotypes.

postconventional level according to Kohlberg, a period during which moral judgments are derived from moral principles and people look to themselves to set moral standards

11-6 **Discuss the roles of the school in adolescence, focusing on dropping out.** In the postconventional level, according to Kohlberg, moral reasoning is based on the person's own moral standards. In Kohlberg's scheme, males reason at higher levels of moral development than females do, but Gilligan argues that this gender difference reflects patterns of socialization, with girls being encouraged to take a more "caring" orientation.

11-7 **Discuss work experience during adolescence.** The transition to middle, junior high, or high school generally involves a shift from a smaller neighborhood elementary school to a larger, more impersonal setting. The transition is often accompanied by a decline in grades and a drop in self-esteem. High school dropouts are more likely to be unemployed and earn lower salaries. Dropouts are more likely to show delinquent behaviors. Truancy and reading below grade level predict school dropout.

self-efficacy expectations beliefs that we will be able to successfully meet the requirements of our situations

12-1 **Discuss the formation of identity in adolescence.** Erikson's adolescent stage of psychosocial development is ego identity versus role diffusion. The primary task of this stage is for adolescents to develop a sense of who they are and what they stand for. Marcia's identity statuses represent the four combinations of the dimensions of exploration and commitment: identity diffusion, foreclosure, moratorium, and identity achievement. Development of identity is more complicated for adolescents who belong to ethnic minority groups. Minority adolescents are faced with two sets of cultural values and might need to reconcile and incorporate elements of both.

Researchers propose a three-stage model of the development of ethnic identity: unexamined ethnic identity, an ethnic identity search, and an achieved ethnic identity. As minority youth move through adolescence, they are increasingly likely to explore and achieve ethnic identity.

Erikson proposed that interpersonal relationships are more important to women's identity than occupational and ideological issues, bur research suggests that U.S. adolescent females and males are equally concerned about careers. Adolescents incorporate psychological traits and social relationships into their self-descriptions. Self-esteem tends to decline as the child progresses from middle childhood into early adolescence, perhaps because of increasing recognition of the disparity between the ideal self and the real self. Then, self-esteem gradually improves.

TABLE 12.1 THE FOUR IDENTITY STATUSES OF JAMES MARCIA

		Exploration: Yes	Exploration: No
Commitment	Yes	**Identity Achievement** • Most developed in terms of identity • Has experienced a period of exploration • Has developed commitments • Has a sense of personal well-being, high self-esteem, and self-acceptance • Cognitively flexible • Sets goals and works toward achieving them	**Foreclosure** • Makes commitments without considering alternatives • Commitments based on identification with parents, teachers, or other authority figures • Often authoritarian and inflexible
	No	**Moratorium** • Actively exploring alternatives • Attempting to make choices with regard to occupation, ideological beliefs, and so on • Often anxious and intense • Ambivalent feelings toward parents and authority figures	**Identity Diffusion** • Least developed in terms of identity • Lacks commitments • Not trying to form commitments • May be carefree and uninvolved or unhappy and lonely • May be angry, alienated, rebellious

ego identity vs. role diffusion Erikson's fifth life crisis, during which adolescents develop a firm sense of who they are and what they stand for (ego identity), or they do not develop a sense of who they are and tend to be subject to the whims of others

psychological moratorium a period when adolescents experiment with different roles, values, beliefs, and relationships

identity crisis a turning point in development during which one examines one's values and makes decisions about life roles

Identity diffusion an identity status that characterizes those who have no commitments and who are not in the process of exploring alternatives

foreclosure an identity status that characterizes those who have made commitments without considering alternatives

moratorium an identity status that characterizes those who are actively exploring alternatives in an attempt to form an identity

Identity achievement an identity status that characterizes those who have explored alternatives and have developed commitments

ethnic identity a sense of belonging to an ethnic group

unexamined ethnic identity the first stage of ethnic identity development; similar to the diffusion or foreclosure identity statuses

ethnic identity search the second stage of ethnic identity development; similar to the moratorium identity status

achieved ethnic identity the final stage of ethnic identity development; similar to the identity achievement status

12-2 **Describe relationships with parents and peers during adolescence.** During adolescence, children spend much less time with parents than during childhood. Although adolescents become more independent of their parents, they generally continue to love and respect them. The role of peers increases markedly during the teen years. Adolescents are more likely than younger children to stress intimate self-disclosure and mutual understanding in friendships. The two major types of peer groups are cliques and crowds. Adolescent peer groups also include peers of the other gender. Romantic relationships begin to appear during early and middle adolescence. Dating is a source of fun, prestige, and experience in relationships. Dating is also a preparation for adult courtship.

cliques a group of five to ten individuals who hang around together and who share activities and confidences

crowds a large, loosely organized group of people who may or may not spend much time together and who are identified by the activities of the group

12-3 **Discuss sexuality during adolescence, focusing on sexual orientation, sexual behavior, and teenage pregnancy.** Some adolescents have a homosexual orientation. The process of "coming out" can be a long and painful struggle. Masturbation is the most common sexual outlet in adolescence. Adolescents today start dating earlier than past generations. Teens who date earlier are

- more likely to engage in sexual activity
- less likely to use contraception
- more likely to become pregnant

Early onset of puberty is connected with earlier sexual activity. Adolescents who have close relationships with parents are less likely to initiate sexual activity early. Peer pressure is a powerful contributor to sexual activity.

Many girls who become pregnant have received little advice about how to resist sexual advances. Most of them do not have access to contraception. Most misunderstand reproduction or miscalculate the odds of conception. Teenage mothers are more likely to have medical complications during pregnancy and birth, largely because of inadequate medical care. The babies are more likely to be premature and to have low birth weight. Teenage mothers have a lower standard of living and a greater need for public assistance. Their children have more academic and emotional problems.

FIG.12.1 NEVER-MARRIED TEENAGERS, AGED 15–19, WHO HAVE HAD SEXUAL INTERCOURSE

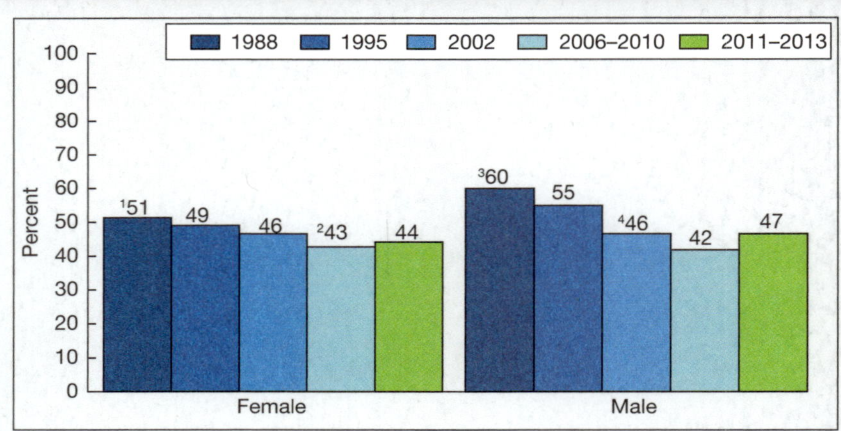

Source: Martinez, G., & Abma, J. C. (2015). Sexual activity, contraceptive use, and childbearing of teenagers aged 15–19 in the United States. U.S. Department of Health and Human Services, National Center for Health Statistics. NCHS Data Brief, No. 209, Figure 1.

Masturbation sexual self-stimulation

Petting kissing and touching the breasts and genitals

homosexual referring to an erotic orientation toward members of one's own gender

Bisexual attracted to individuals of both genders

transgendered psychologically belonging to the other gender—that is, the gender that is inconsistent with one's sexual anatomy

LGBT acronym for *l*esbian, *g*ay, *b*isexual, and *t*ransgendered

sexual identity the label a person uses to signal who she or he is as a sexual being, especially concerning her or his sexual orientation

12-4 **Discuss the characteristics of juvenile delinquents.** Behaviors, such as drinking, that are considered illegal when performed by minors are called status offenses. Boys are more apt to commit crimes of violence, whereas girls are more likely to commit status offenses. Risk factors associated with juvenile delinquency include poor school performance, delinquent friends, early aggressive or hyperactive behavior, substance abuse, low verbal IQ, low self-esteem, impulsivity, and immature moral reasoning. The parents and siblings of delinquents have frequently engaged in antisocial behavior themselves.

juvenile delinquency conduct in a child or adolescent characterized by illegal activities

12-5 **Discuss risk factors in adolescent suicide.** Suicide is the third leading cause of death among adolescents. Most suicides among adolescents and adults are linked to stress, feelings of depression, identity problems, impulsivity, and social problems. Girls are more likely to attempt suicide, whereas boys are more likely to "succeed."

13-1 **Discuss the (theoretical) stage of emerging adulthood.** Emerging adulthood is a period of development, spanning the ages of 18 to 25, in which young people engage in extended role exploration. Emerging adulthood can occur in affluent societies that grant young people the luxury of developing their identities and their life plans.

emerging adulthood a theoretical period of development, spanning the ages of 18 to 25, in which young people in developed nations engage in extended role exploration

13-2 **Describe trends in physical development in early adulthood.** Physical development peaks in early adulthood. Most people are at their height of sensory sharpness, strength, reaction time, and cardiovascular fitness in early adulthood. A higher percentage of men's body mass is made of muscle, and men are normally stronger than women. Peak fitness is followed by gradual declines in the cardiovascular, respiratory, and immune systems. Regular exercise helps maintain cardiovascular and respiratory capacity. As people age, the disease-fighting ability of the immune system declines.

FIG.13.1 SUBJECTIVE CONCEPTIONS OF ADULT STATUS IN RESPONSE TO THE QUESTION, "DO YOU FEEL THAT YOU HAVE REACHED ADULTHOOD?"

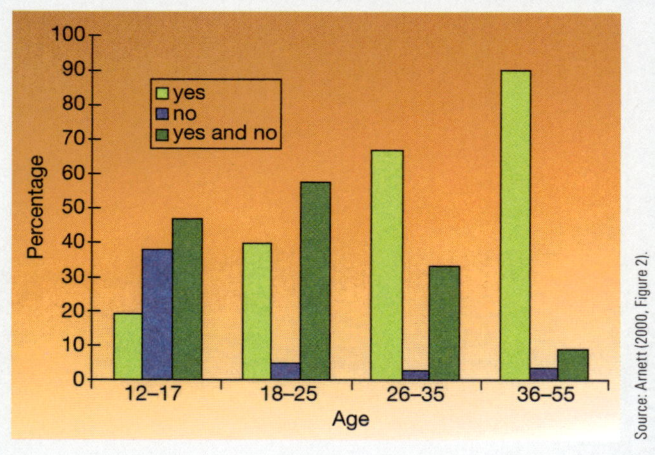

Source: Arnett (2000, Figure 2).

Fertility in both sexes declines as early adulthood progresses; after age 35, women are usually advised to have their fetuses checked for Down syndrome and other abnormalities.

13-3 **Discuss health in early adulthood, focusing on causes of death, diet, exercise, and substance use and abuse.** Accidents are the leading cause of death in early adulthood. Most young adults do not eat the recommended five fruits and vegetables each day. About four in ten report insufficient exercise and being overweight. Sizeable minorities report smoking and binge drinking. Heredity is involved in weight, and adaptive thermogenesis can sabotage dieting efforts. Substance abuse is use of a substance despite related social, occupational, psychological, or physical problems.

Substance dependence is characterized by tolerance and withdrawal symptoms. Depressants such as alcohol, narcotics, and barbiturates are addictive substances that slow the activity of the nervous system. Alcohol also lowers inhibitions, relaxes, and intoxicates. Stimulants such as nicotine, cocaine, and amphetamines accelerate the heartbeat and other bodily functions but depress the appetite. Hallucinogenics such as marijuana and LSD give rise to perceptual distortions called hallucinations. One-third of Americans say they are living with "extreme" stress.

TABLE 13.1 LEADING CAUSES OF DEATH FOR 15- TO 44-YEAR-OLDS

15 – 24	25 – 44
Accidents	Accidents
Suicide	Suicide
Homicide	Homicide
Cancer	Cancer
Heart disease	Heart disease
Congenital problems	Liver disease
Influence & pneumonia	Diabetes
Diabetes	HIV/AIDS
Respiratory disease	Stroke
Stroke	Influenza & pneumonia

Source: National Vital Statistics System, National Center for Health Statistics, CDC. 10 Leading Causes of Death by Age Group, United States–2014. Produced by: National Center for Injury Prevention and Control, CDC.

adaptive thermogenesis the process by which the body converts food energy (calories) to heat at a lower rate when a person eats less, because of, for example, famine or dieting

TABLE 13.2 HAVE YOU USED ________ IN THE PAST YEAR?

Percent of college students and young adults (aged 19–28) saying "yes":

	College students	Young Adults
Alcohol	76.1	82.3
Amphetamines	10.1	8.0
Cigarettes	22.6	27.0
Cocaine	4.4	5.0
Ecstasy	5.0	4.8
Heroin	0.0	0.4
Narcotics other than heroin*	4.8	6.3
LSD	2.2	2.2
Marijuana	34.4	31.6

*e.g., OxyContin, Vicodin

Source: Johnston, L. D., O'Malley, P. M., Bachman, J. G., Schulenberg, J. E. & Miech, R. A. (2015). Monitoring the Future national survey results on drug use, 1975–2014: Volume 2, College students and adults ages 19–55. Ann Arbor: Institute for Social Research, The University of Michigan.

Early Adulthood: Physical and Cognitive Development

13-4 **Discuss sexuality in early adulthood, focusing on homosexuality, STIs, menstrual problems, and sexual coercion.** Sexual activity with a partner tends to peak in the 20s. From a learning theory point of view, early reinforcement of sexual behavior influences sexual orientation. Researchers have found evidence for genetic and hormonal factors in sexual orientation. Sexually transmitted infections (STIs) include bacterial infections such as chlamydia, gonorrhea, and syphilis; viral infections such as HIV/AIDS, HPV, and genital herpes; and some others. Risk factors for contracting STIs include sexual activity with multiple partners and without condoms, and substance abuse. Fifty percent to 75% of women experience at least some discomfort prior to or during menstruation, including dysmenorrhea, menstrual migraines, amenorrhea, premenstrual syndrome (PMS), and premenstrual dysphoric disorder (PMDD). Half a million U.S. women are raped each year, and women aged 16–24 are most likely to be victimized. Rape obviously has sexual aspects, but it is also the male subjugation of women. Social attitudes such as the myth that "Women say no when they mean yes" support rape, as does encouragement of young men to be aggressive.

dysmenorrhea painful menstruation

prostaglandins hormones that cause muscles in the uterine wall to contract, as during labor

Amenorrhea the absence of menstruation

Premenstrual syndrome (PMS) the discomforting symptoms that affect many women during the four–six day interval preceding their periods

Premenstrual dysphoric disorder (PMDD) a condition similar to but more severe than PMS

sexual harassment deliberate or repeated unwanted comments, gestures, or physical contact

13-5 **Discuss cognitive development in early adulthood, focusing on "postformal" developments and effects of college life.** Schaie points out that the cognitive development of adults is strongly tied in to the societal developments of the day. Young adults can be said in some ways to engage in "postformal" thinking: Perry's theory of epistemic cognition concerns the ways in which we arrive at our beliefs, facts, and ideas; e.g., dualistic thinking might be replaced by relativistic thinking. Labouvie-Vief's theory of pragmatic thought notes that "cognitively healthy" adults are more willing than egocentric adolescents to compromise and deal within the world as it is, not as they would like it to be; they develop cognitive–affective complexity that enables them to harbor both positive and negative feelings about their choices. The diversity of college life can also broaden students.

crystallized intelligence one's intellectual attainments, as shown, for example, by vocabulary and accumulated knowledge

fluid intelligence mental flexibility; the ability to process information rapidly

epistemic cognition thought processes directed at considering how we arrive at our beliefs, facts, and ideas

dualistic thinking dividing the cognitive world into opposites, such as good and bad, or us versus them

relativistic thinking recognition that judgments are often not absolute but made from a certain belief system or cultural background

pragmatic thought decision making characterized by willingness to accept reality and compromise

cognitive–affective complexity a mature form of thinking that permits people to harbor positive and negative feelings about their career choices and other matters

13-6 **Describe career choice and development during early adulthood.** People work for extrinsic rewards, such as money and benefits, and for intrinsic rewards, such as self-identity and self-fulfillment. Stages of career development include a fantasy stage, a realistic-choice stage, a maintenance stage, perhaps job-changing or retraining stages, and a retirement stage. Developmental tasks when beginning a job include accepting subordinate status, learning to get along with co-workers and supervisors, finding a mentor, and showing progress.

CHAPTER 14 LEARNING OUTCOMES / KEY TERMS

14-1 **Examine the issues involved in early adulthood separation.** Havighurst's "tasks" for early adulthood include getting started in an occupation and courting a mate. Young adults who enter the job market out of high school might live at home for a while to save money. Other young adults might leave home to attend college or enlist in the military. Traditional or insecure parents might find a child's—especially a daughter's—leaving for college stressful. Young adults need to become individuals by integrating their own values with those of their parents and society.

individuation the young adult's process of becoming an individual by means of integrating his or her own values and beliefs with those of his or her parents and society at large

14-2 **Describe the conflict between intimacy and isolation.** Erikson's core conflict for early adulthood is intimacy versus isolation. Young adults who develop ego identity during adolescence are more ready to marry and develop friendships.

intimacy versus isolation according to Erik Erikson, the central conflict or life crisis of early adulthood, in which a person develops an intimate relationship with a significant other or risks heading down a path toward social isolation

14-3 **Discuss the seasons of life experienced during early adulthood.** Levinson labels the ages of 17 to 33 the entry phase of adulthood—when people leave home and strive for independence. Many young adults adopt "the dream," which serves as a tentative blueprint for life. Young adults undergo an age-30 transition and commonly reassess their lives. Young adults often settle down during the later thirties.

life structure in Levinson's theory, the underlying pattern of a person's life at a given stage, as defined by relationships, career, race, religion, economic status, and the like

the dream according to Daniel Levinson and his colleagues, the drive to become someone, to leave one's mark on history, which serves as a tentative blueprint for the young adult

14-4 **Examine the emotional forces of attraction and love.** Physical appearance is a key in selection of romantic partners. People prefer slenderness in both genders and tallness in males. Women are more likely to prefer socially dominant men, but many men are put off by assertive women. Women find physical attractiveness less important than men do, but they prefer steady workers. Some psychologists believe that gender differences in preferences for mates provide reproductive advantages. People prefer partners who are similar to them in attractiveness and attitudes. People tend to reciprocate feelings of attraction. Berscheid and Hatfield define romantic love in terms of arousal and cognitive appraisal of that arousal as love. Sternberg's "triangular theory" of love includes the building blocks of intimacy, passion, and commitment.

attraction–similarity hypothesis the view that people tend to develop romantic relationships with people who are similar to themselves in physical attractiveness and other traits

reciprocity the tendency to respond in kind when we feel admired and complimented

romantic love a form of love fueled by passion and feelings of intimacy

intimacy the experience of warmth toward another person that arises from feelings of closeness and connectedness

passion intense romantic or sexual desire for another person

commitment the decision to devote oneself to a cause or another person

FIG.14.2 WHY DID THEY DECK HER OUT IN RED?

Cultural conditioning and the human biological heritage provide two good answers.

14-5 **Explain why people get lonely and what they do in response.** Loneliness is connected with low self-confidence, depression, and physical health problems. Lonely people tend to lack social skills, interest in other people, and empathy. Many people remain lonely because of fear of rejection. There are a number of coping strategies for loneliness (see page 298).

14 Early Adulthood: Social and Emotional Development

14-6 **Discuss the lifestyle of being single.** Being single is the most common U.S. lifestyle of people in their early 20s. Many people postpone marriage to pursue educational and career goals. Many cohabit. Some have not found the right partner.

Some single people are lonely, but most are well adjusted. Many singles engage in serial monogamy.

serial monogamy a series of exclusive sexual relationships

celibacy abstention from sexual activity, whether from choice or lack of opportunity

14-7 **Describe the practice of cohabitation.** More than half of today's marriages are preceded by cohabitation. More than half of high school seniors believe that it is a good idea to cohabit before marriage to test compatibility. Cohabitants tend to have less traditional views of marriage and gender roles.

cohabitation living together with a romantic partner without being married

14-8 **Describe the practice of marriage.** Two-thirds of U.S. adults age 35–44 are married. Marriage legitimizes sexual relations, provides an institution for rearing children, and permits the orderly transmission of wealth from one generation to another. Types of marriage include monogamy, polygamy, and arranged marriage. In 2015, the U.S. Supreme Court held that marriage is a fundamental right that cannot be denied to couples of the same sex, legalizing same-sex marriage after decades of debate. Similarity in physical attractiveness, attitudes, background, and interests plays a role in marital choices. Most marriages follow age homogamy. Intimacy and support of one's spouse are connected with marital satisfaction. Gay and lesbian couples are more likely to distribute chores evenly.

FIG.14.11 PERCENT OF AMERICANS WHO SUPPORT AND OPPOSE SAME-SEX MARRIAGE

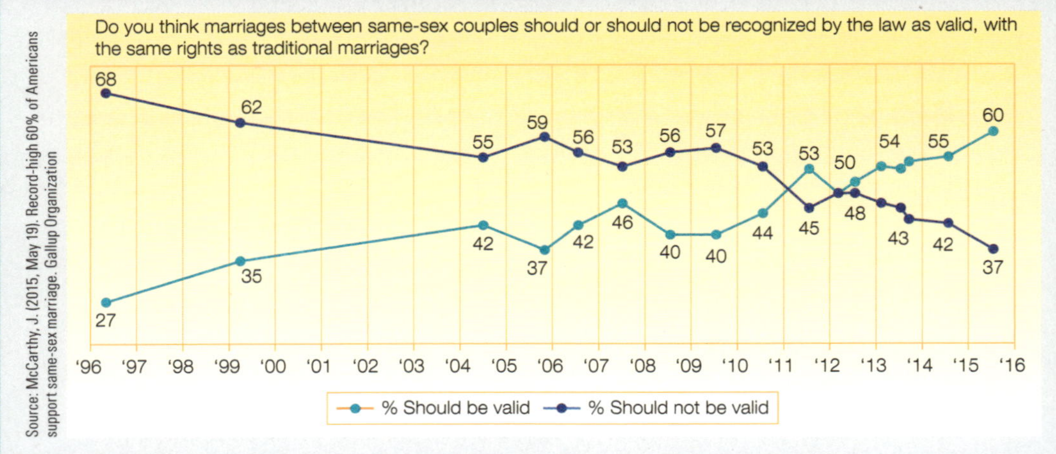

In 2001 57% of Americns opposed same-sex marriage and 35% approved of it. By 2016 those numbers had been in effect reversed, so that 60% of Americans approve of same-sex marriage and 37% are opposed.

monogamy marriage between one person and one other person

polygamy marriage in which a person has more than one spouse and is permitted sexual access to each of them

homogamy the practice of people getting married to people who are similar to them

14-9 **Discuss the state of parenthood.** Young U.S. adults are delaying parenthood into their later 20s. In developed nations, most couples say they choose to have children for personal happiness. In more traditional societies, people say children provide security and social status, assist with labor, and secure property rights. Having a child is unlikely to save a marriage. The mother is usually the primary caregiver and encounters more stress and role overload than the father does when she is also in the workforce. Workplace tension affects home life, and vice versa. It is usually the mother who cuts back on work when families want a parent in the home full time.

14-10 **Discuss divorce and its repercussions.** Nearly half of U.S. marriages end in divorce. No-fault divorce laws and the increased economic independence of women contribute to the divorce rate. Divorce hits women harder in the pocketbook than it does men, especially when they do not have careers. Divorced and separated people have the highest rates of physical and mental illness.

15-1 **Describe trends in physical development in middle adulthood.** Hair begins to gray in middle adulthood, and hair loss accelerates. Ultraviolet rays worsen wrinkling. The skin loses elasticity. It becomes harder to focus on nearby objects or fine print. Reaction time increases. Breathing capacity declines. Fat replaces lean tissue and the basal metabolic rate declines. Strength decreases. Bone begins to lose density and strength. The cardiovascular system becomes less efficient. Sensitivity to insulin decreases, so the pancreas initially produces more; eventually, however, blood sugar levels rise, increasing the risk of adult-onset diabetes.

middle adulthood the stage of adulthood between early adulthood and late adulthood, beginning at 40 to 45 and ending at 60 to 65

interindividual variability the fact that people do not age in the same way or at the same rate

presbyopia loss of elasticity in the eye lens that makes it harder to focus on nearby objects

15-2 **Discuss the major health concerns of middle adulthood, including cancer and heart disease.** In middle adulthood, cancer and heart disease are the two leading causes of death. Cancer is a noncommunicable but malignant disease characterized by uncontrolled growth of cells that invade and destroy surrounding tissue. Risk factors for cancer include heredity, problems in the immune system, hormonal factors, and carcinogens. Smoking and diet cause two out of three U.S. cancer deaths. Men should begin screening for prostate cancer about age 50, women for breast cancer around age 40, and both genders for cancer of the colon and rectum around age 50. African American men are at greater risk for prostate cancer and are advised to start screening earlier. Family history, high blood pressure, high serum cholesterol, smoking, sedentary lifestyle, and arteriosclerosis are risk factors for heart disease.

TABLE 15.1 LEADING CAUSES OF DEATH IN MIDDLE ADULTHOOD, UNITED STATES

45–54	55–64
Cancer	Cancer
Heart disease	Heart disease
Accidents	Accidents
Suicide	Respiratory disease
Liver disease	Diabetes
Diabetes	Liver disease
Stroke	Stroke
Respiratory disease	Suicide
Influenza & pneumonia	Blood poisoning
Blood poisoning	Influenza & pneumonia

Source: National Vital Statistics System, National Center for Health Statistics, CDC. Produced by National Center for Injury Control and Prevention, CDC using WISQARS.

metastasis the movement of malignant or cancerous cells into parts of the body other than where they originated

arteriosclerosis hardening of the arteries

atherosclerosis the buildup of fatty deposits (plaque) on the lining of arteries

15-3 **Discuss the functioning of the immune system.** The immune system combats disease by producing white blood cells (leukocytes), which engulf and kill pathogens. Leukocytes recognize foreign substances (antigens), deactivate them, and mark them for destruction. The immune system also causes inflammation, which rushes leukocytes to a damaged area. Stress suppresses the immune system. Stress hormones connected with anger can constrict the blood vessels to the heart, leading to a heart attack.

leukocyte white blood cell

15-4 **Discuss sexuality in middle adulthood, focusing on menopause and sexual dysfunctions.** Most people in middle adulthood lead rich sex lives, but the frequency of sex tends to decline. Menopause is a normal process that lasts for about two years; perimenopause is usually characterized by months of amenorrhea or irregular periods. The climacteric generally lasts about 15 years and is caused by decline in estrogen production. Lowered estrogen levels can cause night sweats, hot flashes, hot flushes— even dizziness, headaches, joint pain, tingling in the hands or feet, burning or itchy skin, heart palpitations, and, sometimes, brittleness and porosity of the bones (osteoporosis). Men show a more gradual decline in sex hormones and fertility. Sexual dysfunctions are quite common, beginning in middle adulthood. Women more often report painful sex, inability to reach orgasm, and lack of desire. Men often report erectile dysfunction.

menopause the cessation of menstruation

perimenopause the beginning of menopause, usually characterized by 3 to 11 months of amenorrhea or irregular periods

climacteric the gradual decline in reproductive capacity of the ovaries, generally lasting about 15 years

sexual dysfunction a persistent or recurrent problem in becoming sexually aroused or reaching orgasm

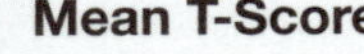

FIG.15.5 LONGITUDINAL CHANGES IN SIX INTELLECTUAL ABILITIES, AGES 25–88

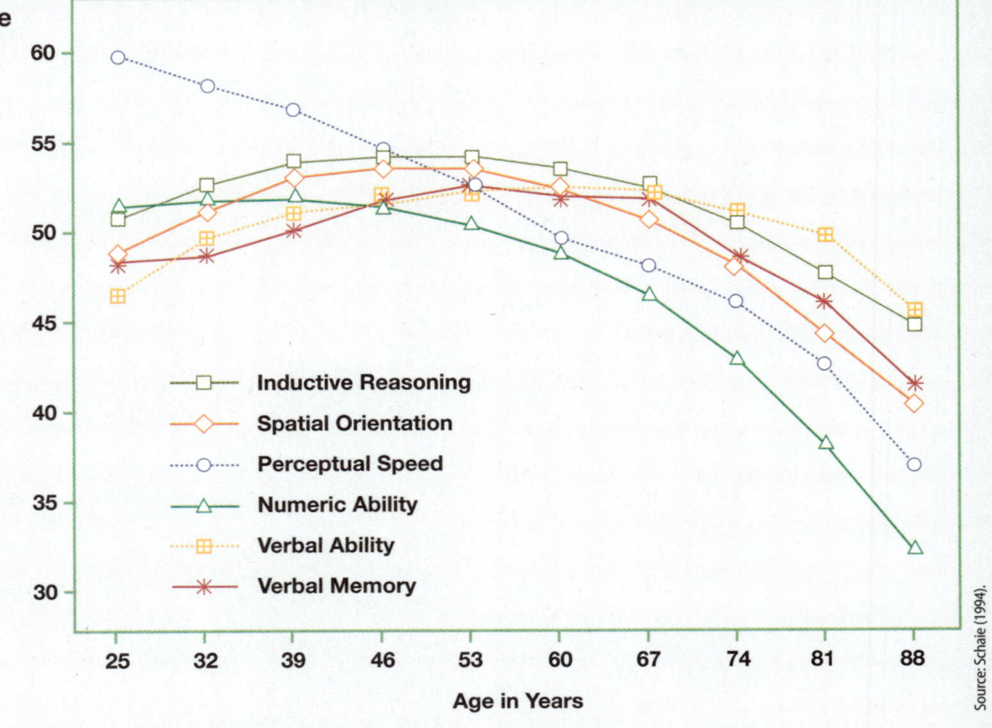

Most intellectual abilities show gains or remain largely stable from early adulthood through middle adulthood. Numeric ability shows a modest decline throughout middle adulthood, and perceptual speed shows a more dramatic drop-off.

15-5 **Describe cognitive development in middle adulthood, distinguishing between crystallized and fluid intelligence.** Intellectual development in adulthood shows multidirectionality, interindividual variability, and plasticity. Flynn found that U.S. IQ scores increased about 18 points between 1947 and 2002. Schaie's Seattle Longitudinal Study found that adults born more recently were superior to those born at earlier times in inductive reasoning, verbal meaning, spatial orientation, and word fluency. The earlier cohorts performed better in numeric ability. Horn distinguished between crystallized and fluid intelligence. Neurological factors apparently play a powerful role in fluid intelligence. Crystallized intelligence tends to increase with age through middle adulthood, but there is a decline in fluid intelligence. Perceptual speed, spatial orientation, and numeric ability are related to fluid intelligence and drop off. Verbal ability and reasoning mainly reflect crystallized intelligence; they increase through middle adulthood and hold up in late adulthood. Good health and staying intellectually active help stem cognitive decline in late adulthood.

multidirectionality in the context of cognitive development, the fact that some aspects of intellectual functioning may improve while others remain stable or decline

plasticity the fact that intellectual abilities are not absolutely fixed but can be modified

crystallized intelligence a cluster of knowledge and skills that depends on accumulated information and experience, awareness of social conventions, and good judgment

fluid intelligence a person's skills at processing information. Skills at processing information

15-6 **Discuss opportunities for exercising creativity and continuing education in middle adulthood.** The middle-age decline in processing speed apparently reflects changes in the nervous system. Most researchers find that people in middle and late adulthood perform less well than young adults at memorizing lists. In later middle adulthood, we are less able to learn by rote repetition and to screen out distractions. Elaborative rehearsal can suffer because we are less capable of rapid classification. Yet we tend to retain or expand general knowledge. We can retain procedural memories for a lifetime. Middle-age people have the verbal abilities of young adults, have lost little fluid intelligence, and have a greater store of expertise.

Mature learners in higher education are likely to be highly motivated and to find the subject matter interesting for its own sake. Ironically, women with the greatest family and work demands are most likely to return to school.

16-1 **Discuss theories of development in middle adulthood.** Havighurst's tasks for middle adulthood include helping our children establish themselves, adjusting to physical changes, and adjusting to caring for aging parents. Erikson believed that the major psychological challenge of the middle years is generativity versus stagnation. Van Hiel finds that generativity and stagnation are independent dimensions rather than opposites. Levinson characterizes the years of 40–45 as a midlife transition that is often accompanied by a midlife crisis, but many people are at the height of their productivity and resilience. Though it was once assumed that women without children in the home would undergo an "empty nest syndrome," this can be a positive event.

FIG.16.2 WOMEN'S ATTITUDES TOWARD HAVING PRENATAL TESTING FOR VARIOUS CONGENITAL DISORDERS

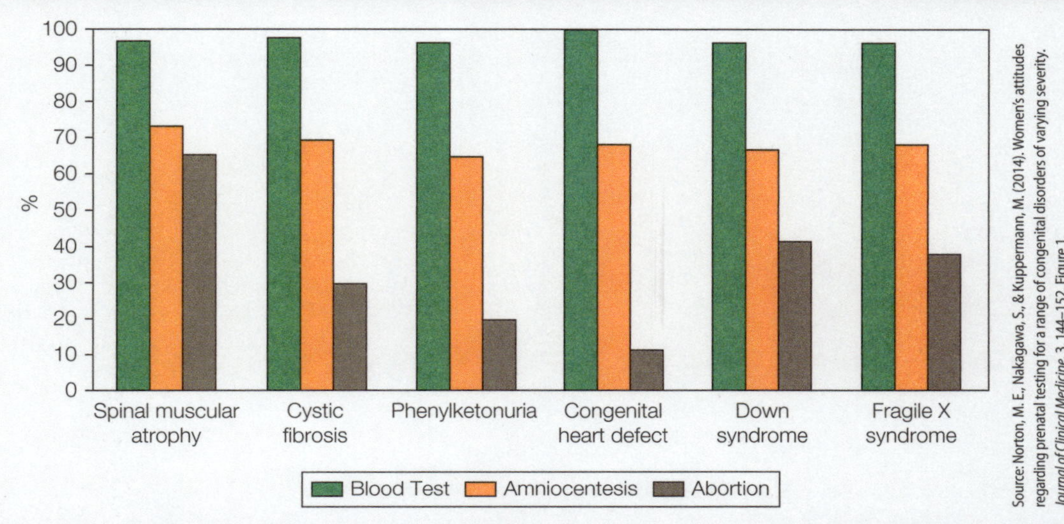

Source: Norton, M. E., Nakagawa, S., & Kuppermann, M. (2014). Women's attitudes regarding prenatal testing for a range of congenital disorders of varying severity. *Journal of Clinical Medicine*, 3, 144–152. Figure 1.

Proportion of women who say they would have a blood test to screen for various fetal health problems, who would have an amniocentesis to test for the problem, and who would have an abortion if the problem were found. Note that the women were more willing to have (less-obtrusive) blood tests than amniocenteses. Moreover, most women said they would not abort a fetus that was shown to have one of these problems.

generativity versus stagnation Erikson's seventh stage of psychosocial development, in which the life crisis is the dichotomy between generativity (as in rearing children or contributing to society) and stagnation (a state characterized by lack of development, growth, or advancement)

midlife transition a psychological shift into middle adulthood that is theorized to occur between the ages of 40 and 45 as people begin to believe they have more to look back upon than forward to

midlife crisis a time of dramatic self-doubt and anxiety during which people sense the passing of their youth and become concerned with their own aging and mortality

empty nest syndrome a feeling of loneliness or loss of purpose that parents, and especially the mother, are theorized to experience when the youngest child leaves home

16-2 **Discuss stability and change in social and emotional development in middle adulthood.** After the age of 30, longitudinal research finds that the "big five" personality traits show a good deal of stability, but the traits of agreeableness and conscientiousness increase somewhat and neuroticism declines.

TABLE 16.1 THE "BIG FIVE": THE FIVE-FACTOR MODEL OF PERSONALITY

Factor	Name	Traits
I	Extraversion	Contrasts talkativeness, assertiveness, and activity with silence, passivity, and reserve
II	Agreeableness	Contrasts kindness, trust, and warmth with hostility, selfishness, and distrust
III	Conscientiousness	Contrasts organization, thoroughness, and reliability with carelessness, negligence, and unreliability
IV	Neuroticism	Contrasts nervousness, moodiness, and sensitivity to negative stimuli with coping ability
V	Openness to experience	Contrasts imagination, curiosity, and creativity with shallowness and lack of perceptiveness

Middle-aged college-educated women show greater identity certainty, confident power, and concern about aging than women in their twenties.

"big five" personality traits basic personality traits derived from contemporary statistical methods: extraversion, agreeableness, conscientiousness, neuroticism (emotional instability), and openness to experience

FIG.16.4 MEAN SCORES OF COLLEGE-EDUCATED WOMEN OF DIFFERENT AGES ACCORDING TO FIVE PERSONALITY THEMES

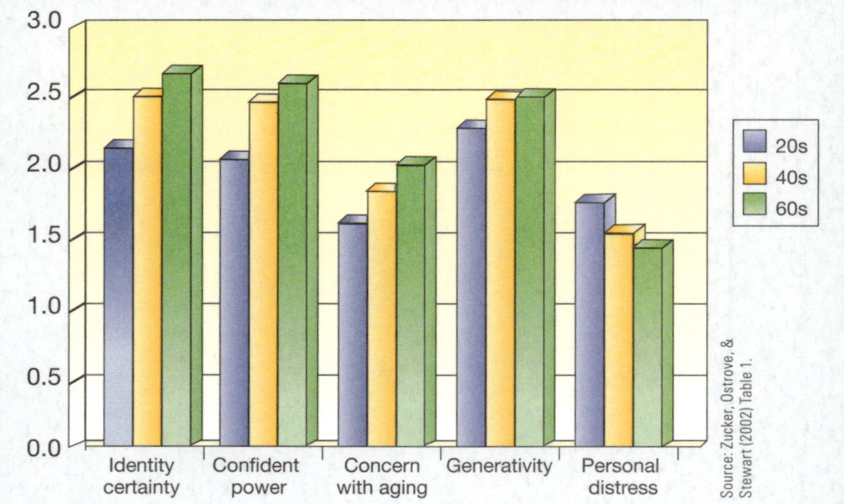

16-3 **Describe career developments typical of middle adulthood.** A study of university employees found that job satisfaction increased through middle adulthood. Most career changes in midlife involve shifts into related fields. Unemployed middle-aged people show lower well-being than unemployed young adults.

16-4 **Discuss trends in relationships in middle adulthood, focusing on grandparenting and on being in the "sandwich generation."** When their children take partners or get married, middle-aged people need to adjust to in-laws. Research generally finds that grandchildren are beneficial to grandparents socially and psychologically. Parents' years with children include their children's time in child care, whereas grandparents spend relatively more time with grandchildren in recreational and educational activities. Grandchildren spend more time in activities with their grandmothers than with their grandfathers, and are relatively more involved with their mother's parents. In some cases, grandparents bear the primary responsibility for rearing grandchildren, and sometimes they are the sole caregivers. Such arrangements typically begin when the grandchild has a single parent. Acting as the parent again can be highly stressful for grandparents.

After working for more than 15 years as a television and film actor, Clint Eastwood made his directorial debut with *The Beguiled* in 1971, at the age of 41. He has continued to make Oscar-nominated and Oscar-winning films through the 2000s.

More than half of the middle-aged people in developed nations have at least one living parent, and most aging parents live near a child. When aging parents need help, the task usually falls to a middle-aged daughter, who then becomes "sandwiched" between caring for or helping her children (and grandchildren) at the same time she is caring for her parents. Most adult sibling relationships are close but can reflect the nature of sibling relationships in childhood. Sisters tend to have more intimate relationships than brothers. Sibling relationships that were antagonistic in childhood can grow closer in middle adulthood if the siblings cooperate in caring for parents. In middle adulthood, the number of friends tends to decline, and people tend to place more value on the friends they retain. The loss of a friend is felt more deeply. Men are less likely than women to have friends or other close social relationships.

sandwich generation the term given to middle-aged people who need to meet the demands of their own children and of aging parents

CHAPTER 17 LEARNING OUTCOMES / KEY TERMS

17-1 **Discuss physical development in late adulthood.** One in eight Americans is older than 65. The life span of a species depends on its genetic programming. Our life expectancy is the number of years we can actually expect to live. Disease prevention and treatment contribute to longevity. The average American baby can expect to live about 78 years, but there are differences because of gender, race, geographic location, and behavior. Men's life expectancy trails women's by about five years. Heart disease develops later in life in women, and men are more likely to die from accidents, cirrhosis of the liver, suicide, homicide, HIV/AIDS, and some forms of cancer. After we reach our physical peak in our twenties, our biological functions gradually decline. Chemical changes of aging can lead to vision disorders such as cataracts and glaucoma. Presbycusis affects one senior citizen in three. Taste and smell become less acute. Osteoporosis results in more than 1 million U.S. bone fractures a year. Insomnia and sleep apnea become more common in later adulthood.

Sexual daydreaming, sex drive, and sexual activity decline with age, but sexual satisfaction can remain high. Many of the physical changes in older women stem from a decline in estrogen production. Women's vaginal walls lose elasticity and they produce less lubrication so that sexual activity may become irritating. Men take longer to achieve erection, and erections become less firm. For both genders, the contractions of orgasm become weaker and fewer. Sexual frequency declines with age.

late adulthood the final stage of development, beginning at age 65

life span (longevity) the maximum amount of time a person can live under optimal conditions

life expectancy the amount of time a person can actually be expected to live in a given setting

ageism prejudice against people because of their age

cataract a condition characterized by clouding of the lens of the eye

glaucoma a condition involving abnormally high fluid pressure in the eye

presbycusis loss of acuteness of hearing due to age-related degenerative changes in the ear

osteoporosis a disorder in which bones become more porous, brittle, and subject to fracture, due to loss of calcium and other minerals

sleep apnea temporary suspension of breathing while asleep

17-2 **Compare programmed and cellular damage theories of aging.** There are two main categories of theories of aging: (1) programmed theories, such as cellular clock theory, hormonal stress theory, and immunological theory, and (2) cellular damage theories, such as wear-and-tear theory, free-radical theory, and cross-linking theory.

Programmed theories of aging views of aging based on the concept that the processes of aging are governed, at least in part, by genetic factors

telomeres protective segments of DNA located at the tips of chromosomes

Immunological theory a theory of aging that holds that the immune system is preset to decline by an internal biological clock

Cellular damage theories of aging views of aging based on the concept that internal bodily changes and external environmental insults, such as carcinogens and poisons, cause cells and organ systems to malfunction, leading to death

wear-and-tear theory a theory of aging that suggests that over time our bodies become less capable of repairing themselves

free-radical theory a theory of aging that attributes aging to damage caused by the accumulation of unstable molecules called free radicals

Cross-linking theory a theory of aging that holds that the stiffening of body proteins eventually breaks down bodily processes, leading to aging

17-3 **Identify common health concerns associated with late adulthood.** The three major causes of death of Americans age 65 and older are heart disease, cancer, and stroke (see Figure 17.4). Hypertension is a major risk factor for heart attacks and strokes. Arthritis becomes more common with advancing age and is more common in women. Many older adults are addicted to prescription drugs; many have adverse drug reactions. Older adults have a greater risk of accidents, especially falls. Dementia is not a normal result of aging (see Figure 17.3). As Alzheimer's disease progresses, people find it harder to manage daily tasks and eventually can no longer recognize family members. Memory loss might be caused by accumulation of plaque.

normal aging processes of aging that represent a gradual decline of systems and body functions, enabling people to enjoy health and vitality well into late adulthood

pathological aging aging in which chronic diseases or degenerative processes, such as heart disease, diabetes, and cancer, lead to disability or premature death

arthritis inflammation of the joints

osteoarthritis a painful, degenerative disease characterized by wear and tear on joints

rheumatoid arthritis a painful, degenerative disease characterized by chronic inflammation of the membranes that line the joints

dementia a condition characterized by deterioration of cognitive functioning

Alzheimer's disease (AD) a severe form of dementia characterized by memory lapses, confusion, emotional instability, and progressive loss of cognitive functioning

FIG.17.4 LEADING CAUSES OF DEATH AMONG U.S. ADULTS, MEN AND WOMEN, 65 YEARS AND OVER

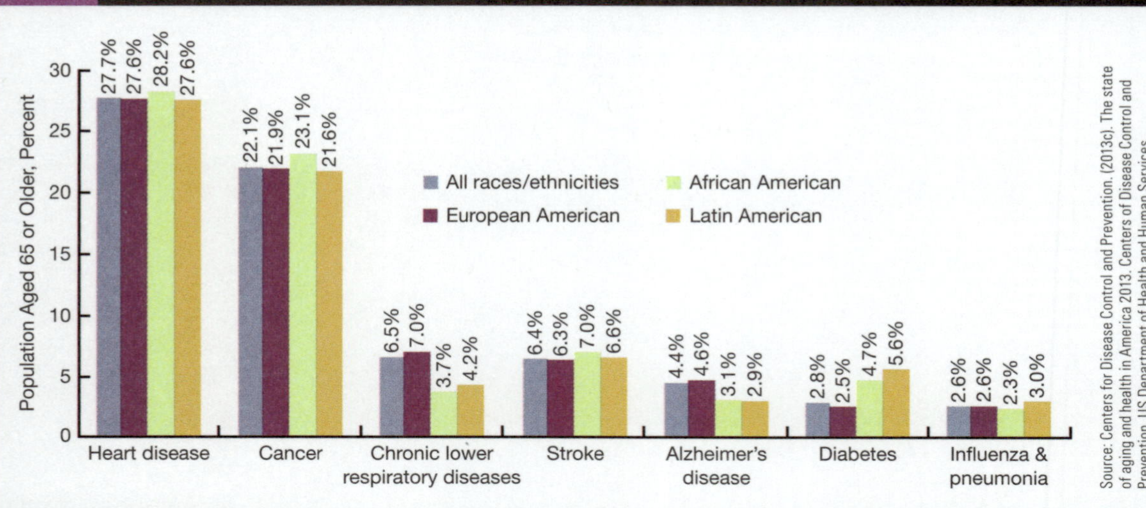

FIG.17.5 CAUSES OF DEMENTIA

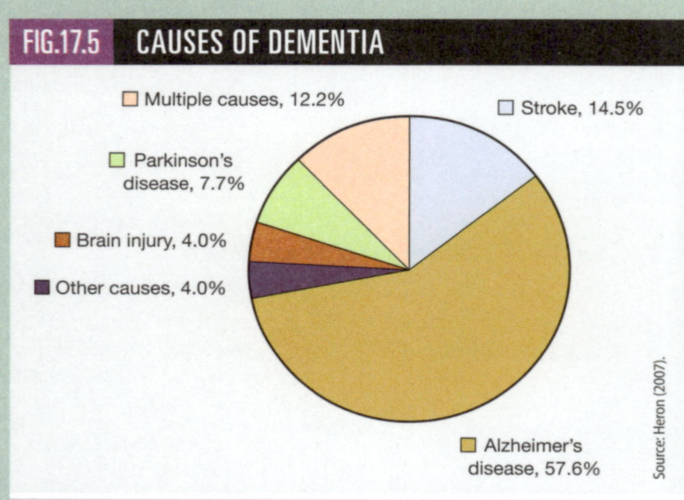

Alzheimer's disease is the leading cause of dementia.

17-4 **Discuss cognitive development in late adulthood.** Fluid intelligence is most vulnerable to decline in late adulthood. Crystallized intelligence can improve throughout much of late adulthood. Older adults have relatively more difficulty naming public figures than uncommon objects. The working memories of older adults hold less information than the working memories of young adults. The temporal memory of older adults might become confused. They might have trouble telling apart memories of actual events and of illusory events. Older adults usually do as well as younger adults in tasks that measure implicit memory, such as memory of multiplication tables or the alphabet. Aging has a more detrimental effect on associative memory than on memory for single items, perhaps because of impairment in binding and in use of strategies for retrieval. Long-term memories are subject to distortion, bias, and even decay. Older people recall events from their teens and twenties in greatest detail and emotional intensity, perhaps because of the effects of sex hormones. Age-related declines in processing speed and working memory (fluid intelligence) impair retrospective memory. Distractibility also plays a role.

Knowledge of meanings of words can improve well into late adulthood, but there is a decline in reading comprehension related to a decrease in working memory. Because of the decline in working memory and also because of impairments in hearing, many older adults find it more difficult to understand the spoken language and to produce language. Older people are more likely to experience the "tip-of-the-tongue" phenomenon.

Problem solving requires executive functioning to select strategies, working memory to hold the elements of the problem in mind, and processing speed to accomplish the task while the elements remain in mind. All of these have fluid components that decline with age. Older adults tend to regulate their emotional responses when they experience conflict.

The greater distractibility of older adults may encourage them to take a broader view of situations, contributing to wisdom. People with wisdom tend to tolerate other people's views and to admit that life has its uncertainties and that we seek workable solutions in an imperfect world.

explicit memory memory for specific information, including autobiographical information, such as what you had for breakfast, and general knowledge, such as state capitals

implicit memories automatic memories based on repetition and apparently not requiring any conscious effort to retrieve

Retrospective memory memory of past events and general knowledge

Prospective memory memory of things one has planned for the future

18-1 **Evaluate various theories of social and emotional development in late adulthood.** Erikson's final stage is ego integrity versus despair; the challenge is to continue to see life as meaningful and worthwhile in the face of physical decline and the approach of death. Peck's three developmental tasks of late adulthood are ego differentiation versus work-role preoccupation, body transcendence versus body preoccupation, and ego transcendence versus ego preoccupation. Butler proposes that reminiscence, or life review, attempt to make life meaningful and accept the end of life. According to disengagement theory, older people and society mutually withdraw from one another, but well-being among older adults is generally predicted by pursuing goals rather than withdrawal. Activity theory argues that older adults are better adjusted when they are more active and involved. According to socioemotional selectivity theory, older people limit their social contacts to regulate their emotional lives.

ego integrity versus despair Erikson's eighth life crisis, defined by maintenance of the belief that life is meaningful and worthwhile despite physical decline and the inevitability of death versus depression and hopelessness

life review looking back on the events of one's life in late adulthood, often in an effort to construct a meaningful narrative

disengagement theory the view that older adults and society withdraw from one another as older adults approach death

activity theory the view that older adults fare better when they engage in physical and social activities

socioemotional selectivity theory the view that we place increasing emphasis on emotional experience as we age but limit our social contacts to regulate our emotions

18-2 **Discuss psychological development in late adulthood, focusing on self-esteem and maintaining independence.** Self-esteem is highest in childhood, dips precipitously with entry into adolescence, rises gradually throughout middle adulthood and declines again in late adulthood, as you can see in Figure 18.2. Life changes such as retirement, loss of a spouse or partner, and declining health might account for age differences in self-esteem. Older adults who are independent see themselves as normal, whereas adults who are dependent on others tend to worry more about physical disabilities and stress. Depression affects some 10% of older adults, and may be connected with neuroticism, imbalances in norepinephrine, illness, loss of loved ones, and cognitive impairment. Depression can lead to suicide. The most common anxiety disorders among older adults are generalized anxiety disorder and phobic disorders.

FIG.18.2 MEAN LEVEL OF SELF-ESTEEM AS A FUNCTION OF AGE: FOR TOTAL SAMPLE, MALES, AND FEMALES

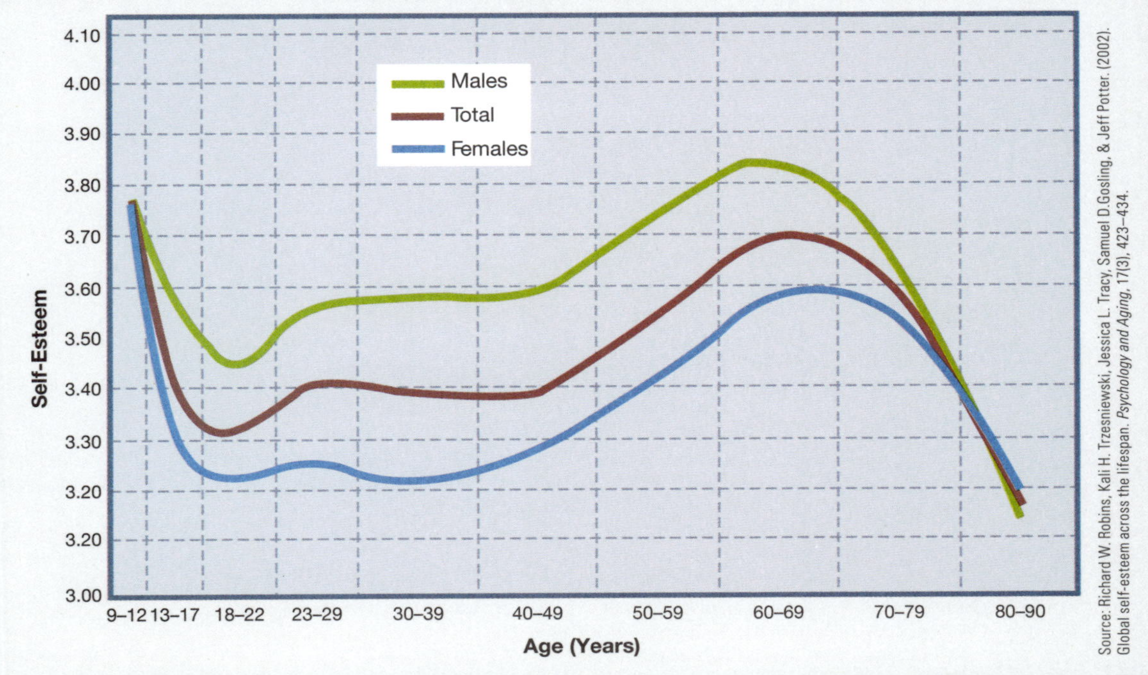

Source: Richard W. Robins, Kali H. Trzesniewski, Jessica L. Tracy, Samuel D Gosling, & Jeff Potter. (2002). Global self-esteem across the lifespan. *Psychology and Aging*, 17(3), 423–434.

generalized anxiety disorder general feelings of dread and foreboding

phobic disorder irrational, exaggerated fear of an object or situation

panic disorder recurrent experiencing of attacks of extreme anxiety in the absence of external stimuli that usually evoke anxiety

agoraphobia fear of open, crowded places

18-3 **Discuss the social contexts in which people age, focusing on housing, religion, and family.** Older Americans prefer to remain in their homes as long as their physical and mental conditions permit. Older people with greater resources and community ties are more likely to remain in their homes. Older city dwellers worry about crime, although they are less likely than younger people to be victimized. Older people who cannot live alone might hire home visiting or live-in helpers, move in with adult children, or enter assisted-living residences or nursing homes. Relocation disrupts social networks. Religious involvement often provides social, educational, and charitable activities as well as the promise of an afterlife. Religious involvement in late adulthood is usually associated with less depression and more life satisfaction. One-fifth to one-quarter of U.S. marriages last at least half a century. A study of the "big five" personality factors and marital satisfaction found that similarity in conscientiousness and extraversion predicts marital satisfaction in the sixties. When couples reach their sixties, many midlife responsibilities such as childrearing and work have declined, and intimacy re-emerges as a central issue. As compared with couples in midlife, older couples are more affectionate when they discuss conflicts, and disagree less. Sharing power in the relationship and dividing household tasks contribute to satisfaction. Older adults are less likely than younger adults to seek divorce. As with heterosexuals, gay men and lesbians in long-term partnerships tend to enjoy higher self-esteem, less depression, fewer STIs, and less substance abuse. Losing one's spouse in late adulthood is a traumatic experience and leads to a decline in health. Widowed men are more likely to remarry. Single older adults without children are as likely as people with children to be socially active. Older sibling pairs tend to shore each other up emotionally. Older people often narrow friendships to people who are most like them. Grandparents and adult grandchildren often have very close relationships.

elder abuse the abuse or neglect of senior citizens, particularly in nursing homes

18-4 **Describe factors that contribute to adjustment to retirement.** Retirement planning is a key to successful retirement—e.g., putting money aside and investigating locales to which one might relocate. Couples in relationships often plan collaboratively. The best-adjusted retirees are involved in a variety of activities. The most satisfied retirees maintain enjoyable leisure activities or replace work with more satisfying activities. Upscale professional workers appear to be well-adjusted as retirees.

TABLE 18.2 FACTOR ANALYSIS OF LEISURE ACTIVITIES OF RETIREES

Factor #	Name	Items
I	Athletic–Competitive–Outdoors	Adventure sports, team sports, hunting & fishing, individual sports, camping & outdoors, building & repair, cards & games, computer activities, collecting
II	Artistic–Cultural–Self-Expressive	Shopping, arts & crafts, entertaining & culinary arts, cultural arts, dancing, literature & writing, socializing, gardening & nature, community involvement, travel
III	Social	Partying

Source: Hansen, Dik, & Zhou (2008).

©shippee/Shutterstock.com

Though late adulthood is often viewed as a time to sit back and rest, it is an excellent opportunity to engage in new challenges and activities, such as going back to school.

18-5 **Discuss factors in "successful aging."** Definitions of successful aging often focus on physical activity, social contacts, the absence of cognitive impairment and depression, and health. Baltes and Carstensen focus on person–environment fit and see successful aging in terms of selective optimization with compensation, which is related to socioemotional selectivity theory. Successful agers also tend to be optimistic and to challenge themselves.

selective optimization with compensation reshaping of one's life to concentrate on what one finds to be important and meaningful in the face of physical decline and possible cognitive impairment

CHAPTER 19 LEARNING OUTCOMES / KEY TERMS

19-1 **Define death and dying, and evaluate views on stages of dying.** Death is the end of life, but *dying* is a part of life. Medical authorities usually use brain death—absence of activity in the cerebral cortex—as the standard for determining whether a person has died. Whole brain death includes death of the brain stem. Kübler-Ross hypothesized five stages of dying: denial, anger, bargaining, depression, and final acceptance. But Kübler-Ross's view applies only to people who have been diagnosed with terminal illness, and other investigators find that dying does not necessarily follow a progression of stages.

Death the irreversible cessation of vital life functions

Dying the end stage of life in which bodily processes decline, leading to death

brain death cessation of activity of the cerebral cortex

whole brain death cessation of activity of the cerebral cortex and brain stem

19-2 **Identify settings in which people die, distinguishing between hospitals and hospices.** About half of U.S. residents die in hospitals. Only a few—usually very old or terminally ill—die at home. About three in four hospice patients die in a private residence, nursing home, or other residential facility. Four hospice patients in nine die of cancer. Hospices provide palliative care rather than curative care, and they help the whole family, not just the patient. People who are dying often want to focus on other things and might enjoy hearing about humorous events or a companion's life experiences.

hospice an organization that treats dying patients by focusing on palliative care rather than curative treatment

palliative care treatment focused on the relief of pain and suffering rather than cure

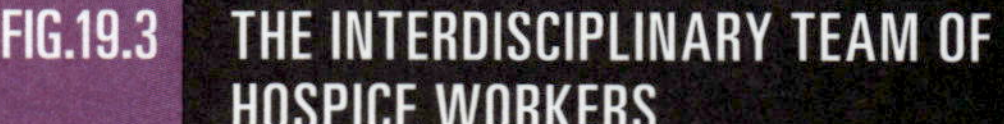
FIG.19.3 THE INTERDISCIPLINARY TEAM OF HOSPICE WORKERS

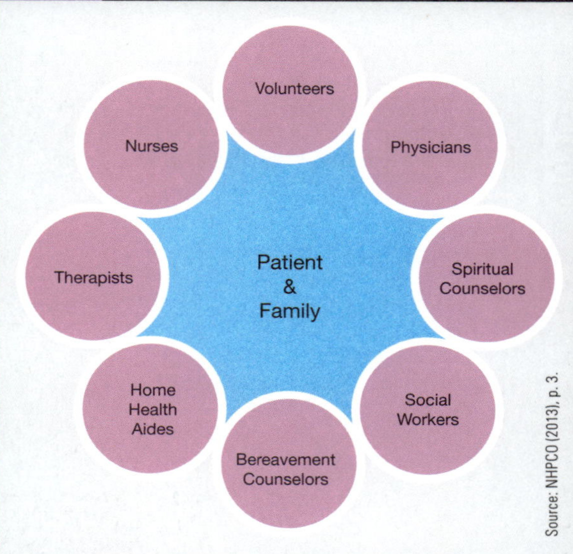

Source: NHPCO (2013), p. 3.

Hospice workers attempt to include the patient and the family as part of the team that will try to ease the passing of the patient.

19-3 **Discuss various kinds of euthanasia and controversies about them.** In active euthanasia, a lethal treatment is administered to cause a quick and painless death. Voluntary active euthanasia, or assisted suicide, is illegal throughout most of the United States. Physicians have assisted some patients with terminal or incapacitating illnesses who wished to die by providing lethal doses of drugs or sometimes administering them. Cases of involuntary euthanasia usually involve irreversibly comatose patients whose guardians believe they would not have wanted to remain alive. Terminal sedation is not intended to cause death. Highly religious physicians are more likely to object to physician-assisted suicide.

A legal form of passive euthanasia is withholding or withdrawing life-support equipment or techniques when terminally ill people do not wish to be kept alive by such aggressive treatment. The declaration of the wish to forgo aggressive treatment can be in the form of a living will.

FIG.19.4 PERCENT OF PHYSICIANS WHO OBJECT TO PHYSICIAN-ASSISTED SUICIDE OR TERMINAL SEDATION, ACCORDING TO RELIGIOSITY

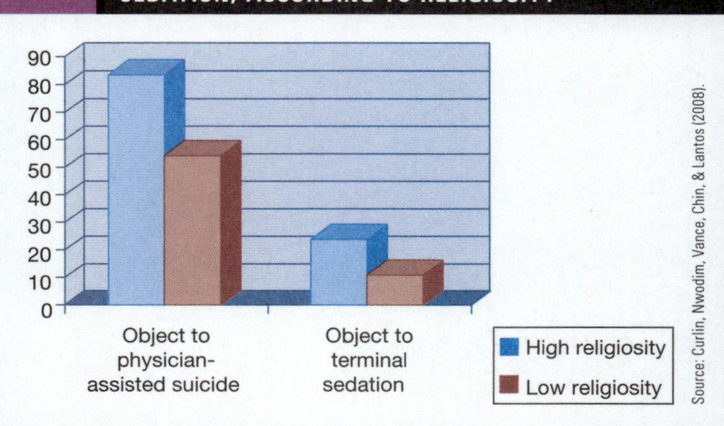

Source: Curlin, Nwodim, Vance, Chin, & Lantos (2008).

euthanasia the purposeful taking of life to relieve suffering

active euthanasia the administration of a lethal treatment (usually a drug) to cause a quick and painless death

voluntary active euthanasia the intentional administration of lethal drugs or other means of producing a painless death with the person's informed consent

(continues)

(continued)

involuntary active euthanasia the intentional administration of lethal drugs or other means of producing a painless death without the person's informed consent

Passive euthanasia the withholding or withdrawal of life-sustaining treatment to hasten death

living will a document prepared when a person is well, directing medical care providers to terminate life-sustaining treatment in the event he or she becomes incapacitated and unable to speak

19-4 **Discuss people's perspectives about death at various stages of development.** Preschoolers may think that death is reversible or temporary, but they become progressively more realistic at the ages of four, five, and six. Death of a parent is usually the most difficult for a child to bear. It is normal for children to fear death. Adolescents know that when someone dies, life cannot be restored, but they might construct magical, spiritual, or pseudoscientific theories as to how some form of life or thought might survive. Most young adults in developed nations need not think too much about death. In middle adulthood, death comes more to the fore, often when screening for various deadly diseases is prescribed. Older people might come to fear disability almost as much as death. Some theorists suggest that ego transcendence enables some people to begin to face death with calmness.

19-5 **Discuss coping with death, focusing on the funeral and possible stages of grieving.** If you are present at someone's death, call the family doctor, the police, or 911. Funerals provide an organized response to death that is tied to religious and cultural traditions. Ritual allows people to grieve publicly and bid farewell to the deceased person. Family can find it difficult to focus on legal and financial matters. A death can lead to bereavement and mourning. Grief can involve a variety of feelings—depression, loneliness, emptiness, numbness, fear, guilt, even anger. Bowlby proposed a stage theory of grief, and Maciejewski and his colleagues found some research evidence for five stages: disbelief, yearning, anger, depression, and acceptance. If you are grieving, allow yourself to feel the loss, do not reject offers of help, and give yourself time to let grieving run its course.

bereavement the state of deprivation brought about by the death of a family member or close friend

grief emotional suffering resulting from a death

mourning customary methods of expressing grief

dual process model the view that people who have suffered the loss of a loved one vacillate between focusing on the death and focusing on reengaging with their own lives.

John & Lisa Merrill/The Image Bank/Getty Images

Selling special *pan de muertos* (bread of the dead) as offerings during the Day of the Dead in Mexico.